World Trade Law

Text, Materials and Commentary

Second Edition

Simon Lester
Bryan Mercurio
and
Arwel Davies

·H A R T·
PUBLISHING

OXFORD AND PORTLAND, OREGON
2012

Published in the United Kingdom by Hart Publishing Ltd.
16C Worcester Place, Oxford, OX1 2JW
Telephone: +44 (0)1865 517530
Fax: +44 (0)1865 510710
E-mail: mail@hartpub.co.uk
Website: http://www.hartpub.co.uk

Published in North America (US and Canada) by
Hart Publishing
c/o International Specialized Book Services
920 NE 58th Avenue, Suite 300
Portland, OR 97213-3786
USA
Tel: +1 503 287 3093 or toll-free: (1) 800 944 6190
Fax: +1 503 280 8832
E-mail: orders@isbs.com
Website: http://www.isbs.com

British Library Cataloguing in Publication Data

Data Available

ISBN: 978-1-84946-222-8

Typeset by Forewords, Oxford
Printed and bound in Great Britain by
TJ International Ltd, Padstow, Cornwall

MIX
Paper from
responsible sources
FSC® C013056

World Trade Law

This newly updated version of one of the leading textbooks on world trade law offers what is in a number of ways a unique perspective on this important subject. Combining the best aspects of both casebook and treatise, this comprehensive textbook provides both detailed explanations and analysis of the law to help understand the issues as well as case extracts to offer a flavour of the judicial reasoning of trade adjudicators. Moreover, the book is truly global in outlook, being equally useful for students of international trade law in the UK, Europe, the US, Asia and elsewhere in the world. This updated edition includes in-depth discussions of the most recent developments in international trade jurisprudence, setting out important precedents that help establish the boundaries between global trade rules and domestic national autonomy. The implications of these rulings will be of great interest to traders, investors, government negotiators and even critics of globalisation.

7 DAY

Publisher's Note

The author and publisher gratefully acknowledge the authors and publishers of extracted material which appears in this book, and in particular the following for permission to reprint from the sources indicated.

AEA Web: *The American Economic Review*: P Krugman, 'The Narrow and Broad Arguments for Free Trade' (1993) 83, (2), 23–6. **American Society of International Law (via the Copyright Clearance Center)**: *American Journal of International Law*: William S Dodge, 'International Decision: Metalclad Corporation v Mexico' (2001), 95, 901; J Pauwelyn, 'The Role of Public International Law in the WTO: How Far Can We Go?' (2001) 95, 535; J Trachtman, 'Conflict of Norms in Public International Law: How the WTO Law Relates to Rules of International Law by J Pauwelyn', Review (2004) 98, 855. **Berkeley Electronic Press**: *The Economists' Voice*: J Stiglitz, 'A New Agenda for Global Warming' (2006) 13. **Blackwell Publishing**: *World Economy,* G R Winham, 'The World Trade Organisation: Institution Building in the Multilateral Trade System' (1998) 21 (3) 353–7. *Modern Law Review*: M Handler, 'The WTO Geographical Indication Dispute' (2006) 69, 70. **Brookings Institution Press:** R Z Lawrence, *Regionalism, Multilateralism and Deeper Integration* (1996). **Brooklyn Law School:** *Brooklyn Journal of International Law*: John H Jackson, 'GATT and the Future of International Trade Institutions' (1992) 8, 11. **Cambridge University Press**: N Lockhart and A Mitchell in Lester and Mercurio (eds) *Bilateral and Regional Trade Agreements: Commentary, Analysis and Case Studies* (2008). **Cambridge University Press Journals:** *World Trade Review,* P Norgaard Pedersen, 'The WTO Decision-Making Progress and Internal Transparency' (2006) 5 (1) 103–31; Arwel Davies, 'Reviewing Dispute Settlement at the World Trade Organisation: A Time to Reconsider the Role/s of Compensation?' (2006) 5 (1) 31. **D Griswold:** extract from his speech 'Trade, Democracy and Peace: The Virtuous Cycle' (2007). **D Rodrik:** 'Globalization for Whom? Time to Change the Rules – and Focus on Poor Workers' (2002) Reprinted with permission from the July-August 2002 issue of *Harvard Magazine*. **Center for Trade Policy and Law:** *Canadian Foreign Policy*: W A Dymond and M M Hart, 'Abundant Paradox: The Trade and Culture Debate' (2002) 9 (2); W Dymond, 'Core Labour Standards and the World Trade Organization: Labour's Love Lost' (2001) 8 (3) 99. **Focus on the Global South**: A Kwa, 'Power Politics in the WTO' (2003). **Fordham Publications**: *Fordham International Law Journal*: extracts from Riyaz Dattu, 'A Journey from Havana to Paris: The Fifty Year Quest for the Elusive MAI' (2000) 24, 275. **Hoover Press:** *Hoover Digest*: M Friedman, 'The Case for Free Trade' (1997). **Institute for International Economics (Peterson Institute):** J Schott and J Watal, *Decision Making in the WTO* (2000). **International Institute for Sustainable Development and the Center for International Environmental Law** H Mann and S Porter, *The State of Trade and Environmental Law – 2003: Implications for Doha and Beyond*, (2004). **Kluwer Law International:** *Journal of World Trade*: L Bartels, 'Applicable Law in WTO Dispute Settlement Proceedings' (2001) 25, 499–519. **Lexington Books:** J J Barceló III, 'Status of

WTO Rules in US Law' in *Rethinking the World Trading System*, J Barceló and H Corbet (forthcoming). **Marquette University Law School:** *Marquette Intellectual Property Law Review*: B Mercurio, 'TRIPS, Patent and Access to Life-Saving Drugs in the Developing World' (2004) 8, 211. **The Melbourne Journal of International Law Inc:** *Melbourne Journal of International Law*: B Mercurio and R Laforgia, 'Expanding Democracy: Why Australia Should Negotiate for Open and Transparent Dispute Settlements in its Free Trade Agreements' (2005) 6, 485. **MIT Press**: *Global Environmental Politics*: E Neumayer, 'The WTO and the Environment: Its Past Record is better than Critics Believe but the Future Outlook is Bleak' (2004) 4 (3) 1. **Northwestern University School of Law**: *Northwestern University Journal of International Human Rights*: B Mercurio, 'Resolving the Public Health Crisis in the Developing World: Problems and Barriers of Access to Essential Medicines', 5, 1. **Oxford University Press**: B Mercurio, 'TRIPS-Plus Provisions in FTAs' in L Bartels and F Ortino (eds) *Recent Trends, Regional Trade Agreements and the WTO Legal System*, (2006) 215–37. **Oxford University Press Journals:** *Journal of International Economic Law*: T Cottier and K N Schefer, 'The Relationship Between World Trade Organisation Law, National and Regional Law' (1998) 83, 91–106; A Davies, 'Connecting or Compartmentalizing the WTO and United States Legal Systems? The Role of the *Charming Betsy* Canon' (1998) 117, 121–33; K Leitner and S Lester, 'WTO Dispute Settlement 1995–2006 – A Statistical Analysis' (2007) 165–179; W J Davey, 'The WTO Looking Forwards' (2006) 9–23; Alan O Sykes, 'The Persistent Puzzles' (2004) 562–3. *European Journal of International Law*: E-U Petersmann, 'Time for a United Nations "Global Compact" for Integrating Human Rights into the Law of Worldwide Organisations: Lessons from European Integration' (2002) 621; P Alston, 'Resisting the Merger and Acquisition of Human Rights by Trade Law: A Reply to Petersmann' (2002) 815. **S Suranovic:** extracts from *International Trade Theory and Policy*. **Sweet and Maxwell:** *International Trade Law and Regulation*: X Zhang, 'Direct Effect of the WTO Agreements: National Survey' (2003) 9, 35, at 40–4. **University of Minnesota Law School**: *Minnesota Journal of Global Trade*: R Hudec, 'The New WTO Dispute Settlement Procedure: An Overview of the First Three Years' (1999) 8, 1, at 5–6. **University of New South Wales:** *University of New South Wales Law Journal*: B Mercurio, 'Should Australia Continue Negotiating Bilateral Free Trade Agreements? A Practical Analysis' (2004) 27, 667. **University of North Carolina School of Law:** *North Carolina Journal of International Law and Commercial Regulation* P M Gerhart and A S Kella, 'Power and Preferences: Developing Countries and the Role of the WTO Appellate Body' (2005) 30, 515. **Werner Publishing Company Ltd:** *Journal of World Investment and Trade*: A Emch, 'The European Court of Justice and WTO Dispute Settlement Rulings: The End of the Flirt' (2006) 7, 563 at 566–9. **World Bank**: extracts from Dollar and Kray, *Trade, Growth and Poverty* (2001) and B Hoekman, *Free Trade and Deep Integration: Antidumping and Antitrust in Regional Agreements* (1998). **World Trade Organisation:** C Trautmann, extract from a Press Release of a speech on the mandate given to the European Commission to preserve the Cultural Exception (1999) and P Lamy extract from a speech entitled 'Globalization and the Environment in a Reformed UN: Charting a Sustainable Development Path' (2007. **Yale University Press:** M Wolf 'Traumatized by Trade' in *Why Globalization Works*.

Contents

Part I

Introduction to the Legal and Economic Aspects of World Trade Regulation

1

Introduction to World Trade Law

The scope of the field of 'World Trade Law' is somewhat difficult to define. In part, this is because a number of terms have been used to describe it: International Economic Law, International Trade Law, Global Trade Law and International Trade Regulation, among others. All seem to refer to generally the same subject matter, although there may be slight variations. There are a wide range of topics that have, to some extent, aspects that are 'global' or 'international' or 'world-wide'; that relate to 'trade' or 'economics'; and that are 'legal' or 'regulatory' in nature. We chose the term 'World Trade Law' in large part because it emphasises the central role of the World Trade Organization (WTO) in regulating the rules of world trade. The WTO is not the only relevant legal instrument or international organisation, but it is the broadest and most comprehensive in its coverage, and to some extent governs other bilateral and regional agreements in this area. In addition, while we address various 'economic' issues in this book, the core focus is on 'trade' issues. To the extent that other issues are discussed, it is in large part because of their connection to trade. Thus, 'World Trade Law' seemed the most appropriate title for this volume.

The 'World Trade Law' covered by this book focuses on the legal instruments that regulate trade flows. This includes international agreements related to trade, as well as certain domestic laws affecting trade flows. The international agreements begin with the WTO Agreement, which established the World Trade Organization. With 155 countries (or customs territories) as members as of this writing (and many more attempting to join), the WTO is almost a fully global agreement at this point. It provides a binding set of rules on a wide range of trade-related topics (including trade in goods and services, intellectual property protection, as well as a few limited rules on investment).

In addition to the WTO, there are the numerous bilateral, regional and plurilateral trade agreements. These agreements are, in a sense, still part of the multilateral system. This is the case because the WTO Agreement establishes conditions which these agreements must meet in order to be permitted under WTO rules. However, these agreements often go further in terms of economic integration than do WTO rules, so there are important substantive differences. The most prominent of the regional agreements are the European Union (EU), the North American Free Trade Agreement (NAFTA), Mercosur (the Southern Common Market) and the ASEAN Free Trade Area (AFTA). Having proliferated in large numbers in recent years, bilateral agreements are increasingly gaining in importance in any 'World Trade Law' discussion or debate.

Investment agreements also play a significant role in trade law. Traditionally, these

3

agreements have taken the form of bilateral investment treaties, under which the signatories promise to give certain treatment to inward investment in their territory. Recently, though, many bilateral and regional trade agreements have now incorporated investment provisions, thus combining both trade and investment into a single agreement.

In terms of domestic law, the key areas covered are the so-called 'trade remedies', where domestic agencies oversee a quasi-judicial process for putting up barriers to both fair and unfair trade (within the boundaries of certain international rules). Also important is customs administration, under which governments collect duties and otherwise regulate imports and exports.

While this book does briefly cover domestic laws, the focus is on the international agreements, with a heavy emphasis on the rules of the WTO. In a sense, WTO rules are an umbrella under which almost everything else falls. The WTO sets the international trade rules and regulates regional and bilateral trade agreements and domestic trade laws.

Before moving on to the substance of this text, it is important that students are first introduced to international trade and economics more generally. We will do so in this chapter by looking at how trade has played, and continues to play, an important role in the world economy. As will be seen, the trend is towards more trade and deeper international integration. The chapter then asks and attempts briefly to answer the following questions: why do nations trade? why is integration increasing? what is the effect of this? In answering these questions, we present several extracts providing various perspectives on globalisation and trade. Finally, we provide an outline of the structure of the book.

I. INCREASED TRADE AND DEEPER INTEGRATION: GLOBALISATION!

'Globalisation' is an often spoken but seldom defined term used by many to describe the growing inter-connectedness of the world. This inter-connectedness, of course, includes but is not limited to trade. The ability to speak on the telephone or send an email to someone in another country, to send a parcel or travel beyond one's borders with relative ease are all the result of 'globalisation'. The ability to purchase a product made in another country, or conversely to sell a product beyond one's own border, as well as the ability to make an investment in a foreign country, are also examples of 'globalisation'.

While some portray 'globalisation' as a new trend, this cannot be farther from the truth. 'Globalisation', in its rawest form, began with the first human migrants from Africa over 60,000 years ago. Continual movement of people, whether by choice, necessity (due to, for instance, natural disaster) or coercion (due to, say, an invading army), as well as the emergence of powerful nations, firmly established the position of 'globalisation' in the world.

It is often the emergence of technological advances that increases the pace of 'globalisation'. For instance, writing in the 1850s, David Livingstone stated:

The extension and use of railroads, steamships, telegraphs, break down nationalities and bring peoples geographically remote into close connection commercially and politically. They make the world one, and capital, like water, tends to a common level.[1]

Today, relatively inexpensive air travel, telephone and computer network coverage, and a host of other recent technological advances, have taken this further and created a world where one can instantly connect to others in every country in the world.

The impact of 'globalisation' on world trade law has run a similar course. New technologies, such as relatively safe ocean-going vessels, created opportunities for explorers to 'discover' new lands and establish trading routes. This, in combination with colonisation, allowed merchants of varying countries to trade their wares while also providing a more diverse range of products to the populace (whether it be food, wine, spices, silk, cloth, etc).

By the 1910s, trade (imports and exports) in goods as a percentage of gross domestic product (GDP)—output—had reached 12 per cent in several colonising nations. This level of trade diminished with increased protectionism and two world wars and, in fact, did not return until the 1970s. Thus, it can unquestionably be stated that 'globalisation' is not new. Instead, it is a new term to describe a very old process.[2]

It can also be stated that the world trade-to-GDP ratio has continued to grow. In other words, the importance of trade to the world is increasing. While part of the growth can be attributed to technological advances, a large part is due to the reduction in trade barriers and trade stability brought about by the GATT/WTO system. As noted, the legal obligations resulting from such international agreements form the substance of this book, but it is worthwhile at this point to provide some statistics on the trends in world trade.

(a) Increased Trade and Increased Importance of Trade

The first statistical point to make is simply that trade, as a whole, is increasing. Table 1.1 shows a consistent rise in exports and imports throughout the decades. Notably, it also shows the rapid rise in trade in the period following the conclusion of the Uruguay Round and advent of the WTO in 1995.

Table 1.2 shows the percentage growth in world merchandise exports and production from 2005 to 2010; of note, while the effects of the global financial crisis were devastating to the 2009 trade figures, the world strongly rebounded in 2010. It is also worth noting the consistently stronger growth in trade relative to GDP, and in the case of 2009

Table 1.1 World Merchandise Trade
(US dollars at current prices (billions))

	1948	1953	1963	1973	1983	1993	2003	2010
World exports	59	84	157	579	1838	3676	7377	14851
World imports	62	85	164	594	1882	3786	7695	15077

[1] As cited in 'The Early Pioneers', *The Economist*, 28 July 2007, 76.
[2] *Ibid.*

Table 1.2 Growth in the volume of world merchandise exports and production, 2005–10
(Annual percentage change)

	2005–10	2008	2009	2010
World merchandise exports	3.5	2.5	–12.0	14.0
Agricultural products	3.5	2.5	–2.5	7.5
Fuels and mining products	1.5	1.0	–5.5	5.5
Manufactures	4.0	2.5	–15.0	18.0
World merchandise production	2.0	1.0	–2.5	4.0
Agriculture	2.0	3.5	0.5	0.0
Mining	0.5	1.5	–1.5	2.0
Manufacturing	2.5	0.0	–4.0	5.5
World GDP	2.0	1.5	–2.5	3.5

the deeper loss of trade volume relative to the decline in GDP. The trade-to-GDP ratio is discussed in more detail below.

This consistently strong growth rate has correspondingly led to rises in GDP in every continent.[3] Not only are global GDP and the level of global trade increasing, but so is trade as a percentage of world output trade, with trade now accounting for approximately 25 per cent of world output, up from 15 per cent in the 1980s.

Moreover, as briefly noted above, the importance of international trade relative to domestic transactions is also increasing. This can be measured by using a trade-to-GDP ratio, which measures the average share of exports and imports of goods and services in GDP. Often referred to as a 'trade openness' ratio, the term is in fact misleading, as a low ratio does not necessarily imply high tariff or non-tariff protection, but may be due to other factors. For instance, international trade seems especially important for smaller countries (whether it be in terms of land mass or population) that are in close proximity to countries with open trade regimes. Larger, as well as more isolated countries tend to have lower trade-to-GDP ratios. Other factors, such as history, culture, trade policy, the structure of the economy and the presence of multinational firms, also help explain differences in trade-to-GDP ratios across countries. Regardless, it is clear that total trade (exports and imports) of both goods and services as a percentage of GDP is increasing. Remembering that the trade-to-GDP ratios of the industrialised countries reached 12 per cent in the 1910s before falling and only recovering to those levels again in the 1970s, the current statistics show the substantial increase in importance of trade over the last three decades, and even a large increase since 1995. Figure 1.1 illustrates not only the consistent rise in the percentage of world exports as well as global GDP, but also highlights the rise in exports as a percentage of global GDP.[4]

---

[3] See WTO, *World Trade Report 2006* (Geneva, WTO, 2006) 2.
[4] See also http://www.wto.org/english/news_e/pres11_e/pr628_e.htm.

Figure 1.1 Volume of world merchandise exports and gross domestic product, 1950-2010
Annual percentage change

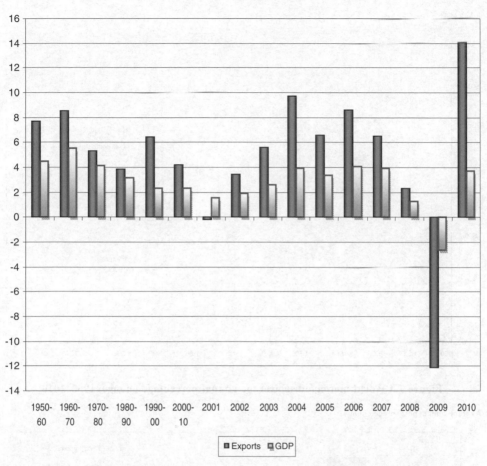

Source: WTO, International Trade Statistics 2011, available at http://www.wto.org/english/res_e/ statis_e/its2011_e/its11_charts_e.htm (visited on 15 April 2012).

(b) What is Traded?

Merchandise accounts for the majority of world trade (approximately 61 per cent), while services (approximately 20 per cent) are playing an increasingly important role in world trade. Meanwhile, mining (approximately 11 per cent) and agriculture (approximately 8 per cent) account for a small, but politically important percentage of world trade.

Figure 1.2 further breaks down the trade in goods statistics and reveals the change in trading volumes from 1950 to 2010, while Figure 1.3 shows the average annual percentage change in trade in agricultural products, fuels and mining, and manufacturing in three periods from 1950 to 2010.

Manufacturing (of all kinds) accounts for a large percentage of all trade in goods, but the prominence of agriculture in world trade continues to diminish. This continues a

Figure 1.2 World merchandise trade volume by major product group, 1950–2010 (volume indices, 1950 = 100)

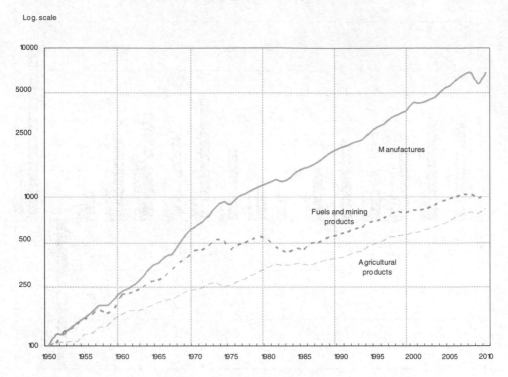

Figure 1.3 World merchandise average annual percentage change, 1950–2010

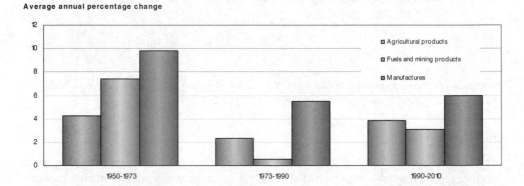

long decline for agriculture as a share of global trade. Thus, despite the prominence of agriculture in the multilateral trade negotiations, its role in the economies of most nations has declined for over 50 years. Figure 1.4 tracks the decline of world agriculture exports as a percentage of total world trade.

This shift from agriculture has disproportionately affected developing countries, many of which have industrialised in the last few decades. Overall, while agriculture accounted for 58 per cent and manufacturing 12 per cent of developing country exports in 1960,

Figure 1.4 Agriculture as percentage share of world merchandise exports

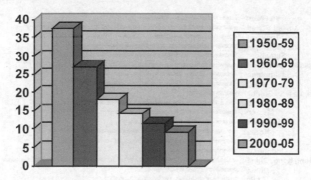

Source: *World Trade Report 2006*, above n 3, 7.

Figure 1.5 Global growth in services

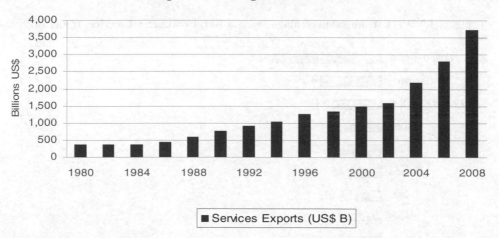

manufacturing exports accounted for 65 per cent and agriculture only 10 per cent of developing country exports in 2001. This trend has been particularly true in many East Asian nations, such as Korea, Hong Kong and Singapore, where rapid industrialisation since the 1960s dramatically shifted output and trading patterns.

Trade in services has also significantly increased its position of prominence in the last few decades. Figure 1.5 shows the rapid post-WTO rise in global service exports.

The service sector significantly contributes to global growth, with its contribution to GDP averaging around 60 per cent in most advanced countries. Figure 1.6 shows the contribution of services to the GDP in select countries, while Figure 1.7 shows the world contribution to the services trade by country.

(c) Who Trades?

It is fair to say that large countries dominate trade—large economics produce more goods and services to sell and generate more income for people to buy more (what economists

Figure 1.6 Services as a percentage of GDP, 2010

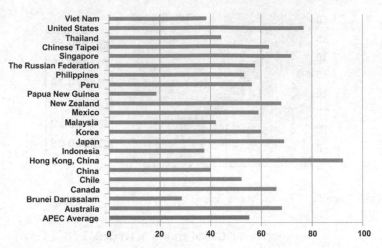

Figure 1.7 WTO Members' percentage share in world commercial services trade, 2010

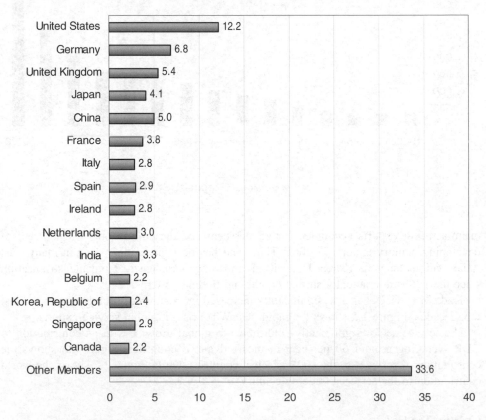

refer to as the 'gravity model'). In this regard, the largest 10 trading partners of the US account for almost 70 per cent of its total trade. But the quantity of trade, and its importance to an economy, is dictated by factors other than size. For instance, proximity (distance in transportation and also communication) and cultural affinity have long been and remain an important determinant. Other factors, such as trade policy, openness to trade and investment and border policies, also play a critical role in the level of imports and exports. For instance, membership of trade agreements promotes trade through the reduction of barriers and lowering of costs to trade. Technology (whether by aeroplane travel, faster shipping lanes or computerised negotiating and transacting) also plays a part in making the world 'smaller', in that it has reduced the barriers of proximity. Moreover, intra-firm and intra-regional trade is playing an important (and growing) role in world trade. In fact, multinational companies currently account for approximately 50 per cent of Chinese exports, 25 per cent of Brazilian exports, 15 per cent of Korean exports and up to 90 per cent of Ireland's exports.[5]

The trading pattern of the largest economy, the US, demonstrates the above, as the top trading partners of the US are a mix of neighbouring countries and large economies, all with relatively open economies (the US's top five trading partners are: Canada, China, Mexico, Japan and Germany). Moreover, almost one-third of US exports and 42 per cent of US imports are the result of multinational companies trading from one division to another.

But trade is also important for developing and least developed countries (LDCs). For instance, since 1978 China has used a liberalised, export oriented trade policy to increase growth and reduce poverty. In so doing, China's economy evolved from being largely agrarian to one of the most dynamic manufacturing based economies. This rise can be demonstrated by the rapid increase in China's share of the world merchandise export market, illustrated in Table 1.3.

Such a rise in total exports has undoubtedly benefited the citizens of China as a whole and lifted millions of people out of extreme poverty. Overall, China's GDP per capita

Table 1.3 China's share in world merchandise exports (percentage)[a]

	1983	1993	2003	2004	2010
Total merchandise	1.2	2.5	6.0	6.7	13
Manufactures	1.0	3.3	7.3	8.3	13.7

Source: WTO, 'Facts and Figures for the Sixth Ministerial Conference', available at http://192.91.247.23/English/thewto_e/minist_e/min05_e/brief24_e.htm (visited 20 July 2012).
[a]WTO, 'Facts and Figures for the Sixth Ministerial Conference', available at http://192.91.247.23/english/thewto_e/minist_e/min05_e/brief_e/brief24_e.htm (visited 20 July 2012); http://www.imf.org/external/pubs/ft/fandd/2010/12/arora.htm; http://www.google.com/url?sa=t&rct=j&q=&esrc=s&source=web&cd=4&sqi=2&ved=0CDkQFjAD&url=http%3A%2F%2Fcomtrade.un.org%2Fpb%2FFileFetch.aspx%3FdocID%3D4204%26type%3Dcommodity%2520pages&ei=CLCOT8WwIsi3iQfojo3pDA&usg=AFQjCNHWge5IgTtwXzwFUC30igRiCqsPng.

---

[5] 'The Emerging Market to Emerging Market Opportunity: Are You Ready To Play?' [January/February 2010] *Global Business*, available at http://www.iveybusinessjournal.com/topics/global-business/the-emerging-market-to-emerging-market-opportunity-are-you-ready-to-play; IDA Ireland, 'Multinational Companies Account for Bulk of Irish Exports' (27 July 2011), available at http://www.idaireland.com/news-media/featured-news/multinationals-exports/; UNCTAD, *World Investment Report 2002* (2003), available at www.unctad.org/en/docs/wir2002_en.pdf (accessed on 20 July 2012).

has increased from $94 in 1960, to $452 in 1980, to $1,411 in 1990 to $3,600 in 2000 to $7,600 in 2010 (US dollars).[6]

Other developing countries have similarly benefited by an increase in trade. For instance, Brazil has emerged from a military dictatorship advocating import-substitution economic policies to become a thriving democracy with open, liberalised and export oriented economic policies. During this same period, the government has also improved the legal and regulatory framework by improving the laws (lowering tariffs, lowering tax rates and improving business regulations and protections), stressing the rule of law and fighting corruption.[7] Brazil now has an annual trade surplus of almost US$50 billion (Brazil exports $140 billion worth of goods and imports $90 billion) and foreign investment is considerable. Moreover, Brazil became a net exporter of capital in 2006. The changes have also had a positive social effect. For instance, the percentage of Brazilians living below the poverty line has been reduced from nearly 36 per cent in 1992 to 23 per cent in 2005. Whereas in the mid-1990s 17 per cent of children aged 7–14 did not go to school, nearly all students are now enrolled in school (the number of graduates has tripled in little more than a decade).[8]

Despite having a miniscule amount of total world trade, least developed countries (LDCs account for approximately 1 per cent of both world exports and world imports) are active members of the world trading community and their performance level is increasing. For instance, between 1990 and 1999, the growth of LDC exports and imports was less than that of world exports, but since then the growth of LDC exports exceeded that of world exports. Of particular note is the significant growth rate of exports posted by LDCs in 2004, which was 34 per cent, compared to 21 per cent for world exports. Figure 1.8 illustrates the growth of LDC trade in merchandise.

Of course, expansion of trade is not the only thing needed for development. While LDCs as a whole are major producers of primary products, fuels, clothing and food products,[9] economic performance varies widely depending upon a number of factors, including civil stability, trade policy and corruption.[10]

Figure 1.9 shows the regional shares of merchandise exports, and further reveals the increasing percentage of Asian exports from 2005 to 2010.

II. WHY TRADE?

It is often stated that there are two main reasons advanced for why countries trade with each other. The first is economics and the second is peace and security.

---

[6] These figures were compiled using A Heston, R Summers and B Aten, Penn World Table Version 7.0, Center for International Comparisons of Production, Income and Prices at the University of Pennsylvania, May 2011; and CIA World Fact Book, available at https://www.cia.gov/library/publications/the-world-factbook/ (accessed on 19 April 2012).

[7] 'A Special Report on Brazil', *The Economist*, 14 April 2007, 3–5, 14.

[8] *Ibid*, 4–13.

[9] *Ibid*, 8, 14.

[10] See, eg B Mercurio, 'Growth and Development: Economic and Legal Conditions' [2007] *University of New South Wales Law Journal* 437.

Figure 1.8 Growth in the value of LDC merchandise trade, 1990–2004
(Indices 1990 = 100)

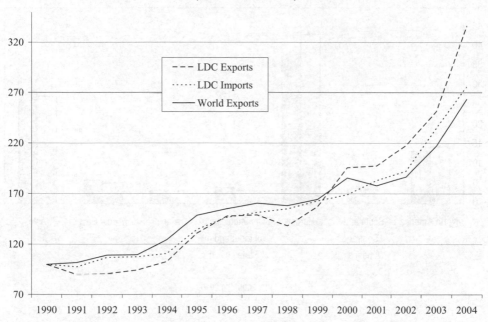

Source: WTO, 'Market Access Issues Related to Products of Export Interest Originating from Least-Developed Countries', Note by the Secretariat, WTO Doc No WT/COMTD/LDC/W/38, TN/MA/S/19 (22 February 2006).

(a) Economics

Trade is a necessary, but not sufficient, condition for growth.[11] No nation has experienced sustained economic growth by closing itself off from international trade and investment. Openness to trade and investment promotes growth in a number of ways, including:

- It encourages economies to specialise and produce in areas where they have a relative cost advantage over other economies. Over time, this helps economies to employ more of their human, physical and capital resources in sectors where they get the highest returns in open international markets, boosting productivity and the returns to workers and investors.
- Trade expands the markets local producers can access, allowing them to produce at the most efficient scale to keep down costs. Even in populous developing economies, low incomes often make producers' potential local market small, so trading with the world is vital.
- Trade diffuses new technologies and ideas, increasing local workers' and managers' productivity. Technology transfers through trade and investment are even more valuable for developing economies which employ less advanced technologies and typically have less capacity to develop new technologies themselves.

[11] See, eg RN Cooper, *'Growth and Inequality: The Role of Foreign Trade and Investment', Annual World Bank Conference on Development Economics 2001/2002* (World Bank, Washington, DC, 2002), available at www.economics.harvard.edu/faculty/cooper/papers/growthinequal.pdf.

Figure 1.9 Regional shares in world merchandise exports, 2005 and 2010 (percentage)

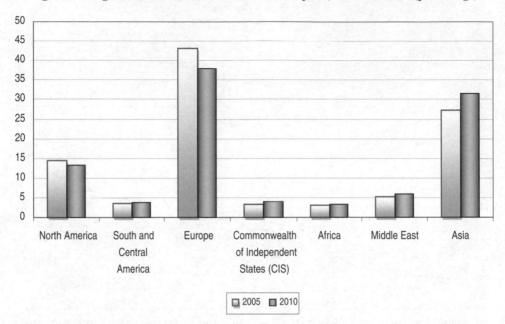

- Removing tariffs on imports gives consumers access to cheaper products, increasing their purchasing power and living standards, and gives producers access to cheaper inputs, reducing their production costs and boosting their competitiveness.[12]

Liberalised trade is, in large part, responsible for much of the reduction in global poverty.[13] Countries that have embraced liberalised trade policies and increased trade have reduced poverty at a far greater rate than those countries which have maintained high barriers to trade.[14] Dollar and Kraay summarise the economic data by stating:

> [E]xamination of individual cases suggests that trade openness leads to declining inequality between countries, and declining poverty within countries. The poor countries that have reduced trade barriers and participated more in international trade over the past twenty years have seen their growth rates accelerate. In the 1990s they grew far more rapidly than the rich countries, and hence reduced the gap between themselves and the developed world. At the same time the developing countries that are not participating in globalization are falling further and further behind. Within the globalizing developing countries there has been no general trend in inequality.

---

[12] AusAid, 'Trade, Development and Poverty Reduction', available at www.ausaid.gov.au/publications/pdf/trade_devel_poverty.pdf.

[13] DFID, 'Trade Matters in the Fight against World Poverty' (2005), available at www.berr.gov.uk/ files/file23498.pdf. In 2004, for the first time since statistics began being counted (1990), the number of people living on under $1 a day was less than one billion. The total, 986 million, represents slightly less than 18% of total population, down from the height of nearly 1.25 billion people—approximately 30% of the population—in 1990: 'Another Day, Another $1.08', *The Economist*, 26 April 2007, 90.

[14] See D Dollar and A Kraay, 'Trade, Growth and Poverty' (2001) World Bank Policy Research Working Paper; D Dollar and A Kraay, 'Growth is Good for the Poor' (2001) World Bank Policy Research Working Paper; M Ravallion, 'Growth, Inequality, and Poverty: Looking Beyond Averages' (2001) 29(11) *World Development* 1803.

Thus, rapid growth has translated into dramatic declines in absolute poverty in countries such as China, India, Thailand, and Vietnam.[15]

When a nation grows, the poor in that nation also benefit. This is the case even when the distribution of growth gains (ie, equity distribution) within a country does not change.[16] For instance, Vietnam has recently experienced huge gains in GDP as it has liberalised the economy, but the equality distribution of the country's wealth has not changed. However, it cannot be said that the poor of Vietnam have not benefited from the nation's growth, as the poverty rate in Vietnam has been reduced from 75 to 37 per cent in the first 10-year period (1989–98) following the beginning of the liberalisation efforts.[17]

It is widely acknowledged that the effects of trade on poverty could be even more far reaching if barriers were further reduced or eliminated entirely. For instance, the World Bank estimates that the reduction of barriers on merchandise trade coupled with the elimination of subsidies could boost global welfare by up to US$290 billion in 2015 (with almost 45 per cent of the gains going to developing countries) and reduce global poverty by 32 million people. Moreover, it is estimated that the removal of developed country barriers could be worth over US$100 billion a year to developing countries (a figure which is almost double the current total amount of aid received by developing countries).[18] The reduction of subsidies, notably agricultural subsidies, would also assist developing countries in gaining from international trade. For instance, market agricultural subsidies have been estimated to reduce world prices by an estimated 3–12 per cent (depending upon the commodity)[19] and reduce the output of East Asia and the Pacific by US$37 billion annually (a figure five times greater than the amount of aid received in those regions).[20] For these reasons, Kofi Annan, former Secretary General of the United Nations, stated: 'No single change could make a greater contribution to eliminating poverty than fully opening up the markets of prosperous countries to the goods produced by poor ones'.

While the reduction of developed country barriers would undoubtedly assist developing countries, that is only half the story. Developing countries must adopt the proper trade and investment policies, including the reduction of their own barriers to trade. In fact, the reduction of developing country barriers to trade would have as large an effect on developing countries as would the removal of developed country barriers.[21] This is due to the fact that the vast majority of developing countries import the bulk of food products, even staple grains, and therefore are subject to the high tariff rates of the developing world. This is particularly the case in agricultural, where tariffs average 62 per cent, and

---

[15] Dollar and Kraay, 'Trade, Growth and Poverty', *ibid*, 12.

[16] *Ibid*, 5.

[17] *Ibid*, 3.

[18] P Collier and D Dollar, *Globalization, Growth, and Poverty: Building an Inclusive World Economy* (Washington, DC, World Bank/Oxford University Press, 2002) 9.

[19] KA Elliot, 'Agriculture and the Doha Round' (January 2007) CGD Brief, 6. See also K Anderson and WMartin, 'Agriculture, Trade, and the Doha Agenda' in K Anderson and W Martin (eds), *Agricultural Trade Reform and the Doha Development Agenda* (Palgrave Macmillan and the World Bank, Washington, DC, 2006).

[20] The Hon A Downer, Minister for Foreign Affairs, 'The Livestock Revolution: A Pathway from Poverty' Speech at the Crawford Fund conference: The Livestock Revolution: A Pathway from Poverty Canberra, 13 August 2003, available at www.ausaid.gov.au/media/release.cfm?BC=Speech&ID=812_6241_5875_6417_7855.

[21] K Anderson and W Martin, *Agricultural Trade Reform and the Doha Development Agenda* (May 2005) World Bank Policy Research Working Paper 3607, 8–9.

are an average of 75 per cent in Africa and 34 per cent in Asia.[22] In total, approximately 70 per cent of tariffs paid by developing country exporters go to other developing countries (resulting in a loss of US$62 billion per annum).[23]

(b) Peace

Another often suggested reason for 'free' trade is that it promotes peace. The thinking behind this theory is that countries which trade with each other are less likely to declare war against each other. By creating ties between the people of each nation, the risk of armed conflict is reduced, as there will be constituencies that oppose war and look for peaceful solutions. In practice, the theory has been borne out—with limited but notable exceptions—not only in modern times, but also as far back as to at least the Egyptians and Phoenicians.[24] In the following extract, Daniel Griswold, director of the Center for Trade Policy Studies at the Cato Institute, links trade, democracy and peace in what he calls a 'virtuous cycle'.

> **D Griswold, 'Trade, Democracy and Peace: The Virtuous Cycle', Presentation delivered at the 'Peace Through Trade' Conference at the World Trade Centers Association, Oslo, Norway on 20 April 2007**
>
> **How Free Trade Tills Soil for Democracy**
>
> In one of my studies for Cato, called "Trading Tyranny for Freedom," I examined the idea of whether free and open markets promote human rights and democracy. Political scientists since Aristotle have long noted the connection between economic development, political reform, and democracy. Increased trade and economic integration promote civil and political freedoms directly by opening a society to new technology, communications, and democratic ideas. Along with the flow of consumer and industrial goods often come books, magazines, and other media with political and social content. Foreign investment and services trade create opportunities for foreign travel and study, allowing citizens to experience first-hand the civil liberties and more representative political institutions of other nations. Economic liberalization provides a counterweight to governmental power and creates space for civil society.
>
> The faster growth and greater wealth that accompany trade promote democracy by creating an economically independent and political aware middle class. A sizeable middle class means that more citizens can afford to be educated and take an interest in public affairs. They can afford cell phones, Internet access, and satellite TV. As citizens acquire assets and establish businesses and careers in the private sector, they prefer the continuity and evolutionary reform of a democratic system to the sharp turns and occasional revolutions of more authoritarian systems. People who are allowed to successfully manage their daily economic lives in a relatively free market come to expect and demand more freedom in the political and social realm.
>
> Wealth by itself does not promote democracy if the wealth is controlled by the state or a small,

---

[22] Australian Department of Foreign Affairs and Trade, *Advancing African Agriculture Through Trade Reform* (Economic Analytical Unit, Canberra, March 2003) 11.

[23] *Ibid,* 4.

[24] See, eg, T Graham, 'Global Trade: War & Peace' (1983) 50 *Foreign Policy* 124; U Albrecht, 'The Study of International Trade in Arms and Peace Research' (1972) 9(2) *Journal of Peace Research* 165. Evidence from archaeological digs traces trade in stones and shells to the ancient peoples. R Guisepi, 'The Stone Age: The General Picture' [2000] *International World History Project, available at* http://history-world.org/stone_age2.htm.

ruling elite. That's why a number of oil-rich countries in the Middle East and elsewhere remain politically repressive despite their relatively high per capita incomes. For wealth to cultivate the soil for democracy, it must be produced, retained, and controlled by a broad base of society, and for wealth to be created in that manner, an economy must be relatively open and free.

In my study for Cato, I found that the reality of the world broadly reflects those theoretical links between trade, free markets, and political and civil freedom.

First, I examined the broad global trends in both trade and political liberty during the past three decades. Since the early 1970s, cross-border flows of trade, investment, and currency have increased dramatically, and far faster than output itself. Trade barriers have fallen unilaterally and through multilateral and regional trade agreements in Latin America, in the former Soviet bloc nations, in East Asia, including China, and in more developed nations as well. During that same period, political and civil liberties have been spreading around the world. Thirty years ago democracies were the exception in Latin America, while today they are the rule. Many former communist states from the old Soviet Union and its empire have successfully transformed themselves into functioning democracies that protect basic civil and political freedoms. In East Asia, democracy and respect for human rights have replaced authoritarian rule in South Korea, Taiwan, the Philippines, and Indonesia.

Freedom House, a human rights think tank in New York, measures the political and civil freedom each year in every country in the world. It classifies countries into three categories: "Free"—meaning countries where citizens enjoy the freedom to vote as well as full freedom of the press, speech, religion and independent civic life; "Partly Free"—those countries "in which there is limited respect for political rights and civil liberties"; and "Not Free"—"where basic political rights are absent and basic civil liberties are widely and systematically denied." According to the most recent Freedom House survey, political and civil freedoms have expanded dramatically along with the spread of globalization and freer trade. In 1973, 35 percent of the world's population lived in countries that were "Free." Today that share has increased to 46 percent. In 1973, almost half of the people in the world, 47 percent, lived in countries that were "Not Free." Today that share has mercifully fallen to 36 percent. The share of people living in countries that are "Partly Free" is the same, 18 percent.

In other words, in the past three decades, more than one-tenth of humanity has escaped the darkest tyranny for the bright sunlight of civil and political freedom. That represents 700 million people who once suffered under the jack boot of oppression who now enjoy the same civil and political liberties that we all take for granted.

Next, I examined the relationship between economic openness in individual countries today and their record of human rights and democracy. To make this comparison, I combined the Freedom House ratings with the ratings for economic freedom contained in the Economic Freedom of the World Report. That study rates more than 120 countries according to the freedom to trade and invest internationally, to engage in business, access to sound money, property rights, and the size of government. The study is jointly sponsored by 50 think tanks around the world, including the Cato Institute, the Fraser Institute in Canada, and Norway's own Center for Business and Society Incorporated, or Civita. When we compare political and civil freedoms to economic freedom, we find that nations with open and free economies are far more likely to enjoy full political and civil liberties than those with closed and state-dominated economies. Of the 25 rated countries in the top quintile of economic openness, 21 are rated "Free" by Freedom House and only one is rated "Not Free." In contrast, among the quintile of countries that are the least open economically, only seven are rated "Free" and nine are rated "Not Free." In other words, the most economically open countries are three times more likely to enjoy full political and civil freedoms as those that are economically closed.

Those that are closed are nine times more likely to completely suppress civil and political freedoms as those that are open.

The percentage of countries rated as "Free" rises in each quintile as the freedom to exchange with foreigners rises, while the percentage rated as "Not Free" falls. In fact, 17 of the 20 countries rated as "Not Free" are found in the bottom two quintiles of economic openness, and only three in the top three quintiles. The percentage of nations rated as "Partly Free" also drops precipitously in the top two quintiles of economic openness.

A more formal statistical comparison shows a significant, positive correlation between economic freedom, including the freedom to engage in international commerce, and political and civil freedom. The statistical correlation remains strong even when controlling for a nation's per capita gross domestic product, consistent with the theory that economic openness reinforces political liberty directly and independently of its effect on growth and income levels. One unmistakable lesson from the cross-country data is that governments that grant their citizens a large measure of freedom to engage in international commerce find it dauntingly difficult to deprive them of political and civil liberties. A corollary lesson is that governments that "protect" their citizens behind tariff walls and other barriers to international commerce find it much easier to deny those same liberties.

Even when we look at reform within individual countries, we see a connection. A statistical analysis of those countries shows a significant and positive correlation between the expansion of the freedom to exchange with foreigners over the past three decades in individual countries and an expansion of political and civil freedoms in the same country during the same period. Countries that have most aggressively followed those twin tracks of reform—reflected in their improved scores during the past two decades in the indexes for freedom of exchange and combined political and civil freedom—include Chile, Ghana, Hungary, Mexico, Nicaragua, Paraguay, Portugal, and Tanzania. Twenty years ago, both South Korea and Taiwan were essentially one-party states without free elections or full civil liberties. Today, due in large measure to economic liberalization, trade reform, and the economic growth they spurred, both are thriving democracies where a large and well-educated middle class enjoys the full range of civil liberties. In both countries, opposition parties have gained political power against long-time ruling parties.

Our best hope for political reform countries that are "Not Free" will not come from confrontation and economic sanctions. In Cuba, for example, expanded trade with the United States would be a far more promising policy to bring an end to the Castro era than the failed, four-decades-old economic embargo. Based experience elsewhere, the U.S. government could more effectively promote political and civil freedom in Cuba by allowing more trade and travel than by maintaining the embargo. The folly of imposing trade sanctions in the name of promoting human rights abroad is that sanctions deprive people in the target countries of the technological tools and economic opportunities that nurture political freedom.

A More Democratic China?

In China, the link between trade and political reform offers the best hope for encouraging democracy and greater respect for human rights in the world's most populous nation. After two decades of reform and rapid growth, an expanding middle class is experiencing for the first time the independence of home ownership, travel abroad, and cooperation with others in economic enterprise free of government control. The number of telephone lines, mobile phones, and Internet users has risen exponentially in the past decade. Tens of thousands of Chinese students are studying abroad each year.

China's entry into the World Trade Organization in 2001 has only accelerated those trends.

So far, the people of mainland China have seen only marginal improvements in civil liberties and none in political liberties. But the people of China are undeniably less oppressed than they were during the tumult of the Cultural Revolution under Mao Tse-Tung. And China is reaching the stage of development where countries tend to shed oppressive forms of government for more benign and democratic systems. China's per capita GDP has reached about $7,600 per in terms of purchasing power parity. That puts China in the upper half of the world's countries and in an income neighborhood where more people live in political and civil freedom and fewer under tyranny. Among countries with lower per capita incomes than China, only 27 percent are free. Among those with higher incomes, 72 percent are free. Only 16 percent are not free, and almost all of those are wealthier than China not because of greater economic freedom but because of oil.

By multiple means of measurement, political and civil freedoms do correlate in the real world with expanding freedom to trade and transact across international borders. Nations that have opened their economies over time are indeed more likely to have opened themselves to political competition and greater freedom for citizens to speak, assemble, and worship freely. And around the globe, the broad expansion of international trade and investment has accompanied an equally broad expansion of democracy and the political and civil freedoms it is supposed to protect.

The Peace Dividend of Globalization

The good news does not stop there. Buried beneath the daily stories about suicide bombings and insurgency movements is an underappreciated but encouraging fact: The world has somehow become a more peaceful place.

A little-noticed headline on an Associated Press story a while back reported, "War declining worldwide, studies say." In 2006, a survey by the Stockholm International Peace Research Institute found that the number of armed conflicts around the world has been in decline for the past half-century. Since the early 1990s, ongoing conflicts have dropped from 33 to 17, with all of them now civil conflicts within countries. The Institute's latest report found that 2005 marked the second year in a row that no two nations were at war with one another. What a remarkable and wonderful fact.

The death toll from war has also been falling. According to the Associated Press report, "The number killed in battle has fallen to its lowest point in the post-World War II period, dipping below 20,000 a year by one measure. Peacemaking missions, meanwhile, are growing in number." Current estimates of people killed by war are down sharply from annual tolls ranging from 40,000 to 100,000 in the 1990s, and from a peak of 700,000 in 1951 during the Korean War.

Many causes lie behind the good news—the end of the Cold War and the spread of democracy, among them—but expanding trade and globalization appear to be playing a major role in promoting world peace. Far from stoking a "World on Fire," as one misguided American author argued in a forgettable book, growing commercial ties between nations have had a dampening effect on armed conflict and war. I would argue that free trade and globalization have promoted peace in three main ways.

First, as I argued a moment ago, trade and globalization have reinforced the trend toward democracy, and democracies tend not to pick fights with each other. Thanks in part to globalization, almost two thirds of the world's countries today are democracies—a record high. Some studies have cast doubt on the idea that democracies are less likely to fight wars. While it's true that democracies rarely if ever war with each other, it is not such a rare occurrence for democracies to engage in wars with non-democracies. We can still hope that has more countries turn to democracy, there will be fewer provocations for war by non-democracies.

A second and even more potent way that trade has promoted peace is by promoting more economic integration. As national economies become more intertwined with each other, those nations have more to lose should war break out. War in a globalized world not only means human casualties and bigger government, but also ruptured trade and investment ties that impose lasting damage on the economy. In short, globalization has dramatically raised the economic cost of war.

The 2005 Economic Freedom of the World Report contains an insightful chapter on "Economic Freedom and Peace" by Dr. Erik Gartzke, a professor of political science at Columbia University. Dr. Gartzke compares the propensity of countries to engage in wars and their level of economic freedom and concludes that economic freedom, including the freedom to trade, significantly decreases the probability that a country will experience a military dispute with another country. Through econometric analysis, he found that, "Making economies freer translates into making countries more peaceful. At the extremes, the least free states are about 14 times as conflict prone as the most free."

By the way, Dr. Gartzke's analysis found that economic freedom was a far more important variable in determining a countries propensity to go to war than democracy.

A third reason why free trade promotes peace is because it allows nations to acquire wealth through production and exchange rather than conquest of territory and resources. As economies develop, wealth is increasingly measured in terms of intellectual property, financial assets, and human capital. Such assets cannot be easily seized by armies. In contrast, hard assets such as minerals and farmland are becoming relatively less important in a high-tech, service economy. If people need resources outside their national borders, say oil or timber or farm products, they can acquire them peacefully by trading away what they can produce best at home. In short, globalization and the development it has spurred have rendered the spoils of war less valuableOf course, free trade and globalization do not guarantee peace. Hot-blooded nationalism and ideological fervor can overwhelm cold economic calculations. Any relationship involving human beings will be messy and non-linier. There will always be exceptions and outliers in such complex relationships involving economies and governments. But deep trade and investment ties among nations make war less attractive.

A Virtuous Cycle of Democracy, Peace and Trade

The global trends we've witnessed in the spread of trade, democracy and peace tend to reinforce each other in a grand and virtuous cycle. As trade and development encourage more representative government, those governments provide more predictability and incremental reform, creating a better climate for trade and investment to flourish. And as the spread of trade and democracy foster peace, the decline of war creates a more hospitable environment for trade and economic growth and political stability.

We can see this virtuous cycle at work in the world today. The European Union just celebrated its 50th birthday. For many of the same non-economic reasons that motivated the founders of the GATT, the original members of the European community hoped to build a more sturdy foundation for peace. Out of the ashes of World War II, the United States urged Germany, France and other Western European nations to form a common market that has become the European Union. In large part because of their intertwined economies, a general war in Europe is now unthinkable.

In East Asia, the extensive and growing economic ties among Mainland China, Japan, South

Korea, and Taiwan is helping to keep the peace. China's communist rulers may yet decide to go to war over its "renegade province," but the economic cost to their economy would be staggering and could provoke a backlash among its citizens. In contrast, poor and isolated North Korea is all the more dangerous because it has nothing to lose economically should it provoke a war.

In Central America, countries that were racked by guerrilla wars and death squads two decades ago have turned not only to democracy but to expanding trade, culminating in the Central American Free Trade Agreement with the United States. As the Stockholm Institute reported in its 2005 Yearbook, "Since the 1980s, the introduction of a more open economic model in most states of the Latin American and Caribbean region has been accompanied by the growth of new regional structures, the dying out of interstate conflicts and a reduction in intra-state conflicts."

Much of the political violence that remains in the world today is concentrated in the Middle East and Sub-Saharan Africa—the two regions of the world that are the least integrated into the global economy. Efforts to bring peace to those regions must include lowering their high barriers to trade, foreign investment, and entrepreneurship.

Finally, those of us who live in countries that have benefited the most from free trade and globalization should rededicate ourselves to expending and institutionalizing the freedom to trade.

On a multilateral level, a successful agreement through the World Trade Organization would create a more friendly climate globally for democracy, human rights and peace. Less developed countries, by opening up their own, relatively closed markets, and gaining greater access to rich-country markets, could achieve higher rates of growth and develop the expanding middle class that forms the backbone of most democracies. A successful conclusion of the Doha Development Round that began in 2001 would reinforce the twin trends of globalization and the spread of political and civil liberties that have marked the last 30 years, and with it the further decline of war as an instrument of foreign policies. To set a good example, the United States, the European Union, Norway and other OECD countries should scrap their farm subsidies and all remaining trade barriers and urge other WTO Members to respond in kind. Failure of the round would delay and frustrate progress and peace for millions of people.

Advocates of free trade and globalization . . . have long argued that trade expansion means more efficiency, higher incomes, and reduced poverty. The welcome spread of representative government and decline of armed conflicts in the past few decades remind us that free trade also comes with its own peace dividend.

... ...

III. THE ECONOMICS OF TRADE

In this section, we discuss a number of economics issues that are central to an understanding of the legal aspects of international trade agreements. Our treatment of these issues is much briefer than that in an economics textbook. Here, we are simply introducing some concepts and ideas that help provide a framework for the trade regime and the current policy debate over trade.

We begin with a discussion of 'comparative advantage', which provides a crucial economic foundation for the idea that trade makes countries better off than self-sufficiency and, in addition, that trade can benefit all countries, even those which are not the most efficient producers. We then turn to several critiques that have been offered of free trade policies. These alternative views do not necessarily disavow the idea of comparative advantage, but rather offer reasons why complete and open trade may not be the right policy in all situations. In this regard, we discuss the following:

• How the harms caused to some from free trade should be weighed against the benefits to others.
• Whether trade between countries at different income levels leads to problems.
• Whether economic development in poor countries is a special situation, for which the traditional free trade rules do not apply.
• Whether broader exceptions from free trade for 'industrial policy', 'strategic trade policy' and similar justifications for protection.

Finally, we talk briefly about whether economics tells us anything about the various 'new' issues in trade agreements, beyond the traditional free trader versus protection debate.

(a) Comparative Advantage

One of the fundamental economic justifications offered by supporters of free trade is the theory of 'comparative advantage', developed by David Ricardo in 1817. In this section, we examine this theory, along with the related concept of 'absolute advantage'. We look at both concepts using a simple example of two countries (England and Portugal), two products (cloth and labour) and one factor of production (labour).[25] The purpose of this section is to demonstrate how comparative advantage supports the notion that trade can increase economic well-being even where one country makes all products more efficiently than its trading partners.

The example is as follows. Assume that England and Portugal produce only cloth and wine and there is no trade between them at the outset (a condition referred to as 'autarky'). Each produces its own wine and cloth, and consumes all of its production domestically. Both countries have 1,000 units of labour to divide between the two products.

Productivity varies as between the countries. In England, for cloth production, assume that 1 unit of labour can produce 3 units of cloth; and for wine production, assume that 1 unit of labour can produce 6 units of wine; in Portugal, for cloth production, assume that 1 unit of labour can produce 1 units of cloth; and for wine production, assume 1 unit of labour can produce 3 units of wine. Without any trade between the two, the production and consumption are as follows. If England divides its labour between the two products so as to get roughly equal amounts to consume, it could end up with 2,100 units of cloth (700 × 3) and 1,800 units of wine (300 × 6) to consume; and if Portugal divides its labour with the same goal in mind, it will end up with 700 units of cloth (700 × 1) and 900 units of wine (300 × 3) to consume.

Now imagine that trade opens up between the two (eg a war between them ends). England has an 'absolute advantage' in both products, as its labour is more efficient at producing each one. If absolute advantage were all that is relevant, there would be no reason for England to trade. It would only make sense for countries to trade when one

---

[25] Our example is loosely based on Ricardo's original explanation of the issue.

country was more efficient at producing one product and the other country was more efficient at producing the other product.

However, comparative advantage illustrates how being *relatively* better at producing a particular product is the key, and that it will almost always be the case that a country has something it is relatively better at (except in the rare circumstance where relative productivity is exactly equal). Thus, trade almost always makes countries better off, and England would benefit from trade with Portugal. Here, even though England is absolutely better at making both products, it is relatively better at producing cloth, in the following sense: it is three times as good at Portugal at producing cloth, but only two times as good at producing wine. Thus, taking into account both products it makes, it is relatively better at making cloth.

As a result of these differences in relative productivity, England can benefit from trade by specialising in cloth production, and then trading with Portugal, who will specialize in wine. To illustrate this, with specialisation, England can use all 1,000 units of labour to make cloth, thus making 3,000 units of cloth; and Portugal can use all 1,000 units of labour to make wine, thus making 3,000 units of wine. As a result, total production of both products is now higher. Prior to specialisation, the total production of cloth was 2,800 units and wine was 2,700 units. Now it is 3,000 of each. If the two countries trade with each other, they can find a rate of exchange which will make both better off. If England were to trade 800 units of its cloth for 1,900 units of Portugal's wine, England would have 2,200 units of cloth and 1,900 units of wine and Portugal would have 800 units of cloth and 1,100 units of wine. Thus, both would have improved their situation for both products in relation to the autarky amounts.

In summary, this example is as follows:

—English productivity: 1L = 3C, 1L = 6W
—Portugal productivity: 1L = 1C, 1L = 3W

(England is twice as good as Portugal at producing wine, but three times as good at producing cloth.)

Pre-Trade (Autarky) Situation

England	**Portugal**
Cloth: 700 × 3 = 2,100	Cloth: 700 × 1 =700
Wine: 300 × 6 = 1,800	Wine: 300 × 3 = 900

Total production prior to specialisation: 2,800 cloth and 2,700 wine

With specialisation, England will produce 3,000 units of cloth and Portugal will produce 3,000 units of wine. Thus, the total output of both products has increased. With trade (800 units of English cloth for 1,900 units of Portuguese wine), both can be made better off:

Post-Trade Situation

England	**Portugal**
Cloth: 2,200	Cloth: 800
Wine: 1,900	Wine: 1,100

Thus, the argument for free trade is that if trade barriers are removed, comparative advantage allows countries to trade their way to increased economic well-being.

To make this concept a little clearer, think about the issue outside the context of international trade. In your personal life, you often have the choice to do things yourself or to pay someone else to do them for you. For example, you could do your own ironing or have the dry cleaner do it. Or you could grow your own food or buy it at the supermarket. You may be better at some of these things than the people you pay to do them. Nevertheless, it makes more sense for you to spend your time on other things, such as your law practice. Most likely, you are only slightly better than they are at ironing or growing food, but you are a lot better at legal work. In essence, this is the same specialisation we saw in the context of international trade. Specialisation takes place in the same way across nations. In a sense, comparative advantage is simply the application of the specialisation principle to the situation where the actors are in different nations.

Moving beyond the simple two-country, two-product model makes things a bit more complicated. When one looks at the actual state of production and trade around the world, it is not immediately obvious that specialisation is occurring exactly as the theory suggests. Take the example of automobile production. Production takes place in many countries, and these countries tend to both export and import the products.

However, while the practice is a good deal messier than the theory, three things must be borne in mind. First, there are a number of distortions in the present system, as governments have intervened in the market in ways that put production in places it might not otherwise exist. (Reasons they might do so are to boost domestic wages and employment or because they are following 'strategic trade' theories or infant industry protection, concepts which are discussed below.) Secondly, keeping with the example of automobiles, not all cars are alike. Because of differences in consumer taste, it may be that there are a wide variety of models produced in various places around the world. As a result, the theory holds up better than it appears to at first glance, as the specialisation may be in a type of car rather than in cars as a whole. Finally, despite the recent trend in 'globalisation', the world is still a very large place. Thus, it may make sense to have a number of regional production centres, rather than one country that makes all automobiles.

An additional economic concept that plays a role here is 'economies of scale'. As the size of an enterprise increases, its average cost per unit falls, as the fixed costs are spread out over more products. Economies of scale can make the benefits of specialisation even greater. As countries specialise, the scale of production increases and the production of specific products becomes more concentrated. Thus, the key economic lesson to take from the comparative advantage discussion is that specialisation combined with economies of scale means that economic welfare, measured in a society as a whole, can be improved through trade. For this reason, comparative advantage provides a powerful basis for the view that free trade is good.

The basic theory of comparative advantage is not very controversial. Even some trade critics have acknowledged its importance, although they do not subscribe to it without reservations.[26] However, while comparative advantage is important, it is not the only consideration when evaluating free trade. There are a number of critiques that acknowledge the point, but take the view that other factors need to be accounted for as well. Several of these are discussed in the subsections that follow.

---

[26] I Fletcher, 'Free Trade Doesn't Work' (US Business & Industry Council, Washington, DC, 2010) 96–123.

(b) Weighing the Harms to Some against the Benefits to Others

The theory of comparative advantage explains at a very general level how nations can be better off with trade than under autarky. However, when you look at the individuals who make up a society, the picture gets more complicated.

Applying traditional economics models to free trade, economists conclude that the benefits to consumers in terms of lower-cost, higher-quality products outweigh the harms to workers who lose their jobs as a result of foreign competition (in the Ricardian example, the cloth producers in Portugal and wine producers in England lose their jobs).[27] But while welfare gains exist when looking at the economy as a whole, this does not change the fact that some people face significant harms from opening up to trade. Tariffs and other barriers 'protect' jobs, and removing them leads to job losses. In addition, these harms are concentrated in a relatively small number of people, whereas the benefits of trade are diffuse, as each person receives a very small benefit (they may not even be aware of it). Moreover, the harms are very noticeable and make the news headlines. For example, when a US factory shuts down in order to move production to Mexico (taking advantage of the zero tariffs that apply due to NAFTA), there are usually loud protests from the affected workers and their supporters. By contrast, a 5 per cent drop in the price of kids' toys makes less of an impact. These factors make the politics of trade very difficult, as those harmed are more likely to organise to make their views known.

Given all this, are there policies that can be used to improve the situation? One typical policy response is that the winners from trade can compensate the losers. In practical terms, this could mean using tax revenues to fund programmes to help those whose jobs were lost to trade, for example through education grants or retraining programmes. However, these programmes have been criticised by those who argue that there are lots of reasons people lose their jobs, so why should trade be a special case? Many people lose their jobs through changes in technology. Do they deserve the same programmes? Furthermore, if the jobs only existed in the first place due to government actions to close the market, perhaps it is consumers who deserve to be compensated for the many years of paying more than they should have.

Generally speaking, most governments recognise the concerns about workers losing jobs due to trade and have programmes of the sort mentioned, although some countries' programmes are more extensive than others. One of the key features of the trade debate in the US is how much 'adjustment assistance' to give those who have suffered job losses due to trade.

(c) Trade between Countries at Different Income Levels

In addition to the general concerns about lost jobs due to trade, there is an additional problem that arises where the trade is between countries at different levels of development. Both sides—that is, the richer countries and the poorer countries—have expressed specific concerns in this regard.

For the richer countries, one concern is that weaker labour and environmental protection in the poorer countries, along with lower wages, give those countries an advantage,

---

[27] S Suranovic, 'International Trade Theory and Policy', available at http://catalog.flatworldknowledge.com/bookhub/reader/28?cid=&e=fwk-61960-ch04#web-199668 (accessed on 17 April 2012)

by lowering their costs. Thus, they contend, companies in rich countries have trouble competing with the lower-cost competitors in poor countries. This issue takes on a very high profile when corporations from rich countries move production to a developing country. There is also a fear that the different income levels will have a direct impact on wages in the richer country, by putting downward pressure on wages. In rich countries, trade that takes place in such situations is sometimes labelled 'unfair', and the low-priced imports that result are sometimes referred to as 'social dumping' (the concept of dumping is more complex, and is discussed in Chapter 11).

On the other side, the poorer countries are concerned about the greater resources and efficiency of the rich country producers. In terms of resources, one concern is the large subsidies that many rich countries give to certain industries, such as agriculture. Even if they wanted to do the same thing, the poor countries could not afford such subsidies, and the resulting situation seems to be an unfair advantage to the producers in rich countries. With regard to efficiency, taking agriculture as an example again, poor countries are worried that their small farms will have trouble competing against the huge, mechanised agri-business companies in rich countries.

In recent years, some bilateral and regional trade agreements have taken some of these concerns into account. In this regard, certain rich countries, such as the US and the EU, have demanded that enforceable provisions on labour and environmental protection be included in their trade agreements. The goal is to limit any possible advantages the poor country may gain from their weaker protections. With regard to poor country concerns, such as subsidies, less progress has been made.

(d) Free Trade and Development

Free trade has been particularly controversial in the context of how countries develop, that is, go from being poor to rich (generally speaking, through industrialisation). It is safe to say that most people would like to see this happen throughout the developing world. However, there is much disagreement as to how to bring it about.

On the one side, free traders argue that it is the openness to trade that has been the key to economic development in the past, whereas protection has left many poor countries with inefficient industries and low economic growth. On the other side, critics of this view contend that all of today's developed countries used protection to give their companies time to catch up to those who were more advanced (and they furthermore contend that today's developed countries are acting badly by trying to take away from poor countries the tools they themselves used to develop). Comparative advantage is a fine theory, they say, but a country's comparative advantage is not always something that it is born with (although in some cases, such as proximity to natural resources, it is). Rather, some kinds of comparative advantage can be created. For example, efficient production techniques can be learned through practice. This practice can only occur if protection gives producers time. In essence, the view is that protection can give 'infant industries' time to learn how to operate efficiently, to catch up to their established competitors. While there is a short-term loss to domestic consumers, who have to put up with shoddy, expensive products for a while, once these companies get up to speed, workers and consumers are both better off. As noted, inherent in this thinking is that comparative advantage is malleable. It is not set in stone. Thus, while a country may not be the relatively best steel producer at the moment, it could be if given time to learn.

The facts of this debate are complex and messy, and we will not go through them all here. It is probably correct to say that all of today's developed countries used protection, to some extent, during their development period. However, showing cause and effect is difficult. Was protection a help or a hindrance to the development process? People on different sides of the issue look at specific examples, such as South Korea and Taiwan, and come to very different conclusions about how development is achieved. And while there are success stories of developed countries which used protection, there are also many examples of countries which used protection but have not progressed very far.

It is worth noting a couple of additional factors. First, the situation today is very different from when early industrialisers, such as the US and Germany, were in their development periods, and even different from the development periods of recently developed countries such as South Korea. Back then, if you wanted your country to have, say, a steel industry, you had only one option: create your own. Now, by contrast, capital flows much more freely across borders, so instead of keeping out all foreign products for a while to let domestic companies learn how to make steel efficiently, a country can now seek out foreign companies to set up shop there.

Secondly, complicating the issue further is that there is little doubt that factors such as education and culture play an important role. As a result, it is difficult to say with great certainty the extent to which protection contributes to development.

Finally, there are serious questions about whether governments are good at figuring out which industries should be protected. And even if they could figure it out, there are additional questions as to whether governments are competent or honest enough to pick the appropriate ones, rather than just favouring well-connected companies (and along the same lines, whether they will remove protection when it is no longer appropriate, or just continue it indefinitely for companies that have now developed a close relationship with the government).

(e) Industrial Policy

Some economists take the idea that governments can bend comparative advantage to develop successful industries even further, applying it beyond the development context. They put forward a number of arguments as to how 'industrial policy' (which can take the form of trade barriers, such as tariffs, quotas, subsidies or other measures) can make a country better off. As one example, they argue that 'strategic trade policy' can be used to make a country the leader in industries that are particularly desirable, due to high wages or other factors. The goal is to provide the most effective support for the country's domestic industry, so that it is left as one of the few (or only) competitors.

This idea can be applied to many industries, but it is perhaps most clear in an industry where it is uncertain whether more than one company can be profitable. An industry that requires high capitalisation, like the aircraft industry, provides a good example. The economies of scale involved mean that it is only feasible to have a small number of companies competing—perhaps only one. A standard game theory model looks at whether government subsidies to the aircraft industry can help a domestic competitor. The two main players here are Airbus (from the EU) and Boeing (from the US). Is it possible for the US or the EU to provide subsidies to their producer, giving them an advantage which allows them to be the sole producer? In principle, the game theory models show that this can be done. In practice, though, both governments have provided billions of dollars worth of subsidies over several decades, and the subsidies provided have recently been litigated over at the WTO (see Chapter 10). Both companies are doing fairly well in terms of profitability. However, it is not clear what the industry would have looked like without all the subsidies, or whether the subsidies have had a positive impact for either side.

More generally, one critique of the idea of strategic trade policy is that the hope is to 'win' the competition with other countries; but not everyone can win. Presumably the idea is that 'we' can play the game better than 'they' do, and thus reap huge benefits. However, it is not clear that 'we' will win, and if all countries play hard, it may be that everyone loses. As in the aircraft example, if all countries subsidise, the companies may split the market, costing the taxpayers without any clear benefit. Thus, the 'winners' may end up in a perpetual subsidy race. Furthermore, the competitive mood created by subsidies in one industry can spread to other industries, leading to a spiralling of trade protection.

There are three points of criticism to note here, two of which were alluded to in the developing country section above: first, it may be that there are better ways to 'win' this competition, ones that do not involve all the possible pitfalls of protection. For example, companies looking to produce high-tech products need highly educated workers. It is possible that one of the most effective ways to attract such production is to create a top-notch education system, from early childhood through specialised graduate programmes. Secondly, it can be very hard to identify the good industries. For example, there is a lot of talk these days about clean energy technology. But should we support solar power, wind power, nuclear, clean coal or something else? Similarly, should a country seek big, dirty manufacturing industries, or would it be better to have architects and software developers? It is easy to choose wrongly in these matters, and doing so could cost the taxpayers quite a lot of money. Finally, with the globalisation of much industry, favouring 'domestic' companies becomes more difficult (both Boeing and Airbus themselves work with a number of foreign partners).

(f) Conclusions on the Free Trade versus Protection Debate

Taking all of these arguments into account, what is the right answer in the free trade versus protection debate? Comparative advantage provides a strong argument for how trade can make people better off. However, by itself, it probably should not lead to the conclusion that all tariffs (and other trade barriers) should be removed. There are other factors to consider, and different countries may have different views on how to weigh and balance these factors. The free trade versus protection debate has been around for a long time, and is likely to continue into the foreseeable future. In some ways, it seems that free trade has won, as there are numerous international agreements designed to reduce tariffs and other barriers. At the same time, many tariffs and barriers remain, and trade-distorting measures, such as subsidies, seem to be growing in number and amount (and others, such as anti-dumping laws, are firmly embedded in the system). The answer of most economists is that free trade is the better policy, but this general statement leaves many important sub-issues in the trade debate—eg economic development, the role of subsidies—unanswered.

(g) The Economics of the 'New' Issues

Most economics and international trade law textbooks cover some or all of the topics above, but then stop. Their focus is on 'free trade' mainly in the sense of lowering tariffs and quotas, and related issues; they do not have much to say about the various issues that have become part of the trade regime starting in the early 1990s. For example, intellectual property rights protection is now firmly entrenched as part of international trade rules. But what is the economics of this area? The WTO's TRIPS Agreement includes a 20-year minimum patent term for patent protection. Does this obligation properly balance the desire to give producers an incentive to innovate against the cost to consumers of a 20-year monopoly? Similarly, certain food safety measures must, under trade rules, be based on sound science. Do the rules in this area give governments the right degree of flexibility in regulating where a product is new and the risks are hard to assess? The traditional economics of trade have not yet been updated to take into account these issues.

IV. FREE TRADE VS PROTECTIONISM

While Section III above introduces the economics (and economic complexities) of trade in some detail, it is useful here to further provide context to the topic. In the following extract, one of the twentieth century's most notable and recognisable economists, Milton Friedman, briefly comments on why economists almost universally regard 'free trade' as one of the necessary conditions for growth and development. In the extract, Friedman introduces arguments for free trade and directly engages with and counters several arguments for protectionism.

M Friedman, 'The Case for Free Trade' [1997] *Hoover Digest* No 4.

It is often said that bad economic policy reflects disagreement among the experts; that if all economists gave the same advice, economic policy would be good. Economists often do disagree, but that has not been true with respect to international trade. Ever since Adam Smith there has been virtual unanimity among economists, whatever their ideological position on other issues, that international free trade is in the best interests of trading countries and of the world. Yet tariffs have been the rule. The only major exceptions are nearly a century of free trade in Great Britain after the repeal of the Corn Laws in 1846, thirty years of free trade in Japan after the Meiji Restoration, and free trade in Hong Kong under British rule. The United States had tariffs throughout the nineteenth century, and they were raised still higher in the twentieth century, especially by the Smoot-Hawley tariff bill of 1930, which some scholars regard as partly responsible for the severity of the subsequent depression. Tariffs have since been reduced by repeated international agreements, but they remain high, probably higher than in the nineteenth century, though the vast changes in the kinds of items entering international trade make a precise comparison impossible.

Today, as always, there is much support for tariffs—euphemistically labeled "protection" a good label for a bad cause. Producers of steel and steelworkers' unions press for restrictions on steel imports from Japan. Producers of TV sets and their workers lobby for "voluntary agreements" to limit imports of TV sets or components from Japan, Taiwan, or Hong Kong. Producers of textiles, shoes, cattle, sugar–they and myriad others complain about "unfair" competition from abroad and demand that government do something to "protect" them. Of course, no group makes its claims on the basis of naked self-interest. Every group speaks of the "general interest," of the need to preserve jobs or to promote national security. The need to strengthen the dollar vis-à-vis the deutsche mark or the yen has more recently joined the traditional rationalizations for restrictions on imports.

One voice that is hardly ever raised is the consumer's. That voice is drowned out in the cacophony of the "interested sophistry of merchants and manufacturers" and their employees. The result is a serious distortion of the issue. For example, the supporters of tariffs treat it as self evident that the creation of jobs is a desirable end, in and of itself, regardless of what the persons employed do. That is clearly wrong. If all we want are jobs, we can create any number— for example, have people dig holes and then fill them up again or perform other useless tasks. Work is sometimes its own reward. Mostly, however, it is the price we pay to get the things we want. Our real objective is not just jobs but productive jobs—jobs that will mean more goods and services to consume.

Another fallacy seldom contradicted is that exports are good, imports bad. The truth is very different. We cannot eat, wear, or enjoy the goods we send abroad. We eat bananas from Central America, wear Italian shoes, drive German automobiles, and enjoy programs we see on our Japanese TV sets. Our gain from foreign trade is what we import. Exports are the price we pay to get imports. As Adam Smith saw so clearly, the citizens of a nation benefit from getting as large a volume of imports as possible in return for its exports or, equivalently, from exporting as little as possible to pay for its imports.

The misleading terminology we use reflects these erroneous ideas. "Protection" really means exploiting the consumer. A "favorable balance of trade" really means exporting more than we import, sending abroad goods of greater total value than the goods we get from abroad. In your private household, you would surely prefer to pay less for more rather than the other way around, yet that would be termed an "unfavorable balance of payments" in foreign trade.

The argument in favor of tariffs that has the greatest emotional appeal to the public at large is the alleged need to protect the high standard of living of American workers from the "unfair" competition of workers in Japan or Korea or Hong Kong who are willing to work for a much lower wage. What is wrong with this argument? Don't we want to protect the high standard of living of our people?

The fallacy in this argument is the loose use of the terms "high" wage and "low" wage. What do high and low wages mean? American workers are paid in dollars; Japanese workers are paid in yen. How do we compare wages in dollars with wages in yen? How many yen equal a dollar? What determines the exchange rate?

Consider an extreme case. Suppose that, to begin with, 360 yen equal a dollar. At this exchange rate, the actual rate of exchange for many years, suppose that the Japanese can produce and sell everything for fewer dollars than we can in the United States–TV sets, automobiles, steel, and even soybeans, wheat, milk, and ice cream. If we had free international trade, we would try to buy all our goods from Japan. This would seem to be the extreme horror story of the kind depicted by the defenders of tariffs–we would be flooded with Japanese goods and could sell them nothing.

Before throwing up your hands in horror, carry the analysis one step further. How would we pay the Japanese? We would offer them dollar bills. What would they do with the dollar bills? We have assumed that at 360 yen to the dollar everything is cheaper in Japan, so there is nothing in the U.S. market that they would want to buy. If the Japanese exporters were willing to burn or bury the dollar bills, that would be wonderful for us. We would get all kinds of goods for green pieces of paper that we can produce in great abundance and very cheaply. We would have the most marvelous export industry conceivable.

Of course, the Japanese would not in fact sell us useful goods in order to get useless pieces of paper to bury or burn. Like us, they want to get something real in return for their work. If all goods were cheaper in Japan than in the United States at 360 yen to the dollar, the exporters would try to get rid of their dollars, would try to sell them for 360 yen to the dollar in order to buy the cheaper Japanese goods. But who would be willing to buy the dollars? What is true for the Japanese exporter is true for everyone in Japan. No one will be willing to give 360 yen in exchange for one dollar if 360 yen will buy more of everything in Japan than one dollar will buy in the United States. The exporters, on discovering that no one will buy their dollars at 360 yen, will offer to take fewer yen for a dollar. The price of the dollar in terms of the yen will go down–to 300 yen for a dollar or 250 yen or 200 yen. Put the other way around, it will take more and more dollars to buy a given number of Japanese yen. Japanese goods are priced in yen, so their price in dollars will go up. Conversely, U.S. goods are priced in dollars, so the more dollars the Japanese get for a given number of yen, the cheaper U.S. goods become to the Japanese in terms of yen.

The price of the dollar in terms of yen would fall, until, on the average, the dollar value of goods that the Japanese buy from the United States roughly equalled the dollar value of goods that the United States buys from Japan. At that price everybody who wanted to buy yen for dollars would find someone who was willing to sell him yen for dollars.

The actual situation is, of course, more complicated than this hypothetical example. Many nations, and not merely the United States and Japan, are engaged in trade, and the trade often takes roundabout directions. The Japanese may spend some of the dollars they earn in Brazil, the Brazilians in turn may spend those dollars in Germany, the Germans in the United States, and so on in endless complexity. However, the principle is the same. People, in whatever country, want dollars primarily to buy useful items, not to hoard, and there can be no balance of payments problem so long as the price of the dollar in terms of the yen or the deutsche mark or the franc is determined in a free market by voluntary transactions.

Why then all the furor about the "weakness" of the dollar? Why the repeated foreign exchange crises? The proximate reason is because foreign exchange rates have not been determined in a free market. Government central banks have intervened on a grand scale in order to influence the price of their currencies. In the process they have lost vast sums of their citizens' money (for the United States, close to two billion dollars from 1973 to early 1979). Even more important, they have prevented this important set of prices from performing its proper function. They have not been able to prevent the basic underlying economic forces from ultimately having their effect on exchange rates but have been able to maintain artificial exchange rates for substantial intervals. The effect has been to prevent gradual adjustment to the underlying forces. Small disturbances have accumulated into large ones, and ultimately there has been a major foreign exchange "crisis."

In all the voluminous literature of the past several centuries on free trade and protectionism, only three arguments have ever been advanced in favor of tariffs that even in principle may have some validity.

First is the national security argument–the argument that a thriving domestic steel industry, for example, is needed for defense. Although that argument is more often a rationalization for particular tariffs than a valid reason for them, it cannot be denied that on occasion it might justify the maintenance of otherwise uneconomical productive facilities. To go beyond this statement of possibility and establish in a specific case that a tariff or other trade restriction is justified in order to promote national security, it would be necessary to compare the cost of achieving the specific security objective in alternative ways and establish at least a prima facie case that a tariff is the least costly way. Such cost comparisons are seldom made in practice.

The second is the "infant industry" argument advanced, for example, by Alexander Hamilton in his Report on Manufactures. There is, it is said, a potential industry that, if once established and assisted during its growing pains, could compete on equal terms in the world market. A temporary tariff is said to be justified in order to shelter the potential industry in its infancy and enable it to grow to maturity, when it can stand on its own feet. Even if the industry could compete successfully once established, that does not of itself justify an initial tariff. It is worthwhile for consumers to subsidize the industry initially–which is what they in effect do by levying a tariff–only if they will subsequently get back at least that subsidy in some other way, through prices lower than the world price or through some other advantages of having the industry. But in that case is a subsidy needed? Will it then not pay the original entrants into the industry to suffer initial losses in the expectation of being able to recoup them later? After all, most firms experience losses in their early years, when they are getting established. That is true if they enter a new industry or if they enter an existing one. Perhaps there may be some special reason why the original entrants cannot recoup their initial losses even though it may be worthwhile for the community at large to make the initial investment. But surely the presumption is the other way.

The infant industry argument is a smoke screen. The so-called infants never grow up. Once imposed, tariffs are seldom eliminated. Moreover, the argument is seldom used on behalf of true unborn infants that might conceivably be born and survive if given temporary protection; they have no spokesmen. It is used to justify tariffs for rather aged infants that can mount political pressure.

The third argument for tariffs that cannot be dismissed out of hand is the "beggar-thy-neighbor" argument. A country that is a major producer of a product, or that can join with a small number of other producers that together control a major share of production, may be able to take advantage of its monopoly position by raising the price of the product (the Organization of Petroleum Exporting Countries cartel is the obvious example). Instead of raising the price directly, the country can do so indirectly by imposing an export tax on the product–an export tariff. The benefit to itself will be less than the cost to others, but from the national point of view, there can be a gain. Similarly, a country that is the primary purchaser of a product–in economic jargon, has monopsony power–may be able to benefit by driving a hard bargain with the sellers and imposing an unduly low price on them. One way to do so is to impose a tariff on the import of the product. The net return to the seller is the price less the tariff, which is why this can be equivalent to buying at a lower price. In effect, the tariff is paid by the foreigners (we can think of no actual example). In practice this nationalistic approach is highly likely to promote retaliation by other countries. In addition, as for the infant industry argument, the actual political pressures tend to produce tariff structures that do not in fact take advantage of any monopoly or monopsony positions.

A fourth argument, one that was made by Alexander Hamilton and continues to be repeated down to the present, is that free trade would be fine if all other countries practiced free trade but that, so long as they do not, the United States cannot afford to. This argument has no validity whatsoever, either in principle or in practice. Other countries that impose restrictions on international trade do hurt us. But they also hurt themselves. Aside from the three cases just considered, if we impose restrictions in turn, we simply add to the harm to ourselves and also harm them as well. Competition in masochism and sadism is hardly a prescription for sensible international economic policy! Far from leading to a reduction in restrictions by other countries, this kind of retaliatory action simply leads to further restrictions.

We are a great nation, the leader of the world. It ill behooves us to require Hong Kong and Taiwan to impose export quotas on textiles to "protect" our textile industry at the expense of U.S. consumers and of Chinese workers in Hong Kong and Taiwan. We speak glowingly of the virtues of free trade, while we use our political and economic power to induce Japan to restrict exports of steel and TV sets. We should move unilaterally to free trade, not instantaneously but over a period of, say, five years, at a pace announced in advance.

Few measures that we could take would do more to promote the cause of freedom at home and abroad than complete free trade. Instead of making grants to foreign governments in the name of economic aid–thereby promoting socialism–while at the same time imposing restrictions on the products they produce–thereby hindering free enterprise–we could assume a consistent and principled stance. We could say to the rest of the world: We believe in freedom and intend to practice it. We cannot force you to be free. But we can offer full cooperation on equal terms to all. Our market is open to you without tariffs or other restrictions. Sell here what you can and wish to. Buy whatever you can and wish to. In that way cooperation among individuals can be worldwide and free.

… … …

It is clear that economists think of trade in terms of overall economic welfare. However, as discussed above in Section III, while the 'whole' may indeed benefit from trade, those that have been left behind have sometimes been given scant attention. In recent times, some commentators have begun to think of trade in different terms, giving greater weight to the negatives of trade. The following extract by Harvard economist Dani Rodrik tends to agree and picks up upon the point that the rules regulating international trade can be improved to benefit even more people. More specifically, Rodrik argues that while globalisation has the potential to help the poor, the current set of rules regulating international trade do not.

D Rodrik, 'Globalization for Whom? Time to Change the Rules—and Focus on Poor Workers' (2002) 104(6) *Harvard Magazine* 29–31.

Globalization has brought little but good news to those with the products, skills, and resources to market worldwide. But does it also work for the world's poor?

That is the central question around which the debate over globalization—in essence, free trade and free flows of capital—revolves. Antiglobalization protesters may have had only limited success in blocking world trade negotiations or disrupting the meetings of the International Monetary Fund (IMF), but they have irrevocably altered the terms of the debate. Poverty is now *the* defining issue for both sides. The captains of the world economy have conceded that progress in international trade and finance has to be measured against the yardsticks of poverty alleviation and sustainable development.

For most of the world's developing countries, the 1990s were a decade of frustration and disappointment. The economies of sub-Saharan Africa, with few exceptions, stubbornly refused to respond to the medicine meted out by the World Bank and the IMF. Latin American countries were buffeted by a never-ending series of boom-and-bust cycles in capital markets and experienced growth rates significantly below their historical averages. Most of the former socialist economies ended the decade at *lower* levels of per-capita income than they started it—and even in the rare successes, such as Poland, poverty rates remained higher than under communism. East Asian economies such as South Korea, Thailand, and Malaysia, which had been hailed previously as "miracles," were dealt a humiliating blow in the financial crisis of 1997. That this was also the decade in which globalization came into full swing is more than a minor inconvenience for its advocates. If globalization is such a boon for poor countries, why so many setbacks?

Globalizers deploy two counter-arguments against such complaints. One is that global poverty has actually decreased. The reason is simple: while *most* countries have seen lower income growth, the world's two largest countries, China and India, have had the opposite experience. (Economic growth tends to be highly correlated with poverty reduction.) China's growth since the late 1970s—averaging almost 8 percent per annum per capita—has been nothing short of spectacular. India's performance has not been as extraordinary, but the country's growth rate has more than doubled since the early 1980s—from 1.5 percent per capita to 3.7 percent. These two countries house more than half of the world's poor, and their experience is perhaps enough to dispel the collective doom elsewhere.

The second counter-argument is that it is precisely those countries that have experienced the greatest integration with the world economy that have managed to grow fastest and reduce poverty the most. A typical exercise in this vein consists of dividing developing countries into two groups on the basis of the increase in their trade—"globalizers" versus "non-globalizers"— and to show that the first group did much better than the second. Here too, China, India, and a few other high performers like Vietnam and Uganda are the key exhibits for the pro-globalization argument. The intended message from such studies is that countries that have the best shot at lifting themselves out of poverty are those that open themselves up to the world economy.

How we read globalization's record in alleviating poverty hinges critically, therefore, on what we make of the experience of a small number of countries that have done well in the last decade or two—China in particular. In 1960, the average Chinese expected to live only 36 years. By 1999, life expectancy had risen to 70 years, not far below the level of the United States. Literacy has risen from less than 50 percent to more than 80 percent. Even though economic development has been uneven, with the coastal regions doing much better than the interior, there has been a striking reduction in poverty rates almost everywhere.

What does this impressive experience tell us about what globalization can do for poor countries? There is little doubt that exports and foreign investment have played an important role in China's development. By selling its products on world markets, China has been able to purchase the capital equipment and inputs needed for its modernization. And the surge in foreign investment has brought much-needed managerial and technical expertise. The regions of China that have grown fastest are those that took the greatest advantage of foreign trade and investment.

But look closer at the Chinese experience, and you discover that it is hardly a poster child for globalization. China's economic policies have violated virtually every rule by which the proselytizers of globalization would like the game to be played. China did *not* liberalize its trade regime to any significant extent, and it joined the World Trade Organization (WTO) only last year; to this day, its economy remains among the most protected in the world. Chinese currency markets were *not* unified until 1994. China resolutely refused to open its financial markets to foreigners, again until very recently. Most striking of all, China achieved its transformation without adopting private-property rights, let alone privatizing its state enterprises. China's policymakers were practical enough to understand the role that private incentives and markets could play in producing results. But they were also smart enough to realize that the solution to their problems lay in institutional innovations suited to the local conditions—the household responsibility system, township and village enterprises, special economic zones, partial liberalization in agriculture and industry—rather than in off-the-shelf blueprints and Western rules of good behavior.

The remarkable thing about China is that it has achieved integration with the world economy *despite* having ignored these rules—and indeed because it did so. If China were a basket case today, rather than the stunning success that it is, officials of the WTO and the World Bank would have fewer difficulties fitting it within their worldview than they do now.

China's experience may represent an extreme case, but it is by no means an exception. Earlier successes such as South Korea and Taiwan tell a similar story. Economic development often requires unconventional strategies that fit awkwardly with the ideology of free trade and free capital flows. South Korea and Taiwan made extensive use of import quotas, local-content requirements, patent infringements, and export subsidies—all of which are currently prohibited by the WTO. Both countries heavily regulated capital flows well into the 1990s. India managed to increase its growth rate through the adoption of more pro-business policies, despite having one of the world's most protectionist trade regimes. Its comparatively mild import liberalization in the 1990s came a decade *after* the onset of higher growth in the early 1980s. And India has *yet* to open itself up to world financial markets—which is why it emerged unscathed from the Asian financial crisis of 1997.

By contrast, many of the countries that *have* opened themselves up to trade and capital flows with abandon have been rewarded with financial crises and disappointing performance. Latin America, the region that adopted the globalization agenda with the greatest enthusiasm in the 1990s, has suffered rising inequality, enormous volatility, and economic growth rates significantly below those of the post-World War II decades. Argentina represents a particularly tragic case. It tried harder in the 1990s than virtually any country to endear itself to international capital markets, only to be the victim of an abrupt reversal in "market sentiment" by the end of the decade. The Argentine strategy may have had elements of a gamble, but it was solidly grounded in the theories expounded by U.S.-based economists and multilateral agencies such as the World Bank and the IMF. When Argentina's economy took off in the early 1990s after decades of stagnation, the reaction from these quarters was not that this was puzzling—it was that reform pays off.

What these countries' experience tells us, therefore, is that while global markets are good for poor countries, the rules according to which they are being asked to play the game are often not. Caught between WTO agreements, World Bank strictures, IMF conditions, and the need to maintain the confidence of financial markets, developing countries are increasingly deprived of the room they need to devise their own paths out of poverty. They are being asked to implement an agenda of institutional reform that took today's advanced countries generations to accomplish. The United States, to take a particularly telling example, was hardly a paragon of free-trade virtue while catching up with and surpassing Britain. In fact, U.S. import tariffs during the latter half of the nineteenth century were higher than in all but a few developing countries today. Today's rules are not only impractical, they divert attention and resources from more urgent developmental priorities. Turning away from world markets is surely not a good way to alleviate domestic poverty—but countries that have scored the most impressive gains are those that have developed their *own* version of the rulebook while taking advantage of world markets.

The regulations that developing nations confront in those markets are highly asymmetric. Import barriers tend to be highest for manufactured products of greatest interest to poor countries, such as garments. The global intellectual-property-rights regime tends to raise prices of essential medicines in poor countries.

But the disconnect between trade rules and development needs is nowhere greater than in the area of international labor mobility. Thanks to the efforts of the United States and other rich countries, barriers to trade in goods, financial services, and investment flows have now been brought down to historic lows. But the one market where poor nations have something in abundance to sell—the market for labor services—has remained untouched by this liberalizing trend. Rules on cross-border labor flows are determined almost always unilaterally (rather than multilaterally as in other areas of economic exchange) and remain highly restrictive. Even a small relaxation of these rules would produce huge gains for the world economy, and for poor nations in particular.

Consider, for example, instituting a system that would allot temporary work permits to skilled and unskilled workers from poorer nations, amounting to, say, 3 percent of the rich countries' labor force. Under the scheme, these workers would be allowed to obtain employment in the rich countries for a period of three to five years, after which they would be expected to return to their home countries and be replaced by new workers. (While many workers, no doubt, will want to remain in the host countries permanently, it would be possible to achieve acceptable rates of return by building specific incentives into the scheme. For example, a portion of workers' earnings could be withheld until repatriation takes place. Or there could be penalties for home governments whose nationals failed to comply with return requirements: sending countries' quotas could be reduced in proportion to the numbers who fail to return.) A back-of-the-envelope calculation indicates that such a system would easily yield $200 billion of income annually for the citizens of developing nations—vastly more than what the existing WTO trade agenda is expected to produce. The positive spillovers that the returnees would generate for their home countries—the experience, entrepreneurship, investment, and work ethic they would bring back with them—would add considerably to these gains. What is equally important, the economic benefits would accrue directly to workers from developing nations. There would be no need for "trickle down."

If the political leaders of the advanced countries have chosen to champion trade liberalization but not international labor mobility, the reason is not that the former is popular with voters at home while the latter is not. They are *both* unpopular. When asked their views on trade policy, fewer than one in five Americans reject import restrictions. In most advanced countries, including the United States, the proportion of respondents who want to expand imports tends to be about the same or lower than the proportion who believe immigration is good for the economy. The main difference seems to be that the beneficiaries of trade and investment liberalization have managed to become politically effective. Multinational firms and financial enterprises have been successful in setting the agenda of multilateral trade negotiations because they have been quick to see the link between enhanced market access abroad and increased profits at home. Cross-border labor flows, by contrast, usually have not had a well-defined constituency in the advanced countries. Rules on foreign workers have been relaxed only in those rare instances where there has been intense lobbying from special interests. When Silicon Valley firms became concerned about labor costs, for example, they pushed Congress hard to be allowed to import software engineers from India and other developing nations.

It will take a lot of work to make globalization's rules friendlier to poor nations. Leaders of the advanced countries will have to stop dressing up policies championed by special interests at home as responses to the needs of the poor in the developing world. Remembering their own history, they will have to provide room for poor nations to develop their own strategies of institution-building and economic catch-up. For their part, developing nations will have to stop looking to financial markets and multilateral agencies for the recipes of economic growth. Perhaps most difficult of all, economists will have to learn to be more humble!

… … …

While the above argument does have populist appeal, many others believe it is oversimplified and overstated. In the following extract, economist Martin Wolf considers and confronts several of the most frequent criticisms of integrated trade and of the WTO.

While he finds most criticisms baseless, he does acknowledge that some reforms are needed (for instance, the WTO rules regarding trade in agriculture). More specifically, Wolf addresses nine complaints against liberalised economic development:

- low-wage developing countries make it impossible for high-wage countries to compete without depressing wage levels;
- rising developing country production threatens a global glut, deflation and depression;
- competitive advantage of developing countries exploits workers (including children);
- global free trade destroys the environment;
- for the reasons above, 'localisation' should replace liberal global trade;
- liberalised trade undermines developing country development strategies, which cannot compete with the advanced technologies of developed countries;
- commodity-based trade is unfair and unrewarding for developing countries;
- the WTO is anti-democratic, run in the interests of transnational companies and a threat to national autonomy, the environment and human welfare; and
- high-income countries are hypocritical, in that they advocate the imposition of free trade while at the same time remaining protectionist themselves, particularly in the areas of interest to developing countries.

While we would like to extract Wolf's analysis on all nine points, space permits us to extract his analysis only on points 1, 6 and 9. Before continuing with the extract, however, we note that Wolf makes what should be a fairly obvious point which is often overlooked:

> It should not escape the reader's attention that these complaints are inconsistent. It makes no sense to argue that everybody is uncompetitive everywhere (though everybody ought to be uncompetitive somewhere). Nor should one complain about barriers against developing-country exports to high-income countries while recommending localization. Nor, again, should one encourage developing countries to pursue their own development strategies *and* high-income countries to pursue self-sufficiency, if the strategy the former wish to pursue is exporting to the markets of the latter. Nor, yet again, should one aspire to freedom for each country or community to frame its own environmental rules *and* seek to impose higher environmental standards everywhere. But consistency is hardly to be expected, since these complaints come from very different sources. The task, instead, is to separate those that make sense from those that do not . . .

M Wolf. 'Traumatized by Trade' in M Wolf, *Why Globalization Works* (2004, Yale University Press, New Haven, Conn)

Fear of pauper labour and the myth of de-industrialization

The scholarly debate on the impact of imports on the distribution of labour incomes in high-income countries, discussed in the previous chapter, has more simplistic counterparts in the popular debate. The 'pauper labour' argument is back. How can workers in high-income countries compete with Chinese workers? How can they find jobs when the ones they have go abroad? How is the world going to avoid a glut of manufacturing capacity, with deflation and mass unemployment? Happily, the answer to all these questions is: easily.

Start then with those overwhelmingly competitive Chinese workers. It is true that, on average, a worker in Chinese manufacturing cost only $730, annually, between 1995 and 1999, while a German worker cost $35,000, an American one $29,000 and a British one $24,000. Is it then not perfectly evident that German, American and British wages will be driven down to Chinese levels? It is not merely not obvious; it is untrue. Chinese labour is cheap because it is unproductive. If an American worker produces $81,000 dollars of value added annually, a German worker $80,000 and a British worker $55,000, while a Chinese worker produces only $2,900, it is not at all difficult for the workers of the high-income countries to compete, even if their wages are vastly higher.

The evidence on the relationship between productivity and wages is overwhelming. Stephen Golub, for example, has analysed the index of unit labour costs, at PPP, which relates the cost of labour to productivity and changes in real exchange rates. Note that if wages rise in line with productivity (and real exchange rates remain unchanged), the unit labour cost remains constant. Looking at seven developing countries, Golub finds that the unit labour cost rose in five from 1970 to 1993 (India, Korea, Malaysia, the Philippines and Thailand) and fell in two (Mexico and Indonesia). In the first five, then, wages rose even faster than productivity. In the last two, they rose more slowly. These deviations could occur for a number of different reasons—initial (or terminal) overvaluation or undervaluation of the real exchange rate or initial (or terminal) labour market disequilibria, for example. But the overall pattern is clear. Golub also analysed forty-nine countries at a point in time and found that productivity growth explained most of the variation in wage growth, again just as one would expect.'

Why are workers in high-income countries so much more productive than those in China (or other developing countries)? One explanation is that they have far more capital at their command than a Chinese worker. In 2000, Chinese gross capital formation per person was only about 4 per cent of US levels, at market exchange rates.S Moreover, because of China's rapid growth, its relative rates of investment were even lower just a few years ago. By comparison with high-income countries, therefore, China has very little capital to spread around. A second explanation is that Americans and Europeans are far better educated, on average, than Chinese. A third explanation is the Chinese people's lack of experience with sophisticated modem management and manufacturing. A final explanation is the different composition of Chinese manufacturing. China specializes in relatively labour-intensive manufacturing, which makes value added per worker lower than in high-income countries. By exporting the products of its cheap but relatively unskilled labour, China gains access to the physical and human capital, and know-how, of high-income countries, embodied in their exports. China does not make Boeing aircraft and the US, by now, makes relatively few garments.

In future, the efficiency of Chinese workers and managers and the capital at their disposal will rise rapidly, generating correspondingly swift increases in productivity. That will not make China invincibly competitive, because, in a competitive economy, wages will rise as well. They have done just that in other rapidly growing east Asian countries, such as South Korea. Today, South Korea's wages are fifteen times as high as China's. Fifty years ago, they would have been much the same. In time, China's wages and so its costs will also rise, together with its productivity. As they do so, its comparative advantage will also change. Today, South Korea has largely left garment manufacture behind. In time, so will China.

At this stage, a sophisticated critic would argue that China is different from South Korea. It has an enormous potential supply of labour, whose wages, in a competitive economy, will be determined not by rising productivity in manufacturing, but by low productivity back home in rural areas. If the latter rises slowly, as it is quite likely to do, then wages in Chinese industry must also rise slowly, if the labour market remains competitive. Since underlying productive efficiency is bound to grow in Chinese manufacturing, will this not make China invincibly competitive after all?

The answer, again, is no. Assume that the real wage does not rise at all, but 'total factor productivity'—the output that can be produced by a unit of capital and labour—does continue to increase. It will then become profitable to take advantage of this productivity increase through rapidly increasing employment of still cheap labour. Increases in productivity per worker will then remain low, but the growth in industrial employment will be rapid. This is exactly as it ought to be in a country so early in its industrialization. Then, when the supply of labour begins to tighten, wages and labour productivity will both explode upwards. That also happened to South Korea after a decade or two of rapid growth.

The same will happen in China, provided it is allowed to do so. If, however, the movement of labour into modern industry is controlled or wages are pushed up prematurely (as is, in fact, happening), China will end up with a dualistic economy instead, with higher wages for a relatively privileged few, but a smaller modern economy and a lower overall standard of living than would be desirable. Given the controls on labour mobility in China, that is quite likely to happen. These are also one of the reasons for the widening income gap between the people of the coastal provinces and the rest of the country. Either way, one can be confident that the relationship between real wages and productivity per worker will hold: either real wages *and* productivity per worker will rise slowly for a long time, or real wages will rise rapidly *and* so will productivity per worker

If developing countries are not so overwhelmingly competitive in manufacturing, why have 'good' manufacturing jobs for unskilled or semi-skilled workers in high-income countries shrunk over the past three decades? Between 1970 and 2000, the US lost 2.5 million jobs in manufacturing, while the share of manufacturing in total employment fell from 26.4 per cent to 14.7 per cent. In the UK, the reduction in employment in manufacturing was 3.5 million between 1970 and 1998, while the share of manufacturing in employment fell from 34.7 to 18.6 per cent. The UK was extreme. But similar patterns can be seen elsewhere: 39.5 per cent of West Germany's workers were in manufacturing in 1970, an extraordinarily high share. By 1999, this had fallen to 24.1 per cent.

To understand why absolute numbers employed and, still more, the share of employment in manufacturing fell in high-income countries over the past two or three decades, one has to go back to underlying causes. Logically, employment depends on output and productivity trends. If growth of labour productivity is higher than the growth of output, employment must shrink. If growth of productivity is sufficiently higher in manufacturing than in the rest of the economy, the employment share in manufacturing will fall, even if the employment level does not. Output, in turn, will depend on the growth in demand and changes in the trade balance. If the deterioration in the trade balance is big enough, positive trends in demand for manufactures can be consistent with a reduction in output

What then are the facts? Paul Krugman, a well-known US trade economist, calculates that the increase in the US trade deficit in manufactures may have accounted for just a quarter of the decline of the share of manufacturing in US GDP, from 25.0 per cent in 1970 to 15.9 per cent in 2000. In 2001, the US ran a trade deficit in manufactures of $300 billion (approximately 3 per cent of GDP), of which $165 billion was with developing countries. The European Union, however, ran an overall surplus in manufactures of $120 billion and a surplus with developing countries of $50 billion. In the US, therefore, trade created a modest gap between growth in demand for manufactures and in domestic output. But this is not true for the EU as a whole, where a negative impact of trade in manufactures with developing countries on jobs in manufacturing can only have come via differences in the labour intensity of what was exported and imported. In other words, balanced trade with developing countries will tend to raise productivity in manufacturing, since labour-intensive manufacturing will shrink and capital-intensive manufacturing rise. That is beneficial in itself, since it raises potential incomes, just as any other productivity increase does. The only requirement is a labour market capable of reallocating workers.

Now turn to output and productivity. Between 1973 and 1995, labour productivity in US manufacturing rose at 2.5 per cent a year, while it grew at only 1.5 per cent a year in the business sector as a whole. Similar gaps exist in every other high-income country. Inevitably, therefore, employment in manufacturing had to shrink, relative to that in the business sector as a whole, if output merely rose at the same rate in the two sectors. But people in high-income countries also tend to spend a declining share of their incomes on manufactures and an increasing share on services.10 The combination of sluggish growth in demand for manufactures with rapid rises in productivity guarantees a steep fall in the share of employment in manufacturing in the years ahead, *regardless of what happens to trade balances.*

Consider the following simple example: an economy with an initial share of manufacturing in employment of 15 per cent; productivity growth at 2.5 per cent a year in manufacturing and 1.5 per cent a year in the rest of the economy; growth in demand for manufactures at 2 per cent a year (in real terms) and in demand for the rest of economic output (overwhelmingly services) at 2.5 per cent a year; and balanced trade in both manufactures and services. Then, after twenty-five years, the share of manufacturing in employment will be 11 per cent; after fifty years, it will be 8 per cent; after a hundred years, it will be 4 per cent. Manufacturing is, in short, the new agriculture.

To think this will be a disaster shows one is prey to the 'lump of labour fallacy'—the view that there exists a fixed number of jobs in an economy. Nobody with any knowledge of economic history could believe such a thing. Two hundred years ago, the share of the population engaged in agriculture in today's high-income countries was about three-quarters. Today it is 2 or 3 per cent in populations that have also increased many times over. Are all the people not required in the fields now unemployed? The answer is: of course not. They do a host of jobs, most of them far more amusing and less arduous than their ancestors could even have imagined in 1800. The same will be true in future.

So far, then, the notion of an insuperable tide of hyper-competitive production laying waste the jobs, industries and economic activity of the high income countries can be seen as hysteria. But this leaves aside one last possible meaning to the notion of competition among countries. When a developing country, such as China, sends goods to the US or the EU, in line with its comparative advantage, the terms of trade—and so real incomes—of the importing countries improve. This means that the prices of their imports fall in relation to exports. That, in turn, means that the importing country can buy more with what it produces. It is better off. That, indeed, is why China's entry into world markets is beneficial for the high-income countries that make the sophisticated goods and services the Chinese wish to buy. Trade is not a zero-sum game. It is mutually enriching.

In a world with many countries, however, it is perfectly possible for the entry of new suppliers—particularly a huge country such as China—to hurt others. But this would come through competition not in the markets of importing countries, but in third markets. As China and other Asian countries continue to grow, the prices of what they export (manufactures, especially labour-intensive manufactures) may well fall relative to the prices of what they import (sophisticated manufactures, energy, other raw materials and food).

This could be quite important . . . over the past three decades, the real prices of primary commodities have been very weak. The only exception is petroleum, whose real price exploded in the 1970s and then fell in the 1980s and 1990s. This has been wonderful for the high-income countries, which are net importers of commodities, and dreadful for many developing countries, which are net exporters. Now suppose that China becomes, in time, the world's largest importer of commodities. This seems rather likely. By doing so, it may reverse these trends in commodity prices. In addition, China will tend to drive down the relative prices of those manufactured goods in which it has a comparative advantage. Although a reduction in the relative prices of labour intensive manufactures benefits high-income countries (which are net importers), while harming other developing country exporters, a reduction in the world prices of sophisticated manufactures, relative to commodities, would tend to worsen the terms of trade of the high-income countries.

As always, however, what matters is the size of these effects. Take an extreme possibility for the US. In 2001, US GDP was close to $10,000 billion, merchandise exports were $730 billion and merchandise imports were $1,180 billion. Net imports of manufactures were $300 billion and net imports of commodities were $150 billion. Now assume that China has no overall impact on the relative prices of different manufactures (though it is more plausible that it lowers the relative prices of US imports and raises those of US exports, which would make the US a bit better off). Assume also that China's rise doubled the relative prices of all commodities (with no differentiation, again, between those the US imports and those it exports), in relation to manufactures (whose price, in dollars, is assumed to remain unchanged). Roughly speaking, this would take the prices of commodities, in dollars, back to where they were in 1980. The net imports of commodities, which cost the US $150 billion in 2001, would now cost $300 billion. Thus the US would be worse off by just 1.5 per cent of GDP—about half a year's normal growth. In the case of the EU, the loss would be fractionally larger, because it is a slightly bigger net importer of commodities ($160 billion, instead of $150 billion). Yet the conclusion in both cases is the same. Even if the relative prices of commodities were to double, neither the US nor the EU would suffer a real income loss as big as 2 per cent pf GDP. Moreover, this relative price assumption is, it should be stressed, an extreme one.

What then are the conclusions? First, an irresistibly competitive China is a figment of the fevered imagination, since the real cost of labour will tend to remain in line with its productivity. Second, the principal determinants of declining employment in manufacturing in the high-income countries have been sluggish demand and rapidly rising productivity, not trade. Third, even a dramatic impact on the terms of trade of high-income countries, via a huge rise in the relative prices of commodities, would have a modest impact on their real incomes. In short, worries about de-industrialization and global competition from pauper labour are nonsense.

...

Concerns about development strategy

Let us turn, at this point, from people who wish to destroy an integrated world economy to more sophisticated analysts who wish to protect developing countries from excessive pressure to move towards free trade. Several scholars argue that the merits of a policy of free trade have been greatly exaggerated and that premature liberalization could significantly damage the prospects of development. Powerful critiques of contemporary orthodoxy on trade and development have been advanced by, among others, Ha-Joon Chang of Cambridge University, Alice Amsden of the Massachusetts Institute of Technology and Dani Rodrik of Harvard University, though other distinguished scholars would argue on similar lines. None of these authors denies the role of trade as 'a handmaiden of growth, in the words of a distinguished economist of an earlier generation, Irving Kravis. On the contrary, all note that successful economies have both increased their integration in the world economy and depended upon it for their success. They are not arguing for a return to the local—or anything like it. Nor are they arguing against use of markets and economic incentives. All recognise that working market institutions are a necessary condition for long-term success. But they resist the idea that across-the-board trade liberalization is a sufficient, or even necessary, condition for rapid economic development. They are right to do so. It is not.

Dr Chang, presumably influenced by the remarkable experience of his own country, South Korea, argues that active 'industrial, trade and technology policies' are 'necessary for socializing the risks involved in the development of infant industries'. He makes this argument on the basis of a historical analysis of the successful economies of today, starting with the first industrializer, the UK. All these economies, notably including the US, Germany, France, Sweden, Belgium and, later on, Japan, South Korea and Taiwan, used a range of active measures to overcome backwardness and promote industrial development. This observation, unquestionably correct, he qualifies in two significant respects: first, this 'does not mean there is only one way of doing it—that is to say, by means of tariff protection'; second, the fact that the use of activist industrial, trade and technology policies 'is necessary does not imply that all countries that use such policies are guaranteed economic success'. What it does mean, however, is that developing countries must be granted the opportunity to use such policies. Otherwise, the incumbent economic powers are 'kicking down the ladder' up which they themselves ascended.

Professor Amsden argues on not dissimilar lines, but from the experience of the developing countries of the post-Second World War period and economic theory. She describes two contemporary strategies for industrial catch-up.

In one set, embracing China, India, Korea and Taiwan, call them the 'independents' (with the understanding that all latecomers have become more global since World War II), long-term growth was premised on the 'make' technology decision, which was synonymous with the build-up of national capabilities and national firms. In another set, embracing Argentina, Brazil, Chile, Mexico and Turkey, call them the 'integrationists' (with the understanding that no country in 'the rest' has completely relinquished its economic or political autonomy), long-term growth was premised on the 'buy' technology decision, and a reliance on both foreign rules of conduct to discipline business (as provided by membership in NAFTA and the EU), and spillovers from foreign investment and technology transfer to generate wealth.

Moreover, she argues, the interventionism of the first category of countries, to which, in her view, all these latecomers belonged before about 1980, was justified by the simple fact that 'none had sufficient knowledge-based assets to compete in modern industry at world prices. Government intervention arose everywhere in response to the lack of competitiveness rather than to simple cronyism, or the need to "coordinate" investment decisions, or the desire to capture "external economies": or some other typical textbook explanation for government intervention: In the absence of perfect knowledge, she argues, potentially highly profitable long-term opportunities will never be exploited. It is this obstacle that governments can (and should) help overcome.

Professor Rodrik's position is rather different. In some respects, on the need for investment co-ordination for example, it is close to one Professor Amsden attacks. His central argument is that the benefits of trade liberalization have been greatly exaggerated by its proponents. Policy-makers should instead 'focus on the fundamentals of economic growth—investment, macroeconomic stability, human resources, and good governance—and not let international economic integration dominate their thinking on development'. Rodrik agrees that successful economies become more open, but, he also argues, making an economy more open, by lowering trade barriers, does not guarantee success. On the contrary, his view is that the old highly protectionist import-substitution strategies did rather well. He points to the fact that growth performance for most developing economies was better before 1973 than afterwards. The reason for the subsequent collapse, he suggests, was the failure to sustain macroeconomic stability in response to a series of shocks, particularly the two oil shocks and the debt crisis of the early 1980s.

These are important critiques of liberal trade. Are they also justified? The right response is 'up to a point'.

It is correct that successful economies have intervened to promote industry in a host of different ways, and continue to do so to this day. But one must avoid the fallacy of *post hoc, propter hoc*—because one event preceded another, it also caused it. While some of those interventionist measures have worked, many have not. Even the benefits of import substitution in the nineteenth century are denied. Moreover, of the instruments for industrial promotion, high levels of infant-industry protection, including total bans on competing imports, particularly in the absence of offsetting incentives to export (or export requirements), are extremely inefficient: they create a strong home market bias in trade policy, thereby taxing competitive exports and limiting the benefits of the support to producers aiming at an uncompetitive and ridiculously small home market. As a result, they have had a well-known and depressing tendency to create perpetual children. As the World Bank has stated, 'typically the long-protected firms have not become efficient and do not in fact survive in the more competitive environment'. The Bank points to the Indian machine-tool industry, long protected with 100 per cent tariffs. When these tariffs were liberalized, Taiwanese producers took a third of the market. Since then, the Indians have fought back, but the successful competitors are new entrants, not the old flabby incumbents.

It is also unquestionably correct that developing countries need to be allowed to use instruments which help them overcome the many obstacles of backwardness and, especially, as Professor Amsden argues, the absence of knowledge of what to do—and how to do it—that is an essential characteristic of that backwardness. They may use them unwisely from time to time. But they have sometimes worked. Sovereign governments should be allowed to take such actions—and, if necessary, learn from their mistakes. But trade measures are, all the same, not the most effective measures to use.

Professor Rodrik's rather different views appear more debatable. But let us first agree with him where agreement is necessary. Trade liberalization, on its own, regardless of the circumstances, will not generate rapid growth. On this, there is no disagreement and never has been, among sensible analysts. No disagreement exists on the need for macroeconomic stability either, nor on the difficulty of achieving it. Nor is there debate on the desirability of 'good government', or higher investment in human and physical resources, other things being equal. For all that, there are good reasons to question both some of Rodrik's propositions and the methods that he—and many other economists—now use to reach their results. Apart from these difficulties, at least two further objections can be made to Rodrik's position.

First, the view that the level of investment *per se* is of overriding importance can be strongly contested. William Easterly, for example, in his masterly analysis of the many failures of development, observes that 'both Nigeria and Hong Kong increased their physical capital stock per worker by over 250 per cent over the 1960 to 1985 time frame. The results of this massive investment were different: 'Nigeria's output per worker rose by 12 per cent from 1960 to 1985, while Hong Kong's rose by 328 per cent. Rodrik shows some awareness of this in remarking that if investment were the crux of the matter, 'centrally planned economies would have been the world's best performers over the longer run. Ultimately, the return on investment matters a great deal too.' Indeed, it does. And among its determinants must be how well market institutions operate and distortions in relative prices in the economy. However, these will affect not just the return on investment, but also its level. It is at the least extremely likely that the investment rates in east Asian economies, to which Rodrik (and others) point, are the consequence of the governments' well-known and well-publicized determination to preserve the profitability of exports. Export markets have, it should be stressed, the benefit that for most developing-country producers they are effectively infinite in size. That provides a huge incentive for a profitable exporter to expand capacity.

Second, Rodrik's conclusions on the relative merits of import-substitution strategies are debatable in several respects. One is that his conclusion on the growth performance of economies under import substitution must be qualified by the fact that this is growth at often highly distorted domestic prices, not world prices. Another is that he cannot legitimately assume that the growth performance of the 1960–80 period would have continued if the policies of the import-substitution period had been sustained. The same absurd conclusion on the superiority of Soviet socialism over the market economy could be reached by contrasting the former's growth between 1960 and 1980 with the performance of the Soviet Union and its successor states during the subsequent two decades of admittedly difficult and often mismanaged reforms.

Also, there are, contrary to Rodrik's view, good reasons to believe that an import-substitution strategy will reach natural limits. As imports fall in relation to GDP, it will become increasingly difficult to find even tolerably economic import-substitution projects. In the end, growth will be limited by export and agricultural performance, both stunted by the incentives to import substitution oriented industry.

Finally, the superior ability of east Asian export-oriented economies to adjust to external shocks is not independent of their export-oriented strategy. As a number of economists have observed, the difficulty Latin American countries have found in coping with macroeconomic shocks (whose size in relation to GDP has often been no larger than those confronting the east Asians) is partly a result of the small size of their sectors that produce tradable goods and services. For this reason, a given degree of expenditure switching, in the technical jargon, requires considerably larger changes in real exchange rates in Latin America than have been necessary in east Asia. South Korea has been remarkable for the ease with which it has been able to push out exports in response to domestic recessions and relatively modest changes in the real exchange rate. This is one of the great benefits of an outward-looking strategy and especially one that finds a strong comparative advantage in easily expandable manufactures.

Yet, despite these powerful criticisms, the views of Professor Rodrik need to be taken into account. In particular, he is right to emphasize that much more is involved in successful development than trade policy. It is also unquestionably right, as Chang and Amsden argue, that some of the most successful developing countries—South Korea and Taiwan—did not all follow policies of free trade, though Hong Kong and Singapore remain important exceptions on this score. The creation of indigenous technological capacities has demanded special efforts by developing countries. Now that most developing countries have eliminated the most damaging non-tariff barriers and the highest tariffs, it is reasonable to conclude that further liberalization is no longer among their immediate priorities. It is also reasonable to ask whether WTO rules impose unreasonable constraints on their policy discretion. We will do that in the penultimate section of this chapter.

...

Hypocrisy of the rich

Now let us turn to the last—and more than justified—charge, that the rich countries are grossly hypocritical in their treatment of developing countries. They call on developing countries to adjust, liberalize and respond to market forces. But this is not advice that the high-income countries themselves adopt. Instead, high-income countries force the developing countries to take greater account of their own concerns than they themselves do of developing-country concerns. Worse, they handicap the world's poor countries with obstacles to trade far bigger than those they impose on one another. But this is not the only obstacle developing countries confront in taking advantage of global market opportunities. They also need to overcome the hurdles to trade created by one another's barriers.

Average tariffs in the high-income countries are around 3 per cent. But average tariffs on agricultural commodities are almost double those for manufactures. Tariff barriers on labour-intensive products are raised through tariff peaks (tariffs exceeding 15 per cent). Imports at such peaks represent about 5 per cent of total imports of Canada, the European Union, Japan and the US (the 'Quadrilateral' or 'Quad' countries) from developing countries and more than 11 per cent of their imports from the world's poorest countries, the least developed countries. In North America, tariff peaks are commonly found in labour-intensive manufactures, particularly textiles and clothing. In the EU and Japan, they are found, more often, in agriculture, especially processed food. Tariff peaks on imports of footwear are found in all these high-income markets and surpass those on textiles and clothing.

In the US, 6.6 per cent of imports from developing countries are subject to tariffs over 15 per cent. The comparable figure for the EU is 4.9 per cent, for Canada 4.8 per cent and for Japan 2.8 per cent. While average tariffs on all manufactured imports into high-income countries are only 3 per cent, tariffs on labour-intensive manufactured imports from developing countries are 8 per cent and on imports of agricultural commodities from developing countries 14 per cent. Unfortunately, developing countries are also damaged by the protectionism of other developing countries. The average tariff applied by developing countries to their imports from other developing countries is more than three times higher than the average imposed by the high-income countries. The World Bank has calculated that the average tariff faced by the poor (those living on less than two dollars a day, at PPP) in all markets is 14 per cent, against 6 per cent for the rest, as a result of barriers in both high income countries and other developing countries.

A study by the Progressive Policy Institute in the US gives dramatic indications of these gross inequities. Exports to the US from Bangladesh, with a GDP per head (at market prices) of $370, paid $331 million in tariffs in 2001, or an average rate of 14.1 per cent. This revenue was as big as that levied on exports from France. But French exports were thirteen times as large, so the average rate they paid was only 1.1 per cent. Similarly, exports from Cambodia, with a GDP per head of $260, paid $152 million in tariffs, an average rate of 15.8 per cent, while Singapore's exports paid $96 million, an average rate of only 0.6 per cent. On average, it concluded, the world's least developed countries face tariffs four to five times higher than the richest economies. This is a disgrace.

As has already been mentioned above, tariffs escalate steeply, especially on processed agricultural commodities. This is especially true for the EU and Japan. On average, the tariff on processed commodities is 2.75 times higher than that on unprocessed commodities in the ED. In Japan, the ratio is 3.75. Such escalation makes protection to domestic value added vastly higher than one might realize. To take a simple example: imagine that a given raw product (coffee) faces a tariff of 5 per cent, while the finished product faces one of 14 per cent. Assume also that value added at world prices is divided, half and half, between the production of the raw product and the processing. The 'effective protection' given to the activity of processing then turns out to be 23 per cent.

This is a substantial subsidy. Today, the UK grinds more cocoa than Ghana. Tariff escalation must be a large part of the reason.

Non-tariff barriers also remain significant obstacles for the developing countries. The true level of protection afforded to European industry rises from 5.1 per cent if tariffs alone are included to 9 per cent if non-tariff barriers are taken into account. Among significant obstacles to developing countries are product standards. A World Bank study, cited by Oxfam, showed that implementation of a new EU standard to protect consumers against aflatoxin (a naturally occurring carcinogen) will cost African exporters of nuts, cereals and dried fruits $670 million a year, without generating significant health benefits. Anti-dumping measures are also a severe obstacle to developing. country exporters, particularly to small and inexperienced companies. Between them the US and EU launched 234 anti-dumping cases against developing countries in the five years following the end of the Uruguay Round. Every well-informed economist knows that anti-dumping lacks all economic justification, even in theory, let alone in its still more indefensible practice. Perhaps the most disgraceful episode in a long and shameless history has been the Byrd amendment in the US, which transfers anti-dumping duty revenue directly to the complaining firms. A better way of corrupting the trade-policy system can hardly be imagined, especially since the rules governing the determination of dumping makes a positive finding so absurdly easy.

Preferential trading arrangements have also exploded in number since the 1980s. The most important for the trading system are those between powerful high-income countries and a selected number of favoured developing countries. The European Union was responsible for starting the flood. But the US has become an increasingly active promoter. These discriminatory arrangements create significant difficulties for the less favoured developing countries. They are put at a disadvantage in the markets of the members. Yet some of those excluded from all such arrangements—Bangladesh, for example—are among the world's poorest countries. These arrangements are also potentially an obstacle to further trade liberalization, since beneficiaries will try to defend their preferences. Last but not least, the granting of such discretionary favours gives powerful high income countries great leverage over weaker trading partners, which they can use, among other things, to ensure support for their positions in the WTO.

In the grand deal of the Uruguay Round, the developing countries agreed, unwillingly, to accept the provisions on trade-related intellectual property, trade-related investment measures and services. The *quid pro quo* was to be liberalization of barriers against exports of textiles and clothing under the multi-fibre arrangement. According to the agreement on textiles and clothing, the high-income countries were to remove quotas from at least 51 per cent of their imports by January 2002. So, ostensibly, they did. But they will in fact have removed quotas from only 12 per cent of the imports that were effectively constrained by quotas. Effectively, the liberalization has been almost entirely back-loaded until 2005. It is now feared that quota restrictions will still apply on more than 80 per cent of developing-country exports in these sectors in 2004. So, instead of a progressive adjustment to the elimination of these restrictions, the cowardly and incompetent authorities of the EU and US have arranged for all the liberalization to occur in a rush in 2005. This undermines the entire idea of phased liberalization—that it compels those affected to adjust in stages. The sudden liberalization at the end of the period is bound to trigger fierce political resistance. That, in turn, is likely to lead to yet more anti-dumping and so-called 'safeguard-protection' actions against surges in exports from developing countries.

Yet perhaps the greatest of all the scandals remains the treatment of agriculture. In this area, one of comparative advantage for many developing countries, they have hardly managed to raise their share of world exports. This is so even though agriculture is, for the high-income countries, of trivial economic importance in terms of GDP, employment and trade. What stops the developing countries is the staggering scale of rich-country subsidies. According to the Organization for Economic Co-operation and Development, total assistance to rich country farmers was $311 billion in 2001, six times as much as all development assistance, indeed more than the GDP of sub-Saharan Africans. In 2000, the EU provided $913 for each cow and $8 to each sub-Saharan African. The Japanese, more generous still, though only to cows, provided $2,700 for each one and just $1.47 to each African. Not to be outdone, the US spent $10.7 million a day on cotton and $3.1 million a day on all aid to sub-Saharan Africa. The priorities shown here are obscene. In order to justify the grotesquerie of its agricultural policy regime, the common agricultural policy, the EU has started to apply the notion of 'multi-functionality'. By this it means that agricultural supports are justified by their ability not only to support farm incomes, but to protect the environment, food security and rural life. The EU is right about the multi-functionality of the CAP, just wrong about the functions its policies serve. The CAP is regressive (since it provides 50 per cent of its benefits to the 17 per cent biggest farmers, who need this help least), wasteful (since it still consumes almost half the EU's budget), environmentally damaging (since it encourages needless intensification of agricultural production) and harmful to developing countries (since it deprives them of markets and undermines the competitiveness of their farmers with its dumping of subsidized surpluses). This is multi-functionality with a vengeance. The picture is little different in the us: only 16 per cent of the support goes to the 80 per cent of the farmers who operate on a relatively small scale

Unfortunately, while the Uruguay Round brought a little discipline to this sector, it was grossly inadequate. Agricultural support in the EU and US was higher in the late 1990s, as measured by the OECD's Producer Support Estimates, than between 1986 and 1988, the base years for the Uruguay Round agreements. Much of the support is still output related. Moreover, many of the subsidies that are supposed not to affect production do so.

Because farm supports are anti-cyclical, they increase the instability of residual world markets, with devastating effects on exporters from developing countries. Moreover, subsidized surpluses are still being dumped on world markets. The US and EU account for around half of all world wheat exports, with prices 46 and 34 per cent respectively below costs of production. In 1998, subsidized exports made up a quarter of global exporters. The EU is the world's largest exporter of skimmed-milk powder, at half the costs of production. It is also the largest exporter of white sugar, at a quarter of the costs of production. Some argue that such dumping can be beneficial to developing countries that are net food importers. With very few exceptions, this is not so. In most developing countries, farmers are not just the majority of the population, but the overwhelming majority of the poor. Thus the dumped products benefit an urban minority at the expense of the rural majority. Often the subsidized food has turned countries into net importers. Without it, they would both be net exporters and possess far healthier rural economies.88 While the transition to a world of higher international food prices needs to be handled carefully— and food aid needs to be available to help food-importing countries and those vulnerable to harvest failure—it is virtually certain that developing countries would gain hugely from the elimination of current farm policies in the high-income countries. The World Bank has estimated the annual welfare losses to developing countries at $20 billion a year—close to 40 per cent of all development assistance.

This is not, alas, the end of the hypocrisy of the high-income countries. The Uruguay Round also saw the introduction of trade-related intellectual property into what subsequently became the WTO. While patent and similar forms of protection may be appropriate for some of the bigger or more economically advanced developing countries (such as Brazil, China and India), it is a rent-extraction device for the rest of them, with potentially devastating consequences for their ability to educate their people (because of copyright), adapt designs for their own use (ditto) and deal with severe challenges of public health. The World Bank estimates that transfers from developing countries in the form of license payments to northern transnational companies, above all those of the US, will rise almost four-fold, from their current level of $15 billion. If so, the sum would fully offset all development assistance. Yet, as was argued in Part II above, there is an obvious inefficiency in restricting the use of knowledge. When it is its use by poor countries that is being restricted, then it is unjust as well. The case of access to medicines is merely the most publicized and egregious example of these costs. It is also remarkable that while the high-income countries have supported their companies in attempts to protect patents abroad, they have no compunction about threatening them at home. The US, for example, threatened Bayer, producer of an effective anti-anthrax medicine, in the aftermath of the anthrax scare in late 2001, unless it reduced its prices. Canada went even further.

Again, while a strong case can be made for liberalization of services, it is noteworthy that the high-income countries have done rather better in securing access for their capital-intensive service providers than in accepting the movement of people as providers of labour-intensive services. This is yet another hypocrisy. Nor is this the end of it. Standards on such matters as customs valuation are burdensome for developing countries, as is meeting the standards of high-income countries in such areas as food safety.

Global trade liberalization offers enormous opportunities for developing countries to expand trade and increase their welfare. Work by the World Bank suggests that world income in 2015 would be $355 billion a year more with merchandise-trade liberalization (in 1997 dollars). The developing countries would gain $184 billion annually. Of this, $121 billion would be the benefits from their own liberalization, while the rest would come from liberalization by high-income countries. Nearly 80 per cent of the gains to developing countries would come from liberalization of agriculture. With dynamic benefits added, the Bank estimates developing-country incomes could rise by more than $500 billion a year, with $390 billion of this coming from agriculture and $120 billion from textiles and clothing. To put this in context, the total GDP, in market prices, of the developing countries was $6,300 billion in 2000.

The Bank also adds huge estimates for the gains from liberalization of trade in services. This is obviously, as the Bank says, 'more art than science'. The barriers in these studies take three forms: a cost penalty reflecting inefficiency; a price mark-up reflecting monopoly; and barriers to cross-border trade. The Bank concludes that reform by developing countries could increase their incomes by nearly $900 billion a year, some 4.5 times greater than their gains from merchandise-trade liberalization—a 9.4 per cent income gain, compared to base levels. Of this, $670 billion would come from cheaper trade and transportation.

Finally, the Bank evaluates the consequences of such liberalization. First, it argues that the unskilled—above all, rural labour—would benefit proportionately most from liberalization that redressed the anti-agriculture bias in most developing-country trade policy regimes and increased access to world markets. Wages of the unskilled would rise more than those of the skilled and returns to capital. Second, there would be substantial displacement of people, which is one reason why liberalization needs to be credible and carried out over a lengthy time period. But the benefits would greatly outweigh costs. Third, under the Bank's baseline scenario world trade would rise to $11,200 billion. With liberalization, this would be $1,900 billion more ($13,100 billion). Developing countries would take the lion's share of this: their exports would be $1,300 billion higher, $600 billion of which would be increased exports to high-income countries and $700 billion increased exports to one another. Developing-country agricultural exports would rise by $200 billion and textiles and clothing by nearly $180 billion. These figures dwarf any conceivable increase in foreign aid.

In sum, the treatment of developing countries by the high-income countries has been a disgrace. Nevertheless, the extent to which the trade route to prosperity has been blocked must also not be exaggerated. Remember how successful export-oriented developing countries have been. At the same time, further liberalization should benefit everybody. The only important proviso is the one discussed above—that developing countries are able to make the policy decisions needed to promote their long-term development.

Conclusion

Liberal trade and the world trading system have become a lightning rod for everything people dislike about our world. But if we look back at the charges discussed in this chapter, we can see that the criticisms fall into a few categories. The first contains charges brought by people who believe that the rise of the developing countries threatens the livelihoods of the privileged citizens of high-income countries. Their complaints are largely, though not entirely, groundless. The second group contains charges brought by people who wish to stop trade everywhere. Their ideas—above all, localization—are both foolish and dangerous, particularly to the people of the developing countries whom they pretend to wish to help. The third group contains charges brought by people who fear that the freedom of action of developing countries is improperly circumscribed, particularly over infant-industry promotion. These arguments are not worthless, though they are exaggerated. It is an issue that needs to be re-examined. The fourth group concerns the WTO as an institution. These complaints are generally wrong and, where not wrong, exaggerated. But the institution is imperfect. It needs to be reformed. The last and much the most persuasive group of charges are complaints about the handicaps now imposed upon the poor, because of the dreadful state of commodity markets and the grotesque hypocrisy of the high-income countries. . . .

… … …

As mentioned above, the term 'globalisation' is often used but, as is demonstrated by the above extracts, its precise scope is not always clear. Certainly trade agreements are an important part of it. However, not all trade agreements are alike. In the following paragraph, Hoekman explores the distinction between 'shallow' and 'deep' integration through trade agreements:

As average tariffs of industrialized countries have fallen (to less than five percent currently) and quantitative restrictions been abolished, international negotiations have increasingly centered on domestic regulatory policies that are alleged to impede the ability of foreign firms and products to contest a market. Examples of the latter include technical regulations that aim to safeguard public health or the environment, and licensing or certification requirements for service providers. Dealing with such "behind the border" policies has been termed "deeper integration" in the literature, in contrast with the "shallow" integration that has been the staple of the General Agreement on Tariffs and Trade (GATT), which revolves around reducing the prevalence of measures applied at the border (tariffs, quotas). Rather than use the border-nonborder distinction, in this paper shallow integration is defined to comprise actions to eliminate discrimination between foreign and domestic firms—i.e., to apply the principle of national treatment. This implies not only zero tariffs and quotas, but also the abolition of contingent protection. Deep integration consists of explicit actions by governments to reduce the market segmenting effect of differences in national regulatory policies that pertain to products, production processes, producers and natural persons. In practice this will require decisions: (i) that a partner's policies are equivalent (mutual recognition); or (ii) to adopt a common regulatory stance in specific areas (harmonization). The latter approach may be complemented by decisions to cede enforcement authority to a supra-national entity.[28]

It is difficult to know what to take from the conflicting views set out above from a number of highly esteemed economists. To a great extent, people's views on the benefit of free trade are governed by their general world view. For example, those who have a general scepticism towards big business will often see existing trade agreements as merely a tool for creating a system that is biased in their favour. And those who are not particularly concerned with environmental and labour protection will be sceptical of the criticisms made by NGOs which specialise in these areas.

---

[28] B Hoekman, 'Free Trade and Deep Integration: Antidumping and Antitrust in Regional Agreements' (World Bank and CEPR, 13 April 1998).

An important point to consider is that regarding the distinctions drawn between shallow and deep integration. The distinction was the focal point of the final extract, but not discussed at all in the excerpts. This illustrates one of the main problems with the current trade debate: people are not always talking about the same thing. A debate about whether or not to use tariffs as protection is very different from a debate about the conditions under which governments may regulate food safety. Yet sometimes these distinctions get blurred through the use of the term 'free trade', which means different things to different people.

In truth, the multilateral trading system is a mix of a number of different policy views and goals, and reflects lobbying from various different actors. The rules in the TRIPS Agreement that promote stricter intellectual property protection were clearly a response to lobbying by Western companies that owned and developed intellectual property, such as pharmaceutical, entertainment and software companies. By contrast, the large number of rules that carve out special treatment for developing countries are the result of demands by the developing world to give them a break in terms of the obligations imposed on them. Weighing and balancing all of the extensive and complex obligations that have been taken on by all of the participating countries to determine who benefited most is an extremely hard task.

This book may not change everyone's pre-existing views on the issue. However, hopefully it will provide some details that stimulate thinking about precisely where the current balance lies and whether your initial impressions were accurate. As you read the book, some key questions to think about are:

- What is free trade? Is free trade desirable? Do trade agreements today strive for or mandate free trade? What are the goals of trade agreements? What purpose does the WTO serve? What effect does it have on nations? On traders? On consumers? How would trade be regulated if there were no WTO? A hundred years, ago free trade was probably best characterised as simply the opposite of protectionism. However, today's trade agreements do much more than limit protectionism. When we talk about free trade and trade agreements, it is important to have a sense of what the specific components involved are.
- How do trade agreements affect sovereignty? As trade agreements move beyond traditional anti-protectionism and expand to new areas of regulation, additional limits are placed on the ability of governments to regulate. There has been some concern expressed that current agreements go too far in this regard.
- Are current trade rules appropriate for developing countries? Generally speaking, today's rich countries industrialised under conditions that were far different from those that exist today. They were not constrained by international trade agreements, and often used substantial protection. The question thus arises whether the current crop of trade agreements appropriately deals with issues related to economic development.

IV. STRUCTURE OF THE BOOK

Following this introduction, Part II of the book then covers additional 'general' issues: the history and institutions of the international trading system; the relationship between international law and world trade law; and the relationship between world trade law and domestic law.

The substantive chapters begin with Part III, which is made up entirely of Chapter 5, on dispute settlement. The WTO's dispute settlement mechanism is a crucial aspect of the international trading regime because it provides a binding adjudicatory system that gives force to WTO rules.

Part IV then turns to the core obligations of the General Agreement on Tariffs and Trade (GATT). These are the rules on the use of border measures like tariffs and quotas, and the non-discrimination principles of Most Favoured Nation (MFN) treatment (non-discrimination among trading partners) and National Treatment (NT) (non-discrimination against foreign products).

Part V covers the key exceptions to the GATT. These include the general exceptions relating to policies such as public morals, health and environmental conservation; and also the exception to MFN for regional trade agreements.

Part VI discusses the so-called 'trade remedies': anti-dumping, countervailing duties and safeguards. These measures are permitted types of protection that can be used in specific circumstances.

Part VII explores several 'new' areas of regulation, beyond trade in goods. While they are not so new any more, most having been around since at least the mid-1990s, these rules are less developed and well understood than the traditional GATT obligations. The new areas are: product standards and health measures; trade in services; investment; government procurement; and intellectual property protection.

Part VIII addresses several issues related to 'social policy', including the role of trade in economic development, as well as controversial issues such as linkages between trade and 'non-trade' policies.

Part II

History, Institutional Aspects and the Relationship between World Trade Law, International Law and Domestic Law

2

The History and Institutions of the Multilateral Trading System

I. INTRODUCTION

In this chapter, we explain the history and background of the WTO as an institution, including its origins as the GATT, its goals, basic structure, decision-making and accession process.

At the outset, it may be useful to offer some general clarifications about the nature of the WTO. Reading about the WTO in the popular press, it is sometimes easy to come away with misconceptions about how the organisation operates. There are frequent references to decisions, both legal and political, made by the 'WTO'. For example, it may be said that the WTO struck down a US tariff law as violating WTO rules or that the WTO admitted China as a Member. In some sense, these statements are true, but they can be misleading without further explanation as to what exactly the 'WTO' is. In this regard, it is important to understand that the WTO is a Member-driven organisation, in that most of the decisions that come out of the WTO are the result of an agreement among all of the countries and customs territories that are WTO Members. That is, nearly all of the decisions reached are in fact made by these countries and territories acting in their capacity as equal members of the WTO. Thus, the WTO is not a global parliament with legislators making decisions that national governments must follow. Rather, it is a tool of the governments themselves, through which they make joint decisions. It does not govern its Members from above, but rather governs through the Members.

In addition to the Members, there is an actual staff of the organisation. These employees play a key role in carrying out the day-to-day work of the organisation. However, generally speaking, they are not the ultimate decision-makers, but merely assist the Members in carrying out their work.

II. THE GATT AS AN INSTITUTION

Before explaining the details of the WTO, it is useful to trace its historical foundation. Such a review will not only provide important context to the modern day trading system, it will also allow the reader to appreciate more fully and understand the reasons why the WTO operates and exists in the form it does.

(a) The Origins of the GATT

Formal trade relationships between countries have existed for centuries. In fact, many of the early explorers discovered new lands in order to seek out new trading opportunities—from the Phoenicians to the Greeks and Romans, the Maghribi to Marco Polo, through to the modern Portuguese, Spanish, Dutch and English explorers of the fifteenth–seventeenth centuries. Generally speaking, these early-modern trading relationships were shaped by colonisation and the corresponding restriction of imports from sources other than the coloniser.

Trade restrictions eased in the late seventeenth and eighteenth centuries, when bilateral Friendship, Commerce and Navigation (FCN) treaties included within their scope non-discrimination provisions calling for conditional 'most-favoured nation' status and 'national treatment'. These treaties were the first step towards more formal trade relationships based on the idea of liberalisation. By the late nineteenth century, numerous bilateral efforts to rein in international trade restrictions were underway. This overall trend of cooperation and liberalisation continued, with a minor hiccup in the 1870s, until World War I. The intervening years between the first and second World Wars initially involved talk of liberalised trade through the League of Nations. However, while these talks were taking place, there was an outbreak of protectionism, led by the US passage of the isolationist Smoot-Hawley Tariff Act (1930), which sharply raised tariff rates. Many believed the ensuing sharp decline in the importation and exportation of goods actually worsened the Great Depression significantly and, in part, led to the beginning of the Second World War. Within a few years of Smoot-Hawley, however, the League discussions seemed to bear fruit, as there was a proliferation of bilateral trade treaties (especially by the US through the Reciprocal Trade Agreements programme) which sought to liberalise trade. These treaties offered some progress towards freer trade, but were limited in terms of the countries involved, and, as noted, were bilateral not multilateral.

In the aftermath of World War II, many Western leaders wanted to reverse the mistakes of economic isolationism that characterised the pre-war years, believing that freer international trade would in the long term be mutually advantageous for economic and security reasons, both to individual nations and the world in general. Desiring to create new world political and economic institutions they viewed as necessary to promote and maintain peaceful international relations, the leaders united in 1944 at the Bretton Woods conference to address monetary and banking issues. At the conference, the Bretton Woods Agreement was negotiated, which established the charters for the International Monetary Fund and the International Bank for Reconstruction and Development (the World Bank). However, trade was not covered. In December 1945, though, the US took the lead in setting up a corresponding institution for trade, publishing a document called 'Proposals for Expansion of World Trade and Employment' and proposing the creation of the International Trade Organisation (ITO).

The US and UK, acting through the United Nations Economic and Social Council, further developed the idea and organised a Preparatory Committee (meeting in London (1946), New York (1947) and Geneva (1947)), to produce a draft charter for the ITO. The proposed charter included specific provisions on trade, development, commodity agreements and other economic issues. It also mandated, at US insistence, dispute settlement provisions involving consultation, arbitration and referral to the International Court of Justice (ICJ). On 21 November 1947, 57 nations met in Cuba as part of the UN Conference on Trade and Employment to finalise drafting of the proposal, which became the Havana Charter.[1] At the same time, the Conference also established an Interim Commission for the ITO and a secretariat.

In December 1945 (only a few months prior to the creation of the United Nations Economic and Social Council), the US also invited several nations to enter into negotiations with a view to concluding a multilateral agreement designed to reduce tariffs. While the two negotiations were technically separate, in truth the negotiators were the same individuals and the negotiations intertwined. In what was sometimes described as a 'three-ring circus', one part of the negotiations focused on drafting the ITO Charter (part of which was a chapter on Commercial Policy); a second part focused on an agreement to reduce tariffs; and a third part focused on drafting the provisions relating to the tariff reductions (much of which was taken from the Commercial Policy chapter of the ITO).[2] Thus, negotiators at the time had a dual purpose: they had to draft an ITO Charter while at the same time negotiating for the reduction and binding of thousands of individual tariff commitments.

The second and third parts of the negotiations eventually came into being as the General Agreement on Tariffs and Trade (GATT). However, the first part never materialised. By 1951, it was clear that the US Congress would not ratify the ITO Charter, and President Truman ceased efforts to generate Congressional support and announce that he would no longer seek approval for the ITO. Without the US, the remaining countries abandoned the effort and the organisation was never formed.

In hindsight, the ITO was too ambitious a proposal for the times. The ITO required significant and meaningful commitments for signatories in such areas as dispute settlement, international commodity arrangements, foreign investment, labour standards and restrictive business practices. By contrast, the GATT was restricted to tariffs and related matters, and thus could be adopted in the United States without formal legislative approval. Thus, while the ITO floundered, 23 nations became signatories to the GATT and eight of those nations (Australia, Belgium, Canada, France, Luxembourg, The Netherlands, the UK and the US) agreed to apply the GATT provisionally as of 1 January 1948 (the remaining 15 did so soon thereafter). The Protocol of Provisional Application (PPA) allowed for full application of Parts I and III of the GATT (which cover Most Favoured Nation treatment and tariff concessions, among other things), but applied Part II (which provides for substantive obligations such as National Treatment and a ban on quotas) only 'to the fullest extent not inconsistent with existing legislation'. This clause became known as 'grandfather rights', and allowed parties with these rights to continue applying measures inconsistent with the obligations under Part II. While such rights were necessary in order for some signatories to avoid having to seek legislative approval, it was not seen by negotiators as a major problem since 'definitive' application of the GATT would occur following the creation of the ITO. The PPA was designed to be temporary and Article

---

[1] The records of these meetings run to over 100 volumes and contain over 27,000 pages. See JH Jackson, *The World Trading System, Law and Policy of International Economic Relations*, 2nd edn (Cambridge, MA, MIT Press, 1997) 37.

[2] *Ibid.* See also JH Jackson, *World Trade and the Law of GATT* (Charlottesville, VA, Bobbs-Merrill, 1969) 42–46.

XXIX:2 of the General Agreement proves just how fleeting the PPA was supposed to be, providing, 'Part II of this Agreement shall be suspended on the day which the Havana Charter comes into force'. As the Havana Charter was expected to come into force rather quickly, existing GATT-inconsistent legislation was not supposed to be tolerated for long. Of course, the ITO never materialised, and 'grandfather rights' did create a problem for a number of years. Although many of these rights were superseded when new legislation was passed or old laws became inoperative, they were never fully removed from the GATT until the completion of the Uruguay Round. Consequently, many of the key GATT obligations survived for 47 years on a 'provisional' basis. Thus the GATT alone, without a constitutional or institutional foundation, was left to function as the world forum for international trade matters. The result of this scheme was an 'organisation' ill-equipped to regulate the broad issues presented in world trade. To address this, the contracting parties continuously sought additions (such as a Council and various committees), revisions, codifications and improvements to the system, leading to constant improvisation. Overall, the GATT proved itself to be successful in reducing certain trade barriers, but the growing complexity of international trading relations coupled with increased membership proved to be too much for the 'organisation'. The contracting parties to the GATT were on the right track towards developing a body regulating international trade, but too many flaws in its initial formation and development exposed the GATT's shortcomings and weaknesses.

Professor John H Jackson wrote during the Uruguay Round about some of the institutional flaws of the GATT:

1) The 'provisional' application of GATT has been very confusing to the public and experts alike. It has also involved the so-called 'grandfather rights' of existing legislation, which have been the subject of the rankest debate.

2) The amending provisions of the GATT treaty structure are inadequate. It is very difficult to amend the GATT (unanimity for some clauses; two-thirds for other clauses), and even when amended, the amendments do not apply to countries that refuse to accept the amendment. Many people have felt that the GATT is impossible to amend, and one result of this feeling in the Tokyo Round of the 1970's, was the establishment of a series of separate treaty 'side agreements,' or 'codes', which added greatly to the complexity of GATT. This rendered the GATT vulnerable to the charge that it was an 'a la carte' system, which reduced the predictability and uniformity of obligations among nations.

3) The relationship of some of these side agreements to the GATT itself, in some cases affected by the most favored nation clause, has been sometimes murky and difficult to apply.

4) The relationship of the GATT treaty system to domestic law in a number of GATT member countries, including the United States, is also a troublesome issue.

5) A number of problems concerning membership, or contracting party status, in the GATT system exist. There are various ways by which a nation or an independent customs territory can become a GATT contracting party, but there are additional troublesome clauses in GATT, such as the opt out clause of Article XXXV by which some contracting parties can opt out of a GATT relationship with other parties.

6) The Contracting Parties have been acting jointly much in the role of an 'assembly' comparable to other international organizations, but the power of the Contracting Parties so acting is very ambiguous, and could be abused (although it has not so far been abused). There are a number of unsettled and disquieting issues such as the power of the Contracting Parties to interpret the

GATT agreement, and the relationship of actions of Contracting Parties to some of the side agreements. It is also very hard to develop a new rule-making process.

7) The dispute settlement processes of GATT have been among the more intriguing and, at least recently, successful experiences of that institution. But there are still some very important problems, including the situation by which a losing party can block acceptance by the Council of a panel report, and the lack of a unified procedure. More attention to this procedure is obviously needed, and to ambiguous GATT phrases such as 'nullification or impairment'.

8) There has long been a problem with respect to the relationship of GATT to the other Bretton Woods institutions such as the International Monetary Fund and the World Bank. The GATT has often been treated as a 'country cousin,' inferior to the other institutions, and there have sometimes developed certain contradictory policies as between these institutions. There is a feeling that more 'coherence' is called for.[3]

(b) GATT Negotiating Rounds

Although the framework and basic legal text of the GATT remained relatively constant throughout the GATT years, several multilateral negotiating rounds were used to further liberalisation in the form of tariff reductions as well as the expansion of topical coverage through plurilateral, voluntary agreements. The eight negotiating rounds of the GATT, subjects covered and number of participating countries and economies are listed in Table 2.1.

While the first five rounds focused solely on reducing tariffs, the purpose of the sixth round (Kennedy Round) expanded to include anti-dumping practices. That round mainly focused on tariff reduction, though, and it was not until the seventh round (Tokyo Round) that non-tariff measures and systemic issues were comprehensively negotiated. While this round failed to achieve agreement on agriculture and safeguards, it did conclude several plurilateral 'codes', on topics including subsidies and countervailing measures, technical barriers to trade (standards), import licensing procedures, government procurement, customs valuation, anti-dumping, bovine meat, international dairy and trade in civil aircraft. Moreover, 'understandings', 'decisions' and 'declarations' were also negotiated on such issues as special and differential treatment, balance-of-payments, safeguards and dispute settlement.

The most ambitious, comprehensive and far-reaching round to date has been the Uruguay Round. Not only did the Uruguay Round continue the goal of liberalising trade through tariff reduction and the elimination of non-tariff barriers to trade, it also expanded the multilateral trading system beyond goods to include, inter alia, trade in services and intellectual property. Significantly, the Round also streamlined and strengthened the dispute settlement system and agreed to abandon most plurilateral agreements in favour of a multilateral approach to almost every topical area. Finally, and most importantly, through this Round Members agreed to the creation of the WTO, a formal organisation that would unify all of the various agreements within one institutional framework. The current WTO negotiating round is called the Doha Round. Launched in 2001, progress in the round has been slow and at present there are serious concerns the round will fail. In fact, Members

---

[3] JH Jackson, 'GATT and the Future of International Trade Institutions' (1992) 8 *Brooklyn Journal of International Law* 11.

Table 2.1 GATT negotiating rounds

Year	Place/name	Subjects covered	Participating countries and economies
1947	Geneva	Tariffs	23
1949	Annecy	Tariffs	13
1951	Torquay	Tariffs	38
1956	Geneva	Tariffs	26
1960–61	Dillon Round	Tariffs	26
1964–67	Kennedy Round	Tariffs and anti-dumping measures	62
1973–79	Tokyo Round	Tariffs, non-tariff measures, 'framework' agreements	102
1986–94	Uruguay Round	Tariffs, non-tariff measures, rules, services, intellectual property, dispute settlement, textiles, agriculture, creation of WTO, etc	123

Source: WTO, *Understanding the WTO* (WTO, Geneva, 2005) 16.

declared the Round was at an 'impasse' at the Eighth Ministerial Conference held in December 2011 and no timeline has been set for formally restarting the negotiations.

III. THE WTO AS AN INSTITUTION

The formation of the WTO was not a smooth process. In fact, the Uruguay Round did not even originally set out to establish an 'organisation'. Instead, the creation of the WTO was the product of over seven years of turbulent negotiation between 127 countries culminating in the most extensive international trade agreement ever concluded. The following extract discusses the negotiating history and formation of the WTO in more detail.

GR Winham, 'The World Trade Organisation: Institution-Building in the Multilateral Trade System' (1998) 21(3) *World Economy* 353

The WTO was an unintended by-product of the Uruguay Round negotiation. It was not included in the negotiating mandate of the Uruguay Round established in the Ministerial Meeting at Punta del Este in 1986. The concept of a new international trade organisation developed as a derivative of other concerns that surfaced during the negotiation process. One such early concern was coherence, which referred generally to international cooperation in all areas of global economic policymaking, and specifically to institutional cooperation between the GATT, IMF and World Bank. The concern for coherence was enunciated by the European Community in the Negotiating Group on Functioning of the GATT System (FOGs) in 1988, and it remained an issue throughout all subsequent discussions.

Another concern was enunciated by academic trade lawyers, mainly Professor John Jackson of the University of Michigan [Ed. Note: Professor Jackson is now at the Georgetown University Law Center]. Jackson noted that the incremental development of the GATT created a system characterised by legal uncertainty and political weakness. The crux of Jackson's argument was that the GATT was not a single treaty instrument, but a large cluster of more than 180 agreements which had differing purposes and memberships and which, in some cases, were not entirely consistent with the GATT itself. Most of the agreements were added during GATT multilateral negotiations.

Jackson's argument had particular force with respect to the Tokyo Round, where nine codes of non-tariff measures and four 'understandings' were produced. The Tokyo Round Codes were open to limited membership, hence they were arguably inconsistent with the principle of non-discrimination in GATT Article I. Moreover, they had separate dispute settlement arrangements, which encouraged 'forum-shopping' among Contracting Parties. Unless efforts were made to achieve a mechanism of coordination, it was possible the Uruguay Round might produce further decentralisation of the GATT system. Such a mechanism might be a charter or constitution for international trade cooperation, which Jackson, 'for simplicity's sake', called a World Trade Organisation.

Initially, Jackson's concerns made little headway with negotiators who felt they did not address the more important substantive issues facing the Uruguay Round. However, government lawyers in the EC and Canada pursued the idea of a WTO and in the process recognised it had valuable political content. For example, the European Community noted that the reasons usually given by the US Government for using unilateral trade sanctions was the absence of an effective and credible multilateral enforcement mechanism: might not a WTO remove the rationale for such unilateralism? Internal discussion in the EC was subsequently aired in public when in February, 1990, Italian Trade Minister Renato Rugiero called for the establishment of an international trade organisation. This call was shortly echoed by Canadian Trade Minister John Crosbie, who evoked postwar institution-building in calling for the creation of an 'institutional architecture' to cope with challenging times.

The concept of an international trade organisation was raised in internal negotiations over the summer of 1990. The EC tabled a formal paper in the FOGs Group calling for the Establishment of a Multilateral Trade Organisation (MTO) in June, 1990. The paper argued: (i) GATT needed a proper legal basis; (ii) the Tokyo Round codes, and the forthcoming Uruguay Round accords, needed a common institutional framework; (iii) a single dispute settlement system would be advantageous; and (iv) the GATT needed a role beyond its limited contractual nature to conduct internal reviews of members' trade policies and to negotiate externally with other international organisations. Throughout the fall, Canadian and EC lawyers worked to draft language for the Final Act to be tabled at the Brussels Ministerial Meeting in December, 1990. However, most delegations felt the MTO – as it was then called – was a nuisance issue, and there was little support for anything at Brussels other than a vague reference to the future creation of an organisation, when, and if, there was an agreement on substantive aspects of the negotiation.

The Brussels meeting, which was intended to conclude the Uruguay Round, failed. Negotiation picked up again in the spring of 1991, and by late fall an Institutions negotiating group had been established under Ambassador Julio Lecarte to work on dispute settlement and other institutional issues. Negotiators worked toward a deadline of mid-December, 1991, imposed by GATT Director-General Arthur Dunkel for the completion of what became known as the Draft Final Act (the Dunkel text). Dispute settlement was the principal preoccupation of the Institutions Group, and by the deadline the main lines of what became the DSU were in place. This included the controversial issue of a 'single integrated dispute settlement system', which would allow for cross-retaliation. India, the principal holdout on this issue, indicated its acceptance on 19 December, 1991, in the last hour of the negotiation.

During the run-up to the Draft Final Act, the Canadian and EC negotiators, now working together, produced successive drafts of an MTO in the Institutions Group. Some of the provisions in these drafts were controversial and attracted resistance from other delegations. For example, the EC-Canadian drafts carried forward the legal voting requirements from the GATT which provided for one country-one vote and majority voting, without acknowledging that historically the GATT operated on the basis of consensus. By December, the efforts of the EC-Canadian negotiators were joined by Mexico. However, the United States and Japan did not accept the principle that a new organisation was needed, even though they participated in the deliberations of the Institutions Group. By the deadline, an unfinished text went forward to be included as an annex in the Draft Final Act of December, 1991. Most delegations made major reservations to the text, except the EC, Canada and Mexico.

In early 1992, Uruguay Round negotiators commenced reviewing and finalising the Draft Final Act (DFA). A Legal Drafting Group was initiated to 'scrub' the DFA, and to work on the MTO text. The Group quickly became, in the words of one participant, 'neither legal nor drafting', but rather a full-blown negotiation that focused on the MTO. Work concentrated on decision-making and structure of a new organisation, with the US delegation proposing a number of ideas that eventually found their way into Article IV (Structure) of the WTO Agreement. Progress was made, but then work was suspended in May, 1992, when a new breakdown on agriculture paralysed work throughout the Uruguay Round.

In November, 1992, the United States and EC concluded the Blair House accord on agriculture, which re-started negotiations in Geneva. Efforts were made to conclude the negotiation before the Republicans, who had lost the White House to the Democrats, left office. About this time the US delegation came forward with major reservations to an MTO, and tabled a proposal for a protocol that could have concluded the Uruguay Round without the need for any new structure (Inside US Trade, 1992). This action puzzled other negotiators, who had assumed following the discussions in 1992 that the United States would be willing to accept a new organisation assuming other things in the negotiation fell into place. The objection in principle appeared to be a turnaround in the US position.

It is clear that US negotiators felt they could not get out in front on the MTO. The MTO was seen as a political lightening rod in Washington, and there was fear that those interests opposed to the Uruguay Round for whatever reason could rally around this issue. Whether this concern was heightened by the Democratic Presidential victory in November, 1992, is a matter of speculation. Whatever the reason, the US action put it at variance with most other delegations, who had come to accept the MTO as an attractive solution to the two basic problems of how to provide for legal consistency and how to administer the forthcoming Uruguay Round agreements. By the end of 1992, major actors like Japan and Brazil lifted reservations to the MTO. The United States was isolated in opposition, with only Switzerland for support.

The negotiation again suffered a hiatus in early 1993, but re-started following the appointment in July of Peter Sutherland to replace Arthur Dunkel as GATT Director General. By August, Sutherland had reconvened the Institutions Negotiating Group under Ambassador Lecarte, and given it a mandate to complete the MTO and a dispute settlement agreement. In a Trade Negotiations Committee meeting on 31 August, 1993, the Director General's mandate was questioned by the representative of the United States, who suggested that the discussion should focus on whether or not it was necessary to create a new organisation since the major objectives of the Round could be achieved without it. This interpretation was not supported by other delegations. Particularly India and the EC argued that—following the previous year's discussions in the Legal Drafting Group—the principle of establishing an MTO was no longer at issue, and they fully supported the initiative of the Director General to complete negotiations on this subject.

Negotiations quickened after September, with an overall deadline set for 15 December, 1993.

The United States again tabled a proposal designed to implement the Uruguay Round with a protocol and ministerial conference in lieu of establishing an MTO. However, it gradually became clear that the United States accepted it had lost the argument, and that despite its concerns on sovereignty it probably would not break the Uruguay Round on this issue. In part, the US position had been one of principle, of putting substance before form, which was reflected in former US Trade Representative Carla Hills oft-repeated dictum: 'You don't build the courthouse until you have the walls in place'. In part, however, the position also had been one of tactics, of seeking quid pro quo, which was evident in US Chief Negotiator John Schmidt's reported comments to European business leaders:

The Administration has told trading partners, he said, that 'if you can solve all the other problems in the Round so we don't have major constituencies that are likely to oppose us, and if you give us enough in terms of the positive side that we can feel comfortable that we will have the kind of support we need to carry it in Congress,' the Administration could rethink its opposition to the MTO.

The United States maintained its opposition in principle to the MTO at what was known as the Heads of Delegation level. Meanwhile, it also negotiated hard in the Institutions Group to weaken the impact of majoritarian voting rules (which were largely drawn from the original GATT accord) in favour of stronger admonitions supporting consensus decision-making. At the end of the Institutions negotiation, Ambassador Lecarte drew aside about four countries (likely these were the United States, the EC, Japan and India) and worked out final changes to the text, and then presented the text on a take-it-or-leave-it basis to about 50 delegation representatives participating in the Institutions Group. Canada spoke first and supported the text, and 'then all the dominoes fell and everyone agreed'. Only Egypt had some minor complaint, but Chairman Lecarte gavelled the text through.

The text subsequently went forward to the Heads of Delegation level and on 15 December, 1993, it was the last issue of the Uruguay Round to be settled between the United States and the EC. The question was whether the United States would lift its reservation in principle to the MTO. The United States agreed to lift its reservation in exchange for an EC concession on computer chips, and on condition that the organisation name be changed from MTO to World Trade Organisation (WTO). This was the name originally proposed by the Canadian delegation, who in turn had lifted it from the writings of Professor Jackson.

… … …

(a) WTO Objectives, Scope and Functions

Unlike the GATT, the WTO is without question an international organisation established by treaty with full legal personality, all 'privileges and immunities' necessary to exercise its functions and the ability and mandate to develop relations with other international organisations.[4] The WTO is the only multilateral international body that creates, regulates and manages the rules of trade between nations. Vital and central to the WTO are the various negotiated agreements, including commitments and concessions on goods and services. Together, these documents—which are essentially binding contracts (some scholars have referred to them as a 'constitution')—supply the international trading community with the legal ground-rules for international commerce. Although it is governments who negotiate, sign and implement the agreements, the ultimate goal of the WTO, the WTO

---

[4] Agreement Establishing the World Trade Organisation, Art VIII.

itself says, is to help producers, importers and exporters conduct business.[5] In this section, we examine in more detail the WTO's official view of its purpose.

(i) Objectives

Defining a specific purpose or purposes for the WTO is difficult. A number of theories have been put forward as to the WTO's actual or appropriate objectives, but there is much disagreement on the issue. Officially, the WTO presents its three main objectives as follows:[6]

- It is a negotiating forum.
- It provides a set of rules.
- It helps settle disputes among Members.

In addition, the WTO elaborates that the world trading system is governed by the following principles:[7]

- non-discrimination
- freer trade through reductions in trade barriers
- predictability through binding trade commitments
- fair and undistorted competition
- special treatment for developing countries

The following extract, part of a document produced by the WTO, more fully develops this view of the WTO's basic objectives and principles.

> **WTO, *Understanding the WTO* (WTO, Geneva, 2005) 8–13**
>
> **Above all, it's a negotiating forum** ... Essentially, the WTO is a place where member governments go, to try to sort out the trade problems they face with each other. The first step is to talk. The WTO was born out of negotiations, and everything the WTO does is the result of negotiations. The bulk of the WTO's current work comes from the 1986-94 negotiations called the Uruguay Round and earlier negotiations under the General Agreement on Tariffs and Trade (GATT). The WTO is currently the host to new negotiations, under the 'Doha Development Agenda' launched in 2001.
>
> Where countries have faced trade barriers and wanted them lowered, the negotiations have helped to liberalize trade. But the WTO is not just about liberalizing trade, and in some circumstances its rules support maintaining trade barriers—for example to protect consumers or prevent the spread of disease.
>
> **It's a set of rules ...** At its heart are the WTO agreements, negotiated and signed by the bulk of the world's trading nations. These documents provide the legal ground-rules for international commerce. They are essentially contracts, binding governments to keep their trade policies within agreed limits. Although negotiated and signed by governments, the goal is to help producers of goods and services, exporters, and importers conduct their business, while allowing governments to meet social and environmental objectives.

---

[5] WTO, *Understanding the WTO* (Geneva, WTO, 2005) 8. It could be argued that this official statement perhaps exaggerates the WTO's role, as the WTO has little bearing on contracts between private companies.
[6] *Ibid.*
[7] *Ibid.*

The system's overriding purpose is to help trade flow as freely as possible—so long as there are no undesirable side-effects. That partly means removing obstacles. It also means ensuring that individuals, companies and governments know what the trade rules are around the world, and giving them the confidence that there will be no sudden changes of policy. In other words, the rules have to be 'transparent' and predictable.

And it helps to settle disputes ... This is a third important side to the WTO's work. Trade relations often involve conflicting interests. Agreements, including those painstakingly negotiated in the WTO system, often need interpreting. The most harmonious way to settle these differences is through some neutral procedure based on an agreed legal foundation. That is the purpose behind the dispute settlement process written into the WTO agreements.

...

Principles of the trading system

The WTO agreements are lengthy and complex because they are legal texts covering a wide range of activities. They deal with: agriculture, textiles and clothing, banking, telecommunications, government purchases, industrial standards and product safety, food sanitation regulations, intellectual property, and much more. But a number of simple, fundamental principles run throughout all of these documents. These principles are the foundation of the multilateral trading system.

The trading system should be . . .

without discrimination—a country should not discriminate between its trading partners (giving them equally 'most-favoured-nation' or MFN status); and it should not discriminate between its own and foreign products, services or nationals (giving them 'national treatment');

freer—barriers coming down through negotiation;

predictable—foreign companies, investors and governments should be confident that trade barriers (including tariffs and non-tariff barriers) should not be raised arbitrarily; tariff rates and market-opening commitments are 'bound' in the WTO;

more competitive—discouraging 'unfair' practices such as export subsidies and dumping products at below cost to gain market share;

more beneficial for less developed countries—giving them more time to adjust, greater flexibility, and special privileges.

A closer look at these principles:

Trade without discrimination

1. Most-favoured-nation (MFN): treating other people equally

Under the WTO agreements, countries cannot normally discriminate between their trading partners. Grant someone a special favour (such as a lower customs duty rate for one of their products) and you have to do the same for all other WTO members.

This principle is known as most-favoured-nation (MFN) treatment. It is so important that it is the first article of the General Agreement on Tariffs and Trade (GATT), which governs trade in goods. MFN is also a priority in the General Agreement on Trade in Services (GATS) (Article 2) and the Agreement on Trade-Related Aspects of Intellectual Property Rights (TRIPS) (Article 4), although in each agreement the principle is handled slightly differently. Together, those three agreements cover all three main areas of trade handled by the WTO.

Some exceptions are allowed. For example, countries can set up a free trade agreement that applies only to goods traded within the group— discriminating against goods from outside. Or they can give developing countries special access to their markets. Or a country can raise barriers against products that are considered to be traded unfairly from specific countries. And in services, countries are allowed, in limited circumstances, to discriminate. But the agreements only permit these exceptions under strict conditions. In general, MFN means that every time a country lowers a trade barrier or opens up a market, it has to do so for the same goods or services from all its trading partners—whether rich or poor, weak or strong.

2. National treatment: Treating foreigners and locals equally

Imported and locally-produced goods should be treated equally—at least after the foreign goods have entered the market. The same should apply to foreign and domestic services, and to foreign and local trademarks, copyrights and patents. This principle of 'national treatment' (giving others the same treatment as one's own nationals) is also found in all the three main WTO agreements (Article 3 of GATT, Article 17 of GATS and Article 3 of TRIPS), although once again the principle is handled slightly differently in each of these.

National treatment only applies once a product, service or item of intellectual property has entered the market. Therefore, charging customs duty on an import is not a violation of national treatment even if locally-produced products are not charged an equivalent tax.

Freer trade: gradually, through negotiation

Lowering trade barriers is one of the most obvious means of encouraging trade. The barriers concerned include customs duties (or tariffs) and measures such as import bans or quotas that restrict quantities selectively. From time to time other issues such as red tape and exchange rate policies have also been discussed.

Since GATT's creation in 1947–48 there have been eight rounds of trade negotiations. A ninth round, under the Doha Development Agenda, is now underway. At first these focused on lowering tariffs (customs duties) on imported goods. As a result of the negotiations, by the mid-1990s industrial countries' tariff rates on industrial goods had fallen steadily to less than 4%.

But by the 1980s, the negotiations had expanded to cover non-tariff barriers on goods, and to the new areas such as services and intellectual property.

Opening markets can be beneficial, but it also requires adjustment. The WTO agreements allow countries to introduce changes gradually, through 'progressive liberalization'. Developing countries are usually given longer to fulfil their obligations.

Predictability: through binding and transparency

Sometimes, promising not to raise a trade barrier can be as important as lowering one, because the promise gives businesses a clearer view of their future opportunities. With stability and predictability, investment is encouraged, jobs are created and consumers can fully enjoy the benefits of competition—choice and lower prices. The multilateral trading system is an attempt by governments to make the business environment stable and predictable.

The Uruguay Round increased bindings

Percentages of tariffs bound before and after the 1986–94 talks

	Developed countries	Developing countries	Transition economies
Before	78	21	73
After	99	73	98

(These are tariff lines, so percentages are not weighted according to trade volume or value)

In the WTO, when countries agree to open their markets for goods or services, they 'bind' their commitments. For goods, these bindings amount to ceilings on customs tariff rates. Sometimes countries tax imports at rates that are lower than the bound rates. Frequently this is the case in developing countries. In developed countries the rates actually charged and the bound rates tend to be the same.

A country can change its bindings, but only after negotiating with its trading partners, which could mean compensating them for loss of trade. One of the achievements of the Uruguay Round of multilateral trade talks was to increase the amount of trade under binding commitments (see table). In agriculture, 100% of products now have bound tariffs. The result of all this: a substantially higher degree of market security for traders and investors.

The system tries to improve predictability and stability in other ways as well. One way is to discourage the use of quotas and other measures used to set limits on quantities of imports—administering quotas can lead to more red-tape and accusations of unfair play. Another is to make countries' trade rules as clear and public ('transparent') as possible. Many WTO agreements require governments to disclose their policies and practices publicly within the country or by notifying the WTO. The regular surveillance of national trade policies through the Trade Policy Review Mechanism provides a further means of encouraging transparency both domestically and at the multilateral level.

Promoting fair competition

The WTO is sometimes described as a 'free trade' institution, but that is not entirely accurate. The system does allow tariffs and, in limited circumstances, other forms of protection. More accurately, it is a system of rules dedicated to open, fair and undistorted competition.

The rules on non-discrimination—MFN and national treatment—are designed to secure fair conditions of trade. So too are those on dumping (exporting at below cost to gain market share) and subsidies. The issues are complex, and the rules try to establish what is fair or unfair, and how governments can respond, in particular by charging additional import duties calculated to compensate for damage caused by unfair trade.

Many of the other WTO agreements aim to support fair competition: in agriculture, intellectual property, services, for example. The agreement on government procurement (a 'plurilateral' agreement because it is signed by only a few WTO members) extends competition rules to purchases by thousands of government entities in many countries. And so on.

Encouraging development and economic reform

The WTO system contributes to development. On the other hand, developing countries need flexibility in the time they take to implement the system's agreements. And the agreements themselves inherit the earlier provisions of GATT that allow for special assistance and trade concessions for developing countries.

Over three quarters of WTO members are developing countries and countries in transition to market economies. During the seven and a half years of the Uruguay Round, over 60 of these countries implemented trade liberalization programmes autonomously. At the same time, developing countries and transition economies were much more active and influential in the Uruguay Round negotiations than in any previous round, and they are even more so in the current Doha Development Agenda.

At the end of the Uruguay Round, developing countries were prepared to take on most of the obligations that are required of developed countries. But the agreements did give them transition periods to adjust to the more unfamiliar and, perhaps, difficult WTO provisions—particularly so for the poorest, 'least-developed' countries. A ministerial decision adopted at the end of the round says better-off countries should accelerate implementing market access commitments on goods exported by the least-developed countries, and it seeks increased technical assistance for them. More recently, developed countries have started to allow duty-free and quota-free imports for almost all products from least-developed countries. On all of this, the WTO and its members are still going through a learning process. The current Doha Development Agenda includes developing countries' concerns about the difficulties they face in implementing the Uruguay Round agreements.

... ...

While the WTO is mainly dedicated to trade liberalisation, the Preamble to the WTO Agreement makes clear that the organisation's mandate extends to additional objectives. The Preamble states:

Recognizing that their relations in the field of trade and economic endeavour should be conducted with a view to raising standards of living, ensuring full employment and a large and steadily growing volume of real income and effective demand, and expanding the production of and trade in goods and services, while allowing for the optimal use of the world's resources in accordance with the objective of sustainable development, seeking both to protect and preserve the environment and to enhance the means for doing so in a manner consistent with their respective needs and concerns at different levels of economic development,

Recognizing further that there is need for positive efforts designed to ensure that developing countries, and especially the least developed among them, secure a share in the growth in international trade commensurate with the needs of their economic development,

Being desirous of contributing to these objectives by entering into reciprocal and mutually advantageous arrangements directed to the substantial reduction of tariffs and other barriers to trade and to the elimination of discriminatory treatment in international trade relations,

Resolved, therefore, to develop an integrated, more viable and durable multilateral trading system encompassing the General Agreement on Tariffs and Trade, the results of past trade liberalization efforts, and all of the results of the Uruguay Round of Multilateral Trade Negotiations,

Determined to preserve the basic principles and to further the objectives underlying this multilateral trading system...

... ...

Thus, the ultimate goals of the WTO include increasing living standards, attaining full employment, growth of real income and effective demand and an expansion of the production of and trade in goods and services. In addition, the Preamble also specifically states that these objectives are to be achieved in accordance with sustainable development and through increasing integration of developing countries, and especially least developed countries, into the world trading system to allow those countries to secure a share in the growth. Importantly, though, the Preamble also notes that these objectives are to be achieved through the reduction of trade barriers and the elimination of discrimination in international trade relations. Thus, despite the mention of these broader goals, trade liberalisation is the focus.

The Preamble also provides that the newly created organisation is designed to provide an integrated, more viable and durable multilateral trading system by building upon and encompassing the GATT and the results of all the previous negotiating rounds. Thus, even though the Uruguay Round created a new organisation, the WTO remains connected to the previous trading system and all of the decisions reached throughout the GATT years.

These objectives were re-affirmed in the Doha Ministerial Declaration (14 November 2001), a key document from the current negotiations. It is worth reprinting the first section of the Declaration in full:

1. The multilateral trading system embodied in the World Trade Organization has contributed significantly to economic growth, development and employment throughout the past fifty years. We are determined, particularly in the light of the global economic slowdown, to maintain the process of reform and liberalization of trade policies, thus ensuring that the system plays its full part in promoting recovery, growth and development. We therefore *strongly reaffirm the principles and objectives set out in the Marrakesh Agreement Establishing the World Trade Organization*, and pledge to reject the use of protectionism.

2. International trade can play a major role in the promotion of economic development and the alleviation of poverty. We recognize the need for all our peoples to benefit from the increased opportunities and welfare gains that the multilateral trading system generates. The majority of WTO members are developing countries. We seek to place their needs and interests at the heart of the Work Programme adopted in this Declaration. Recalling the Preamble to the Marrakesh Agreement, we shall continue to make positive efforts designed to ensure that developing countries, and especially the least-developed among them, secure a share in the growth of world trade commensurate with the needs of their economic development. In this context, enhanced market access, balanced rules, and well targeted, sustainably financed technical assistance and capacity-building programmes have important roles to play.

3. We recognize the particular vulnerability of the least-developed countries and the special structural difficulties they face in the global economy. We are committed to addressing the marginalization of least-developed countries in international trade and to improving their effective participation in the multilateral trading system. We recall the commitments made by ministers at our meetings in Marrakesh, Singapore and Geneva, and by the international community at the Third UN Conference on Least-Developed Countries in Brussels, to help least-developed countries secure beneficial and meaningful integration into the multilateral trading system and the global economy. We are determined that the WTO will play its part in building effectively on these commitments under the Work Programme we are establishing.

4. We stress our commitment to the WTO as the unique forum for global trade rule-making and liberalization, while also recognizing that regional trade agreements can play an important role in promoting the liberalization and expansion of trade and in fostering development.

5. We are aware that the challenges members face in a rapidly changing international environment cannot be addressed through measures taken in the trade field alone. We shall continue to work with the Bretton Woods institutions for greater coherence in global economic policy-making.

6. We strongly reaffirm our commitment to the objective of sustainable development, as stated in the Preamble to the Marrakesh Agreement. We are convinced that the aims of upholding and safeguarding an open and non-discriminatory multilateral trading system, and acting for the

protection of the environment and the promotion of sustainable development can and must be mutually supportive. We take note of the efforts by members to conduct national environmental assessments of trade policies on a voluntary basis. We recognize that under WTO rules no country should be prevented from taking measures for the protection of human, animal or plant life or health, or of the environment at the levels it considers appropriate, subject to the requirement that they are not applied in a manner which would constitute a means of arbitrary or unjustifiable discrimination between countries where the same conditions prevail, or a disguised restriction on international trade, and are otherwise in accordance with the provisions of the WTO Agreements. We welcome the WTO's continued cooperation with UNEP and other inter-governmental environmental organizations. We encourage efforts to promote cooperation between the WTO and relevant international environmental and developmental organizations, especially in the lead-up to the World Summit on Sustainable Development to be held in Johannesburg, South Africa, in September 2002.

7.   We reaffirm the right of members under the General Agreement on Trade in Services to regulate, and to introduce new regulations on, the supply of services.

8.   We reaffirm our declaration made at the Singapore Ministerial Conference regarding internationally recognized core labour standards. We take note of work under way in the International Labour Organization (ILO) on the social dimension of globalization.

9.   We note with particular satisfaction that this conference has completed the WTO accession procedures for China and Chinese Taipei. We also welcome the accession as new members, since our last session, of Albania, Croatia, Georgia, Jordan, Lithuania, Moldova and Oman, and note the extensive market-access commitments already made by these countries on accession. These accessions will greatly strengthen the multilateral trading system, as will those of the 28 countries now negotiating their accession. We therefore attach great importance to concluding accession proceedings as quickly as possible. In particular, we are committed to accelerating the accession of least-developed countries.

10.   Recognizing the challenges posed by an expanding WTO membership, we confirm our collective responsibility to ensure internal transparency and the effective participation of all members. While emphasizing the intergovernmental character of the organization, we are committed to making the WTO's operations more transparent, including through more effective and prompt dissemination of information, and to improve dialogue with the public. We shall therefore at the national and multilateral levels continue to promote a better public understanding of the WTO and to communicate the benefits of a liberal, rules-based multilateral trading system.

11.   In view of these considerations, we hereby agree to undertake the broad and balanced Work Programme set out below. This incorporates both an expanded negotiating agenda and other important decisions and activities necessary to address the challenges facing the multilateral trading system.

… … …

As a final point related to the WTO's objectives, it could be argued that the WTO's official statements of its purpose are somewhat misleading, and tend to gloss over differences in viewpoint with carefully worded statements that avoid some of the controversy. The WTO's official statements of its objectives are not wrong, but they do leave out important parts of the story.

Reading through the WTO rules, as we will do in later chapters, there are a number of policy goals that are pursued. Two of the core goals, promoting non-discrimination and transparency, have widespread support (although defining non-discrimination can be quite difficult and rulings limiting the ability to engage in protectionism have many opponents). In addition, though, there are a number of rules that pursue other principles, sometimes vaguely defined:

- The TRIPS Agreement sets out substantive intellectual property protection rules that governments must enforce.
- The GATS provides for 'market access' rules that go beyond non-discrimination.
- The Telecoms Reference Paper that some Members have incorporated into their GATS Commitments requires pro-competition policies for the telecommunications sector.
- SPS Agreement Article 2.2 requires that SPS Measures be based on 'scientific principles'.
- TBT Agreement Article 2.2 requires that Members ensure that technical regulations are not prepared, adopted or applied with a view to or with the effect of creating unnecessary obstacles to international trade.
- The SPS, TBT and TRIPS Agreements all promote harmonisation and mutual recognition of laws to some extent.

These kinds of rules go far beyond the more limited rules of the GATT, which by and large were limited to issues of tariff reduction and non-discrimination. As the scope of the rules has grown, so has the intrusiveness of these rules into domestic policy-making. This expansion has been one of the main reasons for the increased criticism of trade agreements in recent years. Combined with the absence of clear guidelines and boundaries to the scope of WTO rules, this has caused concern among those who see the WTO as a future 'world government', and also those who worry that it pursues harmful policies that favour corporations over ordinary people.

(ii) Scope and Functions

The scope and functions of the WTO are set out in Articles II and III of the WTO Agreement:

Article II

Scope of the WTO

1. The WTO shall provide the common institutional framework for the conduct of trade relations among its Members in matters related to the agreements and associated legal instruments included in the Annexes to this Agreement.

…

Article III

Functions of the WTO

1. The WTO shall facilitate the implementation, administration and operation, and further the objectives, of this Agreement and of the Multilateral Trade Agreements, and shall also provide the framework for the implementation, administration and operation of the Plurilateral Trade Agreements.

2. The WTO shall provide the forum for negotiations among its Members concerning their

multilateral trade relations in matters dealt with under the agreements in the Annexes to this Agreement. The WTO may also provide a forum for further negotiations among its Members concerning their multilateral trade relations, and a framework for the implementation of the results of such negotiations, as may be decided by the Ministerial Conference.

3. The WTO shall administer the Understanding on Rules and Procedures Governing the Settlement of Disputes (hereinafter referred to as the 'Dispute Settlement Understanding' or 'DSU') in Annex 2 to this Agreement.

4. The WTO shall administer the Trade Policy Review Mechanism (hereinafter referred to as the 'TPRM') provided for in Annex 3 to this Agreement.

5. With a view to achieving greater coherence in global economic policy-making, the WTO shall cooperate, as appropriate, with the International Monetary Fund and with the International Bank for Reconstruction and Development and its affiliated agencies.

(b) Basic Structure of the WTO

While the WTO was created in 1995, many aspects of the organisation are carry-overs from its predecessor, the GATT. Members of the WTO continue to use negotiating rounds to develop the rules of the international trading system and further liberalise through binding tariff and other commitments. Another feature of the GATT carried over to the WTO is the 'consensus' approach to the decision-making process. The WTO remains a Member driven organisation, and consensus decision-making allows Members to retain control of the system and avoids the problems of majority voting, weighted voting and any other method which could see a Member being forced to adhere to something on which it disagrees. That being said, the WTO Agreement does allow for votes to be taken on certain decisions when consensus cannot be reached (see, eg, Articles IX and X of the WTO Agreement, discussed below).

(i) The Basic Rules

The WTO Agreement is a relatively sparse document that merely outlines institutional measures; it contains no substantive trade obligations. Instead, the substantive commitments and rules are contained in four annexes. The substantive rules are made effective through Article XVI:4 of the WTO Agreement, which states:

> Each member shall ensure the conformity of its laws, regulations and administrative procedures with its obligations as provided in the annexed Agreements.

The annex structure of the WTO is significant and, in theory, allows for amendments, additions and subtractions to specific agreements more easily than if all the rules were in only one agreement. Annex 1 is comprised of the Multilateral Trade Agreements (Annex 1A: Goods, Annex 1B: Services and Annex 1C: Intellectual Property). These agreements are 'mandatory', meaning they are binding on all Members. Therefore, and unlike the GATT, the WTO, for the most part, is a 'single package', and Members can no longer 'pick and choose' which agreements to abide by and which to ignore. With the agreements and schedules of concessions on goods and services, Annex 1 contains the bulk of the final text of the Uruguay Round negotiations.

Annex 2 contains the rules of dispute settlement. Unlike the GATT, dispute settlement under the WTO is binding and enforceable. Annex 2 is applicable to the WTO Agreement and to the agreements in Annexes 1 and 4, as well as to the Annex 2 dispute settlement rules themselves.

Annex 3 creates the Trade Policy Review Mechanism (TPRM), under which the WTO reviews and reports on the trade policies and practices of the Members. Trade policy reviews are undertaken to increase the transparency and understanding of trade policies and practices, through regular monitoring, so as to improve the quality of public and intergovernmental debate on the issues and to enable a multilateral assessment of the effects of policies on the world trading system.

Annex 4 contains the four plurilateral (ie, optional membership) agreements which remained following the creation of the WTO. Originally negotiated in the Tokyo Round, these agreements targeted relatively few industries and affected a narrower group of signatories. Only two of the original four plurilateral agreements remain in force today, but the structure of the WTO Agreement allows for additional agreements to be added if the Membership so decides at some point in the future.

The structure of the WTO Agreement annexes is as follows:

Annex 1
Annex 1A Multilateral Agreements on Trade in Goods
—GATT 1994 (which incorporates GATT 1947)
—Agriculture
—Sanitary and Phytosanitary Measures
—Textiles and Clothing (this Agreement terminated on 1 January 2005)
—Technical Barriers to Trade
—Trade-Related Investment Measures
—Anti-dumping
—Customs valuation
—Preshipment Inspection
—Rules of Origin
—Import Licensing
—Subsidies and Countervailing Measures
—Safeguards
Annex 1B General Agreement on Trade in Services (GATS)
Annex 1C Trade-Related Aspects of Intellectual Property Rights (TRIPS)
Annex 2 Dispute Settlement Understanding
Annex 3 Trade Policy Review Mechanism
Annex 4 Plurilateral Trade Agreements
—Annex 4(a) Agreement on Trade in Civil Aircraft
—Annex 4(b) Agreement on Government Procurement
—Annex 4(c) International Dairy Agreement (this Agreement terminated in 1997)
—Annex 4(d) International Bovine Meat Agreement (this Agreement terminated in 1997)

An important point to note is that Annex 1A refers to the 'General Agreement on Tariffs and Trade 1994'. In essence, with the establishment of the WTO, Members formally agreed to a new GATT, called GATT 1994. The GATT 1994 does not provide new substantive obligations, but rather incorporates the original GATT, now called GATT 1947, as well as various other GATT decisions and other instruments. Thus, technically speaking, the current agreement is called the GATT 1994. For ease of reference, however, we use the term 'GATT' in this book.

(ii) Governing Structure / Ministerial Conference

While the governance of the WTO is based upon and similar to the governing structure of the GATT, it does depart from the past in several substantial areas. The 'topmost' decision-making body of the WTO is the Ministerial Conference, which must meet at least every two years. The Ministerial Conference brings all Members of the WTO together and can take decisions on all matters under any of the multilateral trade agreements. Directly under the Ministerial Conference is the General Council. Composed of representatives of all Members, the General Council has overall supervisory authority and carries out many of the functions of the Ministerial Conference between such Conferences. The General Council meets whenever necessary in between meetings of the Ministerial Conference, and in practice meets at least monthly. In addition, in the same way, the Members also act as the Dispute Settlement Body and the Trade Policy Review Mechanism. In essence, these are just the General Council wearing a different 'hat'. The General Council also directs the activities of the other three Councils—the Council for Trade in Goods, the Council for Trade in Services and the Council for the Trade-Related Aspects of Intellectual Property Rights.

Figure 2.1 illustrates the organisation of the WTO.

(iii) WTO Secretariat

The WTO Secretariat, located in Geneva, Switzerland, is headed by a director-general appointed by the General Council. The WTO employs a staff of approximately 600 people (representing at least 70 nationalities) and operates with a budget of approximately CHF196 million (Swiss Francs). The Secretariat is responsible for the day-to-day operation of the WTO. More specifically, the Secretariat is responsible for the administrative and technical support for the WTO bodies (councils, committees, working parties, dispute settlement panels, etc); technical support for developing countries; trade performance and policy analyses; legal assistance to panels hearing trade disputes involving interpretation of WTO rules; advice and organisational infrastructure for accession negotiations.

The Secretariat is funded by assessed contributions on members, calculated on the basis of a Member's share in the total trade of all WTO Members, computed as a three year average of the most recent trade figures. If a Member's share is less than 0.015 per cent, only a minimal contribution is assessed.

(c) Decision-making in the WTO

(i) Ordinary Decisions

Decision-making in the WTO is normally done by consensus. Article IX:1 states: 'The WTO shall continue the practice of decision-making by consensus followed under GATT 1947'. Following GATT custom, consensus is deemed to exist if no Member, present at the meeting when the decision is taken, formally objects to the proposed decision. (This standard is similar, but not the same, as requiring unanimous affirmative

Figure 2.1 Governing structure of the WTO

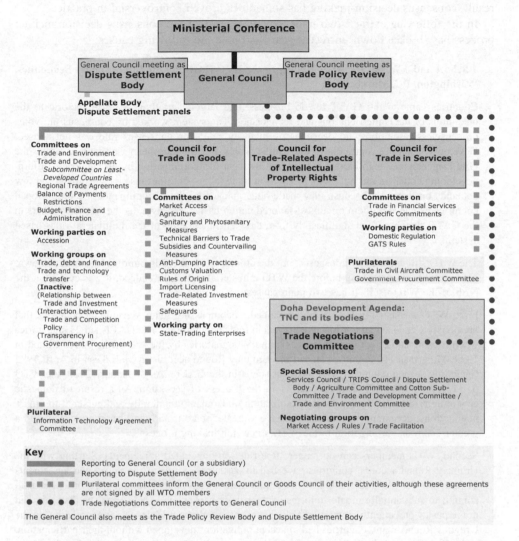

consent.) For instance, when adopting a Ministerial Declaration, the Chair will ask if there are any objections to the adoption of the Declaration and, if there are none, will announce that the Declaration has been adopted. Therefore, any Member, no matter how large or small an economy, has the ability to block any decision by explicitly objecting to a proposed decision.

In practice, Members of all sizes have occasionally used their 'veto' power when the decision would affect their national or economic interests. However, the ever-present threat of a 'veto' creates an environment where only decisions likely to garner consensus are generally brought forward. In such a circumstance, decisions resemble a 'lowest common denominator' and thus are often 'watered down'. In addition, consensus decision-making means that progress is slow and sometimes stalls due to the necessity of getting all Members to agree on the proposed decision. It is also not hard to imagine that pressure is sometimes applied to recalcitrant Members not to block 'progress'. As a result, consensus decision-making has sometimes proven controversial in practice.

In the following extract, two trade experts claim that the consensus decision-making process has 'broken down' in recent years and note the following causes:

J Schott and J Watal, *Decision-Making in the WTO* (Institute for International Economics, Washington, DC, March 2000)

Countries came to the GATT to 'do business' and largely left their political rhetoric to the talkathons of the United Nations and its agencies. The system worked by consensus: no votes on senseless resolutions; no decisions by majority rule. The consensus rule was not abused. Developed countries, particularly the United States and the European Community, drove the GATT agenda and negotiations but did not insist on full participation by all countries. In turn, developing countries did not block progress in trade talks—both because the accords posed few demands on them and because they made huge gains from the commitments of the developed countries extended to them on a most-favored nation basis. Moreover, as the weaker partners in the GATT, they benefited significantly from the well-functioning of the multilateral rules-based system.

The WTO still operates by consensus, but the process of 'consensus-building' has broken down. This problem emerged long before the WTO ministerial in Seattle; indeed, it was evident at the birth of the WTO itself. It has two main causes:

First, WTO membership has greatly expanded, encompassing many developing countries that previously were outsiders or inactive players in trade negotiations. The GATT had 23 signatories when it came into effect in January 1948, and 84 signatories by the end of the Tokyo Round in 1979. More than 110 countries signed the Uruguay Round accords in Marrakesh in April 1994 (including several countries with observer status in the GATT). As of January 2000, the WTO has 135 members with an additional 31 in the process of accession. As a result of domestic economic reforms, including trade liberalization undertaken unilaterally and pursuant to GATT negotiations, developing countries now have a greater stake in the world trading system and a greater claim on participation in the WTO's decision-making process.

Second, WTO members can no longer 'free ride' on negotiated agreements. Starting with the Uruguay Round accords, countries have had to participate in all of the negotiated agreements as part of a 'single undertaking'. This requirement means that developing countries have to commit to substantially greater reforms of their trade barriers and trade practices than they did in the past. Consequently, they need to be better informed about issues under negotiation. In the Uruguay Round, many countries had to accept obligations developed without their participation, and which required the implementation and enforcement of regulatory policies that they have had great difficulty in fulfilling.

In sum, GATT decision making worked in the past because there were fewer countries actively engaged and there was no compulsion for all countries to adhere to the results. Decisions could be taken by the 'Committee of the Whole' because only a few countries were significantly affected by the results. Consensus-building engaged a small group of countries; the rest were relatively passive. This process has fallen victim to the GATT's success in integrating developing countries more fully into the trading system and requiring them to be full partners in new trade agreements.

More active participants, representing more diverse interests and objectives, have complicated WTO decision-making. China's prospective accession will amplify this problem by adding another politically powerful player that will demand a strong voice in the WTO. In addition,

WTO decision-making has become more complicated as member countries face increasingly complex issues (for example, intellectual property rights) on the WTO negotiating agenda.

The traditional 'Green Room' process, in which a relatively small number of self-selected developed and developing countries get together to decide on divisive issues, excluded too many newly active players in WTO negotiations and thus had problems building consensus. In the course of preparations for the Seattle Ministerial, developing countries tabled about half of the proposals made for the WTO agenda. The Geneva decision-making machinery could not accommodate the diversity of views.

... ...

Of course, consensus is not the only option for decision-making. If consensus cannot be reached, Article IX:1 also provides for majority voting on the basis of one Member, one vote. Therefore, unlike in the World Bank system of weighted voting, all Members of the WTO vote in equal proportion.[8]

Decision-making in the GATT and WTO has been criticised over the years as lacking both internal and external transparency, as well as favouring the larger Members. The following extract from a WTO Secretariat employee offers some insight into the decision-making process, details recent changes to the process made in light of criticism, and evaluates the potential effectiveness and impact of alternative forms of decision-making. Ultimately, the author concludes that while the WTO process needs to continue to improve, the alternatives either are not well supported by the Members or will not bring additional benefits or transparency.

P Nørgaard Pedersen, 'The WTO Decision-making Process and Internal Transparency' (2006) 5(1) *World Trade Review* 103

1. Origins of the issue of internal transparency and decision making

Although the GATT decision-making process encountered a number of problems throughout its almost 50 year existence, many of its practices were subsequently institutionalized in the WTO. Whereas the practice of decision making by consensus was not articulated anywhere in the GATT, Article IX of the WTO Charter states 'the WTO shall continue the practice of decision making by consensus followed under GATT 1947'. Significantly, the footnote to this Article actually defines what consensus means. Articles IX and X specify when voting is possible.

The GATT decision-making process relied heavily on informal consultations. Although the practice of the Director-General hosting Green Room meetings among a few delegations had been initiated in the Tokyo Round, these informal consultations became both more frequent and involved more Contracting Parties throughout the Uruguay Round. In addition, numerous informal groups began meeting outside the GATT to discuss how to move the negotiations forward.

There was never any pretence that these groups would engage in actual decision making, but they did perform an important function in terms of gradually exposing ideas and proposals which would have died an instant death had they been aired in meetings among all the Contracting Parties. Such limited meetings also underscore the fact that then, as well as today, effective discussion, debate, and negotiation is impossible when the group exceeds 25–30 Members.

---

[8] During such votes, the EC is entitled to have a number of votes equal to the number of their member States which are Members of the WTO (currently 27).

Informal consultations among a limited number of countries have continued in the WTO, but the practice has become increasingly controversial as a result of two factors in particular. First, with a few exceptions, agreements reached in the WTO impose obligations on all Members. The perception that the trade-offs and compromises discussed in the Green Room meetings will be imposed on other Members without their participation have made delegations outside the room wary of sanctioning the practice. Second, the demand for active participation in WTO decision-making processes has increased drastically among a large number of Members, particularly developing countries. Although small group consultations remain as common in the WTO as in the final years of the GATT, the practice is now under closer scrutiny than ever and has been at the heart of the criticism of a 'democratic deficit ' and a 'legitimacy problem' at the WTO.

It is important to make a clear distinction between the frequent small group consultations held by Chairpersons in the day-to-day work of the WTO and the Green Room. The WTO membership will regularly request a Chairperson of a WTO body to consult on one or more specific issues and report back. Such consultations are encouraged and tolerated because they are recognized as necessary and because they have a better chance of producing results and generating momentum than deliberations among the full membership. The composition and size of small group consultations will vary depending on the specific issue, but it is generally rather predictable. These consultations perform a facilitating or bridge-building role and there is never any pretence that they have some sort decision-making power. The Chairperson will generally announce the intention to hold such consultations and will report back, if not immediately, then at the end of a consultation cycle.

The Green Room, on the other hand, is generally linked to the final stages of a negotiating process, covers a broader agenda, and is therefore more controversial. Traditionally the Director-General has called and chaired such meetings which have provided an effective forum for a few delegations to discuss and negotiate informally. However, over the past four or five years, Green Room consultations among senior Geneva Permanent Representatives have repeatedly ended in grid-lock and failed to make the progress required for eventual ministerial decisions. Although the term Green Room remains part of the Geneva trade vocabulary, such consultations have declined in number and importance. The real Green Room meetings take place among Ministers and address a crosscutting agenda where most outstanding decisions are of a political nature. Ministerial Green Rooms are generally slightly smaller than the comparable consultation among Geneva Permanent Representatives, although developing countries still make up a large majority. The controversy and antagonism they have generated since the creation of the WTO stem from the perception that the outcomes of these meetings are presented as a fait accompli for the membership to accept. The fact that these consultations normally take place under intense time pressure adds to their controversial nature.

The vilification of the Green Room process also stems from criticism on the part of some WTO observers, many of whom have only a rudimentary insight into the role and composition of this process. Occasionally, even the participants of these consultations feel obliged to criticize the process for political reasons or out of solidarity with delegations that were not involved. At the same time, the ability of these Ministerial Green Rooms to deliver has been vastly exaggerated. As indicated previously, the failure of two out of three Ministerial Conferences since 1999 has underscored that a Green Room process offers no guarantee of success.

....

4. Alternative suggestions for reforming decision-making at the WTO

As with the 'in-house' debate on internal transparency, the Seattle debacle sharpened the focus of external observers on this issue. Initial reactions by several observers suggested that the failure of Seattle was a direct result of an undemocratic and un-transparent decision-making process designed to marginalize the less powerful Members of the WTO. Some concluded that the WTO decision-making process was in dire need of a dramatic overhaul. Although the entire Seattle process exposed a number of institutional problems, such conclusions fail to acknowledge that even a perfect process would have been unable to bridge the substantive differences among Members in 1999.

The dedicated discussions on internal transparency among WTO Members in 2000 and 2002 featured very few of the proposals and solutions provided by WTO observers on how to improve WTO's decision-making processes. Below a number of the external proposals for reform of the WTO's decision-making process will be analysed.

Elimination of Green Room type consultations

Over the past two years a number of NGOs have argued that the practice of Green Room meetings has undermined the legitimacy of WTO decisions and that a more democratic model should be adopted. Such a model would rely almost exclusively on open-ended formal meetings for negotiation among WTO Members and would restrict smaller group meetings by Chairpersons, unless explicitly approved by the full membership. While such an approach could theoretically improve transparency, there are a number of problems associated with this model. First, the pre-Seattle experience clearly illustrated that a formal process does not provide an appropriate forum for negotiations. Second, formalizing a preparatory process is unlikely to enhance transparency for those delegations that do not have representation in Geneva, as the formal records, also known as 'Minutes', from a full-day meeting on average take around two weeks to process and translate into the WTO's three working languages. Third, and perhaps most importantly, an increasingly unwieldy and formal process will inevitably lead a number of delegations to take the consultative process outside the framework of the organization. Unlike in-house consultations, these processes will operate with no transparency or reporting obligation. Finally, formalizing the WTO decision-making process would be contrary to the very real concern of many delegations, that the general proliferation of meetings is hampering their efforts to participate effectively.

During the discussion on transparency in 2000 and 2002 some delegations did call for more open-ended meetings at which Chairpersons could report back and this practice is now solidly embedded in the WTO decision-making practices. The debate on transparency among the WTO membership has clearly illustrated that delegations do not believe that fundamental reform to the decision-making processes is necessary.

WTO steering committee/executive board

The idea to establish a steering committee or an executive board with a rotating membership has some historical precedent in the so-called 'Consultative Group of 18' of the GATT. This may, to some extent, explain why this idea continues to receive considerable attention by some WTO pundits. The fundamental idea behind these proposals is that such a body would provide a more transparent and predictable consultative mechanism compared with ad hoc Green Rooms. The proponents of such a mechanism all emphasize that it would not take decisions that bind the full membership, but would rather make recommendations based on thorough consultations.

In October 2003, the European Commission circulated a reflection paper to the 133 Committee on WTO Organizational Improvements, which called for the creation of an advisory group to prepare negotiating options.

An executive board with a pre-determined membership could perhaps add an element of predictability to the consultative process. It has been argued that the creation of such a group would reduce the risk of bigger players abandoning the multilateral approach on certain issues in favour of a bilateral or plurilateral negotiation outside the WTO. However, although the creation of such a mechanism appears to have significant benefits in theory, it is almost certain that questions such as the criteria for representation and the status of the discussions in the body would make its establishment very difficult. The principal opposition to a steering committee or an executive board would most likely come from a sub-set of countries which historically have been able to get into any Green Room they are interested in, but which would struggle to gain their own seat on such a board.

This group might include countries such as Argentina, Australia, Canada, Chile, Colombia, Hong Kong (China), Korea, Mexico, Norway, New Zealand, South Africa, and Thailand. These countries have a long tradition as strong supporters of the multilateral trading system along with the EU, US, and Japan. It is therefore no surprise that the creation of such a mechanism has not been raised in any detail among Members during discussions on internal transparency. In addition, the past few years have seen a much more assertive membership insisting on the WTO being 'member-driven', and it is difficult to see how anything that could be seen to encroach on this notion could be successful. Significantly, the idea of a consultative board would appear to address the issue of efficiency rather than transparency.

Regional representation

The idea of organizing the decision-making process of the WTO around regional representation has often been linked with the creation of a consultative board and the formalization of a consultative forum. This idea has failed to generate any interest among those countries which would be encouraged to organize themselves along regional lines. Despite the proliferation of regional trade agreements regional coordination in the WTO remains a very marginal activity. The notion of regional representation has not been raised in the context of the transparency discussions at the WTO. An important reason why the idea of regional representation is unlikely to flourish is simply that negotiating interests in the WTO do not always coincide with the geographic location of countries.

Weighted voting

The introduction of a variant of weighted voting along the lines of the IMF and the World Bank or even the EU would certainly provide for a more predictable and stable balance between participation and efficiency. However, this idea would fundamentally undermine the rule and practice of decision making by consensus, break with the principle of equality among states, and exacerbate what many countries see as existing asymmetries. It would also seem very unlikely that developing countries would sacrifice their surge in importance at the WTO to a system of weighted voting, e.g. based on share of world trade, which would reduce their influence. Finally, a system of weighted voting would certainly not be the answer to criticism regarding the legitimacy of WTO decisions. It should be recalled that one of the first intermediary conclusions of the consultations on internal transparency in 2000 was that Members did not see the need for any fundamental change to the consensus rule and the issue has not featured in any detail since.

Flexible integration/plurilateral approach

The idea of returning to the more flexible integration or 'a la carte ' approach of the 1970s gained some currency among a limited group of Members recently in the context of the Singapore issues. It was argued that those countries that had the interest and the capacity to move ahead with negotiations should be allowed to do so. The WTO has been down this road before with some success and a recent report by the Consultative Board to the Director-General endorses the idea of 'variable geometry', i.e. allowing some Members to take on more extensive obligations than others.

However, given the strong opposition to any plurilateral negotiations on the Singapore Issues, it seems unlikely that this approach could generate support in the WTO. Developing countries in particular are adamant that they do not wish to see a 'two-tier' WTO. Nevertheless, considering the difficulty of launching comprehensive trade rounds, the possibility of small groups of interested countries seeking a plurilateral deal outside the multilateral framework may not be that far-fetched. The proliferation of Free Trade Agreements over the past few years would suggest that plurilaterism may have a role to play.

Enhancing coalition building—concentric circles model

The basic idea behind the concentric circles model is to work towards a situation where existing coalitions among Members play important roles in building consensus on difficult issues. The work of such groups would support and complement the small group consultations and their coordinators would be closely involved in these. The weakness of this model is its focus on achieving internal agreement in such groups rather than conciliation with groups of opposing views. Viability of this model relies heavily on the extent to which group coordinators are able to 'win' a mandate to represent and, above all, speak for their constituencies. The concentric circles model in many ways reflects what has been happening over the past years in the WTO. The growing influence of such groups as the African Group, the LDC Group, and the ACP in Geneva, and at the ministerial level over the past few years, has been an important feature of the decision-making process in the WTO. Similarly, the emergence of a number of informal coalitions around specific issues or platforms, e.g. the LMG (implementation), the G20 (agriculture), and Friends of The Round would suggest that such groups have a role to play.

The above has shown that there is no shortage of ideas and models for improving the decision-making processes at the WTO. However, it is noteworthy that most of the ideas and suggestions for change articulated by observers of the WTO have only rarely featured in the discussions among Members on the issue of internal transparency. At the recent off-the-record discussion of the report by the Consultative Board to the Director-General, Members appeared to reject some of the recommendations on WTO decision making, including a modification of the consensus principle. Indeed, most observers tend to ignore the significance that WTO Members attach to the notion of a 'Member-driven' organization. In this context it is also significant that WTO observers have rarely bothered to analyse the incremental but nevertheless significant improvements to WTO decision making and internal transparency since 2000.

5. Conclusion

...

The WTO decision-making process remains imperfect and will most certainly require further improvements in the future. However, with internal transparency and decision making now important systemic issues in their own right, there is little doubt that they will continue to be scrutinized by the membership as well as by observers of the WTO.

Contrary to what many observers of the WTO decision-making process argue, WTO Members have spent considerable time and effort on this issue. Much of the criticism of the decision-making process in the WTO is either dismissive of the progress made, or simply chooses to ignore the fact that the membership has engaged substantively to improve the transparency of the multilateral trading system. Discussions on internal transparency in 2000 and 2002 reaffirmed that Members did not believe the fundamental principle of consensus decision making should be changed, but that the informal decision-making processes, particularly in the context of Ministerial Conferences, were in need of reform. The current practices, and the guidelines within which consultations take place at the WTO, are the direct result of what a large number of Members believed was wrong with the decision-making processes. Although these practices have little legal status, their behavioural impact on the way the WTO operates is considerable.

There is enough evidence in the day-to-day work of Chairpersons and the Director-General in the WTO to demonstrate adherence to a culture of increased transparency and participation.

The way in which Members have approached the issue of internal transparency contains a number of parallels to how they have dealt with the challenge of opening up the WTO to greater public scrutiny. The approach to improving the external transparency and the relationship with NGOs over the past decade reflects a similar preference on the part of the WTO membership for improved practices and guidelines, rather than specific institutional amendments. The practices for dealing with civil society groups, developed and refined over the past decade, but with no legal foundation, have become so embedded in the operation of the multilateral trading system that it would be unthinkable that they could be rescinded. Similarly, insistence on specific and formal rules for consultative processes in the WTO would not only result in a lowest common denominator outcome, but would also undermine the moral authority embodied in the current practices and guidelines. It may be argued that what is in place is the least bad of the workable alternatives.

Experience at the WTO shows that the legitimacy of the decision-making process requires that there is an adequate degree of open-ended and inclusive activity to balance other more restrictive consultative processes. Critics of the WTO often appear to single out the decision-making processes of the organization as uniquely exclusive in comparison with other international institutions. This is disingenuous. All international intergovernmental organizations face challenges when it comes to finding the right balance between efficiency and inclusiveness.

Small group consultations by Chairpersons and Green Rooms will continue to play important roles in the overall WTO process, since, on balance, they offer important forums for making progress. WTO Members in general recognize this. However, their legitimacy hinges on the ability to ensure an adequate degree of transparency and inclusiveness, as well as a guarantee that such mechanisms are understood to be coalition building and not decision-making forums. It is also clear that any attempt to short circuit or deviate from the guidelines and practices on transparency will continue to require some general acceptance among WTO Members. Past experience has shown that in some cases, and faced with a high stake substantive agenda, the WTO membership appears willing to accept such a temporary deviation. However, muddling through and experiencing negotiating collapses on a regular basis is unsustainable for the multilateral trading system and the legitimacy of its decisions. In this respect it will be crucially important that the progress made so far on internal transparency and the decision-making processes in the WTO is bolstered by further improvements. Some of these will be relatively straightforward, e.g. previewing organizational features of Ministerial Conferences sufficiently ahead of time and ensuring consistent adherence to the consultative practices of the Geneva process. Other issues, such as the transfer of a workable draft text to Ministers prior to the Ministerial Conference, will be more difficult. Of course, a certain degree of flexibility will always be required, but provided certain practices are maintained such flexibility will most likely also be granted.

... ...

In addition to the normal decision-making process, the WTO also provides for special procedures in certain situations, including interpretations, waivers and amendments. We discuss each of these below.

(ii) Interpretations

According to Article IX:2, the Ministerial Conference and the General Council have the exclusive authority to adopt 'interpretations' of the WTO Agreement and of the Multilateral Trade Agreements ('WTO agreements'). Article IX:2 states:

> The Ministerial Conference and the General Council shall have the exclusive authority to adopt interpretations of this Agreement and of the Multilateral Trade Agreements. In the case of an interpretation of a Multilateral Trade Agreement in Annex 1, they shall exercise their authority on the basis of a recommendation by the Council overseeing the functioning of that Agreement. The decision to adopt an interpretation shall be taken by a three-fourths majority of the Members. This paragraph shall not be used in a manner that would undermine the amendment provisions in Article X.

Interpretations of the agreements are binding on the entire WTO membership and may affect the rights and obligations of the Members.[9] To date, the WTO has not used Article IX:2 to adopt any interpretations (although it has taken actions which effectively are interpretations of the agreements).[10]

(iii) Waivers

In exceptional circumstances, Article IX:3 authorises the Ministerial Conference to decide to waive an obligation imposed by the WTO agreements. In normal circumstances, waiver decisions must be taken by three-quarters[11] of the Members. In addition, paragraph 3 of Article IX adds the following:

> (a) A request for a waiver concerning this Agreement shall be submitted to the Ministerial Conference for consideration pursuant to the practice of decision-making by consensus. The Ministerial Conference shall establish a time-period, which shall not exceed 90 days, to consider the request. If consensus is not reached during the time-period, any decision to grant a waiver shall be taken by three fourths of the Members.

> (b) A request for a waiver concerning the Multilateral Trade Agreements in Annexes 1A or 1B or 1C and their annexes shall be submitted initially to the Council for Trade in Goods, the Council for Trade in Services or the Council for TRIPS, respectively, for consideration during a time-period which shall not exceed 90 days. At the end of the time-period, the relevant Council shall submit a report to the Ministerial Conference.

Notwithstanding the above provisions regarding voting by three quarters of the membership, Members later agreed that decisions on waivers should not ordinarily go to a vote but should remain, if possible, taken by consensus.[12]

---

[9] As discussed in Chapter 5, while the dispute settlement system 'clarifies' the provisions of the WTO agreements, neither panels nor the Appellate Body can 'add to or diminish the rights and obligations' of Members: see DSU Art 3.2. In addition, panel and Appellate Body decisions are only formally binding upon the parties to the dispute.

[10] See, eg 'Implementation of Paragraph 6 of The Doha Declaration on the TRIPS Agreement and Public Health, Decision of 30 August 2003', WTO Doc No WT/L/540 (2 September 2003). See generally C-D Ehlermann and L Ehring, 'The Authoritative Interpretation Under Article IX:2 of the Agreement Establishing the World Trade Organization: Current Law, Practice and Possible Improvements' (2005) 8(4) *Journal of International Economic Law* 803.

[11] Note that a decision to grant a waiver in respect of any obligation subject to a transitional period or a period for staged implementation that the requesting Member has not performed by the end of the relevant period shall be taken only by consensus.

[12] See 'Decision-Making Procedures under Articles IX and XII of the WTO Agreement', WTO Doc No WT/L/93 (24 November 1995). On occasions when the General Council deals with matters related to requests for waivers or accessions to the WTO under Articles IX or XII of the WTO Agreement respectively, the General

As waivers constitute exceptional circumstances, a request for a waiver must be reported to the relevant Council for consideration. As a result, a decision by the Ministerial Conference granting a waiver must state the exceptional circumstances justifying the decision, the terms and conditions governing the application of the waiver and the termination date of the waiver. Moreover, any waiver granted for a period of more than one year is reviewed by the Ministerial Conference not later than one year after it is granted (and thereafter annually until the waiver terminates) to determine whether the exceptional circumstances justifying the waiver still exist and whether the terms and conditions attached to the waiver have been met. On the basis of the annual review, the Ministerial Conference determines whether the waiver will be extended, modified or terminated.[13]

One example of a waiver is that under Article I:1 (Most Favoured Nation Treatment), Article XI:1 (Elimination of Quantitative Restrictions) and Article XIII:1 (Non-Discriminatory Administration of Quantitative Restrictions) of the GATT for trade measures taken under the Kimberley Process Certification Scheme for Rough Diamonds (an international scheme of certification for rough diamonds which provides that participants should 'ensure that no shipment of rough diamonds is imported or exported to a non-Participant').[14] The waiver provides 'legal certainty' to those taking domestic measures under the Kimberley Process to curb the trade in conflict diamonds while at the same time supporting legitimate diamond trade.[15] Another, more recent, example is that of the EU seeking and being granted a waiver in order to grant duty-free treatment to 75 products from Pakistan to help that country recover from the economic effects of the flooding which occurred in the summer of 2010.[16]

(iv) Amendments

The process of amending one of the WTO agreements is complicated and difficult. Article X of the WTO Agreement provides the basis for the amendment process. In particular, paragraph 1 of that provision sets out the basic elements of the process:

> Any Member of the WTO may initiate a proposal to amend the provisions of this Agreement or the Multilateral Trade Agreements in Annex 1 by submitting such proposal to the Ministerial Conference. The Councils listed in paragraph 5 of Article IV may also submit to the Ministerial Conference proposals to amend the provisions of the corresponding Multilateral Trade Agreements in Annex 1 the functioning of which they oversee. Unless the Ministerial Conference decides on a longer period, for a period of 90 days after the proposal has been tabled formally at the Ministerial Conference any decision by the Ministerial Conference to submit the proposed amendment to the Members for acceptance shall be taken by consensus. . . . If consensus

---

Council will seek a decision in accordance with Article IX:1. Except as otherwise provided, where a decision cannot be arrived at by consensus, the matter at issue shall be decided by voting under the relevant provisions of Articles IX or XII. The above procedure does not preclude a Member from requesting a vote at the time the decision is taken.

[13] See Art IX:4 of the WTO Agreement.

[14] Decision, 'Waiver Concerning Kimberley Process Certification Scheme for Rough Diamonds', WTO Doc. No. G/C/W/432/Rev.1 (24 February 2003); see also 'Kimberley Process Certification Scheme for Rough Diamonds—Request for a WTO Waiver', WTO Doc No G/C/W/431 (12 November 2002).

[15] See WTO, 'Agreement Reached on WTO Waiver for "conflict diamonds"' (26 February 2003), available at www.wto.org/english/news_e/news03_e/goods_council_26fev03_e.htm.

[16] See WTO, 'Members Approve EU Waiver Request for Trade Aid to Pakistan' (1 February 2012), available at http://www.wto.org/english/news_e/news12_e/good_02feb12_e.htm.

is reached, the Ministerial Conference shall forthwith submit the proposed amendment to the Members for acceptance. If consensus is not reached at a meeting of the Ministerial Conference within the established period, the Ministerial Conference shall decide by a two-thirds majority of the Members whether to submit the proposed amendment to the Members for acceptance. Except as provided in paragraphs 2, 5 and 6, the provisions of paragraph 3 shall apply to the proposed amendment, unless the Ministerial Conference decides by a three-fourths majority of the Members that the provisions of paragraph 4 shall apply.

In other words, Article X:1 provides that any Member or any of the Councils may initiate the amendment process by submitting a proposal to the Ministerial Conference or General Council. For a period of at least 90 days following the formal tabling of the proposal at the Ministerial Conference or General Council, the proposed amendment may only be accepted by consensus. If consensus cannot be reached within the 90 day period, the Ministerial Conference or General Council opens the process to a vote. In order to be adopted, two-thirds of the membership of the WTO must agree to adopt the proposal. In this circumstance, the amendment becomes effective for all Members at the same time. However, if the proposal will affect Members' rights and obligations, the amendment is only effective for those members who have accepted it. Importantly, the Ministerial Conference may decide by a three-quarters majority of the Members that any amendment is of such a nature that any Member which has not accepted it within a period specified by the Ministerial Conference must either withdraw from the WTO or remain a Member only with the consent of the Ministerial Conference. Furthermore, Article X:2 states that certain fundamental provisions must be unanimously adopted by all Members before they can take effect. These fundamental provisions include Article IX of the WTO Agreement (decision-making); Articles I and II of GATT (MFN and tariff schedules); Article II:1 of GATS (MFN); and Article 4 of TRIPS (MFN). Additionally, amendments to the DSU and TPRM can be made by the Ministerial Conference alone—without Member acceptance—but according to Article X:8, amendments to the DSU can only be made by consensus, and these amendments shall take effect for all Members upon approval by the Ministerial Conference.

The WTO Agreement has been formally amended only once, when the waiver reached on 30 August 2003 granting counties with insufficient or no manufacturing capability the ability to import pharmaceuticals under a compulsory licence ('The Implementation of Paragraph 6 of the Doha Declaration on TRIPS Agreement and Public Health') was converted into a permanent amendment to the TRIPS Agreement.[17] The amendment will come into force following ratification from two-thirds of WTO Members.

(v) Plurilateral Agreements

Decision-making and amendments under these agreements are governed by the rules contained in each agreement.

(d) Membership

As of May 2012, the WTO was comprised of 155 Members, including all major industrialised nations and most developing countries. Following the accession of the People's Republic of China in 2001, the largest economic power not holding WTO membership is Russia. The

---

[17] See 'Amendment of the TRIPS Agreement: Decision on 6 December 2005', WTO Doc No WT/L/641 (8 December 2005).

Eighth Ministerial Conference held in December 2011, however, formally approved Russia's application for membership, and it will become a Member of the WTO 30 days after notifying the Secretariat of the domestic ratification of its Accession Package. This will conclude Russia's 18 year accession process. Approximately 26 other mostly former Soviet Republic, Middle Eastern and Pacific nations are in the process of acceding to the WTO.

(e) Accession and Withdrawal

(i) Accession

Article XI of the WTO Agreement sets out provisions on 'original membership' for those nations or customs territories which were contracting parties to the GATT as of January 1995. All of the GATT contracting parties used these provisions to accede to the WTO. By contrast, countries that were not contracting parties to the GATT must formally accede to the WTO. The accession process remains largely the same as it was under Article XXXIII of the GATT.[18] Article XII of the WTO Agreement now governs the process, providing that '[a]ny state or customs territory having full autonomy in the conduct of its trade policies is eligible to accede to the WTO on terms agreed between it and WTO Members'.[19]

Acceding to the WTO is not a simple and straightforward process. Nations wishing to accede cannot simply declare their interest and intent to join the WTO and sign the accession papers. Instead, in addition to accepting all of the terms of the WTO Agreement and all the multilateral trade agreements, acceding countries must also negotiate specific terms of accession with interested Members of the WTO. These negotiations revolve around the market access commitments and concessions the acceding nation will have to make in order to join the 'club'. This process, while arduous and time-consuming, is considered necessary so that acceding members do not receive the benefit of over 40 years of progressive liberalisation without having to open their own markets.

A nation (or customs territory) wishing to accede to the WTO (the 'applicant' nation) must first submit a formal written request for accession which describes and reports on its trade regime. The General Council then establishes a Working Party to examine the accession request and, ultimately, to submit the findings of the Working Party to the General Council for approval. The Working Party is open to all WTO Members. Thus, in this 'tell us about yourself' phase, a nation describes all aspects of its trade and economic policies which have a bearing on WTO agreements and ultimately submits a memorandum covering all relevant aspects of the above to the WTO.[20] The applicant's memorandum is an important part of the accession process as it forms the basis for detailed fact finding by the Working Party. Based on the information provided in the memorandum, interested WTO Members pose questions to the applicant. While this phase of the accession process is time-consuming, it allows the applicant nation to begin transitioning and amending its

---

[18] One notable difference is the removal of the 'sponsorship' path to membership allowed by Art XXVI:5(c) of the GATT. Under this provision, newly independent nations which had previously been under colonial rule were allowed to accede under the terms of their parent sponsors. Thus, an acceding nation did not have to negotiate its own terms of accession, and it was able to make use of the 'grandfather' rights of the PPA.

[19] As the use of the term 'customs territory' makes clear, membership of the WTO is not limited solely to independent States. Instead, the WTO also includes separate customs unions having full autonomy in the conduct of external trade policies (such as Hong Kong, China and Chinese Taipei (Taiwan)).

[20] WTO Doc No WT/ACC/1 lists all of the major categories of trade and legal policy to be covered by the applicant.

laws in anticipation of future accession. Following this examination process, the substantive phase of the accession process begins. This process ultimately determines the terms and conditions of entry for the applicant—such as the applicant's commitments to observe WTO rules and disciplines upon accession and transitional periods—and is largely based upon the economic development level of the acceding nation.

At the same time, the second phase of parallel bilateral negotiations—the 'work out with us individually what you have to offer' phase—begins between the applicant and interested Working Party members on concessions and market access commitments (eg, tariff concessions and services commitments). As noted, these bilateral negotiations seek to avoid allowing the acceding nation to benefit from over 50 years of multilateral liberalisation undertaken by current Members without having to enter into any corresponding liberalisation. The negotiations are bilateral in nature because different Members will have different interests regarding tariff rates and specific market access commitments, and other policies in goods and services. It must be recalled, however, that all concessions and market access commitments negotiated bilaterally are ultimately applied equally to all Members by virtue of the Most Favoured Nation principle. These bilateral negotiations, which can last for a number of years, become part of the final 'accession package'.

Thirdly, in the 'let's draft membership terms' phase, which begins when the working party completes its examination of the applicant's trade regime and the parallel bilateral negotiations are complete, the working party finalises the terms of accession. The terms of accession appear in a report (containing a summary of proceedings and conditions of entry), a draft membership treaty ('protocol of accession') and lists ('schedules') of the acceding Member's commitments.

The fourth phase—'the decision'—begins when the members of the Working Party are satisfied with the Working Party's Draft Report and the Protocol of Accession (ie draft accession treaty), and when the market access commitments and concessions in goods and services are completed. The Working Party adopts the 'accession package' at a final formal meeting.

The General Council or Ministerial Conference is presented with the 'accession package' for adoption. When adopted, the Decision of the General Council and a Protocol of Accession are annexed to the Final Working Party Report, which states that the country accedes to the WTO Agreement, defines the Schedules and outlines final provisions for timing of acceptance of the Protocol and full membership of the WTO.

Once approved by at least a two-thirds majority of the WTO membership, the applicant may sign the Protocol of Accession stating that it accepts the approved 'accessions package' subject to ratification in its national parliament (if applicable).[21] Under normal circumstances, acceding nations are given three months from the signature of the Protocol of Accession for domestic ratification. Finally, 30 days after the applicant notifies the WTO Secretariat that it has completed its ratification procedures, the acceding nation becomes a full Member of the WTO.

Table 2.2 summarises the current accession process for all acceding nations.

---

[21] A Member can, under Art XIII of the WTO Agreement, decide to non-apply (essentially not treat the acceding nation as a Member) the WTO Agreement to the acceding nation, but to do so the Member must notify the Ministerial Conference of its decision at the time of the approval of the accession agreement. This opt-out provision is modelled on Art XXXV of the GATT. Under the GATT, the provision was utilised over 80 times (most notably by Pakistan and India against South Africa during the period of Apartheid and by several countries against Japan following its accession in the 1950s).

Table 2.2 Ongoing WTO accessions (updated February 2012)

	Application	Working Party Established	Memorandum	First/Latest* Working Party Meeting	Number of Working Party Meetings*	Goods Offer initial	Goods Offer latest*	Services Offer initial	Services Offer latest*	Draft Working Party Report**
Afghanistan	Nov 2004	Dec 2004	Mar 2009	Jan 2011	1					
Algeria	Jun 1987	Jun 1987	Jul 1996	Apr 1998/Jan 2008	10	Feb 2002	Nov 2007	Mar 2002	Nov 2007	Jun 2006
Andorra	Jul 1997	Oct 1997	Mar 1999	Oct 1999	1	Sep 1999		Sep 1999		
Azerbaijan	Jun 1997	Jul 1997	Apr 1999	Jun 2002/Feb 2012	9	May 2005	Jan 2012	May 2005	Oct 2011	Nov 2011 (FS)
Bahamas	May 2001	Jul 2001	Apr 2009	Sept 2010	1					
Belarus	Sep 1993	Oct 1993	Jan 1996	Dec 1997/May 2005	7	Mar 1998	July 2010	Feb 2000	July 2010	Jun 2007 (FS)
Bhutan	Sep 1999	Oct 1999	Feb 2003	Nov 2004/Jan 2008	4	Aug 2005	Nov 2007	Aug 2005	Nov 2007	Dec 2007
Bosnia and Herzegovina	May 1999	Jul 1999	Oct 2002	Nov 2003/Sep 2011	9	Oct 2004	Feb 2007	Oct 2004	Feb 2007	Jun 2011
Comoros	Feb 2007	Oct 2007								
Equatorial Guinea	Feb 2007	Feb 2008								
Ethiopia	Jan 2003	Feb 2003	Jan 2007	May 2008/May 2011	2	Feb 2012				
Iran	Jul 1996	May 2005	Nov 2009		2					
Iraq	Sep 2004	Dec 2004	Sep 2005	May 2007/April 2008	2					
Kazakhstan	Jan 1996	Feb 1996	Sep 1996	Mar 1997/Jul 2008	10	Jun 1997	Dec 2004	Sep 1997	Jun 2004	Jun 2008
Lao People's Democratic Republic	Jul 1997	Feb 1998	Mar 2001	Oct 2004/Jul 2011	7	Nov 2006	Aug 2010	Oct 2007	Jul 2010	Feb 2012
Lebanese Republic	Jan 1999	Apr 1999	Jun 2001	Oct 2002/Oct 2009	7	Nov 2003	Jun 2004	Nov 2003	Jun 2004	Oct 2009
Liberia, Republic of	Jun 2007	Dec 2007	April 2011							
Libya	Jun 2004	Jul 2004								
Montenegro	Dec 2004	Feb 2005	Mar 2005	Oct 2005/Dec 2011	8		Final schedules: December 2011	Final schedules: December 2011		Final Report Dec 2011
Russian Federation	Jun 1993	Jun 1993	Mar 1994	Jul 1995/Nov 2011	31		Final schedules: November 2011	Final schedules: November 2011		Final Report Nov 2011
Samoa	Apr 1998	Jul 1998	Feb 2000	Mar 2002/Oct 2011	2		Final schedules: November 2011	Final schedules: November 2011		Final Report Nov 2011
Sao Tome and Principe	Jan 2005	May 2005								
Serbia	Dec 2004	Feb 2005	Mar 2005	Oct 2005/Sep 2011	11	Apr 2006	Nov 2008	Oct 2006	Nov 2008	Aug 2011
Seychelles	May 1995	Jul 1995	Aug 1996/ May 2009 ***	Feb 1997/Nov 2010	2	Jun 1997	Oct 2010	May 1997	Oct 2010	Jun 1997
Sudan	Oct 1994	Oct 1994	Jan 1999	Jul 2003/Mar 2004	2	Jul 2004	Oct 2006	Jun 2004	Oct 2006	Sep 2004 (FS)
Syrian Arab Republic	Oct 2001	May 2010		Mar 2004/Mar 2012						
Tajikistan	May 2001	Jul 2001	Feb 2003	Jul 2002/Oct 2005	7	Feb 2004	May 2011	Feb 2004	Apr 2011	Feb 2012
Uzbekistan	Dec 1994	Dec 1994	Oct 1998	Jul 1996/May 2011	3	Sep 2005		Sep 2005		
Vanuatu	Jul 1995	Jul 1995	Nov 1995		3		Final schedule: May 2011	Final schedule: May 2011		Final Report May 2011
Yemen	Apr 2000	Jul 2000	Nov 2002	Nov 2004/Sept 2010	8	Sep 2005	Aug 2008	Aug 2005	Aug 2008	Nov 2010

* As of the date of this document.
** Most recent Factual Summary (FS), draft Working Party Report or Elements of draft Working Party Report.
*** Updated Memorandum on the Foreign Trade Regime.

Source: WTO, Summary Table of Ongoing Accessions, available at www.wto.org/english/thewto_e/acc_e/status_e.htm (visited 21 Jan 2007)/

(ii) Withdrawal

According to Article XV of the WTO Agreement, any Member may withdraw from the WTO by simply notifying the Director-General of the WTO of its intent to withdraw. Withdrawal takes effect upon the expiration of six months from the date on which written notice of withdrawal is received by the Director-General. Withdrawal from a Plurilateral Trade Agreement is governed by the provisions of those individual Agreements.

IV. QUESTIONS

1. What is the WTO's purpose? What should it be?

2. When political systems are made of many individual states, they inevitably are faced with the difficulty of allocating votes among the states. Should it be by population? By land mass? By wealth? By trade flows? Does the WTO's voting structure seem reasonable given the specific nature of the organisation?

3. What are the pros and cons of consensus decision-making? What effect would any of the alternatives have on internal and external transparency?

4. Should any nation wanting to accede to the WTO be automatically admitted? What are the pros and cons of the present system of negotiating entry into the organisation?

5. What are the consequences of withdrawal from the WTO?

6. One of the criticisms of the WTO is its failure to take into account the views of 'civil society'. This results from the nature of the WTO as an inter-governmental organisation. Interest groups can lobby the governments which are Members, but they cannot participate directly in the WTO decision-making process. Is this concern a legitimate one? Should there be a mechanism for non-governmental entities to play a more direct role in WTO decision-making?

7. How does the decision-making process of the WTO treat developing countries? Are they better off within the WTO framework than they would be if there were no multilateral framework? Could the WTO decision-making process be improved from the perspective of developing countries?

3

World Trade Law and International Law

I. INTRODUCTION

The relationship of world trade law to international law is a complex and controversial one. Historically, trade lawyers and international lawyers have operated, to a great extent, in different spheres. Trade law consisted mostly of practitioners who dealt with domestic regulatory proceedings in national capitals or GATT specialists working in Geneva. While some practitioners and academics did bridge the gap, the fields were largely separate and little interaction between individuals in the differing spheres took place. As a result, both sides often looked sceptically at each other. For instance, some trade lawyers do not think international law should have much, if any, impact on trade law. They see WTO rules, for example, as a separate, self-contained legal regime. At the same time, some international law specialists see international trade law in general, and WTO law in particular, as having a lesser status than the rest of international law, partly because it deals with mere 'commercial' matters.

In spite of the traditional separation and personal feelings involved, it is clear that trade law and international law have some kind of formal relationship. The WTO is a treaty, and thus it is part of the larger body of international law (one of the sources of international law is treaties).

Nevertheless, the practical considerations that result from the fact that world trade law is a part of public international law are unclear. There are a number of specific ways in which the two fields can overlap, conflict and relate to each other, and there is a great deal of disagreement in this area.

II. WORLD TRADE LAW AND INTERNATIONAL LAW: DIFFERING VIEWPOINTS

In this chapter, we present the views of some leading WTO commentators who offer differing perspectives on how one aspect of this relationship, the role of international law in WTO law, can be interpreted. The first excerpt is by Professor Joost Pauwelyn, who argues for a substantial role for international law in WTO law. The second excerpt is by Professor Joel Trachtman, who, in a review of Professor Pauwelyn's book on the subject, disagrees with Pauwelyn's view and argues for a lesser role. At the end of these two excerpts, we briefly deconstruct the precise scope of their disagreement. We then provide a final excerpt from Professor Lorand Bartels which explains certain uses of 'other' international law in the WTO. Finally, we briefly introduce how a WTO panel exhibits flexibility in dealing with these complex issues.

J Pauwelyn, 'The Role of Public International Law in the WTO: How Far Can We Go?' (2001) 95 *American Journal of International Law* 535, 535–52

THE WTO AS A PART OF PUBLIC INTERNATIONAL LAW

The Creation and Interplay of Rules in Public International Law

International law, unlike domestic legal systems, is "decentralized" in that it has no central legislator creating its rules. The creators of international law are at the same time the main subjects of international law, namely states. States as subjects of international law, unlike individuals in domestic law, do not elect an "international legislator," which is then mandated to make law on their behalf. Moreover, states as creators of law are complete equals. The law created by state *A* and state *B* has the same legal value as that created by state *C* and state *D*. International law is a law of cooperation, not subordination. Its creation depends essentially on the consent of states, be it explicit or only implicit. The lack of consent by a given state generally means that it cannot be held to the rule in question (*pacta tertiis nec nocent nec prosunt*). As a result, since each state is largely its own lawmaker, the legal relationship between states varies enormously depending on the states concerned (much more than the relationship between individuals under domestic law where legislation and other generally applicable law largely outweigh private contracts).

Although international law does not have a central legislator—and is essentially a compilation of varying bilateral legal relationships (even if these relationships are increasingly effected by multilateral treaties)—international law *does* include an element with features of international legislation, namely general international law, composed of general customary international law and general principles of law. The rules of general international law, in principle, are binding on *all* states. Each new state, as well as each new treaty, is automatically born into it. General international law fills the gaps left by treaties. More important, being composed largely of rules on the law of treaties, state responsibility, the interplay of norms, and the settlement of disputes, general international law ensures the existence of international law as a legal system. General international law is not limited, however, to these "secondary" rules of law, as they might be called (or a "toolbox" for the creation, operation, interplay, and enforcement of other rules of law). It also includes "primary" rules of law directly imposing rights and obligations on states (which "secondary" rules impose only indirectly through other rules of law), such as customary law and general principles of law on the use of force, genocide, and human rights. Looked at from this angle, general international law does resemble domestic legislation (or even domestic constitutions).

In contrast, however, to much domestic legislation (and all domestic constitutions), general international law does *not* have an inherent legal value that is superior to other rules of law (sub-federal law, administrative regulations, and contracts in domestic law; treaties in international law). On the contrary, general customary international law and general principles of law are often characterized as vague, whereas treaties are much more explicit. The lack of any inherent hierarchy between general international law and treaties—as well as, more generally, between any two rules of international law—is explained on the ground that both derive, in one way or another, from the will or acquiescence of states. As they derive from the same source (essentially state consent), they must in principle be equal in value. A prominent (but still disputed) exception to this absence of hierarchy in international law is rules of *jus cogens*. Pursuant to the Vienna Convention on the Law of Treaties, rules of *jus cogens* (by their very nature, part of general international law) prevail over all, past and future, treaty norms. One further exception can be found: the rules created by different organs of the same international organization often have an inherent hierarchical status corresponding to the hierarchical status of the organ that made the rule.

This general lack of hierarchy in international law has major consequences. First, by concluding a treaty, states can contract out of or deviate from general international law (other than *jus cogens*). States do so regularly, for example, in the final provisions of treaties on how to amend the treaty (thus contracting out of rules of general international law on the law of treaties) and in treaty provisions setting up a tailor-made enforcement mechanism (thus deviating from certain rules of general international law on state responsibility). Importantly, unless the treaty contracts out of a rule of general international law, this rule is valid and also applies with respect to the newly concluded treaty. As noted earlier, each new state, as well as each new treaty, is automatically born into general international law. The treaty must exclude the rules of general international law that the parties do not want to apply with respect to the treaty, not the reverse (i.e., the treaty does not have to list all such rules that are to apply to it). Just as private contracts are automatically born into a system of domestic law, so treaties are automatically born into the system of international law. Much the way private contracts do not need to list all the relevant legislative and administrative provisions of domestic law for them to be applicable to the contract, so treaties need not explicitly set out rules of general international law for them to be applicable to the treaty (for example, the text of the Vienna Convention does not have to be attached to the new treaty for general international law rules on the law of treaties to be applicable to it). The same applies as regards existing treaties: any new treaty not only is subsumed under general international law, but is created within the wider corpus of public international law, including pre-existing treaties. These pre-existing treaties, insofar as they relate to the new treaty, automatically interact with it.

Second, since treaty rules and rules of customary law have the same binding force and the notion of *acte contraire* is alien to international law, not only can treaties contract out of, or overrule custom (custom being the main source of general international law), but also custom, in principle, can replace a treaty norm. Once a custom has been validly established and proven, an earlier contradictory treaty rule must give way to it unless it can be proved that the earlier treaty continues to apply as *lex specialis*. In practice, this continuing existence is often manifest.

Third, the absence of any inherent hierarchy of treaty norms (other than rules of *jus cogens*) means that, in principle, the treaty norms concluded under the auspices of the United Nations Environment Programme (UNEP) have the same legal status as those concluded in the World Intellectual Property Organization (WIPO), the WTO, or a bilateral treaty. No a priori hierarchy exists between WTO rules and other treaty rules. All treaty rules derive from the consent of the states involved. Deriving from the same source, they must be equally binding in nature. Nevertheless, in practice, treaties themselves, as well as general international law rules on the interaction between them (in particular, the *lex posterior* rule in Article 30 of the Vienna Convention), do set out rules on the priority of different treaty norms. *In abstracto*, however, one treaty norm, once validly concluded, is as legally binding as any other. As a result, in principle, any treaty norm existing today (other than a rule of *jus cogens*) can be changed tomorrow, as between any number of states and with the consent of these states, by another treaty norm. Only explicit prohibitions or conflict rules in pre-existing treaties, and general international law rules on the interplay of norms, can prevent states from thus "changing their minds."

WTO Rules as Rules of Public International Law

With one possible exception, no academic author (or any WTO decision or document) disputes that WTO rules are part of the wider corpus of public international law. Like international environmental law and human rights law, WTO law is "just" a branch of public international law. To public international lawyers, my call in the April 2000 issue of this *Journal* for WTO rules to "be considered as creating international legal obligations that are part of public international law" is a truism. To many negotiators and other WTO experts in Geneva, however, it comes as a surprise. Not a single legal argument has been (or, in my view, can be) put forward in their support. The fact that many negotiators of the WTO treaty (in numerous countries representatives of a trade ministry de-linked from that of foreign affairs) did not *think* of public international law when drafting the WTO treaty is not a valid legal argument. At most, it amounts to an excuse for the WTO treaty not to have dealt more explicitly with the relationship between WTO rules and other rules of international law.

Stating that WTO rules are just a part of public international law is one thing. It is quite another to submit that there is nothing special about WTO rules. In many respects WTO rules are *lex specialis* as opposed to general international law. But contracting out of *some* rules of general international law (for example, as does the WTO dispute settlement mechanism vis-à-vis certain rules of general international law on state responsibility) does not mean that one has contracted out of *all* of them, nor a fortiori that WTO rules were created completely outside the system of international law. Much has been written about so-called self-contained regimes. However, all references to this notion concerned certain international legal regimes (in particular, those of diplomatic immunities, the European Community, and human rights treaties) that, in terms of their compliance mechanism or secondary rules, may somehow be self-contained, without any or only limited "fallback" on general international law. No one has spoken of self-contained regimes in the sense of treaty regimes that are completely isolated from all rules of general international law (including the law on treaties, judicial proceedings, and matters such as the use of force and human rights), let alone treaty regimes concluded completely outside the international legal system. As noted above, states, in their treaty relations, can contract out of one, more, or, in theory, all rules of general international law (other than those of *jus cogens*), but they cannot contract out of the system of international law. As soon as states contract with one another, they do so automatically and necessarily within the system of international law.

WTO rules are thus rules of international law that, in certain respects, constitute *lex specialis* vis-à-vis certain rules of general international law. However, this does not mean that WTO rules are *lex specialis* vis-à-vis all rules of international law. WTO rules regulate the trade relations between states (as well as separate customs territories). Nonetheless, in today's highly interdependent world, a great number, if not most, state regulations in one way or another affect trade flows between states. Hence, WTO rules, essentially aimed at liberalizing trade, have a potential impact on almost all other segments of society and law. For example, liberalizing trade may sometimes jeopardize respect for the environment or human rights. Equally, enforcing respect for human rights or environmental standards may sometimes require the imposition of trade barriers.

Moreover, trade restrictions are resorted to increasingly in pursuit of all kinds of nontrade objectives, ranging from respect for human rights and the environment to confirmation of territorial borders. Such resort creates a huge potential for interaction between WTO rules and other rules of international law, as WTO rules cut across almost all other rules of international law. It also means that in certain respects these "all-affecting" WTO rules are framework rules only or *lex generalis*. Indeed, the WTO forms a general and increasingly universal framework for all (or almost all) of the trade relations between states. Although GATT/WTO rules replaced a myriad of other bilateral and regional arrangements, they do allow for certain more detailed or further-reaching regional and bilateral arrangements, as well as a series of exceptions related to the environment and national security, among other things. In these respects, WTO trade liberalization rules are general or *lex generalis* permitting the continuation or creation of more focused or detailed rules of international law (such as certain rules on the environment, human rights, or the law of the sea, as well as on customs unions and free trade areas). In this sense, WTO rules are not the alpha and omega of all possible trade relations between states. Other, more detailed or special rules of international law (in terms of either subject matter or the number of states bound by them) continue to be highly relevant.

The Relationship Between WTO Rules and Other Rules of International Law

With the preceding two sections in mind, we can now portray the universe of international law relevant to the WTO as consisting of the following:

(1) WTO rules that add previously nonexistent rights or obligations to the corpus of international law (such as nondiscrimination principles in trade in services);

(2) WTO rules that contract out of general international law (such as rules in the Dispute Settlement Understanding on the "suspension of concessions," which contract out of general international law rules on countermeasures) or deviate from, or even replace, other preexisting rules of international law (such as bilateral quota or tariff arrangements and the Tokyo Round codes);

(3) WTO rules that confirm preexisting rules of international law, be they of general international law (such as DSU Article 3.2 confirming that WTO covered agreements are to be interpreted "in accordance with customary rules of interpretation of public international law") or preexisting treaty law (such as GATT 1994 incorporating GATT 1947 and the TRIPS Agreement incorporating parts of certain WIPO conventions);

(4) non-WTO rules that already existed when the WTO treaty was concluded (on April 15, 1994) and that are (a) relevant to and may have an impact on WTO rules; and (b) have not been contracted out of, deviated from, or replaced by the WTO treaty. These non-WTO rules consist mainly of general international law, in particular rules on the law of treaties, state responsibility, and settlement of disputes, but also of other treaty rules that regulate or have an impact on the trade relations between states (such as certain rules in environmental or human rights conventions and customs unions or free trade arrangements); and

(5) non-WTO rules that are created subsequently to the WTO treaty (post-April 1994) and (a) are relevant to and may have an impact on WTO rules; (b) either add to or confirm existing WTO rules or contract out of, deviate from, or replace aspects of existing WTO rules; and (c) if the latter is the case, do so in a manner consistent with interplay and conflict rules in the WTO treaty and general international law.

...

I. The Applicable Law Before a WTO Panel

Once it has been determined that a WTO panel has jurisdiction to hear a case, the panel must ascertain the law to be applied so as to resolve the WTO claims concerned. The applicable law before a WTO panel is delimited by four factors:

(1) *The claims that can be brought before a WTO panel.* Because of the limited substantive jurisdiction of WTO panels, only legal claims under WTO covered agreements may be examined. A panel's mandate covers only claims set out with sufficient clarity in the panel request. Counterclaims are not allowed within the same procedure. A panel may also be required

to make other findings pursuant to its implied jurisdiction or to come to a legal conclusion within the purview of the WTO claims themselves.

(2) *The defenses invoked by the defending party*. Except for matters or defenses that it must consider *ex officio* (such as its own jurisdiction), a WTO panel must limit its examination to defenses invoked by the defending party (*non ultra petita*).

(3) *The scope of the relevant rules* ratione materiae, ratione personae, *and* ratione temporis. Within the framework of the claims and defenses thus before it, a WTO panel can employ only those rules which apply to the facts and circumstances of the case before it.

(4) *Conflict rules in the WTO treaty, general international law and other non-WTO treaties*. If two or more rules apply to the facts and circumstances of the case and are contradictory (pursuant to the definition of conflict described earlier), a WTO panel must apply the relevant conflict rules. When two rules in WTO covered agreements conflict, the WTO treaty states in a series of provisions which one should prevail. For example, conflicts between the WTO Agreement and any of the multilateral trade agreements (such as the GATT, GATS, TRIPS and DSU) must be resolved in favor of the WTO Agreement (Art. XVI:3). In the event of conflict between the GATT 1994 and another agreement on trade in goods in Annex 1A to the WTO Agreement, the other Annex 1A agreement prevails. If no conflict rules can be found for intra-WTO conflicts in the WTO treaty itself or for conflicts between WTO rules and other rules of international law, the conflict rules of general international law must be resorted to, as well as any conflict rules in the non-WTO treaty containing the contradictory rule of international law.

Crucially—and this is one of the main points of this article—the fact that the substantive jurisdiction of WTO panels is limited to claims under WTO covered agreements does not mean that the applicable law available to a WTO panel is necessarily limited to WTO covered agreements. Much has been said above about the creation and continuing existence of the WTO treaty in the wider context of general international law and other non-WTO treaties, be they pre- or post-1994. This context and background (essentially, that WTO rules belong to the rules of international law) does not suddenly evaporate when WTO claims are transferred to a WTO panel. As submitted earlier, there is arguably a "two-class society" between those rules of international law that can be judicially enforced and those that cannot. In that sense, rules of international law may indeed operate at two levels: the first and most general level being that of the entire corpus of public international law where all rules of international law freely interact; and the second and more specific level being that of a court of international law with jurisdiction to enforce only a limited number of rules. Rules in WTO covered agreements operate at both the first and the second levels. However, these two levels do not exist in "splendid isolation". An obvious link joins them. In particular, if at the first, more general level of the entire corpus of international law, WTO rules are somehow changed, that change will necessarily be felt in and penetrate the second, more concrete level of WTO dispute settlement. (The exact consequences of such change will be discussed below.) Like the WTO treaty itself, the WTO dispute settlement system set up by that treaty was not created and does not exist in a legal vacuum. That system is merely an instrument to enforce WTO covered agreements as they were created and necessarily continue to exist in the wider corpus of international law. It is not frozen into April 1994 law or limited to the four corners of WTO covered agreements (even if it is limited to enforcing claims under these agreements). No treaty can be created outside the system of international law, nor can a court or tribunal that enforces claims under a treaty. The *Lockerbie* cases perfectly illustrate this point. There, the ICJ had jurisdiction to consider Libyan claims only under the Montreal Convention. However, this did not stop it from also examining other international law, in particular UN Security Council Resolution 748 invoked in defense by the United Kingdom and the United States, as part of the applicable law.

Relevant DSU provisions and WTO jurisprudence. The DSU limits the jurisdiction of WTO panels and the Appellate Body. It does not limit the potentially applicable law before them. Unlike the LOS Convention and the Statute of the ICJ, the DSU does not include an explicit provision on "applicable law." The repeated references to "providing security and predictability to the multilateral trading system," preserving "the rights and obligations of Members under the covered agreements" (DSU Art. 3.2), protecting the "benefits accruing to it directly or indirectly under the covered agreements," and maintaining the "proper balance between the rights and obligations of Members" (DSU Art. 3.3), as well as the panel function of assessing the "applicability of and conformity with the relevant covered agreements" (DSU Art. 11), relate to the jurisdiction or substantive mandate of WTO panels to judicially enforce only WTO covered agreements, not to the law that may be applied in doing so.

DSU Article 7 is more directed to applicable law. Paragraph 1 sets out the standard terms of reference of panels and instructs them to examine the matter referred to them "in the light of the relevant provisions" of the covered agreement(s) cited by the parties to the dispute. Paragraph 2 obliges panels to "address the relevant provisions in any covered agreement or agreements cited by the parties to the dispute." However, and again crucially for the thesis in this paper, despite this obligation to address and possibly apply these WTO rules, nothing in the DSU or any other WTO rule precludes panels from addressing and, as the case may be, applying other rules of international law so as to decide the WTO claims before them. As outlined earlier with respect to the WTO treaty, the DSU, a judicial system aimed at enforcing certain rules of international law, need not refer explicitly to or confirm all other potentially relevant rules of international law, be they pre- or post-1994. Such reference or confirmation occurs automatically as a result of the simple fact that the DSU was created and continues to exist in the wider context of international law. Thus, other rules of international law apply automatically unless the DSU or any other WTO rule has contracted out of them. As the panel in *Korea—Government Procurement* noted (in a footnote!) about the rules of customary international law that it referred to in examining the non-violation complaint before it: "We do not see any basis for arguing that the terms of reference [in DSU Article 7.1] are meant to exclude reference to the broader rules of customary international law in interpreting a claim properly before the Panel."

Unlike Article 291 of the LOS Convention and Article 38 of the ICJ Statute, the DSU does not explicitly confirm its creation and existence in international law. However, there was no need for the DSU to do so, as it cannot have been otherwise. Implicit confirmation that WTO panels, when examining WTO claims, may be required to refer to and apply other rules of international law can be found in DSU Articles 3.2, 7.1, and 11. The obligation in Article 11 to assess the applicability of WTO rules objectively may require a panel— depending on the claims, defenses, and facts of the matter before it—to refer to and apply other rules of international law. These other rules may show that the relevant WTO rules do not apply and have therefore not been violated. However, failure to look at these other rules would preclude an "objective assessment of . . . the applicability of . . . the relevant covered agreements." The reference in Article 11 to making all "other findings" (or, in the words of DSU Article 7.1, all "such findings") as will assist the DSB in resolving the WTO claims before it further acknowledges that WTO panels may need to resort to and apply rules of international law beyond WTO covered agreements. Hence, to deduce from the explicit references in paragraphs 1 and 2 of DSU Article 7 (quoted above) to some law (i.e., WTO covered agreements) that all other law is thereby implicitly excluded is erroneous. Indeed, in practice the terms of reference of WTO panels do not read as requiring an examination "in the light of the relevant provisions in . . . the covered agreement(s) cited by *the parties to the dispute*" but, rather, an examination in the light of the relevant provisions of the covered agreements cited by *the complainant* in its panel request. Does this exclusive reference to the provisions invoked by the complainant imply that no other law (not even the defenses invoked by the defending party) can be considered? Surely not. The same reasoning applies to the references in the DSU to resort to WTO covered agreements. These references cannot be read as excluding all other law. Or does the law explicitly referred to in Article 38 of the ICJ Statute preclude the Court's consideration and application of other rules of international law? It does not. The ICJ, like WTO panels, as a court under international law, regularly refers to law not explicitly mentioned in Article 38, in particular unilateral acts of states and acts of international organizations.

WTO jurisprudence also confirms that the DSU, or any other WTO rule, should not be interpreted as limiting the applicable law before a WTO panel to WTO covered agreements. In practice, panels and the Appellate Body alike have frequently referred to and applied other rules of international law in examining WTO claims. They have done so not only in interpreting WTO covered agreements. More important, WTO panels and the Appellate Body have applied other rules of international law independently of construing a given WTO provision. In their examination of WTO claims, they have applied rules of general international law, in particular on (1) issues of judicial dispute settlement (such as standing, representation by private counsel, *la compétence de la compétence*, burden of proof, the treatment of municipal law, the acceptability of amicus curiae briefs, authority to draw adverse inferences, and judicial economy); (2) the law of treaties (such as the principle of nonretroactivity and error in treaty formation); and (3) state responsibility (such as provisions on countermeasures and attribution), referring each time to the work of the ILC on the subject. Moreover, WTO panels and the Appellate Body have also applied WTO rules that are not part of WTO covered agreements (such as the Declaration on the Relationship of the WTO and the IMF and acts of WTO organs such as waivers), as well as non-WTO rules that are not part of general international law (such as the Lomé Convention and unilateral acts of WTO members). In the absence of an inherent hierarchy of rules of international law (other than *jus cogens*), there is no reason to apply general international law, but not, for example, non-WTO treaties—always to the extent, of course, that both disputing parties are legally bound by them and it is done in the examination of WTO claims. Finally, confirmation that the WTO judiciary does not apply only WTO covered agreements can be found in its repeated references to GATT/WTO jurisprudence and publicists. These sources do not, in and of themselves, represent rules of international law. However, as noted in Article 38(1)(d) of the ICJ Statute (where they are mentioned as two of the five legal sources that the Court must "apply"), they are "subsidiary means for the determination of rules of law." Clearly, if WTO panels and the Appellate Body were not allowed to refer to or apply any source of law other than WTO covered agreements, all of the WTO cases referenced above would be legally incorrect.

Under the DSU, should WTO rules always prevail? One might ask whether it is even possible, under international law, generally to limit the applicable law before an international court or tribunal. Of course, its jurisdiction can be limited and, depending on the claims, defenses, and facts of a specific case, the applicable law will also be narrowed down in a given dispute. But could a court of international law, generally and *ex ante,* exclude consideration of rules of international law other than those it was asked to enforce? I do not think so. Other international law can be excluded as a result of contracting out by the treaty or a general conflict clause in favor of the treaty. However, such a contracting-out or conflict clause does not concern the potentially applicable law in settling disputes as much as which of several potentially applicable laws is to prevail.

A commentator has suggested that DSU Article 3.2, as confirmed in DSU Article 19.2, is this kind of general conflict clause in favor of WTO rules. The last sentence of Article 3.2 provides: "Recommendations and rulings of the DSB cannot add to or diminish the rights and obligations provided in the covered agreements." Article 19.2 states: "In accordance with paragraph 2 of Article 3, in their findings and recommendations, the panel and Appellate Body cannot add to or diminish the rights and obligations provided in the covered agreements." Should these provisions be read as saying that WTO panels, the Appellate Body, and the DSB cannot ever add to or diminish the rights and obligations explicitly set out in WTO covered agreements? Do these provisions mean that no other law, be it pre- or post-1994, can ever influence WTO covered agreements and that, in the event of conflict between these agreements and another rule of international law, the WTO rule must always prevail? In my view, the answer is no. DSU Articles 3.2 and 19.2 do not address the jurisdiction of panels, the applicable law before them, or the relationship between WTO covered agreements and all past and future law. Rather, they deal with the inherent limits a WTO panel must observe in interpreting WTO covered agreements. In exercising this judicial function of interpretation, WTO panels may clarify the meaning of WTO covered agreements, but they may not "add to or diminish the rights and obligations provided in the covered agreements." To put it differently, as judicial organs, WTO panels may not create new rights and obligations; they must apply those that WTO members agreed to. Once again, this limitation on the function of WTO panels was made *ex abundante cautela*. Even without its enunciation, WTO panels would have been subject to it as an inherent limitation of the judicial function prescribed in general international law.

However, stating what the judiciary can do with the law differs greatly from stating what the legislature (i.e., WTO members) has done, or can do, with the law. Articles 3.2 and 19.2 specify that the WTO judiciary, like any other judiciary, cannot "change" the WTO treaty. A conflict clause, in contrast, would (1) tell us that WTO members, when negotiating the treaty, did not want any other existing rules of international law to prevail over the WTO treaty; and (2) direct WTO members that in their future dealings they must not change or overrule the rights and obligations in the WTO treaty (except pursuant to the amendment procedures and other provisions in the treaty itself). To make an analogy with the ICJ: the Statute prescribed in 1945 that the Court must "decide in accordance with international law"—a phrase interpreted in the *South West Africa* cases to mean that the ICJ's "duty is to apply the law as it finds it, not to make it." This provision can hardly be interpreted to mean that the law the ICJ may look at is limited to that of 1945, nor that international law as it existed in 1945 must always and necessarily prevail over all subsequent rules of international law. The drafters of the WTO treaty could have inserted a conflict clause stating that the WTO treaty is to prevail over all past and future international law, similarly to Article 103 of the UN Charter. Although such a clause would have had only limited effect, the contractual freedom of WTO members would have permitted them to do so (within the limits of *jus cogens* and the principle of *pacta tertiis*). But if the drafters had wanted the WTO treaty to play the role of a second UN Charter, prevailing over all other law, would they not have said so? For example, would they not have put a non-derogation clause in the WTO Agreement itself, instead of twice inserting a sentence at the end of a provision on the interpretive function of WTO panels in a technical instrument, the DSU?

As further evidence of the proposition advanced here that WTO dispute settlement both encompasses more than WTO covered agreements (as well as more than interpreting these agreements in the light of other rules of international law) and does not include a general and automatic conflict clause in favor of WTO covered agreements, consider the following extreme example. Imagine that the WTO treaty included an agreement regulating the slave trade. Would a WTO panel be obliged to apply and enforce this agreement at the request of a WTO member complaining about trade restrictions regarding slaves imposed by another member? If the DSU were read as precluding reference to international law other than WTO covered agreements (i.e., as a mechanism created outside the system of international law) and/or as containing a conflict clause to the effect that WTO rules always prevail, a WTO panel would be so obliged. This example confirms the absurdity of portraying the DSU as some alien mechanism divorced from, and superior to, all other international law. Following the theory put forward in this paper, the defending party in our hypothetical dispute would be allowed to invoke Article 53 of the

Vienna Convention as a legal defense against the WTO slave trade agreement (the applicable law for defenses not being inherently limited). Article 53 provides that "[a] treaty is void if, at the time of its conclusion, it conflicts with a peremptory norm of general international law." On that ground, the WTO panel would be obliged to find the WTO slave trade agreement invalid, hence inapplicable to and unenforceable against the WTO member in question. Nevertheless, given the limited jurisdiction of WTO panels (claims under WTO covered agreements only), the WTO member concerned could not itself bring a complaint to the WTO against the WTO member trading in slaves.

… … …

Therefore, according to Professor Pauwelyn, the fact that legal claims in WTO dispute settlement are limited to WTO covered agreements does not mean that the applicable law available to a WTO panel is found exclusively in these covered agreements. Rather, he argues, WTO rules 'belong to the rules of international law', and thus international law is part of the law that may be, and in fact has been, applied. The following extract offers a differing viewpoint on the issue.

Conflict of Norms in Public International Law: How WTO Law Relates to Other Rules of International Law by Joost Pauwelyn, Review author: J Trachtman, (2004) 98 *American Journal of International Law* 855, 855–61

This authoritative work, *Conflict of Norms in Public International Law,* originated in the author's doctoral dissertation, and it is an impressive record of an education. Like any good dissertation, it begins with a single question: what is the relationship between WTO law and "other" international law? It broadens from there to include many subsidiary questions that are important in their own right. Joost Pauwelyn has performed penetrating and comprehensive research, has looked at this question from every salient angle, and has written the strongest possible argument for the position that (1) general international law (both customary and conventional) is applicable as law in WTO dispute settlement, and (2) most relevant international law will supervene WTO law in the event of a conflict. The central question addressed in this book is whether the WTO dispute resolution system allows broader international law (in particular, but not limited to, human rights, environmental, and labor law) to be used as defenses in relation to alleged violations of WTO obligations.

…

NORMATIVE CRITIQUE

…

Neither the author of *Conflict of Norms* nor anyone else can know whether demotion of WTO law enhances human welfare or whether it is otherwise recommended by ethical considerations. Nevertheless, what one encounters in *Conflict of Norms* is a systematic effort to demote WTO law in favor of less "mercantile" law, such as human rights law and environmental law. In the first sentence of the preface, the author declares: "At heart, this book is inspired by a willingness to see more to life than money" (page xi). While this inspiration cannot be gainsaid, it does not provide a normative basis for the position that human rights or environmental protection should peremptorily trump trade law. There is great nuance here. The rights to trade—including those to a vocation and a livelihood — are not necessarily inferior in priority to certain other rights. We can think of circumstances in which there may be deep normative import, if not normative superiority, attaching to trade law values; for example, trade disciplines may alleviate poverty in a very significant way at the expense of modest incursions on human rights or environmental protection. Not all human rights are peremptory, and some, like the right to health, are dependent on states' financial resources. While there is indeed more to life than money, much of what is good in life becomes available, or enjoyable, only after sufficient resources are secured.

Notwithstanding the above uncertainties concerning the substantive justice of the normative approach pursued in *Conflict of Norms,* that approach is almost certainly incorrect from the perspective of procedural justice. It seems patent that at the conclusion of the Uruguay Round in 1994, states—and especially developing states like India or Brazil—did not intend to agree, and did not agree, that their WTO rights to trade could, within WTO dispute settlement, potentially be nullified in response to requirements of other international law. The equilibrium point of the trade-off between environmental protection or human rights and freedom to trade, as well as the enforcement relationship between these values, cannot merely be intuited from first principles about normativity or about the nature of law. Rather, it is the product of political give-and-take. The WTO treaties represent the results of substantial political negotiation, including democratic approval. We should not lightly reject their clear meaning.

One of the reasons that the world may soon outgrow decentralized global lawmaking and decentralized global adjudication relates directly to the central problem addressed in *Conflict of Norms:* under circumstances of varying and shifting legislative sources, how do we resolve conflicts between rules (which are the legal face of conflicts between different values)? The core issue is a choice-of-law problem, though not between states in a horizontal legal order, and not between component political entities and a central government. Rather, it is an inter-functional choice-of-law problem, between law that arises in different sectors of the international legal system, and in different functional and institutional contexts. These contexts overlap like tectonic plates and sometimes collide with one another, causing discontinuity and disruption. *Conflict of Norms* represents a valiant attempt to lend order to this turbulent world. It is impossible to determine, however, that the system is not optimally disorderly—perhaps the turbulence we see is the best way at this particular historical moment to deal with diverse values at the international level. If this is true, perhaps the relationship between trade law and other law should be left to diplomatic give-and-take outside WTO dispute settlement. Moreover, the order proposed by *Conflict of Norms* has normative implications that are not necessarily consistent with the normative visions of others. Importantly, that order also has distributive implications.

The main normative criticism that can be leveled against *Conflict of Norms* is that it tries too valiantly—and vainly—to impose a particular order where none exists. Most importantly, the doctrinal critique developed below suggests that in an effort to create this order, *Conflict of Norms* seeks to reshape the texts to conform to the author's vision, sacrificing both procedural justice and the balance that distinguishes the strongest analytical work from advocacy. The latter is unconcerned with either textual commitment or doctrinal integrity—with procedural justice. It is willing to sacrifice procedural justice to achieve its vision of substantive justice.

DOCTRINAL CRITIQUE

...

Applicable Law Within WTO Dispute Settlement

Pauwelyn is correct, of course, that the general body of international law applies to the conduct of states, except to the extent that they effectively contract out of it. It is important, however, to recognize the distinction between the law that applies to the conduct of states and the law that is applicable within WTO dispute settlement.

Conflict of Norms confuses these two points (see pp. 461, 465). It therefore argues that because states are subject to the full range of their conventional and customary international legal obligations unless they contract out of them, WTO dispute settlement must apply all international legal obligations unless they are specifically precluded from application (chapter 8). This logic is fundamentally incorrect: it is a non sequitur. The opposite is true. International legal tribunals are authorized only to (1) hear cases and (2) apply law pursuant to their specific, positive mandates. They are not implicitly courts of general jurisdiction, either as to the cases they can hear *or* as to the law they can apply.

From the International Court of Justice down, international legal tribunals are, instead, courts of limited jurisdiction that may apply law only to the extent authorized in their mandates. The ICJ is fastidious about adhering to its mandate, as shown most recently in the *Oil Platforms* case. There the Court was careful to use the laws regarding use of force only for the purpose of interpreting a treaty exception that it was authorized to interpret. It declined to *apply* the laws regarding use of force, either to say that U.S. conduct violated those laws or that those laws somehow modified the treaty in question.

Although *Conflict of Norms* argues that international tribunals such as WTO panels are implicitly authorized to apply all law (see pp. 459-61, 466), the default rule for international law is auto-interpretation, and states are not held under international law to have accepted mandatory jurisdiction of international tribunals to apply law without their consent. The clear and general practice of international tribunals is to limit the scope of applicable law to that specified in their particular mandates. In the case of the DSU, its affirmative mandate is clearly and repeatedly limited to WTO law: the "covered agreements." Therefore, the only law that *WTO* panels and the Appellate Body are authorized to apply (directly) is WTO law. Lest there be any doubt, the international community knows how to provide tribunals with broad jurisdiction to apply a wide variety of law. For example, Article 293(1) of the UN Convention of the Law of the Sea requires the International Tribunal on the Law of the Sea to apply "other rules of international law not incompatible with this Convention." Pauwelyn's argument is difficult to square not only with the mandate contained in the DSU, but also with the decision by the Appellate Body in the *Hormones* case not to determine whether (or not) the precautionary principle is part of customary international law. For if the obligation of the panels and Appellate Body were to apply all international law, surely this obligation would include the requirement to determine whether an asserted rule of international law exists or not? The Appellate Body's flat refusal in the *Poultry* case to apply the bilateral Oilseeds Agreement, since it was not a covered agreement, is further confirmation of this point.

The only possible remaining argument within WTO dispute settlement is that the WTO law applicable in WTO dispute settlement—the "covered agreements"—is modified by pre-existing or subsequent international law. If such a claim were true, the amended covered agreements would indeed be applicable, as amended, in WTO dispute settlement. As we shall see, however, this position is untenable, and as conceded by *Conflict of Norms* (see pp. 26, 456), other international law was not intended by the negotiators to be applicable in WTO dispute settlement.

The WTO Charter specifies the means that can be used to modify WTO law. In particular, Articles IX and X of the Charter contain provisions for waiver and amendment, respectively. Generally, they require formal notice and specify procedure, including majority voting. In practical terms, they require consensus. They do not authorize bilateral or plurilateral waivers and amendments. These provisions seem intended to be exclusive; it is difficult to read them and to think that bilateral amendment or waiver was contemplated. For example, Article X:2 permits these two provisions themselves to be amended only by unanimous vote. This protection would be eviscerated by the possibility for other inter se modification. Thus, while the negotiators did not specifically state that Articles IX and X provide the only way that WTO agreements may be waived or amended, the inference seems inescapable. It can be inferred, in turn, that for an amendment to be understood as part of a "covered agreement" within the meaning of the DSU, it must follow the procedures of the WTO Charter. Consequently, even if other international law were to modify WTO law under international law generally, these modifications would not be applicable law in WTO dispute settlement.

Conflict of Norms argues that it would violate the principle *of pacta sunt servanda* for WTO tribunals to fail to apply other international law. However, it seems that the greater violation of *pacta sunt servanda* would be to require WTO tribunals to apply other international law contrary to the specific *pacta* that gives them their authority. The nonapplication of other international law in WTO dispute settlement violates no other treaty, as no other treaty purports to require application of particular non-WTO legal rules in WTO dispute settlement.

Applicable Law Outside WTO Dispute Settlement

But what is the situation outside WTO dispute settlement—in the general international legal system? It is fair to say that this system is somewhat chaotic, or at least underspecified. Consider the special question of multilateral treaties such as the WTO Charter. Is it possible for an agreement among two or more, but not all, of the parties to the WTO, to modify WTO law inter se? As noted above, within the WTO legal system, Articles IX and X of the WTO Charter would permit inter se modification only after compliance with the multilateral processes set forth in those provisions. But now we are considering the situation *outside* WTO dispute settlement, so we must consider whether this limitation would be respected under general international law.

Consider the situation at customary international law, as expressed in Articles 41 (modification) and 58 (suspension) of the Vienna Convention on the Law of Treaties. These provisions, addressing multilateral agreements, are similar in structure, so I will focus on Article 41. That article allows inter se modifications when they (1) are not prohibited by the multilateral treaty, (2) do not "affect the enjoyment by the other parties of their rights under the treaty or the performance of their obligations," and (3) do "not relate to a provision, derogation from which is incompatible with the effective execution of the object and purpose of the treaty as a whole." I explain below why these provisions do not permit inter se modification of WTO law. But we must also recognize that the WTO Charter was capable of contracting out of these rules of customary international law, so we must investigate whether it did so.

It appears that Articles IX and X of the WTO Charter, possibly combined with Article XVI:4, are best understood as contracting out of any possible permission for inter se modification or waiver under Articles 41 and 58 of the Vienna Convention. Although the WTO provisions do not explicitly prohibit inter se modification, they seem intended to provide an exclusive and preemptive means of modification. Moreover, Article XVI:4 seems to provide a continuing obligation for states to conform their laws, including arguably their international legal obligations, to their WTO obligations.

But even assuming that Articles 41 and 58 of the Vienna Convention apply, inter se modifications and waivers would be permitted only if they were not prohibited by the treaty. As discussed above, there is a strong argument that inter se modification or waiver is prohibited by the WTO treaty.

With respect to the last two conditions of Article 41—effects on third-party rights and consistency with the object and purpose of the treaty—there are strong arguments that many of the kinds of inter se modifications and waivers we are likely to see would violate these conditions. We may even understand Articles IX and X of the WTO Charter—providing third-party rights to approve waivers and amendments—as themselves violated by any inter se modifications or waivers. Importantly, as noted above, Article X:2 specifies that these provisions may be amended only by unanimous decision, making it clear that the member states of the WTO did not think it appropriate to avoid these provisions even by a *majority*. If the provisions for amendment and waiver cannot be amended by a subgroup, how can it be argued that there is room left for amendment or waiver to be effected by the means specified in Articles 41 and 58, respectively, of the Vienna Convention?

Furthermore, there are other third-party rights and other treaty purposes that would be prejudiced by inter se modification or waiver. First, the WTO Charter recites that its purposes include not just bilateral trade relations, but the increase in global standards of living, employment, and demand. If states were to agree inter se to violate WTO law in a manner inconsistent with this goal, it would adversely affect third parties' enjoyment of their rights.

Second, economic analysis shows that import restraints in one country may have important trade effects in third countries. An example of a dispute of this nature is the *Semiconductor* case, where the European Communities complained about a U.S.-Japan voluntary-restraint agreement. Article 3.5 of the DSU requires that any solutions to matters raised thereunder, even if consensual, must be consistent with the covered agreements.

Third, the *Bananas* decision of the Appellate Body recognizes a broad scope of state interest in other states' violations of their obligations. Article 3.8 of the DSU similarly expresses the broad scope of prima facie nullification or impairment, without need for proof of injury by the complainant, arising from violation. *Conflict of Norms* suggests that WTO law is best understood as "reciprocal" rather than "integral," and from this distinction it draws important conclusions to the effect that WTO law can be modified by inter se agreements. The reciprocal-integral distinction should be understood, however, as merely a shorthand description of other features, and as subsidiary to the more specific analysis of the Vienna Convention provided above, as well as to the exclusive provisions for amendment and waiver contained in Articles IX and X. Consequently, neither normative nor doctrinal consequences flow from the mere characterization of an agreement as reciprocal versus integral (and as I have also argued above, it is a mistake to characterize WTO law generally as "reciprocal").

To conclude this argument about what happens outside the WTO dispute settlement system in cases of conflict between WTO law and other international law, it seems quite incorrect to say that WTO law is generally trumped by international environmental, human rights, or labor agreements. Rather, in the general international legal system, we are stuck with the messy and often normatively incoherent rules *of lex posterior,* as reflected in Article 30 of the Vienna Convention, and questions about how multilateral treaties may be modified by custom or by other multilateral treaties with different membership under Articles 41 and 58 of the Vienna Convention.

CONCLUSION

It is not surprising that WTO negotiators in 1994 did not intend other international law to be used as potential defenses to WTO obligations. Most other international law—both treaty and custom—was not entered into with formal dispute settlement in mind. These non-WTO obligations are more extensive, and are also often more imprecise, than they would be if formal dispute settlement were contemplated. The general precautionary principle discussed in *Hormones* (as opposed to the more specific version contained in Article 5.7 of the Agreement on Sanitary and Phytosanitary Measures) is a good example of an imprecise principle often argued to be law. WTO member states sought to establish multilateral balances of trade obligations. The introduction of extra-WTO defenses that were not originally intended to be formally enforced anywhere, let alone in the WTO, would upset this balance. It must also be noted, however, that the WTO agreements are written without a clear obligation to withdraw measures that violate WTO law, and without supplying punitive, as opposed to compensatory, remedies for noncompliance, even after a judgment. This is good news for states that decide to violate WTO obligations in order to take action to promote human rights or environmental protection. So long as they are willing to accept rebalancing within the WTO, little impedes them from acting in "civil disobedience" of their WTO obligations. Again, *Hormones* is a good example.

Over the next 50 years, we may expect to see more negotiations in an effort to integrate different global values, such as trade, environment, and human rights. Hopefully, these negotiations will result in nuanced rules and institutional development that will be superior to the blanket subordination of the trade values incorporated in WTO law to other values, as proposed in *Conflict of Norms*. Those prospective changes will, no doubt, reduce the indeterminacy arising from the current, wide variation in the arrangements for adjudicating disputes in different subject areas—that is, from what is now functionally decentralized international adjudication. But future changes will surely not eliminate that variation entirely. After all, states need the flexibility to create norms of varying binding force. There is also another fundamental problem in international "legislation"—one highlighted by *Conflict of Norms*—that remains unresolved: given the diversity of legislative forums, and of the scope of participation in those forums, how can the international legal system deal with acts of over-lapping, but not identical, groups of states? Joost Pauwelyn is to be applauded for raising these issues and for illuminating them with intensive research and great analytical acuity.

… … …

As a starting point for examining the role of international law in WTO law, we note the following point on which Professors Trachtman and Pauwelyn agree. DSU Article 3.2 states: 'The Members recognize that it serves to preserve the rights and obligations of Members under the covered agreements, and to clarify the existing provisions of those agreements in accordance with customary rules of interpretation of public international law'.

This reference to the 'customary rules of interpretation of public international law' has been taken to mean the treaty interpretation rules in the Vienna Convention on the Law of Treaties. The relevant aspects of these rules for this issue are:

Article 31: General rule of interpretation

1. A treaty shall be interpreted in good faith in accordance with the ordinary meaning to be given to the terms of the treaty in their context and in the light of its object and purpose.

…

3. There shall be taken into account, together with the context:

…

(c) any relevant rules of international law applicable in the relations between the parties.

Professors Trachtman and Pauwelyn would agree that international law is relevant to WTO law under Article 31(3)(c), which provides that the 'relevant rules of international law applicable in the relations between the parties' shall be 'taken into account' together with the 'context'.

Where they disagree, however, is how international law can apply beyond the textual interpretation of Article 31(3)(c). Professor Pauwelyn's view is that international law simply 'applies' in WTO law due to the nature of WTO law as part of the larger body of international law. Of course, this does not mean that a claim can brought in WTO dispute settlement pursuant to non-WTO aspects of international law. But it does mean that international law can be applied as a general matter in the context of WTO disputes.

Drawing a line between 'interpretation' of and 'applying' the law can be quite difficult. The following extract from Lorand Bartels helps to clarify this distinction by classifying three different uses of 'other' international law (that is, non-WTO international law) that can be used in WTO disputes:

L Bartels, 'Applicable Law in WTO Dispute Settlement Proceedings' (2001) 35 *Journal of World Trade* **499**

III. THREE DIFFERENT USES OF "OTHER" INTERNATIONAL LAW

. . . In order to illustrate *how* "other" international law can be applied by Panels and the Appellate Body, it is necessary to draw a distinction between three different ways in which international law can be used in deciding a dispute: (a) as an aid to the interpretation of a given provision of an agreement; (b) as evidence of a Member's compliance with its obligations; and (c) as *law* in the chain of legal reasoning.

A. INTERPRETATION

It is most common for "other" international law to be used by Panels and the Appellate Body to *interpret* a provision in a covered agreement in accordance with the "customary rules of interpretation of public international law" referred to in Article 3.2 of the DSU. This was done, for instance, in *Canada—Term of Patent Protection*, where the Appellate Body supported its interpretation of Article 70 of TRIPS by reference to Article 28 of the Vienna Convention on the Law of Treaties, which establishes a presumption against the retroactive effect of treaties, and in *US—Shrimp*, where it found the Chapeau of Article XX of GATT to be "but one expression of the principle of good faith . . . [which] at once a general principle of law and a general principle of international law, controls the exercise of rights by states". The same thing occurred in *EC—Bananas*, where both the Panel and the Appellate Body interpreted a waiver expressly referring to the Lomé Convention in light of that Convention. They did not, however, *apply* that Convention as law, and so there was no question of any modification of the rights and obligations under the covered agreements. What is essential in these cases is the perhaps obvious point that there is a text to be interpreted. As we shall see, this is not always the case.

B. EVIDENCE OF COMPLIANCE WITH OBLIGATIONS

International law can also be used as *evidence* of a party's compliance with its obligations under the covered agreements. This happened in *US—Shrimp*, where the Appellate Body referred to an international agreement concluded by the United States (the Inter-American Convention for the Protection and Conservation of Sea Turtles) as evidence that other courses of action were reasonably open to it and that its actions therefore constituted unjustifiable discrimination. In *India—Patents*, the Appellate Body stated that municipal law can also constitute evidence of a party's compliance with its international obligations.

C. APPLICATION AS LAW

Third, "other" international law can be applied as *law* in the chain of legal reasoning (or argument). Often a focus on the precise question at issue—in our case the validity of a claim of nullification or impairment—tends to under-emphasise for the fact that a good deal of law is being applied at the subordinate levels of legal argument. That is to say, if to answer Question A one must first answer Question B, the latter is of subordinate logical status in the chain of reasoning, but to the extent that it is essential to the reasoning, it is still being applied as law.

Two cases from the International Court of Justice should serve to illustrate this point. In the first, the *Fisheries* case, the Court refused to make a decision merely on "a set of propositions which, in the form of definitions, principles or rules, purport to justify certain contentions and do not constitute a precise and direct statement of a claim". It said that "these elements may be taken into account only in so far as they would appear to be relevant for deciding the sole question in dispute . . .". Clearly, these "elements" were legal: the problem was that they were not within the Court's jurisdiction in the case at hand. The second case, the *East Timor* case, dealt with the opposite situation, where a decision on one of these "elements" (Indonesian sovereignty over East Timor) would have been so logically necessary to the claim that it constituted the very subject matter of the dispute. Because a decision on this "element" would have affected the legal interests of an absent third party (Indonesia), the "indispensable third parties" rule meant that the dispute could not be decided by the Court.

There may, of course, be some overlap between the *application* of law at the subordinate levels of legal reasoning and the *interpretation* of a particular textual provision. This can be seen in *Turkey—Textiles*, where the Panel used the rules of state responsibility in deciding that the measures at issue were attributable to Turkey and not to the EC—Turkey customs union. The Panel decided that the customs union had no international legal personality (it was also not recognised as a WTO Member) and because—in the absence of a contrary treaty provision—Turkey was to be presumed to be responsible for the acts of a common organ. What is interesting is that while it might have been possible to treat the issue as an interpretation of the "Member" bound by the GATT 1994, the Panel did not phrase its enquiry in this way. And this was presumably not only because to do so would have been unnecessarily strained; but also because it would have changed nothing in the Panel's reasoning. It was simply cleaner to apply the rules of state responsibility directly without attempting to justify these rules as being used to interpret a particular provision of a covered agreement.

... ...

As an additional point, we note that WTO panels have shown some flexibility in how they will take into account international law as part of the Vienna Convention treaty interpretation rules. In the *EC—Biotech* case, after finding that the international law rules in question could not be brought in through Article 31(3)(c), the panel nevertheless considered the relevance of this law as part of the 'ordinary meaning' under Article 31(1):

Panel Report, *European Communities—Measures Affecting the Approval and Marketing of Biotech Products*, Adopted 21 November 2006, WT/DS291, 292, 293/R

(b) Other rules of international law as evidence of the ordinary meaning of terms used in a treaty

7.90 Up to this point, we have examined whether there are other applicable rules of international law which we are required to take into account, in accordance with Article 31(3)(c) of the *Vienna Convention*, in interpreting the WTO agreements at issue in this dispute. We now turn to examine whether other rules of international law could be considered by us in the interpretation of the WTO agreements at issue even if these rules are not applicable in the relations between the WTO Members and thus do not fall within the category of rules which is at issue in Article 31(3)(c).

7.91 The European Communities notes in this regard that in *US—Shrimp* the Appellate Body interpreted WTO rules by reference to treaties which were not binding on all parties to the proceedings. More specifically, the European Communities points out that the Appellate Body in that case invoked treaties in support of arguments made by the United States, even though the United States had either not signed or not ratified these treaties. The European Communities notes that one such treaty was the *Convention on Biological Diversity*.

7.92 The **Panel** recalls that pursuant to Article 31(1) of the *Vienna Convention*, the terms of a treaty must be interpreted in accordance with the "ordinary meaning" to be given to these terms in their context and in the light of its object and purpose. The ordinary meaning of treaty terms is often determined on the basis of dictionaries. We think that, in addition to dictionaries, other relevant rules of international law may in some cases aid a treaty interpreter in establishing, or confirming, the ordinary meaning of treaty terms in the specific context in which they are used. Such rules would not be considered because they are legal rules, but rather because they may provide evidence of the ordinary meaning of terms in the same way that dictionaries do. They would be considered for their informative character. It follows that when a treaty interpreter does not consider another rule of international law to be informative, he or she need not rely on it.

7.93 In the light of the foregoing, we consider that a panel may consider other relevant rules of international law when interpreting the terms of WTO agreements if it deems such rules to be informative. But a panel need not necessarily rely on other rules of international law, particularly if it considers that the ordinary meaning of the terms of WTO agreements may be ascertained by reference to other elements.

7.94 This approach is consistent with the Appellate Body's approach in *US—Shrimp*, as we understand it. In that case, the Appellate Body had to interpret the term "exhaustible natural resources" in Article XX(g) of the GATT 1994. The Appellate Body found that this term was by definition evolutionary and therefore found it "pertinent to note that modern international conventions and declarations make frequent references to natural resources as embracing both living and non-living resources". Thus, as we understand it, the Appellate Body drew on other rules of international law because it considered that they were informative and aided it in establishing the meaning and scope of the term "exhaustible natural resources". The European Communities correctly points out that the Appellate Body referred to conventions which were not applicable to all disputing parties. However, the mere fact that one or more disputing parties are not parties to a convention does not necessarily mean that a convention cannot shed light on the meaning and scope of a treaty term to be interpreted.

7.95 In the present case, in response to a question from the Panel, the European Communities has identified a number of provisions of the *Convention on Biological Diversity* and of the *Biosafety Protocol* which it considers must be taken into account by the Panel. The European Communities has not explained how these provisions are relevant to the interpretation of the WTO agreements at issue in this dispute. We have carefully considered the provisions referred to by the European Communities. Ultimately, however, we did not find it necessary or appropriate to rely on these particular provisions in interpreting the WTO agreements at issue in this dispute.

7.96 Furthermore, we recall that after consulting the Parties, we have requested several international organizations (Codex, FAO, the IPPC Secretariat, WHO, OIE, the CBD Secretariat and UNEP) to identify materials (reference works, glossaries, official documents of the relevant international organizations, including conventions, standards and guidelines, etc.) that might aid us in determining the ordinary meaning of certain terms used in the definitions provided in Annex A to the *SPS Agreement*. The materials we have obtained in this way have been taken into account by us, as appropriate.

... ...

Based on all of the above, it is clear that international law can and will play a role in WTO disputes at times. However, the precise scope for using international law is still unclear, and there is a great deal of disagreement in this regard. Regardless of the theoretical basis for invoking international law in WTO disputes, however, Members are likely to refer to international law whenever they believe it helps their arguments. Thus, even without a clearly defined legal standard in this area, international law is likely to play a role in WTO law.

III. QUESTIONS

1. What is the practical difference between using international law as part of the 'interpretation' process and using it as part of the 'applicable law'? Could it be argued that these are just two ways of doing the same analysis? That is, you can take into account international law as part of the interpretation, or you can wait until later and incorporate it as part of the reasoning. Could it be argued that these two approaches get you to the same point?

2. With regard to Professor Pauwelyn's slave trade agreement example, do you agree with his conclusion that a 'WTO panel would be obliged to find the WTO slave trade agreement invalid' pursuant to Article 53 of the Vienna Convention on the Law of Treaties because 'it conflicts with a peremptory norm of general international law'?

3. What is the significance of the statement in DSU Article 3.2 that the dispute settlement system of the WTO 'serves to . . . clarify the existing provisions of those agreements in accordance with customary rules of interpretation of public international law'? Without this reference to the 'customary rules of interpretation of public international law', on what basis would panels and the Appellate Body 'clarify' the WTO agreements?

4. Professor Pauwelyn explains that each new treaty is 'automatically born into' general international law. Could the WTO be created in a way that puts it outside general international law?

4

World Trade Law and Domestic Law

I. INTRODUCTION

The role of international law in domestic legal systems varies considerably by country, according to the Constitutions, judicial interpretations and specific implementing legislation involved. Some countries are quite willing to incorporate international law into their domestic law, viewing international law as a positive constraint on their actions. Others have a great deal of scepticism about the practice, in part based on concerns that it undermines the democratic aspects of their system because international law has a serious 'democracy deficit'.

In the field of world trade law, questions about the domestic legal status of the WTO agreements have arisen most often in cases brought by private applicants against government agencies, such as the United States Department of Commerce, and institutions such as the European Commission and Council. Broadly speaking, these cases have adjudicated on the direct effect and indirect effect of the WTO agreements in the jurisdiction within which the case is brought. The basic argument in cases where the direct effect of the WTO agreements has been raised is that WTO law should prevail in the event of a clear inconsistency with national or regional law. In such cases, applicants may be able to rely upon a report of a WTO panel or the Appellate Body confirming the presence of a clear inconsistency. On the basis of such inconsistency, applicants will typically seek either the annulment of the challenged measures or a damages remedy. In contrast, indirect effect is synonymous with the idea of consistent interpretation which is recognized in most jurisdictions. The basic argument here is that legislation which is capable of being interpreted consistently with international obligations such as the WTO agreements should be so interpreted. In other words, the principle comes into operation when inconsistency is capable of being avoided by techniques of interpretation. In cases where consistent interpretation is raised, applicants typically argue that national agencies or regional institutions should be required to interpret broad and ambiguous statutory mandates consistently with WTO law.

There is much at stake in this area of study. Private entities frequently have a strong involvement in the domestic procedures which precede the possible commencement of inter-governmental dispute settlement proceedings in the WTO. However, the outcome of this collaboration may well be an eventual refusal on the part of the government to initiate dispute settlement proceedings. Even when proceedings are initiated and run their course, WTO dispute settlement remedies are prospective or forward looking only. Thus, if an anti-dumping duty has been calculated using a methodology which is eventually found to be inconsistent with the ADA by the Appellate Body, the obligation on the respondent state is to cease using this methodology, rather than also to reimburse duties collected before the Appellate Body report or its subsequent national implementation. These characteristics of inter-governmental dispute settlement lead private applicants affected by possible or established WTO violations to seek remedies at the national or regional level. Questions are thereby raised on the extent to which WTO law is enforceable at these levels.

This chapter continues below with an extract that offers some general thoughts on the debate over whether WTO law should have 'direct effect' in domestic law. Some specific aspects of a number of domestic/regional legal systems are then considered.

T Cottier and KN Schefer, 'The Relationship Between World Trade Organisation Law, National And Regional Law' (1998) 1 *Journal of International Economic Law* 83, 91-101

THE RELATIONSHIP OF WORLD TRADE ORGANISATION RULES AND
INCONSISTENT NATIONAL OR REGIONAL RULES: THE PROBLEM OF DIRECT
EFFECT

1. THE CONCEPT OF DIRECT EFFECT

In cases of explicit conflict between WTO rules and national or regional rules (situations which cannot be remedied by consistent interpretation), a situation of conflict exists in a domestic context and with domestic law. While international law clearly prevails as a matter of international relations under state responsibility discussed above, the matter is controversial and unresolved as a matter of domestic or EC law. It is generally addressed under the doctrine of direct effect or self-executing effect of international law rules, these terms being used interchangeably in the present context.

In this study, 'direct effect' is used to mean that a private person in a state (or Union, respectively) may base a claim in, and be granted relief from, the domestic courts of that state against another private person or the state on the basis of the state's obligations under an international treaty. Such claims can be made without a transformation of the obligation by national or regional rule-makers. They may equally be made against implementing legislation on grounds that such legislation is not compatible with international law.

Direct effect brings about the empowerment of three actors: the administration, private actors, and the courts. The administration is empowered to act without specific internal legislation, directly relying upon treaty provisions, provided that the legislator or the government decides to act this way. Private actors directly derive rights and assume obligations under a self-executing treaty. Importantly, they may use such rights and obligations to challenge domestic law. But foremost, the position of courts is reinforced vis-à-vis government and national or regional legislators to the extent that the courts may overrule national or regional rules inconsistent with treaty obligations based upon supremacy of international law. Direct effect, in other words, has a fundamental impact on constitutional power relations among domestic actors, private and public.

Whether or not a rule is apt for such an application has been a matter of national or regional law and doctrine. The issue only exists under constitutions that follow the monist doctrine. It does not come up in dualist systems, absent explicit treaty or statutory provisions which empower authorities to rely directly upon international law. Nevertheless, state practice in monist countries has developed comparable criteria which rely upon intention, context and purpose of the treaty. The criteria centre, explicitly or implicitly, around the precision ('Bestimmtheit') of the rule concerned. Moreover, the matter of direct effect is not one of the entire treaty, but rather focuses on individual provisions. Behind the criteria of sufficient precision we find the concept, often unexpressed, of justiciability of the rule. The rights and obligations of a rule, in other words, need to be of a quality which can be understood and applied by courts within their competences. Thus, obligations of a clearly programmatic nature (e.g., a negotiating programme) which need further work on the international level or by national or regional legislation cannot be self-executing.

Justiciability cannot be determined merely on the basis of the wording of a norm. In many instances, courts have applied and construed broad principles, such as general human rights guarantees. They have done so because the application of such broad rules and principles has been considered to be within the competence of courts of law in determining individual rights and obligations. Such determination may be made by looking at the wording and context of the provision, but it can also be found in the intent of negotiators and national legislators.

Looking at WTO rules, there can be little doubt that most of them are sufficiently precise to be construed by courts. This is equally true for exceptions which do not show structural differences to comparable norms in national or regional law. Moreover, to the extent that principles, rules and exceptions are being applied and legally construed by panels and the Appellate Body – and indeed made more precise by this very process of creating precedents – they can be increasingly applied, and relied upon, by national courts in many instances. The basic problem lies in determining whether these rules are in a national court's competence as set out within the national structures of government and the separation of powers. It can be readily seen, therefore, that the underlying issue (except for clearly programmatic norms) again is a problem of national or regional constitutional law. Answers cannot be found on the level of international law and the WTO.

2. THE ACADEMIC DISCUSSION

Several authors have written excellent articles addressing the implications and potential effects of recognising treaty provisions as having direct effect being self-executing. Their opinions will be heavily relied upon here in an attempt to reiterate the importance of looking to the structural importance the use of direct effect has within a government.

Among the scholars writing on the topic of direct effect of international trade agreements, there are three that stand out as the main proponents of the two schools of thought on the issue: Jan Tumlir and Ernst-Ulrich Petersmann advocating direct effect and John H. Jackson for the critics of direct effect. A fourth author, Piet Eeckhout, has set out what we call an 'intermediate position' on the issue. The many other excellent authors that have considered the question of self-execution do not merely mimic the ideas of the three authors, but for the sake of simplicity, they will be dealt with within the summaries of the principal proponents as needed.

Advocates of the direct effect of World Trade Organisation rules. The late Jan Tumlir, whose main thesis supporting direct effect is followed by Ernst Ulrich Petersmann, looks at the direct effect of trade treaties as a weapon against inherently protectionist tendencies in domestic law systems. Tumlir and Petersmann set forth the idea of 'constitutionalising' international trade principles, elevating the rights of an individual to trade freely with foreigners to the level of a fundamental human right. To prevent the erosion of a state's sovereignty, Tumlir suggests granting individuals the right to invoke treaty provisions in front of their domestic courts. Allowing for standing in this way would be available to those citizens harmed by protectionist national policies put into effect by other national interest groups. Thus, direct effect widely defined 'helps to correct the asymmetries in the political process'.

Ernst-Ulrich Petersmann has written numerous articles that reinforce the need for using the GATT, and now the WTO, system for what he calls 'constitutional restraints' on protectionist behaviour. Sharing Tumlir's viewpoint, Professor Petersmann brings in the political theory of public choice to support his position that the WTO's reciprocal trade rules must be available to individuals to ensure that governments adhere to their international obligations of non-discrimination and liberalised access to their markets. Other authors who support the direct effect of trade rules base their beliefs on quasi-economic arguments. One author explains the idea of 'compliance capital' which in essence translates into benefits deriving from reliability and the protection of legitimate expectations.

Still other authors look to the textual arguments of courts' refusals to apply GATT rules and urge an end to this practice on the grounds that the more detailed and firmer obligations of the WTO Agreements make the arguments invalid. Meinhard Hilf, postulating that governments may be the more legitimate body for developing trade policies, nevertheless rejects the arguments made by some adjudicators that the WTO Agreements are too flexible to apply. Comparing GATT general principles to pertinent provisions of the Treaty of Rome, he cannot discern any difference in justiciablity. Moreover, the possibility to take safeguard or procedures of authoritative interpretation cannot rule out direct effect. Pleading for keeping the possibility of judicial review open to individuals, Jacques Bourgois put it quite bluntly: 'Quite simply, what is in the end the use of making law, also international law, designed to protect private parties, if these private parties cannot rely on it?'

Looking to regional integration mechanisms, Frederick Abbott is one of a handful of Americans who support the direct effect of trade provisions. Abbott does so not only because direct effect would encourage the implementation of market regulations, but more importantly because direct effect would in his view encourage a 'deeper', or social and political, integration in addition to economic integration. He writes:

> [t]his policy preference for deepened integration is based upon the beliefs that such integration enhances regional wealth generation and, with appropriate care, will not result in adverse global welfare effects; that such integration increases social tolerance by facilitating personal interaction; that it enhances the prospects for political maturation and co-operation through the creation of regional political structures.

If one would view the WTO as a very large regional integration mechanism, which given the depth of the members' commitments is not unreasonable, the same arguments can be used for allowing self-execution of the WTO Agreements in each member state.

Finally, it would seem interesting to note that authors from smaller and medium-sized trading nations, heavily depending on the rule of law in international relations, have advocated direct effect of GATT for a number of years. This is particularly true for Switzerland. Under GATT, the argument of one of the authors was essentially founded on the following: (i) the need to secure the rule of law in international economic relations and possible pioneering by smaller countries; (ii) the need to prevent disputes within the EC by securing import regulations compatible with GATT; (iii) practical considerations (no need to transformation); (iv) the possibility to exclude, as a safeguard, direct effect by the legislator where such effects are deliberately excluded or a rule is introduced later in time; and finally (v) that deliberate choices on direct effect by Parliament render trade law more transparent and secure. The approach was essentially endorsed by Olivier Jacot-Guillarmod, now a Supreme Court Judge and a principled supporter of direct effect. More recent arguments under the WTO add the idea in regard to Switzerland that: (i) direct effect is an important element of checks and balances in direct democracy which tends to be open to protectionist arguments; (ii) that the absence of global foreign policy responsibilities renders direct effect more feasible than elsewhere; and finally we argued that (iii) WTO rules which had passed the test of direct democracy (possible referendum) enjoy the same democratic legitimation as national statutes. Direct democracy therefore considerably enlarges the basis for direct effect and renders Switzerland a well-suited candidate to take the lead unilaterally in this matter under WTO law. Daniel Thürer, finally, carefully balanced the pros and cons of direct effect. He concluded in favour of it, subject to the possibility of a 'political question' doctrine as recognised by the Swiss Supreme Court.

Critics of direct effect of World Trade Organisation rules. John Jackson has written several highly differentiated works on the dangers of self-execution, and basically supports US trade policies of denying direct effect due to the imbalances in the institutional balance of government it would cause domestically. His approach considerably deviates from US scholars emphasising the Supremacy Clause (Article VI clause 2 US Const.) and its interpretation containing a strong presumption of direct effect of any treaty, thus also including WTO law. Jackson separates the concept of direct effect into three parts which can be categorised as: self-execution narrowly defined (the incorporation of the treaty into national law); standing of individuals (the right of the individual to invoke treaty provisions before domestic courts); and hierachy of norms (what rank the treaty provisions have with respect to domestic federal legislation and the domestic constitution). Because he sees each of the three aspects as important, Jackson neither vigorously nor universally either supports or denies self-execution narrowly defined. He does, however, find the idea of granting standing and allowing for an international treaty law to be superior to federal legislation (let alone the constitution) to be dangerous to the idea of democracy and democratic representation of individuals.

John Jackson's analysis begins with an overall look at the 'landscape' of treaty-making in the domestic arena: the role of the citizen and the answerability of the treaty-making parts of government are important factors in determining the desirability of allowing treaties to be self-executing. Then he turns to policy reasons for and against direct effect. While Jackson acknowledges that governments have an obligation to abide by international commitments they undertake, direct effect is not necessary to ensure this.

The stronger reasons for denying direct effect are what Jackson calls 'functional arguments'. These functional arguments include the fact that '[s]ome constitutions provide for very little democratic participation in the treaty-making process; for example, by giving no formal role to Parliaments or structuring the government so that control over foreign relations is held by certain elites'. There are also legitimate desires of legislatures to adapt international treaty language to the domestic legal system (such as translating the obligations into the native language, using local terms for legal principles, or further explaining certain provisions). And, some governments may want the opportunity to implement the obligations in a national legislative process because 'the act of transformation sometimes becomes part of a purely internal power struggle, and may be used by certain governmental institutions to enhance their powers vis-à-vis other governmental entities' or 'even, perhaps, . . . the legislature desires to preserve the option to breach the treaty in its method of application'. Even such uses of the separate implementation process are legitimate in Professor Jackson's mind because 'some breaches may be "minor" and therefore preferable to the alternative of refusing to join the treaty altogether'. Finally, Jackson argues that if treaties are given direct effect automatically, the characteristic of direct effect itself will not necessarily guarantee that the national courts will apply the treaty rules.

Ultimately, Jackson believes that the question of direct effect broadly defined must be decided by each government for itself. Depending on the treaty-making process, the national constitutional framework, the characteristics of the legal system, and the policies a particular government wants to promote, direct effect may or may not be the optimal policy for implementing trade rules. These arguments, in the final analysis, do not necessarily only relate to the WTO. They question the doctrine of direct effect for constitutional reasons in a general manner.

In the European Union, critics of direct effect mainly rely upon arguments and concerns of reciprocity in light of the fact that direct effect is not available in most members of the WTO, and in particular the USA. It is an arms' length argument in trade policy. Jan Peter Kuijper expressed what perhaps amounts to predominant thinking in the European Union:

> In the case of [the WTO] treaty, the party whose constitutional and judicial system does not know the mechanism of direct effect of treaty provisions-or worse still, specifically excludes such direct effect-places itself in such favourable position that it becomes fundamentally unfair to its trading partners. In this way it shields itself against what was called above the most powerful enforcement mechanism for treaties, and its negotiators, when discussing interpretation and application of the treaty, arrive with free hands at the table, contrary to their counterparts from countries with direct effect, whose hands are tied by the interpretation of their courts.

The argument, thus is not directed against direct effect as such, and the basic quality of applying WTO rules is not put into question. It is an argument of realpolitik. It recalls that the discussion of direct effect in the law of major trading powers-despite economic and legal arguments in favour of unilateral liberalisation and direct effect-cannot be successfully and realistically dissociated from the status of WTO law abroad.

Another basis for disagreeing with the idea of direct effect is based on a concern for the WTO's consistency. Piet Eeckhout, speaking in terms of 'judicial policy' in the context of the European Union and its member states, warns that multiple national courts interpreting the WTO Agreements independently may reduce the effectiveness of the WTO rules and its dispute settlement procedures. The argument echos concerns of diverging application of the Anti-dumping Agreement by different national authorities. He writes:

> The need to ensure an efficient interconnection between, on the one hand, the legal systems of the Community and the Member States and, on the other, the WTO system seems at first sight an argument in support of granting direct effect. However, I have some doubts whether at the present stage full-scale direct effect would be the best device for ensuring such interconnection. Attention was drawn above to the complex character of the GATT's rules and mechanisms. That complexity is, if anything, increased by the WTO Agreement. It explains why the agreement contains such a full-blown dispute settlement mechanism, which aims to reach legally justified decisions made by competent bodies. It is therefore questionable whether domestic courts . . . should become day-to-day operators and interpreters of the WTO Agreement . . . [I]n my view, the argument of the appropriate forum, namely that disputes concerning the implementation of the WTO Agreement will often give rise to intricate legal questions which are best resolved at the appropriate level (WTO panels and the Appellate Body), is a forceful argument against direct effect.

Similar concerns were equally raised by Wolfgang Benedek, in particular in the wake of the Austrian Supreme Court erring, in his view, in interpreting the Tokyo Round Agreement on Subsidies and Countervailing Duties. These concerns go to the heart of direct effect in general since the potential of diverging interpretation of rules in different member states, of course, cannot be denied. On the other hand, the problem is not unique to international law, and legal systems have found ways to avoid it by means of appeal mechanisms, in particular in federal states. The problem shows that direct effect and procedural issues cannot be dissociated.

INTERMEDIATE POSITIONS

The debate on direct effect has mainly developed two opposite positions. *Tertium non datur*, it would seem. The revision, however, of the GATT dispute settlement system has widened the options. Neither the establishment of a panel, nor the adoption of a report can be blocked any longer. Unlike before, the issue of complying with specific decisions of the Dispute Settlement Body by national or regional courts therefore will arise. This is an issue which legally speaking is separate from direct effect in the traditional sense. It is not a matter of applying general rules, but of complying with a specific ruling arrived by quasi-judicial procedures respecting due process of law.

Differentiating his argument opposing direct effect, Piet Eeckhout eventually argues that if a case has been specifically settled by WTO dispute settlement procedures, domestic effect should be given to the decision:

> Where a violation is established the binding character of the agreement and the principle of legality should in my view trump any lack of direct effect. That may be the only acceptable result if those principles are to be more than mere rhetoric. The reasons for not granting direct effect-whether it is the agreement's flexibility, or the division of powers between the legislature and the judiciary, or the respect of appropriate dispute settlement forum-cease to be valid where a violation is established.

Eeckhout's idea is most interesting as it is an intermediate position and goes beyond the critics of direct effect in the USA and Europe to balance the competing ideas on direct effect's acceptability. It is supported by Meinhard Hilf as at least a minimal standard of granting direct effect:

> No flexibility seems to be left to the discretion of the contracting parties if, in a given dispute, a panel procedure has concluded with a final consent expressed by the GATT Council. The relevant GATT law will then have been stated and clarified. At least in such a situation the ECJ would have safe grounds to apply the relevant GATT law directly.

This intermediate approach provides an important option which deserves further examination in the light of remedies available in WTO law. An obligation to enforce adopted reports in casu in particular removes the possibility to choose not to perform and instead pay compensation or accept retaliations, if this option is deemed to be more favourable. It therefore will be necessary to develop nuanced judicial policies building and explore the interaction between courts and government in cases of compensation.

... ...

II. UNITED STATES

(a) Direct Effect

Before examining the modern law here, it is interesting to note a case from the early GATT era in which a Hawaiian law was held to be inconsistent with the GATT and set aside. The law at issue in the Supreme Court of Hawaii case of *Territory of Hawaii v Henry MY Ho*[1] made it unlawful for any person to sell, offer or expose for sale any

---

[1] 41 Haw 565 (1957).

imported chicken eggs of foreign origin unless a placard bearing the words 'WE SELL FOREIGN EGGS' was displayed in a conspicuous place where the customers entering could see it. Having been charged under this law, the defendant argued in defence that it contravened the GATT 1947 and, therefore, also contravened clause 2 of Article VI of the Constitution of the United States. In part, clause 2 of Article VI provides that 'all Treaties made, or which shall be made, under the Authority of the United States, shall be the supreme Law of the Land; and the Judges in every State shall be bound thereby, any Thing in the Constitution or Laws of any State to the Contrary notwithstanding'. Marumoto J of the Supreme Court of Hawaii confirmed the GATT inconsistency in the following terms:

> Section 5 of Act 167, in requiring a conspicuous display of a placard of origin, singles out chicken shell eggs of foreign origin from domestic eggs. No such requirement is imposed in connection with the sale, or offering or exposing for sale, of chicken shell eggs of local or mainland origin. That its purpose is to protect domestic production is indicated by the following statement in Standing Committee Report No. 482 to the President of the Senate, Twenty-Eighth Legislature: 'Your Committee conducted a public hearing, at which time it was determined that the majority of poultrymen in the Territory were in favor of this measure.' Thus, it contravenes the proscription of Article III, paragraph 1, of the General Agreement on Tariffs and Trade that internal laws affecting the internal sale or offering for sale should not be applied to imported products so as to afford protection to domestic production. Furthermore, in imposing an additional requirement on foreign eggs which is not imposed on domestic eggs, it contravenes Article III, paragraph 4, of the agreement which provides that the products of the territory of any contracting party imported into the territory of any other contracting party shall be accorded treatment no less favorable than that accorded to like products of national origin in respect of all laws affecting their internal sale or offering for sale.[2]

Marumoto J went on to find that the GATT violation was not capable of being justified under GATT Article XX and dismissed the charge against the defendant.

In general terms, the case was an authority for the position that a state law must be set aside when it is irreconcilably in conflict with GATT law, even when GATT law is being relied upon by a private individual as opposed to the US Federal government. As such, it could be said that the direct effect of GATT was recognised. Analogous laws to that at issue in this case have very probably long since been repealed. However, what if a similar case arose today? Would a defendant be able to rely on GATT/WTO law as part of their defence? The answer is contained in the provisions considered below.

The direct effect of the WTO agreements in the US is comprehensively excluded by the Uruguay Round Agreements Act (URAA),[3] which implements and codifies US obligations under the WTO agreements. Also of note here are certain provisions in the Statement of Administrative Action (SAA)[4] which provides a guide for interpreting the URAA.[5]

Within the URAA, 19 USC Section 3512 provides as follows:

---

[2] *Ibid*, 570–71.
[3] Pub L No 103–465, 109 Stat 4809 (1994) (codified at 19 USC SS 3501–624 (1994).
[4] HR Rep 103–316, 1994 USCCAN 4040.
[5] The URAA itself provides that, '[T]he statement of administrative action approved by the Congress under section 3511(a) of this title shall be regarded as an authoritative expression by the United States concerning the interpretation and application of the Uruguay Round Agreements and this Act in any judicial proceedings in which a question arises concerning such interpretation or application.' 19 USC S 3512(d) (1994).

Relationship of agreements to United States law and State law

(a) Relationship of agreements to United States law

(1) United States law to prevail in conflict

No provision of any of the Uruguay Round Agreements, nor the application of any such provision to any person or circumstance, that is inconsistent with any law of the United States shall have effect . . .

(b) Relationship of agreements to State law . . .

(2) Legal challenge

A In general

No State law, or the application of such a State law, may be declared invalid as to any person or circumstance on the ground that the provision or application is inconsistent with any of the Uruguay Round Agreements, except in an action brought by the United States for the purpose of declaring such law or application invalid . . .

(c) Effect of agreement with respect to private remedies

(1) Limitations

No person other than the United States—

(A) shall have any cause of action or defense under any of the Uruguay Round Agreements or by virtue of congressional approval of such an agreement, or

(B) may challenge, in any action brought under any provision of law, any action or inaction by any department, agency, or other instrumentality of the United States, any State, or any political subdivision of a State on the ground that such action or inaction is inconsistent with such agreement.

The most relevant provision in the SAA provides that the decisions of WTO panels and the Appellate Body 'have no binding effect under the law of the United States and do not represent an expression of the US foreign or trade policy',[6] and also that '[o]nly Congress and the Administration can decide whether to implement a WTO panel recommendation and, if so, how to implement it'.[7]

It follows from these provisions that it is not possible for a private applicant before a US court to successfully argue that WTO law should prevail when a federal or state law is contrary to WTO law. When the conflict is with a federal law, the provisions above establish two insurmountable barriers. First is that the conflicting WTO law simply has no effect. This barrier continues to apply even if the Appellate Body has confirmed that there is a conflict as Appellate Body reports have 'no binding effect'. The second barrier is the express reservation of a cause of action or defence to the US. When the conflict is with a state law, only the second barrier applies. Therefore, a defendant charged under a comparable law to that at issue in *Territory of Hawaii v Henry MY Ho* would no longer be able to rely on GATT/WTO law as part of their defence.

---

[6] Above n 4, 4318.
[7] *Ibid*, 4042.

(b) Indirect Effect/Consistent Interpretation

Because the direct effect of WTO law is excluded in such clear terms by the URAA, most of the case law before US courts has involved possible indirect effect' through consistent interpretation. Indirect effect becomes relevant when the domestic statute at issue is ambiguous and capable of being interpreted both consistently and inconsistently with WTO law. In most jurisdictions, a principle of consistent interpretation applies in this situation. In the US, this was articulated in the early Supreme Court case *Murray v The Charming Betsy*, in which Chief Justice Marshall declared that 'an Act of Congress ought never to be construed to violate the law of nations if any other possible construction remains'.[8] Therefore, this canon of statutory interpretation advises that statutes which are capable of being interpreted consistently with international obligations should be so interpreted.

The general rationale for consistent interpretation has been described in these terms: 'If the United States is to be able to gain the benefits of international accords and have a role as a trusted partner in multilateral endeavors, its courts should be most cautious before interpreting its domestic legislation in such manner as to violate international agreements.'[9]

The need for consistent interpretation when the international obligation emanates from the WTO agreements has been explained on the basis that, 'were the agency to construe an ambiguous statute so as to benefit domestic interests in violation of international agreements, retaliatory tariffs would result, a penalty which Congress presumably would wish to avoid'.[10]

(i) The Charming Betsy and its Relationship with Chevron Deference[11]

Applicants before US courts usually raise the *Charming Betsy* canon when challenging the manner is which executive agencies such as the Department of Commerce interpret their statutory mandates. The scope for the canon's operation is closely connected with *Chevron* deference as formulated by the Supreme Court in the following passages. Discussions of *Chevron* deference frequently differentiate between '*Chevron* part 1' and '*Chevron* part 2' so that these terms have been inserted into the passages.

> When a court reviews an agency's construction of the statute which it administers, it is confronted with two questions. **[Part 1]** First, always, is the question whether Congress has directly spoken to the precise question at issue. If the intent of Congress is clear, that is the end of the matter; for the court as well as the agency, must give effect to the unambiguously expressed intent of Congress. **[Part 2]** If, however, the court determines Congress has not directly addressed the precise question at issue, the court does not simply impose its own construction on the statute, as would be necessary in the absence of an administrative interpretation. Rather, if the statute

---

[8] *Murray v Charming Betsy* 6 US (2 Cranch), 118, 2 L Ed 208 (1804).
[9] *Vimar Seguros y Reaseduros, SA v M/V Sky Reefer*, 515 US 528, 115 S Ct 2322, 529.
[10] *Allegheny Ludlum v United States*, 29 CIT 157, 358 F Supp 2d 1334 (2005), 1348.
[11] For further discussion of this area, see G Gattinara, 'The Relevance of WTO Dispute Settlement Decisions in the US Legal Order' (2009) 36(4) *Legal Issues of Economic Integration* 285; A Davies, 'Connecting or Compartmentalizing the WTO and United States Legal Systems? The Role of the *Charming Betsy* Canon' (2007) 10(1) *Journal of International Economic Law* 117.

is silent or ambiguous with respect to the specific issue, the question for the court is whether the agency's answer is based on a permissible construction of the statute.[12]

Under *Chevron* part 1, if the statute is considered to be clear and unambiguous on the 'precise question at issue', this meaning prevails even if it is contrary to WTO law. It follows that, if the part 1 analysis is resolved in this way, there is no scope for the operation of the *Charming Betsy* canon. There are a couple of additional points here which relate to the determination of whether the statute is ambiguous. First, a statute which embodies a detailed and comprehensive regime may be ambiguous. However, the statues in the cases considered below are not of this kind. Rather, they contain very little more than an authorisation for the Department of Commerce to adopt detailed regulations. The statutes are ambiguous in the sense that they do not provide very much guidance on the content of these regulations. Secondly, it is important to bear in mind that different views can be formed on whether any particular statute is ambiguous, depending on the analytical perspective which is adopted. A good example of this point is provided by the manner in which the Court of Appeals decided the *Corus Staal* case considered below.

Chevron part 2 only applies if, under part 1, the statute is considered to be ambiguous. In this situation, there is scope for the *Charming Betsy* canon to operate alongside *Chevron* part 2. Under part 2, the question is whether the agency's answer to the precise question at issue 'is based on a permissible interpretation of the statute'. The argument made possible by the canon is that an answer to the question at issue which is contrary to an international obligation is an impermissible answer.

There is one additional and rather critical question which arises when the canon operates alongside *Chevron* part 2. In the process of interpreting the statute consistently with WTO law, what meaning will be attributed to WTO law? There are several possibilities here with different implications for the strength of canon. One possibility is that ambiguous statutes must be interpreted consistently with WTO law as understood by the WTO panels and the Appellate Body. Were this the position, the canon would be a powerful device for ensuring that US executive agencies act in accordance with panel and Appellate Body interpretations of the WTO agreements, at least when the domestic statute is ambiguous and capable of being interpreted consistently with these interpretations. At the opposite extreme, another possibility is that ambiguous statutes must be interpreted consistently with WTO law as understood by the agency in question and entirely independently of any panel or Appellate Body pronouncements. In this situation, the national court would defer completely to the agency interpretation of WTO law and declare the panel or Appellate Body interpretation to be irrelevant. An intermediate position would be where the national court forms its own independent view of the meaning of WTO law taking into account both any panel and Appellate Body interpretations, and the agency's position.

(ii) Review of the Case Law

A review of the cases reveals a somewhat ambivalent attitude towards the canon. The canon tends to be treated with considerable caution when it is relied upon in order to overturn a preferred agency interpretation. The first and second cases considered (*Hyundai*

---

[12] *Chevron USA, Inc v Natural Res Def Council, Inc*, 467 US 837, 104 S Ct 2778, 842–43.

Electronics and *Corus Staal*) are examples of this cautious approach, with the second case being the stronger example. Both of these cases arose in the area of anti-dumping duties.

In contrast, the courts tend to be more receptive towards the canon when it can be used to confirm a preferred agency interpretation. The third case (*Warren Corporation*) illustrates the more receptive approach.

Hyundai Electronics[13] The background to the *Hyundai Electronics* case was an antidumping order on semiconductors from Korea. The continued operation of this order was reviewed by the Department of Commerce. This review was conducted under Commerce's own regulations which had been adopted under a broad legislative mandate.[14] Under these regulations one of the conditions for the revocation of an antidumping order required Commerce to be satisfied that the producers were 'not likely' to dump in the future. Commerce found that this revocation criterion had not been met. This finding was appealed by a number of Korean producers to the US Court of International Trade (CIT). One of the grounds of appeal was that that Commerce had violated WTO law by formulating and applying the 'not likely' standard.

Under *Chevron* part 1, the CIT found that Congress (not to be confused with Commerce!) had not spoken on the conditions under which antidumping duties could be revoked after an administrative review. Congress had merely conferred broad implementing authority. Therefore, the CIT went on to consider whether Commerce's actions were reasonable. This entailed an examination of whether Commerce's 'not likely' requirement was consistent with WTO law. On this matter, the CIT noted that, "this issue merits more than cursory analysis due in large measure to a WTO panel report that addressed the same question'. It went on to note that, '[W]hen asked to review the same underlying administrative decision, a WTO dispute settlement panel recently found that Commerce's "not likely" requirement violates WTO rules'.[15] In other words, the Commerce decision before the CIT was the same as the one successfully challenged before the WTO panel. This is significant. If WTO panel interpretations of the WTO Agreements are potentially relevant at national level to the process of determining the WTO consistency of national measures, this is the clearest example of a case where the potential relevance should be realised.

The CIT initially gave the impression that its own decision might mirror that of the WTO panel. It did so by explaining the reasoning of the panel which centred on the wording of Article 11.2 of the Anti-Dumping Agreement. This provides that '[I]nterested parties shall have the right to request the authorities to examine whether . . . the injury would be likely to continue or recur if the duty were removed or varied'. In contrast, under the regulations, Commerce can revoke an anti-dumping order if (among other considerations) it is satisfied that dumping is 'not likely' to occur in the future. The CIT summarised passages from the panel report to the effect that the 'not likely' approach in the regulations resulted in a more rigorous standard for companies requesting the removal of antidumping duties, than the 'likely' standard in the Anti-Dumping Agreement. The CIT proceeded to note that, even though it was not bound by the WTO panel report, this

---

[13] *Hyundai Electronics Co v United States*, 23 CIT 302, 53 F Supp 2d 1334 (1999).

[14] Congress provided that Commerce, as the administering authority, 'may revoke, in whole or in part, a countervailing duty order or an antidumping duty order or finding, or terminate a suspended investigation after [an administrative] review'.

[15] *Hyundai*, above n 13, 1342. The relevant WTO case was WTO Panel Report, *United States-Anti-Dumping Duty on Dynamic Random Access Semiconductors (DRAMS) of One Megabit or Above from Korea*, WT/DS99/R, adopted 19 March 1999.

was, 'not to imply that a panel report serves no purpose in litigation before the court. To the contrary, a panel's reasoning, if sound, may be used to inform the court's decisions.'[16] The *Charming Betsy* canon was also affirmed, the court noting that, 'absent express language to the contrary, a statute should not be interpreted to conflict with international obligations'.[17]

Clearly, therefore, the CIT's analysis proceeded beyond *Chevron* part 1. It remained for the CIT to decide upon the critical question which arises when the canon operates alongside *Chevron* part 2. In the process of interpreting the statute consistently with WTO law, what meaning would be given to WTO law? Would the CIT give effect the WTO panel's understanding of WTO law, or would it depart from the panel's understanding and interpret Article 11.2 of the Anti-Dumping Agreement with the result of upholding Commerce's preferred methodology? The latter option prevailed. The CIT noted that, 'operationally, Article 11.2 provides that an administering authority has considerable discretion to make an inherently predictive analysis'. It acknowledged the absence of a 'perfect overlap' between the two standards and concluded its own interpretation of the requirements of Article 11.2 as follows: 'the discretion afforded to predict the state of future dumping erases any clear conflict between the two approaches. So viewed, unless the conflict between an international obligation and Commerce's interpretation of a statute is abundantly clear, a court should take special care before it upsets Commerce's regulatory authority under the *Charming Betsy* doctrine'.[18]

For the WTO panel, the conflict referred to by the court did appear to be abundantly clear. Its finding was that 'the . . . "not" likely criterion (in Commerce's regulations) operates to effectively require the continued imposition of anti-dumping duties, and prevents revocation, in circumstances inconsistent with and outside of those provided by Article 11.2'.[19]

In this case, the *Charming Betsy* canon was clearly applicable and did indeed require that a statute be interpreted consistently with international obligations. Commerce was required to interpret its statutory mandate in light of the requirements of the Anti-Dumping Agreement. As for the meaning of these requirements, the court engaged to a significant extent with the panel report, but ultimately decided not to align its own interpretation with the panel. This resulted in Commerce's preferred methodology being upheld.

Corus Staal[20] *Corus Staal* involved a challenge by a Dutch manufacturer and American importer against the methodology used by Commerce in an anti-dumping investigation against steel imports. Part of the methodology for calculating the dumping margin involved the practice of zeroing. The CIT noted one of its own previous cases, where it had commented that the practice 'introduces a statistical bias in the calculation of dumping margins because it allows Commerce to make an affirmative finding of dumping even if the vast majority of sales made by the subject foreign producers in the US were at prices higher than the average foreign market value'. It went on to find, under *Chevron* part 1, that

---

[16] *Ibid*, 1343.
[17] *Ibid*, 1344.
[18] *Ibid*, 1345.
[19] Panel Report, *United States—DRAMS*, above n 15, para 6.51.
[20] *Corus Staal BV and Corus Staal USA Inc v United States Department of Commerce*, 27 CIT 388, 259 F Supp 2d 1253 (2003); on appeal *Corus Staal BV v Department of Commerce*, 395 F 3d 1343 (Fed Cir 2005).

the relevant US legislation neither requires nor prohibits the practice of zeroing thus raising the *Chevron* part 2 question of whether the use of zeroing was a permissible interpretation of the statute.

In considering this question, the CIT asked whether the Anti-Dumping Agreement clearly prohibits zeroing. This practice was found to be 'technically' compatible with the Anti-Dumping Agreement albeit that the CIT questioned whether the intentional minimization of the impact of non-dumped transactions was consistent with the spirit of the Agreement. The CIT concluded that, '[W]hen faced with an ambiguous statute and an ambiguous international agreement, the court should defer to Commerce's interpretation'.[21] The most striking feature of the case is that the Anti-Dumping Agreement was considered to be ambiguous despite the Appellate Body ruling in the *Bed Linen* case[22] that a zeroing methodology used by the EC was inconsistent with the agreement. The CIT even noted that the 'circumstances and methodology' before them appeared to be 'similar, if not identical' to those previously before the Appellate Body.[23]

The approach of the CIT in this case was therefore much the same as in the *Hyundai* case. As the domestic statute was considered to be ambiguous on the precise question at issue, the analysis proceeded beyond *Chevron* part 1. However, under *Chevron* part 2, the CIT considered that the use of zeroing was a permissible reading of the statute. According to the CIT, this reading was not clearly contrary to WTO law despite strong indications of incompatibility from the WTO Appellate Body. The CIT therefore attributed a meaning to WTO law which upheld the preferred agency approach, even though this approach had been struck down by the WTO Appellate Body.

The CIT decision was appealed by the complainants. By the time the appeal was heard, the Appellate Body in the *Softwood Lumber* case had found Commerce to have violated the Anti-Dumping Agreement when it used zeroing to calculate the weighted-average dumping margin in its investigation of imports of Canadian softwood lumber.'[24] Thus, as a matter of WTO law, the practice of zeroing was clearly becoming increasingly problematic. However, the appellants were again unsuccessful. Indeed, they were further away from success on appeal than before the CIT. The appeal seemed to fail under *Chevron* part 1. It is this aspect of the case which illustrates that point made above that different views can be formed on whether any particular statute is ambiguous, depending on the analytical perspective which is adopted. Unlike the CIT, the Court of Appeals did not seem to think that the statute was ambiguous, so there was no need to proceed to *Chevron* part 2 and consider the possible operation of the *Charming Betsy* canon. This evaluation of the Court of Appeals judgment is based on the following passage, which indicates that the statute provides a list of the relevant considerations when conducting the investigation, and that Commerce was not required to take account of non-listed factors, such as the content of international obligations. It was noted that the US statute 'does not impose any requirements for calculating normal value beyond those explicitly established in the statute and does not carry over to create additional limitations on the calculation of

---

[21] *Ibid*, 1264.

[22] WTO Appellate Body Report, *European Communities—Antidumping Duties on Imports of Cotton-Type Bed Linen from India*, WT/DS141/AB/R, adopted 12 March 2001.

[23] *Corus Staal*, above n 20, 17.

[24] WTO Appellate Body Report, *United States—Final Dumping Determination on Softwood Lumber from Canada*, WT/DS264/AB/R, adopted 31 August 2004, para 117.

dumping margins'.[25] Therefore, for the Court of Appeals, the statute was clear in that it did not require that Commerce take account of non-listed obligations such as the content of international obligations. There was no need to proceed beyond *Chevron* part 1 and the *Charming Betsy* canon was inapplicable. However, the Court of Appeals might have proceeded to a *Charming Betsy* analysis simply by noting that, under *Chevron* part 1, Congress has not spoken to the precise question of whether Commerce was precluded from considering the US Treaty obligations. Like the CIT, the Court of Appeals might also have found the domestic statute to be ambiguous, but it preferred to adopt a different analytical perspective.

There are also other indications of a dismissive approach towards the canon in the Court of Appeals judgment. In particular, there was no statement to the effect that the reasoning of the WTO tribunals, if sound, may be used to inform the decisions of the US courts. For the Court of Appeals, it was sufficient to unequivocally deny any binding effect to WTO reports, in particular noting that: 'Congress has enacted legislation to deal with the conflict presented here. It has authorized the United States Trade Representative, an arm of the Executive branch, in consultation with various congressional and executive bodies and agencies, to determine whether or not to implement WTO reports and determinations and, if so implemented, the extent of implementation'.[26] As the findings in *Softwood Lumber* had not been implemented as per this statutory scheme, they were not binding.

Warren Corporation[27] This case illustrates the more receptive approach towards the canon which applies when it can be used to confirm a preferred agency interpretation. The case arose in the environment/conservation context. Among the complainants were a number of environmental groups arguing that a US statute should be interpreted so as to maximise the level of protection for the environment. Unlike the two cases considered above, the complainants in *Warren Corporation* were not arguing that the statute should be interpreted in conformity with WTO law as understood by the Appellate Body. Indeed, the statue was already being interpreted in this way. Rather, the complainants were opposed to the WTO consistent interpretation on the basis that it coud lead to a lower level of environmental protection than other interpretations.

The relevant statutory provision was contained in the Clean Air Acts Amendments of 1990. This contained a so-called 'anti-dumping'[28] provision requiring that the gasoline of all suppliers (domestic and foreign) remain as clean as it was in 1990. The statute envisaged two ways of ensuring this. The first was to compare the cleanliness of the gasoline of the individual supplier in question with that which it produced in 1990—the individual baseline approach. The statute also conferred a discretion on the Environmental Protection Agency (EPA) to impose a statutory baseline where the EPA 'determines that no adequate and reliable data exist' to set an individual baseline. The first set of standards announced in 1994 required domestic refiners to set individual baselines while foreign refiners were not permitted to do so, based on the view that most foreign refiners would most likely lack the necessary data. In its very first case, the Appellate Body found that

---

[25] *Corus Staal*, above n 20, 1348.
[26] *Ibid*, 1349.
[27] *George E Warren Corporation v US Environmental Protection Agency*, 159 F 3d 616 (DC Cir 1998).
[28] The term dumping in this context is a reference to the transfer of pollutants from reformulated gasoline to conventional gasoline in the refining process.

this differentiation infringed the national treatment obligation in GATT Article III:4. In response to this report, new standards were adopted in 1997 allowing foreign refiners to petition the EPA for permission to establish an individual baseline. It is these new standards which were challenged in *Warren Corporation*. The complainants argued that the EPA had improperly considered factors other than air quality in adopting the new standards. One of these extraneous factors was the Appellate Body's decision.

The Court of Appeals for the District of Columbia responded by noting that there was nothing in the statute to preclude the EPA from considering the treaty obligations of the US. It then stated that, '[U]nder step two of *Chevron*, therefore, we must defer to the agency's construction if it is reasonable'.[29] Citing *Charming Betsy*, the court then confirmed the reasonableness of Commerce's interpretation of the statute in the following terms:

> In the particular circumstances of this case our usual reluctance to infer from congressional silence an intention to preclude the agency from considering factors other than those listed in the statute is bolstered by the decision of the WTO lurking in the background.[30]

The difference in emphasis between this case and *Corus Staal* on the significance of Congressional silence is striking. In *Corus Staal*, the Court of Appeals emphasised that the statute did not require that non-listed factors (such as the content of international obligations) be taken into consideration. In *Warren Corporation*, the court emphasised that the statute did not require that non-listed factors (such as the content of international obligations) be ignored. In both cases, the courts approved the preferred agency interpretations of the statutes.

(iii) Summary of the Case Law

The *Charming Betsy* canon is applicable before US courts in order to provide indirect effect to WTO law. Therefore, it is possible to argue that an ambiguous domestic statute should be interpreted in conformity with WTO law. The operation of the canon will be halted under *Chevron* part 1 if it is determined that the domestic statute is clear. When part 1 is surmounted, the critical question is what meaning the court will give to WTO law. Although panel and Appellate Body reports can be persuasive on this matter, more significant is the deference which US courts afford to the preferred US agency interpretation.

(iv) What if the WTO Dispute Settlement Report has been Implemented by the Time of the Challenge?

Looking back at the reasoning in *Corus Staal*, the Court of Appeals considered that WTO reports lacked binding force because, as a matter of US law, it was for the executive branch 'to determine whether or not to implement WTO reports and determinations and, if so implemented, the extent of implementation'. A little later in the same report, the Court of Appeals added that it 'would not attempt to perform duties that fall within the exclusive province of the political branches, and [that it would] therefore refuse to

---

[29] *Warren Corporation*, above n 27, 623.
[30] *Ibid*, 624.

overturn Commerce's zeroing practice based on any ruling by the WTO or any other international body *unless and until such ruling has been adopted pursuant to the specified statutory scheme*'[31] (emphasis added).

This statement raises questions which apply in cases where the applicant can point towards not only a relevant panel or Appellate Body report, but also domestic measures which purport to implement the adverse report findings. Under *Charming Betsy*, will the US court now require the agency to interpret the statute consistently with WTO law as understood in the relevant report? A possible retort is that this is an unnecessary question. If the WTO report has been fully implemented, domestic law will obviously embody what is required by the WTO agreements so that compliance with domestic law will also entail compliance with WTO law. However, the question is relevant if the private applicant considers that the implementing measures have failed to achieve compliance and wishes the domestic court to assess the implementing measures against provisions of WTO law as understood by the panel or Appellate Body. Does an explicit attempt by the executive to fully implement WTO reports empower US courts to consider whether full implementation has been achieved? Another possibility is where the applicant considers that the implementing measures achieve compliance with WTO obligations but is concerned that the revisions have only prospective effect. The purpose of the action would then be to overturn agency determinations which pre-date the revisions on the basis of the WTO report and the completion of the implementation process.

In this area, there is an interesting divergence of opinion between the US courts and NAFTA Chapter 19 panels. Among the NAFTA Parties, these binational panels replace national judicial review of final antidumping and countervailing duty determinations and decide on the compatibility of agency determinations with the antidumping or counter-vailing duty law of the importing party.[32] The divergence, as further described below, is that the NAFTA panels envisage a stronger role for the *Charming Betsy* canon than US courts.

The present state of the case law emanating from US courts preserves the theoretical possibility of a successful action in the situations noted above. To date, however, one or more of the conditions which need to be present in order for the action to have a possibility of success have been absent. The extent of these conditions is indicated by *Corus Staal II* before the CIT.[33] In this case, the court noted that Corus was now relying on 'changed facts' in arguing that 'the WTO's *Softwood Lumber* decision . . . has been "adopted pursuant to the specified statutory scheme," and therefore, the court should rule zeroing no longer reasonable, not based on the WTO ruling itself, but on Commerce's re-interpretation of its policy in the wake of the adverse *Softwood Lumber* ruling'.[34]

This argument was rejected on several grounds. Among these grounds was that the statutory procedure for implementation was incomplete. Even though Commerce had issued its final determination to implement *Softwood Lumber*, it remained for the United States Trade Representative (USTR) to direct Commerce to implement the determination.[35] The CIT also considered that Corus's action would fail even if the USTR had so directed Commerce. This was based on a distinction in the URAA between implementing

---

[31] *Corus Staal*, above n 20, 1375.

[32] NAFTA Article 1904, paras 1–2.

[33] *Corus Staal BV v US*, 29 CIT 777, 387 F Supp 2d 1291, 19 July 2005.

[34] *Ibid*, 1298.

[35] *Ibid*, 1299.

WTO reports with the broad mandate of adjudicating on a general practice and implementing those with the lesser remit of adjudicating only on the methodology used in the particular case. As the *Softwood Lumber* report had been concerned only with zeroing 'as applied' in that case to Canadian lumber, the subsequent implementation of the report also applied only to this situation. In other words, the implementation would apply neither to the general practice of zeroing nor to the zeroing which was of specific concern to Corus. Finally, even if the implementation had been concerned with the general methodology of zeroing, it would, according to the statutory scheme, have had only a prospective effect.[36] These considerations led the CIT to conclude as follows:

> Had the Government appeared here saying it had lost in the WTO, with respect to this very administrative determination, and it had complied with the entire statutory framework, to the effect that it was reversing its position, even as to a past determination, then the court would have to consider what to do.[37]

As noted above, NAFTA panels have envisaged a stronger role for the *Charming Betsy* canon in cases where the applicant state is able to identify measures which implement WTO reports. In particular, the NAFTA panel in *Softwood Lumber*[38] found that, even though implementing measures have only prospective effect under the statutory scheme, this was not evidence of 'a deliberate Executive/Congressional decision . . . that would insulate the original . . . determination from . . . review'.[39] The statement clearly does not sit very comfortably with the CIT's position in *Corus Staal II* that review of determinations which pre-date the implementing measures is prevented because the statutory scheme envisages that implementation has only prospective effect.

The subsequent NAFTA panel in *Carbon and Alloy Steel Wire Rod*[40] also reached some striking conclusions on the relevance of the statutory scheme for implementing WTO reports, to the scope for reviewing agency determinations based on the *Charming Betsy* canon. It is worth recalling the CIT's view here in *Corus Staal II*. The case involved the zeroing methodology. The CIT considered that the statutory scheme was applicable and that the procedures envisaged had yet to run their course. This was among the reasons for the CIT's refusal to review the zeroing methodology in light of WTO law. In contrast, the NAFTA panel considered that the statutory scheme was simply inapplicable to the implementation of WTO reports dealing with the zeroing methodology, thereby removing a barrier considered by the CIT to preclude any review. Specifically, the NAFTA panel found as follows:

> Section 3533 (g)(1) of 19 USC requires consultation with Congress before Commerce changes only a "regulation or practice" that a WTO panel has found to be inconsistent with the ADA. Zeroing, however, is based on neither a regulation nor a practice; the Statement of Administrative Action [SAA] authoritatively describes "practice" as "a written policy guidance of general applicability." Section 3533 thus does not require Congressional involvement for changes in anything of less definitive authority . . . It follows . . . from the SAA's definition of

---

[36] *Ibid*, 1299–300.

[37] *Ibid*, 1300.

[38] *Certain Softwood Lumber Products from Canada Anti-Dumping Agreement: Final Affirmative Antidumping Determinations*, USA-CDA-2002-1904-02, 9 June 2005.

[39] *Ibid*, 34.

[40] *Carbon and Certain Alloy Steel Wire Rod from Canada: 2nd Administrative Review*, USA-CDA-2006-1904-04, 28 November 2007.

"practice" and the absence of a written policy of general applicability for zeroing in reviews, that Congressional review is not required in order to change the zeroing methodology for reviews.[41]

It followed from the inapplicability of the statutory scheme for implementation that it could have no preclusive effect on review of the zeroing methodology in light of Appellate Body rulings.

(b) Summary of the US Law Position

It is clear from the URAA that direct effect of WTO law is excluded. Private applicants cannot successfully argue before US courts that WTO law should prevail in the event of an irreconcilable conflict with a domestic statute. The URAA does not, however, expressly exclude possible indirect effect which can be relevant when the domestic law is ambiguous and capable of being interpreted consistently with the WTO agreements. Of relevance here is the *Charming Betsy* canon, which raises the sensitive question of whether US courts will require agencies such as Commerce to interpret their statutory mandates consistently with the WTO agreements as understood by WTO panels and the Appellate Body. To date, this has not occurred in cases where the agency does not wish to so align its interpretation. However, the possibility has been kept alive that a US court might, in the future, assess whether an agency interpretation of its statutory mandate is consistent with the Appellate Body's understanding of the WTO agreements. This possibility is best captured by the CIT's statement that it 'would have to consider what to do' in a future case where, inter alia, the process of implementing the adverse report had been completed. In contrast, NAFTA panels have attributed greater weight to Appellate Body reports via the *Charming Betsy* canon to the extent of finding the zeroing methodology to be an impermissible interpretation of Commerce's statutory mandate.

A more generalised summary of the position before US courts is that direct effect is expressly excluded whereas indirect effect is a theoretical possibility which has not, to date, improved the legal position of any applicant. There are strong parallels between this position and that in the European Union, albeit that caution is also required when drawing analogies.

III. EUROPEAN UNION

Questions relating to the direct and indirect effect of WTO law have been adjudicated upon by the courts of the EU mainly in the context of private challenges to EU secondary legislation operating in the trade remedies area, and the EU's banana import regime. These challenges have frequently been brought directly to the EU courts in the form of actions for annulment or damages. In other cases, questions relating to direct and indirect effect have been put to the EU courts by the courts of the Member States via the preliminary reference procedure. A separate treatment of direct effect and indirect effect is provided below.

---

[41] *Ibid*, 31–32.

(a) Direct Effect

The general position is that direct effect in the sense of the explicit review of EU measures with reference to WTO law is not possible. Notable in this respect is a statement in the preamble of the Council Decision which implemented the WTO Agreement and its Annexes. This provides that the WTO Agreement is 'by its nature . . . not susceptible to being directly invoked in Community or Member State courts'.[42] This statement can be likened to those contained in the URAA, although it can be recalled that these statements were described above as a comprehensive denial of direct effect. The EU statement possibly has a less hortatory character by reason of its location, brevity and suggestive (as opposed to unequivocally preclusive) language. This seems to be reflected in the EU case law. While the reasoning is entirely consistent with the statement in the preamble, there is perhaps a stronger sense (relative to the US case law) that the EU courts are independently formulating a policy in this area.

The ECJ first set out its views on the direct effect of the WTO agreements in *Portugal v Council*.[43] The case involved an action to annul the act of an EU organ brought by a Member State. Portugal requested that the Decisions of the European Council on the conclusion of agreements with India and Pakistan concerning market access for textiles be declared null and void based on their alleged incompatibility with the WTO Agreement on Textiles and Clothing. The European Court of Justice (ECJ) decided that WTO rules are not among the rules in the light of which the Court can review the lawfulness of measures adopted by the Community institutions.[44] This view was based first on an assessment of the WTO dispute settlement process and secondly on reciprocity based considerations.

On the first matter, the ECJ acknowledged that the first aim of the DSU is to secure the withdrawal of measures found to be inconsistent with WTO obligations, and that the suspension of concessions or compensation were envisaged to be temporary remedies when immediate withdrawal was impracticable. However, the ECJ was strongly influenced by DSU Article 22(2), which envisages negotiations in order to develop 'mutually acceptable compensation' in the event of a failure to withdraw the offending measure. The ECJ therefore considered that:

> to require the judicial organs to refrain from applying the rules of domestic law which are inconsistent with the WTO agreements would have the consequence of depriving the legislative or executive organs of the contracting parties of the possibility afforded by Article 22 of that memorandum of entering into negotiated arrangements even on a temporary basis.[45]

With regard to the reciprocity considerations, the ECJ noted that some of the EU's main trading partners had concluded 'from the subject-matter and purpose of the WTO agreements that they are not among the rules applicable by their judicial organs when reviewing the legality of their rules of domestic law'.[46] It followed that the judicial enforceability of WTO rules before EU courts would 'deprive the legislative or executive organs of

---

[42] Dec 94/800/EC, [1994] OJ L336/1.

[43] Case C-149/96 *Portugal v Council* [1999] ECR I-8395. See S Grilller, 'Judicial Enforceability of WTO Law in the European Union Annotation to Case C-149/96, *Portugal v Council*' (2000) 3(3) *Journal of International Economic Law* 441.

[44] *Ibid*, para 47.

[45] *Ibid*, para 40.

[46] *Ibid*, para 43.

the Community of the scope for manoeuvre enjoyed by their counterparts in the Community's trading partners'.[47]

Despite the general denial of direct effect in *Portugal v Council*, the ECJ also confirmed the continued availability of the so-called *Nakajmia*[48]/*Fediol*[49] exceptions. Under these exceptions, the legality of EU law can be reviewed in light of WTO law when EU institutions intend to fulfil a particular WTO obligation, or when an EU measure explicitly refers to a particular WTO obligation that is implemented by that measure.

These exceptions are analogous to the possible exception recognized in the US—this being where the process of implementing the adverse WTO report has been completed. It is necessary, however, to add a clarification on the extent of this analogy. The possible exception in the US is an aspect of indirect effect/consistent interpretation. In other words, if the exception applies, the US courts will require agencies to interpret a broad and ambiguous statutory mandate consistently with WTO law. There is no question in the US of the exception also applying to require the non-application, amendment or removal of statutory provisions which cannot be interpreted consistently with WTO law, for this would be plainly contrary to the URAA. In contrast, more is at stake in the EU context when discussing the *Nakajima* exception. The exception operates, not as an aspect of consistent interpretation, but when interpreting EU legislative measures consistently with WTO law is not possible. It follows that recourse to this exception follows on from the inability to reconcile legislative measures with the WTO agreements. Therefore, if the *Nakajima* exception applies, it could result in an EU institution being prevented from applying, or required to amend or withdraw, a legislative measure which contrary to WTO law.

The cases discussed in the extract below deal with the critical question raised by the *Nakajima* exception. In what circumstances will EU institutions be found to have intended to fulfil a particular WTO obligation such as to permit the review of EU law with reference to WTO law? In particular, is there such an intention when an EU measure is amended, or a new measure adopted, with the apparent intention of implementing an adverse WTO report?

A Emch, 'The European Court of Justice and WTO Dispute Settlement Rulings: The End of the Flirt' (2006) 7(4) *Journal of World Investment and Trade* 563

I. INTRODUCTION

The law of the World Trade Organization cannot be invoked to challenge a measure adopted by the European Union—not even after the WTO's dispute settlement body (DSB) has issued a ruling declaring the inconsistency of the EU measure with WTO law. That was the message from the Court of First Instance (CFI) in *Chiquita* and in *FIAMM* and from the European Court of Justice (ECJ) in *Van Parys*.

With the exception of the situation where an EU institution has signalled its intention to implement WTO law or where an EU measure expressly refers to a specific WTO provision, the EU courts have long held that WTO law can neither be invoked by individuals nor by EU Member States to challenge the lawfulness of EU measures. The question has arisen, however, whether the adoption of a DSB ruling, in particular after the expiry of the deadline granted by

[47] *Ibid*, para 47.
[48] Case C-69/89 *Nakajima v Council* [1991] ECR I-2069, para 31.
[49] Case 70/87 *Fediol v Commission* [1989] ECR 1781, paras 19–22.

the DSB for implementing the ruling, might modify the situation to such an extent as to allow WTO law to be invoked.

In a recently decided case, the ECJ itself had nurtured expectations of a move in this direction. In *Van Parys*, *Chiquita* and *FIAMM*, however, the EU courts closed the door on any 'opening-up' in that regard. Moreover, despite recognising that the EU had amended its legislation as a result of the DSB ruling adopted in the *Banana* dispute, the courts found that the applicants in *Van Parys*, *Chiquita* and *FIAMM* could not benefit from the exception to the general rule that WTO law cannot be invoked.

The *Van Parys*, *Chiquita* and *FIAMM* judgments touch upon the issue of how the relationship between WTO law and EU law is to be articulated from the EU's perspective. Nonetheless, the importance of these cases stretches beyond that relationship. On the one hand, the judgments at hand also fundamentally affect the EU's relations with African, Caribbean and Pacific (ACP) countries (whose bananas enjoy preferential access to the EU market). On the other hand, it may be possible to argue that the judgments' scope went beyond the EU's relationship with WTO law to cover its relationship with international law as a whole. Indeed, in the three cases, the disputes were brought before the EU judicature because the EU had failed to properly implement a ruling by the DSB—an organ that comes close to an international tribunal (sometimes dubbed the 'World Trade Court'). Hence, at stake to a limited extent was the EU's pretension that, as an actor in its own right in the field of international relations, its actions are always in compliance with rules of international law.

...

III. THE JUDGMENTS

On 3 February and 1 March 2005, the CFI and the ECJ issued their judgments in *Chiquita* and *Van Parys*. The *FIAMM* case was decided on 14 December 2005. In all three cases, the courts rejected the applicants' pleas in their entirety. Moreover, the content of the arguments used by the courts in the three cases was very similar. Nonetheless, there remain certain differences in the way the courts structured their arguments.

In *Van Parys*, the ECJ first repeated its previous case law on WTO law, stating that the WTO Agreements could not be relied upon before EU courts except where the EU intended to implement a particular WTO obligation (the *Nakajima* exception) or the EU measure explicitly referred to a WTO provision. Then, the Court answered the question raised by the national court and thereby set out the structure of its reasoning. By undertaking to comply with the recommendations of the DSB ruling, the EU did not intend to assume a particular obligation in the context of the WTO. In other words, the ECJ examined whether the applicant's claim fell under the *Nakajima* exception.

The ECJ gave two reasons for rejecting the application of the *Nakajima* exception. First, it began with an analysis of the provisions of the DSU, with frequent quotations of the earlier *Portugal v. Council* case, to find essentially that the recommendations of a DSB ruling are not mandatory. To the contrary, a WTO Member that lost in a dispute could reach a negotiated solution with the complaining WTO Member. Then, the ECJ looked at the facts of the *Banana* case and found that the EU had negotiated agreements with two of the WTO complainants— the United States and Ecuador. The Court held that such an outcome would be in danger if the EU judicature allowed WTO law to be relied upon. Also, the Court implicitly agreed with the idea that compliance with the EU's WTO obligations must be reconciled with the EU's obligations towards the ACP States and with the requirements of the EU's own agriculture policy.

As a second line of argument, it appears that the ECJ repeated its previous case law that the legislative and executive bodies of the EU's major trading partners enjoyed discretion to negotiate the implementation with WTO litigants because the courts of those trading partners did not allow WTO law to be invoked. The ECJ found that, if the EU courts alone allowed WTO law to be invoked, there would be a lack of reciprocity which would result in 'an anomaly in the application of the WTO rules'.

In *Chiquita*, the Court was asked to decide whether the *Nakajima* exception applied, enabling the applicant to rely on WTO law. For the purposes of this article, three main lines of argument in the CFI's reasoning can be highlighted. First, the CFI undertook a discussion, in the abstract, of how the *Nakajima* exception should be interpreted. The most important conclusion of this analysis was that the exception applies only where the lawfulness of an EU measure which 'specifically transposes prescriptions arising from the WTO Agreements into Community law' is at stake.

A second part of the Judgment was dedicated to giving reasons as to why the *Nakajima* exception was not applicable to the *Banana* case. Although the arguments in that part were not explicitly organised in that way, the CFI's reasons were essentially twofold. On the one hand, the Court found that the EU did not intend 'to implement a particular obligation assumed in the context of the WTO', as the *Nakajima* case law requires. This was, first, because the obligations imposed by the DSB ruling (and the underlying GATT and GATS provisions) were of a general, not a particular, nature. Second, the EU did not intend to implement WTO obligations. The Court appeared to have accepted the defendant's restrictive reading of the word 'implement'. In line with its findings in the first part of the Judgment, the CFI essentially held that, because no transposition was required under WTO law, the EU did not intend to implement any WTO obligations. On the other hand, the CFI analysed the provisions of the DSU, finding that they did not oblige the EU to fully comply with a DSB ruling. Similarly to the ECJ's reasoning in *Van Parys*, the Court found that full compliance was only one option, while agreeing on a negotiated solution with other litigants of a dispute would be a viable alternative.

The third relevant part of the *Chiquita* Judgment concerned the applicant's plea relating to the international law principle *pacta sunt servanda*. There, the CFI essentially found this line of argument to overlap with the argument relating to the *Nakajima* exception. For the rest, the CFI concluded that the EU had not acted in bad faith.

In the *FIAMM* case, the Court was requested to decide whether the EU's failure to adopt WTO-consistent measures to comply with the DSB ruling in the *Banana* dispute triggered the EU's liability for its institutions' unlawful and lawful conduct and whether the EU should be held responsible for the payment of compensation for damages. The first part of that analysis (i.e. whether or not the failure to adopt WTO-consistent measures was unlawful) required an examination of whether WTO law can be invoked to challenge the lawfulness of EU measures. The Grand Chamber of the CFI started its analysis with the 'preliminary question as to whether the WTO rules may be relied upon'. For two reasons, its answer was in the negative. First, the Court found, in the same vein as did the ECJ in *Van Parys*, that, because the courts of the EU's most important trading partners did not allow WTO law to be invoked, there would be an unequal application of WTO rules if the EU did so; the EU's legislative and executive organs would be deprived of the same scope of manoeuvre that their counterparts of other WTO Members enjoy. Second, the CFI appeared to argue that a DSB ruling is not compulsory for a WTO Member. Negotiated solutions would also be possible.

In the subsequent analysis, the CFI analysed whether the *Nakajima* exception to the general rule of non-invocability of WTO law should apply. This part of the analysis started with a relatively lengthy discussion of the DSU provisions. The CFI found that the EU had several methods of settling disputes made available by the DSU. The Court concluded that review of the EU measures by EU courts for compliance with a DSB ruling would 'weaken the position of the Community negotiators in the search for a mutually acceptable solution' to a WTO dispute. Thus, negotiations are possible and DSB rulings are not directly enforceable. The CFI then took note of the fact that, in the *Banana* dispute, the EU had reached a truce with the United States which provisionally froze the imposition of increased customs duties. The Court found that this solution would have been in jeopardy if the EU courts allowed reliance upon WTO rules.

In a second line of argument, the CFI more clearly analysed the relevant legislation which the EU had adopted to comply with the DSB ruling and enquired whether that legislation was the result of the EU's intention to implement WTO obligations within the meaning of the *Nakajima* case law. Similarly to the ECJ in *Van Parys*, the CFI found that the legislation had been adopted with the aim 'to reconcile various divergent objectives'. Going beyond the *Van Parys* case, the CFI held that the reference to the EU's intention to comply with rules of international trade expressed in the Preamble of the amended Banana Regulation included the international agreement between the EU and the ACP countries. Similarly, the CFI found that the obligation upon the European Commission (the Commission) to respect international agreements when implementing policy, contained in the text of the EU's banana legislation, covered the agreement with the ACP States in the same way as it covered the WTO Agreements.

... ...

As a postscript to this extract, it is notable that an appeal in the *FIAMM* case to the ECJ was dismissed in 2008.[50] A number of points from these judgments can also be further explained. It is clear that the EU courts consider that WTO Members can choose not to implement panel and Appellate Body reports, but instead seek to develop a mutually acceptable solution with the complaining Member/s. This view can be criticised based on the argument that various provisions of the DSU indicate a clear preference for compliance with panel and Appellate Body reports once they are adopted.[51] For example, DSU Article 22:1 provides that 'neither compensation nor the suspension of concessions or other obligations is preferred to full implementation of a recommendation to bring a measure into conformity with the covered agreements'. While this line of argument has not significantly influenced the EU courts, it has been strongly endorsed by several Advocate Generals responsible for providing Opinions to the ECJ. Their views are explained in the extract below:

N Lavranos, 'The *Chiquita* and *Van Parys* Judgments: An Exception to the Rule of Law' (2005) 32(4) *Legal Issues of Economic Integration* 453

The Opinion of AG Tizzano in the *Van Parys* case started by repeating the acknowledgment of the ECJ that the dispute settlement system had been strengthened by the WTO Agreement as compared to the old GATT 1947. It concurred with the Opinion of AG Alber in the *Biret* case that, at the end of the day, there is no alternative other than full compliance with the WTO dispute settlement report. Consequently AG Alber concluded that after the implementation deadline had lapsed, private parties should have the possibility to rely on a WTO dispute settlement report in order to be able to start a procedure against the EC for damages for failure to implement the WTO dispute settlement report. AG Tizzano fully concurred with this

---

[50] Joined Cases C-120/06 P and C-121/06 P *FIAMM and Fedion v Council and Commissions* [2008] ECR I-6513.

[51] See JH Jackson, 'International Law Status of WTO Dispute Settlement Reports: Obligation to Comply or Option to Buy Out?' (2004) 98 *American Journal of International Law* 109.

conclusion when he argued that in a Community based on the rule of law (*Rechtsgemeinschaft*), it would be impossible *not* to use legally binding WTO dispute settlement reports as a standard for reviewing Community law acts that are apparently inconsistent with WTO law. Indeed, AG Tizzano emphasized the point that in its *Biret*-judgment, the ECJ did not deviate or criticize in any way the conclusions of AG Alber that he drew in his Opinion. Accordingly, AG Tizzano deemed it appropriate to apply them to the *Van Parys* case. As a result thereof, AG Tizzano came to the conclusion that the various Community banana regulations must be considered invalid as they were incompatible with WTO law. AG Tizzano continued his analysis be examining whether this case fell within one of the *Nakajima/Fediol* exceptions. After all, the basic banana regulation 404/93 was amended after the WTO dispute settlement report was adopted that found that regulation to be incompatible with WTO law. AG Tizzano had no difficulties concluding that the amending regulation must be considered to be an act intended to implement the WTO dispute settlement report and thus falls within the *Najajima* exception. Since the subsequent WTO dispute settlement report also found that the amendment of the basic banana regulation was still incompatible with WTO law, AG Tizzano came to the conclusion that the amending banana regulation was invalid. As a result, Van Parys should be allowed to rely on the WTO dispute settlement reports.

... ...

Despite the position of the Advocate Generals, it must be accepted that the present view of the EU courts is that a negotiated settlement can take the place of implementing adverse findings. Based on this view, the EU courts consider that the review of EU measures in light of Appellate Body findings would weaken the position of the EU institutions in any such negotiations, or jeopardise any mutually agreed solution already in place.

There is a convincing rationale for this end point in the analysis, even if the earlier steps are regarded as based on false understandings of the WTO dispute settlement system. In an action for the annulment of an EU measure, if the courts review the measure in light of Appellate Body findings which may not have been properly implemented, and which the EU institutions may not, at least for the present, intend to properly implement, the position is *as if* full implementation has occurred. The applicant is effectively asking the court to confer on it the advantages it would enjoy if implementation had occurred. It can be seen how the position of EU institutions would be undermined if the courts effectively require the WTO dispute settlement findings to be implemented. It becomes rather difficult for the institutions to open negotiations with complainant WTO Members by indicating a disinclination to implement the findings; an option which, according to the EU courts, is permissible. Similarly, if there is already a mutually agreed solution in place based on the premise that implementation will be delayed, it can be seen how this solution would be jeopardised. Should the EU courts effectively require the implementation of dispute settlement findings, the EU provides two remedies to the complaining Member/s (the mutually agreed solution and implementation) when the intention was to provide only one (the mutually agreed solution).

With some adaptation, the same points apply when the applicant seeks damages based on the continued existence of the EU measure which is contrary to WTO law, as opposed to the annulment of this measure. The award of damages does not entail the effective implementation of the Appellate Body findings since the offending measure can remain in place after the award of damages. However, a damages award could weaken the position of the EU institutions in negotiations towards a settlement, or jeopardise any mutually agreed solution already in place. Of relevance here is a remark by Antoniadis:

Had the applicant's claim been upheld in *Chiquita*, the Community would have been subject to damages originating in the same conduct both in the WTO (the US retaliation) and Community (Chiquita's claim for damages) legal orders. As the Commission convincingly argued, after the offer of [trade] compensation or the application of retaliation the overall balance of concessions is re-established.[52]

In other words, the EU would be understandably reluctant to endure the authorized WTO remedy, most likely in the form of suspension of concessions by the US, if the EU courts were to grant an additional damages remedy to a private applicant.

There is also a further problem with the damages remedy. What if the WTO violation impacts upon private traders who then seek a damages remedy, but there are WTO-compatible means to remove the violation which continue to cause injury to these traders? In this situation, the award of a damages remedy presupposes that WTO compliance will be achieved in a manner which restores the trader to the position they were in before the violation. This may be the outcome of some WTO complaint solutions, but not all.[53] Therefore, as with the annulment remedy, there is also a need here to avoid constraining the room for manoeuvre enjoyed by Community institutions on how to achieve conformity.

(b) Indirect Effect/Consistent Interpretation and Beyond

While the EU courts do not attribute any general direct effect to WTO obligations, and while the *Nakajima* exception is narrowly interpreted, there is possible scope in the EU for indirect effect via consistent interpretation. To reiterate, this operates when the legislative measure at issue is ambiguous. If the measure is capable of being interpreted consistently with an international law obligation, it should be so interpreted.

The strongest expression of a consistent interpretation principle is found in *Commission v Germany*.[54] Here, the German government argued that its obligation to follow Community law precluded it from complying with conflicting international obligations under the International Dairy Agreement. The ECJ rejected this argument on the basis of 'the primacy of international agreements concluded by the Community over provisions of secondary law' and the consequent obligation to interpret Community law in a manner consistent with these agreements. A more recent application of the principle in the *Hermes* case[55] made no reference to the primacy of international obligations, but did require national courts to interpret their national law on provisional measures for the protection of intellectual property rights in light of the wording and purpose of Article 50 of the TRIPs Agreement.

It is notable that these cases respectively required a Member State and a national court

---

[52] A Antoniadis, 'The Chiquita and Van Parys Judgments: Rules, Exceptions and the Law' (2005) 32(4) *Legal Issues of Economic Integration*, 461, 471.

[53] For further recent discussion of the possibility of a damages remedy, see A Steinbach, 'EC Liability for Non-compliance with Decisions of the WTO DSB: The Lack of Judicial Protection Persists' (2009) 43(5) *Journal of World Trade* 1047. Note, however, that this contribution is primarily about a damages remedy for indirect victims of WTO violations—those who suffer the suspension of concessions as a result of the failure to remove offending measures. The comments in the main text relate to direct victims—those whose trade opportunities are directly impacted upon by the WTO violation.

[54] Case C-61/94 *Commission v Germany* [1996] ECR I-3989, para 53.

[55] Case C-53/96 *Hermès International v FHT Marketing Choice BV* [1998] ECR I-3603, para 28; affirmed in Case C-300/98 above n 18.

to follow or give effect to international obligations. In contrast, the application of the principle does not seem to have resulted in the sensitive outcome of an EU institution having to revise its preferred interpretation of either an EU measure or a provision of WTO law. Therefore, it is presently not possible to offer a firm view on whether consistent interpretation in the EU is a stronger technique of connecting the EU and WTO legal systems, than the *Charming Betsy* canon in the US.

Despite this observation, there is an interesting possible development in the EU which, strictly speaking, does not exemplify consistent interpretation, but where the ECJ has nevertheless effectively interpreted EU measures such as to avoid conflict with WTO law as interpreted by the Appellate Body. This development is illustrated by the *IKEA* case,[56] which arose from a refusal by UK authorities to reimburse anti-dumping duties on imports of bed linen from Pakistan and India paid by IKEA. These duties had been imposed by a Council Regulation enacted pursuant to the so-called 'basic regulation'. The Council Regulation envisaged the use of a zeroing methodology and was successfully challenged before a WTO panel and the Appellate Body. IKEA's challenge in the UK to the collection of duties under the Council Regulation eventually reached the High Court which referred questions to the ECJ. Among these questions was whether the Council Regulation was valid in light of the basic regulation. Here, the ECJ found a 'manifest error' in the determination of the dumping margin on the basis that the zeroing methodology was not permitted by the basic regulation.

It is significant that, in this section of its analysis, the ECJ does not refer to the Appellate Body's appraisal of the Council Regulation in light of WTO law. Rather the ECJ's analysis is much more straightforward. Independently of anything required by WTO law, the Community basic regulation simply did not permit zeroing. It is this point which reveals why the case does not involve consistent interpretation. The basic regulation was not considered to be ambiguous as to whether zeroing was permitted. Rather, it was considered to unequivocally prevent zeroing. However, it is entirely possible that, in reaching this view on the basic regulation, the ECJ may well have been influenced by the Appellate Body findings. Marco Bronckers has coined the phrase 'muted dialogue' to describe the engagement between the WTO Appellate Body and the ECJ which may have occurred in this case.[57]

(c) Summary of the EU Law Position

The exclusion of the direct effect of WTO law before the EU courts is suggested by the preamble of the Council Decision which implemented the WTO Agreement and its Annexes. This exclusion has been confirmed by the EU courts and the *Nakajima* exception has been interpreted restrictively. Under this exception, a legislative instrument which would not have come into existence were it not for a WTO dispute settlement report will not necessarily be found to indicate an intention to implement a particular WTO obligation, such as to permit the review of EU law in light of WTO law. Therefore, on direct effect, the EU position is very similar to that in the US. This is not surprising,

[56] Case C-351/04 *IKEA v Commissioners of Customs & Excise* (2007) ECR I-7723, [55]–[56].

[57] M Bronckers, 'Private Appeals to WTO Law: An Update' (2008) 42 *Journal of World Trade Law* 245; M Bronckers, 'From "Direct Effect" to "Muted Dialogue" Recent Developments in the European Courts' Case Law on the WTO and Beyond' (2008) 11 *Journal of International Economic Law* 885.

as the reasoning of the EU courts has been explicitly influenced by reciprocity-based considerations. With regard to indirect via consistent interpretation, the crucial question is whether this principle will be used to overturn interpretations of EU law and WTO law which are preferred by the EU institutions. As in the US, there is no clear indication that this has occurred in the EU, though that this may well be because the issue has not arisen in the EU case law. Finally, slightly outside of the field of consistent interpretation, the ECJ held in the *IKEA* case that EU law was clear in not permitting the practice of zeroing. It is possible that the ECJ was influenced by the Appellate Body's views on the impermissibility of zeroing in WTO law.

IV. OTHER JURISDICTIONS

The extract below reviews a number of jurisdictions. It is followed by some general observations drawn from the extract and other academic work.

X Zhang, 'Direct Effect of the WTO Agreements: National Survey' (2003) 9 *International Trade Law & Regulation* 35

Commonwealth Members

Members of the Commonwealth adopt a similar dualist approach to the United Kingdom for the relation between treaty and domestic law. For the vast majority of treaties which entail alteration of the existing domestic law, an implementing legislation should be passed to give effect to treaties in the domestic legal system. Private parties cannot invoke the provision of a treaty before national courts, because the treaty itself has no effect in the domestic law and what creates such effect is the provision of implementing legislation. The hierarchical ranking of treaties in the domestic legal system would be equal to a statute, depending on the status of its implementing legislation, which may not prevail over subsequent conflicting statutes. These general rules also apply to the effect of WTO agreements in their domestic legal system.

Australia

The Parliament has amended a number of statutes to implement the obligations under the WTO agreements. Rather than passing an omnibus implementing legislation, the amendment of each statute serves as the implementing legislation of particular parts of WTO agreements. Examples include the Customs Act 1901, the Customs Legislation (World Trade Organisation Amendments) Act 1994, the Copyright (World Trade Organisation Amendments) Act 1994, the Trade Marks Act 1995, and amendments to the Dairy Produce Act 1986.

Canada

The WTO Agreements were implemented by the 1995 World Trade Organisation Agreement Implementation Act. They are in the form of an omnibus statute enacted by the Parliament of Canada, with legislative amendments necessary to bring existing Canadian legislation into conformity with the WTO obligations. Sections 5 and 6 prohibit a private party from bringing an action against federal or provincial legislative or administrative bodies to enforce or determine any right or obligation arising under this implementing Act or under the WTO Agreement itself, without the consent of the Attorney-General of Canada.

India

International obligations, including those relating to WTO provisions, must be formally incorporated into domestic laws before they can be invoked before national courts. The Parliament takes responsibility for implementing legislation as well as amendments to existing laws. However, in the case that there is no relevant Indian law, provisions of the WTO agreements may be enforced through the Indian courts if they are not in conflict with any other treaty obligations. This position shows a partial flexibility to the direct invocability of WTO agreements.

Singapore

All international treaties signed by the Government (including the WTO Agreements) must be incorporated into Singapore's legislative system through legal amendments or new laws, which are passed by Parliament through subsidiary legislation or under common law, where necessary. As the WTO Agreements do not form part of the domestic legal system, WTO provisions may not be invoked before a national court of law. However, the WTO obligations may be enforced by a national court of law either through implementing legislation or as part of common law.

Hong Kong

Article 151 of the Basic Law stipulates that the HKSAR may, on its own, conclude and implement international trade agreements. Under the common law system in Hong Kong, international agreements do not automatically form part of Hong Kong's domestic legislation without an act of transformation. However, no implementing legislation was necessary to implement the WTO agreements in Hong Kong, except for the amendments to certain laws related to intellectual property rights (completed in May 1996).

Members with civil-law tradition

Members with a civil-law system adopt the monist approach in general. For the issue of direct applicability, the general rule is that the WTO Agreements, once ratified, become automatically a part of domestic law (except for Norway); for the issue of direct invocability, the general rule allows such effect, while the position in some Members (e.g. Japan) is unclear.

Japan

Treaties have the force of law and prevail over statutes (including subsequently enacted statutes), and in theory there is no need for an act of transformation because treaties are capable of regulating the matter directly in Japan as a force of law. It is clear that the WTO Agreements have the force of law in Japan after the ratification by the government, that is, they have direct applicability in Japan.

However, Japanese courts rejected the direct invocability of GATT provisions by private parties, largely because the provision was not precise and unconditional enough to confer rights on individuals. It is unclear whether the WTO agreements have the direct invocability in Japanese courts. Some scholars argue that they are more likely to have direct invocability because of the nature and structure of the WTO, while others observe that there is a general negative attitude toward such effect.

The Republic of Korea

The WTO Agreements were approved by the National Assembly as a single package and subsequently ratified by the President in December 1994. It became part of the domestic law, without the need of separate implementing legislation. The National Assembly also passed the Special Law Implementing the World Trade Organisation Agreement, but only for certain additional implementing matters on a selective basis. However, a newer law will prevail over the WTO Agreements, and a special law with more specific coverage in such areas will override the WTO Agreements as a general law.

For the issue of direct invocability, the Supreme Court affirmed the direct invocability of the GATT provisions in several cases, so it is estimated that the Korean courts will allow for the invocation of provisions of the WTO agreements before them. So far there is no court case examining the conflicts between the WTO agreements and domestic law.

Mali

Mali was formerly a French territory, so its legal system can represent all other former French territories. The National Assembly ratified the WTO Agreements by means of a law, and the President issued a decree promulgating the law. Once approved, the WTO Agreements become a part of domestic law and take precedence over domestic law. The provisions of WTO agreements can be directly invoked before a court.

Mexico

Article 133 of the Mexican Constitution provides that international treaties signed by the President and ratified by the Senate, such as the WTO Agreements, have the status of Supreme Law and are thus inserted into the domestic legal system. The WTO Agreements will have the direct invocability before the domestic courts.

Switzerland

Once a treaty enters into force, it becomes part of Swiss law automatically and will prevail over inconsistent existing or future law. Provisions of a treaty can be directly invoked before a court if they establish rights and obligations of private persons and if they are clear and concrete enough to serve as legal base for a judicial decision. These general principles are also valid for the WTO Agreements. However, the Swiss Federal Court has not held any WTO provision as directly applicable until the year of 2000.

Arabic-country Members

Two Arabic-country Members are selected for analysis: Bahrain and Egypt. Their practice will represent the general practice of Arabic countries, whose legal rules on the issue of direct effect are similar to a great extent. Generally, the Arabic-country Members adopt the monist approach for the relation between the WTO Agreements and domestic law, which allows the direct invocability before courts.

Bahrain

Article 37 of the Constitution provides that trade treaties, once ratified and decreed by the Amir, and subsequently published in the Official Gazette, become part of national law, and supersede any national legislation, despite constitutional provisions that may contradict it. The WTO Agreements became part of Bahrain's laws, after Amiri Decree No.7 of 1994 was passed and ratified by the Amir on July 12, 1994. To the extent that Bahraini legislation is not in accord with its WTO obligations, the WTO Agreements will be definitive, i.e. treaty obligations supersede national legislation and are admissible in national courts.

Egypt

Under Art.151 of the Constitution, any international agreement (including the WTO Agreements), after being ratified by the Assembly and published in the National Gazette, becomes legal in Egypt and cancels thereby all national legislation that may contradict it. The WTO Agreements thus require no further legislative implementation to be invoked before national courts. It is most remarkable that the Constitution of Egypt even allows the application of WTO Agreements to automatically cancel all inconsistent national legislation, which is so far the highest degree of recognising its effect in any domestic legal system.

China

There is no settled law in China concerning direct effect of treaties within the domestic legal system. Ranking as the fifth trading entity of the world trade in goods (2000), China's practice will certainly change the existing countries "map" and affect other Members' future attitude.

Similar to other civil-law countries, China has a monist approach that a treaty becomes part of domestic law automatically upon ratification and will immediately be valid under the Chinese legal system once that treaty enters into force under international law. Therefore, upon China's accession to the WTO, the WTO Agreements and the Accession Protocol constitute part of Chinese domestic law after the ratification by President Jiang Zemin in November 2001.

There is no express rule on the hierarchy ranking of treaties in China's domestic legal system. Scholars suggest that treaties approved by the Standing Committee of National People's Congress (NPC) would have the same status as statutes, because they follow the same parliamentary deliberation and approval procedure that implies the same status between these legal norms, but in case of conflicts between treaties and domestic statutes, China puts into effect the supremacy of treaties over the statutes (including those subsequently enacted). However, this view cannot explain why treaties, though an international obligation on China, should enjoy a higher status than domestic statutes in case of conflicts, if two norms are in the same hierarchy of the Chinese legal system. It might be thought that there is no legal basis to draw such a general conclusion; instead, it might be necessary to probe which statute conflicts with which treaty. While there is no constitutional rule that treaties can take precedence over domestic statutes, there are several statutes which provide in case of conflicts between these statutes and treaties concluded or acceded by China . . . the treaties will prevail. Therefore, only in these contexts can treaties be in a superior status to conflicting domestic statutes. In the absence of such clauses, the normal rule shall apply, that is, the subsequent statute prevails over the former statute, and the statute relating to a specific issue prevails over the statute with general applicability. Applying this rule to the WTO Agreements, the WTO Agreements may take precedence over conflicting statutes if those statutes contain a clause recognising its superiority; if a subsequent statute deliberately violates the WTO Agreements, the statute will apply, although China will breach its international obligation under that circumstance.

Considering the deep doubts on China's intention and ability to implement the widespread WTO commitments, it would surely be an effective weapon to private parties (in particular the foreign parties) to challenge the governmental actions or inactions that are not consistent with the WTO Agreements and China's accession commitments. Similarly, there is no uniform rule on direct invocability of treaties before Chinese courts. Adopting the monist approach, Chinese law contains no prohibition on invoking provisions of treaty by private parties, and there have already occurred some cases involving the application of treaty provisions. On the other hand, there is no rule expressly recognising the issue of direct invocability.

There are heated discussions among academics as to whether or not China should grant the direct invocability to the WTO Agreements, and the prevailing view is that China should refuse to grant such effect, mainly based on the policy consideration that the main WTO Members (United States, EC, Canada and Japan) do not recognise the direct effect of WTO agreements. The Chinese judiciary formally acknowledged this prevailing view in August 2002.

On August 27, 2002, the People's Supreme Court issued a judicial interpretation titled as "Measures on Several Issues Relating to the Adjudication of International Trade Administrative Litigations" ("the Measures"). It is the first authoritative document that sets out the rules for domestic effect of the WTO Agreement in China, which shows not only the latest development of this issue but also the trend of Chinese law in the general treaty practices and in the WTO Agreement per se. The Measures applies to the administrative litigations in the following areas: international trade in goods, international trade in services, international-trade-related intellectual properties, and others concerned with international trade. The Administrative Litigation Chamber in the People's Courts is in charge of adjudicating such international trade administrative litigations, and the court of first instance shall be the Intermediate People's Courts with the jurisdiction. Under the Measures, the individuals, legal persons and other organisations (collectively referred to as "private parties") can bring an "administrative litigation" (xingzheng susong) against an administrative organ if they hold that the organ's specific administrative behaviour concerning international trade (compared to the abstract administrative behaviour such as issuing regulations, rules or orders with general applicability) has infringed their legal interests and benefits.

The most notable part of the Measures is Arts 7 and 8. Article 7 provides that when the courts adjudicate international trade administrative litigations, they shall apply "PRC laws, administrative regulations, and local regulations issued by the local legislatures within the relevant legislative competence that relates to or affects international trade", while Art.8 allows the courts to "make reference to" the ministerial rules issued by the ministries, departments or commissions of the State Council and the local rules issued by the local governments within their legislative competence. Although these articles do not expressly indicate to reject the direct invocability of the WTO Agreement, the literal meaning is clear and unambiguous enough to such an effect, that is, the courts will only apply or refer to PRC laws, regulations and rules and will neither apply nor refer to the provisions of WTO agreements. Consequently, Chinese courts do not recognise the direct invocability of WTO Agreements, which means there is no direct effect of WTO Agreements in the Chinese domestic legal system. This position follows the mainstream of academic views and general practices. It is also the first time that a judicial opinion clarifies the relationship between domestic law and treaties in China, which will greatly contribute to theory and practice in this general topic.

However, the issuance of the Measures does not necessarily mean the absolute denial of direct effect of WTO agreements in China. This view is based on two reasons. First, the Measures are applicable to international trade "administrative" litigations, rather than to all types of litigations with the international trade elements. Hence, it does not express the rejection of direct effect in civil and commercial cases, provided that one WTO provision is invocable by private parties (for example, the TRIPs). Presumably, when the provision concerned grants clear, unambiguous and identifiable rights to or obligations on private parties, one party in relevant civil and commercial cases may invoke this provision provided it is different from the applicable domestic civil or commercial law. Secondly, Art.9 of the Measures establishes the "consistent interpretation" principle for the first time in Chinese law, which reads as:

'When there exist two or more than two reasonable interpretations of the provisions of applicable law or regulation in adjudicating the international trade administrative litigations, and one interpretation is consistent with the relevant provision of international treaties concluded or acceded by [China], the courts shall choose the interpretation consistent with the relevant international treaty, unless relating to clauses declared reservation by China.'

As a result, the courts are now obliged to apply the interpretation consistent with China's commitments under the WTO Agreement. It will not only avoid the conflict between Chinese law and the WTO Agreement, but also imply the judicial attitude to interpret the domestic law as far as possible to be consistent with the international obligations. Consequently, the WTO Agreement may have an indirect effect in China through the back door thanks to the application of this principle.

... ...

V. GENERAL OBSERVATIONS ON OTHER JURISDICTIONS[58]

The single most important point is that direct effect tends to be excluded. This applies regardless of the domestic legal traditions of the state in question, in particular with regard to whether a monist (for example, Japan) or dualist (for example, India) approach towards the reception of international law into the domestic legal system is preferred. In the treatment of the US and EU positions above, it was noted that measures which implement the WTO agreements express a clear view on whether individuals should be permitted to invoke WTO law before the courts. However, the denial of direct effect also applies in some states (for example, Japan) where no such view has been communicated. On the other hand, indirect effect via consistent interpretation is very commonly observed. A further general observation is that, compared to the case law in the US and the EU, the case law in other jurisdictions is relatively underdeveloped. Arguments which have been tested before US and EU courts have yet to be put to courts in other jurisdictions. A related point is that there are frequent references to reciprocity based considerations in the academic literature relating to other jurisdictions. It seems likely that, as courts are confronted with new arguments, they will pay close attention to the already established responses of US and EU courts. A proliferation of the denial of direct effect can therefore be predicted, regardless of the general legal traditions of the state concerned.

On the denial of direct effect, the *Novartis* case[59] heard by the Madras High Court in India is of particular note. Part of the claim by Novartis, a Swiss pharmaceutical company, argued that a provision of the Indian Patent Act was contrary to the TRIPs Agreement. India, as respondent, denied this incompatibility and, more fundamentally, argued that the alleged incompatibility could only be challenged in inter-governmental dispute settlement under the DSU. India therefore considered that the legal challenge could not be sustained in any Indian court of law. The court agreed with India on this issue of jurisdiction, likening the DSB, as the preferred mechanism for dispute settlement among WTO Members, to a contract clause allocating jurisdiction to courts of a

---

[58] These observations are based on the extract provided above and a review of a number of chapters in a recent edited collection. C Dordi (ed), *The Absence of Direct Effect of WTO in the EC and in Other Countries* (Torino G Giappichelli Editore, 2010).

[59] *Novartis AG v Union of India*, (2007) 4 MLJ 1153 [Madras High Court]. On this case, see N Chowdhry, 'The (Absence of) Direct Effect of WTO law: Current Developments within the Indian Legal System' in C Dordi (ed), *ibid*, 345–50; S Basheer and P Reddy, '"Ducking" TRIPS in India: A Saga Involving Navartis and the Legality of Section 3(D)' (2008) 20 *National Law School of India Review* 131.

specified state. Therefore, the competence of the DSB to decide upon the compatibility of the Patent Act with the TRIPs excluded any concurrent competence for the Indian court.

Similar views have been expressed by courts in Japan. In the *Kyoto Necktie* case,[60] a group of necktie producers challenged the Silk Law, which was intended to stabilize the domestic price of raw silk and thereby protect domestic production. This involved import restrictions such that only a government agency and authorised individuals were permitted to import raw silk. This meant that the necktie producers were deprived of the ability to import raw silk from the cheapest sources, so that these producers lost competitiveness relative to European producers. One of the arguments considered by the Kyoto District Court related to inconsistency between the Silk Law and a number of GATT provisions. While the court engaged with this issue, and expressed the view that the Silk Law was GATT consistent, it then went on the hold that:

> A violation of a provision of the GATT pressures the country in default to rectify the violation by being confronted with a request from another member country for consultation and possible retaliatory measures. However, it cannot be interpreted to have more effect than this.

Both the Madras High Court and the Kyoto District Court therefore concurred on two related matters: first, that the WTO DSB (previously the GATT Council) is the exclusive forum at which allegations of inconsistency between national law and GATT/WTO law can be assessed; and, secondly, that the available remedies are exclusively as provided for in the DSU.

VI. QUESTIONS

1. What are the differences between the concepts of the direct effect and indirect effect of world trade law?

2. Explain why private applicants raise arguments about direct and indirect effect before national and regional courts when the WTO itself has a highly developed system of dispute settlement.

3. Consider the following passage from the Cottier and Schefer extract:

> To prevent the erosion of a state's sovereignty, Tumlir suggests granting individuals the right to invoke treaty provisions in front of their domestic courts. Allowing for standing in this way would be available to those citizens harmed by protectionist national policies put into effect by other national interest groups. Thus, direct effect widely defined 'helps to correct the asymmetries in the political process'.
>
> In Tumlir's conception, the complainant is a national of the state which has put in place a protectionist trade measure. Can you identify the possible identity/identities of such complainants? What is the possible problem with extending standing to non-nationals? For examples of the differing nationalities and identities of complainants, see the *Hyundai Electronics* and *Corus Staal* cases above.

---

[60] Judgment of 29 June 1984, Kyoto District Court, Hanrei Times, No 530, 1984, 265. On this case, see F Azuma 'GATT 1947 and WTO Agreements Case Law in Japan' in C Dordi (ed), *ibid*, 373–80.

4. What are some of the arguments for and against recognising the direct effect of WTO law?

5. In connection with the *Intermediate positions* described in the Cottier and Schefer extract, how, if at all, is the case for direct effect strengthened when the applicant is able to rely upon a WTO panel or Appellate Body report?

6. In the US, which overall school of academic thought on direct effect is reflected in the relevant provisions of the URAA and SAA? Do these provisions recognise an intermediate approach?

7. On the possible indirect effect of WTO law in the US legal order, describe the relationship between the *Charming Betsy* canon of statutory interpretation and *Chevron* deference.

8. Based on a review of the case law, analyse whether US courts have struck an appropriate balance between *Charming Betsy* and *Chevron*.

9. Discuss how, if at all, the position of applicants is strengthened if they are able to rely, not only a panel or Appellate Body report, but also the implementation of this report. Your answer should contrast the position before US courts and NAFTA tribunals.

10. Turning to the EU law position, identify and explain the factors which have influenced the policy of the ECJ on the direct effect of world trade law, in particular as evident in the *Portugal v Council* case.

11. Discuss the following: 'Under the *Nakajmia* exception, the legality of EU law can be reviewed in light of WTO law when EU institutions intend to fulfil a particular WTO obligation that is implemented by that measure. Recent cases have rendered this exception virtually inutile, and quite rightly so.'

12. Explain Marco Bronckers' description of the *IKEA* case as evidencing a possible 'muted dialogue' between the WTO Appellate Body and the ECJ.

13. Discuss the following: 'If one were to think of a metaphor to represent the evolution of the US and EU case law on the direct and indirect effects of world trade law, it would be "moving goal posts". This is not necessarily an unwelcome phenomenon.'

14. Discuss the following: 'Based on reciprocity considerations, the absence of direct effect of WTO law is common to most jurisdictions regardless of their legal traditions with regard to the national reception of international law.'

Part III

Dispute Settlement in the WTO

5

The Settlement of Disputes in GATT/WTO

I. INTRODUCTION

The establishment of the WTO significantly reshaped the world trading system, not only by expanding upon the topical coverage of the GATT (as discussed in Chapter 2), but also by creating a system of compulsory, binding and enforceable dispute settlement. The primary legal framework for this system is set out in the Understanding on Rules and Procedures Governing the Settlement of Disputes ('Dispute Settlement Understanding' or 'DSU'). The DSU represents an important change from the dispute settlement system in the GATT. The creation of a broader, more efficient, predictable and reliable dispute resolution process guided by the rule of law has been widely hailed as an improvement over the more diplomatically-based rules and procedures of the GATT. Indeed, reaching agreement to reform the dispute settlement mechanism led Peter Sutherland, the former Director General of the GATT, to state that the DSU is the greatest achievement of the international community since Bretton Woods.[1] More recently, former Director General Mike Moore, during his tenure, frequently described the DSU as the 'crown jewel' of the entire multilateral trading system.[2]

Without question, the WTO dispute settlement system has become one of the most important and widely utilised international tribunals. As of this writing, through the 17 years of its existence the WTO has received over 436 complaints comprising over 320 'matters'[3], and it has adopted over 229 panel and Appellate Body reports. By comparison, the list of Contentious Cases referred to the International Court of Justice (ICJ) since 1946 totals around 115, while Advisory Proceedings total 26.[4] In addition to the high utilisation, the system has also been effective in terms of compliance with decisions. Even though many WTO disputes are highly contentious and politicised, Members recognise that overall the benefits of the process outweigh concerns about specific cases and, for the most part, implement adverse decisions against them without the complainant having to resort to retaliatory measures. The Members' willingness to use and comply with the system as intended shows the confidence and faith they have in the WTO to effectively

---

[1] See J Bacchus, 'Inside the World Trade Organization', speech on 17 April 2002 to the Columbia Business School APEC Study Center, 6, available at http://www.columbia.edu/cu/business/apec/bacchuscf.pdf.

[2] *Ibid.*

[3] The term 'matters' is defined in Section VI below.

[4] For a listing of WTO disputes, see http://www.wto.org/english/tratop_e/dispu_e/dispu_status_e.htm. For a listing of ICJ decisions, see http://www.icj-cij.org/icjwww/idecisions.htm.

resolve disputes. On the other hand, several high-profile cases have tested both the institutional capacity of the WTO to deal with contentious issues as well as Members' resolve towards the multilateral system.

In this chapter, we provide an account of dispute settlement in the WTO. We start by looking at the evolution of dispute settlement under the GATT. We then discuss the advent of the WTO and the DSU before detailing the finer points of the agreement. This discussion includes a basic overview of the dispute process as well as an examination of some of the important procedural and systemic issues that have arisen. Finally, we provide an excerpt of an article discussing the effectiveness of the DSU.

II. DISPUTE SETTLEMENT IN THE GATT

In order to fully appreciate the dispute settlement process of the WTO, it is important to understand dispute settlement in the multilateral trading system as it developed prior to the establishment of the WTO. In particular, one must realise that the GATT evolved during its 47 year existence from a diplomatic-based conciliatory process into a more judicially focused model and that the DSU, far from being an entirely new and separate legal instrument, merely completed the evolutionary process to a system based on the rule of law.

At its inception, the GATT contained few provisions addressing dispute settlement. When the GATT was negotiated, the Contracting Parties anticipated that the more detailed provisions on dispute settlement under the International Trade Organization (ITO) would soon apply. Because these other rules were expected to govern, it was not considered necessary to develop additional dispute rules specific to the GATT. As a result, when the efforts to create the ITO failed, the GATT was left without a detailed dispute mechanism. Instead, the very brief provisions of Articles XXII and XXIII of the GATT provided the foundation of its dispute settlement system.

Article XXII, entitled 'Consultation', provides for consultations regarding 'any matter affecting the operations of this Agreement'. Article XXIII does a bit, but not much, more. Entitled 'Nullification or Impairment',[5] Article XXIII provides that a party can make a written representation or proposal to another party when it considers that any benefit accruing to it directly or indirectly under the GATT is being nullified or impaired or that the attainment of any objective of the GATT is being impeded as the result of: (*a*) the failure of another contracting party to carry out its obligations under the GATT; or (*b*) the application by another contracting party of any measure, whether or not it conflicts with the provisions of the GATT; or (*c*) the existence of any other situation. (We discuss below, in the procedural and systemic issues section, the various claims that can be brought based on this language.) Article XXIII:1 also provides that the Contracting Party approached shall give 'sympathetic consideration' to the representations or proposals.

If a resolution is not reached through consultations within a reasonable period of time, then Article XXIII:2 states that the matter may be referred to the Contracting Parties

---

[5] As will be discussed below, 'nullification or impairment' is, for practical purposes, the basis of all GATT complaints. Under Article XXIII, a complainant alleges that nullification or impairment has occurred as the result of a violation (or in certain other circumstances), rather than merely alleging a violation.

(that is, the GATT membership as a whole), who will promptly investigate and make appropriate recommendations or give a ruling on the matter. In addition, if nullification or impairment is found, Article XXIII:2 permits the Contracting Parties to authorise the complaining party to suspend tariff concessions or other GATT obligations to the party complained against.

As noted, while not intended to play such an important role, Articles XXII and XXIII became the *de facto* basis for the GATT dispute settlement process. However, because these provisions fail to provide clear procedural rules to guide the process, the Contracting Parties were left to discover, invent and reform rules based on their experience with actual disputes.

One unambiguous aspect of the rules was the clear preference for negotiated settlements. The dispute settlement process was initially referred to as 'conciliation', and, as set out in Articles XXII and XXIII, Contracting Parties were mandated to enter into consultation and negotiation before turning to adjudicatory procedures. In such circumstances, the formal process of dispute settlement developed slowly.

In the first case settled under the GATT, the Chairman alone decided the case without discussion or explanation, and the respondent removed the offending measure without complaint.[6] Soon after, the process began to rely on working parties consisting of representatives from various Contracting Parties, who would investigate disputes and, where agreement could be reached, to recommend action.[7] In essence, the working parties were not designed to reach legal decisions, but rather to find consensus where it existed. On issues that could not be resolved, the 'Working Party report simply catalogued the opposing arguments'.[8] One leading GATT scholar, Robert Hudec, described the situation as follows: '[Working parties] were meant to clarify the issues, to discuss them, and hopefully to produce enlightened agreement on the merits. But "agreement" was critical. Without it, working parties could only report on the reasons for disagreement'.[9]

By the 1950s, however, the process had become more legalistic in nature. Disputes were submitted to an ad hoc 'panel' of unbiased, neutral trade experts (usually representatives from Contracting Parties who were not parties to the dispute, acting in their individual capacities) to take evidence, hear arguments, rule on the legal issues and merits of the complaint and submit a written report to the GATT Council to make 'appropriate recommendations'.[10] The legal nature of the proceedings was tempered, however, by political aspects of the process. For example, once the Council received the written decision of the panel, a unanimous vote was needed to adopt, that is, give legal effect to, the panel decision. Because the Council was made up of all the Contracting Parties, the respondent could block, or essentially veto, an adverse panel decision from having any effect.

Throughout these early years, additional procedures were developed. When the Contracting Parties felt the need to codify practice or make minor adjustments to the system,

---

[6] See GATT/CP.2/SR.11 (24 August 1948).

[7] See, eg the Brazilian Taxes Working Party, which included representatives from Brazil and France (the principals), the US and UK (supporters of the complaint) and China, Cuba and India (neutral parties). See GATT/CP.3/SR.10 (26 April 1949).

[8] R Hudec, *Enforcing International Trade Law: The Evolution of the Modern GATT Legal System* (London, Butterworths, 1993) 79.

[9] *Ibid.*

[10] The GATT Council generally met monthly and consisted of all government representatives who wanted to be present. In essence, the Council was all the Contracting Parties acting jointly.

they issued a 'Decision' to supplement Article XXIII.[11] Through these codifications, the system became more rule-oriented in its approach.

Despite the textual ambiguities and other impediments and shortcomings, the process was very successful in peacefully and amicably resolving disputes in the early years. Most panel decisions were observed and implemented by the disputing parties. For this reason, Contracting Parties frequently submitted claims. Indeed, forty claims were submitted in the period 1952–58. Hudec accounts for the early success in the following way:

> Governments understood the legal rulings implicit in its vaguely worded decisions, and once these rulings were approved by the GATT Contracting Parties, defendant governments almost always felt it necessary to comply. The reason these impressionistic half-decisions were successful was that the early GATT of the 1950s was essentially a small "club" of likeminded trade policy officials who had been working together since the 1946-1948 ITO negotiations . . . Thus they did not need a very elaborate decision-making procedure to generate an effective consensus about what particular governments were expected to do.[12]

Eventually the challenges of the changing conditions of international trade, which brought not only more complex cases but also a larger, more diverse group of nations, caught up with the dispute settlement process. The GATT was no longer a small club of like-minded nations, but a large group with diverse viewpoints on a wider range of trade issues. The textual and procedural weaknesses continued to reveal themselves in the difficulties and failures of the system and increasingly led to a large number of disputes that the GATT could not effectively resolve.

The most conspicuous shortcoming of the GATT dispute settlement system stemmed from the complete consensus required for key steps in the process, which meant that a defendant essentially had a veto right at virtually every stage, from the establishment of a panel (until certain modifications to the rules, made in 1989) to the adoption of the panel's recommendation and authorisation of trade sanctions for non-compliance. While parties did not generally use their 'veto' power,[13] differing views and opinions often produced long delays. It must also be noted that as time progressed, the frequency of use of the 'veto' power increased. Partly as a result, smaller and developing nations found it difficult to obtain a successful resolution to the GATT process.

More problems, such as panel delays and a concern regarding the quality of the panel reports, in terms of the reasoning of the vaguely worded decisions, inconsistent panel decisions and an unsound body of case law, further undermined the system. Moreover, transparency was a major issue. For instance, because documents relating to the decision-making process were sometimes unavailable, future claimants lacked notice of what to expect from the process. As a result, many Contracting Parties became increasingly frustrated and disenchanted with the lack of coordination, guidance, and stability of the

---

[11] This occurred five times: See (1) The 1966 Decision on Procedures under Article XXIII, 5 April 1966 (BISD 14S/18); Understanding Regarding Notification, Consultation, Dispute Settlement and Surveillance, 28 November 1979 (BISD 26/210); The 1982 Decision on Dispute Settlement Procedures, 29 November 1982 (BISD 29/9); The 1989 Decision on Improvements to the GATT Dispute Settlement Rules and Procedures, 12 April 1989 (BISD 36/61). These amendments were, in the main, formally adopted later as part of the DSU.

[12] See R Hudec, 'The New WTO Dispute Settlement Procedure: An Overview of the First Three Years' (1999) 8 *Minnesota Journal of Global Trade* 1, 5–6.

[13] This may have been because they recognised the systemic issues which would result from the abuse of the provision, or it may have simply been because a nation knew that if it used the power too much it would very likely be used against it at some stage.

system. Furthermore, increased GATT membership led to differing views on international trade and, thus, international trade law. Perhaps more importantly, some Contracting Parties began abandoning, withdrawing or failing to bring disputes to GATT panels, and instead choosing to resort to unilateral measures to resolve disputes.[14] Therefore, even though the GATT remained a triumph in that it became one of (if not) the most successful international dispute settlement mechanism,[15] it was apparent that wholesale changes were needed. Negotiations on this subject were carried out during the Uruguay Round, and, as part of the overall package of agreements resulting from the Uruguay Round, the DSU was created.

III. DISPUTE SETTLEMENT IN THE WTO: INTRODUCTION

As noted, the primary WTO dispute settlement rules are set out in the DSU. Article 2.1 of the DSU establishes the Dispute Settlement Body (DSB) to administer the DSU's rules and procedures. In essence, the DSB is all the WTO Members acting together. The DSB has the authority to establish dispute settlement panels, adopt panel and Appellate Body reports, maintain surveillance of implementation rulings, and, if necessary, to authorise Members to suspend concessions and other obligations. According to Article 2.3 of the DSU, the DSB meets 'as often as necessary to carry out its functions'. In practice, the DSB regularly meets monthly. Decisions at the meetings are taken by consensus.[16]

Two of the most important changes from the GATT era are the following. First, the WTO created a standing Appellate Body to review panels' legal decisions, partly in response to the concern with the uneven quality of GATT panel reports. Secondly, the DSB automatically adopts, that is, gives legal effect to, panel and Appellate Body reports unless it decides by consensus *not* to adopt the report.[17] This shift to 'reverse consensus' eliminates the ability of one Member to block adoption of a panel/Appellate Body report and means adoption is a virtual certainty because, in order for a report not to be adopted, every Member—including the 'winning' party—would have to object.

In the following sections, we describe a number of aspects of the WTO dispute settlement system. First, we offer a basic overview of the key stages of the DSU process. We then discuss some alternatives to formal dispute procedures. Next, we provide statistics on the usage of the system. Turning to substantive issues, we explain how the DSU rules interact with more specific dispute settlement rules that are present in other agreements.

---

[14] Even the Director-General, in a 1979 report, stated that the scope of cases was too broad for the system and issues too important in terms of national interest. See T Stewart (ed), *The GATT Uruguay Round: A Negotiating History* (The Hague, Kluwer Law International, 1993) p. 2706. See also WTO, *A Handbook on the WTO Dispute Settlement System* (2004) 13–14 (hereinafter *WTO Handbook*).

[15] Professor Hudec's comprehensive study of GATT statistics up to 1989 reveals that complainants reached full satisfaction in 60% of cases and partial satisfaction in 29%. See R Hudec, *Enforcing International Trade Law: The Evolution of the Modern GATT Legal System* (London, Butterworths, 1993) 375–83. At the time, these statistics were unparalleled in any other international dispute settlement forum and today are only rivaled by the DSU statistics.

[16] See Art 2.4 of the DSU.

[17] Arts 16.4 and 17.14 of the DSU.

We also offer brief descriptions of a number of important procedural and systemic issues that have arisen. Finally, we look at whether the DSU has been a 'success'.

IV. BASIC OVERVIEW OF THE DSU PROCESS

The DSU process consists of a number of procedural stages. In this section, we consider the following: consultations, panel, appellate review, implementation, compliance and compensation/retaliation.

Not all of these stages are reached in every dispute, of course. At each stage, there is the possibility for resolution of the dispute. A dispute might be resolved in consultations; the claims might be rejected by the panel; or findings of violation might be implemented immediately. Very few disputes make it all the way to the compensation/retaliation stage.

(a) Consultations

The WTO dispute settlement process formally begins when a Member requests consultations with another Member regarding a perceived 'nullification or impairment' of benefits, usually resulting from an alleged violation of the substantive rules. The consultations phase is intended to provide an opportunity for the parties to discuss the dispute and negotiate a resolution of the matter. In furtherance of this goal, consultations are confidential, and without prejudice to the rights of any Member in any further proceedings.[18]

Parties are given great scope in carrying out the consultations, as the DSU does not provide any guidance on how the consultations are to be conducted. Therefore, the manner and form in which the parties discuss the dispute, interpret the facts and reveal legal arguments is left almost entirely to them.

Consultations may be either 'multilateral' or 'bilateral', at the designation of the complainant. Multilateral consultations are open to other Members with a 'substantial trade interest'. Such Members may request to join in the consultations. By contrast, bilateral consultations are 'private', that is, only the complaining and responding Members may participate.[19]

The DSU also states that special attention should be paid to the particular problems and interests of developing country Members in the context of consultations. For example, under DSU Article 12.10, where a measure taken by a developing country Member is at issue, the parties may agree to extend the timeline established in the DSU, or the Chairman of the DSB can, after consultation with the parties, decide whether to extend the consultations and, if so, for how long.

A large number of disputes are resolved, either through a mutually agreed solution or through abandonment, at the consultations stage of the dispute settlement process. This

---

[18] Art 4.6 of the DSU.

[19] This distinction is not explained clearly in the text, but Art 4.11 of the DSU refers to Art XXII:1 of the GATT and Art XXII:1 of the GATS, and the corresponding provisions of other agreements, as providing for multilateral consultations, in the sense of allowing other Members to join. As a result, under the GATT, for example, consultations requested under Art XXII are multilateral, whereas consultations requested under Art XXIII are bilateral.

suggests that, despite the shift from a conciliatory model of dispute settlement to an adjudicatory model, Members still often use the consultations phase as it is intended and do not simply view it as a necessary delay before proceeding to the panel phase and beyond.

(b) Panels

If consultations fail to resolve the dispute, the complaining party may request the DSB to establish a panel. To do so, the complainant simply puts its request on the agenda of a DSB meeting. A panel will be convened at the latest at the second meeting of the DSB where the request is heard unless the DSB decides by consensus not to establish one (Members still have the option of blocking the request at the first meeting, a carry over from the GATT rules). Therefore, and in contrast to the GATT, a Member effectively has a right to have a panel established, as the only way a panel will not be established is if every Member, including the Member requesting the establishment of a panel, decides not to establish the panel! Obviously, this is unlikely to happen, as the complaining party would simply withdraw its request rather than vote against it.

Panels are composed on an ad hoc basis of three (or if the parties agree, five) well-qualified individuals: generally academics, private lawyers or, quite often, present or former Members of government delegations to the WTO who are not parties to the dispute. Panelists serve in their individual capacity, not as a representative of their government, and Members cannot give instructions to panelists or seek to influence them in any manner.[20]

The parties to the dispute can, by mutual agreement, select the panelists themselves, based on suggestions made by the Secretariat. Parties can oppose the suggestions for 'compelling reasons'. If the parties cannot agree on the composition of the panel within 20 days following the establishment of the panel, either of the parties can request that the Director-General determine its composition. In doing so, the Director-General consults with the parties to the dispute, the chairman of the DSB and the chairman of the relevant Councils and Committees.[21] The staff members of the relevant division of the Secretariat provide guidance in this regard. In practice, the Director-General determines the composition of the panel in over half the disputes.

Once the composition of the panel is determined, the panel process can begin. Article 7 provides the standard terms of reference for panels, which essentially states that the panel should examine the complaint as set out in the panel request and 'make such findings as will assist the DSB in making the recommendations or in giving the rulings provided for in that/those agreement(s)'.

The panel process is similar to that used under the GATT and in most domestic courts. The panel evaluates the factual and legal aspects of the dispute through written submissions from the parties, meetings with the parties, and the power to seek additional information and expert opinions. The panel then makes an 'objective assessment' of the matter by examining the facts of the case and the relevant WTO agreements. In practice,

---

[20] In order to avoid conflict of interests or the appearance of impropriety, the DSB has adopted rules of conduct requiring panelists to be 'independent and impartial' and to 'avoid direct or indirect conflict of interests'. Parties to the dispute can allege a violation of the rules and, if upheld, can remove a panelist from the panel. See WT/DSB/RC/1.

[21] Art 8.10 mandates that, when a dispute involves a developing country, at least one panelist must be from a developing country if the developing country Member so requests.

panels make every effort to reach decisions by consensus, but where a decision cannot be arrived at by consensus, decisions are taken by a majority vote. In such a circumstance, the dissenting or concurring opinion of any panelist is included in the panel report, but the author of the opinion remains anonymous. Based on the evidence presented, the panel reaches conclusions on the legal claims. It then issues an 'interim' report to the parties (the interim report is another new element introduced by the DSU and is intended to improve the quality of panel reports). The parties can (and often do) comment on the findings contained in this report. After the interim review process is complete, the panel issues the final report to the parties, taking into account the interim review comments. After issuance to the parties, the report is translated into the other official WTO languages which were not used in the proceedings (English, French and Spanish are the three) and then circulated to the full WTO membership and to the public. While the DSU provides that, in most circumstances, the panel process is to last for no more than six months, and that in no case should the period from the establishment of the panel to the circulation of the report to the Members exceed nine months, in practice the process normally takes much longer to complete. On average, it takes a little over a year between panel establishment and circulation of a panel report, but this time period varies widely depending on the complexity of the dispute.

After circulation, the panel report can either be appealed by any party to the dispute or adopted by the DSB. If there is an appeal, the appellate review process begins. If no appeal is filed, the panel report is considered for adoption. Upon adoption, the panel's findings have legal force, and thus any findings of violation must be implemented by the responding party (the implementation process is discussed below). Unless the DSB decides by consensus not to adopt the report—meaning all parties, including the 'winning' party, decide to block adoption of the report—the report is automatically adopted.

(c) Appellate Review

Appeals of panel reports are made to the Appellate Body. The Appellate Body is a standing body composed of seven persons with demonstrated expertise in law, international trade and the WTO agreements.

Appellate Body members serve a four-year term, and may be reappointed once for a further four-year term. The DSU requires that Appellate Body members be broadly representative of membership in the WTO (there has always been a member from the EC, the US and three or four members from various developing countries). In addition, Appellate Body members cannot be affiliated with any government nor should they accept or seek instructions from any international, governmental or non-governmental organisation or any private source.[22]

While the Appellate Body is composed of seven members, only three members serve on any one case. The three members selected to adjudicate and review a case are known as a 'division'. Appellate Body members sit on cases on a rotating basis. According to the Working Procedures, divisions are determined through random selection, unpredictability and with opportunity for all members to serve.[23]

Decisions relating to a particular appeal are taken solely by the division. However, a

---

[22] Art 17.3 of the DSU and Rule 2(3) of the Working Procedures for Appellate Review.
[23] Rule 6 of the Working Procedures for Appellate Review.

practice of 'collegiality' has been developed by the Appellate Body and enshrined in its Working Procedures. One aspect of this practice is that the division hearing a particular appeal will 'exchange views' with the other Appellate Body members before finalising their decision in the dispute.[24]

Appeals are limited to issues of law covered in the panel report and legal interpretations and conclusions developed by the panel. The Appellate Body has the authority to uphold, modify or reverse the legal findings and conclusions of the panel. Therefore, it is not the role of the Appellate Body to engage in fact-finding or evaluation of the evidence, and findings of fact are, in principle, not subject to Appellate Body review. As explained below, however, factual findings can be reviewed pursuant to Article 11 of the DSU in limited circumstances.

Like with panels, Appellate Body proceedings are confidential and the opinions expressed anonymous. Where consensus cannot be reached, decisions are taken by a majority vote. Dissenting or concurring opinions of any Appellate Body member are included in the report of the Appellate Body, but the author of the opinion remains anonymous. To date, there has only been one dissenting opinion and one concurrence.

The DSU provides that appellate proceedings are generally to last no more than 60 days following the notification of appeal. When the Appellate Body considers that it cannot provide its report within 60 days, it informs the DSB in writing of the reasons for delay and estimates the date when it will submit its report. According to the DSU, 'in no case shall the proceedings exceed 90 days'. In practice, most cases take around 90 days, although several proceedings have exceeded the 90 day timeline.

After the Appellate Body report is circulated, this report—along with the panel report as upheld, modified or reversed by the Appellate Body report—is placed on the agenda of a DSB meeting and is automatically adopted unless the DSB decides otherwise by consensus. Again, the only circumstance in which the DSB will not adopt the report of the Appellate Body is if all Members—including the 'winning' party—decide by consensus not to adopt the report.

(d) Implementation

When implementing adverse panel/Appellate Body decisions, two of the key issues for the responding party are (1) what needs to be done to come into compliance and (2) when does compliance need to be achieved. With regard to the former, according to Article 3.7 of the DSU, the primary objective of dispute settlement is to secure the modification or withdrawal of the offending measure. Thus, when panels and the Appellate Body make the standard recommendation under Article 19.1 of the DSU, that a Member found to be in violation 'bring the measure into conformity with' WTO rules, the hope is that the implementing Member will withdraw the measure or modify it so that it is consistent. Once adopted, these recommendations become the 'recommendations and rulings' of the DSB. This characterisation is a vestige of the old GATT regime, where the Contracting Parties played a greater role in the process. Today, practically speaking, the 'recommendations and rulings' of the DSB are really those of the panel and Appellate Body, which are then formally endorsed by the DSB through adoption of the reports.

In terms of the timing of compliance, Article 21.1 of the DSU states that 'prompt

---

[24] Rule 4(3) of the Working Procedures for Appellate Review.

compliance' is 'essential'. However, the DSU also recognises that immediate compliance may be 'impracticable' in certain circumstances (eg, when the Member concerned must initiate and pass legislation to amend a law found to be inconsistent with its WTO obligations) and, in such circumstances, allows the Member concerned a 'reasonable period of time' to comply. Article 21.3 outlines three ways of determining a reasonable period of time: (1) the Member concerned proposes a period and the DSB approves (by consensus) the nominated timeline; (2) the complaining party and implementing Member agree on an implementation period within 45 days following adoption of the ruling; or (3) if neither of the first two methods occur, the period can be set by binding arbitration (to be completed within 90 days following adoption of the report). In practice, the Member concerned usually first informs the DSB of its intention to implement the rulings of the DSB. If prompt compliance is impracticable, and in most instances it is or is claimed to be, the Member concerned proposes what it considers to be a reasonable period of time in which to comply with the rulings of the DSB and consults with the other parties to the dispute in an attempt to reach agreement. If agreement cannot be reached, the parties request binding arbitration to determine the reasonable period. In this arbitration, the parties make written submissions to the arbitrator, who is normally a past or present Appellate Body Member. The arbitrator holds a hearing in which the parties present and explain their arguments and respective positions. The arbitrator(s) then make(s) a decision as to the reasonable period, with Article 21.3(c) offering the 'guideline' that the reasonable period should not exceed 15 months from the date the ruling was adopted. However, it 'may be shorter or longer, depending upon the particular circumstances' of the dispute.

In addition to the timing and means of compliance issues, the DSU provides for monitoring of the implementation process. Article 21.6 of the DSU requires the DSB to keep the losing party 'under surveillance' from the onset of the 'reasonable period' until the issue is resolved. More specifically, this provision says that the losing member must provide regular 'status reports' beginning six months into each implementation period and continuing through subsequent DSB meetings. However, the implementing Member is not required to identify the specific changes, such as whether it will remove or amend the measures at issue, that will bring it into compliance with the ruling. Members are not even required to specify any sort of implementation schedule or consult with the winning party over the means of implementation, aside from the reasonable period issues.

Despite the limited requirements imposed on the losing party in terms of how it will come into compliance, the losing party nevertheless often actively consults with the winning party during the implementation period to ensure compliance is reached. On the other hand, a Member could use its reasonable period to delay the process and evade its obligations.

(e) Compliance Review

Article 21.5 provides, 'where there is disagreement as to the existence or consistency with a covered agreement of measures taken to comply with the recommendations and rulings such *dispute shall be decided through recourse to these dispute settlement procedures*, including wherever possible resort to the original panel.' (emphasis added). Article 21.5 also directs the panel to circulate its report within 90 days after the date of referral of the matter, but it provides no other explanation of exactly what the Article means by 'these dispute settlement procedures', when those procedures may or must be invoked or who may invoke them.

In practice, the provision is most often invoked by the complainant state after the expiry of a reasonable period of time for implementation by the respondent state. If compliance has been attempted by the respondent state, the conformity of its compliance measures must be decided by a neutral body before authorisation to suspend concessions can be granted.

The scope of Article 21.5 proceedings has a close relation to the original proceedings, but there are also some differences between them. Article 21.5 specifically refers to the 'measures taken to comply', and it is these measures that will be the focus of the proceedings. Therefore, the claims, arguments and factual circumstances raised in the Article 21.5 compliance review may not necessarily be the same as those that were pertinent or relevant in the original dispute (although there might be some overlap). For instance, the Article 21.5 compliance panel can sometimes make findings even when the provisions of the covered agreements with which violations are alleged were not included in the original case.[25] However, the measures and rulings in the original dispute will play a role in the Article 21.5 proceeding.[26]

To illustrate one of the ways these issues can arise, in *Australia—Salmon*, Australia claimed that one of the measures at issue in the Article 21.5 proceeding was a new measure governing the matter, not a 'measure taken to comply' with the ruling of the DSB, and thus should not be within the terms of reference of the DSU Article 21.5 panel.[27] The panel rejected the argument, holding that measures enacted by a Member (or, in this case, an authority in the territory of a Member) subsequent to the original dispute that are in the 'category of' or 'closely related' to the measures identified in the panel request, namely 'measures to comply with the recommendations and rulings of the DSB' that 'Australia has taken or does take', are within the panel's terms of reference.[28] Furthermore, the panel noted that it could not grant the implementing Member the power to deem whether a measure is 'taken to comply', stating that if this were the rule, then a Member could avoid Article 21.5 scrutiny by simply deeming a measure not to be 'taken to comply', even if the measure was 'clearly connected' to the DSB ruling at issue.[29] The reason behind this approach is simple: the Australian position would have effectively forced Canada to open a new dispute and repeat every formal step of the dispute settlement process. Such a position seems extremely unfair and would result in a circular situation where another new measure could be introduced every time an old measure was deemed to violate a Member's WTO obligations, thereby forcing a new complaint to be filed and the process repeated, with no ultimate resolution reached.

It was noted above that Article 21.5 is most often invoked by complainant states.

---

[25] Panel Report, *United States—FSCs, Article 21.5*, paras 8.123–8.158. The original proceedings did not include a claim under GATT, but the Art 21.5 compliance panel found that the new measures taken by the US were inconsistent with Art III:4 of GATT. See Appellate Body Report, *United States—FSCs, Article 21.5*, paras 197–213.

[26] See Appellate Body Report, *Canada—Aircraft, Article 21.5*, para 41.

[27] See Panel Report, *Australia—Salmon, Article 21.5*, para 7.10, sub-para 27.

[28] *Ibid.*

[29] *Ibid*, para 7.10, sub-paras 22–23.

Following *Canada/US—Continued Suspension*,[30] it is clear that respondent states can also invoke the provision. As noted by the Appellate Body:

> A 'disagreement' as to the consistency with the WTO agreements of a measure taken to comply arises from the existence of conflicting views: the original complainant's view that such a measure is inconsistent with the WTO agreements or brings about only partial compliance, and the original respondent's view that a measure is consistent with the WTO agreements and brings about full compliance with the DSB's recommendations and rulings. Article 21.5 does not indicate which party may initiate proceedings under this provision. Rather, the language of the provision is neutral on this matter, and it is open to either party to refer the matter to an Article 21.5 panel to resolve this disagreement. The text of Article 21.5, therefore, leaves open the possibility that either party to the original dispute may initiate the proceedings. Thus, contrary to the European Communities' argument, the text of Article 21.5 does not preclude an original respondent from initiating proceedings under that provision to obtain confirmation of the consistency with the WTO agreements of its implementing measure.[31]

(f) Compensation and the Suspension of Concessions or Other Obligations

If compliance is not achieved, there are two possibilities for resolution of the dispute: (1) compensation offered by the party who failed to implement; or (2) suspension of concessions or other obligations by the complainant. We discuss each below.

(i) Compensation[32]

If the implementing Member fails to comply fully with the rulings and recommendations of the DSB by the end of the reasonable period of time, Article 22.2 requires that, if so requested, the Member enter into consultations with the complaining party with a view to mutually agreeing on compensation. Compensation, as the term is used in the DSU, does not necessarily mean monetary payment or other remuneration. Instead, the respondent Member will provide additional trade benefits to the complaining Member, often in the form of a reduction of the tariff rate on other products, or greater market access for certain goods of the complaining Member, equivalent to the benefit the respondent Member has nullified or impaired through the ongoing application of its measure. Therefore, compensation is not retroactive, in that it does not compensate the complaining Member for the past harmful effects of the respondent Member's measure. Rather, compensation is prospective in that the respondent Member will 'compensate' the complaining Member for its continued breach of WTO obligations.

In the negotiations, the parties must be mindful of the Article 22.1 mandate requiring the parties to reach an agreement on compensation in a manner which is consistent with the covered agreements. Thus, according to a strict interpretation of this requirement, any agreement on compensation must be in conformity with all WTO obligations – including

---

[30] Appellate Body Reports, *Canada/United States—Continued Suspension of Obligations in the EC—Hormones Dispute*.

[31] *Ibid*, para 347.

[32] For a more complete treatment of this area, see A Davies, 'Reviewing Dispute Settlement at the World Trade Organization: A Time to Reconsider the Role/s of Compensation?' (2006) 5 *World Trade Review* 31. See also B Mercurio, "Why Compensation Cannot Replace Trade Retaliation in the WTO Dispute Settlement Understanding' (2009) 8(2) *World Trade Review* 31.

the most favoured nation clause. Under such an interpretation, any benefit granted to the complaining party (such as a tariff reduction on certain goods) would also have to be granted to all other WTO Members.

In practice, compensation has been used only sparingly, with one of the few examples occurring in the *Turkey—Textiles* dispute.[33] A mutually satisfactory solution involving trade compensation was notified in July 2001. Turkey agreed to tariff reductions on 15 categories of chemicals by way of trade compensation. There is no indication that these tariffs were reduced only in respect of chemicals from the complaining Member (India). The trade compensation appears therefore to have been granted on an MFN basis.

Generally speaking, where it is perceived that compliance has not been achieved, the complaining Member opts for suspension of concessions or other obligations, rather than compensation.

(ii) Suspension of Concessions or Other Obligations

If the Member complained against fails to implement the WTO ruling, and a compensatory agreement cannot be reached within 20 days after the expiration of the 'reasonable period', the complaining Member may, pursuant to Article 22.2 of the DSU, request authorisation from the DSB to suspend the application to the Member complained against of concessions or other obligations under the covered agreements. Article 22.6 further states that in this situation: 'the DSB, upon request, shall grant authorisation to suspend concessions or other obligations within 30 days of the expiry of the reasonable period', unless there is consensus otherwise or the losing party refers the requested suspension amount to arbitration. In practice, these requests are always referred to arbitration. If the suspension request is referred to arbitration, Article 22 instructs the original panel, if available, to determine whether the requested suspension amount is 'equivalent to the level of nullification or impairment' and to issue its determination within 60 days after the expiration of the reasonable period.[34] The procedures followed by the complaining party in making its request may also be challenged as part of the arbitration. Following the arbitration decision, the DSB, upon request, must then authorise a suspension of concessions or other obligations consistent with that decision.

The suspension of concessions or other obligations is commonly referred to as 'retaliation', as concessions or other obligations are suspended only when the Member complained against fails to implement the rulings of the DSB. The suspension can take numerous forms, but, in terms of trade in goods, it usually includes temporary increases in tariff rates by the complaining Member on certain products from the Member complained against.

There is some disagreement as to the goal of retaliation.[35] Some would argue that the objective is to rebalance the tariff concessions and other obligations which Members have agreed to. Thus, if one Member is violating the rules and thereby nullifying or impairing

---

[33] *Turkey—Restrictions on Imports of Textile and Clothing Products.*

[34] The procedure to be used when there is a prohibited or actionable subsidy under the SCM Agreement differs. See SCM Agreement, Arts 4 and 7.

[35] See H Spamann, 'The Myth of "Rebalancing" Retaliation in WTO Dispute Settlement Practice' (2006) 9(1) *Journal of International Economic Law* 31; for the rebalancing view see D Palmeter, 'The WTO Dispute Settlement Mechanism, Compliance with WTO Rulings and other Procedural Problems' (2001) 4(2) *The Journal of World Intellectual Property* 291.

benefits, the other Member can violate the rules as well to restore the original balance. On the other hand, it is also said that the purpose is to induce the Member complained against to comply with its obligations under the covered agreements. In this regard, retaliatory measures often target powerful interest groups from the territory of the Member complained against in order to encourage them to lobby for compliance. For instance, in *EC—Bananas*, one of the complaining parties, the US, suspended the concessions on certain meat products, pecorino cheese, sweet biscuits, candles, bed linen, electrothermic coffee and tea makers and handbags, even though the original matter concerned restrictions on the importation and distribution of bananas.[36] Under this view, the suspension of concessions or other obligations is designed to be a temporary measure pending full implementation of the DSB report. The ultimate goal is to have the offending measure brought into compliance, and suspension is designed to achieve this outcome.[37]

As a general rule, Article 22.3(a) of the DSU provides that complaining parties should first seek to suspend concessions or other obligations with respect to the same sector(s) as that in which the panel or Appellate Body has found a violation or other nullification or impairment. Thus, if the violation relates to the GATT, the retaliatory measures should target goods. However, while all goods are grouped as one sector, this is not the case for every covered agreement. For instance, trade in services (GATS) is classified into 12 sectors (such as business services, communication services, construction and related engineering services, distribution service, educational services, etc), and retaliatory measures should first be sought within the specific sector of the infringing measures.

If the complaining party does not consider it practicable or effective to suspend concessions or other obligations with respect to the same sector(s), it may seek to suspend concessions or other obligations in other sectors under the same agreement. For instance, if the measures taken by the Member concerned relate to the financial services sector of trade in services and suspension in that sector is not practicable or effective for the complaining party, it may target another sector, such as the educational services sector. Likewise, if the measures taken by the Member concerned relate to the patent sector under the TRIPS Agreement, but the complaining party does not consider it practicable or effective to suspend concessions or other obligations with respect to the patent sector, its retaliation may target another sector within TRIPS, such as the trade mark sector.

Finally, if the complaining party does not consider it practicable or effective to suspend concessions or other obligations with respect to other sectors under the same agreement, and the circumstances are serious enough, Article 22.3(c) of the DSU allows the complaining party to suspend concessions or other obligations under another covered agreement. Thus, if the measures taken by the Member complained against relating to financial services are found inconsistent with GATS, and the complaining party does not consider it practicable or effective to suspend concessions or other obligations with respect to any other sector in the GATS, the complaining party's retaliation may target aspects

---

[36] See *EC—Bananas, Recourse by the United States to Article 22.2 of the DSU*, WTO Doc No WT/DS27/43 (14 January 1999) 3.

[37] For a debate on the obligation to implement a DSB decision, see J Bello, 'The WTO Dispute Settlement Understanding: Less Is More' (1996) 90 *American Journal of International Law* 416; JH Jackson, 'The WTO Dispute Settlement Understanding–Misunderstandings on the Nature of Legal Obligation' (1997) 91 *American Journal of International Law* 60; W Schwartz and A Sykes, 'The Economic Structure of Renegotiation and Dispute Resolution in the World Trade Organization' (2002) 31 *Journal of* Legal Studies 179; JH Jackson, 'International Law Status of WTO Dispute Settlement Reports: Obligation to Comply or Option to "Buy Out"?' (2004) 98 *American Journal of International Law* 109.

of another agreement, such as intellectual property rights under the TRIPS Agreement or trade in goods under the GATT. The use of retaliatory measures against a different agreement is commonly referred to as 'cross-retaliation'. The ability to cross-retaliate is of the utmost importance to smaller and developing countries due to: (1) the fact that imports in a particular sector or agreement may not be large enough to have much impact; (2) the asymmetrical relationship that many smaller and developing countries have with larger trading nations; and (3) the fact that many smaller and developing countries rely upon certain imports from larger nations and raising barriers will decrease supply and/or increase the price of the product to its domestic producers and consumers.

The Arbitrators in *EC—Bananas (Ecuador)* clarified the circumstances in which a complaining Member may request the suspension of concessions with respect to a different agreement. In this case, Ecuador requested the suspension of concessions of TRIPS obligations, as opposed to the suspension of obligations under the GATT and/or in service sectors under the GATS other than distribution services (the sectors at issue in the dispute) because it considered that it would not be practicable or effective in the meaning of Article 22.3(b) and (c) of the DSU, and that circumstances in Ecuador's bananas trade sector and the economy on the whole were serious enough to justify suspension under another agreement. In response, the EC argued that in making its request, Ecuador did not follow the principles and procedures set forth in subparagraphs (b) and (c) (arguing that Ecuador had not demonstrated why it is not practicable or effective for it to suspend concessions under the GATT or commitments under the GATS in service sectors other than distribution services; that circumstances were not serious enough for requesting suspension under another agreement; and that Ecuador had not taken into account the parameters in subparagraphs (i) and (ii) of Article 22.3(d)). The Arbitrators found as follows:

Article 22.6 Arbitration Decision, *European Communities—Regime for the Importation, Sale and Distribution of Bananas, Recourse to Arbitration by the European Communities* Circulated 18 May 2000, WT/DS27/ARB/ECU

1. General Interpretation of the Principles and Procedures Set Forth in Article 22.3

69. . . . In this case, our examination of the EC's claim that Ecuador has not followed the principles and procedures set forth in subparagraphs (a-e) of Article 22.3 requires us to analyze the following issues:

(a) First, whether suspension of concessions under the GATT as one of the same sectors as those where violations were found by the reconvened panel is "not practicable or effective";

(b) Second, whether suspension of commitments under the GATS in another subsector than wholesale trade services within the sector of distribution services is "not practicable or effective";

(c) Third, whether suspension of commitments under the GATS in another service sector than distribution services is "not practicable or effective";

(d) Fourth, whether "circumstances are serious enough" to seek suspension under another agreement than those where violations were found;

(e) Fifth, whether the trade in the sector(s) under the agreement(s) under which violations were found and the "importance of such trade to the party" suffering nullification or impairment were taken into account; and

(f) Sixth, whether "broader economic elements" related to nullification or impairment and the "broader economic consequences" of the requested suspension were taken into account.

70. Several of these issues require the party seeking suspension to consider whether an alternative suspension with respect to the same sectors or agreements under which a violation was found is "not practicable or effective". In this regard, we note that the ordinary meaning of "practicable" is "available or useful in practice; able to be used" or "inclined or suited to action as opposed to speculation etc.". In other words, an examination of the "practicability" of an alternative suspension concerns the question whether such an alternative is available for application in practice as well as suited for being used in a particular case.

71. To give an obvious example, suspension of commitments in service sub-sectors or in respect of modes of service supply which a particular complaining party has not bound in its GATS Schedule is not available for application in practice and thus cannot be considered as practicable. But also other case-specific and country-specific situations may exist where suspension of concessions or other obligations in a particular trade sector or area of WTO law may not be "practicable".

72. In contrast, the term "effective" connotes "powerful in effect", "making a strong impression", "having an effect or result". Therefore, the thrust of this criterion empowers the party seeking suspension to ensure that the impact of that suspension is strong and has the desired result, namely to induce compliance by the Member which fails to bring WTO-inconsistent measures into compliance with DSB rulings within a reasonable period of time.

73. One may ask whether this objective may ever be achieved in a situation where a great imbalance in terms of trade volume and economic power exists between the complaining party seeking suspension and the other party which has failed to bring WTO-inconsistent measures into compliance with WTO law. In such a case, and in situations where the complaining party is highly dependent on imports from the other party, it may happen that the suspension of certain concessions or certain other obligations entails more harmful effects for the party seeking suspension than for the other party. In these circumstances, a consideration by the complaining party in which sector or under which agreement suspension may be expected to be least harmful to itself would seem sufficient for us to find a consideration by the complaining party of the effectiveness criterion to be consistent with the requirement to follow the principles and procedures set forth in Article 22.3.

74. A consideration by the complaining party of the practicability and the effectiveness of an alternative suspension within the same sector or under the same agreement does not need to lead to the conclusion that such an alternative suspension is both not practicable and not effective in order to meet the requirements of Article 22.3. This is so because in no instance do subparagraphs of Article 22.3 require that an alternative suspension within the same sector or under the same agreement be neither practicable nor effective. Thus a consideration by the complaining party that an alternative suspension which does not concern other sectors or other agreements is either not practicable or not effective is sufficient for that party to move on to seek suspension under another sector or agreement.

75. In this context, we recall our considerations above concerning the allocation of the burden of proof in arbitration proceedings under Article 22 that in the light of the requirement in Article 22.3(e), the complaining party requesting suspension has to come forward and submit information giving reasons and explanations for its initial consideration of the principles and procedures set forth in Article 22.3 which led it to request authorization under another sector or another agreement than those where a violation was found. However, by the same token, it would then be for the other party to bear the ultimate burden of showing that suspension within the same sector or under the same agreement is both practicable and effective for the party

requesting suspension. This implies for the case before us that once Ecuador has laid out its considerations under Article 22.3, it is ultimately for the European Communities to establish that suspension of concessions on goods under the GATT or suspension of commitments in service sectors other than distribution services under the GATS are both practicable as well as effective for Ecuador given the case-specific and country-specific circumstances.

76. Our interpretation of the "practicability" and "effectiveness" criteria is consistent with the object and purpose of Article 22 which is to induce compliance. If a complaining party seeking the DSB's authorization to suspend certain concessions or certain other obligations were required to select the concessions or other obligations to be suspended in sectors or under agreements where such suspension would be either not available in practice or would not be powerful in effect, the objective of inducing compliance could not be accomplished and the enforcement mechanism of the WTO dispute settlement system could not function properly.

77. In our view, it is important to point out that Article 22.3 sets out the criteria of practicability and effectiveness in the negative. On the one hand, establishing that something does not exist is often deemed more difficult than proving that it does exist. On the other hand, subparagraph (b) implies that Ecuador's considerations need to show that suspension is not practicable or effective with respect to the same sector(s) as those where a violation was found. That provision does not imply establishing that suspension is practicable and effective in other sectors under the same agreement. Likewise, subparagraph (c) implies showing that suspension is not practicable or effective with respect to other sectors under the same agreement(s) as those where a violation was found, it does not imply establishing that suspension is practicable and effective under another agreement.

78. This has important consequences for the examination of the case before us. They imply that our review of the effectiveness and practicability criteria focuses, in the light of the legal and factual arguments submitted by both parties, on Ecuador's considerations why it is not practicable or effective for it (i) to suspend concessions under the GATT or (ii) commitments under the GATS with respect to the distribution service sector for purposes of subparagraph (b), or (iii) to suspend commitments under the GATS with respect to service sectors other than distribution services for purposes of subparagraph (c). We emphasize that Article 22.3(b) and (c) does not require Ecuador, nor us, to establish that suspension of concessions or other obligations is practicable and/or effective under another agreement (i.e. the TRIPS Agreement) than those under which violations have been found (i.e. the GATT and the GATS). The burden is on the European Communities to establish that suspension within the same sector(s) and/or the same agreement(s) is effective and practicable. However, according to subparagraph (c) of Article 22.3, it is our task to review Ecuador's consideration that the "circumstances are serious enough" to warrant suspension across agreements.

79. From a contextual perspective, it should be stressed that the criteria of practicability and effectiveness are not set forth in subparagraphs (b) and (c) in isolation from the other subparagraphs of Article 22.3. These criteria have to be read in combination especially with the factors set out in subparagraphs (i) and (ii) of Article 22.3(d) which, as the introductory clause of subparagraph (d) stipulates, the complaining party seeking authorization for suspension shall take into account in applying the above principles, i.e. those provided for in subparagraphs (a)-(c).

80. We also note that the threshold for considering a request for suspension in another sector under the same agreement (e.g. service sectors other than distribution services) pursuant to subparagraph (b) is lower than the threshold for considering a request for suspension under another agreement pursuant to subparagraph (c) of Article 22.3. Suspension across sectors under the same agreement is permitted if suspension within the same sector is "not practicable

or effective". However, an additional condition applies when the complaining party considers a request for suspension across agreements. Such suspension under another agreement is not justified unless "circumstances are serious enough".

81. The concepts of "circumstances" and the degree of "seriousness" that are relevant for the analysis of this condition remain undefined in subparagraph (c). The provision specifies no threshold as to which circumstances are deemed "serious" enough so as to justify suspension under another agreement. We find useful guidance in the ordinary meaning of the term "serious" which connotes "important, grave, having (potentially) important, especially undesired, consequences; giving cause for concern; of significant degree or amount worthy of consideration". Arguably, the factors listed in subparagraph (d) provide at least part of the context for further defining these meanings.

82. More specifically, subparagraphs (i) of Article 22.3(d) provide that, in applying the principles set forth in subparagraph (a-c), the complaining party seeking authorization shall take into account, inter alia, the trade in the sector or under the agreement under which WTO inconsistencies were found, as well as the "importance of . . . trade" to that party.

83. The European Communities argues that this criterion concerns the trade in the sector(s) and/or the agreement(s) in question in their entirety, i.e. all trade in goods under the GATT, all trade in distribution services and/or all trade in services under the GATS. In contrast, Ecuador implies that in this case the "importance of such trade" refers to trade in goods and services in the bananas sector because the findings of the reconvened panel concern the revised EC regime for the importation, sale and distribution of bananas.

84. We do not exclude the possibility that trade in the relevant sector(s) and/or agreement(s) in their entirety may be relevant under subparagraph (d)(i). In particular, we deem it appropriate to consider the proportion of the trade area(s) affected by WTO-inconsistent measure(s) covered by the terms of reference of the reconvened panel in relation to the entire trade under the sector(s) and/or agreement(s) in question. However, we believe that the criteria of "such trade" and the "importance of such trade" to the complaining party relate primarily to trade nullified or impaired by the WTO inconsistent measure at issue. In the light of this interpretation, we attribute particular significance to the factors listed in subparagraph (i) in the case before us, where the party seeking suspension is a developing country Member, where trade in bananas and wholesale service supply with respect to bananas are much more important for that developing country Member than for the Member with respect to which the requested suspension would apply.

85. In contrast, subparagraph (ii) of Article 22.3(d) requires the complaining party to take into account in addition "broader economic elements" related to the nullification or impairment as well as "broader economic consequences" of the suspension of concessions or other obligations. The fact that the former criterion relates to "nullification or impairment" indicates in our view that this factor primarily concerns "broader economic elements" relating to the Member suffering such nullification or impairment, i.e. in this case Ecuador.

86. We believe, however, that the fact that the latter criterion relates to the suspension of concessions or other obligations is not necessarily an indication that "broader economic consequences" relate exclusively to the party which was found not to be in compliance with WTO law, i.e. in this case the European Communities. As noted above, the suspension of concessions may not only affect the party retaliated against, it may also entail, at least to some extent, adverse effects for the complaining party seeking suspension, especially where a great imbalance in terms of trade volumes and economic power exists between the two parties such as in this case where the differences between Ecuador and the European Communities

in regard to the size of their economies and the level of socio-economic development are substantial.

… … …

In applying the law to the facts of the case, the Arbitrators found that, overall, Ecuador followed the principles and procedures of Article 22.3 in requesting authorisation to suspend certain obligations under the TRIPS Agreement. More specifically, the Arbitrators found that Ecuador followed the principles and procedures of Article 22.3 in its consideration of whether suspension of concessions on primary and investment goods is practicable or effective; however, it concluded that Ecuador did not follow the principles and procedures of Article 22.3 in its consideration of whether suspension of concessions on these goods was practicable or effective with regard to consumer goods. Moreover, the Arbitrators found that Ecuador followed the principles and procedures of Article 22.3 in its consideration of whether suspension of these GATS commitments with respect to both sub-sectors of distribution services other than 'wholesale trade services' and sectors other than distribution services was practicable or effective. Overall, the Arbitrators concluded that Ecuador had acted in accordance with Article 22.3.[38]

(g) The Sequencing Debate

A keen eye would have noticed the apparent contradictory language between Articles 21.5 and 22.6 of the DSU. On the one hand, Article 21.5 provides, 'where there is disagreement as to the existence or consistency with a covered agreement of measures taken to comply with the recommendations and rulings such dispute *shall be decided through recourse to these dispute settlement procedures*' (emphasis added). In such circumstances, the compliance panel is directed to circulate its report within *90 days* after the date of referral of the matter. On the other hand, Article 22.6 of the DSU provides that when the Member concerned fails to implement the recommendations and rulings of the DSB within the compliance period or negotiate mutually acceptable compensation within 20 days after the 'reasonable period' expires, 'the DSB, upon request, shall grant authorization to suspend concessions or other obligations *within 30 days of the expiry of the reasonable period*' (emphasis added)—unless there is consensus otherwise or the losing party refers the requested suspension amount to arbitration. As a result, suspension is to be authorised *prior* to a finding that the Member complained against has not come into complianceThe DSU provides no guidance as to how to reconcile the Article 22.6 timeline with the compliance review procedures pursuant to Article 21.5. The matter is even more precarious when one considers that Article 23 of the DSU prohibits Members from unilaterally deciding if a measure nullifies or impairs its benefits under the WTO Agreement and subsequently taking action. The conflict between Articles 21.5 and 22 came to a head in the *EC—Bananas* dispute when the EC revised its banana import regime six months before the expiration of the reasonable period, but the complaining parties were of the view that the revisions did not bring the EC into compliance with the rulings and recommendations of the DSB.[39]

---

[38] Art 22.6 Arbitration Decision, *EC—Bananas (Ecuador)*, paras 87–138.
[39] The following is largely drawn from B Mercurio, 'Improving Dispute Settlement in the WTO: The DSU Review—Making It Work?' (2004) 38 *Journal of World Trade* 795.

Upon the expiration of the EC's compliance period, the US requested DSB authorisation to suspend concessions. When the request came before the DSB, the EC requested arbitration of the requested suspension amount. The Article 22 arbitrators (being also the Article 21.5 panelists) resolved the situation by compressing a review of the EC's new measures into their analysis of whether the US request amount was equivalent to the level of nullification or impairment.[40] The Arbitrators reasoned that they could not complete their Article 22 task of assessing the equivalence between the proposed suspension and the nullification or impairment at issue without deciding on the consistency of the revised EC regime. Thus, three and a half months after the expiration of the EC's reasonable period of time (almost two months beyond the DSU deadline for arbitral rulings), the arbitrators issued decisions in the Article 21.5 and Article 22 proceedings. Both rulings found the revised EC regime inconsistent with WTO obligations and the Article 22 Arbitrators authorised the US suspension of concessions in the amount of $US191.4 million.[41]

Thus, a tense situation was only resolved by reaching an improvised solution. But this solution did not completely resolve the crisis, as the text of the DSU is still contradictory or, at the very least, uncertain and confusing. Subsequent disputes have relied on equally creative 'voluntary agreements' to solve the textual deficiency of the DSU. Two approaches to allow Members to temporarily avoid the sequencing issue have developed. Under the first approach, the parties agree to initiate concurrent procedures under Article 21.5 and Article 22.6. In this approach, Article 22 proceedings are suspended until the Article 21.5 procedure is complete. If the Article 21.5 proceedings find that the respondent has failed to comply with the original ruling, then the complainant can re-commence Article 22 proceedings.[42]

In the second method of 'voluntary agreements', the parties undertake an Article 21.5 review prior to initiating procedures to suspend concessions, thereby waiving the Article 22 timetable under the condition that if non-compliance were found, the losing party would not object to a suspension request (even though it was made outside the time-period). The undertakings do not prohibit the Member concerned from contesting the level of suspension requested.

While the voluntary agreements have placated the situation, the 'sequencing debate' has assumed a prominent position in the DSU Review taking place in the context of the Doha round.

As a final point, thus far only a handful of disputes have involved an effective admission by the losing party that it had failed to come into compliance.[43] Such an admission enables the complainants to proceed directly to Article 22 following the expiration of the reasonable period of time.

---

[40] Art 22.6 Arbitration Decision, *EC—Bananas*, paras 4.1–4.9 (citing the DSB Chairman's statement of 29 January 1999).

[41] See *ibid*; Panel Report, *EC—Bananas, Article 21.5 (Ecuador)*, WT/DS27/RW/ECU (12 April 1999); Art 22.6 Arbitration Decision, *EC – Bananas*, para 8.1 (citing the DSB Chairman's statement of 29 January 1999). The US had requested $US520 million in suspension of concessions.

[42] This approach was first used in *Australia—Salmon, Recourse to Art 21.5 of the DSU by Canada*, Communication from the Chairman of the Panel, WT/DS18/17 (13 December 1999).

[43] See, eg *EC—Hormones, US—1916 Act, Canada—Aircraft II* and *US—Offset Act*.

V. ALTERNATIVES TO DISPUTE SETTLEMENT: MEDIATION AND ARBITRATION

The DSU complaint procedure is inherently contentious, as it may involve a finding that a Member is in violation of a WTO obligation and it allows for the possibility of trade sanctions (ie retaliation under Article 22 of the DSU). Members who wish to take a less confrontational approach may avail themselves of other dispute resolution techniques under the DSU. In this regard, Article 5 of the DSU provides for the possibility of 'good offices, conciliation and mediation'. In essence, these procedures offer a way for disputing parties to use a neutral arbitrator to find a solution in a more peaceful manner. To date, only one of these possibilities—mediation—has been invoked.[44]

In addition to the alternatives enumerated in Article 5, Members may resolve a dispute through binding arbitration conducted under Article 25 of the DSU. In order for this to occur, the parties involved in the dispute must agree on the issues to be resolved and procedures to be used during the arbitration. Arbitration awards are binding, cannot be appealed and are enforceable through the DSU (ie retaliatory measures can be imposed for non-compliance with an award).

To date, there has been only one arbitration convened under Article 25. The arbitration, involving the US and EC in the *US—Copyright* dispute, arose following the panel decision in the dispute (adopted by the DSB on 27 July 2000), which found US measures relating to royalty payments for the playing of recorded music in certain establishments to be in violation of Article 13 of the TRIPS Agreement and inconsistent with Articles 11*bis*(1)(iii) and 11(1)(ii) of the Berne Convention (1971). Following almost a year of negotiations, the parties notified the DSB of their mutual agreement to resort to arbitration under Article 25 of the DSU. The stated objective of the arbitration was to determine the level of nullification or impairment of benefits to the EC caused by the US measure at issue,[45] and both parties also publicly stated that the less confrontational Article 25 proceedings were chosen in favour of the more formal Article 22 proceedings in order to facilitate a compensatory resolution to the dispute.[46] After reviewing the evidence and determining an appropriate methodology, the Arbitrators held that the level of EC benefits being nullified or impaired as a result of the US measure was € 1,219,900 per year.[47] In contrast to the DSU rules on compensation, the parties planned to use this amount as the basis for calculating a monetary payment from the US to certain groups in the EC.

---

[44] Mediation was successfully utilised in a dispute involving Thailand and the Philippines on one side and the EC on the other, although Art 5 was not mentioned explicitly. See N Xuto, 'Thailand: Conciliating a Dispute on Tuna Exports to the EC' in P Gallagher, P Low and AL Stoler (eds), *Managing the Challenges of WTO Participation: 45 Case Studies* (Cambridge, Cambridge University Press, 2005), ch 40.

[45] Award of the Arbitrators, *US—Copyright*, Recourse to Arbitration under DSU Art 25, WT/DS160/ARB25/1, 9 November 2001, para 1.1.

[46] See US first written submission, para 4, available at http://www.ustr.gov; 'EU and US Agree on Procedures for Exploring Compensation in the Copyright Dispute', IP/01/1098, 25 July 2001, available at http://europa.eu/rapid/pressReleasesAction.do?reference=IP/01/1098&format=HTML&aged=0&language=EN&guiLanguage=en (accessed on 7 August 2007).

[47] Award of the Arbitrators, *US—Copyright*, Recourse to Arbitration under DSU Article 25, WT/DS160/ARB25/1, 9 November 2001, para 5.1.

VI. STATISTICS ON WTO DISPUTE SETTLEMENT

K Leitner and S Lester, 'WTO Dispute Settlement 1995-2011—A Statistical Analysis'
15 *Journal of International Economic Law* (2012) 315

I. WTO COMPLAINTS

Generally, a 'complaint' arises under WTO dispute settlement when one Member requests consultations with another Member pursuant to the DSU. For each 'complaint', the WTO Secretariat assigns an individual dispute settlement (DS) number. As of 1 January 2012, there have been 427 WTO complaints filed under the DSU. Over the past 16 years, the number of complaints filed each year has been as follows:

	1995–99	2000–04	2005–09	2010–11
Complaints	185	139	78	25
Average complaints per year	37	28	16	12.5

It should be noted that some DS numbers relate to complaints that are very similar in terms of the measures and legal claims at issue, such that they could be considered as part of the same 'matter'.[3] For example, of the 37 complaints brought in 2002, eight of these related to the *U.S—.—Steel Safeguards* dispute, with separate complaints filed by eight different Members. Thus, the number of 'matters' is an important alternative measure of the degree of use of the WTO dispute settlement system.

Unfortunately, identifying 'matters' is a bit subjective, as it involves a judgment as to the degree of similarity and overlap between complaints, and therefore it is difficult to provide a precise number. Based on our own assessment, the number of 'matters' that have been subject to WTO dispute settlement is somewhat less than the number of complaints, with a total of 315 over the period 1995–2011, broken down as follows:

	1995–99	2000–04	2005–09	2010–11
Matters	130	109	56	19
Average matters per year	26	22	11	9.5

In terms of the WTO Members that have been involved in disputes, Tabless 1 and 2 break down the number of complaints filed by and against some of the more active WTO Members.

From Tables 1 and 2, it is clear that the heaviest users of the WTO dispute settlement system have been the USA and the European Union. In this regard, we note that 183 complaints have involved either the USA or the European Union as a complaining party, which constitutes 42.9% of the total complaints. Similarly, 184 complaints have involved either the USA or the European Union as the responding party, comprising 43.1% of the total complaints. Furthermore, 51 disputes have been directly between the USA and the European Union. However, the statistics also show that the number of complaints brought by the USA and the European Union has declined in recent years, and that other WTO Members have been consistently active in WTO disputes.

Table 1 Complaining parties in WTO disputes

	1995–99	2000–04	2005–09	2010–11	Total
Brazil	6	16	2	1	25
Canada	15	11	7	0	33
Chile	2	7	1	0	10
China	0	1	5	2	8
EU	47	21	13	4	85
India	9	7	2	1	19
Japan	8	4	1	1	14
Korea	3	9	2	1	15
Mexico	8	5	8	0	21
USA	60	20	13	5	98
Other—developed	12	6	4	0	22
Other—developing	34	40	20	10	104
Other—least developed	0	1	0	0	1
Total	204	148	78	25	455

Table 2 Responding parties in WTO disputes

	1995–99	2000–04	2005–09	2010–11	Total
Brazil	9	3	2	0	14
Canada	10	3	2	2	17
Chile	3	7	3	0	13
China	0	1	16	6	23
EU	28	23	16	3	79
India	13	4	3	0	20
Japan	12	2	1	0	15
Korea	11	2	1	0	14
Mexico	3	9	2	0	14
USA	39	49	20	5	113
Other—developed	20	4	1	0	25
Other—developing	37	32	11	9	89
Other—least developed	0	0	0	0	0
Total	185	139	78	25	427

The heavy use of the system by the USA and the European Union highlights the fact that high income countries are the primary users of the dispute settlement system. However, countries with lower incomes do use the system as well, and this usage has increased in recent years.

...

In terms of the subject-matter of the complaints, a wide range of WTO agreements has been invoked. The break-down of the agreements invoked over the 1995–2011 period is as shown in Table 5.

Table 5 Breakdown of the agreements invoked over the 1995–2010 period

Agreement	1995–99	2000–04	2005–09	2010–11	Total
AD	21	38	21	10	90
Agriculture	33	22	9	0	64
ATC	11	5	0	0	16
Customs	6	5	4	0	15
GATS	10	5	4	1	20
GATT	125	115	70	23	333
GPA	4	0	0	0	4
Licensing	25	8	1	0	34
Rules of origin	3	1	3	0	7
Safeguards	9	22	5	4	40
SCM	31	30	22	5	88
SPS	16	14	6	1	37
TBT	22	11	7	1	41
TRIMs	15	4	6	2	27
TRIPS	20	5	1	2	28

Table 5 shows that in terms of the total number of complaints, the GATT has, by far, been invoked the most frequently. The frequent invocation of the GATT is because many complaints refer to the provisions of other, more specific substantive agreements, as well as to the more general provisions of the GATT. The trend of complaints over the years shows a generally high level of 'trade remedy' complaints brought pursuant to the AD, Safeguards and SCM Agreements. With regard to some of the 'new' areas of regulation—such as services, intellectual property and SPS measures—the number of complaints has been limited, but fairly steady, over this period, although there has been a decline in recent years.

II. WTO 'DECISIONS'

We turn now to an examination of the 'Decisions' reached through WTO dispute settlement proceedings. In particular, we will look at the following: panel reports, Appellate Body reports, DSU Article 22.6 arbitration decisions, DSU Article 21.3(c) arbitration awards, DSU Article 25 arbitration awards and other arbitrations. Except where explicitly indicated, this section does not include panel and Appellate Body reports resulting from DSU Article 21.5 'compliance' disputes, which are considered separately in the next section.

A. Panel reports

The number of panel reports circulated each year since the establishment of the WTO is as follows:

	1995–99	2000–04	2005–09	2010–11
Panel reports	37	55	34	19
Panel reports per year	7.4	11	6.8	9.5

B. Appellate body reports

One of the most important aspects of the DSU is the opportunity for appellate review, a possibility that did not exist under the GATT 1947. Appellate review has been used quite heavily at the WTO. As of 1 January 2011, the total number of circulated panel reports, as set out in the previous section, that were later appealed is as follows (not including circulated panel reports where the deadline for appeal had not yet occurred at the time of this writing):

Year	Total panel reports circulated	Circulated panel reports that were appealed
1995	0	0
1996	4	4
1997	10	10
1998	10	7
1999	13	10
2000	18	11
2001	7	5
2002	10	5
2003	9	6
2004	11	9
2005	13	7
2006	3	2
2007	7	3
2008	8	7
2009	3	1
2010	9	6
2011	8 (there were 10 total panel reports circulated in 2011, as noted in the previous table, but an appeal decision is still pending in 2 of those)	5
Total	132	90

Based on figures presented in the above table, the percentage of panel reports appealed to date is 68%. An appeal of a panel report occurs when one of the parties to the dispute files a notice of appeal. In addition, though, other parties to the dispute may file a notice of 'other' appeal. As of 1 January 2012, 56.31% of completed appellate proceedings have involved an 'other' appeal of this type.

The number of Appellate Body reports circulated each year has been as follows:

	1995–99	2000–04	2005–09	2010–11
Appellate body reports	25	31	22	7
Appellate body reports per year	5	6.2	4.4	3.5

C. Reasonable period of time arbitrations

DSU Article 21.3 provides that where immediate compliance with an adverse panel or Appellate Body report is 'impracticable', implementation must be completed within a reasonable period of time. Where the parties to the dispute cannot agree on the length of this period, Article 21.3(c) establishes an arbitration process. In practice, the arbitrator in all such proceedings has been a past or present Appellate Body Member, although the rules do not require that this be the case.

The number of Article 21.3(c) arbitration awards circulated over the past 16 years is as follows:

	1995–99	2000–04	2005–09	2010–11
Article 21.3.c(3)(c) arbitrations	6	11	8	0

D. Arbitrations on the level of suspension of concessions or other obligations

DSU Article 22.6 provides for the possibility of arbitration in situations where there is a disagreement regarding the proposed level of 'suspension of concessions or other obligations'. Article 22.6 arbitrations are normally conducted by the original panel hearing the dispute. SCM Agreement Articles 4.11 and 7.10 provide special and additional rules for Article 22.6 arbitration proceedings that relate to certain types of subsidies.

The number of Article 22.6 arbitration decisions circulated by year is as follows:

	1995–99	2000–04	2005–09	2010–11
Article 22.(6) arbitrations	3	6	3	0

E. Article 25 arbitrations

DSU Article 25 sets forth a general provision for arbitration. Only one arbitration has been conducted under this provision. This arbitration occurred in the *U.S—.—Copyright* dispute, and it related to the level of nullification or impairment resulting from the findings of violation by the panel in that case.

F. Other arbitrations

In 2005, an arbitration was carried out pursuant to the procedures in the Annex to the ACP-EC Partnership Agreement ('Doha Waiver'). The issue was whether the European Union's 'envisaged rebinding' of its tariff on bananas would result in at least maintaining total market access for MFN banana suppliers, taking into account the relevant EU commitments, as required by the Waiver. A second arbitration was later carried out to determine whether the European Union had 'rectified the matter' based on the first arbitration decision.

III. IMPLEMENTATION DISPUTES UNDER DSU ARTICLE 21.5

A significant improvement to WTO dispute settlement rules agreed to during the Uruguay Round was the inclusion of special dispute settlement provisions that may be invoked '[w]here there is disagreement as to the existence or consistency with a covered agreement of measures taken to comply with the recommendations and rulings . . .'. In this situation, DSU Article 21.5 allows for a complaint under procedures that use a shortened time-frame.

Since the start of the WTO, 41 of these disputes have been initiated, sometimes with a formal request for consultations and sometimes going straight to a panel request. The number of these complaints on a yearly basis is as follows:

	1995–99	2000–04	2005–09	2010–11
Complaints	8	15	18	1

With regard to Article 21.5 panel reports, the following table shows the number of panel reports circulated each year:

	1995–99	2000–04	2005–09	2010–11
Panel Reports	2	11	15	0

As to appellate review of Article 21.5 disputes, the total number of circulated Article 21.5 panel reports that were later appealed is as follows:

Year	Total Article 21.5 panel reports circulated	Circulated Article 21.5 panel reports that were appealed
1995	0	0
1996	0	0
1997	0	0
1998	0	0
1999	2	0
2000	4	2
2001	5	4
2002	2	2
2003	0	0
2004	0	0
2005	5	3
2006	3	3
2007	3	1
2008	3	3
2009	1	1
2010	0	0
2011	0	0
Total	28	19

To date, the percentage of Article 21.5 panel reports appealed is 67.9% . ..

IV.   PANELISTS

As noted above, the USA and the European Union are far and away the biggest users of the WTO dispute settlement system. With regard to the appointment of panelists, DSU Article 8.3 provides:

Citizens of Members whose governments[6] are parties to the dispute or third parties as defined in paragraph 2 of Article 10 shall not serve on a panel concerned with that dispute, unless the parties to the dispute agree otherwise.

[6]In the case where customs unions or common markets are parties to a dispute, this provision applies to citizens of all member countries of the customs unions or common markets.

As a result of the additional hurdle for prospective panelists who are citizens of one of the parties to the dispute, citizens of the USA and of EU Member countries play a relatively small role, in comparison to these Members' participation in disputes, as panelists, as they are unlikely to serve as panelists in disputes where these Members are parties. The consequence is that WTO panelists tend to come from countries who are active in WTO affairs but not the main users of the dispute settlement mechanism. Since 1995, the top 10 countries represented in terms of panelist positions, taking into account circulated panel reports only, has been as shown in Table 6.

Table 6. The top 10 countries represented in terms of panelist positions since 1995

Rank	Country	Number of panelist positions
1	New Zealand	46
2	Switzerland	40
3	Australia	39
4	Canada	27
5	Brazil	23
6	Chile	20
7	Hong Kong	19
8	South Africa	18
9	India	17
10	Mexico	14
10	Poland	14
10	Uruguay	14

Out of 501 total panelist positions, 195 were from six countries/customs territories: New Zealand, Switzerland, Australia, Canada, Brazil and Chile. In contrast, only 12 positions were taken by US citizens. The situation of the European Union is more complicated, as many countries have joined the European Union only recently. For example, note that in the above table Poland has 14 panelist positions. However, all of these were prior to 2004, the year Poland joined the European Union. The total number of panelist positions held by citizens of WTO Members that are now part of the EU is 71.

… … …

VII. INTERACTION OF THE DSU RULES WITH OTHER WTO AGREEMENTS

As noted, the DSU provides the primary rules on dispute settlement, and it applies to all WTO agreements. Article 1 of the DSU establishes that the agreement applies to disputes brought pursuant to the consultation and dispute settlement provisions of the covered agreements listed in Appendix 1 (the 'covered agreements'), including disputes brought under the DSU itself.

However, the DSU does not exclusively provide the rules and procedures guiding dispute settlement in all cases, as the other WTO agreements also have some of their own provisions. For the most part, the provisions on consultation and dispute settlement in the covered agreements simply refer back to or are closely modelled on the DSU and Articles XXII and XXIII of the GATT. In this regard, it can be said that the DSU complements the dispute rules outlined in each of the covered agreements, and it applies to any dispute brought pursuant to these provisions.

Some agreements, however, also include special or additional rules and procedures, as listed in appendix 2 of the DSU. For example, Articles 17.4–17.7 of the Agreement on Implementation of Article VI of GATT 1994 (Anti-dumping Agreement) provide a special standard of review to be used by panels considering disputes about anti-dumping measures. These rules prevail when there is a conflict between the DSU and the special or additional rules.[48] The Appellate Body has explained that the special and additional rules apply only in the case of 'inconsistency' or a 'difference' between these rules and the provisions of the DSU:

> Article 1.2 of the *DSU* provides that the "rules and procedures of this Understanding shall apply *subject to such special or additional rules and procedures* on dispute settlement contained in the covered agreements as are identified in Appendix 2 to this Understanding." (emphasis added) It states, furthermore, that these special or additional rules and procedures "shall prevail" over the provisions of the *DSU* '[t]o the extent that there is a *difference* between' the two sets of provisions (emphasis added) Accordingly, if there is no "difference," then the rules and procedures of the *DSU* apply *together with* the special or additional provisions of the covered agreement. In our view, it is only where the provisions of the *DSU* and the special or additional rules and procedures of a covered agreement *cannot* be read as *complementing* each other that the special or additional provisions are to *prevail*. A special or additional provision should only be found to *prevail* over a provision of the *DSU* in a situation where adherence to the one provision will lead to a violation of the other provision, that is, in the case of a *conflict* between them. An interpreter must, therefore, identify an *inconsistency* or a *difference* between a provision of the *DSU* and a special or additional provision of a covered agreement *before* concluding that the latter *prevails* and that the provision of the *DSU* does not apply.[49]

Generally speaking, the DSU and the special or additional rules in the covered agreements are applied together to form an integrated system and only in specific circumstances ('inconsistency' or 'difference') will the special rules prevail. As many disputes involve more than one covered agreement, there is a possibility that the special rules of one agreement may conflict with the special rules of another covered agreement that has been invoked. In such circumstances, Article 1.2 of the DSU instructs the parties to

---

[48] See, eg Appellate Body Report, *Guatemala—Cement*, para 67.
[49] *Ibid*, para 65. See also Appellate Body Report, *US—FSCs*, para 159.

the dispute to attempt to reach agreement on the applicable rules and procedures to be used in the dispute settlement proceedings. If they cannot, the Chairman of the DSB, in consultation with the parties to the dispute, determines the rules and procedures.

VIII. IMPORTANT PROCEDURAL AND SYSTEMIC ISSUES

Over the years, a number of procedural and systemic issues have arisen in WTO dispute settlement, many of which are not explicitly addressed by the DSU. Some of them are quite complex, and we cannot do justice to them all in the brief space allotted here. However, we do provide a brief overview of the most important issues below.

(a) The Complaint

(i) Types of Complaints: Violation, Non-violation and Situation

As noted above, Article XXIII of the GATT sets out the circumstances in which complaints may be brought. First, it refers to two types of harms: (1) any benefit accruing directly or indirectly under the GATT is being nullified or impaired; and (2) that the attainment of any objective of the GATT is being impeded. It then describes three possible causes of this harm: (1) the failure of another Member to carry out its obligations under the GATT; (2) the application by another Member of any measure, whether or not it conflicts with the provisions of the GATT; or (3) the existence of any other situation. Matching each of these two harms with each of the three causes, there are six possible complaints. In practice, however, the 'attainment of any objective of [the GATT] is being impeded' claim has not been utilised, and thus for practical purposes it is only the three 'nullification or impairment' claims that are relevant.

The GATS and the TRIPS Agreement have similar provisions. The GATS provides for a straightforward violation complaint, with no mention of nullification or impairment, and it also includes a non-violation nullification or impairment complaint. The TRIPS Agreement provides for violation complaints, with a temporary moratorium on non-violation and situation complaints. We focus here on the GATT rules, as they have the most extensive jurisprudence. In this section, we discuss each of the three types of complaints related to 'nullification or impairment' of benefits. The common short names for these three types of complaints are: (1) violation; (2) non-violation; and (3) situation. We cover all three complaints below, but it should be noted that almost all complaints actually filed are violation complaints.

Before turning to this, however, we note the importance of the phrase 'nullification or impairment'. Article XXIII makes clear that a Member does not challenge another Member's measure as violating the rules directly. Rather, the challenge is based on the nullification or impairment of benefits as a result of measures alleged to cause a violation (or even measures that do not violate the rules or any other situation). Thus, the concept of nullification or impairment is, in theory anyway, of prime importance. In practice, though, as described below, nullification or impairment does not generally play a significant role in violation complaints, because there is a presumption that violations will result in nullification or impairment. With non-violation and situation complaints, on the other hand, nullification or impairment is a key issue.

a. Violation Complaint In a violation complaint, the complainant alleges that a measure of another Member breaches an obligation under one of the covered agreements and that this results in direct or indirect nullification or impairment of a benefit accruing to the complainant. The notion of a violation is straightforward, and there is no need to go into great detail here. A violation exists when a measure is inconsistent with WTO rules.

With regard to the requirement of nullification or impairment, Article 3.8 of the DSU states:

> In cases where there is an infringement of the obligations assumed under a covered agreement, the action is considered prima facie to constitute a case of nullification or impairment. This means that there is normally a presumption that a breach of the rules has an adverse impact on other Members' parties to that covered agreement, and in such cases, it shall be up to the Member against whom the complaint has been brought to rebut the charge.

In other words, once a violation has been established, there is a rebuttable presumption that the breach has caused nullification or impairment.

The presumption of nullification or impairment when a violation has been proven has been the subject of several disputes, but it has never been successfully rebutted. The issue arose in *EC—Bananas III*, where the EC attempted to 'rebut the presumption of nullification or impairment on the basis that the United States has never exported a single banana to the European Community, and therefore, could not possibly suffer any trade damage'.[50] In deciding the issue, the Appellate Body noted that the issues of nullification or impairment and of standing are 'closely related'. The Appellate Body then recognised, in relation to the question of whether the EC had rebutted the presumption of nullification or impairment, the fact that the 'United States is a producer of bananas and that a potential export interest by the United States cannot be excluded' and that the internal market of the US for bananas 'could be affected by the EC bananas regime and by its effects on world supplies and world prices of bananas'.[51] The Appellate Body then quoted the GATT panel in *US—Superfund* as follows:

> Article III:2, first sentence, cannot be interpreted to protect expectations on export volumes; it protects expectations on the competitive relationship between imported and domestic products. A change in the competitive relationship contrary to that provision must consequently be regarded *ipso facto* as a nullification or impairment of benefits accruing under the General Agreement. A demonstration that a measure inconsistent with Article III:2, first sentence, has no or insignificant effects would therefore in the view of the Panel not be a sufficient demonstration that the benefits accruing under that provision had not been nullified or impaired even if such a rebuttal were in principle permitted.[52]

For these reasons, the panel in *US—Superfund* decided, 'not to examine the submissions of the parties on the trade effects of the tax differential'.[53] The Appellate Body concluded

---

[50] See Appellate Body Report, *EC—Bananas*, paras 249–250.
[51] *Ibid*, para 251.
[52] *Ibid*, para 252 (quoting GATT Panel Report, *US—Petroleum Taxes*, para 5.1.9).
[53] *Ibid*, para 253.

that the reasoning of '*United States—Superfund* applies equally in this case' and concluded that the EC had not rebutted the presumption.[54]

In another dispute, *Turkey—Textiles*, Turkey attempted to rebut the presumption of
nullification or impairment in relation to its quantitative restrictions on imports of textile
and clothing products from India. In this regard, Turkey produced evidence showing
that imports of textile and clothing from India had actually increased since the Turkish
measures at issue had entered into force. The panel, in a finding that was not appealed,
rejected this argument:

> 9.204 We are of the view that it is not possible to segregate the impact of the quantitative
> restrictions from the impact of other factors. While recognising Turkey's efforts to liberalise
> its import regime on the occasion of the formation of its customs union with the European
> Communities, it appears to us that even if Turkey were to demonstrate that India's overall
> exports of clothing and textile products to Turkey have increased from their levels of previous
> years, is would not be sufficient to rebut the presumption of nullification and impairment caused
> by the existence of WTO incompatible import restrictions. Rather, at minimum, the question
> is whether exports have been what they would otherwise have been, were there no WTO
> incompatible quantitative restrictions against imports from India. Consequently, we consider
> that even if the presumption in Article 3.8 of the *DSU* were rebuttable, Turkey has not provided
> us with sufficient information to set aside the presumption that the introduction of these import
> restrictions on 19 categories of textile and clothing products has nullified and impaired the
> benefits accruing to India under GATT/WTO.[55]

Thus, the panel's view was that even if Turkey demonstrated that India's overall exports
of clothing and textile products to Turkey increased from their levels of previous years,
this would not be sufficient to rebut the presumption of nullification or impairment caused
by the existence of WTO-incompatible import restrictions. Instead, the proper question
in this situation, according to the panel, is whether exports would have been even greater
in the absence of these quantitative restrictions.

b. Non-violation Complaints In addition to the violation complaint, which is the standard
type of complaint, a complainant may also make a 'non-violation' complaint, pursuant to
Article XXIII:1(b) of the GATT. With this complaint, the complainant alleges that even
though there is no violation of any covered agreement, benefits have been nullified or
impaired as the result of the application of a measure of another Member.

The basic reason for the non-violation complaint is simple. There is a concern that
Members might act in a manner that complies with the letter of the law but nevertheless
frustrates an objective or undermines commitments contained in the agreement. In other
words, a non-violation complaint protects certain benefits Members have accrued under
the WTO agreements, and it guarantees that those benefits are not affected by measures
that are not regulated in these agreements and where such measures may not have been
foreseen at the conclusion of the agreement. In a sense, the non-violation remedy is a
way to ensure that Members act in good faith when carrying out their WTO obligations.

The existence of the non-violation remedy is best understood in the context of the
original GATT, which had only limited coverage with regard to trade rules. For example,
subsidies were subject to only minimal regulation at this time. Thus, for example, it

---

[54] *Ibid.*
[55] Panel Report, *Turkey—Textiles*, para 9.204.

was a reasonable concern that Contracting Parties might use subsidies to undermine the tariff concessions they had made. In fact, many of the early non-violation complaints related to subsidies. It has been argued that the expansion of WTO rules to many new areas, including more detailed rule on subsidies, has made the non violation remedy less important.[56]

In terms of the substantive aspects of a non-violation complaint, the panel in *Japan— Film* described three elements that must be proven as part of such a claim: (1) the application of a *measure* by the responding party; (2) the existence of a *benefit* accruing under the agreement (usually related to benefits from tariff concessions); and (3) nullification or impairment of that benefit as the result of the application of the measure (*causal relationship*).[57] The panel also explained that the traditional rules governing the burden of proof in WTO disputes were applicable in non-violation claims. In this regard, the panel stated: 'it is for the party asserting a fact, claim or defence to bear the burden of providing proof thereof'. However, it also noted that, under Article 26.1 of the DSU, the complaining party 'bears the burden of providing a *detailed justification* for its claim in order to establish a presumption that what is claimed is true' (emphasis added), a higher standard than for violation claims.[58]

The application of the non-violation remedy is somewhat complex, and it may vary a bit depending on the specific claims brought. To illustrate, we look briefly at how the three elements described above were interpreted and applied in the *EC—Asbestos* dispute. In that case, the measure at issue was a French decree banning, *inter alia*, the manufacture, use and import of certain asbestos products. In examining the claims, the panel began by concluding that the first element was satisfied because a measure (ie the Decree) was being applied, a fact which was not disputed by the parties.[59] With regard to the third element, whether there was nullification or impairment as a result of the measure, the panel considered that nullification or impairment existed if the measure had the effect of upsetting the competitive relationship between 'Canadian' asbestos and asbestos products and 'substitute' fibres and products. The panel then stated that since this measure was an 'import ban', it could be presumed that this competitive relationship was upset. The panel concluded: '[b]y its very nature, an import ban constitutes a denial of any opportunity for competition, whatever the import volume that existed before the introduction of the ban'.[60]

The majority of the panel's analysis focused on the second element, which was the existence of a benefit accruing under the GATT. As noted, the 'benefits' cited under this provision have typically been tariff concessions. In this regard, the panel noted that tariff concessions on the asbestos products at issue were made (by France or the EC) in 1947, 1962 and at the conclusion of the Uruguay Round.[61] Regarding the concessions made in 1947 and 1962, the panel held that it was Canada's responsibility to present detailed evidence showing why it could legitimately expect the 1947 and 1962 concessions not to

---

[56] See F Roessler and P Gappah, 'A Re-appraisal of Non-violation Complaints under the WTO Dispute Settlement Procedures', in PFJ Macrory, AE Appleton, MG Plummer (eds), *The World Trade Organization: Legal, Economic and Political Analysis*, vol 1 (New York, Springer, 2005).

[57] Panel Report, *Japan—Film*, para 10.41.

[58] *Ibid*, paras 10.28–10.32.

[59] Panel Report, *EC—Asbestos*, paras 8.283–8.284.

[60] *Ibid*, paras 8.288–8.289. In a sense, this third element is really two separate sub-elements: (1) nullification or impairment and (2) causation.

[61] *Ibid*, para 8.290.

be affected by the measure and why it could not reasonably anticipate that France might adopt measures restricting the use of all asbestos products 50 and 35 years, respectively, after the negotiation of the concessions concerned (the consultations request was made in May of 1998). The panel concluded that Canada did not meet its burden of providing a 'detailed explanation' of why it could not reasonably have anticipated that France would not adopt measures 'restricting the use of asbestos'.[62]

The panel next examined whether, at the conclusion of the Uruguay Round, when new concessions were made, 'Canada could reasonably have expected France (a) not to adopt a measure restricting the use of asbestos and (b) not to do so by introducing a total ban'.[63] In deciding the issue, the panel stated that the scientific literature, international regulations and other WTO Members' public policy created a 'context' in which Canada 'could not reasonably not have anticipated that sooner or later chrysotile [asbestos] would be banned by France'.[64] The panel concluded that Canada had 'not presented a detailed justification in support of its claim that it could not reasonably have anticipated that France would, in the light of developments in the scientific evidence and the choices made by other Members, also decide to apply a total ban on asbestos on its market in the short term'.[65]

Therefore, since Canada had not proved the second element of its non-violation claim, the panel rejected the claim.

Turning to some practical issues related to the non-violation remedy, it is important to note that if the responding party loses a non-violation case, it has no obligation to withdraw the measure concerned. Instead, DSU Article 26.1(b) instructs the panel or Appellate Body to recommend that the Member concerned make a 'mutually satisfactory adjustment'. Pursuant to Article 26.1(c), upon the request of either party, arbitration to decide the reasonable period of time may include a determination of the level of nullification or impairment and may also suggest possible ways and means of reaching a mutually satisfactory adjustment (including compensation). However, such suggestions are not binding upon the parties.

As a result of these rules, the non-violation remedy is not as effective as the violation remedy, in terms of inducing another Member to change its measures, which perhaps explains, in part, why so few of these complaints have been filed. The sequencing of the three possible complaints under Article XXIII may also be a sign that non-violation cases are a secondary choice. In this regard, in *EC—Asbestos* the Appellate Body quoted with approval the statements of the panel in *Japan—Film* that non-violation complaints should be 'approached with caution' and should remain an 'exceptional remedy'.[66] In furtherance of this point, the Appellate Body quoted the panel at length:

> Although the non-violation remedy is an important and accepted tool of WTO/GATT dispute settlement and has been "on the books" for almost 50 years, we note that there have only been eight cases in which panels or working parties have substantively considered Article XXIII:1(b) claims. This suggests that both the GATT contracting parties and WTO Members have approached this remedy with caution and, indeed, have treated it as an exceptional instrument of dispute settlement. We note in this regard that both the European Communities and the United

---

[62] *Ibid*, paras 8.292–293.
[63] *Ibid*, para 8.294.
[64] *Ibid*, para 8.301.
[65] *Ibid*.
[66] See Panel Report, *Japan—Film*, para 9.5.

States in the *EEC—Oilseeds* case, and the two parties in this case, have confirmed that *the non-violation nullification or impairment remedy should be approached with caution and treated as an exceptional concept*. The reason for this caution is straightforward. *Members negotiate the rules that they agree to follow and only exceptionally would expect to be challenged for actions not in contravention of those rules.* (emphasis added [by the Appellate Body])[67]

c. 'Situation' Complaints Article XXIII:1(c) provides for the possibility of a complaining party bringing a dispute in relation to 'any other situation' that causes nullification or impairment. In such a circumstance, as with non-violation complaints, the complaining party must present a 'detailed justification' in support of its complaint. The 'situation complaint' was designed to be used in situations such as macro-economic emergencies (ie general depressions, high unemployment, commodity price collapses, balance of payments difficulties)[68] and, although there were a few situation complaints under the GATT (complaints were made regarding the withdrawal of concessions, failed re-negotiations and non-realised trade expectations), none resulted in a panel report.[69] There has not been a situation complaint under the WTO.

For situation complaints, DSU procedures apply only up to and including the point in the proceedings where the panel report is circulated to the Members. For subsequent proceedings, including adoption, surveillance and implementation of recommendations and rulings, the pre-DSU rules and procedures contained in the GATT 'Decision of 12 April 1989' apply. According to this Decision, panel reports are adopted by consensus; in other words, the 'negative consensus' decision-making mechanism of the DSU does not apply in 'situation' disputes. Moreover, the Decision does not include the detailed rules and protections of the DSU concerning the surveillance and implementation of rulings and recommendations and, significantly, panel reports cannot be appealed to the Appellate Body.

(ii) The Panel Request: Identification of the Measures and the Claims

Article 6.2 of the DSU requires that panel requests (1) 'identify the specific measures at issue' and (2) 'provide a brief summary of the legal basis of the complaint sufficient to present the problem clearly'. In an early case, the Appellate Body made clear that it takes these requirements seriously. In *Guatemala—Cement*, which involved claims against an anti-dumping measure and therefore implicated certain Anti-Dumping Agreement dispute settlement provisions in addition to Article 6.2 of the DSU, the panel had made a number of findings of violation. However, on appeal, the Appellate Body concluded that the panel request had not properly identified the measures at issue because it had not explicitly mentioned 'a definitive anti-dumping duty, the acceptance of a price undertaking or a provisional measure'. Instead, it had only referred to actions taken by the investigating authority during the investigation. As a result, the Appellate Body reversed all of the findings of violation, finding that the claims had not been brought properly.[70]

It is difficult to state briefly any general principles in the application of the Article 6.2 requirements. The key is simply to be sufficiently precise in explaining the measures

[67] Appellate Body Report, *EC—Asbestos*, para 186 (quoting Panel Report, *Japan—Film*, para 10.36).
[68] *WTO Handbook*, above n 13, 34.
[69] *Ibid*, 30, 34.
[70] Appellate Body Report, *Guatemala—Cement*, paras 57–89.

that are the subject of the complaint and the legal provisions that are alleged to have been violated. There is an obvious tension between, on the one hand, being very precise and giving away too much of the claim to the respondent versus, on the other hand, being too vague and risking a violation of Article 6.2. One 'exception' of sorts to note is that in some instances where the panel request is found to have been lacking, it may be concluded that the defending party's ability to respond was not 'prejudiced', and therefore there is no violation of Article 6.2.[71]

(iii) The Measure at Issue: What Types of Measures Can be Challenged?

In trying to understand individual WTO disputes, one of the most important aspects is to determine what government action is being challenged. Is it a piece of legislation? An implementing regulation? A judicial or quasi-judicial decision by a court or government agency? These are the main types of government 'measures', a term used in various places in the DSU, that may be the subject of a complaint, but it is possible for other measures to be challenged as well. The precise level of government involvement required for the action to qualify as a 'measure', however, is difficult to define. The Appellate Body has explained that 'acts setting forth rules or norms that are intended to have general and prospective application' are challengeable measures.[72] This provides some useful guidance, although actual application to specific situations may not always be straightforward.

For example, in *US—Zeroing*,[73] the issue was a 'zeroing' methodology applied by the US Department of Commerce in anti-dumping investigations. The report reveals the source of the zeroing methodology as 'certain lines of computer code that are *always* included in the computer program[s] used by [Commerce] in anti-dumping proceedings'.[74] The US argued that the panel

> erred in finding that the zeroing methodology is a 'norm' and, thus, a 'measure' [capable of being challenged in WTO dispute settlement] even though it did not identify any act or instrument of the United States setting forth or creating that rule or norm.[75]

The Appellate Body rejected this argument and instead concluded that 'the evidence before the Panel was sufficient to identify the precise content of the zeroing methodology; that the zeroing methodology is attributable to the United States, and that it does have general and prospective application'.[76]

In contrast, an action as limited as the statement of a parliamentarian is not enough. Thus, for example, a US Senator saying in a television interview 'I encourage my constituents to boycott all Chinese goods' is unlikely to be deemed a 'measure' that can be challenged (even though it might actually have some impact on imports). The areas that are most problematic are often reports and policy statements generated by government agencies, where the force and effect is not clear.

As an additional point in this section, we discuss briefly the so-called 'mandatory/

---

[71] Appellate Body Report, *Korea—Dairy Safeguards*, paras 114–31.
[72] Appellate Body Report, *US—OCTG Sunset Reviews*, para 187.
[73] Appellate Body Report, *US—Zeroing*.
[74] *Ibid*, para 199.
[75] *Ibid*, para 185.
[76] *Ibid*, para 204.

discretionary' distinction.[77] This distinction has a long history in GATT/WTO jurisprudence, although its precise scope and meaning continue to be the subject of debate. A WTO panel in *US—Exports Restraints* explained this issue as follows:

8.4 There is a considerable body of dispute settlement practice under both GATT and WTO standing for the principle that only legislation that *mandates* a violation of GATT/WTO obligations can be found as such to be inconsistent with those obligations. This principle was recently noted and applied by the Appellate Body in *United States—Anti-Dumping Act of 1916* ('*1916 Act*'):

"[T]he concept of mandatory as distinguished from discretionary legislation was developed by a number of GATT panels as a threshold consideration in determining when legislation as such—rather than a specific application of that legislation—was inconsistent with a Contracting Party's *GATT 1947* obligations."

. . .

"[P]anels developed the concept that mandatory and discretionary legislation should be distinguished from each other, reasoning that only legislation that mandates a violation of GATT obligations can be found as such to be inconsistent with those obligations."

8.5 Prior to *1916 Act*, the Panel in *United States—Measures Affecting the Importation, Internal Sale, and Use of Tobacco* ("*United States Tobacco*") summed up the practice of GATT panels in the area as follows:

"[P]anels had consistently ruled that legislation which mandated action inconsistent with the General Agreement could be challenged as such, whereas legislation which merely gave the discretion to the executive authority of a contracting party to act inconsistently with the General Agreement could not be challenged as such; only the actual application of such legislation could be subject to challenge."

Thus, the essence of the distinction is that legislation that mandates action that is inconsistent with WTO rules will result in a violation, whereas legislation that merely contains the discretion to act inconsistently will not result in a violation. As an illustration, consider the following pieces of legislation relating to export subsidies. The first states: 'The responsible agency shall grant export subsidies to promote the automobile industry'. The second states: 'In order to promote the automobile industry, the responsible agency may take actions to encourage exports'. When considering these measures under the SCM Agreement export subsidy provisions (see Chapter 10), it is fairly clear that the first measure mandates action that is inconsistent with the rules. The second, by contrast, simply gives the agency general guidance, under which it could use its discretion to provide export subsidies that violate the rules. Thus, applying a simple form of the 'mandatory/discretionary' distinction, the first measure would violate the rules whereas the second would not. Of course, the second measure could be *applied* in a way that violates the rules, and that application could be challenged as an independent measure. But on the face of the measure, there is no violation.

The mandatory/discretionary distinction has been criticised and called into question in a number of ways. For example, in *US—Section 301*, the panel held that the existence of

---

[77] For a detailed analyses of this distinction, see S Lester, 'A Framework for Thinking About the "Discretion" in the Mandatory/Discretionary Distinction' (2011) 14 *Journal of International Economic Law* 369; N Lockhart and E Sheargold, 'In Search of Relevant Discretion: The Mandatory/Discretionary Distinction in WTO Law' (2010) 13 *Journal of International Economic Law* 379.

'discretion' in a measure was not sufficient to find that there is no violation of particular WTO rules. This panel expressed concern that a rule that discretionary legislation would never violate the rules could lead to a situation where Members explicitly reserve in their legislation the right to violate the rules. The panel considered that the proper approach is to examine each specific WTO legal obligation at issue in relation to the challenged measure to decide whether a violation exists, rather than follow the general mandatory/ discretionary principle in all cases.[78] Secondly, in recent years, the EC has taken the position that the distinction does not even 'exist'.[79] In doing so, it has questioned the usefulness and coherence of the doctrine.[80]

The scope (and existence) of the mandatory/discretionary distinction awaits a definitive clarification from the Appellate Body. To date, the Appellate Body has been somewhat vague in its statements on the issue. While it has stated that the distinction should not be applied 'in a mechanistic fashion', it also said in the same case that it had not yet 'pronounce[d] generally upon the continuing relevance or significance of the mandatory/ discretionary distinction'.[81] Subsequently, the Appellate Body applied what was arguably a form of the mandatory/distinction. Examining a particular aspect of US anti-dumping law on sunset reviews, a panel had found no evidence in the US measures to indicate that the responsible agency would act consistently with the Anti-Dumping Agreement, and on this basis the panel found a violation. On appeal, however, the Appellate Body reversed the panel, concluding that the agency was not 'precluded' under the measures from acting consistently, and thus there was no violation. Arguably, saying that the agency is not 'precluded' from acting in a way that is consistent with WTO rules is the same thing as saying that it has the 'discretion' to act consistently. Thus, without making an explicit statement on the matter of 'mandatory/discretionary', the Appellate Body seems to have implicitly validated part of the underlying theory: it has found that a particular measure does not violate WTO rules 'as such' on the basis that it does not mandate actions which are inconsistent with the rules. However, the Appellate Body carefully avoiding making any general statements on this issue, and it avoided using the terms 'mandatory' and 'discretionary', so its full views are still a bit unclear.[82]

(iv) Burden of proof

As with any litigation proceeding, a key question under the DSU is which party bears the burden of proving its prima facie case. In general, the complaining party in a WTO dispute must present arguments and evidence sufficient to establish a *prima facie* case for each of the various elements of its claims. Once the complaining party has made its case, it is for the respondent to rebut that *prima facie* case. The panel in *Turkey—Textiles* succinctly summarised the established rules on burden of proof:

---

[78] Panel Report, *US—Section 301*, paras 7.53–7.54.

[79] See, eg Appellate Body Report, *US—Zeroing*, para 67.

[80] See EC third party submission in appeal of the *US—OCTG Sunset Reviews, Article 21.5* dispute (available on the EC DG trade website: http://ec.europa.eu/trade/); and Appellate Body Report, *US—OCTG Sunset Reviews, Article 21.5*, para 76.

[81] Appellate Body Report, *US—Corrosion-Resistant Steel Sunset Reviews*, para 93.

[82] Appellate Body Report, *US—OCTG Sunset Reviews, Article 21.5*, paras 87–122.

(a) it is for the complaining party to establish the violation it alleges;

(b) it is for the party invoking an exception or an affirmative defense to prove that the conditions contained therein are met; and

(c) it is for the party asserting a fact to prove it.[83]

In cases of uncertainty as to whether a prima facie case has been made, the panel in *US—Section 301* stated:

7.14 Since, in this case, both parties have submitted extensive facts and arguments in respect of the EC claims, our task will essentially be to balance all evidence on record and decide whether the EC, as party bearing the original burden of proof, has convinced us of the validity of its claims. In case of uncertainty, i.e. in case all the evidence and arguments remain in equipoise, we have to give the benefit of the doubt to the US as defending party.[84]

As a final point, the Appellate Body has held that a panel is not obliged to make an explicit finding that a party has met its burden of proof of making a prima facie case. In *Thailand—H-Beams*, the Appellate Body stated:

134. [A] panel is not required to make a separate and specific finding, in each and every instance, that a party has met its burden of proof in respect of a particular claim, or that a party has rebutted a *prima facie* case.[85]

(b) Participation by WTO Members and Other Interested Groups

(i) 'Standing' to Bring a Complaint

The DSU does not contain particularly onerous 'standing' requirements. In fact, arguably, the DSU does not contain *any* standing requirements. While Article 3.7 of the DSU calls upon Members to 'exercise . . . judgement as to whether action under these procedures would be fruitful', in reality, these rules provide few constraints on Members. In *EC—Bananas III*, the Appellate Body discussed this issue as follows:

132. We agree with the Panel that "neither Article 3.3 nor 3.7 of the DSU nor any other provision of the DSU contain any explicit requirement that a Member must have a 'legal interest' as a prerequisite for requesting a panel". We do not accept that the need for a "legal interest" is implied in the DSU or in any other provision of the *WTO Agreement*. It is true that under Article 4.11 of the DSU, a Member wishing to join in multiple consultations must have "a substantial trade interest", and that under Article 10.2 of the DSU, a third party must have "a substantial interest" in the matter before a panel. But neither of these provisions in the DSU, nor anything else in the *WTO Agreement*, provides a basis for asserting that parties to the dispute have to meet any similar standard. Yet, we do not believe that this is dispositive of whether, in this case, the United States has "standing" to bring claims under the GATT 1994.

133. The participants in this appeal have referred to certain judgments of the International Court of Justice and the Permanent Court of International Justice relating to whether there is a requirement, in international law, of a legal interest to bring a case. We do not read any of these judgments as establishing a general rule that in all international litigation, a complaining party

---

[83] Panel Report, *Turkey—Textiles*, para 9.57.
[84] Panel Report, *US—Section 301*, para 7.14.
[85] Appellate Body Report, *Thailand—H-Beams*, para 134.

must have a "legal interest" in order to bring a case. Nor do these judgments deny the need to consider the question of standing under the dispute settlement provisions of any multilateral treaty, by referring to the terms of that treaty.

134. This leads us to examine Article XXIII of the GATT 1994, which is the dispute settlement provision for disputes brought pursuant to the GATT 1994, most other Annex 1A agreements and the *Agreement on Trade Related Aspects of Intellectual Property Rights* ("*TRIPs*"). The chapeau of Article XXIII:1 of the GATT 1994 provides:

If any Member should consider that any benefit accruing to it directly or indirectly under this Agreement is being nullified or impaired or that the attainment of any objective of the Agreement is being impeded . . .

Of special importance for determining the issue of standing, in our view, are the words "[i]f any Member should consider . . .". This provision in Article XXIII is consistent with Article 3.7 of the DSU, which states:

Before bringing a case, a Member shall exercise its judgement as to whether action under these procedures would be fruitful . . .

135. Accordingly, we believe that a Member has broad discretion in deciding whether to bring a case against another Member under the DSU. The language of Article XXIII:1 of the GATT 1994 and of Article 3.7 of the DSU suggests, furthermore, that a Member is expected to be largely self-regulating in deciding whether any such action would be "fruitful".

136. We are satisfied that the United States was justified in bringing its claims under the GATT 1994 in this case. The United States is a producer of bananas, and a potential export interest by the United States cannot be excluded. The internal market of the United States for bananas could be affected by the EC banana regime, in particular, by the effects of that regime on world supplies and world prices of bananas. We also agree with the Panel's statement that:

. . . with the increased interdependence of the global economy, . . . Members have a greater stake in enforcing WTO rules than in the past since any deviation from the negotiated balance of rights and obligations is more likely than ever to affect them, directly or indirectly.

... ...

In *Mexico—HFCS, Article 21.5* the Appellate Body repeated its statement in *EC—Bananas* that the Article 3.7 requirement to exercise judgment in bringing a dispute is 'largely self-regulating', and it further explained that the provision 'reflects a basic principle that Members should have recourse to WTO dispute settlement in good faith, and not frivolously set in motion the procedures contemplated in the DSU'.[86] As a result, the Appellate Body stated that it must 'presume' that, whenever a panel request is submitted, the submitting Member is acting in good faith, and it reiterated that Article 3.7 'neither requires nor authorizes a panel to look behind that Member's decision and to question its exercise of judgement'.[87]

These decisions of the Appellate Body have far reaching implications, as it is conceivable that all WTO Members have an interest in any other Member's violations of any of the covered agreements, regardless of their commercial interest in the issues. Fortunately, there have not been any claims or assertions of Members abusing the system.

---

[86] Appellate Body Report, *Mexico—HFCS, Article 21.5*, para 73.
[87] *Ibid*, paras 73–75.

(ii) Merged and Parallel Disputes

In the domestic judicial process, disputes may emerge as a result of a single party filing a claim or from several parties filing a claim resulting from the same issue. The dispute settlement system in the WTO is no different. Several Members can (and often do) refer the same matter to the DSB as separate complaints. When this occurs, a single panel will normally be established. For instance, in *US—Steel Safeguards*, the EC, Japan, Korea, China, Switzerland, Norway, New Zealand and Brazil each submitted a complaint relating to the same safeguard measures against steel imports taken by the US, and a single panel was established to examine the dispute.[88] As an alternative approach, multiple Members can sign on to the same complaint, as happened in *EC—Bananas III*.[89]

When a single panel is established for multiple complainants, the panel must ensure that the rights which the parties to the dispute would have enjoyed had separate panels examined the complaints are not impaired by the single panel process. The DSU sets out several requirements in this regard: (1) if one of the parties to the dispute so requests, the panel shall submit separate reports on the dispute concerned;[90] (2) the written submissions by each of the complainants shall be made available to the other complainants; and (3) each complainant shall have the right to be present when any one of the other complainants presents its views to the panel.

However, it is not always feasible to establish a single panel for similar complaints and, when this occurs, separate panels will be established to hear the disputes. For instance, in a dispute concerning India's patent protection of pharmaceuticals, the US requested the establishment of a panel on 7 November 1996, while the EC requested the establishment of a panel around 10 months later, on 9 September 1997. Given the time gap, the DSB established two separate panels to examine the complaints. In *India—Patents (EC)*, the panel rejected India's contention that a single panel should have been established. According to the panel, it was 'impracticable' for the DSB to establish a single panel since the EC had not even requested consultations at the time the US completed the consultation process and had requested that a panel be established.[91] Importantly, the panel stated that Article 9.1 of the DSU is recommendatory rather than mandatory and thus is similar to a 'code of conduct' that does not impact upon the rights and obligations of Members.[92]

If more than one panel is established, to the extent possible, the same persons will serve as panelists on the separate panels and, where appropriate, the timetable for the panel process will be harmonised. In certain circumstances, this can even mean that hearings are conducted simultaneously between the two panels. For instance, the two panels (consisting of the same individuals) in *EC—Hormones* made adjustments to the panel procedures in order to hold a joint meeting with scientific experts and to share the information obtained at this meeting between the two panels.[93]

---

[88] Panel Report, *US—Steel Safeguards*, para 2.7.

[89] WTO Doc No WT/DS27/1 (12 February 1996).

[90] This 'right' is not unlimited however, and the Appellate Body has upheld panel decisions to reject such requests. See, eg Appellate Body Report, *US—Offset Act*, paras 305–17.

[91] Panel Report, *India—Patents (EC)*, paras 7.16–7.19.

[92] *Ibid*, para 7.14.

[93] Panel Report, *EC—Hormones*, paras 8.8, 8.20; Appellate Body Report, *EC—Hormones*, paras 152–55.

(iii) Third Parties

If any Member believes that it has a 'substantial interest' in a matter before a panel, it can generally participate in the case as a third party. The DSU fails to define the term 'substantial interest', but in practice third party participation requests are generally approved at the DSB without substantial comment.

Third parties can play an important role in the dispute settlement process and are encouraged to have meaningful participation. The DSU facilitates this in three different ways: (1) third parties receive the submissions of the parties to the dispute to the first panel meeting in a timely fashion; (2) third parties make submissions to the panel and have their arguments reflected in the panel report; and (3) third parties present their views at a meeting with the panel. Third parties can choose to participate both in writing and orally, or they may choose to simply follow the progress of the case and obtain the relevant documents without observing the third party session.

Members who participate in a dispute as a third party can also participate in any appeal of the panel report as a 'third participant'. Much like the panel process, third participants are allowed to make written and oral submissions to the Appellate Body.[94]

Furthermore, the DSU does not preclude a third party from later bringing a complaint in regard to the same matter. In fact, Article 10.4 provides that any subsequent dispute involving a Member who was a third party in a prior dispute should (where possible) be referred to the 'original panel'. In *India—Patents (EC)*, discussed above, India requested that the panel declare the EC complaint 'inadmissible' under Article 10.4 of the DSU, because, according to India, since the EC was a third party in the earlier dispute brought by the US, the EC should have submitted a complaint to the panel established to hear the US complaint.[95] The panel rejected India's argument, but it did recognise the Indian concern that multiple panels covering the same facts could pose 'serious risks' due to potentially inconsistent rulings, unwarranted harassment and the waste of resources. However, it said that dispute settlement was not 'an appropriate forum to address these issues'.[96]

(iv) Transparency

The WTO dispute settlement system has been criticised a great deal for its lack of transparency. The language of the DSU explicitly provides that many aspects of dispute settlement proceedings are to remain confidential. For instance, and like any court, the internal panel deliberations are confidential. However, unlike most domestic courts, the meeting of the panel with the parties is normally closed off from outside observers. Moreover, opinions expressed by panelists and individual Appellate Body members remain anonymous, and parties are bound to respect the confidentiality of any document so marked.[97] Furthermore, individuals who are not part of the delegations of parties or third parties to a dispute are excluded from panel proceedings, and transcripts of these proceedings are

---

[94] Members who have not participated in the panel process are not given the opportunity of becoming third participants but may side-step this procedural hurdle by submitting an amicus brief, which the Appellate Body may or may not consider. See Appellate Body Report, *EC—Sardines*, paras 161–67.

[95] Panel Report, *India—Patents (EC)*, para 7.19.

[96] *Ibid*, paras 7.22–7.23.

[97] DSU Arts 4, 14, 18.

not publicly available. Consequently, only a small range of the information available to the parties is made public: the final panel reports and non-confidential versions of party submissions.[98] Even these versions are often not available promptly enough to provide a meaningful opportunity for public engagement with the issues under discussion.

Therefore, the DSU can be described as somewhat of a closed system, in that it has several features that prevent or hamper public scrutiny of, or participation in, the dispute settlement process. The current trend, however, is for more transparency. The following extract reviews the developments and Member proposals for even more reform.

B Mercurio and R LaForgia, 'Expanding Democracy: Why Australia Should Negotiate For Open and Transparent Dispute Settlement in Its Free Trade Agreements' 6 *Melbourne Journal of International Law* **485, 495–99**

A *WTO Developments on Transparency and NGO Participation*

While the wording of the *DSU* insists upon a closed system of dispute settlement, it must be noted that the WTO is taking steps to open the system in terms of both transparency of the process and NGO participation. This is being accomplished through parties' own conduct, the recent jurisprudence of the panels and Appellate Body, and as part of the current review of the *DSU*.

1 *The Move towards Internal Transparency*

(a) Developments under Current Provisions

The *DSU* already provides for some limited openness. For instance, while art 18.2 of the *DSU* . . . states that submissions of the parties to panels or Appellate Body proceedings are confidential, Members are not prohibited from making their submissions public if they so desire. In this regard, the US sets a positive example by making its own submissions to the DSB public. In fact, US legislation actually mandates that US submissions shall be public. Other developed countries — including Australia, Canada and the European Communities — likewise make their submissions public and support US proposals for increasing transparency in the *DSU*.

Moreover, under present practice, art 18.3 and appendix 3 of the *DSU* are deemed to provide that, while the parties' submissions are confidential, the possibility of making public summaries remains. Appendix 3 enables a Member to request from another party to the dispute a 'non-confidential summary of information contained in its submissions that could be disclosed to the public', although the rules have not been read to establish a deadline for such submissions. The US is required, by domestic legislation, to request such non-confidential summaries in all cases in which they are a party, third party or third participant. However, common practice is generally not to make such summaries available until very late in the process or only after the case has been decided.

[A recent Panel] weighed into the debate and, in a truly landmark decision, ruled that nothing in the *DSU* specifically prohibits Members from opening up panel and Appellate Body hearings to interested observers. Thus, [] observers [will be allowed] to view proceedings upon the joint request of the parties. Such a request was made by the US, Canada and the EC in a recent compliance hearing in the *EC — Hormones* dispute. In a decision dated 1 August 2005, the [Panel] gave 'careful consideration [to] the existing provisions of the *DSU*' and found that nothing in the rules prohibits the parties from agreeing to open the hearings to observers. In the dispute, the parties agreed to allow 'observation by the public through a closed circuit TV

---

[98] DSU Art 18.2.

broadcast'. This decision provides further evidence that not only is the WTO moving away from the closed system, but that FTAs that narrowly interpret mechanisms based on WTO provisions may now contradict the very system they copied.

(b) Further Developments Proposed in the DSU Review

DSU Review proposals from several democratic developed nations recognise the fact that the current model operates in a manner contrary to their own domestic judicial systems in that it excludes members of the public from participating in or witnessing the proceedings. Collectively, their proposals can be said to recognise the right of all stakeholders, including workers, firms, industry and NGOs, to observe and participate in a more open and transparent dispute settlement system.

For example, US proposals specifically call for all substantive meetings of the panels and Appellate Body and all arbitration to be open to the public; for all submissions to panels, the Appellate Body and arbitrators to be public, except those portions dealing with confidential information; and for the WTO to make a final panel report available to WTO Members and the public once it has been issued to the parties.

The US summarised the arguments of the developed countries advocating for increased transparency in the *DSU* by stating that both the public at large and governments of Member States would benefit by increasing the transparency of the process. More specifically, the US proposal stated that '[t]he public has a legitimate interest in the proceedings', that non-party WTO Members would also 'benefit from being able to observe the arguments and proceedings of WTO disputes' and that open hearings would

assist Members, including developing countries, in understanding the issues involved as well as gaining greater familiarity and experience with dispute settlement. Being better informed about disputes generally could aid Members in deciding whether to assert third party rights in a particular dispute.

Moreover, the proposal stated that the

implementation of the DSB recommendations and rulings may be facilitated if those being asked to assist in the task of implementation, such as the constituencies of legislators, have confidence that the recommendations and rulings are the result of a fair and adequate process.

The US concluded by stating:

A more open and transparent process would be a significant improvement to the *DSU*, in keeping with the commitment by Ministers 'to promote a better public understanding of the WTO', and 'to making the WTO's operations more transparent, including through more effective and prompt dissemination of information'. Such a more open and transparent process could be achieved by providing an opportunity to observe the arguments and evidence submitted in proceedings as well as observing those proceedings, subject to appropriate safeguards such as for confidential information and security. In addition, the final results of those proceedings should be made available to the public as soon as possible.

Of particular importance to the arguments for greater transparency in the bilateral context, the US pointed out that many other international dispute settlement fora and tribunals were open to the public, and noted specifically that the International Court of Justice, the International Tribunal for the Law of the Sea, the International Criminal Tribunal for the Former Yugoslavia, the International Criminal Tribunal for Rwanda, the European Court of Human Rights and the African Court on Human and Peoples' Rights all conduct open hearings and allow for submissions to be distributed to interested observers. The US further observed that those fora dealt with issues that were intergovernmental in nature and were 'at least as sensitive as those involved in WTO disputes', and questioned why the WTO should be different in this respect.

It must be noted that some delegations explicitly disagreed with the proposals of the EC and of the US. Those Members argued that the WTO was an intergovernmental organisation, where Members discussed and kept the balance of rights and obligations among Members, and that openness would undermine this intergovernmental character and severely erode the Member governments' authority and ability to participate effectively in the dispute settlement process. Some specifically stated that allowing observers at hearings would 'lead to trials by media'. For that reason, the above proposals have not as of yet been included in the *Proposed Amendments to the* DSU.

Throughout the course of the *DSU* Review, the US, the EC and others have also repeatedly submitted that art 18.2 of the *DSU* should be amended so as to require the timely preparation and submission of public versions of all DSB submissions and exhibits (with an appropriate exception for business confidential information). More specifically, the proposals recommended that, in order to maintain the spirit of the provision, art 18.2 be amended to require parties to submit a public version of their submissions within a fixed deadline (a majority of the proposals recommended a period of 10 days after the submission to the panel or Appellate Body).

The *Proposed Amendments* recognise the usefulness of the above proposal and include stricter rules on the submission of public versions in the course of the *DSU* Review. If the amendments remain part of the final text, the resulting simple change would increase the transparency of the WTO by keeping the public informed of developments and support Members that currently operate a more transparent system of domestic regulation

… … …

The opening of oral hearings is now a regular occurrence in WTO disputes involving the US, EU and Canada. The WTO's News Archives indicate that public observation was most recently requested by Canada and the US, and approved by the Appellate Body in *United States—Certain Country of Origin Labelling (COOL) Requirements*. Prior to this, the oral hearings of both the panel and the Appellate Body were opened at the request of the US and EU in the Boeing dispute (*United States—Measures Affecting Trade in Large Civil Aircraft (Second Complaint)*).

Transparency in the dispute settlement process remains as a subject of discussion in the DSU review. The most recent report indicates that the disagreement among Members referred to in the extract above is a continuing feature.[99]

(v) Amicus Curiae

One of the most controversial issues that has arisen at the WTO in recent years is whether panels and the Appellate Body may consider unsolicited *amicus curiae* briefs submitted by (normally) non-state actors (such as private industry groups, non-governmental organisations (NGOs) and academics).

Amicus submissions were not accepted by any GATT panel and, without any clear and definitive guidance from the DSU or elsewhere in any of the covered agreements, early panels composed under the DSU also refused to accept the submissions. This view

---

[99] See TN/DS/25, Special Session of the Dispute Settlement Body, 21 April 2011.

has been definitively overruled, and it is now well established that both panels and the Appellate Body may, but are not required to, accept amicus submissions

The issue of amicus submissions came to the fore in the highly visible and controversial *US—Shrimp* dispute. The dispute gained attention when environmental groups worldwide publicised the issues involved, and two NGOs attempted to influence the process by submitting amicus briefs to the panel. The panel refused to consider the content of these submissions, concluding that although it had the authority under Article 13 to seek information from 'any relevant source', it would be 'incompatible' with the DSU to accept unsolicited information from a non-governmental source. Instead, the panel attempted to reach a compromise position by permitting the parties to the dispute to attach the NGOs' briefs as an appendix to their own submissions.[100]

In a landmark decision, the Appellate Body rejected the panel's conclusion and determined that, although NGOs have no *right* under the DSU to have a panel consider the contents of their *amicus* briefs, a panel does have broad authority under Article 13 to 'seek' information, and thus it was permitted to consider such briefs if it chose to do so.[101]

In two subsequent disputes, the Appellate Body held that it too was empowered to accept amicus submissions at its discretion. In *US—Lead and Bismuth II*, the Appellate Body based its decision on the fact that although nothing in the DSU specifically authorises it to accept or consider amicus briefs from outside sources, Article 17.9 of the DSU provides the Appellate Body with 'broad authority to adopt procedural rules which do not conflict with any rules and procedures of the DSU or the covered agreements',[102] and, in addition, Rule 16(1) of the Working Procedures 'authorizes a division to create an appropriate procedure when a question arises that is not covered by the Working Procedures'. It also stated that 'neither the DSU nor the Working Procedures explicitly prohibit acceptance or consideration of such briefs'.[103] Thus, the Appellate Body said that, while it was under no 'legal duty' to accept submissions from non-state actors, it did have 'the legal authority to decide whether or not to accept and consider any information that we believe is pertinent and useful in an appeal'.[104]

In *EC—Asbestos*, the Appellate Body reaffirmed its decision in *US—Lead and Bismuth II*. This time, though, it went further by relying on Rule 16(1) of the Working Procedures to promulgate Additional Procedures for the acceptance of amicus submissions. These Additional Procedures were communicated to all participants and third participants as well as the Chair of the DSB, and provided that 'any person, whether natural or legal, other than a party or a third party to this dispute . . . must apply for leave to file such a brief from the Appellate Body [within eight days of the communication]'.[105] The Additional Procedures explicitly and clearly stated that no *amicus* submissions would be accepted from those organisations or individuals who had failed to file an application for leave and been granted such leave.

Section 3 of the Additional Procedures detailed the necessary information an applica-

---

[100] Panel Report, *US—Shrimp*, para 7.8. The Appellate Body confirmed that a party can attach an *amicus* brief to its submissions and panels may accept it in this manner. See Appellate Body Report, *US—Shrimp*, paras 79–91.

[101] See Appellate Body Report, *US—Shrimp*, paras 107–08.

[102] *Ibid.*

[103] Appellate Body Report, *US—Lead and Bismuth II*, paras 38–39.

[104] *Ibid*, para 39.

[105] See Additional Procedure Adopted Under Rule 16(1) of the Working Procedures for Appellate Review, WTO Doc No WT/DS135/9 (8 November 2000), para 2.

tion for leave should contain, including information about the applicant, its activities, membership and sources of funding, interest of the applicant in the proceedings, disclosure of all information regarding any relationship the applicant may have to any of the parties or third parties, any financial assistance or contribution made to the applicant in preparation of this application or the brief by a party or any third party and identification of the specific legal issues that are the subject of the appeal that the applicant intends to address in its brief.[106] In addition, Part 3(f) of the Additional Procedures required the applicant to 'indicate, in particular, in what way the applicant will make a contribution to the resolution of this dispute that is not likely to be repetitive of what is already submitted by a party or third party to this dispute'. Moreover, the Additional Procedures instructed that 'the grant of leave to file a brief by the Appellate Body does not imply that the Appellate Body will address, in its Report, the legal arguments made in such a brief'.[107]

In the end, the Appellate Body rejected the 18 *amicus* submissions it received in that case. Nonetheless, its decision to set out these procedures was highly controversial. Despite the fact that the Appellate Body stated that the rules were adopted 'for the purposes of this appeal only', and that the rules were not permanent additions to the Working Procedures of the Appellate Body, several Members of the WTO immediately criticised the decision. In fact, the issue sparked so much controversy that a group of Members jointly requested and were granted a Special Session of the WTO General Council regarding the Additional Procedures (the Special Session on the Additional Procedures took place on 22 November 2000). Many Members at the Special Session claimed the Appellate Body overstepped its authority and misinterpreted the DSU provisions covering third parties and outside experts.[108] More significantly, those same Members strongly believed that the Appellate Body's broad interpretation of the term 'working procedures' and interpretative approach permitting conduct which is not explicitly forbidden to the Appellate Body could have undesirable consequences if extended to other WTO provisions. In this regard, it is apparent that broader notions of non-governmental participation (such as NGO representation during negotiations) intruding upon the intergovernmental nature of the organisation were at the forefront of these Members' statements. Finally, Members argued that the issue was not procedural, but a substantive one that only Members could decide through negotiation, rather than through a judicially created right. A statement issued by a group of developing countries in connection with the Special Session stated that while the Appellate Body was entitled to adopt its own working procedures, this decision went beyond that to 'an outreach activity, seeking information from individuals . . . not mandated by the DSU'.[109]

Only one member, the United States, unequivocally supported the Appellate Body's ruling and use of Article 17 of the DSU and Article 16 of the Working Procedures to craft the Additional Procedures.[110] Since the decision, several other developed country

---

[106] See *Ibid*.

[107] See Ibid, para 1.

[108] See, eg Statement by Uruguay at the General Council Meeting on 22 November 2000, WTO Doc No WT/GC/38 (12 December 2000).

[109] See C Raghavan, 'Will Appellate Body Listen to "Strong Signal" from General Council?', *SUNS Online*, 22 November 2000, available at http://www.twnside.org.sg/title/signal.htm (accessed on 7 August 2007).

[110] See, 'Amicus Brief Storm Highlights WTO's Unease with External Transparency' (November–December 2000) 4(9) *ICTSD Bridges Weekly Trade News Digest* 4, available at http://www.ictsd.org/English/BRIDGES4-9.pdf.

Members have expressed support for the right of panels and the Appellate Body to accept unsolicited non-governmental submissions at their discretion.

Thus, even though only a minority of Members initially supported, or continue to support, the decision to allow these submissions, the situation remains that NGOs and other non-state actors can submit unsolicited amicus briefs to both the panels and the Appellate Body.

However, panels and the Appellate Body continue to reject the vast majority of submissions. Interestingly, in *EC—Sardines*, where the Appellate Body 'accepted' part of an amicus submission, the submission was by the government of Morocco, the only time a Member has made an *amicus* submission.[111] Morocco had not been a third party in the panel process and therefore could not become a third participant in the appellate review; instead, it chose to submit an amicus brief to the Appellate Body in order to get its views across. While the legality of the submission was upheld, Morocco's legal arguments did not assist the Appellate Body in rendering its decision.[112]

As part of the DSU Review, the United States proposed the adoption of definitive guidelines and procedures for handling *amicus curiae* submissions to address those procedural concerns that had been raised by Members, panels and the Appellate Body in light of the experience to date. Other Members, however, have proposed to prohibit unsolicited submissions from non-state actors, while a few have expressed the belief that the issue of *amicus curiae* is broader than the issue of transparency and beyond the mandate of the negotiations given by the Doha Declaration.

(c) Panel and Appellate Body Decision-making

(i) Guiding Principles of Treaty Interpretation

The proper interpretation of constitutions, statutes and other legal instruments is very controversial in domestic settings. The situation is no different at the WTO. The DSU provides some explicit guidance on this matter, but that has not stopped controversy from arising.

With regard to the method of interpretation, Article 3.2 of the DSU states:

> The dispute settlement system of the WTO is a central element in providing security and predictability to the multilateral trading system. The Members recognize that it serves to preserve the rights and obligations of Members under the covered agreements, and to clarify the existing provisions of those agreements in accordance with customary rules of interpretation of public international law.

Thus, in dispute settlement, panels and the Appellate Body are to 'clarify' the provisions of the agreements based on the 'customary rules of interpretation of public international law'. However, the last sentence of Article 3.2, along with Article 19.2 of the DSU, makes it clear that these clarifications must not go too far, explaining that panels and the Appellate Body cannot 'add to or diminish the rights and obligations provided in the covered agreements'.

Finding the proper balance between clarifications based on the interpretative rules of public international law and the requirement not to 'add to or diminish' the existing

---

[111] Appellate Body Report, *EC—Sardines*, paras 153–70.
[112] *Ibid*, paras 170 and 314.

rules is an extremely difficult task. Determining the right approach is no doubt influenced implicitly by one's views on the proper role of courts and the particular substantive issues involved, among other things.

There is little controversy about which public international law interpretative rules are to be applied. In practice, the 'customary rules of interpretation of public international law' used by panels and the Appellate Body are Articles 31 and 32 of Vienna Convention on the Law of Treaties.[113] Article 31 of the Vienna Convention states:

1. A treaty shall be interpreted in good faith in accordance with the ordinary meaning to be given to the terms of the treaty in their context and in the light of its object and purpose.

2. The context for the purpose of the interpretation of a treaty shall comprise, in addition to the text, including its preamble and annexes:

(a) any agreement relating to the treaty which was made between all the parties in connection with the conclusion of the treaty;

(b) any instrument which was made by one or more parties in connection with the conclusion of the treaty and accepted by the other parties as an instrument related to the treaty.

3. There shall be taken into account, together with the context:

(a) any subsequent agreement between the parties regarding the interpretation of the treaty or the application of its provisions;

(b) any subsequent practice in the application of the treaty which establishes the agreement of the parties regarding its interpretation;

(c) any relevant rules of international law applicable in the relations between the parties.

4. A special meaning shall be given to a term if it is established that the parties so intended.

Article 32 of the Vienna Convention adds:

Recourse may be had to *supplementary means of interpretation*, including the preparatory work of the treaty and the circumstances of its conclusion, in order to confirm the meaning resulting from the application of article 31, or to determine the meaning when the interpretation according to article 31:

(a) leaves the meaning ambiguous or obscure; or

(b) leads to a result which is manifestly absurd or unreasonable (emphasis added).

Accordingly, a term contained in a covered agreement shall be based on its ordinary meaning, in its context, and in line with the object and purpose of the agreement. In *Japan—Alcoholic Beverages II*, the Appellate Body explained that 'Article 31 of the *Vienna Convention* provides that the words of the treaty form the foundation for the interpretative process: "interpretation must be based above all upon the text of the treaty"'.[114] In *US—Shrimp*, the Appellate Body further clarified this rule when it adopted the following approach:

A treaty interpreter must begin with, and focus upon, the text of the particular provision to be interpreted. It is in the words constituting that provision, read in their context, that the object

---

[113] See, eg Appellate Body Report, *US—Gasoline*, part III.B. *Vienna Convention on the Law of Treaties*, Vienna, 23 May 1969, 1155 UNTS 331; (1969) 8 International Legal Materials 679.

[114] Appellate Body Report, *Japan—Alcoholic Beverages III*, 11.

and purpose of the states parties to the treaty must first be sought. Where the meaning imparted by the text itself is equivocal or inconclusive, or where confirmation of the correctness of the reading of the text itself is desired, light from the object and purpose of the treaty as a whole may usefully be sought.[115]

Therefore, while the other parts of the Vienna Convention rules will also play a role, Article 31:1, and in particular the 'ordinary meaning' of the text, often provides the initial focus. Only under special circumstances may supplementary materials be used to assist in the interpretation.

The Appellate Body has recently commented on, and confirmed the applicability of, Article 31:3(a) in two disputes. In *Clove—Cigarettes*, it considered that paragraph 5.2 of the Doha Ministerial Decision was a 'subsequent agreement between the parties' for the purposes of Article 31:3(a). Therefore, the terms of paragraph 5.2 constituted 'an interpretative clarification to be taken into account in the interpretation of Article 2:12 of the TBT Agreement'.[116] When the two provisions are considered, the applicability of Article 31:3(a) is almost self-evident:

Article 2:12 of the *TBT Agreement*:

Except in those urgent circumstances referred to in paragraph 10, Members shall allow a reasonable interval between the publication of technical regulations and their entry into force in order to allow time for producers in exporting Members, and particularly in developing country Members, to adapt their products or methods of production to the requirements of the importing Member.

Paragraph 5.2 of the Doha Ministerial Decision:

Subject to the conditions specified in paragraph 12 of Article 2 of the Agreement on Technical Barriers to Trade, the phrase 'reasonable interval' shall be understood to mean normally a period of not less than 6 months, except when this would be ineffective in fulfilling the legitimate objectives pursued.

The Appellate Body confirmed that 'paragraph 5.2 *bears specifically* upon the interpretation of the term "reasonable interval" in Article 2:12 of the *TBT Agreement*'.[117]

The Appellate Body also made findings on the applicability of Article IX:2 of the WTO Agreement, and on the relationship between this provision and Article 31:3(a). Article IX:2 provides for the multilateral or authoritative interpretation as follows:

The Ministerial Conference and the General Council shall have the exclusive authority to adopt interpretations of this Agreement and of the Multilateral Trade Agreements. In the case of an interpretation of a Multilateral Trade Agreement in Annex 1, they shall exercise their authority on the basis of a recommendation by the Council overseeing the functioning of that Agreement. The decision to adopt an interpretation shall be taken by a three-fourths majority of the Members. This paragraph shall not be used in a manner that would undermine the amendment provisions in Article X.

---

[115] Appellate Body Report, *US—Shrimp*, para 114. Contra *US—Section 301*, where the panel held that 'the elements referred to in Art 31—text, context and object-and-purpose as well as good faith—are to be viewed as one holistic rule of interpretation rather than a sequence of separate tests to be applied in a hierarchical order'. Panel Report, *US—Section 301*, para 7.22.

[116] Appellate Body Report, *Clove—Cigarettes*, para 269.

[117] *Ibid*, para 266 (emphasis in original).

The US argued that the panel had declined to determine whether paragraph 5.2 of the Doha Ministerial Decision constituted an authoritative interpretation under Article IX:2. The US further argued that the panel had nevertheless applied 'paragraph 5.2 as a "rule" that amended the text of Article 2:12 of the TBT Agreement'.[118] In contrast, Indonesia considered that the panel had determined that paragraph 5.2 constituted an authoritative interpretation under Article IX:2. The Appellate Body considered that the panel had not determined the applicability of Article IX:2 and proceeded to make its own findings on this matter. These findings were presaged with the view that:

> Multilateral interpretations adopted pursuant to Article IX:2 of the *WTO Agreement* have a pervasive legal effect. Such interpretations are binding on all Members. As we see it, the broad legal effect of these interpretations is precisely the reason why Article IX:2 subjects the adoption of such interpretations to clearly articulated and strict decision-making procedures.[119]

This passage signals that the requirements set out in Article IX:2 must be strictly interpreted and clearly satisfied. It was therefore necessary to determine whether paragraph 5.2 had been adopted on the basis of a recommendation from the relevant Council—here the Council for Trade in Goods. On this point, the Appellate Body considered that:

> Whereas the content of paragraph 5.2 of the Doha Ministerial Decision might very well have been based on discussions within the Committee on Technical Barriers to Trade, we are not persuaded that this is sufficient to establish that the Ministerial Conference exercised its authority to adopt an interpretation of the *TBT Agreement* on the basis of a *recommendation* from the Council for Trade in Goods.[120]

Paragraph 5.2 did not therefore have the status of an authoritative interpretation under Article IX:2.

The Appellate Body then proceeded to consider whether this finding should have implications for the applicability of Article 31:3(a). In particular, the US argued that if paragraph 5.2 was not an authoritative interpretation, then it similarly could not be a 'subsequent agreement of the parties' pursuant to Article 31:3(a). This position was dismissed on the basis that authoritative interpretations and subsequent agreements 'serve different functions and have different legal effects in WTO law'.[121] Article IX:2 interpretations were described as 'binding on all Members, including in respect of all disputes in which these interpretations are relevant'. In contrast, Article 31:3(a) was identified as 'a rule of treaty interpretation'. It was added that, '[i]nterpretations developed by panels and the Appellate Body in the course of dispute settlement proceedings are binding only on the parties to a particular dispute'. Despite these statements, it can be questioned whether, in practice, there is likely to be a significant gap between the binding quality of authoritative interpretations and subsequent agreements. It is technically correct that an interpretation of a WTO provision which is influenced by a subsequent agreement will only bind the parties to a particular dispute. However, it would be a most unusual occurrence for the Appellate Body to interpret the same WTO provision differently in a subsequent dispute. It is arguable that this observation raises the practical binding quality of subsequent agreements almost to the level of authoritative interpretations.

---

[118] *Ibid*, para 242.
[119] *Ibid*, para 250.
[120] *Ibid*, para 255.
[121] *Ibid*, para 257.

It is possible to argue that this is a matter of concern. As provided in Article IX:2, authoritative interpretations can only emanate from the WTO's highest decision making bodies—the Ministerial Conference and the General Council. The subsequent agreement in *Clove—Cigarettes* also emanated from the Ministerial Conference, so that there is little cause for concern if this particular subsequent agreement is treated as binding. However, in the subsequent *US—Tuna* ruling, the Appellate Body confirmed that a TBT Committee Decision amounted to a subsequent agreement.[122] This Decision is clearly of lesser provenance than a Decision of a Ministerial Conference. If the argument that authoritative interpretations and subsequent agreements are very similar in terms of their binding quality is accepted, the question is whether this is acceptable when they may be dissimilar in their provenance. This is an important question bearing in mind that Committee Decisions under individual WTO agreements are much greater in number than authoritative interpretations.

The recognition of Committee Decisions as subsequent agreements can also be depicted in a positive light. While there is a difference in provenance between such a Decision and Decisions of the Ministerial Conference and General Council, it must also be considered, as the Appellate Body noted in *US—Tuna* 'that the membership of the TBT Committee comprises all WTO Members and that the Decision was adopted by consensus'.[123] Therefore, the dissimilarity in provenance need not be over-emphasized. The use of Article 31:3(a) can also be located within the broader debate concerning the imbalance between the WTO's dispute settlement process and its relatively inefficient political decision making process. The possibility of authoritative interpretations under Article IX:2 is often presented as a means of redressing this imbalance. However, there has not to date been an instance of recourse to this provision.[124] The use of Article 31:3(a) in the dispute settlement process contributes towards the function which Article IX:2 is intended to serve. The views of the WTO Membership on the proper interpretation of open textured WTO norms are fed into the dispute settlement process.

It is almost inevitable that methods of treaty interpretation will be controversial, as the particular method chosen may lead to a specific outcome on certain issues. For example, there are many 'gaps' in various WTO agreements on issues where the negotiators simply could not agree and different approaches could be taken to fill these 'gaps'. One approach is that panels and the Appellate Body could declare that in the absence of rules there are simply no obligations on the issues.[125] This approach would please governments which may come up with creative ways to take protectionist measures and seek to avoid WTO disciplines. Another approach is to try to stretch the existing rules, by use of their context and other interpretive elements, to discern obligations in these areas. This approach is more likely to lead to findings of violation, which will please the complainants in these cases. Regardless of which approach is taken, however, there is likely to be some criticism of the interpretive method whenever the rules at issue are vague.

---

[122] Appellate Body Report, *US—Tuna*, paras 371–72.

[123] *Ibid*, para 371.

[124] See C-D Ehlermann and L Ehring, 'The Authoritative Interpretation Under Article IX:2 of the Agreement Establishing the World Trade Organization: Current Law, Practice and Possible Improvements' (2005) 8(4) *Journal of International Economic Law* 803.

[125] See L Bartels, 'The Separation of Powers in the WTO: How to Avoid Judicial Activism' (2004) 53(4) *International and Comparative Law Quarterly* 861.

(ii) Precedential Effect of Adopted Panel//Appellate Body Reports

While the WTO dispute settlement system differs from many domestic common law systems in that it does not have a formal system of binding precedent, precedent does play an important role. A quick read of any panel or Appellate Body report shows extensive citation to prior reports. (Note that in this book we have removed footnotes from case extracts in order to improve readability). While it is generally accepted that adopted panel and Appellate Body reports are binding only on the parties to the dispute, there is nonetheless an expectation that prior disputes, where relevant, should be taken into account.

The issue of the precedential effect of adopted reports was first discussed in *Japan—Alcoholic Beverages II*. In that case, the panel found that 'panel reports adopted by the GATT CONTRACTING PARTIES and the WTO Dispute Settlement Body constitute subsequent practice in a specific case', in the sense of 'subsequent practice' under Article 31(3)(b) of the *Vienna Convention*.[126] The Appellate Body overturned this finding, however, concluding that while adopted panel reports are an important part of the GATT *acquis*, that is, the accumulated body of law, they are not binding, except with respect to resolving the particular dispute between the parties to that dispute. On the other hand, the Appellate Body recognised that prior adopted reports are often considered by subsequent panels and create 'legitimate expectations' among Members, and therefore should be 'taken into account where they are relevant to any dispute'. Interestingly, and perhaps recognising the de facto precedential system developing, the Appellate Body noted in a footnote that:

> [T]he Statute of the International Court of Justice has an explicit provision, Article 59, to the same effect. This has not inhibited the development by that Court (and its predecessor) of a body of case law in which considerable reliance on the value of previous decisions is readily discernible.[127]

In a more recent case, the Appellate Body explained its view further, stating:

> [F]ollowing the Appellate Body's conclusions in earlier disputes is not only appropriate, but is what would be expected from panels, especially where the issues are the same.[128]

Generally speaking, it is safe to say that there is at least an informal system of precedent in WTO dispute settlement. While the role of precedent might not be quite as strong as in some common law systems, it is fairly important.

Of course, there are some complications in determining the precise deference to specific precedent. Clearly, a prior Appellate Body finding is the highest level. Adopted GATT and WTO panel reports come next. However, the relative weight to be given to a WTO or GATT panel is open to question. WTO panel reports are more recent, which generally suggests that they are more relevant. On the other hand, GATT panel reports were explicitly endorsed by all of the GATT Contracting Parties (as a result of the positive consensus rules). After adopted panel reports come WTO panel reports that were never put on the agenda for adoption (to date, this has occurred only once),[129] followed by unadopted GATT panel reports. Finally, there are dissenting opinions in panel and

---

[126] Appellate Body Report, *Japan—Alcoholic Beverages III*, 14.

[127] *Ibid*, fn 30.

[128] Appellate Body Report, *US—OCTG Sunset Reviews*, para 188.

[129] Panel Report, *EC—Bananas, Article 21.5 (EC)*. This report was issued in the context of the Bananas dispute. It was based on the EC's request for the Art 21.5 panel to declare the revised EC measures to be in

Appellate Body reports and WTO panel findings that were reversed by the Appellate Body. While these findings were specifically rejected, the fact that they had enough support to form part of the formal jurisprudence suggests that there is a possibility they could be resurrected in the future.

The complexities of this issue and growing pains in the system can be seen in *US—Zeroing (Japan)*, where the panel 'recognize(d) the important systemic considerations in favour of following adopted panel and Appellate Body reports' before declining to adopt the approach used previously by the Appellate Body, and later outlining in detail its reasons for declining to adopt the approach based on the substance of the issue:

> 7.99. We have carefully considered the arguments of Japan in favour of a broader application of the "product as a whole" concept in a manner consistent with the reasoning of the Appellate Body in *US—Zeroing (EC)*. However, while we recognize the important systemic considerations in favour of following adopted panel and Appellate Body reports, we have decided not to adopt that approach for the reasons outlined below. [733]

---

[733] It is well established that panel and Appellate Body reports are not binding, except with respect to resolving the particular dispute between the parties to the dispute, but that such reports create 'legitimate expectations' among WTO Members and should therefore be taken into account where they are relevant to any dispute. . . . The Appellate Body has stated that '. . . following the Appellate Body's conclusions in earlier disputes is not only appropriate, but is what would be expected from panels, especially where the issues are the same'. . . . This notion of an 'expectation' that panels will follow Appellate Body reports (as well as panel reports) is supported by important systemic considerations, including the objective, referred to in Article 3.2 of the DSU, of providing security and predictability to the multilateral trading system. At the same time, a panel is under an obligation under Article 11 of the DSU to 'make an objective assessment of the matter before it, including an objective assessment of the facts of the case and the applicability of and conformity with the relevant covered agreements . . .' Moreover, Article 3.2 of the DSU requires a panel 'to clarify the existing provisions of those agreements in accordance with customary rules of interpretation of public international law' and provides that '[r]ecommendations and rulings of the DSB cannot add to or diminish the rights and obligations provided in covered agreements'.[130]

In essence, the panel stated that while it knew it was supposed to follow Appellate Body precedent, it would not do so in a situation where it felt that a proper interpretation dictated otherwise. Such direct rejection by a panel of an Appellate Body finding is rare, and the decision of this panel probably reflects the extremely controversial nature of the claim at issue, related to the practice of 'zeroing' of dumping margins. On appeal, the Appellate Body reversed the panel's ruling on the substantive issue, but it did not comment on the panel's decision not to follow precedent.[131]

The Appellate Body later expressed its view on this matter in *US—Stainless Steel (Mexico)*. This was also a case in which the panel had declined to follow Appellate Body jurisprudence on zeroing. The Appellate Body responded in terms which were in part familiar, but which also went somewhat beyond previous statements

---

compliance with WTO rules. No other Members participated in the dispute. When the report did not conclude in favour of the EC view, the EC had no incentive to push for adoption.

[130] Panel Report, *US—Zeroing*, para 7.99, fn 733.

[131] Appellate Body Report, *US—Zeroing*.

158. It is well settled that Appellate Body reports are not binding, except with respect to resolving the particular dispute between the parties. This, however, does not mean that subsequent panels are free to disregard the legal interpretations and the *ratio decidendi* contained in previous Appellate Body reports that have been adopted by the DSB.

Three further statements are of particular note:

160 . . . Ensuring 'security and predictability' in the dispute settlement system, as contemplated in Article 3.2 of the DSU, implies that, absent cogent reasons, an adjudicatory body will resolve the same legal question in the same way in a subsequent case.

161 . . . While the application of a provision may be regarded as confined to the context in which it takes place, the relevance of clarification contained in adopted Appellate Body reports is not limited to the application of a particular provision in a specific case.

162. We are deeply concerned about the Panel's decision to depart from well-established Appellate Body jurisprudence clarifying the interpretation of the same legal issues. The Panel's approach has serious implications for the proper functioning of the WTO dispute settlement system . . .

The precise meaning of paragraph 160 was raised in *US—Continued Zeroing*. According to the EC, the correct understanding was that both panels and the Appellate Body could invoke cogent reasons to depart from their own decisions pertaining to a legal question previously before them, but that panels could not invoke cogent reasons to depart from an Appellate Body decision pertaining to the same legal question.[132] The Appellate Body found it unnecessary to address this point.[133] At least one subsequent panel has signalled its willingness to hear arguments on why it should depart from Appellate Body interpretations, finding, however, that the respondent state had not offered any 'convincing arguments' in this regard.[134]

Paragraphs 158 and 161 can be read together as both seem to convey the same two points using different language. By way of explanation, the first point appears to be that the aspect of panel and Appellate Body reports which binds *only* the parties comprise the findings on whether the challenged measure(s) violate any provision(s) of the WTO agreements. The second point is that legal interpretations of the provisions have a binding quality in future disputes involving the same legal question.

(iii) Objective Assessment (Standard of Review Applied to Panels)

Article 11 of the DSU provides guidance for the 'function of panels', establishing that a panel's responsibility is to:

[A]ssist the DSB in discharging its responsibilities under this Understanding and the covered agreements. Accordingly, a panel should make an objective assessment of the matter before it, including an objective assessment of the facts of the case and the applicability of and conformity with the relevant covered agreements, and make such other findings as will assist the DSB in making the recommendations or in giving the rulings provided for in the covered agreements.

In some cases, Members who 'lose' at the panel stage of proceedings (both complainants

---

[132] Appellate Body Report, *US—Continued Zeroing*, para 363.
[133] *Ibid.* para 365.
[134] Panel Report, *Dominican Republic—Bag and Fabric Safeguards*, para 7.129.

and respondents) base an appeal in part on an allegation that the panel failed to make an 'objective assessment' of the matter and the facts. In several early cases, the Appellate Body appeared to set a high standard for such claims, characterising an allegation of the panel failing to conduct an objective assessment as a 'very serious allegation' that challenges the 'very core of the integrity of the WTO dispute settlement process itself'.[135]

In *EC—Hormones*, the EC argued that the panel failed to make an 'objective assessment of the facts' by 'disregard[ing] or distort[ing]' the evidence submitted and the opinions and statements made by the scientific experts advising the panel.[136] The Appellate Body explained that making a claim that a panel has disregarded or distorted evidence is a claim that the panel has denied the party submitting the evidence 'fundamental fairness' or 'due process of law or natural justice'.[137] (It further noted that the issue of whether a panel has made an objective assessment of the facts under Article 11 of the DSU was a 'legal question' and, thus, within the scope of Appellate review under Article 17.6 of the DSU.)[138] The Appellate Body then considered the four evidentiary issues for which the EC claimed that the panel failed to make an objective assessment. In rejecting all of the claims, the Appellate Body made clear that 'it is generally within the discretion of the panel to decide which evidence it chooses to utilize in making findings' and further that 'the Panel cannot realistically refer to all statements made by the experts advising it and should be allowed a substantial margin of discretion as to which statements are useful to refer to explicitly'.[139] In addition, while recognising that the panel misinterpreted a portion of the evidence, the Appellate Body found that the mistakes did not rise to the level of 'deliberate disregard' or 'wilful distortion or misrepresentation' of the evidence.[140]

More recently, however, the Appellate Body seems to have loosened the standard a bit. It now emphasises that panels have a 'margin of discretion' as the trier of facts.[141] It has found that this margin has been exceeded, and thus a violation of Article 11 exists, in a variety of circumstances. For example, in *Chile—Price Band System*, the Appellate Body found that the panel violated Article 11 of the DSU when it ruled on a claim under Article II:1(b), second sentence of the GATT that was neither made nor argued by Argentina during the panel proceeding. In doing so, the Appellate Body said, the panel violated the requirement of 'due process' by depriving Chile (the responding party) of a 'fair right of response'.[142] In so holding, the Appellate Body rejected an Argentinean argument that the panel 'had the right, indeed the duty, to develop its own legal reasoning to support the proper resolution of Argentina's claim'. The Appellate Body distinguished this case from the situation in both *EC—Hormones* and *US—Certain EC Products*, where the capacity of panels to develop their own legal reasoning was affirmed by explaining that the complainants in the prior cases had advanced arguments in support of the finding made by the panels, even though those arguments were not the same as the interpretation ultimately adopted by the panels. By contrast, Argentina never made a claim nor advanced any legal arguments under Article II:1(b), second sentence. Therefore, as Argentina never

---

[135] Appellate Body Report, *EC—Poultry*, para 133.
[136] Appellate Body Report, *EC—Hormones*, para 131.
[137] *Ibid*, para 133.
[138] *Ibid*, paras 132–33.
[139] *Ibid*, paras 135, 138.
[140] *Ibid*, paras 133, 138, 139, 253(e).
[141] See, eg Appellate Body Report, *Dominican Republic—Cigarettes*, para 78.
[142] Appellate Body Report, *Chile—Price Band System*, para 149.

made a claim, the Appellate Body concluded that '[t]he Panel was not entitled to make a claim for Argentina, or to develop its own legal reasoning on a provision that was not at issue'.[143] Thus, while the panel did not act in 'bad faith' and did not 'refuse to consider' or 'distort' or 'misrepresent' any evidence, the Appellate Body pointed out that a panel's obligations under Article 11 'go beyond a panel's appreciation of the evidence before it'. The Appellate Body stated: 'Article 11 obliges panels not only to make "an objective assessment of the facts of the case", but also "an objective assessment of the matter before it"'. In this context, the Appellate Body reasoned that, by making a finding on a claim that was not made, the panel had assessed a provision that 'was not a part "of the matter before it"' and that, because it had made a finding on a provision that was not before it, the panel did not make an objective assessment of the matter: 'the Panel acted *ultra petita* and inconsistently with Article 11 of the *DSU*'.[144]

The Appellate Body has also found violations in situations involving the consideration of evidence. In *US—Cotton Yarn*, for instance, the Appellate Body found that the panel exceeded its mandate under Article 11 of the DSU by considering, in the context of reviewing a safeguard determination under Article 6.2 of the Agreement on Textiles and Clothing, evidence relating to facts which predated the determination and which were not in existence at the time the determination was made.[145]

Thus, despite its early statements on the issue, the Appellate Body appears willing to find violations of Article 11 of the DSU in a number of circumstances. Where it does, the panel's findings will be reversed. (The ultimate outcome of the issue may depend on the ability of the Appellate Body to 'complete the analysis' on the issue, a standard which we discuss below.)

(iv) Standard of Review to be Applied to Actions of Domestic Actors

In the previous section, we discussed how the 'objective assessment' standard in Article 11 of the DSU has been used by the Appellate Body as a standard that panels must meet. In addition Article 11 has also been used to establish the standard that panels themselves are to apply when reviewing certain decisions of domestic government agencies. In a sense, the issue is the level of deference that WTO panels must give to domestic decisions, and has some parallels to the standard of review that domestic appeals courts use when reviewing lower court decisions.

There are two types of decisions that are of most relevance here: decisions of government agencies to apply sanitary and phytosanitary (SPS) measures; and quasi-judicial decisions of government agencies in the context of trade remedies (anti-dumping, countervailing duties and safeguards). The standard has been somewhat controversial in both contexts, with a number of domestic groups taking the view that the WTO has intruded too far into the domestic decision-making process by finding that well-reasoned domestic decisions violate WTO rules.

Standard of Review for Domestic SPS Decisions One of the early WTO decisions in the area of standard of review was in the *EC—Hormones* case, a contentious case involving an EC decision to ban certain meats that had been treated with hormones. The purported

---

[143] *Ibid*, paras 165–68.
[144] *Ibid*, paras 172–73.
[145] Appellate Body Report, *US—Cotton Yarn*, paras 67–80.

reason for the ban was a risk to human health from consuming such meat. Canada and the US challenged the ban as being, *inter alia*, discriminatory and not based on sound science, pursuant to a number of rules, including the SPS Agreement. The WTO panel hearing the case found that the EC actions violated a number of WTO rules. One of the issues raised during the case was the amount of deference that the WTO panel should have given to the EC's internal decision-making process in adopting the ban. The Appellate Body found as follows on this point:

Appellate Body Report, *EC Measures Concerning Meat and Meat Products (Hormones)*, Adopted 13 February 1998, WT/DS26,48/AB/R

111. In the view of the European Communities, the principal alternative approaches to the problem of formulating the "proper standard of review" so far as panels are concerned are two-fold. The first is designated as "*de novo* review". This standard of review would allow a panel complete freedom to come to a different view than the competent authority of the Member whose act or determination is being reviewed. A panel would have to "verify whether the determination by the national authority was 'correct' both factually and procedurally". The second is described as "deference". Under a "deference" standard, a panel, in the submission of the European Communities, should not seek to redo the investigation conducted by the national authority but instead examine whether the "procedure" required by the relevant WTO rules had been followed . . .

114. The first point that must be made in this connection, is that the *SPS Agreement* itself is silent on the matter of an appropriate standard of review for panels deciding upon SPS measures of a Member. Nor are there provisions in the DSU or any of the covered agreements (other than the *Anti Dumping Agreement*) prescribing a particular standard of review. Only Article 17.6(i) of the *Anti-Dumping Agreement* has language on the standard of review to be employed by panels engaged in the "assessment of the facts of the matter". We find no indication in the *SPS Agreement* of an intent on the part of the Members to adopt or incorporate into that Agreement the standard set out in Article 17.6(i) of the *Anti-Dumping Agreement*. Textually, Article 17.6(i) is specific to the *Anti-Dumping Agreement*.

115. The standard of review appropriately applicable in proceedings under the *SPS Agreement*, of course, must reflect the balance established in that Agreement between the jurisdictional competences conceded by the Members to the WTO and the jurisdictional competences retained by the Members for themselves. To adopt a standard of review not clearly rooted in the text of the *SPS Agreement* itself, may well amount to changing that finely drawn balance; and neither a panel nor the Appellate Body is authorized to do that.

116. We do not mean, however, to suggest that there is at present no standard of review applicable to the determination and assessment of the facts in proceedings under the *SPS Agreement* or under other covered agreements. In our view, Article 11 of the DSU bears directly on this matter and, in effect, articulates with great succinctness but with sufficient clarity the appropriate standard of review for panels in respect of both the ascertainment of facts and the legal characterization of such facts under the relevant agreements. Article 11 reads thus:

The function of panels is to assist the DSB in discharging its responsibilities under this Understanding and the covered agreements. Accordingly, a panel should make an objective assessment of the matter before it, including an objective assessment of the facts of the case and the applicability of and conformity with the relevant covered agreements, and make such other findings as will assist the DSB in making the recommendations or in giving the rulings provided in the covered agreements. Panels should consult regularly with the parties to the dispute and give them adequate opportunity to develop a mutually satisfactory solution".

117. So far as fact-finding by panels is concerned, their activities are always constrained by the mandate of Article 11 of the DSU: the applicable standard is neither *de novo* review as such, nor "total deference", but rather the "objective assessment of the facts". Many panels have in the past refused to undertake *de novo* review, wisely, since under current practice and systems, they are in any case poorly suited to engage in such a review. On the other hand, "total deference to the findings of the national authorities", it has been well said, "could not ensure an 'objective assessment' as foreseen by Article 11 of the DSU".

118. In so far as legal questions are concerned—that is, consistency or inconsistency of a Member's measure with the provisions of the applicable agreement—a standard not found in the text of the *SPS Agreement* itself cannot absolve a panel (or the Appellate Body) from the duty to apply the customary rules of interpretation of public international law. It may be noted that the European Communities refrained from suggesting that Article 17.6 of the *Anti-Dumping Agreement* in its entirety was applicable to the present case. Nevertheless, it is appropriate to stress that here again Article 11 of the DSU is directly on point, requiring a panel to "make an objective assessment of the matter before it, including an objective assessment of the facts of the case and the applicability of and conformity with the relevant covered agreements . . .".

119. We consider, therefore, that the issue of failure to apply an appropriate standard of review, raised by the European Communities, resolves itself into the issue of whether or not the Panel, in making the above and other findings referred to and appealed by the European Communities, had made an "objective assessment of the matter before it, including *an objective assessment of the facts* . . .". This particular issue is addressed (in substantial detail) below. Here, however, we uphold the findings of the Panel appealed by the European Communities upon the ground of failure to apply either a "deferential reasonableness standard" or the standard of review set out in Article 17.6(i) of the *Anti-Dumping Agreement*.

… … …

The above excerpt sets out the basic framework of the standard of review issue. There is a continuum of different possible levels of deference. At one end is a *de novo* standard, under which a panel may give no deference to the view of the competent authority of the Member whose act or determination is being reviewed, and may instead substitute its own view. At the other end would be 'total deference', under which domestic decisions could not be reviewed at all. In between are a number of possibilities, such as the 'deference' standard mentioned by the EC under which the WTO panel should not seek to redo the investigation conducted by the national authority but instead examine whether the 'procedure' required by the relevant WTO rules had been followed. The Appellate Body did not explain precisely where on this continuum the standard of review for SPS decisions lies. Instead, it simply referred to the 'objective assessment' standard in Article 11 of the DSU. In the next section, we explore how this standard has been further developed in the trade remedy context.

Standard of Review for Trade Remedy Decisions For trade remedies, unlike SPS measures, the domestic measure at issue is one based on a quasi-judicial decision by a government agency. The decision can be appealed to a domestic court, in which case it will be assessed for compatibility with national laws and regulations using the domestic standard of review. However, a complaint can also be brought at the WTO. The assessment here is whether decisions comply with the obligations contained in the relevant WTO agreements. The applicable standard of review is also a matter of WTO law.

In an early WTO dispute, the panel in *US—Underwear* examined the standard of review to be applied in the context of a safeguard measure imposed pursuant to the Agreement on Textiles and Clothing (ATC). As with the *EC—Hormones* case excerpted in the previous section, this panel also held that a policy of total deference to the findings of the national authorities could not ensure an 'objective assessment' as foreseen by Article 11 of the DSU. The panel stated:

> 7.12 . . . [T]he Panel's function should be to assess objectively the review conducted by the national investigating authority . . . We draw particular attention to the fact that a series of panel reports in the anti-dumping and subsidies/countervailing duties context have made it clear that it is not the role of panels to engage in a *de novo* review. In our view, the same is true for panels operating in the context of the ATC, since they would be called upon, as in the context of cases dealing with anti-dumping and/or subsidies/countervailing duties, to review the consistency of a determination by a national investigating authority imposing a restriction under the relevant provisions of the relevant WTO legal instruments, in this case the ATC. In our view, the task of the Panel is to examine the consistency of the US action with the international obligations of the United States, and not the consistency of the US action with the US domestic statute implementing the international obligations of the United States. Consequently, the ATC constitutes, in our view, the relevant legal framework in this matter.
>
> 7.13 . . . In our view, an objective assessment would entail an examination of whether the [national investigating authority] had examined all relevant facts before it (including facts which might detract from an affirmative determination in accordance with the second sentence of Article 6.2 of the ATC), whether adequate explanation had been provided of how the facts as a whole supported the determination made, and, consequently, whether the determination made was consistent with the international obligations of the United States. . . .[146]

The standard set out in paragraph 7.13 has been elaborated on in many later cases in the context of the Safeguards Agreement, countervailing duties under the SCM Agreement, and the Anti-Dumping Agreement (which has a special standard of review for legal issues). We discuss several of these cases briefly below to illustrate how this standard has been applied to trade remedy decisions generally.

In *Argentina—Footwear Safeguards,* the Appellate Body affirmed that Article 11 of the DSU sets forth the appropriate standard of review for panels under all circumstances except for the Anti-Dumping Agreement, for which Article 17.6 sets out a special standard of review (we discuss the special rules in Article 17.6 later in this chapter and also in Chapter 11). The Appellate Body then emphasised that a panel should not conduct a '*de facto de novo* review' of the findings and conclusions of the investigating authority; in other words, the panel should not substitute its analysis and judgment for those of the investigating authorities. Rather, the Appellate Body held that the panel should examine whether, as required by Article 4 of the Agreement on Safeguards, the investigating authorities had considered all the relevant facts and had adequately explained how the facts supported the determinations that were made. The Appellate Body explained that in the case at hand:

> [W]ith respect to its *application* of the standard of review, we do not believe that the Panel conducted a *de novo* review of the evidence, or that it substituted its analysis and judgement for that of the Argentine authorities. Rather, the Panel examined whether, as required by Article 4 of the *Agreement on Safeguards*, the Argentine authorities had considered all the relevant facts and had adequately explained how the facts supported the determinations that were made.

---

[146] Panel Report, *US—Underwear*, paras 7.12–13.

Indeed, far from departing from its responsibility, in our view, the Panel was simply fulfilling its responsibility under Article 11 of the DSU in taking the approach it did. To determine whether the safeguard investigation and the resulting safeguard measure applied by Argentina were consistent with Article 4 of the *Agreement on Safeguards*, the Panel was obliged, by the very terms of Article 4, to assess whether the Argentine authorities had examined all the relevant facts and had provided a reasoned explanation of how the facts supported their determination.[147]

In a more recent decision involving both anti-dumping and countervailing duties, the Appellate Body offered the following explanation of the standard of review in the trade remedy decision context:

Appellate Body Report, *United States—Investigation of the International Trade Commission in Softwood Lumber from Canada*, Recourse to Article 21.5 of the DSU by Canada, Adopted 9 May 2006, WT/DS277/AB/RW

93. We begin our analysis with an examination of the requirements of Article 11 of the DSU in the context of the review by a panel of determinations made by investigating authorities. As Canada's appeal is primarily focused on the Panel's examination of how the USITC treated the evidence before it, we examine first the duties that apply to panels in their review of the *factual components* of the findings made by investigating authorities. The Appellate Body has considered these duties on several previous occasions. It is well established that a panel must neither conduct a *de novo* review nor simply defer to the conclusions of the national authority. A panel's examination of those conclusions must be critical and searching, and be based on the information contained in the record and the explanations given by the authority in its published report. A panel must examine whether, in the light of the evidence on the record, the conclusions reached by the investigating authority are reasoned and adequate. What is "adequate" will inevitably depend on the facts and circumstances of the case and the particular claims made, but several general lines of inquiry are likely to be relevant. The panel's scrutiny should test whether the reasoning of the authority is coherent and internally consistent. The panel must undertake an in-depth examination of whether the explanations given disclose how the investigating authority treated the facts and evidence in the record and whether there was positive evidence before it to support the inferences made and conclusions reached by it. The panel must examine whether the explanations provided demonstrate that the investigating authority took proper account of the complexities of the data before it, and that it explained why it rejected or discounted alternative explanations and interpretations of the record evidence. A panel must be open to the possibility that the explanations given by the authority are not reasoned or adequate in the light of other plausible alternative explanations, and must take care not to assume itself the role of initial trier of facts, nor to be passive by "simply *accept[ing]* the conclusions of the competent authorities".

...

99. [T]he injunction that panels should not substitute their own conclusions for those of the competent authorities does *not* mean that all a panel needs to do in order to comply with its duties when reviewing a determination is to consider whether the investigating authority's findings or conclusions appear to be "reasonable" or "plausible" in the abstract. To the contrary, a panel can assess whether an authority's explanation for its determination is reasoned and adequate *only* if the panel critically examines that explanation in the light of the facts and the alternative explanations that were before that authority. A panel's consideration of whether a certain inference can reasonably be drawn from individual pieces of evidence and/or from

---

[147] Appellate Body Report, *Argentina—Footwear Safeguards*, para 121. See also Panel Report, *Korea—Dairy Safeguards*, para 7.30.

evidence in its totality is one of the means by which a panel satisfies its duty to examine whether a determination was based on positive evidence on the record. In its assessment, the panel should seek to review the determination while giving due regard to the approach taken by the investigating authority, or it risks constructing a case different from the one put forward by that authority. Finally, in its assessment of whether the conclusions reached by an investigating authority are reasoned and adequate, "[a] panel may not reject an [investigating authority's] conclusions simply because the panel would have arrived at a different outcome if it were making the determination itself."

... ...

Summing up this issue, the standard of review applied in the trade remedy context has extremely important implications. With most WTO complaints outside the trade remedy context, WTO panels will simply consider whether the measure is consistent with WTO rules. Thus, there is no 'deference' to the government actor which adopted the measure, in terms of whether it acted 'reasonably' or provided 'adequate explanations'. By contrast, with trade remedy decisions, WTO panels can be said to review the decision-making *process* as much as the decision itself. Was the agency's decision well-reasoned? Did the agency look at the factors it was supposed to? Did the agency explain itself clearly? If the decision satisfies these and other criteria, it will likely be found consistent with WTO rules, even if the panel itself might not have reached the same conclusion if it had been making the underlying decision.

For the most part, as noted, WTO trade remedy rules do not contain an explicit standard of review. As a result, Article 11 of the DSU has been applied in these cases, as set out in the above excerpts. In essence, the 'objective assessment' standard has been used to require panels to consider the appropriateness of the agency decisions by reviewing certain aspects of those decisions. However, the Anti-Dumping Agreement does set out an explicit standard of review. Article 17.6 provides in part:

(i) in its assessment of the facts of the matter, the panel shall determine whether the authorities' establishment of the facts was proper and whether their evaluation of those facts was unbiased and objective. If the establishment of the facts was proper and the evaluation was unbiased and objective, even though the panel might have reached a different conclusion, the evaluation shall not be overturned;

(ii) the panel shall interpret the relevant provisions of the Agreement in accordance with customary rules of interpretation of public international law. Where the panel finds that a relevant provision of the Agreement admits of more than one permissible interpretation, the panel shall find the authorities' measure to be in conformity with the Agreement if it rests upon one of those permissible interpretations.

Sub-paragraph (ii) establishes the legal standard of review, which is a special standard that applies only to legal interpretations. We discuss this standard further in Chapter 11 on Dumping and Anti-Dumping Measures. Sub-paragraph (i), however, deals with the factual standard of review, and uses similar language to the standard of review jurisprudence noted above. Under sub-paragraph (i), the WTO panel will examine whether the government agency's 'establishment of the facts' was 'proper' and whether 'their evaluation of those facts was unbiased and objective'. This standard has parallels to the Article 11 standard, in that it reviews the agency's reasoning and the approach taken.

(v) Judicial Economy

Panels sometimes exercise 'judicial economy' and only make the findings necessary to support a ruling of inconsistency or otherwise resolve the dispute at issue. The principle of judicial economy is recognised in WTO jurisprudence and, in practice, panels frequently rely on it and do not examine all claims by the complaining party. This occurs despite the language of Article 7.2 of the DSU, which instructs panels to 'address the relevant provisions in any covered agreement or agreements cited by the parties to the dispute'.

The practice was affirmed by the Appellate Body in *US—Shirts and Blouses*. Recalling that previous GATT 1947 and WTO panels have frequently addressed only the issues considered necessary for the resolution of the matter and finding that '[n]othing in this provision or in previous GATT practice requires a panel to examine all legal claims made by the complaining party', the Appellate Body explained:

> [I]f a panel found that a measure was inconsistent with a particular provision of the GATT 1947, it generally did not go on to examine whether the measure was also inconsistent with other GATT provisions that a complaining party may have argued were violated. In recent WTO practice, panels likewise have refrained from examining each and every claim made by the complaining party and have made findings only on those claims that such panels concluded were necessary to resolve the particular matter.[148]

The Appellate Body then discounted the fact that some panels in the past did consider issues that were not absolutely necessary to dispose of the particular dispute by again pointing out that nothing in the DSU requires panels to consider every issue. It further noted that a requirement that panels consider every issue would not be consistent with the aim of the WTO dispute settlement system generally, and specifically Article 3.7 of the DSU, which states: 'The aim of the dispute settlement mechanism is to secure a positive solution to a dispute. A solution mutually acceptable to the parties to a dispute and consistent with the covered agreements is clearly to be preferred'. The Appellate Body also stated that, given the 'explicit aim of dispute settlement that permeates the DSU', Article 3.2 of the DSU is 'not meant to encourage either panels or the Appellate Body to "make law" by clarifying existing provisions of the WTO Agreement outside the context of resolving a particular dispute', but instead the provision means that a panel 'need only address those claims which must be addressed in order to resolve the matter in issue in the dispute'.[149]

In *EC—Poultry*, the Appellate Body recalled and agreed with the finding in *US—Shirts and Blouses* that nothing in Article 11 requires panels to examine every legal claim raised by the complaining party, and it seemingly extended the principle of judicial economy by holding that the panel has similar discretion to 'address only those *arguments* it deems necessary to resolve a particular claim'.[150]

In *Canada—Autos*, the Appellate Body stated its preference for panels to explicitly state that they are exercising judicial economy when they do not address a particular claim. Although the Appellate Body did not question the panel's use of judicial economy, it stated that, 'for purposes of transparency and fairness to the parties, a panel should,

---

[148] Appellate Body Report, *US—Shirts and Blouses*, 18.
[149] *Ibid.*
[150] Appellate Body Report, *EC—Poultry*, para 135 (emphasis added by the Appellate Body).

however, in all cases, address expressly those claims which it declines to examine and rule upon for reasons of judicial economy. Silence does not suffice for these purposes'.[151]

The principle of judicial economy does have its limits. For instance, in *US—Lead and Bismuth II*, the Appellate Body rejected an argument that the panel was *required* to exercise judicial economy and not address issues which did not need to be addressed for resolving the dispute at hand. In its ruling, the Appellate Body underscored the fact that the exercise of judicial economy was within the discretion of a panel, but that a panel was never required to exercise judicial economy. The Appellate Body stated:

> The [Member putting forth the argument] seems to consider that our Report in *United States—Shirts and Blouses* sets forth a general principle that panels may not address any issues that need not be addressed in order to resolve the dispute between the parties. We do not agree with this characterization of our findings. In that appeal, India had argued that it was entitled to a finding by the Panel on each of the legal claims that it had made. We, however, found that the principle of judicial economy allows a panel to decline to rule on certain claims.[152]

In practice, some panels consider additional issues that are seemingly unnecessary to resolve the dispute, as an alternative basis for its findings. They often take this approach so that if the Appellate Body reverses one aspect of the panel's reasoning on an issue, the Appellate Body can still uphold the alternative finding.

The Appellate Body has also explained that panels can misuse the principle of judicial economy. For example, in *Australia—Salmon*, the Appellate Body held that judicial economy could not be exercised where only a partial resolution of a dispute would result:

> 223. The principle of judicial economy has to be applied keeping in mind the aim of the dispute settlement system. This aim is to resolve the matter at issue and 'to secure a positive solution to a dispute'. To provide only a partial resolution of the matter at issue would be false judicial economy. A panel has to address those claims on which a finding is necessary in order to enable the DSB to make sufficiently precise recommendations and rulings so as to allow for prompt compliance by a Member with those recommendations and rulings 'in order to ensure effective resolution of disputes to the benefit of all Members.'

> 224. In this case, for the Panel to make findings concerning violation of Article 5.1 with respect to other Canadian salmon, without also making findings under Articles 5.5 and 5.6, would not enable the DSB to make sufficiently precise recommendations and rulings so as to allow for compliance by Australia with its obligations under the *SPS Agreement*, in order to ensure the effective resolution of this dispute with Canada. An SPS measure which is brought into consistency with Article 5.1 may still be inconsistent with either Article 5.5 or Article 5.6, or with both.[153]

As a final point, it could be argued that Article 17.12 of the DSU prohibits the Appellate Body, as opposed to panels, from exercising judicial economy. Article 17.12 reads, 'The Appellate Body shall address each of the issues raised'. However, the Appellate Body hinted in *US—Shirts and Blouses* that the principle of judicial economy may extend to its own analysis,[154] and in a number of cases has said that it was not 'necessary' to make a finding on a particular issue, although it did not mention the term 'judicial economy'.[155]

---

[151] Appellate Body Report, *Canada—Autos*, paras 116–17.
[152] Appellate Body Report, *US—Lead and Bismuth II*, para 71.
[153] Appellate Body Report, *Australia—Salmon*, paras 223–24.
[154] Appellate Body Report, *US—Shirts and Blouses*, 19.
[155] See, eg *US—Line Pipe Safeguards*, paras 198–99.

(vi) Completing the Legal Analysis/Remand

Under Article 17 of the DSU, the Appellate Body may uphold, modify or reverse the legal findings and conclusions of the panel. Importantly, the DSU does not provide the Appellate Body with the ability to remand an issue back to the panel in a manner well-known in domestic legal systems. The lack of remand authority means that when the Appellate Body reverses a finding of the panel, sometimes the only way to resolve the issue is for the Appellate Body to act like a panel and make its own findings on the issue. The Appellate Body has referred to this practice as 'completing the legal analysis'.

The Appellate Body's authority to 'complete the analysis' cannot be found in the text of the DSU. Instead, it is a creation of judicial activism, as the Appellate Body's mandate is to merely 'uphold, modify or reverse the legal findings and conclusions of the panel'. Thus, completing the analysis is a bit of a 'grey area' in terms of defining its scope.

This process is illustrated in *Canada—Periodicals*, where the Appellate Body reversed one of the panel's conclusions and 'completed the legal analysis' in order to substitute its own ruling on the issue. In the dispute, the Appellate Body reversed the panel's finding on the issue of 'like products', and, in order to successfully adjudicate the case, made its own finding on whether the products concerned were 'directly competitive or substitutable'.[156] In its view, it was imperative that it complete the analysis to ascertain whether there had been a violation; otherwise the case would not have been successfully resolved, and the Appellate Body would not have fulfilled its obligation to promote the prompt settlement of disputes.

In *EC—Asbestos*, the Appellate Body clarified the conditions under which it would complete the analysis by stating that it may do so only if the factual findings of the panel and the undisputed facts in the panel record provide it with a sufficient basis to conduct its own analysis, and its analysis is closely related to the panel's analysis.[157] Subsequent cases have provided additional guidance, but the standard is still somewhat vague.

The EC, as part of the DSU Review, has proposed the introduction of a limited remand procedure, under which any party can, within 10 days after the adoption of the Appellate Body Report, request the DSB to remand back to the panel those issues on which the Appellate Body could not rule.[158] The EC model for remand authority has been included in the draft amendments to the DSU with the hope that it will strengthen the legal foundation of the DSU and end the uncertain status of 'completing the legal analysis'.[159]

(vii) Panel Fact-finding

WTO panel proceedings are less fact-intensive than many domestic proceedings. The focus in WTO complaints is usually the measures themselves, that is, what they say and how they operate. There are no witnesses to call or physical evidence to present (although affidavits have been submitted). Instead, it is mainly just arguments and documentation provided by the parties, with questions from the panel or Appellate Body.

---

[156] Appellate Body Report, *Canada—Periodicals*, ss VI.B, VIII(c)).

[157] Appellate Body Report, *EC—Asbestos*, paras 78–79.

[158] Communication from the European Communities, TN/DS/W/38 (23 January 2003) 6.

[159] See Special Session of the Dispute Settlement Body, Report by the Chairman, Ambassador Péter Balás, to the Trade Negotiations Committee, TN/DS/9 (6 June 2003). The Chairman's Text of 28 May 2003, doc. Job(03)/91/Rev.1, is contained as in annex to doc. TN/DS/9.

Nevertheless, there are some situations where panels request information from outside experts in order to help understand and resolve the dispute. Article 13 of the DSU establishes that panels may 'seek information' in this way. Panels have taken advantage of this privilege to request information from international organisations, from the parties to the dispute, from Members who were not parties and from experts. One notable area in this regard is in disputes under the SPS Agreement, where Article 11.2 of the SPS Agreement sets out special rules for consultation with experts on the highly technical scientific issues involved.

(viii) Adverse Inferences

As noted, Article 13.1 of the DSU grants panels the authority to seek information and technical advice. In *Canada—Aircraft*, the Appellate Body addressed the issue of whether panels have the authority to draw adverse inferences from a party's refusal to provide information. In this dispute, Canada refused during consultations to provide Brazil with information on the financing of its aircraft industry. Canada also subsequently refused the panel's request that Canada provide the information. Brazil appealed the panel's decision not to draw an adverse inference from Canada's refusal to provide the requested information. The Appellate Body held that it is within the discretion of panels to draw adverse inferences, although in this case it concluded that the panel had not abused its discretion by refusing to draw adverse inferences. The Appellate Body stated:

> 202. There is no logical reason why the Members of the WTO would, in conceiving and concluding the *SCM Agreement*, have granted panels the authority to draw inferences in cases involving actionable subsidies that *may* be illegal *if* they have certain trade effects, but not in cases that involve prohibited export subsidies for which the adverse effects are presumed. To the contrary, the appropriate inference is that the authority to draw adverse inferences from a Member's refusal to provide information belongs *a fortiori* also to panels examining claims of prohibited export subsidies. Indeed, that authority seems to us an ordinary aspect of the task of all panels to determine the relevant facts of any dispute involving any covered agreement: a view supported by the general practice and usage of international tribunals.

> 203. Clearly, in our view, the Panel had the legal authority and the discretion to draw inferences from the facts before it—including the fact that Canada had refused to provide information sought by the Panel.

> ...

> 205. . . . Yet, we do not believe that the record provides a sufficient basis for us to hold that the Panel erred in law, or abused its discretionary authority, in concluding that Brazil had not done enough to compel the Panel to make the inferences requested by Brazil. For this reason, we let the Panel's finding of *not proven* remain, and we decline Brazil's appeal on this issue. (emphasis in original)[160]

This ruling was confirmed in *US—Wheat Gluten*, where the EC argued that the panel had failed to 'draw the necessary adverse inferences from the United States' refusal to submit . . . requested information', and it claimed this failure was an error of law and a violation of Article 11 of the DSU. In rejecting the argument, the Appellate Body

---

[160] Appellate Body Report, *Canada—Aircraft*, paras 202–03, 205.

characterised the drawing of inferences as 'a 'discretionary' task falling within a panel's duties under Article 11', and stated:

> 175. In reviewing the inferences the Panel drew from the facts of record, our task on appeal is not to redo afresh the Panel's assessment of those facts, and decide for ourselves what inferences we would draw from them. Rather, we must determine whether the Panel improperly exercised its discretion, under Article 11, by failing to draw certain inferences from the facts before it. In asking us to conduct such a review, an appellant must indicate clearly the manner in which a panel has improperly exercised its discretion. Taking into account the full *ensemble* of the facts, *the appellant should, at least: identify the facts on the record from which the Panel should have drawn inferences; indicate the factual or legal inferences that the panel should have drawn from those facts; and, finally, explain why the failure of the panel to exercise its discretion by drawing these inferences amounts to an error of law under Article 11 of the DSU.* (emphasis added)[161]

Applying the law to the facts of the case, the Appellate Body pointed out that the EC presented 'broad and general statements' claiming the panel erred by not drawing adverse inferences from the facts. However, the Appellate Body stated that the EC:

> 176. [Did] not identify, in any specific manner, *which facts* supported a particular inference. Nor [did] the European Communities identify *what inferences* the Panel should have drawn from those facts, other than that the inferences should have been favourable to the European Communities. Besides the simple refusal of the United States to provide information requested by the Panel, which we have already addressed, the European Communities does not offer any other specific reasons why the Panel's failure to exercise its discretion by drawing the inferences identified by the European Communities amounts to an error of law under Article 11 of the DSU. Therefore, we decline this ground of appeal.[162]

(d) Multilateralism versus Unilateralism

Prior to the WTO, the US was often criticised for making unilateral determinations that other countries were not complying with international trade rules or were otherwise burdening international trade, and imposing trade sanctions in response. Article 23 of the DSU was designed, in part, to limit the use of unilateral trade measures. According to Article 23:

> 1. When Members seek the redress of a violation of obligations or other nullification or impairment of benefits under the covered agreements or an impediment to the attainment of any objective of the covered agreements, they shall have recourse to, and abide by, the rules and procedures of this Understanding.

> 2. In such cases, Members shall:

> (a) not make a determination to the effect that a violation has occurred, that benefits have been nullified or impaired or that the attainment of any objective of the covered agreements has been impeded, except through recourse to dispute settlement in accordance with the rules and procedures of this Understanding, and shall make any such determination consistent with the findings contained in the panel or Appellate Body report adopted by the DSB or an arbitration award rendered under this Understanding;

---

[161] Appellate Body Report, *US—Wheat Gluten*, para 175.
[162] *Ibid*, para 176.

(b) follow the procedures set forth in Article 21 to determine the reasonable period of time for the Member concerned to implement the recommendations and rulings; and

(c) follow the procedures set forth in Article 22 to determine the level of suspension of concessions or other obligations and obtain DSB authorization in accordance with those procedures before suspending concessions or other obligations under the covered agreements in response to the failure of the Member concerned to implement the recommendations and rulings within that reasonable period of time.

Thus, under this provision, Members may not address trade disputes through unilateral determination and action. Rather, they must follow the procedures of the DSU. The following excerpt identifies the rationale for Article 23.

Panel Report, *United States—Import Measures on Certain Products from the European Communities***, Adopted 10 January 2001, WT/DS165/R**

6.14 An important reason why Article 23 of the DSU must be interpreted with a view to prohibiting any form of unilateral action is because such unilateral actions threaten the stability and predictability of the multilateral trade system, a necessary component for "market conditions conducive to individual economic activity in national and global markets" which, in themselves, constitute a fundamental goal of the WTO. Unilateral actions are, therefore, contrary to the essence of the multilateral trade system of the WTO. As stated in the Panel Report on *US— Section 301*:

"7.75 Providing security and predictability to the multilateral trading system is another central object and purpose of the system which could be instrumental to achieving the broad objectives of the Preamble. Of all WTO disciplines, the DSU is one of the most important instruments to protect the security and predictability of the multilateral trading system and through it that of the market-place and its different operators. DSU provisions must, thus, be interpreted in the light of this object and purpose and in a manner which would most effectively enhance it."

6.15 In the *US—Section 301* dispute, the Panel was convinced that the legislation at issue had to be examined both from the perspective of the damage it causes to Member governments and from the perspective of the damages caused to the market-place itself. The following statement regarding the mere existence of a law that would allow for some unilateral actions to be taken, is even more relevant in specific instances of unilateral measures, such as those at issue in the present case:

". . . [unilateral actions] may prompt economic operators to change their commercial behaviour in a way that distorts trade. Economic operators may be afraid, say, to continue ongoing trade with, or investment in, the industries or products threatened by unilateral measures. Existing trade may also be distorted because economic operators may feel a need to take out extra insurance to allow for the illegal possibility that the legislation contemplates, thus reducing the relative competitive opportunity of their products on the market. Other operators may be deterred from trading with such a Member altogether, distorting potential trade . . . ."

... ...

It is clear from the text of Article 23 that the question of whether the provision has itself been violated is closely linked to whether other DSU provisions have been violated. Indeed, as the Appellate Body clarified in *United States/Canada—Continued Suspension*, state conduct which is shown to be consistent with the specific provisions governing the conduct in question will not constitute a violation of Article 23. The case concerned the suspension of concessions by the US and Canada against the EC in connection with the hormones dispute. The issue was whether Canada and the US could continue to suspend concessions following the notification by the EC of a Directive taken to bring the EC into conformity with its WTO obligations. The panel found that the continued application of the suspension of concessions after notification of the Directive violated DSU Article 23.2(a) and 23.1. The Appellate Body found as follows:

Appellate Body Report, *United States/Canada—Continued Suspension of Obligations in the EC—Hormones Dispute*, **Adopted 14 November 2008, WT/DS320/AB/R**

374 . . . the suspension of concessions that has been duly authorized by the DSB will not constitute a violation of Article 23.1, as long as it is consistent with other rules of the DSU, including paragraphs 2 through 8 of Article 22, even if the continued application of the suspension of concessions is regarded as an action or part of a process of 'seeking the redress' . . .

375. This does not mean that Article 23.1 ceases to apply once the suspension of concessions has been authorized by the DSB. Article 23.2(c) specifically refers to Article 22 of the DSU. Paragraph 8 of this provision states that the suspension of concessions shall only be applied until the inconsistent measure has been removed or one of the other two conditions in Article 22.8 is met. Thus, if the Member subject to the suspension of concessions takes an implementing measure and that measure is found in WTO dispute settlement proceedings to bring this Member into substantive compliance, the suspension of concessions would no longer be consistent with Article 22.8 of the DSU, and, as a result, would become a unilateral action prohibited by Articles 23.1 and 23.2. In other words, the requirements in Article 22.8 and Article 23 apply and must be read together in the post-suspension stage of a dispute. Therefore, Article 23 must be seen as containing an ongoing obligation and continues to apply even after the suspension of concessions has been duly authorized by the DSB.

376. With this in mind, we turn to examine the issues raised by the United States and Canada on appeal.

2. The Panel's Alleged Examination of Articles 23.2(a) and 23.1 in Isolation from the Requirements in Article 22.8 of the DSU

377. The United States and Canada submit that the Panel erred by examining the European Communities' claims under Articles 23.2(a), 23.1, and 21.5 independently from the question of whether Article 22.8 required the termination of the suspension of concessions. The United States argues that the Panel ignored the fact that none of the conditions requiring the cessation of the suspension of concessions under Article 22.8 of the DSU had occurred. Thus, the United States maintains, the Panel's findings that the suspension of concessions by the United States is 'without recourse to the procedures under the DSU' would effectively undermine the DSB's authorization to suspend concessions, rendering it 'meaningless'. Canada claims that the '[k]ey to this case is Article 22.8 of the DSU' which, as *lex specialis* in the post-suspension phase of a dispute, sets out the three conditions that must be met in order to have the suspension of concessions terminated, one of the conditions being actual compliance with the DSB's recommendations and rulings. Canada adds that 'the continuous involvement of the DSB', pursuant to the second sentence of Article 22.8, 'suggests that [the DSB] retains jurisdiction over the matter until its recommendations and rulings have been fully implemented.' Thus, in Canada's view, the Panel should have first considered whether Canada was required to discontinue the suspension of concessions pursuant to Article 22.8.

378. We note that the suspension of concessions maintained by the United States and Canada were duly authorized by the DSB subsequent to its adoption of the recommendations and rulings in *EC—Hormones* and an arbitration award resulting from proceedings under Article

22.6 regarding the level of the suspension of concessions. As discussed above, where the suspension of concessions has been duly authorized by the DSB and is applied consistently with the rules of the DSU, including Article 22.8, it does not constitute a violation of Article 23.1, because it is not imposed without recourse to or without abiding by the DSU. The requirements in Article 22 and those in Article 23 must be read together, in the post-suspension stage of the dispute, to determine the legality of the continued suspension when an implementing measure has been taken. Thus, we share the view of the United States and Canada that, in order to determine whether they acted inconsistently with Article 23 by continuing the suspension of concessions subsequent to the notification of Directive 2003/74/ EC, the Panel had to first determine whether the suspension of concessions was being applied consistently with Article 22.8 of the DSU.

...

380. . . . . [A] proper interpretation of Article 22.8, in its context and in the light of the object and purpose of the DSU, indicates that substantive compliance is required before the suspension of concessions must be terminated. Where parties disagree as to whether there is substantive compliance, the duty to cease the suspension of concessions is not triggered until substantive compliance is determined through multilateral dispute settlement proceedings. A unilateral declaration of compliance cannot have the same effect. We note that, as the original respondent, the European Communities has the option to initiate Article 21.5 panel proceedings for purposes of determining whether the DSB's recommendations and rulings have been implemented through the adoption of Directive 2003/74/EC.

...

383. In sum, the suspension of concessions maintained by the United States and Canada has been duly authorized by the DSB and was obtained through recourse to the relevant rules and procedures of the DSU, consistently with Article 23.1 of the DSU. Pursuant to Article 22.8, the legality of the continued suspension of concessions depends on whether the measure found to be inconsistent in *EC—Hormones* has been removed, and this requires substantive compliance. We therefore find that the Panel erred in considering that the European Communities' claims under Articles 23.2(a), 23.1, and 21.5 may be examined 'completely separately' from whether the European Communities implemented the DSB's recommendations and rulings in *EC— Hormones*.

384. The DSB's authorization does not mean that Article 23 becomes irrelevant. Rather, as Article 23.2(c) specifies, the suspension of concessions is subject to Article 22, including the requirement in Article 22.8 that it shall only be applied until such time as the measure found to be inconsistent with the covered agreements has been removed. Therefore, the suspension of concessions by the United States and Canada would be in breach of Article 23.2(c), and consequently Article 23.1, if it were established in WTO dispute settlement that the inconsistent measure has indeed been removed within the meaning of Article 22.8 and the suspension is not immediately terminated. Article 22.8 thus provides relevant context for the analysis of the issues appealed under Article 23. Moreover, the application of DSB-authorized suspension of concessions is temporary and subject to the objective conditions laid down in Article 22.8. The United States, Canada, as well as the European Communities, have the shared responsibility to ensure that the suspension of concessions is not applied beyond the time foreseen in Article 22.8. Consequently, the United States and Canada have a duty to engage actively in dispute settlement proceedings concerning whether the suspension of concessions is applied consistently with such conditions. Failing to do so could be contrary to the overarching principle in Article 23.1 prohibiting Members from seeking redress without having recourse to, or abiding by the rules of, the DSU. Nonetheless, this is not

currently the case, because both the United States and Canada are actively engaged in these proceedings initiated by the European Communities to determine whether the measure found to be inconsistent with a covered agreement in *EC—Hormones* has been removed within the meaning of Article 22.8.

... ...

IX. QUESTIONS

1. Why is there no formal system of binding precedent in GATT/WTO law? Can you define the present situation? What status do adopted and unadopted WTO panel and Appellate Body reports have? What status do adopted GATT panel reports have? Should more deference be shown to adopted GATT panel reports because they were explicitly endorsed by all of the GATT Contracting Parties (as a result of the positive consensus rules in effect at the time)?

2. Should the DSU provide for the possibility of remand authority? What effect will this have on the workload of the panelists? Should this issue be linked to the proposals for permanent panelists?

3. Is it a problem that many WTO panelists are government officials who participate in WTO disputes and negotiations?

4. Is the compensation agreement reached by the EC and US to resolve the *US—Copyright* dispute compatible with the DSU? Is monetary compensation what the DSU envisages? Some FTAs now have explicit provisions regarding monetary compensation. Should this concept be brought into the DSU?

5. Why are panel and Appellate Body proceedings 'closed'? Why is the current trend towards openness perhaps taking hold?

6. Should measures that do not mandate a violation of the rules, but rather are vague enough to allow a violation, be prohibited? Is there one categorical answer to this question, or should it vary depending on the specific nature of the measure and the relevant WTO legal provision? Should measures that are not just vague but explicitly establish the discretion to violate WTO rules be prohibited?

7. What is the 'standard of review' to be applied when WTO panels review decisions of domestic government agencies? How does this standard differ from that used by domestic courts?

8. Is the non-violation remedy still necessary now that WTO rules cover so many areas of government policy? Are there many ways left in which governments could undermine their commitments if they wanted to?

9. Does the 'nullification or impairment' requirement continue to serve a useful purpose?

10. A frequent criticism of the 'retaliation' aspect of DSU disputes is that it imposes trade barriers, which the WTO otherwise tries to reduce due to their negative economic impact. Are there any plausible alternatives to the WTO approach? If monetary fines were used, how would they be enforced?

11. Can smaller, developing countries ever really 'win' a dispute given the nature of 'retaliation'? What factors enter the debate? How does the possibility of cross-retaliation impact the debate?

12. Should WTO Members make use of 'good offices, conciliation and mediation' more often?

13. Do 'situation' complaints serve any purpose? Can you think of any circumstances under which they might be useful?

14. What exactly is the 'upsetting the competitive relationship' standard under the nullification or impairment element of a non-violation claim? How does it relate to a non-discrimination standard

15. Is it unfair for responding parties to have to defend themselves in multiple complaints where the disputes cannot be merged due to time considerations?

16. Is a heavy focus on the ordinary meaning of the terms of a treaty appropriate under the Vienna Convention on the Law of Treaties?

17. If a panel were to draw 'adverse inferences' against a Member due to failure to provide information, and on this basis were to find a violation of WTO rules, how would the Member react? Are panels likely to take this approach?

Part IV

Traditional GATT Obligations

6

Border Measures: Tariffs and Quotas

I. INTRODUCTION

One of the most important aspects of WTO rules is the limitations imposed on the use of import tariffs and quotas. These measures are the two kinds of 'border measures' used to restrict trade in goods. Border measures are, just like they sound, imposed at the border, and stand in contrast to 'internal' measures that apply within the territory of a country.

As will be explained in more detail below, for tariffs each WTO Member has submitted a Schedule of Concessions, under which it 'binds' its tariffs on designated products. This binding represents a commitment by a Member that it will not impose a tariff higher than the listed rate. As to quotas, these are generally prohibited or tightly regulated where they are permitted. The difference in formal treatment between these two types of measures, with more flexibility for using tariffs, is mainly due to a preference for the use of tariffs, which preserve the benefits of free market competition better than do quotas. When countries impose tariffs, imports can still be purchased, just at a higher price. Thus, the benefits to competition offered by trade are not completely eliminated. By contrast, quotas limit the availability of imports as competing products to a greater extent.

Limits placed on the use of tariffs and quotas have almost certainly led to a greater amount of trade liberalisation than any other aspect of WTO rules. Despite their importance, though, the rules for these measures are not very prominent in most of the debates about the role of the WTO. In part, this is because tariffs and quotas are less likely to raise concerns about the various social issues with which many critics and commentators of the WTO are concerned. Border measures tend to be used more for protectionist purposes than to promote other social policies (although there are exceptions). Also, because border measures have traditionally been subject to international trade rules, WTO rules in this area do not raise significant concerns relating to interference with domestic sovereignty, as do regulations on internal measures. Finally, rules on tariffs and quotas often involve esoteric issues that are less 'glamorous' than some other trade issues.

The WTO legal regime for tariffs is set out in Article II of the GATT. For quotas, Articles XI and XIII of the GATT are the key provisions. We examine each in turn. For tariffs, we begin with a discussion of WTO rules and case law in this area, before turning to the administration of tariffs in domestic law. For quotas, we cover the relevant GATT rules. Finally, we conclude with a brief consideration of certain measures that are related to import tariffs and quotas, but sometimes get left out of the standard discussion: the 'tariff quota' and tariffs and quotas imposed on *exports*.

II. TARIFFS

Tariffs (often referred to as 'duties' or 'customs duties') are a long-standing means of protecting domestic industries from foreign competition. An import tariff is a tax on imports imposed when goods cross the border. Through the imposition of an extra cost on foreign goods, domestic producers can gain an advantage over their foreign counterparts.

Tariffs are also a means of raising revenue. One important feature of tariffs in this regard is that they avoid placing a clear and explicit burden on domestic constituencies. Nominally, they are a tax on *foreign goods*, paid by the foreign producer or the importer. Of course, they do impose a burden in the form of higher prices, as the cost of the tariff often leads sellers to increase prices (in order to maintain their profit margin), which ultimately are paid by consumers. However, this price increase is non-transparent, in the sense that it is not evidenced by a separate and identifiable payment for the amount of the tariff (as compared to a domestic sales tax, which is generally imposed more transparently). Thus, tariffs are less likely to be the subject of popular criticism than are general taxes. For this reason, governments may prefer tariffs to other taxes, as they are easier to push through the domestic political process. Raising revenue through tariffs is particularly important in poor countries, where taxing income may not yield the necessary amounts.

There are three types of tariffs. An *ad valorem* tariff is based on a fixed percentage of the value of the good that is being imported. For example, a 10 per cent tariff on the value of an imported car is an *ad valorem* tariff. By contrast, a specific tariff relies on a designated amount of money that does not vary with the price of the product, and is typically based on quantity or weight of the product. For example, a tax of 30 cents per kilogramme of an agricultural product would be a specific tariff. Finally, a third type of tariff is a mixed tariff, which combines the first two types of tariffs, for instance, a tax of 30 cents per kilogramme plus a tax of 10 per cent of value of the product.

In this section, we discuss three issues related to tariffs: (1) the role of negotiations in setting tariff bindings; (2) GATT rules regulating the use of tariffs; and (3) certain aspects of domestic regimes for tariff administration.

(a) GATT/WTO Tariff Negotiations

The process by which lower tariff rates are negotiated is one of the most important aspects of the WTO. As tariffs are the most widely used form of protectionism, their reduction contributes substantially to freer trade. Tariff negotiations usually occur as part of a major 'round' of negotiations, during which reductions are agreed to by all Members.[1] We discuss briefly here the negotiating process used in the major 'rounds', with the caveat that a full discussion of the negotiating process is outside the scope of this book.[2]

Generally speaking, the negotiating process involves give and take among individual WTO Members as they decide what tariff reductions they will offer in exchange for reductions by their trading partners. The resulting tariff 'bindings' become law when they

---

[1] In addition, tariff negotiations may occur in the context of the modification or withdrawal of a particular concession, or with regard to the accession of new Members.

[2] For a discussion of the tariff negotiations process see A Hoda, *Tariff Negotiations and Renegotiations under the GATT and the WTO: Procedures and Practices* (Cambridge, Cambridge University Press, 2002).

are incorporated into Members' Schedules. We discuss the relevant legal rules for these bindings below.

Over the years, the tariff negotiation process has evolved. In the early years of the GATT a product-by-product approach was used, where each participant submitted a request list indicating the products for which it wanted others to make tariff concessions and an offer list indicating the products for which it would be willing to make concessions. Soon thereafter, this approach was replaced by an 'across-the-board' approach in most cases, under which each participating country agreed to cut tariffs by a certain percentage (the 'linear' approach). This linear approach was later modified to include a 'harmonisation' formula, which was designed to account for the varied starting levels of the tariffs to be cut. In essence, this formula resulted in larger reductions for higher duties and smaller reductions for lower duties, to bring the final rates closer together (ie, to 'harmonise' them). Currently, all of these approaches play some role in the negotiating process.

The result of the many rounds of GATT/WTO tariff negotiations has been a significant lowering of the tariff rates that are applied by WTO Members. The average tariff rate on industrial products imported into developed countries has fallen from around 40 per cent at the beginning of the GATT to 3.8 per cent today.[3] In addition, tariff rates have now been 'bound' on many more products, ensuring that the applied tariff rates on these products will not be raised above the designated level in the future. In this regard, during the Uruguay Round developed countries increased the number of imports the tariff rates of which were bound from 78 per cent of product lines to 99 per cent. For developing countries, the increase was from 21 per cent to 73 per cent, and economies in transition from central planning increased their bindings from 73 per cent to 98 per cent.[4]

(b) GATT Rules on Bound Tariffs

The GATT rules on tariffs are set out in Article II, which is entitled 'Schedules of Concessions'. In this section, we discuss several important aspects of these rules. We begin with the basic obligations, which are set out in GATT Article II:1. We then explore the relationship between GATT Articles II and III:2 (ie, between the regulation of tariffs imposed at the border and the regulation of internal tax measures).

(i) Article II:1: The Basic Obligations Relating to Tariff Commitments

a. The Key Provisions Article II:1(a) of the GATT provides: '[e]ach Member shall accord to the commerce of the other Members treatment no less favourable than that provided for in the appropriate Part of the appropriate schedule annexed to this Agreement'. Under this provision, Members commit to offering treatment that is no worse than that promised in their schedule (we discuss schedules in more detail at c below). For example, if in the schedule the bound tariff rate for a certain product is 10 per cent, the Member may not impose a tariff of more than that amount. Charging more than that amount would violate GATT Article II:1(a) (the Member can, of course, charge amounts less than 10 per cent,

---

[3] WTO, *Understanding the WTO: The Agreements: Tariffs: More Bindings and Closer to Zero,* available at www.wto.org/english/thewto_e/whatis_e/tif_e/agrm2_e.htm (accessed on 29 May 2007).

[4] *Ibid.*

and can raise or lower or lower the amount charged, subject to various conditions). In essence, GATT Article II:1(a) is the provision that makes the schedules 'operative', that is, it provides a legal basis for enforcing the commitments made in the schedule.

GATT Article II:1(b) then states the following:

> The products described in Part I of the Schedule relating to any Member, which are the products of territories of other Members, shall, on their importation into the territory to which the Schedule relates, and subject to the terms, conditions or qualifications set forth in that Schedule, be exempt from ordinary customs duties in excess of those set forth and provided therein. Such products shall also be exempt from all other duties or charges of any kind imposed on or in connection with the importation in excess of those imposed on the date of this Agreement or those directly and mandatorily required to be imposed thereafter by legislation in force in the importing territory on that date.

The first sentence of Article II:1(b) offers a more specific version of the Article II:1(a) obligation, requiring that Members not charge 'ordinary customs duties in excess of those set forth and provided' in the schedule. Article II:1(b), first sentence is a rule specific to customs duties, requiring that such duties not exceed what is established in the schedule. By contrast, the 'less favourable treatment' language in Article II:1(a) is written in more general terms and thus is potentially broader.

The second sentence of Article II:1(b) prohibits 'other duties or charges' in excess of those imposed at the time of signing of the GATT. It is designed in part to prevent Members from evading their scheduled commitments by imposing what is effectively an 'ordinary customs duties' under another name. An 'Understanding' on Article II:1(b) was signed as part of the Uruguay Round, and provides, inter alia, that 'other duties or charges' 'shall be recorded in respect of all tariff bindings'. If no 'other duties or charges' are recorded for a product, then none are permitted for that product. That is, they are permitted only to the extent notified as a bound commitment.

b. Important Interpretations We discuss briefly here two important issues related to these provisions arising in dispute settlement. First, with regard to the 'clarification' of the commitments in Members' schedules by panels and the Appellate Body, in *EC—Computer Equipment* the Appellate Body explained that these clarifications are to be carried out using the same method as applied to clarifications of the WTO agreements generally, that is, by using the rules of Articles 31 and 32 of the Vienna Convention on the Law of Treaties. In reaching this conclusion, the Appellate Body rejected the panel's finding in that case that the 'legitimate expectations' of Members are relevant for these interpretations. The Appellate Body emphasised instead that it is the 'common intention' of the parties that is to be examined.[5] A portion of this decision is excerpted in the next section.

Secondly, in *Argentina—Textiles* the Appellate Body explained that Article II:1 does not require that Members impose the same 'type' of duty that is set out in their schedule. Thus, if a Member's schedule refers to a specific duty, it may nonetheless impose an *ad valorem* duty as long as the actual amount of the duties imposed does not exceed the amount bound in the schedule.[6]

c. Schedules As noted, each WTO Member binds its tariffs for designated products and these bindings are set out in each Member's schedule. Each schedule consists of four parts:

---

[5] Appellate Body Report, *EC—Computer Equipment*, paras 74–97.
[6] Appellate Body Report, *Argentina—Textiles*, paras 49–56.

Part I: MFN tariff concessions. This part is further divided into:
—Section 1A—Agricultural products: tariffs
—Section 1B—Agricultural products: tariff quotas
—Section II—Other products

Part II: Preferential concessions (tariffs relating to certain trade arrangements listed in GATT Article I)

Part III: Concessions on non-tariff measures (NTMs) (such as export duties)

Part IV: Specific commitments on domestic support and export subsidies on agricultural products

Of primary relevance here is Part I. For Part I, each schedule contains the following information: tariff item number; description of the product; rate of duty; date on which the present concession was established; Initial Negotiation Rights (or INR); date on which the concession was first incorporated in a GATT schedule; INR on earlier occasions; other duties and charges; and for agricultural products special safeguards may also be defined.[7] Not all information is included for all product entries in a schedule, as some information is not relevant for specific products. For instance, the special safeguard category is only relevant to agricultural products.

The following is an excerpt from Australia's schedule:

SCHEDULE I—AUSTRALIA
PART 1: MOST-FAVOURED-NATION TARIFF
SECTION II—Other Products

Tariff item number	Description of product	Bound rate of duty	Present concession established in	Initial negotiating right (INR) on concession	Concession first incorporated in a GATT Schedule	INRs on earlier concessions
1	2	3	4	5	6	7
... 8715.00	BABY CARRIAGES AND PARTS THEREOF	15%	UR/94		UR/94	

Most of the categories of the schedule are self-explanatory. One that is not is INRs. Put simply, an INR is a right of a particular Member relating to a concession in another Member's schedule. It indicates that the first Member was the country seeking the concession and retains certain rights if modification or withdrawal of the concession is requested. This Member is listed in the other Member's schedule. Countries that have acceded to the WTO more recently have the highest number of INRs recorded in their schedules, as these INRs were demanded as part of the accession process. By contrast, longstanding GATT/WTO Members (such as the US and EC) have few, if any, INRs recorded in the Schedules. In this regard, note that in Australia's schedule above there are no Members

---

[7] WTO, 'Goods Schedules, Members' commitments', available at www.wto.org/english/tratop_e/schedules_e/goods_schedules_e.htm (accessed on 23 May 2007).

listed in the INR column for the product, as Australia is one of the original GATT signatories. Similarly, the holders of INRs tend to be these same longstanding Members.

(ii) Customs Valuation

As explained above, when goods are imported the calculation of the duties owed is based either on the value of the goods or on the specific number of units (either by quantity or weight) imported. Where the value of the goods is used, a determination must be made of the precise value. This calculation is made using the rules set out in GATT Article VII and the Uruguay Round Agreement on Implementation of Article VII of the GATT 1994 ('Customs Valuation Agreement').

The Customs Valuation Agreement establishes a set of alternative valuation methods which must be considered in the following order. First, pursuant to Article 1 of the Agreement, domestic customs authorities must use 'transaction value' as the primary method. 'Transaction value' is 'the price actually paid or payable for the goods when sold for export to the country of importation adjusted in accordance with the provisions of Article 8 [of this Agreement]'. However, Article 1 also sets out a number of conditions that must be met in order to use transaction value. If these conditions are not met, an alternative method must be used. The first two alternatives are the transaction value of 'identical goods' (Article 2) and transaction value of 'similar goods' (Article 3). If Articles 2 and 3 cannot be used, the customs authorities must use 'deductive value' (Article 4), or if that is not possible the 'computed value' (Article 5). These methods are set out in detail in the Agreement. Finally, if none of these methods will work, the customs authorities must apply a 'reasonable means' of valuation. (Article 7)

To date, there has not been any interpretation of these provisions through dispute settlement. In Section II.C below, covering domestic tariff administration, we provide an excerpt of a domestic customs valuation ruling.

(iii) Customs Classification

The classification of a product in one tariff category or another can be extremely important, as tariff rates vary considerably. Unlike with customs valuation, there are no agreed WTO rules for customs classification, that is, for how to determine under which tariff category specific products should be categorised. Thus, the only applicable GATT rules are the general provisions of Article II. In fact, it is the World Customs Organisation ('WCO') that administers the international rules on tariff classification, through the Harmonised Commodity Description and Coding System (generally referred to as the 'Harmonised System' or simply 'HS'). The HS is 'a multipurpose international product nomenclature developed by the World Customs Organization (WCO)', comprising 'about 5,000 commodity groups, each identified by a six digit code, arranged in a legal and logical structure and is supported by well-defined rules to achieve uniform classification'.[8] Despite the WCO's formal role in this area, classification issues can nonetheless arise in WTO disputes. We discuss here two such disputes that have dealt with claims that a Member's classification was inconsistent with the rules, both of which focused on

---

[8] WCO, 'Harmonized System Convention—General information—Countries applying the HS', available at www.wcoomd.org/ie/en/topics_issues/harmonizedsystem/hsconve2.html.

Article II:1. We then briefly examine the relationship of WCO and WTO rules, as well as the possibility of using the non-violation nullification or impairment remedy for tariff classification disputes.

a. *EC—Computer Equipment* The *EC—Computer Equipment* dispute concerned the customs classification in the EC of certain computer equipment associated with local area networks ('LAN'), namely: (1) 'LAN equipment', such as network or adaptor cards, along with devices such as hubs, bridges, routers, repeaters, LAN switches and various cables and modules, and (2) 'multimedia PCs [personal computers]'.

According to the US, during the Uruguay Round negotiations and for a short period after their conclusion, the EC classified LAN equipment and multimedia PCs as automatic data processing ('ADP') machines or parts and accessories thereof. As part of the Uruguay Round negotiations, the EC bound its tariff rates for ADP machines at 4.9 per cent (to be reduced over the following five years to 2.5 per cent for some products or duty-free for others), while the accessories thereof were subject to a 4 per cent duty (to be reduced to 2 per cent over the following five years). However, in May 1995, the European Commission adopted a regulation classifying certain LAN equipment as telecommunications apparatus, a category subject to generally higher duties, in the range of 4.6 to 7.5 per cent (to be reduced to 3 to 3.6 per cent over the following five years). This Regulation was adhered to by EC customs authorities, including those of the United Kingdom and Ireland. Moreover, according to the US, authorities in certain EC Member States began classifying other LAN equipment as telecommunications apparatus as well. With respect to multimedia PCs, in April 1996, a United Kingdom tribunal upheld a customs administration determination classifying a certain type of PC as a television receiver, thereby subjecting those machines to a 14 per cent tariff. Furthermore, in June 1997, the European Commission adopted a regulation that established a general classification of PCs as ADP machines subject to the tariffs noted above, but PCs with multimedia capabilities were subject to higher tariff rates of up to 14 per cent.

The US argued that these changes in classification resulted in tariff rates for the products at issue that were 'less favourable' than those bound in the EC's Schedule, in violation of GATT Article II:1.[9]

In its examination of the claims, the panel hearing the case took into account the 'legitimate expectations' of the US with regard to the tariff classification of these products. It concluded that the EC violated Article II:1 with respect to LAN equipment, but not with respect to multimedia PCs.[10] On appeal, however, the Appellate Body[11] reversed the panel's interpretive approach of looking at 'legitimate expectations' and therefore reversed the panel's conclusion of a violation for LAN equipment. The Appellate Body's reversal focused on the panel's errors, and it did not make its own finding as to whether the EC actions violated Article II. However, in its criticism of the panel, the Appellate Body did offer some guidance as to how the panel should have conducted its analysis:

---

[9] Panel Report, *EC—Computer Equipment*, paras 2.1–2.24, 8.1–8.4.
[10] Panel Report, *EC—Computer Equipment*, paras 8.30–8.68.
[11] Appellate Body Report, *EC—Computer Equipment*, paras 74–99.

Appellate Body Report, *European Communities—Customs Classification of Certain Computer Equipment,* **Adopted 22 June 1998, WT/DS62,67,68/AB/R**

87. In paragraphs 8.20 and 8.21 of the Panel Report, the Panel quoted Articles 31 and 32 of the *Vienna Convention* and explicitly recognized that these fundamental rules of treaty interpretation applied "in determining whether the tariff treatment of LAN equipment . . . is in conformity with the tariff commitments contained in Schedule LXXX". As we have already noted above, the Panel, after a textual analysis, came to the conclusion that:

> . . . for the purposes of Article II:1, it is impossible to determine whether LAN equipment should be regarded as an ADP machine purely on the basis of the ordinary meaning of the terms used in Schedule LXXX taken in isolation.

Subsequently, the Panel abandoned its effort to interpret the terms of Schedule LXXX in accordance with Articles 31 and 32 of the *Vienna Convention.* In doing this, the Panel erred.

88. As already discussed above, the Panel referred to the *context* of Schedule LXXX as well as to the *object and purpose* of the *WTO Agreement* and the GATT 1994, of which Schedule LXXX is an integral part. However, it did so to support its proposition that the terms of a Schedule may be interpreted in the light of the "legitimate expectations" of an exporting Member. The Panel failed to examine the context of Schedule LXXX and the object and purpose of the *WTO Agreement* and the GATT 1994 in accordance with the rules of treaty interpretation set out in the *Vienna Convention.*

89. We are puzzled by the fact that the Panel, in its effort to interpret the terms of Schedule LXXX, did not consider the *Harmonized System* and its *Explanatory Notes.* We note that during the Uruguay Round negotiations, both the European Communities and the United States were parties to the *Harmonized System.* Furthermore, it appears to be undisputed that the Uruguay Round tariff negotiations were held on the basis of the *Harmonized System's* nomenclature and that requests for, and offers of, concessions were normally made in terms of this nomenclature. Neither the European Communities nor the United States argued before the Panel that the *Harmonized System* and its *Explanatory Notes* were relevant in the interpretation of the terms of Schedule LXXX. We believe, however, that a proper interpretation of Schedule LXXX should have included an examination of the *Harmonized System* and its *Explanatory Notes.*

90. A proper interpretation also would have included an examination of the existence and relevance of subsequent practice. We note that the United States referred, before the Panel, to the decisions taken by the Harmonized System Committee of the WCO in April 1997 on the classification of certain LAN equipment as ADP machines. Singapore, a third party in the panel proceedings, also referred to these decisions. The European Communities observed that it had introduced reservations with regard to these decisions and that, even if they were to become final as they stood, they would not affect the outcome of the present dispute for two reasons: first, because these decisions could not confirm that LAN equipment was classified as ADP machines in 1993 and 1994; and, second, because this dispute "was about duty treatment and not about product classification". We note that the United States agrees with the European Communities that this dispute is not a dispute on the *correct* classification of LAN equipment, but a dispute on whether the tariff treatment accorded to LAN equipment was less favourable than that provided for in Schedule LXXX. However, we consider that in interpreting the tariff concessions in Schedule LXXX, decisions of the WCO may be relevant; and, therefore, they should have been examined by the Panel.

91. We note that the European Communities stated that the question whether LAN equipment was bound as ADP machines, under headings 84.71 and 84.73, or as telecommunications equipment, under heading 85.17, was *not* addressed during the Uruguay Round tariff negotiations with the United States. We also note that the United States asserted that:

> In many, perhaps most, cases, the detailed product composition of tariff commitments was *never* discussed in detail during the tariff negotiations of the Uruguay Round . . . (emphasis added)

and that:

> The US-EC negotiation on Chapter 84 provided an example of how two groups of busy negotiators dealing with billions of dollars of trade and hundreds of tariff lines relied on *a continuation of the status quo.* (emphasis added)

This may well be correct and, in any case, seems central to the position of the United States. Therefore, we are surprised that the Panel did not examine whether, during the Tokyo Round tariff negotiations, the European Communities bound LAN equipment as ADP machines or as telecommunications equipment.

92. Albeit, with the mistaken aim of establishing whether the United States "was entitled to legitimate expectations" regarding the tariff treatment of LAN equipment by the European Communities, the Panel examined, in paragraphs 8.35 to 8.44 of the Panel Report, the classification practice regarding LAN equipment in the European Communities during the Uruguay Round tariff negotiations. The Panel did this on the basis of certain BTIs and other decisions relating to the customs classification of LAN equipment, issued by customs authorities in the European Communities during the Uruguay Round. In the light of our observations on "the circumstances of [the] conclusion" of a treaty as a supplementary means of interpretation under Article 32 of the *Vienna Convention*, we consider that the classification practice in the European Communities during the Uruguay Round is part of "the circumstances of [the] conclusion" of the *WTO Agreement* and may be used as a supplementary means of interpretation within the meaning of Article 32 of the *Vienna Convention*. However, two important observations must be made: first, the Panel did *not* examine the classification practice in the European Communities during the Uruguay Round negotiations *as a supplementary means of interpretation* within the meaning of Article 32 of the *Vienna Convention*; and, second, the value of the classification practice as a supplementary means of interpretation is subject to certain qualifications discussed below.

93. We note that the Panel examined the classification practice of only the European Communities, and found that the classification of LAN equipment by the United States during the Uruguay Round tariff negotiations was not relevant. The purpose of treaty interpretation is to establish the *common* intention of the parties to the treaty. To establish this intention, the prior practice of only *one* of the parties may be relevant, but it is clearly of more limited value than the practice of all parties. In the specific case of the interpretation of a tariff concession in a Schedule, the classification practice of the importing Member, in fact, may be of great importance. However, the Panel was mistaken in finding that the classification practice of the United States was *not* relevant.

94. In this context, we also note that while the Panel examined the classification practice during the Uruguay Round negotiations, it did not consider the EC legislation on customs classification of goods that was applicable at that time. In particular, it did not consider the "General Rules for the Interpretation of the Combined Nomenclature" as set out in Council Regulation 2658/87 on the Common Customs Tariff. If the classification practice of the importing Member at the time of the tariff negotiations is relevant in interpreting

tariff concessions in a Member's Schedule, surely that Member's legislation on customs classification at that time is also relevant.

... ...

b. *EC—Chicken Classification* In *EC—Chicken Classification*, Brazil and Thailand complained that various EC measures pertaining to the tariff classification of certain chicken products resulted in treatment less favourable than that provided for in the EC tariff schedule. The relevant concessions were set out in the EC schedule as follows:

Tariff item number	Description of products	Final bound rate of duty	Special safe-guard
0207 (...)	Meat and edible offal, of the poultry of heading No 0105, fresh, chilled or frozen:		
0207.41	-Poultry cuts and offal other than livers, frozen: –Of fowls of the species Gallus domesticus: —Cuts:		
0207.41.10 (...)	——Boneless	1024 ECU/T	SSG
0210 (...)	Meat and edible meat offal, salted, in brine, dried, smoked; edible flours and meals of meat or meat offal		
0210.90	-Other, including edible flours and meals of meat or meat offal: –Meat:		
(...) 0210.90.20	—Other	15.4%	–

Thus, products falling under the tariff line 0207.41.10 were subject to a bound specific duty rate of 1024 ECU/T, or 102.4E/100kg/net, and could be subject to a special safe-guard mechanism provided for in Article 5 of the Agriculture Agreement. By contrast, products falling under the tariff line 0210.90.20 were subject to a final bound duty rate of 15.4 per cent *ad valorem*.

The issue was the following. Tariff heading 02.07.41.10 covered frozen boneless chicken cuts, while 02.10.90.20 covered certain types of 'salted' meat (including 'salted' chicken). In 2002 the EC reclassified frozen boneless chicken cuts impregnated with salt from item number 02.10.90.20 to item number 02.07.41.10. The complainants argued that the products had been properly classified as 'salted' meat under 02.10.90.20, which was the classification that had generally been applied to these products from 1996 to 2002, based on the addition of salt to the chicken. In response, the EC contended that the salting that had taken place did not qualify the products as 'salted' under 02.10.90.20

because it had not been undertaken for the purpose of long-term preservation of the product. The EC adopted new measures to make it clear that this was the legal standard for determining whether a measure is 'salted'. Thus, according to the EC, the products should be classified under 02.07.41.10, as frozen boneless chicken cuts. In essence, the parties disagreed as to which category the salted frozen boneless chicken cuts at issue should fall under, and thus whether the reclassification was permissible under WTO rules. Brazil and Thailand claimed that through these measures the EC acted inconsistently with GATT Article II:1(a) and II:1(b). In particular, they argued that the EC 'changed its customs classification so that those products, which had previously been classified under subheading 0210.90.20 and were subject to an *ad valorem* tariff of 15.4%, are now classified under subheading 0207.14.10 and are subject to a tariff of 102.4E/100kg/net as well as being potentially subject to special safeguard measures pursuant to Article 5 of the Agreement on Agriculture'.[12] According to the complainants, based on this specific rate, the effective *ad valorem* rate for their exports of the products at issue ranged from around 40 to 60 per cent during the period 1997–2003.

Thus, the focus of this dispute was the meaning of one word in heading 02.10 of the EC Schedule: 'salted'. In particular, the issue was whether 'salted' means simply the addition of salt to the meat products at issue (as argued by the complainants), or whether it refers only to salting for the purpose of 'long-term preservation' of the product (as argued by the EC). (Although it was never stated explicitly, the EC view seems to have been that the salting that was carried out was illegitimate because it was done only to take advantage of the lower tariff rate for the 'salted' category.) After an extensive application of the Vienna Convention interpretive process to the word 'salted', both the panel and Appellate Body sided with the complainants on this point, and thus found that the salting that had occurred with the products at issue was sufficient to place the products under heading 02.10. On this basis, it found that the EC had violated Article II:1(a) and II:1(b).

c. Relationship between WCO and WTO Rules on Tariff Classification In *EC— Chicken Classification*, the main focus was on the EC's tariff reclassification of the chicken products at issue from 02.10.90.20 to 02.07.41.10. Because the reclassification constituted a change from the existing classification status, there may have been an underlying feeling on the part of the panel and Appellate Body that the actions taken were intended to apply a higher tariff rate to the imports at issue. Thus, the emphasis was on whether the EC customs authorities acted properly in making the reclassification. In this regard, the panel and Appellate Body spent most of their time evaluating the rationale offered by the EC relating to the notion of 'long-term preservation'. By contrast, the panel and the Appellate Body seemed to avoid the issue of which of the two categories—02.07.41.10 or 02.10.90.20— was actually a better fit for the product at issue in terms of tariff classification. As a result, some important questions relating to the specifics of the classification of this product have been left open.[13]

Along these lines, an interesting issue that was raised, but only briefly discussed, is the relationship between the WTO and WCO in addressing matters of tariff classification. In this case, the panel had sought information from the WCO on issues relating to the dispute. In its response, the WCO stated:

---

[12] Panel Report, *EC—Chicken Classification*, paras 7.1–7.3.
[13] For instance, how much added salt is enough to take a product out of the 02.07.41.10 category and move it into the 02.10.90.20 category?

it appears that the present dispute concerns a classification question involving several contracting parties to the HS Convention. The WCO refers to Article 10 of the HS Convention, which stipulates that "any dispute between Contracting Parties concerning the interpretation or application of this Convention shall, so far as possible, be settled by negotiation between them" and "any dispute which is not so settled shall be referred by the Parties to the dispute to the Harmonized System Committee which shall thereupon consider the dispute and make recommendations for its settlement". The WCO suggests that the settlement procedures contained in the HS Convention should be followed by the parties to this dispute before the Panel makes its decision.[14]

Thus, as the WCO pointed out, the HS Convention has a dispute settlement process of its own, albeit a non-binding one, that can be (and arguably must be) used to resolve classification disputes. In response, the panel nonetheless found it had jurisdiction, noting: '[w]e understand that, once seized of a matter, [DSU] Article 11 prevents a panel from abdicating its responsibility to the DSB. In other words, in the context of the present case, we lack the authority to refer the dispute before us to the WCO or to any other body.'[15] The panel further explained:

> The Panel is mindful of the respective jurisdiction and competence of the WCO and the WTO and, in fact, we specifically raised this issue with the parties during the course of these proceedings. Nevertheless, we consider that we have been mandated by the DSB in this dispute to determine whether the European Communities has violated Article II of the GATT 1994 with respect to the products at issue. As mentioned above in paragraph 7.54, in so doing, we will need to interpret the WTO concession contained in heading 02.10 of the EC Schedule.[16]

The panel's findings on this issue, while noting the role of the WCO, seem to indicate that where WTO Members bring a complaint related to GATT tariff commitments, panels will hear the dispute regardless of the WCO's potential role in the matter. Clearly, there is potential for overlap between the two sets of rules, because the choice of an improper tariff classification could lead to tariffs being imposed above the bound rate for a product. In practice, in the absence of a formal clarification as to how the WTO and WCO rules interact, it seems to be up to the complainant(s) which dispute settlement procedures to invoke when issues such as these arise.

d. The Non-violation Nullification or Impairment Remedy In the *EC—Computer Equipment* complaint discussed above, one of the claims set out in the panel request was that the EC actions led to 'non-violation nullification or impairment'.[17] (See Chapter 5 for an explanation of this remedy.) While this claim was not pursued, it may be that claims related to tariff re-classifications of the sort involved in the two cases discussed in this section are sometimes better brought as non-violation claims, because the absence of detailed rules on tariff classification makes it difficult to prove a violation for these kinds of actions (although not impossible, as demonstrated by the *EC—Chicken Classification* case).

---

[14] Panel Report, *EC—Chicken Classification*, para 7.53.
[15] *Ibid*, para 7.56.
[16] *Ibid*, para 7.59.
[17] See *EC—Computer Equipment* (Request for the Establishment of a Panel by the United States), WTO Doc No WT/DS62/4, 2.

(iv) Article II:2: Relationship between Article II and Article III:2

Article II:2 of the GATT addresses the relationship between Article II and certain other kinds of measures. In this regard, it provides that:

[n]othing in this Article shall prevent any Member from imposing at any time on the importation of any product:

(*a*) a charge equivalent to an internal tax imposed consistently with the provisions of paragraph 2 of Article III in respect of the like domestic product or in respect of an article from which the imported product has been manufactured or produced in whole or in part;

(*b*) any anti-dumping or countervailing duty applied consistently with the provisions of Article VI;

(*c*) fees or other charges commensurate with the cost of services rendered.

The last two items are fairly straightforward. Sub-paragraph (b) means that the imposition of anti-dumping and countervailing duties (discussed in Chapters 10and 11) the bound rate will not violate Article II; and sub-paragraph (c) permits Members to impose fees and charges for services related to importation. By contrast, sub-paragraph (a) is somewhat complicated, addressing the relationship between Articles II and III:2. We explore this issue in more detail here.

At a basic level, Article II of the GATT deals with duties or other charges on imported products that are applied at a Member's border (ie, upon importation). By contrast, Article III:2 of the GATT deals with *internal* taxes or charges on products within a Member's borders. Thus, Article II applies to importation, whereas Article III:2 covers domestically produced goods as well as imports that have already entered the Member's customs territory (ie, after they have passed through customs). Most measures are applied *either* internally *or* at the border, so it is usually clear which of GATT Article II or Article III:2 applies to a particular measure.

The situation becomes more complicated when the duty or charge being applied at the border is related to a similar tax or charge that is applied internally. That is, a measure may have two aspects, one dealing with imports at the border and the other dealing with domestic products internally. For example, a tax may apply to domestically produced cars at the time of sale, but, for convenience and efficiency, apply to imported goods on importation (as they are already subject to tariff duties at that time, it is relatively easy to collect additional fees as well). The GATT recognises the complexity of this situation, and it contains some specific provisions to deal with it. First, a Note to GATT Article III instructs that where there is a tax or charge on imports, and a related tax or charge is also applied internally to domestic like products, the import tax or charge is to be 'regarded as' an *internal* tax or charge. Specifically, the Note provides:

Any internal tax or other internal charge, or any law, regulation or requirement of the kind referred to in paragraph 1 *which applies to an imported product and to the like domestic product and is collected or enforced in the case of the imported product at the time or point of importation, is nevertheless to be regarded as an internal tax or other internal charge*, or a law, regulation or requirement of the kind referred to in paragraph 1, and is accordingly subject to the provisions of Article III. [emphasis added]

Thus, in these situations, Article III applies even though the measure, or part of it, applies to imports at the border.

Article II:2(a) appears to reflect a similar policy in the treatment of import charges that are related to a domestic tax. While Article II:2(a) does not classify such an import charge as an 'internal tax', it does state that import charges that are 'equivalent' to certain internal taxes are not prohibited under Article II. This provision covers both taxes 'in respect of the like domestic product' and taxes 'in respect of an article from which the imported product has been manufactured or produced in whole or in part'.

Note that there is a slightly different scope of coverage under Article II:2(a) and the Article III Note. Under the Note, an import charge will be 'regarded as' an 'internal' tax or charge where it also applies to the 'like' domestic product. As a result, the import charge/internal tax is subject to Article III. By contrast, under Article II:2(a), an import 'charge' is not 'regarded as' an internal tax or charge. Rather, there is an examination of whether this 'charge' is 'equivalent' to a particular 'internal tax'. This 'internal tax', but not the import 'charge' itself, must be consistent with Article III:2. In essence, the inquiry under the Note to Article III is whether the import charge *itself* should be considered an 'internal tax', whereas under Article II:2(a) the question is whether the import 'charge' is 'equivalent' to some *other* internal tax.

Clearly, these two provisions have substantial overlap, and are intended to address some of the same issues. However, because of the different language used, the provisions involve somewhat different examinations of import charges. As a result, a finding under the Note that Article III:2 does not apply to the import charge due to the absence of a 'like' domestic product does not necessarily mean that Article II:2(a) does not apply (although such a conclusion is likely). Rather, the specific conditions set out in Article II:2(a) must be evaluated on a case-by-case basis.

(c) Domestic Tariff Administration

Contrary to the misperception of some people, WTO rules on tariffs do not actually impose tariffs. Rather, they simply govern certain aspects of how domestic authorities run their tariff regime. In this section, we examine some of the elements discussed in the preceding section, but this time from the perspective of the domestic government agencies dealing with tariffs.

(i) Domestic Tariff Schedules

As mentioned above, the Harmonised Commodity Description and Coding System, generally referred to as the 'Harmonised System' or simply the 'HS,' is a product classification system used by more than 190 countries and economies as a basis for their customs tariffs. It is administered by the World Customs Organisation in Brussels. The HS comprises about 5,000 commodity groups, each identified by a six-digit code. It is governed by the International Convention on the Harmonised Commodity Description and Coding System (the HS Convention), which contains rules for interpretation of the HS. The official interpretation of the HS is carried out by the HS Committee, which comprises representatives from the Contracting Parties to the HS Convention.

To illustrate how tariff schedules are implemented in various domestic settings, we look at the US and New Zealand systems.

a. United States Tariff Schedule US tariff rates are set out in the Harmonised Tariff

Schedule of the United States (HTS). The HTS structure sets out duties for all goods and is based upon the HS. The US HTS is broken down into 22 different sections, which are then sub-divided into 99 chapters. Each chapter of the HTS contains notes on classifying products within that chapter. A 10-digit number is used to identify a specific product. The following is a sample excerpt from the 2007 US Schedule:

Chapter 87
Vehicles other than Railway or Tramway Rolling Stock, and Parts and Accessories Thereof

Heading/ subheading	Stat. suffix	Article description	Unit of quantity	Rates of duty		
				1		2
				General	Special	
		... Baby carriages (including strollers) and parts thereof				
		... Baby carriages (including strollers)...				
...	20	Parts	No		Free (A,AU,BH,CA, CL,E,IL,J,JO,MA,M	
8715.00.00	40	...	kg	4.4%	X,P,SG)	45%

The entry at issue is from Chapter 87 of the HTS, which covers 'Vehicles other than Railway or Tramway Rolling Stock, and Parts and Accessories Thereof'. From the first column, it can be seen that 8715.00.00 covers 'Baby carriages (including strollers) and parts thereof'. The second column clarifies that 8715.00.00.20 covers 'Baby carriages (including strollers)' and heading 8715.00.00.20 covers 'parts'. The first two digits (87) of the classification are a reference to the relevant chapter. The first four digits combined (8715) comprise the article's heading within that chapter, while the last six digits (00.00.20 and 00.00.40) break that heading down into subheadings. The fourth column provides the 'Unit of Quantity', and is the US Customs Service's acceptable measure of quantity for a product. This could be a number indicating the number of units of the product itself or a number indicating a quantity by weight. This column only applies where specific duties are used, and thus is blank in the excerpt provided because an *ad valorem* duty is at issue there. Finally, the last column, broken down into several sub-categories, sets out the applicable 'Rates of Duty'. This column determines the amount of duty that must be paid. These rates are generally expressed in a quantity/cost rate (eg, $0.04/kg) (specific duty) or as a percentage of the value of the goods (eg, 2.5 per cent of the value) (*ad valorem* duty). In the example above, *ad valorem* duty rates are used. The duty rate column is further divided into three sub-columns. These columns are interpreted as follows. First, the 'General' column is the typical rate of duty from the majority of the world's countries (the MFN rate). Next, the 'Special' column is a special duty rate assigned mainly to countries which have entered into FTAs with the United States. Each abbreviation represents a country with which the United States has a free trade agreement (eg, SG refers to Singapore). Finally, Column 2 is the duty assigned to countries which do not receive MFN treatment (currently, only Cuba and North Korea are in this category).[18]

b. New Zealand Tariff Schedule New Zealand's tariff schedule is set out in the Working Tariff Document of New Zealand, a portion of which from the 2007 version is excerpted here:

Chapter 87
Vehicles other than railway or tramway rolling-stock, and parts and accessories thereof

Number	Statistical key		Goods	Rates of duty	
	Code	Unit		Normal tariff	Preferential tariff
87.15 8715.00.00			Baby carriages and parts thereof	7 7/2008 5	CA Free LDC 5.5 7/2008 5 TH Free TPA Free
	01F	...	Baby carriages		
	09A	...	Parts		

The explanations provided in the document indicate that the % sign has been omitted in the duty columns, so a number without any other qualification in these columns signifies that an *ad valorem* duty applies at the percentage rate signified by the number. Thus, an entry of '7' means that duty is payable at a rate of 7 per cent of the value of the goods concerned. The document provides two duty columns. First, the 'Normal Tariff' applies to all goods from all countries except those goods entitled to be entered at Preferential Tariff duty rates. A date,eg, 7/2008 in the excerpt, shown under a tariff item, indicates that as from the first day of that month, until notified otherwise, the corresponding rate of duty applies. Thus, in the table above, the rate changes to '5', that is 5 per cent, as of July 2008. Secondly, the 'Preferential Tariff' column indicates rates of duty for certain countries or groups of countries. For example, TH in the excerpt refers to Thailand, with which New Zealand has an FTA. Again, a date shown under a tariff item indicates that as from the first day of that month until notified otherwise the corresponding rate of duty applies.

(ii) Valuation of Goods by Domestic Authorities

As noted above, where tariffs are imposed on an *ad valorem* basis, the amount owed is calculated as a percentage of the value of the goods. Thus, the valuation of imported goods has important implications. The WTO rules described in the previous sections provide some constraints on domestic authorities in carrying out the valuation process.

---

[18] VN Pregelj, CRS Report for Congress, 'Country Applicability of the US Normal Trade Relations (Most-Favored-Nation) Status' (24 March 2005), available at www.opencrs.com/rpts/96-463_20050324.pdf.

Nonetheless, many issues can still arise in relation to customs authorities' valuation methodologies. We provide a US agency ruling dealing with one such issue.

HQ 548161

August 21, 2002 RR:IT:VA 548161 LR CATEGORY: Valuation Port Director U.S. Customs Service Blaine, Washington

RE: Application for Further Review of Protest 300402100086; Goods and Services Tax (GST); taxes paid in country of exportation; Caterpillar Inc. v. United States; HRL 548128

Dear Port Director:

The above-referenced protest was forwarded to this office for further review. We received it on June 24, 2002. The protest was submitted by Border Brokerage Company Inc. on behalf of the importer, Timothy Earl Hostetler ("Protestant"). It concerns the valuation of an automobile purchased in Canada and imported into the United States.

FACTS:

Protestant purchased the subject automobile from Don Docksteader Motors in Canada. A copy of the purchase contract was submitted. One of the items included in the contract price was an amount for "GST" (Goods and Services Tax). This amount is separately shown on the contract. Protestant entered the automobile based on the contract price, but did not include the GST in the entered value. The Customs Service appraised the automobile using the transaction value method and value advanced the entry to include the GST and other amounts not relevant here. Protestant protests the inclusion of the GST amount in the transaction value.

GST is a 7% tax on the sale of most goods and services in Canada. A non-resident visitor can claim a refund to GST paid if certain requirements are met. Among other things, the goods must be removed from Canada within 60 days of the date they were purchased. See www.ccra-adrc. gc.ca/tax/nonresidents/ visitors/tax-e.html, "Welcome to Canada Customs & Revenue Agency's Tax Refund for Visitors Page".

Some time after the automobile was imported, Protestant applied for and received a refund of the GST from the Canadian Government Protestant submitted a copy of the form from the Canadian Commissioner of Customs and Revenue approving the application and a copy of the check from the Government of Canada.

ISSUE:

Whether Customs decision to include the refunded GST in transaction value was proper.

LAW AND ANALYSIS:

Merchandise imported into the United States is appraised in accordance with section 402 of the Tariff Act of 1930, as amended by the Trade Agreement Act of 1979 (TAA; 19 U.S.C. 1401a). The preferred method of appraisement under the TAA is transaction value defined as the "price actually paid or payable for the merchandise when sold for exportation to the United States" plus certain enumerated additions. 19 U.S.C. 1401a(b)(1) The "price actually paid or payable" is defined in 19 U.S.C. 1401a(b)(4)(A) as "the total payment (whether direct or indirect . . .) made, or to be made, for the imported merchandise by the buyer to, or for the benefit of, the seller".

The question of whether refunded internal taxes are part of transaction value was addressed in a court case and a recent Customs ruling. In Caterpillar Inc. v. United States, 20 C.I.T. 1169, 941 F. Supp. 1241 (1996), the Court of International Trade addressed the issue of whether a Value Added Tax (VAT) assessed by the British government was properly included in transaction value. In that case, Caterpillar purchased truck components from a British company and the British revenue authorities assessed a VAT upon the sale of the merchandise. The invoice issued by the seller to Caterpillar included an amount for the merchandise and a separate amount for the VAT. Subsequently, the truck was exported to the United States, and the British government refunded the VAT paid to Caterpillar. Upon importation, Customs appraised the merchandise including the VAT taxes in transaction value.

The court noted that VAT taxes were not explicitly listed as one of the five statutory enumerated additions to transaction value; nor were they one of the listed exclusions to transaction value to 19 U.S.C. §1401a(b)(3). After a comprehensive analysis of the statutory language, the legislative history, and the GATT, the court determined that when VAT taxes are separately identified and are refunded, they may not be included in the transaction value of the merchandise. Part of the reasoning for this result was the court's finding that the drafters of Article VII of the GATT "did not intend for refunded internal taxes to be included in the definition of 'the price actually paid or payable' for purposes of determining transaction value". Caterpillar, Inc., supra, at p. 1175.

In HRL 548128, July 15, 2002, Customs specifically addressed the issue of whether a refunded GST was covered by Caterpillar. In that case, a U.S. resident purchased a automobile in Canada. The submitted bill of sale included an amount to GST and PST (Provincial Sales Tax) in the total price. An amount for each of these taxes was separately listed on the bill of sale. The importer paid the internal Canadian taxes and the claim was made that these amounts were subsequently refunded to the importer. Customs determined that there were no material differences between the facts presented and those in Caterpillar and that the case should be followed. Accordingly, Customs held that neither the GST nor PST should be included in the price actually paid or payable assuming that the taxes paid in the country of exportation were refunded to the importer.

The facts presented in the instant case are essentially the same as those presented in HRL 548128, supra. Here, the imported automobile was purchased by Protestant (presumably, a U.S. resident). The purchase contract sets forth the contract price, and includes an amount for GST. Such amount is separately itemized. The contract also indicates that Protestant paid the entire purchase price. In addition, the evidence presented by Protestant indicates that the GST amount paid to the seller was refunded to Protestant by the Canadian government. Accordingly, based on Caterpillar and HRL 548128, we find that the GST is not properly included in the transaction value as part of the price actually paid or payable. It is also not an addition to the price actually paid or payable.

HOLDING:

The protest should be GRANTED. In accordance with Section 3A11(b) of Customs Revised Protest Directive 099 35500-065, dated August 4, 1993, you are to mail this decision, together with Customs Form 19, to the Protestant no later than 60 days from the date of this letter. Any reliquidation of the entry or entries in accordance with the decision must be accomplished prior to mailing the decision.

Sixty days form the date of the decision, the Office of Regulations and Rulings will make the decision available to Customs personnel, and to the public on the Customs Home Page on the World Wide Web at www.customs.ustreas.gov., by means of the Freedom of Information Act, and other methods of public distribution.

Sincerely,

Virginia L. Brown Chief, Value Branch

… … …

(iii) Classification of Goods by Domestic Authorities

Domestic tariff schedules set out rules of interpretation for the items therein. These rules are based on the General Rules for the interpretation of the Harmonised System in the Harmonised System Nomenclature established through the World Customs Organisation. As an example, the rules set out in New Zealand's tariff schedule are as follows:

General Rules for the Interpretation of Part I of the Tariff

Classification of goods in Part I of the Tariff shall be governed by the following principles:

1. The titles of Sections, Chapters, and sub-Chapters are provided for ease of reference only; for legal purposes, classification shall be determined according to the terms of the headings and any relative Section or Chapter Notes and, provided such headings or Notes do not otherwise require, according to the following provisions:

2. (a) Any reference in a heading to an article shall be taken to include a reference to that article incomplete or unfinished, provided that, as presented, the incomplete or unfinished article has the essential character of the complete or finished article. It shall also be taken to include a reference to that article complete or finished (or falling to be classified as complete or finished by virtue of this Rule), presented unassembled or disassembled.

(b) Any reference in a heading to a material or substance shall be taken to include a reference to mixtures or combinations of that material or substance with other materials or substances. Any reference to goods of a given material or substance shall be taken to include a reference to goods consisting wholly or partly of such material or substance. The classification of goods consisting of more than one material or substance shall be according to the principles of Rule 3.

3. When by application of Rule 2(b) or for any other reason, goods are, *prima facie*, classifiable under two or more headings, classification shall be effected as follows:

(a) The heading which provides the most specific description shall be preferred to headings providing a more general description. However, when two or more headings each refer to part only of the materials or substances contained in mixed or composite goods or to part only of the items in a set put up for retail sale, those headings are to be regarded as equally specific in relation to those goods, even if one of them gives a more complete or precise description of the goods.

(b) Mixtures, composite goods consisting of different materials or made up of different components, and goods put up in sets for retail sale, which cannot be classified by reference to 3(a), shall be classified as if they consisted of the material or component which gives them their essential character, insofar as this criterion is applicable.

(c) When goods cannot be classified by reference to 3(a) or 3(b), they shall be classified under the heading which occurs last in numerical order among those which equally merit consideration.

4. Goods which cannot be classified in accordance with the above Rules shall be classified under the heading appropriate to the goods to which they are most akin.

5. In addition to the foregoing provisions, the following Rules shall apply in respect of the goods referred to therein:

(a) Camera cases, musical instrument cases, gun cases, drawing instrument cases, necklace cases and similar containers, specially shaped or fitted to contain a specific article or set of articles, suitable for long-term use and presented with the articles for which they are intended, shall be classified with such articles when of a kind normally sold therewith. This Rule does not, however, apply to containers which give the whole its essential character;

(b) Subject to the provisions of Rule 5(a) above, packing materials and packing containers presented with the goods therein shall be classified with the goods if they are of a kind normally used for packing such goods. However, this provision is not binding when such packing materials or packing containers are clearly suitable for repetitive use.

6. For legal purposes, the classification of goods in the subheadings, *items and statistical keys* of a heading shall be determined according to the terms of those subheadings, *items and statistical keys* and related Subheading Notes *or New Zealand Notes* and, *mutatis mutandis*, to the above Rules, on the understanding that only subheadings, *items and statistical keys* at the same level are comparable. For the purposes of this Rule the relative Section and Chapter Notes also apply, unless the context otherwise requires.

... ...

Although the specific procedures for classification of goods differ by country, there are many common elements. Generally speaking, the customs authorities take the initial step in determining the classification, with a possibility of appeal of the agency decision to the domestic judicial system.

A US customs classification ruling, made in response to a request by an importer, is excerpted below:

NY L82253

February 8, 2005
CLA-2-83:RR:NC:N1:121 L82253
CATEGORY: Classification
TARIFF NO.: 8715.00.0020

Ms. Marsha L. Dawson
Graco Children's Products Inc.
150 Oaklands BoulevardExton, PA19341

RE: The tariff classification of a "Snugrider" stroller frame from China

Dear Ms. Dawson:

In your letter dated January 25, 2005 you requested a tariff classification ruling.

The merchandise is a frame that a car seat will snap into for easy mobility. The frame, called the Snugrider, consists of a folding stroller frame with wheels and a fabric utility storage basket. The Snugrider will be imported and sold separately, without the car seat.

In your letter, you request classification of this item under HTS 9401.20.00, the provision for seats of a kind used for motor vehicles. You claim that the item is not a stroller as it cannot be used without the car seat, since there is nowhere for a child to sit in this unit unless they are in a car seat. This item, however, is specifically described as an unfinished stroller and therefore is properly classified as a baby carriage under 8715.00.0020.

The applicable subheading for the Snugrider will be 8715.00.0020, Harmonized Tariff Schedule of the United States (HTS), which provides for Baby carriages (including strollers) and parts thereof. The rate of duty will be 4.4% ad valorem.

...

Sincerely,

Robert B. Swierupski

Director,
National Commodity
Specialist Division

Note that in this ruling the imports of the requested classification, HTS 9401.20.00, are duty-free, whereas the ruling places the goods in a classification with a 4.4 per cent duty. Thus, in this case, the importer did not obtain the classification it was hoping for. As noted, where this occurs, the importer may appeal through the domestic courts or special tribunals. Below is an excerpt of an appeal of a ruling by theUS Court of International Trade (CIT) in *BenQ America v US*, in which the court held that LCD monitors are properly classified as video monitors, with the higher duty rate, rather than computer monitors (that is, 'ADP' display units, the term used in the tariff schedule), with the lower rate:[19]

In this action, Plaintiff BenQ America Corporation challenges the decision of the Bureau of Customs and Border Protection denying BenQ's protest concerning the tariff classification of certain liquid crystal display ("LCD") monitors imported from the People's Republic of China in mid-May 2004.

...

The Government maintains that Customs properly classified the merchandise at issue—Dell™ 2001FP Flat Panel Color Monitors—as "video monitors" under heading 8528 of the Harmonized Tariff Schedule of the United States ("HTSUS"), assessing duties at the rate of five percent ad valorem.

...

BenQ contends that the monitors instead should have been classified as display units for automatic data processing ("ADP") machines under HTSUS heading 8471, duty-free.

...

According to a study commissioned by BenQ, which surveyed purchasers of the monitor at issue (and a somewhat earlier model), "[a] very large majority (86.6 percent) of survey respondents . . . purchas[ed] the monitors . . . for use principally as a display unit for computer uses," and "[a]n overwhelming majority (more than 99 percent of survey respondents)" were using the monitors with a computer.

...

[However,] as designed, manufactured, and imported, the monitors at issue are equipped to receive signals from both computers and other non-computer devices.

. . . Asserting that the "principal function" of the imported merchandise is "as a computer monitor," BenQ contends that the merchandise should be classified under HTSUS heading 8471

---

[19] Court of International Trade, 1 March 2010, Slip-Op 10-20.

("Automatic data processing machines and units thereof"), duty-free, as BenQ claimed at the time of importation. . . . In contrast, the Government maintains that Customs correctly classified the monitors under heading 8528 ("Reception apparatus for television . . .; video monitors and video projectors: Video monitors"), dutiable at the rate of five percent ad valorem, and that Customs' denial of BenQ's protest should therefore be sustained.

...

As set forth below, however, under Chapter 84 Note 5 (read in tandem with the relevant Explanatory Notes), the pivotal issue is instead whether the imported merchandise can "perform[ ] a specific function other than data processing"—or, stated differently, whether the monitors "are capable of accepting a signal only from the central processing unit ["CPU"]" of a computer (or whether they can also accept non-computer signals).

...

[Because the monitors at issue are "capable of connection to a video source as video monitors," and thus can "perform[ ] a specific function other than data processing," they] are thus classified under HTSUS heading 8528 under a straightforward GRI 1 analysis.

. . . the imported monitors cannot be classified as display "units" of "automatic data processing machines" under HTSUS heading 8471. . . . By the same token, it is undisputed that the monitors are video monitors . . .. As such, they are classifiable as "video monitors" under the broad *eo nomine* heading 8528, and thus were properly classified thereunder. . . . All that remains now is to ascertain the proper subheading.

...

Customs classified the monitors under subheading 8528.21.70, which covers "Reception apparatus for television, . . .; video monitors . . .: Video monitors: Color: With a flat panel screen: Other: Other." See Subheading 8528.21.70, HTSUS. Here, there is no claim by BenQ that some other subheading of heading 8528 more specifically describes the imported merchandise. An independent review of the potential subheadings confirms that, in fact, there is none. The monitors were thus properly classified under subheading 8528.21.70 of the HTSUS.

III. QUOTAS

Article XI of the GATT is the primary provision governing the use of quotas (or, to use the broader term referred to in the GATT, 'Quantitative Restrictions'). Article XI is entitled 'General Elimination of Quantitative Restrictions', indicating both that quantitative restrictions are generally prohibited, and hinting that they will be permitted in some situations. In this regard, Article XI:1 states:

> No prohibitions or restrictions other than duties, taxes or other charges, whether made effective through quotas, import or export licences or other measures, shall be instituted or maintained by any Member on the importation of any product of the territory of any other Member or on the exportation or sale for export of any product destined for the territory of any other Member.

There are two important aspects to this provision. First, with regard to the types of measures covered, it applies to all 'prohibitions or restrictions . . . whether made effective through quotas, import or export licences or other measures', but excluding 'duties, taxes or other charges' (which are covered by GATT Article II). Secondly, it applies to 'prohibitions or restrictions' *on both export and import*, although in practice import restrictions have been a far greater concern. (Export quotas are discussed briefly in Section V below.)

As noted, quantitative restrictions, while generally prohibited, are permitted in various circumstances. For example, Article XI:2 of the GATT sets out a number of specific exceptions; Article XII provides for restrictions to be used to address balance of payments difficulties; and the general exceptions in Article XX apply. For those situations where a quota is permitted in spite of the Article XI:1 prohibition, Article XIII provides some specific rules to ensure the 'non-discriminatory administration of quantitative restrictions'.

Aside from the complicated Article XIII rules on ensuring that quantitative restrictions are non-discriminatory, Article XI is generally considered a fairly straightforward provision. An import ban represents the most obvious type of measure covered. Thus, in one case, a panel found that '[s]ince the importation of certain foreign products into Canada is completely denied under Tariff Code 9958, it appears that this provision by its terms is inconsistent with Article XI:1'.[20]

On the other hand, one aspect that is not as clear is the extent to which measures other than 'border' measures are covered. As mentioned above, it is generally considered that Articles II and XI deal with 'border' measures, whereas Article III deals with 'internal' measures. However, a limitation on Article XI to 'border' measures could open a loophole for Members to evade their obligations by simply passing internal laws to prohibit the sale of imports once they have been imported (that is, let imports cross the border but then ban their internal sale). In some cases, Article III could deal with this practice. However, where there is no 'like' or 'directly competitive or substitutable' domestic product, Article III may not apply. The panel in *India—Autos* addressed this issue, and concluded that Article XI does not apply solely to 'border' measures, but rather found that it is the 'nature of the measure as a restriction *in relation to importation* which is the key factor to consider in determining whether a measure may properly fall within the scope of Article XI:1'.[21] The following extract shows how the panel applied this view to one of the measures at issue, which was a 'trade balancing' condition requiring that certain companies' exports be equal in value to their imports over a defined period.

Panel Report, *India—Measures Affecting the Automotive Sector*, Adopted 5 April 2002, WT/DS146,175/R

(i) The notion of "restriction . . . on importation"

7.264 Although the title of Article XI refers to the elimination of "quantitative restrictions", the text of the provision makes no distinction between different types of restrictions on importation. On the contrary, the words "No prohibitions or restrictions . . . whether made effective through quotas, import or export licenses or other measures" (emphases added) suggest an intention to cover any type of measures restricting the entry of goods into the territory of a Member, other than those specifically excluded, namely, duties, taxes or other charges. As was noted by the India—Quantitative Restrictions panel,

"the text of Article XI:1 is very broad in scope, providing for a general ban on import or export restrictions or prohibitions 'other than duties, taxes or other charges'. As was noted by the panel in Japan – Trade in Semi-conductors, the wording of Article XI:1 is comprehensive: it

---

[20] Panel Report, *Canada—Periodicals*, para 5.5.
[21] Panel Report, *India—Autos*, paras 7.256–7.262.

applies 'to all measures instituted or maintained by a [Member] prohibiting or restricting the importation, exportation, or sale for export of products other than measures that take the form of duties, taxes or other charges'. The scope of the term 'restriction' is also broad, as seen in its ordinary meaning, which is 'a limitation on action, a limiting condition or regulation'".

7.265 This Panel endorses the ordinary meaning of the term "restriction" as identified by the India – Quantitative Restrictions panel and its view as to the generally broad scope of the prohibition expressed in Article XI:1. As a result, it can be concluded that any form of limitation imposed on, or in relation to importation constitutes a restriction on importation within the meaning of Article XI:1.

7.266 As far as the trade balancing obligation is concerned, it is a condition placed on importation of the product. It results both from the signature of the MOU (whereby the principle of the obligation is agreed to, as part of the conditions to gain the right to import the restricted products) and from the actual importation of products (which determines the "quantum" of the export obligation). The MOUs are signed "on the basis of" projections regarding indigenization and trade balancing. After entering into the MOU, signatories had the opportunity to apply for licenses whenever they wished to import kits or components subject to restrictions. It seems that the licenses themselves, before 1 April 2001, made a reference to the trade balancing obligation.

7.267 Both complainants describe the measure as a "limitation" on imports, and highlight the practical threshold imposed by the export requirement on the value of imports that can be made, which, they assert, amounts to a restriction.

7.268 The trade balancing condition does not set an absolute numerical limit on the amount of imports that can be made. It does, however, limit the value of imports that can be made to the value of exports that the signatory intends to make over the life of the MOU. If all signatories could at all times have an unlimited desire and ability to export, this obligation would be unlikely to have any impact upon import decisions. That is not a realistic scenario, however and was not contended for by India. In reality, therefore, the limit on imports set by this condition is induced by the practical threshold that a signatory will impose on itself as a result of the obligation to satisfy a corresponding export commitment. The amount of imports is therefore linked to a certain amount of anticipated exports. The more a signatory would be concerned about its ability to export profitably at significant levels, the more it would be induced by the trade balancing obligation to limit its imports of the relevant products.

7.269 The question of whether this form of measure can appropriately be described as a restriction on importation turns on the issue of whether Article XI can be considered to cover situations where products are technically allowed into the market without an express formal quantitative restriction, but are only allowed under certain conditions which make the importation more onerous than if the condition had not existed, thus generating a disincentive to import.

7.270 On a plain reading, it is clear that a "restriction" need not be a blanket prohibition or a precise numerical limit. Indeed, the term "restriction" cannot mean merely "prohibitions" on importation, since Article XI:1 expressly covers both "prohibition or restriction". Furthermore, the Panel considers that the expression "limiting condition" used by the India—Quantitative Restrictions panel to define the term "restriction" and which this Panel endorses, is helpful in identifying the scope of the notion in the context of the facts before it. That phrase suggests the need to identify not merely a condition placed on importation, but a condition that is limiting, i.e. that has a limiting effect. In the context of Article XI, that limiting effect must be on importation itself.

7.271 The Panel believes that a substance over form approach should be taken to the analysis of the facts in the context of this test. Such an approach is consistent with that taken by the panel on Japan- Semi-conductors. The panel examined a series of actions taken by the Government of Japan after concluding an Agreement on trade in semi-conductors with the United States. These included requests which the Japanese Government addressed to Japanese producers and exporters of semi-conductors not to export semi-conductors at prices below company-specific costs to contracting parties other than the United States. There was also a statutory requirement for exporters to submit information on export prices and systematic monitoring of company and product-specific costs and export prices by the Government. This was backed up with the use of supply and demand forecasts to impress on manufacturers the need to align their production to appropriate levels. The panel concluded that:

> "the complex of measures exhibited the rationale as well as the essential elements of a formal system of export control. The only distinction in this case was the absence of formal legally binding obligations in respect of exportation or sale for export of semiconductors. However, the Panel concluded that this amounted to a difference in form rather than substance because the measures were operated in a manner equivalent to mandatory requirements. The Panel concluded that the complex of measures constituted a coherent system restricting the sale for export of monitored semi-conductors at prices below company-specific costs to markets other that the United States, inconsistent with Article XI:1".

7.272 This finding suggests that measures which involve no formal restriction but rather a network of strong suggestions can fall within the scope of Article XI:1. It is true that in that instance, exports were being restricted, rather than imports, and the panel referred in its final conclusion to a restriction on "the sale for export". This Panel acknowledges that this phrase has no matching phrase under Article XI:1 with regard to imports. However, the rest of the Semi-conductors panel's conclusions suggest that the restrictions found by the panel also concerned exportation (e.g. "The Panel considered that the complex of measures exhibited the rationale as well as the essential elements of a formal system of export control. The only distinction in this case was the absence of formal legally binding obligations in respect of exportation or sale for export of semi-conductors".). This report thus seems to support a reading of Article XI:1 encompassing import limitations made effective through disincentives to importation, without a formal numerical limit on imports.

7.273 The same panel also found that "export licensing practices by Japan, leading to delays of up to three months in the issuing of licences for semi-conductors destined for contracting parties other than the United States, had been non-automatic and constituted restrictions on the exportation of such products inconsistent with Article XI:1". This finding suggests that a measure that does not preclude any exportation but rather makes it more burdensome can also amount to a restriction on exportation. Mutatis mutandis, the same reasoning could apply to a restriction on importation.

7.274 The Panel Report on EEC—Programme of Minimum Import Prices, Licences and Surety Deposits for Certain Processed Fruits and Vegetables also made a finding on Article XI:1 which is of interest in identifying its scope. In that case, the panel examined a minimum import price and associated security system for tomato concentrate. The United States was arguing that the system prohibited importation of goods below a certain price and was, therefore, a restriction within the meaning of Article XI on the importation of these goods. The EC, on the contrary, was arguing that the system was a non-tariff barrier measure and that, in principle, imports of tomato concentrates into the Community were allowed, but not below the minimum price. The panel found that "the minimum price system, as enforced by the additional security, was a restriction 'other than duties, taxes or other charges' within the meaning of Article XI:1".

7.275 That report was adopted by the CONTRACTING PARTIES and cited by the Japan – Semi-conductors panel as having decided that "the import regulation allowing the import of a product in principle, but not below a minimum price level, constituted a restriction on importation within the meaning of Article XI:1". The Panel also notes, in this regard, the observation made by the panel in Argentina –Hides and Leather that "[t]here can be no doubt, in [its] view, that the disciplines of Article XI:1 extend to restrictions of a de facto nature".

7.276 As noted above, the India—Quantitative Restrictions panel endorsed the broad scope of the provision articulated by Japan—Semi-conductors in finding that a discretionary import licensing scheme, where licenses were not granted automatically but rather on "unspecified" merits, was contrary to Article XI:1. This Panel agrees with and adopts these interpretations. For reasons outlined above, the Panel does not consider that it is a separate requirement of Article XI that a measure can be described as a border measure. It is the impact of a measure by way of a "restriction . . . on importation" that counts, not the physical place of its application.

(ii) Analysis of the trade balancing condition

7.277 With regard to the trade balancing condition, the Panel finds that as at the date of its establishment, there would necessarily have been a practical threshold to the amount of exports that each manufacturer could expect to make, which in turn would determine the amount of imports that could be made. This amounts to an import restriction. The degree of effective restriction which would result from this condition may vary from signatory to signatory depending on its own projections, its output, or specific market conditions, but a manufacturer is in no instance free to import, without commercial constraint, as many kits and components as it wishes without regard to its export opportunities and obligations.

7.278 The Panel therefore finds that the trade balancing condition contained in Public Notice No. 60 and in the MOUs signed thereunder, by limiting the amount of imports through linking them to an export commitment, acts as a restriction on importation, contrary to the terms of Article XI:1. With respect to the European Communities' argument that the MOU signatories that have yet to achieve the 70% indigenization requirement would continue to incur export obligations after 1 April 2001, the Panel notes that no evidence was presented to show that any such new export obligations have in fact accrued.

7.279 The Panel is comforted in this finding by the fact that it appears consistent with Item 2(a) of the Illustrative list of the TRIMs Agreement which suggests that measures linking the amount of imports to a certain quantity or value of exports can constitute restrictions on importation within the meaning of Article XI:1. The Illustrative List thus provides that:

"TRIMS that are inconsistent with the obligation of general obligation of elimination of quantitative restrictions provided for in paragraph 1 of Article XI of GATT 1994 include those which are mandatory or enforceable under domestic law or under administrative rulings, or compliance with which is necessary to obtain an advantage, and which restrict: (a) the importation by an enterprise of products used in or related to its local production, generally or to an amount related to the volume or value of local production that it exports".

7.280 In particular, the Panel notes that this item does not limit the linkage to past exports.

7.281 Nevertheless, the Panel is not ruling on whether the specific type of measure under consideration here is necessarily the precise type of measure envisaged in the Illustrative List or on the extent to which this list may operate as an aid to interpretation of Article XI itself. The Panel also notes that to fall within the terms of item 2(a), the measures in question may in any case need to be characterized as measures that "restrict" imports in certain ways. The essence of our analysis has been to consider the proper meaning of a similar term under Article XI:1 itself. Nonetheless, this item is at least consistent with the finding that a measure linking imports to a certain amount of exports constitutes a restriction on importation within the meaning of Article XI.1.[22]

... ...

Thus, the panel did not limit Article XI to measures imposed at the 'border'. Instead, the panel saw the issue as whether the measure places limitations on importation. In this regard, the panel found that while the 'trade balancing' condition at issue does not set an 'absolute numerical limit' on the amount of imports, it does limit the amount/value of imports by linking them to an export commitment. This latter finding is a fairly broad interpretation of Article XI, and it is not clear whether the Appellate Body would agree with this approach.

Finally, there is one additional issue relating to the line between border measures and internal measures. Where a measure is a pure internal measure, applying generally to the internal regulation or taxation of all goods sold on the domestic market, it is clear that GATT Article III applies (it is entitled 'National Treatment on Internal Taxation and Regulation'). Likewise, where a measure is a pure border measure, applying solely to importation, Article XI applies. But where a measure (or measures) applies to domestic goods and imports through separate mechanisms, the situation is more complicated. For example, a measure may have two separate sets of provisions, one set that applies to imports and one set that applies to domestic products. Alternatively, a Member may in one year adopt a measure that applies to domestic goods; two years later, after additional debate among law-makers, it may adopt a related measure that applies to imports and is imposed at the border. The question is, should the import aspects of the single measure or the import component of the alternative measure be considered a 'border' measure subject to Article XI?

This question is dealt with by the Note to Article III, discussed earlier in the context of tariffs, which provides:

> Any internal tax or other internal charge, or any law, regulation or requirement of the kind referred to in paragraph 1 which applies to an imported product and to the like domestic product and is collected or enforced in the case of the imported product at the time or point of importation, is nevertheless to be regarded as an internal tax or other internal charge, or a law, regulation or requirement of the kind referred to in paragraph 1, and is accordingly subject to the provisions of Article III.

In essence, this provision states that if an internal tax or regulation is imposed on imports at the time of importation (rather than imposed internally, as would be the case with domestic products) it is to be 'regarded as' an internal tax or regulation and is subject to Article III. While some parts of this provision are straightforward, questions about its scope do arise.

First, for the two situations described above, where a measure (or measures) separately addresses domestic products and imports, does the Note (and thus Article III) still apply? In the context of a single measure that contained provisions applying to both imports and domestic products, one panel concluded that Article III does apply.[23] By contrast, another panel, while not explicitly mentioning this issue, found that an import prohibition that

---

[22] Panel Report, *India—Autos*, paras 7.264–7.281.
[23] Panel Report, *EC—Asbestos*, paras 8.86–8.99.

had been imposed after a related domestic regulation violated Article XI.[24] Implicitly, at least, this latter panel does not seem to have considered the existence of a related domestic regulation to exclude the application of Article XI. However, the argument that the measure should have been covered under Article III alone was not made by the parties, which may have led to the panel's decision not to address the issue.

Secondly, the provision makes clear that such measures are 'subject to' Article III. But does this imply that they are not subject to Article XI? That is, are they subject to Article III only, or to both Articles III and XI? One panel noted that '[i]n appropriate circumstances [measures] may have an impact both in relation to the conditions of importation of a product [*i.e.* Article XI] and in respect of the competitive conditions of imported products on the internal market within the meaning of Article III:4'.[25] This seems to mean that the panel considered that both provisions might apply, although under what circumstances it thought this would be the case is unclear.

IV. TARIFF QUOTAS

Tariffs impose additional costs on imports through various types of duties; quotas limit the numerical quantity of imports, often to a specific amount. The tariff quota combines the key features of these measures into one. Essentially, a tariff quota charges a certain duty rate for some set number of imports. Then, when that number is exceeded, a higher duty rate is charged. Thus, with a quota, only a certain number of products may be imported. By contrast, with a tariff quota, only a certain number of products may be imported at the lower duty rate.

Tariff quotas are generally permitted (subject to compliance with any commitments made in the Member's schedule). However, Article XIII:5 makes clear that the rules on non-discriminatory application of quantitative restrictions apply to tariff quotas as well.

V. EXPORT QUOTAS AND EXPORT TARIFFS

In general, when people refer to 'tariffs' and 'quotas' they mean tariffs and quotas imposed on imports, as this is the most common use of these measures. However, tariffs and quotas can also be imposed on exports, often to ensure a sufficient supply of a product that a domestic producer uses as an input. We deal with export quotas first here because the rules in this area are more detailed.

(a) Export Quotas

Although they do not get the attention given to import quotas, export quotas are a fairly common measure used by governments. They can be taken for the following reasons,

---

[24] Panel Report, *US—Shrimp*, paras 7.11–7.17.
[25] Panel Report, *India—Autos*, para 7.296.

among others: national security, by prohibiting export of goods that can be used by a nation's enemies; to help a domestic industry, by limiting export of a product that the industry needs as an input, thereby increasing the supply available; to protect natural resources such as forests; or in response to a trading partner's demands. Export restrictions based on national security concerns could be justified under Article XXI of the GATT. Similarly, restrictions to protect natural resources could fall within the Article XX(g) environmental exception, discussed in Chapter 9 below. On the other hand, certain export restrictions taken in response to a trading partner's demands (often referred to as 'voluntary export restraints'), while once a common practice, are now prohibited.[26]

The main WTO provision on export quotas is Article XI:1 of the GATT, the same one that applies to import quotas. Thus, the legal standard for export quotas is the same as for import quotas. One WTO complaint relying on this provision involved a claim by the EC that Argentina was imposing a de facto export restriction on bovine hides by allowing representatives of the domestic tanning industry, for whom bovine hides are an input, to be present during the customs clearing process, to object to the decisions of the customs officers, and to obtain access to confidential information that could be used to pressure the bovine hides producers not to export. Underlying this claim was the EC's belief that the tanning representatives were interfering with the export process so as to limit exports and thus ensure a greater supply of inputs for their own business. Ultimately, the panel rejected the EC claim, on the basis that the burden of proof had not been met.[27] We extract a key portion of the Panel's reasoning here:

Panel Report, *Argentina— Measures Affecting the Export of Bovine Hides and the Import of Finished Leather*, Adopted 16 February 2001, WT/DS155/R

6. Presence of tanners' representatives, access to confidential information and abuse of such information as an export restriction

11.44 The European Communities has argued that, in fact, the Argentinean tanners do abuse the information to which they have access. According to the European Communities, there is a reason for the *frigoríficos* to be concerned about the release to their domestic customers of their confidential business information, particularly the name of the exporters. The European Communities alleges that there is a cartel of tanners operating in the Argentinean market and that this cartel has as one of its objects the stifling of exports of its raw materials, bovine hides.

11.45 The European Communities has supported these allegations by introducing several pieces of information. Among these are a trade magazine article describing the structure of the Argentinean tanning industry as being concentrated. Also, a statement has been provided from the president of the association of *frigoríficos* to the effect that price collusion is taking place.353 The European Communities also point in particular to an explanation offered by a member of the *Congreso de la Nación* regarding a draft law introduced in 1992 to the effect that there was a pricing cartel among the tanners. The European Communities points out that the member who provided this explanation is now Argentinean Secretary of State for Agriculture. The European Communities also provided a copy of a recent newspaper editorial referring to these restrictions.

11.46 The European Communities also argues that the Panel must take into account the historical context for the measures in question. The European Communities notes that in 1972 Argentina

[26] See Safeguards Agreement, Art 11(1)(b).
[27] Panel Report, *Argentina—Hides and Leather*, paras 11.1–11.55.

imposed a prohibition on exports of raw (wet salted) bovine hides with the stated objective of "protect[ing] the adequate supplies of bovine hides to the tanning industry". In 1979, following a Section 301 petition filed with the U.S. government by the U.S. Tanners council, Argentina committed itself to convert the export prohibition into an export tax which was to have been phased out within a certain time-frame. In 1985, Argentina introduced a "suspension" on exports of raw hides and semi-finished leather in order "to maintain the volume of supply in raw materials adequate to the needs of the domestic market of the leather tanning and manufacturing sector facilitating a smooth flow of supplies while avoiding any undue increase in prices". In 1992, the "suspension" was replaced by an export duty of 15 percent on the exports of raw bovine hides and bovine wet blue as well as an additional tax which was later abolished. In 1993, Argentina authorized the presence of CICA representatives during customs inspection of raw bovine hides and wet blue bovine hides destined for export. This authorization applied to the same products that were subject to the aforementioned export duty. Finally, in 1994, Argentina for the first time authorized ADICMA representatives to participate in the customs inspection not only of raw hides and wet blue hides destined for export, but also of products destined for export which fall under customs position 4104, which includes finished leather and furs.

11.47 According to the European Communities, in light of both the current cartelized tanning industry and the stated goals of the industry as they have been implemented historically, there is a great incentive for the *frigorificos* not to export their products and risk losing their domestic customers. The European Communities argues that the measure in question, Resolution 2235, provides the means for making effective these export restrictions.

11.48 Argentina responds to the European Communities' allegations by claiming that the European Communities has provided no specific evidence to support the allegations. A self-serving statement by the *frigorificos* does not suffice to prove anything. The *frigorificos* do not even provide any evidence themselves of the allegations they are making. Argentina points out that no complaints have been received by the Argentinean competition authority. Furthermore, the European Communities' allegations are not logical. The tanners and the *frigorificos* have essentially equal bargaining power, particularly in light of the fact the value of the raw hides is only about 10 percent of the value of the slaughtered animal. Because hides are a mere by-product for the *frigorificos*, that is the real reason they have not paid much attention to exporting; the risks and costs are not worth the rewards in an ancillary line of business. Furthermore, the *frigorificos* have larger overall sales than the tanners, hardly making them presumptively subject to pressure from the tanners not to export their raw hides.

11.49 We begin by noting that it is possible that there is a cartel operating among the tanners. It is possible that they collude to set prices. But this leads to another question. Namely, it is not at all clear what the relationship is between an alleged price cartel (operating either vertically or horizontally—the European Communities has been vague about this) and the alleged export restrictions. Indeed, even assuming we are looking at a vertically operating cartel (i.e., an agreement by cartel members not to pay more than a certain price for raw materials) imposed on the suppliers of raw hides, there is no direct link to a quantitative export limitation resulting therefrom. More analytical steps are needed to move from one to the other (e.g., the price cartel has created and enforced a surplus domestic supply of hides by restricting exports) and each step would need to be supported by some evidence. The allegations by a parliamentarian (even one who is now a Secretary of State) and the various mentions in newspaper articles do not serve to prove that there is a cartel operating, much less how it operates and why such operation leads to export restrictions.

11.50 It is the case, as we have discussed above, that the levels of exports of hides from Argentina seem to be unusually low. It also seems that the price of hides in Argentina is lower than the world price and does not seem to correlate to the low level of exports. However, this is not enough. As we also discussed, in situations where circumstantial evidence is used, it must lead clearly and convincingly to the conclusion sought. Reasonable alternatives must be eliminated. It is simply not sufficient for the European Communities to assert that there is no *ratio legis* for Resolution 2235 other than for it to be designed to restrict exports. The European Communities must prove it and, in our view, it has not.

11.51 In our view, it is possible that a government could implement a measure which operated to restrict exports because of its interaction with a private cartel. Other points would need to be argued and proved (such as whether there was or needed to be knowledge of the cartel practices on the part of the government) or, to put it as mentioned above, it would need to be established that the actions are properly attributed to the Argentinean government under the rules of state responsibility. But we have not reached that stage here. It may be the case that it will be difficult for one Member to prove that there is a cartel operating within the jurisdiction of another Member. Nonetheless, we cannot ignore the need for sufficient proof of a party's allegations simply because obtaining such proof is difficult.

11.52 The evidence before us is quite thin. We have a newspaper article and opinion piece, a press release from the *frigoríficos* and a statement by a member of the *Congreso de la Nación*. Such evidence would certainly not support a case in a domestic court. While it may be an open question whether the same quantum of evidence is necessary to support such allegations in a WTO dispute under Article XI of the GATT 1994, surely the difference cannot be that great. What is clear is that whatever level of proof may be required, it was not reached here. And we note again that there is no obligation under Article XI for a Member (Argentina in this instance) to assume a full "due diligence" burden to investigate and prevent cartels from functioning as private export restrictions.

11.53 It remains a possibility that individual tanners might abuse the information obtained through participation in the Customs process. However, as the European Communities has implicitly acknowledged in the way its argument has been presented, only collective action can result in an export restriction. If one tanner misuses the information, a *frigorífico* may always sell to another. We must also emphasize that the European Communities has also not provided sufficient evidence to support a claim even of a chilling effect which results in a restriction on exports due to the potential for individual tanners to abuse information.

11.54 As we discussed above, the European Communities must prove that this measure is taken to make an export restriction effective. Indeed, it is entirely possible to conclude that such an export limiting cartel could operate wholly independently of this measure. The European Communities would have had to prove that there was a causal relationship rather than a coincidental one here. Even if we were to agree that there were a cartel operating in this industry, there is simply no proof that Resolution 2235 is what is causing (or making effective) the export restriction.

11.55 Thus, in conclusion, we do not find that the evidence is sufficient to prove that there is an export restriction made effective by the measure in question within the meaning of Article XI of the GATT 1994.

... ...

The more recent case of *China—Raw Materials* involved not only Article XI:1, but also the 'exceptions' clause of Article XI:2, which reads:

2. The provisions of paragraph 1 of this Article shall not extend to the following:

(*a*) Export prohibitions or restrictions temporarily applied to prevent or relieve critical shortages of foodstuffs or other products essential to the exporting contracting party;

(*b*) Import and export prohibitions or restrictions necessary to the application of standards or regulations for the classification, grading or marketing of commodities in international trade;

(*c*) Import restrictions on any agricultural or fisheries product, imported in any form, necessary to the enforcement of governmental measures which operate:[28]

(i) to restrict the quantities of the like domestic product permitted to be marketed or produced, or, if there is no substantial domestic production of the like product, of a domestic product for which the imported product can be directly substituted; or

(ii) to remove a temporary surplus of the like domestic product, or, if there is no substantial domestic production of the like product, of a domestic product for which the imported product can be directly substituted, by making the surplus available to certain groups of domestic consumers free of charge or at prices below the current market level; or

(iii) to restrict the quantities permitted to be produced of any animal product the production of which is directly dependent, wholly or mainly, on the imported commodity, if the domestic production of that commodity is relatively negligible.

In the dispute, China argued that its export quota on refractory-grade bauxite was not inconsistent with GATT Article XI:1 because it was a restriction 'temporarily applied' to prevent or relieve a 'critical shortage' of an essential product in accordance with Article XI:2(a) of the GATT. Therefore, according to China, its measure did not fall within the scope of the general prohibition of quantitative restrictions under Article XI:1. The panel rejected this argument, finding that China failed to demonstrate that the export quota was 'temporarily applied' or that China faced a 'critical shortage' of refractory-grade bauxite.

On appeal, China claimed that the panel erred in its interpretation and application of Article XI:2(a). More specifically, China disagreed with the panel's interpretation and application of the term 'temporarily' and its interpretation of the term 'critical shortages'. Concerning 'temporarily', China asserted that the panel erred in excluding 'long-term' export restrictions from the scope of Article XI:2(a), and also that the panel failed to take into consideration the fact that China's export quota on refractory-grade bauxite is subject to annual review. With respect to 'critical shortages', China argued that the panel erred by interpreting this term to exclude shortages caused by the 'finite' nature or 'limited reserve[s]' of a product. In addition, China advanced two separate claims that the panel failed to make an objective assessment of the matter under DSU Article 11. The Appellate Body's analysis of these issues is extracted below.

---

[28] The Article also notes: 'Any contracting party applying restrictions on the importation of any product pursuant to subparagraph (*c*) of this paragraph shall give public notice of the total quantity or value of the product permitted to be imported during a specified future period and of any change in such quantity or value. Moreover, any restrictions applied under (i) above shall not be such as will reduce the total of imports relative to the total of domestic production, as compared with the proportion which might reasonably be expected to rule between the two in the absence of restrictions. In determining this proportion, the contracting party shall pay due regard to the proportion prevailing during a previous representative period and to any special factors which may have affected or may be affecting the trade in the product concerned.'

Appellate Body Report, *China—Measures Related to the Exportation of Various Raw Materials*, **Adopted 22 February 2012, WT/DS394,395,398/AB/R**

329. As noted above, China argues that the Panel erred in finding that China had not demonstrated that its export quota on refractory-grade bauxite was "temporarily applied", within the meaning of Article XI:2(a) of the GATT 1994, to either prevent or relieve a "critical shortage". With respect to the Panel's interpretation of the term "temporarily", China supports the Panel's finding that the word "temporarily" "suggest[s] a fixed time-limit for the application of a measure". China, however, alleges that the Panel subsequently "adjusted" its interpretation of the term "temporarily" to exclude the "long-term" application of export restrictions. China argues that the term "temporarily" does not mark a "bright line" moment in time after which an export restriction has necessarily been maintained for too long. Instead, Article XI:2(a) requires that the duration of a restriction be limited and bound in relation to the achievement of the stated goal. Furthermore, China argues that the Panel erroneously found that Article XI:2(a) and Article XX(g) are mutually exclusive, and that this finding was a significant motivating factor for the Panel's erroneous interpretation of the term "temporarily" in Article XI:2(a). China submits that the two provisions are not mutually exclusive, and instead apply cumulatively.

330. We note that the Panel found that the word "temporarily" suggests "a fixed time-limit for the application of a measure", and also expressed the view that a "restriction or ban applied under Article XI:2(a) must be of a limited duration and not indefinite". We have set out above our interpretation of the term "temporarily" as employed in Article XI:2(a). In our view, a measure applied "temporarily" in the sense of Article XI:2(a) is a measure applied in the interim, to provide relief in extraordinary conditions in order to bridge a passing need. It must be finite, that is, applied for a limited time. Accordingly, we agree with the Panel that a restriction or prohibition in the sense of Article XI:2(a) must be of a limited duration and not indefinite.

331. The Panel further interpreted the term "limited time" to refer to a "fixed time-limit" for the application of the measure. To the extent that the Panel was referring to a time-limit fixed in advance, we disagree that "temporary" must always connote a time-limit fixed in advance. Instead, we consider that Article XI:2(a) describes measures applied for a limited duration, adopted in order to bridge a passing need, irrespective of whether or not the temporal scope of the measure is fixed in advance.

332. China alleges that the Panel erred in reading the term "temporarily" to exclude the "longterm" application of export restrictions. In particular, China refers to the Panel's statements that Article XI:2(a) cannot be interpreted "to permit the long-term application of . . . export restrictions", or to "permit long-term measures to be imposed". We consider that the terms "long-term application" and "long-term measures" provide little value in elucidating the meaning of the term "temporary", because what is "long-term" in a given case depends on the facts of the particular case. Moreover, the terms "long-term" and "short-term" describe a different concept than the term "temporary", employed in Article XI:2(a). Viewed in the context of the Panel's entire analysis, it is clear, however, that the Panel used these words to refer back to its earlier interpretation of the term "temporarily applied" as meaning a "restriction or prohibition for a limited time". Because the Panel merely referred to its earlier interpretation of the term "temporarily applied" and did not provide additional reasoning, the Panel cannot be viewed as having "adjusted" its interpretation of the term "temporarily" to exclude the "long-term" application of export restrictions.

333. This brings us to China's allegation that the Panel erroneously found that Article XI:2(a) and Article XX(g) are mutually exclusive, and that this finding was a significant motivating factor for the Panel's erroneous interpretation of the term "temporarily" in Article XI:2(a). As we see it, the Panel considered Article XX(g) as relevant context in its interpretation of Article

XI:2(a). It noted that Article XX(g) "incorporates additional protections in its chapeau to ensure that the application of a measure does not result in arbitrary or unjustifiable discrimination or amount to a disguised restriction on international trade". The Panel considered that the existence of these further requirements under Article XX(g) lent support to its interpretation that an exception pursuant to Article XI:2(a) must be of a limited duration and not indefinite, because otherwise Members could resort indistinguishably to either Article XI:2(a) or to Article XX(g). We do not understand the Panel to have found that these two provisions are mutually exclusive. Rather, the Panel sought to confirm the result of its interpretation, and stated that the interpretation proffered by China would be inconsistent with the principle of effective treaty interpretation. We therefore see no merit in China's allegation that the Panel erroneously found that Article XI:2(a) and Article XX(g) are mutually exclusive. Nor do we agree that such a finding was a basis for the Panel's interpretation of the term "temporarily" in Article XI:2(a).

334. In any event, we have some doubts as to the validity of the Panel's concern that, if Article XI:2(a) is not interpreted as confined to measures of limited duration, Members could "resort indistinguishably to either Article XI:2(a) or to Article XX(g) to address the problem of an exhaustible natural resource". Members can resort to Article XX of the GATT 1994 as an exception to justify measures that would otherwise be inconsistent with their GATT obligations. By contrast, Article XI:2 provides that the general elimination of quantitative restrictions *shall not extendto* the items listed under subparagraphs (a) to (c) of that provision. This language seems to indicate that the scope of the obligation not to impose quantitative restrictions itself is limited by Article XI:2(a). Accordingly, where the requirements of Article XI:2(a) are met, there would be no scope for the application of Article XX, because no obligation exists.

335. Turning then to the Panel's application of the term "temporarily applied" in the present case, China alleges that the Panel failed to take into consideration the fact that China's export restrictions on refractory-grade bauxite are subject to annual review. China faults the Panel for "simply assum[ing]" that China's restriction on exports of refractory-grade bauxite will be maintained indefinitely. China submits that, at the close of each year, the factual circumstances are assessed in the light of the legal standard set forth in Article XI:2(a) to establish whether the export restriction should be maintained. We note that China has made parallel claims, under Article XI:2(a), alleging an error of application, and under Article 11 of the DSU, alleging that the Panel failed to make an objective assessment of the facts. We consider China's allegation that the Panel "simply assumed" something to be more in the nature of a claim made under Article 11 of the DSU, and therefore address it below at the end of our analysis in this section.

336. China further argues that the Panel erred in its interpretation and application of Article XI:2(a) by presuming that export restrictions "imposed to address a limited reserve of an exhaustible natural resource" cannot be "temporary" and that a shortage of an exhaustible nonrenewable resource cannot be "critical". The Panel reasoned that, "if there is no possibility for an existing shortage ever to cease to exist, it will not be possible to 'relieve or prevent' it through an export restriction applied on a temporary basis." The Panel further stated that, "[i] f a measure were imposed to address a limited reserve of an exhaustible natural resource, such measure would be imposed until the point when the resource is fully depleted." The Panel added that "[t]his temporal focus seems consistent with the notion of 'critical', defined as 'of the nature of, or constituting, a crisis'".

337. We do not agree with China that these statements by the Panel indicate that the Panel presumed that a shortage of an exhaustible non-renewable resource cannot be "critical" within the meaning of Article XI:2(a). The Panel noted instead, correctly in our view, that the reach of Article XI:2(a) is not the same as that of Article XX(g), adding that these provisions are "intended to address different situations and thus must mean different things". Articles XI:2(a) and XX(g) have different functions and contain different obligations. Article XI:2(a) addresses

measures taken to prevent or relieve "critical shortages" of foodstuffs or other essential products. Article XX(g), on the other hand, addresses measures relating to the conservation of exhaustible natural resources. We do not exclude that a measure falling within the ambit of Article XI:2(a) could relate to the same product as a measure relating to the conservation of an exhaustible natural resource. It would seem that Article XI:2(a) measures could be imposed, for example, if a natural disaster caused a "critical shortage" of an exhaustible natural resource, which, at the same time, constituted a foodstuff or other essential product. Moreover, because the reach of Article XI:2(a) is different from that of Article XX(g), an Article XI:2(a) measure might operate simultaneously with a conservation measure complying with the requirements of Article XX(g).

338. As a final matter, we note that China advances two separate claims that the Panel failed to make an objective assessment of the matter pursuant to Article 11 of the DSU. First, China alleges that the Panel failed properly to assess evidence that China's export restriction is annually reviewed and renewed, and that the Panel's failure to consider this evidence has a bearing on the objectivity of the Panel's factual assessment. China submits that evidence relating to China's annual review procedures demonstrates that the export restriction will be maintained only as long as it is justified to prevent or relieve the critical shortage of refractory-grade bauxite. For China, this evidence demonstrates that the Panel erred in assuming that the restriction "will remain in place until the reserves have been depleted".

339. We note that the Panel identified several reasons for finding that China's export restriction is not temporarily applied to prevent or relieve a critical shortage. The Panel observed that China's restriction on exports of refractory-grade bauxite had "already been in place for at least a decade with no indication of when it will be withdrawn and every indication that it will remain in place until the reserves have been depleted". The Panel also referred to evidence of the existence of an export quota submitted by the parties, as well as China's explanation that its "export quota on refractory grade bauxite forms part of a conservation plan aimed at extending the reserves of refractory-grade bauxite".

340. To us, these elements of the Panel's reasoning indicate that the Panel's finding was not, as China alleges, based on a mere "assumption" that the restriction would remain in effect until depletion of the reserves. Instead, the Panel considered evidence indicating that the measure had been in place for at least a decade and China does not contest the Panel's finding that this was the case. In particular, the Panel noted that "China has had an export quota in place on exports of bauxite classifiable under HS No. 2508.3000 dating back to at least 2000" and found that "China's estimation of a 16-year reserve for bauxite suggests that China intends to maintain its measure in place until the exhaustion of remaining reserves (in keeping with its contention that it needs to restrain consumption), or until new technology or conditions lessen demand for refractory-grade bauxite." In addition, as an indication that the restrictions would remain in place until depletion, the Panel noted China's explanation that its export quota on refractory-grade bauxite forms part of a conservation plan aimed at extending the reserves of refractory-grade bauxite.

341. China's argument appears to be directed mainly at the weight the Panel ascribed to evidence indicating that the export restriction is annually reviewed and renewed. The Appellate Body has consistently recognized that panels enjoy a margin of discretion in their assessment of the facts. This margin includes the discretion of a panel to decide which evidence it chooses to utilize in making its findings, and to determine how much weight to attach to the various items of evidence placed before it by the parties. A panel does not err simply because it declines to accord to the evidence the weight that one of the parties believes should be accorded to it. A panel is entitled "to determine that certain elements of evidence should be accorded more weight than other elements— that is the essence of the task of appreciating the evidence". We

therefore reject China's claim that the Panel failed to make an objective assessment of the matter as required by Article 11 of the DSU.

342. Next, China asserts that the Panel employed internally inconsistent or incoherent reasoning in stating, on the one hand, that "there is no possibility for an existing shortage [of an exhaustible natural resource] ever to cease to exist" such that "it will not be possible to 'relieve or prevent' it through an export restriction applied on a temporary basis" and acknowledging, on the other hand, that "advances in reserve detection or extraction techniques", or the availability of "additional capacity", could "alleviate or eliminate" a shortage of an exhaustible natural resource, or that "new technology or conditions" might "lessen demand" for the resource.

343. The Appellate Body has previously found that a Panel's reasoning may be so internally inconsistent that it amounts to a breach of Article 11 of the DSU. We do not consider this to be the case here. Contrary to what China suggests, the Panel did not find that "'there is no possibility for an existing shortage [of an exhaustible natural resource] ever to cease to exist', such that 'it will not be possible to 'relieve or prevent' it through an export restriction applied on a temporary basis'". Instead, the Panel's statement to which China refers contains a hypothetical. It reads as follows: "*if* there is no possibility for an existing shortage ever to cease to exist, it will not be possible to 'relieve or prevent' it through an export restriction applied on a temporary basis." The Panel did not make such a finding but employed a hypothetical and did not, as China alleges, make two internally inconsistent findings. Therefore, the Panel did not fail to conduct an objective assessment of the matter pursuant to Article 11 of the DSU.

344. For the above reasons, we *uphold* the Panel's conclusion that China did not demonstrate that its export quota on refractory-grade bauxite was "temporarily applied", within the meaning of Article XI:2(a) of the GATT 1994, to either prevent or relieve a "critical shortage", and we dismiss China's allegation that the Panel acted inconsistently with its duty to conduct an objective assessment of the matter as required by Article 11 of the DSU.

... ...

(b) Export Tariffs

With regard to tariffs (or any kind of tax, fee or other charge) on exports, WTO rules do not contain any general obligation prohibiting this practice, although a Member could make commitments in its Schedule not to impose an export tariff.[29] Export duties may be used to serve all the same purposes as noted in the case of export quotas, but in addition they may also serve as a means of raising revenue.[30]

VI. QUESTIONS

1. Are frozen boneless chicken cuts impregnated with salt (in a content of at least 1.2 per cent by weight) better classified as frozen boneless chicken cuts or as salted meat?

---

[29] See, eg, Australia's WTO Sched I, where Pt III, covering 'Non-Tariff Concessions', which states that '[f] or the products listed below, there shall be no export duty': available at www.olis.oecd.org/olis/2002 doc.nsf/4 3bb6130e5e86e5fc12569fa005d004c/233f10f9868ee7f3c1256cbf00361ac7/$FILE/JT00138512.PDF

[30] See generally, J Kazeki, *Analysis of Non-Tariff Measures: The Case of Export Duties*, OECD Working Party of the Trade Committee, TD/TC/WP(2002)54/Final.

How would the General Rules for the interpretation of the Harmonised System apply to this issue? Are WTO panels and the Appellate Body capable of examining tariff classification issues such as this one in the absence of any rules on the subject?

2. The Appellate Body has made clear on a number of occasions that WTO Schedules should be interpreted using Vienna Convention treaty interpretation rules, just as other WTO rules are. But does it make sense to interpret these treaty terms in the same manner? Is the interpretation of, for example, the National Treatment obligation really no different from interpreting the word 'salted'?

3. Should tariff re-classifications that cause a product to be subject to higher duties be looked at with suspicion? Should there be a presumption that such actions violate Article II:1?

4. Is the non-violation nullification or impairment remedy a suitable method for dealing with the issue of tariff re-classifications?

5. In the *EC—Computer Equipment* case, what factors did the Appellate Body emphasise as important for interpreting the terms in the EC schedule?

6. What is the scope of the WCO's competence versus that of the WTO on matters related to tariff classification? Where there is a WTO complaint alleging that a product has been improperly classified, and as a result a tariff has been imposed above the bound rate for the product, is it possible for the WTO to assess the consistency with GATT Article II without determining the proper classification of the product? Would the WCO be a better forum for resolving these issues? Should the WTO take over the WCO's functions in this area?

7. Does a total ban on the sale of a product, covering both domestic products and imports, constitute a quantitative restriction under GATT Article XI:1? What if the ban is imposed through two aspects of the same measure, one of which bans domestic sale or production and the other bans imports? What if the ban is imposed through two separate measures, one applying to domestic products and the other to imports?

8. Do restrictions on production of a natural resource, such as oil, constitute a quantitative restriction on exports under GATT Article XI:1? Under what conditions do you believe they could be justified, and why?

9. Generally speaking, Chile imposes one basic tariff rate for all products, eliminating the need for tariff classification to determine the duty rate. Should this approach be encouraged as a general practice among WTO Members?

10. Should developing countries be permitted to maintain high tariff rates for revenue purposes?

7

Non-Discrimination: MFN and National
Treatment

In this chapter, we address the GATT's non-discrimination requirement. Non-discrimination has long been, and remains, one of the core principles of the GATT. The two most important non-discrimination provisions in the GATT are the Most Favoured Nation (MFN) provision in Article I and the National Treatment provision in Article III. There are additional examples of both MFN and National Treatment in other provisions as well, but these are the provisions that apply most broadly and that have received the most detailed consideration in the case law.

In addition to the GATT, the non-discrimination requirement exists in various other agreements, such as the GATS, the TRIPS Agreement and the SPS/TBT Agreements. We discuss the application of the non-discrimination requirement in the context of those agreements in the substantive chapters on each of those agreements.

This chapter is broken down into three sections. First, we offer a basic overview of the concept of non-discrimination, examining several cross-cutting issues that apply in both the National Treatment and MFN contexts. Secondly, we address the National Treatment provisions in GATT Article III. Finally, we examine the MFN provisions of GATT Article I.

I. OVERVIEW OF NON-DISCRIMINATION

In this brief overview section, we discuss two key issues relating to the non-discrimination principle: (1) how to identify discrimination; and (2) *de facto* versus *de jure* discrimination.

(a) What is Discrimination? The Role of Intent, Effect and Comparisons

Before examining the details of the specific provisions setting out the non-discrimination principle, it is useful to step back and think about the possible components of a legal standard for identifying discrimination against imported products. There are two fundamental elements in this regard: an *intent* to discriminate (also referred to as purpose or motive or aim) and the *effect* of discriminating (also referred to as disparate impact).

In addition to these two elements, there is also the issue of determining what is to be compared in applying a non-discrimination standard in the context of trade in goods. In this regard, discrimination is most likely to occur when there is some degree of similarity between the imported and domestic products at issue. For example, a measure may treat domestic cars better than foreign cars in terms of tax or regulatory policies.

In this section, we briefly explore the possible scope of these elements within the context of a non-discrimination standard. It will be helpful to keep this general discussion in mind when reading the more specific analysis of the GATT provisions below.

(i) Intent

One theory of identifying discrimination is that intent is the key, or even exclusive, element to be used. (Intent can also be referred to as 'aim' or 'motive' or 'purpose'.) Under this view, it is *behaviour* that needs to be deterred through regulation, so it is crucial to focus on that behaviour in crafting the legal standard. However, there is an opposing view that intent is too difficult to ascertain for it to be a useful criterion.

As a result of these opposing views, the use of 'intent' as a factor in GATT non-discrimination standards has been hotly contested over the years. In particular, the so-called 'aim and effect' test, discussed in section II(c)(i)b below, developed by two GATT panels and later rejected by a WTO panel and the Appellate Body, led to much debate about the appropriateness of looking at intent.

In thinking about intent, it is important to distinguish between two categories: subjective and objective intent. *Subjective* intent refers to the motivations of individual legislators or regulators in putting the measure into effect. For example, legislators may make statements during debate on the measure setting out their view of the purpose. By contrast, *objective* intent represents the overall intent of the government in adopting the measure, and is based on the wording of the measure itself.[1] In some instances, a purported non-protectionist intent is offered by the defending party in response to a claim of violation of National Treatment. For example, if it is claimed that the measure promotes environmental protection, the text of the measure will be examined to see if that is really the case. In looking at objective intent in this situation, one possibility is to consider the means–ends relationship of the stated intent and the measure, to determine whether it actually accomplishes what it is claimed to.

(ii) Effect

The other factor commonly associated with discrimination is 'effect', that is, whether a measure has a discriminatory effect (also referred to as disparate impact) against imports.

---

[1] The term 'subjective' is defined as 'existing in the mind; belonging to the thinking subject rather than to the object of thought' in the *Random House Unabridged Dictionary*, available at http://dictionary.reference. com/browse/subjective. JB Sykes (ed), *Concise Oxford Dictionary of Current English*, 6th edn (Oxford, Oxford University Press, 1976) defines this term as 'giving prominence to or depending on personal idiosyncrasy or individual point of view, not producing the effect of literal and impartial transcription of external realities'. The term 'objective' on the other hand, according to the *Random House Unabridged Dictionary*, is defined as 'not influenced by personal feelings, interpretations, or prejudice; based on facts; unbiased'. The *Concise Oxford Dictionary* defines this term as 'belonging not to the consciousness or the perceiving or thinking subject, but to what is presented to this, external to the mind, real'.

This element is more widely accepted as relevant to the discrimination debate than intent, although its particular application has also been contested.

With this element, if, for example, a measure is alleged to result in de facto discrimination—the difference between de facto and de jure discrimination is discussed below—based on the different product classifications in a Member's tax system, it will need to be determined whether the measure has a disproportionate impact on foreign goods as compared to domestic goods. For example, imagine a situation where a luxury tax imposes a 30 per cent tax on cars worth over US$30,000 while cars priced at $30,000 or under are taxed at 10 per cent (a similar measure was the subject of a GATT case discussed in section II(c)(i)b below). If 90 per cent of imported cars fell into the high tax classification, whereas only 20 per cent of domestic cars fell into that classification, a discriminatory effect could be said to exist. Table 7.1 illustrates the examination of discriminatory effect in this situation.

Table 7.1 Assessing whether there is a discriminatory effect on imports

Price of car	Imports	Domestic
More than $30,000 (30% tax)	180 units (90% of imports) [A]	40 units (20% of domestic) [C]
$30,000 or less (10% tax)	20 units (10% of imports) [B]	160 units (80% of domestic) [D]

Comparing the treatment of imports in cells A and B to the treatment of domestic products in cells C and D, it is clear that imports are disproportionately affected by the high tax rate.

It is worth noting at this point that an alternative theory offered in WTO jurisprudence is that there is no need to compare the overall treatment of imports to that of domestic products. Rather, a violation of the non-discrimination requirement exists if there is any individual domestic product in cell D getting the more favourable treatment and any individual imported 'like' product in cell A getting the less favourable treatment. That is, there is a violation if any individual foreign product receives worse treatment than any individual domestic product. If taken to its logical extreme, this approach would find a violation even where most domestic products got the less favourable treatment and most imported products got the more favourable treatment, as long as there was one imported product (or even a product that might potentially be imported) that got less favourable treatment than one domestic product. Thus, even if the percentage figures were reversed, a violation would still be found. Table 7.2 illustrates the examination of discriminatory effect in this situation.

Table 7.2 Assessing whether there is a discriminatory effect on imports

Price of car	Imports	Domestic
More than $30,000 (30% tax)	20 units (10% of imports) [A]	160 units (80% of domestic) [C]
$30,000 or less (10% tax)	180 units (90% of imports) [B]	40 units (20% of domestic) [D]

One commentator has distinguished the approaches as follows. The first approach, in which the treatment of the entire group of domestic products (that is, domestic cars above and below $30,000) is compared to the treatment of the entire group of imports (that is, imported cars above and below $30,000), is referred to as the 'asymmetric impact' test. The second approach, in which imports in the disfavoured product category are compared to domestic products in the favoured category, has been referred to as the 'diagonal' test (as it simply makes a diagonal comparison across cells A and D), without taking into account the overall, or aggregate, impact on the group of imported products.[2] This approach could also be called an 'individual' like product approach, because the existence of any individual (or potential individual) imported product in the disfavoured category would lead to a finding of violation; or a 'strict' like product approach, because once the products are found to be like a violation will almost certainly be found. We discuss this approach in more detail below in the context of the specific provisions where it has been used.

(iii) Conclusions on Intent and Effect

We discuss the role of intent and effect in more detail below in the context of specific GATT provisions. Practically speaking, there are four main possibilities for applying these elements in a non-discrimination standard: Intent alone is sufficient to find a violation; effect alone is sufficient to find a violation; both are required to find a violation; or there is a weighing and balancing of the intent and effect elements, taking into account the strength of the discrimination in each. Of course, it is also possible that none of these elements are to be examined, as is arguably the case with the view of the non-discrimination standard involving the 'diagonal' or 'individual' like product approach, mentioned above and discussed again in various contexts below.

(iv) Comparability

A final point is that any determination of whether discrimination exists must be made in relation to comparable products. Thus, if a government imposed a 20 per cent tax on cars and a 10 per cent tax on lumber, the higher tax imposed on imported cars would not be discriminatory because cars and lumber are completely different products. The higher tax on cars as compared to lumber is unlikely to have much impact on car sales, as the products are completely unrelated (and it clearly does not favour domestic car sales over imported car sales, as both face the tax).

In order for discrimination to exist, the foreign and domestic products at issue must have some degree of similarity. We examine below the specific comparison standards set out in GATT Articles III and I, which use the terms 'like' products and 'directly competitive or substitutable' products.

There is, of course, a possibility that a country's policies may discriminate against foreign products more generally. For example, a government may decide to impose taxes on products that are primarily imported, such as cars and luxury goods, but keep taxes low on products made domestically, such as bananas. But such discriminatory policies

---

[2] L Ehring, 'De Facto Discrimination in World Trade Law: National and Most-Favoured-Nation-Treatment or Equal Treatment?' (2002) 36 *Journal of World Trade* 921.

are probably less prevalent and also harder to identify as protectionist intent, and thus are not covered by the WTO's non-discrimination rules.

(b) *De Facto* versus *De Jure* Discrimination

One of the most important points to be aware of in relation to the non-discrimination standard is the difference between *de jure* (in law) and *de facto* (in fact) discrimination. *De jure* discrimination involves discrimination that is apparent on the face of the measure. For example, a measure may state: 'imported goods are subject to a sales tax of 20% whereas domestically produced goods are subject to a sales tax of 10%'. The discrimination here is explicitly stated in the measure. A discriminatory effect results because all imports face a higher tax rate than all domestic goods.

By contrast, *de facto* discrimination involves measures that do not explicitly differentiate between imports and domestic goods. Rather, these measures may distinguish between different products, based on their physical characteristics. Thus, a measure may impose a variable tax rate on alcoholic beverages, with a higher tax rate imposed on beverages with a higher alcohol content. There is nothing necessarily discriminatory about such a measure, of course. However, if, based on the market situation, imports tend to have a high alcohol content and domestic products a low one, the measure has a disparate impact on imports, and thus discriminates against imports on a *de facto* basis. Much of the GATT/WTO jurisprudence on non-discrimination addresses situations involving *de facto* discrimination claims of this kind.

As a final note here, it is worth emphasising that formally different treatment is not sufficient to find a violation. For instance, in the National Treatment context, the Appellate Body has found that different treatment must actually have an adverse effect on the 'conditions of competition' for imports.[3] Thus, the mere existence of different rules for domestic products and imports does not necessarily lead to a violation of the rules. In order to determine whether a violation exists, there will have to be an examination of whether the differentiation between imports and domestic products actually puts imports at a disadvantage as compared to domestic products.

II. NATIONAL TREATMENT: DOMESTIC TAXES AND REGULATIONS

(a) Introduction

The National Treatment requirement has always been, and remains, one of the core principles of the GATT/WTO, along with the rules on tariff concessions and MFN. These three areas make up the first three Articles of the GATT: Article I is MFN; Article II is tariff concessions; and Article III is National Treatment.

National Treatment and MFN are the two main non-discrimination requirements in WTO rules. Whereas the MFN requirement prohibits discrimination *among* trading partners, the National Treatment requirement prohibits discrimination *against* foreign

[3] Appellate Body Report, *Korea—Beef*, paras 135–38.

products. As will be seen, many aspects of the National Treatment non-discrimination principle are very similar to those discussed in the context of MFN. Thus, some of the concepts used in National Treatment, such as 'likeness' and discriminatory effect, are also relevant for MFN. However, because of a number of differences in the specific language of the two provisions, there are important distinctions as well, as will be seen in this section and the following one on MFN.

Although closely related conceptually, the origins of National Treatment as a principle of international trade agreements differ from those of MFN. As explained in the next section, MFN arose as a way to ensure that tariff and other concessions were provided to all trading partners equally. In essence, this approach to trade negotiations was a way to promote broader trade liberalisation (by extending tariff concessions to all countries, rather than limiting them to just the specific trading partner who had requested them) and to ensure harmonious trade relations (countries would not form alliances that treated some worse than others, causing conflict and tension). By contrast, the idea of National Treatment originated, in part, as a rule against circumvention of tariff concessions by means of discriminatory internal measures. There was a concern that, for example, a country might lower its tariff on a product, but then adopt an internal tax or regulatory measure that treated the foreign product worse than the equivalent domestic one. In doing so, the country might even try to disguise its intentions by adopting a measure with an ostensibly legitimate, non-trade related purpose, which on its face treated foreign and domestic products equally, but nonetheless had an adverse impact on foreign products. The National Treatment rule addressed this concern by prohibiting discriminatory internal measures.

In addition to the concern with undermining the concessions, there was also a problem with discrimination against foreign goods more generally, as internal measures could be used for protectionist purposes outside the context of tariff concessions. After much debate, the drafters of the GATT decided that the National Treatment rule would be applied even where no concessions had been made, thereby creating a broader obligation against discrimination that applied regardless of whether or not circumvention of concessions had occurred.[4]

National Treatment is much more prominent than MFN in GATT/WTO jurisprudence. This is likely because the main reason countries breach the MFN principle is due to free trade agreements and customs unions, which are permitted under GATT Article XXIV, provided certain conditions are met. Aside from this circumstance, however, MFN violations are fairly infrequent, as countries rarely attempt to favour some trading partners over others. By contrast, National Treatment violations are much more common and are very likely to cause friction with trading partners. Where National Treatment issues arise, it is usually due to a perceived attempt to discriminate against foreign products, thereby triggering concerns among competing foreign producers and often leading to formal trade disputes.

Before turning to the specifics of the National Treatment rules, it is worth making some general observations on the importance and complexity of this rule in GATT/WTO jurisprudence. With regard to the importance, because of its effect on the scope of permissible domestic policy-making, the National Treatment rule is one of the most sensitive

---

[4] JH Jackson, *World Trade and the Law of GATT* (Charlottesville, VA, Bobbs-Merrill Company, 1969) 277–78.

of all GATT/WTO rules. The precise scope given to it will have a substantial impact on the ability of WTO Members to regulate in non-trade policy areas. Because *all* domestic tax and regulatory measures coming within the broad scope of the rule must comply, any domestic policy area, from labour rights to environmental protection to income taxes, can be scrutinised under the National Treatment requirement. As we will see below, the scope of Members' discretion under this rule has shifted considerably over the years.

As to the complexity, Article III is more complicated than it may at first appear, due to two factors: (1) the various competing conceptions of the provision that exist; and (2) the lack of clarity with which these conceptions have been expressed. Two people can read the same passage in Article III or in a GATT/WTO panel/Appellate Body report interpreting some part of Article III and come away with completely different ideas of what the rules are. Thus, a panel may state a finding in a specific way, but that finding is interpreted differently by different people, each of whom takes it to support his/her own view of the provision. One of our goals in this Chapter is to explain the different possible meanings that arise based on particular language in Article III and findings by the panels and the Appellate Body.

We divide this section up as follows. First, we set out the key National Treatment provisions in GATT Article III and describe the relationship among them. We then examine each of the main Article III provisions, paragraphs 2 and 4, separately. We begin with Article III:2, first sentence and Article III:2, second sentence, the two provisions dealing with tax measures. We then turn to Article III:4, the provision that addresses regulatory measures. Finally, we sum up by offering some general observations on the non-discrimination requirement.

(b) The National Treatment Provisions of GATT Article III

The main GATT provisions on National Treatment are contained in Article III, which is entitled 'National Treatment on Internal Taxation and Regulation'.[5] The term 'National Treatment', of course, refers to the treatment to be provided to foreign goods, which must be just as good as that given to national (ie domestic) goods. Paragraph 1 states:

> The Members recognize that internal taxes and other internal charges, and laws, regulations and requirements affecting the internal sale, offering for sale, purchase, transportation, distribution or use of products, and internal quantitative regulations requiring the mixture, processing or use of products in specified amounts or proportions, should not be applied to imported or domestic products so as to afford protection to domestic production.

Thus, under this provision, the internal laws described, when they have the effects set out in the provision, 'should not be applied to imported or domestic products *so as to afford protection to domestic production*' (emphasis added). Based on this language, the Appellate Body has explained that '[t]he broad and fundamental purpose of Article III is to avoid protectionism in the application of internal tax and regulatory measures'.[6] Note that paragraph 1 uses the word 'should' and thus does not provide the basis for a claim

---

[5] Other National Treatment provisions are found in various other agreements, eg in the SPS and TBT Agreements and in the GATS and TRIPS Agreement. We discuss those provisions in the relevant chapters.

[6] Appellate Body Report, *Japan—Alcohol*, 16.

of violation on its own.[7] However, it has been used, controversially, to interpret the other provisions of Article III in certain cases, as discussed below.

Paragraph 2 then addresses tax measures, stating:

> The products of the territory of any Member imported into the territory of any other Member shall not be subject, directly or indirectly, to internal taxes or other internal charges of any kind in excess of those applied, directly or indirectly, to like domestic products. Moreover, no Member shall otherwise apply internal taxes or other internal charges to imported or domestic products in a manner contrary to the principles set forth in paragraph 1.

An interpretive note to this provision clarifies that:

> A tax conforming to the requirements of the first sentence of paragraph 2 would be considered to be inconsistent with the provisions of the second sentence only in cases where competition was involved between, on the one hand, the taxed product and, on the other hand, a directly competitive or substitutable product which was not similarly taxed.

Thus, taking paragraph 2, paragraph 1 and the interpretive note together, there are two different obligations in the two sentences of paragraph 2. The first sentence is fairly straightforward, setting out rules where the products at issue are 'like'. Applying the second sentence is more complicated. As explained in more detail below, in combination with the interpretative note and paragraph 1, the second sentence sets out rules for products which are 'directly competitive or substitutable'.

Article III:4 then deals with regulatory measures, providing in relevant part:

> The products of the territory of any Member imported into the territory of any other Member shall be accorded treatment no less favourable than that accorded to like products of national origin in respect of all laws, regulations and requirements affecting their internal sale, offering for sale, purchase, transportation, distribution or use. . . .

Unlike Article III:2, Article III:4 has only one obligation, which requires that 'no less favourable treatment' be accorded to imported products as to domestic 'like products'. There is no separate category of 'directly competitive or substitutable' here.

As a final point, while the second paragraph covers tax measures, it is important to note that some tax measures may fall under Article III:4 if they have a regulatory aspect. For example, if a tax break were conditioned on using local content, the local content part of the measure would fall under Article III:4. (The tax aspect of the measure could be considered under Article III:2 if there were also some discrimination resulting from the tax rates involved, separate from the local content condition.)

Below we discuss the interpretation of these provisions offered in the jurisprudence.

(c) Article III:2: Tax Measures

Article III:2 provides the National Treatment rules for tax measures. As noted above, the first sentence of Article III:2 sets out the standard where the products at issue are 'like', whereas the second sentence establishes a standard where the products are 'directly competitive or substitutable.' We address each provision in turn.

---

[7] *Ibid*, 17–18.

(i) First Sentence: Like Products

Article III:2, first sentence states that imported products 'shall not be subject, directly or indirectly, to internal taxes or other internal charges of any kind in excess of those applied, directly or indirectly, to like domestic products'. There are two key elements to this provision: (1) are the imported products at issue 'like' the domestic products? and (2) are the taxes or charges that have been applied to imported products 'in excess of' those applied the like domestic products? (In addition, the measure at issue must constitute a 'tax' or 'charge'.) We consider each element separately. Then, we examine the use of the so-called 'aim and effects' test under this provision, which was used briefly under the GATT before being rejected by the Appellate Body (at least to some degree and in some contexts).

a. 'Like Products' The 'like products' standard is a particular implementation of the comparability of products issue noted in the previous section. In order to find that imported products are being discriminated against, there must be a similar domestic product the treatment of which can serve as the basis for a comparison. In Article III:2, first sentence, the degree of similarity required is that the products at issue must be 'like'.

The question whether imported and domestic products are 'like' under Article III:2, first sentence, generally arises when a government imposes a tax or other charge that varies among products that are part of a closely related group, such as alcoholic beverages. The government may set a different tax rate for different beverages within this group. For the purposes of claims under Article III:2, first sentence, a key question is whether the products at issue are 'like'.

The issue of 'likeness' was discussed in an early WTO case, *Japan—Alcohol*. The issue there was whether various alcoholic beverages were 'like' shochu, a traditional Japanese drink that was allegedly receiving favourable tax treatment. The panel in that case found as follows:

> 6.23 The Panel next turned to an examination of whether the products at issue in this case were like products, starting first with vodka and shochu. The Panel noted that vodka and shochu shared most physical characteristics. In the Panel's view, except for filtration, there is virtual identity in the definition of the two products. The Panel noted that a difference in the physical characteristic of alcoholic strength of two products did not preclude a finding of likeness especially since alcoholic beverages are often drunk in diluted form. The Panel then noted that essentially the same conclusion had been reached in the 1987 Panel Report, which
>
> > . . . agreed with the arguments submitted to it by the European Communities, Finland and the United States that Japanese shochu (Group A) and vodka could be considered as 'like' products in terms of Article III:2 because they were both white/clean spirits, made of similar raw materials, and the end-uses were virtually identical.

> Following its independent consideration of the factors mentioned in the 1987 Panel Report, the Panel agreed with this statement. The Panel then recalled its conclusions concerning the relationship between Articles II and III. In this context, it noted that (i) vodka and shochu were currently classified in the same heading in the Japanese tariffs, (although under the new Harmonized System (HS) Classification that entered into force on 1 January 1996 and that Japan plans to implement, shochu appears under tariff heading 2208.90 and vodka under tariff heading 2208.60); and (ii) vodka and shochu were covered by the same Japanese tariff binding at the time of its negotiation. Of the products at issue in this case, only shochu and vodka have the same tariff applied to them in the Japanese tariff schedule (see Annex 1). The Panel noted that,

with respect to vodka, Japan offered no further convincing evidence that the conclusion reached by the 1987 Panel Report was wrong, not even that there had been a change in consumers' preferences in this respect. The Panel further noted that Japan's basic argument is not that the two products are unlike, in terms of the criteria applied in the 1987 Panel Report, but rather that they are unlike because the Japanese tax legislation does not have the aim and effect to protect shochu. The Panel noted, however, that it had already rejected the aim-and-effect test. Consequently, in light of the conclusion of the 1987 Panel Report and of its independent consideration of the issue, the Panel concluded that vodka and shochu are like products. In the Panel's view, only vodka could be considered as like product to shochu since, apart from commonality of end-uses, it shared with shochu most physical characteristics. Definitionally [*sic*], the only difference is in the media used for filtration. Substantial noticeable differences in physical characteristics exist between the rest of the alcoholic beverages at dispute and shochu that would disqualify them from being regarded as like products. More specifically, the use of additives would disqualify liqueurs, gin and genever; the use of ingredients would disqualify rum; lastly, appearance (arising from manufacturing processes) would disqualify whisky and brandy. The Panel therefore decided to examine whether the rest of alcoholic beverages, other than vodka, at dispute in the present case could qualify as directly competitive or substitutable products to shochu. The Panel lastly noted that the 1987 Panel Report had also considered these products only under Article III:2, second sentence.[8]

… … …

Thus, the Panel found that vodka is 'like' shochu 'since, in addition to its commonality of end-uses, it shared with shochu most physical characteristics'. By contrast, liqueurs, gin and genever were not 'like' shochu due to 'the use of additives'; rum was not 'like' shochu because of 'the use of ingredients'; and whisky and brandy were not 'like' shochu because of 'appearance (arising from manufacturing processes).'

On appeal, the Appellate Body upheld the Panel's finding that vodka and shochu are 'like', without offering any additional analysis of the 'likeness' of the products at issue.[9] However, the Appellate Body did offer some general guidance on the issue of 'likeness' under Article III:2, first sentence. In this regard, the Appellate Body stated:

> We agree with the practice under the GATT 1947 of determining whether imported and domestic products are "like" on a case-by-case basis. The Report of the Working Party on *Border Tax Adjustments*, adopted by the CONTRACTING PARTIES in 1970, set out the basic approach for interpreting "like or similar products" generally in the various provisions of the GATT 1947:
>
> > . . . the interpretation of the term should be examined on a case-by-case basis. This would allow a fair assessment in each case of the different elements that constitute a "similar" product. Some criteria were suggested for determining, on a case-by-case basis, whether a product is "similar": the product's end-uses in a given market; consumers' tastes and habits, which change from country to country; the product's properties, nature and quality.
>
> This approach was followed in almost all adopted panel reports after *Border Tax Adjustments*. This approach should be helpful in identifying on a case-by-case basis the range of "like products" that fall within the narrow limits of Article III:2, first sentence in the GATT 1994.[10]

… … …

---

[8] Panel Report, *Japan—Alcohol*, para 6.23.
[9] Appellate Body Report, *Japan—Alcohol*, para 24.
[10] *Ibid*, para 20.

Thus, the Appellate Body referred to the following criteria: (1) the product's end-uses in a given market; (2) consumers' tastes and habits; and (3) the product's properties, nature and quality. It later noted that 'tariff classification can be a helpful sign of product similarity', thus setting out a fourth factor.[11]

The Appellate Body also made the following statement on the issue of 'likeness':

> No one approach to exercising judgement will be appropriate for all cases. The criteria in *Border Tax Adjustments* should be examined, but there can be no one precise and absolute definition of what is "like". The concept of "likeness" is a relative one that evokes the image of an accordion. The accordion of "likeness" stretches and squeezes in different places as different provisions of the *WTO Agreement* are applied. The width of the accordion in any one of those places must be determined by the particular provision in which the term "like" is encountered as well as by the context and the circumstances that prevail in any given case to which that provision may apply. We believe that, in Article III:2, first sentence of the GATT 1994, the accordion of "likeness" is meant to be narrowly squeezed.[12]

The Appellate Body made it clear that 'likeness' has a narrow scope in the context of Article III:2, first sentence (but, as noted, it did agree with the panel that vodka and shochu are like).In the more recent decision of *Philippines—Distilled Spirits*, the Appellate Body provided further guidance when it stated:

> 119. While in the determination of "likeness" a panel may logically start from the physical characteristics of the products, none of the criteria that a panel considers necessarily has an overarching role in the determination of "likeness" under Article III:2 of the GATT 1994. A panel examines these criteria in order to make a determination about the nature and extent of a competitive relationship between and among the products.[211]

> 120. We understand that products that have very similar physical characteristics may not be "like," within the meaning of Article III:2, if their competitiveness or substitutability is low, while products that present certain physical differences may still be considered "like" if such physical differences have a limited impact on the competitive relationship between and among the products.

---

[211] In *EC—Asbestos* the Appellate Body found that "a determination of 'likeness' under Article III:4 is, fundamentally, a determination about the nature and extent of a competitive relationship between and among products." (Appellate Body Report, *EC—Asbestos*, para 99)

With these statements, the Appellate Body has seemingly issued a clear and determinative statement that 'likeness' is about the economic competitiveness of products.

Given the wide range of products that can be subject to claims under this provision, it is difficult to come up with any additional direction on this issue except to say that the 'likeness' of any two products must be determined on a case-by-case basis under the criteria referred to by the Appellate Body.

Based on the description offered thus far, the 'likeness' standard might be thought of as a fairly narrow component of the Article III:2, first sentence non-discrimination standard, serving merely to define the range of products to be compared. Under one view of the provision, this is, in fact, the function of 'likeness'. However, there is another view of

---

[11] *Ibid*, paras 20–22.
[12] *Ibid*, para 21.

'likeness' that elevates it to a more prominent role. Under this view, once products have been found to be 'like', there can be no differentiation in the treatment given to them; *any* differentiation will lead to a finding of violation.[13] The basis for such an approach appears to be the following: once the products are established as 'like', and it has been proven that the products receive different treatment, then there will always potentially be at least one individual imported product in the disfavoured category that could receive less favourable treatment than an individual domestic product in the favoured category. This approach was described in the previous section as the 'individual' or 'strict' like product approach, or the 'diagonal' approach. Thus, under this latter view, the 'likeness' element can offer more than just the comparison that provides the first step in the analysis. It can also be the key to the provision. We discuss this approach to 'likeness' further in several places later in the chapter.

b. Imported Products Taxed 'in Excess of' Domestic Like Products Under Article III:2, first sentence, the next element is whether imported products are taxed 'in excess of' domestic like products. This is, in effect, the 'discrimination' element of the provision.

The panel in the *Japan—Alcohol* case addressed this issue as follows in the context of the vodka and shochu taxes noted above:

> The Panel then proceeded to examine whether vodka is taxed in excess of the tax imposed on shochu under the Japanese Liquor Tax Law. The Panel noted that what was contested in the Japanese legislation was a system of specific taxes imposed on various alcoholic drinks. In this respect, it noted that vodka was taxed at 377,230 Yen per kilolitre—for an alcoholic strength below 38°—that is 9,927 Yen per degree of alcohol, whereas shochu A was taxed at 155,700 Yen per kilolitre—for an alcoholic strength between 25° and 26°—that is 6,228 Yen per degree of alcohol. The Panel further noted that Article III:2 does not contain any presumption in favour of a specific mode of taxation. Under Article III:2, first sentence, WTO Members are free to choose any system of taxation they deem appropriate provided that they do not impose on foreign products taxes in excess of those imposed on like domestic products. The phrase "not in excess of those applied . . . to like domestic products" should be interpreted to mean at least identical or better tax treatment. The Japanese taxes on vodka and shochu are calculated on the basis of and vary according to the alcoholic content of the products and, on this basis, it is obvious that the taxes imposed on vodka are higher than those imposed on shochu. Accordingly, the Panel concluded that the tax imposed on vodka is in excess of the tax imposed on shochu.[14]

Thus, the panel found that vodka was taxed more heavily than shochu, concluding that the tax on vodka is 'in excess of' that on shochu.

On appeal, the Appellate Body briefly referred to the issue of 'whether the taxes on imported products are "in excess of" those on like domestic products', and upheld the anel's legal reasoning and conclusions. In this regard, it stated:

> Even the smallest amount of 'excess' is too much. 'The prohibition of discriminatory taxes in Article III:2, first sentence, is not conditional on a 'trade effects test' nor is it qualified by a *de minimis* standard.'[15]

---

[13] L Ehring, 'De Facto Discrimination in World Trade Law: National and Most-Favoured-Nation-Treatment or Equal Treatment?' (2002) 36 *Journal of World Trade* 921.

[14] Panel Report, *Japan—Alcohol*, para 6.24.

[15] Appellate Body Report, *Japan—Alcohol*, para 23.

The absence of a *de minimis* exception makes the standard quite strict, as even the slightest difference will lead to a finding of violation.

There is an aspect of this issue that was not discussed explicitly in the panel or Appellate Body's reasoning, but may nevertheless have great importance. In particular, the panel's finding is not stated as a comparison of taxes imposed on *imported* products as compared to taxes imposed on *domestic* products. Rather, the panel refers to taxes imposed on *vodka* as compared to those imposed on *shochu*. It may be that the panel was simply equating vodka with imports and shochu with domestic products, and thus in effect believed it was comparing imports to domestic products. If this is the case, the panel's finding is simply that there was a discriminatory effect against imports under the measure.

An alternative explanation, however, is that the panel did not believe that the overall impact on imports as compared to domestic products needed to be compared. In this regard, under one view of the 'like product' standard, discussed above, if any *individual* imported product is taxed at a higher rate than any *individual* like domestic product, there is a violation of Article III:2, first sentence, regardless of the overall impact on the *group* of imported products as compared to the *group* of domestic products. Applying that approach here, if any individual imported vodka product was taxed at a higher rate than any individual domestic shochu product, a violation would exist.

Most likely, the panel had the former in mind. However, the panel did find that there was shochu produced outside Japan[16] and that spirits, whisky and brandy were produced in Japan.[17] As a result, the panel's reasoning could support either approach.

c. The 'Aim and Effect' Test Any discussion of Article III:2, first sentence, needs to address, at least briefly, the controversial 'aim and effect' test (also referred to as 'aim and effects', 'aims and effects' and 'aims an effect'). As is clear from the two terms involved, this test relates to the concepts of discriminatory intent and effect noted above. In the early 1990s, two GATT panels developed an approach under which 'likeness', and thus a violation of Article III:2, first sentence, would be found only if the aim and the effect of the measure were to protect domestic goods.[18] We set out below a portion of the findings of the GATT panel in *US—Taxes on Automobiles* in this regard:

GATT Panel Report,*United States—Taxes on Automobiles*, Circulated 11 October 1994 (unadopted), DS31/R

A. Luxury Tax

5.1   The Panel noted that the issues in dispute with respect to the luxury tax arose essentially from the following facts, as described more fully in Part II of this report. In 1990, the United States Omnibus Budget Reconciliation Act imposed a retail excise tax on certain luxury products, amounting to 10 percent of the excess of the retail price over a fixed threshold value. These luxury products included passenger vehicles, boats, aircraft, jewellery and furs. A threshold level of $30,000 was fixed for passenger vehicles, which covered any four-wheeled vehicle manufactured primarily for use on public streets, roads, and highways, and weighing 6,000 pounds or less. The tax did not apply to the sale of any passenger vehicle for trade, business

---

[16] Panel Report, *Japan—Alcohol*, para 6.24.

[17] *Ibid*, para 6.25.

[18] GATT Panel Report, *US—Auto Taxes*, paras 5.5–5.36; GATT Panel Report, *US—Alcoholic and Malt Beverages*, paras 5.23–5.26.

and certain other purposes. In 1993, after the establishment of the Panel, a further Omnibus Budget Reconciliation Act repealed the retail excise tax on boats, aircraft, jewellery and furs. Passenger vehicles, the only product remaining subject to the tax, were made subject to an increased threshold of $32,000 to compensate for inflation.

5.2   The Panel noted the EC view that the luxury tax imposed by the United States on domestic and imported automobiles sold for over $30,000 violated Article III:2 of the General Agreement. The EC argued that automobiles costing over $30,000 were like products to automobiles costing less, since they had the same end use, basic physical characteristics, and tariff classification. Further, a mere difference in price between the imported and domestic products was not sufficient for those products to be considered unlike for the purposes of Article III. The price threshold of $30,000 would in addition have to be shown to be based on objective product differences, and to be part of a general system of internal taxation equally applied in a trade-neutral manner to all like or directly competing automobiles. According to the EC, the United States measure was not based on objective product differences, since luxury cars were found above and below the $30,000 threshold. They were also not applied in a trade-neutral manner, since automobiles were singled out as a product for less favourable tax treatment, and EC automobiles were in particular targeted. The disproportionate burden borne by EC automobiles was shown by the proportion of EC automobiles subject to the tax, the proportion of revenues generated by EC automobiles, and the average tax paid per EC luxury automobile. The EC further considered that, under the terms of Article III:2, second sentence, and the Note ad Article III, domestic automobiles under $30,000 were afforded protection, since they competed with and were 'directly competitive and substitutable' to imported automobiles costing more.

5.3   The Panel noted also the United States view that the luxury tax did not violate Article III. In determining whether automobiles over $30,000 were 'like' those selling for less, the United States argued that it was necessary only to determine whether the threshold had been applied 'so as to afford protection to domestic production.' The purpose of Article III was not to prevent contracting parties from differentiating between products for policy purposes unrelated to the protection of domestic production. Further, the United States argued that Article III only protected expectations on competitive conditions resulting from government measures. It did not guarantee specific levels or proportions of trade, nor the results in the market of particular choices made by companies. The United States also argued that, even if the trade impact of the luxury tax were considered relevant to the determination of obligations under Article III:2, figures showed that automobiles of foreign origin were not disproportionately affected by the measure.

(i) Article III:2, first sentence

5.4   The Panel proceeded to consider whether the luxury tax maintained by the United States was consistent with Article III:2, first sentence, which states:

The products of the territory of any contracting party imported into the territory of any other contracting party shall not be subject, directly or indirectly, to internal taxes or other internal charges of any kind in excess of those applied, directly or indirectly, to like domestic products.

The Panel found, and the parties agreed, that the luxury tax applied by the United States came within the scope of "internal taxes or other internal charges", and that imported automobiles selling for more than $30,000 were subject to the tax. The parties disagreed, however, on whether automobiles selling at prices above and below this threshold were like products in terms of Article III:2. The EC claimed that automobiles above and below the threshold were like products, since they had the same physical characteristics, end-use, and tariff classification. The threshold level was not based on objective product differences, nor applied in a trade-neutral manner. The United States disagreed with this approach, arguing that the tax could be imposed on the basis of a threshold of $30,000, as long as the tax was not applied so as to afford protection to domestic production.

(a) Treatment of like products under Article III

5.5   The Panel noted that the central issue raised by the parties was whether under Article III:2 cars selling for more than $30,000 were "like" products to domestic cars selling for less. The resolution of this issue required a preliminary analysis of the scope of Article III with respect to the treatment to be accorded to a product of foreign origin. The Panel proceeded to examine the terms of Article III. It observed that Article III deals with differences in treatment between products. These differences in treatment resulted from regulatory distinctions made by governments. If regulatory distinctions were drawn explicitly with respect to the origin of the product, or with respect to manifestly different products, then the consistency with Article III:2 or 4 could be determined in a straightforward manner. If the regulatory distinctions were not drawn explicitly with respect to origin, then it had to be determined whether the products were "like". The Panel recalled the EC argument that likeness of products under Article III should be based on factors such as their end use, physical characteristics and tariff classification, and that the disproportionate impact of the measure on a foreign product is relevant in determining the overall consistency of the measure with Article III. The Panel noted, on the other hand, that the United States argued that the key criterion in judging likeness under Article III was whether the measure was applied "so as to afford protection to domestic production".

5.6   The Panel observed that the ordinary meaning of the term "like" in paragraphs 2 and 4 of Article III was "the same" or "similar". The Panel recognized however that two individual products could never be exactly the same in all aspects. They could share common features, such as physical characteristics or end use, but would differ in others. These differences between products formed the basis of regulatory distinctions by governments which could result in less favourable treatment to imported products. Thus the practical interpretative issue under paragraphs 2 and 4 of Article III was: which differences between products may form the basis of regulatory distinctions by governments that accord less favourable treatment to imported products? Or, conversely, which similarities between products prevent regulatory distinctions by governments that accord less favourable treatment to imported products?

5.7   In order to determine this issue, the Panel examined the object and purpose of paragraphs 2 and 4 of Article III in the context of the article as a whole and the General Agreement. The Panel noted that the purpose of Article III is set out in paragraph 1 of the article, which states:

> "The contracting parties recognize that internal taxes and other internal charges, and laws, regulations and requirements affecting the internal sale, offering for sale, purchase, transportation, distribution or use of products, and internal quantitative regulations requiring the mixture, processing or use of products in specified amounts or proportions, should not be applied to imported or domestic products *so as to afford protection to domestic production.*" (emphasis added)

The Panel considered that paragraphs 2 and 4 of Article III had to be read in the light of this central purpose. The Panel reasoned therefore that Article III serves only to prohibit regulatory distinctions between products applied so as to afford protection to domestic production. Its purpose is not to prohibit fiscal and regulatory distinctions applied so as to achieve other policy goals. This view has been expressed in a recent panel report, which states:

> "The purpose of Article III is . . . not to prevent contracting parties from using their fiscal and regulatory powers for purposes other than to afford protection to domestic production. Specifically, the purpose of Article III is not to prevent contracting parties from differentiating

between different product categories for policy purposes unrelated to the protection of domestic production. The Panel considered that the limited purpose of Article III has to be taken into account in interpreting the term "like products" in this Article. Consequently, in determining whether two products subject to different treatment are like products, it is necessary to consider whether such product differentiation is being made "so as to afford protection to domestic production".

5.8   The Panel noted that earlier practice of the Contracting Parties had been to determine the permissibility of regulatory distinctions under Article III on a case-by-case basis, examining likeness in terms of factors such as "the product's end-uses in a given market, consumers' tastes and habits, which change from country to country; the product's properties, nature and quality." The Panel noted that regulatory distinctions based on such factors were often, but not always, the means of implementing government policies other than the protection of domestic industry. Non-protectionist government policies might, however, require regulatory distinctions that were not based on the product's end use, its physical characteristics, or the other factors mentioned. Noting that a primary purpose of the General Agreement was to lower barriers to trade between markets, and not to harmonize the regulatory treatment of products within them, the Panel considered that Article III could not be interpreted as prohibiting government policy options, based on products, that were not taken so as to afford protection to domestic production.

5.9   The Panel noted that the EC had relied in its interpretation of Article III:2 on the findings of an earlier panel. That panel had stated that:

"the ordinary meaning of Article III:2 in its context and in the light of its object and purpose supported the past GATT practice of examining the conformity of internal taxes with Article III:2 by determining, firstly, whether the taxed imported and domestic products are "like" or "directly competitive or substitutable" and, secondly, whether the taxation is discriminatory (first sentence) or protective (second sentence of Article III:2).

This two-step approach implied that less favourable tax treatment could not be imposed on a foreign product consistently with Article III:2 if the domestic and foreign products shared certain common features (likeness) and if the tax measure was discriminatory or protective. However, the first step of determining the relevant features common to the domestic and imported products (likeness) would in the view of the Panel, in all but the most straightforward cases, have to include an examination of the aim and effect of the particular tax measure. Therefore the second step of determining whether the tax measure was discriminatory or protective was simply a continuation of the inquiry under the first step. The Panel concluded that its interpretation was consistent with previous ones, but made explicit that issues of likeness under Article III should be analyzed primarily in terms of whether less favourable treatment was based on a regulatory distinction taken so as to afford protection to domestic production.

5.10   The Panel then proceeded to examine more closely the meaning of the phrase "so as to afford protection." The Panel noted that the term "so as to" suggested both aim and effect. Thus the phrase "so as to afford protection" called for an analysis of elements including the aim of the measure and the resulting effects. A measure could be said to have the *aim* of affording protection if an analysis of the circumstances in which it was adopted, in particular an analysis of the instruments available to the contracting party to achieve the declared domestic policy goal, demonstrated that a change in competitive opportunities in favour of domestic products was a desired outcome and not merely an incidental consequence of the pursuit of a legitimate policy goal. A measure could be said to have the *effect* of affording protection to domestic production if it accorded greater competitive opportunities to domestic products than to imported products. The effect of a measure in terms of trade flows was not relevant for the purposes of Article III, since a change in the volume or proportion of imports could be due to many factors other than government measures. A previous panel had stated:

"Article III:2, first sentence, obliges contracting parties to establish certain competitive conditions for imported products in relation to domestic products. Unlike some other provisions in the General Agreement, it does not refer to trade effects."

The Panel observed that the central objective of the analysis remained the determination of whether the regulatory distinction was made "so as to afford protection to domestic production." The analysis of aims and effects of the measure were elements that contributed to that determination.

(b) The luxury tax threshold

5.11   In the light of the preliminary considerations set out above, the Panel proceeded to examine whether it was consistent with Article III:2 for imported automobiles selling for more than $30,000 to be taxed more highly than domestic automobiles selling for less. This required the Panel to examine whether the threshold distinction was drawn so as to afford protection to domestic production.

5.12   The Panel first considered whether the *aim* of establishing the threshold within the luxury tax was to afford protection to domestic production. It noted that the EC had argued that evidence of statements by legislators suggested that the threshold was intentionally targeted on foreign automobiles. The Panel considered however that an assessment of the aim of the legislation could not be based solely on such statements or on other preparatory work. The aim of the legislation had also to be determined through the interpretation of the wording of the legislation as a whole. In the view of the Panel, the policy objective apparent in the legislation, to raise revenue from sales of perceived "luxury" products, was consistent with setting a price threshold, and setting it at a level at which only a small proportion of automobiles sold within the United States market were taxed. The fact that a large proportion of EC imports (but not necessarily a large proportion of imports from other countries) was affected by the measure did not demonstrate that the legislation was aimed at affording protection to domestic automobiles selling for less than $30,000. The Panel further noted that the conditions of competition accorded to products just above the $30,000 threshold did not differ markedly from those just below the threshold, and that there was considerable uncertainty as to the proportion of foreign and domestic automobiles selling above and below the threshold. This also suggested that the principal aim of the legislation was not to target closely a distinct product category of imported automobile.

5.13   The Panel then considered whether the threshold distinction in the luxury tax had the *effect*, in terms of conditions of competition, of affording protection to domestic production. The Panel noted that the parties submitted extensive data on sales of automobiles above and below the $30,0000 threshold. The data did not accord, due mainly to different assumptions regarding the actual transaction price at which the automobiles were sold. Just below the threshold, EC figures suggested that some 85 percent of automobiles sold in 1991 in the United States were domestic; the United States estimate was 42 percent. Just above the threshold, in the $30,000 to $33,000 range, the EC claimed that some 40 percent of automobiles sold in the United States in 1991 were domestic; the United States put the figure at 90 percent. The Panel noted that large numbers of cars of non-EC (mainly Japanese) origin were also sold at prices just below and just above the threshold level. The Panel did not find that the sales data provided conclusive evidence of a change in the conditions of competition favouring United States automobiles. Under either set of figures, the greater or lesser percentages could have been due to marketing and production decisions by EC manufacturers, by their United States or other foreign competitors, or by decisions of consumers in the market.

5.14   The Panel then considered whether there was evidence, other than sales or trade-flow data, that the threshold had the effect, in terms of conditions of competition, of affording protection to domestic automobiles. The Panel noted that a selling price above $30,000 did not appear from the evidence to be inherent to EC or other foreign automobiles. In particular, no evidence had been advanced that EC or other foreign automobile manufacturers did not in general have the design, production, and marketing capabilities to sell automobiles below the $30,000 threshold, or that they did not in general produce such models for other markets. On the contrary, there was evidence that EC automobile manufacturers produced a wide range of automobiles that, if exported to the United States, could sell for below $30,000. Some EC and many Japanese and other foreign models were in fact exported to the United States and sold for below $30,000. Nor had evidence been advanced that United States manufacturers did not have the capabilities to design, produce and market automobiles costing over $30,000. The Panel also noted that there was no sudden transition to a higher tax at the threshold. The more closely automobiles above and below the threshold competed on price, the less the tax affected their competitiveness. These factors, together with the fact that the threshold did not appear arbitrary or contrived in the context of the policies pursued, indicated to the Panel that in this case, the dominant presence at a particular time of the EC cars in the sector of the market affected by the measure could not be taken as evidence of a discriminatory effect. In the view of the Panel therefore the regulatory distinction of $30,000 did not create conditions of competition that divided the products inherently into two classes, one of EC or other foreign origin and the other of domestic origin.

5.15   The Panel concluded that the threshold distinction of $30,000 in the luxury tax was not implemented so as to afford protection to the domestic production of automobiles, that automobiles above and below that threshold value could not, for the purposes of the luxury tax, be considered as like products under Article III:2, first sentence, and that different treatment could therefore be accorded under the luxury tax to automobiles above and below the threshold.

… … …

The panel in *US—Taxes on Automobiles* based its approach to 'likeness' on the language of Article III:1, stating that 'issues of likeness under Article III should be analyzed primarily in terms of whether less favourable treatment was based on a regulatory distinction taken so as to afford protection to domestic production'. Based on the 'so as to afford protection' language in Article III:1, the panel concluded that both 'aim' and 'effect' must be demonstrated for the products to be deemed 'like' Applying this reasoning to its consideration of whether the products at issue—cars costing $30,000 or more and those costing less than $30,000—were 'like', the panel concluded that there was no protectionist aim or effect, and thus the products were not 'like' for the purposes of Article III:2, first sentence. Therefore, it said, different treatment could be accorded to cars above and below the price threshold.

The panel's reason for taking this approach was probably to avoid intruding too far into domestic policy-making. If, for example, a finding of discriminatory effect were sufficient to find a violation, or if an even broader standard, like the 'individual'/ 'strict' like product approach noted above were used, a wide range of domestic measures could be deemed to violate the rules. The 'aim and effect' approach may have been designed to narrow the scope of Article III by limiting violations to situations where there were both discriminatory intent and effect, so as to avoid the controversial impact this intrusion might have.

It is important to note that 'aim and effect' was used here in relation to the 'likeness' element, rather than the element which considers whether imports are taxed 'in excess of' domestic products. Arguably, an examination of 'aim and effect' fits more naturally with this latter element, as it seems to be the basis for rooting out discrimination, whereas 'likeness' is, textually speaking, related more to the comparison element.

Regardless of where 'aim and effect' might fit best, it was quickly abandoned soon after the establishment of the WTO. In *Japan—Alcohol*, both the United States and Japan argued for this approach to be applied (although they were on different sides of the case, both apparently thought this interpretation would favour the result they were hoping for). However, the Panel rejected their argument, noting:

> [T]he proposed aim-and-effect test is not consistent with the wording of Article III:2, first sentence. The Panel recalled that the basis of the aim-and-effect test is found in the words "so as to afford protection" contained in Article III:1.The Panel further recalled that Article III:2, first sentence, contains no reference to those words.[19]

Thus, because Article III:2, first sentence has no reference to Article III:1, the 'so as to afford protection' language, which had served as the basis for 'aim and effect' in the *US—Taxes on Automobiles* case excerpted above, could not be applied here. On appeal, the Appellate Body affirmed the panel's finding.[20]

The panel and Appellate Body rulings were fairly clear in their rejection of an 'aim and effect' test under Article III:2, first sentence. But, then, what test will be applied under Article III:2, first sentence instead? This question applies to both elements of the provision: 'likeness' and taxed 'in excess of'. As will be seen in later sections, the Appellate Body has recently, under other provisions of Article III, made findings that seem to restore certain elements of the 'aim and effect' test. In this regard, 'effect' seems to play an important role, and intent can, in some circumstances, also be relevant, although not under the 'likeness' element. It is possible, then, that 'likeness' under Article III:2, first sentence will be limited to a product comparison, whereas taxed 'in excess of' will focus on effect and, possibly, some form of intent. However, the Appellate Body's only findings on this issue are those in *Japan—Alcohol*, described above, which are vague enough to allow for a number of approaches.

(ii) Second Sentence: Directly Competitive or Substitutable Products

Article III:2, second sentence does not contain all the elements of an obligation on its own, but rather refers back to paragraph 1 of Article III, which requires that internal taxes and charges (as well as other measures) 'should not be applied to imported or domestic products so as to afford protection to domestic production'. An interpretive note to the second sentence clarifies that this obligation applies where the measure at issue is consistent with the first sentence, and applies only where 'competition was involved between, on the one hand, the taxed product and, on the other hand, a directly competitive or substitutable product which was not similarly taxed'. The resulting standard based on all of these provisions—ie the second sentence of Article III:2, the note to Article III:2, and Article III:1—contains three elements that must be considered under Article III:2, second sentence:

---

[19] Panel Report, *Japan—Alcohol*, para 6.16.
[20] Appellate Body Report, *Japan—Alcohol*, paras 18–23.

(1) whether the imported products and the domestic products are 'directly competitive or substitutable products' which are in competition with each other;

(2) whether the directly competitive or substitutable imported and domestic products are 'not similarly taxed;' and

(3) whether the dissimilar taxation of the directly competitive or substitutable imported domestic products is 'applied . . . so as to afford protection to domestic production.'[21]

We examine each of these elements separately.

a. Directly Competitive or Substitutable The directly competitive or substitutable element is the comparison of products element, under which the similarity of the products at issue is judged. As the early WTO panel in *Korea—Alcohol* noted, in the GATT negotiations, this provision was discussed as follows:

> A review of the negotiating history of Article III:2, second sentence and the *Ad* Article III language confirms that the product categories should not be so narrowly construed as to defeat the purpose of the anti-discrimination language informing the interpretation of Article III. The Geneva session of the Preparatory Committee provided an explanation of the language of the second sentence by noting that apples and oranges could be directly competitive or substitutable. Other examples provided were domestic linseed oil and imported tung oil and domestic synthetic rubber and imported natural rubber. There was discussion of whether such products as tramways and busses or coal and fuel oil could be considered as categories of directly competitive or substitutable products. There was some disagreement with respect to these products.[22]

In the *Japan—Alcohol* case discussed above, the Appellate Body considered the panel's interpretation of 'directly competitive or substitutable' as follows:

> If imported and domestic products are not "like products" for the narrow purposes of Article III:2, first sentence, then they are not subject to the strictures of that sentence and there is no inconsistency with the requirements of that sentence. However, depending on their nature, and depending on the competitive conditions in the relevant market, those same products may well be among the broader category of "directly competitive or substitutable products" that fall within the domain of Article III:2, second sentence. How much broader that category of "directly competitive or substitutable products" may be in any given case is a matter for the panel to determine based on all the relevant facts in that case. As with "like products" under the first sentence, the determination of the appropriate range of "directly competitive or substitutable products" under the second sentence must be made on a case-by-case basis.

> In this case, the Panel emphasized the need to look not only at such matters as physical characteristics, common end-uses, and tariff classifications, but also at the "market place". This seems appropriate. The GATT 1994 is a commercial agreement, and the WTO is concerned, after all, with markets. It does not seem inappropriate to look at competition in the relevant markets as one among a number of means of identifying the broader category of products that might be described as "directly competitive or substitutable".

> Nor does it seem inappropriate to examine elasticity of substitution as one means of examining those relevant markets. The Panel did not say that cross-price elasticity of demand is "*the* decisive criterion" for determining whether products are "directly competitive or substitutable". The Panel stated the following:

---

[21] Appellate Body Report, *Japan—Alcohol*, para 24.

[22] Panel Report, *Korea—Alcohol*, para 10.38.

In the Panel's view, the decisive criterion in order to determine whether two products are directly competitive or substitutable is whether they have common end-uses, *inter alia*, as shown by elasticity of substitution.[23]

... ...

Thus, as explained by the Appellate Body, the 'directly competitive or substitutable' standard is somewhat broader than the 'likeness' standard, covering products that are not similar enough to be deemed 'like'. The additional factor to be considered for the 'directly competitive or substitutable' analysis under Article III:2, second sentence, as compared to the 'likeness' analysis under Article III:2, first sentence, is competition in the market, including elasticity of substitution between products.[24]

Applied to the facts at issue, the panel in *Japan—Alcohol* concluded as follows:

6.32 The Panel then concluded that in deciding whether shochu and the other products [whisky, brandy, gin, genever, rum and liqueurs] in dispute were directly competitive or substitutable products, it noted that the products concerned were all distilled spirits and it would give particular emphasis to the following factors: the findings of the 1987 Panel Report; the studies put forward by the complainants (the ASI study) that contained persuasive evidence that there is significant elasticity of substitution among the products in dispute; the survey submitted by Japan that, notwithstanding the fact that it failed to take into account price distortions caused by internal taxation, still shows elasticity of substitution among the products in dispute; and, lastly, the evidence submitted by complainants concerning the 1989 Japanese tax reform which showed that whisky and shochu are essentially competing for the same market. In the view of the Panel, the conclusions of the 1987 Panel Report, buttressed by any of the other three factors, were sufficient for the Panel to conclude that shochu and the other products subject to dispute are directly competitive or substitutable according to Article III:2, second sentence.[25]

The Appellate Body upheld the panel's conclusion.[26] As with 'likeness', it is hard to provide any additional guidance except to say that the 'directly competitive or substitutable' standard will be applied on a case-by-case basis using the factors noted above.

b. Not Similarly Taxed We turn now to the issue of the standard for whether the imported and domestic products are 'not similarly taxed'. On this issue, we will examine another case involving taxes on alcoholic beverages, this time relating to Chilean taxes on the traditional domestic drink pisco and on various other beverages. The tax measure at issue did not apply a tax based on the products themselves, as in *Japan—Alcohol* where shochu had one tax rate while other products each had specific rates assigned to them. Rather, the Chilean tax measure was based on alcohol content, with the tax rate rising with the increase in alcohol content, as follows[27]:

---

[23] Appellate Body Report, *Japan—Alcohol*, para 25.
[24] Elasticity of substitution measures how likely purchasers are to substitute one product for another.
[25] Panel Report, *Japan—Alcohol*, para 6.28.
[26] Appellate Body Report, *Japan—Alcohol*, para 25.
[27] Panel Report, *Chile—Alcohol*, para 2.6, Table 2.

Alcohol content	Tax rate ad valorem
Less or equal to 35°	27%
Less or equal to 36°	31%
Less or equal to 37°	35%
Less or equal to 38°	39%
Less or equal to 39°	43%
Over 39°	47%

In considering whether the products at issue were 'not similarly taxed', the Appellate Body found as follows:

Appellate Body Report, *Chile—Taxes on Alcoholic Beverages*, Adopted 12 January 2000, WT/DS87, 110/AB/R

49. In *Japan—Alcoholic Beverages*, we stated that "to be 'not similarly taxed', the tax burden on imported products must be heavier than on 'directly competitive or substitutable' domestic products, and that burden must be more than *de minimis* in any given case." Like the Panel, we consider that this is the appropriate legal standard to apply under the second issue of "not similarly taxed". We must, therefore, assess the relative tax burden imposed on directly competitive or substitutable domestic and imported products.

50. The New Chilean System applies a minimum tax rate of 27 per cent *ad valorem* to all distilled alcoholic beverages with an alcoholic content of 35° or less and a maximum rate of 47 per cent *ad valorem* to all such beverages with an alcohol content of more than 39°. The Panel found, as a factual matter, that "roughly 75% of domestic production will enjoy the lowest rate and . . . over 95% of all current (and potential) imports will be taxed at the highest rate . . .".

51. Chile has argued that there is "similar taxation" of domestic and imported production under the New Chilean System because all beverages with a specific alcohol content are subject to identical *ad valorem* tax rates, irrespective of their origin. In making this argument, Chile invites us to focus exclusively on a comparison of the relative tax burden on domestic and imported products *within each fiscal category* and to disregard the differences of tax burden on distilled alcoholic beverages which have different alcohol contents and which are, therefore, in *different fiscal categories*. In other words, Chile asks us to disregard the comparison which the Panel undertook of the relative tax burden on domestic and imported products located in *different fiscal categories*.

52. It is certainly true that, as Chile claims, if we were to focus the inquiry under the second issue solely on a comparison of the taxation of beverages of a specific alcohol content, we would have to conclude that all distilled alcoholic beverages of a specific alcohol content are taxed similarly. However, as we stated at the outset, in our analysis we must assume that the group of directly competitive or substitutable products in this case is broader than simply the products *within each fiscal category*. Chile's argument fails to recognize that the Panel has found, and Chile has not appealed, that imported beverages of a specific alcohol content are directly competitive or substitutable with other domestic distilled alcoholic beverages of a different alcohol content. To accept Chile's argument on appeal would, we believe, disregard the objective of Article III, which is to "provide equality of competitive conditions" for *all* directly competitive or substitutable imported products in relation to domestic products, and not simply for *some* of these imported products. The examination under the second issue must, therefore, take into

account the fact that the group of directly competitive or substitutable domestic and imported products at issue in this case is not limited solely to beverages of a specific alcohol content, falling within a *particular* fiscal category, but covers *all* the distilled alcoholic beverages in *each and every* fiscal category under the New Chilean System.

53. A comprehensive examination of this nature, which looks at *all* of the directly competitive or substitutable domestic and imported products, shows that the tax burden on imported products, most of which will be subject to a tax rate of 47 per cent, will be heavier than the tax burden on domestic products, most of which will be subject to a tax rate of 27 per cent. We agree with the Panel that the difference in the level of the tax burden is clearly more than *de minimis* and, in any event, Chile has not appealed the Panel's finding that the difference between these tax rates is more than *de minimis*.

… … …

On this basis, the Appellate Body upheld the Panel's finding that directly competitive or substitutable imported and domestic products are 'not similarly taxed'.[28] In doing so, it emphasised that on the facts of this case, 'most' imported products will face a heavier tax burden than 'most' domestic products, and that the difference in tax rates is more than *de minimis*. The Appellate Body's approach here appears to reflect a discriminatory effect test, under which imports and domestic products will be considered 'not similarly taxed' if there is a disparate impact on imports as a group as compared to domestic products as a group.[29]

c. Applied so as to Afford Protection On the final element under Article III:2, second sentence, whether the tax measure is 'applied so as to afford protection', we turn again to *Chile—Alcohol*. The Appellate Body found as follows:

Appellate Body Report, *Chile—Taxes on Alcoholic Beverages*, Adopted 12 January 2000, WT/DS87,110/AB/R

61. . . . In our Report in *Japan—Alcoholic Beverages*, we said that examination of whether a tax regime affords protection to domestic production "is an issue of how the measure in question is *applied*", and that such an examination "requires a comprehensive and objective analysis":

> . . . it is possible to examine objectively the underlying criteria used in a particular tax measure, its structure, and its overall application to ascertain whether it is applied in a way that affords protection to domestic products.

62. We emphasized in that Report that, in examining the issue of "so as to afford protection", "it is not necessary for a panel to sort through the many reasons legislators and regulators often have for what they do and weigh the relative significance of those reasons to establish legislative or regulatory intent." The *subjective* intentions inhabiting the minds of individual legislators or regulators do not bear upon the inquiry, if only because they are not accessible to treaty interpreters. It does not follow, however, that the statutory purposes or objectives—that is, the purpose or objectives of a Member's legislature and government as a whole—to the extent that they are given *objective* expression in the statute itself, are not pertinent. To the contrary, as we also stated in *Japan—Alcoholic Beverages*:

---

[28] Appellate Body Report, *Chile—Alcohol*, para 54.
[29] By contrast, in the earlier *Canada—Periodicals* case, the Appellate Body seems to have taken the individual product approach. See Appellate Body Report, *Canada—Periodicals*, para 29. In taking this approach, the Appellate Body cited its own reasoning in *Japan—Alcohol* and that of the GATT Panel in *US—Section 337*.

Although it is true that the aim of a measure may not be easily ascertained, nevertheless its protective application can most often be discerned from the *design*, the *architecture*, and the revealing *structure* of a measure. (emphasis added)

63. We turn, therefore, to the design, the architecture and the structure of the New Chilean System itself. That system taxes *all* alcoholic beverages with an alcohol content of 35° or below on a linear basis, at a fixed rate of 27 per cent *ad valorem*. Thereafter, the rate of taxation increases steeply, by 4 percentage points for every additional degree of alcohol content, until a maximum rate of 47 per cent *ad valorem* is reached. This fixed tax rate of 47 per cent applies, once more on a linear basis, to *all* beverages with an alcohol content in excess of 39°, irrespective of how much in excess of 39° the alcohol content of the beverage is.

64. We note, furthermore, that, according to the Panel, approximately 75 per cent of all domestic production has an alcohol content of 35° or less and is, therefore, taxed at the lowest rate of 27 per cent *ad valorem*. Moreover, according to figures supplied to the Panel by Chile, approximately *half* of all domestic production has an alcohol content of 35° and is, therefore, located on the line of the progression of the tax at the point *immediately before* the steep increase in tax rates from 27 per cent *ad valorem*. The start of the highest tax bracket, with a rate of 47 per cent *ad valorem*, coincides with the point at which most imported beverages are found. Indeed, according to the Panel, that tax bracket contains approximately 95 per cent of all directly competitive or substitutable imports.

65. Although the tax rates increase steeply for beverages with an alcohol content of more than 35° and up to 39°, there are, in fact, very few beverages on the Chilean market, either domestic or imported, with an alcohol content of between 35° and 39°. The graduation of the rates for beverages with an alcohol content of between 35° and 39° does not, therefore, serve to tax distilled alcoholic beverages on a progressive basis. Indeed, the steeply graduated progression of the tax rates between 35° and 39° alcohol content seems anomalous and at odds with the otherwise linear nature of the tax system. With the exception of the progression of rates between 35° and 39° alcohol content, this system simply applies one of two fixed rates of taxation, either 27 per cent *ad valorem* or 47 per cent *ad valorem*, each of which applies to distilled alcoholic beverages with a broad range of alcohol content, that is, 27 per cent for beverages with an alcoholic content of *up to 35°* and 47 per cent for beverages with an alcohol content of *more than 39°*.

66. In practice, therefore, the New Chilean System will operate largely as if there were only two tax brackets: the first applying a rate of 27 per cent *ad valorem* which ends at the point at which most domestic beverages, by volume, are found, and the second applying a rate of 47 per cent *ad valorem* which begins at the point at which most imports, by volume, are found. The magnitude of the difference between these two rates is also considerable. The absolute difference of 20 percentage points between the two rates represents a 74 per cent increase in the lowest rate of 27 per cent *ad valorem*. Accordingly, examination of the design, architecture and structure of the New Chilean System tends to reveal that the application of dissimilar taxation of directly competitive or substitutable products will "afford protection to domestic production."

67. It is true, as Chile points out, that domestic products are not only subject to the highest tax rate but also comprise the major part of the volume of sales in that bracket. This fact does not, however, by itself outweigh the other relevant factors, which tend to reveal the protective application of the New Chilean System. The relative proportion of domestic versus imported products within a particular fiscal category is not, in and of itself, decisive of the appropriate characterization of the total impact of the New Chilean System under Article III:2, second sentence, of the GATT 1994. This provision, as noted earlier, provides for equality of competitive

conditions of *all* directly competitive or substitutable imported products, in relation to domestic products, and not simply, as Chile argues, those imported products within a particular fiscal category. The cumulative consequence of the New Chilean System is, as the Panel found, that approximately 75 per cent of all domestic production of the distilled alcoholic beverages at issue will be located in the fiscal category with the lowest tax rate, whereas approximately 95 per cent of the directly competitive or substitutable imported products will be found in the fiscal category subject to the highest tax rate.

68. The comparatively small volume of imports consumed on the Chilean market may, in part, be due to past protection. We consider that it would defeat the objective of Article III:2, second sentence, of the GATT 1994 if a Member of the WTO were able to avoid a finding that a measure is applied "so as to afford protection" for reasons that could, in part, result from its past protection of domestic production.

69. Before the Panel, Chile stated that the New Chilean System pursued four different objectives: "(1) maintaining revenue collection; (2) eliminating type distinctions [such] as [those which] were found in Japan and Korea; (3) discouraging alcohol consumption; and (4) minimizing the potentially regressive aspects of the reform of the tax system." Chile also stated that the New Chilean System reflected compromises between the four objectives which became necessary in the process of legislative enactment. The Panel did not find any clear relationship between the stated objectives and the tax measure itself and considered the absence of a clear relationship as "evidence *confirming* the discriminatory design, structure and architecture of [the Chilean] measure." (emphasis added)

70. On appeal, Chile argues that the Panel was "wrong to even consider the objectives" underlying the New Chilean System. Chile declines to explain the relationship between the design, architecture and structure of the New Chilean System and the objectives it stated that System sought to realize. At the oral hearing, Chile confirmed that, in its view, the stated objectives of the New Chilean System were not "relevant" in assessing whether that measure would be applied "so as to afford protection".

71. We recall once more that, in *Japan—Alcoholic Beverages*, we declined to adopt an approach to the issue of "so as to afford protection" that attempts to examine "the many reasons legislators and regulators often have for what they do". We called for examination of the design, architecture and structure of a tax measure precisely to permit identification of a measure's objectives or purposes as revealed or objectified in the measure itself. Thus, we consider that a measure's purposes, objectively manifested in the design, architecture and structure of the measure, *are* intensely pertinent to the task of evaluating whether or not that measure is applied so as to afford protection to domestic production. In the present appeal, Chile's explanations concerning the structure of the New Chilean System—including, in particular, the truncated nature of the line of progression of tax rates, which effectively consists of two levels (27 per cent *ad valorem* and 47 per cent *ad valorem*) separated by only 4 degrees of alcohol content—might have been helpful in understanding what *prima facie* appear to be anomalies in the progression of tax rates. The conclusion of protective application reached by the Panel becomes very difficult to resist, in the absence of countervailing explanations by Chile. The mere statement of the four objectives pursued by Chile does not constitute effective rebuttal on the part of Chile.

72. At the same time, we agree with Chile that it would be inappropriate, under Article III:2, second sentence, of the GATT 1994, to examine whether the tax measure is *necessary* for achieving its stated objectives or purposes. The Panel did use the word "necessary" in this part of its reasoning. Nevertheless, we do not read the Panel Report as showing that the Panel did, in fact, conduct an examination of whether the measure is necessary to achieve its stated objectives. It appears to us that the Panel did no more than try to relate the observable structural

features of the measure with its declared purposes, a task that is unavoidable in appraising the application of the measure as protective or not of domestic production.

....

On this basis, the Appellate Body upheld the Panel's finding that the dissimilar taxation at issue is applied 'so as to afford protection to domestic production', and hence it is inconsistent with Article III:2, second sentence.[30] In doing so, it relied on an analysis of the 'objective' purpose of the measure, as revealed by its 'design', 'architecture' and 'structure'.

By contrast, it stated, the 'subjective' intent behind the measure will not be considered. However, it should be noted in an earlier case, the Appellate Body did make apparent reference to these kinds of subjective intent considerations, although it is not clear what weight they were given.[31] Regardless of whether subjective intent is a formal part of the standard, it is likely that some panels will take such evidence into account nonetheless, either explicitly or implicitly. For an example of an explicit reference, the panel in *Mexico—Soft Drinks* stated:

> the declared intention of legislators and regulators of the Member adopting the measure should not be totally disregarded, particularly when the explicit objective of the measure is that of affording protection to domestic production. . . .

> In this respect, the United States has presented a copy of the written record of the debate that took place in December 2001 in the Mexican Congress on the bill that proposed the amendments to the LIEPS that would put in place the measures at issue. During that debate, a member of the Mexican Congress presented the bill on behalf of the committee that had drafted it (the Committee of Treasury and Public Credit of the Chamber of Deputies (*Comisión de Hacienda y Crédito Público*). During his presentation, the representative of the committee declared, after explaining to the chamber the taxes that would be imposed on soft drinks and syrups, "[w] e legislators, however, have the commitment to protect the national sugar industry, because a great number of Mexicans' subsistence depends on it. To that effect, it is proposed that the tax on soft drinks be applied only to those [soft drinks] that for their production utilize fructose instead of cane sugar".[32]

(iii) Article III:2: Conclusions

It is worth noting briefly here the relationship between the standards under the first and second sentences of this provision. Under the first sentence, there is a very strict standard where the products involved are 'like', as even a *de minimis* amount of difference in taxes will violate the provision. By contrast, under the second sentence, the difference in taxes must be greater, and there must also be a showing that the 'objective' purpose of the measure was to afford protection to domestic products. One may ask why there are different standards for varying degrees of similarity between the products at issue. In a sense, it is stricter scrutiny where the products have a higher degree of similarity, perhaps reflecting a view that measures which treat such products differently have a higher probability of being protectionist than measures involving products that are less similar.

---

[30] Appellate Body Report, *Chile Alcohol*, para 76.
[31] Appellate Body Report, *Canada—Periodicals*, paras 30–32.
[32] Panel Report, *Mexico— Soft Drinks*, paras 8.91–8.92.

(d) Article III:4: Regulatory Measures

GATT Article III:4 governs 'laws', 'regulations' and 'requirements' other than taxes or other charges, and thus can be loosely defined as covering 'regulatory' measures. This provision contains the following key elements. There must be (1) a 'law', 'regulation' or 'requirement' (2) affecting the internal sale, offering for sale, purchase, transportation, distribution or use of imported products that (3) accords 'less favourable treatment' to the imported products than to (4) 'like' domestic products. We discuss the first two elements briefly, and then delve more deeply into the latter two. It is these latter two that are generally the key issues in an Article III inquiry: Are the products 'like' for the purposes of Article III:4, and has there been 'treatment no less favourable'? As will be seen below, in considering these questions Article III:1 has played an important and controversial role.

The first element essentially requires that there be a certain degree of formal government involvement before a government action can be challenged under Article III:4. For example, it is unlikely that a statement by a Member of Parliament supporting a boycott of foreign goods would constitute a 'law', 'regulation' or 'requirement'. By contrast, a statute, regulation or a measure with a similar effect would qualify. A 'requirement' is generally thought of as something other than a statute or regulation, but close in terms of nature and impact.

Next, the second element, which requires that the measure 'affect' the internal sale, offering for sale, purchase, transportation, distribution or use of imported products, has been interpreted as having a 'broad scope of application'.[33] In an early GATT case, the *Italian Agricultural Machinery* case, a panel used this term to establish a wide scope for Article III:4:

> 12. In addition, the text of paragraph 4 referred both in English and French to laws and regulations and requirements *affecting* internal sale, purchase, etc., and not to laws, regulations and requirements governing the conditions of sale or purchase. The selection of the word "affecting" would imply, in the opinion of the Panel, that the drafters of the Article intended to cover in paragraph 4 not only the laws and regulations which directly governed the conditions of sale or purchase but also any laws or regulations which might adversely modify the conditions of competition between the domestic and imported products on the internal market.

It is worth noting here that the reference in *Italian Agricultural Machinery* to 'conditions of competition' has played a very important role in establishing the scope of Article III:4. An important consequence of this standard is that actual trade flows do not matter when alleging a National Treatment violation. Rather, a complainant need only show that the measure alters the competitive landscape in favour of the domestic product. Thus, for example, a measure might impose higher standards on imports than comparable domestic products, but, due to surging demand for the particular foreign products, imports actually increase relative to the domestic product. Despite the increase in imports, a violation may still be found based on the adverse change in the competitive conditions for imports. Similarly, a decrease in imports that occurs following the adoption of a measure may not necessarily lead to a finding of violation if the competitive conditions for imports have not been altered.

We turn now to the latter two elements.

---

[33] Appellate Body Report, *US—FSC*, Art 21.5, para 210.

(i) 'Less Favourable Treatment'

Arguably, the most important aspect of Article III:4 is the 'treatment no less favourable' language. In general terms, this part of the provision dictates that foreign products not be treated worse than 'like' domestic products ('likeness' will be discussed in the next section). As explained by a GATT panel, the words 'treatment no less favourable' call for 'effective equality of opportunities' for imported products.[34] This language appears to convey a similar meaning to the 'conditions of competition' language noted above, that is, Article III:4 is about competitive opportunities as opposed to actual trade flows. Both of these phrases—'conditions of competition' and 'equality of opportunities'—have been carried over to WTO jurisprudence.[35]

The difference between *de jure* and *de facto* discrimination, mentioned in the introductory section above, is of particular importance in the context of the 'less favourable treatment' element. Where there is an allegation of *de jure* discrimination, the formally different treatment between imported and domestic products is examined to assess whether it results in imported products being treated 'less favourably' than domestic products. In this regard, the 'conditions of competition' between imported and domestic products are considered. As an example, we extract here the Appellate Body's findings in the *Korea—Beef* case, in which the measure at issue required imported and domestic beef to be sold in separate shops or separate areas of the same shop:

Appellate Body Report, *Korea—Measures Affecting the Importation of Fresh, Chilled and Frozen Beef*, Adopted 10 January 2001, WT/DS161,169/AB/R

143. Korean law in effect requires the existence of two distinct retail distribution systems so far as beef is concerned: one system for the retail sale of domestic beef and another system for the retail sale of imported beef. A small retailer (that is, a non-supermarket or non-department store) which is a "Specialized Imported Beef Store" may sell any meat *except domestic beef*; any other small retailer may sell any meat *except imported beef*. A large retailer (that is, a supermarket or department store) may sell both imported and domestic beef, as long as the imported beef and domestic beef are sold in separate sales areas. A retailer selling imported beef is required to display a sign reading "Specialized Imported Beef Store".

144. Thus, the Korean measure formally separates the selling of imported beef and domestic beef. However, that formal separation, *in and of itself*, does not necessarily compel the conclusion that the treatment thus accorded to imported beef is less favourable than the treatment accorded to domestic beef. To determine whether the treatment given to imported beef is less favourable than that given to domestic beef, we must, as earlier indicated, inquire into whether or not the Korean dual retail system for beef modifies the *conditions of competition* in the Korean beef market to the disadvantage of the imported product.

145. When beef was first imported into Korea in 1988, the new product simply entered into the pre-existing distribution system that had been handling domestic beef. The beef retail system was a unitary one, and the conditions of competition affecting the sale of beef were the same for both the domestic and the imported product. In 1990, Korea promulgated its dual retail system for beef. Accordingly, the existing small retailers had to choose between, on the one hand, continuing to sell domestic beef and renouncing the sale of imported beef or, on the other hand,

---

[34] GATT Panel Report, *US— Section 337*, para 5.11.
[35] Appellate Body Report, *Korea—Beef*, para 135; Appellate Body Report, *Japan—Alcohol*, at 16–17; Appellate Body Report, *US—Section 211*, para 258.

ceasing to sell domestic beef in order to be allowed to sell the imported product. Apparently, the vast majority of the small meat retailers chose the first option. The result was the virtual exclusion of imported beef from the retail distribution channels through which domestic beef (and until then, imported beef, too) was distributed to Korean households and other consumers throughout the country. Accordingly, a new and separate retail system had to be established and gradually built from the ground up for bringing the imported product to the same households and other consumers if the imported product was to compete at all with the domestic product. Put in slightly different terms, the putting into legal effect of the dual retail system for beef meant, in direct practical effect, so far as imported beef was concerned, the sudden cutting off of access to the normal, that is, the previously existing, distribution outlets through which the domestic product continued to flow to consumers in the urban centers and countryside that make up the Korean national territory. The central consequence of the dual retail system can only be reasonably construed, in our view, as the imposition of a drastic reduction of commercial opportunity to reach, and hence to generate sales to, the same consumers served by the traditional retail channels for domestic beef. In 1998, when this case began, eight years after the dual retail system was first prescribed, the consequent reduction of commercial opportunity was reflected in the much smaller number of specialized imported beef shops (approximately 5,000 shops) as compared with the number of retailers (approximately 45,000 shops) selling domestic beef.

146. We are aware that the dramatic reduction in number of retail outlets for imported beef followed from the decisions of individual retailers who could choose freely to sell the domestic product or the imported product. The legal necessity of making a choice was, however, imposed by the measure itself. The restricted nature of that choice should be noted. The choice given to the meat retailers was *not* an option between remaining with the pre-existing unified distribution set-up or going to a dual retail system. The choice was limited to selling domestic beef only or imported beef only. Thus, the reduction of access to normal retail channels is, in legal contemplation, the effect of that measure. In these circumstances, the intervention of some element of private choice does not relieve Korea of responsibility under the GATT 1994 for the resulting establishment of competitive conditions less favourable for the imported product than for the domestic product.

147. We also note that the reduction of competitive opportunity through the restriction of access to consumers results from the imposition of the dual retail system for beef, notwithstanding the "perfect regulatory symmetry" of that system, and is not a function of the limited volume of foreign beef actually imported into Korea. The fact that the WTO-consistent quota for beef has, save for two years, been fully utilized does not detract from the lack of equality of competitive conditions entailed by the dual retail system.

148. We believe, and so hold, that the treatment accorded to imported beef, as a consequence of the dual retail system established for beef by Korean law and regulation, is less favourable than the treatment given to like domestic beef and is, accordingly, not consistent with the requirements of Article III:4 of the GATT 1994.

… … …

In contrast to a situation with formally different treatment for imported and domestic products, a claim under Article III:4 can also be made where the treatment is formally the same but there is an allegation that the measure results in *de facto* 'less favourable treatment' for imports. One of the most important statements by the Appellate Body on the meaning of 'less favourable treatment' that applies to these situations was the following *obiter dicta* in the *EC—Asbestos* case (made in the context of a finding on 'likeness'):

We recognize that, by interpreting the term "like products" in Article III:4 in this way, we give that provision a relatively broad product scope—although no broader than the product scope of Article III:2. In so doing, we observe that there is a second element that must be established before a measure can be held to be inconsistent with Article III:4. Thus, even if two products are "like", that does not mean that a measure is inconsistent with Article III:4. A complaining Member must still establish that the measure accords to the group of "like" *imported* products "less favourable treatment" than it accords to the group of "like" *domestic* products. The term "less favourable treatment" expresses the general principle, in Article III:1, that internal regulations "should not be applied . . . so as to afford protection to domestic production". If there is "less favourable treatment" of the group of "like" imported products, there is, conversely, "protection" of the group of "like" domestic products. However, a Member may draw distinctions between products which have been found to be "like", without, for this reason alone, according to the group of "like" *imported* products "less favourable treatment" than that accorded to the group of "like" *domestic* products. In this case, we do not examine further the interpretation of the term "treatment no less favourable" in Article III:4, as the Panel's findings on this issue have not been appealed or, indeed, argued before us.[36]

The relevance of this statement is that it emphasises a comparison of the 'group' of imported products to the 'group' of 'like' domestic products, rather than a comparison between an individual imported product and an individual 'like' domestic product. It is a fairly strong indication by the Appellate Body that it will not take an 'individual' or 'strict' like product approach—discussed above—in the context of Article III:4. In other words, a discriminatory effect, at the least, must be shown. This statement applies generally to all 'less favourable treatment' situations, of course, but it has particular relevance for *de facto* claims. In a *de jure* claim situation, it is clear that all imports are treated one way and all domestic products are treated a different way. The question is whether this different treatment alters the competitive conditions in favour of domestic products. By contrast, with *de facto* claims, one of the key issues is what percentage of imported and domestic products receives the worse treatment. The Appellate Body's statements in *Asbestos* get at this issue.

This statement can be seen as effectively overturning the panel's finding on this issue. In this regard, the panel found that:

> Inasmuch as the Decree does not place an identical ban on PVA, cellulose or glass fibre and fibro-cement products containing PVA, cellulose or glass fibres, we must conclude that *de jure* it treats imported chrysotile fibres and chrysotile-cement products [i.e. asbestos] less favourably than domestic PVA, cellulose or glass fibre and fibro-cement products.[37]

Thus, the panel did not consider it necessary to examine the treatment of the 'group' of imports and the 'group' of domestic products. Instead, it compared only the *imports of asbestos (and asbestos-containing products)* with the *domestic substitutes* (PVA, cellulose or glass fibre). This is an example of the 'individual' or 'strict' like product approach noted above. By contrast, the 'group' comparison for which the Appellate Body expressed support would have identified *all imports of asbestos and substitutes*, and compared the treatment of these products to the treatment given to *all domestic asbestos (if any) and substitutes*.

---

[36] Appellate Body Report, *EC—Asbestos*, para 100.
[37] Panel Report, *EC—Asbestos*, para 8.155.

As noted, of course, this statement was merely *dicta*. However, it has been widely cited and discussed as setting out the Appellate Body's current view of the provision.[38]

A more recent finding by the Appellate Body on this issue provides some additional guidance. In the *Dominican Republic—Cigarettes* case, at issue was a requirement to post a bond for the sale of both domestic and imported cigarettes. As explained by the panel:

7.234 Under Article 376 of the Dominican Republic Tax Code555 and Article 14 of Decree 79-03, the Dominican Republic imposes the requirement, for both importers and domestic producers of cigarettes, to post a bond (bond requirement).

7.235 According to Article 376 of the Dominican Republic Tax Code: "No alcohol and tobacco products may be manufactured in the Dominican Republic unless the person wishing to do so has previously registered and provided the Tax Administration with a bond to guarantee compliance with all of the tax liabilities established pursuant to this Chapter."

7.236 Article 14 (Bond) of Decree 79-03 extends the requirement to importers of cigarettes and sets the conditions for the bond:

"For the purposes of Article 376 of the Tax Code, the amount of the bond shall be five million pesos (RD$5,000,000) indexed for inflation. Such a bond shall be posted with the DGII [*Dirección General de Impuestos*, Directorate General of Internal Taxes] both by importers and local manufacturers of alcoholic beverages, beers and tobacco products and shall be issued by an insurance company or banking institution accredited in the Dominican Republic."

… … …

One of the arguments that Honduras, the complainant, made in connection with its Article III:4 claim was that the fixed amount of the bond resulted in *de facto* less favourable treatment for imported products, as follows:

(iii) Fixed amount of the bond

7.295 Finally, Honduras claims that the less favourable treatment for imported cigarettes would also result from the fact that the required bond has been set at a fixed amount of RD$5million that must be posted by each importer and domestic producer. In its opinion, there would be no direct relationship between the amount required to be guaranteed (i.e. the fixed amount of the bond) and the actual amount giving rise to the Selective Consumption Tax which would be dependent upon variable factors such as monthly volumes of sales and variations in the retail selling price according to market factors. The two amounts would not be commensurate. Honduras suggests that, since two domestic manufacturers have a higher market share than the importer of Honduran cigarettes, the per unit cost of the bond (the result of dividing the cost of the bond by the number of cigarettes sold) would be higher for imported cigarettes than for domestic cigarettes.

7.296 The Dominican Republic responds that the bond amounts do not have to be linked to the potential tax liabilities of the producers or the importers, or to any other factors. In its opinion, no such link would be reasonable, especially since the underlying tax obligations that the bond is intended to secure are not discriminatory. The Dominican Republic argues that, provided that the amount and the terms of the bond requirement are non-discriminatory, and in the absence of

---

[38] See, eg above n 2; A Porges and J Trachtman, 'Robert Hudec and Domestic Regulations: The Resurrection of Aim and Effects' (2003) 37 *Journal of World Trade* 783.

evidence that demonstrates that the bond is applied in a discriminatory manner, that bond would not be contrary to Article III of the GATT.

... ...

The Panel rejected the Honduran arguments on the following basis:

7.297 The Panel is not convinced by the argument that, in and of itself, the fact that the amount of the bond is the same for domestic producers and importers, creates less favourable treatment for imported cigarettes than for the like domestic products. Honduras has not presented evidence to that effect, other than the assertion that the per unit cost of the bond would be higher for imported than for domestic cigarettes.

7.298 The Panel recalls that the Appellate Body has declared that:

"The broad and fundamental purpose of Article III is to avoid protectionism in the application of internal tax and regulatory measures. . . . Toward this end, Article III obliges Members of the WTO to provide equality of competitive conditions for imported products in relation to domestic products. . . . Article III protects expectations not of any particular trade volume but rather of the equal competitive relationship between imported and domestic products."

7.299 The Panel notes that, under the domestic regulations, the required bond must be issued by an insurance company or banking institution accredited in the Dominican Republic. The effective cost that the bond has on domestic producers and importers is thus the fee charged by the financial institution that issues the bond. According to the evidence provided by Honduras, in the specific case of the importer of cigarettes from that country, the annual fee charged by the insurance company that issued the bond was RD$84,000 (approximately US$1,873). When divided by the annual imports of cigarettes made by that same company, the cost of the bond would be equivalent to RD$0.9 (or approximately 2 cents of a US dollar) per thousand cigarettes. That annual value is equivalent to 0.2 per cent of the value of cigarette imports made by the importer in the year 2003. The Panel also notes that the cost of complying with the bond requirement has been diminishing for the importing company in the recent years, since its imports have increased while the bond amount has remained the same. Had the importer posted a bond in the years 2001 and 2002 for the same cost, the cost of that bond would have represented 0.64 per cent and 0.41 per cent, respectively, of the value of cigarette imports made by the importer in those two years.

7.300 By definition, any expense that is fixed (i.e. not related to volumes of production) may lead to different costs per unit among supplier firms. As long as the difference in costs does not alter the conditions of competition in the relevant market to the detriment of imported products, that fact in itself should not be enough to conclude that the expense creates a less favourable treatment for imported products.

7.301 In light of the preceding arguments, the Panel considers that Honduras has not presented evidence to support its argument that the different cost per unit generated by complying with the bond requirement has a detrimental impact on the competitive conditions for imported products in relation to domestic products in the Dominican Republic cigarette market.

... ...

On appeal, the Appellate Body upheld the panel's findings, stating:

96. Nor do we accept Honduras' argument that the bond requirement accords "less favourable treatment" to imported cigarettes because, as the sales of domestic cigarettes are greater than those of imported cigarettes on the Dominican Republic market, the per-unit cost of the bond requirement for imported cigarettes is higher than for domestic products. The Appellate Body

indicated in *Korea—Various Measures on Beef* that imported products are treated less favourably than like products if a measure modifies the conditions of competition in the relevant market *to the detriment of imported products*. However, the existence of a detrimental effect on a given imported product resulting from a measure does not necessarily imply that this measure accords less favourable treatment to imports if the detrimental effect is explained by factors or circumstances unrelated to the foreign origin of the product, such as the market share of the importer in this case. In this specific case, the mere demonstration that the per-unit cost of the bond requirement for imported cigarettes was higher than for some domestic cigarettes during a particular period is not, in our view, *sufficient* to establish "less favourable treatment" under Article III:4 of the GATT 1994. Indeed, the difference between the per-unit costs of the bond requirement alleged by Honduras is explained by the fact that the importer of Honduran cigarettes has a smaller market share than two domestic producers (the per-unit cost of the bond requirement being the result of dividing the cost of the bond by the number of cigarettes sold on the Dominican Republic market). In this case, the difference between the per-unit costs of the bond requirement alleged by Honduras does not depend on the foreign origin of the imported cigarettes. Therefore, in our view, the Panel was correct in dismissing the argument that the bond requirement accords less favourable treatment to imported cigarettes because the per-unit cost of the bond was higher for the importer of Honduran cigarettes than for two domestic producers.[39]

Thus, the Appellate Body said that a measure's 'detrimental effect' on imports was not sufficient to find a violation 'if the detrimental effect is explained by factors or circumstances unrelated to the foreign origin of the product, such as the market share of the importer in this case'.

There are (at least) three ways to interpret the Appellate Body's reasoning on this point. The first is the most straightforward: that a discriminatory effect on imports is not sufficient to find a violation, and that something more is required'. However, the Appellate Body did not say what else is required. Perhaps it could be discriminatory intent, either objective or subjective; or a certain degree of discriminatory effect, ie a very high one. Or perhaps the Appellate Body had some other additional factor entirely in mind. The Appellate Body's reference to 'factors or circumstances unrelated to the foreign origin of the product' seems important here, but it is not clear what the Appellate Body meant.

The second view of this statement is that the Appellate Body considered the detrimental effect demonstrated here to have been insufficient because the panel did not examine the *overall* impact of the measure on imports. Thus, the Appellate Body referred to the comparison in question as having been with 'some' or 'two' domestic producers. This limited comparison is not enough, under this view. By contrast, a comparison with *all* domestic producers might have been enough for a finding of less favourable treatment if all or most importers were worse off by reason of the measure than all or most domestic producers.

Thirdly, the Appellate Body may have considered that any effect here was *de minimis*. In this regard, the panel had explained that the impact of the bond was quite small.

In a recent case decided under Article 2.1 of the TBT Agreement, the Appellate Body addressed some of these same issues. In that case, the US made arguments that relied on the Appellate Body's findings in *Dominican Republic—Cigarettes*. In response, and in a footnote, the Appellate Body explained its previous ruling as follows:

[39] Appellate Body Report, *Dominican Republic—Cigarettes*, para 96.

We disagree with the United States to the extent that it suggests that *Dominican Republic—Import and Sale of Cigarettes* stands for the proposition that, under Article III:4, panels should inquire further whether "the detrimental effect is unrelated to the foreign origin of the product". (United States' appellant's submission, para. 101 (referring to *Appellate Body Report, Dominican Republic—Import and Sale of Cigarettes*, para. 96)) Although the statement referred to by the United States, when read in isolation, could be viewed as suggesting that further inquiry into the rationale for the detrimental impact is necessary, in that dispute the Appellate Body rejected Honduras' claim under Article III:4 because:

> . . . the difference between the per-unit costs of the bond requirement alleged by Honduras is explained by the fact that the importer of Honduran cigarettes has a smaller market share than two domestic producers (the per-unit cost of the bond requirement being the result of dividing the cost of the bond by the number of cigarettes sold on the Dominican Republic market). (Appellate Body Report, *Dominican Republic—Import and Sale of Cigarettes*, para. 96)

Thus, in that dispute, the Appellate Body merely held that the higher per unit costs of the bond requirement for imported cigarettes did not conclusively demonstrate less favourable treatment, because it was not attributable to the specific measure at issue but, rather, was a function of sales volumes. In *Thailand—Cigarettes (Philippines)*, the Appellate Body further clarified that for a finding of less favourable treatment under Article III:4 "there must be in every case a genuine relationship between the measure at issue and its adverse impact on competitive opportunities for imported versus like domestic products to support a finding that imported products are treated less favourably". (Appellate Body Report, *Thailand—Cigarettes (Philippines)*, para. 134) The Appellate Body eschewed an additional inquiry as to whether such detrimental impact was related to the foreign origin of the products or explained by other factors or circumstances.[40]

To date, a good deal of uncertainty remains as to the exact contours and meaning of the Appellate Body ruling in *Dominican Republic—Cigarettes*. With this statement, not to mention that the Appellate Body's findings were made under Article 2.1 of the TBT Agreement (which has language similar to that of Article III:4), it remains unclear what effect this will have on the interpretation of Article III:4. Chapter 13 on the SPS and TBT agreements provides more information and details in respect of the decision in *United States—Clove Cigarettes*.

As a final point, it is worth recalling the 'aim and effect' test noted above in the context of Article III:2, first sentence. This standard was also applied by a GATT panel in the context of 'likeness' under Article III:4 (see next section).[41] As with Article III:2, first sentence, this approach was rejected by the Appellate Body under Article III:4 in an early case.[42] However, the combined effect of *Asbestos* and *Cigarettes* may be to bring some or all of it back in the context of the 'treatment no less favourable' element.

(ii) 'Like' Products

We have already discussed 'likeness' in the context of Article III:2, first sentence above. While this prior discussion is useful here, of course, as will be seen the standard is somewhat different in the context of Article III:4.

The *EC—Asbestos* case noted above provides guidance on the meaning of 'like' products under Article III:4. The dispute involved a measure that set out a general ban on

---

[40] Appellate Body Report, *United States—Clove Cigarettes*, para 179, fn 372.
[41] GATT Panel Report, *US—Alcoholic and Malt Beverages*, paras 5.70–5.77.
[42] Appellate Body Report, *EC—Bananas*, para 216.

the manufacture, processing, sale, import, placing on the domestic market and transfer of asbestos, both to protect workers and to protect consumers. There was a limited exception to the ban for chrysotile (white) asbestos, but it only applied where there was no substitute product available that had a lower risk for workers. Canada was of the view that the rules for white asbestos, which it produced, were too restrictive, and alleged that the measure violated various provisions of the GATT and the TBT Agreement, including GATT Article III:4. With regard to the Article III:4 claim, the Appellate Body had the following to say about the 'likeness' issue:

Appellate Body Report, *European Communities—Measures Affecting Asbestos and Asbestos-Containing Products*, Adopted 5 April 2001, WT/DS135/AB/R

93. To begin to resolve these issues, we turn to the relevant context of Article III:4 of the GATT 1994. In that respect, we observe that Article III:2 of the GATT 1994, which deals with the internal tax treatment of imported and domestic products, prevents Members, through its first sentence, from imposing internal taxes on imported products "in excess of those applied . . . to *like* domestic products." (emphasis added) In previous Reports, we have held that the scope of "like" products in this sentence is to be construed "narrowly". This reading of "like" in Article III:2 might be taken to suggest a similarly narrow reading of "like" in Article III:4, since both provisions form part of the same Article. However, both of these paragraphs of Article III constitute specific expressions of the overarching, "general principle", set forth in Article III:1 of the GATT 1994.

94. In addition, we observe that, although the obligations in Articles III:2 and III:4 both apply to "like products", the text of Article III:2 differs in one important respect from the text of Article III:4. Article III:2 contains *two separate* sentences, each imposing *distinct* obligations: the first lays down obligations in respect of "like products", while the second lays down obligations in respect of "directly competitive or substitutable" products.

95. For us, this textual difference between paragraphs 2 and 4 of Article III has considerable implications for the meaning of the term "like products" in these two provisions. In *Japan—Alcoholic Beverages*, we concluded, in construing Article III:2, that the two separate obligations in the two sentences of Article III:2 must be interpreted in a harmonious manner that gives meaning to *both* sentences in that provision. We observed there that the interpretation of one of the sentences necessarily affects the interpretation of the other. Thus, the scope of the term "like products" in the first sentence of Article III:2 affects, and is affected by, the scope of the phrase "directly competitive or substitutable" products in the second sentence of that provision. We said in *Japan—Alcoholic Beverages*:

Because the second sentence of Article III:2 provides for a separate and distinctive consideration of the protective aspect of a measure in examining its application to a broader category of products that are not "like products" as contemplated by the first sentence, we agree with the Panel that the first sentence of Article III:2 must be construed narrowly so as not to condemn measures that its strict terms are not meant to condemn. Consequently, we agree with the Panel also that the definition of "like products" in Article III:2, first sentence, should be construed narrowly.

96. In construing Article III:4, the same interpretive considerations do not arise, because the "general principle" articulated in Article III:1 is expressed in Article III:4, not through two distinct obligations, as in the two sentences in Article III:2, but instead through a single obligation that applies solely to "like products". Therefore, the harmony that we have attributed to the two sentences of Article III:2 need not and, indeed, cannot be replicated in interpreting

Article III:4. Thus, we conclude that, given the textual difference between Articles III:2 and III:4, the "accordion" of "likeness" stretches in a different way in Article III:4.

97. We have previously described the "general principle" articulated in Article III:1 as follows:

> The broad and fundamental purpose of Article III is to avoid protectionism in the application of internal tax and regulatory measures. More specifically, the purpose of Article III "is to ensure that internal measures 'not be applied to imported and domestic products so as to afford protection to domestic production'". Toward this end, Article III obliges Members of the WTO to provide *equality of competitive conditions for imported products in relation to domestic products* . . . . Article III protects expectations not of any particular trade volume but rather of the equal competitive relationship between imported and domestic products. . . . (emphasis added)

98. As we have said, although this "general principle" is not explicitly invoked in Article III:4, nevertheless, it "informs" that provision. Therefore, the term "like product" in Article III:4 must be interpreted to give proper scope and meaning to this principle. In short, there must be consonance between the objective pursued by Article III, as enunciated in the "general principle" articulated in Article III:1, and the interpretation of the specific expression of this principle in the text of Article III:4. This interpretation must, therefore, reflect that, in endeavouring to ensure "equality of competitive conditions", the "general principle" in Article III seeks to prevent Members from applying internal taxes and regulations in a manner which affects the competitive relationship, in the marketplace, *between the domestic and imported products involved*, "so as to afford protection to domestic production."

99. As products that are in a competitive relationship in the marketplace could be affected through treatment of *imports* "less favourable" than the treatment accorded to *domestic* products, it follows that the word "like" in Article III:4 is to be interpreted to apply to products that are in such a competitive relationship. Thus, a determination of "likeness" under Article III:4 is, fundamentally, a determination about the nature and extent of a competitive relationship between and among products. In saying this, we are mindful that there is a spectrum of degrees of "competitiveness" or "substitutability" of products in the marketplace, and that it is difficult, if not impossible, in the abstract, to indicate precisely where on this spectrum the word "like" in Article III:4 of the GATT 1994 falls. We are not saying that *all* products which are in *some* competitive relationship are "like products" under Article III:4. In ruling on the measure at issue, we also do not attempt to define the precise scope of the word "like" in Article III:4. Nor do we wish to decide if the scope of "like products" in Article III:4 is co-extensive with the combined scope of "like" and "directly competitive or substitutable" products in Article III:2. However, we recognize that the relationship between these two provisions is important, because there is no sharp distinction between fiscal regulation, covered by Article III:2, and non-fiscal regulation, covered by Article III:4. Both forms of regulation can often be used to achieve the same ends. It would be incongruous if, due to a significant difference in the product scope of these two provisions, Members were prevented from using one form of regulation—for instance, fiscal—to protect domestic production of certain products, but were able to use another form of regulation—for instance, non-fiscal—to achieve those ends. This would frustrate a consistent application of the "general principle" in Article III:1. For these reasons, we conclude that the scope of "like" in Article III:4 is broader than the scope of "like" in Article III:2, first sentence. Nonetheless, we note, once more, that Article III:2 extends not only to "like products", but also to products which are "directly competitive or substitutable", and that Article III:4 extends only to "like products". In view of this different language, and although we need not rule, and do not rule, on the precise product scope of Article III:4, we do conclude that the product scope of Article III:4, although broader than the *first* sentence of Article III:2, is certainly *not* broader than the *combined* product scope of the *two* sentences of Article III:2 of the GATT 1994.

...

101. We turn to consideration of how a treaty interpreter should proceed in determining whether products are "like" under Article III:4. As in Article III:2, in this determination, "[n]o one approach . . . will be appropriate for all cases." Rather, an assessment utilizing "an unavoidable element of individual, discretionary judgement" has to be made on a case-by-case basis. The Report of the Working Party on *Border Tax Adjustments* outlined an approach for analyzing "likeness" that has been followed and developed since by several panels and the Appellate Body. This approach has, in the main, consisted of employing four general criteria in analyzing "likeness": (i) the properties, nature and quality of the products; (ii) the end-uses of the products; (iii) consumers' tastes and habits—more comprehensively termed consumers' perceptions and behaviour—in respect of the products; and (iv) the tariff classification of the products. We note that these four criteria comprise four categories of "characteristics" that the products involved might share: (i) the physical properties of the products; (ii) the extent to which the products are capable of serving the same or similar end-uses; (iii) the extent to which consumers perceive and treat the products as alternative means of performing particular functions in order to satisfy a particular want or demand; and (iv) the international classification of the products for tariff purposes.

102. These general criteria, or groupings of potentially shared characteristics, provide a framework for analyzing the "likeness" of particular products on a case-by-case basis. These criteria are, it is well to bear in mind, simply tools to assist in the task of sorting and examining the relevant evidence. They are neither a treaty-mandated nor a closed list of criteria that will determine the legal characterization of products. More important, the adoption of a particular framework to aid in the examination of evidence does not dissolve the duty or the need to examine, in each case, *all* of the pertinent evidence. In addition, although each criterion addresses, in principle, a different aspect of the products involved, which should be examined separately, the different criteria are interrelated. For instance, the physical properties of a product shape and limit the end-uses to which the products can be devoted. Consumer perceptions may similarly influence—modify or even render obsolete—traditional uses of the products. Tariff classification clearly reflects the physical properties of a product.

103. The kind of evidence to be examined in assessing the "likeness" of products will, necessarily, depend upon the particular products and the legal provision at issue. When all the relevant evidence has been examined, panels must determine whether that evidence, as a whole, indicates that the products in question are "like" in terms of the legal provision at issue. We have noted that, under Article III:4 of the GATT 1994, the term "like products" is concerned with competitive relationships between and among products. Accordingly, whether the *Border Tax Adjustments* framework is adopted or not, it is important under Article III:4 to take account of evidence which indicates whether, and to what extent, the products involved are—or could be—in a competitive relationship in the marketplace.

...

111. We believe that physical properties deserve a separate examination that should not be confused with the examination of end-uses. Although not decisive, the extent to which products share common physical properties may be a useful indicator of "likeness". Furthermore, the physical properties of a product may also influence how the product can be used, consumer attitudes about the product, and tariff classification. It is, therefore, important for a panel to examine fully the physical character of a product. We are also concerned that it will be difficult for a panel to draw the appropriate conclusions from the evidence examined under each criterion if a panel's approach does not clearly address each criterion separately, but rather entwines different, and distinct, elements of the analysis along the way.

112. In addition, we do not share the Panel's conviction that when two products can be used for the same end-use, their "*properties* are then *equivalent*, if not identical." (emphasis added) Products with quite different physical properties may, in some situations, be capable of performing similar or identical end-uses. Although the *end-uses* are then "*equivalent* ", the physical properties of the products are not thereby altered; they remain different. Thus, the physical "uniqueness" of asbestos that the Panel noted does not change depending on the particular use that is made of asbestos.

...

114. Panels must examine fully the physical properties of products. In particular, panels must examine those physical properties of products that are likely to influence the competitive relationship between products in the marketplace. In the case of chrysotile asbestos fibres, their molecular structure, chemical composition, and fibrillation capacity are important because the microscopic particles and filaments of chrysotile asbestos fibres are carcinogenic in humans, following inhalation. In this respect, we observe that, at paragraph 8.188 of its Report, the Panel made the following statements regarding chrysotile asbestos fibres:

> . . . we note that the carcinogenicity of chrysotile fibres has been acknowledged for some time by international bodies.[135] This carcinogenicity was confirmed by the experts consulted by the Panel, with respect to both lung cancers and mesotheliomas, even though the experts appear to acknowledge that chrysotile is less likely to cause mesotheliomas than amphiboles. We also note that the experts confirmed that the types of cancer concerned had a mortality rate of close to 100 per cent. We therefore consider that we have sufficient evidence that there is in fact a serious carcinogenic risk associated with the inhalation of chrysotile fibres. Moreover, in the light of the comments made by one of the experts, the doubts expressed by Canada with respect to the direct effects of chrysotile on mesotheliomas and lung cancers are not sufficient to conclude that an official responsible for public health policy would find that there was not enough evidence of the existence of a public health risk.

> [135] Since 1977 by the IARC (see List of Agents Carcinogenic to Humans, Overall Evaluations of Carcinogenicity to Humans, Monographs of the International Agency for Research on Cancer, Volumes 1-63), see also WHO, IPCS Environmental Health Criteria (203) on Chrysotile, Geneva (1998), cited in para. 5.584 above. On the development of knowledge of the risks associated with asbestos, see Dr. Henderson, para. 5.595.

This carcinogenicity, or toxicity, constitutes, as we see it, a defining aspect of the physical properties of chrysotile asbestos fibres. The evidence indicates that PCG fibres, in contrast, do not share these properties, at least to the same extent. We do not see how this highly significant physical difference *cannot* be a consideration in examining the physical properties of a product as part of a determination of "likeness" under Article III:4 of the GATT 1994.

115. We do not agree with the Panel that considering evidence relating to the health risks associated with a product, under Article III:4, nullifies the effect of Article XX(b) of the GATT 1994. Article XX(b) allows a Member to "adopt and enforce" a measure, *inter alia*, necessary to protect human life or health, even though that measure is inconsistent with another provision of the GATT 1994. Article III:4 and Article XX(b) are distinct and independent provisions of the GATT 1994 each to be interpreted on its own. The scope and meaning of Article III:4 should not be broadened or restricted beyond what is required by the normal customary international law rules of treaty interpretation, simply because Article XX(b) exists and may be available to justify measures inconsistent with Article III:4. The fact that an interpretation of Article III:4, under those rules, implies a less frequent recourse to Article XX(b) does not deprive the exception in Article XX(b) of *effet utile*. Article XX(b) would only be deprived of *effet utile* if that provision could *not* serve to allow a Member to

"adopt and enforce" measures "necessary to protect human . . . life or health". Evaluating evidence relating to the health risks arising from the physical properties of a product does not prevent a measure which is inconsistent with Article III:4 from being justified under Article XX(b). We note, in this regard, that, different inquiries occur under these two very different Articles. Under Article III:4, evidence relating to health risks may be relevant in assessing the *competitive relationship in the marketplace* between allegedly "like" products. The same, or similar, evidence serves a different purpose under Article XX(b), namely, that of assessing whether a *Member* has a sufficient basis for "adopting or enforcing" a WTO-inconsistent measure on the grounds of human health.

116. We, therefore, find that the Panel erred, in paragraph 8.132 of the Panel Report, in excluding the health risks associated with chrysotile asbestos fibres from its examination of the physical properties of that product.

117. Before examining the Panel's findings under the second and third criteria, we note that these two criteria involve certain of the key elements relating to the competitive relationship between products: first, the extent to which products are capable of performing the same, or similar, functions (end-uses), and, second, the extent to which consumers are willing to use the products to perform these functions (consumers' tastes and habits). Evidence of this type is of particular importance under Article III of the GATT 1994, precisely because that provision is concerned with competitive relationships in the marketplace. If there is—or could be—*no* competitive relationship between products, a Member cannot intervene, through internal taxation or regulation, to protect domestic production. Thus, evidence about the extent to which products can serve the same end-uses, and the extent to which consumers are—or would be—willing to choose one product instead of another to perform those end-uses, is highly relevant evidence in assessing the "likeness" of those products under Article III:4 of the GATT 1994.

118. We consider this to be especially so in cases where the evidence relating to properties establishes that the products at issue are physically quite different. In such cases, in order to overcome this indication that products are *not* "like", a higher burden is placed on complaining Members to establish that, despite the pronounced physical differences, there is a competitive relationship between the products such that *all* of the evidence, taken together, demonstrates that the products are "like" under Article III:4 of the GATT 1994. In this case, where it is clear that the fibres have very different properties, in particular, because chrysotile is a known carcinogen, a very heavy burden is placed on Canada to show, under the second and third criteria, that the chrysotile asbestos and PCG fibres are in such a competitive relationship.

119. With this in mind, we turn to the Panel's evaluation of the second criterion, end-uses. The Panel's evaluation of this criterion is far from comprehensive. First, as we have said, the Panel entwined its analysis of "end-uses" with its analysis of "physical properties" and, in purporting to examine "end-uses" as a distinct criterion, essentially referred to its analysis of "properties". This makes it difficult to assess precisely how the Panel evaluated the end-uses criterion. Second, the Panel's analysis of end-uses is based on a "small number of applications" for which the products are substitutable. Indeed, the Panel stated that "[i]t suffices that, for a *given utilization*, the properties are the same to the extent that one product can replace the other." (emphasis added) Although we agree that it is certainly relevant that products have similar end-uses for a "small number of . . . applications", or even for a "given utilization", we think that a panel must also examine the other, *different* end-uses for products. It is only by forming a complete picture of the various end-uses of a product that a panel can assess the significance of the fact that products share a limited number of end-uses. In this case, the Panel did not provide such a complete picture of the various end-uses of the different fibres. The Panel did not explain, or elaborate in any way on, the "small number of . . . applications" for which the various fibres have similar end-uses. Nor did the Panel examine the end-uses for these products

which were not similar. In these circumstances, we believe that the Panel did not adequately examine the evidence relating to end-uses.

120. The Panel declined to examine or make any findings relating to the third criterion, consumers' tastes and habits, "[b]ecause this criterion would not provide clear results". There will be few situations where the evidence on the "likeness" of products will lend itself to "clear results". In many cases, the evidence will give conflicting indications, possibly within each of the four criteria. For instance, there may be some evidence of similar physical properties and some evidence of differing physical properties. Or the physical properties may differ completely, yet there may be strong evidence of similar end-uses and a high degree of substitutability of the products from the perspective of the consumer. A panel cannot decline to inquire into relevant evidence simply because it suspects that evidence may not be "clear" or, for that matter, because the parties agree that certain evidence is not relevant. In any event, we have difficulty seeing how the Panel could conclude that an examination of consumers' tastes and habits "would not provide clear results", given that the Panel did not examine *any* evidence relating to this criterion.

121. Furthermore, in a case such as this, where the fibres are physically very different, a panel *cannot* conclude that they are "like products" if it *does not examine* evidence relating to consumers' tastes and habits. In such a situation, if there is *no* inquiry into this aspect of the nature and extent of the competitive relationship between the products, there is no basis for overcoming the inference, drawn from the different physical properties of the products, that the products are not "like".

122. In this case especially, we are also persuaded that evidence relating to consumers' tastes and habits would establish that the health risks associated with chrysotile asbestos fibres influence consumers' behaviour with respect to the different fibres at issue. We observe that, as regards *chrysotile asbestos and PCG fibres*, the consumer of the fibres is a *manufacturer* who incorporates the fibres into another product, such as cement-based products or brake linings. We do not wish to speculate on what the evidence regarding these consumers would have indicated; rather, we wish to highlight that consumers' tastes and habits regarding *fibres*, even in the case of commercial parties, such as manufacturers, are very likely to be shaped by the health risks associated with a product which is known to be highly carcinogenic. A manufacturer cannot, for instance, ignore the preferences of the ultimate consumer of its products. If the risks posed by a particular product are sufficiently great, the ultimate consumer may simply cease to buy that product. This would, undoubtedly, affect a manufacturer's decisions in the marketplace. Moreover, in the case of products posing risks to human health, we think it likely that manufacturers' decisions will be influenced by other factors, such as the potential civil liability that might flow from marketing products posing a health risk to the ultimate consumer, or the additional costs associated with safety procedures required to use such products in the manufacturing process.

123. Finally, we note that, although we consider consumers' tastes and habits significant in determining "likeness" in this dispute, at the oral hearing, Canada indicated that it considers this criterion to be *irrelevant*, in this dispute, because the existence of the measure has disturbed normal conditions of competition between the products. In our Report in *Korea—Alcoholic Beverages*, we observed that, "[p]articularly in a market where there are regulatory barriers to trade or to competition, there may well be latent demand" for a product. We noted that, in such situations, "it may be highly relevant to examine latent demand" that is suppressed by regulatory barriers. In addition, we said that "evidence from other markets may be pertinent to the examination of the market at issue, particularly when demand on that market has been influenced by regulatory barriers to trade or to competition." We, therefore, do not accept Canada's contention that, in markets where normal conditions of competition have been

disturbed by regulatory or fiscal barriers, consumers' tastes and habits cease to be relevant. In such situations, a Member may submit evidence of latent, or suppressed, consumer demand in that market, or it may submit evidence of substitutability from some relevant third market. In making this point, we do not wish to be taken to suggest that there *is* latent demand for chrysotile asbestos fibres. Our point is simply that the existence of the measure does not render consumers' tastes and habits irrelevant, as Canada contends.

... ...

One aspect of the Appellate Body's analysis that jumps out immediately is the use of the same criteria for likeness as discussed in the context of Article III:2, first sentence. However, the Appellate Body was careful to note a distinction between the two 'likeness' standards, emphasising that 'likeness' under Article III:4 is broader than that under Article III:2, first sentence (although it is not broader than the combined scope of 'like' and 'directly competitive or substitutable'), and involves an examination of the competitiveness between the products at issue.

In *EC—Asbestos*, the likeness issue involved a comparison of asbestos fibres and products containing asbestos, on the one hand, and polyvinyl alcohol, cellulose and glass ('PCG') fibres and products containing these fibres, on the other hand. The panel had found that these products, as well as products in which they are contained, are 'like'. On appeal, the Appellate Body reversed the panel's conclusion based on various flaws in its reasoning, and then attempted to complete the analysis on this issue, as follows:

Appellate Body Report, *European Communities—Measures Affecting Asbestos and Asbestos-Containing Products*, Adopted 5 April 2001, WT/DS135/AB/R

Chrysotile and PCG fibres

134. We address first the "likeness" of *chrysotile asbestos fibres* and *PCG fibres*. As regards the physical properties of these fibres, we recall that the Panel stated that:

> The Panel notes that no party contests that the structure of chrysotile fibres is unique by nature and in comparison with artificial fibres that can replace chrysotile asbestos. The parties agree that none of the substitute fibres mentioned by Canada in connection with Article III:4 has the same structure, either in terms of its form, its diameter, its length or its potential to release particles that possess certain characteristics. Moreover, they do not have the same chemical composition, which means that, in purely physical terms, none of them has the same nature or quality. ....

135. We also see it as important to take into account that, since 1977, chrysotile asbestos fibres have been recognized internationally as a known carcinogen because of the particular combination of their molecular structure, chemical composition, and fibrillation capacity. In that respect, the Panel noted that:

> ... the carcinogenicity of chrysotile fibres has been acknowledged for some time by international bodies. This carcinogenicity was confirmed by the experts consulted by the Panel, with respect to both lung cancers and mesotheliomas, even though the experts appear to acknowledge that chrysotile is less likely to cause mesotheliomas than amphiboles. We also note that the experts confirmed that the types of cancer concerned had a mortality rate of close to 100 per cent. We therefore consider that we have sufficient evidence that there is in fact a serious carcinogenic risk associated with the inhalation of chrysotile fibres. ....

In contrast, the Panel found that the PCG fibres "are not classified by the WHO at the same level of risk as chrysotile." The experts also confirmed, as the Panel reported, that current scientific evidence indicates that PCG fibres do "not present the same risk to health as chrysotile" asbestos fibres.

136. It follows that the evidence relating to properties indicates that, physically, chrysotile asbestosand PCG fibres are very different. As we said earlier, in such cases, in order to overcome this indication that products are *not* "like", a high burden is imposed on a complaining Member to establish that, despite the pronounced physical differences, there is a competitive relationship between the products such that, *all* of the evidence, taken together, demonstrates that the products are "like" under Article III:4 of the GATT 1994.

137. The Panel observed that the end-uses of chrysotile asbestos and PCG fibres are the same "for a small number" of applications. The Panel simply adverted to these overlapping end-uses and offered no elaboration on their nature and character. We note that Canada argued before the Panel that there are some 3,000 commercial applications for asbestos fibres. Canada and the European Communities indicated that the most important end-uses for asbestos fibres include, in no particular order, incorporation into: cement-based products; insulation; and various forms of friction lining. Canada noted that 90 percent, by quantity, of French imports of chrysotile asbestos were used in the production of cement-based products. This evidence suggests that chrysotile asbestos and PCG fibres share a small number of similar end-uses and, that, as Canada asserted, for chrysotile asbestos, these overlapping end-uses represent an important proportion of the end-uses made of chrysotile asbestos, measured in terms of quantity.

138. There is, however, no evidence on the record regarding the nature and extent of the many end-uses for chrysotile asbestos and PCG fibres which are *not* overlapping. Thus, we do not know what proportion of all end-uses for chrysotile asbestos and PCG fibres overlap. Where products have a wide range of end-uses, only some of which overlap, we do not believe that it is sufficient to rely solely on evidence regarding the overlapping end-uses, without also examining evidence of the nature and importance of these end-uses in relation to all of the other possible end-uses for the products. In the absence of such evidence, we cannot determine the significance of the fact that chrysotile asbestos and PCG fibres share a small number of similar end-uses.

139. As we have already stated, Canada took the view, both before the Panel and before us, that consumers' tastes and habits have no relevance to the inquiry into the "likeness" of the fibres. We have already addressed, and dismissed, the arguments advanced by Canada in support of this contention. We have also stated that, in a case such as this one, where the physical properties of the fibres are very different, an examination of the evidence relating to consumers' tastes and habits is an indispensable—although not, on its own, sufficient—aspect of any determination that products are "like" under Article III:4 of the GATT 1994. If there is no evidence on this aspect of the nature and extent of the competitive relationship between the fibres, there is no basis for overcoming the inference, drawn from the different physical properties, that the products are not "like". However, in keeping with its argument that this criterion is irrelevant, Canada presented *no* evidence on consumers' tastes and habits regarding chrysotile asbestos and PCG fibres.

140. Finally, we note that chrysotile asbestos fibres and the various PCG fibres all have different tariff classifications. While this element is not, on its own, decisive, it does tend to indicate that chrysotile and PCG fibres are not "like products" under Article III:4 of the GATT 1994.

141. Taken together, in our view, all of this evidence is certainly far from sufficient to satisfy Canada's burden of proving that chrysotile asbestos fibres are "like" PCG fibres under Article III:4 of the GATT 1994. Indeed, this evidence rather tends to suggest that these products are not "like products" for the purposes of Article III:4 of the GATT 1994.

Cement-based products containing chrysotile and PCG fibres

142. We turn next to consider whether *cement-based products containing chrysotile asbestosfibres* are "like" *cement-based products containing PCG fibres* under Article III:4 of the GATT 1994. We begin, once again, with physical properties. In terms of composition, the physical properties of the different cement-based products appear to be relatively similar. Yet, there is one principal and significant difference between these products: one set of cement-based products contains a known carcinogenic fibre, while the other does not. The Panel concluded that the presence of chrysotile asbestos fibres in cement-based products poses "an undeniable public health risk".

143. The Panel stated that the fibres give the cement-based products their specific function— "mechanical strength, resistance to heat, compression, etc." These functions are clearly based on the physical properties of the products. There is no evidence of record to indicate whether the presence of chrysotile asbestos fibres, rather than PCG fibres, in a particular cement-based product, affects these particular physical properties of the products. For instance, a tile incorporating chrysotile asbestos fibres may be more heat resistant than a tile incorporating a PCG fibre.

144. In addition, there is no evidence to indicate to what extent the incorporation of one type of fibre, instead of another, affects the suitability of a particular cement-based product for a specific end-use. Once again, it may be that tiles containing chrysotile asbestos fibres perform some end-uses, such as resistance to heat, more efficiently than tiles containing a PCG fibre. Thus, while we accept that the two different types of cement-based products may perform largely similar end-uses, in the absence of evidence, we cannot determine whether each type of cement-based product can perform, with *equal* efficiency, *all* of the functions performed by the other type of cement-based product.

145. As with the fibres, Canada contends that evidence on consumers' tastes and habits concerning cement-based products is irrelevant. Accordingly, Canada submitted no such evidence to the Panel. We have dismissed Canada's arguments in support of this contention. We have also indicated that it is of particular importance, under Article III of the GATT 1994, to examine evidence relating to competitive relationships in the marketplace. We consider it likely that the presence of a known carcinogen in one of the products will have an influence on consumers' tastes and habits regarding that product. It may be, for instance, that, although cement-based products containing chrysotile asbestos fibres are capable of performing the same functions as other cement-based products, consumers are, to a greater or lesser extent, not willing to use products containing chrysotile asbestos fibres because of the health risks associated with them. Yet, this is only speculation; the point is, there is no evidence. We are of the view that a determination on the "likeness" of the cement-based products cannot be made, under Article III:4, in the absence of an examination of evidence on consumers' tastes and habits. And, in this case, no such evidence has been submitted.

146. As regards tariff classification, we observe that, for any given cement-based product, the tariff classification of the product is the same. However, this indication of "likeness" cannot, on its own, be decisive.

147. Thus, we find that, in particular, in the absence of any evidence concerning consumers' tastes and habits, Canada has not satisfied its burden of proving that cement-based products containing chrysotile asbestos fibres are "like" cement-based products containing PCG fibres, under Article III:4 of the GATT 1994.

148. As Canada has not demonstrated either that chrysotile asbestos fibres are "like" PCG fibres, or that cement-based products containing chrysotile asbestos fibres are "like" cement-based products containing PCG fibres, we conclude that Canada has not succeeded in establishing that the measure at issue is inconsistent with Article III:4 of the GATT 1994.

… … …

Thus, the Appellate Body found that Canada did not prove that the products are 'like'. The controversial nature of the 'likeness' issue is illustrated by the concurring statement made by one Member of the Appellate Body Division hearing the case, as such statements are quite rare. This Member expressed differing views on two of the key issues:

149. One Member of the Division hearing this appeal wishes to make a concurring statement. At the outset, I would like to make it abundantly clear that I agree with the findings and conclusions reached, and the reasoning set out in support thereof, by the Division, in: Section V (*TBT Agreement*); Section VII (Article XX(b) of the GATT 1994 and Article 11 of the DSU); Section VIII (Article XXIII:1(b) of the GATT 1994); and Section IX (Findings and Conclusions) of the Report. This concurring statement, in other words, relates only to Section VI ("Like Products" in Article III:4 of the GATT 1994) of the Report.

150. More particularly, in respect of Section VI of the Report, I join in the findings and conclusions set out in: paragraphs 116, 126, 128, 131, 132, 141, 147 and 148. I am bound to say that, in truth, I agree with a great deal more than just the bare findings and conclusions contained in these eight paragraphs of the Report. It is, however, as a practical matter, not feasible to sort out and identify which part of which paragraph, of the sixty-odd paragraphs comprising Section VI of our Report in which I join. Nor is it feasible to offer a detailed statement with respect to the portions that would then remain. Accordingly, I set out only two related matters below.

151. In paragraph 113 of the Report, we state that "[w]e are very much of the view that evidence relating to the health risks associated with a product may be pertinent in an examination of 'likeness' under Article III:4 of the GATT 1994." We also point out, in paragraph 114, that "[p]anels must examine fully the physical properties of products. In particular, . . . those physical properties of products that are likely to influence the competitive relationship between products in the market place. In the cases of chrysotile asbestos fibres, their molecular structure, chemical composition, and fibrillation capacity are important because the microscopic particles and filaments of chrysotile asbestos fibres are carcinogenic in humans, following inhalation." This carcinogenicity we describe as "a defining aspect of the physical properties of chrysotile asbestos fibres" , which property is not shared by the PCG fibres, "at least to the same extent." We express our inability to "see how this highly significant physical difference *cannot* be a consideration in examining the physical properties of a product as part of a determination of 'likeness' under Article III:4 of the GATT 1994." (emphasis in the original) We observe also that the Panel, after noting that the carcinogenicity of chrysotile asbestos fibres has been acknowledged by international bodies and confirmed by the experts the Panel consulted, ruled that it "[has] sufficient evidence that *there is in fact a serious carcinogenic risk associated with the inhalation of chrysotile fibres*." (emphasis added) In fact, the scientific evidence of record for this finding of carcinogenicity of chrysotile asbestos fibres is so clear, voluminous, and is confirmed, a number of times, by a variety of international organizations, as to be practically overwhelming.

152. In the present appeal, considering the nature and quantum of the scientific evidence showing that the physical properties and qualities of chrysotile asbestos fibres include or result in carcinogenicity, my submission is that there is ample basis for a definitive characterization, on completion of the legal analysis, of such fibres as *not* "like" PCG fibres. PCG fibres, it may be recalled, have not been shown by Canada to have the same lethal properties as chrysotile asbestos fibres. That definitive characterization, it is further submitted, may and should be made even in the absence of evidence concerning the other two *Border Tax Adjustments* criteria (categories of "potentially shared characteristics") of end-uses and consumers' tastes and habits. It is difficult for me to imagine what evidence relating to economic competitive relationships as reflected in end-uses and consumers' tastes and habits could outweigh and set at naught the

undisputed deadly nature of chrysotile asbestos fibres, compared with PCG fibres, when inhaled by humans, and thereby compel a characterization of "likeness" of chrysotile asbestos and PCG fibres.

153. The suggestion I make is not that *any* kind or degree of health risk, associated with a particular product, would *a priori* negate a finding of the "likeness" of that product with another product, under Article III:4 of the GATT 1994. The suggestion is a very narrow one, limited only to the circumstances of this case, and confined to chrysotile asbestos fibres as compared with PCG fibres. To hold that these fibres are not "like" one another in view of the undisputed carcinogenic nature of chrysotile asbestos fibres appears to me to be but a small and modest step forward from mere reversal of the Panel's ruling that chrysotile asbestos and PCG fibres are "like", especially since our holding in completing the analysis is that Canada failed to satisfy a complainant's burden of proving that PCG fibres are "like" chrysotile asbestos fibres under Article III:4. That small step, however, the other Members of the Division feel unable to take because of their conception of the "fundamental", perhaps decisive, role of economic competitive relationships in the determination of the "likeness" of products under Article III:4.

154. My second point is that the necessity or appropriateness of adopting a "fundamentally" economic interpretation of the "likeness" of products under Article III:4 of the GATT 1994 does not appear to me to be free from substantial doubt. Moreover, in future concrete contexts, the line between a "fundamentally" and "exclusively" economic view of "like products" under Article III:4 may well prove very difficult, as a practical matter, to identify. It seems to me the better part of valour to reserve one's opinion on such an important, indeed, philosophical matter, which may have unforeseeable implications, and to leave that matter for another appeal and another day, or perhaps other appeals and other days. I so reserve my opinion on this matter.[43]

... ...

While the *EC—Asbestos* Appellate Body report may resolve certain issues, it also highlights the continuing disagreement over the proper interpretation of 'likeness'. Two members of the Division seemed to focus on competitiveness between the products as a key factor. By contrast, the third member expressed doubt on this point. In essence, the concurrence had two main concerns: first, that there was too much reliance on the notion of competition in the market in the majority's determination of 'likeness'; and, secondly, that the facts here were sufficient to find that the products at issue were not 'like', rather than simply state that Canada had not proved that they were 'like'.

In two recent cases under other provisions, the Appellate Body has emphasised the importance of competitiveness in the interpretation of 'likeness'. First, as noted above, the Appellate Body focused on competitiveness in *Philippines—Distilled Spirits* under Article III:2, first sentence. Secondly, and further discussed in Chapter 13 on the SPS and TBT Agreements, the Appellate Body looked at competitiveness in the context of the Article 2.1 of the TBT Agreement ('less favourable treatment' standard). These recent rulings strongly suggest that the Appellate Body would now also rely on competitiveness under Article III:4, but there has not yet been a specific ruling in this regard.

Because of the crucial role 'likeness' has played in non-discrimination standards at various times and under various provisions, with a finding of likeness sometimes leading almost inevitably to a finding of violation, the standard to be applied for likeness is understandably controversial. In addition, given the strong feelings among some people that certain products are inherently harmful, it is not surprising that they are concerned when

---

[43] Appellate Body Report, *EC—Asbestos*, paras 149–54.

such products are deemed 'like' other products they consider safe. Arguably, the statements by the *Asbestos* majority about the 'less favourable treatment' standard were an attempt to elevate that standard and reduce the importance of the 'likeness' comparison.

As a final point, it is worth noting here the 'aim and effect' test described above in the context of Article III:2, second sentence, as this test was also briefly the standard under Article III:4 'likeness'.[44] The Appellate Body's findings in *EC—Asbestos* indicate that 'aim and effect' will not be considered as part of the 'likeness' element. However, as noted, effect and possibly aim are likely to be relevant under the 'less favourable treatment' element, as described in the previous section.

(e) Article III: Conclusions and General Observations

As demonstrated above, the different wording in the various provisions of Article III results in several distinct non-discrimination standards. The current state of the law for each can be roughly summarised as follows:

For Article III:2, first sentence, some kind of 'effect' test will be used. However, its parameters are not clear. Most likely, it will be a discriminatory effect test that looks at the overall impact of the measure on the group of imported products as compared to the group of domestic 'like' products. But it is also possible than an 'individual' or 'strict' like products test will be applied. Intent will not be considered here (at least not explicitly, although it may be something the adjudicators are aware of and consider implicitly). The 'likeness' of products will have a very narrow scope under this provision.

Under Article III:2, second sentence, discriminatory effect will be taken into account, as will objective intent. Reference may even be made to subjective intent, but the weight given to this factor is unclear. The standard of directly competitive or substitutable products is fairly broad, and relies heavily on whether the products at issue compete in the market.

For Article III:4, discriminatory effect will play an important role. By contrast, the role of intent is unclear, both in terms of whether it is to be used and, if so, whether objective or subjective intent is relevant (although if anything it is probably objective intent). The like products standard here lies somewhere between likeness under Article III:2, first sentence and directly competitive or substitutable in Article III:2, second sentence. Competition in the market is probably relevant here, although opposing views on this point do exist.

This simple description of the state of law, while it offers a fairly accurate picture, is probably insufficient, however. There are a number of conflicting views out there as to what the National Treatment standard should involve, as well as varying opinions on the interpretation of specific provisions. One of the most important disputed aspects has been mentioned above and is worth recalling here. While the description we offered treats 'likeness' as perhaps a less important component of the National Treatment standard under Article III:2, first sentence and under Article III:4, there is also a view that 'likeness' is, in fact, the key element. An older view was that 'likeness' is the key in the sense that 'aim and effect' come into play in the context of analysing 'likeness'. However, this view has been clearly rejected in the jurisprudence. In addition, though, some people take a view of 'likeness' that is, in a sense, outside the discriminatory intent/effect approach

---

[44] GATT Panel Report, *US—Malt Beverages*, paras 5.70–5.77.

we have noted above, relying instead on the 'individual' or 'strict' like product test. This approach may be based on the notion that any distinction between like products is impermissible, or that discrimination exists if any individual imported product receives worse treatment than an individual comparable domestic product. While this approach has been criticised, it is clearly still a part of the thinking about 'likeness',[45] and cannot be ignored.

It is also worth recalling again the 'aim and effect' test. The current status of intent and effect is fairly clear in Article III:2, second sentence. For the other two provisions, however, things are less clear. Some commentators have contended that the Appellate Body moved toward an 'aim and effect' test for Article III:4 in *EC—Asbestos*[46] and *Dominican Republic—Cigarettes*.[47] In addition, it appears that any use of these factors is now shifting from the 'likeness' criterion to the 'less favourable treatment' criterion. But there has been no definitive statement on this matter under Article III:4, and the situation under Article III:2, first sentence is even less clear.

In addition, there is one other issue under Article III that should be noted here. A line of jurisprudence followed under the GATT indicated that internal laws that regulate the *production process*, as opposed to the *product itself*, do not fall under Article III in relation to their impact on imports and are thus subject to the stricter rules of Article XI (and even if they do fall under Article III, they violate that provision). Thus, for a United States law that regulated domestic tuna fishing practices so as to protect dolphins, and also prevented imports of tuna where no agreement had been reached with the exporting country on dolphin-safe fishing practices, two separate panels found that Article III did not apply. Instead, the measure was found to fall within Article XI, dealing with restrictions on imports.[48] Because Article XI is a strict prohibition with little flexibility, it was therefore widely assumed that any such import prohibition based on the production process would be found to be in violation. This result led to a great deal of criticism of the GATT as being insensitive to non-trade concerns. The current status of the doctrine is unclear. It has come under academic criticism in recent years,[49] but it has not been addressed in WTO dispute settlement.

Finally, we note the complex relationship that Article III has with both Article XI (quantitative restrictions) and Article XX (general exceptions), which we discuss in the chapters dealing with those provisions.

The above description of the GATT/WTO non-discrimination jurisprudence makes clear that there are a number of basic issues for which the law seems to be unsettled. It is perhaps surprising that one of the core principles has not been more clearly defined. In

---

[45] In its arguments in the *EC—Biotech Products* case, Canada argued that its imported products in the disfavoured category had been treated less favourably than 'like' domestic products in the favoured category, thus making the 'diagonal' argument described above. See Panel Report, *EC—Biotech Products*, paras 4.223–4.227.

[46] Porges and Trachtman, above n 38, 783–99.

[47] J Pauwelyn, 'The Unbearable Lightness of Likeness', a review of M Cossy, *Some Thoughts on The Concept of 'Likeness' in the GATS*, WTO Staff Working Paper ERSD-2006-08, available at http://www.law.duke.edu/fac/pauwelyn/pdf/unbearable_lightness.pdf (accessed on 31 July 2007) 10.

[48] GATT Panel Report, *US—Tuna I*, paras 5.1–5.16; GATT Panel Report, *US—Tuna II*, paras 5.2–5.8.

[49] See, eg S Charnovitz, 'The Law of Environmental "PPMs" in the WTO: Debunking the Myth of Illegality' (2002) 27 *Yale Journal of International Law* 1; R Howse and D Regan, 'The Product/Process Distinction—An Illusory Basis for Disciplining "Unilateralism" in Trade Policy' (2000) 11 *European Journal of International Law* 249; R Hudec, 'The Product–Process Doctrine in GATT/WTO Jurisprudence' in M Bronckers and R Quick (eds), *New Directions in International Economic Law* (The Hague, Kluwer Law International, 2000). For an opposing view see JH Jackson's response to the R Howse and D Regan article, 'Comments on Shrimp/Turtle and the Product/Process Distinction' (2000) 11 *European Journal of International Law* 303.

part, this situation is the result of disagreements as to what the law *should* be. In addition, to some extent there may have been an attempt to come up with vague judicial language that accommodates different views so as to make all parties happy in the short term because they can see their position reflected, to some extent, in the decision. Whatever the reason, there is still some doubt as to how core concepts like discriminatory intent and effect will be applied in the different provisions of Article III, and also some confusion as to whether doctrines like the 'individual' or 'strict like product' test and the 'product/ process' distinction will be applied in the various Article III provisions.

III. QUESTIONS

1. Is there any reason to have different National Treatment standards for tax and regulatory measures?

2. Why was the old 'aim and effect' standard included in the 'likeness' element rather than the 'less favourable treatment' or taxed 'in excess of' elements? Which language seems like the more natural place for it?

3. How reliable is subjective intent as a factor in a non-discrimination standard?

4. If discriminatory effect is a factor, how much of an effect is required? If 55 per cent of imports fall into the disfavoured category, whereas only 45per cent of domestic products fall into the disfavoured category, is that sufficient to find that a discriminatory effect exists?

5. If there is no domestic production of any 'like' or 'directly competitive or substitutable' product, would a 100 per cent tax on imports of the products violate Article III:2? What if the measure did not mention imports and just taxed the product itself?

6. Is there any reason to have tax measures broken down into 'like' and 'directly competitive or substitutable' products, whereas regulatory measures only have a 'likeness' category?

7. In *EC—Asbestos*, was the Appellate Body's explanation of 'less favourable treatment' in paragraph 100 an indication that it will use a discriminatory effect test? Did it suggest support for an 'aim and effect' test?

8. In *Dominican Republic—Cigarettes*, what did the Appellate Body mean with its 'unrelated to the foreign origin of the product' language?

9. In *EC—Asbestos*, should asbestos and its substitutes have been found to be 'like' or 'unlike'? Can a health risk be relevant to a competitive relationship in the market place between products? How did the Appellate Body's approach differ from the approach of the panel? In your opinion, should health risks be considered as part of the Article III analysis or only as part of the Article XX exception?

10. Is a panel bound to consider the *Border Tax Adjustments* criteria in its analysis of product likeness?

11. A number of different elements have been proposed as the basis for identifying discrimination. Putting aside the issue of the appropriate part of the provision under which they should be considered, what do you think of a standard that would weigh and balance all of the relevant considerations, as follows. A non-discrimination standard would take into account: (1) the existence of, and degree of, disparate impact on imports; (2) the various subjective intents of the government officials involved in the enactment of the measure; (3) the objective intent of the measure based on its working (including an examination of whether the means–ends relationship of the measure and its stated goals).

IV. THE MOST FAVOURED NATION PRINCIPLE

(a) Introduction

The Most Favoured Nation ('MFN') principle is one of the oldest and most important legal obligations in the area of international economic law, with origins in Medieval times. It became prominent in bilateral commerce and trade treaties negotiated in the eighteenth century.[50] The term itself may be somewhat confusing, as it has been mistakenly construed as indicating that there is a country or countries that are the 'most favoured'.[51] However, the principle is actually a (somewhat) straightforward non-discrimination requirement. The MFN principle means that a country must treat other countries at least as well as it treats the 'most favoured' country. For example, if Australia imposes a 10 per cent tariff on German car imports, it cannot charge 20 per cent on car imports from France or other trading partners, but rather must give these others the 10 per cent rate as well. Thus, a key aspect of the principle is a prohibition on discriminating among trading partners.

But the principle also has broader effects, outside the context of its application to existing tariffs and other laws described in the previous paragraph. For example, it plays an important role in trade negotiations. In the earliest trade negotiations, when two countries exchanged mutual tariff concessions, there was some debate as to the circumstances under which other countries would also benefit from the lower tariff. At this time, there were two very different approaches taken to MFN when negotiating these tariff concessions. One view was that tariff concessions made to one country in a particular trade agreement would apply generally to all other countries as well. The competing view was that concessions in one agreement would only apply to other countries if these other countries offered their own concessions in return. The former was known as 'unconditional' MFN. It was 'unconditional' in the sense that no conditions were placed on granting concessions to other countries. That is, recipient countries need not give anything in

---

[50] 'The Most-Favoured-Nation Clause in the Law of Treaties', Working Paper submitted by Mr E Ustor, Special Rapporteur (A/CN.4/L.127), Extract from the Yearbook of the International Law Commission, 1968, Vol ii, para 6.

[51] In US domestic law, the term has now been officially replaced by 'normal trade relations' in order to clarify the policy behind it (ie the goal is not to favour certain countries by designating them with MFN treatment, but rather to provide those countries with the normal treatment given to others). See, eg US Bill, S 747, 'To amend trade laws and related provisions to clarify the designation of normal trade relations'. See Public Law 105–206, 22 July 1998, 112 Stat 789, Sec. 5003. Clarification of Designation of Normal Trade Relations.

return. The latter was known as 'conditional' MFN. It was 'conditional' in the sense that tariff concessions were granted to other countries only on the condition that they offered compensation in the form of their own concessions. In other words, for 'conditional' MFN, a tariff concession given by Country A to Country B as part of an agreement involving mutual tariff reductions between the two would only be given to Country C if Country C offered its own tariff concessions to Country A. Different countries took different approaches. During the nineteenth century, the United States practised conditional MFN. The United Kingdom, by contrast, followed unconditional MFN, as did much of Europe by the end of the nineteenth century.[52]

One of the key developments in the evolution of MFN was World War I. During the lead up to the war, the European powers formed many alliances, including trade alliances, and it was felt by many that these alliances were a major cause of the war. As a result, in the aftermath of the war, many countries recognised the important role equal treatment in trade relations could play in peace and security more generally. The role of MFN was discussed during the League of Nation economic and financial conferences in the 1920s and 1930s, and an MFN principle was generally included in the various bilateral trade agreements negotiated in the inter-war years.[53] It was during this period that unconditional MFN became the dominant approach, in part, most likely, because the conditional form undermined the goals of promoting peaceful trade relations.[54]

With its long history and strong backing by the major trading nations, it was no surprise that the MFN principle was included in the GATT. Along with National Treatment, discussed in the previous section, MFN was one of the original cornerstones of the GATT. Indeed, it is set out in the first Article of the GATT (as well as in a number of other provisions). While National Treatment is more prominent in both the case law and the academic literature, the importance of MFN should not be underestimated. There are a wide range of economic and political benefits arising from this principle, including:

- It eliminates distortions in production patterns, as companies will produce in the most efficient production location, allowing comparative advantage to work. Without MFN, by contrast, a company may produce in a country favoured with lower tariff rates so as to take advantage of these rates, even if that country is not the most efficient production location.
- It can result in broader trade liberalisation, as any tariff cuts offered to one country will apply to all countries.
- Unconditional MFN can simplify trade negotiations, for example by eliminating the need to gauge reciprocity in tariff concessions, something which is required with conditional MFN.
- It makes for more straightforward and transparent customs policies, as complex rules of origin to determine where products made in multiple countries originate are unnec-

---

[52] Working Paper submitted by Mr E Ustor, above n 49.

[53] Jackson, above n 4, 249–51.

[54] 'In 1922 the United States made a concession to economic liberalism by turning from the conditional to the unconditional type of the most-favoured-nation clause. The reason for this departure from previous practice was explained as follows by the United States Tariff Commission: "the use by the United States of the conditional interpretation of the most-favoured-nation clause has for half a century occasioned, and, if it is persisted in, will continue to occasion frequent controversies between the United States and European countries"'. A/CN.4/L.127, 'The most-favoured-nation clause in the law of treaties', Working Paper submitted by Mr E Ustor, para 10.

essary. This simplicity also helps reduce the opportunities for special interests to lobby for rules that favour them.

- It reduces international tensions, because the possibility of one country being treated worse than other countries is eliminated. Furthermore, it treats all nations equally, regardless of size or power. In this way, it spreads peace and security along with trade liberalisation.

The reason MFN gets less attention than National Treatment is probably because discrimination *among* trading partners does not occur as often today as discrimination *against* trading partners. Countries are more likely to discriminate against imports generally, eg through tariffs, rather than among imports from different countries. In addition, disputes over National Treatment are more prevalent than disputes over MFN. This is because where discrimination among countries does occur, it is usually pursuant to a specific exception, waiver or other justification, which 'legalises' such discrimination. The main type of discrimination among trading partners is through bilateral and regional trade agreements ('FTAs'), which are permitted if they meet the requirements of GATT Article XXIV (see Chapter 8). It is also common for rich countries to offer special tariff preferences to poor countries, for example through a Generalised System of Preferences pursuant to the Enabling Clause (see Chapter 18), or a more specific waiver such as the Lomé Waiver granted to the European Communities to favour the former colonies of various EC Member States.[55] In addition, special duties on specific countries can be set through properly conducted anti-dumping and countervailing duty procedures.

Turning to the substance of the rules, the MFN principle appears in a number of provisions of the GATT and other WTO agreements. The most important of such provisions in the GATT is Article I, which provides for 'General Most-Favoured-Nation Treatment'.[56] The key elements of this provision, as set out in paragraph 1, are the following. First, the types of measures covered by the provision are:

> With respect to customs duties and charges of any kind imposed on or in connection with importation or exportation or imposed on the international transfer of payments for imports or exports, and with respect to the method of levying such duties and charges, and with respect to all rules and formalities in connection with importation and exportation, and with respect to all matters referred to in paragraphs 2 and 4 of Article III . . . [emphasis added]

The broad scope of this provision means that just about every government measure is covered. It applies to the combined scope of the internal measures covered by Article III:2 and III:4, which address domestic tax measures and laws, regulations and requirements; and also applies to border measures like customs duties and charges, and other import and export rules. Of course, customs duties, ie tariffs, are of perhaps the greatest importance for MFN. In the past, trade agreements focused almost exclusively on tariff concessions. Even today, however, with the expanded reach of trade rules, tariffs still

---

[55] The Fourth ACP–EEC Convention of Lomé, Decision of the CONTRACTING PARTIES of 9 December 1994, L/7604, 19 December 1994.

[56] MFN provisions also appear in a number of specific contexts, such as GATT Art XVII governing state trading enterprises, where Art XVII:1(a) states: 'Each Member undertakes that if it establishes or maintains a State enterprise, wherever located, or grants to any enterprise, formally or in effect, exclusive or special privileges, such enterprise shall, in its purchases or sales involving either imports or exports, act in a manner consistent with the general principles of non-discriminatory treatment prescribed in this Agreement for governmental measures affecting imports or exports by private traders' (footnote omitted).

play a key role. In part, this is because today's tariff schedules offer very fine distinctions between products. As seen in the next section, products that are nearly identical may be subject to different duty rates because of the way the tariff schedule is structured.

Note that there are fundamental differences in applying MFN rules to the different types of measures listed. Where a dispute over tariffs is involved, there is usually no question that there is different treatment as it is the difference in tariff rates that is at issue. Rather, the question is whether the different products involved are 'like'. Similarly, with internal measures that result in *de jure* discrimination among imports from various countries, the only question is whether the products involved are 'like'. By contrast, with internal measures that involved allegations of *de facto* discrimination, the existence of different treatment among the imports will be a key issue.

With regard to the type of treatment required, the Article I:1 states:

> any advantage, favour, privilege or immunity granted by any Member to any product originating in or destined for any other country shall be accorded immediately and unconditionally to the like product originating in or destined for the territories of all other Members.

Thus, an 'advantage, favour, privilege or immunity' granted to products of one Member 'shall be accorded immediately and unconditionally' to the 'like product' imported from other Members or exported to other Members. Put simply, treatment offered to one Member must be provided to other Members as well. As stated by the Appellate Body, in relation to the *EC—Bananas* case:

> The essence of the non-discrimination obligations is that like products should be treated equally, irrespective of their origin. . . .

> Non-discrimination obligations apply to all imports of like products, except when these obligations are specifically waived or are otherwise not applicable as a result of the operation of specific provisions of the GATT 1994, such as Article XXIV. In the present case, the non-discrimination obligations of the GATT 1994, specifically Articles I:1 and XIII, apply fully to all imported bananas irrespective of their origin, except to the extent that these obligations are waived by the Lomé Waiver.[57]

But of course, interpretation of legal rules is never simple, and in this chapter we discuss the main issues that have arisen in relation to MFN treatment under GATT Article I:1: (1) are the products at issue 'like products', and (2) is the advantage, favour, privilege or immunity 'accorded' to 'all other Members' immediately and unconditionally (in other words, has there been discrimination)? In addition, an argument has been made that the term 'unconditionally' means that no conditions of any sort can be imposed on the advantages, etc. granted under this provision.[58]

---

[57] Appellate Body Report, *EC—Bananas*, paras 190–91.

[58] Other interpretive issues could also exist with regard to issues like the meaning of 'advantage', 'granted', etc. However, we will focus on the issues that have been the focus of the case law and that seem most fundamental to the MFN principle.

(b) Elements of the Most Favoured Nation Principle: 'Likeness' and Non-discrimination

(i) Like Products

The question of 'like products' generally arises in MFN cases when a government measure makes a distinction between two *products*, rather than between specific *countries*, under which one product receives better treatment, such as a lower tariff rate.[59] Where the product receiving inferior treatment is predominantly made by one Member, that Member may complain that its products are not accorded advantages, etc that 'like products' from the other Members receive, in violation of Article I:1. A key question for such a claim is whether the two products at issue are, in fact, 'like'. On this point, we examine first a GATT case, *Spain—Coffee*, that addressed this issue, which was adopted in 1981.[60] The reasoning is much briefer then would be likely to be seen in a WTO decision, but the fact pattern involved provides a useful illustration of the issue.

Spain—Coffee involved tariff treatment of Brazilian coffee exports to Spain. Before 1979, Spain classified all unroasted, non-decaffeinated coffee under one tariff heading; that is, it charged the same rate for all such coffee. In 1979, however, Spain sub-divided its classification of this type of coffee into five parts:

Product description	Duty rate
1. Columbian mild	Free
2. Other mild	Free
3. Unwashed Arabica	7 percent ad valorem
4. Robusta	7 percent ad valorem
5. Other	7 percent ad valorem

Brazil's exports of unroasted coffee to Spain consisted mainly of 'unwashed Arabica', and also 'Robusta', which were subject to the higher 7 per cent rate. By contrast, the products with the duty free rate tended to come from Spain's former colonies. Brazil argued that by imposing a 7 per cent tariff rate on imports of unwashed Arabica and Robusta coffee, while giving duty-free treatment to other types of 'like' coffee, the new Spanish tariff regime was discriminatory against Brazil. Therefore, Brazil argued, the new regime was in violation of Article I:1.[61] In essence, Brazil's claim was that the products it supplied that were subject to a 7 per cent duty were 'like' those which were subject to no duty, and thus MFN treatment had not been provided.[62] The panel addressed the 'like products' issue as follows:

[59] The issue of 'like' product is merely a formality in cases where the products are agreed to be the same in the various Members, and the real issue is whether the advantage, etc has been 'accorded' to all Members.

[60] GATT Panel Report, *Spain—Coffee*.

[61] *Ibid*, paras 2.2, 2.11, 3.1, 3.9.

[62] Note that this is not a case about tariff bindings. There was no claim that the tariff charged was more than that allowed by Spain's schedule of tariff concessions.

GATT Panel Report, *Spain—Tariff Treatment on Unroasted Coffee,* **Adopted 11 June 1981, BISD 28S/102**

4.5   The Panel, therefore, in accordance with its terms of reference, focused its examination on whether the various types of unroasted coffee listed in the Royal Decree 1764/79 should be regarded as "like products" within the meaning of Article I:1. Having reviewed how the concept of "like products" had been applied by the CONTRACTING PARTIES in previous cases involving, *inter alia,* a recourse to Article I:1 the Panel noted that neither the General Agreement nor the settlement of previous cases gave any definition of such concept.

4.6   The Panel examined all arguments that had been advanced during the proceedings for the justification of a different tariff treatment for various groups and types of unroasted coffee. It noted that these arguments mainly related to organoleptic differences resulting from geographical factors, cultivation methods, the processing of the beans, and the genetic factor. The Panel did not consider that such differences were sufficient reason to allow for a different tariff treatment. It pointed out that it was not unusual in the case of agricultural products that the taste and aroma of the end-product would differ because of one or several of the above-mentioned factors.

4.7   The Panel furthermore found relevant to its examination of the matter that unroasted coffee was mainly, if not exclusively, sold in the form of blends, combining various types of coffee, and that coffee in its end-use, was universally regarded as a well-defined and single product intended for drinking.

4.8   The Panel noted that no other contracting party applied its tariff régime in respect of unroasted, non-decaffeinated coffee in such a way that different types of coffee were subject to different tariff rates.

4.9   In the light of the foregoing, the Panel *concluded* that unroasted, non-decaffeinated coffee beans listed in the Spanish Customs Tariffs under CCCN 09.01 A.1a, as amended by the Royal Decree 1764/79, should be considered as "like products" within the meaning of Article I:1.

… … …

Thus, the panel found that the differences put forward regarding the different types of coffee—geographical factors, cultivation methods, processing and genetic factors—were insufficient to allow for different tariff treatment. It also said that coffee 'in its end-use, was universally regarded as a well-defined and single product intended for drinking'. Finally, it noted, no other GATT contracting party sets up its tariff schedule this way. Therefore, it concluded, all of the types of coffee at issue are 'like'.[63]

The other key GATT case dealing with 'likeness' under Article I:1 was the *Japan— SPF Lumber* case. In this case, Canada filed a complaint alleging that Japan's lumber tariffs violated Article I:1 because Spruce, Pine, Fur (SPF) 'dimension lumber' was subject to an 8 per cent duty, whereas other types of lumber could be imported duty-free. This Panel showed a lot more deference to governments' tariff classification decisions than did the *Spain—Coffee* panel, finding thatcountries have a lot of discretion in setting up tariff classifications, and that 'tariff differentiations' are basically legitimate:

---

[63] *Ibid,* para 4.10. Turning to the other element of Art I:1,'according' advantages, etc to all other Members immediately and unconditionally, the panel then found that because Brazil's exports were 'mainly' of the high tariff coffee products, there was a violation of Art I:1.

GATT Panel Report, Canada / Japan—Tariff on Imports of Spruce, Pine, Fir (SPF) Dimension Lumber, Adopted 19 July 1989, BISD 36S/167

5.8   The Panel noted in this respect that the General Agreement left wide discretion to the contracting parties in relation to the structure of national tariffs and the classification of goods in the framework of such structure (see the report of the Panel on Tariff Treatment of Unroasted Coffee, BISD 28S/102, at III, paragraph 4.4). The adoption of the Harmonized System, to which both Canada and Japan have adhered, had brought about a large measure of harmonization in the field of customs classification of goods, but this system did not entail any obligation as to the ultimate detail in the respective tariff classifications. Indeed, this nomenclature has been on purpose structured in such a way that it leaves room for further specifications.

5.9   The Panel was of the opinion that, under these conditions, a tariff classification going beyond the Harmonized System's structure is a legitimate means of adapting the tariff scheme to each contracting party's trade policy interests, comprising both its protection needs and its requirements for the purposes of tariff- and trade negotiations. It must however be borne in mind that such differentiations may lend themselves to abuse, insofar as they may serve to circumscribe tariff advantages in such a way that they are conducive to discrimination among like products originating in different contracting parties. A contracting party prejudiced by such action may request therefore that its own exports be treated as "like products" in spite of the fact that they might find themselves excluded by the differentiations retained in the importing country's tariff.

5.10   Tariff differentiation being basically a legitimate means of trade policy, a contracting party which claims to be prejudiced by such practice bears the burden of establishing that such tariff arrangement has been diverted from its normal purpose so as to become a means of discrimination in international trade. Such complaints have to be examined in considering simultaneously the internal protection interest involved in a given tariff specification, as well as its actual or potential influence on the pattern of imports from different extraneous sources. The Canadian complaint and the defence of Japan will have to be viewed in the light of these requirements.

… … …

Thus, the panel emphasised that complaints in this area must show that the tariff classification has been 'diverted from its normal purpose' and has become 'a means of discrimination in international trade'. Turning to the facts of the case, the Panel rejected the complaint, saying that 'dimension lumber' does not exist as a category in Japan's tariff schedule, and that Canada did not make any arguments based on the actual categories.[64]

The *Japan—SPF Lumber* panel's findings can be criticised as being a bit formalistic. SPF lumber falls within a particular tariff classification, and the treatment of Canadian products under that classification could have been compared to 'like' products in other classifications. Nevertheless, the panel's concern was likely that an overly aggressive approach to rooting out discrimination in tariff schedules would have invalidated much of current practice in this regard (with fine distinctions being the norm). In this sense, it may have been reasonable for the panel to place some additional burden on complainants to argue very precisely.

Generally speaking, because these panels' reasoning was so brief, they do not offer a great deal of guidance on the issue. Today's legal analysis in WTO disputes is much more extensive. Furthermore, the concept of 'like products' has since been the subject of

---

[64] GATT Panel Report, *Japan—SPF Lumber*, paras 5.14–5.15.

detailed examination under other provisions, such as GATT Article III:4. As discussed in the previous section, an analysis of 'like products' in that context is based on physical properties, end-uses, consumer tastes and habits and tariff classification. While the tariff classification factor could not always be applied productively to Article I:1, an analysis of 'like products' under Article I:1 would almost certainly be more detailed than that of the *Spain—Coffee* and *Japan—SPF Lumber* panels, and would be likely to follow the other Article III:4 factors. Nonetheless, the *Spain— Coffee* and *Japan—SPF Lumber* disputes offer a good illustration of the kind of case that might be brought based on different treatment of 'like products'. Sticking with the coffee theme, other hypothetical examples include:

- Whether different treatment can be provided to 'fair trade' coffee as compared to other coffee. As explained by one NGO: '[t]o become Fair Trade certified, an importer must meet stringent international criteria; paying a minimum price per pound of $1.26, providing much needed credit to farmers, and providing technical assistance such as help transitioning to organic farming'.[65] Such coffee involves the promotion of several policies, but importantly it attempts to provide a minimum wage for the labour involved. Thus, one question becomes whether these 'fair trade' and 'non-fair trade' coffees can be treated as 'un-like' based on differences in their impact on the labour used as an input.

- Whether different treatment can be provided for coffee that is genetically modified as compared to other coffee. For example, producers may be able to engineer coffee that is 'naturally caffeine-free, can be more easily harvested, or better resist drought, frost and disease'.[66] The question here is whether such products can be treated as 'un-like' based on differences in their physical characteristics. A similar question arises with regard to organic and non-organic coffee.

As noted above, tariff lines have become narrower in recent years, as can be seen in the sample tariff schedule excerpted in Chapter 6. In part, this may be the result of attempts to prevent 'free riding' on tariff concessions—that is, allowing countries to benefit from concessions made in response to requests from other countries—by tailoring them to certain categories of products as precisely as possible. Of course, fine tariff distinctions have been with us for quite some time. A famous example of tariff distinctions occurred early in the twentieth century. In 1904 Germany granted a duty reduction on 'large dappled mountain cattle or brown cattle reared at a spot at least 300 metres above sea level and which have at least one month's grazing each year at a spot at least 800 metres above sea level'.[67] Could there really have been a meaningful distinction between these cows and other cows? It was widely presumed that this reduction was intended to benefit Switzerland, with its many mountains, at the expense of others, like Denmark.

The issue of 'likeness' plays a very important role in MFN disputes. Simply stated, if the products in question are considered not 'like', they can be placed in different tariff categories or subjected to other forms of disparate treatment, even if the result is that

---

[65] See www.globalexchange.org/campaigns/fairtrade/coffee/ (accessed on 1 May 2006).

[66] 'GMO Coffee in Laboratories But No Sell-by Date Yet', *Planet Ark*, available at www.planetark.com/dailynewsstory.cfm/newsid/30868/story.htm (accessed on 1 May 2006).

[67] League of Nations, Economic and Financial Section, *Memorandum on Discriminatory Classifications* (Ser LoNP 1927.11.27) 3.

countries which produce mostly the higher tariff goods will be at a disadvantage.[68] A distinction like the one in the *Spain—Coffee* case is usually made for purely commercial reasons, that is, to favour some entity (eg a company or country) that is involved in the production or sale of the favoured product. However, the two hypothetical coffee examples illustrate the other kinds of policies that can lead to distinctions in tariff treatment for products that are very similar. Whether these similar products can be considered 'like' becomes an important issue in determining whether a violation exists.

(ii) Advantage, etc 'Accorded' to 'All Other' Members: Non-discrimination

The non-discrimination aspect of Article I:1 provides:

> any advantage, favour, privilege or immunity granted by any Member to any product originating in or destined for any other country shall be accorded immediately and unconditionally to the like product originating in or destined for the territories of all other Members.

This language requires that advantages, etc granted to products of one Member must also be accorded to products of all other Members. In essence, it requires non-discrimination among Members (with regard to products that are 'like', of course).[69] Issues related to the precise meaning of the GATT non-discrimination requirement are explored in more detail in the introductory section to this chapter and in the section on National Treatment. It is worth noting that Article I:1 applies to both imports from other Members and exports to other Members. We focus here on the non-discrimination rules for imports, which is where the disputes have arisen.

As noted in the introduction, stepping back from the specific provisions of Article I:1, there appear to be two possible elements that can be used to identify discrimination: (1) the *intent* to discriminate (also referred to as 'aim' or 'purpose'), and (2) the *effect* of discriminating (also referred to as 'differential impact'). A finding of discrimination could be based on the existence of *either one* of these two elements, or on the existence of *both* elements. For Article I, based on the recent WTO case law, it does not appear that intent plays any explicit role. While the case law under Article III has, at various times and under various provisions, emphasised the 'aim' or 'intent' or 'purpose' of a measure, this has not been so explicitly under Article I. Thus, it is probably safe to say that the only issue under Article I is how to evaluate the effect of the measure, and we focus on that issue here. However, it is possible that intent will play some role nevertheless, at least implicitly.

Where the discrimination among trading partners is apparent from the face of the measure (ie it is *de jure* discrimination), the inquiry is normally straightforward and uncontroversial. For example, if a US law provides for a 10 per cent tariff on steel from Japan and a 5 per cent tariff on steel from Canada, it is clear that *all* Japanese steel products do not receive an advantage (a lower tariff rate) that is accorded to *all* Canadian

---

[68] For instance, if watches are taxed heavily and cars are taxed lightly, Switzerland may be at a disadvantage as compared to Germany because consumers will spend more on cars than watches as compared to a situation where duties are equal.

[69] Of course, the provision does not use the term 'discrimination', which leads to some interpretive difficulties. However, in *Canada—Autos*, the Appellate Body stated that the 'object and purpose' of Art I:1 is 'to prohibit discrimination among like products originating in or destined for different countries': Appellate Body Report, *Canada—Autos*, para 84.

steel products. In this situation, the existence of a discriminatory effect is fairly obvious. An example of such a case is *EC—Tariff Preferences*. As the panel described it, the situation was the following:

> 7.57 As the Panel understands it, the following facts are not in dispute: (i) the Drug Arrangements, as prescribed in the current Council Regulation (EC) No. 2501/2001, provide lower tariff rates than the MFN bound rates on certain products; and (ii) the treatment of lower tariff rates is only accorded to products originating in 12 beneficiary Members, not to like products originating in other Members.

> 7.58 Article I:1 requires that with respect to custom duties, any advantages granted to any product originating in any one Member shall be accorded immediately and unconditionally to the like products originating in all other Members. The fact is clear that the tariff preferences granted by the European Communities to the products originating in the 12 beneficiary countries are not accorded to the like products originating in all other Members, including those originating in India.

The difficulty arises where a measure is *origin-neutral* on its face, that is, it does not refer to the country of origin of the products. In the *Spain—Coffee* case discussed above, for example, the measure did not explicitly single out a particular country for less favourable tariff treatment. Rather, it identified certain *products* as receiving worse treatment. How should the *de facto* effect of the measure be evaluated in this situation? The most obvious approach is to examine the different categories of treatment accorded to *all* imported like products, and then look at how different countries' products are distributed within the categories. In other words, one would examine whether there is a discriminatory effect against (or 'disparate impact' on) imports from certain countries. In essence, this is what the *Spain—Coffee* panel did when it found discrimination against Brazil based on the fact that 'Brazil exported to Spain mainly "unwashed Arabica" and also Robusta coffee which were both presently charged with higher duties than that applied to "mild" coffee'.[70]

By contrast, another approach would simply look at whether *any individual product* from a Member is not accorded an advantage received by *any individual like product* of another country. Under this approach, it is irrelevant whether the *majority* of products from one country do not receive an advantage accorded to the *majority* of like products from another country. It is enough that *one* product from one country does not receive an advantage that *one* like product from *any other country* is accorded. This approach has been used more explicitly in the context of GATT Article III:4,[71] but could be applied to Article I:1 as well. Based on recent jurisprudence under GATT Article III:4, it is questionable whether this approach would still be used.[72] However, the approach has never been rejected explicitly, and, furthermore, as discussed below there is one Appellate Body decision in the area of Article I:1 that arguably gives credence to the approach.

The following tables illustrate the different approaches based on a hypothetical example: Country A applies a tax of 20 per cent on cars and 40 per cent on SUVs, to penalise the lower gas mileage of SUVs (assuming that cars and SUVs are 'like'). If Country B's exports to Country A are 90 per cent cars, whereas Country C's exports are 90 per cent SUVs, the breakdown would be as shown in Table 7.3.

---

[70] Panel Report, *Spain—Coffee*, para 4.10.
[71] Panel Report, *EC—Asbestos*, paras 8.154–8.155.
[72] Appellate Body Report, *EC—Asbestos*, 100; Appellate Body Report, *Dominican Republic— Cigarettes*, para 96.

Table 7.3 Assessing whether there is a discriminatory effect among imports from different countries

Tax rate	Imports from Country B	Imports from Country C
20% (cars)	[A] 90% of B imports	[C] 10% of C imports
40% (SUVS)	[B] 10% of B imports	[D] 90% of C imports

On these facts, the discriminatory effect approach would examine the distribution of Country B's and Country C's imports in the two tax categories. Because the vast majority of Country B's imports are taxed at the low rate and the vast majority of Country C's imports are taxed at the high rate, there is a discriminatory effect against Country C's imports. Thus, an advantage accorded to Country B is not accorded to Country C. An individual like product approach would reach the same result, but using different logic. This approach would simply compare Cell D to Cell A. Because some of Country C's imports are taxed at a higher rate than some of Country B's imports, there would be a finding that an advantage accorded to Country B is not accorded to Country C.

On the facts above, the individual like product approach does not seem problematic because it reaches the same result. However, with a different set of facts, it could raise concerns. For instance, if the distribution of car and SUV exports from Country B and C was 50 per cent for both, the breakdown would be as shown in Table 7.4.

Table 7.4 Assessing whether there is a discriminatory effect among imports from different countries

Tax rate	Imports from Country B	Imports from Country C
20% (cars)	[A] 50% of B imports	[C] 50% of C imports
40% (SUVS)	[B] 50% of B imports	[D] 50% of C imports

In this situation, the discriminatory effect standard would show no discrimination, ie the advantage of the lower tax is accorded equally to Country B and C. By contrast, an individual like product test, if applied rigidly, would find that some imports from Country C were subject to a higher tax rate than some imports from Country B. Thus, there would be a finding that an advantage accorded to Country B was not accorded to Country C.

Canada—Autos provides a good illustration of these two approaches. In that case, Canada established a complex regime to encourage domestic production of motor vehicles. One aspect of the regime was favourable tariff treatment for Canadian car producers who met various conditions, such as a domestic value added requirement for the production. There were two categories of tariff treatment: a zero tariff and a 6.1 per cent tariff. The duty-free treatment was available if the conditions were met. The complainants, the European Communities and Japan, argued that their producers were less likely to receive the duty free treatment than were the products of certain other countries, such as the United States, thus violating Article I:1.[73]

In addressing the Article I:1 claim, the panel examined the structure of the Canadian automotive industry, and found that, in fact, most imports of certain countries paid a zero tariff, whereas most imports from certain other countries paid the 6.1 per cent tariff. In this regard, it stated:

---

[73] Panel Report, *Canada—Autos*, paras 2.1–2.35, 3.1–3.6.

[The data] reveal very significant differences between the percentages of imports of automobiles from individual countries that have benefitted (sic) from the import duty exemption. The difference between the United States, Mexico, Sweden and Belgium, on the one hand, and other European countries and Japan on the other—not to mention other major motor vehicle producers such as Korea—is particularly striking.[74]

To be more specific about the data, Japan had submitted statistics which purported to show that 'in 1997, 96% of Sweden's imports into Canada, and 94% of Belgium's were imported duty-free (in both cases these were imports of Volvos and of Saabs, the latter partly owned by GM, with Volvo Canada and GM Canada both being eligible manufacturer beneficiaries)', whereas there were 'just under 30% of duty-free imports for the whole of the European Communities, and of just under 5% for Korea and just under 3% for Japan'. Similarly, the European Communities had stated that 'in 1997, imports of automobiles from the United States and Mexico accounted for 97% of all duty-free imports into Canada, when in contrast imports from these two countries accounted for only 80% of all imports of automobiles into Canada'.[75] Thus, by highlighting the effect of the differential tariff on the various exporting Members, and more specifically the percentage breakdown of those receiving duty-free treatment, the panel seems to have taken the discriminatory effect approach (although there were other factors that played a part in the decision as well, as the measure was quite complex).

By contrast, in its findings on this issue, the Appellate Body arguably relied on *both* approaches, although it did not provide a clear explanation of either one. In this regard, the Appellate Body first stated:

> We note next that Article I:1 requires that "*any advantage*, favour, privilege or immunity granted by any Member to *any product* originating in or destined for any other country shall be accorded immediately and unconditionally to the like product originating in or destined for the territories of *all other Members*." (emphasis added) The words of Article I:1 refer not to *some* advantages granted "with respect to" the subjects that fall within the defined scope of the Article, but to "*any advantage*"; not to *some* products, but to "*any product*"; and not to like products from *some* other Members, but to like products originating in or destined for "*all other*" Members.[76]

Thus, the Appellate Body emphasised that Article I:1 requires that '*any advantage*' given to '*any product*' must be provided to '*all other Members*'. The emphasis on the words 'any product' appears to reflect the individual product approach, under which the overall effect on different countries' imports is irrelevant, as each *individual* imported product must receive the 'advantage' received by all other imported products. Then, in the next paragraph, the Appellate Body stated:

> We note also the Panel's conclusion that, in practice, a motor vehicle imported into Canada is granted the "advantage" of the import duty exemption only if it originates in one of a small number of countries in which an exporter of motor vehicles is affiliated with a manufacturer/importer in Canada that has been designated as eligible to import motor vehicles duty-free under the MVTO 1998 or under an SRO.[77]

---

[74] *Ibid*, para 10.48.
[75] *Ibid*, paras 10.32–10.33, 10.48.
[76] *Ibid*, para 79.
[77] *Ibid*, para 80.

Thus, the Appellate Body noted the panel's finding that, in fact, certain countries' products are more likely to receive the import duty exemption than other countries' products. This appears to be an expression of the discriminatory effect approach, under which the distribution of countries' products over the different categories of treatment is the relevant consideration. Having examined the facts of this case under these two approaches, the Appellate Body then concluded in paragraph 81 that:

> from both the text of the measure and the Panel's conclusions about the practical operation of the measure, it is apparent to us that "[w]ith respect to customs duties . . . imposed on or in connection with importation . . .," Canada has granted an "advantage" to some products from some Members that Canada has not "accorded immediately and unconditionally" to "like" products "originating in or destined for the territories of *all other Members*." (emphasis added) And this, we conclude, is not consistent with Canada's obligations under Article I:1 of the GATT 1994.

The reference to 'some products' here is another sign that perhaps the Appellate Body was not taking an overall discriminatory effect approach.

It is difficult to say what this conclusion means for future applications of Article I:1. The Appellate Body did not make a clear statement as to whether it believed these actually were the two possible approaches, and, if so, what it thought of the two approaches. In the meantime, however, in the context of Article III:4 the 'individual product' approach has come under scholarly criticism[78] and the Appellate Body has arguably moved away from this approach as well.[79] A more complete explanation of the standard for de facto-discrimination under Article I:1 will have to await another case.

(c) Unconditional MFN

One of the other features of the GATT Article I:1 MFN clause is that it provides for 'unconditional' MFN treatment. That is, when a Member binds a tariff rate on a particular product as part of a negotiating round, that tariff rate applies to all Members. Thus, although Country A may have bound the tariff rate on that product in response to a request from Country B, all other Members also get the new tariff rate even if they do not offer any concessions of their own in exchange for Country A's tariff concession. This approach to MFN treatment differs from conditional MFN, under which other Members would only get this rate if they also offered their own concession to Country A.

It is generally accepted that the term 'unconditionally' as used in Article I:1 is the textual basis that establishes 'unconditional' MFN in Article I:1, and the concept itself is not controversial. However, this term has also been used as the basis for arguing for a broader obligation. In the *Indonesia—Autos* case, the panel found a violation of Article I:1 using reasoning that seemed to indicate a view that 'advantages', etc. under Article I:1 must be offered *with no conditions that are unrelated to the imported product itself*. In that case, the panel was considering a measure that conditioned tax and customs duty benefits on various domestic content requirements. In this regard, the panel reasoned as follows, relying in part on its view of GATT case law:

---

[78] Ehring, above n 2.
[79] Appellate Body Report, *EC—Asbestos*, para 100.

Panel Report, *Indonesia—Certain Measures Affecting the Automobile Industry*, Adopted 23 July 1998, WT/DS54,55,59,64/R

14.143 We now examine whether the advantages accorded to National Cars and parts and components thereof from Korea are unconditionally accorded to the products of other Members, as required by Article I. The GATT case law is clear to the effect that any such advantage (here tax and customs duty benefits) cannot be made conditional on any criteria that is not related to the imported product itself.

14.144 For instance, in the Panel Report on *Belgian Family Allowances*, the panel condemned a measure which discriminated against imports depending on the type of family allowances that was in place:

> "3. According to the provisions of paragraph 1 of Article I of the General Agreement, any advantage, favour, privilege or immunity granted by Belgium to any product originating in the territory of any country with respect to all matters referred to in paragraph 2 of Article III shall be granted immediately and unconditionally to the like product originating in the territories of all contracting parties. Belgium has granted exemption from the levy under consideration to products purchased by public bodies when they originate in Luxembourg and the Netherlands, as well as in France, Italy, Sweden and the United Kingdom. If the General Agreement were definitively in force in accordance with Article XXVI, it is clear that that exemption would have to be granted unconditionally to all other contracting parties (including Denmark and Norway). The consistency or otherwise of the system of family allowances in force in the territory of a given contracting party with the requirements of the Belgian law would be irrelevant in this respect, and the Belgian legislation would have to be amended insofar as it introduced a discrimination between countries having a given system of family allowances and those which had a different system or no system at all, and made the granting of the exemption dependent on certain conditions." (emphasis added)

14.145 Indeed, it appears that the design and structure of the June 1996 car programme is such as to allow situations where another Member's like product to a National Car imported by PT PTN from Korea will be subject to much higher duties and sales taxes than those imposed on such National Cars. For example, customs duties as high as 200% can be imposed on finished motor vehicles while an imported National Car benefits from a 0% customs duty. No taxes are imposed on a National Car while an imported like motor vehicle from another Member would be subject to a 35% sales tax. The distinction as to whether one product is subject to 0 % duty and the other one is subject to 200% duty or whether one product is subject to 0% sales tax and the other one is subject to a 35% sales tax, depends on whether or not PT [PTN] had made a "deal" with that exporting company to produce that National Car, and is covered by the authorization of June 1996 with specifications that correspond to those of the Kia car produced only in Korea. In the GATT/WTO, the right of Members cannot be made dependent upon, conditional on or even affected by, any private contractual obligations in place. The existence of these conditions is inconsistent with the provisions of Article I:1 which provides that tax and customs duty benefits accorded to products of one Member (here on Korean products) be accorded to imported like products from other Members "immediately and unconditionally".

14.146 We note also that under the February 1996 car programme the granting of customs duty benefits to parts and components is conditional to their being used in the assembly in Indonesia of a National Car. The granting of tax benefits is conditional and limited to the only Pioneer company producing National Cars. And there is also a third condition for these benefits: the meeting of certain local content targets. Indeed under all these car programmes, customs duty and tax benefits are conditional on achieving a certain local content value for the finished car. The existence of these conditions is inconsistent with the provisions of Article I:1 which provides that tax and customs duty advantages accorded to products of one Member (here on Korean products) be accorded to imported like products from other Members "immediately and unconditionally".

14.147 For the reasons discussed above, we consider that the June 1996 car programme which introduced discrimination between imports in the allocation of tax and customs duty benefits based on various conditions and other criteria not related to the imports themselves and the February 1996 car programme which also introduce discrimination between imports in the allocation of customs duty benefits based on various conditions and other criteria not related to the imports themselves, are inconsistent with the provisions of Article I of GATT.[80]

... ...

An important statement by the panel in this regard was that '[t]he GATT case law is clear to the effect that any such advantage (here tax and customs duty benefits) cannot be made conditional on any criteria that is not related to the imported product itself'. Based on this statement, it appears that the panel took a broad view of the scope of the 'unconditionally' obligation. Specifically, it viewed 'unconditionally' as meaning not only that tariff concessions apply equally to all WTO Members, but also that no conditions 'unrelated to the product' could be imposed. However, it did seem to consider other factors as well as support for its ultimate conclusion of a violation, perhaps undermining the force of its earlier statements.

The 'GATT case law' referred to, and quoted, by the panel was the *Belgian Family Allowances* case from the early 1950s. That case involved a complaint by Norway and Denmark regarding the application of a Belgian law which levied a charge on 'foreign goods purchased by public bodies when these goods originated in a country whose system of family allowances did not meet specific requirements'. The panel explained that the levy 'was collected only on products purchased by public bodies for their own use and not on imports as such, and that the levy was charged, not at the time of importation, but when the purchase price was paid by the public body'. Thus, the panel concluded that it was an 'internal charge' within the meaning of Article III:2, to which the provisions of Article I:1 apply. The panel then made the statement quoted by the *Indonesia—Autos* panel above, which reads in part: 'the Belgian legislation would have to be amended insofar as it introduced a discrimination between countries having a given system of family allowances and those which had a different system or no system at all, and made the granting of the exemption dependent on certain conditions'.[81] This passage could be read to incorporate both notions: (1) that Article I prohibits discrimination, and (2) that Article I prohibits conditions.

In the *Canada—Autos* case, by contrast, the panel reached a different conclusion, expressing disagreement with the *Indonesia—Autos* panel's reasoning. There, Japan argued that the import duty exemption at issue was inconsistent with Article I:1 because, 'by conditioning the exemption on criteria which are unrelated to the imported product itself, Canada fails to accord the exemption immediately and unconditionally to like products originating in the territories of all WTO Members'. The duty exemption at issue was conditioned on using domestic value added and on meeting certain product-to-sales ratio requirements. This panel rejected Japan's argument, concluding that 'whether

---

[80] Panel Report, *Indonesia—Autos*, paras 14.143–14.147.
[81] GATT Panel Report, *BelgianFamily Allowances*, para 3.

an advantage within the meaning of Article I:1 is accorded "unconditionally" cannot be determined independently of an examination of whether it involves discrimination between like products of different countries'. In other words, Article I:1 does not impose a requirement of 'unconditionality' that is separate from the general non-discrimination requirement. Rather, any conditions simply need to be imposed on a non-discriminatory basis. In reaching this conclusion, the panel explained that, in its view, the GATT case law does not support Japan's interpretation. Furthermore, it stated that for both the *Indonesia—Autos* and *Belgian—Family Allowances* disputes, the panels had found that discrimination existed, and thus the statements on 'conditionality' must be read in that context.[82]

The issue arose most recently in *EC—Tariff Preferences*. At issue there was a duty exemption, under a GSP scheme, that was conditioned on the designation of a country as having problems with drug production and trafficking. India argued that the MFN principle requires that advantages related to customs duties be extended to all other Members that the extension be immediate and unconditional, and that the drug 'condition' therefore violated Article I:1. In response, the European Communities argued that 'unconditionally' in Article I:1 means that any advantage granted may not be subject to conditions requiring compensation, and that the measures at issue are not conditional because the beneficiaries are not required to provide any compensation to the European Communities. The panel rejected the EC's argument, finding that 'the term "unconditionally" in Article I:1 has a broader meaning than simply that of not requiring compensation'. According to the panel, the "full" and "ordinary" meaning of "unconditionally" under Article I:1 means "not limited by or subject to any conditions." Thus, the panel found that because the tariff preferences at issue 'are accorded only on the condition that the receiving countries are experiencing a certain gravity of drug problems, these tariff preferences are not accorded "unconditionally" to the like products originating in all other WTO Members, as required by Article I:1'.[83]

In essence, the distinction between the two approaches is the following. Either (1) the term 'unconditionally' is part of the non-discrimination standard, and simply means that any conditions imposed on imports must be applied in a way that does not discriminate; or (2) no conditions unrelated to the product itself can be imposed in relation to the advantages, etc set out in Article I:1. Taking the *Indonesia—Autos* measure as an example, the first approach would mean that a tax or duty exemption based on the use of domestic content applied to imports must not discriminate among imports from other Members. By contrast, the second approach would hold that domestic content as a condition for a tax or duty exemption would violate Article I:1 regardless of whether there was any discrimination among Members.

At this point in time, there appears to be a split among panels, and also among Members, as evidenced by the different arguments before these panels as to which approach is the proper one. The Appellate Body has not yet weighed in. We note that an interpretation prohibiting any conditions, even those that are non-discriminatory, would be a strict one, and is certainly broader than the traditional idea of non-discrimination.

---

[82] Panel Report, *Canada—Autos*, para 10.28.
[83] Panel Report, *EC—Tariff Preferences*, paras 7.55–7.60.

(d) Conclusions on the MFN Obligation

A lack of consensus about what is meant by 'non-discrimination', combined with the specific wording of the text of Article I:1, has led to an interpretation and application of this provision that is quite complicated. When thinking about a non-discrimination standard, it is important to keep in mind generally the role of intent, effect and the comparability of the products at issue. For Article I:1, intent has not played much of a role, at least explicitly. Instead, the focus has been on the effect of the measure, although there are different views as to how effect should be measured. As to the comparability of the products at issue through the 'like products' requirement, this issue has not been examined recently under Article I:1, so the analysis of this issue under Article III:4 may provide some useful guidance. Lastly, the use of the term 'unconditionally' in the text has led some panels to go beyond the idea of non-discrimination in their findings on Article I:1.

As a final point, we note that the MFN principle plays an important role in other areas of WTO rules as well. Both the GATS and the TRIPS Agreement, two of the major new areas of regulation developed during the Uruguay Round, contain an MFN provision. MFN also plays a role in many other agreements. For instance, plurilateral agreements like the Agreement on Government Procurement have an MFN provision, giving countries an incentive to join the agreement so as to receive treatment as good as that received by their trading partners. The role of MFN in these other agreements is discussed in the chapters dealing with those agreements.

V. QUESTIONS

1. As a general matter, outside the context of the language of Article I:1, what are the possible factors that can be used to determine whether there is discrimination among trading partners? In your view, which of these are the most relevant for determining whether such discrimination exists?

2. GATT Article I:1 does not use the term 'discrimination'. What specific language of Article I:1 is helpful in identifying the appropriate standard? What factors does the text of Article I:1 indicate are relevant?

3. Other than participation in bilateral or regional trade agreements, in what circumstances would a Member intentionally discriminate against or in favour of specific trading partners?

4. How should the standard of 'likeness' under Article I:1 be assessed? What role should competition between the products in the market place play?

5. With regard to the divided case law on the issue of the meaning of 'conditionally' in Article I:1, which do you think is the better interpretation of this provision: (1) any conditions imposed must not result in discrimination among trading partners, or (2) no conditions of any sort may be imposed on advantages, etc mentioned in Article I:1.

6. In thinking about the precise standard that should be applied here, it is worth noting that under a discriminatory effect test, there is a question as to how much of a discrepancy

between or among the trading partners is required for finding a violation. Assume the following facts:

Tax rate	Imports from Country B	Imports from Country C
20% (cars)	[A] 55% of imports	[C] 45% of domestic
40% (SUVS)	[B] 45% of imports	[D] 55% of domestic

Applying a discriminatory effect test, should these facts lead to a finding that Country C is not being accorded an advantage that is accorded to Country B?

7. Let us say a WTO Member created separate tariff classifications for cars with petrol tanks on the right and cars with petrol tanks on the left. The former are subject to a 10 per cent tariff, the latter 20 per cent. What factors would you take into account in determining whether this classification violated Article I:1? How would you carry out the same analysis if the tariff classification distinguished between cars with high emissions and cars with low emissions?

Part V

GATT Exceptions

8

Bilateral/Regional Trade Agreements

I. INTRODUCTION

As foreshadowed in Chapter 7, one of the more important and controversial exceptions to MFN is Article XXIV of the GATT. This provision authorises the formation of customs unions and free-trade areas (FTAs), in spite of the non-discrimination concepts set down throughout the GATT. Without an exception for such arrangements, they would violate the principle of MFN.

A customs union eliminates or substantially reduces internal tariffs and barriers within the arrangement while also creating common external tariffs and trade policies for the members of the union. The most well known and successful customs union is the European Communities (EC).[1] By contrast, an FTA eliminates or substantially reduces tariffs and trade barriers between members of the agreement but does not affect each member's external trade policy. Therefore, members of a free trade area retain complete autonomy with respect to their external tariffs and trade barriers. A well-known example of an FTA is the North American Free Trade Agreement (NAFTA). Customs unions and free-trade areas can be bilateral, plurilateral or regional, and we will refer to them collectively as 'Preferential Trade Agreements' (PTAs).

In this chapter, we examine PTAs in several parts. First, we discuss the history and development of PTAs both before the GATT and as an 'exception' to the GATT under Article XXIV. Next, we analyse several arguments both for and against regionalism/bilateralism and explore the consequences of regionalism/bilateralism. Then, we examine the requirements set out under Article XXIV that must be followed in order to have a WTO-compatible customs union or FTA, consider the WTO disputes where PTAs became an issue and attempt to draw principles from those cases. Finally, we discuss the effect that PTAs are having on the multilateral system. We conclude by looking at a proposal discussed as part of the Doha Round for improving the regulatory framework for PTAs.

---

[1] The EC, it must be noted, has gone beyond a customs union in creating a political and monetary union as well.

II. HISTORY OF PTAS

Arrangements between two or more nations to reduce or eliminate barriers between or among countries while maintaining barriers against imports from other nations are not a new development. Early versions of PTAs date as far back as the eighteenth century and more coordinated versions appear in the nineteenth century, when the various states of the European empires established numerous agreements between and among each other.[2] PTAs flourished in the first half of the twentieth century, with agreements between European, African and South American states, and a large number of agreements (such as Commonwealth preferences and the Lomé Convention) forged between countries with colonial ties. The US also became involved in bilateral agreements via the Reciprocal Trade Agreements Act of 1934.

Even after the formation of the GATT, PTAs between contracting parties continued to develop at a reasonable rate. However, until the 1980s, regional or bilateral PTAs were quite limited and only extensively used in Western Europe (such as when various members of Western Europe formed the European Economic Community (EEC) (now known as the EU), the European Free Trade Area (EFTA) and the European Economic Area (EEA)), in countries within close geographical proximity (such as Australia and New Zealand in the Australia–New Zealand Closer Economic Relations Agreement), in a handful of developing countries and as preferences granted from developed to developing countries. In fact, at the same time as the EC was deepening its ties within the community and negotiating a common external tariff, the US was strongly committed to the multilateral process and even argued against PTAs. Perhaps as a result of the strife caused by protectionism and fractured trading arrangements throughout the Great Depression and World War II still engrained in its psyche, the US has been referred to as 'champion of a non-discriminatory global trade regime, grounded firmly in the MFN [Most Favoured Nation] principle'.[3]

When the EU resisted American efforts to start the eighth round of multilateral trade negotiations (which eventually became the Uruguay Round) in 1982, the American aversion to bilateralism began to waiver. Believing that PTAs were the only way to further liberalise international trade, the US abandoned its steadfast opposition to preferential agreements and completed two PTAs in the 1980s, one with Israel (1985) and one with Canada (1989) (the agreement with Canada was expanded to include Mexico in 1992, becoming the NAFTA). At the same time, the EU continued its expansion, adding six new members during the 1980s and 1990s and negotiating PTAs with the Western European countries not in the EU, several Eastern and Central European countries and with the Baltic Republics. Moreover, PTA negotiations also began between other regional markets at this time, including smaller nations in Africa, Central and South America, South and Central Asia, Central and Eastern Europe, Oceania, and the Baltic States. In fact, during

---

[2] See C Schonhardt-Bailey, *The Rise of Free Trade* (London, Routledge, 1997), vols i–iv; CP Kindleberger, 'The Rise of Free Trade in Western Europe, 1820–1875' (1975) 35(1) *The Journal of Economic History* 20.

[3] A Panagariya, 'The Regionalism Debate: An Overview', Working Paper, University of Maryland, Faculty of Economics, 1998, 6. Even as early as 1945, the US expressed its dissatisfaction with FTAs. The sentiments of Howard Ellis explain: '[t]here are good reasons for believing that no device portends more restrictions of international trade in the post-war setting than bilateral arrangements': *ibid*, at 10. One explanation for the US's stance against PTAs was that it did not have colonial ties or many neighbours, and therefore it was simply looking after its best interests.

this period, the only region not to embrace PTAs was East Asia and, by the conclusion of the Uruguay Round, all but three members (Hong Kong, Republic of Korea and Japan) were party to at least one of the 62 PTAs in force.

The rise of PTAs, with their inherent discriminatory qualities, led many to question whether they might undermine the multilateral trading system. This growing discontent led to the formation of the WTO Committee on Regional Trade Agreements (CRTA), which was established in 1996 to examine individual PTAs and to consider whether PTAs were systemically compatible with multilateralism. At the same time, the WTO's Singapore Ministerial Declaration stated:

> We note that trade relations of WTO Members are being increasingly influenced by regional trade agreements, which have expanded vastly in number, scope and coverage. Such initiatives can promote further liberalisation and may assist least-developed, developing and transition economies in integrating into the international trading system. In this context, we note the importance of existing regional arrangements involving developing and least-developed countries. The expansion and extent of regional trade agreements make it important to analyse whether the system of WTO rights and obligations as it relates to regional trade agreements needs to be further clarified. We reaffirm the primacy of the multilateral trading system, which includes a framework for the development of regional trade agreements, and we renew our commitment to ensure that regional trade agreements are complementary to it and consistent with its rules. In this regard, we welcome the establishment and endorse the work of the new Committee on Regional Trade Agreements. We shall continue to work through progressive liberalisation in the WTO as we are committed in the WTO Agreement and Decisions adopted at Marrakesh, and in so doing facilitate mutually supportive processes of global and regional trade liberalisation.[4]

Thus, despite some misgivings, the official position of the WTO Membership is that PTAs are compatible with multilateralism and can be used to promote liberalism and development.[5]

Since the establishment of the WTO, however, the number of PTAs has grown rapidly. To be more specific, there were only 124 PTAs during the GATT years, while the succeeding 10 years of the WTO saw an additional 196 notified PTAs.[6] More importantly, the rate at which PTAs are being negotiated has accelerated since the failed Seattle and Cancun Ministerials and the painstakingly slow progress of the Doha Round. This rapid rise in PTAs can be shown by the fact that 43 PTAs were notified to the WTO between January 2004 and February 2005.

At the time of writing this text, there are 228 PTAs notified to the WTO and in force (not including non-reciprocal preferential schemes), with over 12 finalised agreements

---

[4] World Trade Organization: Ministerial Conference, Singapore Ministerial Declaration, adopted on 13 December 1996, WT/MIN(96)/DEC, para 7..

[5] The effects of regionalism have also been studied by the Organisation of Economic Co-operation and Development and by the World Bank. Several academics and commentators have likewise studied the effects of FTAs on member and non-member countries and have disagreed in their conclusions: see, eg S Devos, *Regional Integration and the Multilateral Trading System: Synergy and Divergence* (OECD, Paris, 1995); L Summers, 'Regionalism and the World Trading System', Symposium Sponsored by the Federal Reserve Bank of Kansas City, 22–24 August 1991, 'Policy Implications of Trade and Currency Zones'; A Panagariya, 'The Regionalism Debate: An Overview' (1999) 22 *World Economy* 477; A Krueger, 'Are Preferential Trading Arrangements Trade-Liberalizing or Protectionist?' (1999) 13(4) *Journal of Economic Perspectives* 105.

[6] JA Crawford and RV Florentino, 'The Changing Landscape of Regional Trade Agreements', WTO working paper (Geneva, World Trade Organization, 2005), available at www.wto.org/english/res_e/booksp_e/ discussion_papers8_e.pdf.

due to come into force upon ratification. In addition, approximately 50 additional PTAs are being negotiated or are being investigated (such as by the completion of a feasibility study). This explosion of PTAs appears not to be driven by any particular country, as every WTO Member is now a member of one or more PTAs or is presently negotiating one or more PTAs. This rise in PTAs, and correspondingly the dramatic rise in world share of preferential trade over the last 10 years, has several important consequences as discussed below.

III. THE DEVELOPMENT OF REGIONALISM: WHY (OR WHY NOT) PTAS?

Deeper economic integration accomplished through PTAs has been undertaken for a number of reasons. First, PTAs ease trade between natural trading partners (such as the US and Canada) and encourage trade and investment in developing countries from developed countries. In addition, it has been argued that PTAs can be negotiated much faster than the multilateral process, enable parties to liberalise beyond the levels achievable through multilateral consensus and may be able to address specific issues that do not even register on the multilateral menu. In this regard, the resulting achievements in trade liberalisation substantially complement the WTO and can be an important building block for future multilateral liberalisation.

In addition, bilateral/regional opportunities may help developing countries to gain from regional integration and stronger economic ties to developed countries, improving both the trading regimes and the rule of law while implementing structural reforms necessary to further their integration into the world economy. As a flow on effect, this could serve further to open and liberalise developing country economies on the multilateral stage. PTAs often also force change to several areas not fully covered by the multilateral system (such as trade and the environment, labour and investment) and, in a sense, are laboratories for experimentation.

For example, if the US succeeds in including environmental and labour standards in its PTAs with both developed and developing countries, such provisions may become commonplace and eventually be eased into the multilateral agreements. As it currently stands, strong developing country opposition is blocking the inclusion of any environmental or labour standards into the WTO agreements. But if enough developing countries agree to abide by environmental and labour standards negotiated in PTAs with the US or other developed countries, those developing countries no longer have any reason to oppose their inclusion in the WTO.[7] In fact, those countries have incentive to encourage their inclusion into the multilateral agreements for the simple reason that if they now have to abide by the stringent rules and other developing countries (ie competitors) do not, they lose any competitive advantage they may have had over those countries and are effectively disadvantaged. This aspect of PTAs has been championed by some and condemned by others.

---

[7] For arguments against the inclusion of environmental and labour standards into FTAs see J Bhagwati, 'Preferential Trade Agreements: The Wrong Road' (1996) 27 *Law and Policy in International Business* 865, 865–6.

The feeling among many WTO Members now is that, because multilateralism is stalled, the momentum created by PTAs is needed to underpin the multilateral environment. Therefore, they do not view PTAs as mutually exclusive of the multilateral negotiations, but rather as a tool to influence the multilateral agenda positively by going beyond what is achievable at the present time. Put simply, they feel that PTAs have the ability to establish prototypes for liberalisation in a wide range of trading areas, including services, e-commerce, intellectual property, transparency in government regulations and procurement and better enforcement of labour and environmental protections that are simply not possible on the multilateral stage.

Another, arguably more important, reason why Members are negotiating PTAs is so that they do not get left behind and become disadvantaged in the world trading system. As a result of the increased bilateralism in recent years, nations that remain relatively inactive on the bilateral front, face actual discrimination in many key markets.

To illustrate, Japan and Mexico recently agreed to a bilateral PTA which will see, among other things, Japan lowering its tariffs and increasing market access to Mexican imports of pork, oranges and other agricultural products, while Mexico will import more steel, motor vehicles and other industrial products from Japan. Negotiating this agreement was difficult for Japan, as the powerful Japanese agriculture lobby worried about cheap agricultural imports flooding the Japanese market. But Japan realised that its lack of bilateral activity disadvantaged its exports, as Mexico already had PTAs with the US and the EU, thus rendering Japanese industries uncompetitive in the market. As a result of the agreement, existing Mexican MFN tariff rates, ranging between 18 and 30 per cent on Japanese games, motorcycles, computer peripherals, photocopiers, telecommunications equipment, CD players and musical instruments will be lifted, as will the duty-free export quota for cars; this means that Japanese products will enter Mexico on an equal footing with products originating in the US and EU.

This agreement has ramifications for other nations. For instance, as food products make up a large amount of Australian exports to Japan, many of which are directly competitive with food products from Mexico, Australian exports to Japan are now disadvantaged vis-à-vis Mexican products. Thus, it is thought that Australian agriculture and food exports to Japan will be likely to see slower than expected or even negative growth in the coming years. For this reason, Australia abandoned its longstanding opposition to negotiating a PTA with Japan and commenced negotiations in early 2007. At the time of this writing, the negotiations remain ongoing.

Another example of this occurred as a result of the Canada–Chile Free Trade Agreement (1997), which was negotiated following American resistance to adding Chile to the NAFTA. American businesses soon realised that they were disadvantaged vis-à-vis their Canadian competitors and soon began lobbying Washington to negotiate an FTA with Chile. By no coincidence, the United States–Chile Free Trade Agreement (2003) was one of the first PTAs the US negotiated following its decision to expand its PTAs.

The above scenarios are not unique or even rare, but are now commonplace in the world trading system. It is clear that certain nations have become disadvantaged worldwide, and it is apparent in a number of markets. With the number of PTAs rapidly increasing, and with every major world trading nation negotiating PTAs with multiple countries, the problem can only increase.

In 1999, and thus before the explosion of PTAs which resulted following the failure of the Seattle and Cancun Ministerial, the WTO estimated that 57 per cent of world trade in goods was covered by PTAs; therefore less than half of all trade in goods was covered by the principle of multilateralism.[8] It now seems impossible for any nation to take a stand against bilateralism as that nation would be acting alone and would have virtually no chance of slowing the pace of bilateralism; there are simply too many PTAs in existence or in the pipeline, and such a stand would only serve severely to harm the interests of that nation. Some economists believe that this exclusion from markets, or disadvantage as against competitor nations, is the main reason driving the growth of PTAs.[9]

On the other hand, it has also been posed that PTAs have the potential to threaten the sustainability of the multilateral trading system. PTAs, by their very nature, are inimical to the non-discriminatory principles of the WTO. In this regard, it is clear that PTAs undermine MFN and weaken the transparency and predictability of the entire multilateral trading system, and if the number of PTAs multiplies in too great numbers, critics argue that the entire foundation of the multilateral system could be weakened.[10] Indeed, the line dividing the positives of PTAs (such as using them to spur multilateral progress) and the negatives (such as hampering multilateral progress) is sometimes unclear.

In addition, the economic benefits of bilateralism/regionalism are uncertain.[11] On the one hand, PTAs may lead to 'trade creation', whereby trade is expanded between efficient producers/suppliers within the preferential trading arrangement. On the other hand, PTAs can also lead to 'trade diversion', whereby trade is not created but is shifted from an efficient producer/supplier outside the preferential trading arrangement to a less efficient producer/supplier inside the preferential trading arrangement.

Economist Robert Z Lawrence provides an example to illustrate the difference between trade creation and trade diversion:

---

[8] See WTO, 'Mapping of Regional Trade Arrangements', WT/REG/W/41 (2000). Intra-EC trade accounted for 25% of this total.

[9] This reasoning is commonly called the 'domino effect', where, the more nations that join FTAs the greater the need for non-members to negotiate FTAs just to keep their goods on competitive terms. The domino effect is strongest when a trading partner has negotiated multiple FTAs. For more on the domino effect see R Baldwin, 'A Domino Theory of Regionalism' in R Baldwin, P Haaparnata and J Kiander (eds), *Expanding Membership of the European Union* (Cambridge University Press, Cambridge, 1995).

[10] Economists debate this point. See, eg Summers, above n 5; J Bhagwati, 'Regionalism and Multilateralism: An Overview' in J Melo and A Panagariya (eds), *New Dimensions in Regional Integration* (Cambridge, Cambridge University Press, 1993); A Panagariya and P Krishna, 'On Necessarily Welfare-Enhancing Free Trade Areas' (2002) 57 *Journal of International Economics* 353; P Krishna, 'Regionalism And Multilateralism: A Political Economy Approach' (1998) 113 *Quarterly Journal of Economics* 227.

[11] For findings that PTAs are net welfare-enhancing see Asian Development Bank, *Asian Development Outlook 2002* (Oxford, Oxford University Press, 2002) 175–76; World Bank, *Global Economic Prospects 2005* (Washington, DC, World Bank, 2005) 57–65; DA De Rosa, 'The Trade Effects of Preferential Arrangements: New Evidence from the Australia Productivity Commission', Peterson Institute for International Economics Working Paper Series 07-01, January 2007, available at www.petersoninstitute.org/publications/wp/wp07-1.pdf (analysing and updating the Australian Productivity Commission's findings that PTAs are net trade-diverting and concluding PTAs are net trade-creating). For findings that PTAs decrease net welfare see generally J Bhagwati, *The World Trading System at Risk* (Princeton, NJ, Princeton University Press, 1991); J Bhagwati, *Free Trade Today* (Princeton, NJ, Princeton University Press, 2005). For findings that PTAs have little or no economic effect on trading patterns and the world economy see R Pomfret, 'Is Regionalism an Increasing Feature of the World Economy', Institute for International Integration Studies Discussion Paper No 164 (June 2006), available at http://ssrn.com/abstract=925802.

RZ Lawrence, *Regionalism, Multilateralism and Deeper Integration* (Brookings Institution Press, Washington, DC, 1996)

Assume that prior to implementing a free trade agreement with the United States, all television sets purchased in Mexico are subject to a tariff of 10 percent. Assume that Japan produces TVs under competitive conditions, which it sells at a cost of $100, but the United States could only produce such sets at $105. Initially, all TVs sold in Mexico and elsewhere would be Japanese. These would be imported at a price of $100 from Japan and sold to Mexican consumers for $110, with the additional $10 representing the tariff that would be paid by Mexican consumers to the Mexican government. Assume now that a free trade agreement is signed between Mexico and the United States which removes tariffs between Mexico and the United States but retains Mexican tariffs on other countries. Mexican consumers will now have a choice between buying American TVs, which will sell in Mexico at $105, or Japanese TVs, which will sell at $110. They will buy the U.S. TVs and be better off. However, the Mexican economy as a whole will be worse off. Before the agreement, Mexico bought TVs from Japan. Although consumers paid $110, $10 was just a transfer from Mexican consumers to the Mexican government. The economy as a whole, therefore, spent $100 per TV. After the agreement, however, Mexico is spending $105 per TV. TV prices in Mexico do not reflect their social opportunity costs. The impact of the agreement is to expand TV production in the United States, which is relatively less efficient, and to reduce it in Japan, which is relatively more efficient.

Of course, not all of the increased trade between partners will represent expansion from a less efficient source. Pure trade creation would also result. Assume in the example that initially Mexico could produce TV sets for $107. In this case, prior to the agreement Mexico would not have imported them from Japan, instead it would have supplied these TV sets domestically. In this case, Mexico would benefit from the agreement, which would allow it [to] pay only $105 per TV, although of course it would have done better by liberalizing fully and buying the sets from Japan.[12]

... ...

While the benefits and burdens of each PTA must be studied individually, it is generally presumed that trade diversion can be problematic, that is, diversion outweighs creation and the PTA partners are economically worse off, in two instances:[13] first, when a PTA is reached between two nations which are not already significant trading partners and, secondly, between nations that have significant tariff barriers to trade. Thus, if two nations that have an insignificant trading relationship and high external barriers to trade agree to a PTA, trade diversion is likely to occur. Conversely, when a PTA is reached between 'natural trading partners', that is nations that already have a significant amount of bilateral trade flowing between two countries that have low barriers to trade, diversion is not thought to be a considerable problem.[14]

Another potential downfall of bilateral agreements is the complexity resulting from multiple PTAs. Each PTA contains different conditions and obligations which can sometimes lead to confusing or even conflicting obligations. The differing standards and rules

---

[12] For more on the trade creation and diversion effects see the seminal work of J Viner, *The Custom Union Issue* (London, Carnegie Endowment for International Peace, 1950).

[13] Lipsey and Lancaster developed a theory based on trade diversion called the General Theory of the Second Best: see R Lipsey and K Lancaster, 'The General Theory of the Second Best' (1956–57) 24 *Review of Economic Studies* 11.

[14] For more on when trade creation exceeds trade diversion see D Salvatore, *International Economics* (New York, Wiley, 1995). In reality, it is often hard to predict or even analyse such benefits/detriments due to the range of goods, services, investment and competition issues included in modern-day PTAs.

can create obstacles to trade facilitation by increasing administrative complexity at customs and creating a 'web' of differing rules. This is a major source of concern for the international trading community. One specific example of the complexities that are a by-product of PTAs is the proliferation of differing rules of origin—a prominent source of trade costs and complexity in today's global market place where companies depend on the rapid delivery of products and components from multiple overseas sources.[15]

Rules of origin are designed to prevent a product being exported from a non-member country to a member country before being re-exported to another member country, and thus gaining the reduced tariff rate. To guard against such abuse, PTAs contain some form of a 'rules of origin' requirement; this requires that a minimum level of value added must occur in a member country of the PTA before the preferential tariff or access is granted. The problem is that the standard differs between PTAs and the sometimes arbitrary definitions of which product comes from where and what constitutes local added value resulting in a multiplicity of tariffs depending on the source are extra business costs and detrimental to PTAs.[16] For example, take one specific product, a computer; if a country's import regime imposes different tariff rates for the same computer, depending on the country of origin (and how much value was added (some PTAs require 'substantial transformation') in each of the several countries the product passed through whilst being assembled), it is common for international traders to apply for a preferential rate, honestly believing that their product qualifies for the rate but only to find out later (as a result of a customs audit) that the product did not meet the complex rules of origin standard set in the bilateral PTA. This innocent mistake can and often does result in millions of dollars of back payments owed on top of the significant fines and penalties which the customs service also will impose. With the number of PTAs rapidly increasing, the already bad situation could worsen dramatically.[17]

In addition, overlapping jurisdiction of PTAs can cause further distortions and confusion. For instance, if Chile were to become a member of NAFTA and MERCOSUR, its producers may have to use inputs from a MERCOSUR member in order to satisfy one set of rules of origin requirements and from a NAFTA member to exploit the preferences of the NAFTA. Such rules are not congruent. Harmonisation of standards and rules, through cohesive negotiations or international intervention, and simplification of preferential rules could alleviate some of these obstacles, but the process of harmonising schemes is slow and certainly will not be completed in the next decade. Economist Jagdish Bhagwati refers to the differing standards in PTAs as a 'spaghetti bowl' and uses the complexity and dissimilarity of the various standards to argue against the further development of PTAs.[18]

Another shortfall of PTAs is that while some issues can easily be negotiated bilaterally—industrial tariffs, for example—many problems cannot be solved between two countries, particularly the 'hard core' issues that have survived more than 50 years

---

[15] For instance, the NAFTA contains over 200 pages dealing with rules of origin requirements.

[16] For more on the effects of rules of origin see A Krueger, 'Free Trade Agreements as Protectionist Devices: Rules of Origin', NBER Working Paper No 4352 (1993); A Krueger, 'Free Trade Agreements as Protectionist Devices: Rules of Origin' in JR Melvin, JC Moore and R Riezman (eds), *Trade, Theory, and Econometrics: Essays in Honor of John C Chipman* (London, Routledge, 1999).

[17] In addition, the rules relating to 'special and differential treatment' of products originating from certain developing and least-developing countries and the protective trading rules given to certain 'infant' industries are also difficult to define in a bilateral context.

[18] See J Bhagwati, *The Wind of the Hundred Days: How Washington Mismanaged Globalization* (Cambridge, MA, MIT Press, 2000); Bhagwati, above n 12.

of multilateral trade negotiations.[19] For instance, inefficient agricultural policies, discriminatory sanitary and phytosanitary measures, technical barriers to trade and biased trade remedy rules remain, despite pressure from almost all of the trading nations in the previous eight rounds of intense multilateral trade negotiations and transparent information flowing between all the parties. It may be unrealistic to expect that two nations of unequal economic levels will have the same bargaining knowledge and power on sensitive issues and therefore highly unlikely that a smaller trading nation can convince a larger nation to change its agricultural subsidies scheme or modify anti-dumping rules in a bilateral framework.

Along those same lines, cutting export subsidies preferentially for one's PTA partners, though technically possible, is politically unrealistic because such a move would turn the political logic of preferential trade deals on its head. Reducing tariffs for members of a PTA lowers the competitiveness of non-members, which continue to face tariffs when they sell into PTA markets. That provides a strong incentive to sign PTAs. But if PTA members cut their export subsidies, the competitiveness of non-members which maintain their subsidies instead increases in both PTA and non-PTA markets. Therefore, for both practical and political reasons, one cannot expect that a nation will agree to cut export subsidies in a bilateral framework.

It is clear that bilateralism cannot replace the multilateral trading system. In short, however, many nations deem it to be the best option to liberalise economies and drive the multilateral agenda. In addition, one must accept the reality that non-economic, political interests sometimes motivate the formation of PTAs. For instance, a PTA could be negotiated to bring peace, security and stability to a region (eg EEC and ASEAN), to enhance political and economic influence in the region or internationally (eg MERCOSUR), or for a host of broader foreign policy goals (eg US–Israel, US–Jordan, US–Gulf Cooperation Council (GCC)). A PTA may be negotiated for one or all of the above reasons. Therefore, while economic considerations are always taken into account, the actual motives behind a country entering into a PTA often encompass a wide range of considerations.

IV. GATT ARTICLE XXIV AND GATS ARTICLE V

Having reviewed the history and policy considerations related to PTAs, we now turn to the legal framework established in the WTO. Article XXIV of the GATT establishes the basis for allowing PTAs as an exception to the most favoured nation requirement. Similar provisions were developed for trade in services negotiated during the Uruguay Round, and are found in Article V of the GATS. We focus here on Article XXIV because of its longer history, but we do make occasional reference to the GATS provisions.

At the outset, Article XXIV:4 states:

---

[19] In this regard, FTAs have the ability to set 'bad precedent' as well as the 'good precedent' detailed earlier in the article. One example of 'bad precedent' is the exclusion of some key agricultural products from the Japan–Singapore FTA (which excludes cut flowers and ornamental fish, Singapore's key agricultural exports to Japan, from the FTA). Similarly, the exclusion of sugar in the AUSFTA re-enforces the idea that such carve outs can be part of full-scale FTAs.

> The Members recognize the desirability of increasing freedom of trade by the development, through voluntary agreements, of closer integration between the economies of the countries parties to such agreements. They also recognize that the purpose of a customs union or of a free-trade area should be to *facilitate trade* between the constituent territories and *not to raise barriers* to the trade of other contracting parties with such territories [emphasis added].

This provision refers to 'customs unions' and 'free-trade areas' as ways of achieving 'closer integration'. As mentioned above, we refer to these agreements generally as 'preferential trade agreements' or 'PTAs', but we distinguish between the two where relevant. In this regard, Article XXIV:4 explains that PTAs are 'desirable', but should 'facilitate' rather than raise new barriers. Article V of the GATS does not contain a similar statement regarding the 'desirability' of PTAs, but in paragraph 4 does refer to facilitating trade and not raising barriers. Article XXIV of the GATT also provides three basic rules that WTO members must comply with in order to establish a PTA covering trade in goods. The first is a procedural requirement to notify the WTO of the PTA (with a subsequent review by the relevant WTO committee).

The next rules are substantive in nature: (1) an obligation not to raise the overall level of protection and make access for products and services from Members not participating in the PTA more onerous (the external trade requirement); and (2) an obligation to liberalise substantially all trade among members of the PTA (the internal trade requirement). The reason behind these obligations is clear: the drafters wanted to ensure that each PTA, on the whole, facilitated, as opposed to hindered or burdened, trade and further wanted to ensure that PTAs could not be used merely to disguise preferential arrangements on a select range of goods or economic sectors. We discuss each of these three requirements in detail below.

As a final preliminary point, Article XXIV:5(c) allows for WTO members to enter into interim agreements to enter into a PTAs as long as the PTA is finalised 'within a reasonable period of time'. In such a circumstance, the interim agreement must include a plan or a schedule for the finalisation of the customs union or PTA. As part of the Uruguay Round, WTO members agreed to the Understanding on the Interpretation of Article XXIV of the GATT 1994, which, inter alia, provides that a 'reasonable period of time' shall be construed as not more than 10 years without a full explanation of why a longer period of time is provided for in the interim agreement. The GATS does not contain a similar provision.

(a) The Obligation to Notify to the CRTA

WTO members desiring to enter into a PTA covering trade in goods must notify the Council for Trade in Goods of their intention. As stated in the Understanding on the Interpretation of Article XXIV of the GATT 1994, the Council for Trade in Goods transfers the notification to the CRTA to examine the PTA for its compatibility with WTO rules.[20]

Established by the WTO General Council in 1996, the CRTA is the successor to

---

[20] In the context of PTAs covering trade in services, members of such an agreement must, according to Art V:7(a) of the GATS, 'promptly' notify the Council on Trade in Services of the PTA. The Council may then decide to form a working party or to refer the agreement to the CRTA for examination. The main difference between this and the requirement set out in the GATT is that examination is optional under the GATS where it is mandatory under the GATT. The working party on the NAFTA is, thus far, the only working party to 'examine' a PTA for consistency with the GATS: see 'Council for Trade in Services—North American Free

GATT Article XXIV working parties. Every member of the WTO can participate in the CRTA. Decisions in the Committee are made by consensus. Technically, the scope and mandate of the CRTA are broad and far-reaching. For instance, paragraphs 1(a) and 1(d) of the Decision Establishing the CRTA provide the Committee with authority to 'carry out the examination of [PTAs] . . . and thereafter present [a] report to the relevant body for appropriate action' and further direct the Committee to 'consider the systemic implications of such [PTAs] and regional initiatives for the multilateral trading system'. Furthermore, Article XXIV:7(a) of the GATT requires members to 'make available to them such information . . . as will enable [the working party] to such reports and recommendations to contracting parties as [the working party] deem appropriate'. The language of Article XXIV:7(b) relating to interim agreements is similar, and perhaps even stronger on this point, stating: '[t]he parties shall not maintain or put into force, as the case may be, such agreement if they are not prepared to modify it in accordance with these recommendations'.

These broad powers would seem to encompass the possibility that the CRTA could conclude in its report that the PTA at issue is not compatible with Article XXIV and recommend either its dismantling or alteration. Of course, such determinations would have to be made by consensus, and this requirement has thus far proven insurmountable. Prior to the implementation of the WTO, GATT Article XXIV working parties, for political and theoretical reasons, often disagreed on the compatibility of proposed PTAs and simply declined to make a formal decision. In fact, only one working party ever agreed by consensus on the consistency of a PTA with Article XXIV of GATT.[21] For the other 50-plus agreements, the working parties simply did not reach consensus and no further action was taken.

In that the CRTA, like its predecessor, must make decisions by consensus, the process has remained marginalised and has not effectively enforced the rules of the WTO.[22] For instance, while Article XXIV:7(a) of the GATT contemplates the notification of a PTA to occur prior to the completion of the agreement by requiring any contracting party 'deciding to enter' a PTA or interim agreement 'promptly [to] notify' the CONTRACTING PARTIES and 'make available to them such information . . . as will enable [the working party] to such reports and recommendations to contracting parties as they deem appropriate', the majority of PTAs have in fact been notified to the GATT/WTO after their successful completion. This is contrary to the language of Article XXIV:7(a) of the GATT.

It must be noted, however, that Article XXIV:7(a) of the GATT does not require working party/CRTA *approval* to form a PTA. Therefore, as long as the requirements of Article XXIV of the GATT are met, members are free to enter into PTAs. Nonetheless, what was originally intended to be an *ex ante* review has become an *ex post* review. It should be further noted that in mid-2006 Members agreed, under negotiations stemming from paragraph 29 of the Doha Ministerial Declaration and in accordance with the instructions contained in paragraph II.2 of Annex D to the Hong Kong Ministerial

Trade Agreement—Joint Communication from Canada, Mexico and the United States of America', WTO Doc S/C/N/4 (1 March 1995).

[21] See Working Party on the Customs Union between the Czech Republic and the Slovak Republic, WTO Doc L/7501 (15 July 1994).

[22] That said, the shift from ad hoc working to a standing CRTA may at some point in the future become significant, in that it may create coherent and consistent decisions.

Declaration, to early notification procedures.[23] However, despite Director-General Lamy stating, '[t]his decision will help break the current logjam in the WTO on regional trade agreements [and][t]his is an important step towards ensuring that regional trade agreements become building blocks, not stumbling blocks to world trade', the procedures do not provide consequences or penalties for the failure to abide by the new procedures.[24]

Two questions remain: (1) what is the proper remedy if/when the CRTA finds that a PTA does not meet the requirements as set out in Article XXIV of the GATT?; (2) do dispute settlement panels also have the jurisdiction to assess the overall WTO compatibility of a customs union?

The first question is, of course, purely theoretical. Consensus decision-making in the CRTA requires the members, including all parties to the PTA at issue, to vote against its compatibility in order for the CRTA to find that the PTA is incompatible with the GATT. One cannot easily imagine that such a situation could ever occur.[25] Where consensus cannot be reached, Rule 33 of the Rules and Procedures for Meetings of the CRTA provides that 'the matter at issue shall be referred, as appropriate, to the General Council, the Council for the Trade in Goods, the Council for the Trade in Services or the Committee on Trade and Development'. In practice, the matter is no longer discussed, and the PTA at issue becomes/remains operational.

With regard to the second question, the panel in *Turkey—Textiles* touched upon the institutional balance and roles of the CRTA and dispute settlement panels but ultimately avoided the issue by relying upon the principle of judicial economy:

Panel Report, *Turkey—Restrictions on Imports of Textile and Clothing Products*, Adopted 19 November 1999, WT/DS34/R

9.52 As to the . . . question of how far-reaching a panel's examination should be of the regional trade agreement underlying the challenged measure, we note that the Committee on Regional Trade Agreements (CRTA) has been established, *inter alia*, to assess the GATT/ WTO compatibility of regional trade agreements entered into by Members, a very complex undertaking which involves consideration by the CRTA, from the economic, legal and political perspectives of different Members, of the numerous facets of a regional trade agreement in relation to the provisions of the WTO. It appears to us that the issue regarding the GATT/WTO compatibility of a customs union, as such, is generally a matter for the CRTA since, as noted above, it involves a broad multilateral assessment of any such custom union, i.e. a matter which concerns the WTO membership as a whole.

9.53 As to whether panels also have the jurisdiction to assess the overall WTO compatibility of a customs union, we recall that the Appellate Body stated that the terms of reference of panels must refer explicitly to the "measures" to be examined by panels. We consider that regional trade agreements may contain numerous measures, all of which could potentially be examined by panels, before, during or after the CRTA examination, if the requirements laid down in the DSU are met. However, it is arguable that a customs union (or a free-trade area) as a whole would logically not be a "measure" as such, subject to challenge under the DSU.

---

[23] See 'Negotiating Group on Rules—Negotiating Group on Rules—Report by the Chairman to the Trade Negotiations Committee', WTO Doc No TN/RL/18 (13 July 2006).

[24] WTO, 'Lamy Welcomes WTO Agreement on Regional Trade Agreements', Press Release, 10 July 2006, available at www.wto.org/english/news_e/news06_e/rta_july06_e.htm.

[25] However, due to Art IX of the WTO Agreement, the possibility does exist for members, in the absence of consensus, to vote on an issue. This has never occurred and it is rarely, if ever, going to be a feasible option due to political considerations.

9.54 We consider that the question of whether panels have the jurisdiction to assess the overall compatibility of a customs union is not in any event an issue on which it is necessary for us to reach a decision in this case; we reach this conclusion in light of paragraphs 9.51 to 9.53 above and in recognition of the principle of judicial economy, as initially developed in the *US—Wool Shirts* case and qualified by the Appellate Body in the recent *Australia—Salmon* case, under which panels do not need to address all the claims and arguments raised by the parties to the dispute. We recall the distinction between claims and arguments (*EC—Hormones*) and understand that some latitude is left to panels to address only arguments that they consider are relevant to resolve the dispute between the parties, which is the main purpose of DSU proceedings. Accordingly, we find that, in order to address the claims of India, it will not be necessary for us to assess the compatibility of the Turkey–EC customs union agreement with Article XXIV as such (in the sense of addressing all aspects of the customs union and all the measures adopted by Turkey and the European Communities in the context of their customs union agreement).

9.55 In our view, it will be sufficient for us to address the relationship between the provisions of Article XXIV and those of Articles XI and XIII of GATT and Article 2.4 of the ATC. We shall have to do so as India's claims are based on an alleged violation of those articles, and Turkey's defense is based on the application, and, in its view, the "primacy", of Article XXIV over those provisions. Our examination will be limited to the question whether in this case, on the occasion of the formation of the Turkey–EC customs union, Turkey is permitted to introduce WTO incompatible quantitative restrictions against imports from a third country, assuming *arguendo* that the customs union in question is otherwise compatible with Article XXIV of GATT. We shall thus limit ourselves to addressing the parties' arguments submitted in this context only and refrain from any discussion as to how an overall compatibility assessment of a customs union should be performed. Our analysis of Article XXIV is limited to defining, in particular, its relationship with Articles XI and XIII of GATT (and Article 2.4 of the ATC) and to ensuring that our interpretation of the WTO provisions applicable to the present dispute, does not prevent Turkey from exercising its right to form a customs union.

… … …

On appeal, however, the Appellate Body seemed to indicate that not only are panels permitted to make such determinations, they are, in fact, *required* to do so in cases where customs unions and FTAs are offered as a defence for a measure:

Appellate Body Report, *Turkey—Restrictions on Imports of Textile and Clothing Products*, Adopted 19 November 1999, WT/DS34/AB/R

58. Accordingly, on the basis of this analysis of the text and the context of the chapeau of paragraph 5 of Article XXIV, we are of the view that Article XXIV may justify a measure which is inconsistent with certain other GATT provisions. However, in a case involving the formation of a customs union, this "defence" is available only when two conditions are fulfilled. First, the party claiming the benefit of this defence must demonstrate that the measure at issue is introduced upon the formation of a customs union that fully meets the requirements of sub-paragraphs 8(a) and 5(a) of Article XXIV. And, second, that party must demonstrate that the formation of that customs union would be prevented if it were not allowed to introduce the measure at issue. Again, *both* these conditions must be met to have the benefit of the defence under Article XXIV.

59. We would expect a panel, when examining such a measure, to require a party to establish that both of these conditions have been fulfilled. It may not always be possible to determine whether the second of the two conditions has been fulfilled without initially determining whether

the first condition has been fulfilled. In other words, it may not always be possible to determine whether not applying a measure would prevent the formation of a customs union without first determining whether there *is* a customs union. In this case, the Panel simply assumed, for the sake of argument, that the first of these two conditions was met and focused its attention on the second condition.

60. More specifically, with respect to the first condition, the Panel, in this case, did not address the question of whether the regional trade arrangement between Turkey and the European Communities is, in fact, a "customs union" which meets the requirements of paragraphs 8(a) and 5(a) of Article XXIV. The Panel maintained that "it is arguable" that panels do not have jurisdiction to assess the overall compatibility of a customs union with the requirements of Article XXIV. We are not called upon in this appeal to address this issue, but we note in this respect our ruling in *India—Quantitative Restrictions on Imports of Agricultural, Textile and Industrial Products* on the jurisdiction of panels to review the justification of balance-of-payments restrictions under Article XVIII:B of the GATT 1994. The Panel also considered that, on the basis of the principle of judicial economy, it was not necessary to assess the compatibility of the regional trade arrangement between Turkey and the European Communities with Article XXIV in order to address the claims of India. Based on this reasoning, the Panel assumed *arguendo* that the arrangement between Turkey and the European Communities is compatible with the requirements of Article XXIV:8(a) and 5(a) and limited its examination to the question of whether Turkey was permitted to introduce the quantitative restrictions at issue. The assumption by the Panel that the agreement between Turkey and the European Communities is a "customs union" within the meaning of Article XXIV was not appealed. Therefore, the issue of whether this arrangement meets the requirements of paragraphs 8(a) and 5(a) of Article XXIV is not before us.[26]

… … …

The Appellate Body's reference to the *India—QRs* case is important here. In that case, the Appellate Body concluded: '[f]or the reasons set out above, we conclude that panels have the competence to review the justification of balance-of-payments restrictions. More generally, we conclude that the dispute settlement provisions of the GATT 1994, as elaborated and applied by the DSU, can be invoked with respect to any matters relating to balance-of-payments restrictions.'[27] Thus, applying this conclusion here, panels arguably would have the jurisdiction to assess the overall compatibility of PTAs with the requirements of Article XXIV.

(b) External Trade Requirement

The external trade requirement differs under Article XXIV:5 of the GATT depending upon whether the PTA at issue is a customs union or a free-trade area.

(i) Free-trade Areas

With regard to free-trade areas, Article XXIV:5(b) requires that 'duties and other regulations of commerce . . . applicable at the formation of such free-trade area or the adoption

---

[26] For a critique of this finding see F Roessler, 'The Institutional Balance Between the Judicial and the Political Organs of the WTO' in M Bronckers and R Quick (eds), *New Directions in International Economic Law: Essays in Honour of John H Jackson* (The Hague, Kluwer Law International, 2000) 325–45.

[27] Appellate Body Report, *India—QRs*, para 109.

of such interim agreement to the trade of contracting parties not included in such area or not parties to such agreement shall not be higher or more restrictive than the corresponding duties and other regulations of commerce existing in the same constituent territories prior to the formation of the free-trade area'. In other words, when entering into an PFTA, members of the FTA may not alter their external protection in such a manner as negatively to affect non-FTA members. The reason behind this prohibition is simple: FTAs are aimed at trade liberalisation. Thus, the goals are to remove trade barriers among FTA participants rather than increase barriers with nations not included in the particular FTA at issue.

This is not to say that liberalising internal trade does not affect nations not included in the particular FTA at issue. As described earlier in this chapter, FTAs can and do shift production sources and often result in trade diversion from an efficient producer in an external country to a less efficient producer located internally.

In addition, as mentioned above, FTAs often include a complex set of 'rules of origin' which can significantly affect external protection. Rules of origin requirements are a necessary part of FTAs, as they regulate which goods circulating in an FTA are eligible to receive preferential treatment. In short, the goal is to provide preferential treatment only to goods actually coming from the FTA member nation while excluding other nations from the preferences. While FTAs differ widely in substance, all provide the same basic guidelines. For instance, if a car is made in Japan and exported to Mexico for on-shipment to the United States, the car enters the United States under the normal, MFN tariff rate. On the other hand, if a Japanese company builds a plant in Mexico to assemble the car and then export it to the United States, the car would qualify under NAFTA for a 'certificate of origin' and enter the United States duty-free. Such a situation not only encourages companies to shift production to FTA member countries (and possibly encourages trade diversion), but it also encourages non-FTA members to sign similar agreements or face discrimination in trading terms. This 'choice' has, in large part, encouraged the current FTA explosion.

(ii) Customs Unions

The external trade requirement is a bit more complicated in the case of customs unions. Customs unions have two obligations. First, they have an obligation not to raise the overall level of external protection above a certain threshold. Secondly, they have a specific obligation to compensate external members in cases where the customs duties in some members of the customs union have been raised to match the level deemed appropriate by the customs union.[28]

a. Obligation not to Raise the Overall Level of External Protection Like free-trade areas, customs unions seek further to liberalise trade among the members. However, customs unions go beyond FTAs in that they also require common external protection. In other words, members forming a customs union must adjust their external protection (eg tariffs) so that all members provide the same level of protection. As nations historically provide

---

[28] The GATS does not mention or encompass external protection, but provides that compensation (in a manner such as that set out in Art XXIV:6 of GATT) is to be offered if a WTO Member entering into a PTA modifies its Schedule. See Art V:(5) of the GATS (stating that the relevant modification of Schedule provisions of Art XXI of the GATS applies).

differing levels of protection in various industries due to a variety of factors including, but not limited to, economic rationale, political considerations, level of development, etc, the likelihood that all members forming a customs union will have the exact level of protection is very small.

In adjusting external protection levels when forming a customs union, members of the customs union must be mindful of their Article XXIV:5(a) obligations. Article XXIV:5(a) states:

> [W]ith respect to a customs union, or an interim agreement leading to a formation of a customs union, the duties and other regulations of commerce imposed at the institution of any such union or interim agreement in respect of trade with contracting parties not parties to such union or agreement shall not on the whole be higher or more restrictive than the general incidence of the duties and regulations of commerce applicable in the constituent territories prior to the formation of such union or the adoption of such interim agreement, as the case may be.

The use of the phrases 'on the whole' and 'general incidence' suggests that Article XXIV:5(a) does not require an item-by-item comparison of protection before and subsequent to the formation of the customs union. Instead, a general comparison of overall external protection before and subsequent to the formation of the customs union appears sufficient. This view seems to have had some support in the GATT years, as evidenced by the working party on 'Accession of Greece to the European Communities', which stated that 'Article XXIV required only generalised, overall judgment on this point'. However, the report failed to gain consensus.[29] Other working party reports varied on their interpretation of this statement.[30] As a result, the working parties could not form a clear consensus view on the issue. It must be noted, however, that the drafters intended for this requirement to be interpreted in a broad and generalised manner. The preparatory materials state:

> [T]he phrase 'on the whole' . . . did not mean that an average tariff should be laid down in respect of each individual product, but merely that the whole level of tariffs of a customs union should not be higher than the average level of the former constituent territories.[31]

The WTO Understanding on the Interpretation of Article XXIV of the GATT 1994 should end any lingering debate on the issue. The Interpretation makes clear that the comparison is to a tariff-line basis and is worth quoting at length:

> 2. The evaluation under paragraph 5(a) of Article XXIV of the general incidence of the duties and other regulations of commerce applicable before and after the formation of a customs union shall in respect of duties and charges be based upon an overall assessment of *weighted average tariff rates* and of customs duties collected. This assessment shall be based on import statistics for a previous representative period to be supplied by the customs union, on a *tariff-line basis* and in values and quantities, broken down by WTO country of origin. The Secretariat shall compute the weighted average tariff rates and customs duties collected in accordance with the methodology used in the assessment of tariff offers in the Uruguay Round of Multilateral Trade Negotiations. For this purpose, the duties and charges to be taken into consideration shall be the *applied rates* of duty. It is recognized that for the purpose of the overall assessment of

---

[29] See Accession of Greece to the European Communities, 9 March 1983, GATT BISD (30th Supp, 1984) 168, para 42, and 184.
[30] See, eg Accession of Portugal and Spain to the European Communities, 19–20 October 1988, GATT BISD (35th Supp, 1989) 293, para 6, 295–6 and para 36, 311.
[31] WTO, *GATT Analytical Index* (Lanham, MD, Bernan Press, 1995) 803 (reprinting EPCT/C.II/38 at 9).

the incidence of other regulations of commerce for which quantification and aggregation are difficult, the examination of individual measures, regulations, products covered and trade flows affected may be required [emphasis added]

b. Obligation to Make a Compensatory Adjustment

Under Article XXIV:6 of the GATT, customs unions have a specific obligation to compensate external members in cases where the customs duties in some members of the customs union have been raised to match the level deemed appropriate by the customs union. Specifically, Article XXIV:6 provides:

> If, in fulfilling the requirements of subparagraph 5 (*a*), a Member proposes to increase any rate of duty inconsistently with the provisions of Article II, the procedure set forth in Article XXVIII shall apply. In providing for compensatory adjustment, due account shall be taken of the compensation already afforded by the reduction brought about in the corresponding duty of the other constituents of the union.

When assessing whether compensation must be offered, one looks to the bound, as opposed to actual applied, tariff rate.[32]

Suppose that Antigua, New Zealand and Canada wish to enter into a customs union and that, before its formation, the external protection in the form of bound rates of gardening equipment differed in each nation. For illustrative purposes, suppose that Antigua had a bound rate of 20 per cent, New Zealand a bound rate of 10 per cent and Canada a bound rate of 0 per cent (duty free). By agreeing to bind the tariff rate at 10 per cent the parties, while arguably meeting their obligation under Article XXIV:5, have failed to meet their obligation with respect to Article XXIV:6 for the following reasons.

First, it is important to understand why scrutiny under Article XXIV:6 is necessary; simply stated, Article XXIV:6 must be met because Canada must raise its bound rate from 0 per cent (duty free) to 10 per cent. In such a circumstance, Article XXIV:6 invokes the procedures set out in Article XXVIII, namely, that WTO members having 'initial negotiating rights', 'principal supplying interests' or a 'substantial interest' in the matter may enter into negotiations with the members of the customs union aimed at compensating those WTO members that, by virtue of the customs union, will be disadvantaged as a result of Canada's participation in the customs union.

In the above circumstance, at least one member of the customs union will have to raise its bound tariff rate on a particular item (in this case, gardening equipment), but this does not necessarily mean that compensation will always be warranted. The second sentence of Article XXIV:6 explicitly states that 'due account shall be taken of compensation already afforded' by the reduction of bound tariff rates by another/other member(s) of the customs union (of which the tariff reductions are necessary in order to comply with Article XXIV:5(a)). Thus, the disadvantages brought about by the formation of the customs union may in fact be offset by the advantages gained through the increased market opportunities brought about by the reduction of protection of another member or members in the customs union.

In order to ascertain whether compensation is necessary and warranted, one must look at the actual economic data of the members of the customs union. In the scenario detailed above, Canada, as a nation, has a high per capita income, whereas Antigua is a smaller nation with a lower per capita income. Assume that neither country produces gardening

---

[32] Although it must be noted that this issue caused some acrimony for GATT working parties and a clear consensus never emerged.

equipment or that the domestic production in each nation allows for substantial importation of gardening equipment. In this case, the amount of trade lost with Canada raising its duties is in all likelihood not compensated for by the fact that Antigua lowered its bound rate. Therefore, in accordance with the second sentence of Article XXIV:6, compensation will be offered to WTO members in an Article XXVIII-like procedure whereby WTO members having 'initial negotiating rights', 'principal supplying interests' or a 'substantial interest' in the matter may enter negotiations with the members of the customs union aimed at compensating those WTO members that, by virtue of the customs union, will be disadvantaged as a result of Canada's participation in the customs union.[33] On the other hand, suppose that it is Canada, not Antigua, which has bound its pre-customs union tariff rate on gardening equipment to 20 per cent and that Antigua, not Canada, has a pre-customs union bound rate on gardening equipment of 0 per cent (duty free). In such a scenario, Canada's lowering of its bound rate from 20 to 10 per cent will, in all likelihood, over-compensate for the fact that Antigua is raising its rate from 0 per cent (duty free) to 10 per cent. This is an example of taking into account 'already afforded' compensation; in other words, compensation is already built into the agreement.

(c) Internal Trade Requirement

The most controversial provisions of Article XXIV relating to PTAs are unquestionably the internal trade requirements. For customs unions and free-trade areas, paragraphs 8(a)(i) and 8(b), respectively, provide for the elimination of 'duties and other restrictive regulations of commerce (except, where necessary, those permitted under Articles XI, XII, XIII, XIV, XV and XX)' with respect to 'substantially all the trade' between members of a PTA.

Throughout the years, working parties have repeatedly failed to accomplish their task due to the fact that members could not agree on the meaning of 'substantially all trade' or of 'other restrictive regulations of commerce'. Even now, in the context of a rapid increase in PTAs and renewed interest in the issue, scholars and commentators alike cannot agree on the proper interpretation of the terms. While it might be expected that the working parties would not resolve the interpretive difficulties, one would expect that the nearly 50 years of GATT would have seen at least one dispute settlement proceeding raise the issue. Such an assumption is incorrect. Thus, despite the fact that 62 PTAs were concluded during the GATT years, no dispute settlement panel interpreted the phrase or shed any light on its proper interpretation.

If we were going to attempt to decipher the meaning of this term we would, in accordance with Article 3.2 of the DSU and the Vienna Convention, first examine its ordinary meaning. Unfortunately, this examination does not provide much guidance. While the use of the word 'substantial' indicates that not all trade between members of a PTA necessarily has to be included in the PTA in order for it to be compatible with Article XXIV:8, it does not answer the question of how much trade must be included to meet the

---

[33] The EC recently made such compensatory adjustments following the enlargement of the EU in 2004. The compensatory package included a reduction in certain tariffs, country-specific tariff rate quotas for certain US exports and expanded global tariff rate quotas for several agricultural products. See USTR, 'United States and European Communities Reach Agreement on Enlargement: Compensation Package', Press Release, 30 November 2005, available at www.ustr.gov/Document_Library/Press_Releases/2005/ November/United_States_European_Communities_Reach_Agreement_on_Enlargement_Compensation_Package.html.

Article XXIV:8 obligation. The use of the term 'substantial', however, does imply that there are both quantitative and qualitative aspects to the term. In addition, it appears that a comparison between 'substantially all the trade' and 'all trade' must be made in order to ascertain the compatibility of the PTA with Article XXIV:8.

Next, we would look to the context of Article XXIV:8, the object and purpose of the GATT and subsequent decisions on the issue. Unfortunately, recourse to the above proves unhelpful, as does recourse to the preparatory work. However, as GATT working parties were formed and acted under the authority of the CONTRACTING PARTIES and Article XXIV, they constitute subsequent practice and can be studied for an answer to this problem. Unfortunately, the working party reports also provide little useful guidance on the interpretation of 'substantially all trade'. For instance, one report stated 'there is no exact definition' for the phrase,[34] while another wrote that 'it would be inappropriate to fix a general figure of the percentage of trade which would be subjected to internal barriers'.[35]

In 1957, the EC proposed that substantially all trade should be achieved when 'the volume of liberalised trade reached 80 percent of total trade'.[36] The working party did not accept the recommendation. Another working party held the view that, even if the volume of liberalised trade reached 90 per cent of total trade, it could not be 'considered to be the only factor to be taken into account'.[37] Yet other working parties were of the view that a PTA could never meet the 'substantially all trade' obligation if it excluded a whole sector from its terms.[38]

A panel and the Appellate Body have also recently weighed in on the issue, without fully resolving the uncertainty. Mitchell and Lockhart summarise these positions as follows:

> In *Turkey—Textiles*, the Appellate Body noted that 'substantially all the trade' is not the same as all the trade, but that it 'is something considerably more than merely *some* of the trade'. Therefore, the relevant amount of trade falls somewhere between some and all trade among the PTA parties. Beyond this, the disputes provide little guidance. In order to prove that NAFTA complied with Article XXIV:8(b) in *US—Line Pipe*, the United States submitted evidence that NAFTA eliminated 'duties on 97 percent of the Parties' tariff lines, representing more than 99 percent of the trade among them in terms of volume'. After reviewing the evidence, and without offering any views on the meaning of 'substantially all the trade', the panel held that the United States had established a prima facie case that NAFTA met the definition of an FTA under Article XXIV:8(b). The Appellate Body took the view that it need not address this finding and declared it to be of no legal effect.[39]

---

[34] European Communities—Agreements with Portugal, 19 October 1973, GATT BISD (20th Supp, 1974) 171.

[35] See the Working Party report on EEC, GATT Doc BISD 6S/100, para 34. In addition, the question whether 'substantially all the trade' should refer to past trade between the parties or trade that would occur but for the barriers was debated and differing opinions emerged in some working parties.

[36] See The European Economic Community, 29 November 1957, GATT BISD (6th Supp) at 70, sect D, para 34. The EC now suggests that 'substantially all the trade' should have both a quantitative and qualitative dimension so that an FTA must cover at least 90% of goods and exclude no major sector. See TN/RL/190.

[37] See European Free Trade Association, 4 June 1960, GATT BISD (9th Supp, 1961) 70, para 48.

[38] See, eg Working Party on the Free Trade Agreement between Canada and the United States, 12 November 1991, GATT BISD (38th Supp) 47, para 83.

[39] A Mitchell and N Lockhart, 'Legal Requirements for PTAs Under the WTO' in S Lester and B Mercurio (eds), *Bilateral and Regional Trade Agreements: Commentary, Analysis and Case Studies* (Cambridge, Cambridge University Press, 2009) 96.

Thus, some level of uncertainty still exists as to what constitutes 'substantially all the trade'. Australia has recently submitted that 'substantially all the trade' contains only a quantitative component, recommended that future negotiations attempt to fix the numeric equivalent to the obligation and proposed that 95 per cent of all six-line tariff lines listed in the Harmonised System satisfy 'substantially all trade'.[40] Australia also recognised the arbitrariness of its numeric value and of the potential pitfalls to such a system; however, it re-stated that its aim was to further negotiations leading to an end to the discussion and debate on the topic. Two recent Australian submissions which have attracted much attention and debate are attached to Part VI of this chapter.

In addition to the elimination of internal duties in relation to PTAs, Article XXIV:8 also applies to the elimination of 'other restrictive regulations of commerce (except, where necessary, those permitted under Articles XI, XII, XIII, XIV, XV and XX)' on substantially all the trade between the customs union or FTA members. Unfortunately, Article XXIV provides no further guidance on the proper interpretation of the phrase 'other restrictive regulations of commerce'. On its face, the provision would seem to forbid all regulation which restricts commerce not mentioned in the parenthesised portion of the provision following the formation of a customs union or FTA. Therefore, it would appear that only necessary restrictive regulations relating to Articles XI, XII, XIII, XIV, XV and XX are allowed.

Such an interpretation which would prohibit any restrictive regulations except those of Articles XI, XII, XIII, XIV, XV and XX, and thus view the list in Article XXIV:8 as exhaustive, would mean that the common restrictive regulation contained in Article VI (anti-dumping) is incompatible with the formation of any PTA. Despite the wording of the text, this interpretation cannot be correct. If such an interpretation is correct, this would mean that anti-dumping actions cannot be maintained between members of a WTO-compatible PTA.[41] This further means that only a few of the almost 200 PTAs in operation comply with the obligation (the EC and the Australia– New Zealand CER being longstanding exceptions, and the China–Hong Kong and China–Macao agreements being more recent exceptions to the rule). Every other PTA would breach Article XXIV as they all allow members to retain the right to initiate investigations and levy anti-dumping duties against other members.

Article VI is not the only restrictive regulation which poses interpretive problems for the narrow view of Article XXIV:8. On its face, other regulations, such as those adopted under Article XVIII (governmental assistance to economic development), Article XIX (safeguards) and Article XXI (security exceptions), would also be prohibited under a narrow interpretation of Article XXIV. It is hard to imagine that the exclusion of the

---

[40] See Submission on Regional Trade Agreements by Australia, WTO Doc No TN/RL/W/15 (9 July 2002). Australia has also proposed tightening the rules of FTAs: see Communication from Australia, Negotiations on Regional Trade Agreements: Key Issues for Consideration, WTO Doc No TN/RL/W/2 (24 April 2002).

[41] Interpretation of this provision is, in fact, the subject of long-standing debate, and several high profile trade scholars have written their theses on issues directly related to the point. For instance, while some believe that the exceptions do not apply to Art XXI, others disagree; while some believe the intended exceptions are limited to protective measures, others go beyond that interpretation. Finally, yet others argue that the fact that so many PTAs have been negotiated with other restrictive regulations of commerce beyond those listed is sufficient to constitute 'subsequent practice'. For more on this issue see J Trachtman, 'Toward Open Recognition? Standardization and Regional Integration under Article XXIV of GATT' (2003) 6 *Journal of International Economic Law* 459; JH Mathis, 'Regional Trade Agreements and Domestic Regulation: What Reach for "Other Restrictive Regulations of Commerce"?' in L Bartels and F Ortino (eds), *Regional Trade Agreements and the WTO Legal System* (Oxford, Oxford University Press, 2006) 79.

above Articles was intended. Therefore, it is clear that the exceptions listed in Article XXIV:8 do not form an exhaustive list. This view is confirmed in working party reports where, speaking on the issue of Article XXI, the EEC stated that 'it would be difficult . . . to dispute the right of contracting parties to avail themselves of [Article XXI] which related, among other things, to traffic in arms, fissionable materials, etc., and it must therefore be concluded that the list was not exhaustive'.[42] On the issue of Article XIX (safeguards), like Article VI (anti-dumping) and unlike Article XXI (security exceptions), a reasonable argument could be made out as to why they should not be allowed in a PTA. However, the Appellate Body has on three separate occasions implicitly determined that a member of a PTA may impose safeguards against other members of the PTA.[43] This line of jurisprudence adds further proof to the assertion that the list of exceptions in Article XXIX:8 is not exhaustive.

V. PTAS AND DISPUTE SETTLEMENT IN THE WTO

The Understanding on the Interpretation of Article XXIV of the GATT 1994 provides WTO panels and the Appellate Body with a wide scope to review any matter arising from a PTA notified under Article XXIV. The Understanding reads, in relevant part:

> The provisions of Articles XXII and XXIII of GATT 1994 as elaborated and applied by the Dispute Settlement Understanding may be invoked with respect to any matters arising from the application of those provisions of Article XXIV relating to customs unions, free-trade areas or interim agreements leading to the formation of a customs union or free-trade area.

PTAs had been the subject of GATT dispute settlement previously, but this statement explicitly grants to the DSB the right to review claims regarding PTAs.

While there has been a flood of activity in establishing PTAs since 1995, there has yet to be a dispute in which a claimant has attempted to use GATT Article XXIV or Article V of the GATS to invalidate a PTA as a whole as inconsistent with the PTA rules. Nonetheless, issues relating to PTAs have arisen in several disputes where it was claimed that challenged measures were justified on the basis of a Member's relationship to a PTA. We provide some brief descriptions here of several of these disputes.[44]

(a) *Turkey—Textiles*

In *Turkey—Textiles*, India argued that Turkey's introduction of quantitative restrictions on 19 of its textile and clothing products was not 'necessary' to comply with the terms of the Turkey–EC Association Council adopted Decision 1/952 (1995), which sets out the rules for implementing the final phase of the customs union between Turkey and the European Communities and includes a provision that Turkey apply 'substantially the

[42] European Economic Community, 29 November 1957, GATT BISD (6th Supp) 70, s D, para 26.

[43] In the context of a customs union see Appellate Body Report, *Argentina—Footwear Safeguards*, paras 107–08; in regard to an FTA see Appellate Body Report, *US—Wheat Gluten Safeguards*, paras 98–100; Appellate Body Report, *US—Line Pipe Safeguards*, paras 181–94.

[44] The issue of PTAs was raised in *Canada—Autos* in the context of Art V of the GATS: see Panel Report, *Canada—Autos*, paras 10.265–10.272.

same commercial policy as the [European] Community in the textile sector including the agreements or arrangements on trade in textile and clothing'.[45] Turkey countered by arguing that because its quotas on textiles and clothing were taken pursuant to a customs union, the measures were justified under GATT Article XXIV. More specifically, Turkey argued that Article XXIV:5(a) should be read as permitting the introduction of new trade restrictions, provided that the overall incidence of duties and other regulations of commerce is not higher or more restrictive after the completion of the customs union than before. In essence, the EC had its own set of quotas on the products at issue, and Turkey's actions were designed to limit imports into Turkey so as to maintain the effectiveness of the EC quotas, which otherwise could have been undermined once Turkey and the EC formed a customs union.

Noting that, under the WTO's rules on burden of proof, it is for the party invoking an exception or an affirmative defence to prove that the conditions contained therein are met[46] and analysing the text and context of Article XXIV:5, the Appellate Body stated that Article XXIV may justify a measure that is inconsistent with certain other GATT provisions when two conditions are fulfilled:

> First, the party claiming the benefit of this defence must demonstrate that the measure at issue is introduced upon the formation of a customs union that fully meets the requirements of sub-paragraphs 8(a) and 5(a) of Article XXIV. And, second, that party must demonstrate that the formation of that customs union would be prevented if it were not allowed to introduce the measure at issue.[47]

Thus, in the context of customs unions, in order to meet the burden of establishing an affirmative defence to an inconsistency with the GATT, the invoking party must prove (1) the existence of a customs union; and (2) that the formation of that customs union would be prevented if it were not allowed to introduce the measure at issue. We examine each issue in turn.

(i) The Existence of a Customs Union

In demonstrating that a customs union exists, the party must satisfy both the internal and external trade requirements under Article XXIV:8. As to the internal trade requirement, Article XXIV:8(a)(i) requires that the constituent members of a customs union eliminate 'duties and other restrictive regulations of commerce' with respect to 'substantially all the trade' between the members. While noting that neither the CONTRACTING PARTIES nor the WTO Members have agreed on a standard, the Appellate Body has stated that the sub-paragraph allows for 'some flexibility' and that 'it is clear, though, that "substantially all the trade" is not the same as *all* the trade'.[48] It has also noted that 'substantially

---

[45] Appellate Body Report, *Turkey—Textiles*, para 2.

[46] Appellate Body Report, *Turkey—Textiles*, para 45; Panel Report, *Turkey—Textiles*, paras 9.57–9.59. The Appellate Body also noted that legal scholars have long considered Art XXIV to be an 'exception' or possible 'defence' to claims of a violation of GATT provisions. The Appellate Body did not specifically say that the burden was on Turkey, but it did say that 'Turkey ha[d] not demonstrated' that the measures were necessary.

[47] Appellate Body Report, *Turkey—Textiles*, para 58. The Appellate Body noted that according to para 4, the purpose of a customs union is 'to facilitate trade' between the constituent members and 'not to raise barriers to the trade' with third countries. In this regard, the Appellate Body concluded that para 4 informs the whole of para 5 (including the chapeau) by setting out the overriding and pervasive purpose for Art XXIV which is manifested in operative language in the specific obligations that are found elsewhere in Art XXIV.

[48] *Ibid*, para 48.

all the trade' is 'considerably more than merely *some* of the trade' before cautioning that 'the degree of 'flexibility' that sub-paragraph 8(a)(i) allows is limited by the requirement that 'duties and other restrictive regulations of commerce' be 'eliminated with respect to substantially all internal trade'.[49]

As to the external requirement, sub-paragraph 8(a)(ii) establishes the standard for the trade of constituent members with third countries (ie countries not party to the customs union) needed to satisfy the definition of a 'customs union'. The sub-paragraph requires the constituent members to apply 'substantially the same' duties and other regulations of commerce to external trade with third countries. In other words, the constituent members are required to apply a common external trade regime, relating to both duties and other regulations of commerce. However, the Appellate Body has noted that sub-paragraph 8(a)(ii) 'does *not* require each constituent member of a customs union to apply *the same* duties and other regulations of commerce as other constituent members with respect to trade with third countries; instead, it requires that *substantially the same* duties and other regulations of commerce shall be applied'.[50] In so holding, the Appellate Body agreed with the Panel that 'substantially' (in the context of subparagraph 8(a)) provides for both qualitative and quantitative components.

The Appellate Body agreed with the panel that the phrase 'substantially the same' offers a certain degree of 'flexibility' to the constituent members of a customs union and that exact sameness is not required. But again, the Appellate Body cautioned that the 'flexibility' is limited and that 'the word "substantially" qualifies the words "the same" . . . something closely approximating "sameness" is required by Article XXIV:8(a)(ii)'.[51] The Appellate Body started its analysis of the issue by looking at the chapeau to Article XXIV:5, which states that the provisions of the GATT shall not prevent the formation of a customs union '*provided that*', and it found that the phrase '*provided that*' is an 'essential element' of the chapeau.

The Appellate Body then went to the relevant proviso set out immediately following the chapeau (Article XXIV:5(a) for customs unions), which reads in relevant part:

> with respect to a customs union . . ., the duties and other regulations of commerce imposed at the institution of any such union . . . in respect of trade with contracting parties not parties to such union . . . shall not on the whole be higher or more restrictive than the general incidence of the duties and regulations of commerce applicable in the constituent territories prior to the formation of such union . . .;

> Therefore, in deciding the issue, one must look at whether the 'duties and other regulations of commerce' are 'not on the whole . . . higher or more restrictive than the general incidence of the duties and regulations of commerce applicable in the constituent territories prior to [its] formation'. In respect of 'duties', the Appellate Body relied on paragraph 2 of the Understanding on Article XXIV (the 'Understanding'), which requires that the evaluation under Article XXIV:5(a) of the *general incidence of the duties* applied before and after the formation

---

[49] *Ibid.*

[50] Appellate Body Report, *Turkey—Textiles*, para 49.

[51] *Ibid*, para 50. The Appellate Body disagreed with the panel that 'as a general rule, a situation where constituent members have "comparable" trade regulations having similar effects with respect to the trade with third countries, would generally meet the qualitative dimension of the requirements of sub-paragraph 8(a)(ii)'. A 'comparable trade regulations having similar effects' does not meet the standards set out in Sub-paragraph 8(a) (ii). The Appellate Body found that a 'higher degree of "sameness" is required by the terms of sub-paragraph 8(a)(ii)'.

of a customs union be 'based upon an overall assessment of weighted average tariff rates and of customs duties collected'.[52] The statement of the Understanding clearly indicates that the *applied* rate, not the bound rate, of duty is to be used.[53] With respect to 'other regulations of commerce', the Appellate Body noted that paragraph 2 of the Understanding recognises that the quantification and aggregation of regulations of commerce other than duties may be difficult, and, therefore, establishes that 'for the purpose of the overall assessment of the incidence of other regulations of commerce for which quantification and aggregation are difficult, the examination of individual measures, regulations, products covered and trade flows affected may be required'.[54] The Appellate Body concluded that the terms of Article XXIV:5(a), as elaborated and clarified by paragraph 2 of the Understanding, provide that the effects of the resulting trade measures and policies of a PTA cannot be more trade restrictive, overall, than were the constituent countries' previous trade policies. Further, the test for assessing whether a specific customs union is compatible with Article XXIV is an 'economic' test.[55]

The importance of these statements by the Appellate Body cannot be understated, as they seem to imply that every defence under Article XXIV must show that all of the elements set out in Article XXIV are met.

(ii) The Formation of that Customs Union would be Prevented if It were not Allowed to Introduce the Measure at Issue

On the issue of whether Turkey's measure was consistent with Article XXIV, the Appellate Body focused on the chapeau of Article XXIV:5, examining whether the formation of a customs union would be 'prevented' if it were not allowed to introduce the measure at issue. In the context of the dispute, Turkey argued that if it were not allowed to impose the quantitative restriction, then the EC would exclude all Turkish imports of the products in question in order to prevent the EC restrictions from being circumvented (it was claimed that these amounted to 40 per cent of exports from Turkey to the EC), thereby leading to an inconsistency with paragraph 8(a), as 'substantially all trade' would not be covered. Thus, Turkey asserted that the formation of the customs union would be prevented if it were not allowed to introduce the quantitative restrictions. The Appellate Body rejected that argument, finding that Turkey could have satisfied the terms of paragraph 8(a) without imposing the quantitative restrictions, such as through adopting appropriate rules of origin whereby products originating in Turkey gain duty free access to Europe and products from other countries would not.[56] In such a case, the EC restrictions would not be circumvented and the customs union could be introduced. The Appellate Body stated:

> 62. We agree with the Panel that had Turkey not adopted the same quantitative restrictions that are applied by the European Communities, this would not have prevented Turkey and the European Communities from meeting the requirements of sub-paragraph 8(a)(i) of Article XXIV, and consequently from forming a customs union. We recall our conclusion that the terms of subparagraph 8(a)(i) offer some—though limited—flexibility to the constituent

---

[52] Appellate Body Report, *Turkey—Textiles*, para 53. See the Understanding, para 2.

[53] Before the agreement on the Understanding, there were different views among the GATT Contracting Parties as to whether one should consider, when applying the test of Art XXIV:5(a), the bound rates of duty or the applied rates of duty.

[54] Appellate Body Report, *Turkey—Textiles*, para 54.

[55] *Ibid*, para 55.

[56] *Ibid*, para 62.

members of a customs union when liberalizing their internal trade. As the Panel observed, there are other alternatives available to Turkey and the European Communities to prevent any possible diversion of trade, while at the same time meeting the requirements of sub-paragraph 8(a)(i). For example, Turkey could adopt rules of origin for textile and clothing products that would allow the European Communities to distinguish between those textile and clothing products originating in Turkey, which would enjoy free access to the European Communities under the terms of the customs union, *and* those textile and clothing products originating in third countries, including India. In fact, we note that Turkey and the European Communities themselves appear to have recognized that rules of origin could be applied to deal with any possible trade diversion. Article 12(3) of Decision 1/95 of the EC-Turkey Association Council, which sets out the rules for implementing the final phase of the customs union between Turkey and the European Communities, specifically provides for the possibility of applying a system of certificates of origin. A system of certificates of origin would have been a reasonable alternative until the quantitative restrictions applied by the European Communities are required to be terminated under the provisions of the *ATC*. Yet no use was made of this possibility to avoid trade diversion. Turkey preferred instead to introduce the quantitative restrictions at issue.

63. For this reason, we conclude that Turkey was not, in fact, required to apply the quantitative restrictions at issue in this appeal in order to form a customs union with the European Communities. Therefore, Turkey has not fulfilled the second of the two necessary conditions that must be fulfilled to be entitled to the benefit of the defence under Article XXIV. Turkey has not demonstrated that the formation of a customs union between Turkey and the European Communities would be prevented if it were not allowed to adopt these quantitative restrictions. Thus, the defence afforded by Article XXIV under certain conditions is not available to Turkey in this case, and Article XXIV does not justify the adoption by Turkey of these quantitative restrictions.

In its findings, the Appellate Body essentially sets out a 'necessity' test to examine whether new trade restrictions proposed in conjunction with a customs union (or a free trade area, presumably) are consistent with Article XXIV. That is, according to the Appellate Body's brief findings, in order to meet the requirements of Article XXIV, the Member must show that the requirements to form the agreement cannot be met without the measure at issue. We note that the scope and breadth of such a standard could potentially become problematic, as the 'necessity' standard has been very controversial in other areas of WTO law.

(b) *United States—Line Pipe Safeguards*

In *US—Line Pipe Safeguard,* Korea claimed that by excluding Mexico and Canada from the line pipe safeguard measure in the form of a tariff quota, the United States violated the MFN principle set out in Articles I, XIII:1 and XIX of the GATT and Article 2.2 of the Safeguards Agreement. The United States countered by arguing that its differing treatment of Mexican and Canadian imports (both members of the NAFTA) was justified under the 'limited exception' of Article XXIV of the GATT.

In considering whether the conditions of Article XXIV:5(b) and (c); and 8(b) had been met, the Panel found that the onus was on the party seeking to rely on this 'defence' to demonstrate compliance with these conditions; in this case, the United States therefore had the burden of demonstrating compliance in order to assert an Article XXIV 'defence'. In order to demonstrate that it had met the requirements, the United States submitted documents showing that substantially all duties and other restrictive regulations of commerce would be eliminated under NAFTA, and therefore NAFTA was in compliance with Article XXIV. The United States also referred to various official WTO documents related to the consideration of the NAFTA by the CRTA further to substantiate its claim. Specifically, the United States argued:

> NAFTA provided for the elimination within ten years of all duties on 97 per cent of the Parties' tariff lines, representing more than 99 per cent of the trade among them in terms of volume. This is the basis for our belief that, wherever the threshold established under Article XXIV:8 for elimination of duties on substantially all trade, NAFTA exceeds that threshold.
>
> With regard to eliminating other restrictive regulations of commerce, NAFTA applies the principles of national treatment, transparency, and a variety of other market access rules to trade among the Parties. The NAFTA Parties also eliminated the application of global safeguard measures among themselves under certain conditions. There is also no question of NAFTA raising barriers to third countries, since none of the NAFTA Parties increased tariffs on trade with non-NAFTA measures. The NAFTA Parties also did not place other restrictive regulations of commerce on other WTO Members upon formation of the free-trade area.
>
> Further explanation of the US views on NAFTA and its compliance with Article XXIV appear in the following documents: L/7176, WT/REG4/1 & Corr.1-2, WT/REG4/1/Add.1 & Corr.1, WT/REG4/5, and WT/REG4/6/Add.1. Since these are voluminous materials, we will not append them, but incorporate them into this submission by reference.[57]

In response, Korea argued that the NAFTA was not in compliance with Article XXIV:8 because the CRTA had not yet issued a final decision to that effect.[58] However, the panel found that the information provided by the United States in the proceedings, the information submitted by the NAFTA parties to the CRTA, and the 'absence of effective refutation' by Korea 'establishe[d] a prima facie case that NAFTA was in conformity with Article XXIV:5(b) and (c), and with Article XXIV:8(b)'. In addition, in regards to Article XXIV:8(b), the panel did not consider that the fact that the CRTA had not yet issued a final decision as to NAFTA's compliance with Article XXIV:8 was sufficient to rebut the prima facie case established by the United States. The panel could find nothing in the relevant provisions of the Agreement Establishing the WTO (including, in particular, the Understanding on the Interpretation of Article XXIV of the GATT 1994) as a basis for Korea's claim that a regional trade arrangement is essentially presumed inconsistent with Article XXIV until the CRTA makes a determination to the contrary.

While the findings of the panel in *US—Line Pipe Safeguards* are instructive as a general matter, on appeal the Appellate Body declared the panel's findings and conclusions on this point to be 'moot and as having no legal effect'.[59] As a result, the value of these findings as precedent is probably limited.

As a final point, it is worth mentioning that the *Line Pipe* panel referred to the Appellate Body's finding in *Turkey—Textiles*, where it was stated that for a measure to be justified under Article XXIV the measure must be 'necessary' for the formation of a regional trade agreement (in that case, a customs union was at issue).[60] However, the

---

[57] Panel Report, *US—Line Pipe Safeguards*, para 142 (citing Response to Panel Question 2 to the United States at the second substantive meeting (see Annex B-8)).

[58] See *ibid*, paras 7.142–7.143.

[59] The Appellate Body found that it 'need not address the question whether an Article XXIV defence is available to the United State', as it was not 'required to make a determination on the question of the relationship between Article 2.2 of the Agreement on Safeguards and Article XXIV of the GATT 1994': see Appellate Body Report, *US—Line Pipe Safeguards*, paras 198–99.

[60] Appellate Body Report, *Turkey—Textiles*, para 158.

panel distinguished the factual situation at issue in *Turkey—Textiles* from the this case by pointing to the fact that the Appellate Body in *Turkey—Textiles* addressed a measure which imposed *new restrictions* against third countries (ie countries not party to the regional trade agreement at issue), whereas here the measure was part of the elimination of duties and other restrictive regulations between parties to the free-trade area. Therefore, according to the panel, '[i]f the alleged violation of GATT 1994 forms part of the elimination of "duties and other restrictive regulations of commerce", there can be no question of whether it is necessary for the elimination of 'duties and other restrictive regulations of commerce'. As a result, the panel was not convinced that Members should be required to demonstrate the necessity of this latter type of measure.[61]

VI. RECENT TRENDS: THE FUTURE OF PTAS IN THE WTO

There can be no denying that there has been an explosion of PTAs following the implementation of the WTO and, more specifically, following the failed Seattle and Cancun Ministerials. As outlined earlier in this chapter, the reasons members are pursuing a bilateral track of trade negotiations are many. The fear is that these nations will become inward-looking and be less interested in forwarding the multilateral agenda. Such fear is at the very least premature. Members pursuing PTAs are, without exception, taking a two-pronged approach to multilateral and bilateral trade. But the question whether increased bilateralism can indefinitely sit comfortably next to the multilateral system remains unanswerable. This is especially the case given that the Doha Round of multilateral trade negotiations has reached an impasse and may not be revived.

An important question linked to these issues remains unanswered: whether the WTO will strictly enforce the disciplines of Article XXIV. The Understanding on the Interpretation of Article XXIV of the GATT 1994 expects both the CRTA and the DSB to be active in the monitoring of PTAs. The CRTA has, until this date, proven itself an ineffective Committee due to the constraints of consensus decision-making. The DSB, however, through the action of panels and the Appellate Body, has begun to lay the foundation for effective monitoring and enforcement of Article XXIV. And while the DSB has had only two disputes in which to analyse Article XXIV, it has begun to provide a detailed interpretive framework in which to guide future action.

As part of the Doha Round, members of the 'Negotiating Group on Rules' have been discussing ways to improve the system, including by setting guidelines, timelines and meaningful standards for, among other issues, 'substantially all trade'. Progress has been slow, although the Group did agree in December 2006 on a new transparency mechanism for PTAs providing for early announcement of any PTA and notification to the WTO.[62] Further progress could provide for meaningful obligations, enforceable at the first instance by the CRTA. Two Australian submissions to the Negotiating Group on Rules

---

[61] Panel Report, *US—Line Pipe Safeguards*, paras 7.147–7.148
[62] WTO General Council, 'Transparency Mechanisms for Regional Trade Agreements', WTO Doc No WT/L/671 (18 December 2006), available at http://docsonline.wto.org/imrd/directDocasp?DDFDocuments/t/WT/L/671.doc.

have been heavily debated and now provide a working draft upon which to base future negotiations. The two submissions are reprinted below.

World Trade Organisation, TN/RL/W/15, 9 July 2002 (02-3820), Negotiating Group on Rules

SUBMISSION ON REGIONAL TRADE AGREEMENTS BY AUSTRALIA

The following communication, dated 8 July 2002, has been received from the Permanent Mission of Australia.

This communication is a contribution to the elaboration of possible solutions to the problem of interpreting the meaning of "substantially all the trade", a key term in the WTO rules applying to customs unions and free-trade areas. Its clarification would represent an important step in the WTO's consideration of the rules on regionalism in the Doha Round.

Background

1. An agreed understanding of the meaning of "substantially all the trade" has so far eluded the WTO Membership. The absence of such an understanding is one of the main reasons why most GATT working parties established to examine regional trade agreements, and more recently the Committee on Regional Trade Agreements (CRTA), have not been able to arrive at a clear-cut decision on their WTO-conformity.

2. GATT Article XXIV:8 defines the meaning of "customs union" and "free-trade area". One characteristic in each case is the requirement that the parties eliminate duties and other restrictive regulations of commerce (except, where necessary, those permitted under Articles XI, XII, XIII, XIV, XV and XX) with respect to substantially all the trade between the constituent territories in products originating in such territories.

3. Starting with the examination of the Treaty of Rome in 1957, some GATT working parties attempted to understand "substantially all the trade" in terms of a percentage of trade covered. Others insisted that an agreement leaving out an entire sector cannot be consistent with the requirements of Article XXIV. An examination of the working party reports reveals the gap in perceptions between delegations on the meaning of this phrase, but it does not greatly advance the search for a solution. This issue has continued to confront the CRTA following the Uruguay Round. It was one of the key issues behind the decision of WTO Ministers in Doha to mandate negotiations aimed at clarifying and improving disciplines and procedures under the existing WTO provisions applying to regional trade agreements.

4. The Understanding on the Interpretation of Article XXIV of the General Agreement on Tariffs and Trade 1994 was a helpful step forward. It noted that the contribution to the expansion of world trade through closer integration between the relevant economies is diminished if any major sector of trade is excluded. However, it did not establish any obligations in this regard.

A possible solution

5. Even in ideal circumstances it would be unlikely that more than substantially all the trade is ever subject to the free trade provisions of a regional trade agreement, or that trade in all products would ever occur completely unhindered. GATT Article XXIV:8 makes it quite clear that WTO Members are free, in certain circumstances, to apply the restrictions authorized by a range of GATT articles. Some part of a Member's trade therefore always is potentially subject to restrictive actions. The extent to which this factor would come into play would obviously

vary to a considerable extent. It might therefore not be helpful to use actual or potential trade flows as a criterion.

6. At first glance, it might seem advisable to use actual trade statistics and trade flows in an assessment of the extent to which the "substantially all the trade" criterion has been met. There are, however, difficulties associated with this. GATT working parties and subsequently the CRTA have recognized that any calculation of the percentage of trade not freed from barriers would need to take account of the fact that this trade would be, or would have been, larger if the trade had been allowed freely. In other words, simply looking at trade flows does not take account of the dynamics at work before the conclusion of an arrangement, its implementation and the situation prevailing once it has been fully implemented.

7. There is, however, an alternative. Instead of using trade flows, it is possible to take advantage of the classifications used to examine or regulate aspects of these flows. The Harmonized Commodity Description and Coding System would be particularly suitable as the basis for an assessment of whether substantially all trade is covered by an arrangement. It is aimed specifically at internationally traded goods, and it is therefore well understood by the trade policy community.

8. Our proposal is that "substantially all the trade" should be defined in terms of coverage by a free trade agreement, or an agreement establishing a customs union, of a defined percentage of all the six-digit tariff lines listed in the Harmonized System. This approach would ensure that there is sufficient flexibility to set aside product areas that for one reason or another cannot yet be traded between the partners free of restrictions. Proceeding in this way, it would not be necessary to discover the extent to which trade in a given product may have been affected by other measures in place.

9. Australia considers that such a percentage criterion should be established at a sufficiently high level to prevent the carving-out of any major sector, in terms of its near-complete exclusion of coverage. The Secretariat in its background survey on coverage, liberalization process and transitional provisions in RTAs (WT/REG/W/46) has pointed out the tendency for certain sectors, especially agriculture, to be left out of RTAs to a greater or lesser extent, and this has the potential to distort trade in that sector. At the same time, to allow the incorporation of cases where trade is initially concentrated in relatively few products, it may be necessary to include an assessment of prospective trade flows at various stages of implementation of the RTA. Such an approach would bridge the quantitative and qualitative approaches mentioned earlier.

10. Particular attention would have to be given to the definition of what is covered by an agreement. Coverage would have to be understood clearly to mean that there are no tariffs or non-tariff measures in that product affecting the trade of products originating from Members, or that such measures would be eliminated during the agreed implementation timeframe.

11. Australia believes that this type of approach would take us a long way in the direction of finding a workable definition of "substantially all the trade". It has the great advantage of being easily verifiable without requiring complex econometric work.

12. This approach also takes into account the provision made in Article XXIV for interim agreements leading to the formation of free trade areas or customs unions. It would, in practice, only be possible to measure the precise impact of the elimination of duties and other restrictive regulations of commerce under such an interim agreement once the free trade area or customs union was fully implemented. The Understanding on the Interpretation of Article XXIV of the General Agreement on Tariffs and Trade 1994 defined 10 years as the "reasonable period of time" in which such restrictions should be eliminated on substantially all trade. The CRTA

would find it difficult to make a precise estimation of the impact of measures to be implemented in 10 years' time. On the other hand, a criterion of "substantially all the trade" based on the number of tariff lines on which restrictions were to be eliminated could just as readily be applied to an assessment of the coverage of measures leading to the formation of a free trade area or customs union over a number of years.

… … …

World Trade Organisation, Negotiating Group on Rules, N/RL/W/173/Rev.1*, 3 March 2005 (05-0923), Submission on Regional Trade Agreements by Australia

Revision

The following submission, dated 28 February 2005, is being circulated at the request of the Delegation of Australia.

This communication builds on Australia's first submission on the definition of 'substantially all trade' (TN/RL/W/15) and provides a possible basis to progress the important issue of defining with greater precision the term 'substantially all the trade' as it pertains to Article XXIV of the General Agreement on Tariffs and Trade (GATT). Agreement on the meaning of 'substantially all trade' is important in assessing whether regional trade agreements to which WTO Members are a party are consistent with the WTO commitments of those Members. This submission by Australia responds to the Doha Declaration mandate for negotiations to clarify and improve the WTO disciplines and procedures related to regional trade agreements, and provides a substantive contribution to the development of effective disciplines related to regional trade agreements in the WTO as called for by the report "The Future of the WTO: Addressing Institutional Challenges in the New Millennium".

Background

1. Paragraph 29 of the Doha Declaration states:

We also agree to negotiations aimed at clarifying and improving disciplines and procedures under the existing WTO provisions applying to regional trade agreements. The negotiations will take into account the developmental aspects of regional trade agreements.

This mandate to improve and give certainty of definition and form to the disciplines and procedures of the WTO provisions related to regional trade agreements reflects widely held concerns; specifically, that the current ambiguities have hindered the Committee for Regional Trade Agreements (CRTA) from completing even one assessment of whether an individual trade agreement conforms to WTO provisions.

2. These concerns have most recently been underlined by the report "The Future of the WTO: Addressing Institutional Challenges in the New Millennium" (the Sutherland report). The Sutherland report articulates the importance of ensuring that regional trade agreements improve the "trading and development prospects of beneficiaries." Furthermore, the report makes a strong call for regional trade agreements to "be subject to meaningful review and effective disciplines in the WTO."

3. As highlighted in the Sutherland report, the existing systemic inability to objectively discern whether regional trade agreements involving WTO Members are consistent with the WTO commitments of those Members presents the danger of a proliferation of regional trade agreements with poor trade-liberalising outcomes and trade distorting effects. Deficient regional trade agreements of this nature, particularly those that deliberately exclude entire

sectors, such as agriculture, from liberalising commitments, undermine the multilateral trading system by entrenching protectionism, and give comfort to interest groups that benefit from such protectionism at the expense of the multilateral rules-based international trading system. Conversely, full coverage, high quality RTAs would through their liberalising effect promote further trade liberalisation at the multilateral level.

4. An important element in the development of effective disciplines that apply to regional trade agreements is the definition of 'substantially all trade'. Article XXIV, paragraph 8, GATT requires that, in relation to customs unions and free trade agreements, "duties and other restrictive regulations of commerce . . . are eliminated with respect to substantially all the trade . . .". On any reading of this provision, the term 'substantially all trade' is pivotal to assessing the WTO-consistency of regional trade agreements.

Substantially All Trade: A Proposed Definition

5. The objective of defining 'substantially all trade' in the context of Article XXIV and the examination of regional trade agreements must be to ensure that neither entire sectors nor 'highly traded' products are excluded from regional trade agreements. It is therefore necessary that the definition incorporate quantitative benchmarks in relation to the "duties" aspect of the agreement that preclude such exclusions.

6. In relation to preventing the exclusion of entire sectors, the appropriate quantitative measure needs to be sufficiently ambitious, and yet reflect the reality that some products may be excluded from regional trade agreements, and furthermore, that in some cases, liberalisation commitments may be phased-in over time. An appropriate accommodation of these competing factors could be achieved by prescribing a benchmark of eliminating all duties on a minimum of at least 95 percent of tariff lines at the six digit level in the harmonised system of tariff classification lines. We regard a minimum 95 percent as satisfying the requirements of an effective discipline under Article XXIV, and yet retains sufficient flexibility to accommodate the exclusion of certain product lines.

7. While the benchmark of at least 95 percent of the harmonised system of tariff lines at the six digit level would prevent the exclusion from a regional trade agreement of a particular sector (i.e. at the Chapter or Heading level), it may not be effective in deterring the exclusion of 'highly traded' products. In addressing this issue it is important to first identify clearly what 'highly traded' products are, and in this regard we propose that these products be defined as those that constitute at least, say, 2 percent of trade between the parties. We are open to other views as to an appropriate percentage of trade between the parties that would give appropriate specificity to the term 'highly traded' product. The important point is to come to an agreement on a clear definition that accurately describes the term 'highly traded'.

8. Another aspect of preventing the exclusion of 'highly traded' products is to identify those products in the context of trade governed by the regional trade agreements. This would require statistical information on the trade between the parties on a product specific basis, with a historical reach of at least three years prior to the notification and each subsequent review of the regional trade agreements. Inclusion of this information could be an added requirement in the standard format for notification, and/or a required feature under the 'Trade Analysis' section in the factual presentation produced by the Secretariat.

9. There is also a need to expose to the examination process those products that Members currently do not, but could trade, if it were not for the protectionist measures of one or more the parties. This could involve analysis of the overall export trade of each Member. We would welcome proposals on how this might most appropriately be achieved.

10. Phased-in commitments: A plain reading of Article XXIV.8.(a) and Article XXIV.8.(b) suggests a requirement for regional trade agreements to achieve the elimination of duties and other restrictive regulations of commerce on substantially all trade on entry into force. However, many regional trade agreements to which WTO Members are a party clearly contain significant trade liberalizing commitments that are phased in over time rather than being operative on entry into force. Some WTO Members have sought comfort from the term 'reasonable length of time' in Article XXIV.5(c), but this provision relates specifically to "interim agreements" within the meaning of Article XXIV.5(a) and Article XXIV.5(b). Accordingly, it does not have any direct bearing on commitments related to 'substantially all trade' in Customs Unions or Free Trade Agreements not notified as interim agreements. However, while Article XXIV:5(c) does not directly concern itself with regional trade agreements other than those notified as interim agreements, we believe it nonetheless provides useful guidance when trying to accommodate the common practice of phased-in liberalisation commitments in regional trade agreements by WTO Members.

11. Therefore a pragmatic approach to the development and consistent application of WTO disciplines to regional trade agreements requires the determination of an appropriate period of time after entry into force of the regional trade agreements at which to assess whether the elimination of duties and other restrictive regulations of commerce on substantially all trade has been achieved. As indicated above, we are firmly of the view that the precedent of defining 'a reasonable length of time' in Article XXIV.5(c) as ten years (articulated in the Understanding on the Interpretation of Article XXIV of the General Agreement on Tariffs and Trade 1994, paragraph 3) provides an appropriate model for application to the assessment of the elimination of duties in respect of substantially all trade.

12. The proposed ten year period for the assessment of regional trade agreements has several benefits: it builds on an existing implicit understanding by WTO Members that ten years is a suitable period is consistent with the period described in Article XXIV.5(c); accommodates the majority of existing regional trade agreements that contain phased-in commitments; and is rigorous enough to prevent the erosion of this requirement as an effective discipline.

13. Complementary to this flexibility in accommodating phased-in commitments, it is appropriate to require an ambitious yet pragmatic percentage for the elimination of duties on 'substantially all trade' upon entry into force of regional trade agreements. It is therefore proposed that a minimum level of, say, 70 percent of tariff lines at the HS six-digit level is an appropriate benchmark for the elimination of duties on 'substantially all trade' at the time of entry into force of the regional trade agreement, as it ensures the majority of the trade between the parties is liberalised immediately.

14. The term "Substantially all Trade" calls for comprehensive liberalisation in RTAs. This proposal merely provides a benchmark for this obligation. Accordingly, these obligations should apply to all regional trade agreements currently in force to which WTO Members are a party.

15. The approach outlined in this document has as its key objectives the conscientious implementation of the Doha mandate, the promotion of comprehensive regional trade agreements that deliver genuinely trade-liberalizing and less trade distorting outcomes, and the development of a mutually supportive multilateral, regional and bilateral trade architecture by ensuring that regional trade agreements to which WTO Members are a party accurately reflect their WTO commitments. We are open to discussing S&D treatment for Developing Countries.

… … …

VII. QUESTIONS

1. Are bilateral and regional trade agreements sensible economic policy choices for nations? What factors should be considered when answering this question?

2. What are the differences in terms of economic and foreign policy between free-trade areas and customs unions?

3. Do foreign policy and other concerns outweigh any negative economic impact of PTAs? Should they?

4. What is the role of the CRTA? How effective is it? What changes would make it more effective?

5. Should both the CRTA as well as dispute settlement panels be able to assess whether a PTA meets the requirements of Article XXIV of the GATT?

6. What does 'substantially all the trade' mean? How has the term been defined or dealt with in the case law? How should it be defined?

7. When is compensation offered under Article XXIV:6 of the GATT? Is the system fair to those offering and to those receiving the compensatory adjustment?

8. Are PTAs a threat to the multilateral trading system?

9. How can PTAs act as 'laboratories' to experiment with different kinds of trade agreement provisions, which might then be incorporated into the multilateral system?

10. Do PTAs alter the balance of trade negotiating power in favour of countries with larger economies?

9

The Article XX 'General Exceptions': Health, the Environment, Compliance Measures, Public Morals and More

I. INTRODUCTION

The drafters of the GATT recognised that although trade is important, governments pursue other policy goals as well. Thus, in formulating the rules for world trade, they made sure to preserve the ability of governments to promote these other policies. To this end, the drafters included a set of 'General Exceptions' in Article XX which makes clear that, in limited circumstances, Members are permitted to act inconsistently with their GATT obligations in order to pursue certain designated policies. The specific policy exceptions are listed in sub-paragraphs (a) to (j) of Article XX, covering measures that are:

- necessary to protect public morals (sub-paragraph (a));
- necessary to protect human, animal or plant life or health (sub-paragraph (b));
- relating to the importation or exportation of gold or silver (sub-paragraph (c));
- necessary to secure compliance with laws or regulations which are not inconsistent with the GATT (sub-paragraph (d));
- relating to the products of prison labour (sub-paragraph (e));
- imposed for the protection of national treasures of artistic, historic or archaeological value (sub-paragraph (f));
- relating to the conservation of exhaustible natural resources if such measures are made effective in conjunction with restrictions on domestic production or consumption (sub-paragraph (g));
- undertaken in pursuance of obligations under any intergovernmental commodity agreement which conforms to certain criteria (sub-paragraph (h));
- involving restrictions on exports of domestic materials necessary to ensure essential quantities of such materials to a domestic processing industry during certain periods (sub-paragraph (i));
- essential to the acquisition or distribution of products in general or local short supply (sub-paragraph (j)).

In GATT/WTO dispute settlement, sub-paragraphs (b), (d) and (g) have been invoked the most frequently. In addition, sub-paragraph (a), covering public morals, constitutes a potentially broad exception that could play a larger role in the future. Thus, our focus in this chapter is on these exceptions. We note that it is the disputes relating to issues under (b) and (g) that have been the basis for many of the protests against the WTO, as they have put trade measures into conflict with measures to protect human health and the environment.

The ability to pursue the listed policies is limited by the chapeau[1] to Article XX, which states that the availability of these exceptions is:

> Subject to the requirement that such measures are not applied in a manner which would constitute a means of arbitrary or unjustifiable discrimination between countries where the same conditions prevail, or a disguised restriction on international trade. . . .

Generally speaking, the chapeau is designed to ensure that Members do not abuse the exceptions by using them as a disguised means of discrimination against or among other Members' goods or a trade restriction of some other kind.[2]

There is a fine line to be drawn in striking a balance between allowing Members to pursue various social policies despite possible negative trade effects and preventing them from using these policies in a manner which abuses the basic GATT obligations. The problem is that, if the exception is crafted too broadly, clever law-makers may be able to disguise their intent so as to hide protectionist policies in, for example, a measure ostensibly intended for environmental protection. On the other hand, if it is too narrow, Members may be prevented from adopting legitimate social policies that only incidentally affect trade. In the cases examined in this chapter, we will see how that line has been drawn through the interpretations of the various exceptions and the chapeau.

In this chapter, we examine Article XX as follows. First, we address a number of general interpretive issues related to Article XX. Secondly, we consider more closely the specific policy goals set out as exceptions, focusing on the relevant case law where it exists. Finally, we examine the role of the chapeau.

II. GENERAL INTERPRETIVE ISSUES

(a) Applicability of Article XX to claims under the GATT and under instruments other than the GATT

Article XX provides for 'General Exceptions' to obligations under the GATT, stating that 'nothing in *this Agreement* shall be construed to prevent the adoption or enforcement' of certain measures (emphasis added). At the time of drafting, the GATT was the only multilateral trade agreement. As a result, the reference to 'this Agreement' was unambiguous and uncontroversial. Over time, though, with additional agreements brought within the GATT/WTO framework, the situation becomes less clear. The reference in Article XX to 'this Agreement' has never been altered or amended, but some commentators and governments assert that Article XX can be applied beyond the GATT. Thus, while some

---

[1] 'Chapeau' is French for hat. This term is often used to describe the introductory clause to Art XX because of its position in the text, above the various sub-paras setting out specific exceptions. The Art XX chapeau is sometimes referred to as the introductory clause or introductory clauses.

[2] Appellate Body Report, *US—Gasoline*, at 22; Appellate Body Report, *US—Shrimp*, para 158.

strongly assert that where the exceptions of Article XX of the GATT are meant to apply to other WTO Agreements they must be expressly incorporated (ie Article 3 of the TRIMS Agreement), others just as strongly argue that explicit incorporation is not a precondition for the availability of Article XX.

On its face, the reference to '*this Agreement*' seems to establish a narrow scope for the exception: it applies only to GATT obligations, not to other WTO agreements or legal instruments. However, arguments for applying the Article XX exceptions beyond the GATT have been suggested, and even argued in WTO dispute settlements. China has argued for the extension of Article XX in two separate cases. First, China argued in *China—Publications and Audiovisual Products* that Article XX could serve as a defence to a claim under the 'trading rights commitments' contained in paragraph 5.1 of China's Accession Protocol. The key part of Paragraph 5.1 states:

> Without prejudice to China's right to regulate trade in a manner consistent with the WTO Agreement, China shall progressively liberalize the availability and scope of the right to trade, so that, within three years after accession, all enterprises in China shall have the right to trade in all goods throughout the customs territory of China, except for those goods listed in Annex 2A which continue to be subject to state trading in accordance with this Protocol.

Thus, the legal text in that case referred to consistency with 'the WTO agreement'. Noting that WTO consistency can be achieved either by not violating any WTO obligation or by justification under an exception, the Appellate Body read the phrase 'right to regulate trade in a manner consistent with the WTO Agreement' as a reference to:

> (i) rights that the covered agreements affirmatively recognize as accruing to WTO Members, namely, the power of Members to take specific types of regulatory measures in respect of trade in goods when those measures satisfy prescribed WTO disciplines and meet specified criteria; and (ii) certain rights to take regulatory action that derogates from obligations under the WTO Agreement—that is, to relevant exceptions.[3]

It then concluded that 'China may rely upon the introductory clause of paragraph 5.1 of its Accession Protocol and seek to justify these provisions as necessary to protect public morals in China, within the meaning of Article XX(a) of the GATT'.[4]

In *China—Raw Materials*, the text at issue in China's Accession Protocol was slightly different. Here, Article XX was offered as a defence to a violation of paragraph 11.3, which states that 'China shall eliminate all taxes and charges applied to exports unless specifically provided for in Annex 6 of this Protocol or applied in conformity with the provisions of Article VIII of the GATT 1994'. In this regard, the reference is not to 'the WTO Agreement' but only to one specific article of the GATT. Nonetheless, China argued that because Article XX of the GATT is an available defence to Article VIII of the GATT, Article XX should apply here as well. The Appellate Body rejected this view for at least two separate reasons:

> 291. As noted by the Panel, "the language in Paragraph 11.3 expressly refers to Article VIII, but leaves out reference to other provisions of the GATT 1994, such as Article XX." Moreover, there is no language in Paragraph 11.3 similar to that found in Paragraph 5.1 of China's Accession Protocol—"[w]ithout prejudice to China's right to regulate trade in a manner consistent with the WTO Agreement"—which was interpreted by the Appellate Body in *China—Publications and*

---

[3] Appellate Body Report, *China—Publications and Audiovisual Products*, paras 216–23.
[4] *IbidIbid,*, para 233.

Audiovisual Products. In our view, this suggests that China may not have recourse to Article XX to justify a breach of its commitment to eliminate export duties under Paragraph 11.3 of China's Accession Protocol.[5]

...

293. Paragraph 11.1 of China's Accession Protocol provides that "China shall ensure that customs fees or charges applied or administered by national or sub-national authorities, shall be in conformity with the GATT 1994". Paragraph 11.2 further stipulates that "China shall ensure that internal taxes and charges, including value-added taxes, applied or administered by national or sub-national authorities shall be in conformity with the GATT 1994." Both of these provisions contain the obligation to ensure that certain fees, taxes or charges are "in conformity with the GATT 1994". This is not the case for Paragraph 11.3. We also note that Paragraph 11.1 refers to "customs fees and or charges" in general and Paragraph 11.2 refers in turn to "internal taxes and charges", while Paragraph 11.3 refers specifically to the elimination of "taxes and charges applied to exports". Given the references to the GATT 1994 in Paragraphs 11.1 and 11.2, and the differences in the subject matter and nature of the obligations covered by these provisions, we consider that the absence of a reference to the GATT 1994 in Paragraph 11.3 further supports our interpretation that China may not have recourse to Article XX to justify a breach of its commitment to eliminate export duties under Paragraph 11.3. Moreover, as China's obligation to eliminate export duties arises exclusively from China's Accession Protocol, and not from the GATT 1994, we consider it reasonable to assume that, had there been a common intention to provide access to Article XX of the GATT 1994 in this respect, language to that effect would have been included in Paragraph 11.3 or elsewhere in China's Accession Protocol.

Unfortunately, these decisions did not affirmatively resolve the issue and considerable uncertainty remains as to how an Article XX defence would fare if used in relation to other provisions of non-GATT agreements and legal instruments. To illustrate this uncertainty, we cite a recent amicus curiae submission to the panel in *Canada—Renewable Energy*.

The term 'this Agreement' in the chapeau of Article XX of the GATT 1994 has no clear 'ordinary' meaning of its own. This term was contained in the GATT 1947, prior to the Uruguay Round, when the GATT 1947 itself constituted the primary multilateral trade agreement. The GATT 1947 was carried over into the WTO Agreement essentially as it is, without being rewritten to take into account its new place as one of many related 'goods' agreements, bound together in an annex. The reference to 'this Agreement' must, therefore, necessarily be interpreted in the light of today's placement of this provision and the link of the GATT 1994 to other Annex 1A agreements, as discussed above.

In *China—Audiovisuals*, the Appellate Body did not interpret the reference to 'this Agreement' as limiting the application of Article XX to the GATT 1994. In the earlier *Brazil—Desiccated Coconut* case, the Appellate Body found that the meaning of 'this Agreement' in Article 32.3 of the SCM Agreement refers to the SCM Agreement *and* Article VI of the GATT 1994. Accordingly, the meaning of 'this Agreement' is not inherently limited to the covered agreement that it is used in.[6]

Thus, while we now have two cases where the Appellate Body interpreted whether Article

---

[5] Appellate Body Report, *China—Raw Materials*, para 291.

[6] Amicus curiae submission on International Institute for Sustainable Development (IISD), Canadian Environmental Law Association (CELA) and Ecojustice Canada (Ecojustice) to the panel in *Canada—Renewable Energy*, 10 May 2012, available at http://worldtradelaw.typepad.com/files/amicusds412.pdf.

XX of the GATT could apply to other WTO instruments and agreements, we do not have definite resolution to the issue, nor do we know how the Appellate Body will react to the many and varied references to GATT or its provisions in the various non-GATT agreements and legal instruments.

To take an example, Article 32.1 of the SCM Agreement states: 'No specific action against a subsidy of another Member can be taken except in accordance with the provisions of GATT 1994, as interpreted by this Agreement'. Two parts of this provision are of note. First, the provision refers to measures being 'in accordance with the provisions of GATT 1994'. Based on the decision in *China—Publications*, this would seem to include the GATT exceptions, as a measure satisfying an exception would be in accordance with the GATT. Second, the provision notes that the GATT is 'interpreted by' the SCM Agreement. This suggests, perhaps, that the SCM Agreement can be thought of as a fundamental part of the GATT. On the other hand, unlike an Accession Protocol, the SCM Agreement is an entirely separate agreement, which might lead the Appellate Body to avoid applying Article XX to it in this way. The question of whether Article XX applies outside the context of the GATT is an important one with systemic implications. Perhaps wisely, the Appellate Body has resisted putting forward an overall solution to the issue, instead waiting to see if defendants invoke Article XX and then addressing the issue on a case-by-case basis. As a result, however, it is difficult to draw any broad conclusions on how the issue will be dealt with under specific provisions.

(b) Burden of Proof

It is well established that the kinds of measures listed in Article XX are 'exceptions' to the general GATT rules, and that the burden of proof is on the party invoking a specific Article XX sub-paragraph to show that the measure is justified under that provision.[7] This allocation of the burden applies to both the arguments relating to the specific sub-paragraph relied upon and the arguments concerning the chapeau. The defending party who invokes an Article XX defence therefore has the burden of demonstrating that both of these aspects have been satisfied.

(c) Structure of the Article XX Analysis: Sub-paragraphs First, Chapeau Second

When a defence is raised under Article XX, the Appellate Body has made it clear that the analysis should be carried out as follows. First, it must be determined whether the measure at issue falls within one of the listed exceptions. (For example, under Article XX(b), the relevant issue is whether the measure is 'necessary to protect human, animal or plant life or health'.) Once it is determined that this is the case, the measure is said to be 'provisionally justified' under the sub-paragraph at issue. There is then an examination of whether the measure satisfies the terms of the chapeau.[8] In explaining this point, the Appellate Body has stated that this 'sequence of steps . . . reflects, not inadvertence or random choice, but rather the fundamental structure and logic of Article XX'. Furthermore, the Appellate Body emphasised, '[t]he task of interpreting the chapeau so as to prevent the abuse or misuse of the specific exemptions provided for in Article XX is

---

[7] Appellate Body Report, *EC—Tariff Preferences*, para 95; Appellate Body Report, *US—Shrimp*, para 157.
[8] See *ibid*, para 120.

rendered very difficult, if indeed it remains possible at all, where the interpreter . . . has not first identified and examined the specific exception threatened with abuse'.[9]

(d) 'Necessary' versus 'Relating to'

An important interpretive issue that arises with regard to the listed policy exceptions is that the word 'necessary' is used for some of the sub-paragraphs, but the phrase 'relating to' is used for others.[10] Based on the ordinary usage of these terms, 'necessary' seems to imply a closer connection between the measure and the policy goal. However, it is not clear why the exceptions using 'relating to' would have been singled out by the GATT's drafters as ones that should be easier to satisfy. Regardless, it is fairly well accepted that the different terms should have a different meaning. The full extent of the difference is not completely clear, though.

The interpretation of 'relating to' has been fairly straightforward. In essence, it involves an examination of whether the 'means' and 'ends' of the measure are reasonably related. That is, based on an analysis of the text of the measure itself, it must be determined whether the design and structure of the measure are closely related to the goal of the measure. This inquiry will involve a factual examination of how the measure operates, and the legal standard—the 'means–ends' test—is then applied to the facts. For example, in the *US—Shrimp* case, the Appellate Body concluded that '[t]he means and ends relationship between Section 609 and the legitimate policy of conserving an exhaustible, and, in fact, endangered species, is observably a close and real one'.[11]

By contrast, the interpretation of 'necessary' has been more complex, and also quite controversial. In the *US—Section 337* GATT Panel Report, adopted in 1989, the panel interpreted this requirement as follows in the context of Article XX(d):

> a contracting party cannot justify a measure inconsistent with another GATT provision as 'necessary' in terms of Article XX(d) if an alternative measure which it could reasonably be expected to employ and which is not inconsistent with other GATT provisions is available to it. By the same token, in cases where a measure consistent with other GATT provisions is not reasonably available, a contracting party is bound to use, among the measures reasonably available to it, that which entails the least degree of inconsistency with other GATT provisions.[12]

This statement reflects the traditional GATT interpretation of 'necessary', that a measure is not 'necessary' if there is a reasonably available alternative measure that leads to a lesser degree of inconsistency with GATT rules. Thus, according to the panel in *US—Section 337*, the rule was that a measure is not 'necessary' if there is a reasonably available alternative measure that is less inconsistent with the GATT. If this approach is applied strictly, though, it is likely that there will often be some alternative measure that could have been taken. Thus, very few measures will be justified as 'necessary' under

---

[9] *Ibid*, paras 119–20.

[10] Other provisions not discussed in detail here use the following phrases: 'imposed for the protection of'; 'undertaken in pursuance of'; 'involving restrictions on'; and 'essential to the acquisition or distribution of'.

[11] Appellate Body Report, *US—Shrimp*, paras 135–42. In an earlier case, *US—Gasoline*, the Appellate Body examined whether a measure was 'primarily aimed at' the policy of conserving exhaustible natural resources. However, the Appellate Body also referred to the 'substantial relationship' between the measure and this policy goal, and in *Shrimp* it emphasised this part of the *Gasoline* reasoning: see Appellate Body Report, *US—Gasoline*, 14–19.

[12] GATT Panel Report, *US—Section 337*, para 5.26.

such a standard. As a result of this approach, and of the perceived—by some—bias of the GATT as favouring trade over other policies, there was concern expressed by many environmentalist groups and other NGOs that the Article XX exceptions that use the term 'necessary' would be virtually impossible to satisfy.

The Appellate Body has since modified the statements of the panel in *US—Section 337* in a way that seems to offer more flexibility to take into account non-trade concerns, and is thus probably more satisfactory to some critics of the earlier approach. In the first case in which the Appellate Body addressed this issue, *Korea—Beef*, it considered the meaning of 'necessary' under Article XX(d). In this case, the Appellate Body provided some important clarifications of the meaning of the term. In particular, it recognised that 'necessary' can have a range of meanings, from 'indispensable' to 'making a contribution to', and it considered that, in the context of Article XX(d), the meaning is closer to 'indispensable'. Measures that are actually 'indispensable', it said, are clearly 'necessary'. In addition, though, measures that are not 'indispensable' may be 'necessary' as well. The Appellate Body set out a number of factors that influence whether such measures are 'necessary', summing up these factors as follows:

> In sum, determination of whether a measure, which is not "indispensable", may nevertheless be 'necessary' within the contemplation of Article XX(d), involves in every case a process of weighing and balancing a series of factors which prominently include the contribution made by the compliance measure to the enforcement of the law or regulation at issue, the importance of the common interests or values protected by that law or regulation, and the accompanying impact of the law or regulation on imports or exports.[13]

There is clearly some overlap between the *Section 337* standard and the *Korea—Beef* standard. In its explanation in the above excerpt, the Appellate Body set out the following three relevant factors for determining whether a measure is 'necessary': (1) the contribution made by the compliance measure to the enforcement of the law or regulation at issue; (2) the importance of the common interests or values protected by that law or regulation; and (3) the accompanying impact of the law or regulation on imports or exports. The first and third of these factors seem, to some extent, to be part of the traditional GATT test as well: under the *Section 337* test, it must be considered whether alternative measures are reasonably available to accomplish the desired objectives (first factor), as well as whether such measures are less GATT-inconsistent, that is, less trade-restrictive (third factor). The new element added by the Appellate Body is the second one, the 'importance or the common interests of values protected'. It is not clear where this new element came from (certainly not the text of Article XX). Rather, it appears to be an attempt by the Appellate Body to ensure that the ability to use certain policies set out in the Article XX exceptions is given sufficient flexibility.[14]

After describing these three factors in *Beef*, however, the Appellate Body then, somewhat confusingly, referred to traditional GATT jurisprudence, namely the *Section 337* panel's statement quoted above, as 'encapsulating' these factors.[15] As a result, the precise

---

[13] Appellate Body Report, *Korea—Beef*, para 164.

[14] There is a strong likelihood that the Appellate Body wrote this opinion while anticipating the *EC—Asbestos* case, which involved necessity under Art XX(b) and was soon to come before it. Thus, perhaps the Appellate Body was trying to lay the groundwork for its future consideration of that case, as it ultimately found in *Asbestos* that protection of human health was a value that was 'both vital and important in the highest degree': Appellate Body Report, *EC—Asbestos*, para 172.

[15] Appellate Body Report, *Korea——Beef*, paras 165–66.

test to be applied for the 'necessary' standard was still unclear, in particular the extent to which the inquiry should focus on whether an alternative measure could have been used.

Some additional clarification came in the *Asbestos* case, which is discussed and quoted in detail below in section IV. Briefly, the measure at issue was a French law prohibiting the manufacture, sale, distribution or import of chrysotile asbestos fibres and products containing this kind of asbestos. Canada alleged, among other things, that the prohibition violated GATT Article III, because it discriminated against Canadian asbestos in favour of certain French substitute products, and that it violated GATT Article XI, due to the import ban. The EC put forward a defence under Article XX(d). In considering this defence, the Appellate Body focused on whether a 'reasonably available' alternative measure exists, as follows:

Appellate Body Report, *European Communities—Measures Affecting Asbestos and Asbestos-Containing Products*, Adopted 5 April 2001, WT/DS135/AB/R

170.   Looking at this issue now, we believe that, in determining whether a suggested alternative measure is "reasonably available", several factors must be taken into account, besides the difficulty of implementation. In *Thailand—Restrictions on Importation of and Internal Taxes on Cigarettes*, the panel made the following observations on the applicable standard for evaluating whether a measure is "necessary" under Article XX(b):

> The import restrictions imposed by Thailand could be considered to be "necessary" in terms of Article XX(b) only if there were no alternative measure consistent with the General Agreement, or less inconsistent with it, which Thailand could *reasonably be expected to employ to achieve its health policy objectives*. (emphasis added)

171.   In our Report in *Korea—Beef*, we addressed the issue of "necessity" under Article XX(d) of the GATT 1994. In that appeal, we found that the panel was correct in following the standard set forth by the panel in *United States—Section 337 of the Tariff Act of 1930*:

> It was clear to the Panel that a contracting party cannot justify a measure inconsistent with another GATT provision as "necessary" in terms of Article XX(d) if an alternative measure which it could reasonably be expected to employ and which is not inconsistent with other GATT provisions is available to it. By the same token, in cases where a measure consistent with other GATT provisions is not reasonably available, a contracting party is bound to use, among the measures reasonably available to it, that which entails the least degree of inconsistency with other GATT provisions.

172.   We indicated in *Korea—Beef* that one aspect of the "weighing and balancing process . . . comprehended in the determination of whether a WTO-consistent alternative measure" is reasonably available is the extent to which the alternative measure "contributes to the realization of the end pursued". In addition, we observed, in that case, that "[t]he more vital or important [the] common interests or values" pursued, the easier it would be to accept as "necessary" measures designed to achieve those ends. In this case, the objective pursued by the measure is the preservation of human life and health through the elimination, or reduction, of the well-known, and life-threatening, health risks posed by asbestos fibres. The value pursued is both vital and important in the highest degree. The remaining question, then, is whether there is an alternative measure that would achieve the same end and that is less restrictive of trade than a prohibition.

173.   Canada asserts that "controlled use" represents a "reasonably available" measure that would serve the same end. The issue is, thus, whether France could reasonably be expected to

employ "controlled use" practices to achieve its chosen level of health protection—a halt in the spread of asbestos-related health risks.

174.   In our view, France could not reasonably be expected to employ *any* alternative measure if that measure would involve a continuation of the very risk that the Decree seeks to "halt". Such an alternative measure would, in effect, prevent France from achieving its chosen level of health protection. On the basis of the scientific evidence before it, the Panel found that, in general, the efficacy of "controlled use" remains to be demonstrated. Moreover, even in cases where "controlled use" practices are applied "with greater certainty", the scientific evidence suggests that the level of exposure can, in some circumstances, still be high enough for there to be a "significant residual risk of developing asbestos-related diseases". The Panel found too that the efficacy of "controlled use" is particularly doubtful for the building industry and for DIY enthusiasts, which are the most important users of cement-based products containing chrysotile asbestos. Given these factual findings by the Panel, we believe that "controlled use" would not allow France to achieve its chosen level of health protection by halting the spread of asbestos-related health risks. "Controlled use" would, thus, not be an alternative measure that would achieve the end sought by France.

… … …

The Appellate Body has further clarified its views on the meaning of 'necessary' in a case brought under the GATS. As discussed in more detail in Chapter 14 in *US—Gambling Services* the Appellate Body considered the meaning of 'necessary' under GATS Article XIV(a). In this regard, it first noted that GATS Article XIV 'sets out the general exceptions from obligations under that Agreement in the same manner as does [GATT] Article XX'. Thus, it found previous decisions under GATT Article XX to be 'relevant for [the] analysis under Article XIV of the GATS'.[16] Presumably, the converse is also true, and therefore the *US—Gambling Services* decision is relevant for interpreting 'necessary' under Article XX. With regard to the 'necessary' requirement, the Appellate Body referred to its finding in *Korea—Beef* and said that the weighing and balancing process set out there 'begins with an assessment of the "relative importance" of the interests or values furthered by the challenged measure'. As to the other two factors, which, it noted, are not 'exhaustive' as to the possible factors to be considered, one is 'the contribution of the measure to the realisation of the ends pursued by it', and the other is 'the restrictive impact of the measure on international commerce'. In addition to examining these factors, it said a 'comparison between the challenged measure and possible alternatives should then be undertaken, and the results of such comparison should be considered in the light of the importance of the interests at issue'. The Appellate Body then stated:

> It is on the basis of this "weighing and balancing" and comparison of measures, taking into account the interests or values at stake, that a panel determines whether a measure is "necessary" or, alternatively, whether another, WTO-consistent measure is "reasonably available".[17]

The Appellate Body further clarified that 'it is not the responding party's burden to show, in the first instance, that there are *no* reasonably available alternatives to achieve its objectives', that is, 'a responding party need not identify the universe of less trade-restrictive alternative measures and then show that none of those measures achieves the desired objective'. Rather, 'it is for a responding party to make a *prima facie* case that

[16] Appellate Body Report, *US—Gambling Services,* para 291.
[17] *Ibid*, paras 304–09.

its measure is "necessary" by putting forward evidence and arguments that enable a panel to assess the challenged measure in the light of the relevant factors to be "weighed and balanced" in a given case'. In doing so, the Appellate Body noted, the responding party 'may . . . point out why alternative measures would not achieve the same objectives as the challenged measure, but it is under no obligation to do so in order to establish, in the first instance, that its measure is "necessary"'. However, if the complaining party 'raises a WTO-consistent alternative measure that, in its view, the responding party should have taken, the responding party will be required to demonstrate why its challenged measure nevertheless remains "necessary" in the light of that alternative or, in other words, why the proposed alternative is not, in fact, "reasonably available"'. Finally, if a responding party 'demonstrates that the alternative is not "reasonably available", in the light of the interests or values being pursued and the party's desired level of protection, it follows that the challenged measure must be "necessary" within the terms of Article XIV(a) of the GATS'.[18]

Finally, the Appellate Body in *Brazil—Retreaded Tyres* clarified how the analysis of importance of the contribution made by a challenged measure to the achievement of the objective pursued is to be undertaken. After first recalling its decision in *Korea—Various Measures on Beef* that 'the word "necessary" is not limited to that which is "indispensable"', the Appellate Body went on to state:

> 150. . . . Having said that, when a measure produces restrictive effects on international trade as severe as those resulting from an import ban, it appears to us that it would be difficult for a panel to find that measure necessary unless it is satisfied that the measure is apt to make a material contribution to the achievement of its objective. Thus, we disagree with Brazil's suggestion that, because it aims to reduce risk exposure to the maximum extent possible, an import ban that brings a marginal or insignificant contribution can nevertheless be considered necessary.

> 151. This does not mean that an import ban, or another trade-restrictive measure, the contribution of which is not immediately observable, cannot be justified under Article XX(b). We recognize that certain complex public health or environmental problems may be tackled only with a comprehensive policy comprising a multiplicity of interacting measures. In the short-term, it may prove difficult to isolate the contribution to public health or environmental objectives of one specific measure from those attributable to the other measures that are part of the same comprehensive policy. Moreover, the results obtained from certain actions—for instance, measures adopted in order to attenuate global warming and climate change, or certain preventive actions to reduce the incidence of diseases that may manifest themselves only after a certain period of time—can only be evaluated with the benefit of time. In order to justify an import ban under Article XX(b), a panel must be satisfied that it brings about a material contribution to the achievement of its objective. Such a demonstration can of course be made by resorting to evidence or data, pertaining to the past or the present, that establish that the import ban at issue makes a material contribution to the protection of public health or environmental objectives pursued. This is not, however, the only type of demonstration that could establish such a contribution. Thus, a panel might conclude that an import ban is necessary on the basis of a demonstration that the import ban at issue is apt to produce a material contribution to the achievement of its objective. This demonstration could consist of quantitative projections in the future, or qualitative reasoning based on a set of hypotheses that are tested and supported by sufficient evidence.

> ... ...

---

[18] *Ibid*, paras 309–11.

(e) Relationship of Article XX Chapeau Discrimination to Article I and Article III Discrimination

As noted above, in addition to the specific policy exceptions listed in Article XX, all measures for which a Member seeks justification under Article XX must also meet the terms of Article XX's chapeau. The chapeau states that the use of these measures is '[s]ubject to the requirement that such measures are not applied in a manner which would constitute a means of arbitrary or unjustifiable discrimination between countries where the same conditions prevail, or a disguised restriction on international trade'. Thus, even where the measures are allowed in principle because they meet an accepted Article XX policy goal under one of the sub-paragraphs, there are additional limitations placed on their application.

The reference to 'arbitrary or unjustifiable discrimination' in the chapeau leads to a complex relationship between Article XX and GATT Articles I and III, which set out the core MFN and National Treatment non-discrimination obligations. In particular, it may seem odd to include a non-discrimination requirement in Article XX when discrimination among or against WTO Members is already prohibited more generally. However, the reference in the chapeau to 'arbitrary or unjustifiable' may help to clarify the relationship. The combined effect of these provisions is that there is some discrimination that may violate Article I or III, but will still be consistent with the chapeau because it is not 'arbitrary' or 'unjustifiable'. Defining the precise scope of the discrimination covered by each is difficult, of course. In the substantive discussion of the chapeau in section V below we explore the case law that has dealt with this issue.

(f) Scope of Article XX

An obvious question that arises when one reads through the list of Article XX exceptions is, why only these specific policy goals? It seems strange that policies considered important by many people—for example promoting human or labour rights—have been left out. As a result of these omissions, panels and the Appellate Body would be faced with a choice if such concerns were invoked as a defence. They could interpret the text of Article XX strictly, and reject the defence. Or they could consider the terms very broadly, and try to fit these other concerns under these existing exceptions by stretching the language a bit. For example, 'public morals' in sub-paragraph (a) is potentially very broad, and could, in theory, encompass some or all human rights concerns.

(g) The Consideration of Extraterritorial Measures

Of particular concern under Article XX have been domestic measures that have an extraterritorial impact, that is, they affect private behaviour and government regulation in foreign countries. There are two types of measures in this regard. First, one country's measure may require that all products sold in the domestic market be produced a certain way. For example, a measure taken for purposes of environmental protection may require that production take place in a way that limits carbon emissions, with a justification offered under Article XX(g). The effect of such a measure is that companies making the product abroad would have to adapt their production methods to comply with the measure in order to sell in the market. Secondly, a country's measure may impose trade restrictions on imports if the foreign government does not take specific actions in a particular policy area. For example, a measure may keep out all imports of an agricultural product unless a specific programme of sanitary measures was taken; or a measure may impose trade barriers unless certain human or labour rights policies are adopted.

Both types of measures have been extremely sensitive in the WTO. There are a number of concerns that have been put forward, such as a fear that countries will be subject to conflicting requirements imposed by different countries and that such measures can be abused for protectionist purposes. These issues arise in several of the cases examined below.

III. THE MAJOR LISTED EXCEPTIONS

Article XX sets out a number of specific policy goals that may be used to justify measures that violate the substantive obligations of the GATT. We discuss here the most prominent of these.

(a) Article XX(a): Public Morals

Sub-paragraph (a) allows measures that are 'necessary to protect public morals'. As noted above, this exception is potentially very broad. In theory, it could cover policies addressing a wide range of behaviour, such as measures restricting the import or use of pornography or drugs, and could even possibly include measures to promote human rights abroad. However, the full scope is not clear at this point, as there have only been a couple cases.

A similar provision has been interpreted in the context of GATS Article XIV(a), which provides an exception for measures 'necessary to protect public morals or to maintain public order'. As discussed in more detail in Chapter 14 on the GATS, a panel concluded that 'measures prohibiting gambling and betting services, including the supply of those services by the Internet, could fall within the scope of Article XIV(a) if they are enforced in pursuance of policies, the object and purpose of which is to "protect public morals" or "to maintain public order"'.[19] If gambling is covered, it seems likely that pornography and illegal drugs would also be covered, as well as, possibly, legal but potentially harmful substances like alcohol products and tobacco. The inclusion of the promotion of human rights in foreign countries would be more of a stretch, because it involves protection of non-citizens and thus would allow for extraterritorial regulation, which, as noted above, is a very sensitive matter. However, it is not inconceivable that a panel or the Appellate

---

[19] Panel Report, *US—Gambling Services*, para. 6.474. The panel's finding was upheld on appeal by the Appellate Body: see the Appellate Body Report, paras 296–99.

Body would accept this argument.[20] In this regard, as will be seen in section III(d) below, the Appellate Body has interpreted 'exhaustible natural resources' 'in the light of contemporary concerns of the community of nations about the protection and conservation of the environment'.[21] If 'contemporary concerns' were taken into account under Article XX(a), the scope of this provision could be fairly broad.

In *China—Publications and Audiovisuals*, the panel directly engaged with the concept of 'public morals' under Article XX(a):

Panel Report, *China—Measures Affecting Trading Rights and Distribution Services for Certain Publications and Audiovisual Products*, Adopted 10 January 2010, WT/DS363/R

7.751 China considers that reading materials and finished audiovisual products are so-called "cultural goods", i.e., goods with cultural content. China submits that they are products of a unique kind with a potentially serious negative impact on public morals. China explains that, as vectors of identity, values and meaning, cultural goods play an essential role in the evolution and definition of elements such as societal features, values, ways of living together, ethics and behaviours. China notes in this respect the UNESCO *Universal Declaration on Cultural Diversity*, which China says was adopted by all UNESCO Members, including the United States. In its Article 8, the *Declaration* states that cultural goods are "vectors of identity, values and meaning" and that they "must not be treated as mere commodities or consumer goods". In China's view, it is clear, therefore that, depending on their content, cultural goods can have a major impact on public morals.

7.752 China points out that because of this impact of cultural goods, it put in place an appropriate content review mechanism so as to prevent the dissemination of cultural goods with a content that could have a negative impact on public morals in China. China notes that it implements a content review mechanism in respect of both products imported into China and domestically produced products. In respect of the imported products, China points out that their importation is prohibited if they have content that could have a negative impact on public morals in China. China further notes that the prohibition on content that could have a negative impact on public morals is enforced through dissuasive sanctions, including fines, the revocation of operating licences and criminal sanctions.

7.753 Regarding the types of content which China thinks must be prohibited from cultural products that are distributed in China, China notes that it includes a wide range of content ranging from violence or pornography to other important values, including the protection of the Chinese culture and traditional values. China notes that its measures concerning reading materials and finished audiovisual products contain provisions which specifically define the types of content that relevant products may not contain. Specifically, and having regard to the relevant measures, China identifies Articles 26 and 27 of the *Publications Regulation*, Article 3 of the *2001 Audiovisual Products Regulation* and Article 6 of the *Audiovisual Products Importation Rule*.

7.754 China further argues that in the case of products to be imported it is critical that the content review be carried out at the border. China notes that it has therefore established a system for the selection of import entities directed at protecting public morals in China. According to China, its administrative authorities are not in a position, due to limited resources, to carry out content

---

[20] For a discussion of this view see S Charnovitz, 'The Moral Exception in Trade Policy' (1998) 38 *Virginia Journal of International Law* 689. For an opposing view see D Steger, 'Symposium: The Boundaries of the WTO: Afterword: The "Trade and . . ." Conundrum—A Commentary' (2002) 96 *American Journal of International Law* 144.

[21] Appellate Body Report, *US—Shrimp*, para 129.

review all by themselves without creating undue delays. China maintains that import entities therefore need to be given a role in the content review. China contends that the contribution of the import entities to the content review is a substantial and essential condition for an effective and efficient content review. China considers that the importance of the input by the import entities in the content review process justifies the appropriate selection of those entities by the competent Chinese authorities, even if it may result in restrictions of the right to import. China argues that what is at stake is the effectiveness and efficiency of the content review.

7.755 China submits that, accordingly, the objective behind the Chinese regulations and rules challenged by the United States is to prevent the importation of reading materials and finished audiovisual products with a content that could have a negative impact on public morals in China. China notes that the measures at issue first define which type of content has a negative impact on public morals and must therefore not be allowed for importation into China and then establish a content review mechanism for imported products and a system for the selection of import entities that ensures an effective contribution of these entities to the content review.

7.756 The United States does not specifically argue that the measures at issue are not measures to protect public morals. The United States is challenging the means China has chosen to achieve its objective of protecting public morals. More particularly, the United States argues that it is not "necessary" within the meaning of Article XX(a) for importers to perform content review. According to the United States, content review is independent of importation and can be performed by individuals or entities unrelated to the importation process.

...

7.758 We note China's contention that the types of content which are prohibited under the aforementioned measures could have a negative impact on public morals in China, if brought into China as part of physical products. To consider this contention, we first need to address the meaning of the concept of "public morals" as it appears in Article XX(a).

7.759 We note that the panel and Appellate Body in *US—Gambling* examined the meaning of the term "public morals" as it is used in Article XIV(a) of the GATS, which is the GATS provision corresponding to Article XX(a). The panel in *US—Gambling*, in an interpretation not questioned by the Appellate Body, found that "the term 'public morals' denotes standards of right and wrong conduct maintained by or on behalf of a community or nation". The panel went on to note that "the content of these concepts for Members can vary in time and space, depending upon a range of factors, including prevailing social, cultural, ethical and religious values." The panel went on to note that Members, in applying this and other similar societal concepts, "should be given some scope to define and apply for themselves the concepts of 'public morals' . . . in their respective territories, according to their own systems and scales of values." Since Article XX(a) uses the same concept as Article XIV(a), and since we see no reason to depart from the interpretation of "public morals" developed by the panel in *US— Gambling*, we adopt the same interpretation for purposes of our Article XX(a) analysis.

7.760 Turning to the types of content which are prohibited under the aforementioned measures, we note that, for reading materials, they are set forth in Articles 26 and 27 of the *Publications Regulation*. Pursuant to Article 26, no publication may contain content that:

"(1) Defies the basic principles specified in the Constitution;

(2) jeopardizes the solidarity, sovereignty and territorial integrity of the nation;

(3) divulges national secrets, jeopardizes national security or injures the national glory and interests;

(4) incites hatred or discrimination of the nationalities, undermines the solidarity of the nationalities or infringes upon customs and habits of the nationalities;

(5) propagates evil cults or superstition;

(6) disturbs public order or destroys social stability;

(7) propagates obscenity, gambling or violence, or instigates crimes;

(8) insults or defames others, or infringes upon legitimate interests of others;

(9) jeopardizes social morality or fine cultural traditions of the nationalities;

(10) otherwise prohibited by laws, administrative regulations and provisions of the State."

7.761 Article 27 of the *Publications Regulation* provides: "Publications catering to minors shall not contain any content enticing minors to imitate acts that violate public ethics or acts that are illegal or criminal, nor shall they contain horror and cruelty which harm the physical and mental health of minors."

7.762 In response to questions from the Panel as to whether all of the contents listed as prohibited could have a negative impact on public morals, China stated that, if disseminated within China, all of these types of prohibited content could have a negative impact on public morals in China.542 China stated that all of the listed items reflect standards of right and wrong conduct specific to China. The United States does not specifically contest China's assertion that reading materials and finished audiovisual products containing the types of content prohibited by China could have a negative impact on public morals in China. Thus, our situation is different from that faced by the panel in *US –Gambling,* where Antigua and Barbuda disputed whether Internet gambling was actually contrary to public morals in the United States, given the view of Antigua and Barbuda that the United States was a significant consumer of gambling and betting services.

7.763 In considering China's lists of prohibited content, we recall that the United States has not specifically contested that if content defined by China as prohibited were imported as part of a physical product, this could have a negative impact on public morals in China. We further recall that the content and scope of the concept of "public morals" can vary from Member to Member, as they are influenced by each Members' prevailing social, cultural, ethical and religious values. We note, finally, our ultimate conclusion on the "necessity" of the measures at issue to protect public morals in China. In the light of these elements, we will proceed with our analysis on the assumption that each of the prohibited types of content listed in China's measures is such that, if it were brought into China as part of a physical product, it could have a negative impact on "public morals" in China within the meaning of Article XX(a) of the GATT 1994.

7.764 In addition to specifying the types of prohibited content, the measures in question also prescribe that the content of reading materials and finished audiovisual products to be imported into China must be reviewed prior to importation. To recall, for reading materials, Article 44 of the *Publications Regulation* provides that publication import entities are responsible for examining the content of the publications they wish to import. For finished audiovisual products, Article 28 of the *2001 Audiovisual Products Regulation* provides that import entities are to submit finished audiovisual products to be imported to the MOC for a review of their content. The *Audiovisual Products Importation Rule* contains a corresponding provision in its Article 11.

7.765 We also recall that in accordance with the *Publications Regulation*, import entities make final content review decisions for reading materials (subject to intervention by the GAPP in accordance with Article 44 and 45 of the *Publications Regulation*), whereas, in accordance with the *2001 Audiovisual Products Regulation*, the competent Chinese authority makes final content review decisions for finished audiovisual products. China also pointed out, however, that for finished audiovisual products, the import entities selected by China conduct a preliminary content review, by submitting review reports to the authorities as part of their application for a final content review. China further notes that as a result of their own evaluation of content, import entities may also refrain from submitting manifestly inappropriate content to the competent authorities. China contends that for these products, the import entities "greatly facilitate" the final content review decisions to be made by the competent authorities.

7.766 It is clear to us that the above-mentioned Chinese requirements that the content of reading materials and finished audiovisual products must be examined prior to importation, and that such products cannot be imported if they contain prohibited content, are measures to protect public morals in China.

… … …

On appeal, the Appellate Body found that a defence under Article XX(a) of the GATT is available to China, and having done so it considered several points related to the panel's application of the 'necessity' test under Article XX(a). Here, we consider two such issues: the panel's consideration of 'the restrictive effects' elements of the 'weighing and balancing' test and the panel's treatment of available alternative measures.

Concerning the first issue, the panel had analysed the 'restrictive effect of the measures on international trade' as part of its assessment of whether the measures were 'necessary'. In this regard, the panel referred to 'two different types of restrictive impact': 'the restrictive impact the measures at issue have on imports of relevant products' and 'the restrictive effect they have on those wishing to engage in importing, in particular on their right to trade'.[22] China appealed these findings and in doing so made a number of allegations.

First, China alleged that the panel erred in including 'an assessment of the effect on those wishing to engage in importing in its assessment of the restrictive effect of the measures at issue'. On this issue, the Appellate Body discussed the origins of the 'restrictive effect' element, noting that in *Korea—Beef* it had referred to language in the preamble of the GATT and 'stated that the extent to which a measure produces restrictive effects "on international commerce" should be taken into account in assessing "necessity"'. Similar to this situation, paragraph 84(b) of China's Accession Working Party Report 'includes a commitment that "any requirements for obtaining trading rights . . . would not constitute a barrier to trade'. The Appellate Body then stated that, 'while in principle a panel must assess the restrictive effect of a measure on international commerce, this test must be applied in the light of the specific obligation of the covered agreements that the respective measure infringes'. It continued,

> The assessment of the restrictive effect to be taken into account in a particular dispute may, in appropriate cases, extend beyond an assessment of the restrictive effect on imported products, as this assessment must be undertaken in the light of the measure at issue, the specific obligation of the covered agreements that the measure infringes, and the defence being invoked.

In this case, the panel had found a violation of paragraph 5.1 of the Accession Protocol, which is concerned with 'who' is entitled to engage in trading. Thus, the Appellate Body saw no error in the panel 'tailoring its assessment of the restrictive effect of the provi-

---

[22] Appellate Body Report, *China—Productions and Audiovisuals*, para 300.

sions of China's measures to take into account the restrictive effect on beneficiaries of the right to trade'.[23]

With regard to China's allegation that the panel's reasoning

> is circular because it relied on the restrictive effect of the measures both in finding that the measures at issue constitute a violation of China's obligation to grant the right to trade under paragraph 5.1 of China's Accession Protocol and in finding that the measures are not 'necessary' within the meaning of Article XX(a),

the Appellate Body said that '[t]he fact that the restrictive effect of a measure is relevant in one context does not preclude that it may also be relevant in the other'. Therefore, it said that the panel's approach does not constitute 'circular reasoning'. Finally, it concluded that the panel did not, as China alleged, place an 'unsustainable burden of proof' on China 'merely by deciding to take account of the restrictive effect of the measures at issue on those wishing to engage in importing'.[24] On this basis, the Appellate Body found that the panel

> did not err in taking into account the restrictive effect that the relevant provisions and requirements have on those wishing to engage in importing as part of its assessment of the restrictive effect of the measures found to be inconsistent with China's trading rights commitments.

The Appellate Body then turned to China's appeal with respect to the panel's analysis of 'whether a less restrictive measure is reasonably available to China as an alternative means of realizing its objective of protecting public morals'. In this regard, the panel had found that 'the suitable organization and qualified personnel requirement and the State plan requirement are "necessary" to protect public morals in China, in the absence of reasonably available alternatives'. In order to reach a final determination as to whether China had demonstrated the 'necessity' of these two requirements, the panel had considered alternative measures proposed by the US, 'in particular, the proposal that the Chinese Government be given sole responsibility for conducting content review'. After consideration, the panel found that this proposal is an alternative that would be 'significantly less restrictive and would make a contribution to the protection of public morals in China that is at least equivalent to the contribution made by the suitable organization and qualified personnel requirement and the State plan requirement'. Moreover, the panel concluded that China 'had not demonstrated that this alternative is not "reasonably available"'.

China appealed this finding, arguing that sole responsibility for the Chinese Government to conduct content review is not 'reasonably available', 'because it is merely theoretical in nature and would impose an undue and excessive burden on China'. China alleged that the Panel 'erred in law and failed to properly address arguments it presented for purposes of demonstrating that the proposed alternative is not "reasonably available"'.[25]

The Appellate Body first rejected a Chinese argument that the panel should not have considered the effect on 'those wishing to engage in importing' before considering the 'burden' that would result from this alternative measure. On this point, the Appellate Body concluded that, 'having reviewed the panel's analysis of the limited evidence before it' as well as the additional arguments made by China on appeal, the panel did not err in

---

[23] *Ibid*, paras 301, 304–07.
[24] *Ibid*, paras 301, 308–10.
[25] *Ibid*, paras 312–13.

finding that at least one of the alternative measures proposed by the United States is an alternative 'reasonably available' to China.[26]

Therefore, the Appellate Body upheld the panel's conclusion that China had not demonstrated that the measures are 'necessary' to protect public morals, within the meaning of Article XX(a), and that, as a result, China has not established that the measures are justified under Article XX(a).

(b) Article XX(b): Human, Animal or Plant Life or Health

Sub-paragraph (b) is unquestionably one of the most important of the Article XX exceptions, permitting measures 'necessary to protect human, animal or plant life or health', so important, in fact, that there is now an entirely new agreement that was drafted to address these issues as positive rules in the form of the SPS Agreement (discussed in Chapter 13).

The general approach to examining a defence under this sub-paragraph is to determine first whether the measure at issue is designed to pursue a policy of protecting human, animal or plant life or health, that is, whether the measure falls within the scope of the provision. If it does fall within the scope, it will then be determined whether the measure is 'necessary' to achieve this objective.[27]

To date, six WTO cases have considered defences under Article XX(b). All these cases deal with issues of human life or health, and, not surprisingly, all were very controversial. We now examine the Article XX(b) aspect of three of these cases: *US— Gasoline*, *EC— Asbestos* and *EC—Tariff Preferences*. Note that the Appellate Body's latest clarification of the 'necessary' test was offered in the context of the GATS in the *Gambling* case, subsequent to these decisions. (See section II.d above.) Thus, the legal standard might be applied slightly differently today. However, the fact patterns of these cases offer a good illustration of the kinds of measures that may be considered under this provision.

(i) US—Gasoline

Decided before any of the Appellate Body's clarifications of the 'necessity' standard, the panel in *US—Gasoline* addressed Article XX(b) in the context of a US law that required certain gasoline to be cleaner-burning, so as to reduce motor vehicle emissions. The law had been found to violate GATT Article III:4 based on its different treatment of foreign and domestic products in terms of a methodology for determining the quality of the gasoline at issue. The United States offered several defences under Article XX, one of which was under Article XX(b).

In examining whether the measure fell within the scope of this provision, the panel accepted a US argument that air pollution presents health risks to humans, animals and plants. Because about half of such pollution is caused by vehicle emissions, and the measure reduced these emissions, the panel found that the measure was within the range of policy goals described in Article XX(b). Specifically, the panel agreed that 'a policy

---

[26] *Ibid*, paras 322–32.

[27] See, eg Panel Report, *EC—Tariff Preferences*, paras 7.195–7.199. It could be argued that there is really no need to separate these two elements, as any measure that is 'necessary' to achieve these goals will in all probability also be designed to do so. However, it is possible that a small number of measures could, in theory, be necessary for a particular purpose even though they were not designed for this purpose.

to reduce air pollution resulting from the consumption of gasoline' is a policy within the range of those concerning the protection of human, animal and plant life or health.[28]

As to whether the measure was 'necessary', the panel examined whether *the aspect of the measure found inconsistent with Article III:4* was necessary to achieve the stated policy objectives under Article XX(b). In other words, the panel did not look at the measure *as a whole*, but rather only considered the specific aspect of the measure that was discriminatory. The panel concluded that the manner in which imported gasoline received 'less favourable' treatment was not 'necessary' under Article XX(b).[29] The findings under Article XX(b) were not appealed. However, the US defence offered under Article XX(g) was appealed in the same case, and there the Appellate Body rejected the panel's approach of looking at whether the discriminatory aspect of the measure, rather than the measure itself, can justify a measure under one of the Article XX sub-paragraphs (we discuss this point in more detail in section IV(d) below).

(ii) EC—Asbestos

In the second case to address this issue, *EC—Asbestos*, the measure at issue was a French law prohibiting the manufacture, sale, distribution or import of chrysotile asbestos fibres and products containing this kind of asbestos. Canada alleged, among other things, that the prohibition violated GATT Article III, because it discriminated against Canadian asbestos in favour of certain French substitute products, and that it violated GATT Article XI due to the import ban.

As is widely known, asbestos can be extremely harmful. Canada's complaint was not based on a view that asbestos was safe, but rather that it could be handled safely if proper precautions were established through regulation, and thus a ban was not justified.

On the issue of whether this measure is covered by Article XX(b), the panel ruled that the evidence demonstrated that handling chrysotile asbestos constitutes a health risk, and therefore the French policy was within the range of policies designed to protect life or health, and thus 'falls within the category of measures' covered by this provision.[30]

On the necessity issue, the panel concluded that the French measure banning asbestos was 'necessary'.[31] However, on appeal the Appellate Body essentially carried out its reasoning on this issue from scratch, applying the 'necessity' test it had developed just months before in the context of Article XX(d) in the *Korea—Beef* case. Its reasoning on this issue was as follows:

Appellate Body Report, *European Communities—Measures Affecting Asbestos and Asbestos-Containing Products*, Adopted 5 April 2001, WT/DS135/AB/R

164. On the issue of whether the measure at issue is "necessary" to protect public health within the meaning of Article XX(b), the Panel stated:

In the light of France's public health objectives as presented by the European Communities, the Panel concludes that the EC has made a prima facie case for the non-existence of a reasonably

---

[28] Panel Report, *US—Gasoline*, para 6.21.
[29] *Ibid*, paras 6.21–25.
[30] Panel Report, *EC—Asbestos*, paras 8.184–8.194. The Appellate Body upheld this finding on appeal. See Appellate Body Report, *EC—Asbestos*, paras 157–63.
[31] Panel Report, *EC—Asbestos*, paras 8.196–8.222.

available alternative to the banning of chrysotile and chrysotile-cement products and recourse to substitute products. Canada has not rebutted the presumption established by the EC. We also consider that the EC's position is confirmed by the comments of the experts consulted in the course of this proceeding.

165.   Canada argues that the Panel erred in applying the "necessity" test under Article XX(b) of the GATT 1994 "by stating that there is a high enough risk associated with the manipulation of chrysotile-cement products that it could in principle justify strict measures such as the Decree". Canada advances four arguments in support of this part of its appeal. First, Canada argues that the Panel erred in finding, on the basis of the scientific evidence before it, that chrysotile-cement products pose a risk to human health. Second, Canada contends that the Panel had an obligation to "quantify" itself the risk associated with chrysotile-cement products and that it could not simply "rely" on the "hypotheses" of the French authorities. Third, Canada asserts that the Panel erred by postulating that the level of protection of health inherent in the Decree is a halt to the spread of asbestos-related health risks. According to Canada, this "premise is false because it does not take into account the risk associated with the use of substitute products without a framework for controlled use". Fourth, and finally, Canada claims that the Panel erred in finding that "controlled use" is not a reasonably available alternative to the Decree.

166.   With respect to Canada's first argument, we note simply that we have already dismissed Canada's contention that the evidence before the Panel did not support the Panel's findings. We are satisfied that the Panel had a more than sufficient basis to conclude that chrysotile-cement products do pose a significant risk to human life or health.

167.   As for Canada's second argument, relating to "quantification" of the risk, we consider that, as with the *SPS Agreement*, there is no requirement under Article XX(b) of the GATT 1994 to *quantify*, as such, the risk to human life or health. A risk may be evaluated either in quantitative or qualitative terms. In this case, contrary to what is suggested by Canada, the Panel assessed the nature and the character of the risk posed by chrysotile-cement products. The Panel found, on the basis of the scientific evidence, that "no minimum threshold of level of exposure or duration of exposure has been identified with regard to the risk of pathologies associated with chrysotile, except for asbestosis". The pathologies which the Panel identified as being associated with chrysotile are of a very serious nature, namely lung cancer and mesothelioma, which is also a form of cancer. Therefore, we do not agree with Canada that the Panel merely relied on the French authorities' "hypotheses" of the risk.

168.   As to Canada's third argument, relating to the level of protection, we note that it is undisputed that WTO Members have the right to determine the level of protection of health that they consider appropriate in a given situation. France has determined, and the Panel accepted , that the chosen level of health protection by France is a "halt" to the spread of *asbestos*-related health risks. By prohibiting all forms of amphibole asbestos, and by severely restricting the use of chrysotile asbestos, the measure at issue is clearly designed and apt to achieve that level of health protection. Our conclusion is not altered by the fact that PCG fibres might pose a risk to health. The scientific evidence before the Panel indicated that the risk posed by the PCG fibres is, in any case, *less* than the risk posed by chrysotile asbestos fibres , although that evidence did *not* indicate that the risk posed by PCG fibres is non-existent. Accordingly, it seems to us perfectly legitimate for a Member to seek to halt the spread of a highly risky product while allowing the use of a less risky product in its place. In short, we do not agree with Canada's third argument.

169.   In its fourth argument, Canada asserts that the Panel erred in finding that "controlled use" is not a reasonably available alternative to the Decree. This last argument is based on Canada's assertion that, in *United States—Gasoline*, both we and the panel held that an alternative

measure "can only be ruled out if it is shown to be impossible to implement". We understand Canada to mean by this that an alternative measure is only excluded as a "reasonably available" alternative if implementation of that measure is "impossible". We certainly agree with Canada that an alternative measure which is impossible to implement is not "reasonably available". But we do not agree with Canada's reading of either the panel report or our report in *United States—Gasoline*. In *United States—Gasoline*, the panel held, in essence, that an alternative measure did not *cease* to be "reasonably" available simply because the alternative measure involved *administrative difficulties* for a Member. The panel's findings on this point were not appealed, and, thus, we did not address this issue in that case.

170.   Looking at this issue now, we believe that, in determining whether a suggested alternative measure is "reasonably available", several factors must be taken into account, besides the difficulty of implementation. In *Thailand—Restrictions on Importation of and Internal Taxes on Cigarettes*, the panel made the following observations on the applicable standard for evaluating whether a measure is "necessary" under Article XX(b):

> The import restrictions imposed by Thailand could be considered to be "necessary" in terms of Article XX(b) only if there were no alternative measure consistent with the General Agreement, or less inconsistent with it, which Thailand could *reasonably be expected to employ to achieve its health policy objectives*. (emphasis added)

171.   In our Report in *Korea –Beef*, we addressed the issue of "necessity" under Article XX(d) of the GATT 1994. In that appeal, we found that the panel was correct in following the standard set forth by the panel in *United States—Section 337 of the Tariff Act of 1930*:

> It was clear to the Panel that a contracting party cannot justify a measure inconsistent with another GATT provision as "necessary" in terms of Article XX(d) if an alternative measure which it could reasonably be expected to employ and which is not inconsistent with other GATT provisions is available to it. By the same token, in cases where a measure consistent with other GATT provisions is not reasonably available, a contracting party is bound to use, among the measures reasonably available to it, that which entails the least degree of inconsistency with other GATT provisions.

172.   We indicated in *Korea—Beef* that one aspect of the "weighing and balancing process . . . comprehended in the determination of whether a WTO-consistent alternative measure" is reasonably available is the extent to which the alternative measure "contributes to the realization of the end pursued". In addition, we observed, in that case, that "[t]he more vital or important [the] common interests or values" pursued, the easier it would be to accept as "necessary" measures designed to achieve those ends. In this case, the objective pursued by the measure is the preservation of human life and health through the elimination, or reduction, of the well-known, and life-threatening, health risks posed by asbestos fibres. The value pursued is both vital and important in the highest degree. The remaining question, then, is whether there is an alternative measure that would achieve the same end and that is less restrictive of trade than a prohibition.

173.   Canada asserts that "controlled use" represents a "reasonably available" measure that would serve the same end. The issue is, thus, whether France could reasonably be expected to employ "controlled use" practices to achieve its chosen level of health protection—a halt in the spread of asbestos-related health risks.

174.   In our view, France could not reasonably be expected to employ *any* alternative measure if that measure would involve a continuation of the very risk that the Decree seeks to "halt". Such an alternative measure would, in effect, prevent France from achieving its chosen level of health protection. On the basis of the scientific evidence before it, the Panel found that, in

general, the efficacy of "controlled use" remains to be demonstrated. Moreover, even in cases where "controlled use" practices are applied "with greater certainty", the scientific evidence suggests that the level of exposure can, in some circumstances, still be high enough for there to be a "significant residual risk of developing asbestos-related diseases". The Panel found too that the efficacy of "controlled use" is particularly doubtful for the building industry and for DIY enthusiasts, which are the most important users of cement-based products containing chrysotile asbestos. Given these factual findings by the Panel, we believe that "controlled use" would not allow France to achieve its chosen level of health protection by halting the spread of asbestos-related health risks. "Controlled use" would, thus, not be an alternative measure that would achieve the end sought by France.

175. For these reasons, we uphold the Panel's finding, in paragraph 8.222 of the Panel Report, that the European Communities has demonstrated a *prima facie* case that there was no "reasonably available alternative" to the prohibition inherent in the Decree. As a result, we also uphold the Panel's conclusion, in paragraph 8.223 of the Panel Report, that the Decree is "necessary to protect human . . . life or health" within the meaning of Article XX(b) of the GATT 1994.[32]

. . . .

Summing up briefly, in its findings on 'necessity' the Appellate Body observed that the preservation of human life or health by eliminating a known and life-threatening risk is a value that is both 'vital and important' in the 'highest degree'. The Appellate Body then stated that the question is whether there is an alternative measure that would achieve the same ends but is less trade restrictive than a total prohibition. In this regard, it agreed with the panel that the effectiveness of controlled use of asbestos—that is, the use of asbestos regulated by proper handling and other safety instructions—as an alternative had not been demonstrated, and therefore it found that no reasonably available alternative exists. Specifically, the Appellate Body said that controlled use is not a sufficient alternative because France wants to eliminate the risk entirely, and controlled use has not been proven to achieve this. Accordingly, the Appellate Body upheld the panel's finding that the EC had demonstrated that France's measure was 'necessary to protect human . . . life or health' under Article XX(b).

(iii) EC—Tariff Preferences

Finally, the last case under Article XX(b) is *EC—Tariff Preferences*. There, the measure at issue was certain tariff preferences offered through the EC's Generalised System of Preferences (GSP) programme. The granting of the preferences at issue was tied to the existence of problems relating to drug production and trafficking in specific countries (the 'Drug Arrangements'). In other words, under the Drug Arrangements, preferences were granted to exports from a country only if that country was experiencing such problems. The EC measure was found by the panel to violate the MFN obligation in Article I:1 because it discriminated against certain countries. As one defence, the EC argued that the measure was justified under Article XX(b). In particular, the EC contended that 'it is beyond dispute that narcotic drugs pose a risk to human life and health in the EC and that tariff preferences contribute to the protection of human life and health by supporting the measures taken by other countries against the illicit production and trafficking of those

---

[32] Appellate Body Report, *EC—Asbestos*, paras 164–75.

substances, thereby reducing their supply to the European Communities'. Therefore, the EC contended, the Drug Arrangements are a measure falling within Article XX(b).

On this issue, the panel first considered 'whether the Drug Arrangements are designed to achieve the stated health objectives'. In this regard, the panel considered 'not only the express provisions of the EC Regulations, but also the design, architecture and structure of the measure'. Examining the text of the measure, the panel said that it found 'nothing . . . relating to a policy objective of protecting the health of European Communities citizens'. Rather, it concluded, 'the only objectives set out in the Council Regulation (in the second preambular paragraph) are "the objectives of development policy, in particular the eradication of poverty and the promotion of sustainable development in the developing countries"'. On this basis, the panel found that 'the policy reflected in the Drug Arrangements is not one designed for the purpose of protecting human life or health in the European Communities and, therefore, the Drug Arrangements are not a measure for the purpose of protecting human life or health under Article XX(b)'.[33]

Even though it had already rejected the defence on the aforementioned basis, the panel nonetheless also considered the other prong of Article XX(b), whether the measure is 'necessary' to protect human life or health. Referring to the Appellate Body's reasoning in *Korea—Beef*, the panel examined the extent to which the Drug Arrangements contribute to the EC's health objective.[34] As a result of the 'decreasing trend of GSP benefits', it stated that 'the contribution of the Drug Arrangements to the realization of the European Communities' claimed health objective is insecure for the future'. Furthermore, the panel noted, 'the EC Regulation provides for no monitoring mechanism on the effectiveness of the Drug Arrangements for protecting human life or health in the European Communities'. Finally, the panel considered whether there are 'less WTO-inconsistent or less trade-restrictive measures reasonably available to the European Communities that would achieve the same objective', and in this regard referred to 'financial and technical assistance combined with multilaterally negotiated tariff reductions that provide sufficient tariff reductions on products of export interest to drug-affected countries'. Also, it said, 'multilaterally negotiated tariff reductions on products for which the drug affected countries have a real export interest would provide equivalent benefits to these countries'.[35] Accordingly, the panel found that the Drug Arrangements are not 'necessary to protect human . . . life or health', pursuant to GATT Article XX(b).[36]

(c) Article XX(d): Compliance Measures

Article XX(d) provides an exception for measures 'necessary to secure compliance with laws or regulations which are not inconsistent with the provisions of this Agreement, including those relating to customs enforcement, the enforcement of monopolies operated under paragraph 4 of Article II and Article XVII, the protection of patents, trade marks and copyrights, and the prevention of deceptive practices'. While Article XX(d) is less prominent than some of the other sub-paragraphs, it potentially has a very broad scope, and it has been invoked in thirteen disputes to date. Although examples of certain policies

---

[33] *Ibid*, paras 7.200–7.210.
[34] *Ibid*, para 7.211.
[35] *Ibid*, paras 7.219–7.223.
[36] *Ibid*, para 7.223.

are set out in the provision, these are only illustrations of the types of covered policies, and the non-exhaustive nature of the provision means that all measures 'necessary to secure compliance with [GATT-consistent] laws or regulations' fall within this provision. The key aspects of this provision are whether the measure (1) is designed to 'secure compliance' with (2) laws or regulations that are not inconsistent with the GATT, and (3) is 'necessary' to secure such compliance.[37] We discuss each element below.

The first element is whether the measure is designed to 'secure compliance' with certain laws. With regard to the meaning of 'secure compliance', the Appellate Body has not yet interpreted this phrase. However, panels have emphasised that the phrase means 'to enforce compliance'[38] or 'to enforce obligations under laws and obligations', rather than the broader 'to ensure the attainment of the objectives of the laws and regulations'.[39]

The second element, whether the law with which compliance is being secured is consistent with GATT rules, is fairly straightforward. However, one somewhat unclear issue is the extent of the evidence that needs to be offered by the defending party to show that the law is consistent. In particular, should this always involve a fully fledged set of arguments by both parties regarding the consistency of the measure with all WTO provisions? Or is it sufficient for the defending party to assert that it has not been shown that the measure is inconsistent with any WTO provision, and thus shift the burden to the complainant to make a detailed argument of inconsistency?[40]

Finally, the third element is 'necessity'. The interpretation of 'necessary' was discussed in section II.d above. It was under Article XX(d) that the Appellate Body, in the *Korea—Beef* case, developed the 'weighing and balancing' test involving three specific factors and the availability of alternative measures. We review briefly here the Article XX(d) defence in that case.

The measure at issue in *Korea—Beef* was a 'dual retail system' Korea had set up for sales of imported and domestic beef. For small shops, shop owners had to make a choice between selling domestic and imported beef, that is, they could only sell one or the other. Large shops could sell both, but the different types of beef had to be sold in separate areas of the shop. An Article III:4 violation was found based on adverse effects on the conditions of competition for imported beef. Korea argued that the measure was justified under Article XX(d) because it was necessary to prevent fraud, specifically the practice of passing off less expensive imported beef as more expensive domestic beef.[41]

The panel found that this measure, at least in part, was put in place to secure compliance with Korean legislation against deceptive practices, in particular to prevent passing

---

[37] Appellate Body Report, *Korea—Beef*, para 157.

[38] Panel Report, *Mexico—Soft Drinks*, para 8.175.

[39] See, eg Panel Report, *Canada—Wheat*, para 6.248; Panel Report, *Canada—Periodicals*, para 5.9; *EEC—Parts and Components*, para. 5.17.

[40] The issue has usually been dealt with by panels with a great deal of brevity. As illustrations, in *Korea—Beef* at para 655, the panel simply noted: '[a]t face value, [the measure with which compliance is being secured] is a GATT consistent regulation'; in *Argentina—Hides and Leather*, the complainant did 'not question the consistency with the GATT 1994 of the measures with which compliance was allegedly being secured, and therefore the panel simply "continue[d] … on the basis that the [measures] must be presumed to be consistent with the GATT 1994"': Panel Report, *Argentina—Hides and Leather*, paras 11.297–11.298; in *Dominican Republic—Cigarettes* at paras 7.210–7.211, the panel noted that the measures 'have not been found to be inconsistent with provisions of the GATT' and said it 'may preliminarily assume' that the measures 'are not inconsistent with the provisions of the GATT'.

[41] Panel Report, *Korea—Beef*, para 645.

cheaper imported beef off as domestic beef. Thus, the panel considered that the measure did fall within the policies covered by Article XX(d).[42] This finding was not appealed.

With regard to the 'necessity' requirement, as noted above this is the case where the Appellate Body set out a new standard for 'necessity'. Applying this standard here, the Appellate Body found as follows:

Appellate Body Report, *Korea—Measures Affecting the Importation of Fresh, Chilled and Frozen Beef*, Adopted 10 January 2001, WT/DS161,169/AB/R

169. Korea argues, on appeal, that the Panel, by drawing conclusions from the absence of any requirement for a dual retail system in related product areas, introduces an illegitimate "consistency test" into Article XX(d). For Korea, the proper test for "necessary" under Article XX(d):

> . . . is to see whether another means exists which is less restrictive than the one used and which can reach the objective sought. Whether such means will be applied *consistently* to other products or not is not a matter of concern for the necessity requirement under Article XX(d).

170. Examining enforcement measures applicable to the same illegal behaviour relating to like, or at least similar, products does not necessarily imply the introduction of a "consistency" requirement into the "necessary" concept of Article XX(d). Examining such enforcement measures may provide useful input in the course of determining whether an alternative measure which could "reasonably be expected" to be utilized, is available or not.

171. The enforcement measures that the Panel examined were measures taken to enforce the same law, the *Unfair Competition Act*. This law provides for penal and other sanctions against any "unfair competitive act", which includes any:

> *Act misleading the public to understand the place of origin of any goods* either by falsely marking that place on any commercial document or communication, in said goods or any advertisement thereof *or in any manner of misleading the general public*, or by selling, distributing, importing or exporting goods bearing such mark; (emphasis added)

The language used in this law to define an "unfair competitive act"—"any manner of misleading the general public"—is broad. It applies to all the examples raised by the Panel—domestic dairy beef sold as Hanwoo beef, foreign pork or seafood sold as domestic product, as well as to imported beef served as domestic beef in restaurants.

172. The application by a Member of WTO-*compatible* enforcement measures to the same kind of illegal behaviour—the passing off of one product for another—for like or at least similar products, provides a suggestive indication that an alternative measure which could "reasonably be expected" to be employed may well be available. The application of such measures for the control of the same illegal behaviour for like, or at least similar, products raises doubts with respect to the objective *necessity* of a different, much stricter, and WTO-inconsistent enforcement measure. The Panel was, in our opinion, entitled to consider that the "examples taken from outside as well as within the beef sector indicate that misrepresentation of origin can indeed be dealt with on the basis of basic methods, consistent with the *WTO Agreement*, and thus less trade restrictive and less market intrusive, such as normal policing under the Korean *Unfair Competition Act*".

173. Having found that possible alternative enforcement measures, consistent with the *WTO Agreement*, existed in other related product areas, the Panel went on to state that:

---

[42] *Ibid*, paras 655–658.

. . . it is for Korea to demonstrate that such an alternative measure is not reasonably available or is unreasonably burdensome, financially or technically, taking into account a variety of factors including the domestic costs of such alternative measure, to ensure that consumers are not misled as to the origin of beef.

174.   The Panel proceeded to examine whether the alternative measures or "basic methods"— investigations, prosecutions, fines, and record-keeping—which were used in related product areas, were "reasonably available" to Korea to secure compliance with the *Unfair Competition Act*. The Panel concluded "that Korea has not demonstrated to the satisfaction of the Panel that alternative measures consistent with the WTO Agreement were not reasonably available". Thus, as noted at the outset, the Panel found that the dual retail system was "a disproportionate measure not necessary to secure compliance with the Korean law against deceptive practices". The dual retail system was, therefore, not justified under Article XX(d).

175.   Korea also argues on appeal that the Panel erred in applying Article XX(d) because it did not "pay due attention to the level of enforcement sought". For Korea, under Article XX(d), a panel must:

. . . examine whether a means reasonably available to the WTO Member could have been used in order to reach the objective sought without putting into question the level of enforcement sought.

For Korea, alternative measures must not only be reasonably available, but must also *guarantee* the level of enforcement sought which, in the case of the dual retail system, is the *elimination* of fraud in the beef retail market. With respect to investigations, Korea argues that this tool can only reveal fraud *ex post*, whereas the dual retail system can combat fraudulent practices *ex ante*. Korea contends that *ex post* investigations do not *guarantee* the level of enforcement that Korea has chosen, and therefore should not be considered. With respect to policing, Korea believes that this option is not "reasonably available", because Korea lacks the resources to police thousands of shops on a round-the-clock basis.

176.   It is not open to doubt that Members of the WTO have the right to determine for themselves the level of enforcement of their WTO-consistent laws and regulations. We note that this has also been recognized by the panel in *United States—Section 337*, where it said: "The Panel wished to make it clear that this [the obligation to choose a reasonably available GATT-consistent or less inconsistent measure] does not mean that a contracting party could be asked to change its substantive patent law or its desired *level of enforcement* of that law . . .". (emphasis added) The panel added, however, the caveat that "provided that such law and such *level of enforcement* are the same for imported and domestically-produced products".

177.   We recognize that, in establishing the dual retail system, Korea could well have intended to secure a higher level of enforcement of the prohibition, provided by the *Unfair Competition Act*, of acts misleading the public *about the origin of beef* (domestic or imported) *sold by retailers*, than the level of enforcement of the same prohibition of the *Unfair Competition Act* with respect to *beef served in restaurants*, or the sale by *retailers* of *other meat or food products*, such as *pork or seafood*.

178.   We think it unlikely that Korea intended to establish a level of protection that *totally eliminates* fraud with respect to the origin of beef (domestic or foreign) sold by retailers. The total elimination of fraud would probably require a total ban of imports. Consequently, we assume that in effect Korea intended to *reduce considerably* the number of cases of fraud occurring with respect to the origin of beef sold by retailers. The Panel did find that the dual retail system "does appear to reduce the opportunities and thus the temptations for butchers to misrepresent foreign beef for domestic beef". And we accept Korea's argument that the dual retail

system *facilitates* control and permits combatting fraudulent practices *ex ante*. Nevertheless, it must be noted that the dual retail system is only an *instrument* to achieve a significant reduction of violations of the *Unfair Competition Act*. Therefore, the question remains whether other, conventional and WTO-consistent instruments can not reasonably be expected to be employed to achieve the same result.

179.   Turning to investigations, the Panel found that Korea, in the past, had been able to distinguish imported beef from domestic beef, and had, in fact, published figures on the amount of imported beef fraudulently sold as domestic beef. This meant that Korea was able, in fact, to detect fraud. On fines, the Panel found that these could be an effective deterrent, as long as they outweighed the potential profits from fraud. On record-keeping, the Panel felt that if beef traders at all levels were required to keep records of their transactions, then effective investigations could be carried out. Finally, on policing, the Panel noted that Korea had not demonstrated that the costs would be too high. For all these reasons, the Panel considered "that Korea has not demonstrated to the satisfaction of the Panel that alternative measures consistent with the WTO Agreement were not reasonably available". Thus, as already noted, the Panel found that the dual retail system was "a disproportionate measure not necessary to secure compliance with the Korean law against deceptive practices".

180.   We share the Panel's conclusion. We are not persuaded that Korea could not achieve its desired level of enforcement of the *Unfair Competition Act* with respect to the origin of beef sold by retailers by using conventional WTO-consistent enforcement measures, if Korea would devote more resources to its enforcement efforts on the beef sector. It might also be added that Korea's argument about the lack of resources to police thousands of shops on a round-the-clock basis is, in the end, not sufficiently persuasive. Violations of laws and regulations like the Korean *Unfair Competition Act* can be expected to be routinely investigated and detected through selective, but well-targeted, controls of potential wrongdoers. The control of records will assist in selecting the shops to which the police could pay particular attention.

181.   There is still another aspect that should be noted relating to both the method actually chosen by Korea—its dual retail system for beef—and alternative traditional enforcement measures. Securing through conventional, WTO-consistent measures a higher level of enforcement of the *Unfair Competition Act* with respect to the retail sale of beef, could well entail higher enforcement costs for the national budget. It is pertinent to observe that, through its dual retail system, Korea has in effect shifted all, or the great bulk, of these potential costs of enforcement (translated into a drastic reduction of competitive access to consumers) to imported goods and retailers of imported goods, instead of evenly distributing such costs between the domestic and imported products. In contrast, the more conventional, WTO-consistent measures of enforcement do not involve such onerous shifting of enforcement costs which ordinarily are borne by the Member's public purse.

182.   For these reasons, we uphold the conclusion of the Panel that Korea has not discharged its burden of demonstrating under Article XX(d) that alternative WTO-consistent measures were not "reasonably available" in order to detect and suppress deceptive practices in the beef retail sector , and that the dual retail system is therefore not justified by Article XX(d).

… … …

Thus, in considering whether the dual retail system was 'necessary', the Appellate Body observed that the panel found that Korea does not require a dual retail system in 'related product areas' where deceptive practices may occur, such as in restaurants where 45 per cent of imported beef is sold. Furthermore, it noted that there is no dual retail requirement for pork. Rather, these other areas rely on 'traditional enforcement measures' (eg spot checks by police and fines). In addition, with regard to Korea's argument that it wanted to eliminate fraud entirely and only a dual retail system would do this, the Appellate Body held that normal fraud prevention methods can accomplish this if appropriate resources are devoted to them.[43] On this basis, the Appellate Body found that the measure was not 'necessary' under Article XX(d), and it rejected Korea's defence.

(d) Article XX(g): Conservation of Exhaustible Natural Resources

Article XX(g) provides for an exception for measures 'relating to the conservation of exhaustible natural resources if such measures are made effective in conjunction with restrictions on domestic production or consumption'. Note that this provision does not apply generally to 'environmental protection'. It is written more narrowly to focus on conserving 'exhaustible natural resources'. However, at least in theory the phrase 'conservation of exhaustible natural resources' could be interpreted quite broadly. For example, as discussed below, panels and the Appellate Body have found that both clean air and sea turtles are a natural resource. Thus, the provision has a wide scope.

Article XX(g) has been examined in three WTO disputes: *US—Gasoline*, *US—Shrimp* and *China—Raw Materials*. We discuss each briefly.

(i) US—Gasoline

As discussed above, in *US—Gasoline* the US measure at issue required the use of cleaner-burning gasoline to reduce harmful vehicle emissions. The specific goal was to improve air quality in the most polluted urban areas of the country.

Two WTO Members claimed that the measure treated imported gasoline products less favourably than domestic products based on its different treatment of foreign and domestic gasoline refiners. The US argued that the measures was justified under various provisions of Article XX, including Article XX(g).

In considering this claim, the panel found as follows:

6.36 The Panel noted the US argument that clean air was an exhaustible resource within the meaning of Article XX(g), since it could be exhausted by pollutants such as those emitted through the consumption of gasoline. Lakes, streams, parks, crops and forests were also natural resources that could be exhausted by air pollution. Measures to control air pollution were therefore measures to conserve exhaustible natural resources. Venezuela disagreed, considering that air was not an exhaustible natural resource within the meaning of Article XX(g); rather, its 'condition' changed depending on its cleanliness. Article XX(g) was originally intended to cover exports of exhaustible goods such as petroleum and coal; to expand it to cover 'conditions' of renewable resources was not justified.

6.37 The Panel then examined whether clean air could be considered an exhaustible natural resource. In the view of the Panel, clean air was a resource (it had value) and it was natural. It could be depleted. The fact that the depleted resource was defined with respect to its qualities was not, for the Panel, decisive. Likewise, the fact that a resource was renewable could not be an objection. A past panel had accepted that renewable stocks of salmon could constitute an exhaustible natural resource. Accordingly, the Panel found that a policy to reduce the

---

[43] Appellate Body Report, *Korea—Beef*, paras 168–80.

depletion of clean air was a policy to conserve a natural resource within the meaning of Article XX(g).[44]

This finding was not appealed.

With regard to the 'relating to' element, the panel had examined whether the *discriminatory aspect of the measure* was related to the conservation of exhaustible natural resources. On appeal, the Appellate Body rejected this approach, and said that the *measure itself*, as a whole, must be examined for its relationship to the policy goal. Applying this approach, the Appellate Body considered whether the measure was 'primarily aimed at' the conservation of natural resources for the purposes of Article XX(g). It answered this question in the affirmative, as follows:

> The baseline establishment rules, taken as a whole (that is, the provisions relating to establishment of baselines for domestic refiners, along with the provisions relating to baselines for blenders and importers of gasoline), need to be related to the "non-degradation" requirements set out elsewhere in the Gasoline Rule. Those provisions can scarcely be understood if scrutinized strictly by themselves, totally divorced from other sections of the Gasoline Rule which certainly constitute part of the context of these provisions. The baseline establishment rules whether individual or statutory, were designed to permit scrutiny and monitoring of the level of compliance of refiners, importers and blenders with the "non-degradation" requirements. Without baselines of some kind, such scrutiny would not be possible and the Gasoline Rule's objective of stabilizing and preventing further deterioration of the level of air pollution prevailing in 1990, would be substantially frustrated. The relationship between the baseline establishment rules and the "non-degradation" requirements of the Gasoline Rule is not negated by the inconsistency, found by the Panel, of the baseline establishment rules with the terms of Article III:4. We consider that, given that substantial relationship, the baseline establishment rules cannot be regarded as merely incidentally or inadvertently aimed at the conservation of clean air in the United States for the purposes of Article XX(g).[45]

Thus, the Appellate Body emphasised the substantial relationship between the measure and the policies at issue, and it found the measures to be covered by Article XX(g).

The Appellate Body then examined whether the measure was 'made effective in conjunction with restrictions on domestic production or consumption'. As stated by the Appellate Body, this clause should be read as a requirement that the measures concerned impose restrictions on both imported *and* domestic gasoline, that is, it is an '*even-handedness*' requirement. The Appellate Body qualified this interpretation, adding that this standard does not require 'identical' treatment for imported and domestic products, of course, since if treatment were identical there would probably be no inconsistency with Article III:4 in the first place. The Appellate Body found that the measure at issue here met this 'even-handedness' requirement, as it applied to both imported and domestic products.[46]

On this basis, the Appellate Body found that the measure at issue was 'provisionally justified' under Article XX(g), subject to examining the measure under the chapeau. In section V, we take up the Appellate Body's consideration of this measure under the chapeau.

One point to note about this case is that the Appellate Body seems to have created

---

[44] Panel Report, *US—Gasoline*, paras 6.36–6.37.
[45] Appellate Body Report, *US—Gasoline*, 19.
[46] *Ibid*, 19–21.

a somewhat loose test for Article XX(g). In considering the relationship of the measure to the objective of conservation of natural resources, the Appellate Body considered the measure *as a whole* rather than examine the discriminatory aspect of the measure. In this regard, the Appellate Body stated:

> One problem with the reasoning in that paragraph is that the Panel asked itself whether the "less favourable treatment" of imported gasoline was "primarily aimed at" the conservation of natural resources, rather than whether the "measure", i.e. the baseline establishment rules, were "primarily aimed at" conservation of clean air. In our view, the Panel here was in error in referring to its legal conclusion on Article III:4 instead of the measure in issue. The result of this analysis is to turn Article XX on its head. Obviously, there had to be a finding that the measure provided "less favourable treatment" under Article III:4 before the Panel examined the "General Exceptions" contained in Article XX. That, however, is a conclusion of law. The chapeau of Article XX makes it clear that it is the "measures" which are to be examined under Article XX(g), and not the legal finding of "less favourable treatment".[47]

Thus, as long as the measure *as a whole* is related to the relevant environmental concerns, it will fall within this exception. With such a standard it seems that governments can bury a multitude of discriminatory provisions in a measure and still be covered by Article XX(g). Of course, the measure still has to satisfy the chapeau, and the discriminatory aspect of a measure may not meet this standard. We discuss the chapeau in section V below.

Finally, it is important to note that while the Appellate Body's finding that the prime consideration is whether the 'measure', rather than the discrimination per se, is 'primarily aimed at' the conservation of natural resources has been extended to other sub-paragraphs, where it has regularly been found that the 'measure' must be 'necessary' to achieve the objectives of the relevant subparagraph, the recent Appellate Body decision in *Thailand— Cigarettes* raises some uncertainties. More specifically, the decision, without specifically referencing prior Appellate Body reasoning or jurisprudence, held in the context of an Article XX(d) defence that

> when Article XX(d) is invoked to justify an inconsistency with Article III:4, what must be shown to be 'necessary' is the treatment giving rise to the finding of less favourable treatment. Thus, when less favourable treatment is found based on differences in the regulation of imports and of like domestic products, the analysis of an Article XX(d) defence should focus on whether those regulatory differences are 'necessary' to secure compliance with 'laws or regulations' that are not GATT-inconsistent.[48]

The effect of this decision is yet to be seen, but if such an interpretation continues, it would radically alter the way in which the Appellate Body views and interprets Article XX.

(ii) US—Shrimp

The second WTO dispute under Article XX(g) was *US—Shrimp*. The measure at issue there was somewhat complex. The basic facts were as follows. In 1987, the United States issued regulations, pursuant to a 1973 statute, that required domestic shrimp trawlers

---

[47] *Ibid*, 16.
[48] *Thailand—Cigarettes from the Philippines*, para 177.

to use turtle excluder devices (TEDs) in areas where sea turtles were present. A TED is a grid trapdoor installed inside a trawling net that allows shrimp to pass to the back of the net while directing sea turtles and other unintentionally caught large objects out of the net. In 1989, Congress passed a law that imposed an import ban on shrimp from particular countries unless the foreign government at issue had a programme in place to protect sea turtles during shrimp trawling in a manner similar to the programme applied to US shrimpers. Originally, the implementing regulations that were developed by the State Department pursuant to the statute only applied to certain Caribbean/western Atlantic countries. Those regulations were issued in 1991. However, a December 1995 court decision expanded the rules to apply worldwide. This expansion was applied as of 1 May 1996, and the State Department issued new rules to comply with the court ruling. In response to a WTO complaint brought by several WTO Members, a panel found that the measure violated GATT Article XI. The United States offered a defence under, inter alia, Article XX(g). The Appellate Body addressed this issue as follows:

Appellate Body Report, *United States—Import Prohibition of Certain Shrimp and Shrimp Products*, Adopted 6 November 1998, WT/DS58/AB/R

125. . . . We proceed . . . to the first tier of the analysis of Section 609 and to our consideration of whether it may be characterized as provisionally justified under the terms of Article XX(g).

126. Paragraph (g) of Article XX covers measures:

relating to the conservation of exhaustible natural resources if such measures are made effective in conjunction with restrictions on domestic production or consumption;

"Exhaustible Natural Resources"

127. We begin with the threshold question of whether Section 609 is a measure concerned with the conservation of "exhaustible natural resources" within the meaning of Article XX(g). The Panel, of course, with its "chapeau-down" approach, did not make a finding on whether the sea turtles that Section 609 is designed to conserve constitute "exhaustible natural resources" for purposes of Article XX(g). In the proceedings before the Panel, however, the parties to the dispute argued this issue vigorously and extensively. India, Pakistan and Thailand contended that a "reasonable interpretation" of the term "exhaustible" is that the term refers to "finite resources such as minerals, rather than biological or renewable resources". In their view, such finite resources were exhaustible "because there was a limited supply which could and would be depleted unit for unit as the resources were consumed". Moreover, they argued, if "all" natural resources were considered to be exhaustible, the term "exhaustible" would become superfluous. They also referred to the drafting history of Article XX(g), and, in particular, to the mention of minerals, such as manganese, in the context of arguments made by some delegations that "export restrictions" should be permitted for the preservation of scarce natural resources. For its part, Malaysia added that sea turtles, being living creatures, could only be considered under Article XX(b), since Article XX(g) was meant for "nonliving exhaustible natural resources". It followed, according to Malaysia, that the United States cannot invoke both the Article XX(b) and the Article XX(g) exceptions simultaneously.

128. We are not convinced by these arguments. Textually, Article XX(g) is *not* limited to the conservation of "mineral" or "non-living" natural resources. The complainants' principal argument is rooted in the notion that "living" natural resources are "renewable" and therefore cannot be "exhaustible" natural resources. We do not believe that "exhaustible" natural resources and "renewable" natural resources are mutually exclusive. One lesson that modern biological

sciences teach us is that living species, though in principle, capable of reproduction and, in that sense, "renewable", are in certain circumstances indeed susceptible of depletion, exhaustion and extinction, frequently because of human activities. Living resources are just as "finite" as petroleum, iron ore and other non-living resources.

129.   The words of Article XX(g), "exhaustible natural resources", were actually crafted more than 50 years ago. They must be read by a treaty interpreter in the light of contemporary concerns of the community of nations about the protection and conservation of the environment. While Article XX was not modified in the Uruguay Round, the preamble attached to the *WTO Agreement* shows that the signatories to that Agreement were, in 1994, fully aware of the importance and legitimacy of environmental protection as a goal of national and international policy. The preamble of the *WTO Agreement* -- which informs not only the GATT 1994, but also the other covered agreements -- explicitly acknowledges "the objective of *sustainable development*":

The *Parties* to this Agreement,

> *Recognizing* that their relations in the field of trade and economic endeavour should be conducted *with a view to raising standards of living, ensuring full employment and a large and steadily growing volume of real income and effective demand*, and *expanding the production of and trade in goods and services*, while allowing for the optimal use of the world's resources in accordance with the *objective of sustainable development, seeking both to protect and preserve the environment and to enhance the means for doing so* in a manner consistent with their respective needs and concerns at different levels of economic development, . . . (emphasis added)

130.   From the perspective embodied in the preamble of the *WTO Agreement*, we note that the generic term "natural resources" in Article XX(g) is not "static" in its content or reference but is rather "by definition, evolutionary". It is, therefore, pertinent to note that modern international conventions and declarations make frequent references to natural resources as embracing both living and non-living resources. For instance, the 1982 United Nations Convention on the Law of the Sea ("UNCLOS"), in defining the jurisdictional rights of coastal states in their exclusive economic zones, provides:

Article 56
Rights, jurisdiction and duties of the coastal State in the
exclusive economic zone

1. In the exclusive economic zone, the coastal State has:

(a)   sovereign rights for the purpose of exploring and exploiting, conserving and managing the natural resources, whether living or non-living, of the waters superjacent to the sea-bed and of the sea-bed and its subsoil, . . . (emphasis added)

The UNCLOS also repeatedly refers in Articles 61 and 62 to "living resources" in specifying rights and duties of states in their exclusive economic zones. The Convention on Biological Diversity uses the concept of "biological resources". Agenda 21 speaks most broadly of "natural resources" and goes into detailed statements about "marine living resources". In addition, the Resolution on Assistance to Developing Countries, adopted in conjunction with the Convention on the Conservation of Migratory Species of Wild Animals, recites:

> Conscious that an important element of development lies in the conservation and management of *living natural resources* and that migratory species constitute a significant part of these resources; . . . (emphasis added)

131.   Given the recent acknowledgement by the international community of the importance of concerted bilateral or multilateral action to protect living natural resources, and recalling the explicit recognition by WTO Members of the objective of sustainable development in the preamble of the *WTO Agreement*, we believe it is too late in the day to suppose that Article XX(g) of the GATT 1994 may be read as referring only to the conservation of exhaustible mineral or other non-living natural resources. Moreover, two adopted GATT 1947 panel reports previously found fish to be an "exhaustible natural resource" within the meaning of Article XX(g). We hold that, in line with the principle of effectiveness in treaty interpretation, measures to conserve exhaustible natural resources, whether *living* or *non-living*, may fall within Article XX(g).

132.   We turn next to the issue of whether the living natural resources sought to be conserved by the measure are "exhaustible" under Article XX(g). That this element is present in respect of the five species of sea turtles here involved appears to be conceded by all the participants and third participants in this case. The exhaustibility of sea turtles would in fact have been very difficult to controvert since all of the seven recognized species of sea turtles are today listed in Appendix 1 of the Convention on International Trade in Endangered Species of Wild Fauna and Flora ("CITES"). The list in Appendix 1 includes "all species *threatened with extinction* which are or may be affected by trade". (emphasis added)

133.   Finally, we observe that sea turtles are highly migratory animals, passing in and out of waters subject to the rights of jurisdiction of various coastal states and the high seas. In the Panel Report, the Panel said:

> . . . Information brought to the attention of the Panel, including documented statements from the experts, tends to confirm the fact that sea turtles, in certain circumstances of their lives, migrate through the waters of several countries and the high sea. . . . (emphasis added)

The sea turtle species here at stake, i.e., covered by Section 609, are all known to occur in waters over which the United States exercises jurisdiction. Of course, it is not claimed that *all* populations of these species migrate to, or traverse, at one time or another, waters subject to United States jurisdiction. Neither the appellant nor any of the appellees claims any rights of exclusive ownership over the sea turtles, at least not while they are swimming freely in their natural habitat -- the oceans. We do not pass upon the question of whether there is an implied jurisdictional limitation in Article XX(g), and if so, the nature or extent of that limitation. We note only that in the specific circumstances of the case before us, there is a sufficient nexus between the migratory and endangered marine populations involved and the United States for purposes of Article XX(g).

134.   For all the foregoing reasons, we find that the sea turtles here involved constitute "exhaustible natural resources" for purposes of Article XX(g) of the GATT 1994.

2. "Relating to the Conservation of [Exhaustible Natural Resources]"

135.   Article XX(g) requires that the measure sought to be justified be one which "relat[es] to" the conservation of exhaustible natural resources. In making this determination, the treaty interpreter essentially looks into the relationship between the measure at stake and the legitimate policy of conserving exhaustible natural resources. It is well to bear in mind that the policy of protecting and conserving the endangered sea turtles here involved is shared by all participants and third participants in this appeal, indeed, by the vast majority of the nations of the world. None of the parties to this dispute question the genuineness of the commitment of the others to that policy.

136.   In *United States—Gasoline*, we inquired into the relationship between the baseline establishment rules of the United States Environmental Protection Agency (the "EPA") and the

conservation of natural resources for the purposes of Article XX(g). There, we answered in the affirmative the question posed before the panel of whether the baseline establishment rules were "primarily aimed at" the conservation of clean air. We held that:

> . . . The baseline establishment rules whether individual or statutory, were designed to permit scrutiny and monitoring of the level of compliance of refiners, importers and blenders with the "non-degradation" requirements. Without baselines of some kind, such scrutiny would not be possible and the Gasoline Rule's objective of stabilizing and preventing further deterioration of the level of air pollution prevailing in 1990, would be substantially frustrated. . . . We consider that, given that substantial relationship, the baseline establishment rules cannot be regarded as merely incidentally or inadvertently aimed at the conservation of clean air in the United States for the purposes of Article XX(g).

The substantial relationship we found there between the EPA baseline establishment rules and the conservation of clean air in the United States was a close and genuine relationship of ends and means.

137. In the present case, we must examine the relationship between the general structure and design of the measure here at stake, Section 609, and the policy goal it purports to serve, that is, the conservation of sea turtles.

138. Section 609(b)(1) imposes an import ban on shrimp that have been harvested with commercial fishing technology which may adversely affect sea turtles. This provision is designed to influence countries to adopt national regulatory programs requiring the use of TEDs by their shrimp fishermen. In this connection, it is important to note that the general structure and design of Section 609 *cum* implementing guidelines is fairly narrowly focused. There are two basic exemptions from the import ban, both of which relate clearly and directly to the policy goal of conserving sea turtles. First, Section 609, as elaborated in the 1996 Guidelines, excludes from the import ban shrimp harvested "under conditions that do not adversely affect sea turtles". Thus, the measure, by its terms, excludes from the import ban: aquaculture shrimp; shrimp species (such as *pandalid* shrimp) harvested in water areas where sea turtles do not normally occur; and shrimp harvested exclusively by artisanal methods, even from non-certified countries. The harvesting of such shrimp clearly does not affect sea turtles. Second, under Section 609(b)(2), the measure exempts from the import ban shrimp caught in waters subject to the jurisdiction of certified countries.

139. There are two types of certification for countries under Section 609(b)(2). First, under Section 609(b)(2)(C), a country may be certified as having a fishing environment that does not pose a threat of incidental taking of sea turtles in the course of commercial shrimp trawl harvesting. There is no risk, or only a negligible risk, that sea turtles will be harmed by shrimp trawling in such an environment.

140. The second type of certification is provided by Section 609(b)(2)(A) and (B). Under these provisions, as further elaborated in the 1996 Guidelines, a country wishing to export shrimp to the United States is required to adopt a regulatory program that is comparable to that of the United States program and to have a rate of incidental take of sea turtles that is comparable to the average rate of United States' vessels. This is, essentially, a requirement that a country adopt a regulatory program requiring the use of TEDs by commercial shrimp trawling vessels in areas where there is a likelihood of intercepting sea turtles. This requirement is, in our view, directly connected with the policy of conservation of sea turtles. It is undisputed among the participants, and recognized by the experts consulted by the Panel, that the harvesting of shrimp by commercial shrimp trawling vessels with mechanical retrieval devices in waters where shrimp and sea turtles coincide is a significant cause of sea turtle mortality. Moreover, the Panel did "not question . . . the fact generally acknowledged by the experts that TEDs, when

properly installed and adapted to the local area, would be an effective tool for the preservation of sea turtles".

141.   In its general design and structure, therefore, Section 609 is not a simple, blanket prohibition of the importation of shrimp imposed without regard to the consequences (or lack thereof) of the mode of harvesting employed upon the incidental capture and mortality of sea turtles. Focusing on the design of the measure here at stake, it appears to us that Section 609, *cum* implementing guidelines, is not disproportionately wide in its scope and reach in relation to the policy objective of protection and conservation of sea turtle species. The means are, in principle, reasonably related to the ends. The means and ends relationship between Section 609 and the legitimate policy of conserving an exhaustible, and, in fact, endangered species, is observably a close and real one, a relationship that is every bit as substantial as that which we found in *United States—Gasoline* between the EPA baseline establishment rules and the conservation of clean air in the United States.

142.   In our view, therefore, Section 609 is a measure "relating to" the conservation of an exhaustible natural resource within the meaning of Article XX(g) of the GATT 1994.

3. "If Such Measures are Made Effective in conjunction with Restrictions on Domestic Production or Consumption"

143.   In *United States—Gasoline*, we held that the above-captioned clause of Article XX(g),

> . . . is appropriately read as a requirement that the measures concerned impose restrictions, not just in respect of imported gasoline but also with respect to domestic gasoline. The clause is a requirement of *even-handedness* in the imposition of restrictions, in the name of conservation, upon the production or consumption of exhaustible natural resources.

In this case, we need to examine whether the restrictions imposed by Section 609 with respect to imported shrimp are also imposed in respect of shrimp caught by United States shrimp trawl vessels.

144.   We earlier noted that Section 609, enacted in 1989, addresses the mode of harvesting of imported shrimp only. However, two years earlier, in 1987, the United States issued regulations pursuant to the Endangered Species Act requiring all United States shrimp trawl vessels to use approved TEDs, or to restrict the duration of tow-times, in specified areas where there was significant incidental mortality of sea turtles in shrimp trawls. These regulations became fully effective in 1990 and were later modified. They now require United States shrimp trawlers to use approved TEDs "in areas and at times when there is a likelihood of intercepting sea turtles", with certain limited exceptions. Penalties for violation of the Endangered Species Act, or the regulations issued thereunder, include civil and criminal sanctions. The United States government currently relies on monetary sanctions and civil penalties for enforcement. The government has the ability to seize shrimp catch from trawl vessels fishing in United States waters and has done so in cases of egregious violations. We believe that, in principle, Section 609 is an even-handed measure.

145.   Accordingly, we hold that Section 609 is a measure made effective in conjunction with the restrictions on domestic harvesting of shrimp, as required by Article XX(g).

… … …

In sum, the Appellate Body concluded that sea turtles are a 'natural resource' and are 'exhaustible'. It also found that the measure at issue here was 'reasonably related' to the conservation of sea turtles. Finally, it found that the measure was made effective in conjunction with restrictions on domestic production or consumption. Given that all three elements of Article XX(g) were met, the Appellate Body considered the measure to be provisionally justified under that provision. (We return to the issue of whether the measure met the terms of the chapeau in the next section.)

One final issue under the conservation of exhaustible natural resources exception is whether the resources must be within the jurisdiction of the government whose measure is at issue, or whether they may be in another jurisdiction. That is, can a government take measures to conserve resources outside its own territory or even within another country's territory. In *Shrimp*, this issue arose with regard to a connection between the sea turtles and the United States. In this regard, the Appellate Body observed that sea turtles 'are highly migratory animals, passing in and out of waters subject to the rights of jurisdiction of various coastal states and the high seas', and said that the sea turtle species at issue 'are all known to occur in waters over which the United States exercises jurisdiction'. Thus, the Appellate Body found that 'there is a sufficient nexus between the migratory and endangered marine populations involved and the United States for purposes of Article XX(g)'. However, it explicitly stated that it did 'not pass upon the question of whether there is an implied jurisdictional limitation in Article XX(g), and if so, the nature or extent of that limitation'.[49] Thus, the Appellate Body focused on the narrow facts of this case and avoided the larger issue of protection of someone else's resources. As a result, the legality of a situation in which a country tries to protect resources in another country through trade measures is still somewhat of an open question.

(iii) China—Raw Materials

The most recent dispute invoking Article XX(g) occurred in *China—Raw Materials*. In this dispute, the EU, US and Mexico claimed that China's use of export restraints on various forms raw materials (ie bauxite, coke, fluorspar, magnesium, manganese, silicon carbide, silicon metal, yellow phosphorus and zinc) breached several articles of China's Accession Protocol, China's Working Party Report and the GATT. The panel found several inconsistencies between China's measures and its WTO obligations.

China appealed on several grounds, including by claiming that the panel erred in interpreting the phrase 'made effective in conjunction with' in Article XX(g) to mean that restrictions on domestic production or consumption must 'be applied jointly with the challenged export restrictions', and that 'the purpose of those export restrictions must be to ensure the effectiveness of those domestic restrictions'. In reversing the panel's findings, the Appellate Body went some way towards clarifying the meaning of 'made effective in conjunction with' in the context of Article XX(g).

Appellate Body Report, *China—Measures Relating to the Exportation of Various Raw Materials*, Adopted 22 February 2012, WT/DS394,395,398/AB/R

346. The Panel found that China's export quota on refractory-grade bauxite is inconsistent with Article XI:1 of the GATT 1994. China sought to justify this export quota pursuant to Article XX(g) of the GATT 1994, arguing that refractory-grade bauxite is an exhaustible natural resource that is scarce and requires protection.

---

[49] Appellate Body Report, *US—Shrimp*, para 133.

347. The Panel first addressed the question of whether China's export quota relates to the conservation of refractory-grade bauxite. Based on its review of the evidence and arguments before it, the Panel found this not to be the case. The Panel nevertheless continued its analysis in order to determine whether the export quota on refractory-grade bauxite was "made effective in conjunction with" restrictions on domestic production or consumption, as required under Article XX(g) of the GATT 1994.

348. The Panel considered that, in order for a measure to be justified under Article XX(g), the measure must satisfy two conditions: (i) it must relate to the conservation of an exhaustible natural resource; and (ii) it must be made effective in conjunction with restrictions on domestic production or consumption. With respect to the first requirement, the Panel stated that the words "relate to . . . conservation" have been interpreted by the Appellate Body to require a substantial relationship between the trade measure and conservation, so that the trade measure would be "primarily aimed at" the conservation of exhaustible natural resources. The Panel further noted that the term "conservation" is defined as "the act of preserving and maintaining the existing state of something, in this case 'natural resources' covered by Article XX(g)."

349. With respect to the requirement that conservation measures in the sense of Article XX(g) be "made effective in conjunction with" restrictions on domestic production, the Panel referred to a statement of the GATT panel in *Canada—Herring and Salmon*, that a measure can only be considered to be "made effective in conjunction with" restrictions on domestic production, if it is "primarily aimed at rendering effective these restrictions". The Panel also quoted the Appellate Body's statement in *US—Gasoline* that the phrase "'if such measures are made effective in conjunction with restrictions on domestic products or consumption' is appropriately read as a requirement that the measures concerned impose restrictions, not just in respect of imported [products], but also with respect to domestic [products]." The Panel then found that "restrictions on domestic production or consumption must not only be applied jointly with the challenged export restrictions but, in addition, the purpose of those export restrictions must be to ensure the effectiveness of those domestic restrictions.'

350. China alleges that the Panel erred in its interpretation of the phrase "made effective in conjunction with" in Article XX(g) of the GATT 1994. China maintains that the Panel read this phrase to mean that, in order to be justified under Article XX(g), a challenged measure must satisfy two cumulative conditions: first, it must "be applied jointly" with restrictions on domestic production or consumption; and, second, the "purpose" of the challenged measure must be to make effective restrictions on domestic production or consumption. China argues that the first element of this interpretation is consistent with the ordinary meaning of the phrase "made effective in conjunction with", but that the second is not. China requests the Appellate Body to reverse the erroneous second element of the Panel's interpretation. China does not, however, appeal the Panel's ultimate conclusion that China's export quota on refractory-grade bauxite is inconsistent with Article XI of the GATT 1994 and not justified under Article XX(g).

351. China submits that the Appellate Body's interpretation of the term "in conjunction with" in *US—Gasoline* corresponds to the first element of the meaning that the Panel attributed to that term, namely, that the challenged measures "be applied jointly with" restrictions on domestic production or consumption. China submits, however, that nothing in the phrase "made effective in conjunction with" suggests that the "purpose" of a challenged measure must be to ensure the effectiveness of domestic restrictions. In particular, China argues that Article XX(g) does not require that each set of measures must have, as a separate and independent purpose, the goal of ensuring the effectiveness of the other set of measures. For China, it suffices that the challenged measure is related to the conservation of a natural resource, and that it operates together with domestic restrictions on the production or consumption of the same resource.

352. By contrast, the United States and Mexico request the Appellate Body to uphold the Panel's reasoning. They submit that *US—Gasoline* did not involve the particular interpretive question of how the operation of the challenged measure should be conjoined with the operation of domestic restrictions, and that the present case was the first instance since the GATT panel proceeding in *Canada—Herring and Salmon* that a respondent asserted Article XX(g) as a defence where the challenged measure was distinct from the restrictions on domestic production or consumption. Therefore, the United States and Mexico argue that the Panel appropriately drew upon the *Canada—Herring and Salmon* panel's reasoning. The European Union also supports the Panel's reasoning, arguing that the GATT panel rightly stated that a measure can only be made effective "in conjunction with" domestic restrictions on production if it is primarily aimed at rendering effective these restrictions.

...

355. In order to fall within the ambit of subparagraph (g) of Article XX, a measure must "relat[e] to the conservation of exhaustible natural resources". The term "relat[e] to" is defined as "hav[ing] some connection with, be[ing] connected to". The Appellate Body has found that, for a measure to relate to conservation in the sense of Article XX(g), there must be "a close and genuine relationship of ends and means". The word "conservation", in turn, means "the preservation of the environment, especially of natural resources".

356. Article XX(g) further requires that conservation measures be "made effective in conjunction with restrictions on domestic production or consumption". The word "effective" as relating to a legal instrument is defined as "in operation at a given time". We consider that the term "made effective", when used in connection with a legal instrument, describes measures brought into operation, adopted, or applied. The Spanish and French equivalents of "made effective"—namely "*se apliquen*" and "*sont appliquées*"—confirm this understanding of "made effective". The term "in conjunction" is defined as "together, jointly, (with)". Accordingly, the trade restriction must operate jointly with the restrictions on domestic production or consumption. Article XX(g) thus permits trade measures relating to the conservation of exhaustible natural resources when such trade measures work together with restrictions on domestic production or consumption, which operate so as to conserve an exhaustible natural resource. By its terms, Article XX(g) does not contain an additional requirement that the conservation measure be primarily aimed at making effective the restrictions on domestic production or consumption.

357. The Appellate Body addressed Article XX(g) in *US—Gasoline*. The Appellate Body noted Venezuela's and Brazil's argument that, to be deemed as "made effective in conjunction with restrictions on domestic production or consumption", a measure must be "primarily aimed at" both conservation of exhaustible natural resources and making effective certain restrictions on domestic production or consumption. The Appellate Body, however, found that:

. . . "made effective" when used in connection with a measure—a governmental act or regulation—may be seen to refer to such measure being "operative", as "in force", or as having "come into effect." Similarly, the phrase "in conjunction with" may be read quite plainly as "together with" or "jointly with." Taken together, the second clause of Article XX(g) appears to us to refer to governmental measures like the baseline establishment rules being promulgated or brought into effect together with restrictions on domestic production or consumption of natural resources. Put in a slightly different manner, we believe that the clause "if such measures are made effective in conjunction with restrictions on domestic production or consumption" is appropriately read as a requirement that the measures concerned impose restrictions, not just in respect of imported gasoline but also with respect to domestic gasoline. The clause is a requirement of even-handedness in the imposition of restrictions, in the name of conservation, upon the production or consumption of exhaustible natural resources.

358. Accordingly, in assessing whether the baseline establishment rules at issue in *US—Gasoline* were "made effective in conjunction with" restrictions on domestic production or consumption, the Appellate Body relied on the fact that those rules were promulgated or brought into effect "together with" restrictions on domestic production or consumption of natural resources. However, even though Brazil and Venezuela had presented arguments suggesting that it was necessary that the purpose of the baseline establishment rules be to ensure the effectiveness of restrictions on domestic production, the Appellate Body did *not* consider this to be necessary. In particular, the Appellate Body did not consider that, in order to be justified under Article XX(g), measures "relating to the conservation of exhaustible natural resources" must be primarily aimed at rendering effective restrictions on domestic production or consumption. Instead, the Appellate Body read the terms "in conjunction with", "quite plainly", as "together with" or "jointly with", and found no additional requirement that the conservation measure be primarily aimed at making effective certain restrictions on domestic production or consumption.

359. As noted above, the Panel in the present case appears to have considered that, in order to prove that a measure is "made effective in conjunction with" restrictions on domestic production or consumption in the sense of Article XX(g), it must be established, first, that the measure is applied jointly with restrictions on domestic production or consumption, and, second, that the purpose of the challenged measure is to make effective restrictions on domestic production or consumption. In particular, the Panel's use of the words "not only . . . but, in addition", as well as the reference at the end of the sentence to the GATT panel report in *Canada—Herring and Salmon*, indicate that the Panel did in fact consider that two separate conditions have to be met for a measure to be considered "made effective in conjunction with" in the sense of Article XX(g).

360. As explained above, we see nothing in the text of Article XX(g) to suggest that, in addition to being "made effective in conjunction with restrictions on domestic production or consumption", a trade restriction must be aimed at ensuring the effectiveness of domestic restrictions, as the Panel found. Instead, we have found above that Article XX(g) permits trade measures relating to the conservation of exhaustible natural resources if such trade measures work together with restrictions on domestic production or consumption, which operate so as to conserve an exhaustible natural resource.

361. Based on the foregoing, we *find* that the Panel erred in interpreting the phrase "made effective in conjunction with" in Article XX(g) of the GATT 1994 to require a separate showing that the purpose of the challenged measure must be to make effective restrictions on domestic production or consumption. Accordingly, we *reverse* this interpretation by the Panel in paragraph 7.397 of the Panel Reports.

… … …

IV. THE CHAPEAU

As explained above, where a measure qualifies as one of the types of measures permitted under one of the Article XX sub-paragraphs, it must still satisfy the terms of the Article XX chapeau. The chapeau states that the measures in the listed exceptions are permitted:

Subject to the requirement that such measures are not applied in a manner which would constitute a means of arbitrary or unjustifiable discrimination between countries where the same conditions prevail, or a disguised restriction on international trade . . .

Thus, to be justified under Article XX, measures must not be applied in a manner that constitutes 'arbitrary' discrimination, 'unjustifiable' discrimination or a 'disguised restriction on international trade'.

We examine below the application of this provision in three disputes. It should be noted that the first two disputes have an important distinction between them. In the first, *US—Gasoline*, the measure imposed different standards on foreign companies as compared to domestic companies with regard to a product sold in the domestic market. By contrast, in the second, *US—Shrimp*, the measure attempted to make *foreign governments* adopt a policy programme comparable to that in place in the United States. This distinction played an important part in the reasoning. The third and most recent dispute, *Brazil—Tyres*, provides the most comprehensive appraisal of the chapeau to date.

(a) *US—Gasoline*

In the *US—Gasoline* case, after a violation of Article III:4 was found based on the less favourable treatment of foreign gasoline, the Appellate Body concluded that the measure was provisionally justified under Article XX(g), as a measure related to the conservation of exhaustible natural resources. It then turned to the chapeau to see if the measure met its terms.

Appellate Body Report, *United States—Standards for Reformulated and Conventional Gasoline*, Adopted 20 May 1996, WT/DS2/AB/R, at 22–29

Having concluded, in the preceding section, that the baseline establishment rules of the Gasoline Rule fall within the terms of Article XX(g), we come to the question of whether those rules also meet the requirements of the chapeau of Article XX. In order that the justifying protection of Article XX may be extended to it, the measure at issue must not only come under one or another of the particular exceptions—paragraphs (a) to (j)—listed under Article XX; it must also satisfy the requirements imposed by the opening clauses of Article XX. The analysis is, in other words, two-tiered: first, provisional justification by reason of characterization of the measure under XX(g); second, further appraisal of the same measure under the introductory clauses of Article XX.

The chapeau by its express terms addresses, not so much the questioned measure or its specific contents as such, but rather the manner in which that measure is applied. It is, accordingly, important to underscore that the purpose and object of the introductory clauses of Article XX is generally the prevention of "abuse of the exceptions of [what was later to become] Article [XX]". This insight drawn from the drafting history of Article XX is a valuable one. The chapeau is animated by the principle that while the exceptions of Article XX may be invoked as a matter of legal right, they should not be so applied as to frustrate or defeat the legal obligations of the holder of the right under the substantive rules of the *General Agreement*. If those exceptions are not to be abused or misused, in other words, the measures falling within the particular exceptions must be applied reasonably, with due regard both to the legal duties of the party claiming the exception and the legal rights of the other parties concerned.

The burden of demonstrating that a measure provisionally justified as being within one of the exceptions set out in the individual paragraphs of Article XX does not, in its application, constitute abuse of such exception under the chapeau, rests on the party invoking the exception. That is, of necessity, a heavier task than that involved in showing that an exception, such as Article XX(g), encompasses the measure at issue.

The enterprise of applying Article XX would clearly be an unprofitable one if it involved no more than applying the standard used in finding that the baseline establishment rules were inconsistent with Article III:4. That would also be true if the finding were one of inconsistency with some other substantive rule of the *General Agreement*. The provisions of the chapeau cannot logically refer to the same standard(s) by which a violation of a substantive rule has been determined to have occurred. To proceed down that path would be both to empty the chapeau of its contents and to deprive the exceptions in paragraphs (a) to (j) of meaning. Such recourse would also confuse the question of whether inconsistency with a substantive rule existed, with the further and separate question arising under the chapeau of Article XX as to whether that inconsistency was nevertheless justified. One of the corollaries of the "general rule of interpretation" in the *Vienna Convention* is that interpretation must give meaning and effect to all the terms of a treaty. An interpreter is not free to adopt a reading that would result in reducing whole clauses or paragraphs of a treaty to redundancy or inutility.

The chapeau, it will be seen, prohibits such application of a measure at issue (otherwise falling within the scope of Article XX(g)) as would constitute

(a) "arbitrary discrimination" (between countries where the same conditions prevail);
(b) "unjustifiable discrimination" (with the same qualifier); or
(c) "disguised restriction" on international trade.

The text of the chapeau is not without ambiguity, including one relating to the field of application of the standards its contains: the arbitrary or unjustifiable discrimination standards and the disguised restriction on international trade standard. It may be asked whether these standards do not have different fields of application. Such a question was put to the United States in the course of the oral hearing. It was asked whether the words incorporated into the first two standards "between countries where the same conditions prevail" refer to conditions in importing and exporting countries, or only to conditions in exporting countries. The reply of the United States was to the effect that it interpreted that phrase as referring to both the exporting countries and importing countries and as between exporting countries. It also said that the language spoke for itself, but there was no reference to third parties; while some thought that this was only between exporting countries *inter se,* there is no support in the text for that view. No such question was put to the United States concerning the field of application of the third standard – disguised restriction on international trade. But the United States put forward arguments designed to show that in the case under appeal, it had met all the standards set forth in the chapeau. In doing so, it clearly proceeded on the assumption that, whatever else they might relate to in another case, they were relevant to a case of national treatment where the Panel had found a violation of Article III:4. At no point in the appeal was that assumption challenged by Venezuela or Brazil. Venezuela argued that the United States had failed to meet all the standards contained in the chapeau. So did Norway and the European Communities as third participants. In short, the field of application of these standards was not at issue.

The assumption on which all the participants proceeded is buttressed by the fact that the chapeau says that "*nothing in this Agreement* shall be construed to prevent the adoption or enforcement by any contracting party of measures ..". The exceptions listed in Article XX thus relate to all of the obligations under the *General Agreement*: the national treatment obligation and the most-favoured-nation obligation, of course, but others as well. Effect is more easily given to the words "nothing in this Agreement", and Article XX as a whole including its chapeau more easily integrated into the remainder of the *General Agreement*, if the chapeau is taken to mean that the standards it sets forth are applicable to all of the situations in which an allegation of a violation of a substantive obligation has been made and one of the exceptions contained in Article XX has in turn been claimed.

Against this background, we see no need to decide the matter of the field of application of the standards set forth in the chapeau nor to make a ruling at variance with the common understanding of the participants.

"Arbitrary discrimination", "unjustifiable discrimination" and "disguised restriction" on international trade may, accordingly, be read side-by-side; they impart meaning to one another. It is clear to us that "disguised restriction" includes disguised *discrimination* in international trade. It is equally clear that *concealed* or *unannounced* restriction or discrimination in international trade does *not* exhaust the meaning of "disguised restriction". We consider that "disguised restriction", whatever else it covers, may properly be read as embracing restrictions amounting to arbitrary or unjustifiable discrimination in international trade taken under the guise of a measure formally within the terms of an exception listed in Article XX. Put in a somewhat different manner, the kinds of considerations pertinent in deciding whether the application of a particular measure amounts to "arbitrary or unjustifiable discrimination", may also be taken into account in determining the presence of a "disguised restriction" on international trade. The fundamental theme is to be found in the purpose and object of avoiding abuse or illegitimate use of the exceptions to substantive rules available in Article XX.

There was more than one alternative course of action available to the United States in promulgating regulations implementing the CAA. These included the imposition of statutory baselines without differentiation as between domestic and imported gasoline. This approach, if properly implemented, could have avoided any discrimination at all. Among the other options open to the United States was to make available individual baselines to foreign refiners as well as domestic refiners. The United States has put forward a series of reasons why either of these courses was not, in its view, realistically open to it and why, instead, it had to devise and apply the baseline establishment rules contained in the Gasoline Rule.

In explaining why individual baselines for foreign refiners had not been put in place, the United States laid heavy stress upon the difficulties which the EPA would have had to face. These difficulties related to anticipated administrative problems that individual baselines for foreign refiners would have generated. This argument was made succinctly by the United States in the following terms:

> Verification on foreign soil of foreign baselines, and subsequent enforcement actions, present substantial difficulties relating to problems arising whenever a country exercises enforcement jurisdiction over foreign persons. In addition, even if individual baselines were established for several foreign refiners, the importer would be tempted to claim the refinery of origin that presented the most benefits in terms of baseline restrictions, and tracking the refinery or origin would be very difficult because gasoline is a fungible commodity. The United States should not have to prove that it cannot verify information and enforce its regulations in every instance in order to show that the same enforcement conditions do not prevail in the United States and other countries . . . The impracticability of verification and enforcement of foreign refiner baselines in this instance shows that the "discrimination" is based on serious, not arbitrary or unjustifiable, concerns stemming from different conditions between enforcement of its laws in the United States and abroad.

Thus, according to the United States, imported gasoline was relegated to the more exacting statutory baseline requirement because of these difficulties of verification and enforcement. The United States stated that verification and enforcement of the Gasoline Rule's requirements for imported gasoline are "much easier when the statutory baseline is used" and that there would be a "dramatic difference" in the burden of administering requirements for imported gasoline if individual baselines were allowed.

While the anticipated difficulties concerning verification and subsequent enforcement are doubtless real to some degree, the Panel viewed them as insufficient to justify the denial to foreign refiners of individual baselines permitted to domestic refiners. The Panel said:

> While the Panel agreed that it would be necessary under such a system to ascertain the origin of gasoline, the Panel could not conclude that the United States had shown that this could not be achieved by other measures reasonably available to it and consistent or less inconsistent with the General Agreement. Indeed, the Panel noted that a determination of origin would often be feasible. The Panel examined, for instance, the case of a direct shipment to the United States. It considered that there was no reason to believe that, given the usual measures available in international trade for determination of origin and tracking of goods (including documentary evidence and third party verification) there was any particular difficulty sufficient to warrant the demands of the baseline establishment methods applied by the United States.
>
> …
>
> In the view of the Panel, the United States had reasonably available to it data for, and measures of, verification and assessment which were consistent or less inconsistent with Article III:4. For instance, although foreign data may be formally less subject to complete control by US authorities, this did not amount to establishing that foreign data could not in any circumstances be sufficiently reliable to serve U.S. purposes. This, however, was the practical effect of the application of the Gasoline Rule. In the Panel's view, the United States had not demonstrated that data available from foreign refiners was inherently less susceptible to established techniques of checking, verification, assessment and enforcement than data for other trade in goods subject to US regulation. The nature of the data in this case was similar to data relied upon by the United States in other contexts, including, for example, under the application of antidumping laws. In an antidumping case, only when the information was not supplied or deemed unverifiable did the United States turn to other information. If a similar practice were to be applied in the case of the Gasoline Rule, then importers could, for instance, be permitted to use the individual baselines of foreign refiners for imported gasoline from those refiners, with the statutory baseline being applied only when the source of imported gasoline could not be determined or a baseline could not be established because of an absence of data.

We agree with the finding above made in the Panel Report. There are, as the Panel Report found, established techniques for checking, verification, assessment and enforcement of data relating to imported goods, techniques which in many contexts are accepted as adequate to permit international trade—trade between territorial sovereigns—to go on and grow. The United States must have been aware that for these established techniques and procedures to work, cooperative arrangements with both foreign refiners and the foreign governments concerned would have been necessary and appropriate. At the oral hearing, in the course of responding to an enquiry as to whether the EPA could have adapted, for purposes of establishing individual refinery baselines for foreign refiners, procedures for verification of information found in U.S. antidumping laws, the United States said that "in the absence of refinery cooperation and the possible absence of foreign government cooperation as well", it was unlikely that the EPA auditors would be able to conduct the on-site audit reviews necessary to establish even the overall quality of refineries' 1990 gasoline. From this statement, there arises a strong implication, it appears to the Appellate Body, that the United States had not pursued the possibility of entering into cooperative arrangements with the governments of Venezuela and Brazil or, if it had, not to the point where it encountered governments that were unwilling to cooperate. The record of this case sets out the detailed justifications put forward by the United States. But it does not reveal what, if any, efforts had been taken by the United States to enter into appropriate procedures in cooperation with the governments of Venezuela and Brazil so as to mitigate the administrative problems pleaded by the United States. The fact that the United States Congress might have intervened, as it did later intervene, in the process by denying funding, is beside the point: the United States, of course, carries responsibility for actions of both the executive and legislative departments of government.

In its submissions, the United States also explained why the statutory baseline requirement was not imposed on domestic refiners as well. Here, the United States stressed the problems that domestic refineries would have faced had they been required to comply with the statutory baseline. The Panel Report summarized the United States' argument in the following terms:

> The United States concluded that, contrary to Venezuela's and Brazil's claim, Article XX did not require adoption of the statutory baseline as a national standard even if the difficulties associated with the establishment of individual baselines for importers were insurmountable. Application of the statutory baseline to domestic producers of reformulated and conventional gasoline in 1995 would have been *physically and financially impossible because of the magnitude of the changes required in almost all US refineries; it thus would have caused a substantial delay in the programme.* Weighing the feasibility of policy options in economic or technical terms in order to meet an environmental objective was a legitimate consideration, and did not, in itself, constitute protectionism, as alleged by Venezuela and Brazil. Article XX did not require a government to choose the most expensive possible way to regulate its environment. (emphasis added)

Clearly, the United States did not feel it feasible to require its domestic refiners to incur the physical and financial costs and burdens entailed by immediate compliance with a statutory baseline. The United States wished to give domestic refiners time to restructure their operations and adjust to the requirements in the Gasoline Rule. This may very well have constituted sound domestic policy from the viewpoint of the EPA and U.S. refiners. At the same time we are bound to note that, while the United States counted the costs for its domestic refiners of statutory baselines, there is nothing in the record to indicate that it did other than disregard that kind of consideration when it came to foreign refiners.

We have above located two omissions on the part of the United States: to explore adequately means, including in particular cooperation with the governments of Venezuela and Brazil, of mitigating the administrative problems relied on as justification by the United States for rejecting individual baselines for foreign refiners; and to count the costs for foreign refiners that would result from the imposition of statutory baselines. In our view, these two omissions go well beyond what was necessary for the Panel to determine that a violation of Article III:4 had occurred in the first place. The resulting discrimination must have been foreseen, and was not merely inadvertent or unavoidable. In the light of the foregoing, our conclusion is that the baseline establishment rules in the Gasoline Rule, in their application, constitute "unjustifiable discrimination" and a "disguised restriction on international trade". We hold, in sum, that the baseline establishment rules, although within the terms of Article XX(g), are not entitled to the justifying protection afforded by Article XX as a whole.

… … …

Of significance here is that the Appellate Body noted the following two factors at the end of its reasoning: (1) the United States did not adequately explore ways to cooperate with the complainants to provide equal treatment to foreign refiners, and (2) the United States did not properly account for the costs to foreign refiners from the measure. The Appellate Body said that these omissions go 'well beyond' what was necessary for the Article III:4 violation. Thus, the 'resulting discrimination must have been foreseen, and was not merely inadvertent or unavoidable'. On this basis, the Appellate Body concluded that the rules constitute 'unjustifiable discrimination' or a 'disguised restriction on international trade'.

The *US—Gasoline* case dealt with the interaction of the non-discrimination obligation of Article III and the non-discrimination requirement of the chapeau. As mentioned above, there is a difficult and complex relationship between the two. If discrimination is already prohibited under Article III, what is the scope of the additional non-discrimination requirement of the Article XX chapeau? One possible explanation of the Appellate Body's findings here is that Article III requires only a discriminatory *effect* to find a violation, whereas the introductory clause requires discriminatory *intent* as well. The discriminatory effect of the measure was sufficient for a finding of violation of Article III:4, but would not by itself have violated the chapeau. Because the discrimination at issue was intentional (ie in the words of the Appellate Body, 'must have been foreseen' and 'not merely inadvertent or unavoidable'), however, it did, in fact, violate the chapeau, according to the Appellate Body's findings.

(b) *US—Shrimp*

The second case addressing the chapeau is *US—Shrimp*, the facts of which were described in section III above. In response to a WTO complaint brought by several WTO Members, a panel found that the measure violated GATT Article XI. The panel rejected a US defence under GATT Article XX, but the Appellate Body reversed the panel's reasoning, and conducted its own Article XX analysis. After finding that the measure fell within Article XX(g), as a measure related to the conservation of exhaustible natural resources, the Appellate Body then examined whether the measure satisfied the terms of the chapeau. In doing so, the Appellate Body first considered the 'unjustifiable discrimination' element. In this regard, it emphasised several factors:

- the 'coercive effect' on the specific policies of WTO Member governments, as the measure required these governments to adopt 'essentially the same policy' that the United States followed, without taking into account the different conditions in other countries;
- the measure prohibits imports of shrimp caught using TEDs if they are from a non-certified country, and thus does not take into account the different conditions in different countries;
- the United States engaged in negotiations on these issues with some countries, such as certain Caribbean countries, but not others, including the complainants;
- because of the effect of a court decision, the complainants only had four months in which to implement the rules, whereas Caribbean countries had a lot more time.

On the basis of these factors, the Appellate Body found that 'unjustifiable discrimination' exists.[50]

The Appellate Body also found that 'arbitrary discrimination' exists, based on two factors: the limited flexibility under the measure in how officials made the certification determination, and the fact that the certification process was not transparent or predictable.[51]

In response to the Appellate Body's rulings, the United States modified the measure so as to comply with WTO rules. In particular, it adopted new guidelines in 1999 that

---

[50] Appellate Body Report, *US—Shrimp*, paras 161–76.
[51] *Ibid*, paras 177–83.

allowed for the use of TEDs or a 'comparably effective' sea turtle protection programme to allow for certification, and it tried, albeit unsuccessfully, to negotiate an agreement on sea turtle conservation with certain Indian Ocean countries (where the original complainants were located). Importantly, unlike with the old measure, shrimp caught using TEDs could now be imported even if the country of origin had not been certified under the measure.[52]

Despite this change, Malaysia, one of the four original complainants, complained in Article 21.5 proceedings that the measure still did not satisfy the Article XX exception. With regard to the chapeau, there were two key issues: the relevance of the international negotiations that had taken place and the added flexibility in the new guidelines.

On the first issue, Malaysia argued that the United States was under an obligation to conclude a treaty, not just negotiate one. The Appellate Body rejected this argument, finding that the United States was in compliance with the earlier ruling as long as it continued with good faith negotiations, and that there was no requirement actually to conclude a treaty. Based on the good faith negotiations that had been undertaken, the Appellate Body upheld the Article 21.5 panel's finding that the measure was no longer applied in a manner that constitutes arbitrary or unjustifiable discrimination. In this regard, the Appellate Body noted that Malaysia's interpretation 'would mean that any country party to the negotiations with the United States, whether a WTO Member or not, would have, in effect, a veto over whether the United States could fulfill its WTO obligations'.[53]

With regard to the second issue, Malaysia argued that 'unilateral' measures like the one at issue here, where access to the US market is conditioned on policies and standards 'unilaterally' prescribed by the United States, are never permitted. The Appellate Body rejected the view that the measure violates the chapeau because of its unilateral nature. The Appellate Body explained that the revised measure allows 'comparably effective' measures in foreign countries, rather than measures that are 'essentially the same' as in the old regime, and this additional flexibility means that the measure is permissible.[54]

(c) *Brazil—Tyres*

The measure challenged here was an import ban on retreaded and used tyres. The measure was motivated by the established connection between the accumulation of waste tyres at the end of their useful life and risks to human, animal and plant life and health. Waste tyres provide suitable breeding grounds for disease-carrying mosquitoes and, if burnt, release toxic emissions which cause all manner of human health problems. The import ban eventually came to be incomplete in two respects. An exemption for remoulded tyres (a sub-category of retreaded tyres) from other MERCOSUR countries was incorporated into the measure as a result of a ruling by a MERCOSUR arbitral tribunal. Secondly, significant volumes of used tyre casings were being imported by Brazilian retreaders who had obtained injunctions from their domestic courts preventing the enforcement of the ban against them. Brazilian retreading firms were therefore able to manufacture retreaded tyres made from casings of European origin, even though European firms were unable

---

[52] This aspect of the regulation was found by the US Court of International Trade to be inconsistent with the statute; however, the Court of Appeals for the Federal Circuit overruled it, and found the regulation to be consistent with the statue: *Turtle Island Restoration Network v Evans*, 284 F 3d 1282 (Fed Cir 2002).

[53] Appellate Body Report, *US—Shrimp*, para 123.

[54] *Ibid*, paras 146–52.

to export retreaded tyres to Brazil. Overall, the panel found for the European Communities, confirming its view that the import ban was a quantitative restriction in violation of GATT Article XI:1 which could not be justified under Article XX.

Within the Article XX analysis, the panel found that the import ban could be provisionally justified under paragraph (b) as being 'necessary to protect human, animal or plant life or health'. This finding was upheld on appeal. However, the panel went on to find that the chapeau was not satisfied. Here, the panel considered that the MERCOSUR exemption, and the court injunctions, should be regarded as aspects of the application of the import ban. For the panel, the MERCOSUR exemption did not fall foul of the chapeau, a finding which was successfully appealed by the European Communities. Even the panel, however, considered that the injunctions obtained by Brazilian firms breached the chapeau, a finding which was upheld by the Appellate Body based on modified reasoning. The following excerpt details the contrasting approaches of the panel and the Appellate Body towards the chapeau language.

A Davies, 'Interpreting the Chapeau of GATT Article XX in Light of the "New" Approach in *Brazil—Tyres*' 2009 (43) *Journal of World Trade Law* 507

II. The Panel's Effects Based Approach to the Chapeau

In attributing meaning to the terms used in the chapeau, the panel adopted an effects based approach. What mattered was the extent to which the discrimination was manifesting itself in trade flows, and, therefore, the extent to which the discrimination was undermining the policy objective:

> If such imports were to take place in such amounts that the achievement of the objective of the measure at issue would be significantly undermined, the application of the import ban in conjunction with the MERCOSUR exemption would constitute a means of unjustifiable discrimination. The more imports enter Brazilian territory through the exemption, the more Brazil's declared policy objective of reducing the unnecessary accumulation of waste tyres to the greatest extent possible will be undermined, thereby affecting the justification for the maintenance of the import ban *vis-à-vis* non-MERCOSUR WTO Members . . .

The Panel then based its conclusion of the absence of 'arbitrary or unjustifiable' discrimination' on the finding that, as of the date of its examination, 'volumes of imports of retreaded tyres under the exemption appear not to have been significant'.

The same approach was applied with respect to the injunctions granted to Brazilian importers of used tyres, albeit with a different result. The panel noted that, [T]he granting of injunctions allowing used tyres to be imported . . . effectively allows the very used tyres that are prevented from entering into Brazil *after* retreading to be imported *before* retreading'. The Panel went on to find both that, [T]his has the direct potential to undermine the objective of the prohibition on importation of retreaded tyres', and that the objective had actually been significantly undermined because of the import volumes.

The panel then went on to consider whether the discrimination was occurring 'between countries where the same conditions prevail'. The panel began here by clarifying the nature of the discrimination created by the court injunctions. It seems clear from the passage below that this discrimination was in the nature of a national treatment violation:

> We first recall that the discrimination at issue, which arises from the importation through court injunctions of used tyres, favours tyres retreaded in Brazil using imported casings, to

the detriment of imported retreaded tyres made from the same casings. The discrimination thus arises between Brazil and other WTO Members, including the European Communities.

The Panel then stated a position expressed on a number of occasions in the report that there was no difference from a waste management point of view between imported retreaded tyres, and retreaded tyres made in Brazil from imported casings . . . [T]his is an interesting interpretation of the phrase 'between countries where the same conditions prevail'. The approach clearly signals that prevailing conditions between countries can be compared with reference to the likeness of the products manufactured in these countries. If the products are 'like', this can be a sufficient basis for finding that prevailing conditions between countries are the same . . .

The panel's approach to the chapeau can be summarized in three stages. The first question was whether there was any discrimination. While the panel did not expressly say so, it effectively considered that the import ban was applied in a discriminatory manner in two respects. The MERCOSUR exemption resulted in discrimination in the nature of a most favoured nation treatment violation, since MERCOSUR firms could export retreaded tyres to Brazil, while European firms could not. As noted above, it also seems clear that the court injunctions resulted in discrimination in the form of a national treatment violation. The second question was whether this discrimination was 'unjustifiable' and it is here that the panel developed its effects based approach. There may well be an insurmountable problem with this approach (discussed below), but it at least provides a way of thinking about how discrimination can be exacerbated to such an extent as to become 'unjustifiable' under the chapeau. The third and final question is whether the unjustifiable discrimination occurs between countries where the same conditions prevail . . .

Under the panel's approach, measures can be exonerated under the chapeau based on a finding of limited trade effects, even if there is no acceptable cause or rationale for the discrimination; in other words, even if there is country based discrimination. Once it has been decided that there is discrimination between countries where the same conditions prevail, a further trade effects test applies. This test is conceptually distinct from the other tests . . . As will be discussed . . ., the same observation does not apply to the Appellate Body's alternative approach towards the chapeau. Before coming to this approach, however, the response to the panel's effects based approach will be discussed.

III. The Appellate Body's Response to the Effects Based Approach

One of the Appellate Body's observations about the effects based approach was that, '. . . the Panel's interpretation of the term "unjustifiable" does not depend on the cause or rationale of the discrimination but, rather, is focused exclusively on the assessment of the *effects* of the discrimination'. This is technically correct because the statement only relates to the panel's approach to the second of its tests—whether the discrimination is unjustifiable. However, a more complete assessment of the panel's approach would acknowledge the relevance of the cause or rationale of the discrimination in the third test. In assessing whether the discrimination was between countries where the same conditions prevail, the panel considered whether there was any difference from a waste management point of view between imported retreaded tyres, and retreaded tyres made in Brazil from imported casings. The conclusion that there was no difference, is effectively a conclusion that there was no acceptable cause or rationale for the discrimination. This point becomes clear once it is observed that there *would* have been an acceptable cause or rationale for the discrimination if the tyres receiving the less favourable treatment were somehow more difficult to dispose of safely. The explanation for the discrimination would then have been to protect public health.

However, the Appellate Body's intention was probably to signal its disapproval of the centrally important characteristic of the panel's approach—the possibility of exonerating measures based on their limited trade effects.

Another of the Appellate Body's reasons for rejecting the Panel's approach was provided in note 437, as follows:

> We also observe that the Panel's approach was based on a logic that is different in nature from that followed by the Appellate Body when it addressed the national treatment principle under Article III:4 of the GATT 1994 in *Japan—Alcoholic Beverages II*. In that case, the Appellate Body stated that Article III aims to ensure 'equality of competitive conditions for imported products in relation to domestic products'. The Appellate Body added that 'it is irrelevant that "the trade effects" of the [measure at issue], as reflected in the volumes of imports, are insignificant or even non-existent'. For the Appellate Body, 'Article III protects expectations not of any particular trade volume but rather of the equal competitive relationship between imported and domestic products.'

. . . Let us proceed . . . by accepting that trade effects are irrelevant in the context of the primary violation analysis. Does this mean that trade effects must also be irrelevant under the chapeau?

Arguably, the position is quite the contrary to the extent that trade effects ought to be relevant in the chapeau analysis, for the very reason that they are not relevant in the primary violation analysis. The reason for this relates to the structure of the GATT / WTO legal texts, under which discrimination can be relevant in both the primary violation and chapeau analyses. The need for a clear distinction between the two analyses was recognized by the Appellate Body in the *United States – Gasoline* case, where the primary violation was of Article III:4. A key insight in the Appellate Body's reasoning was the explanation of why a finding of discrimination under Article III, cannot lead to a finding of discrimination under the chapeau:

> The provisions of the chapeau cannot logically refer to the same standard(s) by which a violation of a substantive rule has been determined to have occurred. To proceed down that path would be both to empty the chapeau of its contents and to deprive the exceptions in paragraphs (a) to (j) of meaning. Such recourse would also confuse the question of whether inconsistency with a substantive rule existed, with the further and separate question arising under the chapeau of Article XX as to whether that inconsistency was nevertheless justified.

. . . [I]t can readily be seen how the conditioning of compliance with the chapeau on the absence of a significant undermining of the policy objective, could provide a means of distinguishing the primary violation, and chapeau analyses. The trade effects of measures would only be considered within the chapeau analysis.

Might there be other reasons for regarding the consideration of trade effects as an unsound basis for determining the 'unjustifiable' nature of discrimination under the chapeau? Surprisingly, the most obvious reason for avoiding trade effects was not referred to by the Appellate Body within its own reasoning, even though the European Communities, and all but one of the third parties in the dispute, presented arguments based on this reason. These arguments were brought together in the extract from a third party submission provided below, the final sentence of which raises an interesting point, which was not explicitly raised in the other submissions:

> The Separate Customs Territory of Taiwan, Penghu, Kinmen, and Matsu further suggests that the Panel's findings in this dispute might cause confusion for WTO Members when assessing whether a specific measure is WTO-consistent, create a tendency for WTO Members to initiate a multiplicity of WTO disputes, and undermine the security and predictability needed to conduct future trade. These problems stem from the Panel's failure to provide

clear criteria for determining what volume of imports or increase in import volumes would be considered 'significant'. Moreover, since import volumes are generally determined by supply and demand, the Panel's significance test, if adopted, would make it difficult for WTO Members, who do not have the power to control trade flows into their domestic markets, to adopt WTO-consistent measures or to eliminate WTO-inconsistent measures.

This passage requires little explanation, although it is worth adding that, even if it were possible to provide clear criteria, the WTO consistency of the measure could vary from year to year (or any shorter or longer a time period considered to be appropriate) as trade flows fluctuate. The uncertainty inherent in the Panel's approach is illustrated by Australia's views. While perhaps not wholly opposed to the quantitative approach, Australia (unlike the panel) considered that the import levels by reason of the MERCOSUR exemption 'did not appear to be insignificant or without practical impact.' . . .

IV. The Appellate Body's Alternative Approach and its Provenance

The crucial passage in the Appellate report was as follows:

. . . there is arbitrary or unjustifiable discrimination when a measure provisionally justified under a paragraph of Article XX is applied in a discriminatory manner "between countries where the same conditions prevail", and when the reasons given for this discrimination bear no rational connection to the objective falling within the purview of a paragraph of Article XX, or would go against that objective.

In terms of provenance, this approach can be traced back to a view presented by the US in *Shrimp* on how it should be determined whether discrimination under the chapeau is 'unjustifiable'. This view was set out by the Appellate Body as follows:

> An evaluation of whether a measure constitutes "unjustifiable discrimination [between countries] where the same conditions prevail" should take account of *whether differing treatment between countries relates to the policy goal of the applicable Article XX exception. If a measure differentiates between countries based on a rationale legitimately connected with the policy of an Article XX exception*, rather than for protectionist reasons, *the measure does not amount to an abuse of the applicable Article XX exception.* (emphasis in original)

As with the key passage in *Tyres*, the intention here is clearly to link the concept of 'unjustifiable' discrimination under the chapeau, with the policy goals under which a measure can be provisionally justified. A useful shorthand version of the test is that there will be 'unjustifiable' discrimination in the absence of a 'rational connection' between the reasons for the discrimination, and the objectives reflected in the heads of provisional justification [these being the specific policy exceptions listed in sub-paragraphs (a) to (j) of Article XX].

In *United States—Shrimp*, the Appellate Body displayed an ambivalent attitude towards this suggested approach. In fact, the approach was both explicitly rejected and implicitly applied. The explicit rejection was informed by a desire to avoid blurring the boundary within Article XX between the initial stage of provisional justification and the second stage of applying the chapeau. It was noted that:

the policy goal of a measure cannot provide its rationale or justification under the standards of the chapeau of Article XX. The legitimacy of the declared policy objective of the measure, and the relationship of that objective with the measure itself and its general design and structure, are examined under [the heads of provisional justification].

A few pages into the report, however, the rejected test is applied:

. . . shrimp caught using methods identical to those employed in the United States have been excluded from the United States market solely because they have been caught in waters of countries that have not been certified by the United States. The resulting situation is difficult to reconcile with the declared policy objective of protecting and conserving sea turtles. (emphasis in original)

The concern in this passage is that the measure, as applied, amounted to country based discrimination. In other words, imports were discriminated against purely because of their origin, rather than on the basis of any legitimate criteria. The rejected test is applied in the closing sentence of the passage. The Appellate Body effectively identifies the absence of a rational connection between the reason for the discrimination, (being the fact that some exporting countries had not been certified) and the conservation objective reflected in Article XX(g). Indeed, the *Brazil—Tyres* report confirms that the now endorsed test was applied in *United States—Shrimp* [para 228].

In the first case to be heard by the Appellate Body, *United States—Gasoline*, it would be an overstatement to claim that the 'new' test was clearly applied. However, the chapeau findings in *Gasoline* can easily be reconciled with the test, so providing further evidence that the test is only new in the sense that it was first explicitly endorsed in *Tyres*.

In *Gasoline*, the United States had provided explanations for why it was not possible to align the treatment of domestic and imported gasoline such as to avoid the initial violation of GATT Article III:4. Imported gasoline could not be granted the same treatment as domestic gasoline because of administrative problems connected with verification of origin and enforcement actions. Although this explanation was not linked to any particular part of the chapeau's language, the United States effectively seemed to be arguing that the difference in treatment was not discriminatory under the chapeau, because it was not as 'between countries where the same conditions prevail'. In other words, prevailing domestic conditions presented less difficulty, with respect to verification of origin and enforcement, than prevailing foreign conditions . . .

The Appellate Body responded by pointing towards the limited efforts by the United States to surmount these difficulties by entering into arrangements with foreign governments. Therefore, the view was that alleged differences in prevailing conditions do not suffice to exonerate measures under the chapeau, and that the United States had failed to establish that these alleged differences actually existed.

It can quickly be appreciated how the *Tyres* approach could be applied here to reach the same result of a failure to meet the terms of the chapeau. The primary explanation for the discrimination was the unsubstantiated claim about difficulties with verification and enforcement. There is no 'rational connection' between this explanation and the environmental policy objective, since the unsubstantiated claims do not support the policy objective to any extent at all. In contrast, had the claims been substantiated, there would have been a connection between the explanation and the policy objective. Subjecting foreign gasoline to the less favourable regime would have been a difficult situation to avoid, and would have been done in the name of conserving an exhaustible natural resource—clean air.

V. Contrasting the Panel and Appellate Body Approaches

As noted above, under the panel's approach, measures can be exonerated under the chapeau based on a finding of limited trade effects, even if the explanation for the discrimination undermines the policy objective. The Appellate Body's alternative approach does not permit this possibility. A finding that the discrimination undermines the policy objective will bring the chapeau analysis to an end without considering the possibly exonerating quality of limited trade effects. As will now be explained, the absence of this independent test means that the Appellate Body has not attributed distinct meaning to the different phrases within the chapeau.

By its formulation, the Appellate Body's test (as set out above) is clearly intended to reveal only the 'arbitrary or unjustifiable' nature of measures already found to have been applied in a discriminatory manner 'between countries where the same conditions prevail'. However, the Appellate Body's test for the 'arbitrary or unjustifiable' element is the same as the panel's test to determine whether the discrimination is 'between countries where the same conditions prevail'. This point has already been illustrated twice in the discussion above. In *Gasoline*, the United States argued that the chapeau was not breached because it was not possible to align the treatment of domestic and imported gasoline. In explaining why this was not possible, the (unsuccessful) argument was effectively that prevailing conditions differed, so that there was a valid explanation for the discrimination connected with a recognized Article XX objective. It has also been explained that the panel in *Tyres* explicitly considered whether the discrimination resulting from the court injunctions occurred 'between countries where the same conditions prevail'. The panel's positive finding here was effectively a finding of the absence of a valid explanation for the discrimination.

It follows that, under the Appellate Body's approach, once it is known that the discrimination is 'unjustifiable', it is also known whether there is discrimination 'between countries where the same conditions prevail', and vice versa. In contrast, the panel's approach in *Tyres* has the relative advantage that distinct tests apply in the two areas. Trade flows are considered only in connection with the 'unjustifiable' standard. Therefore, the panel's approach could be depicted as more responsive to the need to 'give meaning and effect to all the terms of a treaty' first recognised by the Appellate Body in *Gasoline*. However, this surely cannot be something which must be achieved even at the expense of introducing an unworkable test. The panel's approach could also be depicted as preserving more regulatory autonomy for WTO members, since the additional test provides an extra opportunity for measures to be exonerated under the chapeau. However, the inherent uncertainty of considering trade flows only preserves additional regulatory autonomy in a very limited and unpredictable sense which is outside the control of governments.

In any event, there seems to be little wrong in principle with thinking about the chapeau as posing the single question of when there is 'arbitrary or unjustifiable discrimination between countries where the same conditions prevail', and deciding this question with a single test . . .

... ...

This excerpt illustrates that the meaning of the chapeau terms is rather complex. This is particularly so if a high value is attached to giving each of the terms an independent meaning such as to maintain distinct boundaries both within Article XX, and between the chapeau and any discrimination analysis when deciding on the primary violation.

V. CONCLUSIONS

Article XX has been one of the more controversial aspects of GATT/WTO rules. In particular, there are two main areas of contention. First, there has been criticism by many environmental and other NGOs that the rules have not been interpreted flexibly enough to allow for appropriate use of 'non-trade' policies. For many years it was pointed out that no measure had been found to be justified under an Article XX exception. While this is no longer the case, there is still concern that the trade specialists who adjudicate on WTO disputes do not give enough credence to arguments that a measure serves an important non-trade goal.

Secondly, a number of developing countries have complained about the use of 'unilateral' environmental and health policies, particularly by the United States, as a means of disguised protectionism, and they have argued that Article XX should not be interpreted so as to allow these measures. Their concerns relate to both internal measures that set high standards which are difficult for developing country exporters to meet, as well as measures that try to coerce foreign governments to adopt particular policies.

Because much of the language of Article XX is somewhat broad and vague, panels and the Appellate Body have a good deal of discretion in interpreting the provisions in relation to these issues. Thus, depending on the interpretation, the rules could favour different sides.

At the same time, other aspects of the rules are fairly clear, such as the exclusion of labour rights and human rights as covered policies. It would take a very strained interpretation of the provisions to bring these concerns within the current provisions. As a result, this is perhaps an area where the negotiators need to address the issue in order to change the current approach. For more discussion of these issues see Chapter 19 on Trade and Social Policies.

VI. QUESTIONS

1. How different are the 'related to' and 'necessary' standards in the various Article XX exceptions? Is there any policy justification for using the apparently looser 'related to' standard for 'conservation of exhaustible natural resources'?

2. In order to cover policies other than those explicitly set out in Article XX exceptions, what are the advantages and disadvantages of using either negotiations among the WTO Members or expansive dispute settlement clarifications of the existing provisions? Which, in your view, is ultimately preferable? Given the general changes in society since the original GATT was signed, and the specific changes that have occurred in the nature of the countries that make up the WTO membership, is it time for the WTO Members to re-evaluate which policies they would like to see covered by GATT Article XX?

3. In order to ensure that Members have sufficient discretion to implement non-trade policies, what are the differences between developing a broad scope for the Article XX (and other) exceptions and developing a narrow interpretation of GATT obligations such as Article III? Which, in your view, is preferable?

4. The Appellate Body has said that examination of a measure under one of the listed exceptions should take into account the measure as a whole, not just the part of the measure that was found to be in violation (eg a discriminatory aspect of the measure that was found to violate Article III). Is this the right approach? Why not a stricter approach

that considers such measures to fall under an exception only when the discrimination aspect itself was necessary?

5. Does the 'arbitrary' or 'unjustifiable' discrimination standard target intentional discrimination? If not, what does it target? What is the proper relationship between Article III discrimination and Article XX chapeau discrimination?

6. Was it appropriate for the Appellate Body to criticise the 'coercive' nature of the measures at issue in the original *US—Shrimp* dispute as a factor indicating that unjustifiable discrimination was present? What does coercion have to do with discrimination?

7. In the GATT *Thailand—Cigarettes* case, in order to achieve certain health objectives Thailand prohibited the importation of cigarettes and other tobacco products, but authorised the sale of domestic cigarettes. The panel found that the import restrictions could not be considered 'necessary' in terms of Article XX(b) because there were alternative measures consistent with the GATT, or less inconsistent with it, which Thailand could reasonably have been expected to employ to achieve its health policy objectives. There were various measures consistent with the GATT, it said, which were reasonably available to Thailand to control the quality and quantity of cigarettes smoked and which, taken together, could have achieved the health policy goals pursued by Thailand. For instance, the panel suggested that a ban on cigarette advertising could curb the demand while meeting the requirements of Article III:4. How would this case be examined under the current 'necessary' standard set out by the Appellate Body?

8. In paragraph 161 of *Korea—Beef*, the Appellate Body stated, 'We believe that, as used in the context of Article XX(d), the reach of the word "necessary" is not limited to that which is "indispensable" or "of absolute necessity" or "inevitable"'. Then, in applying the 'necessity' standard in Article XX(b) and XX(d), in *Korea—Beef* and *EC—Asbestos* respectively, the Appellate Body seems to have focused on different elements. Is there a reason for applying different standards for these provisions? Did the Appellate Body intend there to be different standards?

9. In the *US—Shrimp* case, the Appellate Body discussed the relevance of whether the sea turtles at issue were physically within the jurisdiction of the US, the Member imposing the measure. The Appellate Body concluded that there was a 'sufficient nexus' between the US and the migrating turtles—which, it said, 'are all known to occur in waters over which the US exercises jurisdiction'—for the US goal of protecting sea turtles to be covered by Article XX(d). To what extent should Members be able to take actions under Article XX to promote the policies set out in Article XX *in foreign jurisdictions*? Does your answer vary by sub-provision? With regard to the issue of extraterritorial jurisdiction, discuss the following examples:

- Canada imposes a trade ban on lumber imports against countries that do not take measures to protect their forests, and it offers a justification under Article XX(g) arguing that it is trying to conserve these forests.
- New Zealand bans the sale or import of products made using energy from dirty coal burning power plants, and it offers a justification under Article XX(g) arguing that it is trying to conserve clean air.
- The US bans the import of products from countries where the human rights record

does not meet certain standards, and it offers a justification under Article XX(a) arguing that human rights violations offend 'public morals'.

10. In *Brazil—Tyres*, how did the Appellate Body's interpretation of the chapeau differ from that of the panel? Which approach should be preferred?

11. The generally accepted purpose of the chapeau is to prevent abuse of the specific policy exceptions listed in sub-paragraphs (a) to (j). Does the chapeau have much of a role to play in this regard when the policy exception at issue uses the 'necessary to' standard as opposed to the 'relating to' standard?

Part VI

Remedies for Fair and Unfair Trade

10

Subsidies and Countervailing Measures

I. INTRODUCTION

In the early years of the GATT, the focus of trade negotiations was on cutting tariffs. At the time, tariffs were the primary form of protection used. Subsidies and other measures that could be used for protectionist purposes were also addressed, but the rules were limited and somewhat vague. Rules on subsidies, set out in Articles XVI and VI of the GATT, provided weak multilateral disciplines and authorised GATT Contracting Parties to take domestic action against injurious subsidies in the form of countervailing duties. As time went by, however, the concern with subsidies as an alternative form of protection grew. In part, this shift was due to the large reduction in tariffs that had occurred over the years, leaving tariffs as less of a problem in relative terms. It may also have been the result of the increased use of subsidies (again, possibly due to the new restrictions that had been imposed on the use of tariffs, or due to more active and wealthy governments in many countries) and the inability of countervailing duties to limit the use of subsidies. At the same time, there were concerns that countervailing duties themselves were being abused, in spite of the GATT rules governing their use. There were some attempts to tighten up the disciplines as part of the Tokyo Round, through the Subsidies Code, but significant progress in this area did come until the Agreement on Subsidies and Countervailing Measures (the 'SCM Agreement') was completed as part of the Uruguay Round. The SCM Agreement contains the primary rules on the use of subsidies and countervailing duties.

In many ways, regulating subsidies is more difficult than regulating tariffs. Tariffs, by their very nature, act as barriers to trade. Thus, in the context of negotiations to lower trade barriers, which has always been an important objective of the GATT/WTO, eliminating or reducing tariffs is a clear and obvious goal to pursue. While tariffs may, in some limited instances, be a legitimate tool to promote other policy goals, in general their strong negative effects on trade outweigh other policy considerations. By contrast, although subsidies can be used in ways that cause economic harm to the recipient company's foreign competitors, and thus cause trade friction, they can also be used for a wide range of important social and economic policies, often in ways that do not distort trade much at all. As a leading economics textbook states, a 'subsidy' is '[a] payment by a government to a firm or household that provides or consumes a commodity. For example, governments often subsidise food by paying for part of the food expenditures of low-income households.'[1] Based on this definition and the accompanying example, it is clear that there are subsidies that have little effect on trade and promote policies that are widely considered to be desirable. Thus, in crafting rules for subsidies, the negotiators could not simply call for their elimination or reduction, as had been the approach to tariffs. Instead, they needed to create a regulatory framework that addressed the problems subsidies may cause in terms of trade-distortions and economic harm to trading partners, without limiting the ability of governments to use subsidies for important policy goals.

As a first step in establishing such rules, the negotiators needed to define the problem. There were two key aspects to doing so. First, what exactly were the 'subsidies' with which they were concerned, that is, what kinds of government actions constitute 'subsidies'? Secondly, which of these subsidies had trade-distorting effects that merited some disciplines?

On the first question, as noted above, the essence of the economics definition of the term 'subsidy' is a government payment to a private entity. The precise scope of this concept, however, is more complicated than it appears at first glance. In their most obvious form, subsidies are fairly easy to identify and regulate. For example, where a government gives money to a specific private company with no expectation of repayment, it is clear that this would constitute a subsidy. However, rules prohibiting direct payments to private entities would be insufficient, as subsidies could be provided in various other ways. Furthermore, moving on to the second question, relating to trade effects, such a rule would be overbroad, as not all direct payments have trade-distorting effects that cause concern.

Thus, in order to establish an appropriate trade regulation framework for subsidies, the key questions are: what are subsidies and when should they be prohibited? In this chapter, we review the provisions of the SCM Agreement that address these questions. In addition to the SCM Agreement rules, we also discuss various other provisions of the WTO Agreement that address subsidies in a narrower and more limited way. The rules set out in all of these subsidies provisions seek to find the right balance between allowing subsidies for legitimate policy goals, on the one hand, and restricting their use when the trade-distorting effects become too great, on the other.

The chapter is broken down into several parts, following the general structure of the SCM Agreement. First, we review the rules that identify which subsidies are subject to the SCM Agreement. The Agreement defines the term subsidy, thereby limiting its regulation to the forms of government assistance set out therein. Only those subsidies defined in the Agreement are subject to such rules. It then further limits regulation to subsidies that are 'specific' to certain entities, thus excluding general government programmes such as aid for the poor. Then, we examine three subsidy categories established by the SCM Agreement: (1) prohibited subsidies; (2) actionable subsidies; and (3) non-actionable subsidies. We also discuss the role of special remedies available for prohibited and actionable subsides. In addition, we examine the relationship of the SCM Agreement to provisions on subsidies in various other agreements, namely the Agriculture Agreement, the GATT and the TRIMs Agreement. Finally, we examine SCM Agreement rules regulating the ability of governments to impose countervailing duties on foreign goods pursuant to domestic law.

As a final point at the outset, it is worth noting briefly a number of institutional and other provisions in the SCM Agreement. Article 24 establishes a Committee on Subsidies

---

[1] P Samuelson and W Nordhaus, *Economics* (New York, McGraw-Hill, 1989) 982.

and Countervailing Measures, composed of representatives from each of the Members, which is to carry out responsibilities as assigned to it under the Agreement. The Committee established a Permanent Group of Experts composed of five independent persons, highly qualified in the fields of subsidies and trade relations, who may be requested to assist certain dispute settlement panels. Articles 25 and 26 then provide for a notification procedure, under which 'Members shall notify any subsidy as defined in paragraph 1 of Article 1, which is specific within the meaning of Article 2, granted or maintained within their territories'. Special, less stringent rules are also established for certain countries under Article 27 (developing countries) and Article 29 ('Members in the process of transformation from a centrally-planned into a market, free-enterprise economy').

II. IDENTIFICATION OF SUBSIDIES THAT ARE SUBJECT TO THE SCM AGREEMENT

As noted, the SCM Agreement limits the scope of its coverage to government assistance that meets the definition of a 'subsidy' and to subsidies that are 'specific'. We discuss each of these aspects of the Agreement below.

(a) The Definition of 'Subsidy'

As explained above, a standard economics definition of 'subsidy' involves the notion of payments by a government to a private entity. However, subsidies can be offered through other means as well. The SCM Agreement recognises this, and sets out the following rules for identifying subsidies.

Article 1.1 states that a subsidy shall be 'deemed to exist' if two conditions are met. First, there must either be 'a financial contribution by a government or any public body' or 'any form of income or price support'. Secondly, a 'benefit' must 'thereby' (ie, by the financial contribution or the income/price support) be 'conferred'. It is important to emphasise that the existence of a financial contribution or price/income support alone is not sufficient to constitute a subsidy. Rather, the financial contribution or price/income support must also confer a benefit.

We now look closely at the following three elements: (i) government of public body; (ii) financial contribution; and (iii) benefit.

(i) Government or Public Body

In many contexts under WTO rules, the issue of the nature of the government's involvement arises. For example, does the impact on trade result from actions by the government or actions by private parties? Or, is the entity at issue part of the government or not? Under the SCM Agreement, this issue comes up in relation to the requirement that financial contribution comes from 'a government or any public body'.

In the *US—Anti-Dumping and Countervailing Duties (China)* case, the Appellate Body considered the meaning of 'public body'. 'We see the concept of "public body" as sharing certain attributes with the concept of "government"; 'A public body within the meaning of Article 1.1.(a)(1) of the SCM Agreement must be an entity that possesses, exercises or is vested with governmental authority'; however, 'just as no two governments are exactly alike, the precise contours and characteristics of a public body are bound to differ from entity to entity, State to State, and case to case'; 'Panels or investigating authorities confronted with the question of whether conduct falling within the scope of Article 1.1.(a)(1) is that of a public body will be in a position to answer that question only by conducting a proper evaluation of the core features of the entity concerned, and its relationship with government in the narrow sense'. In this regard, it added that while this determination may be straightforward when a statute or other legal instrument expressly vests authority in the entity concerned, such a determination may be more complex in other cases where the picture is 'more mixed'. For example, it explained that it does not 'consider that the absence of an express statutory delegation of authority necessarily precludes a determination that a particular entity is a public body'. Rather, '[w]hat matters is whether an entity is vested with authority to exercise governmental functions, rather than how that is achieved'. It continued, '[i]t follows, in our view, that evidence that a government exercises meaningful control over an entity and its conduct may serve, in certain circumstances, as evidence that the relevant entity possesses governmental authority and exercises such authority in the performance of governmental functions'. It stressed, however, that 'apart from an express delegation of authority in a legal instrument, the existence of mere formal links between an entity and government in the narrow sense is unlikely to suffice to establish the necessary possession of governmental authority' (paras 317–18). In this regard, it stated that '[i]n all instances, panels and investigating authorities are called upon to engage in a careful evaluation of the entity in question and to identify its common features and relationship with government in the narrow sense, having regard, in particular, to whether the entity exercises authority on behalf of government' (para 319).

Here, the Appellate Body recalled that 'the Panel interpreted the term "public body" in Article 1.1(a)(1) of the SCM Agreement to mean "any entity controlled by a government", but that the panel never clarified its notion of control. The Appellate Body said that its interpretation above 'indicates that control of an entity by a government, in itself, is not sufficient to establish that an entity is a public body', and it therefore disagreed with the panel's interpretation (para 320).

Thus, the Appellate Body rejected the panel's view that a public body is 'any entity controlled by a government', and instead focused on whether the entity possesses, exercises or is vested with governmental authority.

(ii) Financial Contribution

The 'financial contribution' element is elaborated upon in Article 1.1(a)(1) through four categories. Under this provision, there will be a financial contribution by a government or any public body where:

(i) There is a government practice involving a direct transfer of funds (eg grants, loans, and equity infusion) or a potential direct transfer of funds or liabilities (eg loan guarantees).
(ii) Government revenue that is otherwise due is foregone or not collected (eg fiscal incentives such as tax credits).

(iii) A government provides goods or services other than general infrastructure, or purchases goods.

(iv) A government makes payments to a funding mechanism, or entrusts or directs a private body to carry out one or more of the type of functions illustrated in (i) to (iii) above which would normally be vested in the government, and the practice, in no real sense, differs from practices normally followed by governments.

We examine each of these four categories in more detail, setting out the relevant case law where it is helpful to understand the provision.

a. Direct and Potential Direct Transfers of Funds The first type of financial contribution is fairly easy to understand. Whenever money is transferred from the government to a private company, there will be a financial contribution. The agreement identifies 'grants, loans and equity infusion' as examples. In addition, when the government promises to transfer money under certain conditions, this transfer is considered 'potential' and also constitutes a financial contribution. The agreement identifies 'loan guarantees' as an example.

b. Foregone or Uncollected Revenue that is Otherwise Due The second type of financial contribution is more complicated. The example given in the text of the Agreement is a 'fiscal incentive' such as a 'tax credit'. So, for example, if there is a US$500 rebate given on income taxes for every purchase of a domestic car, this would qualify as a financial contribution under the second type. Under the terms of the provision, this US$500 is revenue that is 'otherwise due', in the sense that it would be due in the absence of a purchase of a domestic car, but has been 'foregone' by the government because the car purchase was made. Similarly, taking an example from the case law, an exemption from customs duties would also be covered. In *Canada—Autos*, the Appellate Body examined a duty exemption that was intended to assist the domestic industry. This duty exemption was given to companies who used a designated amount of domestic value added and met certain other requirements. The Appellate Body found as follows:

> Canada has established a normal MFN duty rate for imports of motor vehicles of 6.1 per cent. Absent the import duty exemption, this duty would be paid on imports of motor vehicles. Thus, through the measure in dispute, the Government of Canada has, in the words of *United States— FSC*, "given up an entitlement to raise revenue that it could 'otherwise' have raised". More specifically, through the import duty exemption, Canada has ignored the "defined, normative benchmark" that it established for itself for import duties on motor vehicles under its normal MFN rate and, in so doing, has foregone "government revenue that is otherwise due".[2]

Thus, where the current tax or customs regime has a 'defined, normative benchmark', and this benchmark is not applied in specific circumstances, in a manner that collects less revenue, government revenue that is otherwise due has been foregone. The Appellate Body elaborated on this standard in *US—FSC, Article 21.5*, stating:

> In identifying the normative benchmark, there may be situations where the measure at issue might be described as an "exception" to a "general" rule of taxation. In such situations, it may be possible to apply a "but for" test to examine the fiscal treatment of income absent the contested measure. We do not, however, consider that Article 1.1(a)(1)(ii) always *requires* panels to identify, with respect to any particular income, the "general" rule of taxation prevailing

---

[2] Appellate Body Report, *Canada—Autos*, para 91.

in a Member. Given the variety and complexity of domestic tax systems, it will usually be very difficult to isolate a "general" rule of taxation and "exceptions" to that "general" rule. Instead, we believe that panels should seek to compare the fiscal treatment of legitimately comparable income to determine whether the contested measure involves the foregoing of revenue which is "otherwise due", in relation to the income in question.[3]

So, in addition to looking for a departure from a 'defined, normative benchmark' with which to compare tax or customs treatment, it is also important to compare the treatment at issue with that given to 'legitimately comparable income'.

In contrast to the above examples, a reduction of the general income tax rate—for example, from 30 per cent to 20 per cent—would not be covered. While this reduction would constitute a 'tax break', it is not covered by the 'foregone revenue' provision because the 10 per cent revenue differential is not 'otherwise due', that is, under the new tax regime it is simply not due at all. The 'defined, normative benchmark' is now 20 per cent under the current rules, so taxing income at 20 per cent does not 'forego' revenue in the sense of Article 1.1(a)(1)(ii).

c. Government Purchase of Goods or Provision of Goods and Services The third type of financial contribution is straightforward. Where a government *purchases goods*, it will generally do so with a transfer of funds. This situation is similar to, and perhaps overlapping with, the first type, which covers a 'direct transfer of funds'. For example, the government may buy military aircraft built by private companies. In addition, a government's *provision of goods or services* other than general infrastructure, such as roads, is also covered. An example from the case law is that certain Canadian provinces provided standing timber to timber harvesters, to be processed into lumber (see section VII below for more details on this case).

Another example comes from the recent *EC—Aircraft* case. In that dispute, the US argued that 'the main runway at Bremen airport was extended by German authorities in 1988–89 to accommodate transport flights for Airbus wings manufactured in Bremen'.[4] In this regard, the US contended that 'the extension of the Bremen airport runway and the provision of the runway to Airbus for its exclusive use, including the implementation of noise reduction measures, constitutes the provision of goods and services other than general infrastructure within Article 1.1(a)(1)(iii)'.[5] The panel explained the factual background as follows:

> According to the European Communities, German authorities require a safety margin at either end of commercial runways, consisting of a 300 meter area free of all obstacles. In Bremen, the implementation of this requirement had resulted in the shortening of the usable length of the runway. In May 1988, an extension of the runway by 300 meters at either end was authorized. Consequently, in 1989–90, the runway was extended from its existing length of 2034 meters to 2634 meters. At the same time, noise reduction measures were put in place. It is undisputed that, with the exception of emergencies, only 2034 meters of the runway's length is available for general aviation use. Regular use of the entire length of the runway, including the 600 meters of extension, is permitted only for flights transporting Airbus wings from Bremen.

---

[3] Appellate Body Report, *US—FSC, Article 21.5*, para 91.
[4] Panel Report, *EC—Aircraft*, para 7.1098.
[5] *Ibid*, para 7.1102; SCM Agreement Art 1.1(a)(1)(iii).

The cost of the runway extension and noise reduction measures was borne by the City of Bremen. The United States asserts that Bremen paid DM 40 million to extend the runway and a further DM 10 million for noise reduction measures. [6]

The panel concluded as follows: '[i]t is clear from the evidence before us that the extension of the runway at Bremen airport, and the associated noise reduction measures, were undertaken by the Bremen city authorities specifically for Airbus' needs'. It concluded that 'the entire project, extending the runway, the associated noise reduction measures, and the right of exclusive use, constitute a financial contribution to Airbus, within the meaning of Article 1.1(a)(1)(iii)'. Thus, it said, 'in view of the specific limitations on access to, i.e., use of the extended runway, and the clear evidence demonstrating that the runway extension was undertaken for the use of Airbus', the measures do not constitute a measure of general infrastructure, but rather constitute 'a financial contribution in the form of the provision of goods or services other than general infrastructure, within the meaning of Article 1.1(a)(1)(iii)'.[7]

d. Payments to Funding Mechanism/Entrustment or Direction of a Private Body Finally, the last type of financial contribution is where a government involves private entities in the provision of one of the above types of financial contributions. The government may either make payments to a 'funding mechanism', which then distributes the money, or it may 'entrust or direct' a private body to carry out one of the three listed types. The Appellate Body has clarified that 'entrustment' occurs where a government gives responsibility to a private body, and 'direction' refers to situations where the government 'exercises its authority over a private body'. In this regard, it noted that 'one would expect entrustment or direction of a private body to involve some form of threat or inducement, which could, in turn, serve as evidence of entrustment or direction'. By contrast, it said, 'mere policy pronouncements' are insufficient, and 'entrustment and direction' 'imply a more active role than mere acts of encouragement' and cannot be 'inadvertent or a mere by-product of government regulation'.[8] In practice, a determination of whether 'entrustment' or 'direction' exists tends to be very fact-intensive, and requires a close look at the specific government actions at issue to determine the degree of force behind the government's effort to get the private industry to act. In one WTO dispute where 'entrustment' or 'direction' was found to exist, the panel considered the following factors in reaching its conclusions: the extent of government ownership of the banks involved; the weak financial situation of the recipient of the financing at the time; the recognised public interest considerations of certain banks in deciding to participate in the programmes; the fact that the restructuring took place in the framework of a formal government act; and the withholding of information in the subsidy investigation.[9]

(iii) Income or Price Support

As an alternative to a financial contribution, a subsidy may also involve 'any form of income or price support in the sense of' Article XVI of the GATT. Article XVI does not

---

[6] Panel Report, *EC—Aircraft*, paras 7.1100–7.1101 (citations omitted).
[7] See Panel Report, *EC—Aircraft*, paras 7.1113–7.1121.
[8] Appellate Body Report, *US—Countervailing Duty Investigation on DRAMS*, paras 113–14.
[9] Panel Report, *EC—Countervailing Measures on DRAMS Chips*, paras 7.74–7.84, 7.118–7.146.

define the terms 'income support' and 'price support', but rather limits the covered support to that 'which operates directly or indirectly to increase exports of any product from, or to reduce imports of any product into, [a Member's] territory'. Generally speaking, income and price support are used in the context of agricultural products, and serve to guarantee farmers' incomes at a certain level through government payments, or to support prices of products at a certain level through government guarantees to buy the product if the price should fall below that level.

(iv) Benefit

As emphasised above, the existence of a financial contribution or income/price support is not sufficient for there to be a subsidy. Rather, the financial contribution or income/price support must confer a benefit. The Appellate Body has spoken fairly clearly on this issue, explaining that determination of whether a 'benefit' exists implies some kind of comparison, and that the 'marketplace' provides an appropriate basis for comparison. For instance, in *Canada—Aircraft* it stated: 'the marketplace provides an appropriate basis for comparison in determining whether a "benefit" has been "conferred", because the trade-distorting potential of a "financial contribution" can be identified by determining whether the recipient has received a "financial contribution" on terms more favourable than those available to the recipient in the market'.[10]

This principle applies to the different types of financial contributions in different ways. For example, for the first type of financial contribution, a direct or potential direct transfer of funds, if the government offers a loan at a 6 per cent interest rate, whereas private banks are offering 7 per cent, a benefit has likely been conferred. This conclusion depends, of course, on a comparison of the other terms of the loan (such as any fees, repayment period, etc) to market benchmarks as well. In practice, the interest rate is only one of many terms relevant to a loan, so a determination will not always be this straightforward, but the basic concept is fairly clear. Similarly, for equity infusions, the terms of the transaction must be compared to what could have been obtained in the market. With grants, on the other hand, it can probably be assumed that there is a benefit, as these are not available in the market.

For the second type of financial contribution, the foregoing of tax revenue that is otherwise due, the analysis would be similar to that for grants, as tax breaks of this sort are not available in the market.

Finally, in respect of the third type of financial contribution, government purchase of goods or provision of goods and services, the analysis would be similar to that for loans, as the purchase price or terms of provision would be compared to what is available in the market.

Once the existence of a financial contribution or income/price support along with the conferment of a benefit have been established, a subsidy is deemed to exist. However, only subsidies that are 'specific' are subject to regulation by the SCM Agreement. We now turn to a discussion of the concept of specificity.

---

[10] Appellate Body Report, *Canada—Aircraft*, para 157.

(b) Specificity

Article 1.2 of the SCM Agreement provides that subsidies are 'subject to' the rules on prohibited and actionable subsidies, as well as the rules on countervailing duties, only if they are 'specific', as defined in Article 2. Thus, subsidies that are not 'specific' are not regulated as either prohibited or actionable and also cannot be countervailed. The main point of the specificity requirement is to exclude broadly based general welfare programmes, such as aid to the poor, from regulation. Presumably, this exclusion is made for two reasons. First, such programmes are much less likely to have trade-distorting effects, as it is subsidies to individual companies or industries that would most effectively favour domestic companies over their foreign competitors. Secondly, even though broadly based subsidies may in some instances have negative trade effects, they are nonetheless considered necessary to promote legitimate policy goals.

Article 2 of the SCM Agreement sets out the rules for when specificity exists. As explained there, the existence of specificity will be based on the following 'principles'. First, under the introductory clause to Article 2.1(a), specificity will exist where the granting authority or relevant legislation explicitly limits access to a subsidy to 'an enterprise or industry or group of enterprises or industries'. Recalling the Bremen runway extension discussed above, after finding that this measure constitutes a subsidy, the panel considered whether it is specific and concluded:

> As Airbus is the only company entitled to regular use of the extended runway, and in view of the fact that the extension was undertaken by the Bremen authorities explicitly to fulfil Airbus' needs in transporting aircraft wings, we find that the subsidy in question is specific to Airbus within the meaning of Article 2.1(a) of the *SCM Agreement*.[11]

Secondly, Article 2.1(b) then establishes that specificity will *not* be found in certain circumstances: where a measure 'establishes objective criteria or conditions governing the eligibility for, and the amount of, a subsidy', there will be no specificity 'provided that the eligibility is automatic and that such criteria and conditions are strictly adhered to'.

Article 2.1(c) then provides, '[i]f, notwithstanding any appearance of non-specificity resulting from the application of the principles laid down in subparagraphs (a) and (b), there are reasons to believe that the subsidy may in fact be specific, other factors may be considered'. It then sets out the following factors for the consideration of whether a subsidy is specific: 'use of a subsidy programme by a limited number of certain enterprises, predominant use by certain enterprises, the granting of disproportionately large amounts of subsidy to certain enterprises, and the manner in which discretion has been exercised by the granting authority in the decision to grant a subsidy'.

An inquiry into whether a particular subsidy measure is *de facto* specific under Article 2.1(c) is very fact-intensive, and depends on the specific aspects of the measure and actions by the government in implementing the measure. As an example, the panel in *US—Lumber CVDs Final ('Lumber IV')* upheld the US Department of Commerce's determination of *de facto* specificity in a countervailing duty investigation relating to government provision of standing timber, on the following basis:

---

[11] Panel Report, *Canada—Aircraft*, para 7.1134.

Panel Report, *United States—Final Countervailing Duty Determination with Respect to Certain Softwood Lumber from Canada*, **Adopted 17 February 2004, WT/DS257/R**

7.119 We recall that a subsidy is specific under Article 2 SCM Agreement, if it is specific to an enterprise or industry or group of enterprises or industries (referred to in the SCM Agreement as "certain enterprises"). The SCM Agreement does not define an "industry" nor does it provide for any other rules concerning which enterprises could be considered to form an industry for the purposes of Article 2 SCM Agreement or whether a group of industries have to produce certain similar products in order to be considered a "group".

7.120 The *New Shorter Oxford Dictionary* defines an industry as "a particular form or branch of productive labour; a trade, a manufacture". Both parties seem to agree that the common practice is to refer to industries by the type of products they produce. It seems therefore that the term "industry" in Article 2 SCM Agreement is not used to refer to enterprises producing specific goods or end-products. Indeed, even Canada agrees that a single industry may make a broad range of end products and still remain a "industry" within the meaning of Article 2 SCM Agreement. We note in this respect that Canada considers that "it may be completely appropriate to find that producers of a wide variety of steel products (or automobile products or textile products, etc) are a group of 'steel industries' (or 'automobile industries', 'textile industries', etc.) because of the similarity and the relatedness of their output products". Canada also does not dispute that a subsidy limited to a single large industry (such as "steel", "autos", "textiles", "telecommunications", or the like) could be found specific, even though the producers make a diversity of products.

7.121 The USDOC Determination considered that only a group of wood product industries, consisting of the pulp and paper mills and the sawmills and re-manufacturers which are producing the subject merchandise used the stumpage programmes. It does not seem that USDOC simply labelled an aggregation of producers as a group of industries merely because they use a particular programme. In our view, the opposite was the case. As Canada recognized, the stumpage programme can clearly only benefit certain enterprises in the wood product industries which can harvest and / or process the good provided, standing timber. In sum, the text of Article 2 SCM Agreement does not require a detailed analysis of the end-products produced by the enterprises involved, nor does Article 2.1 (c) SCM Agreement provide that only a limited number of *products* should benefit from the subsidy. In our view, it was reasonable of the USDOC to reach the conclusion that the use of the alleged subsidy was limited to an industry or a group of industries. We consider that the "wood products industries" constitutes at most only a limited group of industries—the pulp industry, the paper industry, the lumber industry and the lumber remanufacturing industry—under any definition of the term "limited". We do not consider determinative in this respect the fact that these industries may be producing many different end-products. As we discussed above, specificity under Article 2 SCM is to be determined at the enterprise or industry level, not at the product level.

7.122 Canada argues that there were other users of the programmes than the ones identified by the USDOC. We understand Canada to be arguing that not only "the pulp and paper mills and the saw mills and remanufacturers which are producing the subject merchandise" are using the stumpage programmes, but also the pulp and paper mills and the sawmills and remanufacturers which are *not* producing the subject merchandise. In our view, all these producers can reasonably be found to form part of the same industries, which produce both the subject merchandise and other merchandise. It is evident that in order to countervail a specific subsidy it is necessary that the subsidy benefits the producers of the subject merchandise, but that does not mean that the subsidies should be specific to these producers only, nor is it required under Article 2 SCM Agreement that the subsidy be specifically targeted at subsidizing only the subject merchandise of producers who produce both subject merchandise and non-subject merchandise.

7.123 Canada also argues that an authority is required to examine all four factors mentioned in Article 2.1 (c) SCM Agreement in order to determine *de facto* specificity. We note in this respect that Article 2.1 (c) SCM Agreement provides that if there are reasons to believe that the subsidy may in fact be specific, other factors *may* be considered. The use of the verb "may" rather than "shall", in our view, indicates that if there are reasons to believe that the subsidy may in fact be specific, an authority *may* want to look at any of the four factors or indicators of specificity. We note the difference in language between Article 2.1 (c) SCM Agreement and, for example, Article 15.4 SCM Agreement concerning injury which provides that "the examination of the impact of the subsidized imports on the domestic industry *shall include* an evaluation of all relevant economic factors and indices having a bearing on the state of the industry *including* . . .", and then lists the factors which have to be included in the evaluation. Article 15.4 SCM Agreement is almost identical in language to Article 3.4 Anti-Dumping Agreement, which it is well established, contains an obligation on the part of the investigating authority to at a minimum examine and evaluate all factors listed in the provision. In our view, if the drafters had wanted to impose a formalistic requirement to examine and evaluate all four factors mentioned in Article 2.1 (c) SCM Agreement in all cases, they would have equally explicitly provided so as they have done elsewhere in the SCM Agreement. They did not do so. We conclude therefore that there was no obligation on the USDOC to examine whether disproportionately large amounts of the subsidy were granted to certain enterprises or the manner in which discretion has been exercised by the granting authority in the decision to grant a subsidy, the two factors mentioned in Article 2.1 (c) SCM Agreement which the USDOC did not explicitly examine.

... ...

Importantly, specificity need not be established in this way for prohibited subsidies, which are defined in Article 3. Rather, Article 2.3 states that '[a]ny subsidy falling under the provisions of Article 3 shall be deemed to be specific'. This rule is presumably based on the very strong trade-distorting effects of such subsidies, which prompted Members to call for their prohibition even where they do not meet the substantive requirements of specificity. Thus, an export subsidy that is available to all companies would not be specific under the terms of Article 2.1 but is deemed to be specific because it falls under Article 3.

III. REGULATION OF SPECIFIC SUBSIDIES UNDER THE SCM AGREEMENT

The previous section explained that only certain forms of government assistance—those that meet the definition of 'subsidy' and are 'specific'—are regulated under the SCM Agreement. In this section, we discuss how the SCM Agreement rules apply to the covered subsidies. There are three components to this regulation: rules on prohibited subsidies; rules on actionable subsidies; and rules on non-actionable subsidies. This regulatory structure has been referred to as the 'traffic light' system: 'prohibited subsidies' are never allowed, and are thus faced with a red light; 'actionable subsidies' are permitted as long as they do not have 'adverse' trade effects, and are therefore faced with a yellow or amber light (depending on your particular country's traffic signal colours); and non-actionable subsidies, the provisions of which have since lapsed but were permitted in the early years of the WTO, faced a green light. We discuss each in turn below.

(a) Prohibited Subsidies

Part II of the SCM Agreement addresses so-called 'prohibited subsidies'. 'Prohibited' subsidies are just like they sound: banned in all cases. Article 3 of the SCM Agreement sets out two kinds of prohibited subsidies: export subsidies and domestic content subsidies. Article 3.2 provides that Members 'shall neither grant nor maintain' these subsidies. As elaborated in the concluding part of this section, these two kinds of subsidies are singled out for harsher treatment under the rules because of their strongly trade-distorting effects. All subsidies have the potential to have such effects, but these two have effects that are considered particularly egregious. Export subsidies can harm foreign competitors in markets around the world; and domestic content subsidies limit foreign companies' access to a Member's domestic market. The SCM Agreement rules do not require any demonstration of actual adverse effects here (as they do with actionable subsidies). Rather, as long as the elements of the particular subsidy are demonstrated, it qualifies as 'prohibited'.

We examine below the two different types of prohibited subsidies. The analysis is concentrated on export subsidies, where there is more case law. Note, however, that due to the similarity in language between the two provisions, the interpretations of the export subsidy provisions may also be relevant for the domestic content subsidy provisions.

(i) Export Subsidies

Article 3.1(a) of the SCM Agreement addresses export subsidies. In particular, it prohibits 'subsidies contingent, in law or in fact, whether solely or as one of several other conditions, upon export performance, including those illustrated in Annex I'. (The use of 'in law' or 'in fact' corresponds with the commonly used Latin phrases *de jure* and *de facto*.) Footnote 4, coming after the word 'fact', clarifies: '[t]his standard is met when the facts demonstrate that the granting of a subsidy, without having been made legally contingent upon export performance, is in fact tied to actual or anticipated exportation or export earnings'. This footnote also states that '[t]he mere fact that a subsidy is granted to enterprises which export shall not for that reason alone be considered to be an export subsidy within the meaning of this provision'. Thus, while these subsidies are commonly referred to by the shorthand name 'export subsidies', a more precise description of the subsidies at issue is provided in the Agreement, focusing on the concept of export 'contingency'. This 'contingency' requires some degree of link or relationship between export and the subsidy.

The Appellate Body has made a number of statements providing some guidance as to the specific meaning of Article 3.1(a). First, it has explained that the ordinary connotation of 'contingent' is 'conditional' or 'dependent for its existence on something else'. In addition, it has stated that the legal standard expressed by the word 'contingent' is the same for both 'in law' and 'in fact' contingency. It also clarified that footnote 4 of the SCM Agreement gives further guidance, providing, inter alia, that the ordinary meaning of 'tied to' in footnote 4 confirms the linkage of the words 'contingency' and 'conditionality' in Article 3.1(a) and emphasises that a relationship of conditionality or dependence must be demonstrated.[12] Finally, it clarified that because the legal standard is the same for 'in

---

[12] Appellate Body Report, *Canada—Aircraft*, paras 166–71.

fact' and 'in law' export contingency, a 'tie' between export performance and a subsidy meets the standard for 'in law' contingency.[13]

In this section, we consider: (a) the Appellate Body's recent clarifications of the export subsidies standard in *EC—Aircraft*; (b) the application of the standard for 'in fact' subsidies; (c) **the treatment of 'separate** but equal' **regimes for** export and **domestic subsidies**; and (d) the role of the Illustrative List of Export **Subsidies**.

a. The Appellate Body's Clarification of the 'In Fact' Export Subsidy Standard in *EC—Aicraft* In *EC—Aircraft*, one kind of subsidy at issue was the so-called 'Launch Aid' given by the EU and its Member States to support the European aircraft maker Airbus. One of the claims against Launch Aid was that it was an 'in fact' export subsidy. In examining this issue, the Appellate Body stated that the interpretative issue is '*what* must be demonstrated in order to establish that a subsidy is "*in fact tied to . . . anticipated exportation*" within the meaning of footnote 4 of the *SCM Agreement*'.[14]

Beginning its interpretation, the Appellate Body recalled its past precedent that the word 'anticipated' means 'expected' and that 'it is the granting authority that "anticipates" that exportation will occur after the granting of the subsidy, and that grants a subsidy *on the condition* of such anticipated exportation'. Given that anticipated exportation 'alone is not proof that the granting of the subsidy is *tied to* the anticipation of exportation', it emphasized that the legal standard 'further requires that there exists a relationship of conditionality between the granting of the subsidy and anticipated exportation'. It explained, '[w]here a subsidy is alleged to be "in fact tied to . . . anticipated exportation," the relationship of conditionality is, unlike in the case of *de jure* export contingency, not expressly or by necessary implication provided in the terms of the relevant legal instrument granting the subsidy'. In these circumstances, it said, 'we consider that the factual equivalent of such conditionality can be established by recourse to the following test: is the granting of the subsidy geared to induce the promotion of future export performance by the recipient?'[15]

In reaching this interpretation, the Appellate Body said that it was *not* suggesting that the standard is met 'merely because the granting of the subsidy is designed to increase a recipient's production, even if the increased production is exported in whole', nor that a finding of *de facto* export contingency would be precluded by the fact that the granting of the subsidy may, in addition to increasing exports, also increase domestic sales. Rather, it considered that the standard would be met 'when the subsidy is granted so as to provide an incentive to the recipient to export in a way that is not simply reflective of the conditions of supply and demand in the domestic and export markets undistorted by the granting of the subsidy'.[16]

The Appellate Body recalled that the existence of de facto export contingency 'must be *inferred* from the total configuration of the facts constituting and surrounding the granting of the subsidy', and it explained that this may include the following factors: '(i) the design and structure of the measure granting the subsidy; (ii) the modalities of operation set out in such a measure; and (iii) the relevant factual circumstances surrounding the granting of the subsidy that provide the context for understanding the measure's design,

---

[13] Appellate Body Report, *Canada—Aircraft*, para 107.
[14] Appellate Body Report, *EC—Aircraft*, para 1042 (emphasis in original).
[15] *Ibid*, paras 1043–44.
[16] *Ibid*, para 1045.

structure, and modalities of operation'. In addition, it pointed out that where relevant evidence exists, 'the assessment could be based on a comparison between, on the one hand, the ratio of *anticipated* export and domestic sales of the subsidized product that would come about in consequence of the granting of the subsidy, and, on the other hand, the situation in the absence of the subsidy'. In this regard, it noted that '[t]he situation in the absence of the subsidy may be understood on the basis of historical sales of the same product by the recipient in the domestic and export markets before the subsidy was granted' and that, in the event that there are no historical data untainted by the subsidy, or the subsidized product is a new product for which no historical data exists, 'the comparison could be made with the performance that a profit-maximizing firm would hypothetically be expected to achieve in the export and domestic markets in the absence of the subsidy'. It concluded, '[w]here the evidence shows, all other things being equal, that the granting of the subsidy provides an incentive to skew anticipated sales towards exports, in comparison with the historical performance of the recipient or the hypothetical performance of a profit-maximizing firm in the absence of the subsidy, this would be an indication that the granting of the subsidy is in fact tied to anticipated exportation within the meaning of Article 3.1(a) and footnote 4 of the *SCM Agreement*'.[17]

The Appellate Body then set out numerical examples to illustrate 'when the granting of a subsidy may, or may not, be geared to induce promotion of future export performance by a recipient' comparing the historical ratio of exports to production to that ratio after the subsidy. It explained that the subsidy would meet the legal standard if it is 'designed in such a way that it is expected to skew the recipient's future sales in favour of export sales, even though the recipient may also be expected to increase its domestic sales'. However, the Appellate Body also pointed out that it was not suggesting that the issue of whether the granting of a subsidy is tied to anticipated exportation could be based on an assessment of the actual effects of that subsidy, emphasizing instead that 'it must be assessed on the basis of information available to the granting authority at the time the subsidy is granted'.[18]

It further explained that '[t]he standard for determining whether the granting of a subsidy is "in fact tied to . . . anticipated exportation" is an objective standard, to be established on the basis of the total configuration of facts constituting and surrounding the granting of the subsidy, including the design, structure, and modalities of operation of the measure granting the subsidy'. That is, 'the conditional relationship between the granting of the subsidy and export performance must be objectively observable on the basis of such evidence in order for the subsidy to be geared to induce the promotion of future export performance by the recipient'. Thus, it considered that the standard is 'not satisfied by the subjective motivation of the granting government to promote the future export performance of the recipient'. Noting that, in past cases, the Appellate Body and panels have 'cautioned against undue reliance on the intent of a government behind a measure to determine the WTO-consistency of that measure', and recalling its past statement in *US—Offset Act*, at paragraph 259, that '"the intent, stated or otherwise, of the legislators *is not conclusive*" as to whether a measure is consistent with the covered agreement', the Appellate Body said that this 'same understanding applies in the context of a determination on export contingency, where the requisite conditionality between the subsidy and anticipated exportation under Article 3.1(a) and footnote 4 of the *SCM Agreement* must be established on the basis of objective evidence, rather than subjective intent'. It added, however, that 'while the standard for *de facto* export contingency cannot be satisfied by the subjective motivation of the granting government, objectively review- able expressions of a government's policy objectives for granting a subsidy may . . . constitute relevant evidence in an inquiry into whether a subsidy is geared to induce the promotion of future export performance by the recipient'.[19] In this regard, the Appellate Body made clear that 'the standard does not require a panel to ascertain a government's reasons(s) for granting a subsidy'. Instead, the issue must be determined 'by assessing *the subsidy itself,* in the light of the relevant factual circumstances, rather than by reference to the granting authority's reasons for the measure'. However, it cautioned that this does not mean 'that evidence regarding the policy reasons of a subsidy is necessarily excluded from the inquiry into whether a subsidy is geared to induce the promotion of future export performance by the recipient'.[20]

The Appellate Body summarized its interpretation as follows:

> it is clear that a subsidy that is neutral on its face, or by necessary implication, and does not differentiate between a recipient's exports and domestic sales cannot be found to be contingent, in law, on export performance within the meaning of Article 3.1(a) of the *SCM Agreement*. Such a subsidy may nonetheless constitute a subsidy contingent in fact upon export performance within the meaning of the same provision if it is 'in fact tied to actual or anticipated exportation or export earnings' in accordance with footnote 4 of the *SCM Agreement*. The interpretation set out above indicates that the granting of the subsidy may be tied to anticipated exportation, and thus contingent in fact upon export performance under Article 3.1 and footnote 4 of the *SCM Agreement* if it is geared to induce the promotion of future export performance by the recipient. The issue of whether this standard is met must be assessed on the basis of an examination of the measure granting the subsidy and the facts surrounding the granting of the subsidy, including the design, structure, and modalities of operation of the measure. Finally, the fact alone that the recipient of a subsidy exports is insufficient for a finding of *de facto* export contingency. Rather, this fact must be considered together with all other relevant evidence relating to the granting of the subsidy for purposes of determining whether the subsidy is contingent in fact upon export performance.

In thinking about the Appellate Body's findings, it is important to understand the alterna- tive approach, which can perhaps be seen in the arguments of the US in this case. The US argued as follows:

> 487. The United States maintains that, before the Panel, it established that the member States expected certain levels of export performance in return for the provision of LA/MSF, and that these expectations "were based not only on the significant export-oriented nature of Airbus, but also on assurances provided by Airbus forecasts and existing orders for certain models at the time the member States committed to provide {LA/MSF}." The United States further argues that "{t}hese expectations, and Airbus' commitment to meet or exceed them, were codified in the form of {LA/MSF} contracts signed by each member State for a particular model of aircraft" and that, "{w}ithout these contracts, {LA/MSF} would not have been provided." Thus, each of the LA/MSF contracts reflects an "exchange of commitments", whereby the governments committed to provide the loans in exchange for Airbus' commitment to repay the

---

[19] *Ibid*, para 1050.
[20] *Ibid*, para 1051.

loans on the basis of a specified number of aircraft sales that could not be achieved without exports.

488. The United States emphasizes that "it is the particular structure of the {LA/MSF} contracts that provides the 'conditionality' required under Article 3.1(a) and footnote 4". Specifically, the member States "could have structured these contracts in other ways", for example, "by establishing a repayment calendar based on specific dates without regard to the deliveries made by Airbus" or by requiring "repayment over much smaller numbers of deliveries" that "could be reached without necessarily exporting". Instead, "by tying repayment of . . . loans to a specific number of deliveries that required exportation", the LA/MSF contracts reflect an exchange of commitments that "is the essence of 'conditionality'" between the granting of a subsidy and export performance, within the meaning of Article 3.1(a) and footnote 4 of the SCM Agreement.

While the US argument could be taken to mean different things, one possible meaning is that, in the US view, it might be enough to prove export contingency if the subsidy encourages more exports, even if it applies equally to domestic sales and encourages them as well. In other words, if you have a subsidy that will, by its nature, result in more exports, that is enough to demonstrate export contingency. In the situation described by the US here, the contracts require a certain level of sales, one that can only be met if there are export sales. In the US view, this is enough to show export contingency, even if domestic sales increase as well. Such a standard would have been broader than that adopted by the Appellate Body, in the sense that more subsidies would have been found to be export subsidies.

b. Application of the Export Contingency Standard for 'In Fact' Subsidies With regard to the application of the export contingency 'in fact' standard, the standard set out by the Appellate Body in *EC—Aircraft* is too new to have much experience with it (and in that case the Appellate Body concluded that the panel's factual findings and undisputed facts on the record do not provide a sufficient basis to complete the analysis).[21] Nonetheless, an earlier case involving allegations of 'in fact' export subsidies helps illustrate the nature of the inquiry. In the *Canada—Aircraft* case, the standard was applied as follows to the Technology Partnerships Canada ('TPC') programme, one of the subsidy programmes at issue:

Appellate Body Report, *Canada—Measures Affecting the Export of Civilian Aircraft*, Adopted 20 August 1999, WT/DS70/AB/R

175. . . . [W]e turn next to the Panel's application of that legal standard to the facts relating to assistance provided by TPC to the Canadian regional aircraft industry. The Panel set out in some detail the various facts that it took into account in concluding that TPC assistance was "contingent . . . in fact . . . upon export performance". Indeed, the Panel took into account sixteen different factual elements, which covered a variety of matters, including: TPC's statement of its overall objectives; types of information called for in applications for TPC funding; the considerations, or eligibility criteria, employed by TPC in deciding whether to grant assistance; factors to be identified by TPC officials in making recommendations about applications for funding; TPC's record of funding in the export field, generally, and in the aerospace and defence sector, in particular; the nearness-to-the-export-market of the projects funded; the importance of

---

[21] See *Ibid*, para 1104.

projected export sales by applicants to TPC's funding decisions; and the export orientation of the firms or the industry supported.

176. From our scrutiny of the Panel Report, we are unable to agree with Canada that the Panel made the export orientation of the regional aircraft industry the "effective test". In keeping with the standard set forth in footnote 4, the fact of the Canadian industry's export orientation seems to us not to have been given undue emphasis by the Panel. Rather, this fact was simply one of a number of facts that, when considered together, the Panel found demonstrated that the granting of subsidies by TPC was "tied to" actual or anticipated exports.

177. We recall our finding that the Panel could be understood as having treated the nearness-to-the-export-market factor as giving rise to a legal presumption in determining whether TPC assistance was "contingent . . . in fact . . . upon export performance". However, we also have said that this factor may, in certain circumstances, be a relevant factor in making such a determination. In our view, in the circumstances of this case, the Panel did not err in taking this nearness-to-the-export-market factor into consideration, together with all the other facts that the Panel considered. Moreover, in our view and in light of all the facts the Panel considered, the Panel would, in all probability, have concluded that TPC assistance to the Canadian regional export industry was "contingent . . . in fact . . . upon export performance", even if it had not taken this factor into account.

178. Canada also asserts that the Panel "confused" *considerations*—that is, the eligibility criteria set out in the TPC Handbook that TPC took into account in making its funding decisions—with *conditions* based on export performance. We do not agree. The Panel did *not* find that the TPC eligibility criteria *were* conditions, but, rather, it found that those criteria helped to *demonstrate* the existence of *de facto* contingency upon export performance. We consider it perfectly possible that such considerations, especially when taken together with other facts, could demonstrate that a subsidy is "contingent . . . in fact . . . upon export performance". Indeed, in many cases, the eligibility criteria used by a granting authority, and their application in practice, may provide particularly good evidence of whether the granting of a subsidy is "contingent . . . in fact . . . upon export performance".

179. We note, finally, that the Panel took into account a number of facts related to the TPC programme as a whole. Therefore, we do not agree with Canada's assertion that "[t]here is no indication that the Panel considered the operation of the TPC programme as a whole". Moreover, the fact that some of TPC's contributions, in some industry sectors, are *not* contingent upon export performance, does not necessarily mean that the same is true for all of TPC's contributions. It is enough to show that one or some of TPC's contributions do constitute subsidies "contingent . . . in fact . . . upon export performance".

180. For all these reasons, we uphold the Panel's legal finding that "TPC assistance to the Canadian regional aircraft industry is 'contingent . . . in fact . . . upon export performance' within the meaning of Article 3.1(a) of the SCM Agreement".

. . . .

This kind of 'in fact' analysis will vary, of course, depending on the subsidy measure at issue, but the above excerpt provides a good illustration of the types of factors that will be considered.

An important issue that arises in export subsidy cases is how Members are to implement adverse decisions. In particular, the question is whether the Member can maintain the subsidy by modifying the terms under which it is offered, for example by removing the export contingency. In the Article 21.5 proceedings in the *Canada— Aircraft* case extracted above, the Appellate Body examined this issue:

Appellate Body Report, *Canada—Measures Affecting the Export of Civilian Aircraft, Recourse by Brazil to Article 21.5 of the DSU*, Adopted 4 August 2000, WT/DS70/AB/RW

IV. Technology Partnerships Canada

25. The original panel found, for the reasons enumerated in paragraph 9.340 of the original panel report, that TPC assistance to the Canadian regional aircraft industry involved subsidies that were contingent, in fact, upon export performance and, thus, inconsistent with Article 3.1(a) of the *SCM Agreement*. The Article 21.5 Panel summarized, as follows, the steps taken by Canada to implement the recommendations and rulings of the DSB regarding TPC:

> 5.3 Canada has taken two types of action in order to implement the recommendation of the DSB concerning TPC assistance to the Canadian regional aircraft industry. First, Canada has terminated existing TPC activities in the Canadian regional aircraft sector. Thus, Canada (1) has cancelled funding under five TPC transactions identified by Canada, (2) has withdrawn approvals-in-principle for two new TPC funding projects in the regional aircraft sector, and (3) has closed all TPC files in the regional aircraft sector.

> 5.4 Second, Canada has restructured the TPC programme and documentation so that, in its opinion, most of the factual considerations forming the basis for the Panel's finding of *de facto* export contingency no longer apply. According to Canada, the only factual consideration still applicable is the export orientation of the Canadian regional aircraft industry.

26. Brazil's complaint, in the Article 21.5 proceedings, regarding TPC was limited to the second type of action taken by Canada to comply with the recommendations and rulings of the DSB, namely the restructuring of the TPC programme. Brazil does not disagree with the manner in which Canada has terminated existing TPC activities in the Canadian regional aircraft sector, and the Article 21.5 Panel did not examine those termination measures.

27. Before the Article 21.5 Panel, Brazil made four different arguments to establish that the revised TPC programme involves *de facto* export contingent subsidies that are inconsistent with Article 3.1(a) of the *SCM Agreement*. The Panel considered each of these arguments in turn. For the reasons quoted below, the Article 21.5 Panel declined to examine the substance of the first of the four arguments made by Brazil, namely that the revised TPC programme "specifically targeted" the Canadian regional aircraft industry for assistance because of its export-orientation:

> . . . the "specific targeting" concept (in those or other words) *did not form part of our reasoning regarding contingency in fact on export performance in that dispute.* . . . That is, of the factual considerations enumerated by us at para. 9.340 of our Report, **none** concerned the alleged targeting of the Canadian aerospace industry generally, or the Canadian regional aircraft industry in particular, by TPC, **none** concerned the amount of total TPC funding directed at the Canadian aerospace or regional aircraft industries, and **none** concerned the fact that the aerospace or regional aircraft industries were eligible for TPC assistance. . . . Indeed, we consider that the question of whether TPC assistance is "specifically targeted" to the aerospace and regional aircraft industries is not relevant to the present dispute, which concerns the issue of *whether or not Canada has implemented the DSB recommendation* on TPC assistance to the Canadian regional aircraft industry. (italics added)

28. The Article 21.5 Panel next stated that the recommendations and rulings of the DSB:

> . . .cannot have required Canada to take implementation action to ensure that TPC assistance is not "specifically targeted" at the aerospace and regional aircraft industries, *because such alleged "specific targeting" did not form part of the basis for the finding of de facto export contingency that gave rise to that recommendation.* (emphasis added)

29. The Article 21.5 Panel then held, as regards this argument of Brazil, that:

> . . . we do not consider it necessary to examine Brazil's argument that "nothing has changed" because TPC assistance continues to "specifically target" the Canadian aerospace and regional aircraft industries.

...

39. In conducting its review under Article 21.5 of the DSU, the Article 21.5 Panel declined to examine Brazil's argument that "the Canadian regional aircraft industry continues to be 'specifically targeted' for TPC assistance because of its undisputed export orientation." The Article 21.5 Panel stated that this argument "did not form part" of the reasoning of the original panel and was "not relevant to the present dispute, which concerns the issue of whether or not Canada *has implemented the DSB recommendation* . . .". (emphasis added)

40. We have already noted that these proceedings, under Article 21.5 of the DSU, concern the "consistency" of the revised TPC programme with Article 3.1(a) of the *SCM Agreement*. Therefore, we disagree with the Article 21.5 Panel that the scope of these Article 21.5 dispute settlement proceedings is limited to "the issue of whether or not Canada *has implemented the DSB recommendation*". The recommendation of the DSB was that the measure found to be a prohibited export subsidy must be withdrawn within 90 days of the adoption of the Appellate Body Report and the original panel report, as modified—that is, by 18 November 1999. That recommendation to "withdraw" the prohibited export subsidy did not, of course, cover the new measure—because the new measure did not exist when the DSB made its recommendation. It follows then that the task of the Article 21.5 Panel in this case is, in fact, to determine whether the new measure—the revised TPC programme—is consistent with Article 3.1(a) of the *SCM Agreement*.

41. Accordingly, in carrying out its review under Article 21.5 of the DSU, a panel is not confined to examining the "measures taken to comply" from the perspective of the claims, arguments and factual circumstances that related to the measure that was the subject of the original proceedings. Although these may have some relevance in proceedings under Article 21.5 of the DSU, Article 21.5 proceedings involve, in principle, not the original measure, but rather a new and different measure which was not before the original panel. In addition, the relevant facts bearing upon the "measure taken to comply" may be different from the relevant facts relating to the measure at issue in the original proceedings. It is natural, therefore, that the claims, arguments and factual circumstance which are pertinent to the "measure taken to comply" will not, necessarily, be the same as those which were pertinent in the original dispute. Indeed, the utility of the review envisaged under Article 21.5 of the DSU would be seriously undermined if a panel were restricted to examining the new measure from the perspective of the claims, arguments and factual circumstances that related to the original measure, because an Article 21.5 panel would then be unable to examine fully the "consistency with a covered agreement of the measures taken to comply", as required by Article 21.5 of the DSU.

42. Consequently, in these proceedings, the task of the Article 21.5 Panel was not limited solely to determining whether the revised TPC programme had been rid of those aspects of the original measure—the TPC programme, as previously constituted—that had been identified in the original proceedings, in the context of all of the facts, as not being consistent with Canada's WTO obligations. Rather, the Article 21.5 Panel was obliged to examine the revised TPC programme for its consistency with Article 3.1(a) of the *SCM Agreement*. The fact that Brazil's argument in these Article 21.5 proceedings "did not form part" of the original panel's reasoning relating to the *previous* TPC programme does not necessarily mean that this argument is "not relevant" to the Article 21.5 proceedings, which relate to the *revised* TPC programme. In our view, the Article 21.5 Panel should have examined the merits of Brazil's argument as

it relates to the *revised* TPC programme. We conclude, therefore, that the Article 21.5 Panel erred by declining to examine Brazil's argument that the revised TPC programme "specifically targeted" the Canadian regional aircraft industry for assistance because of its export-orientation.

43. With a view to resolving this dispute, and considering that the undisputed facts on the record are adequate for this purpose, we believe that we should complete the Article 21.5 Panel's analysis by examining this argument. In so doing, we observe that the essence of Brazil's argument is that the Canadian regional aircraft industry is "specifically targeted" for assistance in two different ways under the revised TPC programme.

44. First, Brazil notes that the "Eligible Areas" for TPC assistance include "Aerospace and Defence", and that these industrial sectors are the sole such sectors to be identified expressly as eligible for TPC assistance. The other two "Eligible Areas" are "Environmental Technologies" and "Enabling Technologies", which could involve projects drawn from any industrial sector, including "Aerospace and Defence". In Brazil's view, the express identification of "Aerospace and Defence" as "Eligible Areas" puts these industrial sectors, which include the Canadian regional aircraft industry, in a privileged position and represents "specific targeting" of the Canadian regional aircraft industry. Second, Brazil maintains that the Canadian regional aircraft industry is also "specifically targeted", in practice, through the allocation of TPC funding assistance. According to Brazil, 65 per cent of TPC funding has, in the past, "gone to the [Canadian] aerospace industry".

45. Brazil maintains that the reason for these two types of "targeting" is the high export-orientation of the industry. In support of this argument, Brazil relies on a series of statements made by Canadian Government Ministers, Members of Parliament, other government officials, and by the TPC itself, regarding the objectives of TPC. Brazil acknowledges that the statements it relies upon were made in connection with the *old* TPC programme, as *previously* constituted. Brazil argues, nevertheless, that the "specific targeting" is a fact that tends to establish that the revised TPC programme involves subsidies which are *de facto* export contingent.

46. Canada does not contest any of the factual assertions made by Brazil in presenting its "specific targeting" argument. However, Canada emphasizes that the statements Brazil relies upon were made in relation to the *old* TPC programme, not to the *revised* programme. Canada also states that no TPC assistance has been granted or committed under the *revised* TPC programme to the Canadian regional aircraft industry. In other words, Canada asserts that there have been, thus far, no transactions involving the Canadian regional aircraft industry under this new measure. Brazil does not contest this assertion.

47. It is worth recalling that the granting of a subsidy is not, in and of itself, prohibited under the *SCM Agreement*. Nor does granting a "subsidy", without more, constitute an inconsistency with that Agreement. The universe of subsidies is vast. Not all subsidies are inconsistent with the *SCM Agreement*. The only "prohibited" subsidies are those identified in Article 3 of the *SCM Agreement*; Article 3.1(a) of that Agreement prohibits those subsidies that are "contingent, in law or in fact, upon export performance". We have stated previously that "a subsidy is prohibited under Article 3.1(a) if it is 'conditional' upon export performance, that is, if it is 'dependent for its existence on' export performance." We have also emphasized that a "relationship of conditionality or dependence", namely that the granting of a subsidy should be "tied to" the export performance, lies at the "very heart" of the legal standard in Article 3.1(a) of the *SCM Agreement*.

48. To demonstrate the existence of this "relationship of conditionality or dependence", we have also stated that it is *not* sufficient to show that a subsidy is granted in the knowledge, or with the anticipation, that exports will result. Such knowledge or anticipation does not, taken alone, demonstrate that the granting of the subsidy is "contingent upon" export performance.

The second sentence of footnote 4 of the *SCM Agreement* stipulates, in this regard, that the "*mere fact* that a subsidy is granted to enterprises which export shall not *for that reason alone* be considered to be an export subsidy . . .". (emphasis added) That fact, by itself, does not, therefore, compel the conclusion that there is a "relationship of conditionality or dependence", such that the granting of a subsidy is "tied to" export performance. However, we have also said that the export-orientation of a recipient "may be taken into account as *a* relevant fact, provided it is one of several facts which are considered and is not the only fact supporting a finding" of export contingency. (underlining added)

49. Recalling all this, at its core, we see Brazil's argument about "specific targeting" essentially as a contention that the *SCM Agreement* precludes the two types of targeting Brazil identifies simply because of the high export-orientation of the Canadian regional aircraft industry. However, in our view, the fact that an industrial sector has a high export-orientation is not, by itself, sufficient to preclude that sector from being expressly identified as an eligible or privileged recipient of subsidies. Nor does the high export-orientation of an industry limit, in principle, the amount of subsidies that may be granted to that industry. As we have said, granting subsidies, in itself, is not prohibited. Under Article 3.1(a) of the *SCM Agreement*, the subsidy must be *export contingent* to be prohibited. The two "targeting" factors *may* very well be relevant to an inquiry under Article 3.1(a) of the *SCM Agreement*, but they do not necessarily provide conclusive evidence that the granting of a subsidy is "*contingent*", "*conditional*" or "*dependent*" upon export performance. In these proceedings, we do not see the two "targeting" factors, by themselves, as adequate proof of prohibited export *contingency*.

50. Moreover, the evidence that Brazil relies upon in seeking to demonstrate that the Canadian regional aircraft industry is "specifically targeted" *because of* its high export-orientation relates to the TPC as *previously* constituted, and not to the *revised* TPC programme. In particular, Brazil relies upon evidence of the high proportion of TPC funding allocated to the Canadian regional aircraft industry under the *old* TPC programme and on statements made in connection with that programme by Canadian Government Ministers, Members of Parliament, officials, and by TPC itself. The burden of explaining the relevance of the evidence, in proving the claim made, naturally rests on whoever presents that evidence. Brazil has not offered any convincing explanation as to why the evidence relating to the *old* TPC programme continues to be relevant to the *revised* TPC programme. We do not believe we should simply assume that this particular evidence is relevant in respect of the revised TPC programme.

51. For all these reasons, we find that Brazil has not sufficiently established that the Canadian regional aircraft industry is "specifically targeted" *because of* its high export-orientation.

52. We conclude that Brazil has failed to establish that the revised TPC programme is inconsistent with Article 3.1(a) of the *SCM Agreement*. We also conclude that Brazil has failed to establish that Canada has not implemented the recommendations and rulings of the DSB. The outcome of the present proceedings does not, of course, preclude possible subsequent dispute resolution proceedings regarding the WTO-consistency of the revised TPC programme, or of specific instances of assistance actually granted under that programme.

… … …

c. Treatment of Separate Regimes for Exports and Domestic Production With regard to the third issue, the treatment of separate regimes for domestic and export subsidies, in the *US—Cotton Subsidies* case the measure at issue applied to both exporters and domestic users, and therefore, at least on the face of the measure, there was arguably no conditionality at all, nor was there an incentive to export. (Although an analysis of how the measure was actually applied may have indicated something different.) Rather, the subsidy was offered to both possible avenues of sale: export and domestic use. Nevertheless, the Appellate Body found that export contingency existed despite the fact that subsidies were available to domestic users as well as exporters. In doing so, it emphasised that the statute and regulations at issue 'do not establish a 'single class' of recipients of the payments; rather, the statute and regulations clearly distinguish between two types of eligible recipients, namely, eligible exporters and eligible domestic users'. In addition, 'the statute and regulations establish different conditions that eligible exporters and eligible domestic users must meet to receive . . . payments', along with different 'documentation'.[22] (While this finding was technically under Article 9.1(a) of the Agriculture Agreement, the Appellate Body referred to the language of Article 3.1(a) of the SCM Agreement (and the similar language of Agriculture Agreement Article 1(e)), and applied its reasoning to SCM Agreement Article 3.1(a) as well.)

It is not clear how far the Appellate Body would take this approach. Arguably, the Appellate Body's focus on the formal separation of treatment between exports and products for domestic use means that even where the subsidy measure does not create an incentive to export, and has no negative trade effects, there will be a violation of Article 3.1(a) where there is formally different treatment of exports and domestic products, even if this formal difference is merely for administrative convenience. This conclusion would seem to be contrary to the framework of the SCM Agreement, under which only measures that have a clear trade-distorting effect fall into the prohibited category. But perhaps if faced with this issue, the Appellate Body would try to distinguish the *Cotton* measures from one that was purely for administrative convenience.

d. The Role of the Illustrative List In addition to using the 'contingency' standard for determining whether measures constitute export subsidies, Article 3.1(a) also states that export subsidies include 'those illustrated in Annex I'. Annex I is entitled 'Illustrative List of Export Subsidies'. The list included therein was created during the GATT era, and was carried over into the SCM Agreement. The basic function of the list is to establish that export subsidies exist in certain defined circumstances. As examples, we set out here several of the items from the List.

The first item, item (a), is actually similar to Article 3.1(a): '[t]he provision by governments of direct subsidies to a firm or an industry contingent upon export performance'. Thus, it is the same 'contingency' standard discussed above, but with the limitation that subsidies be 'direct' and to a 'firm or industry'. Three other examples are as follows:

Item (e):   'The full or partial exemption remission, or deferral specifically related to exports, of direct taxes or social welfare charges paid or payable by industrial or commercial enterprises'.

Item (j):   'The provision by governments (or special institutions controlled by governments) of export credit guarantee or insurance programmes, of insurance or guarantee programmes against increases in the cost of exported products or of exchange risk programmes, at premium rates which are inadequate to cover the long-term operating costs and losses of the programmes'.

Item (k), first paragraph: 'The grant by governments (or special institutions controlled by and/or acting under the authority of governments) of export credits at rates below those which they actually have to pay for the funds so employed (or would have to pay

---

[22] Appellate Body Report, *US—Cotton Subsidies*, paras 554–84.

if they borrowed on international capital markets in order to obtain funds of the same maturity and other credit terms and denominated in the same currency as the export credit), or the payment by them of all or part of the costs incurred by exporters or financial institutions in obtaining credits, in so far as they are used to secure a material advantage in the field of export credit terms'.

In addition to its primary purpose of setting out examples of measures that constitute export subsidies, the List also offers a few examples of measures that affirmatively *do not* constitute export subsidies, that is, they are permissible practices which do not violate the SCM Agreement. In this regard, footnote 5, which is at the end of the text of Article 3.1(a), provides: '[m]easures referred to in Annex I as not constituting export subsidies shall not be prohibited under this or any other provision of this Agreement'. One such example is the second paragraph of item (k), which narrows the scope of the first paragraph (quoted above) by stating: '[p]rovided, however, that if a Member is a party to an international undertaking on official export credits to which at least twelve original Members to this Agreement are parties as of 1 January 1979 (or a successor undertaking which has been adopted by those original Members), or if in practice a Member applies the interest rates provisions of the relevant undertaking, an export credit practice which is in conformity with those provisions shall not be considered an export subsidy prohibited by this Agreement'. This defence has been invoked on three occasions, once successfully.[23]

Finally, the List has also been used in other way to argue that a particular measure does not constitute an export subsidy. In the *Brazil—Aircraft* dispute, Brazil argued that measures that fall within the terms of item (k), first paragraph, but do not meet the conditions for being an export subsidy set out there, are affirmatively *not* export subsidies and are therefore permitted. In other words, Brazil argued, if the measure meets all the terms of item (k), first paragraph, it is an export subsidy; by contrast, if it is the kind of measure that is covered by this provision, but does not meet the terms, then, *a contrario*, it is not an export subsidy. Specifically, Brazil argued that the measure at issue constituted 'payment by [governments] of all or part of the costs incurred by exporters or financial institutions in obtaining credits' under the last part of the first paragraph of item (k). However, because the measure was not 'used to secure a material advantage in the field of export credit terms', Brazil asserted that it was therefore not an export subsidy. The panel hearing this case rejected this argument in the original proceedings and also in the subsequent Article 21.5 proceedings.[24] On appeal, however, the Appellate Body seems to have taken a different view, stating:

> If Brazil had demonstrated that the payments made under the revised PROEX were not "used to secure a material advantage in the field of export credit terms", and that such payments were "payments" by Brazil of "all or part of the costs incurred by exporters or financial institutions in obtaining credits", then we would have been prepared to find that the payments made under the revised PROEX are justified under item (k) of the Illustrative List.[25]

While this statement is a bit unclear, the Appellate Body's explanation that if the other

---

[23] It was successfully invoked in *Brazil—Aircraft* (Panel Report, *Brazil—Aircraft, Article 21.5 II*, paras 5.58–5.207). It was rejected in *Canada—Aircraft* and *Canada—Aircraft II* (Panel Report, *Canada— Aircraft*, Article 21.5, paras 5.54–5.153; and Panel Report, *Canada—Aircraft II*, paras 7.154–7.182).

[24] Panel Report, *Brazil—Aircraft*, paras 7.15–7.37; Panel Report, *Brazil—Aircraft, Article 21.5*, paras 6.21–6.106.

[25] *Ibid*, para 80.

two elements had been demonstrated it 'would have been prepared to find that the payments made under the revised PROEX are justified under item (k) of the Illustrative List' arguably implies that it would accept such a defence. But the absence of any reasoning on the issue undermines the strength of this implication. Thus, when the issue arose again in the second Article 21.5 proceedings, the panel rejected Brazil's *a contrario* argument in spite of the Appellate Body's statements.[26] This second Article 21.5 panel report was not appealed. In addition, a later panel also rejected the argument in the context of both items (k) and (j).[27]

(ii) Domestic Content Subsidies

Article 3.1(b) of the SCM Agreement addresses domestic content subsides (sometimes called 'local content' or 'import substitution' subsidies). Specifically, it prohibits 'subsidies contingent, whether solely or as one of several other conditions, upon the use of domestic over imported goods'. Thus, the 'contingency' standard explained in the context of Article 3.1(a) is used in Article 3.1(b) as well. The case law on this provision has been limited and relatively straightforward.

The one key textual difference between the two provisions is that Article 3.1(a) explicitly refers to subsidies both 'in law' and 'in fact', whereas Article 3.1(b) does not. However, the Appellate Body has clarified that Article 3.1(b) nevertheless covers both kinds of domestic content subsidies.[28]

As explained in section VI, subsidies that violate this provision could also violate GATT Article III:4 and paragraph 1(a) of the Illustrative List of the TRIMs Agreement.

(iii) Prohibited Subsidies: Final Thoughts

The categorisation of export subsidies and domestic content subsidies as prohibited may reflect the view that the trade effects of these types of subsidies are inherently so discriminatory that these subsidies should be per se illegal. That is, there is no need to evaluate their actual effects in specific cases, as with the actionable subsidies discussed in the next section, because these effects can be presumed. This approach is fairly persuasive, as export subsidies always have the effect of giving an advantage to exports by domestic producers at the expense of foreign competitors in foreign markets, and domestic content subsidies always have the effect of giving an advantage to domestic producers at the expense of foreign competitors in the home market. By contrast, most other types of subsidies may or may not have these kinds of trade effects, depending on various factual circumstances.

Finally, we note that there is a distinction between two types of subsidy measures, which can be particularly important in the case of Prohibited Subsidies: subsidy programmes versus one-time subsidies. A subsidy programme is a regime established by a government to provide subsidies under certain conditions over time. By contrast, a one-time subsidy is a single, independent subsidy given by a government. The distinction can be important because for Prohibited Subsidies, the analysis of claims against subsidy *programmes* will

---

[26] *Ibid*, paras 5.211–5.277.
[27] Panel Report, *Korea—Vessels*, paras 7.193–7.207; 7.309–7.329.
[28] Appellate Body Report, *Canada—Autos*, paras 135–43.

be different from claims against one-time subsidy payments. For subsidy programmes, the mandatory/discretionary distinction will apply (see Chapter 5 for a discussion of this distinction) Under this doctrine, as long as the programme can be operated in a manner consistent with SCM Agreement rules, it will be found consistent. Of course, if particular subsidies provided under the programme violate the rules, these individual subsidies may still be found to be in violation. However, the programme itself will not be found to be in violation unless it *requires* that subsidies be provided in contravention of the rules, ie, unless it requires the provision of subsidies that are export contingent or contingent on the use of domestic over imported goods.[29]

(b) Actionable Subsidies

Part III of the SCM Agreement addresses actionable subsidies. In essence, the use of the term 'actionable' means that under this provision subsidies are not prohibited outright, as with prohibited subsidies, but rather an action may be brought challenging such subsides as having certain negative trade effects. Where the existence of such effects is shown, the subsidies violate the SCM Agreement.

The trade effects in question are set out in Article 5, which refers to subsidies that cause 'adverse effects to the interests of other Members'. This provision refers to three types of 'adverse effects':

(a) injury to the domestic industry of another Member;
(b) nullification or impairment of benefits accruing directly or indirectly to other Members under GATT, in particular the benefits of concessions bound under GATT Article II;
(c) serious prejudice to the interests of another Member.

With regard to 'injury,' footnote 11 to the Agreement clarifies that 'injury to the domestic industry' is used in the same sense as in Part V dealing with countervailing duties (addressed in section VII below). Footnote 45, in Part V, then provides: 'injury' shall, unless otherwise specified, be taken to mean material injury to a domestic industry, threat of material injury to a domestic industry or material retardation of the establishment of such an industry and shall be interpreted in accordance with the provisions of this Article'.

As to 'nullification or impairment', footnote 12 explains that this phrase is used in the same sense as under the GATT. However, by and large 'nullification or impairment' is simply presumed where a violation has been shown under the GATT, so the footnote does not provide much guidance.

Finally, 'serious prejudice' is explained in the SCM Agreement in extensive detail, and has also been the subject of a number of disputes. With regard to the explanation in the Agreement, footnote 13 states that 'serious prejudice' is used in the same sense as it is used in GATT Article XVI:1, and that it includes 'threat' of serious prejudice. Article 6.1 sets out several situations where serious prejudice will be 'deemed to exist'. However, this provision lapsed pursuant to Article 31 when it was not renewed after five years.

Article 6.3 then explains that 'serious prejudice' 'may arise in any case where one or several of the following apply':

---

[29] See, eg Panel Report, *Brazil—Aircraft, Article 21.5 II*, paras 5.42–5.50.

(a) the effect of the subsidy is to displace or impede the imports of a like product of another Member into the market of the subsidising Member;
(b) the effect of the subsidy is to displace or impede the exports of a like product of another Member from a third country market;
(c) the effect of the subsidy is a significant price undercutting by the subsidised product as compared with the price of a like product of another Member in the same market or significant price suppression, price depression or lost sales in the same market;
(d) the effect of the subsidy is an increase in the world market share of the subsidising Member in a particular subsidised primary product or commodity as compared to the average share it had during the previous period of three years, and this increase follows a consistent trend over a period when subsidies have been granted.

Thus, if a panel concludes that any of these four scenarios is met, this provides a sufficient basis for finding serious prejudice.[30]

An examination of claims under these provisions will tend to be very fact-intensive. For instance, to show that there has been 'significant price undercutting' under sub-paragraph (c), data on prices must be gathered and evaluated. This kind of examination goes beyond traditional legal interpretation, and may require the economic analysis typical of trade remedy injury investigations. Nonetheless, legal analysis of these provisions remains important, and some of these provisions have been interpreted by panels or the Appellate Body. We highlight some of the important clarifications here.

Sub-paragraphs (a) and (b) both address situations where the subsidy has the effect of, ie causes, displacing or impeding another Member's sales, either in the other Member's home market or a third country market. An examination of claims under these provisions may look, for example, at market share data of the product at issue, or non-introduction of a product, in the relevant market, to determine whether sales have been displaced or impeded.[31] Additional guidance on paragraph (b) is provided in Article 6.4, and on both paragraphs (a) and (b) in Article 6.7. In considering the issue of 'displacement' in *EC—Aircraft*, the Appellate Body seemed to discuss this concept in terms similar to this in the non-discrimination context, focusing on competition in the marketplace:

> [D]isplacement is a situation where imports or exports of a like product are replaced by the sales of the subsidized product. The mechanism by which displacement operates is, in our view, essentially an economic mechanism, the existence of which is to be assessed by reference to events that occur in the relevant product market. We construe the concept of displacement as relating to, and arising out of, competitive engagement between products in a market. Aggressive pricing of certain products may, for example, lead to displacement of exports or imports in a particular market. This, however, can only be the case if those products compete in the same market. An examination of the competitive relationship between products is therefore required so as to determine whether such products form part of the same market. We conclude therefore that a 'market', within the meaning of Articles 6.3(a) and 6.3(b) of the SCM Agreement, is a set of products in a particular geographical area that are in actual or potential competition with each other. An assessment of the competitive relationship between products in the market is required in order to determine whether and to what extent one product may displace another. Thus, while a complaining Member may identify a subsidized product and the like product by reference to footnote 46, the products thereby identified must be analyzed under the discipline of the

---

[30] Panel Report, *US—Cotton Subsidies*, paras 7.1368–7.1390.
[31] Panel Report, *Indonesia—Autos*, paras 14.212–14.235.

product market so as to be able to determine whether displacement is occurring. Ordinarily, the subsidized product and the like product will form part of a larger product market. But it may be the case that a complainant chooses to define the subsidized and like products so broadly that it is necessary to analyze these products in different product markets. This will be necessary so as to analyze further the real competitive interactions that are taking place, and thereby determine whether displacement is occurring.[32]

Sub-paragraph (c) addresses situations where the subsidy has the effect of 'significant price undercutting' by the subsidised products as compared with like products of other Members in the 'same market', or significant price suppression, price depression or lost sales in the same market. There are a number of issues that arise under this provision. For price undercutting, suppression and depression, an examination of actual price levels for the products at issue will be important. In addition, the Appellate Body has said that the word 'significant' in the context of 'significant price suppression' in Article 6.3(c) means 'important, notable or consequential'.[33] In addition, the Appellate Body has clarified that the 'same market' could be both a national market and the world market.[34] We focus here, though, on the 'causation' issue, that is, whether significant price undercutting, suppression, depression or lost sales is the 'effect' of the subsidy. This issue will be a key element of all the Article 6.3 situations, as they all refer to the 'effect' of the subsidy. The *US—Cotton Subsidies* panel found that a causal link did exist between the subsidy and significant price suppression, based on the following reasoning (which was upheld on appeal):

Panel Report, *United States—Subsidies on Upland Cotton*, Adopted 21 March 2005, WT/DS267/R

i Is there a causal link?

7.1347 There are four main, cumulative, grounds why we believe that a causal link exists between certain of the challenged United States subsidies and the significant price suppression.

7.1348 First, as we have already indicated, we believe that the United States exerts a substantial proportionate influence in the world upland cotton market. This substantial proportionate influence flows, *inter alia*, from the magnitude of the United States production and export of upland cotton. We recall again that the United States does not disagree with the proposition that a Member's proportionate magnitude in world production and consumption of upland cotton might be a relevant consideration here. Nor does the United States disagree with the proposition that increased production and supply of upland cotton which reaches the world markets will have an effect on prices.

7.1349 Second, we recall our examination of the nature of the United States subsidies at issue. In particular, we recall that several of the United States subsidies—marketing loan programme payments, the user marketing (Step 2) payments, MLA payments and CCP payments—are directly linked to world prices for upland cotton, thereby insulating United States producers from low prices. We believe that the structure, design and operation of these three measures constitutes evidence supporting a causal link with the significant price suppression we have found to exist. Furthermore, while we do not believe that it is strictly necessarily to calculate precisely the amount of the subsidies in question, we observe that we have readily available

---

[32] Appellate Body Report, *EC—Aircraft*, para 1119.
[33] Appellate Body Report, *US—Cotton Subsidies*, para 426.
[34] *Ibid*, paras 400–14.

information on the record showing us that the price-contingent subsidies in question involve very large amounts of United States government money benefiting United States upland cotton production. We agree with the United States that "the question is one of the nature of the subsidy examined and the degree of any predicted effect, which could range from significant to negligible". These price-contingent subsidies were, in our view, sufficient to cause the significant price suppression that we have found to exist in the same world market.

7.1350 It is true that PFC payments, DP payments and crop insurance payments were/are also granted contemporaneously with these price-contingent subsidies. However, in our view, Brazil has not established that, in light of their structure, design and operation, these measures—which are more concerned with income support than directly with world price effects—had a sufficient nexus with the marketing of the subsidized product and the price suppression effects as to render their inclusion or non-inclusion in our price suppression analysis legally determinative in respect of the significant price suppression that we have found in the same world market. We nevertheless observe that they did not have the effect of diminishing, or cancelling out, the significant price suppression. However, because of the different nature and effect of these subsidies, we decline to aggregate them and their effects with those of the price-contingent subsidies in our serious prejudice analysis. In our view, Brazil has not established that the significant price suppression we have found was "the effect of" these non-price- contingent subsidies within the meaning of Article 6.3(c).

7.1351 Third, there is a discernible temporal coincidence of suppressed world market prices and the price-contingent United States subsidies. Looking at the period, we see the following:

- United States production of upland cotton increased from MY 1998 to MY 2001 and, while production dropped in MY 2002, there was still an overall increase in MY 2002 compared to MY 1998;
- the United States' share of world upland cotton production increased to and remained at a level of approximately 20 per cent;
- United States prices received by United States upland cotton producers decreased by 34 per cent between MY 1998 and MY 2001;
- the A-Index in MY 1999—MY 2002 was, on average, 29.5 per cent below its 1980-1998 average;
- United States exports increased by approximately 160 per cent from MY 1998 to MY 2001 and by an even greater percentage from MY 1998-MY 2002;
- United States share of world exports of upland cotton increased; and
- United States imports of upland cotton remained at comparatively low levels.

7.1352 These data reveal that, over the same period that the subsidies in question were being granted, the United States market generated large supplies of upland cotton. Over this same time period, market revenue of United States upland cotton producers decreased. So did world market prices. There was also a marked increase in United States exports, both absolute and in terms of relative share of world exports. Even taking into account that in 1998, production may have been driven downward by drought and high levels of crop abandonment and that, in 2001, production may have been driven upward by high yields, we see a strong temporal coincidence between the United States subsidies and the drop in United States prices, the drop in—and suppression of—world market prices, the increase in United States exports.

7.1353 Fourth, we find credible evidence on the record concerning the divergence between United States producers' total costs of production and revenue from sales of upland cotton since 1997. This supports the proposition that United States upland cotton producers would not have been economically capable of remaining in the production of upland cotton had it not been for the United States subsidies at issue and that the effect of the subsidies was to allow

United States producers to sell upland cotton at a price lower than would otherwise have been necessary to cover their total costs.

7.1354 If market revenue alone is compared to United States upland cotton producers' total costs of production, the information before us reveals that United States upland cotton producers would on average have lost money for each planted acre in every year since MY 1998, and made a small profit in MY 1997. We do not believe the utility of the record data is fundamentally undermined by any of the criticisms levied by the United States for the purposes of this dispute, particularly as the data are calculated in accordance with a methodology which the USDA itself has deemed to be a sufficiently reliable reflection of United States upland cotton producers' costs and revenues. That the figures before us are cumulated to show a result over the six-year period from 1997-2002 also lends itself to an assessment of the medium- to longer- term examination of developments in the United States upland cotton industry. We believe that the existence of this gap between upland cotton producers' total production costs and market revenue, on the one hand, and the effect of the subsidies, on the other hand, was to sustain a higher level of output than would have occurred in the absence of the United States subsidies at issue.

7.1355 While there may well have been other factors affecting prices in the world market over this time period, on the basis of the above examination of these four factors, taken together, we find that a causal link exists between the mandatory United States price-contingent subsidies at issue—marketing loan programme payments, user marketing (Step 2) payments, MLA payments and CCP payments—and the significant price suppression that we have found to exist. However, no such causal link has been established in respect of the non-price contingent subsidies before us, that is, PFC and DP payments and crop insurance subsidies.

... ...

Furthermore, it said, other alleged causal factors that were put forward 'do not attenuate the genuine and substantial causal link' that it had found.[35]

While the Appellate Body upheld this finding, it did, however, state that 'the Panel could have provided a more detailed explanation of its analysis of the complex facts and economic arguments arising in this dispute, . . . in order to demonstrate precisely how it evaluated the different factors bearing on the relationship between the price-contingent subsidies and significant price suppression'.[36] The Appellate Body's criticism illustrates the inherent difficulty with causation analysis. It is easy to show a correlation between two events. Causation, on the other hand, is much more difficult to prove. Trade remedy specialists have known this for years, and with the establishment of an 'adverse effects' claim in the SCM Agreement WTO panels are discovering it as well. In all likelihood, the use of sophisticated economic analysis to analyse the issue of causation will increase as more disputes in this area are brought to the WTO.

Issues related to causation are complicated further when multiple subsidies have been used. In this situation, there is a question as to when and whether a combined analysis of the various subsidies may be undertaken. In *US—Aircraft*, the Appellate Body discussed this issue in some detail.

---

[35] Panel Report, *US—Cotton Subsidies*, paras 7.1357–7.1363.
[36] Appellate Body Report, *US—Cotton Subsidies*, para 458.

Appellate Body Report, *United States—Measures Affecting Trade in Large Civil Aircraft,* Adopted 23 March 2012, WT/DS353/AB/R

Assessment of the European Union's Claims of Error on Appeal

(a) Introduction

1282. Over the course of these appellate proceedings, the submissions made by the participants and third participants with respect to the collective assessment of the effects of multiple subsidy measures have focused heavily on the approaches employed in the *US—Upland Cotton* and *EC and certain member States—Large Civil Aircraft* disputes. Moreover, following circulation of the Appellate Body report in the latter dispute, the core disagreement between the participants shifted from their different understandings of what was done by the panel in *US—Upland Cotton* to their different understandings of the Appellate Body's findings in *EC and certain member States—Large Civil Aircraft*. For these reasons, we consider it useful to outline key elements of the approaches taken by the panels in these two disputes. As explained below, and accepted by the participants, two distinct means of undertaking a collective assessment of the effects of multiple subsidies have been used, namely: (i) an *ex ante* decision taken by a panel to undertake a single analysis of the effects of multiple subsidies whose structure, design, and operation are similar and thereby to assess in an integrated causation analysis the collective effects of such subsidy measures; and (ii) an examination undertaken by a panel *after* it has found that at least one subsidy has caused adverse effects as to whether the effects of other subsidies complement and supplement those adverse effects. The former type of approach was employed by the panel in *US—Upland Cotton*, and the latter approach was employed by the panel in *EC and certain member States—Large Civil Aircraft*. For the sake of convenience, we will refer to the first type of approach as a decision to "aggregate" the subsidies, or "aggregation", and to the second type of approach as a decision to "cumulate" the effects of the subsidies, or "cumulation".

1283. Before turning to the European Union's two grounds of appeal, we outline, in subsection (b), the different approaches that have been and that may be taken to a collective assessment of the effects of multiple subsidies. In subsection (c), we identify the approach taken by the Panel in this dispute. In subsection (d), we consider whether the Panel erred in declining to assess collectively the effects of the aeronautics R&D subsidies and the effects of the B&O tax rate reductions. Finally, in subsection (e), we evaluate whether the Panel erred in declining to assess collectively the effects of the tied tax subsidies and the effects of the remaining subsidies and, if so, whether we can complete the analysis and ourselves undertake a collective assessment of the effects of these subsidies.

(b) Different approaches to collective assessment

1284. Articles 5(c) and 6.3 of the *SCM Agreement* do not require that a serious prejudice analysis "clinically isolate each individual subsidy and its effects". Rather, the way in which a panel structures its evaluation of a claim that multiple subsidies have caused serious prejudice will necessarily vary from case to case. Relevant circumstances that will bear upon the appropriateness of a panel's approach include the design, structure, and operation of the subsidies at issue, the alleged market phenomena, and the extent to which the subsidies are provided in relation to a particular product or products. A panel must also take account of the manner in which the claimant presents its case, and the extent to which it claims that multiple subsidies have similar effects on the same product, or that the effects of multiple subsidies manifest themselves collectively in the relevant market. A panel enjoys a degree of methodological latitude in selecting its approach to analyzing the collective effects of multiple subsidies for purposes of assessing causation. However, a panel is never absolved from having to establish a "genuine and substantial relationship of cause and effect" between the impugned subsidies and the alleged market phenomena under Article 6.3, or from assessing whether such causal link is diluted by the effects of other factors. Moreover, a panel must take care not to segment unduly its analysis such that, when confronted with multiple subsidy measures, it considers the effects of each on an individual basis only and, as a result of such an atomized approach, finds that no subsidy is a substantial cause of the relevant adverse effects. At least two ways of conducting a collective causation analysis may be pursued by panels.

1285. First, a panel may group together subsidy measures that are sufficiently similar in their design, structure, and operation in order to ascertain their aggregated effects in an integrated causation analysis and determine whether there is a genuine and substantial causal relationship between these multiple subsidies, taken together, and the relevant market phenomena identified in Article 6.3 of the *SCM Agreement* (such as significant price suppression, lost sales, displacement or impedance). In such circumstances, the panel is not required to find that each subsidy measure is, individually, a genuine and substantial cause of the relevant phenomenon. Nor is it required to assess the relative contribution of each subsidy within the group to the resulting effects. When such an analysis is appropriate in the light of the design, structure, and operation of multiple subsidies, a panel may also add together the *amounts* of the subsidies as part of its analysis of the collective effects of that group of subsidies. Whether such an analysis is appropriate will depend upon the particular features of the subsidies at issue and the case presented by the complainant. The causal mechanism through which a subsidy produces effects is one criterion that will be relevant to the issue of whether aggregation is appropriate in any given instance.

1286. The approach of the panel in *US—Upland Cotton* illustrates this first method of collectively assessing the effects of multiple subsidies (aggregation). That panel noted that the question of whether the effects of the various subsidies should be considered on an aggregated basis was linked to the issue of possible interrelationships among them, and explained that, in analyzing Brazil's claim of significant price suppression, it would conduct its analysis as follows:

> To the extent a sufficient nexus with these exists among the subsidies at issue so that their effects manifest themselves collectively, we believe that we may legitimately treat them as a "subsidy" and group them and their effects together.

In applying this test to the US subsidies challenged by Brazil, the panel divided the subsidies at issue into two general groups: "those that are directly price-contingent, and those that are not". The panel identified certain characteristics shared by the price-contingent subsidies and found that they had "a nexus with the subsidized product and the single effects-related variable— world price", so as to warrant consideration of their effects in the aggregate, given that such effects are "manifest in the movements in upland cotton prices in the same world market during the reference period." In contrast, the panel identified certain characteristics of the non-price contingent subsidies that suggested a much more attenuated nexus between those subsidies and the world price for cotton and, therefore, declined to aggregate the non-price-contingent subsidies with the price-contingent subsidies in its price suppression analysis.

1287. Second, a panel may begin by analyzing the effects of a *single* subsidy, or an *aggregated* group of subsidies, in order to determine whether it constitutes a genuine and substantial cause of adverse effects. Having reached that conclusion, a panel may then assess whether *other* subsidies —either individually or in aggregated groups—have a *genuine* causal connection to the same effects, and complement and supplement the effects of the *first* subsidy (or group of subsidies) that was found, alone, to be a *genuine* and *substantial* cause of the alleged market phenomena. The other subsidies have to be a "genuine" cause, but they need not, in themselves, amount to a "substantial" cause in order for their effects to be combined with those of the first subsidy or group of subsidies that, alone, has been found to be a genuine and substantial cause of the adverse effects.

1288. This second way of collectively assessing the effects of multiple subsidies (cumulation) was adopted by the panel in *EC and certain member States—Large Civil Aircraft*, a dispute that involved challenges to a large number of subsidy measures. Those that were relevant to the panel's analysis of adverse effects fell into four main categories: (i) "launch aid" or "member State financing" ("LA/MSF") for the development of various Airbus LCA models; (ii) research and technological development ("R&TD") funding granted to Airbus companies by the European Communities and member State governments at central and regional levels; (iii) infrastructure and infrastructure-related grants by the member State governments; and (iv) equity infusions and corporate restructuring measures undertaken by the French and German Governments. In its adverse effects analysis, the panel first assessed the effects of one of the categories of subsidies—namely, LA/MSF subsidies—that the United States had contended were the primary subsidies affecting Airbus' commercial behaviour. The panel determined that through their "product effect"—namely, enabling Airbus to launch each of its LCA models at the time that it did—the LA/MSF caused displacement of imports within the meaning of Article 6.3(a), displacement of exports within the meaning of Article 6.3(b), and significant lost sales within the meaning of Article 6.3(c) of the *SCM Agreement*. The panel then turned to assess the effects of non-LA/MSF subsidies, and considered whether the "product" effect of LA/MSF was "complemented and supplemented" by the remaining three types of subsidies. The panel also referred to the test for aggregation of the effects of subsidies set out by the panel in *US—Upland Cotton* in expressing its view that it was "appropriate to undertake {its} analysis of the effects of the subsidies on an aggregated basis".

1289. In reviewing the panel's approach on appeal, the Appellate Body first observed that, notwithstanding that the panel had stated that, like the *US—Upland Cotton* panel, it would undertake an aggregated analysis of the effects of all of the relevant subsidies, that was not in fact what the panel had done. The Appellate Body nevertheless considered that the approach that the panel had taken was in principle permissible provided that, in its analysis, the panel had established a *genuine* causal link between each group of non-LA/MSF subsidies and the relevant adverse effects. Accordingly, the Appellate Body reviewed the panel's individual assessment of each group of non-LA/MSF subsidies in order to determine whether the panel's analysis revealed that it had determined that each such group had a genuine causal connection with the relevant market effects and had thereby identified a sufficient basis for its finding that the effects of each such group "complemented and supplemented" the product effects of the LA/MSF "in that they similarly contributed to Airbus' ability to bring to the market its models of LCA, thereby causing displacement . . . and significant lost sales". The Appellate Body found the panel's approach to have been satisfactory with respect to two of the three groups of non-LA/MSF subsidies, but that the panel had erred in cumulating the effects of the third group of non-LA/MSF subsidies (the R&TD subsidies) with the effects of the LA/MSF subsidies, because it had not established a genuine causal link between those subsidies and Airbus' ability to launch and bring to the market its models of LCA.

1290. Thus, at least two approaches to a collective assessment of the effects of multiple subsidy measures may be used, namely, aggregation and cumulation. Whether either, or both, or neither of these approaches is appropriate in a particular case will be a function of the specific subsidy measures at issue and their effects on prices and sales in the relevant market, as well as upon the manner in which a complainant presents its claim and the panel decides to structure its causation analysis. In deciding how to undertake its analysis of serious prejudice, however, a panel is subject to the constraint that it must employ an approach that will enable it to take due account of all of the subsidies that provide a relevant and identifiable competitive advantage to the recipient and its products in the market and that relate to alleged adverse effects phenomena. Only by doing so can a panel ensure a full appreciation of all of the challenged subsidies that may be contributing, or conducing, to the serious prejudice. At the same time, a panel must be careful not to combine multiple measures in such a way as to absolve a complainant of its burden of proving that each challenged measure is a genuine cause of, or genuinely contributes to producing, the market phenomena identified in Article 6.3 and that the challenged subsidies, taken together, are a genuine and substantial cause of such adverse effects.

1291. A decision to aggregate subsidies that share a similar design, structure, and operation is both a useful tool that a panel can use to avoid having to repeat the same analysis for each and every measure and a substantive recognition that the measures in question are of such kind that they are likely to conduce to the same result. Indeed, an aggregate analysis of such a group of subsidies may establish a genuine and substantial causal link in circumstances where no such link could have been established for each subsidy measure, analyzed in isolation. A decision by a panel to aggregate multiple subsidy measures represents an exercise of judgement by the panel to the effect that, given the degree of similarity among the subsidy measures, there is a reasonable likelihood that the examination of the causal relationship between each such subsidy and the alleged effects will be largely similar, and that it can be anticipated that the effects of the subsidy measures and their causal relationship to the serious prejudice alleged will be largely the same. In adopting such an approach, a panel must explain why it considers such similarity to exist. Such explanation should be grounded in the characteristics of the particular subsidies at issue, particularly the nature and design of those subsidy measures, the implications of that nature and design for the operation of the subsidies, their relationship to the subsidized product, and the structure of the market in which that product competes.

1292. In contrast, a decision as to whether the *effects* of different subsidies can be cumulated can be taken only *after* there has been a determination, for at least one subsidy or group of aggregated subsidies, that it has a genuine and substantial link to the alleged market phenomena. Once such a causal link has been established, then a panel will have to address the question of whether other subsidies have a genuine connection to such phenomena. Considerations that may bear upon a panel's assessment of whether a genuine causal connection exists include the design, structure, magnitude, and operation of the subsidy, as well as the nexus between the subsidy and the subsidized product. In our view, a genuine causal connection may be established in different ways. One way is to demonstrate that the subsidy or subsidies cause effects that follow the same causal pathway as a subsidy that has already been found to be a genuine and substantial cause of the alleged market phenomena under Article 6.3 of the *SCM Agreement*. We do not, however, consider that this is the only way in which the requisite genuine causal connection can be established. A genuine causal connection may also be found when a complainant succeeds in demonstrating that, even though other subsidies do not operate along the same causal pathway, those subsidies nevertheless, either singly or in combination, meaningfully contribute to, and thereby complement and supplement, the adverse effects, within the meaning of Article 6.3, caused by the first subsidy. In other words, the effects of such other subsidy or group of subsidies must be shown to be non-trivial in order to be found to supplement or complement effects for which a genuine and substantial connection has already been established.

1293. We further observe that the characteristics of the market within which the subsidized products compete may affect the analysis of whether the effects of different subsidies complement and supplement each other, and that panels should give consideration to whether the specific market at issue enhances the scope for complementarity among subsidies—even those subsidies that differ in nature. For example, when a subsidy recipient exercises market power, it may be more likely to be able to take advantage of potential interaction between different subsidies, and to exploit these effects to the disadvantage of its competitors, than would be the case in a perfectly competitive market.

… … …

(c) Non-actionable Subsidies

Part IV of the SCM Agreement addresses non-actionable subsidies. These provisions are no longer in force, having lapsed five years after the WTO's entry into force, pursuant to Article 31 of the SCM Agreement. In part, the failure to renew the provisions might have been the result of the Seattle Ministerial Conference debacle that took place around this time, which made any decision-making difficult. In addition, it may have been difficult to generate the necessary support for the substantive issues involved. We discuss these issues here briefly nevertheless to illustrate the context it provides in the overall SCM Agreement framework.

SCM Agreement Article 8 identifies certain subsidies as 'non-actionable'. Specifically, Article 8.1 notes that, in addition to non-specific subsidies, subsidies which meet one of three sets of conditions described in Article 8.2 are non-actionable. Article 8.2 clarifies at the outset that these subsidies are non-actionable '[n]otwithstanding the provisions of Parts III [Actionable Subsidies] and V [Countervailing Measures]'. Thus, the term 'non-actionable' means that subsidies meeting the conditions are not subject to the action-able subsidies provisions or to countervailing duties. These subsidies were granted an exemption because they are likely to have minimal trade distorting effects and because the policy goals they pursue were considered desirable. Article 8.2 sets out the following types of subsidies that are 'non-actionable':

- Paragraph (a): Research and Development ('assistance for research activities conducted by firms or by higher education or research establishments on a contract basis with firms' where certain conditions are met.)
- Paragraph (b): Regional Development ('assistance to disadvantaged regions within the territory of a Member given pursuant to a general framework of regional development and non-specific (within the meaning of Article 2) within eligible regions' where certain conditions are met.)
- Paragraph (c): Environmental Protection ('assistance to promote adaptation of existing facilities to new environmental requirements imposed by law and/or regulations which result in greater constraints and financial burden on firms'.)

The elimination of the 'non-actionable' category of subsidies does not mean that these policies cannot be pursued. Rather, it simply means that when providing these kinds of subsidies, governments must be careful to do so in a way that does not lead to the subsidies falling into the 'prohibited' category, or having a trade impact that would constitute 'adverse effects' or lead to injurious imports that may be countervailed.

IV. DISPUTE SETTLEMENT AND REMEDIES

As explained earlier in Chapter 5, the DSU establishes general time-frames that apply to WTO disputes. It also contains provisions designed to ensure compliances with DSB recommendations and rulings. The SCM Agreement, however, contains several 'special and additional' rules that apply to the various subsidy categories described above. We discuss several of these here.

For prohibited subsidies, pursuant to Article 4 of the SCM Agreement the time-frames are much shorter than those under the DSU. For example, under Article 4.6 circulation of the panel report is to take place within 90 days of composition of the panel and establishment of the terms of reference. In addition, Article 4.10 allows Members to take 'appropriate countermeasures' where there has been non-compliance with DSB recommendations and rulings. This language appears to give Members greater leeway to retaliate than the 'suspension of concessions or other obligations' language in the DSU. Similarly, for actionable subsidies, pursuant to Article 7 there are also shortened time-frames, although not as short as for prohibited subsidies, and Article 7.9 authorises 'countermeasures, commensurate with the degree and nature of the adverse effects determined to exist'.

For both prohibited and actionable subsidies, the question also arises as to what is required substantively to achieve implementation. Under the DSU, Article 19.1 provides for a recommendation that the Member 'bring the measure into conformity' with the relevant agreement. By contrast, Article 4.7 of the SCM Agreement provides that for prohibited subsidies, the panel 'shall recommend that the subsidising Member withdraw the subsidy without delay'. In practice, panels have usually set this period as 90 days from the date of adoption of the panel/Appellate Body reports.[37] For actionable subsides, Article 7.8 provides that for adopted reports where 'adverse effects' were found, the Member 'granting or maintaining such subsidy shall take appropriate steps to remove the adverse effects or shall withdraw the subsidy'. Thus, for prohibited subsidies, a Member must 'withdraw the subsidy', whereas for actionable subsidies it can either 'remove the adverse effects' or 'withdraw the subsidy'. In terms of timing, Article 7.9 states: '[i]n the event the Member has not taken appropriate steps to remove the adverse effects of the subsidy or withdraw the subsidy within six months from the date when the DSB adopts the panel report or the Appellate Body report, and in the absence of agreement on compensation, the DSB shall grant authorisation to the complaining Member to take countermeasures, commensurate with the degree and nature of the adverse effects determined to exist, unless the DSB decides by consensus to reject the request'.

The phrase 'withdraw the subsidy' in Article 4.7 has been interpreted in a controversial manner in one WTO dispute. In the DSU Article 21.5 compliance proceeding in the *Australia—Leather* case, a panel ruled that in order to satisfy the 'withdraw the subsidy' requirement, the recipient company must re-pay the subsidy to the government. Because that had not occurred, the panel ruled that compliance with the original ruling had not been achieved. The panel reasoned as follows:

Panel Report, *Australia—Subsidies Provided to Producers and Exporters of Automotive Leather, Recourse to Article 21.5 of the DSU by the United States*, Adopted 11 February 2000, WT/DS126/RW

(d) Is repayment in full of the prohibited subsidy necessary in this case?

6.46 Australia argues in the first instance that no repayment is required in this case, and that it could have fully complied with the recommendation to withdraw the subsidy in this case by releasing Howe from the remaining obligations under the grant contract. In Australia's view, this action would have eliminated the export contingency on which was based the determination that the subsidies granted to Howe were prohibited, and would bring the prohibited subsidies

---

[37] See, eg Panel Report, *Korea—Vessels*, para 8.5. However, there are some exceptions: see, eg Panel Report, *US—FSC*, paras 8.5–8.8.

into conformity with Article 3.1(a) of the SCM Agreement, thus "withdrawing" the prohibited subsidies.

6.47 We are not persuaded by Australia's argument that it is possible to change, *ex post facto*, the export contingency associated with the prohibited subsidy in this case. Our determination of the existence of in fact export contingency was based on the "facts that existed at the time the contract establishing the conditions for the grant payments was entered into". Where, as here, the prohibited subsidy is a onetime, past event, and its retention is not contingent upon export performance yet to be achieved, it is a logical impossibility to change the facts and circumstances surrounding the decision to provide the subsidy which led to the conclusion that the subsidy was prohibited. While in this case, the period covered by the sales performance targets has not yet ended, releasing Howe from any obligations with respect to those targets cannot change the fact that there was a close tie between anticipated exportation and the grant of the subsidies **at the time the subsidies were provided**. We noted in our original determination that the fact that anticipated exports did not come to pass in the volumes anticipated did not affect the conclusion that the subsidies were contingent upon export performance. Similarly, the removal of the sales performance targets today cannot change the fact that, at the time the subsidies were provided, they were contingent upon anticipated export performance. The purely prospective remedy proposed by Australia of changing after the fact the conditions on which the subsidy was provided, essentially by erasing the sales performance targets from the grant contract, in our view would be completely ineffective in this case.

6.48 Thus, we conclude that, in the circumstances of this case, repayment is necessary in order to "withdraw" the prohibited subsidies found to exist. As discussed above, we do not find any basis for repayment of anything less than the full subsidy. We therefore conclude that repayment in full of the prohibited subsidy is necessary in order to "withdraw the subsidy" in this case.

6.49 In our view, the required repayment does not include any interest component. We believe that withdrawal of the subsidy was intended by the drafters of the SCM Agreement to be a specific and effective remedy for violations of the prohibition in Article 3.1(a). However, we do not understand it to be a remedy intended to fully restore the *status quo ante* by depriving the recipient of the prohibited subsidy of the benefits it may have enjoyed in the past. Nor do we consider it to be a remedy intended to provide reparation or compensation in any sense. A requirement of interest would go beyond the requirement of repayment encompassed by the term "withdraw the subsidy", and is therefore, we believe, beyond any reasonable understanding of that term.

… … …

The panel's approach is certainly understandable. Without a requirement of repayment, Members are essentially free to make one-time subsidy payments, safe in the knowledge that all they need to do to achieve compliance is refrain from paying out more subsidies. On the other hand, the panel's approach is fairly intrusive in terms of interference with domestic affairs because it requires not just government action, but also action by private companies. The Appellate Body has not yet addressed this issue, and it is not clear whether it would take the same approach as that of the *Australia— Leather* panel. At the DSB meeting where this report was adopted, the panel's approach was criticised by a number of WTO Members.[38]

As an additional note, if an 'interest component' is *not* included with the repayment,

---

[38] Even the US, the winning party in the case, noted that '[t]he Panel's remedy went beyond that sought by the United States': WT/DSB/M/75, 7 March 2000.

as found by the panel, then, arguably, governments essentially have the ability to provide interest-free loans consistently with WTO rules, by simply offering the money as a grant and then accepting repayment without interest when ordered to by the DSB.

V. SPECIAL RULES FOR CERTAIN COUNTRIES

The SCM Agreement provides special rules for certain categories of countries. First, recognising the 'important role' subsidies may plan in the economic development of developing country Members, Article 27 sets out a number of exceptions. Some of these special rules were set up to last only for a limited time and have since expired. Similarly, under Article 29 it is recognised that 'Members in the process of transformation from a centrally-planned into a market, free-enterprise economy may apply programmes and measures necessary for such a transformation'. Aside from any special exemptions that are granted, however, these latter provisions have expired.

VI. SUBSIDIES PROVISIONS IN OTHER WTO AGREEMENTS

While the SCM Agreement contains a core set of rules on subsidies, several other WTO agreements include additional disciplines. In this section, we discuss briefly the rules in the Agriculture Agreement, the GATT and the TRIMs Agreement.

(a) Agriculture Agreement

The great importance of agriculture to certain domestic interest groups, mainly in developed countries, has led to special rules on subsidies for agricultural products. The Agriculture Agreement establishes subsidy commitment schedules, similar to the tariff schedules for goods, for both domestic support and export subsidies. Where a commitment has been made in the schedule for a particular product, the Member agrees not to provide more than the committed amount of subsidies. Where no commitment has been made, no subsidies are permitted for that product. Thus, the approach of the Agriculture Agreement in addressing subsidies is, at least formally, different from that of the SCM Agreement. Whereas the SCM Agreement explicitly focuses on the trade-distorting effects of subsidies, the Agriculture Agreement, aside from its distinction between export and domestic subsidies, does not.

For a time, the Agriculture Agreement provided an exception to the stricter SCM Agreement disciplines. Under Article 13 of the Agriculture Agreement, the so-called 'Peace Clause', Members agreed not to challenge agricultural subsidies under the SCM Agreement where certain conditions were met. However, this limitation has now expired, and thus both Agreements now apply simultaneously. Thus, domestic subsidies to agriculture must be within the Agriculture Agreement domestic support commitments, and they must also not cause 'adverse effects' pursuant to Part III of the SCM Agreement. For export subsidies, subsidies on agricultural products that violate Article 3.1(a) of the SCM Agreement are prohibited, although due to the different language of the SCM Agreement export subsidy provisions, export subsidies within the commitment levels do not violate Article 3.1(a).

At the same time, though, the Agriculture Agreement goes further in identifying export subsidies by setting out various specific examples of export subsidies in Article 9.1. These examples go beyond the subsidy definition of Article 1 of the SCM Agreement and the 'contingent upon export performance' language of Article 3.1(a) of the SCM Agreement and thus constitute a broader prohibition. With regard to the scope of the export component, for instance, Article 9.1(b) refers to 'sale or disposal *for export*' and Article 9.1(c) refers to 'payments *on the export*'. Arguably, these phrases imply a looser connection between the subsidy and export than the 'contingent upon export perform-ance' language in this agreement.[39]

As an illustration of the difference in the standard for export subsidies under the Agriculture Agreement, as compared to the SCM Agreement, the Appellate Body's interpretation of Article 9.1(c) of the Agriculture Agreement is particularly striking. This provision sets out the following example of an export subsidy:

> payments on the export of an agricultural product that are financed by virtue of governmental action, whether or not a charge on the public account is involved, including payments that are financed from the proceeds of a levy imposed on the agricultural product concerned or on an agricultural product from which the exported product is derived;

There is nothing about the language of this provision to indicate that it would be inter-preted much differently from the SCM Agreement's subsidy provisions. However, in examining the term 'payments', the Appellate Body introduced a new concept into the subsidy analysis. In essence, it concluded that domestic support could result in a 'pay-ment' under Article 9.1(c) where 'the producer charges prices that do not recoup the total cost of production, over time'. It reasoned that where the total cost of production is not recouped, the loss 'must be financed from some other source, possibly "by virtue of gov-ernmental action".[40] Making the existence of a subsidy, that is, a 'payment', contingent on the pricing decisions of private companies clearly broadens the subsidy disciplines beyond those of the SCM Agreement. The effect of the ruling is that a government could give money to private industry but not know whether a subsidy exists until the producer decides what price to charge.

Finally, Article 10.1 of the Agriculture Agreement also provides a potentially broader scope for export subsidy disciplines in the context of agriculture, stating: '[e]xport subsi-dies not listed in paragraph 1 of Article 9 shall not be applied in a manner which results in, or which threatens to lead to, circumvention of export subsidy commitments; nor shall non-commercial transactions be used to circumvent such commitments'. Both parts of this provision could be interpreted as encompassing a broader range of measures than the 'contingent upon export performance' language used elsewhere in the Agreement.

---

[39] In support see Panel Report, *EC—Sugar (Brazil, Thailand, Australia)*, paras 7.271–7.279. For a view that 'on the export' is the same standard as export contingency see Panel Report, *Canada—Dairy*, paras 7.90–7.101.
[40] Appellate Body Report, *Canada—Dairy*, Article 21.5, paras 87–96.

(b) GATT

The GATT contains limited subsidy rules in Article XVI. Article XVI:1 refers to subsidies that operate 'directly or indirectly to increase exports of any product from, or to reduce imports of any product . . . into' a Member's territory, and it provides for consultations where 'it is determined that serious prejudice to the interests of any other Member is caused or threatened by any such subsidisation'. Article XVI:3 then states that Members 'should seek to avoid the use of subsidies on the export of primary products' and, if they are granted, 'such subsidy shall not be applied in a manner which results in that contracting party having more than an equitable share of world export trade in that product'.

(c) TRIMs Agreement

Paragraph 1 of the TRIMs Agreement Annex provides examples of measures that violate GATT Articles III:4 and XI:1, including measures 'compliance with which is necessary to obtain an advantage' and which require certain actions, such as the purchase of domestic goods. Since subsidies appear to provide an 'advantage', the use of such subsidies could violate these provisions. A violation of this sort was found in *Indonesia—Autos* in the context of tax and customs duty reductions where domestic content was used.[41]

VII. COUNTERVAILING MEASURES

In addition to establishing multilateral disciplines on subsidies, the SCM Agreement also sets limits on the ability of WTO Members to impose restraints on subsidised imports through 'countervailing measures', in particular tariff duties. The use of 'countervailing' tariff duties to limit subsidised imports has a long history under the domestic law of many WTO Members. Along with 'dumped' imports, discussed in Chapter 11, subsidised imports are considered by some to be a form of 'unfair' trade. In response, tariff duties have been used to 'countervail', in others words 'offset' or 'counteract', these imports. As with anti-dumping duties, countervailing duties are additional duties imposed in addition to the standard applied tariff rate. Whereas anti-dumping duties are calculated based on the amount of dumping, countervailing duties are determined based on the amount of subsidy.

The GATT has accepted the legality of countervailing duties since its inception, but at the same time it recognises, in Article VI:3, that these duties must not be abused for protectionist purposes. For instance, Article VI:3 makes it clear that such duties are not to be imposed in excess of the subsidy amount. Over the years, as concerns grew that the use of countervailing duties was being abused, countries attempted to develop additional rules to ensure that these duties were only imposed in legitimate cases and in appropriate amounts. The current rules are provided in Part V of the SCM Agreement, read together with Article VI. The specific domestic procedures for imposing these duties vary among WTO Members. However, all Members must abide by the SCM Agreement rules. These rules mirror, to some extent, the rules on anti-dumping duties

---

[41] Panel Report, *Indonesia—Autos*, paras 14.58–14.92.

established in the Anti-Dumping Agreement, but there are some important differences, so it should not be assumed that the rules on particular subjects are identical in the two agreements.

In essence, countervailing duty proceedings include the following steps. First, a domestic industry petitions a government agency for an investigation into the subsidisation of specific imported products from certain countries. If the agency finds sufficient evidence to go forward, it carries out an investigation. The investigation considers several issues. The most important of these are:

- The existence and amount of the subsidy
- Whether the domestic industry has suffered injury
- Whether the subsidised imports caused the injury

If it is determined that subsidisation exists and that subsidised imports have caused injury to the domestic industry, a countervailing duty may be imposed in the amount of the subsidy, calculated in terms of subsidisation per unit of the subsidised product. The specific procedures that follow differ by country, but the agency will then impose the duty on the imports at issue for a specific period of time. It will review the duty rate periodically in subsequent years, based on the amount of subsidy given in those years.

The key concepts of injury and causation will be discussed in detail in Chapter 11 in the context of dumping. The counterpart provisions of the SCM Agreement, found in Article 15, are very similar. Because the injury and causation standards have been elaborated a great deal in the context of disputes under the Anti-Dumping Agreement, we do not discuss these provisions here, but simply refer to the anti-dumping discussion in Chapter 11 for general guidance on these concepts. We focus here on the concept of 'subsidy'.

A government agency's investigation of the *existence* of a subsidy is based on the definition in Article 1 of the SCM Agreement, which includes the 'financial contribution' and 'benefit' issues discussed in section II(a) above. In other words, when determining whether a subsidy exists, governments must follow the Article 1 rules. With regard to the calculation of the subsidy *amount*, Article 14 of the SCM Agreement entitled 'Calculation of the Amount of a Subsidy in Terms of the Benefit to the Recipient', sets out additional rules. In this regard, Article 14 provides that 'any such method shall be consistent with the following guidelines':

(a) government provision of equity capital shall not be considered as conferring a benefit, unless the investment decision can be regarded as inconsistent with the usual investment practice (including for the provision of risk capital) of private investors in the territory of that Member;

(b) a loan by a government shall not be considered as conferring a benefit unless there is a difference between the amount that the firm receiving the loan pays on the government loan and the amount the firm would pay on a comparable commercial loan which the firm could actually obtain on the market. In this case the benefit shall be the difference between these two amounts;

(c) a loan guarantee by a government shall not be considered as conferring a benefit unless there is a difference between the amount that the firm receiving the guarantee pays on a loan guaranteed by the government and the amount that the firm would pay on a comparable commercial loan absent the government guarantee. In this case the benefit shall be the difference between these two amounts adjusted for any differences in fees;

(d) the provision of goods or services or purchase of goods by a government shall not be considered as conferring a benefit unless the provision is made for less than adequate remuneration, or the purchase is made for more than adequate remuneration. The adequacy of remuneration shall be determined in relation to prevailing market conditions for the good or service in question in the country of provision or purchase (including price, quality, availability, marketability, transportation and other conditions of purchase or sale).

Thus, Article 14 refers to some of the financial contributions listed in Article 1.1, and it explains how the 'amount of the subsidy' in terms of the 'benefit' to the recipient is to be determined for each.

We now examine a domestic countervailing duty determination on subsidisation in the long-standing, extremely contentious *Lumber* dispute between Canada and the United States. Briefly, the US position has been that Canadian provincial governments offer 'stumpage' rights, that is, the right to harvest timber on government land, at below market prices. As a result, US agencies have concluded that the Canadian action constitutes the 'provision of goods' in a way that confers a 'benefit' and therefore constitutes a subsidy. We excerpt some aspects of recent proceedings in this dispute before the US Department of Commerce. The Department's final determination was published in the US Federal Register. However, the reasoning behind the decision was set out in an unpublished Issues and Decision Memorandum,[42] which is referred to in the Federal Register Notice. The portions of the Issues and Decision Memorandum dealing with the Department's reasoning on the 'financial contribution' issue and stating the conclusion on the 'amount of a subsidy in terms of the benefit' issue are excerpted below:

ANALYSIS OF PROGRAMS:

I. Provincial Stumpage Programs Determined To Confer Subsidies

Petitioners have alleged that the stumpage programs administered by the Provinces of British Columbia, Quebec, Ontario, Alberta, Manitoba, and Saskatchewan provide Canadian softwood lumber producers with countervailable benefits. Specifically, petitioners allege that, through the Provincially-administered stumpage systems, the Provinces provide softwood lumber producers with wood fiber for less than adequate remuneration through the selling of rights to harvest timber on government-owned (or Crown) forest lands.

Petitioners have also made the same allegation with respect to the Yukon Territory, Northwest Territories, and timber sold on federal land. However, we have not examined these stumpage programs in this determination because the amount of exports to the United States from the two Territories and from federal land is insignificant. Thus, these programs would have no measurable effect on any subsidy rate calculated for this investigation.

In accordance with section 771(5) of the Act, to find a countervailable subsidy, the Department must determine that a government made a financial contribution and that a benefit was thereby conferred, and that the benefit is specific within the meaning of section 771(5A) of the Act. We address each of these requirements below.

---

[42] Issues and Decision Memorandum: Final Results of the Countervailing Duty Investigation of Certain Softwood Lumber Products from Canada, C-122-839 (21 March 2002), available at http://ia.ita.doc.gov/frn/summary/canada/02-.7849-1.txt (accessed on 27 July 2007).

Financial Contribution

...

Section 771(5)(B) of the Act provides that a subsidy exists if an authority "provides a financial contribution" to a person and a benefit is thereby conferred. See section771(5)(B). "Financial contribution" is defined as:

(i) the direct transfer of funds, such as grants, loans, and equity infusions, or the potential direct transfer of funds or liabilities, such as loan guarantees,

(ii) foregoing or not collecting revenue that is otherwise due, such as granting tax credits or deductions from taxable income,

(iii) providing goods or services, other than general infrastructure, or

(iv) purchasing goods.

Section 771(5)(D)(i)–(iv) of the Act.

At issue in this case is subsection (iii). Thus, we must first determine whether Canada is providing a good or service to lumber producers. The debate over this issue has centered around the nature of "stumpage," i.e., is it a good or a right? To begin, some clarification of the term "stumpage" is necessary. The term "stumpage" can mean standing timber; the value of standing timber; a license to cut timber; or the fee paid for the right to cut timber. Black's Law Dictionary 1437 (7th ed. 1999). Given the multiple meanings of the term stumpage, we realize that its use could confuse the current analysis. Therefore, we will use the precise meanings of the term, as appropriate, to avoid any confusion over which meaning is intended.

The ordinary meaning of "goods" is broad, encompassing all "property or possessions" and "saleable commodities". The New Shorter Oxford English Dictionary, L. Brown, ed., at 1116. Nothing in the definition of the term "goods" indicates that things that occur naturally on land, such as timber, do not constitute "goods". To the contrary, as petitioners point out, the term specifically includes "… growing crops, and other identified things to be severed from real property". Black's Law Dictionary 701-02 (7th ed. 1999). Therefore, we determine that stumpage, i.e., timber, is a "good" within the meaning of section 771(5)(B)(iii) of the Act.

Respondents concede that timber is a "market asset" and that through forest tenures and licenses the Provincial governments relinquish ownership of those assets while retaining ownership of other forest assets. See Respondents' February 22, 2002 Joint Case Brief: Stumpage, Volume 2 at B6. Nevertheless, respondents argue that Provincial governments are not providing timber (a good), but rather are merely granting a right of access and a right to harvest timber. We find this argument unpersuasive.

An examination of the Provincial tenure systems set forth in this memorandum demonstrates that the sole purpose of tenures is to provide lumber producers with timber. To "provide" means to "supply or furnish for use; make available". The New Shorter Oxford English Dictionary at 2393. Thus, regardless of whether the Provinces are supplying timber or making it available through a right of access, they are providing timber within the meaning of Section 771(5)(B)(iii).

This conclusion is supported by an examination of Provincial tenures. As noted in respondents' case brief, the Provinces collect stumpage fees based "on the volume of timber harvested". See Respondents' February 22, 2002 Joint Case Brief: Stumpage, Volume 2 at B6. Softwood lumber producers are charged a set price per cubic meter of timber ($C/m3). Moreover, the per cubic meter fees are charged only for harvested timber. Tenure holders do not pay for timber that they do not harvest. Thus, regardless of the form of the transaction between the Provincial governments and those who harvest the timber, in substance it is a sale of timber. We decline to elevate form over substance.

The fact that tenure holders are required to meet certain obligations with respect to the forests from which they harvest the timber does not alter this conclusion. In the course of selling one asset, the Provinces are merely taking steps to protect other assets. Furthermore, the Provinces factor in these obligations when calculating per cubic meter fees charged for the harvested timber. In effect, these obligations become part of the price paid for the timber.

Finally, we note that, even assuming arguendo that the Provinces are providing stumpage in the form of a license or right to cut timber, Section 771(5)(B)(iii) would still apply. As noted above, the term "goods" encompasses all "property". The term "property" includes "the right to possess, use, and enjoy a determinate thing (either a tract of land or a chattel). . . [and] [a]ny external thing over which the rights of possession, use, and enjoyment are exercised. . . . In its widest sense, property includes all a person's legal rights of whatever description". Black's Law Dictionary at 1232. Therefore, the sale of a license or right to harvest timber also constitutes the provision of a good within the meaning of Section 771(5)(B)(iii) of the Act. Finally, assuming arguendo that we were to accept respondents' argument that tenure holders are merely acquiring a right to the use of the land, including cutting the trees, a financial contribution may still exist in the form of the provision of a service.

In sum, we determine that the Provincial governments provide a good (timber) to lumber producers within the meaning of Section 771(5)(B)(iii) of the Act.

...

TOTAL AD VALOREM RATE:

In accordance with 777A(e)(2)(B) of the Act, we have calculated a single country-wide subsidy rate to be applied to all producers and exporters of the subject merchandise from Canada. This rate is summarized in the table below:

Producer/Exporter	Net Subsidy Rate
All Producers/Exporters	19.34 % ad valorem

... ...

In reading this decision, notice how the DOC applies the US statutory provisions as the relevant law. These provisions closely mirror those in the SCM Agreement, but it is the US law that is applied here.

The DOC's determination was challenged by Canada in a WTO complaint, on a number of grounds. On the 'financial contribution' issue, the WTO panel concluded that the DOC's determination that the Canadian provinces are making a financial contribution in the form of the provision of goods by providing standing timber to timber harvesters through the stumpage programmes is 'not inconsistent' with Article 1.1(a)(1)(iii) of the SCM Agreement. As a comparison with the US decision, we extract a portion of the panel's finding on this matter:

Panel Report, *United States—Final Countervailing Duty Determination with Respect to Certain Softwood Lumber from Canada*, Adopted 17 February 2004, WT/DS257/R

7.9 Canada claims that the USDOC erred in finding that the provision of stumpage by Canadian provincial governments constitutes a financial contribution in the form of the provision of a good in the sense of Article 1.1 (a) (1) (iii) SCM Agreement. According to Canada, the USDOC thus failed to properly determine the existence of a subsidy to the producers of the subject merchandise as defined in Article 1 SCM Agreement, and the measures imposed on the basis of this flawed subsidy determination are therefore inconsistent with Articles 10, 32.1, 19.1, 19.4 SCM Agreement and Article VI:3 GATT 1994.

7.10 Canada's claim thus concerns the definition of a subsidy in Article 1.1 SCM Agreement, and the existence of a financial contribution under Article 1.1 (a) (1) (iii) SCM Agreement in particular. Our analysis of Canada's claim begins of course with the text of that Article. Article 1.1 SCM Agreement provides that:

Article 1

Definition of a Subsidy

"1.1 For the purpose of this Agreement, a subsidy shall be deemed to exist if:

(a)(1) there is *a financial contribution by a government* or any public body within the territory of a Member (referred to in this Agreement as 'government'), i.e. where:

(i) a government practice involves a direct transfer of funds (e.g. grants, loans, and equity infusion), potential direct transfers of funds or liabilities (e.g. loan guarantees);

(ii) government revenue that is otherwise due is foregone or not collected (e.g. fiscal incentives such as tax credits);

(iii) a government provides goods or services other than general infrastructure, or purchases goods;

(iv) a government makes payments to a funding mechanism, or entrusts or directs a private body to carry out one or more of the type of functions illustrated in (i) to (iii) above which would normally be vested in the government and the practice, in no real sense, differs from practices normally followed by governments;

Or

(a)(2) there is any form of income or price support in the sense of Article XVI of

GATT 1994;

And

(b) a benefit is thereby conferred".

7.11 In the Final Determination, the USDOC found that the Canadian provinces provide a good to Canadian producers of softwood lumber through the licence and tenure agreements concluded with companies that harvest standing timber. Canada focuses on the terms of the tenure agreements which confer *harvesting rights* to log producers. According to Canada, such a *right* is not a "good", it certainly is not timber. The United States is of the view that this is form over substance: what Canada is really doing is providing cheap timber to the lumber producers as it allows such producers access to cheap timber through agreements that provide harvesting rights.

7.12 The Final Determination first discusses the meaning of the term "stumpage" and examines the ordinary meaning of the term "goods" to conclude that "stumpage, i.e. timber, is a 'good' within the meaning of section 771 (5) (B) (iii) of the Act". The USDOC then rejects the argument that the provincial governments are not providing timber (a good) but are merely granting a right to harvest timber as it considers that the sole purpose of the tenure systems is to provide lumber producers with timber. The USDOC concludes that the provision of stumpage by the provincial governments constitutes the provision of a good under Section 771 (5) (D) (iii) of the Act.

(a) What do the stumpage programmes provide: the *right* to harvest or *standing timber* ?

7.13 Canada asserts that a tenure or licence carries current and future obligations such as forest management planning, fire protection, etc. which are independent of any harvest, and the right to harvest Crown timber is thus fundamentally different from the simple ownership right in trees. Canada argues that a timber sales contract identifies individual standing trees to be cut, while, in contrast, a tenure or licence grants a right of harvest in an area of land in return for certain rights and obligations, but that no specific trees are identified to be cut. The tenure agreements may even concern trees which have yet to be planted.

7.14 We asked Canada to explain what it considers to be the distinction between the provision of the right to harvest a tree and the right to own the harvested tree. In response, Canada stated that "most forms of tenure confer a right to harvest standing timber that is *in the nature of a proprietary interest*". We read Canada's acknowledgement that the right to harvest timber is in the nature of a proprietary interest, to imply that the tenure holder which has the right to harvest the timber, in fact receives proprietary rights over the standing timber. Canada further discussed, in response to our questions, how various types of tenures or licences operate and when ownership of the timber is transferred to the tenure holder. In light of Canada's answers, it appears that the United States is correct when it argues that "there is no record evidence of stumpage contracts under which the contracting party (tenure holder or licensee) does not have ownership rights to the harvested timber".

7.15 We also asked Canada whether the contractual rights to harvest could be sold without the permission of the provincial governments. Canada stated that the answer to this question varies from province to province, and it provided information concerning British Columbia, Alberta, Ontario and Quebec. On the basis of this information provided by Canada we conclude that, in fact, in each province such rights cannot be sold without government permission, and that various types of tenures or licences are not transferable at all. We wish to emphasise that for purposes of Article 1.1 (a) (1) (iii) SCM Agreement, the exact legal nature of the stumpage contracts is not what is important. Rather, what is important for purposes of the Agreement is whether, through the stumpage programmes, the Canadian provincial governments are "providing a good" to the timber harvesters. We consider that, in essence, the stumpage programmes provide *standing timber* to the harvesters. Canada acknowledges that the provinces own the forests and the trees that grow in them. The only way for harvesters to obtain the trees standing on government-owned Crown land for harvesting and processing is by concluding stumpage agreements (tenures or licences) with the governments concerning these trees. The only way for the government to provide the standing timber that it owns to the harvesters and the mills for processing is by allowing the harvesters to come on the land and harvest the trees. Such legal rights and obligations are transferred through the stumpage agreements. It is thus through the stumpage agreements that the governments provide the standing timber to the harvesters. The price to be paid for the timber, in addition to the volumetric stumpage charge for the trees harvested, consists of various forest management obligations and other in-kind costs relating to road-building or silviculture for example. In return, the tenure holders receive ownership rights over the trees during the period of the tenure. In other words, with the stumpage agreements, ownership over the trees passes from the government to the tenure holders. Standing timber has thus been provided to the tenure holders.

7.16 This conclusion does not change whether one looks at it from the perspective of the recipient, the tenure holder, or from the perspective of the provider, the government. As noted by the Panel in the *US—Softwood Lumber III* case, from the perspective of the tenure holder, the only reason to enter into tenure agreements with the provincial governments is to obtain the timber. The minimum cut requirements for tenure holders under certain stumpage programmes, the requirements to qualify as a tenure holder, such as the requirement to own a processing facility and other processing requirements, are just some examples that demonstrate that the provision and processing of standing timber is what the stumpage programmes are all about. This is not to say that the governments may not at the same time be pursuing certain other social, economic or environmental policies by imposing certain forest management obligations as conditions of sale. However, these conditions of sale or the costs that companies assume for obtaining the stumpage cannot alter the fundamental conclusion that the stumpage programmes provide standing timber, and not just a right to harvest such timber, to the tenure holders. In return, the tenure holders accept to pay a volumetric stumpage fee for the trees actually harvested and assume certain management and other obligations in order to obtain such timber.

7.17 In our view, the right to harvest standing timber is not severable from the right over the standing timber and providing the right to harvest timber is therefore no different from providing standing timber. In this respect we find illustrative the example given by the United States of someone who wants to buy the trees in his neighbour's backyard and the neighbour agrees that he can have the trees if he paints that person's house and pays him $100. As the United States correctly points out, "inherent in the contract is the buyer's right to cut down the trees and haul them away, if he fulfils the conditions of purchase, i.e., paints the house and pays the $100. Nevertheless, this is a contract for the sale of goods—the standing trees in the neighbour's backyard—not the sale of the 'right' to harvest the trees".

7.18 We do not consider relevant the distinction that Canada makes between a contract which identifies individual trees to be cut, and an agreement concerning harvesting rights over a certain area of forest land. In our view, in both cases, trees are provided. In any case, it appears to us that, although a tenure agreement may not provide for a precise number of identified trees to be cut, the tenure holder knows all too well how many trees and which species of trees can be found on the area of land covered by his tenure. In sum, we consider that in this context there is no meaningful distinction between the provision of a right to harvest timber and the provision of standing timber itself, and therefore find that the Canadian provincial stumpage programmes provide standing timber to the tenure or licence holders.

(b) Is standing timber a "good" in the sense of Article 1.1 (a) (1) (iii) SCM Agreement?

7.19 In order to determine whether the USDOC correctly found that through these stumpage programmes Canadian provincial governments provide goods in the sense of Article 1.1 (a) (1) (iii) SCM Agreement, we next consider whether standing timber is a "good" in the sense of Article 1.1 (a) (1) (iii) SCM Agreement.

7.20 Canada argues that standing timber, i.e., trees rooted in the ground, are not "goods" within the meaning of Article 1.1 SCM Agreement. In Canada's view trees do not fall within the ordinary meaning of the term "goods". Moreover, Canada is of the view that the term "goods" in the particular context of Article 1 SCM Agreement refers to tradeable products with an actual or potential tariff line and standing timber which cannot be traded across borders is therefore not a good in the sense of Article 1.1 (a) (1) (iii) SCM Agreement.

7.21 According to the United States, standing timber is clearly included within the broad ordinary meaning of the term "goods". In the view of the United States, the context in which the term is used in the WTO Agreement and the SCM Agreement in particular does not provide a basis to limit its application, for the purpose of Article 1.1 (a) (1) (iii) SCM Agreement, to products for which there is an actual or potential tariff line.

7.22 We recall that Article 3.2 DSU requires a panel to interpret the Agreement in accordance with customary rules of interpretation of public international law, which, it is well-accepted, include in particular Articles 31 and 32 of the Vienna Convention on the Law of Treaties. Article 31 of the Vienna Convention on the Law of Treaties provides that "a treaty shall be interpreted in good faith in accordance with the ordinary meaning to be given to the terms of the treaty in their context and in light of its object and purpose". We will thus examine the ordinary meaning of the word "goods" used in Article 1.1 (a) (1) (iii) SCM Agreement—in its context and in light of the object and purpose of the Agreement.

7.23 The New Shorter Oxford Dictionary defines "goods" as, *inter alia*, "saleable commodities, merchandise, wares". Black's Law Dictionary, to which both parties refer in search of the ordinary meaning of the term "goods", defines "goods" as follows:

"1. Tangible or movable personal property other than money; esp. articles of trade or items of merchandise <goods and services>. The sale of goods is governed by Article 2 of the UCC. 2. Things that have value, whether tangible or not <the importance of social goods varies from society to society>.

"Goods' means all things, including specially manufactured goods that are movable at the time of identification to a contract for sale and future goods. The term includes the unborn young of animals, growing crops, and other identified things to be severed from real property ... . The term does not include money in which the price is to be paid, the subject-matter of foreign exchange transactions, documents, letters of credit, letter-of-credit rights, instruments, investment property, accounts, chattel paper, deposit accounts, or general intangibles". UCC § 2—102 (a) (24).

7.24 The ordinary meaning of the term "goods" as "tangible or movable personal property other than money" is thus very broad and includes standing timber, as trees are tangible objects which are capable of being owned. This is further confirmed by the explanation in Black's Law Dictionary that a "good" includes "an identified thing to be severed from real property". Standing timber indeed seems to us to be an excellent example of an identified thing that can be severed from real property. We note that in its Sale of Goods Act, the Canadian province of British Columbia, the prime exporter of softwood lumber to the United States, itself defines "goods" as including "growing crops, [...], and things attached to or forming part of the land that are agreed to be severed before sale or under the contract of sale". In our view, this definition of a good certainly includes standing timber.

7.25 Article 31 Vienna Convention requires the interpreter to determine the ordinary meaning of the terms of the treaty *in their context and in the light of its object and purpose*. The immediate context of the term "goods" in Article 1.1 (a) (1) (iii) SCM Agreement is "goods or services, other than general infrastructure". We note that the term "goods" in this context is not qualified in any way and its use in the combination "goods or services", in our view, confirms that the term is to be understood broadly. We find further confirmation of this broad meaning in the fact that the drafters of the Agreement considered it necessary to explicitly exclude "general infrastructure". This implies that "goods or services" is sufficiently broad as to include "general infrastructure"; if not, there would have been no reason to explicitly exclude it. At the same time, "general infrastructure" is the only "good or service" which is excluded from the broad scope of Article 1.1 (a) (1) (iii) SCM Agreement. In our view, if the drafters had wanted to exclude other items such as natural resources or non-tradeable goods, they would have also explicitly excluded such "goods or services".

7.26 Article 1.1 SCM Agreement defines a subsidy for the purposes of the SCM Agreement. It provides that the first element of a subsidy is a "financial contribution by the government". Subparagraphs (i) through (iv) explain that a financial contribution can exist in a wide variety of circumstances including of course the direct transfer of funds.102 A financial contribution will also exist if the government does not collect the revenue to which it is entitled or when it does something for ("provides a service") or supplies something to ("provides a good") a recipient. We are of the view that Article 1.1 (a) (1) (iii) SCM Agreement, in its context, clarifies that a *financial* contribution also exists where, instead of a money-transferring action, goods or services are provided. The context in which the term "goods" is used in Article 1.1 (a) (1) (iii) SCM Agreement as well as the purpose of Article 1 SCM Agreement in our view confirm the broad and unqualified meaning of the term "goods".

7.27 We consider Canada's interpretation, that the reference in Article 1.1 SCM Agreement to the provision of "goods" refers to tradeable products for which there is a tariff line, to be excessively narrow. We understand Canada to argue that, since on several occasions in the SCM and other WTO Agreements the term "goods" is qualified as "imported" or is understood to be tradable, and since for many goods there exists a tariff line, this necessarily implies that all "goods" have to be capable of being imported, and must therefore be tradeable.

7.28 We consider that the ordinary meaning of the term "goods", in its context and in light of the object and purpose of the Agreement, does not place the limitations on the meaning of the term suggested by Canada ("tradeable products with a potential or actual tariff line"). In our view, that in many cases in the GATT and the WTO Agreements the general term "good" is used as an equivalent of the term "products", does not imply that this is necessarily always the case. Precisely because of its broad ordinary meaning, the specific content of the term will be determined by the adjective accompanying the term as a sort of qualifier. In the absence of any such limitations placed on the term, as in Article 1.1 (a) (1) (iii) SCM Agreement, we consider that the term "goods" keeps its broad ordinary meaning. All that the text of Article 1.1 (a) (1) (iii) SCM Agreement suggests is that the goods or services are capable of being *provided* by a government; it does not address whether they can be imported or traded. The fact that the SCM Agreement relates to subsidies in the trade in goods context only, and does not cover services, does not mean that the "goods" provided by the government necessarily have to be goods that can be traded or that are covered by the GATT as products under Article II. We note in this respect that Article 1.1 (a) (1) (iii) SCM Agreement also mentions the provision of *services* by the government as constituting a financial contribution while the disciplines of the SCM Agreement, as discussed, only apply to trade in *goods*.

7.29 We agree with Canada that the definition of a subsidy in Article 1 SCM Agreement reflects the Members' agreement that only certain types of government action are subject to the SCM Agreement, and also that not all government actions that may affect the market come within the ambit of the SCM Agreement. When the government provides goods or services, however, such action is clearly covered by the SCM Agreement. Standing timber, a physical and tangible object, is the log and lumber producers' prime input, and the action by the government to supply this input to the producers of logs and lumber, is the provision of a good and therefore covered by the SCM Agreement.

7.30 In the absence of any textual basis for limiting the broad ordinary meaning of the term "goods" in the context of Article 1.1 (a) (1) (iii) SCM Agreement, we find that the USDOC Determination that the Canadian provinces are providing a financial contribution in the form of the provision of a good by providing standing timber to the timber harvesters through the stumpage programmes is not inconsistent with Article 1.1 (a) (1) (iii) SCM Agreement. We therefore reject all of Canada's claims of violation of the SCM Agreement and GATT 1994 in this respect.

… … …

This finding was upheld on appeal.[43]

We conclude with two final points regarding domestic countervailing duties. First, pursuant to Article 23 of the SCM Agreement, agency decisions must be subject to judicial review. This requirement helps to address concerns regarding bias by government agencies in favour of domestic industries, by providing an independent review mechanism. (In addition, in response to concerns regarding the impartiality of domestic courts, for NAFTA countries there is a special review procedure set up outside the traditional court system, in which an arbitral panel made up of nationals of both involved countries hear the case.)

Secondly, footnote 35 to the SCM Agreement makes it clear that action against foreign subsidies can be taken under the SCM Agreement and domestic countervailing duty law simultaneously, stating: '[t]he provisions of Part II or III may be invoked in parallel with the provisions of Part V'. However, it also states that actual remedies may be imposed under only one or the other: 'with regard to the effects of a particular subsidy in the domestic market of the importing Member, only one form of relief (either a countervailing duty, if the requirements of Part V are met, or a countermeasure under Articles 4 or 7) shall be available'.

VIII. QUESTIONS

1. What is the purpose of subsidies regulation through the SCM Agreement? Is it to restrain protectionism? Is it to fight all subsidies with negative effects on trade? Is it to fight all market distorting subsidies? What is the difference between these goals?

2. A government provides a loan to a company on terms that are below market value, but on the condition that the company source its inputs only from domestic companies, which cost significantly more than the competitive foreign goods. Under Article 1.1(b) of the SCM Agreement, can the higher cost of these inputs negate the 'benefit' conferred by the below market loan?

2. A government provides low-interest loans to foreign purchasers of domestically built aeroplanes. What is the benefit, if any, to the domestic producer? Must there be a benefit to this producer, or is a benefit to the purchaser sufficient to find the existence of a subsidy under the SCM Agreement?

3. Is the decision of the Article 21.5 compliance panel in *Canada—Aircraft* satisfactory? Does anything prevent a Member from circumventing the rules on 'export subsidies' by simply 'targeting' the high export-orientation of the industry in a way that does not explicitly make reference to export?

4. A government sets up a programme under which a cash grant is offered to companies that export a certain percentage of their sales. Ten companies receive money under the programme. However, in response to pressure by trading partners, the programme is disbanded (no formal WTO complaint was brought, however). Immediately thereafter,

---

[43] Appellate Body Report, *US—Lumber CVDs Final*, paras 46–76.

the government sets up a new subsidy programme that identifies eight specific companies as recipients, but it does not mention export as a condition. Instead, it purports to help domestic companies in the high technology industry. All eight were among the 10 that received the subsidy under the original programme, and all eight can credibly be considered to be part of the high-tech sector. The two companies from the original group that no longer receive subsidies are in the agriculture sector. Is the new subsidy programme export contingent under Article 3.1(a)?

5. In a pure 'territorial' income tax system, the tax law may be written so as to tax domestic income, while not addressing income earned abroad at all. Do these regimes 'forego' revenue on foreign-earned income that is 'otherwise' due? How would the Appellate Body's 'legitimately comparable income' standard apply to this situation? Could the income of an individual company earned at home and abroad be considered 'legitimately comparable'?

6. What is the appropriate standard for export contingency? How close a link should there be between the subsidy and export? What do you think of the Appellate Body's standard that finds export contingency whenever the subsidy gives domestic producers an 'incentive' to export? What do you think of the alternative approach offered by the US, which focuses on whether the subsidy encourages more exports? What are the positives and negatives of each approach?

7. A US subsidy programme identifies two sets of transactions: sales by a domestic US producer to a US consumer, and sales by a domestic US producer to an exporter. There are different forms and reporting requirements for the two types of sales in order to receive the subsidy. Are the subsidies provided on export sales 'contingent upon export performance'?

8. A law is enacted under which subsidies are paid to all companies for which exports make up at least 10 per cent of their sales. The law is challenged in WTO dispute settlement before any money is paid out. Can a violation be found in relation to the law itself?

9. If 'withdraw' the subsidy under SCM Agreement Article 4.7 is interpreted to mean something other than a requirement to pay the subsidy back to the government, what deterrents are there to prevent governments from offering one-time subsidies whenever they choose?

10. Are WTO panelists, Appellate Body members and the WTO Secretariat qualified, in terms of a background in quantitative economics, to carry out the kind of economic analysis that could be used to assess the existence of 'adverse effects'?

11. Was the *US—Cotton Subsidies* panel's causation analysis and conclusion correct?

12. With the creation of WTO rules on actionable subsidies, has the domestic countervailing duty remedy become unnecessary? What considerations guide industries and governments in deciding whether to address foreign subsidies under domestic countervailing duty law as opposed to invoking the SCM Agreement 'prohibited' or 'actionable' subsidies provisions in a WTO complaint?

13. Given its statements on the matter, what are the chances that the Appellate Body will

find that an *a contrario* defence can be made under item (k), first paragraph of the Illustrative List of Export Subsidies?

14. Many economists would argue that a country's subsidies are, on balance, beneficial to other countries, because the benefits to consumers in the other countries outweigh the harms to producers. Does it make sense for the SCM Agreement to focus on preventing subsidies that have this sort of a trade impact? Why do you think the agreement does focus on these subsidies? Regardless of any benefits to specific consumers, would it be desirable, in terms of economic efficiency, for all countries to stop providing most of their 'specific' subsidies?

15. Why are there stricter remedies for subsidies, such as withdrawal 'without delay' for prohibited subsidies, than for other measures?

11

Dumping and Anti-dumping Measures

I. INTRODUCTION

Issues related to the 'dumping' of products in international trade, and the responses taken through 'anti-dumping' measures, have long been controversial among economists, lawyers, government officials and corporations. The basic concept behind dumping is that when companies sell products in a foreign market at too low a price, the imported products may cause economic harm to the domestic producers in that market because they will have trouble competing. Responses to such pricing are taken in the form of anti-dumping measures, which are normally additional import tariff duties imposed on the dumped products, thus raising the price of the imported products and helping to eliminate the harm to the domestic industry.

In terms of the underlying policies involved, there is a great deal of contention over many of the fundamental issues. The full scope of the debate cannot be set out here, but the main positions are as follows. First, some people take the view that these low-priced sales are 'unfair' and are often the result of a protected home market. The excess profits from the home market sales are said to allow the reduced price foreign sales. Thus, measures to penalise such sales are appropriate.

On the opposing side, others believe that such sales are based on normal business decisions and should be appreciated for the benefits they give to consumers (in the form of lower prices), rather than punished. Furthermore, it is argued, the anti-dumping laws set up to stop dumping are susceptible to protectionist abuse. And finally, they contend, if there is a problem with protected home markets, such protection can be challenged directly through international trade agreements like the WTO.

For those who have studied antitrust/competition policy, this description of dumped sales is likely to be somewhat familiar. Antitrust/competition policy addresses low-priced sales in the context of both predatory pricing and price discrimination. Indeed, there is some overlap between the concepts of dumping and predatory pricing/price discrimination. Anti-dumping laws sometimes consider whether there are different prices charged in different markets, as do price discrimination laws. Similarly, anti-dumping laws sometimes consider whether sales are below cost, as do predatory pricing laws. However, there are many differences between anti-dumping and antitrust/competition policy as well, so it should not be assumed that the concepts from one can be carried over to the other. Anti-dumping laws are somewhat anomalous in their goals and their substance. The current system of domestic and international rules in this area tries to balance the competing views on the value and harm of dumping and anti-dumping measures. If it looks at times as if there is no coherent framework, it is probably because various governments and other interested actors do not agree on many of the underlying policy issues.

Economists, who tend to favour free trade over protectionism, often oppose anti-dumping laws. However, the politics of the issue is very contentious, and anti-dumping has been referred to as the 'third rail of trade policy'.[1]

Moving beyond general policy issues and into the practical impact of anti-dumping measures, it is helpful to understand which countries make use of anti-dumping measures and against whom they are used. In this regard, the WTO Secretariat reported the following basic statistics relating to new initiations:

> The Members reporting the highest number of new initiations during January—June 2010 were India, reporting 17 new initiations, followed by the European Union, reporting 8 new initiations, Argentina (7), Brazil and Israel (5 each). Other Members reporting initiations were Australia and China (4 each), Indonesia and Korea (3 each), Colombia, Thailand and the United States (2 each), and Canada, Chile, Jamaica, Mexico, Chinese Taipei, Turkey and Ukraine (1 each). These figures represented increases for India, the European Union, Brazil and Israel, and declines for Argentina, China, Indonesia, Colombia, the United States, Canada, Turkey and Ukraine. The number of initiations by Australia and Mexico remained unchanged compared with the numbers reported for January—June 2009. Chile, Jamaica, Korea, Chinese Taipei and Thailand, which did not report new initiations for January—June 2009, reported new initiations for the first semester of 2010, while Costa Rica, Pakistan, Peru and South Africa, which reported new initiations for the first half of 2009, did not report new initiations for the first half of 2010.
>
> During the first half of 2010, China was the most frequent subject of the new investigations, with 23 new initiations directed at its exports. This was a 30% decrease from the 33 new investigations opened in respect of exports from China during January—June 2009. The European Union (including individual member States) was next with 11 new investigations directed at its exports, followed by the United States (5), Korea and Thailand (4 each), Malaysia and Chinese Taipei (3 each), Brazil and Japan (2 each), and Belarus, Bosnia & Herzegovina, Chile, Dominican Republic, India, Indonesia, Mexico, Norway, Singapore, South Africa, Ukraine, and Vietnam (one each).[2]

The Secretariat data shows that a wide range countries make use of anti-dumping measures. Keep in mind that the number of new anti-dumping measures in a given year provides only a partial picture, as such measures can remain in effect for years. Thus, anti-dumping measures imposed many years ago may continue to be in place and have an impact.

It is also helpful to know which countries are the subject of anti-dumping measures. It is perhaps unsurprising that China is clearly the leader in this regard. China's role in world trade has grown over the years, and it has faced many allegations of unfair pricing behaviour. One reason for this may be its treatment as a 'non-market economy' by some

---

[1] NG Mankiw and PL Swagel, 'Antidumping: The Third Rail of Trade Policy', *Foreign Affairs*, July/August 2005. The authors argue: 'Although few U.S. politicians will admit it, antidumping policy has strayed far from its original purpose of guarding against predatory foreign firms. It is now little more than an excuse for a few powerful industries to shield themselves from competition—at great cost to both American consumers and American business.'

[2] 'WTO Secretariat Reports Drop in Anti-dumping Investigations and Measures', WTO Press Release, PRESS/623, 6 December 2010.

governments due to the heavy governmental involvement in its economy. Based on this status, governments are able to impose anti-dumping measures under more flexible rules until 2016, pursuant to China's WTO Accession Protocol, at which time the 'non-market economy' categorisation will end and it will have to be treated like other countries.

Given the number of anti-dumping measures, it is not surprising that more than 20 per cent of all WTO dispute settlement complaints relate to anti-dumping measures.

As a final note, concerns with dumped imports are often linked closely to concerns with subsidised imports, discussed in the previous chapter. Together, dumped goods and subsidised goods are sometimes characterised as 'unfair' trade.

The chapter is set out as follows. First, we offer a basic overview of the policies behind, and the history of, anti-dumping rules. Secondly, we discuss the key portions of an anti-dumping investigation and the three main elements: dumping, injury and causation. Thirdly, we examine the various types of anti-dumping measures. Finally, we briefly cover several issues related to challenging anti-dumping measures in the WTO dispute process.

II. ANTI-DUMPING: A BASIC OVERVIEW

As noted above, responses to dumping are taken in the form of anti-dumping measures. In this section, we offer a brief overview of domestic anti-dumping laws and the WTO rules that govern these laws.

(a) Domestic Anti-dumping Rules

The GATT/WTO rules on anti-dumping measures are extremely important, and provide much of the focus of this chapter. However, to a great extent anti-dumping law is domestic in nature. National governments enact domestic anti-dumping laws and regulations, and implement them through specialised agencies. Thus, to understand fully how anti-dumping law works, reference must be made to the domestic rules as well.

Because WTO rules offer flexibility as to how anti-dumping proceedings should be carried out at the domestic level, different approaches to imposing anti-dumping duties can be consistent with the rules. Indeed, the domestic procedures and institutions used take a wide variety of forms in different countries. For example, some governments use separate agencies to conduct the dumping and injury analyses. Others, by contrast, have one agency that conducts both inquiries. Another significant difference is between prospective and retrospective systems. In prospective systems like that used by the EC, the dumping margin—that is, the margin by which export sales are less than the comparison sales—established by the initial investigation applies to all future sales until a review is requested or the order is terminated. By contrast, in a retrospective system like that of the US, specific import sales are reviewed by investigators after the fact to determine the actual dumping margin for a past time period. These variations make the study of the subject difficult. What we try to do in this section is offer a very general sense of how the rules work across the different domestic systems.

The anti-dumping process begins with an investigation of whether injurious dumping is occurring in relation to specific products from specific countries. Most of the time, this investigation commences on the basis of a complaint filed by a domestic industry. However, it is also possible for the responsible government agencies to initiate investigations on their own. There are three basic issues to consider: (1) is there dumping? (2) is there injury? and (3) is there a causal link between the dumping and the injury? All three must be proved in order for anti-dumping measures to be imposed.

During the investigation, the responsible government agencies (often referred to as the 'investigating authorities') consider information submitted by the domestic industry and the foreign exporters and producers accused of dumping (as well as other interested parties). Both sides submit information on the dumping, injury and causation issues. However, most of the information submitted by the foreign companies relates to dumping (eg sales prices in various markets as well as distribution and other costs), whereas much of the domestic industry's information relates to whether it is suffering injury (eg information on its financial condition). In a sense, the foreign companies try to show that they are not dumping, and the domestic industry tries to show that it is injured. On dumping, the domestic industry responds with information to prove that dumping is occurring; and, on injury, the foreign companies respond with information to prove that there is no injury.

Based on this evidence, the investigating authorities reach a decision as to whether dumping and injury exist (for a specific time period), and whether there is a causal link between them. With regard to dumping, they reach a determination on the amount by which export prices in the investigating country's markets are lower than a comparison price. If they find that there is no (or de minimis) dumping, no injury or no causation, then no anti-dumping duties will be imposed. However, if dumping, injury and causation are found, anti-dumping duties will be imposed. Generally speaking, these duties are imposed in the amount of the dumping margin for each product (although it is possible for them to be imposed in lesser amounts).

The decision on whether to impose duties can be appealed to domestic courts, many of which have developed detailed jurisprudence on a number of issues related to dumping calculations and injury determinations. Moreover, there is a special review mechanism in the NAFTA under which decisions relating to NAFTA parties can be appealed to a panel of trade experts outside the normal court systems.

After an anti-dumping investigation is completed and duties are imposed, various reviews can occur over the ensuing years to determine whether duties should continue to be imposed and at what rate. For example, the exporter can request a review based on any 'changed circumstances' that have occurred. In addition, as part of the Uruguay Round, a 'sunset' clause was introduced for anti-dumping duties. Under this provision, after five years the duties will be terminated automatically unless the government agency shows that termination of the duty is likely to lead to the continuation or recurrence of dumping.

All of the domestic rules on anti-dumping must conform to the international rules in this area. The main international rules on dumping and anti-dumping measures are contained in the GATT/WTO. Additional rules may also be found in bilateral and regional trade agreements, but to the extent that they address these issues, most of these agreements simply refer to the GATT/WTO rules. Therefore, our focus is on the GATT/WTO rules. The following provides a general overview of these rules. In the later sections, we provide a more detailed analysis.

(b) History of GATT/WTO Rules on Dumping

Canada enacted the first anti-dumping legislation in 1904 (over concern with US steel imports) and other nations quickly followed with their own laws. By the 1920s many countries were as concerned with anti-dumping laws as they were with dumping, as these laws were thought to have been abused for protectionist purposes in some cases. By the time of the GATT negotiations in the mid-1940s, views on the issues were quite polarised and thus it was difficult to come up with comprehensive rules in this area.

The result of the negotiations was Article VI of the GATT, which deals with both anti-dumping and countervailing duties. We focus here on the anti-dumping aspect, with countervailing duties having been discussed in Chapter 10. Article VI:1 reads, in part:

> The contracting parties recognize that dumping, by which products of one country are introduced into the commerce of another country at less than the normal value of the products, is to be condemned if it causes or threatens material injury to an established industry in the territory of a contracting party or materially retards the establishment of a domestic industry.

Thus, Article VI explains that 'dumping . . . is to be condemned' if it 'causes or threatens material injury to an established industry in the territory of a contracting party or materially retards the establishment of a domestic industry'. However, while injurious dumping is 'condemned', it is not prohibited. Rather, Article VI permits WTO Members to take certain actions against dumping, to limit its impact. In this regard, paragraph 2 states: '[i]n order to offset or prevent dumping, a Member may levy on any dumped product an anti-dumping duty not greater in amount than the margin of dumping in respect of such product'. Article VI then offers a few more details of a general framework for responding to dumping through anti-dumping duties. However, the article is brief and vague, and the need to agree upon more specific standards quickly became apparent.

The Kennedy Round Anti-Dumping Code (1967), signed by 18 nations, attempted to respond to the inadequacies by specifying minimal procedural standards for anti-dumping cases and by requiring that 'dumping' be the 'principal' cause of the injury to the domestic industry. Later, the Tokyo Round Anti-Dumping Code (1979) developed additional rules on dumping (and omitted the requirement that dumping be the principal cause of injury). However, disagreement continued as to the proper use of anti-dumping procedures and the issue was addressed again during the Uruguay Round.

The Uruguay Round negotiations in this area were quite contentious, with the users and targets of anti-dumping measures facing off on many issues. For instance, the US and EC expressed concern with the circumvention of anti-dumping laws by producers accused of dumping (such as by shifting production to different countries) and argued for rules which would more easily facilitate the imposition of anti-dumping duties in such instances. Others, by contrast, particularly Asian nations such as Japan and Korea, as well as the Scandinavian nations, wanted to impose stricter disciplines on the imposition of anti-dumping duties in order to make the rules less susceptible to protectionist abuse.

The result of the negotiations was the Agreement on the Implementation of Article VI of the GATT (Anti-Dumping Agreement). The Anti-Dumping Agreement provides detail and clarification to Article VI of the GATT and governs its application. Thus, today, the Anti-Dumping Agreement, together with Article VI, contains the substantive rules and procedures on dumping and anti-dumping duties. The Anti-Dumping Agreement provides detailed rules on these issues, but Article VI sets out some broad principles and thus remains relevant.

Unfortunately, the differing views on many systemic issues, such as the basic definition of dumping, led to vague and confusing provisions, requiring further clarification. While several ambiguities have already been resolved by the dispute settlement system, other issues are yet to be clarified.

We turn now to a more detailed look at the domestic anti-dumping investigation process.

III. ANTI-DUMPING INVESTIGATIONS

In this section, we discuss a number of aspects of domestic anti-dumping investigations, with reference to the WTO rules where relevant. In this regard, we cover the following: the initiation process; the evidence to be considered by the agencies carrying out these investigations; and the core substantive aspects of anti-dumping proceedings—dumping, injury and causation.

A complete understanding of anti-dumping requires detailed knowledge of concepts from accounting, statistics and economics. We do not go into such detail here. Instead, we try to offer an overview of the different stages of the proceedings, the important legal standards, and some key issues that have arisen.

(a) Initiation

An investigation into whether a foreign product is being dumped is generally initiated in response to a request by the domestic industry. In essence, the domestic industry acts as a private enforcer of the law by filing a formal complaint with the relevant government agencies.[3] In order for the investigation to go forward in response to such a complaint, two key elements must be met: (1) the 'application' for the investigation must be 'by or on behalf of the domestic industry'; and (2) there must be evidence of dumping, injury and causation. We consider each issue in turn.

(i) Domestic Industry

In order for an investigation to be initiated, there must be a certain level of support among the domestic industry. Under Article 5.4 of the Anti-Dumping Agreement, '[t]he application shall be considered to have been made "by or on behalf of the domestic industry" if it is supported by those domestic producers whose collective output constitutes more than 50 per cent of the total production of the like product produced by that portion of the domestic industry expressing either support for or opposition to the application'. This provision also states that 'no investigation shall be initiated when domestic producers expressly supporting the application account for less than 25 per cent of total production

---

[3] Pursuant to Art 5.6 of the Anti-Dumping Agreement, in 'special circumstances' the investigating authorities may initiate an investigation on their own.

of the like product produced by the domestic industry'. Thus, there must be broadly representative support from the relevant industry in order for the application to go forward. This requirement is intended to ensure that the overall impact of an anti-dumping proceeding is positive for the industry. If a certain level of support cannot be generated, this may be an indication that there will be limited benefits or significant harms from imposing anti-dumping measures. It also serves as a constraint on abuse of the system, for example, by individual domestic producers hoping to burden foreign competitors with legal proceedings.

(ii) Sufficient Evidence to Go Forward with the Investigation

With regard to the evidence required, Article 5.2 states that the 'application' 'shall include evidence of (a) dumping, (b) injury within the meaning of Article VI of GATT 1994 as interpreted by this Agreement and (c) a causal link between the dumped imports and the alleged injury'. It further specifies that 'information as is reasonably available to the applicant' shall be included on the following points: (1) identity of the applicant and a description of the volume and value of the domestic production of the like product by the applicant; (2) description of the allegedly dumped product, the names of the country or countries of origin or export in question, the identity of each known exporter or foreign producer and a list of known persons importing the product in question; (3) information on prices at which the product in question is sold; and (4) information on the evolution of the volume of the allegedly dumped imports, the effect of these imports on prices of the like product in the domestic market and the consequent impact of the imports on the domestic industry. Article 5.3 then provides that '[t]he authorities shall examine the accuracy and adequacy of the evidence provided in the application to determine whether there is sufficient evidence to justify the initiation of an investigation'.

On the basis of these provisions, there are, in essence, two requirements imposed in relation to initiation. First, the domestic industry must include certain evidence as part of its application.[4] Secondly, the investigating authority must review this evidence and carry out an examination of whether the evidence supports proceeding with the investigation. Pursuant to Article 5.8, the application must be rejected and the investigation terminated if there is not sufficient evidence of either dumping or injury.

As with the 'domestic industry' requirement, this provision serves to weed out unsupported and frivolous cases, preventing abuse of the system.

(b) Evidence Used in the Investigation

Article 6 of the Anti-Dumping Agreement provides detailed rules pertaining to evidence gathered as part of an investigation. For instance, the provision requires that notices of initiation be provided to the companies involved, sets time limits for replies to questionnaires from the investigating authority, provides parties with general rights to defend their interests, and establishes rules for the treatment of confidential information.

In undertaking an investigation, the authorities must normally satisfy themselves as to the accuracy of the information supplied by interested parties upon which their find-

---

[4] While WTO rules do not apply directly to the domestic industry, they do impose an obligation on the relevant government agencies not to initiate an investigation without the requisite evidence.

ings are based. In order to verify information provided or to obtain further details, the investigating authorities may conduct on-site visits and investigations of the foreign companies involved, provided they obtain the agreement of the firms concerned and notify the representatives of the government of the Member in question, and unless that Member objects.[5] These kinds of verifications are a standard part of anti-dumping investigations, with the investigating government agency officials travelling to the foreign country to meet the exporters/producers (and their lawyers) in order to review and verify the accuracy of the submitted information.

While the use of information, especially pertaining to dumping, submitted by the exporters/producers is the norm, pursuant to Article 6.8 if any interested party significantly impedes the investigation or refuses access to, or otherwise does not provide, necessary information within a reasonable period, determinations may be made on the basis of the 'facts available'. Annex II to the Anti-Dumping Agreement provides more detailed rules on this possibility. These rules are controversial, as the 'facts available' will often be worse for the exporters/producers than their own submitted information. One aspect of these provisions that has been of particular concern to exporters/producers is paragraph 7 of Annex II, which allows investigating authorities to make determinations that are 'less favourable' to interested parties who fail to cooperate with the investigation. The possibility of using 'less favourable' treatment could be the subject of abuse by investigating authorities looking to impose a high level of anti-dumping duties. There are some constraints on such behaviour, though, as this provision does not release investigating authorities from other general requirements on how they conduct their investigation.

(c) Key Substantive Issues: Dumping, Injury and Causation

As noted, the three core issues in an anti-dumping investigation are: (1) the existence of dumping; (2) the existence of injury; and (3) a causal link between the dumping and injury. These are the main substantive aspects of anti-dumping law, and we cover each in detail here.

(i) Dumping

We have noted above the basic concept of dumping, which is that a product is allegedly being sold at too low a price in a foreign country, resulting in economic harm to the importing country's competing domestic industry. In the more precise and technical language of the Anti-Dumping Agreement, Article 2.1 provides that 'a product is to be considered as being dumped, ie introduced into the commerce of another country at less than its normal value, if the export price of the product exported from one country to another is less than the comparable price, in the ordinary course of trade, for the like product when destined for consumption in the exporting country'. The key elements in this definition are the 'normal value' and the 'export price'. We now elaborate on each of the elements, as well as the comparison between them. We also examine a particularly controversial aspect of the dumping calculation methodology, often referred to as 'zeroing', and conclude with an excerpt from a domestic dumping determination.

---

[5] Anti-dumping Agreement, Art 6.6 and 6.7.

a. Normal Value Determinations regarding the 'normal value' of a product are guided by Article 2.1 of the Anti-Dumping Agreement, which indicates that the 'normal value' of a product will ordinarily be:

> [T]he comparable price, in the ordinary course of trade, for the like product when destined for consumption in the exporting country.

Simply stated, the 'normal value' of a product is the price for which it is sold in its home market, ie the market of the producer or exporter. (As described below, however, the home market price cannot always be used, and in such instances alternative methods must be found.) In *US—Hot Rolled Steel*, the Appellate Body explained that Article 2.1 'expressly imposes four conditions on [domestic] sales transactions in order that they may be used to calculate normal value: first, the sale must be "in the ordinary course of trade"; second, it must be of the "like product"; third, the product must be "destined for consumption in the exporting country"; and, fourth, the price must be "comparable"'.[6]

The first condition is that a sales transaction must be 'in the ordinary course of trade'. In *US—Hot Rolled Steel*, the Appellate Body elaborated on the meaning of this term as follows:

> 139. The *Anti-Dumping Agreement* does not define the term 'in the ordinary course of trade'. Before the Panel, Japan referred with approval to the definition of this term given by USDOC in its questionnaire and, for the purposes of this appeal, we are content to work with this definition. That USDOC definition states:
>
>> Generally, sales are in the ordinary course of trade if made *under conditions and practices* that, for a *reasonable period of time prior to the date of sale* of the subject merchandise, have been *normal* for sales of the foreign like product. (emphasis added by the Appellate Body)
>
> 140. In terms of the above definition, Article 2.1 requires investigating authorities to exclude sales not made 'in the ordinary course of trade', from the calculation of normal value, precisely to ensure that normal value is, indeed, the 'normal' price of the like product, in the home market of the exporter. Where a sales transaction is concluded on terms and conditions that are incompatible with 'normal' commercial practice for sales of the like product, in the market in question, at the relevant time, the transaction is not an appropriate basis for calculating 'normal' value.[7]

In such a circumstance, the normal value is determined on the basis of the remaining sales so long as there is sufficient quantity of sales to permit a proper comparison with the export price.

A common basis for finding that a transaction was *not* in the ordinary course of trade is when the transaction takes place for less than the cost of production. Thus, if for a particular transaction a product is sold for below the cost of production (to be determined in accordance with Article 2.2.1 of the Anti-Dumping Agreement), that transaction is deemed to be outside the 'ordinary course of trade' and is thus excluded when determining the normal value of the product.

Another reason why a transaction may be considered outside the 'ordinary course of trade' is if the sale takes place between affiliated parties. In such a circumstance, 'the sale effectively involves a transfer of goods within a *single* economic enterprise [and thus]

---

[6] Appellate Body Report, *US—Hot Rolled Steel from Japan*, para 165.
[7] Appellate Body Report, *US—Hot Rolled Steel from Japan*, paras 139–40.

there is reason to suppose that the sales price *might* be fixed according to criteria which are not those of the marketplace'.[8] In addition, sales may occur at abnormally high or abnormally low prices (including sales below the cost of production) for one reason or another (such as clearing inventory or seasonal changeover). However, the determination of whether a particular sales price is higher or lower than the 'ordinary course of trade' price is not simply a matter of comparing *prices*. Instead, the price must be assessed 'in light of the other terms and conditions of the transaction, such as the volume of the product involved and whether the seller undertook additional responsibilities like transport or insurance'.[9]

The second requirement under the home market 'normal value' standard is that the transactions chosen must relate to a 'like product'. Article 2.6 of the Anti-Dumping Agreement defines the term 'like product' as follows:

> Throughout this Agreement the term 'like product' ('produit similaire') shall be interpreted to mean a product which is identical, i.e. alike in all respects to the product under consideration, or in the absence of such a product, another product which, although not alike in all respects, has characteristics closely resembling those of the product under consideration.

The definition of 'like product' is vague and allows for some discretion by the national authorities.

The third condition is that the product must be 'destined for consumption in the exporting country'; the last condition is that the price must be 'comparable'.

While the domestic price in the exporting country is the preferred figure to use as a 'normal value' for the purposes of comparison with the export price, Article 2.2 of the Anti-Dumping Agreement also provides methods of calculating a 'normal value' when the domestic price is not appropriate—such as when there are no domestic sales or the volume of sales in the domestic market is at such a low level as to prevent a proper comparison. Where domestic price cannot be used, Article 2.2 provides that the margin of dumping shall be determined by comparison of the export price with a comparable price of the like product when exported to an *appropriate third country, provided that this price is representative*, or with the *cost of production in the country of origin* plus a reasonable amount for administrative, selling and general costs and for profits ('constructed price'). Thus, when the domestic price is inappropriate as normal value, the investigating authorities may choose either a third country price or a constructed price as the normal value. Despite the fact that Article 2.2 lists the third country price before the constructed price, it has not been interpreted as expressing a preference for one alternative over the other; thus, the investigating authorities may choose either alternative without regard to hierarchy.

With third country price, the authorities will look for sales by the producers in similar countries. For example, in a case involving exports of canned pineapple from Thailand to the United States, sales to Germany were used as the third country market. Besides pointing out that the third country used should be 'appropriate' and that its normal value price 'representative', the Anti-Dumping Agreement does not provide any additional criteria, direction or interpretive guidance to investigating authorities.

With regard to a 'constructed price', Members have considerable leeway with this

---

[8] *Ibid*, para 141.
[9] *Ibid*, paras 142–44.

method. The Anti-Dumping Agreement does provide that, if possible, the constructed price must be based on *actual data* pertaining to production and sales in the ordinary course of trade of the *like product* by the exporter/producer under investigation.[10] If this is not possible, the amounts may be determined on the basis of:

(i) the actual amounts incurred and realised by the exporter or producer in question in respect of production and sales in the domestic market of the country of origin of the same general category of products;

(ii) the weighted average of the actual amounts incurred and realised by other exporters or producers subject to investigation in respect of production and sales of the like product in the domestic market of the country of origin;

(iii) any other reasonable method, provided that the amount for profit so established shall not exceed the profit normally realised by other exporters or producers on sales of products of the same general category in the domestic market of the country of origin.[11]

b. Export Price Under normal circumstances, the export price is simply the transaction price at which the product is sold by the exporting producer to the importer in the importing country. However, there are circumstances in which the export transaction may not offer an appropriate price, such as where the transaction involves barter or internal transfers between related companies, or where it appears to the authorities concerned that the export price is unreliable because of association or a compensatory arrangement between the exporter and the importer or a third party. In these situations, Article 2.3 of the Anti-Dumping Agreement provides for the export price to be *constructed* on the basis of the price at which the imported products are *first resold to an independent buyer*, or if the products are not resold to an independent buyer, or not resold in the condition as imported, *on such reasonable basis as the authorities may determine.*

c. Comparing the Export Price and the Normal Value: Calculating a Dumping Margin To determine whether dumping exists and, if so, the 'margin' of dumping, the export price is compared with the normal value. Article 2.4 of the Anti-Dumping Agreement elaborates on and sets the conditions for the comparison:

> A fair comparison shall be made between the export price and the normal value. This comparison shall be made at the same level of trade, normally at the ex-factory level, and in respect of sales made at as nearly as possible the same time. Due allowance shall be made in each case, on its merits, for differences which affect price comparability, including differences in conditions and terms of sale, taxation, levels of trade, quantities, physical characteristics, and any other differences which are also demonstrated to affect price comparability.[7] In the cases referred to in paragraph 3 [ed: where a constructed price is necessary], allowances for costs, including duties and taxes, incurred between importation and resale, and for profits accruing, should also be made. If in these cases price comparability has been affected, the authorities shall establish the normal value at a level of trade equivalent to the level of trade of the constructed export price, or shall make due allowance as warranted under this paragraph. The authorities shall indicate

---

[10] See Art 2.2.2 of the Anti-Dumping Agreement.
[11] See Art 2.2.2 (i)–(iii) of the Anti-Dumping Agreement.

to the parties in question what information is necessary to ensure a fair comparison and shall not impose an unreasonable burden of proof on those parties.

---

[7] It is understood that some of the above factors may overlap, and authorities shall ensure that they do not duplicate adjustments that have been already made under this provision.

Article 2.4 therefore demands a 'fair comparison' between the export price and the normal value. In comparing the export price with the normal value, adjustments are to be made to the export price, the normal value, or to both, based on the conditions set out above (differences in conditions and terms of sale, taxation, levels of trade, quantities, physical characteristics) as well as 'any other differences' which may affect price comparability. One of the main points of this provision is to make sure that the particular prices used provide a useful comparison. For example, an export sale price to a wholesaler may not offer a fair comparison with a domestic sale at the retail level. Thus prices may be adjusted to take such differences into account.

In practice, calculating the margin of dumping is an extremely difficult and controversial process, and there are many differences in the methodology to be used from country to country. Some basic guidelines are set out in Article 2.4.2 of the Anti-Dumping Agreement, which provides:

> [T]he existence of margins of dumping during the investigation phase shall normally be established on the basis of a comparison of a weighted average normal value with a weighted average of prices of all comparable export transactions or by a comparison of normal value and export prices on a transaction-to-transaction basis. A normal value established on a weighted average basis may be compared to prices of individual export transactions if the authorities find a pattern of export prices which differ significantly among different purchasers, regions or time periods, and if an explanation is provided as to why such differences cannot be taken into account appropriately by the use of a weighted average-to-weighted average or transaction-to-transaction comparison.

In other words, calculating a dumping margin normally requires either a comparison of the weighted average 'normal value' with that of the weighted average of all comparable export transactions *or* a transaction-to-transaction comparison of normal value and export price. However, a weighted average normal value may be compared to prices of individual export transactions (1) if authorities find targeted dumping ('a pattern of export prices which differ significantly among different purchasers, regions or time periods'); *and* (2) if the investigating authorities explain why such differences cannot be taken into account appropriately by the use of a weighted average-to-weighted average or transaction-to-transaction comparison.

The wide range of methodological variations involved in carrying out such comparisons is beyond the scope of this book. In the next section, we focus on one particularly controversial methodology that has been used: 'zeroing'.

d. Zeroing During the Uruguay Round negotiations, 'zeroing' was discussed in the following context. It had been the practice of some Members to calculate dumping margins on the basis of comparing **weighted-average** normal value to **individual** export prices. Under this methodology, the difference between normal value and export price would be calculated for each export transaction. Positive margins (where export price was lower than normal value) were taken as is. By contrast, negative margins (where export price was higher than normal value) were counted as zero. In this way, countries applying anti-dumping duties were sometimes able to find that dumping existed even when prices were on average the same in both the home and export markets. Table 11.1 demonstrates how this would occur (in a very basic example).

Table 11.1 Basic zeroing example

A	B	C	D	E	F
				Margin before zeroing	Margin after zeroing
Compari-sons	Home market sales (individual transactions)	Home market sales (average price)	Export market sales (individual transactions)	(average-to-transaction)	(average-to-transaction)
1	500	300	500	−200	0
2	400	300	400	−100	0
3	300	300	300	0	0
4	200	300	200	100	100
5	100	300	100	200	200
			Total dumping:	0	300

In this example, five comparisons are made between a home market sales transactions and export sales transaction. Column B shows the prices for each of the five home market transactions. Column C shows an average price for the five home market transactions (ie the five transactions averaged together). Column D shows the prices for each of the five export market transactions. If the sales for the home market and the export market are compared on an average-to-transaction basis (that is, if an average of the home market sales price in Column C is compared to the price for individual transactions in the export market in Column D), the resulting dumping margin depends on whether zeroing is used. Without zeroing, as shown in Column E, there is no dumping, as the positive and negative dumping margins cancel each other out. By contrast, when zeroing is used, the negative margins are treated as zero, and the result is a total—that is, for all sales combined—dumping margin of 300, shown in Column F.

At the heart of the zeroing debate lies a fundamental disagreement over the nature of dumping. On one side are those who contend that dumping exists only when the *average* price of all the exported products at issue is less than the *average* normal value price. On the other side are those who argue that *each individual* dumped export sale constitutes an instance of dumping. For the latter, then, it is enough that one sale is dumped, and offsetting positive dumping margins from dumped sales with the negative margins from sales where export price equals or exceeds normal value makes no sense.

The Anti-Dumping Agreement did not resolve the issue explicitly. However, as a result of a number of disputes brought first against the EC and later against the US, the Appellate Body has generally concluded that most, if not all, forms of zeroing are prohibited under Article 2.4.2 and various other provisions of the Anti-Dumping Agreement.

In the first case to address the issue, *EC—Bed Linen*, the comparison involved the weighted average to weighted average methodology in which the products at issue were grouped into 'models' and the normal value and export price for sales of specific models were compared. The Appellate Body found that the zeroing used as part of this calculation was not consistent with the Anti-Dumping Agreement, stating in part:

54. With this in mind, we recall that Article 2.4.2, first sentence, provides that "the existence of margins of dumping" for the product under investigation shall normally be established according to one of two methods. At issue in this case is the first method set out in that provision, under which "the existence of margins of dumping" must be established:

. . . on the basis of a comparison of a weighted average normal value with a weighted average of prices of all comparable export transactions . . .

55. Under this method, the investigating authorities are required to compare the weighted average normal value with the weighted average of prices of *all* comparable export transactions. Here, we emphasize that Article 2.4.2 speaks of "all" comparable export transactions. As explained above, when "zeroing", the European Communities counted as zero the "dumping margins" for those models where the "dumping margin" was "negative". As the Panel correctly noted, for those models, the European Communities counted "the weighted average export price to be equal to the weighted average normal value . . . despite the fact that it was, in reality, higher than the weighted average normal value." By "zeroing" the "negative dumping margins", the European Communities, therefore, did *not* take fully into account the entirety of the prices of *some* export transactions, namely, those export transactions involving models of cotton-type bed linen where "negative dumping margins" were found. Instead, the European Communities treated those export prices as if they were less than what they were. This, in turn, inflated the result from the calculation of the margin of dumping. Thus, the European Communities did *not* establish "the existence of margins of dumping" for cotton-type bed linen on the basis of a comparison of the weighted average normal value with the weighted average of prices of *all* comparable export transactions—that is, for *all* transactions involving *all* models or types of the product under investigation. Furthermore, we are also of the view that a comparison between export price and normal value that does *not* take fully into account the prices of *all* comparable export transactions—such as the practice of "zeroing" at issue in this dispute—is *not* a "fair comparison" between export price and normal value, as required by Article 2.4 and by Article 2.4.2.[12]

The focus of the Appellate Body's reasoning here was the 'all comparable' transactions language of Article 2.4.2, which applies only to weighted average to weighted average comparisons. In the later *US—Softwood Lumber V* case, however, the Appellate Body changed the focus of its reasoning, so as to prohibit zeroing under the transaction-to-transaction methodology as well. The following is an extract from that case.

Appellate Body Report, *United States—Final Dumping Determination on Softwood Lumber from Canada*, Adopted 31 August 2004, WT/DS264/AB/R

2. "All Comparable Export Transactions" in Article 2.4.2

86. Article 2.4.2 requires that the existence of margins of dumping "shall normally be established on the basis of a comparison of a weighted average normal value with a weighted average of prices of *all comparable export transactions*". (emphasis added) It is clear from the language of Article 2.4.2 that a weighted average normal value is to be compared with a weighted average of the prices of "comparable" export transactions, and not with prices of "non-comparable" export

---

[12] Appellate Body Report, *EC—Bed Linen*, paras 54–55.

transactions. At the same time, the word "all" in "all comparable export transactions" makes it clear that Members cannot exclude from a comparison any transaction that is "comparable". Thus, we agree with the Panel that the term "all comparable export transactions" means that a Member "may only compare those export transactions which are comparable, but [] it must compare *all* such transactions."

87. It is not in dispute in this case that, in the calculation of the weighted average export price for each sub-group, USDOC took into account "all comparable export transactions", and thus no comparable export transactions were excluded at the sub-group level.

88. However, the participants have divergent views with respect to the aggregation of the results of the multiple comparisons of "all comparable export transactions". The United States is of the view that Article 2.4.2 does not require the aggregation of the results of such comparisons, and that, even if there were such a requirement, it would be permissible to exclude the results of those comparisons where the weighted average normal value is less than the weighted average export price (which comparisons according to the United States constitute "non-dumped comparisons"). The United States emphasizes that Article VI:1 of the *General Agreement on Tariffs and Trade 1994* (the "GATT 1994") "explicitly condemns dumping" and that the *Anti-Dumping Agreement* "does not recognize a 'negative dumping margin'." As we understand it, the United States is of the view that a requirement to include results of "non-dumped" comparisons at the aggregation stage would amount to giving offsets unjustifiably to "dumped" amounts from "non-dumped" amounts.

89. In contrast, Canada, the European Communities, India, and Japan are of the view that the terms "dumping" and "dumping margins" in the *Anti-Dumping Agreement* apply to the product under investigation *as a whole* , and that, therefore, the results of multiple comparisons must be aggregated in their entirety to establish the existence of margins of dumping for the product *as a whole*. In their view, the *Anti-Dumping Agreement* does not permit a determination of "dumping" at the level of a product type or model. Moreover, according to Canada and the European Communities, treating comparisons at the sub-group level as "dumped" or "non-dumped" is inconsistent with Article 2.4.2 and amounts to "prejudging" the outcome of an analysis to determine whether dumping exists for the product under investigation as a whole.

90. There is no basic disagreement among the participants that "all comparable export transactions" must be taken into account in establishing margins of dumping. Rather, the participants' disagreement centres on how the results of multiple comparisons are interpreted and aggregated when all comparable transactions have admittedly been taken into account at the sub-group level. And this disagreement flows, in essence, from the participants' respective interpretations of the terms "dumping" and "margins of dumping" in the *Anti-Dumping Agreement*—whether these terms apply at the product or sub-product level. We therefore turn now to an analysis of these terms as used in Article 2.4.2 of the *Anti-Dumping Agreement*.

3. "Margins of Dumping" in Article 2.4.2

91. As we noted above, the United States' position rests on the proposition that "margins of dumping" can be established, and "dumping" can be found, at the *sub-group level*. According to the United States, the term "margins of dumping" in Article 2.4.2 refers to the results of those multiple comparisons "in which the normal value exceeds the export price". In addressing this argument, we turn first to Article VI:1 of the GATT 1994 and Article 2.1 of the *Anti-Dumping Agreement*, which define "dumping" in the context of the GATT 1994 and the *Anti-Dumping Agreement*, respectively.

92. Specifically, Article VI:1 defines "dumping" as occurring where "*products* of one country are introduced into the commerce of another country at less than the normal value of the *products*".

(emphasis added) This definition is reiterated in Article 2.1 of the *Anti-Dumping Agreement*, which provides that:

Article 2
Determination of Dumping

2.1 For the purpose of this Agreement, a *product* is to be considered as being dumped, i.e. introduced into the commerce of another country at less than its normal value, if the export price of the *product* exported from one country to another is less than the comparable price, in the ordinary course of trade, for the like *product* when destined for consumption in the exporting country. (emphasis added)

93. It is clear from the texts of these provisions that dumping is defined in relation to a product as a whole as defined by the investigating authority. Moreover, we note that the opening phrase of Article 2.1—"[f]or the purpose of this Agreement"—indicates that the definition of "dumping" as contained in Article 2.1 applies to the entire Agreement, which includes, of course, Article 2.4.2. "Dumping", within the meaning of the *Anti-Dumping Agreement*, can therefore be found to exist only for the product under investigation as a whole, and cannot be found to exist only for a type, model, or category of that product.

94. Other provisions of the *Anti-Dumping Agreement* confirm this view. For example, Article 9.2 (as well as Article VI:2 of the GATT 1994) stipulate that an anti-dumping duty is to be imposed in respect of the *product* under investigation. In addition, Article 6.10 of the *Anti-Dumping Agreement* provides that the investigating authorities "shall, as a rule, determine an individual margin of dumping for each known exporter or producer concerned *of the product under investigation*". (emphasis added)

95. Having examined the definition of "dumping", we now turn to examine the term "margin of dumping" as defined in Article VI:2 of the GATT 1994, second sentence, which provides that: . . . the margin of dumping is the price difference determined in accordance with the provisions of paragraph 1 [of Article VI of the GATT 1994]. (footnote omitted)

96. The Appellate Body found in *EC—Bed Linen* that "[w]hatever the method used to calculate the margins of dumping . . . these margins must be, and can only be, established for the *product* under investigation as a whole." While "dumping" refers to the introduction of a product into the commerce of another country at less than its normal value, the term "margin of dumping" refers to the magnitude of dumping. As with dumping, "margins of dumping" can be found only for the product under investigation as a whole, and cannot be found to exist for a product type, model, or category of that product.

97. It is clear that an investigating authority may undertake multiple averaging to establish margins of dumping for a product under investigation. In our view, the results of the multiple comparisons at the sub-group level are, however, not "margins of dumping" within the meaning of Article 2.4.2. Rather, those results reflect only intermediate calculations made by an investigating authority in the context of establishing margins of dumping for the product under investigation. Thus, it is only on the basis of aggregating *all* these "intermediate values" that an investigating authority can establish margins of dumping for the product under investigation as a whole.

98. We fail to see how an investigating authority could properly establish margins of dumping for the product under investigation as a whole without aggregating *all* of the "results" of the multiple comparisons for *all* product types. There is no textual basis under Article 2.4.2 that would justify taking into account the "results" of only some multiple comparisons in the process of calculating margins of dumping, while disregarding other "results". If an investigating

authority has chosen to undertake multiple comparisons, the investigating authority necessarily has to take into account the results of *all* those comparisons in order to establish margins of dumping for the product as a whole under Article 2.4.2. Thus we disagree with the United States that Article 2.4.2 does not apply to the aggregation of the results of multiple comparisons.

99. Our view that "dumping" and "margins of dumping" can only be established for the product under investigation as a whole is in consonance with the need for consistent treatment of a product in an anti-dumping investigation. Thus, having defined the product under investigation, the investigating authority must treat that *product* as a whole for, *inter alia* , the following purposes: determination of the volume of dumped imports, injury determination, causal link between dumped imports and injury to domestic industry, and calculation of the margin of dumping. Moreover, according to Article VI:2 of the GATT 1994 and Article 9.2 of the *Anti-Dumping Agreement*, an antidumping duty can be levied only on a dumped product. For all these purposes, the product under investigation is treated as a whole, and export transactions in the so-called "non-dumped" sub-groups (that is, those sub-groups in which the weighted average normal value is less than the weighted average export price) are not excluded. We see no basis, under the *Anti-Dumping Agreement*, for treating the very same sub-group transactions as "non-dumped" for one purpose and "dumped" for other purposes. Indeed, in the anti-dumping investigation at issue in this dispute, the product as a whole—softwood lumber—has been treated as a "dumped" product, except at the stage of zeroing.

100. Moreover, we observe that Article 2.4.2 contains no express language that permits an investigating authority to disregard the results of multiple comparisons at the aggregation stage. Other provisions of the *Anti-Dumping Agreement* are explicit regarding the permissibility of disregarding certain matters. For example, Article 2.2.1 of the *Anti-Dumping Agreement*, which deals with the calculation of normal value, sets forth the *only* circumstances under which sales of the like product may be disregarded. Similarly, Article 9.4 of the *Anti-Dumping Agreement* expressly directs investigating authorities to "disregard" zero and *de minimis* margins of dumping, under certain circumstances, when calculating the weighted average margin of dumping to be applied to exporters or producers that have not been individually investigated. Thus, when the negotiators sought to permit investigating authorities to disregard certain matters, they did so explicitly.

101. We now turn to the implications of zeroing as applied in this case. Zeroing means, *in effect*, that at least in the case of *some* export transactions, the export prices are treated as if they were less than what they actually are. Zeroing, therefore, does not take into account the *entirety* of the *prices* of *some* export transactions, namely, the prices of export transactions in those sub-groups in which the weighted average normal value is less than the weighted average export price. Zeroing thus inflates the margin of dumping for the product as a whole.

102. We understand the United States to argue that a prohibition of zeroing would amount to a requirement to compare "dumped" and "non-dumped" transactions at the aggregation stage. The United States contends that results of multiple comparisons in which the weighted average normal value exceeds the weighted average export price may be excluded because they do not involve "dumping". As we have stated earlier, the terms "dumping" and "margins of dumping" in Article VI of the GATT 1994 and the *Anti-Dumping Agreement* apply to the product under investigation as a whole and do not apply to sub-group levels. The treatment of comparisons for which the weighted average normal value is less than the weighted average export price as "non-dumped" comparisons is therefore not in accordance with the requirements of Article 2.4.2 of the *Anti-Dumping Agreement*.

103. For all these reasons, we do not agree with the United States that the results of comparisons at the sub-group level constitute margins of dumping. Nor do we agree with the United States

that the results of the comparisons in which the weighted average normal value is less than the weighted average export price could be excluded in calculating a margin of dumping for the product under investigation as a whole .

... ...

A key part of the Appellate Body's reasoning was its statement in paragraph 93 that '[i]t is clear from the texts of these provisions that dumping is defined in relation to a product as a whole as defined by the investigating authority'. Whether it is, in fact, 'clear' from the texts is debatable, but regardless the Appellate Body seems to have come out on the side of those who feel that dumping must be calculated based on an average of all sales, as opposed to a comparison of individual sales. In subsequent cases, the Appellate Body has extended this finding to prohibit zeroing in various other aspects of anti-dumping proceedings as well, and it seems likely to rule against zeroing in most, if not all, contexts. The Appellate Body's reasoning on this issue was the subject of a good deal of controversy, as several subsequent panels took a different view and decided not to follow the Appellate Body's reasoning. However, in the appeals of those cases, the Appellate Body maintained its position, and at this point it appears that the general prohibition on zeroing has been accepted by the WTO's judicial decision-makers, although the issue has not been dealt with under all relevant provisions, so there may still be some scope for arguing that particular forms of zeroing are permitted.

The initial case finding zeroing to violate the Anti-Dumping Agreement was in a decision concerning a complaint brought against the EC (the *EC—Bed Linen* case quoted above). Although it contested the issues there, the EC has since come around to the view that zeroing is generally prohibited by the Anti-Dumping Agreement. At this stage, the US is the primary country defending zeroing, and has proposed, as part of the current WTO negotiations, amending the Anti-Dumping Agreement to allow for zeroing.[13] Most Members take the view that zeroing violates WTO rules in almost all circumstances and are not in favour of amending the Agreement to allow for its application. Recently, however, the US indicated that it will implement the Appellate Body's findings on zeroing, although there is some question as to how it will do so. Meanwhile, the US continues to press for zeroing to be permitted as part of any new rules negotiated during the Doha Round.

As a final point, while some exporters involved in US anti-dumping proceedings have argued that the WTO rulings noted above require the US to change its zeroing methodology pursuant to US domestic law, US courts have rejected this argument, as shown in the following extract from a US appeals court decision:

Corus Staal BV v Dep't of Commerce, 395 F 3d 1343 (Fed Cir 2005)

II.

Corus alternatively argues that Commerce unreasonably refused to interpret the statute in a manner consistent with U.S. international obligations under the Charming Betsy doctrine of claim construction, which states that courts should interpret U.S. law, whenever possible, in a manner consistent with international obligations. Murray v. The Schooner Charming Betsy, 6 U.S. (2 Cranch) 64, 118 (1804). Corus asserts that, by disregarding the prices of certain U.S.

---

[13] See 'Offsets for Non-dumping Comparisons', TN/RL/W/208 (5 June 2007); 'Proposal on Offsets for Non-dumped Comparisons', TN/RL/GEN/147 (27 June 2007).

transactions that are made at nondumped prices, Commerce violated its obligation under Article 2.4.2 of the Agreement on the Implementation of Article VI of the General Agreement on Tariffs and Trade ("Antidumping Agreement" or "ADA") to fairly consider all comparable export transactions. This "fair comparison" argument is the same argument offered by the appellant in Timken. In that case, we held that the appellant's invocation of the ADA's "fair comparison" language was misplaced because section 1677b(a)'s fair comparison language and explicit scheme for calculating NV governed. 354 F.3d at 1344. Because "[section] 1677b(a) does not impose any requirements for calculating normal value beyond those explicitly established in the statute and does not carry over to create additional limitations on the calculation of dumping margins," id., we likewise dismiss Corus' invocation of the "fair comparison" language.

Corus further claims that Commerce violated the ADA by failing to discontinue its zeroing methodology in light of WTO Appellate Body interpretations in European Communities—Antidumping Duties on Imports of Cotton-Type Bed Linen from India, WT/DS141/AB/R (Mar. 1, 2001) ("EC-Bed Linen"), United States—Sunset Review of Antidumping Duties on Corrosion-Resistant Carbon Steel Flat Products from Japan, WT/DS244/AB/R (Dec. 15, 2003) ("Corrosion-Resistant Steel"), and United States—Final Dumping Determination on Softwood Lumber from Canada, WT/DS264/AB/R (Aug. 11, 2004) ("Softwood Lumber"). In EC-Bed Linen, a case in which the United States was not a party, the Appellate Body determined that the EC practice of zeroing during an antidumping investigation was inconsistent with Article 2.4.2 of the ADA. WT/DS141/AB/R ¶ 66. In Corrosion-Resistant Steel, the Appellate Body hypothesized (without finding) that Commerce had used zeroed margins from administrative reviews in its sunset review of antidumping orders on Japanese steel products, and suggested that any such use would violate the ADA. WT/DS244/AB/R ¶ 135. In Softwood Lumber, the Appellate Body found that Commerce violated Article 2.4.2 when it used zeroing to calculate the weighted-average dumping margin in its investigation of imports of Canadian softwood lumber. WT/DS264/AB/R ¶ 7.224.

WTO decisions are "not binding on the United States, much less this court." Timken, 354 F.3d at 1344. Further, "[n]o provision of any of the Uruguay Round Agreements [e.g., the ADA], nor the application of any such provision to any person or circumstance, that is inconsistent with any law of the United States shall have effect." 19 U.S.C. § 3512(a) (2000). Neither the GATT nor any enabling international agreement outlining compliance therewith (e.g., the ADA) trumps domestic legislation; if U.S. statutory provisions are inconsistent with the GATT or an enabling agreement, it is strictly a matter for Congress. See Suramerica de Aleaciones Laminads, C.A. v. United States, 966 F.2d 660, 668 (Fed. Cir. 1992); see also 19 U.S.C. § 2504(a) (2000) ("No provision of any trade agreement . . . nor the application of any such provision to any person or circumstance, which is in conflict with any statute of the United States shall be given effect under the laws of the United States."). Congress has enacted legislation to deal with the conflict presented here. It has authorized the United States Trade Representative, an arm of the Executive branch, in consultation with various congressional and executive bodies and agencies, to determine whether or not to implement WTO reports and determinations and, if so implemented, the extent of implementation. See 19 U.S.C. §§ 3533(f), 3538 (2000); see also 19 U.S.C. § 3533(g) (2000) (defining a statutory scheme that Commerce must observe in order to change its policy to conform to a WTO ruling).

We therefore accord no deference to the cited WTO cases. EC-Bed Linen is no more persuasive here than it was for the appellant in Timken, and we now reject it for the same reasons cited in that case. See Timken, 354 F.3d at 1344. Corrosion-Resistant Steel is nonbinding because the Appellate Body did not make a finding regarding Commerce's zeroing methodology. WT/DS244/AB/R ¶ 138. Finally, we reject Softwood Lumber as nonbinding because the finding therein was not adopted as per Congress's statutory scheme.

"[T]he conduct of foreign relations is committed by the Constitution to the political departments of the Federal Government . . . ." United States v. Pink, 315 U.S. 203, 222-23 (1942). In this case, section 1677(35) presented Commerce with a choice as to how it calculates weighted-average dumping margins. We give Commerce substantial deference in its administration of the statute because of the foreign policy implications of a dumping determination. See Fed. Mogul Corp. v. United States, 63 F.3d 1572, 1582 (Fed. Cir. 1995). We will not attempt to perform duties that fall within the exclusive province of the political branches, and we therefore refuse to overturn Commerce's zeroing practice based on any ruling by the WTO or other international body unless and until such ruling has been adopted pursuant to the specified statutory scheme.

… … …

e. A Domestic Dumping Determination A full understanding of how dumping determinations are made requires experience with certain specialised statistical programmes that are used to make these calculations. We will not go into such detail here, but we do offer an extract of a determination by a domestic agency, the Canada Customs and Revenue Agency, on the issue of dumping. This document offers a summary of the calculations carried out by the agency.

Ottawa, 9 December 2002

STATEMENT OF REASONS

Concerning the making of a final determination of dumping with respect to

CERTAIN WATERPROOF FOOTWEAR AND WATERPROOF FOOTWEAR BOTTOMS, ORIGINATING IN OR EXPORTED FROM HONG KONG, CHINA; MACAO, CHINA; AND VIETNAM

…

SUMMARY

On April 26, 2002, the Commissioner of Customs and Revenue (Commissioner) initiated an investigation respecting the alleged injurious dumping of certain waterproof footwear and waterproof footwear bottoms, originating in or exported from Hong Kong, China; Macao, China; and Vietnam. The investigation was initiated in response to a complaint filed by the Shoe Manufacturers' Association of Canada (SMAC) of Beaconsfield, Quebec.

On receiving notice of the investigation, the Canadian International Trade Tribunal (Tribunal) started its preliminary injury inquiry. On June 25, 2002, the Tribunal made a preliminary determination that the evidence disclosed a reasonable indication that the alleged dumping of the subject goods has caused injury to the domestic industry.

On July 17, 2002, pursuant to paragraph 39(1)(a) of the Special Import Measures Act (SIMA), the Commissioner extended to 135 days the time period for rendering a preliminary determination or for terminating the investigation in whole or in part, due to the complexity and novelty of the issues presented by the investigation. On September 9, 2002, the Commissioner made a preliminary determination of dumping.

The Canada Customs and Revenue Agency (CCRA) continued its investigation and, on the basis of the results, the Commissioner is satisfied that the subject goods have been dumped and that the margins of dumping were not insignificant. Consequently, on December 9, 2002, the Commissioner made a final determination of dumping pursuant to paragraph 41(1)(a) of SIMA.

The Tribunal's inquiry into the question of injury to the Canadian industry is continuing. Until the Tribunal renders its decision, provisional duties will continue to be imposed on the subject goods originating in or exported from Hong Kong, China (hereinafter referred to as Hong Kong, except in the definition of the subject goods); Macao, China (hereinafter referred to as Macao, except in the definition of the subject goods); and Vietnam.

INTERESTED PARTIES

Complainant and the Canadian Industry

The complainant, SMAC, acts as a representative for the footwear manufacturing industry in Canada. The complaint is supported by six producers who are members of SMAC: Acton International Inc. (Acton), Baffin Inc. (Baffin), Genfoot Inc. (Genfoot), Les Chaussures Régence (Régence), Rallye Footwear Inc. (Rallye) and Chaussures Yeti Inc. (Yeti). These six firms account for more than 95 per cent of all Canadian production of the subject goods. The complainant and the supporting producers are listed with their addresses in Appendix 1.

Exporters

The CCRA has identified 77 exporters of the subject goods located not only in the named countries, but in other countries as well. Where there were a large number of exporters in a named country of export, the CCRA limited its examination of dumping to a sampled number of exporters, pursuant to subsection 30.3(1) of SIMA. The sampling was based on exporters whose combined shipments to Canada represent a substantial portion of the subject goods exported from that country, during the calendar year 2001.

Importers

The CCRA identified 57 importers of subject goods. The CCRA also limited its detailed examination of imports to those importers whose combined importations represent a substantial portion of the subject goods imported into Canada during the calendar year 2001.

BACKGROUND

An anti-dumping complaint was filed on behalf of SMAC on March 6, 2002. On March 27, 2002, the CCRA informed SMAC that its complaint was properly documented. At the same time, the governments of Hong Kong, Macao, and Vietnam were notified that a properly documented complaint had been received.

On April 26, 2002, the Commissioner initiated a dumping investigation and notified the Tribunal of that decision. The Tribunal subsequently initiated a preliminary injury inquiry into whether the evidence disclosed a reasonable indication of injury, retardation or threat of injury caused by the dumping of the goods. On June 25, 2002, the Tribunal concluded that the evidence disclosed a reasonable indication that the alleged dumping has caused injury.

On July 17, 2002, pursuant to paragraph 39(1)(a) of SIMA, the Commissioner extended to 135 days the time period for rendering a preliminary determination or for terminating the investigation in whole or in part, due to the complexity and novelty of the issues presented in the investigation. On September 9, 2002, the Commissioner made a preliminary determination of dumping in accordance with subsection 38(1) of SIMA.

There have been two past findings concerning waterproof footwear. The footwear covered by the findings is described in the Tribunal's expiry review inquiry RR-2001-005 (October 19, 2002) and the Tribunal's finding NQ-2000-004 (December 8, 2000). The anti-dumping measures in both cases apply to imports from the People's Republic of China (China). The Tribunal's order in expiry review RR-2001-005 reflects a twenty-year-old finding by the Anti-dumping Tribunal (ADT-2-82) on April 23, 1982, which covered waterproof rubber footwear only, as plastic was not widely used in the manufacture of waterproof footwear at that time. As waterproof footwear items of other materials appeared, the Anti-dumping Tribunal finding could not be broadened to include them. Consequently, pursuant to another anti-dumping investigation, the Tribunal's inquiry (NQ-2000-004) dealt with waterproof plastic footwear and certain items of waterproof rubber footwear that had either been omitted from the original inquiry in 1982 or excluded by the Tribunal's expiry review RR-97-001 in 1997.

Product Information

Product—Subject Goods Definition

For the purpose of this investigation the subject goods are defined as:

"waterproof footwear and waterproof footwear bottoms, constructed wholly or in part of rubber or plastic, worn over the foot or shoe, originating in or exported from Hong Kong, China; Macao, China; and Vietnam. The distinctive feature of waterproof footwear is that both the sole portion and a portion of the upper, sufficient to give waterproof protection to the foot, are incorporated in a waterproof component that may be made of rubber or plastic. The goods subject to this investigation include moulded clogs, waterproof safety footwear and waterproof footwear made of waterproof footwear bottoms combined with tops made of leather, textiles or other materials. They may be constructed with or without liners, linings, fasteners or safety features."

Excluded from the definition of subject goods are equestrian riding boots, ski boots and skating boots.

The product information and definitions that follow are an integral part of the description of the goods that are subject to this investigation.

Product Information

Waterproof footwear described as "waterproof rubber footwear" is produced, wholly or in part of natural rubber and/or synthetic rubber, by vulcanization, injection moulding or other processes. The term synthetic rubber includes thermoplastic rubber (TPR).

Waterproof footwear described as "waterproof plastic footwear" is constructed wholly or in part of plastic. It is made from plastic resins by injection moulding or other processes. The term "plastic" includes polyvinyl chloride (PVC), polyurethane (PU) and other plastics. PVC is the plastic most commonly used to date in this class of footwear.

Waterproof rubber footwear and waterproof plastic footwear include footwear worn over the foot or shoe, with or without liners, linings, fasteners or safety features. These include red sole rubber boots, city boots, rain boots, hunting and fishing boots, hip waders and chest waders. In certain styles, such as duck shoes or winter boots, a boat-like (or shell-like) waterproof bottom may have trimmings, attachments, liners, cuffs or tops of nylon or other materials.

The product range of subject goods includes footwear manufactured for men, women, youth, misses and children.

Definitions

The following are specific definitions respecting the footwear that are subject to this investigation.

"Footwear with waterproof bottoms" is characterized by two major components: a "bottom" of plastic or rubber that is waterproof, and a "top". In such footwear, the waterproof bottom comprises the sole and the lower portion of the upper. The term "bottoms" should not be confused with "sole", a portion of footwear that extends from the ground to the sole of the foot. "Top", which comprises the top portion of the upper in certain styles, varies greatly in height and design, and may be made of leather, plastic, fabrics, coated fabrics or other materials. The bottoms and tops of waterproof footwear may be joined by stitching. The tops, which in many instances are assembled by stitching, have seams that may or may not be treated with an adhesive or other substance to inhibit the entry of water. In other cases, waterproof bottoms may be affixed to tops by other means such as direct-injection. Refer to related definition of "Waterproof footwear bottoms" below.

"Moulded clogs" are typically made from plastic or rubber by moulding to produce a clog designed for use in gardening or similar pursuits. Clogs may be open or closed at the heel.

"Thermoplastic rubber" is a thermoplastic elastomer, developed in the 1970s, that has been used in the manufacture of waterproof footwear since the early 1980s. This material has many of the physical properties of rubber but, unlike conventional rubber, it is processed as a thermoplastic material and is not vulcanized. Vulcanization, a thermosetting process, is slow and irreversible. With TPR, the process from molten material to a solid, rubber-like object, which is rapid and reversible, takes place upon cooling.

"Waterproof footwear", for the purpose of this investigation, includes most of the footwear classified under the Harmonized System (HS) heading 6401. It also includes certain footwear with waterproof bottoms and tops of any material, assembled by stitching or other means, that are classified in Chapter 64 under subheadings of 6402, 6403 and 6404, and not under HS 6401.

"Waterproof footwear bottoms" for use in the manufacture of subject footwear are classified as incomplete footwear under HS subheading 6401.99, and more specifically, under HS classification numbers 6401.99.21 if rubber or 6401.99.30 if plastic. Waterproof footwear bottoms are boat-like (or shell-like) components that are combined with tops made of leather, nylon, plastic, coated fabrics or other materials to form articles of finished waterproof footwear. The distinctive feature of waterproof bottoms is that both the outer sole portion and a portion of the upper, sufficient in height to give waterproof protection to the foot, are incorporated into a waterproof component. Waterproof footwear bottoms may be made by the traditional process of cutting components from sheets of rubber, assembling by cement and vulcanizing. Alternatively, waterproof footwear bottoms may be made of thermoplastic rubber by injection moulding. Waterproof footwear bottoms may also be made from plastic resins by injection moulding.

"Waterproof plastic footwear" is made of plastic resins by injection moulding or other moulding processes. The external surface may be made entirely of plastic, as in the case of rain boots. In other styles, such as duck shoes, footwear of moulded plastic may be provided with trimmings or attachments of other materials. Waterproof plastic footwear styles, which are frequently designed to resemble rubber footwear, are widely sold and used as substitutes for rubber footwear.

"Waterproof rubber footwear" is made in many instances by the traditional method commonly referred to as "lay-up" or "vulcanized". Alternatively, waterproof rubber footwear can be made of thermoplastic rubber by the injection moulding process.

"Waterproof safety footwear" includes waterproof footwear made with safety features, whether or not it meets established CSA standards. Safety features include any reinforcement made to the footwear either by adding extra layers of material or by incorporating other materials to reinforce the footwear.

Footwear Excluded from this Investigation

The following are specific definitions respecting the footwear that are excluded from this investigation:

"Equestrian riding boots" designed for use in horse riding are excluded from this complaint. They may be made from either rubber or plastic and are classified under the HS classification number 6401.10.11.00 or 6401.91.11.00 if made of rubber and under the HS classification number 6401.91.20.00 if made of plastic.

"Ski boots" are boots designed for use in downhill skiing.

"Skating boots" are designed to be fitted with skate blades and used for ice skating.

Other Industry Definitions

"Sole" refers to that portion of an item of footwear which extends from the ground to the bottom of the foot.

"Top" refers to that component or portion of an upper which is attached to a waterproof footwear bottom by stitching or other means.

"Upper" refers to that part of any footwear that extends upward from the sole to the uppermost part of the finished product. For the purposes of this investigation the relevant definition of "the upper", its constituent material and the terms "rubber" and "plastics" are found in the HS general notes of Section XII, Chapter 64, notes (D) and (E).

Production Processes

The goods subject to this investigation may be manufactured by the traditional lay-up and vulcanization process, by moulding processes such as injection-moulding, by the direct injection process or by other processes.

Waterproof footwear may be produced using the injection-moulding process alone or in combination with the stitched product process. An example of a product made solely by injection-moulding is a PVC rain boot. On the other hand, the injection-moulding process and stitching could be used in combination to produce a rubber-bottom, nylon-top winter boot.

The following provides an overview of various processes which may be used in manufacturing waterproof footwear:

In the vulcanization process (occasionally referred to as "lay-up"), natural and synthetic rubber are compounded with specialty chemicals and formed into sheets. Footwear parts are then cut from the sheets of rubber. The parts are then laid up on forms and secured with rubber cement. The laid-up footwear is then vulcanized in an oven so that the rubber is irreversibly cured.

In the injection moulding process, a granulated chemical compound of either PVC or TPR, is heated and injected into steel moulds installed in moulding machines. Each mould dictates the size, style and number of colours of a moulded item. When the chemical is forwarded to the moulding machine, it is vacuumed into the hopper and pushed into a heated barrel. A screw inside the barrel generates additional heat to melt the compound and then injects it into a mould. The resulting product may consist of an unfinished waterproof bottom or an item of waterproof footwear such as a rain boot. The moulded items are then cooled, extracted and trimmed. Components and markings are added before the finished footwear is packed for shipping.

In the direct injection process, a suitable material such as polyurethane is injected into a mould that is fitted to a lasted footwear upper typically made of leather. The result is that a directly injected waterproof bottom is affixed permanently to the upper without stitching.

Complex waterproof footwear, such as winter boots, consists of waterproof bottoms that are attached by the simple process of stitching to tops that may be made of leather, textiles or other materials.

Classification of Imports

The subject goods in finished form are normally classified under HS headings 6401, 6402, 6403 and 6404.

The following are the 26 specific 10-digit HS classification numbers under which the subject goods are imported:

...

Canadian Industry

The Canadian industry for the subject footwear is now composed of the six producers listed in Appendix 1. Five years ago this was an industry of nine producers. Since then, four firms have left the industry and one has joined it.

Carlaw Manufacturing Ltd. and Maple Leaf Shoe Company closed in 1998 after years of financial difficulty. Bata Shoe Company Ltd. closed all of its domestic manufacturing operations in the second half of 1999. Kaufman Footwear, a large producer of high-end products that it marketed under the name Sorel, declared bankruptcy in July 2000. Régence, an established producer of women's footwear, acquired certain assets of Maple Leaf Shoe Company and began producing waterproof footwear in 1999.

Imports of Subject Goods

Before making a preliminary determination of dumping, the Commissioner must be satisfied that the actual and potential volume of dumped goods is not negligible. If the volume of dumped goods from a country is less than 3 per cent of the total volume of like goods released into Canada from all countries during the period of investigation, the volume is considered to be negligible.

In its complaint, SMAC identified 26 10-digit HS classification numbers under which subject waterproof footwear may be properly classified (these numbers are listed above). Under the 10-digit classification numbers of headings 6401, 6402, 6403, and 6404, the complainant indicated that broad varieties of subject and non-subject goods may be found within the same 10-digit classification numbers. Accordingly, SMAC compiled and analysed monthly data since January 1998, under each of the 26 10-digit HS classification numbers for Hong Kong, Macao, Vietnam and the rest of the world.

SMAC concluded its examination of imports by focusing closely on the six 10-digit HS classification numbers believed to capture most of the subject imports for men (6402.91.00.91, 6403.91.00.91 and 6404.19.90.91) and for children (6402.91.00.93, 6403.91.00.93 and 6404.19.90.93). Imports from subject countries, as well as from the rest of the world, were also estimated on this basis. Based on a review of the information presented by the complainant and other available information, the CCRA was satisfied at initiation that the complainant's approach in estimating the total volume of imports was reasonable.

In order to further examine the issue of volumes of subject goods, supplementary questionnaires were sent during the preliminary phase of the investigation to all identified importers and exporters of footwear under the 26 10-digit HS classification numbers identified by the complainant. The purpose was to obtain the total volume of goods that are of the same description as the dumped goods that were released into Canada from all countries. The questionnaires asked the importers and exporters to provide the total volume and value of footwear imported from each subject country and from the rest of the world during the period of investigation, and to provide information separately on like goods and non-subject goods.

A limited number of complete submissions were received in response to the supplementary questionnaire. As a result, the CCRA was unable to determine an accurate estimate of the true volume of imports of subject goods based on exporter and importer submissions.

For purposes of the final decision on dumping, import volumes have been calculated based on the information provided by the complainant, and verified by data retrieved from the CCRA's own internal information system, the Facility for Information Retrieval Management (FIRM). The CCRA's analysis was limited to importations under the six 10-digit HS classification numbers mentioned above, that are believed to capture most of the subject goods for men's and children's models.

Hong Kong Import Volume

Prior to the preliminary determination, the Hong Kong government made representations to the CCRA that Hong Kong should not be included in the investigation, as import volumes were negligible.

Verification visits to exporters located in Hong Kong and meetings with Hong Kong government and industry officials were held during July 2002. The government officials and the exporters that were visited by the CCRA provided information respecting shipments of subject goods to Canada. During the verification meetings in Hong Kong, two industry associations, the Hong Kong Leather Shoe and Shoe Material Merchants Association Ltd. and the Hong Kong Rubber and Footwear Manufacturers' Association agreed to petition their members to obtain additional information for the CCRA. That information had not been provided at the time of the CCRA's preliminary determination. As such, for purposes of the preliminary determination of dumping, the volume of imports from Hong Kong was not considered to be negligible.

The CCRA continued to research the matter subsequent to the preliminary determination. A follow-up meeting was held with the Hong Kong Rubber and Footwear Manufacturer's Association in September 2002, during which the association indicated that none its members export subject goods to Canada. However, no written confirmation was provided.

For purposes of the preliminary determination of dumping, the Commissioner has responsibility for determining whether the actual and potential volume of dumped goods is negligible. After a preliminary determination of dumping, the Tribunal assumes this responsibility. In accordance with subsection 42(4.1) of SIMA, the Tribunal is required to terminate its inquiry in respect of any goods if the Tribunal determines that the volume of dumped goods from a country is negligible.

THE INVESTIGATION

The investigation covered subject goods shipped to Canada during the period of investigation, from January 1, 2001 to March 31, 2002.

Generally, normal values are based on the domestic selling prices of the goods in the country of export, or the total cost of the goods (cost of production, administrative, selling and all other costs), plus an amount for profit. The export price of subject goods shipped to Canada is normally the lesser of the exporter's ex-factory selling price or the importer's purchase price. When the export price is less than the normal value, the difference is the margin of dumping.

Importers

All known importers of subject goods were contacted at the initiation of the investigation and were requested to respond to a questionnaire concerning subject goods imported into Canada during the period of investigation. In response, complete submissions were received from only five importers of subject goods. Based on a lack of response to the initial request for information, the CCRA issued supplementary requests for information to all listed importers. Again, only a limited number of responses were received by the CCRA. As a result, an additional set of requests for information was sent to those importers who had previously failed to submit a complete response to the previous two CCRA requests. This was done in accordance with subsection 78(1) of SIMA, which indicates that in any investigation under SIMA, the Commissioner may require a person to provide the Commissioner, under oath or otherwise, with the evidence requested, for the purpose of facilitating the enforcement or administration of the Act.

Eight importers responded to the questionnaires sent under section 78 of SIMA, but the majority of responses were incomplete or did not provide sufficient information regarding import volumes. Thus, the CCRA was unable to use the information collected from importers of subject goods to further substantiate the import statistics for subject goods calculated at the initiation of this investigation. However, as mentioned previously, the CCRA is satisfied that the import volumes collected from the FIRM system, limited to the six relevant HS classification numbers, are an accurate representation of the actual volume of imports of subject goods.

Exporters

In view of the large number of exporters, the CCRA limited the number of exporters to be investigated pursuant to the sampling provisions outlined in subsection 30.3(1) of SIMA. A questionnaire was sent to those exporters that collectively account for a substantial quantity by volume of subject goods exported to Canada from each of the named countries during the calendar year 2001. The exporters that were sent questionnaires were considered to be mandatory respondents. Further, where a mandatory respondent was not the producer of the goods, the CCRA requested such a respondent to forward a copy of the CCRA's questionnaire to all of their unrelated producers or suppliers.

Other exporters, who were not included in the CCRA's sample, were advised of the initiation of this investigation. These exporters were advised that if they wanted to make a full voluntary submission, they could have done so by requesting a copy of the exporter questionnaire from the CCRA.

For purposes of the final determination, margins of dumping were determined in the following manner, in accordance with the provisions of Special Import Measures Regulations (SIMR) section 25.2:

• for imports from an exporter who was part of the sampling of exporters and was sent a request for information, and who has fully complied with the CCRA's request for information and permitted the verification of the information, the margins of dumping were based on the weighted average margin of dumping determined for that exporter;

- for imports from an exporter who was not part of the sampling and who did not make a submission, the margins of dumping were based on the weighted average margin of dumping for sampled exporters in the same country of export, that cooperated, as outlined in SIMR paragraph 25.2(2)(c);
- for imports from an exporter who was not part of the sampling and who did not make a submission, and who is from a country where no complete submissions were received from sampled exporters in that country, the margin of dumping was based on the weighted average margin of dumping determined for all cooperative exporters in the investigation, as outlined in SIMR paragraph 25.2(2)(c); and,
- where the CCRA was unable to determine margins of dumping because of late submissions, incomplete submissions or lack of cooperation by exporters in the sample in any of the named countries, the margin of dumping was based on the highest margin of dumping determined for the investigation, as specified by the Minister under section 29 of SIMA.

In this investigation, the Government of Vietnam and exporters in Vietnam were given the opportunity to provide information so that the Commissioner could form an opinion concerning the applicability of section 20 of SIMA to exports of subject goods. Section 20 of SIMA provides a methodology to determine normal values in respect of dumping investigations of goods exported to Canada from countries whose governments monopolize export trade and control domestic prices in the market sector being investigated.

The Government of Vietnam provided a response to the questionnaire sent by the CCRA at the initiation of the investigation. In response to the exporter questionnaire, submissions were received from one exporter in Macao, and three exporters in Vietnam. No complete responses to the exporter questionnaire were received from exporters in Hong Kong. Determinations of normal values, export prices and margins of dumping are explained in the next section.

RESULTS OF THE INVESTIGATION

Vietnam

a. Section 20 Analysis

In the past, the CCRA has considered that the Government of Vietnam retained a monopoly on its export trade and controlled domestic prices. Under such conditions, domestic market selling prices in Vietnam were not a reliable basis for determining normal values in the market sector being investigated. As such, section 20 of SIMA required that normal values be established on a surrogate country basis.

In the last few years, Vietnam has taken a number of measures to reform its economic structure, seeking to liberalize its economy. Accordingly, in this investigation, the CCRA requested information from the Vietnamese government and all exporters involved to determine whether sufficient progress had been made in economic reforms such that there is an absence of government monopoly in the export trade of waterproof footwear, or the absence of control of domestic prices in the footwear sector.

The CCRA received complete responses to its questionnaires from the Vietnamese government and three exporters in Vietnam: Lac Ty Hung Hiep Co. Ltd. (Lac Ty); Pou Yuen Enterprises Ltd. (Pou Yuen); and The General Shoes Company (General Shoes). Following a review of these submissions and publicly available information collected by the CCRA, additional information was requested from the Government of Vietnam and the exporters. As well, verification visits were held with government officials and exporters.

Meetings with the Government of Vietnam included representatives from the Vietnamese Ministry of Finance, the Ministry of Trade, the Ministry of Industry, and the Ministry of Planning and Investment.

Based on an analysis of the responses received from the government and the three cooperative exporters, and from publicly available information collected by the CCRA, as well as on information collected during the verification visits, the Commissioner is of the opinion that the Government of Vietnam does not have a monopoly or substantial monopoly over its export trade in the waterproof footwear industry. Consequently, the CCRA could now determine normal values for Vietnamese subject goods on the basis of the domestic selling prices and full costs of production, plus an amount for profit.

b. Exporters

Generally, when an exporter provides sufficient information, normal values are based on that exporter's actual domestic market selling prices, under section 15 of SIMA, or on the full cost of production of the goods plus a reasonable amount for profit, under section 19. Export prices are established on the basis of information provided by the exporter and importer.

However, none of the three Vietnamese exporters that cooperated with the CCRA have domestic market sales of subject goods. Therefore, normal values could not be determined on the basis of domestic sales under section 15 of SIMA. For one of the cooperative exporters, Pou Yuen, Vietnam, normal values were calculated under the `cost-plus' provisions of paragraph 19(b) of SIMA. Normal values for the other two Vietnamese exporters, Lac Ty and General Shoes, were determined under ministerial specification. The methodologies used to determine normal values for the three cooperative Vietnamese exporters are outlined below.

Pou Yuen Enterprise Ltd.

Normal Values—For Pou Yuen, normal values were calculated based on the total cost of production of the subject goods, plus a reasonable amount for selling and administrative expenses, plus a reasonable amount for profit, in accordance with paragraph 19(b) of SIMA.

SIMR paragraph 11(b) outlines a hierarchy of methodologies to be used in determining a reasonable amount for profit in calculating normal values under the `cost-plus' provisions of SIMA paragraph 19(b). These methods focus on using profit found for like goods or the next general category of similar goods, which have been sold in the domestic market, by that individual exporter or by another producer. For Pou Yuen, a reasonable amount for profit was found on domestic sales of component footwear parts, the category of goods next largest to the subject goods, in accordance with SIMR subparagraph 11(b)(v).

Export Price—The subject goods were sold to unrelated importers in Canada. Consequently, export prices were determined pursuant to section 24 of SIMA, based on the lesser of the exporter's selling price or importer's purchase price.

Margins of Dumping—Of the goods imported into Canada from Pou Yuen during the period of investigation, 100 per cent were dumped. The weighted average margin of dumping was equal to 10.3 per cent, expressed as a percentage of export price, with margins ranging from 4.1 per cent to 17.1 per cent.

Lac Ty Hung Hghiep Co. Ltd.

Normal Values—Lac Ty did not have sales of like goods in its domestic market on which to base normal values under section 15 of SIMA, or to determine a reasonable amount for profit in calculating normal values under section 19. In such circumstances, where the required information has not been provided or is otherwise not available, section 29 of SIMA provides for the minister to specify the manner in which normal values and export prices are to be calculated. In this case, normal values were determined by ministerial specification under section 29 of SIMA, employing a paragraph 19(b), 'cost-plus' approach. Normal values were calculated based on the sum of the cost of production of the goods, plus a reasonable amount for administrative, selling and all other costs, plus a reasonable amount for profit. A reasonable amount for profit was determined to be the company's overall profit on the production and sale of footwear.

Export Price—The subject goods were sold to unrelated importers in Canada. Consequently, export prices were determined pursuant to section 24 of SIMA, based on the lesser of the exporter's selling price or importer's purchase price.

Margins of Dumping—Of the goods imported into Canada from Lac Ty during the period of investigation, 100 per cent were dumped. The weighted average margin of dumping was equal to 34.4 per cent, expressed as a percentage of export price, with margins ranging from 6.5 per cent to 46.3 per cent.

The General Shoes Corporation

Normal Values—General Shoes did not have sales of like goods in its domestic market on which to base normal values under section 15 of SIMA, or to determine a reasonable amount for profit in calculating normal values under section 19. Thus, as with Lac Ty, normal values were determined by ministerial specification under section 29 of SIMA, employing a paragraph 19(b), 'cost-plus' approach. Normal values were calculated based on the sum of cost of production of the goods, plus a reasonable amount for administrative, selling and all other costs, plus a reasonable amount for profit. A reasonable amount for profit was determined to be the company's overall profit on the production and sale of footwear.

Export Price—The subject goods were sold to unrelated importers in Canada. Consequently, export prices were determined pursuant to section 24 of SIMA, based on the lesser of the importer's purchase price or exporter's selling price.

Margins of Dumping—Of the goods imported by General Shoes into Canada during the period of investigation, 87.8 per cent were dumped. The weighted average margin of dumping was equal to 9.7 per cent, expressed as a percentage of export price, with margins ranging from 0.4 per cent to 31.9 per cent.

Macao

Sunrise Footwear Ltd. (Sunrise) was the sole exporter from Macao that provided a complete response to the CCRA's requests for information. Verification visits were held at the offices of Sunrise's parent company, Symphony Holdings Ltd., in Hong Kong, as well as at Sunrise's facilities in Macao, during the period of July 15 to July 19, 2002.

Normal Values—As with two of the Vietnamese exporters, Sunrise did not have sales of like goods in its domestic market on which to base normal values under section 15 of SIMA, or to determine a reasonable amount for profit in calculating normal values under section 19. Thus, normal values were determined by ministerial specification under section 29 of SIMA, employing a paragraph 19(b) 'cost-plus' approach. Normal values were calculated as the aggregate of cost of production, plus a reasonable amount for administration, selling and all other costs, plus a reasonable amount for profit. The company's overall profit found on the production and sale of footwear was determined to be a reasonable amount for profit.

Export Prices—The subject goods were sold to unrelated importers in Canada. Consequently, export prices were determined pursuant to section 24 of SIMA, based on the lesser of the exporter's selling price or importer's purchase price.

Margins of Dumping Of the goods imported into Canada from Sunrise during the period of investigation, 100 per cent were dumped. The weighted average margin of dumping was 25.5 per cent, expressed as a percentage of export price, with margins ranging from 10.8 per cent to 60.8 per cent.

Hong Kong

No complete submissions were received from exporters of subject goods located in Hong Kong.

Thus, margins of dumping for exporters of subject goods in Hong Kong were determined based on information received from other exporters during the investigation, following the guidelines of the sampling provisions outlined in section 30.3 of SIMA.

For exporters of subject goods in Hong Kong that were requested to provide a complete response to the request for information, and failed to do so, the margin of dumping is 60.8 per cent. This is equal to the highest margin of dumping found for a cooperative exporter in the investigation, as authorized by the ministerial specification granted under section 29 of SIMA, where the CCRA was unable to determine margins of dumping because of lack of cooperation of sampled exporters in the country.

For exporters in Hong Kong that were not requested to provide a complete response to the request for information, the margins of dumping were based on the weighted average margin of dumping for sampled exporters in the investigation, that cooperated, in accordance with SIMR subsection 25.2(1).

Other Exporters

The treatment of imports of subject goods from exporters in countries other than Hong Kong, including Vietnam and Macao, who did not respond to the CCRA's request for information is also based on section 30.3 of SIMA, which is used to determine margins of dumping for other exporters when sampling techniques are employed. For non-sampled exporters who did not provide a response, margins of dumping are equal to the weighted average margin of dumping for sampled exporters in that country, pursuant to SIMR paragraph 25.2(2)(c).

For non-sampled exporters in a country where no submissions were received in order to determine a weighted average margin of dumping for that country, margins of dumping are equal to the weighted average margin of dumping for sampled exporters in the investigation, that cooperated. This is done in accordance with SIMR subsection 25.2(1).

Summary

During the period of investigation, 100 per cent of the subject goods imported into Canada from Hong Kong were dumped by a weighted average margin of dumping of 51.5 per cent; 100 per cent of the subject goods imported into Canada from Macao were dumped by a weighted average margin of dumping of 25.5 per cent; and 98.4 per cent of the subject goods imported into Canada from Vietnam were dumped by a weighted average margin of dumping of 30.9 per cent. All margins of dumping are expressed as a percentage of export price. Overall, 99.2 per cent of the subject goods imported into Canada during the investigation were dumped by a weighted average margin of dumping of 29.4 per cent, when expressed as a percentage of export price.

In making a final determination of dumping, the Commissioner must be satisfied that the subject goods have been dumped and that the margin of dumping is not insignificant. Subsection 2(1) of SIMA stipulates that the margin of dumping is insignificant if it is less than 2 per cent of the export price of the goods. As indicated in Appendix 2, the margin of dumping for the total imports of subject goods is above the 2 per cent threshold.

DECISION

Based on the results of the investigation, the Commissioner is satisfied that the subject goods originating in or exported from Hong Kong, Macao, and Vietnam have been dumped, and that the margin of dumping is not insignificant.

Accordingly, on December 9, 2002, the Commissioner has made a final determination of dumping pursuant to paragraph 41(1)(a) of SIMA.

… … …

(ii) Injury

In addition to a product being introduced into the market of another country for less than normal value, an affirmative finding of 'injury' to the domestic industry is also necessary in order to impose anti-dumping measures. Thus, it is not 'dumping' by itself that is at issue, but rather 'injurious dumping'. The rules on injury determinations are set out in Article 3 of the Anti-Dumping Agreement.

According to the Anti-Dumping Agreement, 'injury' means either: (1) material injury to a domestic industry; (2) threat of material injury to a domestic industry; or (3) material retardation of the establishment of a domestic industry.[14] In a layperson's terms, the question is whether the dumped imports cause, or may soon cause, some degree of economic harm to the domestic industry. The Agreement provides further clarification and guidance on the meaning and consideration of injury, as follows.

At the outset, Article 3.1 of the Anti-Dumping Agreement provides the basic guiding principle of an injury determination, stating that a determination of injury must be:

> based on positive evidence and involve an objective examination of both *(a)* the *volume* of the dumped imports and the *effect* of the dumped imports on prices in the domestic market for like products, and *(b)* the consequent *impact* of these imports on domestic producers of such products [emphasis added].

In *Thailand—H-Beams*, the Appellate Body referred to Article 3.1 as the 'overarching provision that sets forth a Member's fundamental, substantive obligation [with respect to the determination of injury]' and 'informs the more detailed obligations in succeeding paragraphs'.[15]

In a sense, Article 3.1 is a procedural requirement, establishing how investigating authorities must consider the substantive issues, requiring that investigating authorities base their determinations on 'positive evidence' and that they conduct an 'objective examination'. In *US—Hot Rolled Steel*, the Appellate Body held that the term 'positive evidence' relates to the 'quality of the evidence that authorities may rely upon in making a determination'. Further defining the term 'positive', the Appellate Body

---

[14] Anti-Dumping Agreement, n 9.
[15] Appellate Body Report, *Thailand—H-Beams*, para 106.

stated that 'the evidence must be of an affirmative, objective and verifiable character, and that it must be credible'.[16] In terms of an 'objective examination', the Appellate Body said that this term 'aims at a different aspect of the investigating authorities' determination', stating:

> 193. While the term "positive evidence" focuses on the facts underpinning and justifying the injury determination, the term "objective examination" is concerned with the investigative process itself. The word "examination" relates, in our view, to the way in which the evidence is gathered, inquired into and, subsequently, evaluated; that is, it relates to the conduct of the investigation generally. The word "objective", which qualifies the word "examination", indicates essentially that the "examination" process must conform to the dictates of the basic principles of good faith and fundamental fairness. In short, an "objective examination" requires that the domestic industry, and the effects of dumped imports, be investigated in an unbiased manner, without favouring the interests of any interested party, or group of interested parties, in the investigation. The duty of the investigating authorities to conduct an "objective examination" recognizes that the determination will be influenced by the objectivity, or any lack thereof, of the investigative process.

Thus, in order to comply with the 'objective examination' component of Article 3.1, investigating authorities must identify, investigate and evaluate all the relevant factors taken into account in an even-handed manner.

We turn now to some of the key substantive aspects of the injury standard. With regard to the volume of the dumped imports, Article 3.2 of the Anti-Dumping Agreement elaborates on the general Article 3.1 obligation. Article 3.2 directs investigating authorities to consider whether there has been a *significant increase* in dumped imports, either in absolute terms or relative to production or consumption in the importing Member. Thus, the increase can be in absolute terms (increase in quantity) or in relative terms (same quantity but there is a reduction in domestic production, thus increasing the market share of the imports). Moreover, investigating authorities also are directed to look at the effect of the dumped imports on prices by considering whether there has been *significant price undercutting* by the dumped imports as compared with the price of a like product of the importing Member, or whether the effect of such imports is otherwise to depress domestic prices to a significant degree or prevent domestic price increases, which otherwise would have occurred, to a significant degree.

Article 3.4 elaborates on what factors an investigating authority may consider in relation to the 'impact of the dumped imports on the domestic industry':

> The examination of the impact of the dumped imports on the domestic industry concerned shall include an evaluation of *all relevant economic factors* and indices having a bearing on the state of the industry, *including* actual and potential decline in sales, profits, output, market share, productivity, return on investments, or utilization of capacity; factors affecting domestic prices; the magnitude of the margin of dumping; actual and potential negative effects on cash flow, inventories, employment, wages, growth, ability to raise capital or investments. This list is *not exhaustive*, nor can one or several of these factors necessarily give decisive guidance.

Based on this provision, investigating authorities are given wide scope to consider relevant economic factors and indices affecting the domestic industry. In practice, the factors listed in Article 3.4 have been interpreted to be a minimum standard, meaning

---

[16] Appellate Body Report, *US—Hot-Rolled Steel from Japan*, para 192.

that investigating authorities must, at the very least, collect, interpret and analyse data relating to each of the enumerated factors. In addition, though, Article 3.4 mandates investigating authorities to collect, interpret and evaluate data relating to all other relevant factors and indices having a bearing on the state of the domestic industry. As the panel in *Thailand—H-Beams* stated:

> 7.225 We note Thailand's argument that the list of factors in Article 3.4 is illustrative only, and that no change in meaning was intended in the change in drafting from the "such as" that appeared in the corresponding provision in the Tokyo Round Antidumping Code to the "including" that now appears in Article 3.4 of the AD Agreement. The term "such as" is defined as "[o]f the kind, degree, category being or about to be specified" . . . "for example". By contrast, the verb "include" is defined to mean "enclose"; "contain as part of a whole or as a subordinate element; contain by implication, involve"; or "place in a class or category; treat or regard as part of a whole". We thus read the Article 3.4 phrase "shall include an evaluation of all relevant factors and indices having a bearing on the state of the industry, including . . ." as introducing a mandatory list of relevant factors which must be evaluated in every case. We are of the view that the change that occurred in the wording of the relevant provision during the Uruguay Round (from "such as" to "including") was made for a reason and that it supports an interpretation of the current text of Article 3.4 as setting forth a list that is not merely indicative or illustrative, but, rather, mandatory. Furthermore, we recall that the second sentence of Article 3.4 states: "This list is not exhaustive, nor can one or several of these factors necessarily give decisive guidance." Thus, in a given case, certain factors may be more relevant than others, and the weight to be attributed to any given factor may vary from case to case. Moreover, there may be other relevant economic factors in the circumstances of a particular case, consideration of which would also be required.[17]

To illustrate how domestic agencies conduct an injury analysis, we provide an extract of an injury decision by the Canadian International Trade Tribunal:

WATERPROOF FOOTWEAR AND WATERPROOF FOOTWEAR BOTTOMS ORIGINATING IN OR EXPORTED FROM HONG KONG, CHINA; MACAO, CHINA; AND VIETNAM

Inquiry No. NQ-2002-002

Injury

Pursuant to section 42 of SIMA, the Tribunal is required to "make inquiry . . . as to whether the dumping . . . of [waterproof footwear and bottoms] . . . has caused injury or retardation or is threatening to cause injury". Injury is defined in subsection 2(1) as "material injury to a domestic industry".

Subsection 37.1(1) of the Special Import Measures Regulations prescribes certain factors that the Tribunal may consider in determining whether the dumping of goods has caused material injury to the domestic industry. These factors include the volume of dumped goods, their effect on prices in the domestic market for like goods and the impact of the dumped goods on the domestic industry, including actual or potential declines in domestic sales, market share, profits and financial performance. Subsection 37.1(3) of the Regulations also requires the Tribunal to consider other factors not related to the dumping to ensure that any injury caused by those other factors is not attributed to the dumped imports.

---

[17] Panel Report, *Thailand—H-Beams*, paras 7.224–7.225.

Background

The Tribunal notes that the train of events that preceded the emergence, in 2001, of imports of the subject goods from Macao and Vietnam began in July 2000, when Kaufman, one of the oldest and best-known Canadian producers of waterproof footwear, declared bankruptcy. Over its long history, Kaufman had been a major producer of waterproof footwear and owned one of the most recognized brands in this footwear category, namely, Sorel. According to the evidence, sales of the Sorel brand comprised the overwhelming majority of Kaufman's total sales of waterproof footwear.

In September 2000, Columbia acquired the Sorel trademark and associated intellectual property rights from Kaufman's receiver in bankruptcy for a sum of about $12 million. Columbia is a vendor of various brand-name products, including apparel and footwear and, generally, the goods that it markets are manufactured by others under supply arrangements. This is also the case for the subject goods. Having acquired the Sorel trademark, Columbia had to decide where to source its supply of Sorel products. This decision pertained to supply for the 2001 winter season and thereafter, as, by September 2000, there was too little time to bring Columbia's Sorel products to market for the 2000 winter season.

After considering its options, Columbia decided to source its supply of Sorel products for the Canadian market entirely from Macao and Vietnam. This decision is reflected in the data collected by the Tribunal. In 2001 and 2002 to date, the vast majority of the subject goods imported from Macao and Vietnam were imported by Columbia. Furthermore, most of the subject goods from these two sources are comprised of Sorel winter waterproof footwear.

Against the foregoing background, SMAC has focused its claims of injury on the importation of Sorel waterproof footwear by Columbia from Macao and Vietnam, in 2001 and thereafter. More particularly, SMAC claims that the volume of subject goods from these two sources is substantial, that the prices at which Sorel footwear is being sold are both depressing and suppressing domestic prices and that, as a consequence, the domestic industry has suffered injury.

Volume of Subject Goods

According to both industry and retailer witnesses, Kaufman had been expecting to produce and deliver Sorel boots that had been ordered by its customers for the 2000 winter season right up until the time of its bankruptcy in July 2000. However, as a result of the financial difficulties that ultimately resulted in its bankruptcy, Kaufman was unable to produce Sorel or any other waterproof footwear for the 2000 winter season. When it became clear that Kaufman could not deliver, there was confusion in the market, as both retailers and domestic suppliers scrambled to fill the void.

According to the evidence, Sears was able to arrange for a supply of some Sorel products to be manufactured by a domestic producer under a licensing arrangement with Kaufman's receiver in bankruptcy. In addition, there were some Sorel boots available in 2000 from Kaufman's inventory of 1999 production. However, overall, the demand for Sorel boots in 2000 could not be met, according to the evidence.

As a result, going into 2001, domestic retailers were quite anxious to have a supply of the Sorel brand for their customers. Many of these retailers had offered Sorel winter waterproof footwear to their customers for years and considered it to be a "must have" item for their shelves. Indeed, according to several retailer witnesses, the Sorel brand had very strong customer loyalty and, frequently, shoppers asked specifically for it. In the view of one major retailer witness, customers were indifferent to, or unaware of, where the Sorel products were made. The brand name and its quality are what drew customers to Sorel products.

Given the foregoing, in the Tribunal's opinion, it is not surprising that, when Sorel products again became available from Columbia in 2001 through imports from Macao and Vietnam, Columbia quickly captured a certain percentage of the Canadian waterproof footwear market. This simply reflected the strong pent-up demand for the Sorel brand.

In the Tribunal's opinion, the market share captured by Columbia from imports of the subject goods, in 2001, must be evaluated in light of the historical market share held by Kaufman. In this regard, the evidence shows that, in Kaufman's last year of production, 1999, it held somewhere between 10 and 15 percent of the total Canadian market for waterproof footwear, driven in large part by sales of Sorel products. Against this benchmark, the share of the Canadian market captured by the Sorel brand under Columbia, in 2001, fell considerably short of its historical place in the market.

The Tribunal notes that, given the timing of this inquiry, data on imports of the subject goods for all of 2002 were not available. However, as part of a pricing survey conducted in November 2002, the Tribunal's staff gathered information on sales of major Sorel products and of domestic styles that compete with Sorel products. This survey indicates that Columbia's sales volumes of major Sorel styles were proceeding at about the same pace in 2002 as in 2001. This suggests to the Tribunal that the return of Sorel products to the market in 2001 filled the void created by Kaufman's bankruptcy and that the current demand for Sorel products is being met in a stable, measured and orderly manner.

The Tribunal also notes that Columbia has refocused its approach to the market by reducing the number of Sorel styles that it is selling in Canada from the number that was sold by Kaufman and that these styles are being marketed to a much narrower range of retailers. The evidence also shows that major Kaufman accounts have been dropped because Columbia felt that they would not represent the premium nature of the Sorel brand and that, of the Kaufman accounts that were kept, Columbia is currently doing a smaller volume of business compared to that of Kaufman. All these steps support Columbia's assertion that it has taken a responsible approach to marketing the Sorel brand in Canada following its acquisition from Kaufman.

Accordingly, the Tribunal does not find that there has been an increase in the volume of imports of the subject goods, such that it caused injury to the domestic industry.

Prices

The Tribunal notes that the evidence submitted in this case shows that, in 2001, Columbia reduced the suggested retail price for several Sorel styles from the levels that were established by Kaufman in the price lists that it published in 1999 for the 2000 winter season. SMAC argued that the domestic industry had to reduce the prices of its competing brands and that this caused injury. Columbia argued that Kaufman's wholesale and suggested retail prices were, for some Sorel styles, unrealistically high and that it adjusted them accordingly. Columbia further argued that Sorel is a premium brand that is not priced in relation to, and is not a cause of any price erosion or suppression of, domestic brands.

In addressing these claims and counterclaims, the Tribunal will first examine the issue of whether Kaufman's price lists for the 2000 winter season are an appropriate benchmark for evaluating Columbia's pricing decisions in 2001. In this connection, the Tribunal notes that four major retailers testified at the inquiry, two called by Columbia, and two by the Tribunal. Three of these witnesses testified that some of Kaufman's Sorel styles typically sold in their stores at lower than Kaufman's suggested retail prices. In fact, one witness testified that it was common knowledge among retailers that Kaufman's suggested retail prices were high and that most retailers had communicated their concerns on this matter to the manufacturer over the years.

In the Tribunal's estimation, the testimony of these witnesses fully supports Columbia's explanation for the price reductions that it made on certain Sorel styles in 2001 and why the corresponding wholesale prices were reduced to make room for the "keystone" retail margin that Columbia aims to provide for its customers. In the Tribunal's opinion, Columbia's price adjustments in 2001 were appropriate in the circumstances and based on sound business practice. Further, the Tribunal is not persuaded that these adjustments were disruptive to domestic pricing, as claimed by the industry. Columbia brought its price structure into conformity with the actual retail prices that the market had already established, in prior years, for the relevant Sorel styles produced by Kaufman. This means that the industry would have had to compete in relation to these actual retail prices before Columbia ever entered the picture.

In the Tribunal's opinion, there is another factor that makes it problematic to compare Kaufman's 2000 prices with Columbia's 2001 prices. Although Kaufman declared bankruptcy in July 2000, it is clear from the evidence that this was preceded by a number of major financial and other difficulties that had played out for a number of years prior to the actual bankruptcy. Accordingly, the reliability of Kaufman's pricing strategy in 2000 is open to question.

However, regardless of how realistic Kaufman's Sorel prices were or why Columbia decided to lower certain of those prices, there is the question of how closely related the prices of Sorel waterproof footwear are to prices of domestic brands. On this point, the Tribunal finds the testimony of the retailer witnesses, whose combined sales of waterproof footwear, including Sorel and domestic brands, comprise a substantial proportion of the Canadian market, to be clear, consistent and compelling. The witnesses testified that Sorel was a premium brand that was generally a best-in-class line of winter waterproof footwear. They also maintained that, when buying Sorel products for their stores, the Sorel name and its reputation for quality and reliability were more important considerations than price. In this regard, one of the witnesses testified that, on a scale of 1 (least important) to 10 (most important), the pricing of Sorel products rated only 5 in terms of its importance to the purchase decisions made in that retailer's stores.

Further, the retailer witnesses, each of whose stores carried both the Sorel brand and various domestic brands of waterproof footwear, affirmed that the price that they paid for Sorel products had no effect on the price that they paid for domestic brands. In elaborating on this point, one witness testified that, in considering and comparing Sorel prices, the retailer was more concerned with the pricing of Sorel products by its major competitor than with the pricing of domestic brands within its own stores. In the witness's view, the price of a Sorel product could be reduced without necessarily affecting the price of domestic brands.

In sum, in the Tribunal's estimation, the testimony of these witnesses was unanimous that there was not a close relationship between Sorel prices and the prices of domestic brands. The weakness of this link is also evident in the data on prices collected by the Tribunal's staff in the course of the inquiry. More particularly, at the most aggregated level, the data show that average domestic prices for rubber waterproof footwear rose in each year of the period reviewed. The average price of imports of the subject goods from Macao and Vietnam also rose from 2001 through the first half of 2002, but it was about twice as high as average domestic prices. At a more disaggregated level, the Tribunal compared prices for similar categories of winter waterproof footwear, such as children's rubber or TPR bottom boots with fabric uppers, a high volume category for both the domestic industry and Columbia. In all the categories examined, the cumulated average sales values for imports of the subject goods are above corresponding average domestic values. As well, cumulated average import values are increasing, while average domestic values are declining somewhat.

At the most specific and disaggregated level, the Tribunal's staff conducted the survey, cited earlier, of the prices of various styles of Sorel and domestic brands of waterproof footwear.

This survey requested Columbia and the domestic producers to identify their top selling competing styles and to provide the volume and value of sales for each one. The survey shows that Columbia's average unit prices rose consistently, from 2001 to 2002, for all Sorel styles that were reported. These results are consistent with evidence submitted by Columbia that its wholesale prices either increased or remained stable in 2002 for all but one of its styles, which accounted for only 64 pairs. In contrast, the prices of some competing domestic brands rose, while others fell over the same two-year period. In addition, over the three-year period starting in 2000, the study shows that the prices of some competing domestic styles rose each year, some fell each year, and others showed no consistent pattern of rising or falling.

Furthermore, according to the survey, in some cases, the Sorel style is the most expensive product among the competing styles, while, in other cases, a domestic style is the highest-priced item. Moreover, the absolute difference in price between a particular Sorel style and corresponding domestic styles is, in some cases, quite large. Indeed, in general, the overall range of prices between the highest-priced item and the lowest-priced item, among the competing styles, is quite substantial. This suggests to the Tribunal that, even with so-called "competing styles", the different prices between the various Sorel styles and the domestic styles reflect substantial product differentiation. In sum, on the basis of the evidence, the Tribunal can find no apparent correlation between Sorel prices and domestic prices nor can it conclude that the subject goods that are imported from Macao and Vietnam, have undercut, depressed or even suppressed the pricing of like goods by the domestic industry.

Impact on the Industry

The Tribunal's view that the volumes and prices of the subject goods from Macao and Vietnam have not injured the domestic industry is reinforced when the performance of the domestic industry is examined. In this connection, the evidence shows that the industry's production of like goods rose steadily in each full year of the period reviewed and was some 20 percent higher in 2001 than it was in 1999. Its share of the domestic market was up by 6 percentage points, sales volumes by some 10 percent, and sales values by about 15 percent, over the same three-year period. The volume and value of the industry's exports were both higher by almost 30 percent in 2001 compared to 1999.

Further, the industry's combined financial statement shows that its average unit value of net domestic sales has risen each year since 1999. In terms of its domestic business, the industry operated at reasonable levels of profitability in 2000 and 2001 compared to 1999, when it operated at a loss. Interim results for 2001 and 2002 suggest continued profitability for 2002. Export sales were also profitable throughout the period. Employment, hours worked, capacity utilization and investments were all higher in 2001 than they were in 1999.

In short, virtually all the industry's key performance indicators showed improvements in 2000 and 2001 and, in some cases, the improvements were substantial. Moreover, this strong performance was achieved despite what several industry and retailer witnesses described as relatively poor selling seasons in 2000 and again in 2001 because of the late and mild winter conditions that prevailed. This evidence suggests to the Tribunal that the industry has, in fact, been a net beneficiary of Kaufman's demise in 2000. Indeed, the aggregate market data indicate that the industry captured a certain portion of the market that became available with Kaufman's disappearance in 2000. Although the industry appears to have given back some of its gains following the re-introduction of the Sorel brand under Columbia in 2001, the industry continues to hold a substantial proportion of the market share that it initially captured.

In the Tribunal's opinion, the fact that the industry has been able to retain some of Kaufman's former market share is, in some measure, related to Columbia's decision to sell fewer Sorel styles to fewer customers within a narrower and more focused premium brand marketing strategy than that of Kaufman.

The Tribunal notes that, in support of their case, three of the six domestic producers have made injury allegations at specific accounts. The Tribunal has examined the evidence pertaining to these allegations and does not find it to be persuasive. In one case, the evidence indicates that an alleged lost sale was the result of competition between two domestic producers, not with Columbia. In another case, the evidence indicates that some repeat business was not given to a domestic producer because of certain quality concerns.

One of SMAC's principal allegations of lost sales concerned Columbia's decision to have Sorel boots manufactured in Macao and Vietnam rather than by Rallye, which produced them for Sears in 2000. The Tribunal notes that Rallye produced the Sorel boots for Sears, in 2000, under an agreement with the receiver in bankruptcy that held the rights to the trademark at the time. Once the trademark was sold to Columbia, Columbia was under no obligation to continue the arrangement with Rallye, and its decision to have the Sorel boots manufactured in Macao and Vietnam was made for its own corporate reasons. Under the circumstances, the Tribunal does not see this as a lost sale, since Rallye had no right to produce the goods.

More generally, many of the allegations lack relevant details about competing Sorel products and prices. Others appear erroneous, as they allege injury at accounts to which Columbia does not sell waterproof footwear. In other cases, they refer to lost sales at accounts where the industry had never sold its products.

The Tribunal notes that, as further evidence of the injury that the industry was experiencing, SMAC has alluded to the fact that some domestic producers are importing uppers to reduce their costs of production and that, in one case, a producer has begun importing some waterproof footwear in lieu of producing it domestically. According to SMAC, domestic producers have also been injured by reason of the fact that they have had to add more features to their products to compete with the Sorel brand. In the Tribunal's estimation, none of these developments are proof of injury. In the Tribunal's view, the industry's decision to import finished footwear or certain components is consistent with a rationalization and more efficient use of its factors of production that renders it more competitive and more immune to injury. As for the "bells and whistles" that domestic producers may have had to add to their brands to compete with premium-priced Sorel products, this, in the Tribunal's opinion, is a reflection of the strength of the Sorel brand.

In sum, the Tribunal concludes from the evidence provided that the industry, as a whole, was not injured by the subject goods over the period reviewed.

… … …

As noted, an injury determination can be based not just on material injury but also on a 'threat' of material injury. Such determinations are inherently speculative, as, by definition, no injury is actually occurring. Rather, the determination is based on a prediction that injury will occur in the future.

Article 3.7 of the Anti-Dumping Agreement provides that a determination of a threat of material injury shall be *based on facts and not merely on allegation*, conjecture or remote possibility. In addition, the change in circumstances which would create a situation in which the dumping would cause injury must be *clearly foreseen and imminent*. Furthermore, the authorities should consider, inter alia, such factors as:

(i) a significant rate of increase of dumped imports into the domestic market indicating the likelihood of substantially increased importation;

(ii) sufficient freely disposable, or an imminent, substantial increase in, capacity of the exporter indicating the likelihood of substantially increased dumped exports to the importing Member's market, taking into account the availability of other export markets to absorb any additional exports;

(iii) whether imports are entering at prices that will have a significant depressing or suppressing effect on domestic prices, and would be likely to increase demand for further imports; and

(iv) inventories of the product being investigated.

No one of these factors by itself can necessarily give decisive guidance. Instead, according to Article 3.7, the totality of the factors considered must lead to the conclusion that further dumped exports are imminent and that, unless protective action is taken, material injury will occur. In addition, in *Mexico—HFCS*, the panel agreed with an argument by the United States that, in reaching a determination that a threat of material injury exists, an investigating authority must consider not only the factors set out in Article 3.7, but also the factors listed in Article 3.4 governing 'injury' that are relevant to the particular determination.[18]

(iii) Causation

Article 3.5 of the Anti-Dumping Agreement requires that in order for there to be a positive determination of dumping, the dumped imports must, through the effects of dumping, *cause* 'injury'. This provision states:

> It must be demonstrated that the dumped imports are, through the effects of dumping, as set forth in paragraphs 2 and 4, causing injury within the meaning of this Agreement. The demonstration of a causal relationship between the dumped imports and the injury to the domestic industry shall be based on an examination of all relevant evidence before the authorities. The authorities shall also examine any known factors other than the dumped imports which at the same time are injuring the domestic industry, and the injuries caused by these other factors must not be attributed to the dumped imports. Factors which may be relevant in this respect include, *inter alia*, the volume and prices of imports not sold at dumping prices, contraction in demand or changes in the patterns of consumption, trade restrictive practices of and competition between the foreign and domestic producers, developments in technology and the export performance and productivity of the domestic industry.

Thus, the first element of a causation analysis is the demonstration of a causal relationship between the dumped imports and the injury to the domestic industry. There are various different possibilities in terms of the degree of causation required: *more than* de minimis cause; *important* cause; *principal* cause; *substantial* cause; *significant* cause and *sole* or *exclusive* cause. However, the specific degree is not stated in the agreement. In the context of safeguards, discussed in Chapter 12 below, the Appellate Body has rejected the 'exclusive' cause standard, explaining the term 'causal link' (the term used in the Safeguards Agreement) as follows:

> the term "the causal link" denotes, in our view, a relationship of cause and effect such that increased imports contribute to "bringing about", "producing" or "inducing" the serious injury. Although that contribution must be sufficiently clear as to establish the existence of "the causal

---

[18] Panel Report, *Mexico—HFCS*, paras 7.124–7.131.

link" required, the language in the first sentence of Article 4.2(b) does *not* suggest that increased imports be *the sole* cause of the serious injury, or that "*other* factors" causing injury must be excluded from the determination of serious injury. To the contrary, the language of Article 4.2(b), as a whole, suggests that "the causal link" between increased imports and serious injury may exist, *even though other factors are also contributing, "at the same time", to the situation of the domestic industry.*

...

... the competent authorities determine, as a final step, whether "the causal link" exists between increased imports and serious injury, and whether this causal link involves a genuine and substantial relationship of cause and effect between these two elements, ...[19]

Thus, in the context of the Safeguards Agreement causation is to be determined through a vaguely defined 'genuine and substantial relationship of cause and effect' standard. The specific causation language of the Anti-Dumping Agreement differs from that of the Safeguards Agreement, of course, but nevertheless it informs the analysis. While the Appellate Body has not had occasion to examine the anti-dumping causation standard in detail, it did recently criticise a panel because the panel 'did not examine whether the [investigating authority] identified and explained the positive evidence establishing a genuine and substantial relationship of cause and effect between imports and threat of injury'.[20]

Finally, Article 3.5 also establishes a 'non-attribution' requirement, under which the investigating authority must examine other possible causes of the injury that exists in order to make sure that the injury is not more properly attributed to these other causes. That is, investigating authorities must examine all other known causes of injury to the domestic injury and must separate out the injury caused by those other causes. The Appellate Body, in *US—Hot Rolled Steel from Japan*, has explained:

223. The non-attribution language in Article 3.5 of the *Anti-Dumping Agreement* applies solely in situations where dumped imports and other known factors are causing injury to the domestic industry *at the same time*. In order that investigating authorities, applying Article 3.5, are able to ensure that the injurious effects of the other known factors are not "attributed" to dumped imports, they must appropriately assess the injurious effects of those other factors. Logically, such an assessment must involve separating and distinguishing the injurious effects of the other factors from the injurious effects of the dumped imports. If the injurious effects of the dumped imports are not appropriately separated and distinguished from the injurious effects of the other factors, the authorities will be unable to conclude that the injury they ascribe to dumped imports is actually caused by those imports, rather than by the other factors. Thus, in the absence of such separation and distinction of the different injurious effects, the investigating authorities would have no rational basis to conclude that the dumped imports are indeed causing the injury which, under the *Anti-Dumping Agreement*, justifies the imposition of anti-dumping duties.

This process of 'separating and distinguishing' other factors that have caused injury serves to ensure that the role of dumped imports as a causal factor reaches a certain degree by removing the effects of any other causes from the equation.

We now turn to the rules for the imposition of anti-dumping measures.

---

[19] Appellate Body Report, *US—Wheat Gluten*, paras 67 and 69.
[20] Appellate Body Report, *US—Lumber ITC Investigation ('Softwood LumberVI'), Article 21.5*, para 132.

IV. ANTI-DUMPING MEASURES

After an affirmative finding of dumping, injury and causation, an investigating authority may impose anti-dumping measures in the form of higher tariff duties. We discuss several issues relating to these measures. In this regard, we examine: (1) provisional measures; (2) price undertakings; (3) the imposition and collection of duties; (4) the duration and review of duties; and (5) the use of anti-dumping measures other than increased tariff duties.

(a) Provisional Measures

Article 7 of the Anti-Dumping Agreement permits the imposition of 'provisional' anti-dumping duties. The goal of provisional measures is to ensure payment of anti-dumping duties on goods that are imported during an investigation. Before an affirmative anti-dumping determination has been made, anti-dumping duties cannot be collected. However, after the determination, duties can be collected on imported goods which have entered the country for a defined period prior to the determination (only in situations where injury, as opposed to threat, has been found, though). Provisional measures make sure these duties can be collected by imposing a provisional duty or, 'preferably', a security—by cash deposit or bond—equal to an estimated amount of the anti-dumping duty.[21]

Provisional measures put importers on notice that imports after a certain date may be subject to anti-dumping duties. The imposition of such measures prevents importers from trying to increase sales significantly prior to the determination, in an effort to avoid anti-dumping duties. There is an additional mechanism that allows for collection of duties prior to the date of the provisional measures in certain circumstances.[22]

(b) Price Undertakings

As an alternative to anti-dumping measures, Article 8 of the Anti-Dumping Agreement provides for the possibility of voluntary undertakings from exporters to increase export prices or otherwise to cease dumping. The reason the Anti-Dumping Agreement allows such a remedy is simple: anti-dumping investigations are costly and burdensome to exporters, the domestic industry and the investigating authority. As a result, negotiated settlements between the parties can save time and resources.

Investigating authorities can only seek or accept a price undertaking from exporters following a preliminary affirmative determination of dumping and injury. If the undertaking is accepted, a Member cannot under normal circumstances simultaneously continue anti-dumping proceedings alongside the implementation of price undertakings. The investigation is therefore suspended.

If an undertaking is accepted, the exporter can request, or the authorities can decide on their own, that the investigation of dumping and injury be completed. Normally, if a negative determination of dumping or injury is made, the price undertaking has no effect. In addition, the authorities can require exporters to provide periodic information relating

---

[21] Art 7.2 of the Anti-Dumping Agreement.
[22] *Ibid*, Art 10.6.

to the fulfilment of the undertaking and, if the terms of the price undertaking are violated, the investigating authorities may resume the investigation and may be able immediately to impose provisional measures.[23]

(c) Imposition and Collection of Duties

When an affirmative final determination is made by the investigating authorities, it means that anti-dumping duties will be imposed and collected. Article 9 of the Anti-Dumping Agreement provides the rules and procedures in this regard. At the outset, the provision explains that the decision whether to impose anti-dumping duties, even where the requirements for the imposition have been fulfilled, is left to the discretion of the investigating authorities of the importing Member. In other words, the imposition of such duties is optional. Furthermore, Article 9 states that it is 'desirable' that the imposed duty be less than the margin if such lesser duty would be adequate to remove the injury to the domestic industry. Some Members' domestic laws follow this rule, whereas others do not.

According to Article 9.3, the amount of the anti-dumping duty cannot exceed the margin of dumping. The provision establishes rules for two separate duty collection methods: retrospective and prospective. While the various methods used vary across systems, generally speaking they work as follows. In a retrospective system, dumping margins are calculated for a period that has passed already, with the calculation based on actual export sales during that period as compared to normal value for actual comparison sales. Duties are then assessed on those actual sales in the amount of the dumping margin. New assessment proceedings are then conducted for future periods. The US uses a retrospective system. By contrast, in a prospective system like that of the EC, the dumping margin is first calculated based on a specific period. This margin is then applied (prospectively) to future imports, with the duties assessed on such imports at this rate. Provided that the importer requests a review, refunds are possible for duties collected above the appropriate rate.

Anti-dumping investigations often involve multiple foreign producers/importers. Investigating authorities must generally determine an individual margin of dumping for each known exporter or producer concerned of the product under investigation.[24] However, the Agreement recognises that individual determinations may be impractical in cases where the number of exporters, producers, importers or types of products involved is large.[25] In such a circumstance, the investigating authorities may limit their examination either to a reasonable number of interested parties or products by using statistically valid samples based on information available at the time of the selection, or to the largest percentage of the volume of the exports from the country in question which can reasonably be investigated.[26] Anti-dumping duties are then imposed on uninvestigated sources on the basis of the weighted average margin of dumping established for the investigated (selected) exporters or producers (the so-called 'all others' rate). However, the investigating authorities must calculate individual duties or normal values (margins) for any

---

[23] *Ibid*, Art 8.6.
[24] *Ibid*, Art 6.10.
[25] *Ibid*.
[26] *Ibid*.

exporter or producer who provides the necessary information during the course of the investigation.[27]

(d) Duration and Review of Duties

As noted, anti-dumping investigations cover only a specific period. Over time, circumstances may change, in terms of both dumping and injury. As a result, new determinations may need to be made. Article 11 sets out a number of rules in this regard.

Article 11.1 of the Anti-Dumping Agreement establishes the general rule that '[a]n anti-dumping duty shall remain in force only as long as and to the extent necessary to counteract dumping which is causing injury'.[28] Article 11.2 then provides more specific obligations:

> The authorities shall review the need for the continued imposition of the duty, where warranted, on their own initiative or, provided that a reasonable period of time has elapsed since the imposition of the definitive anti-dumping duty, upon request by any interested party which submits positive information substantiating the need for a review. Interested parties shall have the right to request the authorities to examine whether the continued imposition of the duty is necessary to offset dumping, whether the injury would be likely to continue or recur if the duty were removed or varied, or both. If, as a result of the review under this paragraph, the authorities determine that the anti-dumping duty is no longer warranted, it shall be terminated immediately.

Under this provision, the investigating authorities and interested parties can request reviews of the determination. Exporters and foreign producers are likely to request a review if they believe they can prove that they are no longer dumping or injury no longer exists. This is the most common type of review. In addition, the domestic industry may request a review if it believes the dumping margin has increased.

Article 11.3 provides for 'five year' or 'sunset' reviews. Under this provision, duties will terminate five years after imposition unless a review is conducted and a determination is made that 'the expiry of the duty would be likely to lead to continuation or recurrence of dumping and injury'. In theory, this provision helps to eliminate anti-dumping duties that are no longer necessary or desired by the domestic industry. In practice, though, duties have not often been revoked under this provision, as a likelihood of continuation or recurrence is usually found.

(e) The Use of Anti-dumping Measures Other than Tariff Duties

The Anti-Dumping Agreement rules discussed above set out requirements for imposing tariff duties as a response to dumping. But can measures other than duties be taken against dumping? In *US—1916 Act*, there was a claim against an old and little used US law that imposed criminal and civil penalties using a different legal standard for dumping from those described above. The US argued that 'Article VI of the GATT 1994 regulates only the imposition of anti-dumping duties and does not apply to other measures taken to counteract dumping'. In this regard, the US noted that Article VI:2 states that Members '*may* levy on any dumped product an anti-dumping duty' (emphasis added). The US contended that 'the verb "may" indicates that while Members "may" choose to impose

---

[27] For further details see Appellate Body Report, *US—Hot Rolled Steel from Japan*, para 126.
[28] Panel Report, *US—DRAMS*, para 6.42

anti-dumping duties and thereby be bound by the rules of Article VI, Members may also choose to impose other types of anti-dumping measures, in which case they are not bound by the rules of Article VI'.[29] The Appellate Body rejected this view, noting that under Article VI:2, the word 'may' is 'properly understood as giving Members a choice between imposing an anti-dumping duty *or not*, as well as a choice between imposing an anti-dumping duty equal to the dumping margin or imposing a lower duty'.[30]

As a result of its overall analysis of the text of Article VI, however, the Appellate Body said that this provision is inconclusive as to whether Article VI regulates *all measures* taken to counteract dumping or only *duties*. Therefore, the Appellate Body turned to other provisions of the Anti-Dumping Agreement for context. The Appellate Body explained that Article 1 of the Anti-Dumping Agreement makes clear that an 'anti-dumping measure' must be taken in a manner consistent with Article VI of GATT. In this regard, it noted that Article 18.1 of the Anti-Dumping Agreement clarifies the scope of Article VI of GATT. Specifically, Article 18.1 provides: '[n]o *specific action against* dumping of exports from another Member can be taken except in accordance with the provisions of GATT 1994, as interpreted by this Agreement' (emphasis added by the Appellate Body). Under this provision, the Appellate Body considered that a 'specific action against dumping' can be taken only when the constituent elements of 'dumping' are present. Moreover, it concluded that it follows from this provision that GATT Article VI 'is applicable to any "specific action against dumping" of exports, ie action that is taken in response to situations presenting the constituent elements of "dumping"'.[31]

Therefore, the Appellate Body examined 'whether the 1916 Act provides for "specific action against dumping" of exports from another Member, and, thus, falls within the scope of application of Article VI of the GATT 1994'. The United States had argued that the 1916 Act does not 'specifically target' dumping, but rather targets predatory pricing. However, based on the text of the 1916 Act, the Appellate Body found that 'the civil and criminal proceedings and penalties contemplated by the 1916 Act require the presence of the constituent elements of "dumping"', and, therefore, it follows that they are a 'specific action against dumping'. The Appellate Body concluded that GATT Article VI applies.[32] It thus found: 'Article VI, and, in particular, Article VI:2, read in conjunction with the *Anti-Dumping Agreement*, limit the permissible responses to dumping to definitive anti-dumping duties, provisional measures and price undertakings. Therefore, the 1916 Act is inconsistent with Article VI:2 and the *Anti-Dumping Agreement* to the extent that it provides for "specific action against dumping" in the form of civil and criminal proceedings and penalties'.[33]

In a later case, *US—Offset Act (Byrd Amendment)*, the Appellate Body elaborated on this issue. The Offset Act case dealt with a controversial provision that had been added to US anti-dumping law, under which anti-dumping duties that were collected pursuant to a particular anti-dumping determination were distributed to the companies who filed the anti-dumping petition. (Previously, anti-dumping duties were placed in the general treasury fund, where normal duties are deposited, as is the case in all other countries.) US trading partners were concerned about the impact of this change, as it would seem to

---

[29] Appellate Body Report, *US—1916 Act*, para 112.
[30] *Ibid,* para 116.
[31] *Ibid*, paras 117–26.
[32] *Ibid*, paras 127–30.
[33] *Ibid*, para 137.

give companies an added incentive to bring anti-dumping petitions. A number of these countries brought WTO complaints against the US measure. The main issue was whether WTO rules prohibit the distribution of these duties to the domestic petitioners in this way. The following extract from the case discusses the issue:

Appellate Body Report, *United States—Continued Dumping and Subsidy Offset Act of 2000*, Adopted 27 January 2003, WT/DS217,234/AB/R

A. The Term "Specific" in the Phrase "Specific Action Against" Dumping or a Subsidy

...

238. . . . [I]n *US—1916 Act*, we interpreted the phrase "specific action against dumping" in Article 18.1 of the *Anti-Dumping Agreement*. We said:

In our view, the ordinary meaning of the phrase "specific action against dumping" of exports within the meaning of Article 18.1 is action that is taken in response to situations presenting the constituent elements of "dumping". "Specific action against dumping" of exports must, at a minimum, encompass action that may be taken *only* when the constituent elements of "dumping" are present.[66]

[66] We do not find it necessary, in the present cases, to decide whether the concept of "specific action against dumping" may be broader.

Given that Article 18.1 of the *Anti-Dumping Agreement* and 32.1 of the *SCM Agreement* are identical except for the reference in the former to dumping, and in the latter to a subsidy, we are of the view that this finding is pertinent for both provisions.

239. We recall that, in *US—1916 Act*, the United States argued that the 1916 Act did not fall within the scope of Article VI of the GATT 1994 because it targeted predatory pricing, as opposed to dumping. We disagreed, and determined that the 1916 Act was a "specific action against dumping" because the constituent elements of dumping were "built into" the essential elements of civil and criminal liability under the 1916 Act. We also found that the "wording of the 1916 Act . . . makes clear that these actions can be taken *only* with respect to conduct which presents the constituent elements of 'dumping'." Accordingly, a measure that may be taken only when the constituent elements of dumping or a subsidy are present, is a "specific action" in response to dumping within the meaning of Article 18.1 of the *Anti-Dumping Agreement* or a "specific action" in response to subsidization within the meaning of Article 32.1 of the *SCM Agreement*. In other words, the measure must be inextricably linked to, or have a strong correlation with, the constituent elements of dumping or of a subsidy. Such link or correlation may, as in the 1916 Act, be derived from the text of the measure itself.

240. This leads to the question of how to determine what are the constituent elements of dumping or a subsidy. We recall that, in *US—1916 Act*, we said the constituent elements of dumping are found in the definition of dumping in Article VI:1 of the GATT 1994, as elaborated in Article 2 of the *Anti-Dumping Agreement*. As regards the constituent elements of a subsidy, we are of the view that they are set out in the definition of a subsidy found in Article 1 of the *SCM Agreement*.

241. We turn now to determine whether the CDSOA is a "specific action" against dumping or subsidization within the meaning of Article 18.1 of the *Anti-Dumping Agreement* or Article 32.1 of the *SCM Agreement*.

242. In our view, the Panel was correct in finding that the CDSOA is a specific action related to dumping or a subsidy within the meaning of Article 18.1 of the *Anti-Dumping Agreement* and Article 32.1 of the *SCM Agreement*. It is clear from the text of the CDSOA, in particular

from Section 754(a) of the Tariff Act, that the CDSOA offset payments are inextricably linked to, and strongly correlated with, a determination of dumping, as defined in Article VI:1 of the GATT 1994 and in the *Anti-Dumping Agreement*, or a determination of a subsidy, as defined in the *SCM Agreement*. The language of the CDSOA is unequivocal. *First*, CDSOA offset payments can be made *only* if anti-dumping duties or countervailing duties have been collected. *Second*, such duties can be collected *only* pursuant to an anti-dumping duty order or countervailing duty order. *Third*, an anti-dumping duty order can be imposed *only* following a determination of dumping, as defined in Article VI:1 of the GATT 1994 and in the *Anti-Dumping Agreement*. *Fourth*, a countervailing duty order can be imposed only following a determination that exports have been subsidized, according to the definition of a subsidy in the *SCM Agreement*. In the light of the above elements, we agree with the Panel that "there is a clear, direct and unavoidable connection between the determination of dumping and CDSOA offset payments", and we believe the same to be true for subsidization. In other words, it seems to us unassailable that CDSOA offset payments can be made only following a determination that the constituent elements of dumping or subsidization are present. Therefore, consistent with the test established in *US—1916 Act*, we find that the CDSOA is "specific action" related to dumping or a subsidy within the meaning of Article 18.1 of the *Anti-Dumping Agreement* and of Article 32.1 of the *SCM Agreement*.

243. In its appellant's submission, the United States argues that the CDSOA is not specific action related to dumping or to a subsidy because, contrary to the 1916 Act examined in a previous appeal, the language of the CDSOA does not refer to the constituent elements of dumping (or of a subsidy), and dumping (or subsidization) is not the trigger for application of the CDSOA. The United States suggested at the oral hearing that the CDSOA is not "specific" because the constituent elements of dumping or of a subsidy do not form part of the essential components of the CDSOA. In addition, the United States submits that, according to the Panel's reasoning, *any* expenditure of collected anti-dumping (or countervailing) duties, including expenditure for international emergency relief, would be characterized as specific action against dumping (or a subsidy). For the United States, the Panel's approach "cannot withstand scrutiny."

244. We disagree with these arguments. The criterion we set out in *US—1916 Act* for specific action in response to dumping is not whether the constituent elements of dumping or of a subsidy are explicitly referred to in the measure at issue, nor whether dumping or subsidization triggers the application of the action, nor whether the constituent elements of dumping or of a subsidy form part of the essential components of the measure at issue. Our analysis in *US—1916 Act* focused on the strength of the link between the measure and the elements of dumping or a subsidy. In other words, we focused on the degree of correlation between the scope of application of the measure and the constituent elements of dumping or of a subsidy. In noting that the "wording of the 1916 Act also makes clear that these actions can be taken *only* with respect to conduct which presents the constituent elements of 'dumping'", we did not *require* that the language of the measure include the constituent elements of dumping or of a subsidy. This is clear from our use of the word "also", which suggests that this aspect of the 1916 Act was a supplementary reason for our finding, and not the basis for it. Indeed, we required that the constituent elements of dumping (or of a subsidy) be "present", which in our view can include cases where the constituent elements of dumping and of a subsidy are implicit in the measure. Thus, we agree with the European Communities, India, Indonesia and Thailand that the "test" established in *US—1916 Act* "is met not only when the constituent elements of dumping are 'explicitly built into' the action at issue, but also where . . . they are implicit in the express conditions for taking such action." In fact, the presence of the constituent elements of dumping and of a subsidy is implied by the very words of the CDSOA, which refer to "[d]uties assessed pursuant to a countervailing duty order, an antidumping duty order, or a finding under the Antidumping Act of 1921 . . .".

245. We also disagree with the submission of the United States that, under the Panel's reasoning, any expenditure of the collected anti-dumping (or countervailing) duties would be characterized as a specific action against dumping (or a subsidy). This submission does not take into account the express terms of Article 18.1 of the *Anti-Dumping Agreement* and Article 32.1 of the *SCM Agreement*, which, as we said earlier, contain two conditions precedent, namely that the action be "specific" to dumping or a subsidy, and that it be "against" dumping or a subsidy. To refer to the example given by the United States, international emergency relief financed from collected antidumping or countervailing duties would not, in our opinion, be subject to the prohibitions of Article 18.1 of the *Anti-Dumping Agreement* and Article 32.1 of the *SCM Agreement*, because such action would have no effect whatsoever on dumping or subsidization and, therefore, could not be characterized as operating "against" dumping or a subsidy. As the Panel noted, we did not focus on the word "against" in our ruling in *US—1916 Act*, because there was no dispute there that the measure (imposing civil and criminal liabilities on importers) was indeed "against" something—the question there was whether the action was against dumping, or some other conduct (predatory pricing).

B. The Term "Against" in the Phrase "Specific Action Against" Dumping or a Subsidy

...

247. ... In order to identify the ordinary meaning of the term "against" as used in Article 18.1 of the *Anti-Dumping Agreement* and Article 32.1 of the *SCM Agreement*, the United States posits three definitions of that term: (1) "of motion or action in opposition"; (2) "in hostility or active opposition to"; and (3) "in contact with".

248. In our view, the first and second definitions invoked by the United States could, arguably, have some relevance in identifying the ordinary meaning of the term "against" as used in Article 18.1 of the *Anti-Dumping Agreement* and Article 32.1 of the *SCM Agreement*. However, we do not believe the third definition is appropriate given the substance of Articles 18.1 and 32.1. Indeed, the third definition refers to physical contact between two objects and, thus, in our view, is irrelevant to the idea of opposition, hostility or adverse effect that is conveyed by the word "against" as used in Article 18.1 of the *Anti-Dumping Agreement* and Article 32.1 of the *SCM Agreement*. It should be remembered that dictionaries are important guides to, not dispositive statements of, definitions of words appearing in agreements and legal documents.

249. We also note that the third dictionary definition cited by the United States is incomplete; not only does that dictionary definition refer to "in contact with", it also refers to "supported by". This latter element is difficult to reconcile with any idea of opposition, hostility or adverse bearing.

250. Therefore, as the definition "in contact with" cannot be used to ascertain the ordinary meaning of "against" as used in Article 18.1 of the *Anti-Dumping Agreement* and in Article 32.1 of the *SCM Agreement*, we do not believe the United States is justified in using that definition to support its view that an action against dumping or a subsidy must have direct contact with the imported good, or the entity responsible for the dumped or subsidized good. More generally, we fail to see how such a meaning can be given to the term "against", which, given the substance of Article 18.1 of the *Anti-Dumping Agreement* and Article 32.1 of the *SCM Agreement*, must relate to an idea of opposition, hostility or adverse effect.

251. A textual analysis of Articles 18.1 and 32.1 supports, rather than defeats, the finding of the Panel that these provisions are applicable to measures that do not come into direct contact with the imported good, or entities responsible for the dumped or subsidized good. We note that Article 18.1 refers only to measures that act against "dumping", and that there is no express requirement that the measure must act against the imported dumped product, or entities

responsible for that product. Likewise, Article 32.1 of the *SCM Agreement* refers to specific action against "a subsidy", not action against the imported subsidized product or a responsible entity. The United States' contention is further contradicted by the contextual consideration that the *SCM Agreement* authorizes multilaterally-sanctioned countermeasures "against" a subsidy, which may consist of indirect action affecting other products.

252. Turning to considerations of object and purpose, we do not consider that the object and purpose of the *Anti-Dumping Agreement* and of the *SCM Agreement*, as reflected in Article 18.1 of the *Anti-Dumping Agreement* and in Article 32.1 of the *SCM Agreement*, support the incorporation into these provisions, through the term "against", of a requirement that the measure must come into direct contact with the imported good, or the entity responsible for it. Both provisions fulfil a function of limiting the range of actions that a Member may take unilaterally to counter dumping or subsidization. Excluding from Article 18.1 of the *Anti-Dumping Agreement* and Article 32.1 of the *SCM Agreement* actions that do not come into direct contact with the imported good or the entity responsible for the dumped or subsidized good, would undermine that function.

253. We, therefore, agree with the Panel that in Article 18.1 of the *Anti-Dumping Agreement* and Article 32.1 of the *SCM Agreement*, there is no requirement that the measure must come into direct contact with the imported product, or entities connected to, or responsible for, the imported good such as the importer, exporter, or foreign producer. We also agree with the Panel that the test should focus on dumping or subsidization as *practices*. Article 18.1 refers only to measures that act against "dumping"; there is no express requirement that the measure must act against the imported dumped product, or entities responsible for that product. Likewise, Article 32.1 of the *SCM Agreement* refers to specific action against "a subsidy", not to action against the imported subsidized product or a responsible entity.

254. Recalling the other two elements of the definition of "against" from the *New Shorter Oxford Dictionary* relied upon by the United States, namely "of motion or action in opposition" and "in hostility or active opposition to", to determine whether a measure is "against" dumping or a subsidy, we believe it is necessary to assess whether the design and structure of a measure is such that the measure is "opposed to", has an adverse bearing on, or, more specifically, has the effect of dissuading the practice of dumping or the practice of subsidization, or creates an incentive to terminate such practices. In our view, the CDSOA has exactly those effects because of its design and structure.

255. The CDSOA effects a transfer of financial resources from the producers/exporters of dumped or subsidized goods to their domestic competitors. This is demonstrated by the following elements of the CDSOA regime. *First*, the CDSOA offset payments are financed from the anti-dumping or countervailing duties paid by the foreign producers/exporters. *Second*, the CDSOA offset payments are made to an "affected domestic producer", defined in Section 754(b) of the Tariff Act as "a petitioner or interested party in support of the petition with respect to which an anti-dumping duty order, a finding under the Antidumping Act of 1921, or a countervailing duty order has been entered" and that "remains in operation". In response to our questioning at the oral hearing, the United States confirmed that the "affected domestic producers" which are eligible to receive payments under the CDSOA, are necessarily competitors of the foreign producers/exporters subject to an anti-dumping or countervail order. *Third*, under the implementing regulations issued by the United States Commissioner of Customs ("Customs") on 21 September 2001, the "qualifying expenditures" of the affected domestic producers, for which the CDSOA offset payments are made, "must be related to the production of the same product that is the subject of the related order or finding, with the exception of expenses incurred by associations which must relate to a specific case." *Fourth*, Customs has confirmed that there is no statutory or regulatory requirement as to how a CDSOA offset payment to an affected

domestic producer is to be spent, thus indicating that the recipients of CDSOA offset payments are entitled to use this money to bolster their competitive position *vis-à-vis* their competitors, including the foreign competitors subject to anti-dumping or countervailing duties.

256. All these elements lead us to conclude that the CDSOA has an adverse bearing on the foreign producers/exporters in that the imports into the United States of the dumped or subsidized products (besides being subject to anti-dumping or countervailing duties) result in the financing of United States competitors—producers of like products—through the transfer to the latter of the duties collected on those exports. Thus, foreign producers/ exporters have an incentive not to engage in the practice of exporting dumped or subsidized products or to terminate such practices. Because the CDSOA has an adverse bearing on, and, more specifically, is designed and structured so that it dissuades the practice of dumping or the practice of subsidization, and because it creates an incentive to terminate such practices, the CDSOA is undoubtedly an action "against" dumping or a subsidy, within the meaning of Article 18.1 of the *Anti-Dumping Agreement* and of Article 32.1 of the *SCM Agreement*.

257. We note that the United States challenges what it views as the Panel's incorporation of a "conditions of competition test" in Article 18.1 of the *Anti-Dumping Agreement* and in Article 32.1 of the *SCM Agreement*. In our view, in order to determine whether the CDSOA is "against" dumping or subsidization, it was not necessary, nor relevant, for the Panel to examine the conditions of competition under which domestic products and dumped/subsidized imports compete, and to assess the impact of the measure on the competitive relationship between them. An analysis of the term "against", in our view, is more appropriately centred on the design and structure of the measure; such an analysis does not mandate an economic assessment of the implications of the measure on the conditions of competition under which domestic product and dumped/subsidized imports compete.

258. As mentioned above, the finding of the Panel that the CDSOA is a measure against dumping or a subsidy is also based on the view that the CDSOA provides a financial incentive for domestic producers to file or support applications for the initiation of anti-dumping and countervailing duty investigations, and that such an incentive will likely result in a greater number of applications, investigations and orders. We agree with the United States that this consideration is not a proper basis for a finding that the CDSOA is "against" dumping or a subsidy; a measure cannot be against dumping or a subsidy simply because it facilitates or induces the exercise of rights that are WTO consistent. The Panel's reasoning would give Article 18.1 of the *Anti-Dumping Agreement* and Article 32.1 of the *SCM Agreement* a scope of application that is overly broad. For example, the Panel's reasoning would imply that a legal aid program destined to support domestic small-size producers in anti-dumping or countervailing duty investigations should be considered a measure against dumping or a subsidy within the meaning of Article 18.1 of the *Anti-Dumping Agreement* and of Article 32.1 of the *SCM Agreement*, because it could be argued that such legal aid is a financial incentive likely to result in a greater number or applications, investigations and orders.

259. The United States also argues that the Panel erred in relying on the stated purpose of the CDSOA, as expressed in the "Findings of Congress" set forth in Section 1002 of the CDSOA, to support its finding that the CDSOA is a measure against dumping or a subsidy. We note that the Panel referred to the "Findings of Congress", not as a *basis* for its conclusion that the CDSOA constitutes a specific action against dumping or subsidies, but rather as a consideration confirming that conclusion. We agree with the Panel that the intent, stated or otherwise, of the legislators is not conclusive as to whether a measure is "against" dumping or subsidies under Article 18.1 of the *Anti-Dumping Agreement* or Article 32.1 of the *SCM Agreement*. Thus, it was not necessary for the Panel to inquire into the intent pursued by United States legislators in enacting the CDSOA and to take this into account in the analysis. The text of the CDSOA

provides sufficient information on the structure and design of the CDSOA, that is to say, on the manner in which it operates, to permit an analysis whether the measure is "against" dumping or a subsidy. Specifically, the text of the CDSOA establishes clearly that, by virtue of that statute, a transfer of financial resources is effected from the producers/exporters of dumped or subsidized goods to their domestic competitors. This essential feature of the CDSOA constitutes, in itself, the decisive basis for concluding that the CDSOA is "against" dumping or a subsidy—because it creates the "opposition" to dumping or subsidization, such that it dissuades such practices, or creates an incentive to terminate them. Therefore, there was no need to examine the intent pursued by the legislators in enacting the CDSOA. In our view, however, the Panel did not err in simply noting that the stated legislative intent, which appears in the statute itself, confirms the conclusion it had reached as to the scope of the measure.

C. Footnote 24 of the Anti-Dumping Agreement and Footnote 56 of the SCM Agreement

260. The United States challenges the way the Panel addressed footnote 24 of the *Anti-Dumping Agreement* and footnote 56 of the *SCM Agreement*, arguing that the Panel erred in declining to examine the import of the footnotes because it had already determined that the CDSOA was a "specific action" under Article 18.1 of the *Anti-Dumping Agreement* and under Article 32.1 of the *SCM Agreement*. The United States contends that these footnotes permit actions involving dumping or subsidies consistent with GATT 1994 provisions and not addressed by Article VI of the GATT 1994, and that these actions are not encompassed by the prohibitions against "specific action" in Article 18.1 of the *Anti-Dumping Agreement* and Article 32.1 of the *SCM Agreement*. In other words, according to the United States, an action that falls within footnotes 24 and 56 cannot be characterized as a "specific action" within the meaning of Article 18.1 of the *Anti-Dumping Agreement* and Article 32.1 of the *SCM Agreement*, and such action would, therefore, not be WTO inconsistent.

261. We disagree with this argument. We note, first, that, in *US—1916 Act*, we commented on footnote 24 as follows:

Footnote 24 to Article 18.1 of the *Anti-Dumping Agreement* states:

This is not intended to preclude action under other relevant provisions of GATT 1994, as appropriate.

We note that footnote 24 refers generally to "action" and not, as does Article 18.1, to "specific action against dumping" of exports. "Action" within the meaning of footnote 24 is to be distinguished from "specific action against dumping" of exports, which is governed by Article 18.1 itself.

262. The United States' reasoning is tantamount to treating footnotes 24 and 56 as the primary provisions, while according Articles 18.1 and 32.1 residual status. This not only turns the normal approach to interpretation on its head, but it also runs counter to our finding in *US—1916 Act*. In that case, we provided guidance for determining whether an action is specific to dumping (or to a subsidy): an action is specific to dumping (or a subsidy) when it may be taken *only* when the constituent elements of dumping (or a subsidy) are present, or, put another way, when the measure is inextricably linked to, or strongly correlates with, the constituent elements of dumping (or of a subsidy). This approach is based on the *texts* of Article 18.1 of the *Anti-Dumping Agreement* and of Article 32.1 of the *SCM Agreement*, and not on the accessory footnotes. Footnotes 24 and 56 are clarifications of the main provisions, added to avoid ambiguity; they confirm what is implicit in Article 18.1 of the *Anti-Dumping Agreement* and in Article 32.1 of the *SCM Agreement*, namely, that an action that is *not* "specific" within the meaning of Article 18.1 of the *Anti-Dumping Agreement* and of Article 32.1 of the *SCM Agreement*, but is nevertheless related to dumping or subsidization, is

not prohibited by Article 18.1 of the *Anti-Dumping Agreement* or Article 32.1 of the *SCM Agreement*.

... ...

Thus, the Appellate Body concluded that the distribution of tariff duties to petitioners was a specific action against dumping, pursuant to Article 18.1. It later found in that same case that the measure was inconsistent with Article VI of the GATT because the distributions do not represent one of the permitted responses to dumping.[34]

V. CHALLENGING ANTI-DUMPING MEASURES IN WTO DISPUTE SETTLEMENT

Decisions and actions of investigating authorities on anti-dumping matters can be challenged in two ways: (1) in domestic courts through an appeal by the private companies involved; or (2) at the WTO by the government of the foreign exporters/ producers. (In addition, bilateral or regional trade agreements may also include provisions (such as NAFTA Chapter 19) which provide an alternative to an appeal to domestic courts, under which a bi-national panel of trade experts will hear the appeal instead of the domestic court.) In this section, we examine three issues of importance in WTO dispute settlement relating to complaints regarding domestic anti-dumping determinations: (1) the standard of review; (2) requirements for framing the complaint in relation to the measures to be challenged; and (3) the concept of good faith and challenges under GATT Article X.

(a) Standard of Review

For the most part, normal DSU rules apply to WTO disputes regarding anti-dumping. However, a key distinction is the special standard of review to be used in anti-dumping cases. When a WTO panel hears a complaint regarding a domestic anti-dumping proceeding, it is, in a sense, acting as a court of appeal reviewing a lower court determination. Thus, as with domestic appeals courts, the standard of review to be applied is an important consideration. In this regard, Article 17.6 states:

> (i) in its assessment of the facts of the matter, the panel shall determine whether the authorities' establishment of the facts was proper and whether their evaluation of those facts was unbiased and objective. If the establishment of the facts was proper and the evaluation was unbiased and objective, even though the panel might have reached a different conclusion, the evaluation shall not be overturned;

> (ii) the panel shall interpret the relevant provisions of the Agreement in accordance with customary rules of interpretation of public international law. Where the panel finds that a relevant provision of the Agreement admits of more than one permissible interpretation, the panel shall find the authorities' measure to be in conformity with the Agreement if it rests upon one of those permissible interpretations.

Under Article 17.6(i), for issues of fact, the panel must determine whether the authorities'

---

[34] Appellate Body Report, *US—Offset Act*, paras 263–73.

'establishment of the facts' was proper and whether their 'evaluation' of the facts was 'objective and unbiased'. In practice, this standard has not been too different from that used in the context of disputes regarding safeguards and countervailing duties, which do not have a special standard (the normal DSU standard applies).

For issues of law pursuant to Article 17.6(ii), there are some similarities with the standard DSU provisions. As with DSU Article 3.2, panels and the Appellate Body must construe the Anti-Dumping Agreement according to rules of interpretation in public international law (this has been interpreted to mean the Vienna Convention on the Law of Treaties). However, the Article 17.6(ii) standard of review goes a bit further, stating: '[w]here the panel finds that a relevant provision of the Agreement admits of more than one permissible interpretation, the panel shall find the authorities' measure to be in conformity with the Agreement if it rests upon one of those permissible interpretations'. Thus, the agreement indicates that there may be more than one 'permissible interpretation' of the agreement. There is no equivalent of this provision in the DSU or in other agreements. It has been suggested that this provision was added at the request of the US, in an attempt to create a standard similar to that applied in appeals of agency decisions under US law, where a certain amount of deference is given to agency decisions if the statute is unclear and the agency decision is 'reasonable'.[35] However, as applied to date Article 17.6(ii) does not seem to have led to the level of deference the US might have desired, as there have been few instances where the provision has been applied to find that there is more than one permissible interpretation.[36] Although the Appellate Body has indicated that, in principle, there can be more than one permissible interpretation,[37] to date it has never found a measure not to violate WTO rules on the basis that the agency interpretation at issue was a 'permissible' one.

(b) The Measures to be Challenged

Another important aspect of the Anti-Dumping Agreement dispute settlement rules is that there are certain formal requirements that must be met when bringing a complaint against another Member's anti-dumping measure. Specifically, the complaint must identify one of the three measures described in the Anti-Dumping Agreement: a definitive measure, a provisional measure or a price undertaking. A challenge to specific actions taken during the investigation—for instance, the decision to use a specific methodology—will not be sufficient. Rather, one of the three formal measures cited above must be identified in the panel request.[38] Of course, a complaint can also challenge the anti-dumping legislation or regulations themselves, outside the context of these three kinds of measures.[39]

(c) Good Faith, Even-handedness, Impartiality

In addition to arguments against the fundamental economic logic behind anti-dumping laws, there have been complaints voiced over the years that these laws are applied in a

---

[35] See S Croley and JH Jackson, 'WTO Dispute Procedures, Standard of Review, and Deference to National Governments' (1996) 90 *American Journal of International Law* 193.

[36] For one example see Panel Report, *Argentina—Poultry AD Duties*, paras 7.340–7.341 and 7.361.

[37] Appellate Body Report, *US—Hot Rolled Steel from Japan*, para 59.

[38] Appellate Body Report, *Guatemala—Cement*, para 80.

[39] Appellate Body Report, *US—1916 Act*, paras 51–81.

manner that is biased against foreign producers. The decisions are made by government agencies, it is argued, and these agencies sometimes act as political bodies, bending the rules to provide protection to domestic industries. As a result, it has sometimes been argued in WTO disputes that the investigating authorities have not acted fairly towards the foreign companies and importers involved. In this regard, complainants have sometimes raised challenges under GATT Article X:3(a), arguing that the investigative authorities failed to administer their domestic anti-dumping rules in a 'reasonable, uniform and impartial' manner (for example, they might argue that the authorities altered a methodology that they had used in the previous 50 investigations, thereby resulting in an inflated dumping margin). Along the same lines, they have also argued that the investigating authorities failed to follow the general principle of international law to carry out treaty obligations in good faith (eg based on Article 26 of the Vienna Convention on the Law of Treaties). Panels and the Appellate Body have been hesitant to find violations on this basis, preferring to rely on the clearer, substantive obligations of the Anti-Dumping Agreement to find violations. However, the Appellate Body has held that investigating authorities must carry out their anti-dumping procedures in an 'even-handed' manner, implying a general obligation to deal with the foreign and domestic interests involved in a neutral manner.[40]

VI. 'DOUBLE REMEDIES' IN RELATION TO CONCURRENT ANTI-DUMPING AND COUNTERVAILING DUTIES

Anti-dumping and countervailing duties are often discussed together, as two similar mechanisms designed to address 'unfair' trade. GATT Article VI, which was the original multilateral trade provision authorsing their use, is titled 'Anti-Dumping and Countervailing Duties', thus covering both of these kinds of 'trade remedies' in one set of provisions. In relation to both domestic law and multilateral oversight for both types of duties, many of the procedures are the same, and in terms of the substance both contain an 'injury' requirement.

However, despite some close links, the two remedies are different in many ways, and are to a great extent separated in WTO rules. Although GATT Article VI deals with both types of remedies, it often does so in different provisions. Paragraphs 1 and 2 are key provisions addressing anti-dumping duties, while paragraph 3 is an important provision addressing countervailing duties. Separate WTO agreements address each: the AD Agreement and the SCM Agreement. Thus, while there is some overlap in a number of the issues related to both, they are, to some degree, formally separate. Of great importance is the fact that the activities they target are very different: dumping versus subsidisation. Dumping deals with the pricing practices of private firms, whereas subsidies are financial support provided by governments.

In most instances, anti-dumping and countervailing duty cases are not brought against the same product simultaneously; generally, it is one type of case or the other. However,

---

[40] Appellate Body Report, *US—Hot Rolled Steel from Japan*, para 148.

it is possible to bring allegations of both dumping and subsidisation for the same product, and on a number of occasions this has occurred, resulting in concurrent investigations. Where this happens, it has been suggested that an affirmative determination on both kinds of remedies (that is, a determination that both dumping and subsidisation exist) could, in certain instances, lead to 'double remedies' being imposed, meaning that two remedies are imposed for what is essentially the same action.

In this section, we discuss two aspects of the issue of double remedies which can be seen in the *US—Anti-Dumping and Countervailing Duties (China)* case. First, we discuss the distinction between *export* and *domestic* subsidies for the purpose of the double remedies issue. Secondly, we talk about how the issue of double remedies arises through adjustments made to costs (or prices) used for normal value, such as with the treatment of the non-market economies (NMEs) at issue in this case, in a way that allegedly provides a remedy for subsidies through the dumping calculation.

(a) Domestic/Export Subsidies and Lower Export Prices

While many WTO provisions make anti-dumping and countervailing duties seem completely separate, as noted above, there are a few provisions that indicate a degree of overlap. In the context of 'double remedies', a key provision is GATT Article VI, paragraph 5, which states: 'No product of the territory of any WTO Member imported into the territory of any other WTO Member shall be subject to both anti-dumping and countervailing duties to compensate for the same situation of dumping or export subsidization'. Implicit in the prohibition on 'double remedies' in these circumstances seems to be an assumption that export subsidies lead to lower priced exports. In essence, some or all of the subsidy can be 'passed through' to the export price, allowing that export price to be reduced. In a fairly simple example, involving a comparison of home market prices to export prices, an exporter may use subsidies to finance lower priced export sales, and these lower export prices may lead to a finding of dumping. In this situation, it has been argued, a remedy against the export subsidies would also address any resultant dumping, as both arise from the same source. Thus, concurrent remedies against both the dumping and the subsidies would constitute a 'double remedy'.

The extent to which this 'pass through' happens in practice is unclear. Subsidies can be used in a number of ways, some of which affect prices and some of which do not; and the way subsidies can affect prices is not always direct and obvious. It can depend on the type of subsidy and the business strategy of the subsidy's recipient. Nevertheless, at least in theory, it is possible for subsidies to result in lower export prices, and thus lead to a finding that dumping exists. Article VI:5 seems to reflect this possibility in the context of export subsidies, and attempts to preclude any double remedies that might result. Some domestic trade remedy laws (such as the US and EU) also recognise this, and provide for deductions of those countervailing duties taken in response to export subsidies as part of the dumping margin calculation.

While there is a presumption that *export* subsidies lead to lower export prices, it could be argued that lower export prices can occur regardless of whether the subsidy in question is classified as an 'export subsidy'. In reality, the divide between export subsidies and domestic subsidies may not be as clear as suggested by Article VI:5. Export subsidies could be used to lower prices on export sales, but might not always be used in this way; and domestic subsidies themselves could be used for this purpose. Thus, rather than this explicit separation of export subsidies and domestic subsidies, if there is a concern about double remedies where subsidies lead to lower export prices, another approach to the issue might be to eliminate this blanket rule in the case of export subsidies and instead investigate each instance of subsidisation where a concurrent remedy is sought, to determine if the subsidies were used to lower export prices. The burden could be placed either on the investigating authority to make a finding on this issue in all such cases, or on the respondent to prove that a concurrent remedy is not appropriate because the subsidies were the cause of the dumping. In practice, however, determining how the subsidies were used could be extremely difficult, and it may not be possible to come up with a definitive answer to how a particular subsidy was used.

The panel and Appellate Body in the *US—Anti-Dumping and Countervailing Duties (China)* case both discussed this issue, but they did not question the export versus domestic subsidy distinction. The panel discussed this issue in paras 14.71–14.72, and in particular fn 972. There, the panel stated:

> Certain statements of the USDOC in market economy anti-dumping investigations illustrate why a similar 'double remedy' arises in the context of export subsidies, and why it generally does not in the context of domestic subsidies granted by market economies: in *Cold-Rolled Corrosion-Resistant Carbon Steel Flat Products from Korea* (quoted in *LEU from France*), the USDOC wrote that 'domestic subsidies presumably lower the price of the subject merchandise both in the home and the US markets, and therefore have no effect on the measurement of any dumping that might also occur.' The USDOC contrasted this situation with that of export subsidies, which, 'benefit only exported merchandise' and therefore brings about 'the potential for double remedies.'

The Appellate Body seemed to agree, citing the panel's statements on the issue, and then saying:

> 568. We recall that, in principle, an export subsidy will result in a pro rata reduction in the export price of a product, but will not affect the price of domestic sales of that product. By comparison, domestic subsidies will, in principle, affect the prices at which a producer sells its goods in the domestic market and in export markets in the same way and to the same extent. Since any lowering of prices attributable to the subsidy will be reflected on both sides of the dumping margin calculation, the overall dumping margin will not be affected by the subsidization.

It is worth noting two additional points about the domestic versus export subsidies distinction. First, in the context of discussing the NME situation at issue, the Appellate Body made clear that domestic subsidies could lead to lower export prices:

> 599. we agree with the statement by the Panel that double remedies would *likely* result from the concurrent application of anti-dumping duties calculated on the basis of an NME methodology and countervailing duties, but we are not convinced that double remedies *necessarily* result in every instance of such concurrent application of duties. This depends, rather, on whether and to what extent domestic subsidies have lowered the export price of a product, and on whether the investigating authority has taken the necessary corrective steps to adjust its methodology to take account of this factual situation.

The Appellate Body's statements were restricted to the NME situation, but there may also be situations with market economies where third country surrogate data is used. As a result, the same logic would apply there, and thus domestic subsidies may lead to the same problem with double remedies, even outside the NME context. On this issue, the Panel noted the following in fn 972:

> While the question is not before us, it would seem that a double remedy could arise in investigations involving market economy imports, depending on the costs that are used to calculate the normal value: a double remedy may arise when the normal value of a market economy producer is constructed using costs that do not reflect the subsidies that this producer received.

Secondly, and more generally, while the distinction has its difficulties, it seems to be fairly well enshrined in WTO and domestic law. Thus, even though the case for a complete separation in the treatment of domestic versus export subsidies—with export subsidies presumed always to lead to double remedies and domestic subsidies presumed never to do so—may seem flawed, it may be difficult to overcome these assumptions in any future litigation. In an ideal world, it might be desirable to measure the precise extent to which all export/domestic subsidies pass through and result in lower prices, but this will be difficult to achieve in practice.

(b) Adjustments in the Dumping Calculation Which Take Subsidies into Account: The NME Calculation

A second area where the double remedy issue arises is with adjustments made to costs (or prices) in determining normal value in the dumping calculation in a way that takes subsidies into account. The *US—Anti-Dumping and Countervailing Duties (China)* case dealt with the special situation of a non-market economy (NME). In this context, the normal value side of the dumping margin calculation is considered unreliable because of government distortions in the domestic market, and it is therefore replaced by surrogate values from a market-based third country. By using the third country figures, the costs now reflect unsubsidised amounts. When these unsubsidised costs are compared to the producer's export price (which is not adjusted and thus reflects the subsidies), the resulting dumping margin reflects both any price discrimination (ie dumping) and the extent to which the producer benefited from subsidies. Thus, it is argued, the anti-dumping remedy, in effect, counteracts the subsidy as well as the dumping. As a result, a countervailing duty imposed in this situation would constitute a 'double remedy'.

In the case at hand, the panel considered that a 'double remedy' was a real possibility in this situation:

> 14.69 It follows from this description of NME methodologies that, conceptually, the dumping margin calculated under an NME methodology—ie the difference between the constructed normal value and the export price—reflects not only price discrimination by the investigated producer between the domestic and export markets ('dumping'), but also, in addition, the economic distortions that affect the producer's costs of production. Specific domestic subsidies granted to the producer of the good in question, in respect of that good—ie the same subsidies which are countervailed in the context of a countervailing duty investigation—are one of these economic distortions that are 'captured' in the NME dumping margin calculation. Expressed differently, the dumping margin calculated under an NME methodology generally is higher than would be the case otherwise because it results from a comparison of the export price to market-determined, and hence *unsubsidized*, costs of production, rather than to the producer's actual, subsidized (or distorted) costs of production.

The Panel went on to state there is the 'potential' for a double remedy here.

It is worth noting that, unlike with the treatment of export subsidies under Article VI:5, a double remedy may exist in the NME context regardless of a price effect from the subsidies. The price effect may lead to a greater amount of double remedy than otherwise, by pushing the export price down. But even without any such effect on export prices, the NME calculation can lead to a double remedy.

Despite indicating that there is a potential problem with double remedies, when turning to the specific claims, the panel concluded that the GATT and SCM Agreement provisions cited by China do not address the issue. It therefore did not examine 'the extent to which the concurrent imposition of antidumping duties determined under the USDOC's NME methodology and of countervailing duties resulted in the imposition of "double remedies" in the four investigations at issue'.[41]

On appeal, the Appellate Body agreed with the panel that double remedies were a problem, but it disagreed that the cited SCM Agreement provisions do not address it. At the outset, the Appellate Body found it 'useful to outline the concept of "double remedies" at issue in this dispute'. It explained that the issue 'may arise when both countervailing duties and anti-dumping duties are imposed on the same imported products'. It observed that the term does not refer 'simply to the fact that both an anti-dumping and a counter-vailing duty are imposed on the same product'. Rather, '"double remedies," also referred to as "double counting," refers to circumstances in which the simultaneous application of anti-dumping and countervailing duties on the same imported products results, at least to some extent, in the offsetting of the same subsidization twice'. It noted that '"[d]ouble remedies" are "likely" to occur in cases where an NME methodology is used to calculate the margin of dumping', on the following basis. When a dumping margin is calculated for a product from an NME, investigating authorities 'compare the export price to a normal value that is calculated based on surrogate costs or prices from a third country'. In the dumping margin calculation, 'investigating authorities compare the product's constructed normal value (not reflecting the amount of any subsidy received by the producer) with the product's actual export price (which, when subsidies have been received by the producer, is presumably lower than it would otherwise have been)'. The resulting dumping margin is 'thus based on an asymmetric comparison and is generally higher than would otherwise be the case'. The dumping margin calculated under an NME methodology '"reflects not only price discrimination by the investigated producer between the domestic and export markets ('dumping')," but also "economic distortions that affect the producer's costs of production," including specific subsidies to the investigated producer of the relevant product in respect of that product'. The Appellate Body explained that, as a result, '[a]n anti-dumping duty calculated based on an NME methodology may, therefore, "remedy" or "offset" a domestic subsidy, to the extent that such subsidy has contributed to a lowering of the export price'. Put another way, 'the subsidization is "counted" within the overall dumping margin'.[42]

On appeal, China argued that 'the Panel erred in its interpretation of the relevant provisions of the *SCM Agreement* and the GATT 1994, and in reasoning that, because these provisions do not *expressly* prohibit a Member from offsetting the same domestic subsidies through the imposition of two different duties, it was the intention of the drafters to

---

[41] Panel Report, *US—Anti-Dumping and Countervailing Duties (China)*, para 14.76
[42] Appellate Body Report, *US—Anti-Dumping and Countervailing Duties (China)*, paras 541–43.

authorize such actions'. In this regard, China asserted that 'an importing Member is under an affirmative legal obligation to ensure that it does not impose countervailing duties to offset a subsidy that is simultaneously offset through the manner in which it calculates anti-dumping duties in respect of the same imported product'. It contended that such an obligation arises from:

(i) Article 19.3 of the *SCM Agreement*, which requires investigating authorities to impose countervailing duties in the 'appropriate' amounts; (ii) Article 19.4 of the *SCM Agreement* and Article VI:3 of the GATT 1994, which prohibit Members from levying countervailing duties in excess of the amount of the subsidy found to exist; (iii) Article 10 of the *SCM Agreement*, which requires Members to 'take all necessary steps to ensure that the imposition of a countervailing duty . . . is in accordance with the provisions of Article VI of [the] GATT 1994 and the terms of [the SCM] Agreement,'; and (iv) Article 32.1 of the *SCM Agreement*, which prohibits Members from taking 'specific action against a subsidy of another Member . . . except in accordance with the provisions of [the] GATT 1994, as interpreted by [the SCM] Agreement.'[43]

The Appellate Body began its analysis with SCM Agreement Article 19.3, which provides in relevant part:

When a countervailing duty is imposed in respect of any product, such countervailing duty shall be levied, in the appropriate amounts in each case, on a non-discriminatory basis on imports of such product from all sources found to be subsidized and causing injury, except as to imports from those sources which have renounced any subsidies in question or from which undertakings under the terms of this Agreement have been accepted.

In its analysis of this provision, the panel had found that

(i) countervailing duties are collected 'in the appropriate amounts' insofar as the amount collected does not exceed the amount of subsidy 'found to exist,' (ii) 'the imposition of anti-dumping duties calculated under an NME methodology has no impact on whether the amount of the concurrent countervailing duty collected is 'appropriate' or not'; and (iii) 'it was not the intention of the drafters [of] the SCM Agreement to address the question of double remedies in Article 19.3.'

On this basis, the panel had concluded that China failed to establish that the DOC's

use of its NME methodology in the anti-dumping determinations at issue in this dispute, concurrently with its determination of subsidization and the imposition of countervailing duties on the same products in the four countervailing duty determinations at issue, was inconsistent with Article 19.3.[44]

In addressing these issues, the Appellate Body explained that

the main interpretative question before us concerns the meaning of the phrase 'in the appropriate amounts in each case' in Article 19.3 of the *SCM Agreement* and whether, as China contends, it would *not* be appropriate, within the meaning of that provision, to levy countervailing duties that result in, or are likely to result in, the imposition of double remedies.

Examining dictionary definitions of the term 'appropriate', the Appellate Body found them to suggest that the term 'is not an autonomous or absolute standard, but rather something that must be assessed by reference or in relation to something else'/ It con-

---

[43] *Ibid*, para 545.
[44] *Ibid*, para 547.

tinued, '[t]hey suggest some core norm—'proper,' 'fitting,' 'suitable'—and at the same time adaptation to particular circumstances'.[45]

Turning to the context of the term 'appropriate amounts', the Appellate Body observed that the panel 'appears to have ascribed great significance to' Article 19.4, which provides that '[n]o countervailing duty shall be levied on any imported product in excess of the amount of the subsidy found to exist, calculated in terms of subsidization per unit of the subsidized and exported product'. The Appellate Body noted that the Panel's finding 'points to Article 19.4 as the key determinant of what is an "appropriate" amount, for purposes of Article 19.3'. While the Appellate Body shared the panel's view that Article 19.4 provides relevant context, it said that it was not as persuaded as the panel seems to have been that 'Article 19.4, alone, defines when the amount of duty is "appropriate"'. It explained,

> Indeed, if any amount of countervailing duty that does not exceed the amount of the subsidy is an 'appropriate' amount within the meaning of Article 19.3, then the requirement in Article 19.3 would be rendered redundant, as Article 19.4 already prescribes that duties not be levied in excess of the amount of the subsidy found to exist.[46]

Rather, the Appellate Body considered Article 19.2 to be more relevant to this question. While leaving discretion to the investigating authorities as to whether the amount of the countervailing duty to be imposed shall be the full amount of the subsidy or less, this provision 'nevertheless states that it is "desirable" that "the duty should be less than the total amount of the subsidy if such lesser duty would be adequate to remove the injury"'. Article 19.2 thus encourages 'authorities to link the actual amount of the countervailing duty to the injury to be removed'. Moreover, the Appellate Body pointed out, 'once a causal link between the subsidized imports and injury has been demonstrated, the imposition and levying of countervailing duties are not hermetically isolated from any consideration related to injury'. It found the link between the amount of the countervailing duty and the injury that the subsidized imports are found to be causing to be 'reflected in Article 19.3 itself, which provides that a "countervailing duty shall be levied, in the appropriate amounts in each case . . . on imports of such product . . . found to be subsidized and *causing injury*"' (emphasis added by Appellate Body). The Appellate Body found additional contextual support in Articles 10, 19.1, 21.1 and 32.1.[47]

Ultimately, the Appellate Body found a violation of SCM Agreement Article 19.3 due to the DOC's failure 'to establish whether or to what degree it would offset the same subsidies twice by imposing anti-dumping duties calculated under its NME methodology, concurrently with countervailing duties'.[48]

The Appellate Body's finding on this issue were criticised by those who accuse the Appellate Body of 'overreaching', as occurred with many of the Appellate Body's findings on 'zeroing'. There are a number of reasons for this criticism. First, the panel had found there to be no violation, which indicates that three very knowledgeable trade experts took a different view than did the Appellate Body. Secondly, the provision relied on by the Appellate Body does not address the issue explicitly. Whether the term 'appropriate amounts' places constraints on the use of double remedies is not very clear from

---

[45] *Ibid*, para 550–52.
[46] *Ibid*, para 554–55.
[47] *Ibid*, paras 557–63.
[48] *Ibid*, para 604.

the text. And thirdly, an examination of the third parties' views on this issue (see paras 14.60–14.66 of the Panel Report) seems to indicate some disagreement on the issue among WTO Members.

Regardless of any criticism of the decision, though, the US will now have to implement the Appellate Body's ruling on double remedies in the investigations at issue, and more generally some WTO Members may have to adjust their practices in this regard. This may not be an easy task. As the panel noted:

> 14.75 . . . the arguments put forward by the United States reinforce the idea that ascertaining the precise extent of double remedy in specific investigations would be a complex task, a fact which is highlighted by both the GAO, in its 2005 Report, and by the CIT in *GPX*.

The challenge of identifying the specific degree to which subsidies contribute to a finding of dumping will no doubt be very high. What is not clear at this point is exactly how detailed an analysis the Appellate Body expects, and what its components should be. For example, do export prices need to be related to the subsidies at issue, to see how much, if at all, prices were lowered due to the subsidies? Clearly, some type of examination of the issue is required—but what exactly is required may only be known after a couple rounds of trying to come up with a test, and then having it challenged in WTO dispute settlement.

As a final point, with regard to the more general policy issue of putting constraints on double remedies, it is worth noting that there is a counter-argument to all of these suggestions of a double remedy problem, based on either NME-type calculations or effects on export prices. Opponents of restrictions on double remedies might say that there is, in fact, no issue that needs to be addressed. In this regard, it could be argued that anti-dumping and countervailing duties address different issues, and thus there is no need to reconcile them or worry about an overlap. In this view, a countervailing duty is designed to provide a remedy for the use of an injurious subsidy, regardless of any price effects. Also, anti-dumping duties are designed to provide a remedy for injurious dumping, regardless of the cause. Therefore, the fact that subsidies may cause dumping is completely irrelevant, due to the nature of each remedy. To some extent, this view is undermined by the existence of Article VI:5. Clearly, the mid-twentieth-century drafters of this provision were worried about this overlap. As a result, proponents of the view that double remedies should be allowed can argue either that Article VI:5 is wrong, and should be eliminated or limited in some way, or, at the least, that its erroneous approach should not be spread any further.

In addition, it could be argued, as noted above, that the task of identifying how particular subsidies were used is a near-impossible one. Money is fungible, and as a result tracing its various uses will be enormously difficult, even with a large investigative team looking into it. If the burden is placed on respondents, they will be unable to prove that the money was not used to lower the export price; and if the burden is placed on the investigating authorities, they will not be able to prove that it was used to lower the export price. Thus, the entire process would be of little use.

The Appellate Body has, in effect, rejected these counter-arguments in the context of the specific double remedies issue in this case. However, they may still play a role in the discussions over implementation of this case and the possible extension of the reasoning to other areas. These issues will unfold over the next few years as implementation takes place.

VI. QUESTIONS

1. Is dumping 'unfair'? Why does GATT Article VI say it is to be 'condemned'? Do anti-dumping laws target bad behaviour, or are they simply protectionist measures?

2. What is the relationship of 'dumping' to 'price discrimination' or 'predatory pricing' under antitrust/competition law? Could a domestic law enforcement action relating to predatory pricing or price discrimination by foreign companies be considered a 'specific action against dumping' to which WTO anti-dumping rules apply?

3. Should findings of dumping be restricted to situations where the foreign industry has a protected home market or has 'market power' in the home market (in the antitrust/competition policy sense)?

4. Was the Appellate Body correct in its conclusion that 'Article VI, and, in particular, Article VI:2, read in conjunction with the *Anti-Dumping Agreement*, limit the permissible responses to dumping to definitive anti-dumping duties, provisional measures and price undertakings'?

5. Is 'zeroing' unfair? Should dumping be considered to exist when the average price of *all* subject imports is less than the average price for the relevant comparison sales, or when any *individual* product is sold at less than the relevant comparison price?

6. Should zeroing be found to violate WTO rules in all circumstances?

7. Some countries, most notably China, have been deemed to be 'non-market economies', due to the level of government involvement in their economies. As a result, special rules have been applied in carrying out dumping margin calculations for these countries. For example, when using a constructed normal value, the costs used in the calculation are taken from countries that are similar, because the costs reported in the non-market economy are considered unreliable. Given that there is government involvement in the economy of every country, can countries be distinguished on the basis of 'non-market' versus 'market' in any meaningful way? What degree of government involvement would make a country a 'non-market' economy?

8. Does the comparison between sales in one market and sales in another make sense as the basis for finding that 'dumping' exists? Are there legitimate reasons that companies may charge different prices in different markets?

9. Would a company know if it is 'dumping' prior to an agency determination to that effect? Are there actions companies can take to avoid 'dumping'? If the domestic market at issue is very competitive and, as a result, has low prices, will foreign companies sometimes have to dump in order to compete effectively in that market?

10. Does it matter whether Members use a retrospective or prospective system? What are the differences between the two?

11. Would the result in *US—Offset Act (Byrd Amendment)* have been the same if the measure at issue was adopted at the same time as the overall anti-dumping/countervailing duty law, rather than added later in a fairly obvious attempt to make US anti-dumping law more favourable to domestic industries?

12. What causation standard should apply under Article 3.5 of the Anti-Dumping Agreement? Is the Appellate Body's statement about a 'genuine and substantial relationship of cause and effect' appropriate? Should a 'principal' or 'sole' cause standard be used instead?

13. Are there likely to be many situations where there is more than one 'permissible interpretation' of the Anti-Dumping Agreement? The panel in *US—Lumber AD Determination, Article 21.5* concluded that 'neither the ordinary meaning of the first sentence of Article 2.4.2 as a whole, nor the ordinary meaning of the phrase "margins of dumping" in particular, require that all transaction-specific comparisons under the T-T comparison methodology must be treated as "intermediate values" and aggregated, without zeroing, in order to arrive at a single margin of dumping for the product as a whole'. Therefore, it found that that use of 'zeroing' by the US in these circumstances rested on a 'permissible' interpretation of Article 2.4.2. On appeal, the Appellate Body reversed the panel's finding. In this regard, it said that having found that Article 2.4.2 'does not admit an interpretation that would allow the use of zeroing under the transaction-to-transaction comparison methodology', 'the contrary view is not a permissible interpretation of Article 2.4.2 within the meaning of Article 17.6(ii) of the *Anti-Dumping Agreement*'. Do you agree with the panel or Appellate Body?

14. Would it be possible to come up with multilateral rules on 'dumping,' similar to the WTO rules on subsidies established in the SCM Agreement?

12

Safeguards

I. INTRODUCTION

Safeguard measures are intended to shelter troubled industries from economic harm caused by unexpected surges in imports. The types of economic harm at issue here include decreased production and price, which may in turn lead to increased unemployment. Safeguards provide protection on a temporary basis via the raising of bound tariff levels, tariff quotas or quantitative restrictions.

Such measures clearly run contrary to the idea of trade liberalisation, and can therefore be viewed as a form of inefficient protectionism. Rather than erect trade barriers, the economic harm caused by increased imports ought preferably to be remedied with superior policy instruments. For example, displaced workers can be re-trained and receive financial assistance pending their move to more efficient economic sectors. However, such programmes must, of course, be funded from domestic tax revenues, and it is therefore easier for governments to respond to increased import competition by raising tariffs or imposing quotas. Understood in this light, the availability of safeguard measures represents an acknowledgement of political realities, and the notion that trade liberalisation improves overall welfare, but also leaves some worse off.

A further view is that safeguards provide a 'breathing space' during which the protected industry can improve its competitiveness.[1] Of course, the value of this breathing space depends on how productively it is used by the industry concerned to engage in a serious restructuring effort. It must also be borne in mind that the competing industry, whose exports are subject to safeguard measures, will be under direct pressure to improve competitiveness; a consideration which reinforces the need for the productive use of the 'breathing space'.[2] However, the 'breathing space' can also be seen as a possible means of lowering adjustment costs. If competitiveness is to be enhanced through job losses, there could plausibly be a limit on the number of newly unemployed workers which the economy can absorb. The staggering of redundancies over an extended period better

---

[1] The rationale is reflected in the Preamble of the WTO *Agreement on Safeguards* which refers to 'the importance of structural adjustment'.

[2] See MJ Hahn, 'Balancing or Bending? Unilateral Reactions to Safeguard Measures' (2005) 39 *Journal of World Trade* 301 at 303.

enables the economy to offer new opportunities for workers, and reduces the need for these workers to be financially assisted by the state.[3]

A different justification for safeguards is that they facilitate the granting of trade concessions. Trade negotiators are more able to enter into commitments when they understand that these commitments can be relaxed in the future should this unexpectedly prove to be necessary. In this light, safeguards can be viewed as a valuable, perhaps even an indispensable, 'exit' option.

Along with anti-dumping and anti-subsidy measures, safeguard measures form part of the suite of trade remedies at the disposal of WTO Members. These measures are, to some extent, substitutable, especially when the comparison is between anti-dumping and safeguard measures. There are close analogies between these areas, most obviously the need for measures to be preceded by a national investigation. The substantive requirements which national authorities are required to examine in the three areas also overlap to a considerable extent. The main point of distinction between safeguards and both anti-dumping and anti-subsidy measures is that there is no allegation of any unfair trade practice in the safeguards context. Safeguard measures are more directly concerned with increases in the level of imports——something which occurs naturally as a result of trade liberalisation——rather than with the unacceptably low price of imports or the receipt of subsidies. This distinction is reflected in the relevant Treaty provisions. For example, Article 8 of the Safeguards Agreement envisages trade compensation or the suspension of concessions as a means of rebalancing trade concessions during the application of safeguard measures. There is no equivalent provision in the Anti-Dumping Agreement. Additionally, the injury standard in safeguard investigations is 'serious injury', while the lesser 'material injury' standard applies in the anti-dumping context. Both differences can be seen as reflecting the notion that safeguards are a response to fairly traded imports. It is likely that the slightly more permissive standards under which anti-dumping duties can be imposed is part of the explanation for greater recourse to these duties. While 101 safeguard measures were notified between 1996 and 2010, the figure for notified anti-dumping measures in the same period is 2503.[4]

In the GATT, safeguard measures were, and continue to be, regulated by Article XIX, entitled *Emergency Action on Imports of Particular Products*. This provision was supplemented during the Uruguay Round with the Agreement on Safeguards, which is one of the multilateral agreements on trade in goods contained in Annex 1A of the WTO Agreement. The procedural and substantive requirements in these instruments have been strictly interpreted by panels and the Appellate Body. In all the WTO complaints brought in this area, there has been at least one finding to the effect that national investigating authorities acted inconsistently with WTO rules. The interpretations developed through the dispute settlement process have been severely criticised,[5] but have also been defended.[6] The dif-

---

[3] PA Messerlin and H Fridh, 'The Agreement on Safeguards: Proposals for Change in the Light of the EC Steel Safeguards' (2006) 40 *Journal of World Trade* 713 at 715.

[4] See the statistical information available on the WTO's web pages: http://www.wto.org/english/tratop_e/safeg_e/safeg_e.htm for safeguards; http://www.wto.org/english/tratop_e/adp_e/adp_e.htm for anti-dumping.

[5] See A Sykes, *The WTO Agreement on Safeguards: A Commentary* (Oxford, Oxford University Press, 2006); A Sykes, 'The Persistent Puzzles of Safeguards: Lessons From the Steel Dispute' (2004) 7 *Journal of International Economic Law* 523; J Pauwelyn, 'The Puzzle of WTO Safeguards and Regional Trade Agreements' (2004) 7 *Journal of International Economic Law* 109.

[6] Y-S Lee, 'Not Without a Clue: Commentary on "the Persistent Puzzles of Safeguards"' (2006) 40 *Journal of World Trade* 385.

ficulty is to know where the balance lies between allowing Members to use safeguards and keeping a tight reign on their over-use. The task of panels and the Appellate Body is made no less difficult by the text of the Safeguards Agreement, which, according to several commentators, is incoherent in a number of important respects when evaluated from an economics perspective.[7] It is also generally accepted that the Agreement lacks clarity on some issues of key importance, and, therefore, leaves much to be decided through the dispute settlement process.

Also of importance in the regulation of safeguards are the terms on which China acceded to the WTO Agreement via its Accession Protocol.[8] Section 16 of this Protocol is entitled Transitional Product-Specific Safeguard Mechanism, and establishes a special safeguard procedure that WTO Members can apply with respect to imports from China. Section 16.9 provides that the Section is set to expire on 11 December 2013. The rules here make it easier for safeguard measures to be imposed on imports from China, relative to the equivalent rules in GATT Article XIX and the Agreement on Safeguards. For example, while the general threshold for safeguard measures is the presence of 'serious injury' to the domestic industry, this is reduced to 'material injury' under paragraph 16.4 of the Accession Protocol. As Zang notes, a 'buffering mechanism' of this kind was used in the GATT era upon the accession of the so-called state trading countries or non-market economies.[9] However, as this practice ceased after the establishment of the WTO, its revival for China is plausibly attributable as much to the size of its economy as its nature. The imposition of safeguard measures by the US under Section 16 was challenged by China in *United States—Measures Affecting Imports of Certain Passenger and Light Truck Tyres from China*. The panel exonerated the US on all the grounds of challenge raised by China and the panel findings appealed by China were upheld by the Appellate Body. The case therefore stands in stark contrast to those brought under the Agreement on Safeguards, in all of which, one more of the grounds of challenge have been substantiated.

The Chapter is presented as follows. Section II considers the procedural requirements connected with the application of safeguards, which, broadly speaking, are intended to enhance the transparency of the entire process of imposing safeguard measures through notification and consultation obligations. Section III examines the various conditions which must be examined by national authorities in order to determine whether it is possible to apply safeguards. Section IV considers the standard of review applied by panels and the Appellate Body when examining challenges to the methodologies and findings of national authorities. Section V covers the permissible scope of application of safeguard measures, while Section VI deals with the obligation to maintain the balance concessions via compensation and the suspension of concessions.

---

[7] This theme provides the foundation for much of Sykes' work and, for the non-economist, is explained in the most accessible manner in A Sykes 'The Fundamental Deficiencies of the Agreement on Safeguards: A Reply to Professor Lee' (2006) 40 *Journal of World Trade* 979.

[8] WT/L/432, Accession of the People's Republic of China, Decision of 10 November 2001.

[9] MQ Zang, 'The WTO Contingent Trade Instruments Against China: What Does Accession Bring?' (2009) 58 *International and Comparative Law Quarterly* 321, 322.

II. PROCEDURAL REQUIREMENTS

The procedural requirements which must be satisfied in connection with the application of safeguard measures are briefly considered in this section. These are set out primarily in Article 3 of the Safeguards Agreement, dealing with the 'Investigation' which must precede the application of measures, and Article 12, dealing with obligations of notification and consultation. It is notable that one of the functions of the WTO Committee on Safeguards under Article 13.1(b) is 'to find, upon request of an affected Member, whether or not the procedural requirements of this Agreement have been complied with in connection with a safeguard measure, and report its findings to the Council for Trade in Goods'.

In October 2011, Colombia and India invoked this provision for the first time in connection with safeguard measures taken by Ecuador on glass windshields and by Turkey on cotton yarn, respectively. The views expressed in the Committee on Safeguards[10] illustrate the difficulties in applying the provision with the minutes of the meeting recording disagreement on the factual circumstances and calls from a number of Members for procedures to be drafted to guide the Committee's work under Article 13.1(b). Attention was also drawn to the provision's limitation to findings of compliance with 'procedural requirements' as opposed also to compliance with substantive requirements which remain under the exclusive purview of panels and the Appellate Body.

Under Article 3.1, safeguard measures can only be applied following a national investigation. '[R]easonable public notice' of the investigation must be provided and interested parties such as importers and exporters must have the opportunity to present evidence, and their views, via a public hearing or other appropriate means. It is further provided that '[t]he competent authorities shall publish a report setting forth their findings and reasoned conclusions reached on all pertinent issues of fact and law'. These reports have frequently been subject to intense scrutiny by panels and the Appellate Body when called upon to examine whether the substantive requirements of the Safeguards Agreement have been satisfied.

The primary notification obligation under Article 12 relates to the provision of information to the Committee on Safeguards which is established by Article 13. The Committee must be notified of such matters as the decision to initiate an investigation and the decision to apply or extend a safeguard measure. Under Article 12.2, the Committee must be provided with 'all pertinent information' relating to the above decisions. In particular, evidence of the 'serious injury or threat thereof caused by increased imports' must be disclosed.

The main consultation obligation is contained in Article 12.3. This requires the application or extension of a safeguard measure to be preceded by 'consultations with those Members having a substantial interest as exporters of the product concerned'. The most important purpose of these consultations is to reach an understanding on how to restore the balance of negotiated concessions which would inevitably be disturbed by the application of the safeguard measure. Restoring this balance via trade compensation or the suspension of concessions is considered further in section VI.

---

[10] G/SG/M/40, Committee on Safeguards—minutes of the regular meeting held on 27 October 2011.

III. CONDITIONS TO BE SATISFIED IN ORDER TO APPLY SAFEGUARD MEASURES

The Appellate Body has emphasised the distinction between 'two basic inquiries that face an interpreter of the *Agreement on Safeguards*'.[11] First, the national investigating authority must determine whether the conditions for the application of safeguards can be satisfied. Secondly, it must then consider the permissible scope of application of the safeguard measure. This section deals with the first inquiry.

The conditions which must be satisfied before a safeguard measure can be applied are set out in the provisions below.

GATT 1994, Article XIX.1(a)

Emergency Action on Imports of Particular Products

If, as a result of unforeseen developments and of the effect of the obligations incurred by a Member under this Agreement, including tariff concessions, any product is being imported into the territory of that Member in such increased quantities and under such conditions as to cause or threaten serious injury to domestic producers in that territory of like or directly competitive products, the Member shall be free, in respect of such product, and to the extent and for such time as may be necessary to prevent or remedy such injury, to suspend the obligation in whole or in part or to withdraw or modify the concession.

Safeguards Agreement Article 2.1

A Member may apply a safeguard measure to a product only if that Member has determined, pursuant to the provisions set out below, that such product is being imported into its territory in such increased quantities, absolute or relative to domestic production, and under such conditions as to cause or threaten to cause serious injury to the domestic industry that produces like or directly competitive products.

The term 'unforeseen developments' appears in GATT Article XIX.1(a), but is not reiterated in Article 2.1, or any other provision of the Safeguards Agreement. This difference led to uncertainty over the relationship between GATT Article XIX and the Safeguards Agreement; the question being whether the 'unforeseen developments' requirement continued to be applicable. The Appellate Body has relied on two provisions in the Safeguards Agreement to support its view that Article XIX 'continues in full force and effect' so that safeguard measures must conform with both instruments.[12] First, Article 1 defines safeguard measures as 'those measures provided for in Article XIX of GATT 1994'. More tellingly, Article 11.1(a) prohibits 'emergency action . . . unless such action conforms with the provisions of [GATT Article XIX] applied in accordance with this Agreement'. These provisions led the Appellate Body to affirm a panel's view that the two instruments must 'be read as representing an inseparable package of rights and disciplines which have to be considered in conjunction'.[13]

---

[11] Appellate Body Report, *US— Line Pipe Safeguards*, para 225.

[12] Appellate Body Report, *Argentina—Footwear Safeguards*, para 83.

[13] *Ibid*, para 81. This statement was again approved in Appellate Body Report, *US—Steel Safeguards*, para 275. The Appellate Body's view that the existence of unforeseen developments must be specifically demonstrated has been criticised as inconsistent with the intent of the Uruguay Round negotiators. See Y-S Lee, above n 6, 389.

With the benefit of this clarification, the provisions above can helpfully be thought of as setting out four conditions for the imposition of safeguard measures, relating to:

- increased imports;
- unforeseen developments;
- serious injury; and
- causation.[14]

We examine these conditions separately below.

(a) Increased Imports

Article 2.1 states that the increase in imports can be 'absolute or relative to domestic production'. Similar language is used in Article 4.2(b). It follows that the increased imports condition can potentially be satisfied when imports have not increased in absolute terms, and even when imports have decreased in absolute terms, as long as they have increased in relative terms. These relative increases in imports could occur when levels of domestic production decline.

The leading statement by the Appellate Body on the increased imports requirement was given in *Argentina—Footwear*:

> . . . the determination of whether the requirement of imports "in such increased quantities" is met is not a merely mathematical or technical determination. In other words, it is not enough for an investigation to show simply that imports of the product this year were more than last year – or five years ago . . . There must be "such increased quantities" as to cause or threaten to cause serious injury to the domestic industry in order to fulfil this requirement for applying a safeguard measure. And this language in both Article 2.1 of the *Agreement on Safeguards* and Article XIX:1(a) of the GATT 1994, we believe, requires that the increase in imports must have been *recent enough, sudden enough, sharp enough, and significant enough*, both quantitatively and qualitatively, to cause or threaten to cause "serious injury".[15] (emphasis added)

The Appellate Body re-affirmed this passage in *United States—Steel Safeguard*.[16] In this case the United States had undertaken an end-point to end-point analysis of imports of certain steel products, and determined that imports of these products were higher at the end of the period of investigation than at its commencement. The question arose as to whether such an analysis can be a sufficient basis to demonstrate compliance with Articles 2.1 and 4.2(a). It is interesting to note that, in the opening paragraph of the extract below, the United States appears to be suggesting that the Appellate Body engaged in judicial activism in elaborating the test for increased imports in *Argentina—Footwear*. However, the Appellate Body was able to justify its views on the increased imports requirement by referring to the language used in Article 4.2(a).

---

[14] Closely related to the causation requirement, is the 'non attribution' requirement set out in Art 4.2(b). As such, causation and non-attribution are examined together in section III(d) below.

[15] Appellate Body Report, *Argentina—Footwear Safeguards*, para 131.

[16] Appellate Body Report, *US—Steel Safeguards*, para 354.

Appellate Body Report, *United States—Definitive Safeguard Measures on Imports of Certain Steel Products,* **aAdopted 10 December 2003, WT/DS248,249,251,252,253,254,258,259/AB/R**

352. We turn next to examine the United States' argument that, as "the words recent, sudden, sharp or significant" do not appear in Article 2.1, "the phrase 'in such increased quantities' simply states the requirement that, in general, the level of imports at (or reasonably near to) the end of a period of investigation be higher than at some unspecified earlier point in time."

353. Article 4.2 of the *Agreement on Safeguards* elaborates on the prerequisites for the application of a safeguard measure that are set out in Article 2.1. Article 4.2(a) provides context for interpreting the meaning of the requirement relating to increased imports in Article 2.1. Article 4.2(a) provides, in relevant part, that:

> In the investigation to determine whether increased imports have caused or are threatening to cause serious injury to a domestic industry under the terms of this Agreement, *the competent authorities shall evaluate . . . the rate and amount of the increase in imports of the product concerned in absolute and relative terms . . . .*

354. We concluded in *Argentina – Footwear (EC)* that "the competent authorities are required to consider the trends in imports over the period of investigation (rather than just comparing the end points) under Article 4.2(a)." A determination of whether there is an increase in imports cannot, therefore, be made merely by comparing the end points of the period of investigation. Indeed, in cases where an examination does not demonstrate, for instance, a clear and uninterrupted upward trend in import volumes, a simple end-point-to-end-point analysis could easily be manipulated to lead to different results, depending on the choice of end points. A comparison could support either a finding of an increase or a decrease in import volumes simply by choosing different starting and ending points.

355. For instance, if the starting point for the period of investigation were set at a time when import levels were particularly low, it would be more likely that an increase in import volumes could be demonstrated. The use of the phrase "such increased quantities" in Articles XIX:1(a) and 2.1, and the requirement in Article 4.2 to assess the "rate and amount" of the increase, make it abundantly clear, however, that such a comparison of end points will not suffice to demonstrate that a product "is being imported in such increased quantities" within the meaning of Article 2.1. Thus, a demonstration of "any increase" in imports between any two points in time is not sufficient to demonstrate "increased imports" for purposes of Articles XIX and 2.1. Rather, as we have said, competent authorities are required to examine the trends in imports over the entire period of investigation.

... ...

From these paragraphs, it is certain that a challenged investigation will be found to be inadequate if it does not proceed beyond comparing import levels at two points in time. The requirement in Article 4.2(a) to assess the 'rate and amount' of the increase requires that consideration be given to fluctuations in import levels between these two points. Understandably, however, the Appellate Body has not attempted to provide very much advice on when investigating authorities can confidently conclude that there are increased imports, having considered any fluctuations during the investigating period. Paragraph 354 clearly signals that the increased imports requirement would be met when there are no fluctuations, and the investigation reveals 'a clear and uninterrupted upward trend in import volumes'. However, there is uncertainty over what pattern of fluctuations might lead the Appellate Body to strike down a finding of increased imports, in particular, where imports are declining towards the end of the investigation.

Finally, it can be suggested that even an investigation which carefully considers fluctuations might not necessarily be free from the risk of manipulation referred to in paragraph 354. The pattern of fluctuations would seem to depend on the start and end points for the investigation selected by the investigating body. However, the requirement that the increase in imports must have been 'recent' certainly guards against this risk of manipulation to a significant extent.

(b) Unforeseen Developments

Under Article XIX.1(a), the increased imports must, first, be 'a result of unforeseen developments' and, secondly, be a result 'of the effect of the obligations incurred by a Member under this Agreement, including tariff concessions'.

The two tests in this phrase were first interpreted in the 1951 *Hatters' Fur* case.[17] The dispute arose from the increased imports of fur felt hats from Czechoslovakia with special, as opposed to plain, finishes. On the first test, the United States argued that the increase in imports was due to unforeseen developments in the form of a change in fashion and taste towards special finishes. The Working Party considered that the change in hat styles in itself did not constitute an 'unforeseen development'; something which the United States acknowledged.[18] However, the Working Party also considered 'that the United States negotiators in 1947 could not reasonably be expected to foresee *this* style change in favour of velours would in fact subsequently take place, and would do so on as large a scale and last for as long a period as it in fact did'[19] (emphasis added). The Working Party therefore distinguished between changes in fashion, which are eminently foreseeable, and the direction in which they change, together with the extent to which fashion will change, which may, or may not be, foreseeable. On the facts, the Working Party found that the direction and extent of the change were not foreseeable, although one can have some sympathy with Czechoslovakia's opposition to this finding. There was evidence that this particular change in taste had taken hold in Europe at the time of the tariff reduction.[20] Czechoslovakia had also argued that the change 'resulted mainly from the enterprise of the exporters (with their selling organization in the United States) and of the American milliners, who deliberately produced the new designs and created the demand for them by advertisement and good salesmanship'.[21]

Regarding the second test, it was found that the increase in imports was due to the effect of the substantial tariff reduction negotiated in 1947. The Working Party found that the concession reduced the price differential between imported special finishes and domestic plain finishes thereby reinforcing the preference for imports.[22]

The introduction of the Safeguards Agreement led to some uncertainty over the status and relevance of the two tests in GATT Article XIX.1(a). In the *Korea—Dairy* case, the panel was of the view that Article XIX.1(a) was still generally applicable,[23] but also that

---

[17] Report on the Withdrawal by the United States of a Tariff Concession under Art XIX of the General Agreement on Tariffs and Trade, GATT/CP/106 adopted 22 October 1951.

[18] *Ibid*, paras 8 and 11.

[19] *Ibid*, para 11.

[20] *Ibid*, para 8.

[21] *Ibid*, para 10(b).

[22] *Ibid*, para 11(iii).

[23] Panel Report, *Korea—Dairy Safeguards*, para 7.39.

the 'unforeseen developments' clause did not 'add conditions for any measures to be applied pursuant to Article XIX'.[24] According to the panel, the clause merely 'describes generally the situations where the binding nature of the obligations contained in Articles II and XI of GATT may need to be set aside (for a certain period)'.[25] On the appeal of these findings by the European Communities, the Appellate Body found as follows:

> Although we do not view the first clause in Article XIX.1(a) as establishing independent *conditions* for the application of a safeguard measure, additional to the conditions set forth in the second clause of that paragraph, we do believe that the first clause describes certain *circumstances* which must be demonstrated as a matter of fact in order for a safeguard measure to be applied consistently with the provisions of Article XIX of the GATT 1994.[26] (emphasis added)

The extent of the Appellate Body's disagreement with the panel is subtle, but nevertheless important. The Appellate Body almost agrees fully with the panel. The 'unforeseen developments' clause does not establish an independent condition for the application of safeguard measures. Rather, it merely describes the situations, or circumstances, in which safeguard measures can be applied. However, the crucial difference is the Appellate Body's view that the existence of the circumstances must be specifically demonstrated. There is therefore a pronounced difference of approach here to the extent that the panel's view was effectively overruled. Greater clarity might have been achieved by avoiding the somewhat illusory distinction between the absence of independent conditions and the presence of circumstances which must be demonstrated.

This view was reinforced in *United States—Steel Safeguard*, in which one of the issues was whether a single determination on 'unforeseen development' can suffice where the importing Member wishes to impose safeguard measures on a range of products. The Appellate Body found that:

> when an importing Member wishes to apply safeguard measures on imports of several products, it is not sufficient merely to demonstrate that "unforeseen developments" resulted in increased imports of a broad category of products that included the specific products subject to the respective determinations by the competent authority. If that could be done, a Member could make a determination and apply a safeguard measure to a broad category of products even if imports of one or more of those products did not increase and did not result from the "unforeseen developments" at issue . . . [Therefore] the demonstration of "unforeseen developments" must be performed for each product subject to a safeguard measure.[27]

The Appellate Body was also clearly of the view that the United States International Trade Commission (ITC) report had not provided a reasoned and adequate explanation of the connection between the unforeseen developments and increased imports. It agreed with the view of European Communities that, '[i]n the present case where the ITC relied upon macroeconomic events having effects across a number of industries, it was for the ITC to demonstrate the 'logical connection' between the alleged unforeseen development[s] and the increase in imports in relation to each measure, not for the Panel to read into the report linkages that the ITC failed to make'.[28]

---

[24] *Ibid*, para 7.42.
[25] *Ibid*, para 7.43.
[26] Appellate Body Report, *Korea—Dairy Safeguards*, para 85.
[27] Appellate Body Report, *US—Steel Safeguard*, para 319.
[28] *Ibid*, para 322.

The macroeconomic events referred to here were the Asian and Russian financial crises combined with a strong American dollar. Financial crises can lead to increased imports through market displacement. In other words, steel which would otherwise have been sold in Asia and Russia is diverted to the United States. States with strong currency can suffer a reduction in their exports and a consequent decline in domestic production. Both these factors can readily fall under the heading of unforeseen developments, as can changes in fashion in a particular direction, and technological developments. However, in order to satisfy GATT Article XIX.1(a), it is not enough for investigating authorities to describe circumstances which could not reasonably have been foreseen at the time the tariff concession was last negotiated. It must also be explained how the unforeseen developments have resulted in increased imports of each of the products the importing Member wishes to impose safeguard measures on.

Finally, it is notable that the second phrase in Article XIX.1(a)—that the increased imports must be a result 'of the effect of the obligations incurred by a Member under this Agreement, including tariff concessions—has been interpreted by the Appellate Body such as to be capable of satisfaction with reasonable ease. In *Korea—Dairy*, the Appellate Body considered that 'this phrase simply means that it must be demonstrated, as a matter of fact, that the importing Member has incurred obligations under the GATT 1994, including tariff concessions'.[29] Nevertheless, it is possible to fall foul of this obligation. The panel in *Dominican Republic—Bag and Fabric Safeguard* noted the agreement of the parties that the Dominican Republic had granted a tariff concession and that it had therefore undoubtedly 'incurred obligations under the GATT 1994' with respect to the relevant products. Indeed, the investigating authority's report had referred to these obligations, albeit in a cursory manner. However, the panel's key finding here was that the report had failed to refer to these obligations, 'as obligations linked with the increase in imports said to have caused serious injury to its domestic industry'.[30] Therefore, investigating authority reports must both clearly identify a WTO obligation such as a tariff concession and establish a link between this obligation and the increase in imports.

(c) Serious Injury or Threat Thereof

A further prerequisite for the application of safeguard measures is the existence of 'serious injury or threat thereof' to the domestic industry producing like or directly competitive products. There are two issues here. The first issue relates to the identity of the 'domestic industry' which must be sustaining, or threatened by, serious injury. The second relates to when this relevant domestic industry can be understood as sustaining, or threatened by, serious injury.

(i) Identifying the Relevant Domestic Industry

Under Article 2.1, the relevant domestic industry is that which is producing 'like or directly competitive products' to those being imported in increased quantities. This is

---

[29] Appellate Body Report, *Korea—Dairy Safeguards*, para 84. Exactly the same language was used by the Appellate Body in *Argentina—Footwear*, para 91. The Appellate Body reports in these cases were both circulated and adopted on the same dates, respectively 14 December 1999 and 12 January 2000.

[30] Panel Report, *Dominican Republic—Bag and Fabric Safeguard*, para 7.147.

reiterated in Article 4.1(c) which also provides a fuller definition of the relevant domestic industry:

> in determining injury or threat thereof, a "domestic industry" shall be understood to mean the producers as a whole of the like or directly competitive products operating within the territory of a Member, or those whose collective output of the like or directly competitive products constitutes a major proportion of the total domestic production of those products.

In practice, national investigating authorities can be inclined, in some cases, to take a narrow view of the 'domestic industry' and, in other cases, to take a broad view. The tendency towards a narrow view might arise where some of the domestic industry, producing like or directly competitive products, is *not* being injured by the increased imports. If the position of this portion of the domestic industry must be considered, it becomes more difficult for the authority to make a determination of serious injury. Article 4.1(c) requires, as a minimum, that the authority assess the position of the domestic industry, 'whose collective output of the like or directly competitive products constitutes a major proportion of the total domestic production of those products'. There is no guidance to date on what proportion of the domestic industry constitutes a 'major proportion'.

The panel in *Dominican Republic—Bag and Fabric Safeguard* found that an impermissibly narrow view of the domestic industry had been adopted. The relevant imported product was polypropylene bags with no differentiation depending on the starting point and materials from which the imported bags were produced. Therefore the domestic industry ought also to have been defined in this undifferentiated manner. However, it was defined as excluding producers beginning from a stage 'subsequent to the processing of resin'.[31] Therefore, producers which did not themselves undertake the early stages of the bag manufacturing process were excluded from the 'domestic industry', even though their output was like or directly competitive with the investigated imports.

In contrast, the broad view arises from the tendency of authorities to sometimes define the domestic industry as *all* the domestic industry which is being injured by the increased imports, rather than *only* the domestic industry producing like or directly competitive products. In *US Lamb*, the US had imposed safeguard measures on imported lamb meat, and argued that the relevant domestic industry included not only packers and breakers of lamb meat, but also growers and feeders of live lambs. It can readily be seen how the growers and feeders of live lambs could be adversely affected by increased imports of lamb meat. Indeed, it is difficult to disagree with one of the findings in the USITC report that 'there was a substantial coincidence of economic interests between and among the growers and feeders of live lambs, and the packers and breakers of lamb meat'.[32] However, the Appellate Body considered that there was no basis for this consideration in the Safeguards Agreement. There was also no basis for the related consideration that there was a 'continuous line of production from the raw to the processed product'.[33] The Appellate Body explained the correct methodology for identifying the domestic industry as follows:

> According to the clear and express wording of the text of Article 4.1(c), the term "domestic industry" extends solely to the "producers . . . *of the like or directly competitive products*". The

---

[31] *Ibid*, paras 7.188—190.
[32] Appellate Body Report, *US—Lamb*, para 77.
[33] *Ibid.*

definition, therefore, focuses exclusively on the producers of a very specific group of products. Producers of products that are not "like or directly competitive products" do not, according to the text of the treaty, form part of the domestic industry.[34]

The Appellate Body proceeded to set out its conclusion based on the USITC's own findings on the 'like or directly competitive products' at issue:

> . . . [I]n this case, the USITC determined that the like products at issue were domestic and imported lamb meat and that the USITC did not find that live lambs or any other products were directly competitive with lamb meat. On the basis of this finding of the USITC, we consider that the "domestic industry" could only include the "producers" of lamb meat. By expanding the "domestic industry" to include producers of other products, namely, live lambs, the USITC defined the "domestic industry" inconsistently with Article 4.1(c) of the *Agreement on Safeguards*.[35]

Despite the indication in this passage that the USITC might have found lamb meat and live lamb to be directly competitive products, it seems unlikely that such a finding, if challenged, would have been allowed to stand based on the familiar tests for determining the nature and extent of the competitive relationship between products.[36]

(ii) The Injury Determination

Having identified the relevant domestic industry, it must be determined whether this industry is experiencing, or threatened by, serious injury. Article 4.1 defines serious injury, as 'a significant overall impairment in the position of a domestic industry'. Threat of serious injury is defined as 'serious injury that is clearly imminent'. It is further provided that the 'determination of the existence of a threat of serious injury shall be based on facts and not merely on allegation, conjecture or remote possibility'. This provision clearly gives the impression that the existence of a threat of serious injury must be demonstrated by a careful and rigorous investigation, to protect against abuse of the 'threat' provision. This impression is reinforced by the provision below:

Article 4.2(a)

> In the investigation to determine whether increased imports have caused or are threatening to cause serious injury to a domestic industry under the terms of this Agreement, the competent authorities shall evaluate all relevant factors of an objective and quantifiable nature having a bearing on the situation of that industry, in particular, the rate and amount of the increase in imports of the product concerned in absolute and relative terms, the share of the domestic market taken by increased imports, changes in the level of sales, production, productivity, capacity utilization, profits and losses, and employment.

The Appellate Body has interpreted this provision to require that authorities evaluate 'each of the factors listed in Article 4.2(a) as well as all other factors that are relevant to the situation of the industry concerned'.[37] Only when all the listed factors, as well as all other relevant factors, have been evaluated can the authority determine whether there is 'a significant overall impairment in the position of a domestic industry' as required

---

[34] *Ibid*, para 84.
[35] *Ibid*, para 95.
[36] On these tests see Chapter 7.
[37] Appellate Body Report, *Argentina—Footwear Safeguards*, para 136.

by Article 4.1. It is possible for the 'overall picture' to demonstrate 'significant overall impairment' even when some of the examined factors are not in decline.[38]

Further guidance on the nature of the obligation to consider 'all relevant factors' was provided by the Appellate Body in *United States—Wheat Gluten*:

[C]ompetent authorities may [not] limit their evaluation of "all relevant factors", under Article 4.2(a) . . . to the factors which the interested parties have raised as relevant. The competent authorities must, in every case, carry out a full investigation to enable them to conduct a proper evaluation of all of the relevant factors expressly mentioned in Article 4.2(a) of the *Agreement on Safeguards*. Moreover, Article 4.2(a) requires the competent authorities—and not the interested parties—to evaluate fully the relevance, if any, of "other factors". If the competent authorities consider that a particular "other factor" may be relevant to the situation of the domestic industry, under Article 4.2(a), their duties of investigation and evaluation preclude them from remaining passive in the face of possible short-comings in the evidence submitted, and views expressed, by the interested parties. In such cases, where the competent authorities do not have sufficient information before them to evaluate the possible relevance of such an "other factor", they must investigate fully that "other factor", so that they can fulfill their obligations of evaluation under Article 4.2(a) . . .

Thus, we disagree with the Panel's finding that the competent authorities need only examine "other factors" which were "*clearly* raised before them as relevant by the interested parties in the domestic investigation." However, as is clear from the preceding paragraph of this Report, we also reject the European Communities' argument that the competent authorities have an open-ended and unlimited duty to investigate all available facts that might possibly be relevant.[39]

Read as a whole, this passage strengthens the obligation to evaluate the relevance of factors not listed in Article 4.2(a), by specifying that the responsibility lies with the investigating authority rather than the interested parties. However, the passage also relaxes the obligation by indicating that investigating authorities have some discretion to decide on the relevance, or otherwise, of non-listed factors.

(d) Causation and Non-attribution

The causation and non-attribution requirements are set out in Article 4.2(b). The case law has provided guidance on both requirements and how they relate to each other. However, it also raises questions relating to the strictness of the causation test as a condition for the imposition of safeguard measures.

Article 4.2(b):

The determination referred to in subparagraph (a) shall not be made unless this investigation demonstrates, on the basis of objective evidence, the existence of the causal link between increased imports of the product concerned and serious injury or threat thereof. When factors other than increased imports are causing injury to the domestic industry at the same time, such injury shall not be attributed to increased imports.

---

[38] *Ibid*, para 139.
[39] Appellate Body Report, *US—Wheat Gluten Safeguards*, paras 55–56.

(i) The Causation Test

Under the first sentence of Article 4.2(b), the investigating authority must establish 'the existence of the causal link between increased imports of the product concerned and serious injury or threat thereof'. The Appellate Body in *US—Wheat Gluten* commented that 'the term "the causal link" denotes, in our view, a relationship of cause and effect such that increased imports contribute to "bringing about", "producing" or "inducing" the serious injury'.[40] When considered in isolation, this passage gives the impression that the causation threshold is set at a low level. It can clearly be read as indicating that the 'increased imports [merely need to] contribute to "bringing about", "producing" or "inducing" the serious injury'. However, the Appellate Body further explained that the investigating authority must establish

> whether 'the causal link' exists between increased imports and serious injury, and whether this causal link involves a genuine and substantial relationship of cause and effect between these two elements, as required by the *Agreement on Safeguards*.[41]

The two stage test indicated by this passage imposes a heavier burden on the investigating authority than the first passage. The existence of the causal link is not sufficient in itself. The causal link must be sufficiently strong to demonstrate the 'genuine and substantial relationship of cause and effect' indicated.

Both passages were repeated by the Appellate Body in the *US—Lamb* case.[42] In this case, greater emphasis was placed on the second passage. The Appellate Body clarified that

> [t]he primary objective of the process we described in *United States – Wheat Gluten Safeguard* is, of course, to determine whether there is "a genuine and substantial relationship of cause and effect" between increased imports and serious injury or threat thereof.[43]

These passages (and the Safeguards Agreement) leave unanswered the question of what methodology national investigating authorities should use to assess the existence of the required causal link. Panels and the Appellate Body have tended to guardedly endorse a methodology which is commonly used by national investigating authorities. This methodology, which can be described as the 'correlation' or 'coincidence' approach, involves authorities searching for a correlation between increased imports and indicators of industrial decline such as falling profits and employment levels.[44] The panel in *Argentina—Footwear* noted that

> it is the *relationship* between the movements in imports (volume and market share) and the movements in injury factors that must be central to a causation analysis and determination . . . [I]f causation is present, an increase in imports normally should coincide with a decline in the relevant injury factors. While such a coincidence by itself cannot *prove* causation (because, *inter alia*, Article 3 requires an explanation—i.e., 'findings and reasoned conclusions'), its absence

---

[40] *Ibid*, para 66.

[41] *Ibid*, para 69.

[42] Appellate Body Report, *US—Lamb*, paras 166, 168, 177, 179.

[43] *Ibid*, para 179.

[44] A number of authors have referred to the common usage of the correlation approach. In the European context, see E Vermulst, M Pernaute and K Lucenti, 'Recent European Community Safeguards Policy: "Kill Them All and Let God Sort Them Out"?' (2004) 38 *Journal of World Trade* 955 at 962. In the US context, see A Sykes, 'The Persistent Puzzles', above n 5, 531. Sykes also discusses the relative merits of the other methodologies used by the USITC.

would create serious doubts as to the existence of a causal link, and would require a *very* compelling analysis of why causation still is present.[45]

These comments, which were approved by the Appellate Body,[46] have been criticised as coming too close to the conflation of correlation and causation. The objection is that increased imports are deemed to cause injury merely because there is a 'coincidence in time'[47] between injury indicators and increased imports. In this situation, there might well be a genuine causal link. On the other hand, as Sykes points out, the explanation for both the injury and the increased imports might be a domestic recession, or an increase in the costs of domestic producers.[48] Put simply, correlation is not causation. A possible response to this objection is to question whether it might remain appropriate to regard increased imports as the cause of injury, even if the increased imports have themselves been caused by the conditions suggested by Sykes.[49]

An interesting aspect of the *US—Tyres* case decided under Section 16 of China's Accession Protocol provides a good illustration of this question. One of the arguments made by China was that the US tyre industry had voluntarily reduced its investment in the US and had 'outsourced' production to China. According to this view, the voluntary outsourcing was the cause of the increased imports and any possible injury, rather than a response to increased imports from China. Had China been able to substantiate this claim, the panel would have been faced with a difficult question. Can injury to the US industry be confirmed as being caused by increased imports when the increased imports result from voluntary outsourcing by the same US industry? The panel did not, however, directly address this question. Rather, the panel took note of the different views taken by the majority and by dissenting commissioners in the national investigation. The majority considered that the outsourcing was itself a response to increased imports and 'not an alternative cause that prevented the increasing imports from China to be a significant cause' of the injury. In contrast, the dissenting commissioners took the view that 'the business strategy of relocating production to China was an independent business strategy that began before imports were increasing'. In these circumstances, the panel said 'it would be inappropriate for the Panel simply to make a choice between the views of the majority and the dissenting commissioners'. The panel noted that its own assessment of the record 'indicates that it is difficult to separate out the business strategy from the increasing imports' so that there was no basis for a finding that the USITC had erred in its analysis.[50]

(ii) The Non-Attribution Requirement

Under Article 4.2(b), injury caused by factors other than increased imports, must not be attributed to injury caused by increased imports. This provision clearly envisages that

[45] Panel Report, *Argentina—Footwear Safeguards*, paras 8.237—8.238.

[46] Appellate Body Report, *Argentina—Footwear Safeguards*, para 144.

[47] This phrase is used by J Miranda in 'Causal Link and Non-attribution as Interpreted in WTO Trade Remedy Disputes' (2009) 43(5) *Journal of World Trade* 729.

[48] Sykes, above n 5, 532.

[49] In posing this question, the intention is to refer readers to an interesting debate featured in the following contributions: Sykes, above n 5; Lee, above n 6; Sykes, above n 7; Y-S Lee, 'Comments on the Recent Debate on Safeguards-Difference in Perspective, Not a Failure of Appreciation' (2006) 40 *Journal of World Trade* 1145.

[50] Panel Report, *US—Tyres*, paras 7.320—22.

the injury may have several causes apart from increased imports. The provision does not contain an illustrative list of factors of injury other than increased imports along the same lines as Article 3.5 of the Anti-DumpingAgreement and Article 15.5 of the Agreement on Subsidies and Countervailing Measures. However, various 'other' possible causes can be envisaged, including rising input costs, decreases in capacity utilisation, changes in consumer preferences, technological developments which reduce demand for obsolete products, the removal of subsidy payments and inadequate marketing. The Appellate Body has explained the basic framework of how investigating authorities can comply with the requirement in these terms:

> Under the last sentence of Article 4.2(b), we are concerned with the proper "attribution", in this sense, of "injury" caused to the domestic industry by "factors other than increased imports". Clearly, the process of attributing "injury", envisaged by this sentence, can only be made following a separation of the "injury" that must then be properly "attributed". What is important in this process is separating or distinguishing the effects caused by the different factors in bringing about the "injury".

> Article 4.2(b) presupposes, therefore, as a first step in the competent authorities' examination of causation, that the injurious effects caused to the domestic industry by increased imports are distinguished from the injurious effects caused by other factors. The competent authorities can then, as a second step in their examination, attribute to increased imports, on the one hand, and, by implication, to other relevant factors, on the other hand, "injury" caused by all of these different factors, including increased imports. Through this two stage process, the competent authorities comply with Article 4.2(b) by ensuring that any injury to the domestic industry that was actually caused by factors other than increased imports is not "attributed" to increased imports and is, therefore, not treated as if it were injury caused by increased imports, when it is not.[51]

(iii) The Relationship between the Causation Test and the Non-attribution Requirement

The rationale for the non-attribution requirement, and the reason it is set out in the same paragraph as the causation test, is that the causation test cannot be meaningfully applied unless the non-attribution requirement has been met. This can be explained with reference to the following hypothetical situation. Suppose that the report of the national investigating authority indicates that the injury is being simultaneously caused by increased imports, rising input costs and a decrease in capacity utilisation. However, the report does not give a clear impression of the proportion of the overall injury attributable to each of the factors. Without knowing what proportion of the overall injury is being caused, for example, by rising input costs, the risk is that some of the injury caused by this factor will be incorrectly attributed to increased imports. The risk, in other words, is that the investigating authority will incorrectly conclude that a greater proportion of the overall injury is being caused by the increased imports than is actually the position.

The causation test can now be recalled. There must be 'a genuine and substantial relationship of cause and effect between increased imports and serious injury or threat thereof'. This test cannot be properly applied if it is not known what proportion of the overall injury is attributable to increased imports, as opposed to other factors. The proper application of the non-attribution requirement is, therefore, a precondition to the application of the causation test.

---

[51] Appellate Body Report, *US—Wheat Gluten Safeguards*, paras 68–69.

(iv) To What Extent Must the Increased Imports Contribute Towards the Serious Injury?

The question considered here is the extent to which the increased imports must contribute towards the serious injury in order for the causation requirement to be met. This question arises where the non-attribution investigation reveals that serious injury is being caused by the combined effect of increased imports, and other factors. Effectively, the question is how demanding the causation test is as a threshold requirement for the imposition of safeguard measures.

As was noted in Chapter 11 (Dumping and Anti-Dumping Measures), there are various different possibilities in terms of the degree of causation required: *more than* de minimis cause; *important* cause; *principal* cause; *substantial* cause; *significant* cause; *sole* or *exclusive* cause. It was also noted that the specific degree required is not stated in the Anti-Dumping Agreement, and the same applies in the safeguards context. For ease of exposition, and by reason of the legal issues which have arisen in the case law, the choices are reduced to three in this chapter.

Statements (1) and (3) represent the opposite extremes, with (1) being the strictest and most difficult to satisfy, and (3) being the least strict and easiest to satisfy. Statement (2) is an intermediate position.

(1) The causation test is satisfied only when the increased imports, considered in isolation, are causing serious injury.
(2) The causation test is satisfied even when the increased imports, considered in isolation, are not causing serious injury, provided that the increased imports make a genuine and substantial contribution towards the factors which, when considered together, are causing serious injury.
(3) The causation test is satisfied even when the increased imports, considered in isolation, are not causing serious injury, provided that the increased imports make a contribution towards the factors which, when considered together, are causing serious injury.

The Appellate Body has rejected the view of panels that the strict approach represented by statement (1) applies. Between the least strict (3) and intermediate (2) approaches, it appears that the Appellate Body prefers the intermediate approach. It can be argued, however, that a preference for the least strict approach could be preferred without creating any increased risk that safeguard measures would be misused. Put differently, it is arguable that the choice between the least strict approach and the intermediate approach is not especially sensitive from the perspective of balancing the need to allow states to use safeguard measures against maintaining liberalisation commitments. These points are explained further below.

The panel in the *US—Wheat Gluten* case considered that

> where a number of factors, one of which is increased imports, are sufficient collectively to cause a "significant overall impairment of the position of the domestic industry", but increased imports alone are not causing injury that achieves the threshold of "serious" within the meaning of Article 4.1(a) of the Agreement, the conditions for imposing a safeguard measure are not satisfied.[52]

[52] Panel Report, *US—Wheat Gluten Safeguards*, para 8.138.

This finding, which corresponds with the strictest approach (1) above, was reversed by the Appellate Body:

Appellate Body Report, *United States—Definitive Safeguard Measures on Imports of Wheat Gluten from the European Communities*, **Adopted 19 January 2001, WT/DS166/AB/R**

70. The need to ensure a proper attribution of "injury" under Article 4.2(b) indicates that competent authorities must take account, in their determination, of the effects of increased imports as distinguished from the effects of other factors. However, the need to distinguish between the effects caused by increased imports and the effects caused by other factors does not necessarily imply, as the Panel said, that increased imports on their own must be capable of causing serious injury, nor that injury caused by other factors must be excluded from the determination of serious injury.

71. We consider that Article 4.2(a) of the *Agreement on Safeguards*, which is explicitly referred to in Article 4.2(b), indicates that "other factors" have to be taken into account in the competent authorities' determination of serious injury. Article 4.2(a) sets forth the factors which the competent authorities *"shall evaluate"* in "determin[ing] whether increased imports have caused or are threatening to cause serious injury to a domestic industry". Under that provision, the competent authorities must evaluate "all relevant factors having a *bearing* on the situation of [the] industry" . . .

72. The use of the word "all" in the phrase "all relevant factors" in Article 4.2(a) indicates that the effects of any factor may be relevant to the competent authorities' determination, irrespective of whether the particular factor relates to imports specifically or to the domestic industry more generally. This conclusion is borne out by the list of factors which Article 4.2(a) stipulates are, "in particular", relevant to the determination. This list includes factors that relate both to imports specifically and to the overall situation of the domestic industry more generally. The language of the provision does not distinguish between, or attach special importance or preference to, any of the listed factors. In our view, therefore, Article 4.2(a) of the *Agreement on Safeguards* suggests that all these factors are to be included in the determination and that the contribution of each relevant factor is to be counted in the determination of serious injury according to its "bearing" or effect on the situation of the domestic industry. Thus, we consider that Article 4.2(a) does not support the Panel's conclusion that some of the "relevant factors" – those related exclusively to increased imports – should be counted towards an affirmative determination of serious injury, while others – those not related to increased imports – should be excluded from that determination.

... ...

Based on this textual analysis, the Appellate Body was firmly of the view that the panel had erred. Indeed, it was emphasised, in paragraph 71, that factors other than increased imports must (rather than can) be taken into account in the determination of serious injury.

It can be questioned whether the Appellate Body's approach accommodates, or ignores, the concern which led the panel to interpret the provisions in a different manner. This concern was that the non-attribution exercise would be undermined if factors other than increased imports were included in the determination of serious injury. It is submitted that the Appellate Body's textual analysis accommodates this concern. After the non-attribution exercise, the investigating authority ought to have an impression of the extent to which each factor is contributing to the injury. The proportions attributed to each factor are not lost, once and for all, merely by reason of their aggregation for the purpose of determining whether there is serious injury. After it has been determined whether the various factors are collectively causing serious injury, the contribution towards that injury represented by the increased imports can still be reverted to for the purpose of applying the causation test. The Appellate Body's approach does not have the advantage of simplicity. It requires investigating authorities to segregate the factors causing injury for the purpose of the non-attribution test, to then aggregate the factors for the determination of serious injury and, finally, to segregate the factors again in order to apply the causation test. However, the approach does facilitate recourse to safeguard measures, relative to the panel's approach.

Now that the rationale and implications of the Appellate Body's rejection of the strictest approach have been explained, the question of whether it preferred the least strict or an intermediate approach can be considered. The Appellate Body's language seems to indicate a preference for the intermediate approach.

As already noted, the test is not merely 'whether "the causal link" exists between increased imports and serious injury', but also 'whether this causal link involves a genuine and substantial relationship of cause and effect between these two elements'.[53] It is unlikely that this test would be satisfied if the increase in imports is merely a very small factor which, together with other factors, causes serious injury.

It is arguable, however, that investigating authorities should be given broad discretion to determine whether the necessary causal link exists. If demonstrated that any proportion (or perhaps a more than de minimis proportion) of the serious injury is being caused by the increase in imports, this ought to be sufficient to satisfy the causation requirement.[54] Two reasons can be used to justify this view. First, it does not present a risk that safeguard measures will be misused, at least if another vital provisions in the Safeguards Agreement is complied with. As discussed below, under Article 5.1, safeguard measures can only be applied to the extent necessary to remedy the portion of the serious injury caused by increased imports. Thus, if increased imports are found to be a 5 per cent contributing factor to the range of factors which, together, are causing serious injury, there would seem to be no reason to prevent a state from applying a safeguard measure to remove the 5 per cent contribution made by increased imports. Secondly, this interpretation removes some of the uncertainty about how demanding the causation test is as a threshold requirement. If 5 per cent is not enough, approximately how high would the proportion need to be?

The most obvious objection to this suggested approach is that it might be regarded as rendering the causation requirement inutile, or reading it out of the text. However, it is also possible to regard this approach as consistent with a causation requirement which is easy to satisfy—subject to the crucial proviso that the non-attribution requirement has been met. This objection could also be met if the Appellate Body were to specify that the increased imports should be a more than de minimis causal factor. It is argued that

---

[53] Appellate Body Report, *US—Wheat Gluten Safeguards*, para 69.

[54] It is interesting to note a contrasting recent reform proposal whereby the increase in imports should be established as a 'serious cause of the injury' and under which 'at least half of the injury should be attributable to imports' (see Messerlin and Fridh above n 3, 750). The proposal seems to be illogical in the immediate context in which it appears. According to the authors, safeguards have been found to be inconsistent with the Safeguards Agreement because of the 'flawed idea that imports as such cause injury'. The reform proposal mentioned is presented as a means of solving this problem. The view that imports do not cause injury has been understood by economists for some time, and it is one which the legal community is in the process of internalising, primarily as a result of Sykes' work. However, the problem with the reform proposal is that it seems to reinforce the flawed view that increased imports cause injury.

this would be a sensible development simply because the protective role of the causation requirement does not depend on the level at which the causation threshold is set. Whether the contribution towards serious injury made by increased imports is small or large, the safeguard measure must be limited to that portion of the injury caused by increased imports.

IV. STANDARD OF REVIEW[55]

The extent to which the Safeguards Agreement regulates the ability of Members to impose safeguard measures obviously depends on the content of the obligations which are imposed on national investigating authorities. A further, and no less important, consideration when evaluating the regulatory strength of the Agreement is the standard of review applicable in dispute settlement proceedings when there is doubt as to whether authorities have complied with these obligations. Under what circumstances can panels or the Appellate Body strike down, for example, a determination that the increase in imports resulted form 'unforeseen development', or that injury caused by factors other than increased imports have not been attributed to increased imports?

The standard of review for all the WTO agreements, with the exception of the Anti-Dumping Agreement, is set out in Article 11 of the DSU. This provision obliges a panel to 'make an objective assessment of the matter before it, including an objective assessment of the facts of the case and the applicability of and conformity with the relevant covered agreements'.

From this explanation of the general standard of review, the Appellate Body has elaborated the standard which applies to the determinations made by investigating authorities in the safeguards context. The following passage, from the *United States—Steel Safeguards* case, consolidates the approach which has been referred to in a number of the sections above:

> We explained in *US—Lamb*, in the context of a claim under Article 4.2(a) of the *Agreement on Safeguards*, that the competent authorities must provide a "reasoned and adequate explanation of how the facts support their determination". More recently, in *US—Line Pipe*, in the context of a claim under Article 4.2(b) of the *Agreement on Safeguards*, we said that the competent authorities must, similarly, provide a "reasoned and adequate explanation, that injury caused by factors other than increased imports is not attributed to increased imports". Our findings in those cases did not purport to address solely the standard of review that is appropriate for claims arising under Article 4.2 of the *Agreement on Safeguards*. We see no reason not to apply the same standard generally to the obligations under the *Agreement on Safeguards* as well as to the obligations in Article XIX of the GATT 1994.[56]

The Appellate Body proceeded to explain the logical link between the standard of review set out in DSU Article 11 and the need for the 'reasoned and adequate explanation' referred to. If conclusions reached by investigating authorities are not accompanied

---

[55] A fuller treatment of this topic is provided in Chapter 5 on Dispute Settlement.
[56] Appellate Body Report, *US—Steel Safeguards*, para 276.

by such explanations, panels would be unable, under Article 11, to make an 'objective assessment' of the conformity of determinations with the Safeguards Agreement.[57]

The rigour with which the Appellate Body has applied the standard of review has led to concern over what is sometimes perceived as its failure to provide guidance on the circumstances in which safeguards can be permissibly imposed. This view is defended throughout a controversial article by Alan O Sykes which sums up as follows:

> What emerges from the steel dispute is a renewed sense of how difficult it will be for WTO Members to use safeguards going forward without a prospect of near-certain defeat when complaint is brought against them. Members must demonstrate the existence of unanticipated developments, persuade that they were "unforeseen", convincingly trace their impact on increased imports, demonstrate that much of the import surge is sufficiently "recent", convincingly show the relation between the imports and serious injury, and convincingly show the relation between the imports and serious injury, and convincingly show that "other factors" have not caused the injury attributed to increased imports, . . . all in a way that will stand up to analytical quibbles on review . . . In the face of all these hurdles to the opportunity to employ safeguards, one might hope for some clear guidance as to what is required to pass muster on each of them. Instead, the decisions to date . . . simply find that the analysis of national authorities is not "reasoned and adequate", without saying what alternative reasoning will suffice.[58]

V. APPLICATION OF SAFEGUARD MEASURES

This section discusses the permissible scope of application of safeguard measures. The issues here include whether some WTO Members can, or must, be excluded from safeguard measures, and for how long measures can be imposed. The permissible scope of application is the second basic inquiry which follows from the inquiry into whether the conditions for the application of safeguard measures are present. The following limits on the application of safeguard measures are applicable.

(a) The Extent of Safeguard Measures

Article 5.1 on the *Application of Safeguard Measures* provides as follows:

> A Member shall apply safeguard measures only to the extent necessary to prevent or remedy serious injury and to facilitate adjustment. If a quantitative restriction is used, such a measure shall not reduce the quantity of imports below the level of a recent period which shall be the average of imports in the last three representative years for which statistics are available, unless clear justification is given that a different level is necessary to prevent or remedy serious injury. Members should choose measures most suitable for the achievement of these objectives.

The first sentence of this provision can be interpreted in two ways:

• Members can apply safeguard measures to address the serious injury caused by increased imports, as well as other factors.

---

[57] *Ibid*, para 279.
[58] Sykes, 'The Persistent Puzzles', above n 5, 562–63.

- Members can apply safeguard measures to address only the contribution towards the serious injury caused by the increased imports.

The Appellate Body has confirmed the correctness of the second interpretation in *United States—Line Pipe*. In this case, the US argued for the first interpretation. The US reasoned that, because the Appellate Body had previously found in *United States—Wheat Gluten* that 'serious injury' in Article 4.2(a) was a reference to the injury being caused by all factors, it followed that the 'serious injury' referred to in Article 5.1 should also be understood as a reference to the injury being caused by all factors.[59] The Appellate Body responded to this argument by noting that its ruling in *Wheat Gluten* was concerned with whether it was permissible to apply a safeguard measure at all, and did not touch upon the permissible scope of application of safeguard measures under Article 5.1. On the correct interpretation of Article 5.1, the Appellate Body reasoned as follows:

Appellate Body Report, *United States—Definitive Safeguard Measures on Imports of Circular Welded Carbon Quality Line Pipe from Korea*, Adopted 8 March 2002, WT/DS202/AB/R

249. In our view, the "serious injury" to which Article 5.1, first sentence, refers is, in any particular case, necessarily the same "serious injury" that has been determined to exist by competent authorities of a WTO Member pursuant to Article 4.2. We think it reasonable to assume that, as the Agreement provides only one definition of "serious injury", and as the Agreement does not distinguish the "serious injury" to which Article 5.1 refers from the "serious injury" to which Article 4.2 refers, the "serious injury" in Article 5.1 and the "serious injury" in Article 4.2 must be considered as one and the same. On this, we agree with the United States. But, contrary to what the United States argues, the fact that these two provisions refer to the same "serious injury" does not necessarily lead to the conclusion that a safeguard measure may address the "entirety" of the "serious injury", including the part of the "serious injury" that is attributable to factors other than increased imports.

250. This is because Article 5.1, first sentence, sets out the maximum permissible extent to which a safeguard measure may be applied. With its emphasis on the "entirety" of the "serious injury", the United States seems to read the word "all" as if it were between the word "remedy" and the words "serious injury" in this provision, so that the phrase would be "remedy all serious injury". But the word "all" is not there. And, as we have said more than once, words must not be read into the Agreement that are not there.

251. We do not see the text of Article 5.1, first sentence, alone, as indicating one certain meaning. Therefore, in keeping with our customary approach, we must seek the meaning of the terms of this provision in their context and in the light of the object and purpose of the Agreement.

252. We observe here that the non-attribution language of the second sentence of Article 4.2(b) is an important part of the architecture of the *Agreement on Safeguards* and thus serves as necessary context in which Article 5.1, first sentence, must be interpreted. In our view, the non-attribution language of the second sentence of Article 4.2(b) has two objectives. First, it seeks, in situations where several factors cause injury at the same time, to prevent investigating authorities from inferring the required "causal link" between increased imports and serious injury or threat thereof on the basis of the injurious effects caused by factors other than increased imports. Second, it is a benchmark for ensuring that only an appropriate share of the overall injury is attributed to increased imports. As we read the Agreement, this latter objective, in turn, informs the permissible extent to which the safeguard measure may be applied pursuant

---

[59] Appellate Body Report, *US—Line Pipe Safeguards*, para 243.

to Article 5.1, first sentence. Indeed, as we see it, this is the only possible interpretation of the obligation set out in Article 4.2(b), last sentence, that ensures its consistency with Article 5.1, first sentence. It would be illogical to require an investigating authority to ensure that the "causal link" between increased imports and serious injury not be based on the share of injury attributed to factors other than increased imports while, at the same time, permitting a Member to apply a safeguard measure addressing injury caused by all factors.

... ...

(b) Parallelism

The term parallelism does not appear in the Agreement. Rather, it has resulted from the Appellate Body's interpretation of certain provisions of relevance to the permissible scope of application of safeguard measures. Put simply, the requirement is that there must be a parallel, or correspondence, between the imports which are investigated as causing (or threatening) serious injury and the imports on which safeguard measures are imposed. That is, the same imports must be considered for both. The Appellate Body has made this clear in a number of cases where imports from certain states have been excluded from safeguard measures, even though they were included in the investigation and, therefore, contributed to the injury determination. In these cases, the states applying safeguard measures are WTO Members and also members of a free trade agreement or customs union. These arrangements require liberalisation commitments beyond those associated with WTO membership and, therefore, normally prohibit internal tariffs and quotas, even when a Member might wish to impose them in an economic emergency situation. This prohibition explains why WTO Members imposing safeguards need to exclude their trading partners within free trade areas or customs unions.

The parallelism requirement, and its relationship with other GATT / WTO provisions, raises fundamental, and unresolved, questions. Can WTO Members exclude some states from the application of safeguard measures, when these states are both WTO Members, and members of free trade agreements or customs unions? In particular, is this permissible when the investigating authority clearly determines that imports from states other than the free trade area or customs unions are causing serious injury?[60] These questions should be borne in mind while studying the extract below from the Appellate Body report in *United States—Line Pipe*.

Appellate Body Report, *United States—Definitive Safeguard Measures on Imports of Circular Welded Carbon Quality Line Pipe from Korea*, Adopted 8 March 2002, WT/DS202/AB/R

179. The concept of parallelism is derived from the parallel language used in the first and second paragraphs of Article 2 of the *Agreement on Safeguards*. Article 2 provides as follows:

Conditions

1. A Member may apply a safeguard measure to a product only if that Member has determined, pursuant to the provisions set out below, that such product is being imported into its territory in such increased quantities, absolute or relative to domestic production, and under such conditions as to cause or threaten to cause serious injury to the domestic industry that produces like or directly competitive products.

---

[60] These questions, and several other related questions, are considered in detail by Pauwelyn, above n 5.

2. Safeguard measures shall be applied to a product being imported irrespective of its source.

180. In *US – Wheat Gluten*, we explained:

The same phrase—"product . . . being imported"—appears in *both* . . . paragraphs of Article 2. In view of the identity of the language in the two provisions, and in the absence of any contrary indication in the context, we believe that it is appropriate to ascribe the *same* meaning to this phrase in both Articles 2.1 and 2.2. To include imports from all sources in the determination that increased imports are causing serious injury, and then to exclude imports from one source from the application of the measure, would be to give the phrase "product being imported" a *different meaning* in Articles 2.1 and 2.2 of the *Agreement on Safeguards*. In Article 2.1, the phrase would embrace imports from all sources whereas, in Article 2.2, it would exclude imports from certain sources. This would be incongruous and unwarranted. (original emphasis)

181. As we then stated in *US – Wheat Gluten*, "the imports included in the determinations made under Articles 2.1 and 4.2 should correspond to the imports included in the application of the measure, under Article 2.2." We added that a gap between imports covered under the investigation and imports falling within the scope of the measure can be justified only if the competent authorities "establish explicitly" that imports from sources covered by the measure "satisf[y]" the conditions for the application of a safeguard measure, as set out in Article 2.1 and elaborated in Article 4.2 of the *Agreement on Safeguards*." And, as we explained further in *US – Lamb*, in the context of a claim under Article 4.2(a) of the *Agreement on Safeguards*, "establish[ing] explicitly" implies that the competent authorities must provide a "reasoned and adequate explanation of how the facts support their determination".

182. Before the Panel, Korea claimed that the United States violated Articles 2 and 4 of the *Agreement on Safeguards* by including Canada and Mexico in the USITC analysis of serious injury but by excluding Canada and Mexico from the application of the safeguard measure.

The Appellate Body then noted the panel's finding that Korea had failed to establish a prima facie case that the US had excluded imports from Canada and Mexico from the line pipe measure, without establishing explicitly that imports from sources other than Canada and Mexico satisfied the conditions for the application of a safeguard measure. Korea's challenge of this finding was upheld:

187. In our view, Korea has demonstrated that the USITC considered imports from all sources in its investigation. Korea has also shown that exports from Canada and Mexico were excluded from the safeguard measure at issue. And, in our view, this is enough to have made a prima facie case of the absence of parallelism in the line pipe measure. Contrary to what the Panel stated, we do not consider that it was necessary for Korea to address the information set out in the USITC Report, or in particular, in footnote 168 in order to establish a prima facie case of violation of parallelism. Moreover, to require Korea to rebut the information in the USITC Report, and in particular, in footnote 168, would impose an impossible burden on Korea because, as the exporting country, Korea would not have had any of the relevant data to conduct its own analysis of the imports.

188. Having determined that Korea did establish a prima facie case of violation of parallelism of the line pipe measure, we now examine whether the United States rebutted Korea's argument. To do so, it would be necessary for the United States to demonstrate, consistent with our ruling in *US – Wheat Gluten*, that the USITC provided a reasoned and adequate explanation that establishes explicitly that imports from non-NAFTA sources "satisfied the conditions for the application of a safeguard measure, as set out in Article 2.1 and elaborated in Article 4.2 of the *Agreement on Safeguards*."

189. Before the panel and on appeal, the United States has relied on footnote 168 of the USITC Report. In the oral hearing in this appeal, the United States stressed footnote 168, which reads, in its entirety, as follows:

> We note that we would have reached the same result had we excluded imports from Canada and Mexico from our analysis. Imports from non-NAFTA sources increased significantly over the period of investigation, in absolute terms and as a percentage of domestic production. Non-NAFTA imports fell from *** tons in 1994 to *** tons in 1996, but then rose sharply to *** tons in 1997 and *** tons in 1998. While non-NAFTA imports fell from *** tons in interim 1998 to *** tons in interim 1999, they remained at a very high level in interim 1999, exceeding in just 6 months the level of full year 1995 and 1996 imports. These imports also increased significantly in terms of market share at the end of the period of investigation, rising from *** percent in 1996 to *** percent in 1998, and from *** percent in interim 1998 to *** percent in interim 1999. Moreover, the non-NAFTA imports were among the lowest-priced imports. Except for 1994, the average unit value of imports from Canada exceeded the average import unit value throughout the period of investigation, and the volume of imports was relatively small. The average unit value of imports from Mexico exceeded the average for all imports in 1998 and interim 1999, the period in which the serious injury occurred, and the volume of imports from Mexico declined during this period. Moreover, in the 244 possible product-specific price comparisons, non-NAFTA imports undersold domestic line pipe in 194 instances (about 80 percent), and Korean product accounted for by far the largest number of instances of underselling (95 of the 194). Data are based on those in Table C-1 adjusted to exclude certain imports of Arctic-grade and alloy line pipe.

190. The Panel examined footnote 168 and concluded that:

> . . . note 168 contains *a finding* by the ITC that imports from non-NAFTA sources increased significantly over the period of investigation, in absolute terms and as a percentage of domestic production. Note 168 also contains *the basis for a finding* that non-NAFTA [imports] caused serious injury to the relevant domestic industry . . . (emphasis added by the Appellate Body)

192 . . . What we must determine, then, is whether, as the United States submits, footnote 168 satisfies the requirement of parallelism . . .

194. Although footnote 168 contains a determination that imports from non-NAFTA sources increased significantly, footnote 168 does not, as we read it, establish explicitly that increased imports from non-NAFTA sources alone caused serious injury or threat of serious injury. Nor does footnote 168, as we read it, provide a reasoned and adequate explanation of how the facts would support such a finding. To be explicit, a statement must express distinctly all that is meant; it must leave nothing merely implied or suggested; it must be clear and unambiguous . . .

195 . . . Footnote 168 may, as the Panel found, provide a basis for a finding that imports from non-NAFTA sources, alone, caused serious injury, but this is not enough. Footnote 168 does not establish explicitly that imports from sources covered by the measure "satisf[y] the conditions for the application of a safeguard measure, as set out in Article 2.1 and elaborated in Article 4.2 of the *Agreement on Safeguards*." Footnote 168 does not amount to a "reasoned and adequate explanation of how the facts support [the] determination." Therefore, by referring to footnote 168, the United States did not rebut the prima facie case made by Korea . . .

197. Therefore, we reverse the Panel's finding . . . that Korea has not established a prima facie case of the absence of parallelism in the line pipe measure. And, we find that the United States has violated Articles 2 and 4 of the *Agreement on Safeguards* by including Canada and Mexico in the analysis of whether increased imports caused or threatened to cause serious injury, but excluding Canada and Mexico from the application of the safeguard measure, without providing

a reasoned and adequate explanation that establishes explicitly that imports from non-NAFTA sources by themselves satisfied the conditions for the application of a safeguard measure.

198. In doing so, we do not prejudge whether Article 2.2 of the *Agreement on Safeguards* permits a Member to exclude imports originating in member states of a free-trade area from the scope of a safeguard measure. We need not, and so do not, rule on the question whether Article XXIV of the GATT 1994 permits exempting imports originating in a partner of a free-trade area from a measure in departure from Article 2.2 of the *Agreement on Safeguards*. The question of whether Article XXIV of the GATT 1994 serves as an exception to Article 2.2 of the *Agreement on Safeguards* becomes relevant in only two possible circumstances. One is when, in the investigation by the competent authorities of a WTO Member, the imports that are exempted from the safeguard measure are not considered in the determination of serious injury. The other is when, in such an investigation, the imports that are exempted from the safeguard measure are considered in the determination of serious injury, and the competent authorities have also established explicitly, through a reasoned and adequate explanation, that imports from sources outside the free-trade area, alone, satisfied the conditions for the application of a safeguard measure, as set out in Article 2.1 and elaborated in Article 4.2. The first of these two possible circumstances does not apply in this case . . . The second of these two possible circumstances also does not apply in this case. The competent authority—in this case, the USITC—has not provided in its determination a reasoned and adequate explanation that "establish[es] explicitly" that imports from non-NAFTA sources satisfied the conditions for the application of a safeguard measure, as set out in Article 2.1 and elaborated in Article 4.2 of the *Agreement on Safeguards*.

199. Given these conclusions, we need not address the question whether an Article XXIV defence is available to the United States. Nor are we required to make a determination on the question of the relationship between Article 2.2 of the *Agreement on Safeguards* and Article XXIV of the GATT 1994.

... ...

As the result of the Appellate Body's approach, the question of what the outcome would have been had the USITC provided the 'reasoned and adequate explanation' referred to in paragraph 198 is left unanswered. It is known for certain that, had the 'reasoned and adequate explanation' been provided, the parallelism requirement would have been met.[61] However, compliance with the parallelism requirement does not, in itself, automatically mean that imports from free trade agreement sources can be excluded from the application of safeguard measures. This is because the exclusion involves discrimination as between importing nations and, as such, probably amounts to a violation of the GATT Article I *General Most-Favoured-Nation Treatment* obligation, and Article 2.2 of the *Agreement on Safeguards*. It follows that the parallelism requirement is a necessary, but not a sufficient, precondition for exclusion of free trade agreement states. After the parallelism requirement is met, any exclusion would still be discriminatory. The question then becomes whether this discrimination can be justified under Article XXIV.

The panel's analytical approach in this case was the mirror image of the Appellate Body's approach, in that the panel started with the role of GATT Article XXIV. As can be seen from the extract below, the panel was firmly of the view that Article XXIV can provide a defence against the discriminatory application of safeguard measures caused by the exclusion of imports from free trade area partners.

---

[61] This proposition follows from para 197. The Appellate Body clearly states here why the parallelism requirement was breached, and therefore also reveals how to avoid a breach.

Panel Report, *United States—Definitive Safeguard Measures on Imports of Circular Welded Carbon Quality Line Pipe from Korea,* **Adopted 8 March 2002, WT/DS202/AB/R**

7.137 Korea asserts that the non-discriminatory application of safeguard measures is required by Articles I, XIII:1 and XIX. To the extent that these provisions impose an MFN requirement, the United States relies on the "limited exception" set forth in [GATT] Article XXIV. We must decide to what extent, if at all, any such Article XXIV defence is available to the United States.

7.138 We begin our analysis with Article XXIV:5, which provides in relevant part:

> Accordingly, the provisions of this Agreement shall not prevent, as between the territories of Members, the formation of . . . a free-trade area . . .; Provided that: . . .

By virtue of Article XXIV.5, therefore, Members are entitled to form free-trade areas (provided the conditions set forth in sub-paragraphs (b) and (c) of that provision are met).

7.139 Article XXIV.8(b) defines a free-trade area as:

> a group of two or more customs territories in which the duties and other restrictive regulations of commerce (except, where necessary, those permitted under Articles XI, XII, XIII, XIV, XV and XX) are eliminated on substantially all the trade between the constituent territories in products originating in such territories.

7.140 In light of this definition of a free-trade area, we understand Article XXIV.5 to mean that Members are authorised, under certain prescribed circumstances, to eliminate "duties and other restrictive regulations of commerce (except, where necessary, those permitted under Articles XI, XII, XIII, XIV, XV and XX) . . . on substantially all the trade" between them and their free-trade area partners. This authorisation exists, despite the fact that the formation of a free-trade area will necessarily result in more favourable treatment for free-trade area partners than for non-free-trade area partners (in respect of whom "duties and other restrictive regulations of commerce" are not eliminated).

7.141 As noted above, the alleged violation of GATT 1994 arises from the exemption of imports from Canada and Mexico from the scope of the line pipe safeguard measure. Since the line pipe measure introduces a tariff quota, we consider that the line pipe measure constitutes a "dut[y] [or] other restrictive regulation[] of commerce" within the meaning of Article XXIV.8(b). *As the exclusion of imports from Canada and Mexico therefore forms part of the elimination of "duties and other restrictive regulations of commerce" between NAFTA members, it is in principle authorised by Article XXIV.5,* provided the relevant conditions are fulfilled. Having regard to paragraphs 5 and 8 of Article XXIV, the relevant conditions are that NAFTA must (1) comply with Article XXIV.5(b) and (c), and (2) eliminate duties and other restrictive regulations of commerce on "substantially all" intra-NAFTA trade. (emphasis added)

7.142 As the party seeking to rely on an Article XXIV defence (or "limited exception"), the onus is on the United States to demonstrate compliance with these conditions.

... ...

The panel found that the US had established a prima facie case of compliance with these conditions which Korea had failed to rebut. It therefore found that the US was 'entitled to rely on an Article XXIV defence against Korea's claims under Articles I, XIII and XIX regarding the exclusion of imports from Canada and Mexico from the scope of the line pipe measure'.[62] The panel then proceeded to consider whether GATT Article XXIV

---

[62] Panel Report, *US—Line Pipe Safeguards*, para 7.146.

also provided a defence to a claim of discrimination under Article 2.2 of the Safeguards Agreement.

> 7.149 . . . We must determine whether, given the non-discrimination requirement in Article 2.2, the United States should have included imports from Canada and Mexico in the scope of the line pipe measure.

> 7.150 Having found that the United States is entitled to rely on the Article XXIV defence in respect of a violation of the non-discrimination requirement in inter alia Article XIX, we consider it would be incongruous if the United States were precluded from relying on the Article XXIV defence in respect of a violation of the non-discrimination requirement in Article 2.2. A contrary interpretation would ignore the close interrelation between Article XIX and the Safeguards Agreement. This interrelation is evidenced in particular by Article 1, whereby the Safeguards Agreement

>> . . . establishes rules for the application of safeguard measures which shall be understood to mean those measures provided for in Article XIX of GATT 1994.

> By virtue of this provision, therefore, safeguard measures subject to the provisions of the Safeguards Agreement are understood to be Article XIX measures. Thus, if an Article XXIV defence is available for Article XIX measures, by definition it must also be available for measures covered by the disciplines of the Safeguards Agreement. To deny this is to deny the fact that, by virtue of Article 1, measures covered by the Safeguards Agreement and measures provided for in Article XIX are essentially one and the same thing. Thus, to the extent that an Article XXIV defence is available against claims brought under Article XIX, it must necessarily also be available against claims brought under the provisions of the Safeguards Agreement . . .

The panel therefore expressed clear views on the scope for using Article XXIV as a defence against allegations of discriminatory application of safeguard measures. The most crucial paragraph above is 7.141. To put the panel's point in different language, the exclusion of regional partners from safeguard measures fits very well with the definitional element in Article XXIV.8 of eliminating 'duties and other restrictive regulations of commerce . . . with respect to substantially all the trade between the constituent territories'. The Appellate Body has yet to express a view, although it is notable that support for the panel's approach has been expressed in the literature.[63]

(c) Measures in the Form of Quantitative Restrictions

Article 5 aims to limit the permissible extent of safeguard measures in the form of quantitative restrictions on the basis that measures in this form inhibit trade more than tariffs and tariff quotas. The second sentence of Article 5.1 imposes a cap on the level by which a quantitative restriction can reduce the volume of imports. This level must not be less than 'the average of imports in the last three representative years for which statistics are available, unless clear justification is given that a different level is necessary to prevent or remedy serious injury'. The panel in *United States—Line Pipe* found that this provision does not apply to tariff quotas which involve the imposition of a higher tariff on imports above a specified quantitative level—so called 'out of quota imports'.[64] As the panel

---

[63] See Pauwelyn, above n 5, 135–38.
[64] Panel Report, *US—Line Pipe Safeguards*, paras 7.66—7.75.

noted, it would make little sense to apply the provision to tariff quotas on the basis that these do not limit the overall volume of imports.[65]

Article 5.2(a) deals with the situation where a quota is allocated among supplying countries and seeks to ensure the equitable allocation of shares in the quota. If it is 'not reasonably practicable' to obtain the agreement of all Members, the state imposing the safeguard measure 'shall allot to Members having a *substantial interest in supplying the product* shares based upon the proportions, supplied by such Members during a previous representative period, of the total quantity or value of imports of the product' (emphasis added).

It follows from the wording used in this provision that Members without the *substantial interest* referred to need not be allocated any portion of the quota. As Article 5.2(a) is difficult to reconcile with a number of other provisions (such as GATT Article XIII.1, and Safeguards Agreement Article 2.2), it can be regarded as a *lex specialis*.

Article 5.2(b) provides that a departure from paragraph (a) can be justified if various conditions are present including that 'imports from certain Members have increased in disproportionate percentage in relation to the total increase of imports of the product concerned in the representative period'. Reliance on paragraph (b) would result in particular Members being allocated a lower proportion of the quota than would result from the application of paragraph (a) alone.

(d) Excluding Developing Country Members

WTO Members are required to exclude *de minimis* developing country exports from the application of safeguard measures where certain conditions are present. Under Article 9.1:

> Safeguard measures shall not be applied against a product originating in a developing country Member as long as its share of imports of the product concerned in the importing Member does not exceed 3 per cent, provided that developing country Members with less than 3 per cent import share collectively account for not more than 9 per cent of total imports of the product concerned.

Korea alleged a violation of this provision in the *United States—Line Pipe* case. Under the challenged measure, the first 9,000 tons of imports from all sources were excluded from the duty increase. Imports above 9,000 tons were subject to an additional duty of 19 per cent ad valorem in the first year. The measure neither distinguished between developed and developing countries, nor excluded developing countries from its application. Although the Appellate Body expressed a preference for an express exclusion, it found that Article 9.1 did not mandate such exclusion.[66] The Appellate Body then considered the manner in which the measure applied in practice, noting the argument of the US that compliance was achieved by structuring the safeguard duty 'so that it automatically would not apply to developing countries accounting for less than three percent of imports'.[67] The crucial question was whether the 9,000 tons limit was a sufficiently large quantity to represent at least 3 per cent of the total imports of the product concerned. Had this question been answered in the affirmative, it is possible that there would not have

---

[65] *Ibid*, para 7.70.
[66] Appellate Body Report, *US—Line Pipe Safeguards*, paras 127–28.
[67] *Ibid*, para 130.

been a violation, as countries with an import share of 3 per cent or less would have been completely excluded from the measure. The Appellate Body found otherwise, noting that:

> according to the latest data available at the time the line pipe measure took effect . . . the 9,000 short-ton exemption from the over-quota duty imposed by the line pipe measure did not represent three percent of the total imports. Rather, the exemption represented only 2.7 percent of total imports.[68]

It followed that countries whose import share was 2.7 per cent or greater were subject to the over-quota duty. In respect of developing countries, this amounted to an Article 9.1 violation.

(e) Duration of Safeguard Measures

Even though safeguard measures respond to temporary emergency situations, Article 7.1 sets the general maximum period for their application at four years. Under Article 7.2, this period can be extended provided that (among other conditions) the national investigating authority determines that the 'measure continues to be necessary and that there is evidence that the industry is adjusting'. The absolute maximum period of application is eight years for developed country Members, and 10 years for developing country Members.[69] Under Article 7.3, this period encompasses the total life span of the measure from its provisional application (if any), through to its definitive application, and, finally, any extension of the measure.

While these periods are rather long, Article 7.4 requires the gradual reduction of the measure where the period of application exceeds one year. Should the measure still be in force after three years, an interim review must be conducted to assess the feasibility of its withdrawal, or to accelerate its reduction. Article 7.4 envisages that these steps are intended 'to facilitate adjustment'. Article 7.5 prevents the imposition of new safeguard measures on products recently subject to them. For developed country Members, the usual period which must elapse between the expiry of one measure and the imposition of a new measure is the length of time of the original measure. For developing country Members, this time period is halved.[70] However, for all Members, the elapsed period cannot be less than two years. Therefore, if the original measure was applied for one year, a period of two years must elapse before the imposition of a new measure on the same products. Article 7.6 qualifies this general rule in the situation where the original measure lasts for 180 days or less. A new safeguard measure may be applied after the elapse of at least one year, 'provided a safeguard measure has not been applied on the same product more than twice in the five-year period immediately preceding the date of introduction of the measure'.

(f) Provisional Safeguard Measures

Under Article 6, Members can apply provisional safeguard measures in the form of tariff increases 'where delay would cause damage which it would be difficult to repair'. Pro-

---

[68] *Ibid.*
[69] With regard to developing country Members, see Art 9.2.
[70] *Ibid.*

visional measures must be based on a 'preliminary determination that there is clear evidence that increased imports have caused or are threatening to cause serious injury'. They must not be applied for more than 200 days. During this period, the full investigation to determine whether the conditions for the application of safeguard measures are satisfied must be conducted, and the Article 12 notification and consultation obligations must be met. If the full investigation does not establish that the conditions for applying a safeguard measure are satisfied, the increased duties collected must be 'promptly refunded'. The time periods set out in Article 7 commence when provisional measures are applied.

A question raised by Article 6 is how detailed a justification must be provided before the application of provisional measures. The same question arises in the anti-dumping context, albeit that there is a hint here that provisional measures ought not to be applied without very careful consideration. It is provided that such measures cannot be applied 'sooner than 60 days from the date of initiation of the investigation'.[71] There is no equivalent provision in the safeguards context. The only relevant guidance is therefore provided by the standard of review discussed above. A 'reasoned and adequate explanation' of how the facts support the preliminary determination would need to be provided by investigating authorities.

V. MAINTAINING AN EQUIVALENT LEVEL OF CONCESSIONS

The application of safeguard measures inevitably produces an imbalance of negotiated trade concessions. Under Article 8.1, Members seeking to apply, or extend, a safeguard measure must 'endeavour to maintain a substantially equivalent level of concessions and other obligations to that existing under GATT 1994 between it and the exporting Members which would be affected by such a measure'. This requirement reflects the notion that there is no allegation of an unfair trade practice by exporters or foreign governments when safeguards are applied. Article 8.1 refers to Article 12.3, which requires Members 'to provide adequate opportunity for prior consultation with those Members having a substantial interest as exporters of the product concerned, with a view to' achieving the rebalancing objective. A failure to provide this 'adequate opportunity' under Article 12.3 results in a breach of Article 8.1.[72]

As for how rebalancing is achieved, Article 8.1 provides that 'the Members concerned may agree on any adequate means of trade compensation for the adverse effects of the measure on their trade'. Trade compensation will normally entail the Member applying the safeguard measure lowering tariffs on goods other than those affected by the safeguard measure. Article 8.2 provides that where agreement on compensation cannot be reached within 30 days of the commencement of consultations, the affected exporting Members may suspend concessions against the trade of the Member applying the safeguard measure, provided the Council for Trade in Goods does not disapprove. Suspension is also a rebalancing device. Its application normally involves the Members affected by

---

[71] Anti-Dumping Agreement Art 7.3.
[72] Appellate Body Report, *US—Wheat Gluten Safeguards*, paras 144–46.

the safeguard measure raising their tariff levels on goods from the Member applying the safeguard measure. From the point of view of trade liberalisation, trade compensation is the preferred option, since it has the effect of both rebalancing concessions and promoting trade. In contrast, suspension rebalances concessions by contracting trade levels.

Under Article 8.3, if the safeguard measure is responding to an absolute increase in imports and it conforms with the Safeguards Agreement, the right to suspend cannot be exercised for the first three years that the measure is in effect.[73] This provision creates an additional incentive for Members affected by the safeguard measure to seek trade compensation. Unfortunately, it also seems to provide an incentive towards recalcitrance in the consultations on trade compensation by Members applying safeguards. Indeed, it has recently been observed that compensation remains little more than a theoretical possibility and has yet to be agreed in any case.[74] While this is clearly a cause for concern, the weakening of the right to suspend concessions under Article 8.3, serves the purpose of encouraging the use of regulated safeguard measures rather than so-called 'grey-area' measures such as voluntary export restraints.

These 'grey-area' measures would typically follow on from informal communications between governments whereby an importing nation would indicate the possibility of invoking anti-dumping laws, and invite the exporting nation to monitor prices and reduce the quantity of exports. They were problematic from a number of perspectives. As they were entered into outside of any regulated legal framework, they lacked transparency and were of indeterminate duration. The term 'voluntary export restraint' was also something of a misnomer. Even when the nations concerned were of comparable economic power, the voluntary nature of these arrangements could be questioned. Finally, 'grey-area' measures were of dubious legality under GATT Article XI, a matter which was tested in the case of *Japan—Trade in Semi-Conductors*.[75] Growing concern over the proliferation of these arrangements represented an important part of the motivation for the Safeguards Agreement.

As a result of these problems, Article 11.1(b) of the Safeguards Agreement prohibits Members from seeking, taking or maintaining 'any voluntary export restraints, orderly marketing arrangements or any other similar measures on the export or the import side'.

---

[73] It follows from this provision that the three-year moratorium on the right to suspend concessions *does not* apply if the measures are *inconsistent* with the Safeguards Agreement. This raises the question of whether the consistency or otherwise of the measures can only be decided through dispute settlement, or can be unilaterally determined by Members affected by the measures. Hahn argues in favour of the latter option on the basis that 'the introduction of new substantive standards for the adoption of unilateral re-balancing measures must not be read as turning the very notion of a right to take autonomous compensatory measures on its head . . . Rather, a proper reading leads to an understanding of Article 8 according to which affected Members states themselves examine *bona fide* whether the legal requirements established by the WTO treaty for the adoption of compensatory measures have been fulfilled' (Hahn, above n 2, 321–22). In contrast, PM Rodríguez, 'Safeguards in the World Trade Organization Ten Years After: *A Dissociated State of the Law?*' (2007) 41 *Journal of World Trade* 159, 177–78, notes that, with a few notable exceptions, state practice regards Art 8.3 as preventing retaliation for the first three years unless the measures are found to be WTO inconsistent through the dispute settlement system:.

[74] Rodríguez, *ibid*, 176–78 and 180.

[75] GATT Panel Report, *Japan—Semi-Conductors*. The background to the case involved a voluntary arrangement entered into by the Japanese government at the behest of the US government. Pursuant to this arrangement, the Japanese government met with semi-conductor producers and exporters to request that dumping should be avoided. Companies were informed that it was in their own self-interest to avoid dumping and, indeed, the voluntary arrangement was linked to the suspension of anti-dumping procedures initiated in the US. The EC successfully challenged this non-binding request as a measure restricting the sale for export of semi-conductors contrary to GATT Art XI.

VI. QUESTIONS

1. Explain the possible justifications for allowing WTO Members to impose safeguards against 'fairly traded' imports.

2. Explain why the end-point to end-point analysis used by the US was found to be inconsistent with the Safeguards Agreement in the *United States—Steel* case. Does the Appellate Body's reasoning in this case leave unanswered questions?

3. Explain how a financial crisis in WTO Member B might result in increased imports in WTO Member C from WTO Members B and D. Would such a financial crisis ordinarily amount to an 'unforeseen development' under GATT Article XIX.1(a)? Under what circumstances, if any, might the crisis not amount to an 'unforeseen development'?

4. Explain why a correlation/coincidence between increased imports and injury can be regarded as an insufficient basis for fulfilling the causation requirement in Article 4.2(b) of the Safeguards Agreement. As part of your answer, consider whether the causation requirement would be satisfied in the event of a coincidence in time between increased imports, a decline in injury factors and the outsourcing of production to the states from which imports have increased. How could such a scenario be described as an 'own goal' for the domestic industry?

5. Explain how applying the non-attribution requirement can be regarded as a pre-condition for the application of the causation requirement.

6. Evaluate the view that if it demonstrated that any proportion (or perhaps a more than de minimis proportion) of the serious injury is being caused by the increase in imports, this ought to be sufficient to satisfy the causation requirement.

7. One of the findings in the *United States—Line Pipe* case was that the US had not met the parallelism requirement. In other words, there was a gap between the imports which were investigated and the imports upon which the safeguard measure was imposed. Why, in practice, might an investigating authority be reluctant to exclude imports from some sources when there is no intention to apply the safeguard measure to imports from these sources? You might find that the following passage from the panel report will help you to think of a plausible answer:

> 7.129 Korea asserts that the exemption of Mexico was particularly egregious in this case since Mexico was the second largest supplier to the US market during the ITC's period of investigation. Mexico is now the largest supplier to the US market, and Canada has increased its imports three-fold to become the number three supplier to the US market.

8. What advice would you give to a WTO Member wanting to impose a WTO consistent safeguard measure, but not wanting to apply this measure to regional trading partners under a free trade agreement?

9. Examine the view that Article 8.3 of the Safeguards Agreement gives Members free reign to use safeguard measures as short term protectionist measures.

10. Advise State C on the compatibility of the following practices with GATT Article XIX and the WTO Agreement on Safeguards:

(a) In assessing whether imports have increased, State C evaluates only whether the level of imports was higher at the end of the period of investigation, than at its commencement.

(b) In assessing whether the domestic industry has been seriously injured, State C takes account of domestic industries having a substantial coincidence of economic interests with the domestic industry producing a like product to that being imported in increased quantities. In a recent case involving an increase in imports of frozen beef, State C therefore considered whether this increase was causing serious injury to the domestic growers of live cattle.

(c) In assessing whether the domestic industry has been seriously injured, State C does not differentiate the injury caused by increased imports from the injury caused by other factors, such as rising input costs and shifts in consumer preferences.

(d) State C applies safeguard measures at a sufficient level to remedy the serious injury caused by increased imports and other factors.

(e) State C investigates whether imports from all sources are causing serious injury, but excludes State D from the safeguard measure. State C has a bilateral free trade agreement with State D which prohibits the imposition of safeguard measures.

Part VII

Beyond Trade in Goods: Domestic Regulation, Services, Investment, Procurement and Intellectual Property

13

The SPS and TBT Agreements

I. INTRODUCTION

Earlier chapters of this book discuss the concept of 'disguised protectionism', which refers to measures with an ostensibly legitimate policy purpose that are actually designed as a hidden means of protection for domestic industries. Of particular concern have been measures taken in the areas of product regulation and health measures. Over the years, the rules of the GATT, in particular the National Treatment obligation, were stretched in order to deal with these issues. However, as time went on, some of the GATT Contracting Parties became convinced that the GATT rules were insufficient to address these issues, and that new disciplines with more specific requirements designed to root out disguised protection were needed.

The first formal agreement in this regard, the Agreement on Technical Barriers to Trade (generally referred to as the 'Standards Code'), was concluded as part of the Tokyo Round negotiations. This agreement applied to all 'technical regulations' and 'standards', including those established in relation to health measures. The Uruguay Round built upon the Standards Code by introducing a new agreement on the same subject. While the formal title of the agreement is the same, the agreement is now generally referred to as the 'TBT Agreement'.

In addition, a separate agreement covering, inter alia, health measures, the Agreement on the Application of Sanitary and Phytosanitary Measures (the 'SPS Agreement') was also negotiated during the Uruguay Round. Previously, such measures had been subject to the more general requirements of the Standards Code, but now specific rules have been written with SPS measures in mind. In terms of the relationship between the two agreements, pursuant to Article 1.5 of the TBT Agreement, if something is covered by the SPS Agreement, the TBT Agreement does not apply. Thus, for SPS measures, the SPS Agreement takes precedence.

As we will see, in some ways these agreements are merely an elaboration of GATT rules on non-discrimination. In other ways, however, they have the potential to go much further. (Of course, the GATT still applies to these measures as well.)

In terms of their scope, the TBT and SPS Agreement rules only apply to certain kinds of measures. Above we used the terms 'product regulations' and 'health measures'. More specifically, though, the TBT Agreement, like the Standards Code, regulates the use of 'technical regulations', 'standards' and 'conformity assessment procedures'; the SPS

Agreement regulates 'sanitary measures', which relate to human or animal health, and 'phytosanitary measures', which deal with plant health. We examine the precise scope of each set of measures in more detail below.

Since the TBT and SPS Agreements are mutually exclusive in their scope, it may seem odd to group them together. However, they have a shared origin (in the Tokyo Round Standards Code), and there are many similarities in the substance of their rules. Therefore, we address them both in this chapter, beginning with the SPS Agreement and then moving to the TBT Agreement. We first examine the key provisions of each of these agreements, as well as their elaboration through the case law. We then briefly discuss the object and purpose of these agreements, how they fit within the overall objectives of the WTO system, and the manner in which they constrain domestic policy-making.

II. THE SPS AGREEMENT

As noted, the scope of the SPS Agreement is limited to 'sanitary' and 'phytosanitary' measures, which in essence means measures related to human, animal and plant life or health. More specifically, Annex A of the SPS Agreement defines 'Sanitary or phytosanitary measure' as any measure applied:

> (a) to protect animal or plant life or health within the territory of the Member from risks arising from the entry, establishment or spread of pests, diseases, disease-carrying organisms or disease-causing organisms;
> (b) to protect human or animal life or health within the territory of the Member from risks arising from additives, contaminants, toxins or disease-causing organisms in foods, beverages or feedstuffs;
> (c) to protect human life or health within the territory of the Member from risks arising from diseases carried by animals, plants or products thereof, or from the entry, establishment or spread of pests; or
> (d) to prevent or limit other damage within the territory of the Member from the entry, establishment or spread of pests.

Annex A sets out some very specific risks to human, animal or plant life or health that Members might be concerned with, and therefore take measures to prevent. Only measures that are taken for these purposes are covered by the SPS Agreement. Thus, to determine whether a particular measure is an SPS measure, there will need to be an inquiry into its purpose, which can be a difficult issue. Some kinds of measures that have been challenged as SPS measures in WTO dispute settlement are: measures that restrict salmon imports based on a fear that domestic salmon will be infected with diseases found in foreign salmon; measures that restrict apple imports based on a fear that domestic apples will be infected with diseases found in foreign applies; and measures that restrict sales of meat treated with hormones and products that are made with or contain genetically modified organisms.

Article 1.1 of the SPS Agreement provides a further qualification to the scope of the agreement, specifying that '[t]his Agreement applies to all sanitary and phytosanitary measures which may, directly or indirectly, affect international trade'. In practice, this provision might not provide much limitation on the scope, though. Many SPS measures take the form of import bans or restrictions, which clearly affect trade. Other such measures are more general bans or restrictions that apply to all products but, even where a measure applies on a non-discriminatory basis, it seems likely that it would be considered to affect trade, as sales of foreign products would be affected.

We turn now to the key substantive provisions of the SPS Agreement, to examine the disciplines that apply to these measures. As we will see, some of these provisions have counterparts in the GATT, such as a number of provisions that related to non-discrimination and trade restrictions, whereas others are new and significantly expand on traditional GATT obligations by taking on issues related to the soundness of the science used as the basis for regulation.

(a) Basic Rights and Obligations

Article 2 of the SPS Agreement establishes certain 'Basic Rights and Obligations'. The key substantive aspects of this provision are the following:

(i) Article 2.1

Article 2.1 provides Members with an apparent 'right'. It states: 'Members have the right to take sanitary and phytosanitary measures necessary for the protection of human, animal or plant life or health, provided that such measures are not inconsistent with the provisions of this Agreement'. However, despite the initial reference to a 'right', the latter part of the provision makes clear that this 'right' is contingent on the measures in question not being inconsistent with the SPS Agreement. Thus, the reference seems to have somewhat of a political element, designed to present the Agreement as respecting the protection of human, animal or plant life or health. In truth, the SPS Agreement is no different from other WTO agreements, in that Members must act consistently with the obligations stated therein, as the latter part of the provision makes clear. On the other hand, the explicit reference to a 'right' to take such measures could influence the interpretation of the other provisions, possibly leading to conclusions more favourable to Members taking such measures than would otherwise be the case.

(ii) Article 2.2

Article 2.2 provides that Members shall ensure that SPS measures are 'applied only to the extent necessary to protect human, animal or plant life or health' and that they are 'based on scientific principles' and 'not maintained without sufficient scientific evidence'. The first part of this provision sounds very similar to the GATT Article XX(b) exception discussed above in Chapter 9. The difference, of course, is that Article XX(b) is a defence that can be invoked in order to justify a measure that would otherwise violate GATT rules, such as non-discrimination. By contrast, Article 2.2 is a general obligation that applies to all SPS measures, regardless of their impact on trade. Thus, the first part of Article 2.2 requires that all SPS measures meet these requirements.

The second part of the provision, requiring the use of 'scientific principles' and 'sufficient scientific evidence', is arguably even broader, as it establishes a general requirement that measures be based on sound science.

To date, the case law has not examined the 'necessary' requirement under Article 2.2.

However, several disputes have elaborated on the 'sound science' part of this provision. For example, in *Australia—Salmon*, the panel found that where there is a violation of the 'more specific Article 5.1 or 5.2 such finding can be presumed to imply a violation of the more general provisions of Article 2.2'.[1] In addition, in *Japan—Agricultural Products*, the Appellate Body agreed with the panel that the obligation in Article 2.2 not to maintain an SPS measure without 'sufficient scientific evidence' requires that 'there be a rational or objective relationship between the SPS measure and the scientific evidence'.[2] It further explained that whether there is a rational relationship 'is to be determined on a case-by-case basis and will depend upon the particular circumstances of the case, including the characteristics of the measure at issue and the quality and quantity of the scientific evidence'.[3]

As indicated in the quotation from the *Australia—Salmon* panel, 'sound science' rules are also found in Article 5, which we discuss below.

(iii) Article 2.3

Article 2.3 requires that Members 'ensure' that their SPS measures do not 'arbitrarily or unjustifiably discriminate between Members where identical or similar conditions prevail, including between their own territory and that of other Members', and it also states that SPS measures 'shall not be applied in a manner which would constitute a disguised restriction on international trade'. This provision reads more like a traditional trade obligation, focusing on both MFN and National Treatment-type discrimination, as well as on more general trade 'restrictions' that do not necessarily involve discrimination. In fact, it is very similar to the language of the chapeau of Article XX of the GATT.

Article 2.3 has been the subject of only limited interpretation through dispute settlement. As with Article 2.2, it is the related rules in Article 5.5 that establish this obligation in more detail.

(iv) Article 2.4

Finally, Article 2.4 provides: '[s]anitary or phytosanitary measures which conform to the relevant provisions of this Agreement shall be presumed to be in accordance with the obligations of the Members under the provisions of GATT 1994 which relate to the use of sanitary or phytosanitary measures, in particular the provisions of Article XX(b)'. This provision illustrates that the SPS Agreement is in some ways an elaboration of the Article XX(b) exception. In addition to providing substantive disciplines, compliance with the SPS Agreement can also be used to justify measures as an exception to GATT obligations.

(b) Harmonisation

Article 3 of the SPS Agreement is entitled 'Harmonization'. Its provisions promote the use of international standards, guidelines and recommendations as the basis for domestic

---

[1] Panel Report, *Australia—Salmon*, para 8.52. This finding was upheld on appeal. See Appellate Body Report, *Australia—Salmon*, para. 138.
[2] Appellate Body Report, *Japan—Agricultural Products*, para 84.
[3] *Ibid.*

SPS measures. In this regard, Article 3.1 states that Members 'shall base their sanitary or phytosanitary measures on international standards, guidelines or recommendations, where they exist, except as otherwise provided for in this Agreement, and in particular in paragraph 3'. Article 3.2 then creates a presumption of consistency for measures that 'conform to' international standards, guidelines or recommendations, stating that such measures 'shall be deemed to be necessary to protect human, animal or plant life or health'. Article 3.3 further elaborates that Members may introduce or maintain SPS measures 'which result in a higher level of sanitary or phytosanitary protection than would be achieved by measures based on the relevant international standards, guidelines or recommendations, if there is a scientific justification, or as a consequence of the level of sanitary or phytosanitary protection a Member determines to be appropriate in accordance with the relevant provisions of paragraphs 1 through 8 of Article 5'. Thus, Members may, under certain circumstances, provide *more* protection than international standards, guidelines or recommendations offer. Generally speaking, the goal of these provisions is to promote harmonisation of domestic regulations around international rules. Thus, international standards, guidelines and recommendations act as a basic standard for the level of protection that is to be followed.

The one dispute addressing claims under these provisions is *EC—Hormones*. In that dispute, the Appellate Body first explained that under Article 3.1, the term 'based on' is a looser standard than 'conform to' (as the panel in that case had found), which is found in Article 3.2. In this regard, it said that '[a] thing is commonly said to be "based on" another thing when the former "stands" or is "founded" or "built" upon or "is supported by" the latter.'[4]

In addition, the Appellate Body provided some general guidance on the relationship of the provisions of Article 3. It rejected the panel's characterisation of Article 3.3 as an exception to Article 3.1, instead concluding that Article 3.1, 3.2 and 3.3 apply together, each addressing a separate situation.

(c) Equivalence

Article 4 provides for mutual recognition of other Members' laws in certain circumstances. In this regard, Article 4.1 states:

> Members shall accept the sanitary or phytosanitary measures of other Members as equivalent, even if these measures differ from their own or from those used by other Members trading in the same product, if the exporting Member objectively demonstrates to the importing Member that its measures achieve the importing Member's appropriate level of sanitary or phytosanitary protection. For this purpose, reasonable access shall be given, upon request, to the importing Member for inspection, testing and other relevant procedures.

This provision is similar to the Article 3 harmonisation provisions, but does not go quite as far. The harmonisation provisions encourage all Members to adopt the same or similar measures: by requiring Members to base their measures on international standards, guidelines or recommendations; by giving a presumption of consistency to those measures that conform thereto; and forcing Members to justify measures that provide for a higher level of protection. By contrast, Article 4 requires Members to recognise other Members'

---

[4] Appellate Body Report, *EC—Hormones*, paras 157–68.

measures that accomplish the same goals they are trying to promote and to treat them as if they were the same as their own. This approach tries to achieve goals that are similar to harmonisation, by allowing companies of one Member to sell their products intended for their own domestic market in other Members as well, in the same form with no modifications required to meet different regulatory standards. In essence, it helps integrate the markets by reducing burdens caused by different regulatory systems.

In *US—Poultry*, the panel recently discussed Article 4 as follows:

> 7.134 We note that equivalence regimes adopted pursuant to Article 4 have never been the subject of a dispute before the DSB. There is however, a decision from the SPS Committee entitled "*Decision on the Implementation of Article 4 of the Agreement on the Application of Sanitary and Phytosanitary Measures*" (the Decision). This Decision was adopted under the authority of the SPS Committee to carry out the functions necessary to implement and further the objectives of the *SPS Agreement* under Article 12.1. Its preamble provides that the Decision was adopted "[d]esiring to make operational the provisions of Article 4" of the *SPS Agreement*.

> 7.135 The Decision sets out guidelines for any Member who requests the recognition of equivalence of their SPS measures and for the importing Member who is the addressee of such request. As contemplated in the Decision, upon a request for equivalence, the importing Member should explain the objective and rationale of the SPS measure and identify clearly the risks that the relevant measure is intended to address. The Decision further explains that the importing Member should indicate the ALOP which its SPS measure is designed to achieve. Such an explanation should be accompanied by a copy of the risk assessment on which the SPS measure is based or a technical justification based on a relevant international standard, guideline or recommendation. The exporting Member should then provide appropriate science-based and technical information to support its objective demonstration that its measure achieves the ALOP identified by the importing Member. The importing Member should analyse such information with a view to determining whether the exporting Member's SPS measure achieves the ALOP provided by its own relevant SPS measure.

> 7.136 The Panel notes, that while this decision is not binding and does not determine the scope of Article 4, we do consider that this Decision expands on the Members' own understanding of how Article 4 relates to the rest of the *SPS Agreement* and how it is to be implemented. The Panel sees nothing in Article 4 or the Decision which suggests that Article 4 is the only provision in the *SPS Agreement* which regulates the operation of equivalence regimes, including their "procedural requirements" or that it should be applied in isolation from other relevant provisions of the *SPS Agreement*. In fact, the Decision states that the importing Member should explain its SPS measures by identifying the risk and provide a copy of the risk assessment or technical standard on which the measure is based. Further, it requires the importing Member to analyse the science-based and technical information provided by the exporting Member with respect to that Member's own SPS measure(s) to examine if the measure achieves the importing Member's ALOP.

> 7.137 The Decision refers *inter alia* to risk assessments, international standards and ALOPs, which are governed by Article 2 which embodies the "Basic Rights and Obligations", Article 3 governing harmonization with international standards and Article 5 which regulates the assessment of risk and determination of the ALOP. The Decision, therefore, implies that measures taken as part of an equivalence regime, subject to Article 4, should also comply with the other relevant provisions of the *SPS Agreement*.

> 7.138 In addition, there is nothing in the text of Article 4 that suggests that it should be applied in a vacuum, isolated from other relevant provisions of the *SPS Agreement*. This is further

reinforced by the fact that, as stated by the panel in *Japan—Apples*, Article 4 is not a defence against violations of other provisions of the *SPS Agreement*.

7.139 The Panel does not intend to exhaustively explain the relationship between Article 4 and other provisions of the *SPS Agreement*. Suffice it to say that we do not believe that Article 4 is to be applied to the exclusion of other relevant provisions of the *SPS Agreement*. A determination of which particular provisions are applicable to a given measure, must be done on a case-by-case basis. It is the Panel's view that nothing in Article 4 *a priori* precludes a given measure from being subject to the disciplines of Article 2, 4 and 5 at the same time.

… … …

(d) Assessment of Risk and Determination of the Appropriate Level of Sanitary or Phytosanitary Protection

Article 5 covers a variety of topics. As seen above in the sections on Articles 2 and 3, a number of the provisions of Article 5 have been found to be more specific applications of the general provisions of Articles 2 and 3. Article 5.1–5.3, as well as Article 5.7, elaborate on the 'sound science' provisions of Article 2.2 (and also Article 3.3). Similarly, Article 5.4–5.6 addresses trade restrictions in detail, expanding on Article 2.3. We now examine the key aspects of these provisions in detail, beginning with the 'sound science' provisions of Article 5.1, 5.2 and 5.7, and then turning to the 'trade' provisions of Article 5.5 and 5.6.

(i) Article 5.1—5.3—Risk Assessment

Article 5.1 requires that 'Members shall ensure that their sanitary or phytosanitary measures are based on an assessment, as appropriate to the circumstances, of the risks to human, animal or plant life or health, taking into account risk assessment techniques developed by the relevant international organizations'. In essence, this provision requires that all SPS measures be based on a 'risk assessment'. Paragraph 4 of Annex A defines 'risk assessment' as follows:

> The evaluation of the likelihood of entry, establishment or spread of a pest or disease within the territory of an importing Member according to the sanitary or phytosanitary measures which might be applied, and of the associated potential biological and economic consequences; or the evaluation of the potential for adverse effects on human or animal health arising from the presence of additives, contaminants, toxins or disease-causing organisms in food, beverages or feedstuffs.

In a sense, the risk assessment requirement is a more specific formulation of the 'sound science' requirement in Article 2.2. In effect, a risk assessment is a scientific evaluation that must be undertaken, which is then used as the basis for the measures. If a proper scientific evaluation is carried out as the basis for the measure, there is arguably a high probability that the measure is 'based on scientific principles' and 'not maintained without sufficient scientific evidence' (the language of Article 2.2).

Claims have been brought under this provision in a number of cases. In examining these claims, the Appellate Body has explained that 'based on' is 'appropriately taken to refer to a certain *objective relationship* between two elements, that is to say, to an *objective situation* that persists and is observable between an SPS measure and a risk assessment'. Thus, it found that Article 5.1 requires that there be a 'rational relationship' between the measure at issue and the risk assessment.[5] Applying the provision to specific measures under challenge, violations have been found for all the claims under this provision, on the basis either that there was no proper risk assessment at all or that measures were not 'based on' the risk assessment that did exist.

Article 5.2 and 5.3 elaborates on the conduct of risk assessments. Article 5.2 states: '[i]n the assessment of risks, Members shall take into account available scientific evidence; relevant processes and production methods; relevant inspection, sampling and testing methods; prevalence of specific diseases or pests; existence of pest- or disease-free areas; relevant ecological and environmental conditions; and quarantine or other treatment'. Article 5.3 further provides: '[i]n assessing the risk to animal or plant life or health and determining the measure to be applied for achieving the appropriate level of sanitary or phytosanitary protection from such risk, Members shall take into account as relevant economic factors: the potential damage in terms of loss of production or sales in the event of the entry, establishment or spread of a pest or disease; the costs of control or eradication in the territory of the importing Member; and the relative cost-effectiveness of alternative approaches to limiting risks'.

(ii) Article 5.7—Provisional Measures where Scientific Evidence is Insufficient

Article 5 contains another provision related to science. Article 5.7 provides: '[i]n cases where relevant scientific evidence is insufficient, a Member may provisionally adopt sanitary or phytosanitary measures on the basis of available pertinent information, including that from the relevant international organisations as well as from sanitary or phytosanitary measures applied by other Members'. However, it also states: '[i]n such circumstances, Members shall seek to obtain the additional information necessary for a more objective assessment of risk and review the sanitary or phytosanitary measure accordingly within a reasonable period of time'. Thus, Article 5.7 allows Members to take 'provisional' measures where there is insufficient scientific evidence to be sure of the risks involved. The Appellate Body has stated that this provision reflects the 'precautionary principle',[6] in essence a view that a lack of reliable information justifies some degree of regulation even in the absence of evidence of harm.

Below we provide an extract of the application of this provision, from the Appellate Body report in *Japan—Apples*. This case involved a claim by the United States that measures taken by Japan to prevent the spread of 'fire blight' to its own apples were too restrictive. Under these measures, apples could be imported in Japan, but only if a number of conditions were met. These conditions included: (1) apple fruit must be produced in 'designated fire blight-free orchards', with the designation made by the US Department of Agriculture (in practice, only orchards in the states of Oregon and Washington have been designated as such); (2) the fire blight-free orchard must be surrounded by a 500-metre fire blight-free 'buffer zone'; (3) the orchard and buffer zone must be inspected at least three times annually, with additional inspections following any strong storm; (4) harvested apples must be treated by surface disinfection by soaking in sodium hypochlorite solution for one minute or longer; and (5) fruit destined for Japan must be

---

[5] Appellate Body Report, *EC—Hormones*, paras 178–209.
[6] Appellate Body Report, *EC—Hormones*, para 124.

kept separated post-harvest from other fruit. The US position was that it was exporting only mature, symptomless apples, which could not transmit the disease to Japanese apple orchards. One of Japan's arguments in its defence was that, due to the insufficiency of existing scientific evidence, it was permitted to adopt the measures at issue as 'provisional' measures under Article 5.7. The panel rejected Japan's arguments, and Japan appealed. The Appellate Body found as follows.

Appellate Body Report, *Japan—Measures Affecting the Importation of Apples,* Adopted 10 December 2003, WT/DS245/AB/R

169 We turn to the issue whether the Panel erred in finding that Japan's phytosanitary measure was not imposed in respect of a situation where "relevant scientific evidence is insufficient" within the meaning of Article 5.7 of the *SPS Agreement*.

170 Article 2.2 of the *SPS Agreement* stipulates that Members shall not maintain sanitary or phytosanitary measures without sufficient scientific evidence "except as provided for in paragraph 7 of Article 5". Before the Panel, Japan contested that its phytosanitary measure is "maintained without sufficient scientific evidence" within the meaning of Article 2.2. Japan claimed, in the alternative, that its measure is a provisional measure consistent with Article 5.7.

171 Article 5.7 of the *SPS Agreement* reads as follows:

Assessment of Risk and Determination of the Appropriate Level of Sanitary or Phytosanitary Protection

...

In cases where relevant scientific evidence is insufficient, a Member may provisionally adopt sanitary or phytosanitary measures on the basis of available pertinent information, including that from the relevant international organizations as well as from sanitary or phytosanitary measures applied by other Members. In such circumstances, Members shall seek to obtain the additional information necessary for a more objective assessment of risk and review the sanitary or phytosanitary measure accordingly within a reasonable period of time.

172 The Panel found that Japan's measure is not a provisional measure justified under Article 5.7 of the *SPS Agreement* because the measure was not imposed in respect of a situation where "relevant scientific evidence is insufficient".

173 The Panel identified the "phytosanitary question at issue" as the risk of transmission of fire blight through apple fruit. It observed that "scientific studies as well as practical experience have accumulated for the past 200 years" on this question and that, in the course of its analysis under Article 2.2, it had come across an "important amount of relevant evidence". The Panel observed that a large quantity of high quality scientific evidence on the risk of transmission of fire blight through apple fruit had been produced over the years, and noted that the experts had expressed strong and increasing confidence in this evidence. Stating that Article 5.7 was "designed to be invoked in situations where little, or no, reliable evidence was available on the subject matter at issue", the Panel concluded that the measure was not imposed in respect of a situation where relevant scientific evidence is insufficient. The Panel added that, even if the term "relevant scientific evidence" in Article 5.7 referred to a *specific aspect* of a phytosanitary problem, as Japan claimed, its conclusion would remain the same. The Panel justified its view on the basis of the experts' indication that, not only is there a large volume of general evidence, but there is also a large volume of relevant scientific evidence on the specific scientific questions raised by Japan.

174   Japan challenges the Panel's finding that the measure is not imposed in respect of a situation where "relevant scientific evidence is insufficient" within the meaning of Article 5.7 of the *SPS Agreement*. Moreover, Japan submits that its measure meets all the other requirements of Article 5.7. Accordingly, Japan requests us to reverse the Panel's finding and to complete the analysis regarding the consistency of its measure with the other requirements set out in Article 5.7.

1. The Insufficiency of Relevant Scientific Evidence

175   As noted above, Japan's claim under Article 5.7 was argued before the Panel in the alternative. Japan relied on Article 5.7 only in the event that the Panel rejected Japan's view that "sufficient scientific evidence" exists to maintain the measure within the meaning of Article 2.2. It is in this particular context that the Panel assigned the burden of proof to Japan to make a *prima facie* case in support of its position under Article 5.7.

176   In *Japan—Agricultural Products II*, the Appellate Body stated that Article 5.7 sets out four requirements that must be satisfied in order to adopt and maintain a provisional phytosanitary measure. These requirements are:

(i)   the measure is imposed in respect of a situation where "relevant scientific evidence is insufficient";

(ii) the measure is adopted "on the basis of available pertinent information";

(iii) the Member which adopted the measure "seek[s] to obtain the additional information necessary for a more objective assessment of risk"; and

(iv) the Member which adopted the measure "review[s] the . . . measure accordingly within a reasonable period of time".

These four requirements are "clearly cumulative in nature"; as the Appellate Body said in *Japan—Agricultural Products II*, "[w]henever *one* of these four requirements is not met, the measure at issue is inconsistent with Article 5.7."

177   The Panel's findings address exclusively the first requirement, which the Panel found Japan had not met. The requirements being cumulative, the Panel found it unnecessary to address the other requirements to find an inconsistency with Article 5.7.

178   Japan's appeal also focuses on the first requirement of Article 5.7. Japan contends that the assessment as to whether relevant scientific evidence is insufficient should not be restricted to evidence "in general" on the phytosanitary question at issue, but should also cover a "particular situation" in relation to a "particular measure" or a "particular risk". Hence, Japan submits that the phrase "[w]here relevant scientific evidence is insufficient", in Article 5.7, "should be interpreted to relate to a particular situation in respect of a particular *measure* to which Article 2.2 applies (or a particular risk), but not to a particular *subject matter* in general, which Article 2.2 does not address." According to Japan, the Panel "erred by interpreting the applicability of [Article 5.7] too narrowly' and too 'rigid[ly]".

179   It seems to us that Japan's reliance on the opposition between evidence "in general" and evidence relating to specific aspects of a particular subject matter is misplaced. The first requirement of Article 5.7 is that there must be insufficient scientific evidence. When a panel reviews a measure claimed by a Member to be provisional, that panel must assess whether "relevant scientific evidence is insufficient". This evaluation must be carried out, not in the abstract, but in the light of a particular inquiry. The notions of "relevance" and "insufficiency" in the introductory phrase of Article 5.7 imply a relationship between the scientific evidence and something else. Reading this introductory phrase in the broader context of Article 5 of the

SPS Agreement, which is entitled "Assessment of Risk and Determination of the Appropriate Level of Sanitary or Phytosanitary Protection", is instructive in ascertaining the nature of the relationship to be established. Article 5.1 sets out a key discipline under Article 5, namely that "Members shall ensure that their sanitary or phytosanitary measures are based on an assessment . . . of the risks to human, animal or plant life or health". This discipline informs the other provisions of Article 5, including Article 5.7. We note, as well, that the second sentence of Article 5.7 refers to a "more objective assessment of risks". These contextual elements militate in favour of a link or relationship between the first requirement under Article 5.7 and the obligation to perform a risk assessment under Article 5.1: "relevant scientific evidence" will be "insufficient" within the meaning of Article 5.7 if the body of available scientific evidence does not allow, in quantitative or qualitative terms, the performance of an adequate assessment of risks as required under Article 5.1 and as defined in Annex A to the *SPS Agreement*. Thus, the question is not whether there is sufficient evidence of a general nature or whether there is sufficient evidence related to a specific aspect of a phytosanitary problem, or a specific risk. The question is whether the relevant evidence, be it "general" or "specific", in the Panel's parlance, is sufficient to permit the evaluation of the likelihood of entry, establishment or spread of, in this case, fire blight in Japan.

180   The Panel found that, with regard to the risk of transmission of fire blight through apples exported from the United States—"normally", mature, symptomless apples—"not only a large quantity but a high quality of scientific evidence has been produced over the years that describes the risk of transmission of fire blight through apple fruit as negligible", and that "this is evidence in which the experts have expressed strong and increasing confidence."

181   Japan also raised specific questions related to endophytic bacteria in mature apple fruit and regarding the completion of contamination pathways. In relation to these specific questions, the Panel made the finding of fact, based on indications of the experts retained by the Panel, that there is a large volume of relevant scientific evidence regarding these questions as well. Moreover, Japan did not persuade the Panel that this scientific evidence is not conclusive or has not produced reliable results.

182   These findings of fact by the Panel suggest that the body of available scientific evidence permitted, in quantitative and qualitative terms, the performance of an assessment of risks, as required under Article 5.1 and as defined in Annex A to the *SPS Agreement*, with respect to the risk of transmission of fire blight through apple fruit exported from the United States to Japan. In particular, according to these findings of fact by the Panel, the body of available scientific evidence would allow "[t]he evaluation of the likelihood of entry, establishment or spread" of fire blight in Japan through apples exported from the United States. Accordingly, in the light of the findings of fact made by the Panel, we conclude that, with respect to the risk of transmission of fire blight through apple fruit exported from the United States to Japan ("normally", mature, symptomless apples), the 'relevant scientific evidence' is not "insufficient" within the meaning of Article 5.7.

2. Japan's Argument on "Scientific Uncertainty"

183   Japan challenges the Panel's statement that Article 5.7 is intended to address only "situations where little, or no, reliable evidence was available on the subject matter at issue" because this does not provide for situations of "unresolved uncertainty". Japan draws a distinction between "new uncertainty" and "unresolved uncertainty", arguing that both fall within Article 5.7. According to Japan, "new uncertainty" arises when a new risk is identified; Japan argues that the Panel's characterization that "little, or no, reliable evidence was available on the subject matter at issue" is relevant to a situation of "new uncertainty". We understand that Japan defines "unresolved uncertainty" as uncertainty that the scientific evidence is not able

to resolve, despite accumulated scientific evidence. According to Japan, the risk of transmission of fire blight through apple fruit relates essentially to a situation of "unresolved uncertainty". Thus, Japan maintains that, despite considerable scientific evidence regarding fire blight, there is still uncertainty about certain aspects of transmission of fire blight. Japan contends that the reasoning of the Panel is tantamount to restricting the applicability of Article 5.7 to situations of "new uncertainty" and to excluding situations of "unresolved uncertainty"; and that, by doing so, the Panel erred in law.

184   We disagree with Japan. The application of Article 5.7 is triggered not by the existence of scientific uncertainty, but rather by the insufficiency of scientific evidence. The text of Article 5.7 is clear: it refers to "cases where relevant scientific evidence is insufficient", not to "scientific uncertainty". The two concepts are not interchangeable. Therefore, we are unable to endorse Japan's approach of interpreting Article 5.7 through the prism of "scientific uncertainty".

185   We also find no basis for Japan's argument that the Panel's interpretation of Article 5.7 is too narrow for the reason that it excludes cases where the quantity of evidence on a phytosanitary question is "more than little" , but the available scientific evidence has not resolved the question. The Panel's statement that Article 5.7 is intended to address "situations where little, or no, reliable evidence was available on the subject matter at issue", refers to the availability of *reliable* evidence. We do not read the Panel's interpretation as excluding cases where the available evidence is more than minimal in quantity, but has not led to reliable or conclusive results. Indeed, the Panel explicitly recognized that such cases fall within the scope of Article 5.7 when it observed, in the Interim Review section of its Report, that under its approach, Article 5.7 would be applicable to a situation where a lot of scientific research has been carried out on a particular issue without yielding reliable evidence.

3. The Panel's Reliance on a "History of 200 Years of Studies and Practical Experience"

186   Japan contends that the conclusion of the Panel regarding Article 5.7 is based on its assessment that, as regards fire blight, "scientific studies as well as practical experience have accumulated for the past 200 years". Japan submits that the Panel was not authorized to rule on the basis of a "'history' of 200 year[s] of studies and practical experience" because "the United States did not raise any objection to application of Article 5.7 on the basis of [a] 'history' of 200 year[s] of studies and practical experience." In other words, according to Japan, the Panel was not entitled to draw a conclusion regarding Article 5.7 on the basis of such "history" unless the United States had raised an objection based on "history", something that the United States had not done.

187   In the course of its reasoning, the Panel mentioned that, as regards the risk of transmission of fire blight through apple fruit, "scientific studies as well as practical experience have accumulated for the past 200 years". This statement was relevant to the debate under Article 5.7 and was based on the evidence before the Panel. Accordingly, it was appropriate for the Panel to make such a statement irrespective of whether the United States had explicitly advanced an argument based on "history".

188   In the light of these considerations, we uphold the findings of the Panel, in paragraphs 8.222 and 9.1(b) of the Panel Report, that Japan's phytosanitary measure at issue was not imposed in respect of a situation "where relevant scientific evidence is insufficient", and, therefore, that it is not a provisional measure justified under Article 5.7 of the *SPS Agreement*. We note that Japan requested us, in the event we were to reverse the Panel's finding on Article 5.7, to complete the analysis in respect of the other requirements set out in Article 5.7 of the *SPS Agreement*. Given our conclusion, there is no need to do so.

... ...

Thus far, panels and the Appellate Body have strictly enforced the specific language of Article 5.7. This can be seen not only through the level of care shown in the Appellate Body decision above, but also in an earlier case, *Japan—Agricultural Products*, where (after failing to meet the requirements set out in Article 2.2) Japan argued that its testing requirement for agricultural products was justified by Article 5.7. In that case, the Appellate Body agreed with the panel that Japan failed to take action under the second sentence of Article 5.7 to (1) 'seek to obtain the additional information necessary for a more objective assessment of risk'; and (2) 'review the . . . measure accordingly within a reasonable period of time'.[7]

As a final point, in the *EC—Hormones* case the Appellate Body explained that the 'precautionary principle' 'finds reflection' in Article 5.7. This principle has been a particularly contentious issue. We extract the relevant portions of the Appellate Body report here, and discuss the impact of the *EC—Hormones* case further towards the ends of the chapter.

Appellate Body Report, *EC—Measures Concerning Meat and Meat Products (Hormones)*, Adopted 13 February 1998, WT/DSD26,48/AB/R

120. We are asked by the European Communities to reverse the finding of the Panel relating to the precautionary principle. The Panel's finding and its supporting statements are set out in the Panel Reports in the following terms:

> The European Communities also invokes the precautionary principle in support of its claim that its measures in dispute are based on a risk assessment. To the extent that this principle could be considered as part of customary international law *and* be used to interpret Articles 5.1 and 5.2 on the assessment of risks as a customary rule of interpretation of public international law (as that phrase is used in Article 3.2 of the DSU), we consider that this principle would not override the explicit wording of Articles 5.1 and 5.2 outlined above, in particular since the precautionary principle has been incorporated and given a specific meaning in Article 5.7 of the SPS Agreement. We note, however, that the European Communities has explicitly stated in this case that it is not invoking Article 5.7.

> We thus find that the precautionary principle cannot override our findings made above, namely that the EC import ban of meat and meat products from animals treated with any of the five hormones at issue for growth promotion purposes, in so far as it also applies to meat and meat products from animals treated with any of these hormones *in accordance with good practice*, is, from a substantive point of view, not *based on* a risk assessment. (italics added)

121. The basic submission of the European Communities is that the precautionary principle is, or has become, "a general customary rule of international law" or at least "a general principle of law". Referring more specifically to Articles 5.1 and 5.2 of the *SPS Agreement*, applying the precautionary principle means, in the view of the European Communities, that it is not necessary for *all* scientists around the world to agree on the "possibility and magnitude" of the risk, nor for *all* or most of the WTO Members to perceive and evaluate the risk in the same way. It is also stressed that Articles 5.1 and 5.2 do not prescribe a particular type of risk assessment and do not prevent Members from being cautious in their risk assessment exercise. The European Communities goes on to state that its measures here at stake were precautionary in nature and satisfied the requirements of Articles 2.2 and 2.3, as well as of Articles 5.1, 5.2, 5.4, 5.5 and 5.6 of the *SPS Agreement*.

---

[7] Appellate Body Report, *Japan—Agricultural Products*, paras 86–94.

122. The United States does not consider that the "precautionary principle" represents customary international law and suggests it is more an "approach" than a "principle". Canada, too, takes the view that the precautionary principle has not yet been incorporated into the corpus of public international law; however, it concedes that the "precautionary approach" or "concept" is "an *emerging* principle of law" which may in the future crystallize into one of the "general principles of law recognized by civilized nations" within the meaning of Article 38(1)I of the *Statute of the International Court of Justice*.

123. The status of the precautionary principle in international law continues to be the subject of debate among academics, law practitioners, regulators and judges. The precautionary principle is regarded by some as having crystallized into a general principle of customary international *environmental* law. Whether it has been widely accepted by Members as a principle of *general* or *customary international law* appears less than clear. We consider, however, that it is unnecessary, and probably imprudent, for the Appellate Body in this appeal to take a position on this important, but abstract, question. We note that the Panel itself did not make any definitive finding with regard to the status of the precautionary principle in international law and that the precautionary principle, at least outside the field of international environmental law, still awaits authoritative formulation.

124. It appears to us important, nevertheless, to note some aspects of the relationship of the precautionary principle to the *SPS Agreement*. First, the principle has not been written into the *SPS Agreement* as a ground for justifying SPS measures that are otherwise inconsistent with the obligations of Members set out in particular provisions of that Agreement. Secondly, the precautionary principle indeed finds reflection in Article 5.7 of the *SPS Agreement*. We agree, at the same time, with the European Communities, that there is no need to assume that Article 5.7 exhausts the relevance of a precautionary principle. It is reflected also in the sixth paragraph of the preamble and in Article 3.3. These explicitly recognize the right of Members to establish their own appropriate level of sanitary protection, which level may be higher (i.e., more cautious) than that implied in existing international standards, guidelines and recommendations. Thirdly, a panel charged with determining, for instance, whether "sufficient scientific evidence" exists to warrant the maintenance by a Member of a particular SPS measure may, of course, and should, bear in mind that responsible, representative governments commonly act from perspectives of prudence and precaution where risks of irreversible, e.g. life terminating, damage to human health are concerned. Lastly, however, the precautionary principle does not, by itself, and without a clear textual directive to that effect, relieve a panel from the duty of applying the normal (i.e. customary international law) principles of treaty interpretation in reading the provisions of the *SPS Agreement*.

125. We accordingly agree with the finding of the Panel that the precautionary principle does not override the provisions of Articles 5.1 and 5.2 of the *SPS Agreement*.

... ...

Thus, the Appellate Body rejected the EC argument based on the 'precautionary principle'. In resolving the issue, the Appellate Body did not attempt to decide whether the precautionary principle has been accepted as a principle of general or customary international law.

(iii) Article 5.5—Discrimination or Disguised Restrictions on Trade

Turning to the 'trade' related provisions of Article 5, Article 5.5 requires that 'each Member shall avoid arbitrary or unjustifiable distinctions in the levels it considers to be appropriate in different situations, if such distinctions result in discrimination or a disguised restriction on international trade'. This provision uses wording that is similar, although not identical, to that of the Article XX chapeau (discussed in Chapter 9). Article 5.5 targets two types of measures: those that 'discriminate', and those that constitute a 'disguised restriction on international trade'. The reference to 'discrimination' has all the same interpretive difficulties as discussed above in that chapter. Moreover, the specific wording used here is arguably even more difficult to apply, as both 'discrimination' and 'disguised restrictions' must be the result of 'distinctions'.

In *EC—Hormones*, the Appellate Body explained that there that there are three required elements necessary for a finding of violation of Article 5.5:

(1) the Member imposing the measure must have adopted its own appropriate levels of sanitary protection against risks to human life or health in several 'different situations';

(2) those *levels of protection* must exhibit 'arbitrary or unjustifiable' differences in their treatment of the different situations; and

(3) the arbitrary or unjustifiable differences result in 'discrimination or a disguised restriction of international trade'.[8]

To illustrate the application of this provision, we turn to the *Australia—Salmon* dispute. In that case, the Appellate Body addressed an Australian measure that banned imports of salmon unless the salmon has been heat-treated (ie, cooked). Australia had identified 24 'disease agents' which might be present in Canadian salmon and were considered to be a threat to the health of the Australian salmon population. The heat-treatment requirement was designed to eliminate the threat from these disease agents. The panel found that the measure constituted a 'disguised restriction' under Article 5.5, and Australia appealed. The Appellate Body decided this issue as follows:

Appellate Body Report, *Australia—Measures Affecting Importation of Salmon*, Adopted 6 November 1998, WT/DS18/AB/R

139. The next issue we address is whether the Panel erred in law in finding that Australia has acted inconsistently with Article 5.5 of the *SPS Agreement*.

140. Following our Report in *European Communities—Hormones*, the Panel considered:

that three elements are required in order for a Member to act inconsistently with Article 5.5:

— the Member concerned adopts different appropriate levels of sanitary protection in several "different situations";

— those levels of protection exhibit differences which are "arbitrary or unjustifiable"; and

— the measure embodying those differences results in "discrimination or a disguised restriction on international trade".

141. The Panel found that all three conditions are fulfilled and therefore concluded that:

Since all three elements of Article 5.5 are present in this case, we find that Australia, by maintaining the measure at issue, acts inconsistently with its obligations under Article 5.5. Given our earlier finding—that a violation of the more specific Article 5.5 can be presumed to

---

[8] Appellate Body Report, *EC—Hormones*, paras 210–46.

imply a violation of the more general Article 2.3—we find that Australia, to that extent, also acts inconsistently with Article 2.3.

142. Australia appeals from this finding of inconsistency with Article 5.5 and, by implication, Article 2.3 of the *SPS Agreement*. Without challenging the Panel's three-step legal test for inconsistency with Article 5.5 as such, Australia contends that the Panel has made a series of errors of law in the interpretation and application of the test. Australia argues that the Panel, in its application of Article 5.5, exceeded its terms of reference, erred in the allocation and application of the burden of proof, failed to make an objective assessment of the matter as required by Article 11 of the DSU and made a number of substantive errors in its interpretation and application of Article 5.5. The first of these claims has already been dealt with in Part IV of our Report; the second and third claims are dealt with in Sections A and B of Part VI. In this section we focus exclusively on the substantive errors of law Australia claims the Panel made in its interpretation and application of each of the three elements of Article 5.5 of the *SPS Agreement*.

1. First element of Article 5.5

143. With regard to the first element of Article 5.5, namely, the existence of distinctions in appropriate levels of protection in different situations, the Panel cited our Report in *European Communities—Hormones*, where we stated that "situations . . . cannot, of course, be compared, unless they are comparable, that is, unless they present some common element or elements sufficient to render them comparable". The Panel found that:

> . . . in the circumstances of this dispute, we can compare situations under Article 5.5 if these situations involve either a risk of "entry, establishment or spread" of the same or a similar disease *or* of the same or similar "associated biological and economic consequences" and this irrespective of whether they arise from the same product or other products. (emphasis added)

144. On this basis, the Panel determined that the import prohibition on fresh, chilled or frozen salmon for human consumption *and* the admission of imports of (i) uncooked Pacific herring, cod, haddock, Japanese eel and plaice for human consumption; (ii) uncooked Pacific herring, Atlantic and Pacific cod, haddock, European and Japanese eel and Dover sole for human consumption; (iii) herring in whole, frozen form used as bait ('herring used as bait'); and (iv) live ornamental finfish, are "different" situations which can be compared under Article 5.5 of the *SPS Agreement*.

145. Australia argues that the Panel erred by considering that situations are "different", i.e., "comparable", if these situations involve *either* a risk of entry, establishment or spread of the same or a similar disease, *or* a risk of the same or similar "associated potential biological and economic consequences". Australia contends that the Panel has imputed a meaning to the term "risk" which conflicts with the ordinary meaning of the term as used in its context and in the light of the object and purpose of the *SPS Agreement*. According to Australia, the "risk" to be examined is the risk evaluated in the risk assessment, namely, the risk of entry, establishment or spread of several different diseases *and* of the associated potential biological and economic consequences.

146. Situations which involve a risk of entry, establishment or spread of the same or a similar disease have some common elements sufficient to render them comparable under Article 5.5. Likewise, situations with a risk of the same or similar associated potential biological and economic consequences also have some common elements sufficient to render them comparable under Article 5.5. We, therefore, consider that for "different" situations to be comparable under Article 5.5, there is no need for both the disease *and* the biological and economic consequences

to be the same or similar. We recognize that, as pointed out by Australia, the risk which needs to be examined in a risk assessment, pursuant to Article 5.1 and the first definition of risk assessment of paragraph 4 of Annex A, is the risk of *both* the entry, establishment or spread of a disease *and* the associated potential biological and economic consequences. However, we fail to see how this can be of relevance to the question of comparability of different situations under Article 5.5 which is the issue addressed by the Panel. We, therefore, conclude that the Panel was correct in stating that situations can be compared under Article 5.5 if these situations involve *either* a risk of entry, establishment or spread of the same or a similar disease, *or* a risk of the same or similar "associated potential biological and economic consequences".

147. Moreover, we note that the Panel examined and concluded, with respect to each of the four comparisons, that there is a risk of entry, establishment or spread of the same or similar diseases *and* that the risk of associated potential biological and economic consequences is the same or similar.

148. Australia also argues that the Panel erred by examining the biological and economic consequences of the "introduction" of diseases rather than the biological and economic consequences of the "entry, establishment or spread" of diseases. According to Australia, the Panel's interpretation of "entry, establishment or spread" as "introduction" is contrary to the SPS provisions on risk assessment, i.e., Articles 5.1 to 5.3 and Annex A. We note that it is clear from the context of the relevant Panel discussion, that the Panel merely used the word "introduction" as a *short hand expression* for "entry, establishment or spread". It explicitly defined the consequences of disease introduction as "the consequences of a disease once established in a country".

149. Furthermore, even if there were to be a difference between the consequences of "disease introduction" and the consequences of the "entry, establishment and spread of a disease", we note that for the comparability of situations under Article 5.5, nothing requires us to look at the latter and not at the former. We recognize that the definition of a risk assessment requires a risk assessment to evaluate the consequences of the "entry, establishment and spread of a disease" but we fail to see how this can be of relevance to the question of the comparability of different situations under Article 5.5.

150. Australia finally contends that the Panel erred in determining that its examination on the comparability of different situations must be limited solely to those disease agents positively detected. According to Australia, the Panel diminished Australia's right to a cautious approach to determine its own appropriate level of protection. Australia argues that the Panel failed to interpret the provisions of Article 5.5 in their context and in the light of the object and purpose of the *SPS Agreement*. According to Australia, the terms "likelihood" and "potential" in regard to the definition of "risk assessment" contained in paragraph 4 of Annex A, and the terms "scientific principles" and "sufficient scientific evidence" contained in Article 2.2, make it clear that the basic SPS right set out in Article 2.1 to take SPS measures necessary for the protection of animal life or health, is not contingent on positive scientific evidence of disease detection.

151. We note that, contrary to what Australia argues, the Panel did not limit its examination under Article 5.5 to diseases positively detected in fresh, chilled or frozen ocean-caught Pacific salmon. On the contrary, it appears clearly from Annex 1 to the Panel Report, entitled "The Four Comparisons under Article 5.5", that the Panel examined diseases of concern which, according to Australia, may be carried by fresh, chilled or frozen ocean-caught Pacific salmon but which have not yet been positively detected in this type of salmon. We also note that the Panel stated explicitly that:

.. To the extent that both the other products and the salmon products further examined are known to be hosts to one of these disease agents or—for the salmon products—*give rise to an alleged concern for that disease agent*, they can be associated with the same kind of risk, namely a risk of entry, establishment or spread of that disease. (emphasis added)

152. In addition, we believe that for situations to be comparable under Article 5.5, it is sufficient for these situations to have in common a risk of entry, establishment or spread of *one* disease of concern. There is no need for these situations to have in common a risk of entry, establishment or spread of *all* diseases of concern. Therefore, even if the Panel had excluded from its examination *some* diseases of concern not positively detected in fresh, chilled or frozen ocean-caught Pacific salmon, this would not invalidate its finding in paragraph 8.121 on comparable situations under Article 5.5.

153. We, therefore, uphold the Panel's finding in paragraph 8.121 of its Report that the import prohibition on fresh, chilled or frozen salmon for human consumption *and* the admission of imports of other fish and fish products are "different" situations which can be compared under Article 5.5 of the *SPS Agreement*.

5. Second element of Article 5.5

154. With regard to the second element of Article 5.5, namely, the existence of arbitrary or unjustifiable distinctions in appropriate levels of protection in different situations, the Panel began its analysis by noting that in view of the difference in SPS measures and corresponding levels of protection for salmon products, on the one hand, and the four categories of other fish and fish products, on the other, one might expect some justification for this difference, such as a higher risk from imported salmon. However, as the Panel noted:

> . . . the arguments, reports, studies and expert opinions submitted to us in this respect—rather than pointing in the direction of a *higher* risk related to . . . [ocean-caught Pacific salmon], in order to justify the stricter sanitary measures imposed for these products—all provide evidence that the two categories of non-salmonids [herring used as bait and live ornamental finfish], for which more lenient sanitary measures apply, can be presumed to represent at least as high a risk—if not a higher risk—than the risk associated with . . . [ocean-caught Pacific salmon].

155. The Panel, therefore, found that, on the basis of the evidence before it, the distinctions in levels of sanitary protection reflected in Australia's treatment of, on the one hand, ocean-caught Pacific salmon and, on the other, herring used as bait and live ornamental finfish, are "arbitrary or unjustifiable" in the sense of the second element of Article 5.5.

156. Australia argues that the Panel erred in determining that its examination under Article 5.5, second element, must be limited solely to those disease agents positively detected in ocean-caught Pacific salmon. Australia raises the same objections to this limitation as it did in the context of the first element discussed above.

157. We do not agree with Australia that the Panel excluded diseases of concern which have not been positively detected in ocean-caught Pacific salmon from its examination under Article 5.5. The Panel explicitly took into account diseases which have not been positively detected in ocean-caught Pacific salmon but had been detected in herring used as bait and live ornamental finfish. In addition, we observe that the inclusion in the examination under Article 5.5, second element, of *all* diseases of concern which have not been positively detected in ocean-caught Pacific salmon would logically have led to the inclusion of all diseases of concern which have not been positively detected in herring used as bait and live ornamental finfish. Due to the lack of reliable scientific information, this exercise would have become highly speculative and, moreover, would probably not have changed the Panel's finding in paragraph 8.141 on the "arbitrary or unjustifiable" character of the distinctions in the levels of protection.

158. Australia determined explicitly that its appropriate level of protection with respect to ocean-caught Pacific salmon is "a high or very conservative" level of sanitary protection aimed at reducing risk to "very low levels", "while not based on a zero-risk approach". The level of protection reflected in Australia's treatment of herring used as bait and live ornamental finfish is definitely lower. We note the Panel's factual finding that herring used as bait and live ornamental finfish can be presumed to represent at least as high a risk—if not a higher risk—than the risk associated with ocean-caught Pacific salmon. Therefore, we uphold the Panel's finding in paragraph 8.141 of its Report to the extent that the Panel found that the second element of Article 5.5 is fulfilled.

6. Third element of Article 5.5

159. With regard to the third element of Article 5.5, i.e., that the arbitrary or unjustifiable distinctions in levels of protection result in "discrimination or a disguised restriction on international trade", we note that the Panel identified three "warning signals" as well as three "other factors more substantial in nature" ("additional factors"). The Panel considered that each of these "warning signals" and "additional factors" can be taken into account in its decision on the third element of Article 5.5. In paragraph 8.159 of its Report, it concluded:

> On the basis of all "warning signals" and factors outlined above, *considered cumulatively*, . . . the distinctions in levels of protection imposed by Australia for, on the one hand, . . . [ocean-caught Pacific salmon] and, on the other hand, herring . . . use[d] as bait and live ornamental finfish, . . . result . . . in "a disguised restriction on international trade", in the sense of the third element of Article 5.5. (emphasis added)

160. Australia contends that the Panel made a number of substantive errors of law in using these "warning signals" and "additional factors" to come to its conclusion on the third element of Article 5.5.

161. The first "warning signal" the Panel considered was the arbitrary or unjustifiable character of the differences in levels of protection. It noted what we stated in *European Communities—Hormones*:

> . . . the arbitrary or unjustifiable character of differences in *levels of protection* . . . may in practical effect operate as a "warning" signal that the implementing *measure* in its application *might* be a discriminatory measure or *might* be a restriction on international trade disguised as an SPS measure for the protection of human life or health.

The Panel, therefore, considered that:

> . . . In this dispute, . . . the arbitrary character of the differences in levels of protection is a "warning signal" that the measure at issue results in "a disguised restriction on international trade".

162. According to Australia, the Panel erred in according the first "warning signal", the status of evidence which demonstrates that the measure results in a disguised restriction on international trade. We note however, that it appears clearly from the Panel Report, and in particular, from the reference therein to our Report in *European Communities—Hormones*, that the Panel considered the arbitrary or unjustifiable character of differences in levels of protection as a "warning signal" for, and not as "evidence" of, a disguised restriction on international trade.

163. The second "warning signal" considered by the Panel was the *rather substantial difference* in levels of protection between an import prohibition on ocean-caught Pacific salmon, as opposed to tolerance for imports of herring used as bait and of live ornamental finfish. The Panel noted our statement in *European Communities—Hormones* that:

. . . the degree of difference, or the extent of the discrepancy, in the levels of protection, *is only one kind* of factor which, along with others, may cumulatively lead to the conclusion that discrimination or a disguised restriction on international trade in fact results from the application of a measure. (emphasis added)

On that basis, the Panel stated:

. . . we do consider that the rather substantial difference in levels of protection is one of the factors we should take into account in deciding whether the measure at issue results in "a disguised restriction on international trade", as argued by Canada.

164. Australia contends that this second "warning signal" is effectively no different in character from the first "warning signal" and should therefore be discounted. We note, however, that in this case the degree of difference in the levels of protection (prohibition *versus* tolerance) is indeed, as the Panel stated, "rather substantial". We, therefore, consider it legitimate to treat this difference as a separate warning signal.

165. The third "warning signal" the Panel considered was the inconsistency of the SPS measure at issue with Articles 5.1 and 2.2 of the *SPS Agreement*. The Panel considered that its earlier finding of inconsistency with Articles 5.1 and 2.2:

. . . may, together with other factors, lead to the conclusion that the measure at issue results in a "disguised restriction on international trade". Indeed, considering these violations of Articles 5.1 and 2.2 it would seem that the measure at issue constitutes an import prohibition, i.e., a restriction on international trade, "disguised" as a sanitary measure. We do stress, however, that this additional "warning signal" as such cannot be sufficient to conclude that the measure results in a "disguised restriction on international trade".

166. Australia objects to the use of this inconsistency as a warning signal in the context of the third element of Article 5.5. It argues that inconsistency with Article 5.1 cannot "presume" or pre-empt a finding under Article 5.5. We note that a finding that an SPS measure is not based on an assessment of the risks to human, animal or plant life or health—either because there was no risk assessment at all or because there is an insufficient risk assessment—is a strong indication that this measure is not really concerned with the protection of human, animal or plant life or health but is instead a trade-restrictive measure taken in the guise of an SPS measure, i.e., a "disguised restriction on international trade". We, therefore, consider that the finding of inconsistency with Article 5.1 is an appropriate warning signal for a "disguised restriction on international trade".

167. The first "additional factor" considered by the Panel is the fact that the two substantially different SPS measures that Australia applies (import prohibition versus import tolerance) lead to discrimination between salmon, on the one hand, and herring used as bait and live ornamental finfish on the other. In the Panel's view, the concept of "disguised restriction on international trade" in Article 5.5 includes, among other things, restrictions constituting arbitrary or unjustifiable discrimination between certain products.

168. Australia contends that this first "additional factor" is merely a combination of the first two "warning signals" and does not, therefore, constitute additional "evidence". Furthermore, Australia argues that this first "additional factor" is based on an inappropriate analogy to Article III of the GATT 1994 and a wrong concept of discrimination which, in the context of Article 5.5, means, in its view, discrimination between countries. According to Australia, the first "additional factor" should therefore be excluded.

169. We believe that the first "additional factor" should indeed be excluded from the examination of the third element of Article 5.5. All "arbitrary or unjustifiable distinctions" in levels of

protection will lead logically to discrimination between products, whether the products are the same (e.g., discrimination between imports of salmon from different countries or between imported salmon and domestic salmon) or different (e.g., salmon versus herring used as bait and live ornamental finfish). The first "additional factor" is therefore not different from the first warning signal, and should not be taken into account as a *separate factor* in the determination of whether an SPS measure results in a "disguised restriction on international trade".

170. The second "additional factor" considered by the Panel was the substantial, but unexplained change in conclusion between the 1995 Draft Report (which recommended allowing the importation of ocean-caught Pacific salmon under certain conditions) and the 1996 Final Report (which recommended continuing the import prohibition). The Panel suggested that the decisive reason for the reversal of the 1995 draft recommendation "might well have been inspired by domestic pressures to protect the Australian salmon industry against import competition".

171. Australia argues that the Panel erred in considering this difference as a factor to be taken into account in the examination of the third element of Article 5.5. Australia contends that the Panel has incorrectly accorded a draft recommendation the status of an SPS measure and that no provision of the *SPS Agreement* requires WTO Members to implement draft recommendations absent new scientific evidence. Moreover, Australia argues that the Panel refused to consider its arguments and evidence on the role of draft reports and recommendation in the decision-making process of governments. Australia contends that the Panel mischaracterized the reasons for the introduction of QP86A. In Australia's view, the Panel also erred in speculating about the presence and role of lobbying in Australia's decision to adopt the 1996 Final Report.

172. We consider Australia's arguments to be without merit. First, we note that paragraph 1 of Annex A of the *SPS Agreement* defines a sanitary measure of the type relevant in this dispute as a measure applied to protect animal life or health within the territory of a Member from risks arising from the entry, establishment or spread of diseases. In the light of this definition, the Panel was correct to consider the recommendation of the 1995 Draft Report to allow *under certain conditions* the importation of ocean-caught Pacific salmon to be a recommendation of an SPS measure.

173. Second, we note that the Panel did not at any point state that WTO Members are obliged to implement draft recommendations absent new scientific evidence. It did not introduce such obligation. We note that the Panel explicitly acknowledged that the substantial but unexplained reversal of the 1995 draft recommendation does not constitute, in itself, sufficient proof that the measure results in a disguised restriction on trade. The Panel merely considered that this factor "can be taken into account cumulatively with other factors" in the examination under the third element of Article 5.5. We agree with the Panel. We do not share Australia's criticism on the Panel's use of the 1995 Draft Report, which the Panel used correctly as "part of the architecture" or "part of a process" leading to the 1996 Final Report. We also do not see the relevance of the historical reasons for the introduction of QP86A in 1975 to the examination of the substantial changes in conclusion between the 1995 Draft Report and the 1996 Final Report.

174. The third "additional factor" considered by the Panel was the absence of controls on the internal movement of salmon products within Australia compared to the prohibition of the importation of ocean-caught Pacific salmon. The Panel did not come to a conclusion on the existence or nature of this alleged difference, but considered that its doubts whether Australia applies similarly strict sanitary standards, "though probably not conclusive as such, can also be taken into account, cumulatively with other factors, in [its] decision on whether the measure at issue results in a 'disguised restriction on international trade'."

175. Australia contends that the Panel erred in implying that consistency with Article 5.5, requires either restrictions on the internal movement of salmon products within Australia or, alternatively, that Australia apply import zoning to grant access to Australia for ocean-caught Pacific salmon.

176. We note that, as acknowledged by Australia, the Panel did not conclude that the alleged absence of internal controls constituted a violation of Article 5.5 or any other provision of the *SPS Agreement*. The Panel merely stated its doubts on whether Australia applies similarly strict sanitary standards on the internal movement of salmon products within Australia as it does on the importation of salmon products and considered that as *a* factor which can be taken into account in the examination under the third element of Article 5.5. We consider that these doubts do not carry much weight, but we agree with the Panel that they can nevertheless be taken into consideration.

177. In the above analysis, we have upheld the Panel's findings on the first, second and third "warning signals" as well as its findings on the second and third "additional factors". We have only reversed the Panel's finding on the first "additional factor". We consider, however, that this reversal does not affect the validity of the Panel's conclusion in paragraph 8.159 of its Report, that the "warning signals" and "other factors", *considered cumulatively*, lead to the conclusion that the distinctions in the levels of protection imposed by Australia result in a disguised restriction on international trade.

178. We, therefore, uphold the Panel's finding that, by maintaining the measure at issue, Australia has acted inconsistently with its obligations under Article 5.5, and, by implication, Article 2.3 of the *SPS Agreement*.

...   .

The Appellate Body's consideration of the various factors discussed above provides some insights into the determination of whether there is a 'disguised restriction on international trade'. The first point to be noted is that the existence of a 'restriction on international trade' was not really contested. Clearly, the measure at issue restricted trade, as it allowed salmon imports only where they had been heat-treated. Instead, the main issue was whether this was a 'disguised' restriction. In essence, this inquiry is about whether the restriction really had a legitimate purpose, or whether it was just a hidden means of hindering imports. To answer this question, the Appellate Body considered five factors that had been set out by the panel (it rejected another of the factors used):

1.   the arbitrary or unjustifiable character of the differences in levels of protection.
2.   the *rather substantial difference* in levels of protection between an import prohibition on ocean-caught Pacific salmon, as opposed to tolerance for imports of herring used as bait and of live ornamental finfish.
3.   the inconsistency of the SPS measure at issue with Articles 5.1 and 2.2 of the SPS Agreement.
4.   the substantial but unexplained change in conclusion between the 1995 Draft Report (which recommended allowing the importation of ocean-caught Pacific salmon under certain conditions) and the 1996 Final Report (which recommended continuing the import prohibition).
5.   the absence of controls on the internal movement of salmon products within Australia compared to the prohibition of the importation of ocean-caught Pacific salmon.

Overall, this analysis appears to focus more on the reasonableness and appropriateness of the measure than any effect it had on trade, which is not too surprising because the key issue was whether the measure was 'disguised' as something other than what it was claimed to be.

(iv) Article 5.6—No More Trade-restrictive Than Necessary

The final 'trade' related requirement of Article 5 is in Article 5.6, which states:

> when establishing or maintaining sanitary or phytosanitary measures to achieve the appropriate level of sanitary or phytosanitary protection, Members shall ensure that such measures are not more trade-restrictive than required to achieve their appropriate level of sanitary or phytosanitary protection, taking into account technical and economic feasibility.

A footnote clarifies that:

> a measure is not more trade-restrictive than required unless there is another measure, reasonably available taking into account technical and economic feasibility, that achieves the appropriate level of sanitary or phytosanitary protection and is significantly less restrictive to trade.

This requirement appears to be very similar to the 'necessary' test used in certain sub-paragraphs of GATT Article XX. In a sense, it is a codification of the 'necessary' standard as it existed in 1994, when the SPS Agreement was concluded. Thus, based on this provision, and as with the Article XX analysis, claims under Article 5.6 examine whether there is a measure that is 'reasonably available taking into account technical and economic feasibility' which achieves the Member's appropriate level of protection, and is 'significantly less restrictive to trade' than the measure being challenged.[9] These are the three elements that must be established when a complainant alleges a violation of Article 5.6. The following discussion of this issue from the *Australia—Salmon, Article 21.5* dispute helps illustrate the application of this standard.

In the Article 21.5 proceedings in *Australia—Salmon*, Australia had revised the measure discussed above and adopted a new measure under which, in order to be imported, salmon had either to have been heat-treated (ie cooked) or be 'consumer ready', that is be ready to cook or consume and be in cutlets weighing less than 450 grammes. The purported goal of this policy was to prevent the further processing of uncooked salmon in Australia in such a way that the discharge from this processing could contaminate Australian salmon stocks with foreign disease agents. By allowing only cooked or 'consumer-ready' salmon to be imported, further processing would be avoided because no additional processing would be carried out. Canada, the complainant, proposed that instead of imposing a requirement that imported salmon be 'consumer-ready', Australia could simply ensure that imported salmon that undergoes further processing is processed in facilities that do not discharge untreated waste. In this regard, Canada pointed to New Zealand's packaging requirements, which allow for import without a permit if the salmon is packaged for sale only to certain designated outlets at which further processing will not take place.[10]

The panel considered the claim under each of the three elements of Article 5.6. Beginning its analysis with the second element, whether there is another measure which

---

[9] However, it is not clear to what extent the recent Art XX jurisprudence of the Appellate Body involving the 'common interests of values' pursued applies here. See Ch 9 above.

[10] Panel Report, *Australia—Salmon, Article 21.5*, paras 7.119–7.127.

achieves the appropriate level of protection, the panel considered two alternatives: (1) application of the current regime, but without the consumer-ready requirements; and (2) application of the current regime, but with the development of different consumer-ready requirements. Applying the second element, the panel examined whether a regime with no consumer-ready requirements could provide Australia's appropriate level of protection. In this regard, the panel noted that none of the scientific experts consulted could find a justification for the consumer-ready requirements. Furthermore, options like evisceration (gutting), thorough cleaning and inspection would already 'significantly' reduce risk. The panel stated, without coming to a definitive conclusion, that Australia's appropriate level of protection might be achieved without imposing the consumer-ready requirements at all. The panel then considered whether the current regime, but with different consumer-ready requirements, would achieve Australia's appropriate level of protection. Recognising that the current consumer-ready requirements are intended to prevent commercial processing of imported salmon in a way that could lead to risk of the spread of disease through waste discharge, the panel stated that, in its view, there are ways to ensure that commercial processing could be done in a 'controlled manner', thereby eliminating the need for the consumer-ready requirement. For example, Australia could make use of the requirements utilised by New Zealand, which allow the sale of products that have been individually and commercially packaged in a way that makes commercial processing unattractive. Alternatively, Australia could condition the issue of an import permit on the specific end-use of the product, or could ensure that salmon is commercially processed only in facilities that do not discharge untreated waste.[11]

On this basis, the panel concluded that there were other options available to Australia that would meet its appropriate level of protection. Therefore, it found that the second element of Article 5.6 was met.

The panel next considered the *first* element, whether there was another measure reasonably available taking into account technical and economic feasibility. In this regard, the panel noted that since the current regime was reasonably available, a modification of that regime to eliminate the consumer-ready requirements would be even more reasonably available. In addition, the requirement of special packaging would be reasonably available, as New Zealand imposes a similar requirement. Therefore, the panel concluded that the second element of Article 5.6 was met.[12]

Finally, the panel examined the *third* element, whether there was another measure that is significantly less restrictive to trade. The panel noted that all of the options referred to would result in significantly more imported salmon being available for sale. Because of this 'increased market access,' the panel considered that the third element of Article 5.6 was met.[13]

Since all three elements of Article 5.6 were met, the Panel found that Australia acted inconsistently with that provision.[14]

---

[11] *Ibid*, paras 7.138–7.143.
[12] *Ibid*, paras 7.146–7.149.
[13] *Ibid*, paras 7.150–7.152.
[14] *Ibid*, paras 7.115–7.153.

(e) Transparency

Article 7 of the SPS Agreement provides:

> Members shall notify changes in their sanitary or phytosanitary measures and shall provide information on their sanitary or phytosanitary measures in accordance with the provisions of Annex B.

This provision, in combination with Annex B to the SPS Agreement, reflects the long-standing GATT principle of transparency, allowing other Members to become familiar with a Member's SPS measures.

(f) Standard of Review under the SPS Agreement

As discussed in Chapter 5, standard of review has been an important issue in WTO dispute settlement. It has played a particularly prominent role in SPS disputes, but the decisions have sometimes been criticised for lacking precision and clarity.

In *Canada/US—Continued Suspension (Hormones)*, the Appellate Body attempted to clarify the standard of review to be applied in relation to panels' review of 'risk assessments' under SPS Agreement Article 5.1. In essence, the Appellate Body's took an approach which treats a risk assessment like the decision of a government entity such as a court or quasi-judicial agency. Thus, a WTO panel's review of this decision should not re-evaluate the risk assessment decision de novo. Rather, it should simply examine the reasoning behind the decision. Generally speaking, as long as the reasoning is 'coherent and objective', it should be upheld.

In *Australia—Apples*, the panel was forced to apply the SPS Agreement standard of review in a number of situations. For this reason, the case is particularly helpful in clarifying the standard of review in the context of the SPS. With regard to Article 5.1, which focuses on the 'risk assessment', there is a domestic 'decision' that the panel must review. Under other provisions, by contrast, the decision reflected by the risk assessment does not play as great a role, although it may still be relevant. The question arises as to what standard should be applied in relation to each of the various obligations. In this section, we consider how the standard was applied in a number of contexts: Articles 5.1, 5.5 and 5.6. As we explain below, the panel had taken an approach that seemed to extend the more deferential Article 5.1 standard to Article 5.6. However, the Appellate Body criticised this approach, and seems to establish a standard for Article 5.6 that is much less deferential.

We start with Article 5.5. The second element of Article 5.5 relates to whether there are arbitrary or unjustifiable distinctions in the appropriate level of protection (ALOP) achieved by the measures applied in different situations. In *Australia—Apples*, the panel declared it would 'assess this by comparing the risks involved in the comparable situations and the measures applied by Australia against such risks'. In this regard, the panel noted that this

> requires a very delicate balancing act between carrying out a meaningful and objective analysis of the Parties' arguments and evidence, and refraining from a *de novo* review of the risks involved in the different situations, in particular in the context of nashi pears, which is only a comparator product in this dispute.

To address this issue, the panel stated it would 'weigh the evidence put forward by New

Zealand and Australia and decide whether New Zealand has made a prima facie case, not rebutted by Australia, that it can be presumed that one product is riskier than the other'. It further explained that it would compare the risks involved in each of the two pairs of comparable situations in this dispute.[15]

Thus, at least on the surface, the panel's review of the measures under this part of Article 5.5 does not seem to have been deferential in the same way as the 'coherent and objective' standard, which, as noted above, applies to an Article 5.1 'risk assessment'. Instead of according the kind of deference to the domestic decision that is applied under Article 5.1, the panel simply considered whether the measures were consistent with the relevant legal standard. (At the same time, though, it may be worth noting that the Panel rejected the claims.) The panel's Article 5.5 finding was not appealed.

Turning to the claims under Article 5.6, the panel agreed with Australia that its review should not be a de novo one, but also stated that it 'cannot read Article 5.6 out of the SPS Agreement'. In this regard, it stated it would follow the Appellate Body's guidance in *Australia—Salmon* and 'assess "whether [the] . . . alternative SPS measures . . . meet the appropriate level of protection as determined by [Australia]"'.[16]

Ultimately, the panel's actual analysis of the Article 5.6 claims seems to include both a deferential and a non-deferential approach. In considering 'whether New Zealand has demonstrated that Australia's calculation of the fire blight risk resulting from the importation of New Zealand apples is exaggerated', the panel first recalled that it had already found this to be the case through its findings under Article 5.1. In light of its findings under Articles 5.1 and 5.2, the panel concluded that, for the purposes of the Article 5.6 claim, 'New Zealand has made the case that Australia's IRA overestimates the fire blight risk resulting from imports of New Zealand apples', such that 'New Zealand has cast doubt on whether the fire blight risk would exceed Australia's ALOP to the extent calculated by the IRA, and warrant as strict risk management measures as those developed by the IRA'.[17] Thus, here the panel referred back to its Article 5.1 'risk assessment' findings, which relied on the 'coherent and objective' standard.

In addition, though, the panel assessed 'more directly whether, assuming that risk management measures are necessary, New Zealand has raised a presumption, not successfully rebutted by Australia, that its alternative measure sufficiently reduces the fire blight risk to, or below, Australia's ALOP'. The panel considered the opinions expressed by the experts on this matter, and, in light of that testimony, found that both experts 'consider the overall risk of fire blight entry, establishment and spread through mature, symptomless apples imported from New Zealand to be very low—both overall and in regard to specific key points in the import scenario assessed by the IRA'. The panel emphasised as well that its legal analysis is different from the scientific assessment and certainty that scientific experts might prefer. It noted that if it 'tried to achieve the same scientific certainty as scientific experts, it would slip into conducting a *de novo* review'. It then said that if it were 'to recoil from carrying out its legal analysis merely because it could not achieve the same scientific certainty, it would not be acting in conformity with Article 11 of the DSU'. The panel also recalled its earlier findings that New Zealand demonstrated that the IRA does not constitute a proper risk assessment under Articles 5.1 and 5.2, and that the

---

[15] See Panel Report, Australia—Apples, paras 7.988–7.990.
[16] *Ibid*, paras 7.1133–7.1137.
[17] *Ibid*, paras 7.1145–7.1153.

IRA overestimates the probability of entry, establishment and spread of fire blight. On this basis, the panel concluded that 'New Zealand has raised a sufficiently convincing presumption, not successfully rebutted by Australia, that the alternative fire blight measure of restricting imports of New Zealand apples to mature, symptomless apples would meet this ALOP', such that 'this alternative measure fulfils the second condition of the Article 5.6 test in the context of fire blight'.[18]

In its analysis, the panel seemed to be, in a somewhat delicate manner, applying a standard of review that is less deferential than merely looking at whether the reasoning related to the government's actions was 'coherent and objective'. It examined the scientific evidence itself, based on input from the experts, and it reached a conclusion on the specific issue of whether the alternative measure sufficiently reduces the fire blight risk to, or below, Australia's ALOP. The panel did, however, qualify this conclusion by referring back to its Article 5.1 finding, leaving some question as to exactly how, in its view, the Article 5.6 standard of review relates to that for 'risk assessments'.

On appeal, the Appellate Body reversed the panel's Article 5.6 finding, and in doing so criticised the panel's application of the standard of review. The Appellate Body noted that '[c]aution not to conduct a *de novo* review is appropriate where a panel reviews a risk assessment conducted by the importing Member's authorities in the context of Article 5.1', but 'the situation is different in the context of an Article 5.6 claim'. Under that provision, 'the legal question is whether the importing Member could have adopted a less trade-restrictive measure', which 'requires the panel itself to objectively assess, *inter alia*, whether the alternative measure proposed by the complainant would achieve the importing Member's appropriate level of protection'. On this basis, the Appellate Body considered that 'the panel's approach to its analysis of New Zealand's Article 5.6 claim was in error'. Because the panel 'unduly relied on findings that it had made in reviewing the IRA under Article 5.1 and failed to find affirmatively that New Zealand's alternative measures would meet Australia's appropriate level of protection', the Panel's Article 5.6 finding 'lacks a proper legal basis'.[19]

The Appellate Body's clear criticism of the approach taken by the panel suggests the following distinction—panels must show some degree of deference to 'decisions' made by domestic agencies when those decisions are set out in the text of the WTO agreements. Thus, under Article 5.1, there is an 'assessment' of the risks that is to be carried out by the domestic authorities. This 'assessment' is a decision that the authorities make, and must be given deference. (Similar terms implying a decision by a domestic entity would be 'examination' or 'determination'.) In *Australia—Apples*, in the context of Article 5.1, the Appellate Body upheld the panel's approach to the standard of review.[20]

By contrast, where the text does not use such terms, WTO panels should not give much deference to domestic measures, even if the same evidence as used with a particular 'decision' is at issue. Taking this case as an example, even though the Article 5.1 risk assessment might play a role in the Article 5.6 analysis, the Appellate Body did not consider that deference should be given in the same way. Rather, under Article 5.6, the panel should evaluate the science on its own, even though this is the same science that was given deference under Article 5.1. This approach perhaps suggests a strict set of

---

[18] *Ibid*, 7.1154–7.1197.
[19] Appellate Body Report, *Australia—Apples*, paras 356–59.
[20] *Ibid*, 217–31.

obligations in many SPS Agreement provisions other than Article 5.1, with only a limited amount of deference given to domestic decision-makers.

(g) Summary of the SPS Agreement's Provisions

There are several broad principles running through the SPS Agreement. Some of these have been carried over from the GATT, whereas others appear to be new. With regard to GATT principles, the principle of non-discrimination, one of the cornerstones of the GATT, is reflected in Articles 2.3 and 5.5. The application of this principle under the SPS Agreement is likely to be very similar to that under the GATT, although the slightly different wording of certain SPS Agreement provisions could lead to different results. Secondly, there is the broader prohibition on trade 'restrictions'. This principle is also found in the GATT, in Article XI and, for 'disguised' restrictions, the chapeau of Article XX. Under the SPS Agreement, rules governing trade restrictions are found in some form in Articles 2.2, 2.3, 5.5 and 5.6. Finally, the principle of 'transparency' is also very important under the GATT, in particular under Article X, and is reflected in Article 7 of and Annex B to the SPS Agreement.

In addition, there are two principles in the SPS Agreement that were not part of the GATT, at least not in direct and explicit terms. First, there is the requirement that SPS measures be based on sound science. Articles 2.2, 3.3, 5.1 and 5.7 reflect this principle. To the extent that these provisions require science-based regulation, they go well beyond what was required under the GATT. Secondly, there are the provisions of Article 3 encouraging harmonisation and of Article 4 on equivalence. These measures also go beyond what was required under the GATT.

III. THE TBT AGREEMENT

As explained above, the TBT Agreement covers three kinds of measures: 'technical regulations', 'standards' and procedures taken by governments related to the assessment of conformity with technical regulations and standards ('conformity assessment procedures'). These measures are defined in Annex 1 as follows:

1. Technical regulation

Document which lays down product characteristics or their related processes and production methods, including the applicable administrative provisions, with which compliance is mandatory. It may also include or deal exclusively with terminology, symbols, packaging, marking or labelling requirements as they apply to a product, process or production method.

2. Standard

Document approved by a recognized body, that provides, for common and repeated use, rules, guidelines or characteristics for products or related processes and production methods, with which compliance is not mandatory. It may also include or deal exclusively with terminology, symbols, packaging, marking or labelling requirements as they apply to a product, process or production method.

3. Conformity assessment procedures

Any procedure used, directly or indirectly, to determine that relevant requirements in technical regulations or standards are fulfilled.

These definitions are written in fairly dense 'legalese'. In an attempt to explain the terms in plain English, we offer the following.

A technical regulation is, in essence, a product regulation. It can cover a variety of aspects of the product, such as the physical characteristics, labelling or production process. The following examples are instructive: a measure that requires that automobile emissions not exceed a certain level; a measure that requires that products not be manufactured in a way that harms the environment surrounding the factory; or a measure that requires a label indicating whether toys contain parts that could harm young children. Note that while the definition refers to 'documents,' which could be interpreted narrowly, in practice the provision has been presumed to cover laws and other measures generally. A standard does basically the same things as a technical regulation. The main difference is that standards are not mandatory.

Because technical regulations are mandatory, their impact is felt more greatly. In that sense, technical regulations are more important than standards, and the TBT Agreement rules for technical regulations are more detailed and strict. We focus here on the rules for technical regulations.

The key provisions relating to technical regulations are in Article 2, which is entitled: 'Preparation, Adoption and Application of Technical Regulations by Central Government Bodies'. As indicated by its title, Article 2 applies only to central governments. However, Article 3, which applies to local government bodies and non-governmental bodies, refers back to Article 2, stating: 'Members shall take such reasonable measures as may be available to them to ensure compliance by such bodies with the provisions of Article 2'.

The provisions of Article 2 have a great deal in common with the SPS Agreement provisions examined in the preceding section. Like the SPS Agreement provisions, Article 2 addresses issues of discrimination and other trade effects, as well as harmonisation around international standards. However, there is no equivalent to the 'sound science' provisions of the SPS Agreement.

Article 2.1 begins by setting out a basic non-discrimination requirement: 'Members shall ensure that in respect of technical regulations, products imported from the territory of any Member shall be accorded treatment no less favourable than that accorded to like products of national origin and to like products originating in any other country'. This provision covers both forms of non-discrimination, MFN and National Treatment.

Article 2.2 then addresses other, non-discriminatory trade measures:

Members shall ensure that technical regulations are not prepared, adopted or applied with a view to or with the effect of creating unnecessary obstacles to international trade. For this purpose, technical regulations shall not be more trade-restrictive than necessary to fulfil a legitimate objective, taking account of the risks non-fulfilment would create. Such legitimate objectives are, *inter alia:* national security requirements; the prevention of deceptive practices; protection of human health or safety, animal or plant life or health, or the environment. In assessing such risks, relevant elements of consideration are, *inter alia:* available scientific and technical information, related processing technology or intended end-uses of products.

As with Article 5.6 of the SPS Agreement, this provision is similar to the 'necessary' test in some of the sub-paragraphs of Article XX of the GATT.

Article 2.4 establishes the importance of international standards for technical regulations. It states: '[w]here technical regulations are required and relevant international standards exist or their completion is imminent, Members shall use them, or the relevant parts of them, as a basis for their technical regulations except when such international standards or relevant parts would be an ineffective or inappropriate means for the fulfilment of the legitimate objectives pursued'. This provision arguably strays a bit from the issue of 'trade', and instead encourages harmonisation as a general policy. It requires the use of international standards as a basis for technical regulations, except where they are 'ineffective or inappropriate means for the fulfilment of the legitimate objectives pursued'.

Until recently, there was not much jurisprudence addressing these provisions. We now have several cases which add to the understanding and interpretation of the TBT Agreement. Moreover, it is also clear that the Appellate Body's interpretation of Article 2.1 and Article 2.2 will provide general guidance on the Appellate Body's overall thinking and approach to many of the core WTO obligations.

(a) TBT Agreement Article 2.1—National Treatment and Most Favoured Nation Treatment

As noted, Article 2.1 provides for a National Treatment and Most Favoured Nation (MFN) treatment obligation in a single provision. We previously discussed these principles at length in the context of the GATT (Chapter 7) and the GATS (Chapter 14), and, while the GATT obligations inform Article 2.1 (and there are clear parallels between them), the different context may lead to different interpretations.

The Appellate Body recently interpreted Article 2.1 in three separate cases: *US—Clove Cigarettes*, *US—Tuna II* and *US—COOL*. These cases provide important insights on Article 2.1 and, as mentioned above, perhaps other WTO provisions containing National Treatment and MFN obligations. Here we describe briefly the first two of these cases and how the Appellate Body applied Article 2.1 in those cases.

The first case is *US—Clove Cigarettes*, where the issue was a tobacco-control measure taken by the US that prohibits cigarettes with 'characterizing flavours' other than tobacco or menthol. The measure at issue was Section 907(a)(1)(A) of the Federal Food, Drug and Cosmetic Act (FFDCA), which was added to the FFDCA by Section 101(b) of the Family Smoking Prevention and Tobacco Control Act ('FSPTCA'). Section 907(a)(1)(A) reads as follows:

SEC. 907. TOBACCO PRODUCT STANDARDS.

(a) IN GENERAL.—

(1) SPECIAL RULES.—

(A) SPECIAL RULE FOR CIGARETTES.—Beginning 3 months after the date of enactment of the Family Smoking Prevention and Tobacco Control Act, a cigarette or any of its component parts (including the tobacco, filter, or paper) shall not contain, as a constituent (including a smoke constituent) or additive, an artificial or natural flavor (other than tobacco or menthol) or an herb or spice, including strawberry, grape, orange, clove, cinnamon, pineapple, vanilla, coconut, licorice, cocoa, chocolate, cherry, or coffee, that is a characterizing flavor of the tobacco product or tobacco smoke. Nothing in this subparagraph shall be construed to limit the

Secretary's authority to take action under this section or other sections of this Act applicable to menthol or any artificial or natural flavor, herb, or spice not specified in this subparagraph.

The FSPTCA entered into force on 22 September 2009.

Of great importance for this dispute was the fact that the ban on flavoured cigarettes applied to clove cigarettes but not to menthol cigarettes. From the data submitted by the parties, the panel understood that the vast majority of US smokers use two types of cigarettes—regular (ie tobacco-flavoured) cigarettes and menthol cigarettes—with approximately one-quarter of the smoking population smoking menthol cigarettes. By contrast, clove cigarette consumption accounted for approximately 0.1 per cent of the US market between 2000 and 2009. During the period 2007–09, virtually all clove cigarettes were imported from Indonesia. (However, there was at least one US company, Nat Sherman, that manufactured a clove-flavoured cigarette prior to the entry into force of the FSPTCA.) According to a Congressional Committee Report related to the measure, the measure's objectives are 'to provide the Secretary [of Health and Human Services] with the proper authority over tobacco products in order to protect the public health and to reduce the number of individuals under 18 years of age who use tobacco products'. Non-binding guidance from the Food and Drug Administration (FDA) noted that 'flavored products make it easier for new smokers to start smoking by masking the unpleasant flavor of tobacco', and thus '[r]emoving these flavored products from the market is important because it removes an avenue that young people can use to begin regular tobacco use'. As regards menthol cigarettes, which are specifically excluded from the prohibition imposed by Section 907(a)(1)(A), the FSPTCA directed the Tobacco Products Scientific Advisory Committee (TPSAC) 'to deliver a report to FDA on the public health impact of menthol in cigarettes' within a year of the committee's establishment. The March 2011 TPSAC Report recommends to the FDA that the '[r]emoval of menthol cigarettes from the marketplace would benefit public health in the United States'. According to the US, the FDA will 'further consider the recommendations given by the TPSAC'.[21]

Indonesia claimed that the measures is discriminatory in violation of Article 2.1. In examining the Article 2.1 claim, the Appellate Body considered two issues: whether the products at issue were 'like' and whether there was 'less favorable treatment' for imports.

With regard to 'like' products, the Appellate Body made clear that this inquiry is fundamentally about whether the products compete in the market place. By contrast, the 'objective' of the measure is not to be considered. In this case, the Appellate Body concluded that the clove and menthol cigarettes were 'like'. Turning to 'less favourable treatment', the Appellate Body's findings established several important general principles relating to the TBT Agreement (and its relationship to the GATT).

Appellate Body Report, *United States—Measures Concerning the Production and Sale of Clove Cigarettes,* **Adopted 24 April 2012, WT/DS406/AB/R**

2. "Treatment No Less Favourable" under Article 2.1 of the TBT Agreement

166. Referring to the Appellate Body's interpretation of Article III:4 of the GATT 1994, the United States and Indonesia agree that the "treatment no less favorable" standard of Article 2.1 of the *TBT Agreement* requires a panel to determine whether the technical regulation at issue modifies the conditions of competition in the relevant market to the detriment of the

---

[21] Panel Report, *US—Clove Cigarettes*, paras 2.1–32.

imported products. However, Indonesia considers that the existence of any detrimental effect on competitive opportunities for imported products is sufficient to establish less favorable treatment under Article 2.1. In contrast, the United States argues that the existence of a detrimental effect on competitive opportunities for imports is necessary, but not sufficient, to establish a violation of Article 2.1. Referring to the Appellate Body report in *Dominican Republic—Import and Sale of Cigarettes*, the United States argues that Article 2.1 requires further inquiry into whether "the detrimental effect is explained by factors or circumstances unrelated to the foreign origin of the product".

167. Article 2.1 of the *TBT Agreement* provides that, with respect to their central government bodies:

> Members shall ensure that in respect of technical regulations, products imported from the territory of any Member shall be accorded treatment no less favourable than that accorded to like products of national origin and to like products originating in any other country.

168. As already set out above, for a violation of the national treatment obligation in Article 2.1 to be established, three elements must be satisfied: (i) the measure at issue must be a "technical regulation"; (ii) the imported and domestic products at issue must be like products; and (iii) the treatment accorded to imported products must be less favourable than that accorded to like domestic products. In this part of its appeal, the United States challenges only the Panel's finding that Section 907(a)(1)(A) of the FFDCA violates the national treatment obligation provided in Article 2.1 of the *TBT Agreement*, insofar as it accords to imported clove cigarettes less favourable treatment than that accorded to like domestic products.

169. The "treatment no less favourable" requirement of Article 2.1 of the *TBT Agreement* applies "in respect of technical regulations". A technical regulation is defined in Annex 1.1 thereto as a "[d]ocument which lays down product characteristics or their related processes and production methods . . . with which compliance is mandatory". As such, technical regulations are measures that, by their very nature, establish distinctions between products according to their characteristics or their related processes and production methods. This suggests, in our view, that Article 2.1 should not be read to mean that *any* distinction, in particular those that are based *exclusively* on particular product characteristics or their related processes and production methods, would *per se* accord less favourable treatment within the meaning of Article 2.1.

170. We next observe that Article 2.2 of the *TBT Agreement* provides, in relevant part, that:

> Members shall ensure that technical regulations are not prepared, adopted or applied with a view to or with the effect of creating unnecessary obstacles to international trade. For this purpose, technical regulations shall not be more trade-restrictive than necessary to fulfil a legitimate objective, taking account of the risks non-fulfilment would create.

171. The context provided by Article 2.2 suggests that "obstacles to international trade" may be permitted insofar as they are not found to be "unnecessary", that is, "more trade-restrictive than necessary to fulfil a legitimate objective". To us, this supports a reading that Article 2.1 does not operate to prohibit *a priori* any obstacle to international trade. Indeed, if *any* obstacle to international trade would be sufficient to establish a violation of Article 2.1, Article 2.2 would be deprived of its *effet utile*.

172. This interpretation of Article 2.1 is buttressed by the sixth recital of the preamble of the *TBT Agreement*, in which WTO Members recognize that:

> . . . no country should be prevented from taking measures necessary to ensure the quality of its exports, or for the protection of human, animal, or plant life or health, of the environment, or

for the prevention of deceptive practices, at the levels it considers appropriate, subject to the requirement that they are not applied in a manner that would constitute a means of arbitrary or unjustifiable discrimination between countries where the same conditions prevail or a disguised restriction on international trade, and are otherwise in accordance with the provisions of this Agreement.

173. The language of the sixth recital expressly acknowledges that Members may take measures necessary for, *inter alia*, the protection of human life or health, provided that such measures "are not applied in a manner which would constitute a means of arbitrary or unjustifiable discrimination" or a "disguised restriction on international trade" and are "otherwise in accordance with the provisions of this Agreement". We consider that the sixth recital of the preamble of the *TBT Agreement* provides relevant context regarding the ambit of the "treatment no less favourable" requirement in Article 2.1, by making clear that technical regulations may pursue the objectives listed therein, provided that they are not applied in a manner that would constitute a means of arbitrary or unjustifiable discrimination between countries where the same conditions prevail, or a disguised restriction on international trade, and are otherwise in accordance with the provisions of the *TBT Agreement*.

174. Finally, as noted earlier, the object and purpose of the *TBT Agreement* is to strike a balance between, on the one hand, the objective of trade liberalization and, on the other hand, Members' right to regulate. This object and purpose therefore suggests that Article 2.1 should not be interpreted as prohibiting any detrimental impact on competitive opportunities for imports in cases where such detrimental impact on imports stems exclusively from legitimate regulatory distinctions.

175. Accordingly, the context and object and purpose of the *TBT Agreement* weigh in favour of reading the "treatment no less favourable" requirement of Article 2.1 as prohibiting both *de jure* and *de facto* discrimination against imported products, while at the same time permitting detrimental impact on competitive opportunities for imports that stems exclusively from legitimate regulatory distinctions.

176. Like the participants, we also find it useful to consider the context provided by the other covered agreements. In particular, we note that the non-discrimination obligation of Article 2.1 of the *TBT Agreement* is expressed in the same terms as that of Article III:4 of the GATT 1994. In the context of Article III:4, the "treatment no less favourable" requirement has been widely interpreted by previous GATT and WTO panels and by the Appellate Body. Beginning with the GATT panel in *US—Section 337 Tariff Act*, the term "treatment no less favourable" in Article III:4 was interpreted as requiring "effective equality of opportunities for imported products". Subsequent GATT and WTO panels followed a similar approach, and found violations of Article III:4 in cases where regulatory distinctions in enforcement procedures, distribution channels, statutory content requirements, and allocation of import licenses resulted in alteration of the competitive opportunities in the market of the regulating Member to the detriment of imported products vis-à-vis domestic like products.

177. In *Korea—Various Measures on Beef*, the Appellate Body agreed that the analysis of less favourable treatment under Article III:4 focuses on the "conditions of competition" between imported and domestic like products. The Appellate Body further clarified that a formal difference in treatment between imported and like domestic products is:

> . . . neither necessary, nor sufficient, to show a violation of Article III:4. Whether or not imported products are treated "less favourably" than like domestic products should be assessed instead by examining whether a measure modifies the *conditions of competition* in the relevant market to the detriment of imported products. (original emphasis)

178. Subsequently, in *EC—Asbestos*, the Appellate Body explained that imports will be treated less favourably than domestic like products when regulatory distinctions disadvantage the group of imported products vis-à-vis the group of domestic like products. The Appellate Body reasoned that the "treatment no less favourable" clause of Article III:4:

. . . expresses the general principle, in Article III:1, that internal regulations "should not be applied . . . so as to afford protection to domestic production." If there is "less favourable treatment" of the group of "like" imported products, there is, conversely, "protection" of the group of "like" domestic products. However, a Member may draw distinctions between products which have been found to be "like", without, for this reason alone, according to the group of "like" *imported* products "less favourable treatment" than that accorded to the group of "like" *domestic* products. (original emphasis)

179. Thus, the "treatment no less favourable" standard of Article III:4 of the GATT 1994 prohibits WTO Members from modifying the conditions of competition in the marketplace to the detriment of the group of imported products vis-à-vis the group of domestic like products.

180. Although we are mindful that the meaning of the term "treatment no less favourable" in Article 2.1 of the TBT Agreement is to be interpreted in the light of the specific context provided by the TBT Agreement, we nonetheless consider these previous findings by the Appellate Body in the context of Article III:4 of the GATT 1994 to be instructive in assessing the meaning of "treatment no less favourable", provided that the specific context in which the term appears in Article 2.1 of the TBT Agreement is taken into account. Similarly to Article III:4 of the GATT 1994, Article 2.1 of the TBT Agreement requires WTO Members to accord to the group of imported products treatment no less favourable than that accorded to the group of like domestic products. Article 2.1 prescribes such treatment specifically in respect of technical regulations. For this reason, a panel examining a claim of violation under Article 2.1 should seek to ascertain whether the technical regulation at issue modifies the conditions of competition in the market of the regulating Member to the detriment of the group of imported products vis-à-vis the group of like domestic products.

181. However, as noted earlier, the context and object and purpose of the TBT Agreement weigh in favour of interpreting the "treatment no less favourable" requirement of Article 2.1 as not prohibiting detrimental impact on imports that stems exclusively from a legitimate regulatory distinction. Rather, for the aforementioned reasons, the "treatment no less favourable" requirement of Article 2.1 only prohibits *de jure* and *de facto* discrimination against the group of imported products.

182. Accordingly, where the technical regulation at issue does not *de jure* discriminate against imports, the existence of a detrimental impact on competitive opportunities for the group of imported vis-à-vis the group of domestic like products is not dispositive of less favourable treatment under Article 2.1. Instead, a panel must further analyze whether the detrimental impact on imports stems exclusively from a legitimate regulatory distinction rather than reflecting discrimination against the group of imported products. In making this determination, a panel must carefully scrutinize the particular circumstances of the case, that is, the design, architecture, revealing structure, operation, and application of the technical regulation at issue, and, in particular, whether that technical regulation is even-handed, in order to determine whether it discriminates against the group of imported products.

... [editors' note: the Appellate Body then applied this reasoning to the facts of this case, as set out below.]

5. *Detrimental Impact on Imported Products*

213. Finally, the United States claims that, even if the Appellate Body were to agree with the comparison undertaken by the Panel in its less favourable treatment analysis, the Panel nonetheless erred in finding that the detrimental effect on competitive opportunities for imported clove cigarettes was not "explained by factors unrelated to the foreign origin of those products".

214. The United States does not challenge on appeal the Panel's findings that Section 907(a)(1)(A) of the FFDCA accords different treatment to imported clove cigarettes and to domestic menthol cigarettes, and that such differential treatment is to the detriment of the imported product, insofar as clove cigarettes are banned while menthol cigarettes are permitted. Accordingly, the Panel's conclusion that Section 907(a)(1)(A) modifies the conditions of competition in the US market to the detriment of imported clove cigarettes stands.

215. However, as noted earlier, the existence of a detrimental impact on competitive opportunities in the relevant market for the group of imported products vis-à-vis the group of domestic like products is not sufficient to establish a violation of the national treatment obligation contained in Article 2.1 of the *TBT Agreement*. Where the technical regulation at issue does not *de jure* discriminate against imports, a panel must carefully scrutinize the particular circumstances of the case, that is, the design, architecture, revealing structure, operation, and application of the technical regulation at issue, and, in particular, whether that technical regulation is even-handed, in order to determine whether the detrimental impact on imports stems exclusively from a legitimate regulatory distinction rather than reflects discrimination against the group of imported products.

216. Before the Panel, the United States argued that the exemption of menthol cigarettes from the ban on flavoured cigarettes is unrelated to the origin of the products, because it addresses two distinct objectives: one relates to the potential impact on the US health care system associated with the need to treat "millions" of menthol cigarette addicts with withdrawal symptoms; and the other relates to the risk of development of a black market and smuggling to supply the needs of menthol cigarette smokers.

217. The Panel considered that "the potential impact on the health care system and the potential development of a black market and smuggling of menthol cigarettes" did not constitute legitimate objectives, because:

These reasons which the United States has presented as constituting a legitimate objective by themselves, appear to us as relating in one way or another to the costs that might be incurred by the United States were it to ban menthol cigarettes. Indeed, the United States is not banning menthol cigarettes because it is not a type of cigarette with a characterizing flavour that appeals to youth, but rather because of the costs that might be incurred as a result of such a ban. We recall that at the time of the ban, there were no domestic cigarettes with characterizing flavours other than menthol cigarettes which accounted for approximately 25 per cent of the market and for a very significant proportion of the cigarettes smoked by youth in the United States. It seems to us that the effect of banning cigarettes with characterizing flavours other than menthol is to impose costs on producers in other Members, notably producers in Indonesia, while at the same time imposing no costs on any U.S. entity. (footnotes omitted)

218. On appeal, the United States claims that the Panel erred in concluding that any detriment to the competitive opportunities for imported clove cigarettes could not be explained by factors unrelated to the foreign origin of the products. In addition, the United States claims that the Panel failed to make an objective assessment of the matter under Article 11 of the DSU in finding that there were no costs imposed on any US entity.

(a) Application of Article 2.1

219. We begin with the United States' claim that the Panel erred in concluding that any detriment to the competitive opportunities for imported clove cigarettes could not be explained by factors unrelated to the foreign origin of the products. The United States argues that, "even where a technical regulation adversely affects the competitive situation of imported products compared to like domestic products, this does not constitute less favourable treatment when the detrimental effect is unrelated to the foreign origin of the product." According to the United States, many factors affect the costs associated with a technical regulation, such as transportation costs, production methods, the age of the producer's facility, size, efficiency, productivity, and marketing strategy. As a result, Article 2.1 does not prohibit the imposition of costs on imported products as compared to domestic products, where those costs are not related to the origin of the product. The Panel did not examine the "architecture, structure and design" of Section 907(a)(1)(A), including the fact that it allows Indonesia to import and sell regular and menthol cigarettes in the United States. For the United States, reference to unspecified "costs" on foreign producers does not establish that the effects of Section 907(a)(1)(A) on competitive opportunities for imported products are related to their origin. The United States underscores that the costs that Section 907(a)(1)(A) allegedly avoids would be incurred by the US regulatory enforcement and health care systems (and not by domestic menthol cigarette producers), even if all menthol cigarettes were imported.

220. For Indonesia, the Panel's finding that Section 907(a)(1)(A) modifies the conditions of competition in the United States to the detriment of imported clove cigarettes vis-à-vis domestic menthol cigarettes was sufficient to establish a violation of Article 2.1. Although Indonesia maintains that an additional "national origin" test was not required, Indonesia argues that, nevertheless, the Panel was correct in concluding that Section 907(a)(1)(A) had a "discriminatory intent", because menthol cigarettes accounted for 25 per cent of the market, and for a significant proportion of the cigarettes smoked by youth in the United States. The Panel correctly rejected the potential costs on the US health care and enforcement systems as "legitimate reasons" for exempting menthol cigarettes from the ban on flavoured cigarettes. The Panel also appropriately found that the disproportionate allocation of costs between Indonesian and US entities evidenced *de facto* discrimination against imports.

221. At the outset, we agree with the United States that the Panel did not clearly articulate its reasons for concluding that "the effect of banning cigarettes with characterizing flavours other than menthol is to impose costs on producers in other Members, notably producers in Indonesia, while at the same time imposing no costs on any US entity." To the extent that actual or potential costs are relevant to the analysis of less favourable treatment under Article 2.1, the Panel did not elaborate on why, in its view, Section 907(a)(1)(A) does not impose costs "on any US entity" beyond observing that, "at the time of the ban, there were no domestic cigarettes with characterizing flavours other than menthol cigarettes" on the US market.

222. Nonetheless, we are not persuaded that the Panel erred in ultimately finding that Section 907(a)(1)(A) is inconsistent with Article 2.1. By design, Section 907(a)(1)(A) prohibits all cigarettes with characterizing flavours other than tobacco or menthol. In relation to the cigarettes that are banned under Section 907(a)(1)(A), the Panel made a factual finding that "virtually all clove cigarettes" that were imported into the United States in the three years prior to the ban came from Indonesia. The Panel also noted that the "vast majority" of clove cigarettes consumed in the United States came from Indonesia. Although the United States stated that it was "unable to attain market share data for all non-clove products banned under Section 907(a)(1)(A)", the Panel did not find evidence that these products had "any sizeable market share in the United States prior to the implementation of the ban in 2009". In response to a Panel question, the United States confirmed that non-clove-flavoured cigarettes banned under

Section 907(a)(1)(A) "were on the market for a relatively short period of time and represented a relatively small market share".

223. With respect to the cigarettes that are *not* banned under Section 907(a)(1)(A), the record demonstrates that, in the years 2000 to 2009, between 94.3 and 97.4 per cent of all cigarettes sold in the United States were domestically produced, and that menthol cigarettes accounted for about 26 per cent of the total US cigarette market. Information on the record also shows that three domestic brands dominate the US market for menthol cigarettes: Kool, Salem (Reynolds American), and Newport (Lorillard), with Marlboro having a smaller market share.

224. Given the above, the design, architecture, revealing structure, operation, and application of Section 907(a)(1)(A) strongly suggest that the detrimental impact on competitive opportunities for clove cigarettes reflects discrimination against the group of like products imported from Indonesia. The products that are prohibited under Section 907(a)(1)(A) consist primarily of clove cigarettes imported from Indonesia, while the like products that are actually permitted under this measure consist primarily of domestically produced menthol cigarettes.

225. Moreover, we are not persuaded that the detrimental impact of Section 907(a)(1)(A) on competitive opportunities for imported clove cigarettes does stem from a legitimate regulatory distinction. We recall that the stated objective of Section 907(a)(1)(A) is to reduce youth smoking. One of the particular characteristics of flavoured cigarettes that makes them appealing to young people is the flavouring that masks the harshness of the tobacco, thus making them more pleasant to start smoking than regular cigarettes. To the extent that this particular characteristic is present in both clove and menthol cigarettes, menthol cigarettes have the same product characteristic that, from the perspective of the stated objective of Section 907(a)(1)(A), justified the prohibition of clove cigarettes. Furthermore, the reasons presented by the United States for the exemption of menthol cigarettes from the ban on flavoured cigarettes do not, in our view, demonstrate that the detrimental impact on competitive opportunities for imported clove cigarettes does stem from a legitimate regulatory distinction. The United States argues that the exemption of menthol cigarettes from the ban on flavoured cigarettes aims at minimizing: (i) the impact on the US health care system associated with treating "millions" of menthol cigarette smokers affected by withdrawal symptoms; and (ii) the risk of development of a black market and smuggling of menthol cigarettes to supply the needs of menthol cigarette smokers. Thus, according to the United States, the exemption of menthol cigarettes from the ban on flavoured cigarettes is justified in order to avoid risks arising from withdrawal symptoms that would afflict menthol cigarette smokers in case those cigarettes were banned. We note, however, that the addictive ingredient in menthol cigarettes is nicotine, not peppermint or any other ingredient that is exclusively present in menthol cigarettes, and that this ingredient is also present in a group of products that is likewise permitted under Section 907(a)(1)(A), namely, regular cigarettes. Therefore, it is not clear that the risks that the United States claims to minimize by allowing menthol cigarettes to remain in the market would materialize if menthol cigarettes were to be banned, insofar as regular cigarettes would remain in the market.

226. Therefore, even though Section 907(a)(1)(A) does not expressly distinguish between treatment accorded to the imported and domestic like products, it operates in a manner that reflects discrimination against the group of like products imported from Indonesia. Accordingly, despite our reservations on the brevity of the Panel's analysis, we agree with the Panel that, by exempting menthol cigarettes from the ban on flavoured cigarettes, Section 907(a)(1)(A) accords to clove cigarettes imported from Indonesia less favourable treatment than that accorded to domestic like products, within the meaning of Article 2.1 of the *TBT Agreement*.

… … …

The measure at issue in *US—Cloves Cigarettes* may not be an obvious case of a National

Treatment violation, based on the facts. However, taking into account both the impact on Indonesian cigarettes and the arguments related to the alleged purpose of the law (ie whether it based on a 'legitimate regulatory distinction'), the Appellate Body concluded that the measures were a violation of Article 2.1 of the TBT Agreement. In doing so, it established some important general principles setting out how an analysis of Article 2.1 should be conducted. In this regard, paragraph 182 quoted above sets out key aspects of the legal standard, and paragraphs 222–26 show how the Appellate Body applied the standard.

For further clarification of Article 2.1, we can look to *US—Tuna II*, which was decided shortly after *US—Cloves Cigarettes*. This dispute relates to various US measures concerning the importation, marketing and sale of tuna and tuna products. In particular, these measures set out the parameters for when tuna products can be labelled as 'dolphin-safe'. According to the US, through the 'dolphin-safe' label, its measures were intended to give information to consumers on whether tuna had been caught in a way that was harmful to dolphins. The US believed that providing such information would discourage the purchase of such tuna, and therefore help protect dolphins. By contrast, Mexico took the position that the measures interfered with Mexican tuna exports and ignored the provisions of a multilateral treaty, the Agreement on the International Dolphin Conservation Program (AIDCP), which in part protects dolphins during tuna fishing.

The measures at issue were certain provisions of the 'Dolphin Protection Consumer Information Act' (DPCIA), together with related regulations and a ruling by a US federal appeals court in *Earth Island Institute v Hogarth*. Together, these measures set out the conditions for when tuna products sold in the US may be labelled as 'dolphin-safe'.

The DPCIA provisions refer to four criteria which describe the circumstances in which tuna may be caught. These criteria are:

- location (inside or outside the eastern tropical Pacific Ocean (ETP));
- fishing gear (with or without the use of purse seine nets);
- type of interaction between tuna and dolphins schools (there is or is not a regular or significant association between tuna and dolphins schools); and
- the level of dolphin mortalities or injuries (there is or is not a regular and significant mortality or serious injury).

Of crucial importance to this dispute was the treatment of tuna caught by 'setting on dolphins', that is, the 'intentional deployment on or encirclement of dolphins with purse seine nets', a practice commonly used by Mexican fleets in the ETP. Pursuant to the DPCIA, the Department of Commerce (DOC) reviewed the situation of dolphins in the ETP, and found that 'the intentional deployment on or encirclement of dolphins with purse seine nets [was] not having a significant adverse effect on any depleted dolphin stock in the ETP'. As a result, the requirements for the use of the 'dolphin-safe' label were loosened, in the sense that tuna caught by setting on dolphins using purse-seine nets could use the 'dolphin-safe' label, if certain conditions were met. However, the *Hogarth* court ruling vacated the DOC findings, and thus the requirements were tightened. After the ruling, tuna could not be labelled 'dolphin-safe' if purse-seine nets were intentionally deployed on or used to encircle dolphins during that fishing trip. It was the tightening of these requirements that led Mexico to raise trade concerns. In particular, it was the treatment of tuna caught in the ETP (where Mexican fleets operate) as compared to that of tuna caught outside the ETP, where the requirements to use the label were less strict.

In addition to the US labelling requirements, also of relevance is an international agreement on dolphin protection that has its own set of requirements. The Inter-American Tropical Tuna Commission began in 1976, and eventually led to the creation of the International Dolphin Conservation Program. These efforts were later reflected in a series of multilateral agreements that were negotiated in response to the evidence that many dolphins were dying in the ETP each year. These agreements were the La Jolla Agreement (1992), the Panama Declaration (1995) and the Agreement on the International Dolphin Conservation Program (AIDCP) (1999). Both Mexico and the US are signatories to the La Jolla Agreement and the Panama Declaration, and parties to the AIDCP. Under the AIDCP, there is a set of 'dolphin-safe' labelling requirements that differ from those in the US measures at issue. In this regard, the AIDCP does not focus on whether setting on dolphins with purse-seine nets was used, but rather on the mortality and serious injury to dolphins.

This case, decided just over a month after the ruling in *US—Cloves Cigarettes*, applies the standard the Appellate Body had recently developed:

Appellate Body Report, *United States—Measures Concerning the Importation, Marketing and Sale of Tuna and Tuna Products*, Adopted 13 June 2012, WT/DS381/AB/R

D. *Whether the US Measure Is Inconsistent with Article 2.1 of the TBT Agreement*

...

231. Our analysis of this issue proceeds in two parts. First, we will assess whether the measure at issue modifies the conditions of competition in the US market to the detriment of Mexican tuna products as compared to US tuna products or tuna products originating in any other Member. Second, we will review whether any detrimental impact reflects discrimination against the Mexican tuna products.

232. Our analysis will scrutinize, in particular, whether, in the light of the factual findings made by the Panel and undisputed facts on the record, the US measure is even-handed in the manner in which it addresses the risks to dolphins arising from different fishing methods in different areas of the ocean.

1. *Whether the Measure Modifies the Conditions of Competition in the US Market to the Detriment of Mexican Tuna Products*

233. The Panel found that the "dolphin-safe" label has "significant commercial value on the US market for tuna products". The Panel further found that Mexico had presented evidence concerning retailers' and final consumers' preferences regarding tuna products, which, in the Panel's view, confirmed the value of the "dolphin-safe" label on the US market. On this basis, the Panel agreed with Mexico that access to the "dolphin-safe" label constitutes an "advantage" on the US market. These findings have not been appealed.

234. The Panel further found that: (i) "the Mexican tuna cannery industry is vertically integrated, and the major Mexican tuna products producers and canneries own their vessels, which operate in the ETP"; (ii) "at least two thirds of Mexico's purse seine tuna fleet fishes in the ETP by setting on dolphins" and is "therefore fishing for tuna that would not be eligible to be contained in a 'dolphin-safe' tuna product under the US dolphin-safe labelling provisions"; (iii) "the US fleet currently does not practice setting on dolphins in the ETP"; (iv) "as the practices of the US and Mexican tuna fleets currently stand, most tuna caught by Mexican vessels, being caught in the ETP by setting on dolphins, would not be eligible for inclusion in a dolphin-safe product

under the US dolphin-safe labelling provisions", while "most tuna caught by US vessels is potentially eligible for the label".

235. In our view, the factual findings by the Panel clearly establish that the lack of access to the "dolphin-safe" label of tuna products containing tuna caught by setting on dolphins has a detrimental impact on the competitive opportunities of Mexican tuna products in the US market.

236. Mexico and the United States disagree as to whether any detrimental impact on Mexican tuna products results from the measure itself rather than from the actions of private parties. In assessing whether there is a genuine relationship between the measure at issue and an adverse impact on competitive opportunities for imported products, the relevant question is whether governmental action "affects the conditions under which like goods, domestic and imported, compete in the market within a Member's territory". In *Korea—Various Measures on Beef*, the Appellate Body reasoned that:

> . . . the dramatic reduction in number of retail outlets for imported beef followed from the decisions of individual retailers who could choose freely to sell the domestic product or the imported product. The legal necessity of making a choice was, however, imposed by the measure itself. The restricted nature of that choice should be noted. The choice given to the meat retailers was *not* an option between remaining with the pre-existing unified distribution set-up or going to a dual retail system. The choice was limited to selling domestic beef only or imported beef only. Thus, the reduction of access to normal retail channels is, in legal contemplation, the effect of that measure. In these circumstances, the intervention of some element of private choice does not relieve Korea of responsibility under the GATT 1994 for the resulting establishment of competitive conditions less favourable for the imported product than for the domestic product. (original emphasis)

237. The relevant question is thus whether the *governmental* intervention "affects the conditions under which like goods, domestic and imported, compete in the market within a Member's territory". In this regard, we recall that it is the measure at issue that establishes the requirements under which a product can be labelled "dolphin-safe" in the United States. As noted by the Panel:

> . . . access to the label is controlled by compliance with the terms of the measures. Therefore, to the extent that access to the label is an advantage on the marketplace, this advantage is provided by the measures themselves. The exact value of the advantage provided by access to the label on the marketplace will depend on the commercial value attributed to it by operators on the market, including retailers and final consumers.

238. Moreover, while the Panel agreed with the United States that "US consumers' decisions whether to purchase dolphin-safe tuna products are the result of their own choices rather than of the measures", it noted that:

> . . . it is the measures themselves that control access to the label and allow consumers to express their preferences for dolphin-safe tuna. An advantage is therefore afforded to products eligible for the label by the measures, in the form of access to the label.

239. These findings by the Panel suggest that it is the governmental action in the form of adoption and application of the US "dolphin-safe" labelling provisions that has modified the conditions of competition in the market to the detriment of Mexican tuna products, and that the detrimental impact in this case hence flows from the measure at issue. Moreover, it is well established that WTO rules protect competitive opportunities, not trade flows. It follows that, even if Mexican tuna products might not achieve a wide penetration of the US market in the absence of the measure at issue due to consumer objections to the method of setting on dolphins, this does not change the fact that it is the measure at issue, rather than private actors, that denies most Mexican

tuna products access to a "dolphin-safe" label in the US market. The fact that the detrimental impact on Mexican tuna products may involve some element of private choice does not, in our view, relieve the United States of responsibility under the *TBT Agreement*, where the measure it adopts modifies the conditions of competition to the detriment of Mexican tuna products.

240. In the light of the above, we consider that it is the measure at issue that modifies the competitive conditions in the US market to the detriment of Mexican tuna products. We turn next to the issue of whether this detrimental impact reflects discrimination.

2. *Whether the Detrimental Impact Reflects Discrimination*

241. Mexico's claim of discrimination may be summarized as follows:

> The U.S. dolphin-safe labelling provisions are discriminatory. Imports of tuna products produced from tuna harvested outside the ETP—in other words, virtually all of the tuna products currently sold in the U.S. market—can be labelled as dolphin-safe under relaxed compliance standards even though there are no protections for dolphins outside the ETP. Meanwhile, tuna products from Mexican producers—who have taken extensive and demonstratively highly successful measures to protect dolphins—are prohibited from using the label.

242. The Panel found that the US measure pursues the following objectives: (i) "ensuring that consumers are not misled or deceived about whether tuna products contain tuna that was caught in a manner that adversely affects dolphins"; and (ii) "contributing to the protection of dolphins, by ensuring that the US market is not used to encourage fishing fleets to catch tuna in a manner that adversely affects dolphins". The Panel accepted these objectives as legitimate within the meaning of Article 2.2 of the *TBT Agreement*. The Panel further noted that "as described by the United States itself, its measures seek to address a range of adverse effects of fishing techniques on dolphins", including "situations in which dolphins are killed or seriously injured."

243. The Panel made factual findings and reviewed a fair amount of evidence and arguments in the context of its analysis under Article 2.2 that are relevant to the issue of whether the detrimental impact to Mexican tuna products reflects discrimination and thus are pertinent to our assessment of the measure at issue under Article 2.1. We begin by reviewing the uncontested facts on the record of the Panel proceedings, and factual findings by the Panel that are not challenged on appeal, before turning to other findings made by the Panel which are subject to claims brought by the United States under Article 11 of the DSU.

...

251. In sum, the participants do not contest the following findings by the Panel. First, setting on dolphins within the ETP may result in a substantial amount of dolphin mortalities and serious injuries and has the capacity of resulting in observed and unobserved effects on dolphins. Further, the use of certain fishing techniques other than setting on dolphins causes harm to dolphins. With respect to tuna fishing outside the ETP, the participants do not contest that the vast majority of tuna caught in the western Pacific Ocean is caught with FADs, trolls, or gillnets, and that US and foreign vessels use these fishing techniques. It is also uncontested that the tuna-dolphin association does not occur outside the ETP as frequently as it does within the ETP, and that there are no records of consistent and widespread fishing effort on tuna-dolphin associations anywhere other than in the ETP. Finally, the participants do not contest that, as currently applied, the US measure does not address mortality (observed or unobserved) arising from fishing methods other than setting on dolphins outside the ETP, and that tuna caught in this area would be eligible for the US official label, even if dolphins have in fact been killed or seriously injured during the trip.

(c) Whether the Measure Is Calibrated

282. The United States argued before the Panel that to the extent that there are any differences in criteria that must be satisfied in order to substantiate "dolphin-safe" claims, they are "calibrated" to the risk that dolphins may be killed or seriously injured when tuna is caught. In this regard, the United States emphasized the uniqueness of the ETP in terms of the phenomenon of tuna-dolphin association, which is used widely and on a commercial basis to catch tuna, and causes observed and unobserved mortalities that, in the United States' view, are not comparable to dolphin mortalities outside the ETP. The United States further alleged that there is a clear relationship between the objectives of the measure and the conditions under which tuna products may be labeled "dolphin-safe". This clear relationship, the United States argued, does not support the conclusion that the "dolphin-safe" labelling provisions are inconsistent with Article 2.1 of the *TBT Agreement*.

283. As an initial matter, we note that, in *Japan—Apples*, the Appellate Body pointed out that "[i]t is important to distinguish, on the one hand, the principle that the complainant must establish a *prima facie* case of inconsistency with a provision of a covered agreement from, on the other hand, the principle that the party that asserts a fact is responsible for providing proof thereof." Although the burden of proof to show that the US "dolphin-safe" labelling provisions are inconsistent with Article 2.1 of the *TBT Agreement* is on Mexico as the complainant, it was for the United States to support its assertion that the US "dolphin-safe" labelling provisions are "calibrated" to the risks to dolphins arising from different fishing methods in different areas of the ocean.

284. In the light of the findings of fact made by the Panel, we concluded earlier that the detrimental impact of the measure on Mexican tuna products is caused by the fact that most Mexican tuna products contain tuna caught by setting on dolphins in the ETP and are therefore not eligible for a "dolphin-safe" label, whereas most tuna products from the United States and other countries that are sold in the US market contain tuna caught by other fishing methods outside the ETP and are therefore eligible for a "dolphin-safe" label. The aspect of the measure that causes the detrimental impact on Mexican tuna products is thus the difference in labelling conditions for tuna products containing tuna caught by setting on dolphins in the ETP, on the one hand, and for tuna products containing tuna caught by other fishing methods outside the ETP, on the other hand. The question before us is thus whether the United States has demonstrated that *this* difference in labelling conditions is a legitimate regulatory distinction, and hence whether the detrimental impact of the measure stems exclusively from such a distinction rather than reflecting discrimination.

… … …

These cases provide good, recent examples of Appellate Body thinking about 'less favourable treatment' issues under Article 2.1, in particular the complex issue of de facto discrimination. Although the language used can be vague at times, it seems clear that, in some sense and to some extent, the Appellate Body will take into account both the discriminatory effect of the measure and its intent. In this regard, note the two-step process described by the Appellate Body in paragraph 231.

As a final note, we must again stress that these cases are the most recent explanations of the Appellate Body on the scope of the National Treatment obligation. As a result, they may have implications for similar provisions, such as GATT Article III:4, which have not been interpreted as recently. At the same time, every provision has a different context, which may lead the Appellate Body to interpret similarly worded provisions in a different way.

(b) TBT Agreement Article 2.2—More Trade-Restrictive than Necessary

Unlike Article 2.1, Article 2.2 has no counterpart in the GATT. To some extent, Article 2.2 looks like GATT Article XX, and one reading is that the TBT Agreement turns the exceptions into a free-standing obligation. Given the potential of such an obligation to intrude into domestic policy-making, interpretation and application of the provision is very sensitive. The *US—Tuna II* case provided the Appellate Body with its first opportunity explore these issues and interpret the provision.

Appellate Body Report, *United States—Measures Concerning the Importation, Marketing and Sale of Tuna and Tuna Products*, **Adopted 13 June 2012, WT/DS381/AB/R**

312. The first sentence of Article 2.2 requires WTO Members to ensure that their technical regulations are not prepared, adopted, or applied with a view to, or with the effect of, creating unnecessary obstacles to international trade. The second sentence explains that "[f]or this purpose, technical regulations shall not be more trade restrictive than necessary to fulfil a legitimate objective, taking account of the risks non-fulfilment would create". We will address the different elements set out in the text of Article 2.2 in turn below, in particular the meaning of the terms "legitimate objective" and "fulfilment", as well as of the phrases "not . . . more trade-restrictive than necessary" and "taking account of the risks non-fulfilment would create".

313. Considering, first, the meaning of the term "legitimate objective" in the sense of Article 2.2 of the *TBT Agreement*, we note that the word "objective" describes a "thing aimed at or sought; a target, a goal, an aim". The word "legitimate", in turn, is defined as "lawful; justifiable; proper". Taken together, this suggests that a "legitimate objective" is an aim or target that is lawful, justifiable, or proper. Furthermore, the use of the words "*inter alia*" in Article 2.2 suggests that the provision does not set out a closed list of legitimate objectives, but rather lists several examples of legitimate objectives. We consider that those objectives expressly listed provide a reference point for which other objectives may be considered to be legitimate in the sense of Article 2.2. In addition, we note that the sixth and seventh recitals of the preamble of the *TBT Agreement* specifically recognize several objectives, which to a large extent overlap with the objectives listed in Article 2.2. Furthermore, we consider that objectives recognized in the provisions of other covered agreements may provide guidance for, or may inform, the analysis of what might be considered to be a legitimate objective under Article 2.2 of the *TBT Agreement*.

314. Accordingly, in adjudicating a claim under Article 2.2 of the *TBT Agreement*, a panel must assess what a Member seeks to achieve by means of a technical regulation. In doing so, it may take into account the texts of statutes, legislative history, and other evidence regarding the structure and operation of the measure. A panel is not bound by a Member's characterization of the objectives it pursues through the measure, but must independently and objectively assess them. Subsequently, the analysis must turn to the question of whether a particular objective is legitimate, pursuant to the parameters set out above.

315. Next, we consider the meaning of the word "fulfil" in the context of the phrase "fulfil a legitimate objective" in Article 2.2 of the *TBT Agreement*. We note, first, that the word "fulfil" is defined as "provide fully with what is wished for". Read in isolation, the word "fulfil" appears to describe complete achievement of something. But, in Article 2.2, it is used in the phrase "to fulfil a legitimate objective" and, as described above, the word "objective" means "a target, goal, or aim". As we see it, it is inherent in the notion of an "objective" that such a "goal, or aim" may be something that is pursued and achieved to a greater or lesser degree. Accordingly, we consider that the question of whether a technical regulation "fulfils" an objective is concerned

with the degree of contribution that the technical regulation makes toward the achievement of the legitimate objective.

316. We see support for this reading of the term "fulfil a legitimate objective" in the sixth recital of the preamble of the *TBT Agreement*, which provides relevant context for the interpretation of Article 2.2. It recognizes that a Member shall not be prevented from taking measures necessary to achieve its legitimate objectives "at the levels it considers appropriate", subject to the requirement that such measures are not applied in a manner that would constitute a means of arbitrary or unjustifiable discrimination between countries where the same conditions prevail or a disguised restriction on international trade, and are otherwise in accordance with the *TBT Agreement*. As we see it, a WTO Member, by preparing, adopting, and applying a measure in order to pursue a legitimate objective, articulates either implicitly or explicitly the level at which it seeks to pursue that particular legitimate objective.

317. A panel adjudicating a claim under Article 2.2 of the *TBT Agreement* must seek to ascertain to what degree, or if at all, the challenged technical regulation, as written and applied, actually contributes to the legitimate objective pursued by the Member. The degree of achievement of a particular objective may be discerned from the design, structure, and operation of the technical regulation, as well as from evidence relating to the application of the measure. As in other situations, such as, for instance, when determining the contribution of a measure to the achievement of a particular objective in the context of Article XX of the GATT 1994, a panel must assess the contribution to the legitimate objective actually achieved by the measure at issue.

318. We turn next to the terms "unnecessary obstacles to international trade" in the first sentence and "not . . . more trade-restrictive than necessary" in the second sentence of Article 2.2 of the *TBT Agreement*. Both the first and second sentence of Article 2.2 refer to the notion of "necessity". These sentences are linked by the terms "[f]or this purpose", which suggests that the second sentence qualifies the terms of the first sentence and elaborates on the scope and meaning of the obligation contained in that sentence. The Appellate Body has previously noted that the word "necessary" refers to a range of degrees of necessity, depending on the connection in which it is used. In the context of Article 2.2, the assessment of "necessity" involves a relational analysis of the trade-restrictiveness of the technical regulation, the degree of contribution that it makes to the achievement of a legitimate objective, and the risks non-fulfilment would create. We consider, therefore, that all these factors provide the basis for the determination of what is to be considered "necessary" in the sense of Article 2.2 in a particular case.

319. What has to be assessed for "necessity" is the trade-restrictiveness of the measure at issue. We recall that the Appellate Body has understood the word "restriction" as something that restricts someone or something, a limitation on action, a limiting condition or regulation. Accordingly, it found, in the context of Article XI:2(a) of the GATT 1994, that the word "restriction" refers generally to something that has a limiting effect. As used in Article 2.2 in conjunction with the word "trade", the term means something having a limiting effect on trade. We recall that Article 2.2 does not prohibit measures that have any trade-restrictive effect. It refers to "unnecessary obstacles" to trade and thus allows for some trade-restrictiveness; more specifically, Article 2.2 stipulates that technical regulations shall not be "more trade-restrictive than necessary to fulfil a legitimate objective". Article 2.2 is thus concerned with restrictions on international trade that exceed what is necessary to achieve the degree of contribution that a technical regulation makes to the achievement of a legitimate objective.

320. The use of the comparative "more . . . than" in the second sentence of Article 2.2 suggests that the existence of an "unnecessary obstacle to international trade" in the first sentence may be established on the basis of a comparative analysis of the above mentioned

factors. In most cases, this would involve a comparison of the trade restrictiveness and the degree of achievement of the objective by the measure at issue with that of possible alternative measures that may be reasonably available *and* less trade restrictive than the challenged measure, taking account of the risks non-fulfilment would create. The Appellate Body has clarified that a comparison with reasonably available alternative measures is a conceptual tool for the purpose of ascertaining whether a challenged measure is more trade restrictive than necessary.

321. Article 2.2 of the *TBT Agreement* further stipulates that the risks non-fulfilment of the objective would create shall be taken into account, and that, in assessing such risks, relevant elements of consideration are "*inter alia*: available scientific and technical information, related processing technology or intended end-uses of products". As we see it, the obligation to consider "the risks non-fulfilment would create" suggests that the comparison of the challenged measure with a possible alternative measure should be made in the light of the nature of the risks at issue and the gravity of the consequences that would arise from non-fulfilment of the legitimate objective. This suggests a further element of weighing and balancing in the determination of whether the trade-restrictiveness of a technical regulation is "necessary" or, alternatively, whether a possible alternative measure, which is less trade restrictive, would make an equivalent contribution to the relevant legitimate objective, taking account of the risks non-fulfilment would create, and would be reasonably available.

322. In sum, we consider that an assessment of whether a technical regulation is "more trade restrictive than necessary" within the meaning of Article 2.2 of the *TBT Agreement* involves an evaluation of a number of factors. A panel should begin by considering factors that include: (i) the degree of contribution made by the measure to the legitimate objective at issue; (ii) the trade restrictiveness of the measure; and (iii) the nature of the risks at issue and the gravity of consequences that would arise from non-fulfilment of the objective(s) pursued by the Member through the measure. In most cases, a comparison of the challenged measure and possible alternative measures should be undertaken. In particular, it may be relevant for the purpose of this comparison to consider whether the proposed alternative is less trade restrictive, whether it would make an equivalent contribution to the relevant legitimate objective, taking account of the risks non-fulfilment would create, and whether it is reasonably available.

323. With respect to the burden of proof in showing that a technical regulation is inconsistent with Article 2.2, the complainant must prove its claim that the challenged measure creates an unnecessary obstacle to international trade. In order to make a *prima facie* case, the complainant must present evidence and arguments sufficient to establish that the challenged measure is more trade restrictive than necessary to achieve the contribution it makes to the legitimate objectives, taking account of the risks non-fulfilment would create. In making its *prima facie* case, a complainant may also seek to identify a possible alternative measure that is less trade restrictive, makes an equivalent contribution to the relevant objective, and is reasonably available. It is then for the respondent to rebut the complainant's *prima facie* case, by presenting evidence and arguments showing that the challenged measure is not more trade restrictive than necessary to achieve the contribution it makes toward the objective pursued and by demonstrating, for example, that the alternative measure identified by the complainant is not, in fact, "reasonably available", is not less trade restrictive, or does not make an equivalent contribution to the achievement of the relevant legitimate objective.

The Appellate Body applied Article 2.2 to the measure at issue as follows:

A. *The Panel's Findings*

302. The Panel concluded that the measure at issue is inconsistent with Article 2.2 of the *TBT Agreement*, because it is more trade restrictive than necessary to fulfil the legitimate objectives

pursued by the United States, taking account of the risks non-fulfilment would create. This conclusion is based on a number of intermediate findings by the Panel. First, the Panel assessed the United States' objectives based on the description of those objectives by both parties, as well as on the basis of the design, structure, and characteristics of the measure at issue, and found the objectives to be the following:

(a) "ensuring that consumers are not misled or deceived about whether tuna products contain tuna that was caught in a manner that adversely affects dolphins" (the "consumer information objective");

and

(b) "contributing to the protection of dolphins, by ensuring that the US market is not used to encourage fishing fleets to catch tuna in a manner that adversely affects dolphins" (the "dolphin protection objective").

303. The Panel then ascertained whether these objectives are "legitimate" within the meaning of Article 2.2 of the *TBT Agreement*. The Panel noted that the elaboration of legitimate objectives is the prerogative of the Member establishing a measure. The Panel also recalled the Appellate Body's finding in *US—Gambling* that a panel is not bound by a Member's characterization of the objectives of its own measures, but that a panel must make such characterization in an independent and objective fashion, based on the evidence in the record. The Panel also recalled the Appellate Body's finding in *EC—Sardines* that there must be an examination and a determination on the legitimacy of the objectives of the measures. The Panel considered the list of legitimate objectives in Article 2.2 and found that the consumer information objective falls within the broader goal of preventing deceptive practices, and that the dolphin protection objective may be understood as intended to protect animal life or health or the environment. Accordingly, the Panel found "that the objectives of the US dolphin-safe provisions, as described by the United States and ascertained by the Panel, are legitimate" within the meaning of Article 2.2 of the *TBT Agreement*.

304. The Panel then assessed whether the measure at issue is more trade restrictive than necessary to achieve the United States' objectives. The Panel stated that, in order to do so, it would assess "the manner in which and the extent to which the measures at issue fulfil their objectives, taking into account [the] Member's chosen level of protection, and compare this with a potential less trade restrictive alternative measure, in order to determine whether such alternative measure would similarly fulfil the objectives pursued by the technical regulation at the Member's chosen level of protection." The Panel further stated that, "[t]o the extent that a measure is capable of contributing to its objective, it would be more trade-restrictive than necessary if an alternative measure that is less trade-restrictive is reasonably available, that would achieve the challenged measure's objective at the same level."

305. Turning to the measure at issue, the Panel assessed whether the US "dolphin-safe" labeling provisions fulfil the consumer information objective and whether, as Mexico claimed, this objective could also be fulfilled by allowing the AIDCP label to coexist with the US "dolphin-safe" label in the US market. The Panel found that the measure at issue could only partially fulfil the consumer information objective, because, *inter alia*, under the US "dolphin-safe" label, consumers might be misled into thinking that a tuna product did not involve injury or killing of dolphins, even though this may in fact have been the case. The Panel considered that allowing compliance with the "dolphin-safe" labelling requirements of the AIDCP in conjunction with the existing US "dolphin-safe" label would be a less trade restrictive alternative that would achieve a level of protection equivalent to that of the measure at issue. Accordingly, the Panel concluded that the measure at issue is more trade restrictive than necessary to fulfil the consumer information objective.

306. The Panel subsequently considered whether the measure at issue fulfils the dolphin protection objective and whether this objective could also be fulfilled by allowing the AIDCP label to coexist with the US "dolphin-safe" label in the US market. The Panel concluded that the measure at issue could "at best, only partially fulfil [its] stated objective of protecting dolphins". The Panel reasoned that, although the measure was capable of protecting dolphins within the ETP, in other fisheries the measure was "capable of achieving [its] objective only in relation to the practices of setting on dolphins and using high seas driftnets", and "in relation to all other fishing techniques used outside the ETP" the measure is "not able to contribute to the protection of dolphins".

307. The Panel noted that significant dolphin mortality arises outside the ETP from the use of fishing techniques other than setting on dolphins. The Panel considered that, "in some cases, the risks arising from setting on dolphins under controlled circumstances may be lower than the risks arising from other fishing techniques applied without controlling for dolphin mortality or other adverse impacts." The Panel considered that "the alternative suggested by Mexico does not seem to create greater risks to dolphins in the ETP than those accepted by the United States under the challenged measures in relation to other fishing techniques used outside the ETP." Thus, the Panel found that "Mexico's alternative would achieve a level of protection equal to that achieved by the US dolphin-safe provisions outside the ETP". Recalling its earlier conclusion that Mexico's alternative "is less trade-restrictive than the US dolphin-safe provisions", the Panel found that Mexico had identified a reasonably available less trade-restrictive alternative that would achieve the dolphin protection objective at the same level as the measure at issue.

308. Consequently, in relation to both the consumer information objective and the dolphin protection objective, the Panel found the measure at issue to be more trade restrictive than necessary to fulfil its legitimate objectives and thus inconsistent with Article 2.2 of the *TBT Agreement*.

...

2. The Panel's Application of Article 2.2

324. We turn next to the review of the Panel's application of Article 2.2 of the *TBT Agreement*. The United States alleges that the Panel erred in finding that the "coexistence" of the US "dolphin-safe" label and the AIDCP label provides a reasonably available, less trade-restrictive means of achieving the objectives pursued by the United States at its chosen level. According to the United States, allowing the AIDCP label to coexist with the US "dolphin-safe" label would not address risks to dolphins outside the ETP, since by its terms it only applies to tuna caught inside the ETP. The United States further points out that the AIDCP label allows the practice of setting on dolphins to catch tuna, which is harmful to dolphins, and would therefore frustrate the dolphin protection objective. Moreover, in the United States' view, coexistence of the two labels would be confusing for consumers, because the AIDCP and the US official "dolphin-safe" label are virtually identical, and consumers would have difficulty appreciating the difference in what each label signifies so as to make an informed decision about the tuna they buy. Finally, the United States alleges that the Panel erred by implying that the United States is required to fulfil its objective to the same level inside and outside the ETP, regardless of the costs, and that this approach does not respect "well-established approaches to policymaking", such as weighing costs and benefits, which are also consistent with the *TBT Agreement*.

325. In reviewing the Panel's application of Article 2.2 to the facts of this case, we recall its finding that the objectives at issue are, first, "ensuring that consumers are not misled or deceived about whether tuna products contain tuna that was caught in a manner that adversely affects dolphins"; and, second, "contributing to the protection of dolphins, by ensuring that the US

market is not used to encourage fishing fleets to catch tuna in a manner that adversely affects dolphins".

326. Before the Panel, Mexico argued that "a 'reasonably available alternative measure' for the United States would be to permit the use in the US market of the AIDCP 'dolphin safe' label." It was for the Panel, therefore, in assessing Mexico's claim that the US "dolphin-safe" labeling provisions "are more trade-restrictive than necessary" within the meaning of Article 2.2, to examine, *inter alia*, the contribution that the US measure makes to the achievement of its objectives; the trade-restrictiveness of the US "dolphin-safe" labelling provisions; whether Mexico had identified a "reasonably available" and less trade-restrictive alternative measure, and to compare the degree of the US measure's contribution with that of the alternative measure, which is reasonably available and less trade restrictive, taking account of the risks non-fulfilment would create.

327. With respect to the degree to which the measure at issue contributes to the United States' consumer information objective, we recall the Panel's finding that the measure at issue "can only *partially* ensure that consumers are informed about whether tuna was caught by using a method that adversely affects dolphins". This conclusion is based on the Panel's finding that fishing methods other than setting on dolphins or high-sea driftnet fishing outside the ETP may cause adverse effects on dolphins, and that to the extent tuna caught under such circumstances may be labeled "dolphin-safe" pursuant to the US "dolphin-safe" labelling provisions, consumers may be misled about whether tuna was caught using a technique that does not adversely affect dolphins. Similarly, regarding the question of the degree to which the measure at issue contributes to the United States' dolphin protection objective, the Panel found that the US "dolphin-safe" labelling provisions are capable of protecting dolphins by ensuring that the US market is not used to encourage fishing practices that may kill or seriously injure dolphins, only within the ETP. The Panel further found that, in other fisheries, the measure at issue is capable of achieving its objective only in relation to the fishing practices of setting on dolphins and of using high seas driftnets, and that, in relation to all other fishing techniques used outside the ETP, the measure at issue is not able to contribute to the protection of dolphins. Accordingly, the Panel concluded that US "dolphin-safe" labelling provisions "may, at best, only partially fulfil their stated objective of protecting dolphins by ensuring that the US market is not used to encourage fishing fleets to catch tuna in a manner that adversely affects dolphins".

328. The Panel then considered the extent to which the proposed alternative measure would fulfill the United States' objectives and concluded, first, with respect to the consumer information objective, that "the extent to which consumers would be misled as to the implications of the manner in which tuna was caught would not be greater if the AIDCP label were allowed to co-exist with the US dolphin-safe provisions". Second, with respect to the dolphin protection objective, the Panel found that "allowing compliance with the AIDCP labelling requirements to be advertised on the US market would discourage observed dolphin mortality resulting from setting on dolphins to the same extent as the existing US dolphin-safe provisions do and would involve no reduction in the level of protection in this respect." It appears to us, however, that the Panel's analysis of whether Mexico had demonstrated that the US "dolphin-safe" labelling provisions are "more trade-restrictive than necessary" within the meaning of Article 2.2 was based, at least in part, on an improper comparison. With respect to the dolphin protection objective, the Panel contrasted the AIDCP labeling requirements with the US "dolphin-safe" labelling provisions, stating that "allowing compliance" with the former "to be advertised on the US market would discourage observed dolphin mortality resulting from setting on dolphins to the same extent as the existing US dolphin-safe provisions do". Similarly, with respect to the consumer information objective, the Panel noted, *inter alia*, that,

"under the US measures", it is possible that tuna caught during a trip where dolphins were in fact killed or injured may be labelled "dolphin-safe". The Panel compared that to the scenario "under the AIDCP", where "a label would only be granted if no dolphins [were] killed, but where certain unobserved adverse effects could nonetheless have been caused to dolphins". This comparison, however, fails to take into account that the alternative measure identified by Mexico is *not* the AIDCP regime, as such, but rather the *coexistence* of the AIDCP rules with the US measure.

329. In any event, it would appear that, in respect of the conditions for labelling as "dolphin safe" tuna products containing tuna harvested *outside* the ETP, there is no difference between the measure at issue and the alternative measure identified by Mexico, namely, the coexistence of the US "dolphin-safe" labelling provisions with the AIDCP rules. We recall that the geographic scope of application of the AIDCP rules is limited to the ETP. Thus, the conditions for fishing outside the ETP would be identical under the alternative measure proposed by Mexico, since only those set out in the US measure would apply. Therefore, for fishing activities *outside* the ETP, the degree to which the United States' objectives are achieved under the alternative measure would not be higher or lower than that achieved by the US measure, it would be the same. *Inside* the ETP, however, the measure at issue and the alternative measure set out different requirements. Under the alternative measure identified by Mexico, tuna that is caught by setting on dolphins would be eligible for a "dolphin-safe" label if the prerequisites of the AIDCP label have been complied with. By contrast, the measure at issue prohibits setting on dolphins, and thus tuna harvested in the ETP would only be eligible for a "dolphin-safe" label if it was caught by methods other than setting on dolphins.

330. It would seem, therefore, that the Panel's comparison of the degree to which the alternative measure identified by Mexico contributes to the United States' objectives should have focused on the conditions inside the ETP. In particular, for tuna harvested inside the ETP, the Panel should have examined whether the labelling of tuna products complying with the requirements of the AIDCP label would achieve the United States' objectives to an equivalent degree as the measure at issue. We note, in this regard, the Panel's finding, undisputed by the participants, that dolphins suffer adverse impact beyond observed mortalities from setting on dolphins, even under the restrictions contained in the AIDCP rules. Since under the proposed alternative measure tuna caught in the ETP by setting on dolphins would be eligible for the "dolphin-safe" label, it would appear, therefore, that the alternative measure proposed by Mexico would contribute to both the consumer information objective and the dolphin protection objective to a lesser degree than the measure at issue, because, overall, it would allow more tuna harvested in conditions that adversely affect dolphins to be labelled "dolphin-safe". We disagree therefore with the Panel's findings that the proposed alternative measure would achieve the United States' objectives "to the same extent" as the existing US "dolphin-safe" labeling provisions, and that the extent to which consumers would be misled as to the implications of the manner in which tuna was caught "would not be greater" under the alternative measure proposed by Mexico.

331. For these reasons, we find that the Panel's comparison and analysis is flawed and cannot stand. Therefore, the Panel erred in concluding, in paragraphs 7.620 and 8.1(b) of the Panel Report, that it has been demonstrated that the measure at issue is more trade restrictive than necessary to fulfill the United States' legitimate objectives, taking account of the risks non-fulfilment would create. Accordingly, we *reverse* the Panel's findings that the measure at issue is inconsistent with Article 2.2 of the *TBT Agreement*.

… … …

(c) TBT Agreement Article 2.4—International Standards

Article 2.4 has been addressed in the *EC—Sardines* case, which provides a good illustration of the types of measures that may be at issue under this agreement. The facts of the case were as follows. There were two types of fish that had, at some point, been marketed in the EC as 'sardines':

* *Sardina pilchardus* is found mainly around the coasts of the Eastern North Atlantic, in the Mediterranean Sea and in the Black Sea;
* *Sardinops sagax* is found mainly in the Eastern Pacific along the coasts of Peru and Chile.

In 1989, the EC decided that *sardinops sagax* could not be called 'sardines', but had to go by the more technical term '*sardinops sagax*'. Clearly, such a change would make it harder to sell the product.

The relevant international standards for the marketing of sardines were established by the Codex Alimentarius Commission of the United Nations Food and Agriculture Organisation and the World Health Organisation. In 1978, Codex adopted a standard for these products, Codex Stan 94. Article 2.1 of Codex Stan 94 provides that canned sardines or sardine-type products are prepared from fresh or frozen fish from a list of 21 species, including *sardina pilchardus* and *sardinops sagax*. Article 6 of Codex Stan 94 sets out specific labelling provisions for these products, as follows:

6.1 NAME OF THE FOOD

The name of the products shall be:

6.1.1 (i) 'Sardines' (to be reserved exclusively for *Sardina pilchardus* (Walbaum)); or

(ii) 'X sardines' of a country, a geographic area, the species, or the common name of the species in accordance with the law and custom of the country in which the product is sold, and in a manner not to mislead the consumer.

Thus, the international standard allows for the marketing of the *sardinops sagax* as 'X sardines', *eg* 'Peruvian sardines'. By contrast, under the EC measure, only *sardina pilchardus* can be called just 'sardines'.[22]

The EC made a number of arguments in defence of its measure. We focus here on three. First, the EC argued that Codex Stan 94 was not a '*relevant* international standard' because its product coverage was different from that of the EC Regulation. In particular, it argued that while the EC Regulation dealt only with *sardina pilchardus*, Codex Stan 94 also covered other preserved fish that were 'sardine-type'. On this issue, the Appellate Body expressed agreement with the panel's reasoning that, to be a 'relevant international standard', Codex Stan 94 would have to 'bear upon, relate to, or be pertinent to the EC Regulation'. Then, in response to the EC's argument, the Appellate Body stated that even if it were accepted that the EC Regulation related only to *sardina pilchardus*, Codex Stan 94 also related to this product. Thus, in its view, Codex Stan 94 could be said to 'bear upon, relate to, or be pertinent to the EC Regulation because both refer to preserved *Sardina pilchardus*'. In addition, the Appellate Body recalled its earlier finding that the EC Regulation 'has legal consequences for other fish species that could be sold as preserved

---

[22] Panel Report, *EC—Sardines*, paras 2.1–2.7.

sardines, including preserved *Sardinops sagax*'. Therefore, it concluded that Codex Stan 94 'bears upon, relates to, or is pertinent to the EC Regulation'.[23]

Secondly, the EC argued that Codex Stan 94 was, in fact, used 'as a basis for' the EC Regulation, because under paragraph 6.1.1(ii) of Codex Stan 94, each country where the product is sold has the option of choosing between 'X sardines' and the common name of the species. Specifically, it contended that 'the common name of the species in accordance with the law and customs of the country in which the product is sold' is intended to be a self-standing option independent of the formula 'X sardines'. In response, the Appellate Body found that a comparison between sections 6.1.1(ii) and 2.1.1 of Codex Stan 94, on the one hand, and Article 2 of the EC Regulation, on the other hand, leads to the conclusion that a contradiction exists between these provisions. In particular, the effect of Article 2 is to prohibit preserved fish products prepared from the 20 species of fish other than *Sardina pilchardus* to which Codex Stan 94 refers— including *Sardinops sagax*—from being identified and marketed under the name 'sardines', even with one of the four qualifiers set out in the Codex standard. Codex Stan 94, by contrast, permits the use of the term 'sardines' for these species with any of the four qualifiers. Thus, it said, the EC Regulation and Codex Stan 94 are 'manifestly contradictory'.[24]

Finally, the EC argued that Codex Stan 94, by allowing for the use of the word 'sardines' for products other than *Sardina pilchardus*, is ineffective or inappropriate to fulfil the objectives of consumer protection, market transparency and fair competition. Specifically, it argued that its consumers expect that products of the same nature and characteristics will always have the same trade description, and that consumers in most EC Member States have always, and in some Member States have for at least 13 years, associated 'sardines' exclusively with *Sardina pilchardus*. We set out here the panel's findings on this issue (which were upheld by the Appellate Body on appeal).[25]

Panel Report, *European Communities—Trade Description of Sardines*, Adopted 23 October 2002, WT/DS231/R

5. *Whether Codex Stan 94 would be an ineffective or inappropriate means for the fulfilment of the legitimate objectives pursued*

7.113   The European Communities contends that Codex Stan 94, by allowing for the use of the word "sardines" for products other than *Sardina pilchardus*, is ineffective or inappropriate to fulfil the objectives of consumer protection, market transparency and fair competition. The European Communities argues that its consumers expect that products of the same nature and characteristics will always have the same trade description, and that consumers in most member States of the European Communities have always, and in some member States have for at least 13 years, associated "sardines" exclusively with *Sardina pilchardus*. With respect to the objective of promoting fair competition, the European Communities argues that Peru should not be able to take advantage of the reputation associated with the term "sardines", but that Peru should "develop its own reputation with its own name and persuade the consumer to appreciate its product with its own characteristics".

7.114   In paragraph 7.50, we determined that the European Communities, as the party asserting that Codex Stan 94 is ineffective or inappropriate to fulfil the legitimate objectives pursued by

---

[23] Appellate Body Report, *EC—Sardines*, paras 228–32.
[24] *Ibid*, paras 235–58.
[25] Appellate Body Report, *EC—Sardines*, paras 284–91.

the Regulation, has the burden of proving this assertion. Although the burden of proof rests with the European Communities to prove that Codex Stan 94 is an ineffective or inappropriate means for the fulfilment of the legitimate objectives pursued, we note that Peru has provided sufficient evidence and legal arguments, as set out below, to demonstrate that Codex Stan 94 is not an ineffective or inappropriate means to fulfil the legitimate objectives pursued by the EC Regulation.

7.115   In assessing the arguments presented by the European Communities, we must first determine what should be understood by the term "ineffective or inappropriate" and what the "legitimate objectives" referred to by this provision are.

7.116   Concerning the terms "ineffective" and "inappropriate", we note that "ineffective" refers to something which is not "having the function of accomplishing", "having a result", or "brought to bear", whereas "inappropriate" refers to something which is not "specially suitable", "proper", or "fitting". Thus, in the context of Article 2.4, an ineffective means is a means which does not have the function of accomplishing the legitimate objective pursued, whereas an inappropriate means is a means which is not specially suitable for the fulfilment of the legitimate objective pursued. An inappropriate means will not necessarily be an ineffective means and vice versa. That is, whereas it may not be *specially suitable* for the fulfilment of the legitimate objective, an inappropriate means may nevertheless be *effective* in fulfilling that objective, despite its "unsuitability". Conversely, when a relevant international standard is found to be an effective means, it does not automatically follow that it is also an appropriate means. The question of effectiveness bears upon the *results* of the means employed, whereas the question of appropriateness relates more to the *nature* of the means employed.

7.117   We note that the terms "ineffective" and "inappropriate" are separated in the text by the disjunctive "or". Thus, it is clear that the party invoking the affirmative defence under Article 2.4 need not establish that a relevant international standard is both ineffective and inappropriate. If it is established by a party that the relevant international standard is either an ineffective or inappropriate means for the fulfilment of the legitimate objective pursued, that party would not have to use the international standard as a basis for its technical regulation.

7.118   The next question we address concerns the phrase "legitimate objectives pursued". We first consider that the "legitimate objectives" referred to in Article 2.4 must be interpreted in the context of Article 2.2, which lists examples of objectives which are considered legitimate under the TBT Agreement. As indicated by the phrase "*inter alia*", this list is illustrative and allows for the possibility that other objectives, which are not explicitly mentioned, may very well be legitimate under the TBT Agreement.

7.119   We also note in this respect that the WTO Members expressed in the preamble to the TBT Agreement their desire that:

> . . . technical regulations and standards . . . do not create *unnecessary obstacles* to trade . . .;
> (emphasis added)

and recognized that:

> no country should be prevented from taking measures to ensure the quality of its exports, or for the protection of human, animal or plant life or health, of the environment, or for the prevention of deceptive practices, *at the levels it considers appropriate,* subject to the requirement that they are not applied in a manner which would constitute a means of *arbitrary or unjustifiable discrimination* between countries where the same conditions prevail or a *disguised restriction on international trade* . . . .. (emphasis added)

7.120   Article 2.2 and this preambular text affirm that it is up to the Members to decide which policy objectives they wish to pursue and the levels at which they wish to pursue them. At the same time, these provisions impose some limits on the regulatory autonomy of Members that decide to adopt technical regulations: Members cannot create obstacles to trade which are unnecessary or which, in their application, amount to arbitrary or unjustifiable discrimination or a disguised restriction on international trade. Thus, the TBT Agreement, like the GATT 1994, whose objective it is to further, accords a degree of deference with respect to the domestic policy objectives which Members wish to pursue. At the same time, however, the TBT Agreement, like the GATT 1994, shows less deference to the means which Members choose to employ to achieve their domestic policy goals. We consider that it is incumbent upon the respondent to advance the objectives of its technical regulation which it considers legitimate.

7.121   Article 2.4 refers to "the legitimate objective pursued". The ordinary meaning of "to pursue" is "to try to obtain or accomplish" and "to aim at". Thus, a "legitimate objective pursued" is a legitimate objective which a Member aims at or tries to accomplish. Only the Member pursuing the legitimate objective is in a position to elaborate the objective it is trying to accomplish. Panels are, however, required to determine the legitimacy of those objectives. We note in this regard that the panel in *Canada—Pharmaceuticals Patents*, in defining the term "legitimate interests", stated that it must be defined "as a normative claim calling for protection of interests that are 'justifiable' in the sense that they are supported by relevant public policies or other social norms".

7.122   Thus, we are obliged to examine whether the objectives outlined by the European Communities are legitimate in the context of Article 2.4 of the TBT Agreement. We note, however, that in this case Peru acknowledged that the objectives identified by the European Communities are legitimate and we see no reason to disagree with the parties' assessment in this respect. Accordingly, we will proceed with our examination based on the premise that the objectives identified by the European Communities are legitimate.

7.123   We now turn to the arguments presented by the European Communities in support of its position that Codex Stan 94 is ineffective or inappropriate for the fulfilment of the three legitimate objectives pursued by its Regulation. We recall that the three legitimate objectives pursued by the EC Regulation are market transparency, consumer protection and fair competition and these objectives, as argued by the European Communities, are interdependent and interact with each other. In this regard, we are mindful of the European Communities' argument that providing accurate and precise names allows products to be compared with their true equivalents rather than with substitutes and imitations whereas inaccurate and imprecise names reduce transparency, cause confusion, mislead the consumer, i.e., make consumers believe that they are buying something they are not, allow products to benefit from the reputation of other different products, give rise to unfair competition and reduce the quality and variety of products available in trade and ultimately for the consumer. In light of the fact that the three objectives are closely interrelated, if we were to find that Codex Stan 94 allows for precise labelling of products so as to improve market transparency, such finding would have a bearing upon whether Codex Stan 94 is effective or appropriate in protecting consumers and promoting fair competition, that is, not misleading consumers and confusing them into believing that they are buying something that they are not. We also note that the European Communities' stated objectives are based on the factual premise that the consumers in the European Communities associate "sardines" exclusively with *Sardina pilchardus*. Thus, the persuasiveness of European Communities' argument will be affected by the extent to which this factual premise is supported by the evidence and established to be valid.

7.124   Under Codex Stan 94, if a hermetically sealed container contains fish of species *Sardina pilchardus*, the product would be labelled "sardines" without any qualification. A product containing preserved *Sardinops sagax*, however, would be labelled "X sardines" with the "X" representing the name of a country, the name of a geographic area, the name of the species or the common name in accordance with the law and custom of the country in which the product is sold. If a hermetically sealed container is labelled simply as "sardines" without any qualification, the European consumer would know that it contains European sardines. However, if the product is labelled, for example, "Pacific sardines", the European consumer would be informed that the product does not contain sardines originating from Europe. We note that preserved sardines from Morocco, which contains *Sardina pilchardus*, sold in the European Communities is labelled "Sardines Marocaines". Although the product could simply be called "sardines" because it contains *Sardina pilchardus*, the label containing the name of a country provides a precise trade description by informing the European consumers of the provenance of the preserved *Sardina pilchardus*.

7.125   The European Communities, however, argued that "X sardines" is ineffective or inappropriate to fulfil the legitimate objectives pursued by the EC Regulation because European consumers associate the term "sardines" exclusively with *Sardina pilchardus* and even if "sardines" is combined with a qualification, it would suggest to European consumers that the products are the same but come from different countries or geographic areas. As noted above, the argument advanced by the European Communities in support of its claim that Codex Stan 94 is ineffective or inappropriate is based on the underlying factual assumption that consumers in most member States of the European Communities have always associated the common name "sardines" exclusively with *Sardina pilchardus* and that the use of "sardines" in conjunction with "Pacific", "Peruvian" or "*Sardinops sagax*" would therefore not enable the European consumer to distinguish products made from *Sardinops sagax* as opposed to *Sardina pilchardus*. The European Communities summarizes its argument as follows:

> In most parts of the European Communities, especially in the production countries, the term "sardine" has historically made reference only to the *Sardina pilchardus*. However, other species like sprats (*Sprattus sprattus*) were sold in tiny quantities on the European Communities market with the denomination "brisling sardines". In view of the confusion that this created in the market place, the European Communities has constantly tried to clarify the situation, both externally (note of 16/04/73 to Norway) and internally (Regulation 2136/89).
>
> *This situation has now created uniform consumer expectations throughout the European Communities,* the term "sardine" referring only to a preserve made from *Sardina pilchardus*.

7.126   Thus, the European Communities asserted, on the one hand, that in most member States the term "sardines" has historically responded to the particular consumer expectations which in its view underlie its Regulation, and acknowledged, on the other hand, that in some member States, it is the Regulation which "created" those "uniform" consumer expectations. The European Communities therefore made a factual distinction between two situations, and we will address these two situations separately.

7.127   The European Communities acknowledged that it is the Regulation which in certain member States "created" the consumer expectations which it now considers require the maintenance of that same Regulation. Thus, through regulatory intervention, the European Communities consciously would have "created" consumer expectations which now are claimed to affect the competitive conditions of imports. If we were to accept that a WTO Member can "create" consumer expectations and thereafter find justification for the trade-restrictive measure which created those consumer expectations, we would be endorsing the permissibility of "self-justifying" regulatory trade barriers. Indeed, the danger is that Members, by shaping consumer expectations through regulatory intervention in the market, would be able to justify thereafter the legitimacy of that very same regulatory intervention on the basis of the governmentally created consumer expectations. Mindful of this concern, we will proceed to examine whether the evidence and legal arguments before us demonstrate that consumers in most member States of the European Communities have always associated the common name "sardines" exclusively with *Sardina pilchardus* and that the use of "sardines" in conjunction with "Pacific", "Peruvian" or "*Sardinops sagax*" would therefore not enable European consumers to distinguish between products made from *Sardinops sagax* and *Sardina pilchardus*.

7.128   As indicated above, the European Communities asserted that in most member States the consumer expectations allegedly underlying the EC Regulation existed before the EC Regulation introduced an EC-wide regime. To that effect, the European Communities submitted copies of pre-1989 Spanish and French regulations prescribing the common name "sardines" for products made from *Sardina pilchardus*. The European Communities also submitted copies of the 1981 and 1996 United Kingdom Food Labelling Regulations and a copy of the 2000 German *Lebensmittelbuch*, which the European Communities has described as constituting "only a guideline". These documents prescribe the common name "sardines" for *Sardina pilchardus*, and "Pacific pilchard" or "pilchard" for *Sardinops sagax*. Thus, the European Communities argued that for those four European Communities' member States, domestic regulations reserving the common name "sardines" for *Sardina pilchardus* is to be considered probative of consumer perceptions at that time and thereafter. In other words, governments in those countries would have "codified" consumer expectations in their domestic regulations. Although it may be debatable as to whether this will always be so, we will proceed on the assumption that domestic legislation pre-dating the EC Regulation may indeed have such probative value regarding consumer expectations.

7.129   Concerning the pre-1989 versions of Spanish, French and United Kingdom regulations, we consider that these do indeed demonstrate that the legislative or regulatory authorities in those countries considered that the common name "sardines" without any qualification was to be reserved for products made from *Sardina pilchardus*, even before the EC Regulation entered into force. We note, however, that these documents, which concern three European Communities' member States, are not probative of the assertion that the use of a qualifying term, such as "Pacific", "Peruvian" or "*Sardinops sagax*", in combination with "sardines" would not enable European consumers to distinguish products made from *Sardinops sagax* as opposed to *Sardina pilchardus*.

7.130   We also note that in the United Kingdom, which imports 97% of all Peruvian exports of preserved *Sardinops sagax* to the European Communities, the 1981 Food Labelling Regulations also allowed for the use of the common name "pilchards" for *Sardina pilchardus* and prescribed the common name "Pacific pilchards" for *Sardinops sagax*. Thus, United Kingdom consumers did not associate *Sardina pilchardus* exclusively with the common name "sardines", and were able to distinguish *Sardinops sagax* from *Sardina pilchardus* by the simple indication of a geographical region (i.e., "Pacific"). If the insertion of the geographic area "Pacific" with the word "pilchard" was used in the United Kingdom to distinguish between *Sardina pilchardus* and *Sardinops sagax*, we fail to see why the inclusion of the name of a country, name of a geographic area, name of the species or the common name with the term "sardines" to refer to *Sardina sagax* would be ineffective or inappropriate to fulfil the legitimate objectives pursued by the EC Regulation.

7.131   Contrary to the European Communities' assertion, Peru submitted evidence to demonstrate that European consumers do not associate "sardines" exclusively with *Sardina pilchardus*. It did so by demonstrating that the term "sardines" either by itself or combined with the name of a country or the geographic area, is a common name for *Sardinops sagax* in the European Communities. In support of its assertion that "sardines" by itself or combined with the name of a country or geographic region is a common name for *Sardinops sagax* in the European

Communities, Peru referred to the *Multilingual Illustrated Dictionary of Aquatic Animals and Plants*, published in close cooperation with the European Commission and the member States of the European Communities for the purpose of, *inter alia*, *improving market transparency*, which lists the common name of *Sardinops sagax* in nine European languages as "sardines" or the equivalent thereof in the national language combined with the country or geographic area of origin. Similarly, Peru submitted copies of the electronic publication, *Fish Base*, produced with the support of the European Commission, which indicates that a common name for *Sardinops sagax* in Italy, the Netherlands, Germany, France, Sweden and Spain is "sardines" or its equivalent in the national language combined with the country or geographical area of origin. In addition, Peru relied on the *Multilingual Dictionary of Fish and Fish Products* prepared by the Organisation for Economic Cooperation and Development ("OECD") which indicates that a common name of *Sardinops sagax* is "sardines", either by itself or combined with the name of a country or geographic area. According to this *Multilingual Dictionary of Fish and Fish Products*, one of the common names in English is "Pacific Sardine", or "Sardine du Pacifique" in French. Even the European Communities acknowledged that one of the common names for *Sardinops sagax* is "sardines" or its equivalent thereof in the national language combined with the country or geographical area of origin.

7.132 According to the Consumers' Association, "a wide array of sardines were made available to European consumers for many decades prior to the imposition of this restrictive Regulation". Canada submitted evidence showing that a Canadian company exported *Clupea harengus harengus* under the trade description "Canadian sardines" to the Netherlands for thirty years, until 1989. Canada also submitted evidence showing that there have been exports of *Clupea harengus harengus* under the trade description "[company name] sardines in hot tabasco" to the United Kingdom for forty years, until 1989. We note in this regard that with respect to the objective of promoting fair competition, the aim of which is to prevent producers of one product from benefitting from the reputation associated with another product, the underlying premise is that the term "sardines" is associated only with *Sardina pilchardus*. However, as species other than *Sardina pilchardus* also contributed to the reputation of the term "sardines" and in light of the fact that "sardines", either by itself or combined with the name of a country or a geographic area, is a common name for *Sardinops sagax* in the European Communities, we do not consider that only *Sardina pilchardus* developed the reputation associated with the term "sardines".

7.133 Even if we were to assume that the consumers in the European Communities associate the term "sardines" exclusively with *Sardina pilchardus*, the concern expressed by the European Communities, in our view, was taken into account when Codex Stan 94 was adopted. By establishing a precise labelling requirement "in a manner not to mislead the consumer", the Codex Alimentarius Commission considered the issue of consumer protection in countries producing preserved sardines from *Sardina pilchardus* and those producing preserved sardines from species other than *Sardina pilchardus* by reserving the term "sardines" without any qualification for *Sardina pilchardus* only. The other species enumerated in Codex Stan 94 are to be labelled as "X sardines" with the "X" denoting the name of a country, name of a geographic area, name of the species or the common name in accordance with the law and custom of the country in which the product is sold. Thus, Codex Stan 94 allows Members to provide precise trade description of preserved sardines which promotes market transparency so as to protect consumers and promote fair competition.

7.134 Negotiating history confirms that Codex Stan 94 takes into account the European Communities' concern that consumers might be misled if a distinction were not made between *Sardina pilchardus* and other species. The Report of Codex Committee on Fish and Fishery Products on the Seventh Session states:

The traditional canners of this fish [*Sardina pilchardus*] were adamant that no other species should be allowed to use "sardines" without some form of qualification. Nor were they disposed to agree to qualifications which in their view could lead to confusion as to the species . . . For [countries producing fish of other species] any distinction was discriminatory and would result in their consumers being misled . . .. *The Committee agreed upon the need to protect the consumer.* (emphasis added)

7.135   At the Twelfth Session of the Codex Alimentarius Commission where the Commission adopted the draft standard for canned sardines and sardine-type products, a proposal was made to include *Engraulis mordax* and *Sardinella longiceps*. In response to this proposal, it is recorded that:

France stated that, in its opinion, the list of species (2.1.2) covered too broad range of fish which could place the consumer at a disadvantage with regard to making a sound choice between different products. It was pointed out that the present standard was a group standard and that the labelling section contained adequate provisions to safeguard the consumer.

7.136   Moreover, a 1969 Synopsis of Governments Replies on the Questionnaire on "Canned Sardines", prepared by the Codex Committee on Fish and Fishery Products, demonstrates that the governments of several current European Communities' member States, such as Denmark, Sweden and the United Kingdom, responded affirmatively to the question "[i]s it accepted that existing practices whereby sardine-type products are often labelled as sardines but with an appropriate qualifying phrase should be fully taken into account and provided for so long as the consumer is not deceived?". These governments considered "that this way of designating the sardine-type products as sardines has been in use for about one century in many countries". France was recorded as stating that "only the species recognized as sufficiently near to *Sardina pilchardus* might be designated as 'sardine' followed or preceded by a qualifying term", adding that "a geographic qualifying term could be acceptable on the condition that the consumer is not deceived (i.e., Atlantic sardine can mean either *Sardina pilchardus*, or another species caught in the Atlantic Ocean)". Of all current European Communities' members States, only the Federal Republic of Germany, Portugal and Spain stated that their domestic legislation did "not accept any designation of 'sardines' even with a qualifying term for species other than *Sardina pilchardus* (Walbaum)".

7.137   In light of our considerations above and based on our review of the available evidence and legal arguments, we find that it has not been established that consumers in most member States of the European Communities have always associated the common name "sardines" exclusively with *Sardina pilchardus* and that the use of "X sardines" would therefore not enable the European consumer to distinguish preserved *Sardina pilchardus* from preserved *Sardinops sagax*. We also find that Codex Stan 94 allows Members to provide precise trade description for preserved sardines and thereby promote market transparency so as to protect consumers and promote fair competition.

7.138   We therefore conclude that it has not been demonstrated that Codex Stan 94 would be an ineffective or inappropriate means for the fulfilment of the legitimate objectives pursued by the EC Regulation, i.e., consumer protection, market transparency and fair competition. We conclude that Peru has adduced sufficient evidence and legal arguments to demonstrate that Codex Stan 94 is not ineffective or inappropriate to fulfil the legitimate objectives pursued by the EC Regulation.

… … …

The basic point to be taken from *EC—Sardines* is that a Member must follow international standards unless that Member has a valid justification for not doing so. The justification offered by the EC was considered illegitimate because the international standard would have achieved similar results in terms of consumer protection as the EC measure purported to do. (The implication, of course, is that the EC was using the measure as disguised protectionism, to provide an advantage to domestically produced sardines. However, a finding that this was in fact the case is not required by Article 2.4.)

Articles 2.5–2.7 provide additional rules in favour of harmonisation around international standards, or mutual recognition of other Members' similar regulations. Article 2.5 states: '[w]henever a technical regulation is prepared, adopted or applied for one of the legitimate objectives explicitly mentioned in paragraph 2, and is in accordance with relevant international standards, it shall be rebuttably presumed not to create an unnecessary obstacle to international trade'. Article 2.6 further provides: '[w]ith a view to harmonizing technical regulations on as wide a basis as possible, Members shall play a full part, within the limits of their resources, in the preparation by appropriate international standardizing bodies of international standards for products for which they either have adopted, or expect to adopt, technical regulations'. Finally, Article 2.7 provides for recognition of equivalent standards of other Members: 'Members shall give positive consideration to accepting as equivalent technical regulations of other Members, even if these regulations differ from their own, provided they are satisfied that these regulations adequately fulfil the objectives of their own regulations'.

Articles 5–9 provide similar rules for conformity assessment procedures, which are procedures used, directly or indirectly, to determine that relevant requirements in technical regulations or standards are fulfilled, and include, inter alia, procedures for sampling, testing and inspection; evaluation, verification and assurance of conformity; registration, accreditation and approval as well as their combinations.

In addition to these substantive provisions, Article 10 requires Members to provide information to the WTO about their Technical Regulations, Standards and Conformity Assessment Procedures, and thus serves to promote transparency.

IV. CLOSING THOUGHTS: THE OBJECT AND PURPOSE OF THE SPS AND TBT AGREEMENTS

As noted above, GATT rules still apply to measures covered by the SPS and TBT Agreements. Thus, the basic non-discrimination rules of the GATT, as well as the rules on trade restrictions and transparency, already apply to these measures. What, then, is the purpose of the SPS and TBT Agreement rules?

One answer is that the GATT rules were considered too general and vague to address the specific problems occurring with product regulations and health measures, and that more detailed rules were needed to catch protection or otherwise trade-distorting measures in these areas. It is certainly true that technical regulations, standards and SPS measures may be used as a disguised means of protectionism. Now that tariffs have been limited through extensive bindings during the Uruguay Round, domestic producers may have a more difficult time obtaining protection from foreign competitors. One way for them to do this is to persuade the appropriate regulatory authorities in their country to use concern with product safety or health as a basis for imposing import restrictions. Along these lines, the WTO Secretariat explains the purpose of the SPS Agreement as follows:

> The basic aim of the SPS Agreement is to maintain the sovereign right of any government to provide the level of health protection it deems appropriate, *but to ensure that these sovereign rights are not misused for protectionist purposes and do not result in unnecessary barriers to international trade*[26] [emphasis added].

Under this theory, it could be argued, for example, that the SPS prohibition on measures not based on 'scientific principles' is an attempt to identify certain characteristics that indicate that a measure constitutes disguised protectionism. In other words, if the measure is not based on scientific principles, then it can be deemed to be protectionist. While the absence of scientific justification could, in theory, have been taken into account when examining a discrimination claim, by making the rule explicit, WTO Members ensured that this factor would have to be considered. Similarly, these rules could be said to target 'trade barriers' more generally, even where they were not discriminatory. For instance, the existence of different regulatory rules in different Members hinders trade by forcing companies to adjust to these varying regimes, resulting in significant additional costs.

Another answer, though, is that the SPS and TBT Agreement rules target measures that could be described as 'inefficient' or 'unreasonable'. Thus, in the example of SPS measures not based on scientific principles, it could be argued that these measures are prohibited simply because they constitute bad policy, based on the presumption that all such measures should be based on 'sound science'. Similarly, both agreements encourage harmonisation of laws around international standards. A policy of harmonisation could be taken as effort to promote effective domestic law-making through the establishment of 'best practices'.

It is difficult to say what is the 'true' purpose of the SPS and TBT Agreements. The substantive provisions of the agreements arguably reflect both. It may be that different negotiators had different purposes in mind, which, of course, makes the interpretation of these provisions particularly difficult. Regardless of the purpose, however, the effect of these rules is to intrude quite far into domestic policy-making, which has made these agreements, and the SPS Agreement in particular, somewhat controversial. There are two cases in particular that have been the cause of concern, both brought against the EC: *EC—Hormones* and *EC—Biotech Products*.[27] The *EC—Hormones* dispute involved measures taken by the EC to restrict the sale of beef products that had been treated with certain hormones. The measures were found to violate SPS Agreement Article 5.1 because they were not 'based on' a risk assessment. Similarly, in *EC—Biotech*, the EC measures restricted the sale of products that were, or contained, genetically modified organisms. Some of the measures at issue were found to violate Article 5.1 (and 2.2), and others were found to have caused 'undue delay' in the approval procedures, in violation of SPS Agreement Annex C(1)(a), first clause. In both cases, the EC invoked the 'precautionary principle', arguing that there was insufficient scientific evidence on possible harms from hormone-treated beef and GMOs, and thus it should be permitted to take restrictive measures as a precaution. This argument was rejected, however, in both cases.

---

[26] See WTO, 'Understanding the WTO Agreement on Sanitary and Phytosanitary Measures', available at www.wto.org/english/tratop_e/sps_e/spsund_e.htm (visited 6 June 2007).
[27] See *EC—Hormones* and *EC—Biotech*.

The ruling that these measures violate WTO rules led to strong negative reactions from many NGOs and illustrates the potential problems that arise when trade agreement rules go beyond traditional non-discrimination rules.

V. QUESTIONS

1. In what ways, if any, were existing GATT rules insufficient to deal with the issues addressed by the SPS and TBT Agreements? Do the non-discrimination rules of the SPS and TBT Agreements differ from those under the GATT? Was it appropriate to carve out SPS and TBT measures, but not other measures, from the normal rules?

2. Is the goal of harmonisation of laws a good one? What are the advantages and disadvantages? If harmonisation is a useful goal, why limit it to the measures covered by the SPS and TBT Agreements?

3. Under the SPS and TBT Agreements, what do you think the purpose of the provisions promoting harmonisation is? What is the purpose of the provisions in the SPS Agreement requiring measures to be based on sound science?

4. How much deference should WTO panels give to the decisions of government agencies when they adopt SPS measures? Do SPS Agreement rules allow for an appropriate amount of deference?

5. Both the SPS and TBT Agreements often involve complex scientific and technical issues. As a result, both agreements provide the opportunity for dispute settlement panels to consult experts (see SPS Agreement Article 11.2 and TBT Agreement Article 14.2). Is consultation with scientific experts sufficient for the trade experts who serve on panels to decide these complex issues?

6. In the *EC—Hormones* case under the SPS Agreement and the *EC—Sardines* cases under the TBT Agreement, the Appellate Body made important findings relating to the burden of proof. In *EC—Hormones*, the issue was Article 3.1 and 3.3. In the *EC—Sardines* case, the issue was Article 2.4. In both cases, the Appellate Body found that the burden was on the complaining party for a particular element, despite the use of the word 'except' right before the relevant language, which could have been taken to mean that the element was an exception, and thus the burden should have been placed on the party invoking the exception had the burden of proving the element. Is it possible that the Appellate Body's decision to place the burden on the complainants was due to a recognition of the intrusiveness of these rules into domestic policy-making, and an attempt to mitigate the problems this might cause?

7. Is it appropriate to rely on international standards created by bodies like Codex as the source of binding international trade rules? Does it matter what sort of decision-making process was used to create these standards?

8. As noted, there has been some debate over the role of the 'precautionary principle' in relation to SPS measures. The issue has arisen in WTO disputes relating to regulation of beef treated with hormones and products that are, or that contain, genetically modified

organisms (GMOs). One statement of the precautionary principle is: '[w]hen an activity raises threats of harm to the environment or human health, precautionary measures should be taken even if some cause and effect relationships are not fully established scientifically'. The Appellate Body has said that SPS Agreement Article 5.7 reflects this principle. Is Article 5.7 a sufficient implementation of the principle, or should WTO rules allow Members more discretion to follow the precautionary principle? How much scientific evidence should be required for Members to take action against products like hormone-treated beef or GMO products?

9. How does the Appellate Body's standard for national treatment under Article 2.1 of the TBT Agreement compare to the standard developed under Article III:4 of the GATT? What are the implications of the Appellate Body's findings under Article 2.1 of the TBT Agreement for the similar provisions of Article III:4 of the GATT?

10. How does the Appellate Body's standard under Article 2.2 of the TBT Agreement compare to the 'necessary' standard used under Article XX of the GATT?

11. Unlike with the GATT, there are no explicit exceptions to violations of the SPS and TBT Agreements. Should there be?

12. In the *US—COOL* Appellate Body report, circulated just after the *Cloves* and *Tuna* reports, the Appellate Body said the following when examining the 'discrimination' element of 'less favourable treatment': 'we consider the manner in which the COOL measure seems to provide information to consumers on origin . . . to be arbitrary, and the disproportionate burden imposed on upstream producers to be unjustified' (para 347). Should arbitrariness and proportionality be factors in a 'discrimination' analysis? What other factors might be considered?

14

Trade in Services

I. INTRODUCTION

Services currently represent more than two thirds of World Gross Domestic Product (GDP) (73 per cent in high-income countries against 54 per cent and 47 per cent respectively in middle- and low-income countries). Although due to their nature, as discussed in section II below, services can be more difficult to trade internationally than are goods. World exports of commercial services amounted to US$3,350 billion in 2009, after growing on average at around 7.9 per cent per year in value terms since 1980. In 2009, services trade accounted for approximately 21 per cent of total world trade.[1]

Given the substantial role that services play in the world economy, excluding them from world trade rules would leave a major gap in the system. Until 1994, though, they were not covered at all. This changed as part of the Uruguay Round trade talks. While not as important as they are today, services had been growing in prominence for many years by the time the Uruguay Round negotiations began in 1986, especially in the economies of developed countries. As a result, there was a great deal of interest among these countries in increasing sales of services to foreign markets by encouraging liberalisation in this area. Negotiations on trade in services were therefore established, and the result was the General Agreement on Trade in Services (GATS), which provides a set of rules and commitments on trade in services.

While the GATS rules mirror those for goods in many respects, there are some differences that arise due to the specific nature of trade in services. Thus, in studying the GATS, while it is helpful to have first mastered the basic principles and interpretations of the GATT, it is also necessary to understand how trade in services differs from trade in goods.

We structure this chapter as follows. First, we discuss the nature of services: what is a service and how do services differ from goods? Next, we examine the scope of the GATS, including the methods by which services are traded. We then turn to certain general obligations and disciplines in the GATS. Finally, we explain the concept of 'commitments' made in the GATS Schedules and examine some of the key substantive rules in this regard.

---

[1] WTO, 'Measuring Trade in Services: A Training Module Produced by WTO/OMCs', November 2010, 7–9, available at http://www.wto.org/english/res_e/statis_e/services_training_module_e.pdf (accessed on 29 May 2012).

II. THE NATURE OF SERVICES

Because of their tangible, physical nature, goods are relatively easy to identify and classify. By contrast, services are conceptually more difficult to understand. Thus, it is helpful first to explain the nature of services. In exploring the 'nature' of services, we start with some definitions, and then offer a few examples.

A standard law dictionary defines services in a relatively straightforward manner: '[t]hings purchased by consumers that do not have physical characteristics'.[2] Along the same lines, services have been described more colloquially as 'everything you cannot drop on your foot'.[3] In explaining the term 'trade in services', a WTO Secretariat note provides a more detailed statement: '[i]nternational trade in services is any service or labour activity across national borders to provide satisfaction to the needs of the recipient or consumer other than the satisfaction provided by physical goods (although they might be incorporated in physical goods), or to furnish an input for a producer of goods and/or services other than physical inputs (although the former might be incorporated in the latter)'.[4] All of these definitions emphasise the non-physical nature of services.

For the GATS, an important classification system for services is the UN Central Product Classification (CPC), which categorises services in specific groups and sub-groups. Essentially, the CPC is a description of all the different kinds of goods and services that may be offered. As explained by the Appellate Body: '[t]he CPC is a detailed, multi-level classification of goods and services. The CPC is *exhaustive* (all goods and services are covered) and its categories are *mutually exclusive* (a given good or service may only be classified in *one* CPC category).'[5] Since a version of this system was used by many WTO Members in setting up their GATS Schedules, it plays a special role in interpreting these Schedules.[6]

In Table 14.1, we set out a number of examples of purchases that involve services, along with the services category into which they fall, based on the most recent version of the UN CPC.[7]

Distinguishing between goods and services is not always easy.[8] The definitions above are useful, but there will always be some items that have characteristics of both. Simply stated, some purchased items clearly have both a goods and a services component. For

---

[2] *Black's Law Dictionary*, 6th edn (St Paul, MN, West Publishing, 1990) 1369.

[3] 'Public Citizen's Lori Wallach and EU Trade Commissioner Pascal Lamy Sound Off on GATS', available at www.citizen.org/trade/wto/gats/articles.cfm?ID=10940 (accessed on 28 June 2007).

[4] WTO, *Draft Glossary of Terms*, GNS/W/43 (8 July 1988), available at www.wto.org/gatt_docs/English/SULPDF/92050117.pdf.

[5] Appellate Body Report, *US—Gambling Services*, para 172.

[6] The Appellate Body has explained: '[t]he Scheduling Guidelines thus underline the importance of using a common format and terminology in scheduling, and express a clear preference for parties to use W/120 and the CPC classifications in their Schedules. At the same time, the Guidelines make clear that parties wanting to use their own subsectoral classification or definitions—that is, to disaggregate in a way that diverges from W/120 and/or the CPC—were to do so in a "sufficiently detailed" way "to avoid any ambiguity as to the scope of the commitment"': ibid, para 203. Document W/120 is a GATT Secretariat note entitled 'Services Sectoral Classification List', MTN.GNS/W/120 (10 July 1991).

[7] UN CPC, ver 1.1, available at http://unstats.un.org/unsd/cr/registry/regcst.asp?Cl=16 (accessed on 15 May 2007).

[8] For a discussion of the distinction between goods and services see F Smith and L Woods, 'A Distinction Without a Difference: Exploring the Boundary Between Goods and Services in The World Trade Organization and The European Union' (2005–06) 12 *Columbia Journal of European Law* 1, 47–58.

Table 14.1 Services and service categories

Service	UN CPC Code and examples
Dental cleaning	**93123—Dental services** —orthodontic services, eg, treatment of protruding teeth, crossbite, overbite, etc, including dental surgery even when given in hospitals to inpatients —services in the field of oral surgery —other specialised dental services, eg, in the field of periodontics, paedodontics, endodontics and reconstruction —diagnosis and treatment services of diseases affecting the patient or aberrations in the cavity of the mouth, and services aimed at the prevention of dental diseases
Taxi cab	**64321—Taxi services** —motorised taxi services, including urban, suburban and interurban. These services are generally rendered on a distance-travelled basis and to a specific destination. Connected reservation services are also included —non-scheduled airport shuttle services
Museum	**96411—Museum services except for historical sites and buildings** —display services of collections of all kinds (art, science and technology, history) —management and conservation services for the collections —organisation of travelling collection exhibitions
Ski pass	**96520—Sports and recreational sports facility operation services** —operation of and access services to indoor and outdoor sports and recreational sports facilities, such as stadiums, arenas, rinks, swimming pools, sports fields, tracks, ski hills, golf courses, bowling alleys, tennis courts, etc. —services of riding academies —recreation park and beach services
Legal defence for murder trial	**82111—Legal advisory and representation services concerning criminal law** —advice, representation, drafting of documents and related services (defence, search for evidence, witnesses, experts, etc) concerning criminal law
Internet access	**84220—Internet access services** —provision of a direct connection to the internet. The internet service provider (ISP) may also provide free services along with Internet access such as e-mail, space for the customer's web page, tools for simple web page design, chat, and technical support. This service may also include remote access or other types of Internet access and package upgrades such as international roaming and extra e-mail boxes, usually for additional charges to customers.
Construction of an office building	**54122—General construction services of commercial buildings** —construction services of commercial or administrative buildings such as office buildings, bank buildings, parking garages, petrol and service stations, shopping centres and air, rail or road transport terminals

example, when you pay for 'construction services', you have paid for certain services that are involved, such as design of the building, but in the end you also have a physical structure. Similarly, when buying a car, the car itself is a product, but part of the cost covers distribution, marketing and labour inputs. Nonetheless, the goods and the services aspects of the purchase can usually be distinguished and separated conceptually, allowing for separate regulations of goods and services.

III. THE SCOPE OF THE GATS

There are several issues concerning the scope of the GATS that should be considered before we turn to the substantive obligations: (1) what services are covered? (2) how are services traded? and (3) what is the relationship between the rules on trade in services and the rules on trade in goods?

(a) What Services are Covered?

Part I of the GATS is entitled 'Scope and Definition'. In this section, we examine several aspects of the scope of coverage of the GATS.

First, Article I of the GATS states that the GATS applies to measures 'affecting trade in services'. The Appellate Body has said that the word 'affecting' has a 'broad scope of application'.[9] Clearly, there must be some connection between a measure and trade in services to satisfy the 'affecting' standard. However, the boundaries have not been tested in dispute settlement to see exactly how expansive the provision is. For instance, the examples noted in the preceding section illustrate that virtually all goods have a services component. Among other things, they generally require distribution services to get the product to the customer. This raises the question whether all measures affecting the sale of goods—such as a tariff, for example—affect the distribution of those goods, and therefore affect trade in distribution services. In a sense, they do. They affect the price, which affects the ability to sell and thus to distribute. However, it is likely that a more direct connection between the measure and trade in services would be required to satisfy the 'affecting' requirement.

In addition, the scope of the GATS is limited by Article I:3, which states that '"services" includes any service in any sector except services supplied in the exercise of governmental authority'. The provision further explains that 'a service supplied in the exercise of governmental authority' means 'any service which is supplied neither on a commercial basis, nor in competition with one or more service suppliers'. Clearly, the drafters were trying to exclude some types of services with these provisions, but which ones? According to the WTO website, examples of such issues are 'social security schemes and any other public service, such as health or education, that is provided at non-market conditions'.[10] However, the full scope of the provision, in particular the circumstances in which these public services are not covered by the GATS, is unclear.[11]

(b) How are Services Traded?

Due to the nature of services, international trade in services is very different from trade in goods. As a result, 'trade' in services is conceptually more difficult to understand than trade in goods. For trade in goods, the basic process can be illustrated as follows:

---

    [9] Appellate Body Report, *EC—Bananas III*, para 220.

    [10] WTO, 'The General Agreement on Trade in Services (GATS): Objectives, Coverage and Disciplines', available at www.wto.org/english/tratop_e/serv_e/gatsqa_e.htm (visited 15 May 2007).

    [11] Partly as a result of this uncertainty, a number of NGOs have expressed concern that the GATS will force the privatisation or deregulation of public services. See: eg, Global Trade Watch at www.citizen.org/ trade/ wto/gats/.

Produced in Country X → Shipped to Country Y → Sold in Country Y

Thus, goods are traded internationally through the manufacture in one country and the eventual sale in another country (sometimes going through an intermediary company that provides export/import trading services). The process becomes a bit more complicated where, for example, inputs are shipped to another country for additional manufacturing and then sold to consumers in other countries. The resulting goods will then be comprised of products of multiple national origins. However, the basic concept is still the same.

Trade in services, on the other hand, works very differently. GATS Article I:2 sets out four modes of supply for 'trade in services':

(a) *'from the territory of one Member into the territory of any other Member' (cross-border supply)*

This mode is the one that is most analogous to trade in goods, in that a service (like an exported good) crosses a national frontier. Examples are: a U.S. trade lawyer doing work from an office in Washington, DC for the Japanese government; or an international telephone call from Chile to Mexico, where a caller located in Chile uses the Mexican telecommunications network to connect the call. Basically, this mode involves a situation where the service crosses the border, but neither the consumer nor the supplier does.

(b) *'in the territory of one Member to the service consumer of any other Member' (consumption abroad)*

This mode involves the movement of consumers to the territory of a supplier. Examples include: the purchase of services by consumers while travelling abroad as tourists, such as an Australian citizen going to a restaurant or exchanging money for local currency in France; in the education field, a U.S. student attending Oxford University; or the repair of a ship in a foreign port. Thus, in this mode, the consumer crosses the border to consume a service abroad.

(c) *'by a service supplier of one Member, through commercial presence in the territory of any other Member' (commercial presence)*

This mode of supply effectively means foreign investment, which can take various forms. For example, when McDonalds operates a restaurant in China, there is a U.S. company providing restaurant services to Chinese (and other) citizens. Further examples include: a foreign bank or other financial institution establishes a branch or subsidiary in the territory of a country and supplying financial services; and Eurodisney's amusement park in France, which involves a U.S. company providing entertainment services to the French (and others).

(d) *'by a service supplier of one Member, through presence of natural persons of a Member in the territory of any other Member' (presence of natural persons)*

This mode involves services provided through the movement of citizens of one country to another country. For example, when a U.S. fashion model walks a runway in Italy, she is providing services abroad. Or, a company offering biking vacations abroad would have its employees travel to the destination to provide guide services there.

As will be seen below, the existence of these four modes has important implications for Members' GATS obligations and commitments. In this regard, Members may limit the modes of supply to which their commitment applies, that is, they may make commitments for specific modes only.

A final issue related to how services are traded is determining the nationality of the entities involved. As seen in the description of the various modes of supply, the nationality of the supplier and consumer is of great importance. The GATS provides definitions of 'natural persons' and 'juridical persons' to help establish nationality.[12] These issues can get quite complicated when one is dealing with multinational corporations which have subsidiaries in some countries but a parent located in another. The issue has not been explored in great detail in the jurisprudence, but it has come up on occasion. For example, the panel in *Canada—Autos* stated:

> In our view, DaimlerChrysler Canada Inc. is a service supplier of the United States within the meaning of Article XXVIII(m)(ii)(2) of the GATS, because it is controlled by DaimlerChrysler Corporation, a juridical person of the United States according to subparagaph (i) of Article XXVIII(m). What is relevant, therefore, is that DaimlerChrysler Corporation is a juridical person of the United States. The fact that, in turn, DaimlerChrysler Corporation may be controlled by a juridical person of another Member is not relevant under Article XXVIII of the GATS. In order to define a "juridical person of another Member" Article XXVIII(m) of the GATS does not require the identification of the ultimate controlling juridical or natural person: it is sufficient to establish ownership or control by a juridical person of another Member, defined according to the criteria set out in subparagraph (i).[13]

Thus, the panel found that the Canadian subsidiary of DaimlerChrysler was a US service suppler because it was controlled by a US company, even though the parent company may have been controlled by an entity in Germany (this was prior to DaimlerChrysler's sale of Chrysler).

(c) The Relationship of Trade in Goods (the GATT) with Trade in Services (the GATS)

A final issue related to the relationship between goods and services is how the GATT and the GATS overlap for issues that may affect both. In two early cases, *Canada—Periodicals* and *EC—Bananas III*, the Appellate Body explained that these agreements are not mutually exclusive, and thus both may apply. As explained in *Bananas*:

> Given the respective scope of application of the two agreements, they may or may not overlap, depending on the nature of the measures at issue. Certain measures could be found to fall exclusively within the scope of the GATT 1994, when they affect trade in goods as goods. Certain measures could be found to fall exclusively within the scope of the GATS, when they affect the supply of services as services. There is yet a third category of measures that could be found to fall within the scope of both the GATT 1994 and the GATS. These are measures that involve a service relating to a particular good or a service supplied in conjunction with a particular good. In all such cases in this third category, the measure in question could be scrutinized under both the GATT 1994 and the GATS. However, while the same measure could be scrutinized under both agreements, the specific aspects of that measure examined under each agreement could be different. Under the GATT 1994, the focus is on how the measure affects the goods involved. Under the GATS, the focus is on how the measure affects the supply of the service or the service suppliers involved. Whether a certain measure affecting the supply of a

---

[12] See GATS Art XXVIII(k)–(n).
[13] Panel Report, *Canada—Autos*, para 10.257.

service related to a particular good is scrutinized under the GATT 1994 or the GATS, or both, is a matter that can only be determined on a case-by-case basis.[14]

IV. GENERAL OBLIGATIONS AND DISCIPLINES

Part II of the GATS is entitled 'General Obligations and Disciplines'. In this section, we discuss some of the more prominent rules in this Part.

(a) Most-Favoured Nation Treatment (MFN)

GATS Article II requires that most favoured nation treatment be provided to all trading partners. In many ways, this provision is the same non-discrimination requirement discussed in the context of the GATT. However, the wording of Article II is slightly different from that of its the MFN counterpart under the GATT. Article II:1 provides:

> With respect to any measure covered by this Agreement, each Member shall accord immediately and unconditionally to services and service suppliers of any other Member treatment no less favourable than that it accords to like services and service suppliers of any other country.

Due to the different wording, the interpretation of this provision may not be identical to that under the GATT. The GATS MFN obligation actually reads more like the GATT Article III:4 obligation, as it uses the phrase 'treatment no less favourable'.

Pursuant to Article II:2 of the GATS, Members were allowed to notify exemptions from the GATS MFN requirement as of the GATS' entry into force. For example, the United States has listed as one of its MFN exemptions the following: 'Canadian small businesses, but not small businesses of other countries, may use simplified registration and periodic reporting forms with respect to their securities'.[15] This example illustrates one of the main reasons countries choose to derogate from MFN treatment: regional integration. Here, the United States gives special treatment to companies from its neighbour to the North. Other common reasons for not granting MFN treatment are to provide favourable treatment for developing countries; requirements that benefits be given only to countries that offer reciprocal treatment; special treatment under Friendship, Commerce and Navigation or investment treaties; or the result of political cooperation between countries on various issues that lead to special treatment.

(b) Transparency

Article III of the GATS provides obligations on the transparency of laws regulating services. Transparency is particularly important for services due to the often extensive regulation in this area. In this regard, paragraph 1 of this provision states: '[e]ach Member shall publish promptly and, except in emergency situations, at the latest by the time of their entry into force, all relevant measures of general application which pertain to or

---

[14] Appellate Body Report, EC—Bananas III, para 221; See also Appellate Body Report, *Canada—Periodicals*, para 19.

[15] United States of America, 'Final List of Article II (MFN) Exemptions', GATS/EL/90 (15 April 1994) 11.

affect the operation of this Agreement. International agreements pertaining to or affecting trade in services to which a Member is a signatory shall also be published'.

(c) Domestic Regulation

Article VI of the GATS is entitled 'Domestic Regulation'. From the title alone, it appears that this provision could have a broad impact on Members' ability to regulate services. The full scope of GATS Article VI is not clear, however, as some parts of the provision are still being negotiated (as discussed below).

The first paragraph of Article VI states: '[i]n sectors where specific commitments are undertaken, each Member shall ensure that all measures of general application affecting trade in services are administered in a reasonable, objective and impartial manner'. This provision is similar to Article X:3(a) of the GATT, although slightly more limited in scope, as it applies only to 'sectors where specific commitments are undertaken'. As with the similar obligation in Article X:3(a), the impact of this provision is potentially quite broad. However, it has not yet been interpreted in the case law.

Article VI:4 has even broader implications. It provides:

> With a view to ensuring that measures relating to qualification requirements and procedures, technical standards and licensing requirements do not constitute unnecessary barriers to trade in services, the Council for Trade in Services shall, through appropriate bodies it may establish, develop any necessary disciplines. Such disciplines shall aim to ensure that such requirements are, *inter alia*:
>
> (a) based on objective and transparent criteria, such as competence and the ability to supply the service;
>
> (b) not more burdensome than necessary to ensure the quality of the service;
>
> (c) in the case of licensing procedures, not in themselves a restriction on the supply of the service.

While these disciplines are still in development, they have the potential to restrict greatly the ability to adopt domestic regulations in the area of services. A key aspect of this provision is sub-paragraph (b), which requires that the covered measures not be 'more burdensome than necessary to ensure the quality of the service'. This requirement imposes a potentially high standard on all domestic services regulation related to the covered measures (qualification requirements and procedures, technical standards and licensing requirements). As discussed in Chapter 9, the use of 'necessary' standards in Article XX of the GATT has come under great criticism as being too narrowly defined and not flexible enough to accommodate non-trade concerns. On the other hand, recent jurisprudence on the 'necessary' standard, including under the GATS as discussed in section (d) below, seems to involve a loosening of the standard. The application of the 'necessary' standard in this context will be of great importance for defining the scope of the intrusion of the GATS into domestic regulation.

To date, the only services sector where disciplines under paragraph 4 have been developed is accountancy. In that context, the following requirement has been established through a Decision of the Council for Trade in Services:

> Members shall ensure that measures not subject to scheduling under Articles XVI or XVII of the GATS, relating to licensing requirements and procedures, technical standards and qualification

requirements and procedures are not prepared, adopted or applied with a view to or with the effect of creating unnecessary barriers to trade in accountancy services. For this purpose, *Members shall ensure that such measures are not more trade-restrictive than necessary to fulfil a legitimate objective*. Legitimate objectives are, inter alia, the protection of consumers (which includes all users of accounting services and the public generally), the quality of the service, professional competence, and the integrity of the profession[16] [emphasis added].

Thus, in defining which measures are 'necessary', the decision explains that covered measures must not be 'more trade-restrictive than necessary to fulfil a legitimate objective'. It is important to note that this standard does not exist as a general obligation, but, rather, applies only where Members have scheduled specific commitments on accountancy. However, pursuant to paragraph 3 of the Decision, there is a 'standstill' provision that obligates all Members not to take *new* measures that would conflict with this accountancy decision 'to the fullest extent consistent with their existing legislation'.

As disciplines are still being developed under paragraph 4 for most service sectors, paragraph 5 currently applies in place of paragraph 4. This provision states:

5. (a) In sectors in which a Member has undertaken specific commitments, pending the entry into force of disciplines developed in these sectors pursuant to paragraph 4, the Member shall not apply licensing and qualification requirements and technical standards that nullify or impair such specific commitments in a manner which:

(i) does not comply with the criteria outlined in subparagraphs 4(a), (b) or (c); and

(ii) could not reasonably have been expected of that Member at the time the specific commitments in those sectors were made.

(b) In determining whether a Member is in conformity with the obligation under paragraph 5(a), account shall be taken of international standards of relevant international organizations applied by that Member.

Thus, paragraph 5 establishes a looser version of the paragraph 4 standard, applying only where commitments have been made, and only where the measure 'could not reasonably have been expected of that Member at the time the specific commitments in those sectors were made'.

(d) Exceptions

Part II contains a number of exceptions, including: Article V (Economic Integration), Article XII (Restrictions to Safeguard the Balance of Payments), Article XIV (General Exceptions) and Article XIV*bis* (Security Exceptions). The Economic Integration exception is the counterpart to the GATT Article XXIV exception for customs unions and free trade areas. We will not discuss this exception in detail here, but rather simply refer back to Chapter 8 on bilateral/regional trade agreements. Articles XII and XIV*bis* also have counterparts in the GATT. There has been little discussion of these issues in the case law, so we focus here on the 'General Exceptions' provision of Article XIV. Note that these

---

[16] Working Party on Professional Services, 'Disciplines on Domestic Regulation in the Accountancy Sector', S/WPPS/W/21 (30 November 1998), at para 2, adopted by the Council for Trade in Services on 14 December 1998, Decision on Disciplines Relating to the Accountancy Sector, S/L/63 (15 December 1998).

exceptions also apply to the obligations related to specific commitments, as discussed in the next section.

Article XIV of the GATS states:

Subject to the requirement that such measures are not applied in a manner which would constitute a means of arbitrary or unjustifiable discrimination between countries where like conditions prevail, or a disguised restriction on trade in services, nothing in this Agreement shall be construed to prevent the adoption or enforcement by any Member of measures:

(a) necessary to protect public morals or to maintain public order;

(b) necessary to protect human, animal or plant life or health;

(c) necessary to secure compliance with laws or regulations which are not inconsistent with the provisions of this Agreement including those relating to:

(i) the prevention of deceptive and fraudulent practices or to deal with the effects of a default on services contracts;

(ii) the protection of the privacy of individuals in relation to the processing and dissemination of personal data and the protection of confidentiality of individual records and accounts;

(iii) safety;

---

[10] The public order exception may be invoked only where a genuine and sufficiently serious threat is posed to one of the fundamental interests of society.

The substantive rules and wording are very similar to those of the GATT Article XX exceptions (with slightly different language here and there). As with the GATT, only certain policies are listed (environmental protection is not included in the GATS). In addition, as also seen with the GATT, there is a chapeau to the provision, requiring that any such measures not be applied as 'a means of arbitrary or unjustifiable discrimination between countries where like conditions prevail, or a disguised restriction on trade in services'.

To date, only one dispute, *US—Gambling Service,* has involved the application of this provision. The measures at issue there were a series of US laws regulating internet gambling (as well as other forms of 'remote' gambling, such as over the telephone) that were alleged to violate several GATS provisions. As discussed in section IV(a) below, the panel found the measures to violate GATS Article XVI in relation to the US market access commitments. As a defence, the United States invoked Article XIV(a) and (c), arguing that restrictions on 'remote' gambling were justified as necessary to protect public morals and to maintain public order (sub-section (a)) and also to secure compliance with other WTO-consistent laws (sub-section (b)). The panel rejected both defences, but on appeal the Appellate Body reversed some of the panel's key legal reasoning, and it then carried out its own analysis (for reasons of judicial economy, it made findings only under (a) and not (c)). We excerpt the relevant portion of the Appellate Body's findings under Article XIV(a) here:

Appellate Body Report, *United States—Measures Affecting the Cross-Border Supply of Gambling and Betting Services*, Adopted 20 April 2005, WT/DS285/AB/R

291. Article XIV of the GATS sets out the general exceptions from obligations under that Agreement in the same manner as does Article XX of the GATT 1994. Both of these provisions

affirm the right of Members to pursue objectives identified in the paragraphs of these provisions even if, in doing so, Members act inconsistently with obligations set out in other provisions of the respective agreements, provided that all of the conditions set out therein are satisfied. Similar language is used in both provisions, notably the term "necessary" and the requirements set out in their respective chapeaux. Accordingly, like the Panel, we find previous decisions under Article XX of the GATT 1994 relevant for our analysis under Article XIV of the GATS.

292. Article XIV of the GATS, like Article XX of the GATT 1994, contemplates a "two-tier analysis" of a measure that a Member seeks to justify under that provision. A panel should first determine whether the challenged measure falls within the scope of one of the paragraphs of Article XIV. This requires that the challenged measure address the particular interest specified in that paragraph and that there be a sufficient nexus between the measure and the interest protected. The required nexus—or "degree of connection"—between the measure and the interest is specified in the language of the paragraphs themselves, through the use of terms such as "relating to" and "necessary to". Where the challenged measure has been found to fall within one of the paragraphs of Article XIV, a panel should then consider whether that measure satisfies the requirements of the chapeau of Article XIV.

1. Justification of the Measures Under Paragraph (a) of Article XIV

293. Paragraph (a) of Article XIV covers:

. . . measures . . . necessary to protect public morals or to maintain public order. (footnote omitted)

294. In the first step of its analysis under this provision, the Panel examined whether the measures at issue—the Wire Act, the Travel Act, and the IGBA—are "designed" to protect public morals and to maintain public order. As a second step, the Panel determined whether these measures are "necessary" to protect public morals or to maintain public order, within the meaning of Article XIV(a). The Panel found that:

. . . the United States has not been able to provisionally justify, under Article XIV(a) of the GATS, that the Wire Act, the Travel Act (when read together with the relevant state laws) and the Illegal Gambling Business Act (when read together with the relevant state laws) are necessary to protect public morals and/or public order within the meaning of Article XIV(a). We, nonetheless, acknowledge that such laws are designed so as to protect public morals or maintain public order. (footnotes omitted)

295. Our review of this conclusion proceeds in two parts. We address first Antigua's challenge to the Panel's finding that the three federal statutes are "measures that are designed to 'protect public morals' and/or 'to maintain public order' in the United States within the meaning of Article XIV(a)." We then address the participants' respective challenges to the Panel's finding that the three federal statutes are not "necessary" to protect public morals and to maintain public order.

(a) "Measures . . . to protect public morals or to maintain public order"

296. In its analysis under Article XIV(a), the Panel found that "the term 'public morals' denotes standards of right and wrong conduct maintained by or on behalf of a community or nation." The Panel further found that the definition of the term "order", read in conjunction with footnote 5 of the GATS, "suggests that 'public order' refers to the preservation of the fundamental interests of a society, as reflected in public policy and law." The Panel then referred to Congressional reports and testimony establishing that "the government of the United States consider[s] [that the Wire Act, the Travel Act, and the IGBA] were adopted to address concerns

such as those pertaining to money laundering, organized crime, fraud, underage gambling and pathological gambling." On this basis, the Panel found that the three federal statutes are "measures that are designed to 'protect public morals' and/or 'to maintain public order' within the meaning of Article XIV(a)."

297. Antigua contests this finding on a rather limited ground, namely that the Panel failed to determine whether the concerns identified by the United States satisfy the standard set out in footnote 5 to Article XIV(a) of the GATS, which reads:

> [t]he public order exception may be invoked only where a genuine and sufficiently serious threat is posed to one of the fundamental interests of society.

298. We see no basis to conclude that the Panel failed to assess whether the standard set out in footnote 5 had been satisfied. As Antigua acknowledges, the Panel expressly referred to footnote 5 in a way that demonstrated that it understood the requirement therein to be part of the meaning given to the term "public order". Although *"no further mention"* was made in the Panel Report of footnote 5 or of its text, this alone does not establish that the Panel failed to assess whether the interests served by the three federal statutes satisfy the footnote's criteria. Having defined "public order" to include the standard in footnote 5, and then applied that definition to the facts before it to conclude that the measures "are designed to 'protect public morals' and/or 'to maintain public order'", the Panel was not required, in addition, to make a separate, explicit determination that the standard of footnote 5 had been met.

299. We therefore *uphold* the Panel's finding, in paragraph 6.487 of the Panel Report, that "the concerns which the Wire Act, the Travel Act and the Illegal Gambling Business Act seek to address fall within the scope of 'public morals' and/or 'public order' under Article XIV(a)."

(b) The Requirement that a Measure be "Necessary" Under Article XIV(a)

300. In the second part of its analysis under Article XIV(a), the Panel considered whether the Wire Act, the Travel Act, and the IGBA are "necessary" within the meaning of that provision. The Panel found that the United States had not demonstrated the "necessity" of those measures.

301. This finding rested on the Panel's determinations that: (i) "the interests and values protected by [the Wire Act, the Travel Act, and the IGBA] serve very important societal interests that can be characterized as 'vital and important in the highest degree'"; (ii) the Wire Act, the Travel Act, and the IGBA "must contribute, at least to some extent", to addressing the United States' concerns "pertaining to money laundering, organized crime, fraud, underage gambling and pathological gambling"; (iii) the measures in question "have a significant restrictive trade impact"; and (iv) "[i]n rejecting Antigua's invitation to engage in bilateral or multilateral consultations and/or negotiations, the United States failed to pursue in good faith a course of action that could have been used by it to explore the possibility of finding a reasonably available WTO-consistent alternative."

302. Each of the participants appeals different aspects of the analysis undertaken by the Panel in determining whether the "necessity" requirement in Article XIV(a) was satisfied. According to Antigua, the Panel failed to establish a sufficient "nexus" between gambling and the concerns raised by the United States. In addition, Antigua claims that the Panel erroneously limited its discussion of "reasonably available alternatives". In its appeal, the United States argues that the Panel departed from the way in which "reasonably available alternative" measures have been examined in previous disputes and erroneously imposed "a procedural requirement on the United States to consult or negotiate with Antigua before the United States may take measures to protect public morals [or] protect public order".

303. We begin our analysis of this issue by examining the legal standard of "necessity" in Article XIV(a) of the GATS. We then turn to the participants' appeals regarding the Panel's interpretation and application of this requirement.

(i) Determining "necessity" under Article XIV(a)

304. We note, at the outset, that the standard of "necessity" provided for in the general exceptions provision is an *objective* standard. To be sure, a Member's characterization of a measure's objectives and of the effectiveness of its regulatory approach—as evidenced, for example, by texts of statutes, legislative history, and pronouncements of government agencies or officials—will be relevant in determining whether the measure is, objectively, "necessary". A panel is not bound by these characterizations, however, and may also find guidance in the structure and operation of the measure and in contrary evidence proffered by the complaining party. In any event, a panel must, on the basis of the evidence in the record, independently and objectively assess the "necessity" of the measure before it.

305. In *Korea – Various Measures on Beef*, the Appellate Body stated, in the context of Article XX(d) of the GATT 1994, that whether a measure is "necessary" should be determined through "a process of weighing and balancing a series of factors". The Appellate Body characterized this process as one:

> . . . comprehended in the determination of whether a WTO-consistent alternative measure which the Member concerned could "reasonably be expected to employ" is available, or whether a less WTO-inconsistent measure is "reasonably available".

306. The process begins with an assessment of the "relative importance" of the interests or values furthered by the challenged measure. Having ascertained the importance of the particular interests at stake, a panel should then turn to the other factors that are to be "weighed and balanced". The Appellate Body has pointed to two factors that, in most cases, will be relevant to a panel's determination of the "necessity" of a measure, although not necessarily exhaustive of factors that might be considered. One factor is the contribution of the measure to the realization of the ends pursued by it; the other factor is the restrictive impact of the measure on international commerce.

307. A comparison between the challenged measure and possible alternatives should then be undertaken, and the results of such comparison should be considered in the light of the importance of the interests at issue. It is on the basis of this "weighing and balancing" and comparison of measures, taking into account the interests or values at stake, that a panel determines whether a measure is "necessary" or, alternatively, whether another, WTO-consistent measure is "reasonably available".

308. The requirement, under Article XIV(a), that a measure be "necessary"—that is, that there be no "reasonably available", WTO-consistent alternative—reflects the shared understanding of Members that substantive GATS obligations should not be deviated from lightly. An alternative measure may be found not to be "reasonably available", however, where it is merely theoretical in nature, for instance, where the responding Member is not capable of taking it, or where the measure imposes an undue burden on that Member, such as prohibitive costs or substantial technical difficulties. Moreover, a "reasonably available" alternative measure must be a measure that would preserve for the responding Member its right to achieve its desired level of protection with respect to the objective pursued under paragraph (a) of Article XIV.

309. It is well-established that a responding party invoking an affirmative defence bears the burden of demonstrating that its measure, found to be WTO-inconsistent, satisfies the requirements of the invoked defence. In the context of Article XIV(a), this means that the

responding party must show that its measure is "necessary" to achieve objectives relating to public morals or public order. In our view, however, it is not the responding party's burden to show, in the first instance, that there are *no* reasonably available alternatives to achieve its objectives. In particular, a responding party need not identify the universe of less trade-restrictive alternative measures and then show that none of those measures achieves the desired objective. The WTO agreements do not contemplate such an impracticable and, indeed, often impossible burden.

310.   Rather, it is for a responding party to make a *prima facie* case that its measure is "necessary" by putting forward evidence and arguments that enable a panel to assess the challenged measure in the light of the relevant factors to be "weighed and balanced" in a given case. The responding party may, in so doing, point out why alternative measures would not achieve the same objectives as the challenged measure, but it is under no obligation to do so in order to establish, in the first instance, that its measure is "necessary". If the panel concludes that the respondent has made a *prima facie* case that the challenged measure is "necessary"—that is, "significantly closer to the pole of "indispensable" than to the opposite pole of simply "making a contribution to"—then a panel should find that challenged measure "necessary" within the terms of Article XIV(a) of the GATS.

311.   If, however, the complaining party raises a WTO-consistent alternative measure that, in its view, the responding party should have taken, the responding party will be required to demonstrate why its challenged measure nevertheless remains "necessary" in the light of that alternative or, in other words, why the proposed alternative is not, in fact, "reasonably available". If a responding party demonstrates that the alternative is not "reasonably available", in the light of the interests or values being pursued and the party's desired level of protection, it follows that the challenged measure must be "necessary" within the terms of Article XIV(a) of the GATS.

(ii) Did the Panel err in its analysis of the "necessity" of the measures at issue?

312.   In considering whether the United States' measures are "necessary" under Article XIV(a) of the GATS, the Panel began by considering the factors set out by the Appellate Body in *Korea – Various Measures on Beef* as they apply to the Wire Act, the Travel Act, and the IGBA. Antigua claims that the Panel erred in concluding, in the course of its analysis of these factors, that the three federal statutes contribute to protecting the interests raised by the United States.

313.   The Panel set out, in some detail, how the United States' evidence established a specific connection between the remote supply of gambling services and each of the interests identified by the United States except for organized crime. In particular, the Panel found such a link in relation to money laundering, fraud, compulsive gambling, and underage gambling. Considering that the three federal statutes embody an outright prohibition on the remote supply of gambling services, we see no error in the Panel's approach, nor in its finding, in paragraph 6.494 of the Panel Report, that the Wire Act, the Travel Act, and the IGBA "must contribute" to addressing those concerns.

314.   In addition, the United States and Antigua each appeals different aspects of the Panel's selection of alternative measures to compare with the Wire Act, the Travel Act, and the IGBA. The United States argues that the Panel erred in examining the one alternative measure that it did consider, and Antigua contends that the Panel erred in failing to consider additional alternative measures.

315.   In its "necessity" analysis under Article XIV(a), the Panel appeared to understand that, in order for a measure to be accepted as "necessary" under Article XIV(a), the responding Member must have first *"explored and exhausted"* all reasonably available WTO-compatible alternatives before adopting its WTO-inconsistent measure. This understanding led the Panel to conclude

that, in this case, the United States had "an obligation to consult with Antigua before and while imposing its prohibition on the cross-border supply of gambling and betting services". Because the Panel found that the United States had not engaged in such consultations with Antigua, the Panel also found that the United States had not established that its measures are "necessary" and, therefore, provisionally justified under Article XIV(a).

316. In its appeal of this finding, the United States argues that "[t]he Panel relied on the 'necessity' test in Article XIV as the basis for imposing a procedural requirement on the United States to consult or negotiate with Antigua before the United States may take measures to protect public morals [or] protect public order". The United States submits that the requirement in Article XIV(a) that a measure be "necessary" indicates that "necessity is a property of the measure itself" and, as such, "necessity" cannot be determined by reference to the efforts undertaken by a Member to negotiate an alternative measure. The United States further argues that in previous disputes, the availability of alternative measures that were "merely theoretical" did not preclude the challenged measures from being deemed to be "necessary". Similarly, the United States argues, the fact that measures might theoretically be available after engaging in consultations with Antigua does not preclude the "necessity" of the three federal statutes.

317. In our view, the Panel's "necessity" analysis was flawed because it did not focus on an alternative measure that was reasonably available to the United States to achieve the stated objectives regarding the protection of public morals or the maintenance of public order. Engaging in consultations with Antigua, with a view to arriving at a negotiated settlement that achieves the same objectives as the challenged United States' measures, was not an appropriate alternative for the Panel to consider because consultations are by definition a process, the results of which are uncertain and therefore not capable of comparison with the measures at issue in this case.

318. We note, in addition, that the Panel based its requirement of consultations, in part, on "the existence of [a] specific market access commitment [in the United States GATS Schedule] with respect to cross-border trade of gambling and betting services". We do not see how the existence of a specific commitment in a Member's Schedule affects the "necessity" of a measure in terms of the protection of public morals or the maintenance of public order. For this reason as well, the Panel erred in relying on consultations as an alternative measure reasonably available to the United States.

319. We turn now to Antigua's allegation that the Panel improperly limited its examination of possible alternative measures against which to compare the Wire Act, the Travel Act, and the IGBA. Antigua claims that the Panel "erred in limiting" its search for alternatives to the universe of *existing* United States regulatory measures. Antigua also alleges that the Panel erred by examining only those measures that had been explicitly identified by Antigua even though "Antigua was never given the opportunity to properly rebut the Article XIV defence."

320. We observe, first, that the Panel did not state that it was limiting its search for alternatives in the manner alleged by Antigua. Secondly, although the Panel *began* its analysis of alternative measures by considering whether the United States already employs measures less restrictive than a prohibition to achieve the same objectives as the three federal statutes, its inquiry did not end there. The Panel obviously did consider alternatives *not* currently in place in the United States, as evidenced by its (ultimately erroneous) emphasis on the United States' alleged failure to pursue consultations with Antigua. Finally, we do not see why the Panel should have been expected to continue its analysis into additional alternative measures, which Antigua itself failed to identify. As we said above, it is not for the responding party to identify the universe of alternative measures against which its own measure should be compared. It is only if such an alternative is raised that this comparison is required. We therefore dismiss this aspect of Antigua's appeal.

321.   In our analysis above, we found that the Panel erred in assessing the necessity of the three United States statutes against the possibility of consultations with Antigua because such consultations, in our view, cannot qualify as a reasonably available alternative measure with which a challenged measure should be compared. For this reason, we *reverse* the Panel's finding, in paragraph 6.535 of the Panel Report, that, because the United States did not enter into consultations with Antigua:

> . . . the United States has not been able to provisionally justify, under Article XIV(a) of the GATS, that the Wire Act, the Travel Act (when read together with the relevant state laws) and the Illegal Gambling Business Act (when read together with the relevant state laws) are necessary to protect public morals and/or public order within the meaning of Article XIV(a).

322.   Having reversed this finding, we must consider whether, as the United States contends, the Wire Act, the Travel Act, and the IGBA are properly characterized as "necessary" to achieve the objectives identified by the United States and accepted by the Panel. The Panel's analysis, as well as the factual findings contained therein, are useful for our assessment of whether these measures satisfy the requirements of paragraph (a) of Article XIV.

323.   As we stated above, a responding party must make a *prima facie* case that its challenged measure is "necessary". A Panel determines whether this case is made through the identification, and weighing and balancing, of relevant factors, such as those in *Korea – Various Measures on Beef*, with respect to the measure challenged. In this regard, we note that the Panel: (i) found that the three federal statutes protect "very important societal interests"; (ii) observed that "strict controls may be needed to protect [such] interests"; and (iii) found that the three federal statutes contribute to the realization of the ends that they pursue. Although the Panel recognized the "significant restrictive trade impact" of the three federal statutes, it expressly tempered this recognition with a detailed explanation of certain characteristics of, and concerns specific to, the remote supply of gambling and betting services. These included: (i) "the volume, speed and international reach of remote gambling transactions"; (ii) the "virtual anonymity of such transactions"; (iii) "low barriers to entry in the context of the remote supply of gambling and betting services"; and the (iv) "isolated and anonymous environment in which such gambling takes place". Thus, this analysis reveals that the Panel did not place much weight, in the circumstances of this case, on the restrictive trade impact of the three federal statutes. On the contrary, the Panel appears to have accepted virtually all of the elements upon which the United States based its assertion that the three federal statutes are "indispensable".

324.   The Panel further, and in our view, tellingly, stated that

> . . . the United States has legitimate specific concerns with respect to money laundering, fraud, health and underage gambling that are specific to the remote supply of gambling and betting services, *which suggests that the measures in question are "necessary" within the meaning of Article XIV(a).* (emphasis added)

325.   From all of the above, and in particular from the summary of its analysis made in paragraphs 6.533 and 6.534 of the Panel Report, we understand the Panel to have acknowledged that, *but for* the United States' alleged refusal to accept Antigua's invitation to negotiate, the Panel would have found that the United States had made its *prima facie* case that the Wire Act, the Travel Act, and the IGBA are "necessary", within the meaning of Article XIV(a). We thus agree with the United States that the "sole basis" for the Panel's conclusion to the contrary was its finding relating to the requirement of consultations with Antigua.

326.   Turning to the Panel's analysis of alternative measures, we observe that the Panel dismissed, as irrelevant to its analysis, measures that did not take account of the specific concerns associated with *remote* gambling. We found above that the Panel erred in finding

that consultations with Antigua constitutes a measure reasonably available to the United States. Antigua raised no other measure that, in the view of the Panel, could be considered an alternative to the prohibitions on remote gambling contained in the Wire Act, the Travel Act, and the IGBA. In our opinion, therefore, the record before us reveals no reasonably available alternative measure proposed by Antigua or examined by the Panel that would establish that the three federal statutes are not "necessary" within the meaning of Article XIV(a). Because the United States made its *prima facie* case of "necessity", and Antigua failed to identify a reasonably available alternative measure, we conclude that the United States demonstrated that its statutes are "necessary", and therefore justified, under paragraph (a) of Article XIV.

327.   For all these reasons, we *find* that the Wire Act, the Travel Act, and the IGBA are "measures . . . necessary to protect public morals or to maintain public order", within the meaning of paragraph (a) of Article XIV of the GATS.

... ...

The findings under Article XIV(a) in *US—Gambling Services* offer important clarifications of two issues. First, in its reasoning on the scope of 'public morals' and 'public order', the panel had expressed the view that 'the term "public morals" denotes standards of right and wrong conduct maintained by or on behalf of a community or nation'. The panel further found that the definition of the term 'order', read in conjunction with footnote 5 to the GATS, 'suggests that "public order" refers to the preservation of the fundamental interests of a society, as reflected in public policy and law'.[17] The only appeal of this point was a narrow one that the Appellate Body rejected, so the panel's statements on this issue stand as the only interpretations of these terms.

Secondly, the Appellate Body provided some elaboration on how it will apply the 'necessary' standard for GATS exceptions. In doing so, the Appellate Body built upon its earlier jurisprudence on the necessity standard in the context of Article XX, emphasising that the interpretations of both sets of exceptions inform each other. Briefly, as set out in more detail in paragraphs 304–311 above, the Appellate Body explained that an evaluation of whether a measure is 'necessary' 'begins with an assessment of the "relative importance" of the interests or values furthered by the challenged measure.' Then, other factors like the 'contribution of the measure to the realization of the ends pursued by it' and 'the restrictive impact of the measure on international commerce' should be 'weighed and balanced' along with these 'interests or values'. Finally, '[a] comparison between the challenged measure and possible alternatives should then be undertaken'.

While the United States was successful in its argument that the measures at issue were justified under Article XIV(a), there was still the matter of satisfying the terms of the Article XIV chapeau. The panel and Appellate Body considered a number of arguments in this regard. Ultimately, the Appellate Body found that the United States had not satisfied this provision. In this regard, the Appellate Body considered the relevance of certain other United States measures that were alleged to permit remote gambling services supplied by domestic entities related to horseracing. In light of these measures, the Appellate Body found that the United States had not demonstrated that the challenged measures 'are applied consistently with the requirements of the chapeau'.[18]

---

[17] Panel Report, *US—Gambling Services*, paras 6.465–6.467.
[18] Appellate Body Report, *US—Gambling Services*, paras 361–69.

V. SPECIFIC COMMITMENTS

Part III of the GATS covers 'specific commitments' made by Members. There are three types of commitments: 'market access', 'national treatment' and 'additional' commitments. There is no requirement to make commitments. The decision to make commitments or not is part of the negotiating process, similar to the process for tariff concessions. However, where Members have made commitments, they must abide by them. The existence of commitments for national treatment illustrates an important difference between the GATT and the GATS. Under the GATT, national treatment is a general obligation that applies to all measures. By contrast, under the GATS national treatment only applies where a commitment has been made.

GATS commitments are set out in individual Members' Schedules. These commitments are made either horizontally (across all services sectors) or for specific sectors only. Part I of the commitments Schedule deals with horizontal commitments; Part II deals with sector-specific commitments. For both kinds of commitments, the Member indicates in the Schedule which commitments have been made for each mode of supply in relation to market access, national treatment and any additional commitments. We set out in Table 14.2 a brief excerpt from the United States' GATS Schedule, dealing with the commitments at issue in the *US—Gambling Services* dispute. The extract covers the commitment for 'Other Recreational Services (except sporting)', which was the main commitment at issue there.

Table 14.2 Sector-specific Commitments

Modes of supply: 1) Cross-border supply 2) Consumption abroad 3) Commercial presence 4) Presence of natural persons

Sector or subsector	Limitations on market access	Limitations on national treatment	Additional commitments
10. RECREATIONAL, CULTURAL, & SPORTING SERVICES ...			
D. OTHER REC- REATIONAL SERVICES (except sporting)	1) None 2) None 3) The number of concessions available for commercial operations in federal, state and local facilities is limited 4) Unbound, except as indicated in the horizontal section	1) None 2) None 3) None 4) None	

GATS Schedules work as follows. For each specific sector included, the Schedule sets out the commitments made for *each mode of supply* in relation to the market access and national treatment (and 'additional' where they exist) categories of commitment. As shown in the extract, the four modes of supply are listed at the top, and numbered 1 to

4. The numbers 1 to 4 are then entered in the columns for market access and national treatment commitments, with the commitment for each mode of supply specified.

Three general types of entries are found in the schedules. First, 'None' means that there is a full commitment, with no limitations on national treatment or market access. Secondly, 'Unbound' means no commitment has been made, and thus the Member has no obligations with respect to the mode of supply and particular type of commitment at issue for that sector. Finally, a partial commitment, or a commitment with limitations, may be made, through a specific explanation in the text. Modes 3 and 4 under market access in the excerpt above illustrate partial commitments. As seen with mode 4 in the excerpt, the explanation may be combined with 'unbound' or 'none' at the outset, and then 'except' a specific circumstance.

Market access commitments are fairly straightforward. For example, if a Member inscribes 'None' in its Schedule for 'Cross-Border Supply', then the Member has made a full commitment to this mode, and thus must not maintain or adopt any of the measures set out in Article XVI:2 in relation to that mode of supply (the meaning of these 'market access' provisions is discussed in the next subsection below).

National treatment commitments are somewhat more complicated because they involve a comparison of the treatment of foreign services and service suppliers to domestic services and service suppliers. Thus, taking the example of cross-border supply, a full commitment (ie, inscribing 'None' in the Schedule) means that the Member will not treat foreign services or service suppliers using this mode less favourably than 'like' domestic services or service suppliers.[19] As with the GATT, defining a precise scope for this non-discrimination standard is somewhat complicated, and the issue is made more difficult by the existence of the four modes of supply. We discuss this issue in subsection (b) below.

As a final point, with regard to clarification of these Schedules through dispute settlement, interpreting Members' commitments in their Schedules is no different from interpreting the WTO agreements themselves. As the Appellate Body explained in *US—Gambling Services*, the Vienna Convention on the Law of Treaties interpretation rules apply to the GATS Schedules.[20]

(a) Market Access

We have made reference above to commitments on 'market access'. This term is used in many different contexts, with different meanings. We now explain in more detail what this concept means in the context of the GATS. The term is defined in Article XVI, which states in relevant part:

2. In sectors where market-access commitments are undertaken, the measures which a Member shall not maintain or adopt either on the basis of a regional subdivision or on the basis of its entire territory, unless otherwise specified in its Schedule, are defined as:

(a) limitations on the number of service suppliers whether in the form of numerical quotas, monopolies, exclusive service suppliers or the requirements of an economic needs test;

(b) limitations on the total value of service transactions or assets in the form of numerical quotas or the requirement of an economic needs test;

---

[19] Panel Report, *Canada—Autos*, para 10.307.
[20] Appellate Body Report, *US—Gambling Services*, para 159.

(c) limitations on the total number of service operations or on the total quantity of service output expressed in terms of designated numerical units in the form of quotas or the requirement of an economic needs test;

(d) limitations on the total number of natural persons that may be employed in a particular service sector or that a service supplier may employ and who are necessary for, and directly related to, the supply of a specific service in the form of numerical quotas or the requirement of an economic needs test;

(e) measures which restrict or require specific types of legal entity or joint venture through which a service supplier may supply a service; and

(f) limitations on the participation of foreign capital in terms of maximum percentage limit on foreign shareholding or the total value of individual or aggregate foreign investment.

In a sense, this provision defines 'market access' through the above examples. However, it does not provide a general definition or standard for the term. The absence of a clear definition raises a question: what is the purpose of the market access provision? One answer is that the difficulties with applying a national treatment type of non-discrimination standard in the context of trade in services led the drafters to elaborate on specific circumstances involving discrimination about which they were concerned. Thus, the market access provisions could be thought of as a proxy for rooting out discrimination. Another possibility is that the drafters envisaged these provisions as going beyond the non-discrimination provisions to reach certain internal measures the trade impact of which was a concern even though no discrimination was present. The specific examples set out in Article XVI do not answer the question of the drafters' intent. Instead, they are likely to be the result of specific negotiating demands by Members who were trying to promote the interests of particular constituents. Based on these examples, circumstances can be envisaged in which a measure actually helps foreign service suppliers and disadvantages domestic suppliers, yet may still violate the rules. For example, in sub-paragraph (a), it may be the case that the number of service suppliers is limited to 10, and all 10 suppliers are foreign. In this situation, it may be the domestic industry that is harmed most by the measure. Thus, searching for a coherent purpose to these provisions may be fruitless. The rules simply are what they say.

The main dispute dealing with these provisions is *US—Gambling Services*. As discussed above, the measures at issue in that case restricted the ability of companies to provide 'remote' gambling and betting services (eg, gambling over the internet), prohibiting such activity in most circumstances. The focus of the allegations was Article XVI:2(a) and XVI:2(c). The Appellate Body's findings on these points were as follows:

Appellate Body Report, *United States—Measures Affecting the Cross-Border Supply of Gambling and Betting Services*, Adopted 20 April 2005, WT/DS285/AB/R

214. Article XVI of the GATS sets out specific obligations for Members that apply insofar as a Member has undertaken "specific market access commitments" in its Schedule. The first paragraph of Article XVI obliges Members to accord services and service suppliers of other Members "no less favourable treatment than that provided for under the terms, limitations and conditions agreed and specified in its Schedule." The second paragraph of Article XVI defines, in six sub-paragraphs, measures that a Member, having undertaken a specific commitment, is not to adopt or maintain, "unless otherwise specified in its Schedule". The first four sub-paragraphs concern quantitative limitations on market access; the fifth sub-paragraph covers measures that

restrict or require specific types of legal entity or joint venture through which a service supplier may supply a service; and the sixth sub-paragraph identifies limitations on the participation of foreign capital.

215. The Panel found that the United States' Schedule includes specific commitments on gambling and betting services, and we have upheld this finding. The Panel then considered the consistency of the measures at issue with the United States' obligations under Article XVI of the GATS. The scope of those obligations depends on the scope of the specific commitment made in the United States' Schedule. In this case, the relevant entry for mode 1 supply in the market access column of subsector 10.D of the United States' Schedule reads "None". In other words, the United States has undertaken to provide full market access, within the meaning of Article XVI, in respect of the services included within the scope of its subsector 10.D commitment. In so doing, it has committed not to maintain any of the types of measures listed in the six sub-paragraphs of Article XVI:2.

216. Before the Panel, Antigua claimed that, in maintaining measures that prohibit the cross-border supply of gambling and betting services, the United States is maintaining quantitative limitations that fall within the scope of sub-paragraphs (a) and (c) of Article XVI and that are, therefore, inconsistent with the market access commitment undertaken in subsector 10.D of the United States' Schedule. The Panel took the view that a prohibition on the supply of certain services effectively "limits to zero" the number of service suppliers and number of service operations relating to that service. The Panel reasoned that such a prohibition results in a "zero quota" and, therefore, constitutes a "limitation on the number of service suppliers in the form of numerical quotas within the meaning of Article XVI:2(a)" and "a limitation 'on the total number of service operations or on the total quantity of service output . . . in the form of quotas' within the meaning of Article XVI:2(c)".

217. In consequence, the Panel found that, by maintaining the following measures, the United States acts inconsistently with its obligations under Article XVI of the GATS:

(i) Federal laws

(1) the Wire Act;

(2) the Travel Act (when read together with the relevant state laws); and

(3) the Illegal Gambling Business Act (when read together with the relevant state laws).

(ii) State laws:

(1) *Louisiana*: Section 14:90.3 of the Louisiana Revised Statutes (Annotated);

(2) *Massachusetts*: Section 17A of chapter 271 of the Annotated Laws of Massachusetts;

(3) *South Dakota*: Section 22-25A-8 of the South Dakota Codified Laws; and

(4) *Utah*: Section 76-10-1102(b) of the Utah Code (Annotated).

A. Preliminary Matters

218. The United States appeals both the Panel's interpretation of sub-paragraphs (a) and (c) of Article XVI, as well as its application of those provisions to the measures at issue. We have already determined that the Panel should not have made findings under Article XVI with respect to certain state laws because Antigua had not made out a *prima facie* case in respect of these measures. Having already reversed the Panel's findings regarding these state laws, we need not consider them further in our assessment of this part of the United States' appeal. Accordingly, our analysis below is limited to a review of the Panel's interpretation of sub-

paragraphs (a) and (c) of Article XVI:2, as well as to its application of that interpretation to the three *federal* statutes at issue in this case.

219.   We also note that the Notice of Appeal filed by the United States appears to indicate a separate, independent challenge to:

The Panel's finding that a WTO Member does not respect its GATS market access obligations under Article XVI:2 if it limits market access to any part of a scheduled sector or subsector, or if it restricts any means of delivery under mode 1 with respect to a committed sector.

220.   The United States did not, however, adduce any arguments in support of such a challenge in its appellant's submission. Nor did the United States expressly refer to, or request us to reverse, any paragraph of the Panel Report in which the 'finding' referred to in the above excerpt is found. Accordingly, we understand that the United States does *not* challenge separately the Panel's findings as regards restrictions on the supply of *part of a sector*, or as regards restrictions on *part of a mode of supply* (that is, on one or more means of supplying a given service). In response to questioning at the oral hearing, the United States confirmed that its appeal focuses on the Panel's interpretation of sub-paragraphs (a) and (c) of Article XVI:2, and we shall limit our examination accordingly.

B. The Meaning of Sub-paragraphs (a) and (c) of Article XVI

221.   The chapeau to Article XVI:2, and sub-paragraphs (a) and (c), provide:

In sectors where market-access commitments are undertaken, the measures which a Member shall not maintain or adopt either on the basis of a regional subdivision or on the basis of its entire territory, unless otherwise specified in its Schedule, are defined as:

(a) limitations on the number of service suppliers whether in the form of numerical quotas, monopolies, exclusive service suppliers or the requirements of an economic needs test; ...

(c) limitations on the total number of service operations or on the total quantity of service output expressed in terms of designated numerical units in the form of quotas or the requirement of an economic needs test; [9]

---

[9] Subparagraph 2(c) does not cover measures of a Member which limit inputs for the supply of services.

222.   In its appeal, the United States emphasizes that *none* of the measures at issue states any numerical units or is in the form of quotas and that, therefore, *none* of those measures falls within the scope of sub-paragraph (a) or (c) of Article XVI:2. The United States contends that the Panel erred in its interpretation of sub-paragraphs (a) and (c) of Article XVI:2 by failing to give effect to certain elements of the text of these provisions, notably to key terms such as "form" and "numerical quotas". According to the United States, the Panel appears to have been influenced by a "misguided" concern that prohibitions on foreign service suppliers should not escape the application of Article XVI simply because they are not expressed in numerical terms. The United States asserts that the Panel ignored the fact that such prohibitions remain subject to other provisions of the Agreement, including Articles XVII and VI, and contends that, in its approach, the Panel improperly expanded the obligations in Article XVI. For the United States, Members that have made a specific commitment under Article XVI have committed themselves not to maintain the precisely defined limitations set out in Article XVI:2; Members have *not* committed themselves to eliminate all other limitations or restrictions that may impede the supply of the relevant services.

1. Sub-paragraph (a) of Article XVI:2

223.   In interpreting sub-paragraph (a) of Article XVI:2, the Panel determined that:

[a prohibition on one, several or all means of delivery cross-border] is a "limitation on the number of service suppliers in the form of numerical quotas" within the meaning of Article XVI:2(a) because it totally prevents the use by service suppliers of one, several or all means of delivery that are included in mode 1.

224.   The United States submits that this interpretation ignores the text of sub-paragraph (a), in particular the meaning of "form" and "numerical quotas", and erroneously includes within the scope of Article XVI:2(a) measures that have the *effect* of limiting the number of service suppliers or output to zero. Although the Panel opined that any other result would be absurd", the United States stresses the opposite—that a contrary result would be consistent with the balance between liberalization and the right to regulate that is reflected in the GATS.

225.   Article XVI:2(a) prohibits "limitations on the number of service suppliers whether in the form of numerical quotas, monopolies, exclusive service suppliers or the requirements of an economic needs test." In interpreting this provision we observe, first, that it refers to restrictions "on the *number* of service suppliers", as well as to "*numerical* quotas". These words reflect that the focus of Article XVI:2(a) is on limitations relating to numbers or, put differently, to *quantitative* limitations.

226.   The United States urges us to give proper effect to the terms "in the form of" in sub-paragraph (a) and, to that end, refers to dictionary definitions to establish the meaning of "form" in Article XIV(a). Yet even these definitions suggest a degree of ambiguity as to the scope of the word "form". For example, "form" covers both the mode in which a thing "exists", as well as the mode in which it "manifests itself". This suggests a broad meaning for the term "form".

227.   The words "in the form of" in sub-paragraph (a) relate to all four of the limitations identified in that provision. It follows, in our view, that the four types of limitations, themselves, impart meaning to "in the form of". Looking at these four types of limitations in Article XVI:2(a), we begin with "numerical quotas". These words are not defined in the GATS. According to the dictionary definitions provided by the United States, the meaning of the word "numerical" includes "characteristic of a number or numbers". The word "quota" means, *inter alia*, "the maximum number or quantity belonging, due, given, or permitted to an individual or group"; and "numerical limitations on imports or exports". Thus, a "numerical quota" within Article XVI:2(a) appears to mean a quantitative limit on the number of service suppliers. The fact that the word "numerical" encompasses things which "have the characteristics of a number" suggests that limitations "in the form of a numerical quota" would encompass limitations which, even if not in themselves a number, have the characteristics of a number. Because zero is *quantitative* in nature, it can, in our view, be deemed to have the "characteristics of" a number—that is, to be "numerical".

228.   The second type of limitation mentioned in sub-paragraph (a) is "limitations on the number of service suppliers . . . in the form of . . . monopolies". Although the word "monopolies", as such, is not defined, Article XXVIII(h) of the GATS defines a "monopoly supplier of a service" as:

. . . any person, public or private, which in the relevant market of the territory of a Member is authorized or established formally *or in effect* by that Member as the sole supplier of that service. (emphasis added)

229.   The term "exclusive service suppliers", which is used to identify the third limitation in Article XVI:2(a) ("limitations on the number of service suppliers . . . in the form of exclusive service suppliers"), is defined in Article VIII:5 of the GATS, as:

   . . . where a Member, formally *or in effect*, (*a*) authorizes or establishes a small number of service suppliers and

   (*b*) substantially prevents competition among those suppliers in its territory. (emphasis added)

230.   These two definitions suggest that the reference, in Article XVI:2(a), to limitations on the number of service suppliers "in the form of monopolies and exclusive service suppliers" should be read to include limitations that are in form *or in effect*, monopolies or exclusive service suppliers.

231.   We further observe that it is not clear that "limitations on the number of service suppliers . . . in the form of . . . the requirements of an economic needs test" must take a particular "form." Thus, this fourth type of limitation, too, suggests that the words "in the form of" must not be interpreted as prescribing a rigid mechanical formula.

232.   This is not to say that the words "in the form of" should be ignored or replaced by the words "that have the effect of". Yet, at the same time, they cannot be read in isolation. Rather, when viewed as a whole, the text of sub-paragraph (a) supports the view that the words "in the form of" must be read in conjunction with the words that precede them—"limitations on the *number* of service suppliers"—as well as the words that follow them, including the words "*numerical* quotas". (emphasis added) Read in this way, it is clear that the thrust of sub-paragraph (a) is not on the *form* of limitations, but on their *numerical*, or *quantitative*, nature.

233.   Looking to the context of sub-paragraph (a), we observe that the chapeau to Article XVI:2, refers to the purpose of the sub-paragraphs that follow, namely, to define the measures which a Member shall not maintain or adopt for sectors *where market access commitments are made*. The chapeau thus contemplates circumstances in which a Member's Schedule *includes* a commitment to allow market access, and points out that the function of the sub-paragraphs in Article XVI:2 is to define certain limitations that are prohibited unless specifically entered in the Member's Schedule. Plainly, the drafters of sub-paragraph (a) had in mind limitations that would impose a maximum limit of *above* zero. Similarly, Article II:1(b) of the GATT 1994 prohibits Members from imposing duties "in excess of" the bound duty rate. Such bound duty rate will usually be *above* zero. Yet this does not mean that Article II:1(b) does not also refer to bound rates set at zero.

234.   It follows from the above that we find the following reasoning of the Panel to be persuasive:

   [t]he fact that the terminology [of Article XVI:2(a)] embraces lesser limitations, in the form of quotas greater than zero, cannot warrant the conclusion that it does not embrace a greater limitation amounting to zero. Paragraph (a) does not foresee a 'zero quota' because paragraph (a) was not drafted to cover situations where a Member wants to maintain full limitations. If a Member wants to maintain a full prohibition, it is assumed that such a Member would not have scheduled such a sector or subsector and, therefore, would not need to schedule any limitation or measures pursuant to Article XVI:2.

235.   As for the first paragraph of Article XVI, we note that it does not refer expressly to any requirements as to form, but simply links a Member's market access obligations in respect of scheduled services to "the terms, limitations and conditions agreed and specified in its Schedule". Neither this provision, nor the object and purpose of the GATS as stated in its preamble, readily

assists us in answering the question whether the reference in Article XVI:2(a) to "limitations on the number of service suppliers . . . in the form of numerical quotas" encompasses the type of measure at issue here, namely, a prohibition on the supply of a service in respect of which a specific commitment has been made.

236.   In our view, the above examination of the words of Article XVI:2(a) read in their context and in the light of the object and purpose of the GATS suggests that the words "in the form of" do not impose the type of precisely defined constraint that the United States suggests. Yet certain ambiguities about the meaning of the provision remain. The Panel, at this stage of its analysis, observed that any suggestion that the "form" requirement must be strictly interpreted to refer *only* to limitations "explicitly couched in numerical terms" leads to "absurdity". In either circumstance, this is an appropriate case in which to have recourse to supplementary means of interpretation, such as preparatory work.

237.   We have already determined that the 1993 Scheduling Guidelines constitute relevant preparatory work. As the Panel observed, those Guidelines set out an example of the type of limitation that falls within the scope of sub-paragraph (a) of Article XVI:2, that is, of the type of measures that will be inconsistent with Article XVI if a relevant commitment has been made and unless the Member in question has listed it as a condition or limitation in its Schedule. That example is: "nationality requirements for suppliers of services (equivalent to zero quota)". This example confirms the view that measures equivalent to a zero quota fall within the scope of Article XVI:2(a).

238.   For the above reasons, we are of the view that limitations amounting to a zero quota are quantitative limitations and fall within the scope of Article XVI:2(a).

239.   As we have not been asked to revisit the other elements of the Panel's reasoning on this issue—in particular its findings regarding limitations on market access in respect of part of a committed sector, and limitations on one or more means of cross-border delivery for a committed service—we therefore, *uphold* the Panel's finding that:

> [a prohibition on one, several or all means of delivery cross-border] is a "limitation on the number of service suppliers in the form of numerical quotas" within the meaning of Article XVI:2(a) because it totally prevents the use by service suppliers of one, several or all means of delivery that are included in mode 1.

2. Sub-paragraph (c) of Article XVI:2

240.   In interpreting sub-paragraph (c) of Article XVI:2, the Panel observed that the wording of the provision "might perhaps be taken to imply that any quota has to be expressed in terms of designated numerical units". However, after further analysis and, in particular, after comparing the English version of the provision with its French and Spanish counterparts, the Panel found that sub-paragraph (c) does *not* mean that any quota must be expressed in terms of designated numerical units if it is to fall within the scope of that provision. Instead, according to the Panel, the "correct reading of Article XVI:2(c)" is that limitations referred to under that provision may be: (i) in the form of designated numerical units; (ii) in the form of quotas; *or* (iii) in the form of the requirement of an economic needs test.

241.   The Panel then found that, where a specific commitment has been undertaken in respect of a service, a measure prohibiting one or more means of delivery of that service is:

> . . . a limitation "on the total number of service operations or on the total quantity of service output . . . in the form of quotas" within the meaning of Article XVI:2(c) because it . . . results in a 'zero quota' on one or more or all means of delivery include[d] in mode 1.

242.   The United States asserts that, in so finding, the Panel used an incorrect reading of the French and Spanish texts to arrive at an interpretation that is inconsistent with the ordinary meaning of the English text. Specifically, the Panel relied upon the presence of commas in the French and Spanish versions of the text—but not in the English version—in order to find that sub-paragraph (c) identifies *three* types of limitations. The United States argues that, when properly interpreted, sub-paragraph (c) identifies only *two* types of limitations. The United States adds that the measures at issue in this case cannot in any way be construed as falling within the scope of either of the *two* limitations defined in sub-paragraph (c).

243.   Sub-paragraph (c) refers to the following measures:

> limitations on the total number of service operations or on the total quantity of service output expressed in terms of designated numerical units in the form of quotas or the requirement of an economic needs test.

244.   The Panel essentially determined that, *notwithstanding* the absence of a comma between "terms of designated numerical units" and "in the form of quotas" in the *English* version, the phrase should, in order to be read in a manner consistent with the French and Spanish versions, be read *as if* such a comma existed—that is, as if expressed in "terms of designated numerical units" and "in the form of quotas" were disjunctive phrases, each of which modifies the word "limitations" at the beginning of the provision. The Panel relied on the fact that such a comma *does* exist in both the French and Spanish versions of the provision. The United States argues, however, based on a detailed analysis of French grammar, that the existence of the comma in the French version is, in fact, consistent with the absence of a comma in the English version, and that both versions mean that Article XVI:2(c) identifies only *two* limitations.

245.   Ultimately, we are not persuaded that the key to the interpretation of this particular provision is to be found in a careful dissection of the use of commas within its grammatical structure. Regardless of which language version is analyzed, and of the implications of comma placement (or lack thereof), *all* three language versions are grammatically ambiguous. All three can arguably be read as identifying two limitations on the total number of service operations or on the total quantity of service output. All three can also arguably be read as identifying *three* limitations on the total number of service operations or on the total quantity of service output. The mere presence or absence of a comma in Article XVI:2(c) is not determinative of the issue before us.

246.   We find it more useful, and appropriate, to look to the language of the provision itself for its meaning. Looking at the provision generally, we see that the first clause of sub-paragraph (c) deals with the *target* of the limitations covered by that provision. There are two such types of limitations: on the number of service operations; and on the quantity of service output. Both are *quantitative* in nature. The second part of the provision provides more detail as to the *type* of limitations—relating to those service operations or output—that fall within sub-paragraph (c). These are: "designated numerical units in the form of quotas or the requirement of an economic needs test". The second part of the provision clearly modifies the first part of the provision (service operations, service output). Yet certain elements of the second part apply differently to the two elements of the first part. For example, in its ordinary sense, the term "numerical units" is more naturally used to refer to "output" than to "operations".

247.   In our view, by combining, in sub-paragraph (c), the elements of the first clause of Article XVI:2(c) and the elements in the second part of the provision, the parties to the negotiations sought to ensure that their provision covered certain types of limitations, but did not feel the need to clearly demarcate the scope of each such element. On the contrary, there is scope for overlap between such elements: between limitations on the number of service operations and limitations on the quantity of service output, for example, or between limitations in the form

of quotas and limitations in the form of an economic needs test. That sub-paragraph (c) applies in respect of all four modes of supply under the GATS also suggests the limitations covered thereunder cannot take a single form, nor be constrained in a formulaic manner. Nonetheless, all types of limitations in sub-paragraph (c) are quantitative in nature, and all restrict market access. For these reasons, we are of the view that, *even if* sub-paragraph (c) is read as referring to only *two* types of limitations, as contended by the United States, it does not follow that sub-paragraph (c) would not catch a measure equivalent to a zero quota.

248.   To the extent that the above interpretation leaves a degree of ambiguity as to the proper meaning of Article XVI:2(c), we consider it useful to resort to supplementary means of interpretation. The market access obligations set forth in Article XVI were intended to be obligations in respect of *quantitative*, or "quantitative-type", measures. The difficulties faced by the negotiating parties concerned not *whether* Article XVI covered quantitative measures—for it was clear that it did—but rather how to "know where the line should be drawn between quantitative and qualitative measures".

249.   We also consider it appropriate to refer to the 1993 Scheduling Guidelines as preparatory work. These Guidelines set out an example of the type of measure covered by sub-paragraph (c) of Article XVI:2. They refer to '[r]estrictions on broadcasting time available for foreign films', without mentioning numbers or units.

250.   The strict interpretation of Article XVI:2(c) advanced by the United States would imply that only limitations that contain an express reference to numbered units could fall within the scope of that provision. Under such an interpretation, sub-paragraph (c) could not cover, for example, a limitation expressed as a percentage or described using words such as "a majority". It is neither necessary nor appropriate for us to draw, in the abstract, the line between quantitative and qualitative measures, and we do not do so here. Yet we are satisfied that a prohibition on the supply of services in respect of which a full market access commitment has been undertaken is a quantitative limitation on the supply of such services.

251.   In this case, the measures at issue, by prohibiting the supply of services in respect of which a market access commitment has been taken, amount to a "zero quota" on service operations or output with respect to such services. As such, they fall within the scope of Article XVI:2(c).

252.   For all of these reasons, we *uphold* the Panel's finding, in paragraph 6.355 of the Panel Report, that a measure prohibiting the supply of certain services where specific commitments have been undertaken is a limitation:

> . . . within the meaning of Article XVI:2(c) because it totally prevents the services operations and/or service output through one or more or all means of delivery that are included in mode 1. In other words, such a ban results in a "zero quota" on one or more or all means of delivery include in mode 1.

D. Application of Article XVI to the Measures at Issue

257.   Having upheld the Panel's interpretation of Article XVI:2(a) and (c), we now consider its application of that interpretation to the measures at issue in this case. In so doing, we consider, for the reasons already explained, only that part of the Panel's analysis relating to the three *federal* laws, and not its analysis relating to state laws.

258.   The Panel's explanation of the three federal laws is set out in paragraphs 6.360 to 6.380 of the Panel Report. It is, in our view, useful to set out briefly the relevant part of each statute, as well as the Panel's finding in respect of that statute. The relevant part of the Wire Act states:

Whoever being engaged in the business of betting or wagering knowingly uses a wire communication facility for the transmission in interstate or foreign commerce of bets or wagers or information assisting in the placing of bets or wagers on any sporting event or contest, or for the transmission of a wire communication which entitles the recipient to receive money or credit as a result of bets or wagers, or for information assisting in the placing of bets or wagers shall be fined under this title or imprisoned not more than two years, or both.

259. With respect to this provision, the Panel found that "the Wire Act prohibits the use of at least one or potentially several means of delivery included in mode 1", and that, accordingly, the statute "constitutes a 'zero quota' for, respectively, one, several or all of those means of delivery." The Panel reasoned that the Wire Act prohibits service suppliers from supplying gambling and betting services using remote means of delivery, as well as service operations and service output through such means. Accordingly, the Panel determined that "the Wire Act contains a limitation 'in the form of numerical quotas' within the meaning of Article XVI:2(a) and a limitation 'in the form of a quota' within the meaning of Article XVI:2(c)."

260. As regards the Travel Act, the Panel quoted the following excerpt:

(a) Whoever travels in interstate or foreign commerce or uses the mail or any facility in interstate or foreign commerce, with intent to –

(1) distribute the proceeds of any unlawful activity; or

(2) commit any crime of violence to further any unlawful activity; or

(3) otherwise promote, manage, establish, carry on, or facilitate the promotion, management, establishment,

or carrying on, of any unlawful activity,

and thereafter performs or attempts to perform–

(A) an act described in paragraph (1) or (3) shall be fined under this title, imprisoned not more than 5 years, or both; or

(B) an act described in paragraph (2) shall be fined under this title, imprisoned for not more than 20 years, or both, and if death results shall be imprisoned for any term of years or for life.

(b) As used in this section (i) 'unlawful activity' means (1) any business enterprise involving gambling . . .

in violation of the laws of the State in which they are committed or of the United States.

261. The Panel determined that "the Travel Act prohibits gambling activity that entails the supply of gambling and betting services by 'mail or any facility' to the extent that such supply is undertaken by a 'business enterprise involving gambling' that is prohibited under state law and provided that the other requirements in subparagraph (a) of the Travel Act have been met." The Panel further opined that the Travel Act prohibits service suppliers from supplying gambling and betting services through the mail, (and potentially other means of delivery), as well as services operations and service output through the mail (and potentially other means of delivery), in such a way as to amount to a "zero" quota on one or several means of delivery included in mode 1. For these reasons, the Panel found that "the Travel Act contains a limitation 'in the form of numerical quotas' within the meaning of Article XVI:2(a) and a limitation' in the form of a quota' within the meaning of Article XVI:2(c)."

262. The Panel considered the relevant part of the Illegal Gambling Business Act to be the following:

(a) Whoever conducts, finances, manages, supervises, directs or owns all or part of an illegal gambling business shall be fined under this title or imprisoned not more than five years, or both.

(b) As used in this section –

(1) 'illegal gambling business' means a gambling business which –

(i) is a violation of the law of a State or political subdivision in which it is conducted;

(ii) involves five or more persons who conduct, finance, manage, supervise, direct, or own all or part of such business; and

(iii) has been or remains in substantially continuous operation for a period in excess of thirty days or has a gross revenue of $2,000 in any single day.

(2) 'gambling' includes but is not limited to pool-selling, bookmaking, maintaining slot machines, roulette wheels or dice tables, and conducting lotteries, policy, bolita or numbers games, or selling chances therein.

263. The Panel then determined that because the IGBA "prohibits the conduct, finance, management, supervision, direction or ownership of all or part of a 'gambling business' that violates state law, it effectively prohibits the supply of gambling and betting services through at least one and potentially all means of delivery included in mode 1 by such businesses"; that this prohibition concerned service suppliers, service operations and service output; and that, accordingly, the IGBA "contains a limitation 'in the form of numerical quotas' within the meaning of Article XVI:2(a) and a limitation 'in the form of a quota' within the meaning of Article XVI:2(c)."

264. The United States' appeal of the Panel's findings with respect to the consistency of its measures with sub-paragraphs (a) and (c) of Article XVI:2 rests on two pillars: (i) that the Panel erred in interpreting those provisions; and (ii) that the measures at issue do not contain any limitations that explicitly take the form of numerical quotas or designated numerical units. The United States does *not* appeal the Panel's findings as to the various activities that are prohibited under these statutes. We have upheld the Panel's interpretation of sub-paragraphs (a) and (c) of Article XVI:2 and, in particular, its determination that these provisions encompass measures equivalent to a zero quota. In these circumstances, the fact that the Wire Act, the Travel Act and the IGBA do not explicitly use numbers, or the word "quota", in imposing their respective prohibitions, does not mean, as the United States contends, that the measures are beyond the reach of Article XVI:2(a) and (c). As a result, there is no ground for disturbing the above findings made by the Panel.

265. We have upheld the Panel's finding that the United States' Schedule to the GATS includes a specific commitment in respect of gambling and betting services. In that Schedule, the United States has inscribed "None" in the first row of the market access column for subsector 10.D. In these circumstances, and for the reasons given in this section of our Report, we also *uphold* the Panel's ultimate finding, in paragraph 7.2(b)(i) of the Panel Report, that, by maintaining the Wire Act, the Travel Act, and the Illegal Gambling Business Act, the United States acts inconsistently with its obligations under Article XVI:1 and Article XVI:2(a) and (c) of the GATS.

... ...

Briefly summarising the extract, the Appellate Body found violations of both Article XVI:2(a) and XVI:2(c). The sub-section (a) finding was based on the view that the US measures constitute limitations on the number of service suppliers through a ban on certain means of delivery that acts as a numerical quota of zero. Similarly, the sub-section

(c) finding was based on the view that the measures constituted limitations on the number of service operations or output through a ban on certain means of delivery that acts as a zero quota.

As noted above, the underlying purpose of the prohibitions on the market access measures listed in Article XVI:2 is hard to discern. As a result, interpretation of specific terms can be difficult. Here, a key issue was how broadly to interpret the reference to 'in the form of numerical quotas' in Article XVI:2(a) and 'designated numerical units in the form of quotas' in Article XVI:2(c). The United States argued that these provisions cover only measures that actually specify a numeric quantity of service suppliers, or service operations or output. Thus, it asserted, a *ban* on a certain method of service supply is not covered because it does not specify a numeric quantity, even though the 'effect' of the measure may limit the supply of the service through this method to zero. The panel and Appellate Body rejected this argument. The panel's finding on this issue was that such a ban is, in effect, a 'zero quota', and is therefore covered by these provisions.[21] The Appellate Body agreed with the panel and upheld the finding of violation.[22]

The full scope of the panel's and Appellate Body's findings is unclear at this point. It may take further disputes in this area to flesh out the precise boundaries of the market access obligations, in particular in relation to areas such as domestic regulation under Article VI of the GATS. One concern is that the interpretation in *Gambling* could lead to the prohibition of some legitimate regulations, targeting consumer protection for example. In its appellant's submission, the United States argued that the panel's interpretation could lead to attempts at domestic regulation of e-mail 'spam' being found in violation of GATS Article XVI where Members have made commitments on advertising services.[23] The Appellate Body did not address this issue, but the United States' concerns seem justifiable. The panel's findings emphasised that a 'zero quota' on 'one, several or all means' of delivery was prohibited by Article XVI. Thus, arguably, under this finding any regulation that bans a particular method of service delivery, such as e-mail, would constitute a 'zero quota', in violation of Article XVI:2(a) and (c). In essence, this approach converts certain regulations that govern the means of service delivery from 'qualitative' regulations covered by Article VI of the GATS into 'quantitative' regulations covered by Article XVI. The Appellate Body's views on this point are unclear. While it quoted the panel's language relating to 'one, several or all means', it also noted that this issue had not been appealed.[24]

On the other hand, the United States' interpretation, under which only measures that specify a numeric quantity are covered, is somewhat narrow, and could allow Members to evade their GATS commitments by simply banning a certain method of service delivery through ostensibly legitimate regulations as a substitute for imposing a numerical quota.

(b) National Treatment

The GATS provisions on national treatment are set out in Article XVII, which states:

---

[21] Panel Report, *US—Gambling Services*, paras 6.362–6.365.

[22] Appellate Body Report, *US—Gambling Services*, paras 224–39.

[23] See para 128 of US appellant's submission, available at www.ustr.gov/assets/Trade_Agreements/Monitoring_Enforcement/Dispute_Settlement/WTO/Dispute_Settlement_Listings/asset_upload_file50_5581.pdf (accessed on 1 Aug 2007).

[24] Appellate Body Report, *US—Gambling Services*, para 220.

1. In the sectors inscribed in its Schedule, and subject to any conditions and qualifications set out therein, each Member shall accord to services and service suppliers of any other Member, in respect of all measures affecting the supply of services, treatment no less favourable than that it accords to its own like services and service suppliers.

2. A Member may meet the requirement of paragraph 1 by according to services and service suppliers of any other Member, either formally identical treatment or formally different treatment to that it accords to its own like services and service suppliers.

3. Formally identical or formally different treatment shall be considered to be less favourable if it modifies the conditions of competition in favour of services or service suppliers of the Member compared to like services or service suppliers of any other Member.

Thus, as noted, pursuant to Article XVII:1, national treatment applies only where commitments have been scheduled. Turning to the substance, this provision is worded differently from the GATT Article III obligations. In effect, Article XVII of the GATS appears to codify some of the GATT Article III jurisprudence through its explicit statement that both formally identical and formally different treatment is covered, and its reference to modification of the 'conditions of competition'.

Article XVII has been the subject of some interpretation in the case law. However, we will not go into detail regarding Article XVII, but simply note that, as with GATT Article III, there are a number of views as to the meaning of non-discrimination, and thus the interpretation and application of Article XVII may not always be clear and consistent.

One important difference between the GATT and the GATS, as noted above, is the differences in modes of delivery. For the GATT, there is only one mode of delivery: cross-border. For the GATS, however, there are four modes of delivery, as explained earlier in this chapter. The question arises how the GATS national treatment obligations should apply to foreign services or services suppliers using different modes. Recall that commitments are made for each individual mode. Thus, there could be a situation where the only national treatment commitment is for one mode, for example, cross-border supply. In this situation, examination of a claim of violation of the national treatment provisions would require a comparison of the foreign service or service supplier at issue with the various competing domestic services and service suppliers, to determine whether they are 'like'. The four modes do not apply to service supply by domestic entities, so the modes are not directly relevant for this aspect of the comparison. Rather, the characteristics of the foreign service or service supplier at issue must be compared with those of the particular domestic service or service supplier at issue. The means of service supply will certainly be a factor in considering 'likeness', but its relevance and impact will vary depending on the service at issue.

(c) Additional Commitments

Article XVIII of the GATS states that 'Members may negotiate commitments with respect to measures affecting trade in services not subject to scheduling under Articles XVI or XVII, including those regarding qualifications, standards or licensing matters', and that '[s]uch commitments shall be inscribed in a Member's Schedule'. A prominent example of such commitments is the so-called Telecoms Reference Paper, which contains 'a set of pro-competitive regulatory principles applicable to the telecommunications sector'.[25] A number of WTO Members included this Paper as an 'additional commitment' in their GATS schedules, and Mexico's implementation of these commitments was challenged successfully by the United States in *Mexico—Telecoms*.

(d) Withdrawal of Commitments

As with tariff concessions under the GATT, there is a mechanism for modifying or withdrawing GATS commitments. They cannot simply be removed, of course. Pursuant to the process set out in GATS Article XXI, a Member may choose to modify or withdraw a commitment by offering some kind of compensatory trade liberalisation. The existence of this possibility illustrates the importance of balanced trade liberalisation reflected in WTO rules. The WTO does not prohibit all protectionism, but rather aims to achieve a degree of trade liberalization that all Members find acceptable.

VI. CLOSING THOUGHTS

GATS has become a fairly controversial part of the WTO, and it has been a focal point of many of the WTO's critics. There are two aspects of the GATS that are often raised in this regard.

First, it has been suggested that the continued push for trade liberalisation in certain sectors will lead to the *privatisation* and *deregulation* of sectors that are often government-owned, with negative consequences for certain segments of society. Clearly, the merits of privatisation and deregulation as a policy choice are controversial issues. However, it is less clear whether the GATS promotes these policies. On the one hand, governments are only bound by the commitments they make under the GATS, so there is no need to privatise or deregulate if the government does not wish to. As an example of where this issue has arisen, the global financial crisis of 2008–09 led to calls for governments to regulate the financial sector more strictly. During the discussion of possible regulations, the issue of whether such regulation would be consistent with the GATS was raised (that is, whether the GATS would prevent such regulation). The various substantive rules above—Article VI (domestic regulation), Article XVI (market access) and Article XVII (national treatment)—were all mentioned in relation to concerns that proposed financial regulation might conflict with the GATS. In response, defenders of the system pointed to a so-called 'prudential carve out' in Article 2(a) of the GATS Annex on Financial Services, which reads as follows:

> 2. Domestic Regulation
>
> (a) Notwithstanding any other provisions of the Agreement, a Member shall not be prevented from taking measures for prudential reasons, including for the protection of investors, depositors, policy holders or persons to whom a fiduciary duty is owed by a financial service supplier, or to ensure the integrity and stability of the financial system. Where such measures do not conform with the provisions of the Agreement, they shall not be used as a means of avoiding the Member's commitments or obligations under the Agreement.

---

[25] Panel Report, *Mexico—Telecoms*, para 7.5.

As is often the case with trade agreements (and, to be fair, domestic laws as well), the meaning of the text is not completely clear. It seems that in drafting this provision the negotiators had in mind some kind of exception for financial regulation designed to protect consumers of financial services. But whether this particular language was broad enough to allow for the necessary domestic regulation has been subject to debate. Unless and until a WTO complaint is brought on this matter, some uncertainty will remain.

A second area of concern for trade critics is the use of the *necessity standard* in the GATS. As discussed in this chapter as well as Chapter 9 on Article XX of the GATT, the 'necessity' standard under WTO rules has long been a source of criticism. In the late 1980s and early 1990s, the 'necessity' defence under the GATT exceptions was interpreted by GATT panels in a manner that allowed only the 'least-trade restrictive' measures, and this interpretation was considered by some to be extremely narrow and impossible to satisfy. In recent years, the Appellate Body appears to have loosened the standard a bit, taking into account factors such as the importance of the interests pursued. However, there is still a concern that the 'necessity' standard under discussion for 'Domestic Regulation' under GATS Article VI will make it very difficult for Members to adopt domestic regulations where there is any impact on foreign trade.

These concerns appear to have some legitimacy, in two senses. First, there are genuine debates that need to take place as to what are the appropriate policies to pursue in terms of privatisation and deregulation and with regard to balancing trade and non-trade concerns. Secondly, with both the 'necessity' standard and the 'prudential carve-out', the scope of the legal standard is unclear. When the rules are uncertain, it becomes difficult for governments to know what they can and cannot do, and it creates an atmosphere that lends itself to exaggeration in terms of the effects the GATS may have on domestic policy-making.

VII. QUESTIONS

1. Would a tariff duty constitute a measure that 'affects' trade in services based on its impact on the ability to distribute the product?

2. Under GATS Article I:3(c), a service supplied in the exercise of governmental authority means any service which is supplied neither on a commercial basis, nor in competition with one or more service suppliers. Based on this provision, are taxpayer-supported, government-run schools 'supplied in the exercise of governmental authority'?

3. Under the Annex on Financial Services, paragraph 1(b)(ii) states that 'services supplied in the exercise of governmental authority' includes 'activities forming part of a statutory system of social security or public retirement plans'. However, paragraph 1(c) qualifies this provision by stating: '[f]or the purposes of subparagraph 3(b) of Article I of the Agreement, if a Member allows any of the activities referred to in subparagraphs (b)(ii) or (b)(iii) of this paragraph to be conducted by its financial service suppliers in competition with a public entity or a financial service supplier, "services" shall include such activities'. If the proposal in the United States that part of social security contributions could be invested in private accounts were to become law, would the

social security system still constitute 'services supplied in the exercise of governmental authority'?

4. If domestic regulation is very burdensome on trade, but in a non-discriminatory manner, should trade rules be concerned with it all?

5. Based on the Appellate Body's findings in *US—Gambling Services*, would a government measure that banned the placing of any bets by all US citizens over the internet violate GATS Article XVI (Market Access) or Article XVII (National Treatment), assuming that a full commitment had been made for the cross-border supply mode? If it were found to be in violation, could it be justified under Article XIV?

6. Does the GATS encourage privatisation and deregulation? If so: (1) is this a good policy and (2) does it fall in with the proper mission of the WTO?

7. In determining whether services or service suppliers are 'like', how much of a consideration is the method (not mode) of supply? For example, are gambling services supplied over the internet 'like' gambling services supplied in a casino?

8. In paragraph 6.305, the panel in *US—Gambling* stated: '[u]nder Article VI and Article XVI, measures are either of the type covered by the disciplines of Article XVI or are domestic regulations relating to qualification requirements and procedures, technical standards and licensing requirements subject to the specific provisions of Article VI. Thus, Articles VI:4 and VI:5 on the one hand and XVI on the other hand are mutually exclusive.' What is the relationship of the Article VI:4 and Article VI:5 rules on 'domestic regulation', on the one hand, and the Article XVI rules on 'market access' on the other hand? Was the panel correct that these are mutually exclusive categories? Is there some overlap? Does the text of these provisions clarify the relationship at all? Can you think of measures that might fall within both?

9. What is the relationship between GATS Articles VI (domestic regulation), XVI (market access) and XVII (national treatment)? How much overlap is there between the three? Why do you think the GATS drafters thought a simple national treatment requirement was insufficient?

15

Trade and Investment

I. INTRODUCTION

There are a number of close links between trade and investment. For instance, investment and trade are the two ways to sell in foreign markets. With goods, a company can either export its products to a foreign country or open a factory in that country to produce and sell there. Thus, the goals of trade and investment overlap to some extent. In addition, foreign investment often spurs an increase in trade. As multinational corporations seek the ideal location for their production, they often plan for that production to service regional or even global demand. As a result, foreign investment often leads to increased exports from the host country. Furthermore, in some instances it is trade barriers (such as tariffs) that lead to foreign investment, as companies may use investment as a way to sell in a foreign market so as to get round these barriers (and conversely countries may use trade barriers to encourage foreign investment). The rising number of preferential trade agreements makes these kinds of production shifts more likely, as companies often find themselves up against competitors who have preferential access to a particular foreign market.

In this chapter, we discuss the various ways investment rules have have been addressed in the multilateral system. We begin with the issue of trade and investment in the GATT/WTO, focusing on the Agreement on Trade-Related Investment Measures (TRIMs Agreement). Next, we look at the issue of investment and trade outside the WTO context, such as in recent bilateral and regional agreements and an attempt by the OECD to negotiate a multilateral agreement on investment (MAI). Finally, we conclude by looking briefly at the treatment of these issues in the Doha Round.

II. INVESTMENT IN THE GATT/WTO

The ITO Charter (discussed in Chapter 2) contained several meaningful provisions on the treatment of foreign investment as part of a chapter on economic development. However, the Charter was never ratified and only some of its provisions were incorporated into the GATT, and investment was not included. The issue soon resurfaced, though, as the GATT CONTRACTING PARTIES adopted a resolution in 1955 on International Investment for

Economic Development, in which they 'urged' countries to conclude bilateral agreements protecting foreign investment as a way to encourage greater trade.[1] As we will see later in this chapter, the modern Bilateral Investment Treaties (BITs), which comprehensively regulate investment, began to be negotiated shortly thereafter and continue to have a significant presence today.

While GATT rules did not have much more to say about investment regulation in and of itself in the ensuing years, a 1984 GATT panel ruling made clear that measures related to investment USwere covered to the extent they affected trade. In the *Canada—Administration of the Foreign Investment Review Act (FIRA)* case, a GATT dispute settlement panel considered a complaint by the US relating to certain types of undertakings which were required from foreign investors as conditions for the approval of investment projects. These undertakings required the purchase of certain products from domestic sources (local content requirements) and to the export of a certain amount or percentage of output (export performance requirements). The panel concluded that the local content requirements were inconsistent with the national treatment obligation of Article III:4, but that the export performance requirements were not inconsistent with GATT obligations. The panel emphasised that at issue in the dispute before it was the consistency with the GATT of specific trade-related measures taken by Canada under its foreign investment legislation and not Canada's right to regulate foreign investment per se.

During the Uruguay Round, there were some limited efforts to bring investment more fully into the GATT system. First, a specific negotiating group addressed 'trade related' investment measures (along the lines of the reasoning of the *FIRA* panel). The result was a very limited agreement, the Agreement on Trade-Related Investment Measures (the 'TRIMs Agreement'). Secondly, investment is also addressed in the GATS through the commitments offered by Members under the 'commercial presence' mode. This issue was covered in Chapter 14 and we will not discuss it further here.

In this section, we discuss the Uruguay Round negotiations in this area of TRIMs; the substance of the TRIMs Agreement; and some issues related to TRIMs that have arisen in WTO dispute settlement.

(a) The TRIMs Agreement Negotiations

Hesitant to add investment as a negotiating topic, the GATT Contracting Parties carefully worded the Punta del Este Ministerial Declaration (launching the Uruguay Round) language relating to investment measures as follows:

> Following an examination of the operation of GATT Articles related to the trade-restrictive and trade-distorting effects of investment measures, negotiations should elaborate, as appropriate, further provisions that may be necessary to avoid such adverse effects on trade.[2]

Based upon this statement, it is clear that the Uruguay Round negotiations were not intended to be used to draft a comprehensive agreement on investment measures per se, but were only intended to address the 'trade-distorting' effects of such measures. Even with this limitation, though, the Uruguay Round negotiations in this area were the subject

---

[1] International Investment for Economic Development Resolution, 4 Mar 1955, GATT BISD (3rd Supp) 49–50.
[2] Ministerial Declaration on the Uruguay Round (MIN.DEC, 20 September 1986).

of much debate, as the negotiators disagreed on the coverage, scope and nature of the potential TRIMS Agreement.

Arguing that TRIMs were a significant intrusion into a properly functioning liberal trade regime, most developed countries believed that the TRIMS Agreement should prohibit a wide range of measures, going far beyond merely prohibiting the local content requirements that the GATT panel in *Canada—FIRA* found to be inconsistent with GATT Article III. For instance, the EC proposed a comprehensive agreement which included clauses on local content requirements, export performance requirements, trade balancing requirements, product mandating requirements, domestic sales restrictions, foreign exchange and remittance restrictions and investment incentives.[3] The US proposal was even more far reaching, as it included potential clauses on technology transfer requirements and local equity restrictions.[4] Another key player in the negotiations, Japan, supported the entirety of the US proposals, less the clauses on local equity restrictions.[5]

On the other hand, most developing countries opposed the extension of coverage beyond that addressed in *Canada—FIRA*, partly on the basis that TRIMs are necessary to counter the abusive practices of multinational corporations, and that an agreement addressing TRIMS without an agreement regulating, inter alia, certain business practices (part of which would include competition policy) would result in an unbalanced system. These same developing countries also objected to an agreement on an issue which, in their view, did not have direct and significant adverse trade effects, which limited the ability of nations to channel foreign investment to national priority objectives, and that introduced other restrictive clauses which could possibly limit a government's response to an emergency or crisis.

(b) The TRIMs Agreement

The compromise eventually emerging from the negotiations most resembles the developing country position. Generally speaking, the TRIMS Agreement merely interprets and clarifies the GATT provisions on national treatment for imported goods (Article III) and on quantitative restrictions on imports or exports (Article XI) as they relate to investment measures, and does not cover many of the specific TRIMs that were identified by the developed countries and discussed in the Uruguay Round negotiations. Thus, the agreement has a limited focus which relates merely to existing GATT disciplines on trade in goods; it does not regulate foreign investment per se; and it does not address measures such as local equity requirements, technology transfer and licensing requirements, local manufacturing requirements, personnel entry restrictions and local employment requirements.

The objectives of the Agreement, as stated in the Preamble, include 'the expansion and progressive liberalisation of world trade and to facilitate investment across international frontiers so as to increase the economic growth of all trading partners, particularly developing country members, while ensuring free competition'. The limitation of the TRIMS Agreement to those measures 'affecting trade in goods' is clearly stated in Article 1 of the

---

[3] EM Graham, *Global Corporations and National Governments* (Washington, DC, Peterson Institute, 1996) 72.

[4] KE Maskus and DR Eby, 'Developing New Rules and Disciplines on Trade-Related Investment Measures' (1990) 13 *World Economy* 523, 527.

[5] Graham, above n 3, 70.

Agreement. Much like other WTO agreements, the principles of national treatment, prohibition on quantitative restrictions, and transparency run through the TRIMs Agreement.

The main substantive provisions are found in Article 2.1 of the Agreement and an Illustrative List of TRIMs set out in an Annex. Article 2.1 prohibits Members from applying any TRIMs inconsistently with Articles III and XI of the GATT. While the term 'TRIMs' is left undefined, in lieu of a definition, the Agreement contains in an annex an Illustrative List of investment measures that are inconsistent with Article III:4 or Article XI:1 of GATT. The Illustrative List states:

> 1. TRIMs that are inconsistent with the obligation of national treatment provided for in paragraph 4 of Article III of GATT 1994 include those which are mandatory or enforceable under domestic law or under administrative rulings, or compliance with which is necessary to obtain an advantage, and which require:
>
> > (a) the purchase or use by an enterprise of products of domestic origin or from any domestic source, whether specified in terms of particular products, in terms of volume or value of products, or in terms of a proportion of volume or value of its local production; or
> >
> > (b) that an enterprise's purchases or use of imported products be limited to an amount related to the volume or value of local products that it exports.
>
> 2. TRIMs that are inconsistent with the obligation of general elimination of quantitative restrictions provided for in paragraph 1 of Article XI of GATT 1994 include those which are mandatory or enforceable under domestic law or under administrative rulings, or compliance with which is necessary to obtain an advantage, and which restrict:
>
> > (a) the importation by an enterprise of products used in or related to its local production, generally or to an amount related to the volume or value of local production that it exports;
> >
> > (b) the importation by an enterprise of products used in or related to its local production by restricting its access to foreign exchange to an amount related to the foreign exchange inflows attributable to the enterprise; or
> >
> > (c) the exportation or sale for export by an enterprise of products, whether specified in terms of particular products, in terms of volume or value of products, or in terms of a proportion of volume or value of its local production.

Investment measures identified in paragraph 1 of the Illustrative List concern the purchase or use of products by an enterprise. The WTO website explains paragraph 1 as follows:

> Paragraph 1(a) of the Illustrative List covers local content TRIMs, which require the purchase or use by an enterprise of products of domestic origin or domestic source (local content requirements) while paragraph 1(b) covers trade-balancing TRIMs, which limit the purchase or use of imported products by an enterprise to an amount related to the volume or value of local products that it exports. In both cases, the inconsistency with Article III:4 of GATT 1994 results from the fact that the measure subjects the purchase or use by an enterprise of imported products to less favourable conditions than the purchase or use of domestic products.[6]

The investment measures listed in paragraph 2 concern the importation or exportation of products by an enterprise. The WTO explains:

---

[6] WTO, 'Technical Information on Trade and Investment', available at www.wto.org/English/tratop_e/invest_e/invest_info_e.htm.

Paragraph 2(a) of the Illustrative List covers measures which limit the importation by an enterprise of products used in its local production in general terms or to an amount related to the volume or value of local production exported by the enterprise. There is a conceptual similarity between this paragraph and paragraph 1(b) in that they both cover trade-balancing measures. The difference is that paragraph 1(b) deals with internal measures affecting the purchase or use of products after they have been imported, while paragraph 2(a) deals with border measures affecting the importation of products.

Measures identified in paragraph 2(b) of the list involve a restriction of imports in the form of a foreign exchange balancing requirement, whereby the ability to import products used in or related to local production is limited by restricting the enterprise's access to foreign exchange to an amount related to the foreign exchange inflows attributable to the enterprise.

Finally, paragraph 2(c) covers measures involving restrictions on the exportation of or sale for export by an enterprise, whether specified in terms of particular products, volume or value of products or in terms of a proportion of volume or value of its local production. Since paragraph 2 applies the provisions of Article XI:1 of GATT 1994, it deals only with measures that restrict exports. Other measures relating to exports, such as export incentives and export performance requirements, are therefore not covered by the TRIMs Agreement.[7]

The Agreement contains certain transparency obligations. For instance, Article 5.1 requires Members to notify the Council for Trade in Goods of any TRIMs that are not in conformity with the Agreement. Article 5.2 obliges developed country Members to eliminate those notified measures within two years after the date of the entry into force of the WTO Agreement, while developing countries had five years to eliminate the measures, and least developed countries had seven years to eliminate the inconsistent measures.[8] However, Article 5.3 provides for the possible extension of the transitional periods for developing countries which demonstrate particular difficulties in implementing the provisions of the Agreement. In a sense, these transitional provisions allowed developing countries to impose TRIMs that might, in the absence of the TRIMs Agreement, have been found inconsistent with Article III:4 or Article XI:1 of the GATT.

(c) Dispute Settlement

To date, issues relating to the TRIMS Agreement have been raised in several disputes, most notably *Indonesia—Autos*, *Canada—Wheat*, *Canada—Autos* and *EC—Bananas*. The following extract from *Indonesia—Autos* provides some insights into the relationship between the TRIMs Agreement and Article III:4 of the GATT, as well as the process by which a panel analyses issues under the TRIMs Agreement.

Panel Report, *Indonesia—Certain Measures Affecting the Automobile Industry*, Adopted 23 July 1998, WT/DS54,55,59,64/R

D. *Claims of Local Content Requirements*

14.58 The European Communities and the United States claim that the 1993 car programme, by providing for local content requirements linked to tax benefits for finished cars incorporating a

---

[7] *Ibid.*

[8] TRIMs introduced less than 180 days before the date of the entry into force of the WTO Agreement do not benefit from these transitional periods. Thus, the transitional provisions of the TRIMs Agreement do not permit the introduction of new TRIMs that are inconsistent with the Agreement.

certain percentage value of domestic products, and to customs duty benefits for imported parts and components used in cars incorporating a certain percentage value of domestic products, violates the provisions of Article 2 of the TRIMs Agreement, and Article III:4 of the GATT.

14.59 Japan, the European Communities and the United States also claim that the 1996 car programme, by providing for local content requirements linked to tax benefits for National Cars (which by definition incorporate a certain percentage value of domestic products), and to customs duty benefits for imported parts and components used in National Cars, violates the provisions of Article 2 of the TRIMs Agreement and Article III:4 of the GATT.

...

14.63 As to which claims, those under Article III:4 of GATT or Article 2 of the TRIMs Agreement, to examine first, we consider that we should first examine the claims under the TRIMs Agreement since the TRIMs Agreement is more specific than Article III:4 as far as the claims under consideration are concerned. A similar issue was presented in *Bananas III*, where the Appellate Body discussed the relationship between Article X of GATT and Article 1.3 of the Licensing Agreement and concluded that the Licensing Agreement being more specific it should have been applied first. This is also in line with the approach of the panel and the Appellate Body in the *Hormones* dispute, where the measure at issue was examined first under the SPS Agreement since the measure was alleged to be an SPS measure.

2. The application of the TRIMS Agreement

14.64 Article 2.1 of the TRIMs Agreement provides that

"... no Member shall apply any TRIM that is inconsistent with the provisions of Article III or Article XI of GATT 1994."

By its terms, Article 2.1 requires two elements to be shown to establish a violation thereof: first, the existence of a TRIM; second, that TRIM is inconsistent with Article III or Article XI of GATT. No claims have been raised with reference to a violation of Article XI of GATT.

....

14.66 We note also that Article 2.2 of the TRIMs Agreement provides:

"2.2 An Illustrative List of TRIMs that are inconsistent with the obligations of national treatment provided for in paragraph 4 of Article III of GATT 1994 . . . is contained in the Annex to this Agreement.

....

(a) Are the Indonesian measures "investment measures"?

14.73 We note that the use of the broad term "investment measures" indicates that the TRIMs Agreement is not limited to measures taken specifically in regard to *foreign* investment. Contrary to India's argument, we find that nothing in the TRIMs Agreement suggests that the nationality of the ownership of enterprises subject to a particular measure is an element in deciding whether that measure is covered by the Agreement. We therefore find without textual support in the TRIMs Agreement the argument that since the TRIMs Agreement is basically designed to govern and provide a level playing field for foreign investment, measures relating to internal taxes or subsides cannot be construed to be a trade-related investment measure. We recall in this context that internal tax advantages or subsidies are only one of many types of advantages which may be tied to a local content requirement which is a principal focus of the TRIMs Agreement. The TRIMs Agreement is not concerned with subsidies and internal taxes as such but rather with local content requirements, compliance with which may be encouraged through providing any type of advantage. Nor, in any case, do we see why an internal measure would necessarily not govern the treatment of foreign investment.

14.74 We next consider whether the Indonesian measures are investment measures. In this regard, we consider the following extracts (emphases added) from the official Indonesian legislation relevant and instructive.

14.75 With regard to the 1993 car programme, we note:

– The "considerations section" of the Decree of the Ministry of Industry announcing the 1993 car programme states:

"a. that within the framework of supporting and promoting the development of the automotive industry and/or the component industry in the future, it is deemed necessary to regulate the local content levels of domestically produced motor vehicles or components in connection with the grant of incentives in the imposition of import duty rates;

b. that in order to further strengthen domestic industrial development by taking into account the trend of technological advance and the increase of the capability and mastering of industrial design and engineering, it is necessary to improve the relevant existing regulations already laid down;"

– The "considerations section" of the 1995 amendment to the 1993 car programme states:

"That in the framework of further promoting of the development of the motor vehicles industry and /or domestically produced components, it is considered necessary to amend . . ."

14.76 With regard to the February 1996 car programme, we note the following:

– The title of the Presidential Instruction for the National Car programme (No.2) is "The Development of the National Automobile Industry".

– Paragraph a) of the "Considering" section of the Government Regulation No.20 states:

"that in the effort to promote the growth of the domestic automotive industry, it is deemed necessary to enact regulations concerning the Sales Tax on Luxury Goods upon the delivery of domestically produced motor vehicles".

– In addition, the State Minister for Mobilization of Investment Funds/Chairman of the Investment Coordinating Board issued a decree entitled "Investment Regulations within the Framework of the Realisation of the Establishment of the National Automobile Industry" which emphasized that the new measures were intended to promote investment, stating in its fifth considering:

"5. that it is therefore necessary to issue *a decree for the regulation of investment in the national automobile industry*."

– Article 2 of that same Investment Regulation by the Minister of State for Mobilization of Investment Funds/Chairman of the Investment Coordinating Board provides:

"In order *to realise the development of the national automobile industry* as meant in Article 1:

1. . . .

2. *In the endeavour to realise the development of such national car industry, the investment approval will be issued to the automobile industry sector with tax facilities in accordance with legal provisions enacted specifically for such purpose.*"

– The Decision relating to the investment facilities regarding the Determination of PT. Timor Putra National to Establish and Produce a National Car, entitled "Decision of the State Minister for the Mobilization of Investment Funds/Chairman of the Capital Investment Coordinating Board" states:

"1. That *in implementing a national car industry it is deemed necessary to determine investment approval* for a car industry which will build and produce a national car.

2. That in the framework of investment for the car industry, PT.Timor Putra National has submitted an application and working program to build a national car industry and *has obtained domestic investment approval* (PMDN) NO.607/PMDN/1995, dated 9 November 1995".

14.77 With regard to the June 1996 car programme, we note that the "Considering" section of the Decree of the President of the Republic No. 4267677 on the Extension (June) to the February 1996 car programme provides:

"a. that the development of the national car is aimed at improving the nation's self-reliance . . . and to achieve this solid preparations and continuous support are necessary;

b. that the preparation for domestic production of national cars require the *availability of huge financing* and therefore will be carried out in stages;

c. that in connection with the preparations, it is considered necessary to establish a policy on the implementation stage of the production of national cars."

– The "Considering" section of the Government Regulation No. 3667678 states:

"That within the *framework of promoting the development of the automotive industry in the increased use of domestically produced automotive components*, it is deemed necessary to grant Sales Tax on Luxury Goods facilities to the group of luxury goods upon delivery of certain motor vehicles"

– The Elucidation to the Government Regulation No. 36 states:

"Within the *framework of speeding up the realisation of production of national motor vehicles using domestically made automotive components, it is necessary to promote the domestic automotive industry* in order to further its growth particularly in the face of global competition. *One of the endeavours which can be exerted is the provision of a tax incentive in the form of exemption* from the assessment of Sales Tax on Luxury Goods on the delivery of certain motor vehicles which have achieved certain levels of local content."

14.78 We note also that Indonesia indicates that the objectives of the National Car programme include the following:

– To improve the competitiveness of local companies and strengthen overall industrial development;

– To develop the capacity of multiple-source auto parts and components;

– To encourage the development of the automotive industry and the automotive component industry;

– To bring about major structural changes in the Indonesian automobile industry;

– To encourage the transfer of technology and contribute to large-scale job creation;

– To encourage car companies to increase their local content, resulting in a rapid growth of investment in the automobile industry.

14.79 Indonesia has also stated that PT TPN is a "domestic capital investment company"

14.80 On the basis of our reading of these measures applied by Indonesia under the 1993 and the 1996 car programmes, which have investment objectives and investment features and which refer to investment programmes, we find that these measures are aimed at encouraging the development of a local manufacturing capability for finished motor vehicles and parts and components in Indonesia. Inherent to this objective is that these measures necessarily have a significant impact on investment in these sectors. For this reason, we consider that these measures fall within any reasonable interpretation of the term "investment measures". We do not intend to provide an overall definition of what constitutes an investment measure. We emphasize that our characterization of the measures as "investment measures" is based on an examination of the manner in which the measures at issue in this case relate to investment. There may be other measures which qualify as investment measures within the meaning of the TRIMs Agreement because they relate to investment in a different manner.

14.81 With respect to the arguments of Indonesia that the measures at issue are not investment measures because the Indonesian Government does not regard the programmes as investment programmes and because the measures have not been adopted by the authorities responsible for investment policy, we believe that there is nothing in the text of the TRIMs Agreement to suggest that a measure is not an investment measure simply on the grounds that a Member does not characterize the measure as such, or on the grounds that the measure is not explicitly adopted as an investment regulation. In any event, we note that some of the regulations and decisions adopted pursuant to these car programmes were adopted by investment bodies.

(b) *Are the Indonesian measures "trade-related"?*

14.82 We now have to determine whether these investment measures are "trade-related". We consider that, if these measures are local content requirements, they would necessarily be "trade-related" because such requirements, by definition, always favour the use of domestic products over imported products, and therefore affect trade.

(c) *Illustrative List of the TRIMs Agreement*

14.83 An examination of whether these measures are covered by Item (1) of the Illustrative List of TRIMs annexed to the TRIMs Agreement, which refers amongst other situations to measures with local content requirements, will not only indicate whether they are trade-related but also whether they are inconsistent with Article III:4 and thus in violation of Article 2.1 of the TRIMs Agreement.

ANNEX

ILLUSTRATIVE LIST

1. TRIMs that are inconsistent with the obligation of national treatment provided for in paragraph 4 of Article III of GATT 1994 include those which are mandatory or enforceable under domestic law or under administrative rulings, or compliance with which is necessary to obtain an advantage, and which require:

(a) the purchase or use by an enterprise of products of domestic origin or from any domestic source, whether specified in terms of particular products, in terms of volume or value of products, or in terms of a proportion of volume or value of its local production;"

14.85 We note that all the various decrees and regulations implementing the Indonesian car programmes operate in the same manner. They provide for tax advantages on finished motor vehicles using a certain percentage value of local content and additional customs duty advantages on imports of parts and components to be used in finished motor vehicles using a certain percentage value of local content. We also note that under the June 1996 car programme, the local content envisaged in the February 1996 car programme could be performed through an undertaking by the foreign producer of National Cars to counter-purchase Indonesian parts and components.

14.86 For instance, the Decision to issue the Decree of the Minister of Industry Concerning The Determination of Local Content Levels of Domestically Made Motor Vehicles or Components attached to the Decree of the Ministry of Industry announcing the 1993681 car programme states in its Article 2:

"(1) The Automotive Industry and/or the Components Industry *may obtain certain Incentives* within the framework of importing needed Components, Sub-Components, basic materials and semi-Finished Goods, originating in one source as well as various sources (multi sourcing), *if the production has reached/can achieve certain Local Content levels.* . . .

(3) The *Local Content levels* of domestically made Motor Vehicles and/or Components which are *eligible for Incentives* including their Incentive rates shall be those listed in Attachment I to this decree." (emphasis added)

The Instruction of the President of the Republic of Indonesia No.2 of 1996 of the National Car programme (dated 19 February 1998) states in its "INSTRUCT . . . SECONDLY:

"WITHIN the framework of establishment of the National Car Industry:

1. The Minister of Industry and Trade will foster, guide and grant facilities in accordance with provisions of laws in effect such that the national car industry:

a. uses a brand name of its own;

b. uses components produced domestically as much as possible;

c. is able to export its products." (emphasis added)

More specifically Regulation No. 20/1996 established the following sales tax structure where passenger cars of more than 1600cc and jeeps with local content of less than 60% would pay 35% tax; passenger cars of less than 1600cc, jeeps with local content of more than 60%, and light commercial vehicles (other than jeeps using gas) would pay 20% tax; and National Cars would pay 0% tax.682 We recall that one of the requirements for designation as a "National Car" is that the local content rate must be 20% at the end of the first year, 40% at the end of the second year and 60% at the end of the third year.

14.87 We also note with reference to the June 1996 car programme, that the Decree of the President of the Republic of Indonesia Number 42 of 1996684 on the production of National Cars provides in Article 1:

"National Cars which are made overseas by Indonesian workers and fulfil the local content stipulated by the Minister of Industry and Trade will be treated equally to those made in Indonesia."

The Decree of the Minister of Industry and Trade adopted pursuant to this Presidential Decree 42 states in Articles 1, 2 and 3:

"Article 1

Within the framework of preparations, the production of national cars can be carried out overseas for a one-time maximum period of 1 (one) year on the condition that Indonesian made parts and components are used.

Article 2

The procurement of Indonesian made parts and components shall be performed through a system of counter purchase of parts and components of motor vehicles by the overseas company carrying out the production and re-exporting of national cars to Indonesia.

Article 3

The value of the Counter purchase referred to in Article 2 shall be fixed at the minimum of 25% (twenty-five percent) of the import value of the national cars assembled abroad (C&F value)".

14.88 We believe that under these measures compliance with the provisions for the purchase and use of particular products of domestic origin is necessary to obtain the tax and customs duty benefits on these car programmes, as referred to in Item 1(a) of the Illustrative List of TRIMs.

14.89 We need now to decide whether these tax and customs duty benefits are "advantages" in the meaning of the chapeau of paragraph 1 of that Illustrative List. In the context of the claims under Article III:4 of GATT, Indonesia has argued that the reduced customs duties are not internal regulations and as such cannot be covered by the wording of Article III:4. We do not consider that the matter before us in connection with Indonesia's obligations under the TRIMs Agreement is the customs duty relief as such but rather the internal regulations, i.e. the provisions on purchase and use of domestic products, compliance with which is necessary to obtain an advantage, which advantage here is the customs duty relief. The lower duty rates are clearly "advantages" in the meaning of the chapeau of the Illustrative List to the TRIMs Agreement and as such, we find that the Indonesian measures fall within the scope of the Item 1 of the Illustrative List of TRIMs.

14.90 Indonesia also argues that the local content requirements of its car programmes do not constitute classic local content requirements within the meaning of the *FIRA* panel (which involved a binding contract between the investor and the Government of Canada) because they leave companies free to decide from which source to purchase parts and components. We note that the Indonesian producers or assemblers of motor vehicles (or motor vehicle parts) must satisfy the local content targets of the relevant measures in order to take advantage of the customs duty and tax benefits offered by the Government. The wording of the Illustrative List of the TRIMs Agreement makes it clear that a simple advantage conditional on the use of domestic goods is considered to be a violation of Article 2 of the TRIMs Agreement even if the local content requirement is not binding as such. We note in addition that this argument has also been rejected in the Panel Report on *Parts and Components*.

14.91 We thus find that the tax and tariff benefits contingent on meeting local requirements under these car programmes constitute "advantages". Given this and our earlier analysis of whether these local content requirements are TRIMs and covered by the Illustrative List annexed to the TRIMs Agreement, we further find that they are in violation of Article 2.1 of the TRIMs Agreement.

14.92 We note that a violation of Article 2.1 of the TRIMs Agreement may be justified under Articles 3, 4 or 5 of the TRIMs Agreement. However, Indonesia has not invoked any of the general exceptions of GATT as referred to in Article 3 of the TRIMs Agreement, nor the provisions available to developing countries referred to in Article 4. In addition, Indonesia does not claim that the measures in dispute benefit from the transitional period under Article 5 of the TRIMs Agreement.

... ...

It is worth emphasising one aspect of this extract. Investment issues are generally talked about in the context of *foreign* investment, that is, where a company of one country invests in another country. However, in the context of certain TRIMs, such as local content requirements, the focus is not on the source of the investment, but rather on the trade effects of the investment. As a result, it could be argued that it should not matter whether the investment is foreign or domestic, as local content requirements will have a trade-distorting impact regardless of whether they are imposed on foreign or domestic investors. The *Indonesia—Autos* panel took this view, stating: '[w]e note that the use of the broad term "investment measures" indicates that the TRIMs Agreement is not limited to measures taken specifically in regard to *foreign* investment. Contrary to India's argument, we find that nothing in the TRIMs Agreement suggests that the nationality of the ownership of enterprises subject to a particular measure is an element in deciding whether that measure is covered by the Agreement'.[9]

III. INTERNATIONAL INVESTMENT REGULATION OUTSIDE THE WTO CONTEXT

(a) Bilateral Investment Treaties and Investment Provisions of Free Trade Agreements

UNCTAD provides the following definition of BITs:

> Bilateral investment treaties (BITs) are agreements between two countries for the reciprocal encouragement, promotion and protection of investments in each other's territories by companies based in either country. Treaties typically cover the following areas: scope and definition of investment, admission and establishment, national treatment, most-favoured-nation treatment, fair and equitable treatment, compensation in the event of expropriation or damage to the investment, guarantees of free transfers of funds, and dispute settlement mechanisms, both state-state and investor-state.[10]

Therefore, unlike the TRIMs Agreement, BITs are comprehensive agreements which cover a wide range of issues involving investment between nations. The modern bilateral investment treaty (BIT) dates back only to 1959, with the conclusion of an agreement between Germany and Pakistan. Since that time, and especially of late, the number of BITs has dramatically increased. While there were 385 BITs at the end of the 1980s, the number jumped to 1,857 (involving 173 nations) at the end of the 1990s.[11] By 2003, 2,265 BITs had been concluded, and at present there are more than 2,750 BITs in existence.[12] Additionally, a number of recent FTAs also have detailed sections on investment which, for all intents and purposes, are BITs. The following extract provides a historical overview of the development of BITs before briefly detailing several bilateral and regional FTAs and other agreements.

---

[9] Panel Report, *Indonesia—Autos*, para 14.73.

[10] UNCTAD, 'What are BITs?', available at www.unctadxi.org/templates/Page____1006.aspx.

[11] UNCTAD maintains a database of over 1800 BITs, available at www.unctadxi.org/templates/DocSearch____779.aspx.

[12] See UNCTAD, 'UNCTAD Analysis of BITS', available at www.unctadxi.org/templates/Page____1007.aspx.

**R Dattu, 'A Journey from Havana to Paris: The Fifty-Year Quest for the Elusive MAI'
(2000) 24 *Fordham International Law Journal* 275, 303–14**

A. Bilateral Investment Agreements

The precursor to the modern version of the bilateral investment treaty ("BIT") was the Treaty of Amity and Commerce signed between the United States and France in 1778, which governed their commercial relations. This was followed by a number of treaties of Friendship, Commerce and Navigation ("FCN") entered into by the United States prior to World War II, which also governed the commercial relations between the United States and each respective signatory. While the FCNs were mainly concerned with the shipping and trading rights and obligations of the parties, they also provided general obligations to protect the property of the nationals of the other state.

After World War II and Europe's economic recovery, European countries negotiated investment protection treaties with non-market economies and their former colonies. Germany signed the first of these Bilateral Investment Protection Agreements ("BIPAs") with Pakistan in 1959 and many other European countries followed thereafter.

While the United States increasingly began including provisions for the protection of investments in its FCN treaties after the war, the expansion of the European network of BIPAs was the driving force behind the BITs that the United States entered into in the 1960s and thereafter. The increasing number of BITs provided greater protection for United States nationals' investment in foreign countries. As of January 1997, however, the United States was not among the ten countries that had signed the largest number of BITs.

Since the 1960s, BITs—called BIPAs in Europe and Foreign Investment Protection and Promotion Agreements ("FIPAs") in Canada—have spread as the principal means of ensuring reciprocal protection of foreign, direct investment between countries. At the end of 1996, 155 countries had signed 1330 BITs, 822 of which had been concluded by developed countries. By 1999, the number of BITs signed was 1856. Of these 1856 BITs, the United States has signed 46 BITs, in addition to its commitments, vis-à-vis Canada and Mexico, with respect to foreign investment contained in Chapter 11 of NAFTA.

This web of bilateral agreements for the protection of investment offers each signatory reciprocal rights and obligations that are negotiated on a case-by-case basis in accordance with the needs and requirements of the signatory to a particular agreement. While it may be more costly and time-consuming for each country to enter into a multitude of bilateral agreements, it provides a means, particularly for countries that are hosts of foreign investment, to attract investment flows from the investor country in exchange for relinquishing a certain degree of autonomy over their economic policy.

B. Regional Investment Agreements

The trend noted at the bilateral level of the proliferation of BITs is replicated in the regional sphere across all continents. The willingness of countries to enter into regional investment treaties, therefore, contrasts sharply with the reluctance of those same countries to sign onto an MAI.

1. North America and Europe

In the Western hemisphere, NAFTA was the first regional treaty that contained far-reaching investment provisions, including an investor-state dispute settlement procedure. What is also significant about NAFTA is the fact that its membership, composed of Canada, the United

States, and Mexico, combines developed and developing countries, which are all bound by high standards of investment protection.

The investment provisions that provide for the regulation and liberalization of investment within the EU are contained in Title III of the Treaty Establishing the European Community, entitled "Free Movement of Persons, Services and Capital." In particular, Chapter Four sets out the requirement that all restrictions be removed on the movement of capital and on payments, not only among EC Member States, but also between Member States of the European Community and third countries.

In addition to the foregoing agreements, the 1990s also saw a sharp increase in the number of regional economic arrangements between developing countries that included investment clauses as part of their co-operation initiatives.

2. South and Central America

In South America, the member countries of the Andean Community approved on March 21, 1991, Decision 291 on the Treatment of Foreign Capital of the Cartagena Agreement. On January 17, 1994, members of the Southern Cone Common Market ("MERCOSUR") approved the Colonia Protocol for the Promotion and Protection of Investments in MERCOSUR. The endorsement of a Framework Agreement for the Creation of a Free Trade Area between the Andean Community and MERCOSUR on April 16, 1998, achieved further economic integration, coupled with investment regulation.

The Caribbean Community ("CARICOM") approved the Principles and Guidelines on Foreign Investment at the CARICOM Heads of Government Conference in 1982. During the 1990s, two Protocols—Protocols II (Establishment, Services and Capital) and III (Industrial Policy) Amending the Treaty Establishing the Caribbean Community—were introduced, which include liberalizing investment provisions.

In turn, members of CARICOM entered into a Free Trade Agreement with the Dominican Republic, which contains an Agreement on Reciprocal Promotion and Protection of Investments. Earlier agreements between CARICOM and Colombia, on the one hand, and Venezuela, on the other, contain provisions that recognize the importance of investment stimulation; however, no specific investment rules are provided for in those agreements.

The so-called Group of Three (Colombia, Mexico, and Venezuela) entered into a free trade agreement in 1995 that includes a chapter exclusively dedicated to investment. Mexico also entered into a free trade agreement with El Salvador, Guatemala, and Honduras, which contains an investment chapter. In addition, the Free Trade Agreement between Central America and the Republic of Chile dedicates a chapter to the regulation of investment.

3. Asia

The previously discussed trend in Latin America toward regional economic integration arrangements, and the inclusion of investment measures in such agreements, is now prevalent in Asia. As such, the Ministers of the Association of South East Asian Nations ("ASEAN") signed on October 7, 1998, a Framework Agreement on the ASEAN Investment Area ("AIA"), which had been ratified by all ASEAN members. This Framework Agreement complements the 1987 ASEAN Agreement for the Promotion and Protection of Investments and its 1996 Protocol. The commitments set out under the AIA include the opening of all industries and the grant of national treatment—other than those excluded under a Temporary Exclusion List ("TEL") or a Sensitive List ("SL")—to ASEAN investors by 2010, and to all investors by 2020.

The South Asian Association for Regional Cooperation ("SAARC") is currently considering a Regional Agreement on Promotion and Protection of Investments within the region as a trade facilitation measure. Similarly, BIMSTEC ("Bangladesh, India, Myanmar, Sri Lanka, Thailand Economic Cooperation"), a unique organization in that it groups two members of ASEAN with three countries from South Asia, was formed in late 1997 for the purpose of facilitating economic cooperation among its members. BIMSTEC is currently discussing a Free Trade Agreement that would include rules on investment liberalization.

4. Africa

Even in Africa, which is characterized for its historical opposition to the liberalization of foreign direct investment, a number of regional organizations have begun to include investment provisions in their existing trade agreements, or to discuss stand-alone investment agreements to attract more foreign direct investment.

Members of the Central African Economic and Monetary Community ("CEMAC"), which succeeded the Central African Customs and Economic Union in 1999, are currently negotiating the CEMAC Community Charter on Investment, as part of CEMAC's ultimate goal of attaining the free circulation of capital and goods among its members.

On October 31, 2000, the Common Market for Eastern and Southern Africa ("COMESA"), established in 1994, launched the first ever African Free Trade Area ("COMESA FTA"), which includes rules on investment. The previously negotiated Treaty Establishing the Southern African Development Community ("SADC"), signed in 1992, binds all countries of the region to coordinate, harmonize, and rationalize their policies and strategies for sustainable development in all areas of human endeavour. The SADC created a Finance and Investment Sector working group charged with drafting a Protocol on Finance and Investment to be developed over a period of five years from July 1999, and culminating in the Protocol's ratification by July 2004. Furthermore, sectoral sub-committees are currently developing memoranda of understanding in each of their respective areas that will feed into the development of the Protocol and specific annexes.

The West African Economic and Monetary Union ("UEMOA"), whose founding treaty came into force on August 1, 1998, was drafting a Community Code on Investment scheduled for adoption on January 1, 2000. Finally, the Treaty establishing the East African Community ("EAC"), signed on November 30, 1999, includes certain investment rules.

… … …

The scope of the modern BITs and FTAs is quite extensive and provides for, inter alia, national treatment, most favoured nation treatment, fair and equitable treatment, restrictions on performance requirements (similar to TRIMs) and limitations on expropriations. The national treatment and most favoured nation provisions are similar to those discussed in the context of the WTO, although there are some potentially important differences. With regard to fair and equitable treatment and expropriation, we quote here from the NAFTA provisions on these issues:

Article 1105: Minimum Standard of Treatment

1. Each Party shall accord to investments of investors of another Party treatment in accordance with international law, including fair and equitable treatment and full protection and security.

…

Article 1110: Expropriation and Compensation

1. No Party may directly or indirectly nationalize or expropriate an investment of an investor of another Party in its territory or take a measure tantamount to nationalization or expropriation of such an investment ("expropriation"), except:

(a) for a public purpose;

(b) on a non-discriminatory basis;

(c) in accordance with due process of law and Article 1105(1); and

(d) on payment of compensation in accordance with paragraphs 2 through 6.

To a great extent, it is the scope of intrusion of these kinds of provision into domestic law-making that has caused controversy of investment rules. The substance of these provisions—in particular, "fair and equitable treatment" and the idea of measures "tantamount to expropriation"—is quite vague, creating the potential for broad restrictions on government regulation of business.

In addition to the substance, the dispute procedures have also been an issue. Whereas trade agreements rely exclusively on state–state dispute settlement, investment rules often contain investor–state dispute settlement as well, under which investors can bring claims directly against states in various arbitration fora. The absence of a government filter to weed out controversial and contentious complaints from resulting in litigation has led to a number of cases of concern for critics of trade and investment liberalisation.

The following extract reviews a dispute arising between an American investor and the government of Mexico, pursuant to a complaint filed under the NAFTA investment provisions, where the rights of an investor arguably clashed with certain aspects of Mexican governmental public policy and decision-making abilities concerning the protection of the environment. As has become typical of decisions under BITs or FTAs, the tribunal—and later a Canadian federal court hearing an appeal from the tribunal's decision—was called upon to adjudicate on matters that extend beyond the treaty and into the purview of international law.

WS Dodge, 'INTERNATIONAL DECISION: *Metalclad Corporation v Mexico*, **ICSID Case No ARB (AF)/97/1. 40 ILM 36 (2001), NAFTA Chapter 11 Arbitral Tribunal, 30 August 2000' (2001) 95** *AJIL* **910, 910–19**

In 1993, Metalclad Corporation purchased the Mexican company Confinamiento Tecnico de Residuos Industriales, S.A. de C.V. (COTERIN) in order to build and operate a hazardous-waste transfer station and landfill in Guadalcazar, San Luis Potosi. Although the federal government of Mexico and the state government of San Luis Potosi had granted COTERIN permits to construct and operate the landfill, the municipality of Guadalcazar denied a municipal construction permit, and the governor of San Luis Potosi subsequently declared an area encompassing the landfill to be an ecological reserve. An arbitral tribunal (Tribunal), convened under Chapter 11 of the North American Free Trade Agreement (NAFTA), found that the lack of transparency in Mexico's regulatory requirements constituted a denial of fair and equitable treatment in violation of NAFTA Article 1105, and that Mexico's actions to prevent Metalclad from operating the landfill constituted an expropriation under Article 1110. On Mexico's application to set aside the award, the Supreme Court of British Columbia--the provincial trial court--held that the Tribunal's findings concerning fair and equitable treatment and also concerning expropriation based on Mexico's conduct prior to the creation of the ecological reserve were beyond the scope of the submission to arbitration, but that the award could be sustained on the ground that the ecological decree itself was an expropriation.

The complex history of the case began in April 1993, when Metalclad obtained a six-month option to purchase COTERIN, which had previously obtained federal permits to build a hazardous-waste transfer station and hazardous-waste landfill in the valley of La Pedrera, seventy kilometers from the city of Guadalcazar. In May, the state government of San Luis Potosi granted COTERIN a land-use permit for the landfill. In August, the federal government issued a permit to operate the landfill. In September, having been assured by federal officials that it had all the permits required, Metalclad exercised its option to purchase COTERIN.

Metalclad began construction of the landfill in May 1994. In October, the municipality of Guadalcazar ordered that construction stop because no municipal construction permit had been issued. In November, on the advice of federal officials, Metalclad applied for a municipal permit and resumed construction. The landfill was completed in March 1995, but demonstrations prevented its opening. In November, Metalclad and the federal government entered an agreement (*Convenio*) that provided for operation of the landfill while requiring Metalclad to remediate deficiencies that had been detected by an environmental audit and to designate thirty-four hectares as a buffer zone for the conservation of endemic species. The governor of San Luis Potosi, however, opposed the *Convenio*, and in December, the municipality denied Metalclad's application for a construction permit. The municipality subsequently filed an administrative complaint with the federal government challenging the *Convenio*. When this complaint was denied, the municipality filed an *amparo* proceeding in Mexican courts challenging the denial, and an injunction was issued barring Metalclad from operating the landfill.

After further negotiations with the state of San Luis Potosi failed, Metalclad brought its arbitral claim under Chapter 11 of NAFTA on January 2, 1997. In September, three days before the end of his term, the governor of San Luis Potosi issued an Ecological Decree declaring an area encompassing the landfill to be a Natural Area for the protection of rare cactus.

As an initial matter, the Tribunal held that Mexico was responsible under NAFTA for the acts of San Luis Potosi and Guadalcazar, noting that this holding was in accordance with both the text of NAFTA and established rules of customary international law. The Tribunal then turned to Metalclad's claim that Mexico had breached its obligation under NAFTA Article 1105(1) to "accord to investments of investors of another Party treatment in accordance with international law, including fair and equitable treatment and full protection and security." In interpreting the phrase "fair and equitable treatment," the Tribunal followed Article 102(2)'s instruction to look to NAFTA's stated objectives. "These objectives specifically include transparency and the substantial increase in investment opportunities in the territories of the Parties." The Tribunal interpreted transparency as imposing two related obligations. First, all relevant legal requirements for the purpose of initiating, completing and successfully operating investments made, or intended to be made, under the Agreement should be capable of being readily known to all affected investors of another Party. There should be no room for doubt or uncertainty on such matters.

Second, "Once the authorities of the central government of any Party . . . become aware of any scope for misunderstanding or confusion in this connection, it is their duty to ensure that the correct position is promptly determined and clearly stated . . ."

The Tribunal noted that Metalclad had been assured by federal officials prior to purchasing COTERIN that it had all the permits necessary. The Tribunal further interpreted Mexico's General Ecology Law of 1988 as giving the federal government exclusive authority over hazardous-waste landfills and as limiting the municipal government's authority to "construction considerations." The Tribunal faulted the municipality of Guadalcazar for its delay in asserting the need for a municipal permit, for denying Metalclad the opportunity to appear at the meeting where the permit application was considered, and for denying that permit on environmental grounds.

The absence of a clear rule as to the requirement or not of a municipal construction permit, as well as the absence of any established practice or procedure as to the manner of handling applications for a municipal construction permit, amounts to a failure on the part of Mexico to ensure the transparency required by NAFTA.

The Tribunal further held that Guadalcazar's conduct constituted an expropriation in violation of Article 1110. It observed that expropriation under NAFTA includes not only open, deliberate and acknowledged takings of property, such as outright seizure or formal or obligatory transfer of title in favour of the host State, but also covert or incidental interference with the use of property which has the effect of depriving the owner, in whole or in significant part, of the use or reasonably-to-be-expected economic benefit of property even if not necessarily to the obvious benefit of the host State.

The Tribunal held that by permitting Guadalcazar's unfair and inequitable treatment, Mexico had "taken a measure tantamount to expropriation" and that Guadalcazar's conduct, when considered "together with the representations of the Mexican federal government, on which Metalclad relied, and the absence of a timely, orderly or substantive basis for the denial by the Municipality of the local construction permit, amount[s] to an indirect expropriation."

Finally, "although not strictly necessary for its conclusion," the Tribunal found that the "implementation of the Ecological Decree" issued by the governor of San Luis Potosi "would, in and of itself, constitute an act tantamount to expropriation." The Tribunal considered the "motivation or intent" of the decree irrelevant to the question of expropriation.

With respect to compensation, the Tribunal found that damages under Articles 1105 and 1110 would be the same since Metalclad had completely lost its investment. The Tribunal rejected a discounted cash-flow analysis "because the landfill was never operative and any award based on future profits would be wholly speculative." Instead, the Tribunal awarded damages based on "Metalclad's actual investment" in the project, plus 6 percent interest from the date that Guadalcazar denied the municipal construction permit, for a total award of $ 16,685,000.

Mexico then sought to have the award set aside. Because the site of the arbitration had been Vancouver, British Columbia, Mexico filed its application with the Supreme Court of that province. Justice David Tysoe held that his review of the award was governed by British Columbia's International Commercial Arbitration Act (ICAA), which is based on the UNCITRAL [UN Commission on International Trade Law] Model Law on International Commercial Arbitration. He reasoned that "the primary relationship between Metalclad and Mexico was one of investing" and that the ICAA applied to relationships of investing. He rejected Mexico and Canada's argument that the standard of review under the ICAA be determined by a "pragmatic and functional approach." He held that the court's review of the award was limited to the grounds set forth in ICAA Section 34(2) and, more specifically, to whether "the Tribunal made decisions on matters beyond the scope of the submission to arbitration by deciding upon matters outside Chapter 11."

Justice Tysoe then held that the Tribunal's finding of unfair and inequitable treatment based on a lack of transparency went "beyond the scope of the submission to arbitration because there are no transparency obligations contained in Chapter 11." Agreeing with the Chapter 11 tribunal's award in *S.D. Myers, Inc. v. Canada*, and disagreeing with a different tribunal's award in *Pope & Talbot, Inc. v. Canada*, he reasoned that the text of Article 1105 prohibited only such unfair or inequitable treatment as violated international law. He further reasoned that "in using the words 'international law', Article 1105 is referring to customary international law" rather than to treaty law. He faulted the Tribunal for citing "no authority . . . to establish that transparency has become part of customary international law." In his view, the Tribunal improperly imported into Chapter 11 a transparency obligation from Chapter 18.

On the question of expropriation prior to the Ecological Decree, Justice Tysoe found that "the Tribunal's analysis of Article 1105 infected its analysis of Article 1110" because the measures deemed to constitute an expropriation were Mexico's failures to ensure transparency. He held that the award could be sustained, however, on the ground that the Ecological Decree itself constituted an expropriation. He noted that "the Tribunal gave an extremely broad definition of expropriation for the purposes of Article 1110." But he also observed that "the definition of expropriation is a question of law with which this Court is not entitled to interfere under the *International [Commercial Arbitration Act]*." Since the Tribunal found that the Ecological Decree "had the effect of barring forever the operation of Metalclad's landfill," its "conclusion that the issuance of the Decree was an act tantamount to expropriation is not patently unreasonable."

After rejecting Mexico's arguments that the award should be set aside because of Metalclad's improper acts or because of the Tribunal's failure to address all the questions presented to it, Justice Tysoe set aside the award only to the extent of the interest accrued between December 5, 1995 (the date on which Guadalcazar denied the municipal construction permit, which was the point at which the Tribunal had determined that Mexico breached Articles 1105 and 1110) and September 20, 1997 (the date of the Ecological Decree that Justice Tysoe held to be an expropriation). Because Metalclad had successfully resisted Mexico's application to have the award set aside in its entirety, he ordered Mexico to pay Metalclad 75 percent of its costs in the proceeding. Mexico filed a notice of appeal to the British Columbia Court of Appeal at the end of May, 2001, but the parties reached a preliminary agreement in June to settle the case for $ 15,626,260.

* * * *

One often thinks of courts as being concerned with setting precedents to guide future conduct, and of arbitrators as being both less concerned with the content of the law and more willing to fashion compromises to satisfy the parties. In *Metalclad*, however, those roles were reversed. The arbitral tribunal tried hard to advance international law concerning foreign investment by finding that "fair and equitable treatment" required transparency and by adopting an expansive definition of expropriation. It was Justice Tysoe who gave each party what it wanted most-- setting aside for Mexico the transparency aspects of the award, while giving Metalclad most of its money--but at the cost of consistency in the application of British Columbia's ICAA. More broadly, the case may lead one to wonder whether it is appropriate to allow national courts to review Chapter 11 awards.

Although the relevant part of the award has now been set aside, *Metalclad* appears to have been the first arbitral decision to have found a breach of the duty of "fair and equitable treatment." Provisions establishing such a duty have been included in a large number of bilateral investment treaties. To give content to this general concept, the Tribunal looked to other NAFTA provisions, specifically references in its statement of objectives and in Article 1802 to transparency, and in its preamble and statement of objectives to creating a "predictable commercial framework" for investment and to increasing "investment opportunities." It was this reasoning, of course, that led Justice Tysoe to conclude that the Tribunal had made "decisions on matters beyond the scope of Chapter 11."

Justice Tysoe's ultimate conclusion, however, depended on two propositions: (1) that the phrase "international law" in Article 1105 means customary international law and not treaty law; and (2) that the Tribunal was not applying customary international law when it concluded that "fair and equitable treatment" required transparency. On the first point, neither the text of Article 1105 nor the Tribunal's award is completely clear. Assuming, however, that the Tribunal did read "international law" to include treaty law, this interpretation would seem to involve an issue of law on which Justice Tysoe had no authority under the ICAA to second-guess the Tribunal. Having concluded that Article 1105 was limited to customary international law, he then faulted the Tribunal for citing "no authority . . . to establish that transparency has become part of customary international law." In fact, arbitrators have based international responsibility on a lack of transparency in a number of prior decisions, and if the Tribunal had taken the trouble to cite them, Justice Tysoe would have had a much more difficult time setting aside this part of the award.

On the issue of expropriation, the Tribunal read Article 1110 to prohibit "covert or incidental interference with the use of property which has the effect of depriving the owner, in whole or in significant part, of the use or reasonably-to-be-expected economic benefit of property even if not necessarily to the obvious benefit of the host State." Although Justice Tysoe characterized this definition as "extremely broad," it is worth noting that the award requires at least a "*significant*" deprivation of economic benefit, which is arguably more than the *Restatement (Third) of Foreign Relations Law* definition on which another Chapter 11 tribunal has relied. It is unfortunate that the Tribunal did not make clear whether it read the phrase "take a measure tantamount to nationalization or expropriation" in Article 1110 as going beyond the protections of customary international law. It would have required, however, neither a particularly broad definition of expropriation nor an interpretation of Article 1110 as extending beyond customary international law to find that a decree that "had the effect of barring forever the operation of the landfill" was an expropriation.

Although the *Metalclad* Tribunal could have written a clearer and more persuasive award, it could hardly have written one more favorable to foreign investors. Justice Tysoe, by contrast, fashioned a compromise, setting aside the transparency portion of the award for Mexico but letting Metalclad keep most of the money that the Tribunal had awarded it. Yet he could not accomplish this result without some inconsistency. He correctly held that British Columbia's ICAA governed the award, which meant that he was not entitled to review the Tribunal's legal decisions. Accordingly, he observed that he could not interfere with the Tribunal's definition of expropriation because it was a legal issue. Nevertheless, he overrode the Tribunal on another legal issue: the question whether "international law" in Article 1105 is limited to customary international law. This inconsistency may have been expedient, but it was not principled.

In a prior case report, I suggested that it might be advisable to create an appellate body for Chapter 11 cases. *Metalclad* illustrates this need. A national court's review of a Chapter 11 award during a proceeding to set aside or to enforce the award will typically be limited to such questions as whether the tribunal decided matters outside the scope of the submission to arbitration. A national court typically will not be able to correct errors of law made by the tribunal, whereas an appellate body could be given such authority. Both for this reason and because different Chapter 11 awards will come before different national courts, national-court review also cannot ensure a consistent interpretation of NAFTA. Moreover, as *Metalclad* itself illustrates—on issues ranging from the meaning of "fair and equitable treatment" under Article 1105 to the definition of expropriation under Article 1110— there are numerous questions on which Chapter 11 tribunals have reached different interpretations. An appellate body to which all Chapter 11 awards were appealable could provide needed consistency. It would also bring to bear greater expertise on questions of international law than is typically found in municipal courts. Finally, an appellate body would ensure neutrality in the review of Chapter 11 awards. It was fortunate that in *Metalclad* the place of arbitration, and thus the court that was asked to review the award, was in neither the claimant's nor the respondent's country. In *S.D. Myers v.*

Canada, by contrast, the place of arbitration was Toronto, and Canada has applied to the Federal Court of Canada to set aside the award to the U.S. claimant. This application may create the appearance of bias if Canada is successful.

One hopes that the NAFTA parties will see fit to remedy this situation, either by amending NAFTA itself or by providing for an appellate body in the investment chapter of the instruments establishing a free trade area of the Americas, which might supersede NAFTA Chapter 11.

... ...

After some early decisions which were criticised as being overly friendly to investors, a number of recent decisions have gone the other way, leading to concerns that tribunals are going too far to uphold the challenged government measures. The future of investor–state dispute settlement is uncertain, and is currently the subject of domestic political debate in Australia, the US, the EU and elsewhere.

(b) A Multilateral Agreement on Investment?

As one would expect, with the increase in the number of BITs being concluded, differing levels of protection, standards and enforcement options exist in the various agreements. This creates a level of uncertainty and confusion among investors as well as governments. For this reason, a Multilateral Agreement on Investment (MAI) has often been posed as a way of setting uniform standards and simplifying investment rules. The following extract describes the latest failed attempt to negotiate an MAI, by the OECD in the 1990s.

> **R Dattu, 'A Journey from Havana to Paris: The Fifty-Year Quest for the Elusive MAI'**
> **(2000) 24 *Fordham International Law Journal* 275, 295–303**
>
> Despite the negotiations and achievements of the TRIMs Agreement, GATS, and TRIPs during the Uruguay Round, most industrialized countries, particularly the members of the OECD, left the Uruguay Round with a sense that they had been defeated by the developing world in their quest to achieve a high degree of investment liberalization within the WTO. In the view of the OECD Members, the proliferation of bilateral investment treaties and regional economic integration agreements, which included high standards of investment protection (e.g., the North American Free Trade Agreement ("NAFTA") and the Energy Charter), demonstrated that the time was ripe to negotiate a multilateral investment treaty.
>
> As a result, in May 1995, the OECD Ministers established a negotiating group to begin consultations on an MAI that would set out high standards for the liberalization of investment and protection of investors. While the MAI would be open for signature to all countries, the OECD Members opted to negotiate within their organization while granting other interested countries, such as Brazil and Argentina, observer status. The motive for confining the MAI negotiations to the OECD, with the stated objective of a stipulated time frame for the conclusion of the MAI (May 1997), was to achieve an investment agreement within the confines of industrialized countries, which would then be opened for signature to other countries.
>
> III. THE OECD MULTILATERAL AGREEMENT ON INVESTMENT
>
> Prior to the decision to initiate negotiations on the MAI, the OECD undertook a number of initiatives to promote the liberalization of foreign investment among its members. From its inception, the OECD received the mandate from its members to work toward the liberalization of cross-border flows of goods, capital, and services. As such, in 1961, the year of the OECD's inception, the Code of Liberalisation of Capital Movements and the Code of Liberalisation

of Current Invisible Operations (together the "Codes of Liberalisation") were proclaimed. Although the Codes of Liberalisation are not identical in all respects, they share the general objective of the removal of restrictions on specified lists of current invisible operations and capital movements. The ultimate goal is that residents of different OECD members be "as free to transact business with each other as are residents of a single country."

While the Codes of Liberalisation have the legal status of an OECD decision, which is binding on all OECD members, implementation of the Codes of Liberalisation entails "peer pressure" exercised through policy reviews and country examinations. The aim is to encourage members to undertake unilateral, rather than negotiated, liberalization. As a result, enforcement of the Codes of Liberalisation consists of a framework of notification, examination, and consultation, with the purpose of monitoring observance with the liberalizing prescriptions. Furthermore, the commitments made by OECD members under the Codes of Liberalisation do not bind them to specific liberalizing measures. In accordance with this principle of autonomy, members are also permitted under Article 2 of both Codes to enter their own list of reservations, so that they will not be bound to introduce liberalizing measures in certain sectors of their choosing. In addition, Article 7 of the Codes entitles members to register temporary derogations for which specific justifications must be presented.

Despite the Codes' shortcomings, when OECD members left the Uruguay Round feeling that their aspirations with respect to investment protection and liberalization had not been fulfilled, they believed the OECD had the most extensive expertise in the area of investment liberalization.

A. The Start of the OECD MAI Negotiations

In May 1995, the Committee on International Investment and Multinational Enterprises ("CIME") and the Committee on Capital Movements and Invisible Transactions ("CMIT") presented a report at an OECD Council meeting at the Ministerial level. This report indicated that the time was "ripe to negotiate an MAI in the OECD." The conclusion of the CIME and CMIT was based on work conducted by both committees since 1991, and by five working groups which had been set up in 1994 to undertake technical and analytical work on (i) liberalization obligations under existing OECD instruments, (ii) liberalization obligations in new areas, (iii) investment protection, (iv) dispute settlement, and (v) the involvement of non-members of the OECD. The solutions devised by these working groups were partly inspired by investment-related agreements negotiated during that period, such as NAFTA, the Energy Charter, and bilateral investment agreements. Based on its report, the CIME and the CMIT requested and obtained, from the OECD Council, the mandate to begin negotiations with the aim of concluding an MAI by the time of the Ministerial-level OECD Council meeting in 1997.

B. The Objectives of the OECD MAI

In light of the WTO's perceived failure to create a framework for the regulation of foreign, direct investment, the objectives for the MAI, reaffirmed by the OECD Ministers at the May 1996 OECD Council, were as follows:

(i) the creation of a strong and comprehensive multilateral legal framework for foreign direct investment ("FDI") among participating countries;

(ii) the reduction of barriers to FDI and an increase in legal security for international investors;

(iii) "level the playing field" by providing for national treatment;

(iv) a legally binding treaty containing effective provisions for the settlement of disputes; and

(v) a free-standing treaty open to all OECD countries and the European Union, and to accession by non-OECD countries.

As is evident from the tight timeline for completion of the treaty, the OECD Members had anticipated a smooth negotiation of the MAI in light of the involvement of industrialized economies in the process, who seemed to agree on the main goals for the agreement. However, the large amount of square brackets and footnotes in the MAI Negotiating Text of April 1998 proves that the contrary was true. Some of the most relevant aspects of the draft MAI Negotiating text included the following.

1. Scope of the Treaty

MAI negotiators set out an extremely broad definition of investment, which included every kind of asset owned or controlled, directly or indirectly, by an investor, including direct and portfolio investments, real estate, intellectual property rights, rights under contracts, and rights conferred under authorizations and permits. Most importantly, the MAI was designed to cover established, as well as future investments. All such investments would have received the better of national and MFN treatment.

2. Investment Protection

As in most bilateral investment agreements between industrialized countries, the MAI would have required that all investments receive fair and equitable treatment, and full and constant protection and security. Furthermore, expropriations or other measures tantamount to expropriation were not to be permitted, except where such measures were taken in the public interest, in a non-discriminatory fashion, accompanied by the payment of prompt, adequate, and effective compensation and in accordance with due process of law. Compensation would have to be paid without delay, equal the fair market value of the investment before the expropriation occurred, and be fully conceivable and freely transferable. The standards of compensation adopted in the MAI negotiating text provide a codification of developed countries' views on the customary international law on expropriation and compensation.

Despite the general agreement among MAI negotiators to the terms of investment protection, a number of non-governmental organizations ("NGOs") forcefully opposed these provisions in light of the increasing number of NAFTA Chapter 11 challenges brought by U.S. businesses with respect to Canada's environmental regulations under the investor-state dispute resolution mechanism. In their view, the protection of investment against government environmental regulatory measures would provide higher priority to individual property rights and the profit-making capacity of corporations over the right of the state to regulate in the area of environment or labor.

3. Performance Requirements and Investment Incentives

The MAI negotiators agreed to prohibit the use of performance requirements (e.g., export and local sourcing requirements) under the agreement. In addition to the similar prohibitions contained in the TRIMs Agreement and in NAFTA, the MAI's Negotiating Text extended the prohibition to trade in services and to non-trade related performance requirements, such as technology transfers.

The prohibition on investment incentives was a much more controversial issue among MAI negotiators. While some parties believed that such a prohibition avoided costly programs whereby countries compete to attract foreign investment, others argued that certain incentives were needed to promote regional, social, environmental, and developmental goals.

4. Exceptions and Reservations

The availability of certain exceptions and reservations to the MAI was the source of a great deal of disagreement among MAI negotiators. Even with respect to the standard national security and international peace exception, some parties expressed concern about the scope of this exception. In particular, MAI negotiators were concerned with the repeated use of this ground for non-compliance with treaty obligations.

Other grounds for non-compliance with the MAI discussed during the negotiations were the exclusion of fiscal and taxation measures from the MAI's realm, prudential measures in relation to the financial services industry, as well as temporary derogation for balance-of-payment reasons.

Canada was the most vocal proponent of a general cultural exception clause in the MAI that would have exempted any measure to regulate investment of foreign companies and the conditions of activity of these companies, so long as such measures were taken "to preserve and promote cultural and linguistic diversity." In addition to Canada's sweeping proposal, a number of negotiators, including those from France, suggested that cultural industries be excluded from the MAI. However, the parties never agreed on the scope to be granted to a cultural exception.

Finally, the availability and scope of country-specific exceptions continued to be the source of heated debate even at the time that the Negotiating Text was made public. The MAI envisaged a List A of country-specific exceptions that would include existing non-conforming measures. In addition, there was a proposal contemplating a List B of exceptions. This category would include a limited number of new, but unspecified, non-conforming measures to be excepted from the MAI obligation of national and MFN treatment. Among potential areas to be covered by List B were preferential economic policies for aboriginal peoples, minorities, and cultures.

5. Dispute Settlement

Like most bilateral investment agreements and Chapter 11 of NAFTA, the MAI was to provide for both state-to-state and investor-state dispute settlement mechanisms by means of arbitration. The MAI would be governed by the procedures established by the International Centre for the Settlement of Investment Disputes ("ICSID"), the United Nations Commission on International Trade Law ("UNCITRAL"), or the International Chamber of Commerce ("ICC") Court of Arbitration. As of the publication of the Negotiating Text, there had not been an agreement among the MAI negotiators on whether certain MAI provisions (e.g., the pre-establishment rights of investors and investments) would be excluded from the private dispute resolution mechanism.

6. Sub-national Authorities

With respect to sub-national authorities, divergent views arose with respect to two issues. First, federal states, such as Canada, referred to the constitutional difficulty of binding their provinces to the MAI without a prior consultation process. Second, and more controversial, was the question raised by the United States as to whether the MAI's national treatment requirements would be met by applying the treatment accorded to investors in any one of the other states.

7. Regional Economic Integration Organizations

The EU proposed the addition of a regional economic integration organization exception, dubbed the "REIO clause," to the treaty, whereby the EU would have been allowed to grant preferential treatment to its members without having to extend the same treatment to all MAI signatories. While the EU argued that this clause would apply to fields not covered by the MAI, the disagreement continued until the end of the MAI negotiations, as the other parties felt that a REIO clause ran counter to the main goals of the MAI.

8. Labor and Environmental Issues

In response to the vociferous concerns raised by NGOs with respect to the social and environmental impact of the MAI, negotiators began to consider the possibility of including provisions on labor and the environment to the agreement. The issue, including whether a commitment not to lower labor and environmental standards in the MAI would be binding on governments, and thus subject to the MAI's dispute resolution mechanisms, remained unresolved at the end of 1998 when MAI negotiations broke down.

As the foregoing discussion reveals, despite the absence of developing countries from the negotiating process—a factor that had been anticipated to facilitate agreement among all parties—the like-minded economies of the OECD and the EU were unable to overcome a large number of the obstacles that arose in a number of areas of the MAI.

C. The Lessons from the MAI's Failure at the OECD

The lessons of the MAI's failure at the OECD are:

1. The willingness of countries to enter into regional and bilateral investment agreements does not necessarily signify the unconditional willingness to sign onto a global investment agreement that grants all states, and all investors of all states, rights vis-à-vis all other potential host states of investments.

2. An attempt to negotiate an MAI that provides high standards of liberalization and protection among countries that already have well-established, liberal, and transparent foreign investment policies is likely to result in failure, because the benefits to be yielded from such an agreement are expected to be marginal. However, the political cost to the governments of the negotiating countries can be quite significant.

3. The WTO, with its broad mandate over trade matters (and the give and take that this permits during trade negotiations), rather than the OECD, is a more conducive forum for negotiating an MAI that is likely to yield relatively significant benefits, which can then be expected to provide the necessary political impetus to the governments of signatory countries.

4. Furthermore, it is to be expected that in a difficult and controversial area, such as investment liberalization and protection, patience and diligence will be required. This is confirmed by the recent experience of the Uruguay Round negotiations, which at least resulted in pared-down versions of investment liberalization and protection measures in the TRIMs Agreement, GATS, and TRIPs. On the other hand, the OECD's overly ambitious and fast-paced negotiations in Paris could not arrive at any sort of agreement even among like-minded countries.

... ...

IV. INVESTMENT AND THE DOHA ROUND

Article 9 of the TRIMS Agreement stipulated that, not later than five years after the date of entry into force of the Agreement, the Council for Trade in Goods was to review the operation of the TRIMs Agreement. In this review, consideration was to be given to whether the Agreement should be supplemented with provisions on investment policy and competition policy. The first WTO Ministerial Conference, held in Singapore in 1996, established Working Groups on trade and investment and on trade and competition 'having regard to the existing WTO provisions on matters related to investment and competition policy and the built-in agenda in these areas, including under the TRIMs Agreement'. The relevant portion of the Singapore Declaration states:

20. Having regard to the existing WTO provisions on matters related to investment and competition policy and the built-in agenda in these areas, including under the TRIMs Agreement, and on the understanding that the work undertaken shall not prejudge whether negotiations will be initiated in the future, we also agree to:

establish a working group to examine the relationship between trade and investment; and

establish a working group to study issues raised by Members relating to the interaction between trade and competition policy, including anti-competitive practices, in order to identify any areas that may merit further consideration in the WTO framework.

These groups shall draw upon each other's work if necessary and also draw upon and be without prejudice to the work in UNCTAD and other appropriate intergovernmental fora. As regards UNCTAD, we welcome the work under way as provided for in the Midrand Declaration and the contribution it can make to the understanding of issues. In the conduct of the work of the working groups, we encourage cooperation with the above organizations to make the best use of available resources and to ensure that the development dimension is taken fully into account. The General Council will keep the work of each body under review, and will determine after two years how the work of each body should proceed. It is clearly understood that future negotiations, if any, regarding multilateral disciplines in these areas, will take place only after an explicit consensus decision is taken among WTO Members regarding such negotiations.

The Doha Declaration built upon the above statement, but more importantly simply reintroduced the subject to the WTO negotiations (investment, along with trade and competition policy, transparency in government procurement and trade facilitation comprise what is known as the 'Singapore' Issues due to their original inclusion in the Singapore Declaration), despite the fact that a working party had been looking at the issue since 1996. The Doha Declaration states:

Relationship between trade and investment

20. Recognizing the case for a multilateral framework to secure transparent, stable and predictable conditions for long-term cross-border investment, particularly foreign direct investment, that will contribute to the expansion of trade, and the need for enhanced technical assistance and capacity-building in this area as referred to in paragraph 21, we agree that negotiations will take place after the Fifth Session of the Ministerial Conference on the basis of a decision to be taken, by explicit consensus, at that session on modalities of negotiations.

21. We recognize the needs of developing and least-developed countries for enhanced support for technical assistance and capacity building in this area, including policy analysis and development so that they may better evaluate the implications of closer multilateral cooperation for their development policies and objectives, and human and institutional development. To this end, we shall work in cooperation with other relevant intergovernmental organisations, including UNCTAD, and through appropriate regional and bilateral channels, to provide strengthened and adequately resourced assistance to respond to these needs.

22. In the period until the Fifth Session, further work in the Working Group on the Relationship Between Trade and Investment will focus on the clarification of: scope and definition; transparency; non-discrimination; modalities for pre-establishment commitments based on a GATS-type, positive list approach; development provisions; exceptions and balance-of-payments safeguards; consultation and the settlement of disputes between members. Any framework should reflect in a balanced manner the interests of home and host countries, and take due account of the development policies and objectives of host governments as well as their right to regulate in the public interest. The special development, trade and financial needs of developing and least-developed countries should be taken into account as an integral part of any framework, which should enable members to undertake obligations and commitments commensurate with their individual needs and circumstances. Due regard should be paid to other relevant WTO provisions. Account should be taken, as appropriate, of existing bilateral and regional arrangements on investment.

The Doha Declaration does not, therefore, immediately commence negotiations on investment. Rather, the Declaration merely states that 'negotiations will take place after the Fifth Session of the Ministerial Conference on the basis of a decision to be taken, by explicit consensus, at that session on modalities of negotiations [ie how the negotiations are to be conducted]'. Additionally, the Declaration instructs the Working Group to focus on clarifying certain specific issues in the lead up to the Cancun Ministerial (2003). Interestingly, the Declaration also specifically stated that any future negotiated commitments would be modelled on those made in the GATS, where commitments are being made via 'positive lists' rather than making broad commitments and listing exceptions ('negative lists').

Despite the Declaration's call for a balance of interests to be taken into account as well as cooperation with other international organisations, Members failed to reach consensus on investment (or any of the 'Singapore' Issues). Ultimately, it was agreed that investment would be dropped from the agenda of the Doha Round (trade facilitation remained the lone 'Singapore' Issue to remain on the agenda).[13] While the decision has more to do with the lack of progress on other issues (such as services, agriculture and non-agricultural market access), it is important to note the wide range of Members' views and deep levels of disagreement on the subject of investment.

VI. QUESTIONS

1. In terms of the appropriate scope of investment agreements, should domestic investment be covered? If there are concerns with the trade effects of domestic investment measures, are such issues not already covered by trade rules?

2. How do the investment provisions that prohibit measures that are 'tantamount to expropriation' relate to domestic laws on the taking of private property? Is it problematic if investment agreements create more protections for foreign investors than domestic

---

[13] WTO, 'The Doha Declaration Explained', available at www.wto.org/english/tratop_e/dda_e/doha explained_e.htm#investment.

laws provide for nationals? Does the *Metalcad* tribunal's approach to these issues seem reasonable?

3. To what extent do bilateral agreements drive the current system of investment regulation? Would multilateral rules on investment be preferable? What are the pros and the cons to developed countries and to developing countries? Or are these classifications insufficient now that developing countries are increasing their own investments abroad?

4. Is investor–state dispute settlement a good idea? Should investment disputes restricted to those claims brought by states? Should trade disputes be expanded to cover complaints brought by individual traders?

16

Government Procurement

I. INTRODUCTION

Government procurement is the activity whereby public bodies purchase goods and services from private suppliers in order to carry out their functions and responsibilities. The range of goods and services purchased by governments is of course vast, there being a near complete overlap between purchases by public bodies on the one hand, and private firms and consumers on the other hand. Additionally, hard defence materials, such as tanks and missiles, can only (at least in stable political systems) be purchased by governments. Procurement is a highly significant economic activity. It has been estimated that, in developed countries, procurement accounts for around 7–14 per cent of Gross Domestic Product, depending on such factors as whether utilities and military procurement are taken into account. These figures may be higher for developing countries.[1] It follows that discrimination in government procurement, whereby foreign suppliers are somehow given less favourable treatment than domestic suppliers, can amount to a highly significant non-tariff barrier to trade.

By way of explanation, consider the example of a state in which health care is largely a matter of state provision and suppose that there is no quantitative restriction or high import tariff imposed on hospital equipment. Market access opportunities for foreign suppliers will nevertheless be extremely limited if this state only purchases hospital equipment from domestic suppliers. While there is strong empirical evidence of discrimination in government procurement,[2] it is also important to consider that governments also frequently purchase foreign goods and services independently of any international obligation to conduct procurement in a non-discriminatory manner. This is because the main national priority in procurement is generally to obtain value for money in expenditure of revenues raised through taxation. Value for money entails the purchase of the technically

---

[1] See S Arrowsmith, *Government Procurement in the WTO* (The Hague, Kluwer Law International, 2003) 3 and studies cited therein.

[2] A study of a number of EU Member States by Trionfetti compared the import-penetration rate in government markets with that of comparable private markets and found that this rate was consistently around a third lower in government markets. Bearing in mind that this study was conducted in the context of a sophisticated system of procurement regulation, it is plausible that the disparity in import-penetration rates may be higher for countries whose efforts to liberalise procurement markets are at an earlier stage of development. See F Trionfetti, 'Discriminatory Procurement and International Trade' (2000) 23(1) *The World Economy* 57, 61–64.

optimum products at the best available price, which may of course require the awarding of contracts to foreign suppliers.

The questions of whether and how government procurement should be regulated are among the most challenging which GATT and WTO negotiators have faced. The sensitivity of the area became clear at a very early point in the history of international procurement regulation. It is striking that the Suggested Charter for an International Trade Organisation drafted by the US, and published in 1946, originally proposed that government procurement should be subject to the general national treatment obligation.[3] However, it quickly became apparent that this would not be possible because of the prevalence of discriminatory laws and practices involving preferences for domestic suppliers. Indeed, the Charter's initial inclusion of procurement was substituted with an exclusion to the effect that national treatment would not apply to the procurement by governmental agencies of supplies for governmental use. The exclusion survives to this day in GATT Article III:8(a).

The rejection of a multilateral national treatment obligation in the procurement context might have led to the abandonment of attempts at regulation. However it was recognised that this would have undermined commercial opportunities for private suppliers created by liberalisation in this area. The approach therefore adopted was not to abandon the ideal of national treatment for procurement, but rather to acknowledge that it was acceptable to only some GATT contracting parties. The Tokyo Round Agreement on Government Procurement (GPA), which entered into force on 1 January 1981, was therefore plurilateral in character. In other words, accession to the GPA was optional.

The Tokyo Round GPA was a fully fledged Agreement which went significantly beyond declaring that national treatment would apply to procurement conducted by its limited number of members. Positive regulation was also provided for in the form of procedural rules dealing with various aspects of tendering procedures such as the need to publish procurement opportunities and the permissible criteria for awarding contracts. This reflected the view of negotiators that while national treatment alone would catch overtly discriminatory laws, it would be unlikely to have a pronounced impact on discriminatory practices in individual procurement procedures. Minimum procedural safeguards were therefore introduced to enhance the transparency of procedures which in turn would make it more difficult to discriminate.

The most significant weaknesses of the Tokyo Round GPA were that its coverage was restricted to central government contracts for the supply of goods, and its membership was limited, especially with regard to developing countries.[4] The first of these limitations was addressed by the Uruguay Round GPA which entered into force on 1 January 1996. Coverage was significantly extended both in relation to the level of the procuring entity within the state structure, and in relation to the subject matter of the contract. With regard to the level of the entities covered, the GPA is now capable of applying to central government bodies and sub-central government bodies such as individual states in federal

---

[3] National treatment was provided for in Art 9 and was to extend to, 'laws and regulations governing the procurement by governmental agencies of supplies for public use other than by or for the military establishment'.

[4] The original signatories to the Tokyo Round Agreement were Austria, Canada, the then nine Member States of the European Community (Belgium, France, Denmark, Italy, Luxembourg, Netherlands, Republic of Ireland, UK, West Germany), the European Community itself, Finland, Hong Kong, Japan, Norway, Singapore, Sweden, Switzerland and the US. The Agreement became applicable to Greece, Spain and Portugal upon their later accession to the EC, and Israel joined in 1983.

systems or city councils. In addition, the GPA is also capable of applying to bodies cryptically identified as 'other entities'. This phrase implicates entities providing utility functions such as the generation and supply of energy and public transport services. These entities may be subject to the same legal structures as private companies but also be subject to government ownership or control which might give rise to the tendency to discriminate. With regard to the subject matter of the contract, the GPA can now apply to services and construction services contracts as well as goods contracts.

The second limitation referred to above—that of limited membership—remains to a significant extent.[5] While the list of GPA parties is now much expanded, this is explained primarily by EU expansion. The most compelling explanation for the continued modest membership is the desire of states to retain the discretion to favour national suppliers. Procurement is viewed by most states as a useful instrument for promoting national objectives of an industrial and social character, such as preferences for infant industries or firms owned by previously disadvantaged groups. Membership of the GPA does not completely prevent states from pursuing such national objectives, but the GPA's emphasis on removing discrimination does entail that such objectives move towards becoming the exception rather than the norm.

It can be forecasted that the GPA's membership will rise significantly in the foreseeable future as nine WTO Members, including China, are presently negotiating accession.[6] A further five WTO Members, including the Russian Federation, have provisions regarding accession to the Agreement in their respective Protocols of Accession to the WTO.[7]

The GPA's limited (albeit expanding) membership and plurilateral status ought not necessarily be depicted in a negative light. Phrases such as 'variable geometry' and 'multiple-speed' are now a part of the WTO lexicon. Commentators have started to question the merits of the Single Undertaking and to evaluate whether WTO Members which are able to move forward relatively quickly with trade liberalisation should be encouraged to do so.[8] The debate was triggered by the decision taken in 2004 to drop the 'Singapore Issues'—investment, competition, transparency in government procurement and trade facilitation—from the Doha Round, and the suspension of the Doha Round negotiations in mid 2006. The GPA is significant because it is the WTO's foremost example of variable geometry. Indeed, the GPA's development shows the potential benefits of this concept. Just as the multilateral negotiations towards transparency in government procurement were abandoned, separate negotiations towards clarifying and improving the plurilateral GPA and further expanding its coverage were continuing apace. The mandate for these negotiations was provided by Article XXIV:7 of the Uruguay Round GPA. This provision required the Parties to undertake negotiations 'with a view to improving the Agreement and achieving the greatest possible extension of its coverage among all Parties'.

---

[5] The present GPA Parties, numbering 42 in total, are Armenia; Canada; the EU, with its 27 Member States; Hong Kong; Iceland; Israel; Japan; Korea; Liechtenstein; Netherlands with respect to Aruba; Norway; Singapore; Switzerland; Chinese Taipei; and the US.

[6] These nine WTO Members are Albania, China, Georgia, Jordan, Kyrgyz Republic, Moldova, Oman, Panama and Ukraine. For discussion of China's accession, see P Wang 'China's Accession to the WTO Government Procurement Agreement—Challenges and the Way Forward' (2009) 12 *Journal of International Economic Law* 663.

[7] These five WTO Members are Croatia, the Former Yugoslav Republic of Macedonia, Mongolia, Saudi Arabia and the Russian Federation.

[8] For discussion on this issue see the mini-symposium on 'The Future Geometry of WTO Law' in (2006) 9 *Journal of International Economic Law*.

The first milestone in these negotiations corresponded with the first aspect of the negotiations—improvement of the GPA. A revised draft text was published in December 2006.[9] The revised text has been re-structured to make it more user-friendly. Apart from this, electronic forms of disseminating procurement information, and even electronic forms of purchasing, are now expressly provided for. A further significant development is that the importance of 'avoiding conflicts of interests and corrupt practices' is recognised for the first time in both a Preamble recital and a new provision.[10] The GPA's non-discrimination and transparency-based obligation have always had a potential impact in reducing corruption since following the GPA makes it more difficult to conceal practices which lack integrity. With the new recital and provision, it can now be said that tackling corruption is among the GPA's direct objectives.

Significantly, the revised text was not immediately opened for acceptance among the GPA parties. Rather, the opening for acceptance and the process of submitting the new text for approval by national parliaments was delayed until the completion of the second aspect of the Article XXIX:7 negotiations—extension of coverage. This aspect of the negotiations was completed at the political level by way of a Ministerial Decision of 15 December 2011.[11] The results of all aspects of the negotiations were later adopted on 30 March 2012 and are embodied in an extensive document setting out the final version of the revised text and the final coverage offers of each Party.[12]

A final introductory point relates to states which are unlikely to join the GPA in the immediately foreseeable future. International procurement regulation is nevertheless of high relevance to these states. A significant proportion of free trade agreements contain rules which very closely resemble those set out in the GPA.[13] For example, while Australia is not a GPA Member, Chapter 15 of the Australia–United States Free Trade Agreement sets out rules which are virtually identical to those contained in the GPA. An understanding of the GPA is therefore valuable from the perspective of understanding procurement rules in free trade agreements.

The chapter is presented in several parts. In section II, the process of determining whether the GPA applies to any particular contract is discussed. Section III assesses the relationship between the Buy American provisions in the US 'Stimulus Package' and the GPA. Section IV deals with the general principles and specific rules which regulate contracts to which the GPA applies. Section V deals with the exceptions provision and section VI covers domestic review procedures for supplier challenges. Section VII deals with the negotiations towards multilateral procurement rules.

---

[9] See GPA/W/297 of 11 December 2006. The final version of the revised text is set out in GPA/113 of 2 April 2012.

[10] Art IV:4(b) and (c).

[11] Decision on the Outcomes of the Negotiations under Article XXIV:7 of the Agreement on Government Procurement, GPA/112, 15 December 2011. See RD Anderson, 'The Conclusion of the Renegotiation of the World Trade Organization Agreement on Government Procurement: What it Means for the Agreement and for the World Economy' 2012(3) *Public Procurement Law Review* 83.

[12] Adoption of the Results of the Negotiations under Article XXIV:7 of the Agreement on Government Procurement, Following their Verification and Review, as Required by the Ministerial Decision of 15 December 2011 (GPA/112), paragraph 5, GPA/113, 2 April 2012.

[13] See RD Anderson, AC Müller, K Osei-Lah, JP De León and P Pelletier, 'Government Procurement Provisions in Regional Trade Agreements: a Stepping Stone to GPA Accession?' in S Arrowsmith and RD Anderson (eds), *The WTO Regime on Government Procurement: Challenge and Reform* (Cambridge, Cambridge University Press, 2011) 561.

By way of clarification, further references to the GPA in this chapter relate to the present text of 2012 unless otherwise stated.

II. ISSUES RELATING TO CONTRACT COVERAGE

As explained more fully in section III, the primary purpose of the rules set out in the GPA is to deter discrimination against suppliers, goods and services from the GPA parties. However, these rules only apply to contracts which fall within the coverage of the GPA and the issue of coverage is determined mainly by the outcome of negotiations which are usually conduced on a bilateral basis, and with reciprocity considerations in mind. Therefore, when applying the GPA, the first question is whether the particular contract is covered.

The issue of coverage is now more complicated than it was under the Tokyo Round GPA. As the Tokyo Round GPA only covered central government goods contract, a strong presumption of universal coverage could be made, thereby enabling suppliers from all GPA Parties to participate in such contracts. The position remains relatively straight forward for central government goods contracts. However with the expansion of coverage introduced by the Uruguay Round GPA, the market access dimension below the central level of government is rather complex, especially when the subject matter of the contract is services or construction services as opposed to goods. The fact that suppliers from one or more GPA Parties can participate in these contracts does not mean that suppliers from all GPA Parties can participate. As noted, access to the contracts depends mainly on the outcome of coverage negotiations which are set out in Appendix I of each Party. Article II:4 of the GPA sets out what must be contained in each Party's Appendix I as follows:[14]

Each Party shall specify the following information in its annexes to Appendix I:

(a) in Annex 1, the central government entities whose procurement is covered by this Agreement;
(b) in Annex 2, the sub-central government entities whose procurement is covered by this Agreement;
(c) in Annex 3, all other entities whose procurement is covered by this Agreement;
(d) in Annex 4, the goods covered by this Agreement;
(e) in Annex 5, the services, other than construction services, covered by this Agreement;
(f) in Annex 6, the construction services covered by this Agreement; and
(g) in Annex 7, any General Notes.

The GPA's coverage has been more contentious than deciding upon the rules which apply to covered contracts. This is indicated by the negotiations on improvement of the Uruguay Round GPA described above in which there was an interval of five years between the publication of the draft revised text of the GPA and the completion of the coverage negotiations. It is also notable that the only case brought under the Uruguay Round GPA

---

[14] The revised content of each party's Appendix I is set out in GPA/113 of 2 April 2012.

(considered below) adjudicated on disagreement over whether the procuring entities in question were covered.

The sections below focus on the various considerations which are relevant to whether the GPA covers a particular contract. A helpful position to keep in mind here is that of a supplier from a particular GPA Party. The question is whether this supplier can apply to participate in a contract award procedure of another GPA Party.

(a) The Definition of Covered Procurement

Covered procurement is defined in GPA Article II:2 as follows:

> For the purposes of this Agreement, covered procurement means procurement for governmental purposes:
>
> (a) of goods, services, or any combination thereof:
>
> (i) as specified in each Party's Appendix I; and
>
> (ii) not procured with a view to commercial sale or resale, or for use in the production or supply of goods or services for commercial sale or resale;
>
> (b) by any contractual means, including purchase; lease; and rental or hire purchase, with or without an option to buy;
>
> (c) for which the value, as estimated in accordance with paragraphs 6 through 8, equals or exceeds the relevant threshold specified in Appendix I, at the time of publication of a notice in accordance with Article VII;
>
> (d) by a procuring entity; and
>
> (e) that is not otherwise excluded from coverage in paragraph 3 or in a Party's Appendix I.

Four aspects of this definition will be considered:

- Is the subject matter of the contract covered be it goods, services or construction services?
- Is the procurement above the specified thresholds?
- Is the procurement 'by a procuring entity'?
- Is the procurement 'excluded from coverage'?

(i) Procurement of Goods, Services or any Combination Thereof as Specified in each Party's Appendix I

Contracts for the supply of goods are covered by the GPA unless expressly excluded. Exceptions are normally found in the area of defence procurement. While defence ministries are usually covered entities, their purchase of defence oriented supplies tends to be excluded from coverage.[15]

In contrast, services tend only to be covered if they are expressly listed in Appendix I, Annex 5 of each Party. Annex 5 of the United States differs in that all services are covered except those that are expressly excluded; the most significant express exclusions being

---

[15] For example, the EU's Appendix 1, Annex 4 provides that the procurement of 'vehicles' is covered, but excludes, among others, 'tanks and other armoured vehicles' and 'military vehicles'.

all transportation services and telecommunications. Beyond this, significant variations in the level of coverage provided by different Parties have prompted reciprocity-based derogations. For example, Appendix 1, Annex 7 (para 7) of the United States provides that, '[a] service listed in Annex 5 is covered with respect to a particular Party only to the extent that such Party has included that service in its Annex 5'.

With regard to construction services, a standard definition is used in the Annex 6 of each Party: 'A construction service contract is a contract which has as its objective the realization by whatever means of civil or building works, in the sense of Division 51 of the Central Product Classification (CPC)'. Most Parties have committed to coverage of all categories of constructions services within Division 51 so that derogations of the kind found in the services context are not prevalent. As noted below, however, the fact that financial thresholds vary considerably between Parties has prompted reciprocity based derogations.

(ii) Financial Thresholds

As indicated by GPA Article II:2(c) above, the GPA only applies to contracts which are above certain financial values set out in Appendix I of each GPA Party. As the GPA's objective is to open up procurement markets to competition, these financial thresholds are intended to approximately identify contracts of cross-border interest.

For central government entities procuring goods or services, the threshold for almost all Parties is SDR 130,000 (approximately USD 196,000). Below the central level of government, different Parties maintain different thresholds which tend to be higher. For example, the threshold of the US at sub-central level for construction services is SDR 5 million, but it is SDR 15 million for Korea. Reciprocity derogations sometimes apply to financial thresholds so that Parties which have relatively low thresholds do not extend the benefit of these thresholds to Parties with higher thresholds. The coverage offer of the US therefore provides that, '[f]or construction services of the Republic of Korea and suppliers of such services, the threshold for procurement of construction services by the entities included in Annexes 2 or 3 is 15,000,000 SDRs'.[16]

A problem caused by the use of thresholds is the possibility of splitting up contracts so that they fall below the relevant thresholds. As there are several possible explanations for contract splitting, the question of precisely how it should be regulated presents difficulties. Clearly, contract splitting is a regulatory concern if done primarily to evade the GPA and place contracts with domestic suppliers. However, entities might also calculate that their overall expenditure might be reduced by making a larger number of smaller purchases. At first sight, this point seems to be counter intuitive. Small and frequent purchases conducted on an informal basis might result in price increases relative to larger and less frequent purchases subject to formal competitive tendering. However, entities might consider that any price savings achieved through formal competitive tendering would be outweighed by the cost of operating these formal procedures. This view is reflected in the growing use of purchasing cards whereby end users make purchases informally and without the agency of specialist procurement units. The regulatory dilemma is therefore to find the balance between upholding the GPA and allowing Parties to use procurement methods which enhance commercial objectives such as process efficiency.

---

[16] United States, Appendix I, Annex 7 *General Notes*, para 5.

The GPA contains two relevant provisions in this regard. Article II:6 provides that a procurement should not be divided with the intention of excluding it from the application of the Agreement. Given that this provision refers to the motive for dividing the contract, it will be extremely difficult to establish that it has been breached. Of more importance therefore is Article II:7 which recognises that an 'individual requirement' may result in the award of 'more than one contract or in the award of contracts in separate parts'. Where there are such 'recurring procurements' the value of all such contracts over a 12 month period must be aggregated. This provision does not require that recurring procurements which are part of an individual requirement must be awarded as one contract. Rather, if the provision applies, the below threshold recurring procurements must be deemed to be above threshold procurements.

The difficulty, however, is to know whether the provision applies. This question depends on the amount of leeway entities have to decide if a requirement is an 'individual requirement'. It has been strongly argued that considerable leeway should be preserved:

> [S]eparate purchases should only be considered as part of an individual requirement . . . if no *reasonable* purchaser would have chosen to procure items separately. In assessing it is necessary to consider not merely the subject matter of the procurement but also organisational factors. For example, it is submitted that purchases do not generally constitute an individual requirement when made by independent units of a procuring entity. In many entities, purchasing is decentralised to local offices, or other autonomous units, for sound reasons of administrative organisation, in particular to improve efficiency and accountability. If separate units were required to aggregate purchases, entities' ability to implement optimal organisational structures would be curtailed.[17]

(iii) Procurement 'by a Procuring Entity'

Under Article II:2(d) above, the procurement must be 'by a procuring entity'. Article 1(o) defines a procuring entity as 'an entity covered under a Party's Annex 1, 2 or 3 to Appendix I'. These Annexes mostly use a positive list approach so that entities are only covered if they are listed.

Annex 1 covers central government entities. For all parties, there is near universal coverage at this level. Annex 2 covers sub-central government entities. Most GPA Parties have accepted a level of coverage at this level falling somewhere between substantial and complete. In countries with a federal structure, the de facto or formal autonomy of the states or provinces in deciding whether to undertake coverage commitments can have an impact. In the US, it remains the position that 13 states are not listed. In contrast, one of the highlights of the coverage negotiations completed in December 2011 is the listing of Canada's 10 provinces and two of its three territories for the first time.[18] Annex 3 is entitled 'All Other Entities Whose Procurement is Covered by This Agreement'. This Annex mainly covers bodies which carry out utility functions such as the production and supply of drinking water and electricity and the provision of public transportation services. Entities in these sectors are usually excluded from coverage if privatised. Thus, note 1 to the EU's Annex 3 specifies that procurement related, for example, to electricity supply is not covered 'when exposed to competitive forces in the market concerned'.

---

[17] Arrowsmith, above n 1, 139.

[18] On Canada's GPA commitments, see D Collins, 'Canada's Sub-Central Government Entities and the Agreement on Government Procurement: Past and Present' in Anderson and Arrowsmith (eds), above n 13, 175.

This policy is consistent with the GPA. The principal ground for removing an entity from coverage under Article XIX is that 'government control or influence over the entity's covered procurement has been effectively eliminated'.

In terms of the overall expansion of entity coverage achieved in the coverage negotiations, it has been estimated that 'more than 200 additional central, local and other government agencies' have been added.[19]

The interpretation of the Annexes can give rise to difficulties where the procurement is carried out by an entity which is not itself an expressly listed entity, but which is nevertheless, to some extent, associated with an expressly listed entity.

This situation was considered by the panel in *Korea—Measures Affecting Government Procurement*. The case concerned the procurement of construction services for the Inchon International Airport (IIA). The project was managed by the Korean Airports Authority (KAA) and later by the Inchon International Airport Corporation (IIAC). Having interpreted Korea's Annex, the panel found that these entities were not expressly listed.[20] The panel then proceeded to consider the US' argument that these non-listed entities should nevertheless be regarded as covered entities by reason of the control exercised over them by an expressly listed entity—the Ministry of Construction and Transport (MOCT). Reference is also made in the extract below to the New Airport Development Group (NADG), an organisation which was an internal part of the MOCT.

Korea—Measures Affecting Government Procurement, WT/DS163/R adopted 19 June 2000

7.49 . . . [W]e next will examine whether the relationship between MOCT and KAA was such that KAA's procurement is covered . . . even though KAA is not explicitly included. As noted in paragraph 7.29 above, there is a remaining question as to whether there exists the possibility of the inclusion of certain procurements of an entity which is not listed, due to its relationship with a listed entity. These arguably are general issues which arise with respect to any Member's Schedule regardless of the structure and content of the Schedule and any qualifying Notes.

(iii) Evaluation of the Parties Arguments: The Issue of "Control"

7.50 The United States argues that KAA may be considered a part of MOCT because it is controlled, at least for the purposes of the IIA project, by MOCT. As noted in paragraph 7.29 above, a question is raised whether, regardless of what is specifically in a Schedule, an entity which is deemed "controlled" by a listed entity is also covered by the Member's GPA commitments? If so, as a follow-on to this second question, does KAA fall within this category?

7.51 Korea has discussed this issue in a slightly different manner. Korea has argued that if we were to adopt the US proposed control test, it would cause a number of entities included within Korea's (and other Members') Annex 3 commitments to be put by operation of law under Annex 1 because such entities would arguably be under the "control" of Annex 1 entities. This is important because it would change the threshold levels negotiated with respect to the Annex 3 entities . .

(iv) Evaluation of the Relationship of the Entities Concerned

7.58 As discussed above, we do believe that entities that are not listed in an Annex 1 to the GPA whether in the Annex list or through a Note to the Annex, can, nevertheless, be covered

---

[19] Anderson, above n 11, 84.
[20] Panel Report, *Korea—Measures Affecting Government Procurement*, paras 7.30–7.49.

under the GPA. We believe that this flows from the fact that an overly narrow interpretation of "central government entity" may result in less coverage under Annex 1 than was intended by the signatories. On the other hand, an overly broad interpretation of the term may result in coverage of entities that were never intended to be covered by signatories.

7.59 In the present case, our view is that the relevant questions are: (1) Whether an entity (KAA, in this case) is essentially a part of a listed central government entity (MOCT)—in other words, are the entities, legally unified? and (2) Whether KAA and its successors have been acting on behalf of MOCT. The first test is appropriate because if entities that are essentially a part of, or legally unified with, listed central government entities are not considered covered, it could lead to great uncertainty as to what was actually covered because coverage would be dependent on the internal structure of an entity which may be unknown to the other negotiating parties. The second test is appropriate because procurements that are genuinely undertaken on behalf of a listed entity (as, for example, in the case where a principal/agent relationship exists between the listed entity and another entity) should properly be covered under Annex 1 because they would be considered legally as procurements by MOCT. In our view, it would defeat the objectives of the GPA if an entity listed in a signatory's Schedule could escape the Agreement's disciplines by commissioning another agency of government, not itself listed in that signatory's Schedule, to procure on its behalf.

Are the Entities Legally Unified?

7.60 With respect to the first question, in our view, KAA is not legally unified with or a part of MOCT. There are a number of factors leading to this conclusion. Among them are: KAA was established by law as an independent juristic entity; it authored and adopted its own by-laws; it had its own management and employees who were not government employees; it published bid announcements and requests for proposals of its own accord; it concluded contracts with successful bidders on its own behalf; and it funded portions of the IIA project with its own monies.

7.61 There are, nonetheless, some indicia of a relationship between MOCT and KAA and its successors. The senior members of KAA's board of directors are appointed by MOCT and the rest of the directors are appointed by these senior members. There are indicia of control, at least with respect to the IIA project, that indicate some level of oversight or monitoring of KAA by MOCT. We will discuss this in more detail below with respect to the second question, but, in our view, these levels of "control" relate to oversight or monitoring and not to the common identity of the entities. These sorts of relationships exist throughout the public sector. Without them, it would be difficult for governmental functions to be coordinated effectively. But not all such relationships lead to a finding that one entity is, in effect, a part of another entity. Certainly for purposes of the GPA, such a result would lead to a great deal of uncertainty in the coverage of the Schedules. The GPA has always been based on what is affirmatively included in Schedules and extending the coverage further without clear indicia of effective unity between entities is not warranted by the structure and purpose of the GPA. On balance, we are persuaded by the indicia of independence of KAA and its successors and find that these entities are not a part of MOCT.

Legal responsibility for the IIA project

7.62 The second question is whether or not KAA and its successors were acting on behalf of MOCT, at least with respect to the IIA project. That is, was the IIA project really the legal responsibility of MOCT. In answering these questions, we must review the laws governing construction of the IIA . . .

The panel proceeded to review these domestic laws and upheld Korea's view that the Seoul Airport Act was the ultimate controlling statute rather than the Aviation Act. It continued as follows:

7.66 We agree with Korea's reading of these statutes. It seems clear to us that the Aviation Act provides for at least two methods of airport construction. One is by MOCT, in which case the whole of the Aviation Act applies. A second is by other entities as provided otherwise by law. The Seoul Airport Act is such a law . . .

7.67 The Seoul Airport Act has many provisions relating to the relationship between KAA and MOCT. These provisions, as noted in the previous paragraph, would be at the very least unnecessary if the Aviation Act were the controlling statutory authority. Moreover, Article 4 of the Seoul Airport Act provides for MOCT to draw up a master plan of the project including the general direction of construction, an outline of the construction plan, the construction period and a financing plan, as well as other matters deemed necessary by MOCT. These issues of a general nature are not uncommon elements of a Ministry's oversight of a project but do not render the other entity its agent.

7.68 Article 6 of the Seoul Airport Act provides that the master plan shall be implemented by the state and local governments and by what was later designated as KAA. Article 7 then required KAA to develop an execution plan and have it approved by MOCT along with any alterations other than minor ones. There obviously is a relationship of some degree between MOCT and KAA. MOCT has specific responsibilities of continued oversight. However, we are not persuaded that this oversight was such that KAA was acting as a mere agent of MOCT on a project that was still within the procurement responsibility of MOCT.

7.69 Importantly for purposes of analysis under the GPA, procurement appears to be the responsibility of KAA. The United States has provided examples of bid requests that identify MOCT or the Office of Supply, but we do not find these isolated instances that have been shown to us as sufficient evidence that MOCT is responsible for procurement for the IIA. We note that the currently responsible entity, IIAC, has 557 employees and the NADG is staffed by 30 MOCT officials. While we recognize that a smaller entity can utilize a larger agent, it does not appear that IIAC is a mere empty shell. We also take note of Korea's statement that MOCT has no role in IIA procurements. We see no evidence that would cast doubt on this statement.

7.70 The United States has pointed out that the MOCT website states that NADG has responsibility for the IIA project. As discussed previously, we also take note of Korea's caution that a Ministry's website is not a legal document and that in this case it was prepared by the public relations department of MOCT which might have other motivations in describing the Ministry's business other than technical accuracy. There certainly is a role under Korean law for MOCT in the IIA project. It appears to be a role of oversight. We do not think oversight by one governmental entity of a project which has been delegated by law to another entity (which we have already found to be independent and not covered by GPA commitments) results in a conclusion that there is an agency relationship between them.

Conclusion

7.71 In our view, after reviewing the issues raised in this subsection, we return to our previous conclusion that the answer must be that Members generally may, pursuant to negotiations, decide which entities (and procurement covered by those entities) are included in their Schedules and in which Annex they will be included. The question of "control" or other indicia of affiliation is not an explicit provision of the GPA. Rather, it is a matter of interpretation for the content of the Schedules themselves. Therefore, the issue of whether a Party can use a Note to exclude an entity which would otherwise appear to be covered within the concession contained in a particular Annex is precisely the sort of issue appropriate for qualifications through Notes . . .

7.72 We must also note, however, that this ability to define the scope of commitments is not absolute. The United States pointed out that procurement by NADG was unarguably covered by the GPA even though it was neither listed explicitly nor directly within the definition of a subordinate linear organization or otherwise in Note 1 to Annex 1. Korea responded that NADG was merely an ad hoc task force within MOCT. But this response of Korea somewhat avoids the challenge of this example. There can be something else beyond the strict confines of the language of the Schedule which must be examined. If a Party explicitly excludes an entity in a Note, that is conclusive. A Member may also affirmatively put entities in another Annex from an affiliated entity. But if the Schedule is completely silent on an entity, it may be necessary to look somewhat further to see if there is an affiliation of two entities such that they could be considered legally the same entity (which appears to be the case between MOCT and NADG) or one could be acting on behalf of another.

. . . .

The question considered by the panel in this extract is whether procurement conducted by a non-listed entity should be regarded as covered by reason of the degree of connection between this entity and a listed entity. This question can arise in different circumstances. In the case itself, Korea had not made any relevant changes to its coverage Annexes after the completion of coverage negotiations. It was rather a matter of interpreting these Annexes to discover the extent of Korea's market access commitments.

A different scenario is where a GPA Party transfers responsibility for procurement after the completion of negotiations from a listed entity to a non-listed entity. Here, too, the same question might be asked and the 'legal unity' and 'legal responsibility' tests might be applied to determine whether the non-listed entity is covered. It is submitted, however, that a different approach should apply in these circumstances by reason of the shift in responsibility occurring after the completion of coverage negotiations. This would amount to a modification to coverage regulated by Article XIX. Such modifications must be notified to the Committee on Government Procurement and indicate 'the likely consequences of the change for the mutually agreed coverage provided in this Agreement'. Provision is made for 'compensatory adjustment' in order to 'maintain a balance of rights and obligations'.

The legal unity and legal responsibility tests lead to uncertainty thereby raising the question of how their application might be avoided in the future. One suggestion is that the more vigilant a Party is in coverage negotiations, the less likely reliance on the tests becomes as a last resort to secure coverage. Similarly, recourse to the tests becomes less likely when full and frank answers are provided to questions posed during coverage negotiations. As pointed out by the panel, while the coverage Annexes are structured in terms of entities, Parties negotiate for coverage of the procurements which are the responsibility of the covered entities.[21] Parties can only gain a thorough understanding of which entities in other Parties are responsible for certain procurements by asking questions of those other Parties. In this case, the panel considered that Korea had been less than forthright in its responses to questions posed, and that the US had not done enough to protect its own interests.[22] Had these circumstances not been present, the US would have understood

---

[21] *Ibid*, para 7.109.
[22] *Ibid*, para 7.103–7.119.

that MOCT was not responsible for the IIA procurement. It might then have endeavoured to secure the express listing of the responsible entity—KAA. Failing this, it would have adjusted its own entity coverage. Indeed, armed with a more accurate understanding of Korea's commitments, several of its other trading partners took this step.[23]

(iv) Excluding Procurement from Coverage

GPA Article II:2(e) indicates that Parties can specify exclusions from coverage in their Annexes. Various examples of reciprocity-based derogations have been provided above. Another category of derogations is those which are necessary to allow parties to use procurement to further national objectives of an industrial or social character—also referred to as secondary or (more recently) horizontal policies. For example, Canada's Annex 7 *General Notes* specifies that the GPA 'does not apply to set asides for small and minority owned businesses'. Similarly, Korea's Annex 1 Note 2 excludes from coverage, 'any set-asides for small and medium-sized businesses according to the Act Relating to Contracts to Which the State is a Party and its Presidential Decree'. Derogations of this kind create problems of transparency since their scope depends on the content of national laws. This in turn further complicates coverage negotiations.

(b) Coverage from the Developing *Country* Perspective[24]

In an effort to make GPA membership more attractive to developing countries, Article V requires the Parties to 'give special consideration to the development, financial, and trade needs and circumstances of developing countries'. The new text has been strengthened in terms of identifying additional possible transitional measures for developing countries upon accession to the GPA. Under Article V:3, these measures are price preferences for domestic suppliers, offsets, the phased-in addition of specific entities and sectors, and a financial threshold that is higher than the permanent threshold. The extent to which developing countries can secure these transitional measures depends on the 'agreement of the other Parties'.[25] Therefore, there are no definite entitlements here and much depends on the approach of the existing GPA Parties when new developing country WTO members negotiate GPA accession.

Other provisions give the impression of 'giving with one hand while taking with the other'. For example, Article V:2 provides as follows:

> Upon accession by a developing country to this Agreement, each Party shall provide immediately to the goods, services and suppliers of that country the most favourable coverage that the Party provides under its annexes to Appendix I to any other Party to this Agreement, subject to any terms negotiated between the Party and the developing country in order to maintain an appropriate balance of opportunities under this Agreement.

The notion that Article V does not provide definite benefits which developing countries would otherwise lack is reinforced by the ability of all Parties to negotiate for coverage

---

[23] *Ibid*, para 7.116.

[24] For a fuller treatment of this area, see AC Müller, 'Special and Differential Treatment and Other Special Measures for Developing Countries Under the Agreement on Government Procurement: the Current Text and New Provisions' in Arrowsmith and Anderson (eds), above n 13, 339.

[25] Art V.3.

exclusions in order to further national objectives. Indeed, it has been pointed out that the ability of Parties to secure exclusions depends to some extent on the size of their economies. Derogations have a market closing effect and they have to be 'paid for' with market access opportunities in other areas. Linarelli has recently noted that only states with a substantial import market in public procurement have the capacity to open large procurement markets while also keeping substantial markets closed. Larger developed economies are therefore likely to have a higher capacity than smaller developing economies to pay for derogations.[26] On the other hand, the additional transitional measures now identified in Article V have received a broadly positive reception in the recent literature[27] and can be thought of as providing a framework for the conduct of good faith negotiations. It is presently a matter of waiting to see whether the new text will encourage and facilitate developing country accession.

III. THE UNITED STATES 'STIMULUS PACKAGE' BUY AMERICAN PROVISIONS AND THE GPA[28]

'Buy American' requirements recently came under intense scrutiny as a result of provisions in the American Recovery and Reinvestment Act (ARRA) of 2009.[29] This enactment is commonly referred to as the Stimulus Package, based on its rationale of stimulating the US economy at a time of depressed economic growth. Such packages generally increase the proportion of GDP which is attributable to government procurement as funds are made available for public construction and infrastructure projects.

The discussion below deals with the relationship between the Stimulus Package Buy American provisions and the GPA. The main matter to consider is the compatibility of the Buy American provisions with the GPA. Buy American requirements obviously involve nationality-based discrimination in procurement, and can therefore violate the GPA's national treatment obligation. This creates a need to ensure scope for extending the benefits of Buy American requirements to GPA parties. This extension does not occur on a blanket basis. Rather, it is necessary to know whether the contract in question is covered by the GPA. When the contract is not covered, the Buy American provisions can be applied unencumbered by any GPA obligation.

The most significant of the ARRA Buy American provisions provides as follows:

SEC. 1605. USE OF AMERICAN IRON, STEEL, AND MANUFACTURED GOODS

(a) None of the funds appropriated or otherwise made available by this Act may be used for a project for the construction, alteration, maintenance, or repair of a public building or public

---

[26] J Linarelli, 'The WTO Agreement on Government Procurement and the UNCITRAL Model Procurement Law: A View From Outside the Region' (2006) 1 *Asian Journal of WTO and Health Law and Policy* 62, 79.
[27] See Müller, above n 24.
[28] For a fuller treatment of this area, see J Linarelli, 'Global Procurement Law in Times of Crisis: the Buy American Policies and Options in the WTO Legal System' in Arrowsmith and Anderson (eds), above n 13, 773.
[29] Most significantly, the provisions were extensively discussed in the WTO's Committee on Government Procurement. See, for example, GPA/W/304, 27 April 2009, Responses of the United States to Questions of the European Communities with Respect to the "Buy American" Provisions.

work unless all of the iron, steel, and manufactured goods used in the project are produced in the United States.

(b) Subsection (a) shall not apply in any case or any category of cases in which the head of the Federal department or agency involved finds that

(1) applying subsection (a) would be inconsistent with the public interest;

(2) iron, steel, and the relevant manufactured goods are not produced in the United States in sufficient and reasonably available quantities and of a satisfactory quality; or

(3) inclusion of iron, steel, and manufactured goods produced in the United States will increase the cost of the overall project by more than 25 percent.

(c) If the head of a Federal department or agency determines that it is necessary to waive the application of subsection (a) based on a finding under subsection (b) the head of the department or agency shall publish in the Federal Register a detailed written justification as to why the provision is being waived.

(d) This section shall be applied in a manner consistent with United States obligations under international agreements.

Paragraph (d) above is the most important for the relationship between section 1605 and the GPA. The legislative history of this provision and its operation are considered below.

(a) Section 1605(d)—Legislative History

The provision was inserted during the Senate debate on the Stimulus Package bill as a result of concerns expressed by US trading partners. The amendment was proposed by Senator Dorgan.[30] Speaking in favour of the amendment, Senator Grassley commented as follows:

> The original Buy American language in the bill doesn't specifically provide an exemption for countries that provide reciprocal access for the US in the area of government procurement. But we are obligated under international agreements to provide such a carveout. This amendment will fix this problem.[31]

Senator McCain was alone in speaking in opposition, although this was not motivated by a desire to strengthen the Buy American policy. On the contrary, the Senator was strongly opposed to this policy and introduced his own amendment to strike out the existing Buy American provision and replace it with a limitation on the Buy American clause. The thinking was that an equivalent of paragraph (d) would not be required to secure compliance of the limitation clause with international agreements. Senator McCain spoke at length in defence of his position:

> The Buy American provision in the current bill has echoes of the disastrous Smoot Hawley tariff act. It prohibits the use of funds in this bill for projects unless all of the iron, steel, and manufactured goods used in the project are produced in the United States. These anti-trade measures may sound welcome to Americans who are hurting in the midst of our economic troubles and faced with the specter of layoffs. Yet shortsighted protectionist measures like Buy American risk greatly exacerbating our current economic woes. Already, one economist at the

---

[30] Congress Record for 4 February 2009, S1528.
[31] *Ibid.*

Peterson Institute for International Economics has calculated that the Buy American provisions in this bill will actually cost the United States more jobs than it will generate.

Some of our largest trading partners, including Canada and the European Union—who account for hundreds of billions of dollars in annual trade—have warned that such a move could invite protectionist retaliation, further harming our ability to generate jobs and economic growth. And it seems clear that this provision violates our obligations under more than one international agreement, including the WTO Agreement on Government Procurement and the procurement chapter of the North American Free Trade Agreement . . .

Even President Obama himself spoke out against the Buy American provision. "I think that would be a mistake right now," he said yesterday. "That is a potential source of trade wars that we can't afford at a time when trade is sinking all across the globe."[32]

A letter in support of this position signed by over a hundred US industries was also entered into the record. However, the McCain amendment was rejected and the Dorgan amendment was agreed.

(b) Section 1605(d)—Operation

Paragraph (d) requires that section 1605 be applied in a manner consistent with US international obligations. The GPA is the most significant single source of these obligations. If it applies to the particular contract under examination, the basic national treatment obligation under GPA Article IV:1 is to treat the goods of any GPA Party no less favourably than domestic goods. This obligation indicates that it aids understanding to think of paragraph (d) as an extension of the Buy American requirement, rather than the commonly used terms 'exemption' or 'carveout' as favoured by Senator Grassley above. Paragraph (d) operates as an extension because the favourable treatment given to domestic goods must be extended to goods of the GPA parties.

Of course, this extension only needs to occur when funds made available by the Stimulus Package are used on contracts which are covered by the GPA. A few points on coverage which are specific to the present context can be mentioned here. Appendix I, Annex 2 of the United States indicates that a total of 37 states have commitments under the GPA. However, the GPA does not apply to procurement of production-grade steel in a number of states, including Pennsylvania, in which the domestic production of steel is concentrated.[33] Therefore, when procuring entities in these states are using funds made available under the Stimulus Package, and assuming that there is no commitment under a trade agreement other than the GPA, all steel purchased must be produced in the US.

Assuming that the particular contract is covered by the GPA, a further matter to consider relates to the applicable rule of origin. GPA Article IV:1 will only operate to require the extension of the Buy American obligation to goods of GPA parties if, under the applicable rule of origin, the goods are deemed to originate from a GPA Party. Goods will not necessarily be deemed to so originate merely because they can be imported from a GPA Party. The applicable rule of origin for the operation of paragraph (d) is contained in a section of the Federal Acquisition Regulation (FAR) which was added in

---

[32] S1529–S1529.
[33] Appendix 1 to the GPA, Annex 2 of the United States, note 1.

order to implement section 1605. FAR 25.602-1(2) provides that, 'if trade agreements apply, the manufactured construction material shall either be [produced or manufactured in the US] or be wholly the product of or be substantially transformed [in a GPA Party]'. The threshold test is therefore substantial transformation. As a subsequent FAR section clarifies, construction materials satisfy this test even if they '[consist] in whole or in part of materials from [a non-GPA country provided these materials have] been substantially transformed in a WTO GPA country into a new and different construction material distinct from the materials from which it was transformed'.[34] For example, if steel slab originates in a non-GPA country and this slab is transformed into a beam to support a roof in a GPA country, the beam would probably be deemed to originate in a GPA country and be eligible for purchase using funds made available by the Stimulus Package.

(c) Section 1605(b)—the Waiver

Under the section 1605(b) waiver, the Buy American obligation does not apply if, for example, 'iron, steel, and the relevant manufactured goods are not produced in the United States in sufficient and reasonably available quantities and of a satisfactory quality'. As indicated in section 1605(c), a written justification for the waiver must be provided in the Federal Register. By far the most common ground for waiver is on the ground of the unavailability of the product in the US.

Waivers have also occasionally been granted on the public interest ground, which has been the subject of discussion in the WTO Committee on Government Procurement.[35] The US has indicated that there are no plans to issue guidelines on the scope for waivers on public interest grounds. It is therefore helpful to provide an example from the Federal Register. The Environmental Protection Agency granted a project specific waiver to Gwinnett County Department of Water Resources, Georgia for the purchase of submersible pumps manufactured in Sweden.[36] For some time before the enactment of the ARRA, the county had been requiring contractors to use the Swedish pump to 'avoid the increased costs of inventory, service, maintenance, and engineering associated with using several different brands of pumps'. Applying the Buy American requirement in the ARRA would have resulted in a loss of these advantages so that a waiver was justified. It is also interesting to explain why a waiver was required for goods originating in Sweden—an EU Member State and therefore a GPA Party. This was simply because Georgia is among the states which are not covered at all by the GPA. Therefore the ARRA does not infringe the GPA in requiring entities in Georgia to purchase only domestic goods, or, put differently, the GPA does not extend the application of the Buy American requirement to goods produced in Sweden. A waiver was therefore required.

---

[34] FAR Section 52.225–23.
[35] GPA/W/304, 27 April 2009, questions 11–15.
[36] Federal Register, Vol 75, No 13, Thursday, 21 January 2010—Notice of a Regional Project Waiver of Section 1605 (Buy American) of the American Recovery and Reinvestment Act of 2009 (ARRA) to Gwinnett County Department of Water Resources, Gwinnett County, GA.

IV. RULES APPLYING TO COVERED CONTRACTS

Covered contracts must be awarded in compliance with the general principles and specific rules set out the in the GPA. The main general principles relate to non-discrimination. The specific rules also relate to non-discrimination, in the sense that their main purpose is to make discrimination more difficult by requiring that competitive tendering procedures be conducted in a transparent manner.

The existence of the specific rules reduces the importance of problems connected with general principles of non-discrimination, such as identifying the precise scope of these principles and difficulties in establishing that discrimination has occurred. By comparison, it is a relatively straightforward matter to understand the scope of specific rules and to establish that they have been breached. To put this point in a different way, in most cases involving alleged breaches of the GPA the question of whether the general principles of non-discrimination have been breached, *and* that of whether the specific rules have been breached are likely to be considered. The question of compliance with the general principles will therefore not very often be pivotal to the overall success or failure of a case.

These points are illustrated below, although it is appropriate to mention that it will be for panels and the Appellate Body to develop a perspective on the nature of the relationship between the general principles and the specific rules. It may well emerge in future case law that, if a specific rule intended to make discrimination more difficult is found to have been breached, it will follow almost automatically that the general principles of non-discrimination will also be found to have been breached. The specific rules could then be regarded as a proxy for identifying discrimination.

(a) General Principles of Non-discrimination

Article IV:1 provides as follows:

Non-Discrimination

With respect to any measure regarding covered procurement, each Party, including its procuring entities, shall accord immediately and unconditionally to the goods and services of any other Party and to the suppliers of any other Party offering the goods or services of any Party, treatment no less favourable than the treatment the Party, including its procuring entities, accords to:

(a) domestic goods, services and suppliers; and

(b) goods, services and suppliers of any other Party.

A number of interpretative issues related to this provision are discussed below.

(i) 'Goods and Services of Any Other Party'/'Suppliers of Any Other Party Offering the Goods or Services of Any Party'

Article IV:1 applies first to the 'goods and services of any other Party' and secondly to the 'suppliers of any other Party offering the goods or services of any Party'. It is not immediately obvious what the first phrase adds to the second phrase. However, the first phrase is necessary because the supplier of foreign goods and services could of course be a national supplier. Without the first phrase, discrimination against foreign goods and services provided by a national supplier would be permitted.

(ii) Most Favoured Party Treatment

Article IV:1(a) clearly provides for a national treatment obligation. In contrast, paragraph (b) provides for what might be described as most favoured Party treatment, rather than the broader most favoured nation obligation. The use of most favoured Party treatment reflects the GPA's plurilateral status and prohibits discrimination between suppliers, goods and services from the GPA Parties. On the other hand, GPA Parties are entitled to give relatively favourable treatment to the goods, services and suppliers of non-Parties without extending the same treatment to suppliers of the Parties.

However, the use of most favoured Party treatment, as opposed to most favoured nation treatment is of little practical significance. It is true that a GPA Party might wish to extend relatively favourable treatment to a non-GPA Party. This could occur in the setting of a bilateral free trade agreement, with procurement obligations between a state which is a GPA Party and another state which is not. However, such favourable treatment will normally be related to contract coverage. Suppliers from the non GPA Party will be given access under the bilateral agreement to contracts which GPA Parties do not have access. Article IV:1 (along with all other GPA provisions) applies only to 'covered procurement'. Therefore, even if Article IV:1 did provide for most favoured nation treatment, it would not require the benefit of the bilaterally agreed market access under the free trade agreement to be extended to all GPA Parties.

(iii) 'Treatment No Less Favourable'

In what circumstances is a supplier of a Party treated less favourably than a national supplier or a supplier of any other Party? The phrase 'treatment no less favourable' is found in various WTO agreements including the GATT and the GATS and it has been interpreted as applying to both *de jure* and *de facto* discrimination. There is no reason to suppose that the phrase should be interpreted any differently in the GPA context. *De jure* discrimination occurs where the measure is plainly discriminatory on its face. An obvious example would be a price preference whereby national suppliers are favoured even if their tenders are, for example, up to 5 per cent more expensive than those of foreign suppliers. *De facto* discrimination occurs where the same treatment of all suppliers nevertheless results in domestic suppliers gaining an unacceptable advantage in practice. For example, the conditions of participation of procuring entities in a GPA Party might specify that suppliers must have previous experience of performing contracts in that Party. This measure does not explicitly distinguish between domestic and foreign suppliers but it will be relatively easy for domestic suppliers to meet the condition.

The difficulties with applying the 'treatment no less favourable' standard have been considered elsewhere in this volume. We have noted that there is continuing uncertainty over whether discrimination must be both the aim and effect of the measure, or whether one or other will suffice, or whether there might even be some other as yet unidentified criteria. These questions are equally relevant in the procurement context, especially as conditions which national suppliers can more readily meet might be motivated by legitimate commercial objectives such as reducing unnecessary public expenditure. For example, a procuring entity might specify that tenders must be submitted in its national language. The allocation of any translation costs to suppliers both makes it more difficult for foreign suppliers to participate, and reduces public expenditure. It is at least arguable, however, that this condition would not breach Article IV:1. The Appellate Body's views in the *Dominican Republic—Cigarettes* case would seem to be relevant here:

> the existence of a detrimental effect on a given imported product resulting from a measure does not necessarily imply that this measure accords less favourable treatment to imports if the detrimental effect is explained by factors or circumstances unrelated to the foreign origin of the product . . .[37]

This passage can be read with reference to an earlier opinion expressed by Arrowsmith that conditions such as a language requirement 'reflect legitimate and reasonable interests of the procuring entity and, of course, generally apply in private markets'. Therefore they do not so much modify the conditions of competition as reflect normal market conditions.[38]

The issue of whether the 'treatment no less favourable' standard has been met is less likely to be pivotal in the procurement context than it is in GATT and GATS disputes. As has been noted, the GPA sets out rules which are intended to enhance the transparency of procurement procedures thereby making covert discrimination more difficult. These rules either prohibit or authorise certain practices in explicit terms, and can therefore be applied with greater certainty. With respect to the examples above, the requirement of previous experience on the entity's home market is now clearly prohibited by Article VIII:2(a), while the language requirement is clearly permitted by Article VII:2(i).

A further example of an express prohibition is contained in Article IV:6 which relates to the use of offsets by procuring entities. These are defined as, 'any condition or undertaking that encourages local development or improves a Party's balance-of-payments accounts, such as the use of domestic content, the licensing of technology, investment, counter-trade, and similar actions or requirements'. Conditions in a GPA Party to use raw materials or components from that Party, or engage that Party's labour force on a construction project would breach this provision. The first of these conditions would also breach Article IV:1 since it involves *de jure* discrimination against foreign goods. The second condition would also very probably breach Article IV:1 by reason of *de facto* discrimination against foreign suppliers. It is somewhat easier for a GPA Party's suppliers to use that Party's labour force. A final point to reiterate on offsets is that developing countries are permitted under Article V:3 to use them during a transitional period provided the consent of the Parties can be obtained.

We now move from the general principles on non-discrimination to the specific rules contained in the GPA.

(b) Methods of Procurement

The GPA envisages three procurement methods: open, selected and limited tendering procedures. Under the open procedure, all interested suppliers can submit a tender[39] whereas,

---

[37] Para 96.
[38] Above n 1 160.
[39] Art I(m).

under the selected procedure, suppliers must first satisfy the conditions for participation before being invited to submit a tender. The entity can also pick suppliers from among those which meet the conditions for participation to submit tenders.

No preference is expressed in the GPA as between open and selected procedures. In practice, the choice between open and selected procedures (and whether it is made by a Party itself as opposed to individual procuring entities) depends significantly upon the level of professsionalisation of procurement officials and their tendency towards practices which lack integrity. The open procedure limits the amount of discretion exercised by procurement officials and therefore also limits the scope for corrupt practices. There is no scope in the open procedure for accepting payment in return for being among the selected suppliers.[40] Concern about such practices might lead some GPA Parties to implement the Agreement so as to generally require the use of the open procedure. In contrast, Parties with greater confidence in the integrity of public officers are more likely to leave the choice of procedure to entities. Where entities are given the freedom to choose, the open procedure is more likely when the cost of evaluating individual tenders is low. This will be the position with basic 'off the shelf' items such as office stationery where price could realistically be the sole contract award criterion. In this situation, price savings achieved from evaluating a large number of tenders might not be outweighed by the cost of this evaluation process. In contrast, the selected procedure becomes a more likely option for more complex projects such as the supply of an IT system. Here, price would be one of several award criteria and not necessarily the most important one, thereby raising the cost of evaluating individual tenders to a point which might outweigh any price saving generated by the open procedure.

In contrast to open and selected procedures, limited tendering is a non-competitive process under which the entity contacts suppliers individually. This procedure can only be used on the grounds specified in Article XIII. The first grounds set out here relate to the failure of the open or selected procedure for reasons such as the absence of any tenders or the absence of responsive tenders conforming to the essential requirements of the tender documentation. Other grounds include 'extreme urgency brought about by events unforeseeable by the entity' and 'purchases made under exceptionally advantageous conditions which only arise in the very short term . . . [such as] those arising from liquidation, receivership, or bankruptcy'.

Because of the circumstances in which limited tendering can be used, the specific rules examined below do not apply. For example, rules under which interested suppliers must be given a specified period to submit tenders in response to advertised contracts are clearly inconsistent with the idea of taking advantage of a liquidation sale. Regulation of limited tendering is therefore by general principles alone. Article XIII:1 provides that it should not be used 'for the purpose of avoiding competition among suppliers or in a manner that discriminates against suppliers of the other Parties or protects domestic

---

[40] This explains why instruments such as the UNCITRAL Model Law on Procurement of Goods Construction and Services have 'promoted so far traditional open tendering as a "gold standard", whose fundamental principles included prohibition of negotiations and a single opportunity for a supplier to submit its best tender'. Report of Working Group I (Procurement) on the work of its ninth session A/CN.9/595, para 87. The preference for open tendering referred to in the passage above emerges most clearly from the Guide to Enactment which accompanies the Model Law. para 16 of its Introduction provides that '[s]ome of the key features of tendering as provided for in the Model Law include: as a general rule unrestricted solicitation of participation by suppliers or contractors'.

suppliers'. Possible abuse of limited tendering is reduced by Article XIII:2 in that entities must indicate the circumstances and conditions that justified each recourse to limited tendering.

(c) Advertisement of Procurement Opportunities—Notices

A key element in reducing the risk of discrimination is the requirement that contract opportunities are advertised. This area is regulated mainly by Article VII.

There are three forms of notices which can be used to alert suppliers of present or future procurement opportunities. For reasons which will be explained, these three notices will be referred to as different types of invitations to participate, even though this term is no longer used in the GPA 2012.

- Notice of Intended Procurement
- Notice of Planned Procurement
- Notice of a Multi-Use List

The GPA clearly indicates that all entities can use the first type of notice, but that only Annex 2 and 3 entities can use the second and third types.[41] Less flexibility is therefore provided to Annex 1 entities (central government entities) than Annex 2 and 3 entities (respectively sub-central government entities and 'other entities' the latter of which are mainly in the utilities sectors). The only plausible explanation for this is that, if there are central government tendencies or policies to buy national, their influence diminishes as we move away from the central government level.

Some commentators are sceptical about whether this rationale is sufficiently compelling to deprive Annex 1 entities of what amounts to a modest amount of increased flexibility. According to this view, the reduced cost of operating more flexible procedures would not come at the expense of transparency, competition and any increased risk of discrimination, so that the same flexibility should be available to all entities.[42] This view seems to be reflected in recent developments. For example, in the Australia—United States Free Trade Agreement,[43] which came into force on 1 January 2005, the procurement rules apply to central and regional government entities and government enterprises. However, the rules apply in the same way to all entities so that all entities have the same level of flexibility.

(i) Notice of Intended Procurement

All entities can use the notice of intended procurement, which must be published in the paper or electronic medium specified by each Party. The nature of the information which must be provided indicates that the purpose of this notice is to commence a procurement procedure in respect of a specific and imminent need. Under Article VII:2, information must, for example, be provided about the nature and quantity of the products or services required. Suppliers must also be informed of the procurement method to be used and

---

[41] See Arts VII:5 and IX:12.
[42] See Arrowsmith, above n 1, 189.
[43] The Agreement can be viewed in the Bilateral and Regional Trade Agreements on www.worldtradelaw. net. The procurement rules are contained in Chapter 15.

whether it will involve negotiation or electronic auction. Where the selected procedure is used, the criteria for selecting suppliers to be invited to tender must be specified.

(ii) Notice of Planned Procurement

The notice of planned procurement is intended to give advanced notice of procurement plans for each fiscal year. Article VII:4 provides that this notice 'should include the subject-matter of the procurement and the planned date of publication of the notice of intended procurement'. From this provision, it is clear that the notice of planned procurement and the notice of intended procurement are distinct. If a notice of planned procurement is initially used, it must indicate when the notice of intended procurement will follow. The clarity achieved by Article VII:4 is, however, placed in doubt by Article VII:5:

> A procuring entity covered under Annex 2 or 3 may use a notice of planned procurement as *a notice of intended procurement* provided that the notice of planned procurement includes as much of the information referred to in paragraph 2 as is available to the entity and a statement that interested suppliers should express their interest in the procurement to the procuring entity. (emphasis added)

This provision undermines the clear distinction between the two notices. However, the provision can be readily explained by looking back at the terminology used in the GPA 1994. Here, all three different types of notices were referred to as forms of invitation to participate. This phrase is no longer used. However if the emphasised words in the provision above are replaced with 'an invitation to participate', the true meaning of the provision becomes clear. The idea is that Annex 2 and 3 entities can publish a notice of planned procurement, and then dispense with the need to separately publish notices of intended procurement on each occasion an actual need arises. The single notice of planned procurement serves as the invitation to participate.

(iii) Notice of a Multi-use List

The term multi-use list is defined by Article 1 as 'a list of suppliers that a procuring entity has determined satisfy the conditions for participation in that list, and that the procuring entity intends to use more than once'. Multi-use lists are regulated by Article IX:7–13. The lists can be seen as useful streamlining devices since they enable entities to identify suppliers with the basic attributes which are necessary to carry out the type of contracts covered by the lists. The burden of having to evaluate basic attributes for individual procurements is minimised.

Various conditions apply to all entities which use lists. For example, a notice inviting suppliers to join the list must ordinarily be published annually. However all entities can choose to publish the notice only once every three years provided that the notice, for example, states its period of validity and is published via electronic means and made continuously available. All notices must indicate such matters as the categories of goods and services for which the list will be used.

Article IX:12 then provides that Annex 2 and 3 entities can use the notice of the list as a notice of intended procurement. For clarity, it is again better to think of the notice of the list as the invitation to participate. This means that Annex 2 and 3 entities can permissibly dispense with the need to publish notices of intended procurement for individual require-ments, provided that there is a valid list in operation. When individual needs arise, it would be sufficient to contact only the suppliers on the list. However, it is also important to note that, under Article IX:10, access to the list must be kept open at all times and all entities must include qualified suppliers on the lists within a reasonably short time.

(d) Conditions for Participation

At some point before a contract is awarded, the entity will need to ensure that suppliers have the basic attributes which will enable them to perform the contract. The GPA refers to the permissible criteria for assessing basic attributes as conditions for participation. These conditions are verified in qualification procedures. Sometimes all aspects of these procedures will be conducted on an ad hoc basis for individual procurements. As noted above, the cost inherent in repeating the same procedures can also be reduced by inviting suppliers to join a multi-use list.

When the 'open tendering' procedure is used, entities are not permitted to impose any conditions for participation or operate any kind of qualification system before tenders are submitted. This follows from the definition of the open procedure under which 'all interested suppliers may submit a tender'.[44] The process of verifying whether suppliers meet the conditions for participation can only therefore commence after the expiry of the time for receipt of tenders. There is much greater flexibility with the selective procedure to the extent that the qualification process may be conducted even before the precise procurement requirement is known by inviting suppliers to apply for inclusion on lists.

The key obligation in Article VIII:1 with regard to conditions for participation is that they should be limited to those which are 'essential to ensure that a supplier has the legal and financial capacities and the commercial and technical abilities to undertake the relevant procurement'. The further specific rules demonstrate that the concern is to deter discrimination. Thus, capacity and technical ability must be evaluated based on the 'supplier's business activities both inside and outside' of the procuring entity's territory, and it is not permissible to require that 'the supplier has previously been awarded one or more contracts by a procuring entity of a given Party'. It follows that when the selective procedure is used, and when the application of permissible criteria does not sufficiently whittle down the field, it would be permissible for the entity to select the suppliers with, for example, the most experience of performing comparable contracts, provided that no preference is given to suppliers with experience of performing comparable contracts in the procuring entity's own territory.

As for the question of how many suppliers should be invited to tender, Article X:1 of the GPA 1994 referred to the need to 'ensure optimum effective international com-petition under selective tendering procedures'. This was to result in the invitation of tenders from 'the maximum number of domestic suppliers and suppliers of other Parties, consistent with the efficient operation of the procurement system'. These provisions have been omitted from the GPA 2012, giving the impression that it is a matter for individual Parties or entities to decide on the point at which increased competition is likely to be outweighed by the cost of evaluating tenders.

---

[44] Art I(m).

(i) The Scope for Excluding Firms which Can 'Undertake the Relevant Procurement'

Uncertainty exists over whether the application of conditions for participation can result in the exclusion of firms which, in general terms, lack integrity but which are nevertheless capable of undertaking the relevant procurement. This depends on the relationship between Article VIII paragraphs 1 and 4:

Article VIII Conditions for Participation

1. A procuring entity shall limit any conditions for participation in a procurement to those that are essential to ensure that a supplier has the legal and financial capacities and the commercial and technical abilities to undertake the relevant procurement . . .

4. Where there is supporting evidence, a Party, including its procuring entities, may exclude a supplier on grounds such as:

(a) bankruptcy;

(b) false declarations;

(c) significant or persistent deficiencies in performance of any substantive requirement or obligation under a prior contract or contracts;

(d) final judgments in respect of serious crimes or other serious offences;

(e) professional misconduct or acts or omissions that adversely reflect on the commercial integrity of the supplier; or

(f) failure to pay taxes.

The question is whether suppliers can be excluded on grounds such as bankruptcy or false declarations under paragraph 4, even if their ability, under paragraph 1, to undertake the relevant procurement is not affected. Bankruptcy might well prevent suppliers from undertaking the contract. However, the same cannot be said of false declarations or analogous grounds such as convictions for equal opportunities or environmental legislation unless the national penalty in the legal system of the supplier or the procuring entity happens to involve preventing firms found to have committed these misdemeanours from participating in government contracts. If this happened to be the position, then suppliers would arguably lack the legal capacity to undertake the contract so that the exclusion under paragraph 4 would be consistent with paragraph 1.

It is possible to argue that action taken under paragraph 4 must be consistent with paragraph 1. Support for this argument can be found in the fact that paragraph 4 is not set up as an exception to paragraph 1. The opening phrase in paragraph 4 might have, but does not say, 'where there is supporting evidence *and notwithstanding paragraph 1 . . .*'. It would then follow, for example, that a supplier can only be excluded on the basis of final judgments in respect of serious crimes if, under the national law of either the supplier or the procuring entity, the supplier is thereby deprived of the legal capacity to undertake the relevant procurement.

It is submitted, however, that this is a rather odd interpretation since exclusion would depend on the arbitrary factor of whether this is required or permitted under national law. The view that paragraph 1 constrains discretion under paragraph 4 is also weakened by the safeguard in paragraph 4 in the form of the need for 'supporting evidence'. It is improbable that the intention of the Parties was to permit exclusion under paragraph 4 where there is supporting evidence, but only if this happens to be a sanction envisaged by national law. The better interpretation is therefore that the two paragraphs operate independently of each other so that suppliers can be excluded on such grounds as those listed in Article VIII:4, even if they are fully capable of undertaking the procurement under Article VIII:1. This position is confirmed by the fact that the equivalent provisions in the GPA 1994 were clearly intended to operate independently of each other.[45]

(ii) Minimizing Differences in Qualification Procedures and Avoiding Unnecessary Obstacles to the Participation of Foreign Suppliers

Article IX:2 requires each Party to 'ensure that its procuring entities make efforts to minimize differences in their qualification procedures'. Arrowsmith has suggested that this is an unusual provision in that it does not seem to be concerned with either enhancing transparency or reducing the risk of discrimination.[46] In respect of transparency, entities might operate very different procedures but also openly publicise and clearly explain these procedures. In respect of discrimination, all suppliers, domestic and foreign, are equally subject to the various different procedures. The suggestion is, therefore, that this provision is directed towards 'the removal of trade restrictions that are not justifiable in the light of the objectives that those restrictions seek to achieve'[47] but also that this is a 'best efforts provision that cannot be legally enforced'.[48]

Some doubt, in particular, about the non-enforceability point is created by a new provision in the GPA 2011, Article IX.3:

> A Party, including its procuring entities, shall not adopt or apply any registration system or qualification procedure with the purpose or the effect of creating unnecessary obstacles to the participation of foreign suppliers in its procurement.

The task with this provision is to identify the circumstances in which a qualification procedure has the effect of creating the unnecessary obstacles referred to. Might there be an unnecessary obstacle when foreign suppliers have to comply with both the qualification procedures of their domestic entities and those of other Parties? To put this question another way, if a supplier is registered as qualified to build schools in its own state, must it also be recognised as qualified to build schools by the entities of other Parties? In general terms, the answer is almost certainly that Article IX:3 is not breached merely because a foreign supplier is subject to the qualification procedure of foreign entities and its home entities. However, if the procedure before a supplier's domestic entities happens to closely resemble that used by a foreign entity, there would seem to be an argument that the 'double exposure' amounts to a violation.

Greater certainty awaits developments in WTO case law, not only under the GPA, but also under similar provisions such as Article 2.2 of the Agreement on Technical Barriers to Trade (TBT) (See Chapter 14).

---

[45] GPA 1994, Arts VIII(b) and VIII(h).
[46] Arrowsmith, above n 1, 171.
[47] *Ibid.*
[48] *Ibid*, 19.

(e) Time Limits for Award Procedures

The purpose of time limits is to give foreign suppliers adequate opportunity to overcome their potential lack of familiarity with foreign procurement procedures, while also recognising that entities need to progress procurement procedures with reasonable speed. It is notable that one of the grounds on which the US challenged Korea's procurement practices in the case noted above related to allegedly improper time limits. However, as the panel found there was no 'covered procurement' in this case, the panel did not proceed to the question of whether the GPA had been breached. On the whole, the rules on time limits are not difficult to understand, although it is sometimes not altogether clear how the relevant provisions fit together.

Time limits come into operation after the publication of the notice of intended procurement. The question is how long suppliers have to prepare and submit, first, their request to participate and, secondly, their tenders. If the open procedure is used the only relevant time limit is that for submitting tenders. As all interested suppliers must be allowed to submit tenders under the open procedure, there is no question of having to first submit a request to participate. However, when the selected procedure is used, an initial time limit to request participation will be followed by a further time limit to submit the tender.

Article XI regulates time limits with both general and specific obligations. The general obligation requires that time limits be sufficient for suppliers 'to prepare and submit requests for participation and responsive tenders'. Relevant considerations for determining the sufficiency of time limits include 'the nature and complexity of the procurement and the extent of subcontracting anticipated'. Article XI then proceeds to set out minimum periods.

(i) From the Notice of Intended Procurement to the Request to Participate

Under Article XI:2, if selective tendering is used, suppliers must be given at least 25 days after the publication of the notice of intended procurement by the entity to submit their requests to participate. This period can be reduced to not less than 10 days in only one situation: 'where a state of urgency duly substantiated by the procuring entity renders this [25 day] time-period impracticable'.

Applying this provision to Annex 1 entities presents no difficulty since they cannot dispense with the need to publish a notice of intended procurement when individual requirements arise. Therefore, the 25 day period commences each time one of these notices is published. The position is not so straightforward for Annex 2 and 3 entities since (as noted in section IV.C) they can use both a notice of planned procurement[49] and a notice of a multi-use list[50] as the notice of intended procurement. It is thus arguable that the 25 day period commences when the notice of planned procurement or the notice of the multi-use list is published. Arguably, this interpretation will sometimes be unworkable. As a practical matter, suppliers will not be able to fully ascertain their level of interest in an individual requirement until the details of this requirement are known. It therefore seems sensible for the 25 day period to commence when suppliers are noti-

---

[49] Art VII:5.
[50] Art IX:12.

fied of individual requirements rather than from the earlier publication of the notice of planned procurement or the notice of a multi-use list.

(iii) From the Request to Participate to the Submission of Tenders

After suppliers have been notified of individual requirements, at least some will respond with a request to participate. Under Article XI:3, the suppliers then invited to submit tenders must be given at least 40 days to do so.

Article XI:4 permits a reduction of this 40 day period to not less than 10 days where entities publish a notice of planned procurement containing, for example, as much of the information required under a notice of intended procurement as is available at the time. It is notable that this reduced deadline is available to all entities which clearly provides an incentive towards using notices of planned procurement.

A significant modernisation in the GPA 2012 is that electronic forms of communication are now envisaged. Article XI:5 provides for a reduction in the time limit for submitting tenders of five days where the notice of intended procurement is published by electronic means. Further reductions of five days each are permitted if tender documentation is made available electronically from the date of publication of the notice of intended procurement and if tenders can be received electronically. In total therefore, use of electronic means of communication can result in the deadline for receipt of tenders being reduced from 40 days to 25 days from the date suppliers are invited to submit tenders.

Article XI:6 regulates the situation where both electronic means are used, and another ground for reduction of the time limit is present, such as the publication of a notice of planned procurement. It is provided that this, 'shall in no case result in the reduction of the time-period for tendering set out in paragraph 3 [40 days] to less than 10 days *from the date on which the notice of intended procurement is published*' (emphasis added). There is a slight drafting error here since the provision only makes sense if open tendering is used. If selective tendering is used, the notice of intended procurement will be followed by requests to participate from suppliers and, in turn, the invitation to submit tenders from the entity. The lapse of time between the notice of intended procurement and the invitation to submit tenders will normally be significantly greater than 10 days. Under the wording presently used, entities could therefore set a period for tender submission of less than 10 days from the invitation to submit tenders. This anomaly would be removed by the deletion of the emphasised words. Paragraph 3 sets out when the time period should commence in both open and selective procedures and the reference to paragraph 3 in paragraph 6 incorporates this difference.

Finally, Article XI:8 provides increased flexibility for Annex 2 and 3 entities only. When these entities select 'all or a limited number of qualified suppliers, the time-period for tendering may be fixed by mutual agreement between the procuring entity and the selected suppliers'. Even without agreement entities can specify a period of not less than 10 days.

(f) Awarding of Contracts

Article XV:5 states:

Unless a procuring entity determines that it is not in the public interest to award a contract, it shall award the contract to the supplier that the entity has determined to be fully capable of undertaking the contract and, based solely on the evaluation criteria specified in the notices and tender documentation, has submitted:

(a) the most advantageous tender; or

(b) where price is the sole criterion, the lowest price.

(i) The Most Advantageous Tender

Parties have broad discretion over the content of specific evaluation criteria under the overall criterion of 'most advantageous tender' provided, of course, that the specific criteria are specified in advance. This transparency requirement makes it more difficult for discrimination to occur through communicating the criteria only to national suppliers. Article X:9 provides guidance on the type of criteria that might be used. The criteria 'may include, among others, price and other cost factors, quality, technical merit, environmental characteristics, and terms of delivery'.

The inclusion of 'environmental characteristics' on this illustrative list raises the question of whether such characteristics can only permissibly relate to the products or services themselves (for example requirements that any materials used are recyclable) or also to the supplier's production methods (for example relating to its emissions standards). When Article X:9 is read in context, it is revealed that the latter and broader approach is to be preferred. Article I(t) defines the term technical specification as a requirement which 'lays down the characteristics of goods or services to be procured, including quality, performance, safety, and dimensions, or the *processes and methods for their production or provision*' (emphasis added). Additionally, Article X:6 is a new provision under which, 'for greater certainty, a Party, including its procuring entities, may, in accordance with this Article, prepare, adopt, or apply technical specifications to promote the conservation of natural resources or protect the environment'. The utility of these provisions would be reduced if production methods could not be considered at the award stage. It is therefore submitted that it would be permissible to rank tenders partly on the basis of the extent to which the suppliers improve upon international standards on emissions.

(ii) Ranking of Evaluation Criteria

Unlike the GPA 1994, the GPA 2012 requires the tender documentation to indicate the 'relative importance' of 'all the evaluation criteria'.[51] As the evaluation criteria must be ranked and published in tender documentation, the opportunity for tacitly communicating the ranking only to a favoured supplier is removed. The ranking requirement would seem to be flexible and would probably be satisfied by a list of evaluation criteria in order of importance. It would certainly be satisfied by providing approximate percentage values for all the criteria.

However, if an electronic auction is used, entities will in practice be required to give an exact percentage weighting or value to all evaluation criteria. This does not have to be included in the tender documentation. Rather, Article XIV(a) effectively requires the

---

[51] Art X:7(c).

precise weightings to be communicated before the auction commences as part of the 'mathematical formula' referred to in this provision.

(iii) Electronic Auctions

A possible alternative to opening confidential tenders and awarding the contract to the best tender is to conduct an electronic auction. The auction phase of the award procedure involves the participants having the opportunity to improve their tenders which are then continuously re-ranked by electronic means. Electronic auctions can assist in the reduction of pubic expenditure since suppliers have an incentive to improve tenders. Transparency is also enhanced, particularly if participants have information on the characteristics of other tenders, as well as the ranked position of their own tender, during the auction.

The GPA 2012 makes express provision for electronic auctions. Article I(f) defines them as an, 'iterative process[52] that involves the use of electronic means for the presentation by suppliers of either new prices, or new values for quantifiable non-price elements of the tender related to the evaluation criteria, or both, resulting in a ranking or re-ranking of tenders'.

Article XIV deals with auctions in the following terms:

> Where a procuring entity intends to conduct a covered procurement using an electronic auction, the entity shall provide each participant, before commencing the electronic auction, with:
>
> (a) the automatic evaluation method, including the mathematical formula, that is based on the evaluation criteria set out in the tender documentation and that will be used in the automatic ranking or re-ranking during the auction;
>
> (b) the results of any initial evaluation of the elements of its tender where the contract is to be awarded on the basis of the most advantageous tender; and
>
> (c) any other relevant information relating to the conduct of the auction.[53]

The reference to 'any initial evaluation' in paragraph (b) indicates that an initial evaluation of tenders prior to the auction is not mandated. The obligation is rather that the result of any initial evaluation which *is* conducted must be communicated before the auction phase. This is in sharp contrast to the EU public sector directive which requires that, where the most economically advantageous award criterion is used, the invitation to participate in the auction be accompanied by the 'outcome of a full evaluation of the relevant tenderer [*sic*]'.[54] However, this difference is unlikely to have very much impact. When the overall award criterion is the most advantageous tender, an 'initial evaluation' would at least sometimes, if not usually, occur in practice for the following reasons.

Paragraph (a) above refers to 'the automatic evaluation method' and the 'automatic ranking or re-ranking during the auction'. The need for automation rules out any intervention and exercise of subjective judgement by the entity during the auction. It follows that the non-price factors which can be improved upon during the auction must be 'quantifi-

---

[52] Perhaps more helpfully Art 1(7) of the new EU public sector directive (Directive 2004/18/EC [2004] OJ L134/1) uses the phrase 'repetitive process'.

[53] No guidance is provided on what this other relevant information might be although it could most obviously relate to when and how the auction will end.

[54] New public sector directive (above n 52), Art 54(5). The reference in this provision to 'tenderer' is an error, the correct term being 'tender'.

able' and capable of being expressed in 'figures and percentages'. These expressions are from the EU public sector directive,[55] but they are also implicit GPA requirements because of the limits of what can be automatically evaluated via electronic means. Many non-price factors are capable of being automatically evaluated. For example, an aspect of quality might be service intervals for a machine. It could be specified that for every extra month of operation beyond one year during which the machine does not require a service, the entity will pay an extra £100. However, the entity might also choose to undertake an initial evaluation of this factor, and other non-price factors even though they are capable of automatic evaluation. Indeed, it is common for all non-price factors to be evaluated before the auction and for price alone to be subjected to the auction. It is also the position that some non-price factors are not capable of automatic evaluation. It would not be possible, for example, to improve the artistic merit of the construction to be delivered during the auction since the question of how many points to allocate here necessitates human judgement.[56] It can therefore be seen how the Article XIV(b) obligation to disclose the 'results of any initial evaluation' will frequently be triggered.

A possible means of avoiding the obligation might be for the entity to evaluate non-price factors excluded from the auction only after the conclusion of the auction. This practice is probably not permitted. The definition of electronic auctions in Article I(f) refers to a 'ranking or re-ranking of tenders'. The most natural interpretation of this requirement is that participants must know during the auction whether their tender is the winning tender, and must know at the end of the auction whether their tender has won. If this is the position, then the ranking must be based both on the factors which can be revised during the auction and those that have been fixed and inputted after the initial evaluation but before the commencement of the auction. This would enhance both transparency and the incentive to improve tenders.

A final point is that it is clear from the wording of paragraph Article XIV that 'each participant' is only entitled to receive information about 'the results of any initial evaluation of the elements of *its tender*'. There is no obligation to disclose to participants how their tenders relate to other tenders. However, such disclosure is probably also not prohibited provided it occurs in a transparent and non-discriminatory manner. This would involve the ranking after the initial evaluation being made available to all participants. Some doubt on this point is created by the need to guarantee the confidentiality of tenders under Article XV:1. However, this safeguard probably does not apply to any part of an award procedure which culminates in an electronic auction. This interpretation seems to be confirmed by the GPA 1994 Article XIV:3 which supplements the need to treat tenders in confidence with a prohibition against providing 'information intended to assist particular participants to bring their tenders up to the level of other participants'. This, of course, is the entire rationale for the electronic auction.

---

[55] Art 54:3(a)
[56] S Arrowsmith, *The Law of Public and Utilities Procurement* (Sweet & Maxwell, 2005) 1202.

V. THE EXCEPTIONS PROVISION

As in all areas of trade regulation, there is a balance to be achieved between trade liberalisation and allowing states to pursue legitimate non-trade objectives. The GPA sets out an exceptions provision which largely corresponds with GATT Article XX. GPA 2012 Article III:2 provides:

> Subject to the requirement that such measures are not applied in a manner that would constitute a means of arbitrary or unjustifiable discrimination between Parties where the same conditions prevail or a disguised restriction on international trade, nothing in this Agreement shall be construed to prevent any Party from imposing or enforcing measures:
>
> (a) necessary to protect public morals, order, or safety;
>
> (b) necessary to protect human, animal or plant life or health;
>
> (c) necessary to protect intellectual property; or
>
> (d) relating to goods or services or persons with disabilities, philanthropic institutions, or prison labour.

It has been suggested that some human rights oriented policies might fall under paragraph (a).[57] The debate here was triggered by legislation enacted by the Commonwealth of Massachusetts to restrict the award of government contracts to domestic and foreign firms having business links with Burma on the basis that this state is considered to have a poor human rights record. The EU and Japan requested a WTO panel to examine the compatibility of this legislation with the GPA 1994, and a panel was established on 21 October 1998.[58] This might have been a highly significant case in terms of providing guidance on the meaning and scope of several GPA 1994 provisions including Articles VIII(b) (now VIII:1 and 2 GPA 2012) and XIII:4(b) (now XV:5 GPA 2012). Had a violation of these provisions been established, it is reasonable to suppose that the scope for justifying the legislation under the 'public morals, order or safety' exception would have been considered. However, panel proceedings were suspended in February 1999, and the complaint was later allowed to lapse.[59]

Notwithstanding the possible scope of the public morals exception, none of other grounds would seem to permit Parties to provisionally justify the use of procurement for the pursuit of industrial and social policies such as preferences for domestic infant industries, or businesses owned by disadvantaged groups.[60] Only paragraph (d) is of limited relevance to social policies.

---

[57] See C McCrudden, 'International Economic Law and the Pursuit of Human Rights: A Framework for Discussion of the Legality of "Selective Purchasing" Laws Under the WTO Government Procurement Agreement' (1999) 2 *Journal of International Economic Law* 3, 38–42.

[58] *US—Measures Affecting Government Procurement*.

[59] The WTO proceedings were allowed to lapse because the constitutionality of the Massachusetts Burma law was successfully challenged by a non-profit corporation, 34 of whose members had been placed on a restricted purchase list to indicate their business involvement in Burma. The main basis for the Supreme Court decision was that the state legislation was an obstacle to the achievement of Congress's objectives under a later federal statute dealing with sanctions against Burma. *Crosby v. National Foreign Trade Council* 120 S.Ct. 2288 (2000).

[60] One of the matters discussed in the 1997 Green Paper on Public Sector Procurement Reform in South Africa is the need '[t]o realise the potential of public sector procurement as an instrument of policy in the socio-economic transformation process': see http://www.info.gov.za/greenpapers/1997/publicproc.htm (accessed on 29 April 2012) at 3.1.2. For an analysis of subsequent legislative developments, see P Bolton 'An Analysis of

Until recently, this limited scope for justifying horizontal policies might have been explained on the basis that little attention was given to this question during the Uruguay Round negotiations. This is indicated by McCrudden's account of the GPA 1994 negotiations which indicates that discussions focused on derogations to remove certain policies from the GPA's reach, rather than requiring Parties to justify their horizontal policies.[61] However, the GPA 2012 does not implement a reform proposal, suggested by Arrowsmith, which might have facilitated the pursuit of horizontal policies. This proposal is to require all horizontal policies to be justified 'but to remove limitations on the possible *types* of public interest justification' along the lines of the TBT.[62] On the assumption that this proposal was considered in the negotiations which led to the GPA 2012, it is interesting to speculate as to what might have led to its rejection. Some Parties might have considered that implementing the proposal would have done more to undermine than facilitate the horizontal uses of procurement. As noted in Section II.A(4) above, the practice at present is for horizontal policies to be accommodated by derogations in coverage. Policies can therefore operate even if they clearly or potentially breach the GPA. The thrust of the proposal is for this practice to be substituted by the exposure of horizontal policies to a necessity requirement[63] and the chapeau. Given the strictness with which these requirements have been interpreted by WTO panels and the Appellate Body, some parties might have preferred to retain the derogation route.

VI. DOMESTIC REVIEW PROCEDURES FOR SUPPLIER CHALLENGES

When suppliers consider that the GPA has not been properly implemented, or that it has been breached in the context of a particular award procedure, they can take advantage of the requirement to provide for national challenge procedures. Significantly, suppliers can resort to these procedures independently of their governments so that this form of enforcement is fundamentally different to intergovernmental dispute settlement under the Dispute Settlement Understanding (DSU).

Article XVIII:1 provides that:

Each Party shall provide a timely, effective, transparent, and non-discriminatory administrative or judicial review procedure through which a supplier may challenge:

(a) a breach of the Agreement; or

---

the Preferential Procurement Legislation in South Africa' (2007) *Public Procurement Law Review* 36. For an analysis of domestic preferences in Malaysia, see C McCrudden and S Gross, 'WTO Government Procurement Rules and the Local Dynamics of Procurement Policies: A Malaysian Case Study' (2006) 17 *European Journal of International Law* 151.

[61] Above n 57, 20–21.

[62] S Arrowsmith, 'Reviewing the GPA: The Role and Development of the Plurilateral Agreement After Doha' (2002) 5 *Journal of International Economic Law* 761, 782.

[63] TBT Art 2.2 imposes a necessity requirement in the sense that 'technical regulations shall not be more trade-restrictive than necessary to fulfil a legitimate objective'.

(b) where the supplier does not have a right to challenge directly a breach of the Agreement under the domestic law of a Party, a failure to comply with a Party's measures implementing this Agreement,

arising in the context of a covered procurement, in which it has, or has had, an interest. The procedural rules for all challenges shall be in writing and made generally available.

The GPA 1994 did not contain paragraph (b) above, so that suppliers apparently had to be given the opportunity to challenge 'a breach of the Agreement'. Some commentators interpreted this language as indicating that the GPA was intended to have direct effect in the legal systems of all its Parties.[64] Had this been correct, national review bodies would be required to apply the GPA itself, rather than national implementing measures in the event of a conflict. For example, if the standard period for submission of tenders under the GPA is 40 days, but, in national law, the period is 30 days, there would clearly be an implementation failure. The question for the national review body is whether it is required to apply only national law, or whether the international law obligation takes priority. In other words, the question is whether the GPA has direct effect.

It is now clear from the inclusion of paragraph (b) that direct effect is a matter for individual Parties. Therefore, where the supplier's complaint is that the GPA has not been properly implemented by a state which does not recognise the direct effect of the WTO agreements, the appropriate course of action would be for the supplier to petition its government to institute intergovernmental proceedings under the DSU.

In contrast, where the GPA has been properly implemented, but has not been followed by an entity in a specific procurement, suppliers can usefully have recourse to domestic review procedures. Indeed, the requirement for Parties to provide for these procedures stems from the inadequacy of the DSU in providing a meaningful solution where the complaint relates to a specific procurement. The timetable for resolving disputes under the DSU is understandably protracted[65] and there is no provision for interim remedies, such as the suspension of the award procedure, at the start of the dispute. Indeed, there would be little point in providing for suspension, unless a panel could order the recommencement of the procedure in the event of a breach being confirmed. It is generally understood, however, that the standard recommendation under DSU Article 19 has only prospective effect. The requirement to 'bring the [inconsistent] measure into conformity' is a forward looking remedy which does not entail reparations for injury caused by WTO violations.[66]

In the procurement context, the *Trondheim* case, decided under the Tokyo Round GPA, confirms that remedies following intergovernmental proceedings at the WTO cannot have an impact on past conduct.

The case involved the Norwegian Public Roads Administration which awarded a contract relating to electronic toll collection equipment for a toll system around the city of Trondheim to a Norwegian company, Micro Design. As limited tendering was used, (then

---

[64] T Cottier 'A Theory of Direct Effect in Global Law' in A Von Bogdandy, PC Mavroidis and Y Mény (eds), *European Integration and International Co-ordination* (The Hague, Kluwer Law International, 2002).

[65] The GPA 1994 Art XXII.6 had provided that '[e]very effort should be made to accelerate the proceedings to the greatest possible extent' and then went on to recommend specific reduced deadlines. Interestingly, this provision has been jettisoned from the GPA 2012, which probably reflects the view that breaches of the GPA in the context of a specific procurements can only realistically be challenged at the national level.

[66] See A Davies 'Reviewing Dispute Settlement at the World Trade Organization: a Time to Reconsider the Role/s of compensation' (2006) 5 *World Trade Review* 31.

referred to as single tendering) the award was not preceded by any competitive tendering procedure. This was challenged by the US on the basis that the use of limited tendering had excluded 'viable and eager competition from a capable United States supplier'. The panel first found that the use of limited tendering was not justified under the governing provisions in effect at that time.[67] Therefore the national treatment provision then contained in Article II:1 (now Article IV:1) was found to have been breached. The panel then considered the remedies which the US had requested:

Norway—Procurement of Toll Collection Equipment for the City of Trondheim **panel report adopted by the Committee on Government Procurement 13 May 1992, BISD 40S/319**

4.17 The Panel then turned its attention to the recommendations that the United States had requested it to make. In regard to the United States' request that the Panel recommend that Norway take the necessary measures to bring its practices into compliance with the Agreement with regard to the Trondheim procurement, the Panel noted that all the acts of non-compliance alleged by the United States were acts that had taken place in the past. The only way mentioned during the Panel's proceedings that Norway could bring the Trondheim procurement into line with its obligations under the Agreement would be by annulling the contract and recommencing the procurement process. The Panel did not consider it appropriate to make such a recommendation. Recommendations of this nature had not been within customary practice in dispute settlement under the GATT system and the drafters of the Agreement on Government Procurement had not made specific provision that such recommendations be within the task assigned to panels under standard terms of reference. Moreover, the Panel considered that in the case under examination such a recommendation might be disproportionate, involving waste of resources and possible damage to the interests of third parties.

4.18 The United States had further requested the Panel to recommend that Norway negotiate a mutually satisfactory solution with the United States that took into account the lost opportunities in the procurement of United States' companies, including Amtech. Finally, the United States had requested the Panel to recommend that, in the event that the proposed negotiation did not yield a mutually satisfactory result, the Committee be prepared to authorise the United States to withdraw benefits under the Agreement from Norway with respect to opportunities to bid of equal value to the Trondheim contract. Norway had argued that, even if the Panel were to find that the procurement had been conducted inconsistently with the Agreement, such requests should be rejected because they were outside the scope of the complaint referred to the Panel and outside the tasks assigned to dispute settlement panels under the Agreement.

4.19 In examining these requests, the Panel first noted that, as instructed in its terms of reference, it had given Norway and the United States full opportunity to develop a mutually satisfactory solution. The Panel also noted that nothing prevented the two governments from negotiating at any time a mutually satisfactory solution that took into account the lost opportunities of United States' suppliers, provided such solution was consistent with their obligations under this and other GATT agreements. The issue was whether the Panel should recommend this and further recommend that the Committee be prepared to authorise the withdrawal of benefits under the Agreement from Norway if such a solution were not negotiated.

4.20 The Panel noted that the United States had indicated that it was not asking the Panel to recommend the negotiation of compensation for past losses. However, if this was not the case, it was not evident to the Panel what it was being asked to recommend that Norway negotiate with the United States. Clearly the "lost opportunities" referred to were past opportunities

---

[67] Art V:15(e) of the Tokyo Round GPA.

and the remedial action that might be negotiated taking into account these lost opportunities would have to be in the future and therefore in all probability compensatory. The request concerning withdrawal of benefits also confirmed to the Panel that the practical effect of the recommendations sought by the United States would be to invite Norway to offer compensation, in one form or another, to the United States for past losses. Given that the United States had indicated that this was not what it was seeking, the Panel had some difficulty in responding to this request, despite having made efforts to explore its implications with the parties.

4.21 Moreover, the Panel observed that, under the GATT, it was customary for panels to make findings regarding conformity with the General Agreement and to recommend that any measures found inconsistent with the General Agreement be terminated or brought into conformity from the time that the recommendation was adopted. The provision of compensation had been resorted to only if the immediate withdrawal of the measure was impracticable and as a temporary measure pending the withdrawal of the measures which were inconsistent with the General Agreement. Questions relating to compensation or withdrawal of benefits had been dealt with in a stage of the dispute settlement procedure subsequent to the adoption of panel reports.

4.22 The Panel then considered whether there were reasons that would justify dispute settlement panels under the Agreement on Government Procurement differing from the above practice under the General Agreement. In this respect, the Panel noted the argument of the United States that, because benefits accruing under the Agreement were primarily in respect of events (the opportunity to bid), rather than in respect of trade flows, and because government procurement by its very nature left considerable latitude for entities to act inconsistently with obligations under the Agreement in respect of those events even without rules or procedures inconsistent with those required by the Agreement, standard panel recommendations requiring an offending Party to bring its rules and practices into conformity would, in many cases, not by themselves constitute a sufficient remedy and would not provide a sufficient deterrent effect.

4.23 In considering this argument, the Panel was of the view that situations of the type described by the United States were not unique to government procurement. Considerable trade damage could be caused in other areas by an administrative decision without there necessarily being any GATT inconsistent legislation, for example in the areas of discretionary licensing, technical regulations, sanitary and phytosanitary measures and subsidies. Moreover, there had been cases where a temporary measure contested before the GATT had been lifted before a Panel had been able to report. (See, for example, Report of the Panel on European Economic Community Restrictions on Imports of Dessert Apples: Complaint by Chile, adopted on 22 June 1989 (BISD 36S/93)).

4.24 The Panel also believed that, in cases concerning a particular past action, a panel finding of non-compliance would be of significance for the successful party: where the interpretation of the Agreement was in dispute, panel findings, once adopted by the Committee, would constitute guidance for future implementation of the Agreement by Parties.

4.25 Moreover, the Panel was not aware of any basis in the Agreement on Government Procurement for panels to adopt with regard to the issues under consideration a practice different from that customary under the General Agreement, at least in the absence of special terms of reference from the Committee.

4.26 In the light of the above, the Panel did not consider that it would be appropriate for it to recommend that Norway negotiate a mutually satisfactory solution with the United States that took into account the lost opportunities of United States companies in the procurement or that, in the event that such a negotiation did not yield a mutually satisfactory result, the Committee be prepared to authorise the United States to withdraw benefits under the Agreement from Norway with respect to opportunities to bid of equal value to the Trondheim contract. The Panel had recognised, however, that nothing prevented the United States from pursuing these matters further in the Committee or from seeking to negotiate with Norway a mutually satisfactory solution provided that it was consistent with the provisions of this and other GATT agreements.

4.27 The Panel also recognised that it would be possible for the United States to raise in the Committee its concerns of a more general nature referred to in paragraph 4.22 above. The Panel noted that certain proposals for challenge procedures open to suppliers that were under consideration in the context of the negotiations on a revision of the Agreement on Government Procurement were intended to address the difficulty felt to exist in obtaining effective redress in respect of complaints about specific procurements.

… … …

The negotiations referred to in the paragraph above resulted in revisions to the Uruguay Round GPA which are now found in Article XVIII of the GPA 2012. This provision first advises that aggrieved suppliers should seek to resolve the complaint through consultations with the entity. It then sets out requirements on the identity and attributes of the review body, and the remedies which it should have at its disposal.

(a) The Identity and Attributes of the Review Body

Article XVIII:4 provides that '[e]ach Party shall establish or designate at least one impartial administrative or judicial authority that is independent of its procuring entities to receive and review a challenge by a supplier arising in the context of a covered procurement'. Paragraph 5 goes on to provide that 'a body other than an authority referred to in paragraph 4 can initially review a challenge'. It may therefore be permissible for the procuring entity complained of to initially review the challenge, although this could be regarded as an unnecessary procedural formality bearing in mind that consultations between the entity and the supplier will have failed before recourse to more formal proceedings. It might therefore be preferable for challenges to be initially reviewed by the government entity with oversight of the entity complained of.

Where there is an initial review by a non-independent authority, Parties must provide for an appeal against the initial decision to an impartial administrative or judicial authority. Paragraph 6 provides that where this review body is not a court, it must either be subject to judicial review or operate with what might be described as 'court-like' procedures. Participants must, for example, have the right to be heard prior to a decision and have access to all proceedings. It is not expressly provided that entities must follow review body recommendations, although this would seem to be implicit in the need to provide for access to courts or court-like procedures. Some international rules are not as strict in this respect. For example, the North America Free Trade Agreement rule states that entities should 'normally' follow the recommendations of the review body.[68]

(b) Remedies

With regard to remedies which the review body should have at its disposal, the first principle is to provide for 'rapid interim measures to preserve the supplier's opportunity to

---

[68] NAFTA Art 1017(l).

participate in the procurement'.[69] The rationale here is that if the procurement process is permitted to continue during the challenge procedures, the final remedy is unlikely to be very helpful in terms of encouraging suppliers to complain, and deterring breaches. This is because a contract might be concluded or even performed during the review procedure. Should these events be permitted to occur, any remedy, other than a declaration that a breach has occurred, becomes unlikely because of prejudice to the successful supplier and the public interest in the prompt delivery of government functions. In contrast, if the procurement process can be suspended at an early stage, the possibility of re-commencement being ordered is preserved. The GPA leaves the question of interference with concluded and performed contracts to individual Parties or entities. The importance of rapid interim measures has been underlined in the GPA 2012 by a new provision which provides that '[j]ust cause for not acting shall be provided in writing'[70]

The final remedies envisaged by the GPA are either, 'corrective action or compensation for the loss or damages suffered, which may be limited to either the costs for the preparation of the tender, or the costs relating to the challenge, or both'.[71] It has been argued that review bodies must have both remedies (correction and compensation) at their disposal on the basis that 'effective' challenge procedures are required by Article XVIII:1.[72] Of these two remedies, corrective action will generally be by far the most important, given that the compensation remedy can permissibly be a very limited one.[73] Corrective action might involve advertising a covered contract which ought originally to have been advertised, or evaluating a wrongfully excluded tender properly submitted before the deadline. However, we again note that whether meaningful corrective action can be provided depends on how early the procurement procedure can be suspended.

VII. DISCUSSIONS TOWARDS MULTILATERAL PROCUREMENT DISCIPLINES

As between its existing Members, the GPA can be seen as a valuable instrument of trade liberalisation. As has been noted, however, the GPA's membership is both limited and unbalanced towards developed countries. This is explicable mainly on the basis that states desire to retain the use of procurement for the pursuit of horizontal policies, which involve preferences for national suppliers. It follows that the GPA's non-discrimination obligations present a barrier to expanded membership. Discussions have therefore taken place with a view to developing multilateral procurement disciplines at the WTO which would be applicable to all Members. It was intended that this possible new agreement would have operated alongside the existing GPA rather than replace it. The two agreements would have differed in that the goal of the multilateral agreement would have been to enhance the transparency of national procurement procedures, but would not

---

[69] Art XVIII:7(a).

[70] *Ibid.*

[71] Art XVIII:7(b).

[72] Arrowsmith, above n 1, 400.

[73] It notable that the Israel–Mexico Free Trade Agreement provides that compensation 'shall [rather than may] be limited to costs for tender preparation or protest': Art 6.17.7(c).

have included obligations of non-discrimination. WTO Members would therefore have been permitted to retain domestic preference, but would have been required to ensure the transparent operation of these preferences. For example, the agreement might have required WTO Members to publish and explain the manner of operation, and extent of domestic preferences in a specified and publicly available medium. Foreign suppliers would then be able to ascertain the likely conditions of competition on the procurement markets of WTO Members more accurately.

The discussions were conducted within a Working Group on Transparency in Government Procurement which was set up at the December 1996 Ministerial Conference in Singapore. This Working Group produced seven annual reports between 1997 and 2003. A spur to this work was provided by the Doha Declaration in November 2001 which envisaged multilateral negotiations to build on progress made within the Working Group.[74] These negotiations were to commence on the basis of a decision taken by explicit consensus, and were to be, 'limited to the transparency aspects and therefore will not restrict the scope for countries to give preferences to domestic supplies and suppliers'. However, the consensus requirement for the multilateral negotiations was not obtained. Indeed, the decision adopted by the General Council in August 2004 in order to restart the Doha Round negotiations after the failure of the WTO's Fifth Ministerial Conference at Cancún dropped the 'Singapore' issues (transparency in government procurement, trade and investment, and competition policy) from the Doha Round.[75]

Despite the eventual demise of discussions within the Working Group, it is possible to give an impression of the kind of transparency based obligations which might have featured in a new multilateral agreement. An obvious source of inspiration is the GPA, which contains obligations (not discussed above) clearly linked to transparency. It is also notable that both the EU and (jointly) Hungary, Korea, Singapore and the US tabled draft agreements on transparency within the Working Group.[76]

As for the GPA, Article VI is entitled *Information on the Procurement System*. Paragraph 1 requires the publication of laws, regulations, judicial decisions and administrative rulings regarding covered procurement via a specified medium to which the public has access. Article XVI is entitled *Transparency of Procurement Information*. Under paragraph 1, participating suppliers must be informed of the entity's contract award decision. Unsuccessful suppliers can also request 'an explanation of the reasons that the entity did not select its tender and the relative advantages of the successful supplier's tender'. This provision is supplemented by Article XVII entitled *Disclosure of Information*. Under paragraph 1, a GPA Party (as opposed to suppliers) can request any information from another Party, 'necessary to determine whether a procurement was conducted fairly, impartially and in accordance with the Agreement, including information on the characteristics and relative advantages of the successful tender'. It is further provided that the Party receiving the information 'shall not disclose it to any supplier, except after consultation with, and agreement of, the Party that provided the information'. Article XVII:3 also sets out the circumstances in which a Party and its entities can decline to release

---

[74] WT/MIN(01)/DEC/1 adopted on 14 November 2001, para 26.

[75] Decision Adopted by the General Council on 1 August 2004, WT/L/579, para 1(g).

[76] See Elements for an Agreement on Transparency in Government Procurement, Communication from the European Communities, WT/WGTGP/W/26 of 5 November 1999; Communication from Hungary, Korea, Singapore, and the United States, Preparations for the 1999 Ministerial Conference, The WTO's Contribution to Transparency in Government Procurement, WT/GC/W/384, WT/WGTGP/W/27 of 9 November 1999.

confidential information. This provision applies whether the information is requested by another Party or a supplier. The confidential information can be withheld if its release, for example, 'might prejudice fair competition between suppliers' or 'would prejudice the legitimate commercial interests of particular persons, including the protection of intellectual property'.[77]

Provisions of this nature also feature in the two draft texts for a transparency agreement.[78] A further and controversial feature of the draft texts is that both domestic review procedures, and intergovernmental dispute settlement subject to the DSU are envisaged.[79]

It has been reported that several developing countries were strongly opposed to the draft texts 'on the basis that they could undermine the ability of such states to use procurement for social policy purposes'.[80] At first sight, this concern seems to be unfounded. As noted above, the Doha Declaration limited the negotiating mandate to aspects of transparency and explicitly excluded the issue of discriminatory domestic preferences. However, it must also be appreciated how transparency based principles might have severely restricted the pursuit of discriminatory secondary policies. Under a transparency agreement, these policies would merely have been acceptable in principle, subject to compliance with the transparency principles. For many developing countries, implementing such unfamiliar principles would involve significant cost and resource allocation. It is not therefore altogether surprising that the draft texts met with opposition especially when it is recalled that both texts envisaged the enforceability of the transparency principles.

Additionally, some developing countries might have suspected that their domestic preference policies would have come under direct scrutiny despite the limitation of the discussion mandate to transparency. Concern might have been engendered by a rather cryptic statement accompanying the EU draft text:

> The European Communities appreciate that the mandate of the Working Group is limited to elements on transparency in government procurement. *Nevertheless, during this exercise it became clear that introducing multilateral rules on transparency in procurement will not be sufficient to resolve possible distortions in procurement practices.* Therefore, further work on additional multilateral rules on government procurement is necessary. Obviously, commencing any such negotiations does not imply an automatic opening of procurement markets, but it will create a rules-based environment. (emphasis added)

VIII. QUESTIONS

1. Explain the rationale for the international regulation of government procurement.

---

[77] There is an obvious connection between information disclosure obligations and enforcement proceedings, whether instituted by suppliers via domestic review procedures, or GPA Parties via intergovernmental dispute settlement. The information which must be provided will assist in the discovery of any impropriety or inadvertent breach of the GPA.

[78] In both draft agreements, Art 3 provides for Public Accessibility of Domestic Legislation, while Art 7.2 provides: 'Once the contract is awarded, the participating suppliers shall be informed of the rejection of their bid. Unsuccessful bidders can, on request, obtain more detailed information as to why their bid was rejected and/or the winning bid was chosen.'

[79] See Arts 8 and 13 of both draft agreements.

[80] See McCrudden and Gross, above n 60, 178.

2. Explain the concept of the GPA's coverage. Why is the matter of determining the GPA's coverage now a more difficult and sensitive task than it was under the Tokyo Round GPA?

3. Why does the GPA in Article II:6 seek to regulate the practice of 'contract splitting'? Explain how GPA Article II:7 could be interpreted so as to have a detrimental effect on the ability of procuring entities to pursue objectives such as efficiency and accountability.

4. With reference to the case of *Korea—Measures Affecting Government Procurement* (referred to in section II.A.3), explain the scope for finding that a non-listed procuring entity is nevertheless a covered procuring entity. Following the case, what advice would you give to a WTO Member involved in GPA accession negotiations?

5. Identify and explain the matters which have to be taken into account in deciding on the compatibility with the GPA of the Buy American provision in Section 1605 of the American Recovery and Reinvestment Act 2009.

6. On the matter of Conditions for Participation, explain the relationship between Articles VIII:1 and VIII:4. Must any steps taken under paragraph 4 satisfy the requirements of paragraph 1 or do the paragraphs operate independently of each other?

7. Explain the possible advantages of electronic auctions over traditional tendering. Where an electronic auction is used, why might an initial evaluation of tenders normally occur in practice even though it is not mandated by Article XIV?

8. Had the dispute involving the Massachusetts legislation (referred to in section V) been heard by the panel, do you think that violations of the GPA would have been found? Recall that, under the legislation, persons on a restricted purchase list by reason of their business links with Burma could not be awarded government contracts. The legislation applied equally to foreign and domestic firms. The European Communities and Japan considered that provisions now contained in GPA 2012, Articles VIII:1 and 2, and XV:5 had been breached. What is your point of view? You should also examine whether the legislation might have breached Article IV:1 and 2.

9. Suppliers considering that they have been affected by a possible GPA violation can either petition their governments to commence intergovernmental dispute settlement proceedings, or independently institute domestic review procedures. Explain the relative advantages and disadvantages of these options.

10. In the *Trondheim* case (referred to in section VI), the panel noted that 'nothing prevented the two governments from negotiating at any time a mutually satisfactory solution that took into account the lost opportunities of United States' suppliers, provided such solution was consistent with their obligations under this and other GATT agreements' (para 4.19). Interestingly the US had indicated that this solution could take a number of forms 'such as annulment of the contract, the provision of additional opportunities to bid for future contracts, assurances about future conduct etc' (para 3.35). Would these suggested solutions have been compatible with the GPA?

11. How might a multilateral agreement on transparency in government procurement differ from the GPA? What concerns led to the suspension of negotiations in this area?

17

Trade and Intellectual Property: the TRIPS Agreement

I. INTRODUCTION

The Agreement on Trade-Related Aspects of Intellectual Property Rights ('TRIPS Agreement') is perhaps the most controversial agreement included in the WTO Agreement. The GATT contained only occasional references to intellectual property (IP) and the merit of the inclusion of this agreement in the Uruguay Round is still debated.[1] In this chapter, we briefly discuss the history of IP and the international trading system before turning to the framework, principles, and scope and coverage of the TRIPS Agreement. We next discuss the enforcement and remedy provisions of the agreement and the dispute settlement and transitional arrangements. Finally, we provide examples of some of the criticism of the agreement.

II. HISTORICAL TREATMENT OF INTELLECTUAL PROPERTY

Protection of intellectual property in the form of a period of exclusive usage and exclusive exploitation has long been accorded to inventors and creators. Traditionally, countries only recognised registration/production of IP rights (IPRs) by nationals and actually encouraged the copying of IP produced by non-nationals; that is, they did not recognise nor protect the IPRs of non-nationals. By the nineteenth century, however, most nations recognised that protection of IPRs beyond national boundaries should exist. Initially, this took the form of bilateral recognition agreements. However, nations realised that the complex web of agreements was difficult to administer and follow, and thus negotiated to formalise and codify protection standards through multilateral international agreements. This process culminated in the Paris Convention for the Protection of Industrial Property (1883) and the Berne Convention for the Protection of Literary and Artistic Works (1886).

---

[1] See Articles XII:3(c)(iii), AXVIII:10 and XX(d) of the GATT. See also GATT Negotiating Group on Trade-Related Aspects of Intellectual Property, Including Trade in Counterfeit Goods, *GATT Provisions Bearing on Trade-Related Aspects of Intellectual Property Rights*, MTN.GNG/NG11/W/6, 22 May 1987.

Both treaties attempt to standardise at least a part of the IP regimes of signatories. For example, the Paris Convention details basic patent principles, industrial design protection and trade mark protection. Likewise, the Berne Convention requires signatories to meet certain minimum standards of protection before acceding to the treaty. The World Intellectual Property Organisation (WIPO), a specialised agency of the United Nations, was subsequently created to, inter alia, administer these and other agreements.

However, WIPO treaties proved to be ineffective at standardising and harmonising IP law. Therefore, the situation prior to the establishment of the TRIPS Agreement was that IP was largely unregulated internationally and only minimally protected through the WIPO administered agreements. Thus, despite the efforts of WIPO, IP regimes of nations differed widely in a number of important areas. For example:

> [S]ome nations granted patents of relatively long duration, while others granted shorter-term protection; some nations granted patents for processes and products, and some protected only products; some nations legislated for compulsory licensing of drugs, while others prohibited the measure; some nations required that patent holders produce and sell the drug in the country granting the patent or the holder would lose the protection, and others protected the patent regardless of where production and sales occurred; and some nations did not protect or grant pharmaceutical patent protection, while others fully protected the industry.[2]

Not only did this system of regulation lead to varying standards and interpretations, but, perhaps more importantly, it did not provide an adequate dispute settlement mechanism. This led some countries, most notably the US, to begin strengthening the links between IP protection and international trade regulation. In this regard, bilateral negotiations were undertaken; countries were listed on the US Trade Representative (USTR) 'priority watch' list for their lack of adequate IP protection; legal cases were filed; and favourable decisions or negotiated concessions (in the form of the other nation increasing levels of IP protection) were obtained on the basis of sections 301–310 of the US Trade Act of 1974,[3] even though the actions of the foreign company/country may not have violated international law.

At the same time, the US and other developed countries (most notably the EU, Switzerland and Japan) sought to consolidate the gains achieved in the bilateral agreements on IP and shift the multilateral focus from WIPO, which was seen as being dominated by and representing developing countries, to the GATT, as part of the Uruguay Round. Initially, most developing countries expressed the position that such a system would not be in their best interests, in that it would be likely to be interpreted to favour developed country interests while at the same time ignoring the differing levels of needs and flexibilities demanded and needed by certain developing countries. Nonetheless, in search of a more uniform, harmonised and institutionalised system that would not only provide more protection for their nationals, but also provide an adequate remedy in the form of a binding and enforceable dispute settlement mechanism, the developed countries pressed on and, with the threat of continued unilateral action, decreased trade aid and exclusion from increased market access granted by the Generalised System of Preferences (GSP), developing countries finally agreed to the inclusion of IP in the Uruguay Round

---

[2] B Mercurio, 'TRIPS, Patents and Access to Life-Saving Drugs in the Developing World' (2004) 8 *Marquette Intellectual Property Law Review* 211, 215–16.

[3] See the Trade Act of 1974, 19 USC 2251 (2002). See 19 USC 2252 (2002) (s 301 is now part of Public Law 103-465, passed in 1994).

in exchange for concessions in other areas of negotiation, particularly in the area of agriculture and textiles.[4]

III. THE FRAMEWORK OF THE TRIPS AGREEMENT: GENERAL PROVISIONS AND PRINCIPLES

(a) Overview

Broadly speaking, the TRIPS Agreement focuses on and regulates five main IP-related concerns:

(1) how basic principles of the trading system and other international intellectual property agreements should be applied;
(2) how to give adequate protection to intellectual property rights;
(3) how countries should enforce those rights adequately in their own territories;
(4) how to settle disputes on intellectual property between members of the WTO;
(5) special transitional arrangements during the period when the new system is being introduced.[5]

As with other covered agreements of the WTO, a fundamental principle of the TRIPS Agreement is non-discrimination in the form of most-favoured-nation status and national treatment. However, the TRIPS Agreement also establishes minimum levels of IP protection that each Member must provide to other Members. It is important to understand that such a regulatory, harmonised approach to this issue is unlike the approaches of the other covered agreements of the WTO. Additionally, Article 1.1 makes clear that Members are 'free to determine the appropriate method of implementing the provisions of [the TRIPS] Agreement within their own legal system and practice, provided that such protection does not contravene the provisions of this Agreement'.[6]

Substantively, the TRIPS Agreement not only sets out the subject matter to be protected, but also sets out obligations on Members, rights to be conferred, the permissible exceptions to those rights and the minimum duration of protection. In formulating standards, the TRIPS Agreement incorporates most of the substantive obligations of WIPO (namely the Paris Convention and Berne Convention) and certain provisions of the Treaty on Intellectual Property in Respect of Integrated Circuits and the Rome Convention (see Articles 2.1 and 9.1). In addition, the TRIPS Agreement goes beyond the scope of the aforementioned conventions and treaties and also sets standards in areas which were either not addressed or, according to Members, were not sufficiently or properly covered. The

---

[4] For analysis of the alleged lack of 'democratic bargaining' during the TRIPS negotiations see P Drahos, 'Negotiating Intellectual Property Rights: Between Coercion and Dialogue' in P Drahos and R Maybe (eds), *Global Intellectual Property Rights: Knowledge, Access and Development* (Basingstoke and New York, Palgrave Macmillan, 2002) 163–72.

[5] See WTO, *Understanding the WTO* (WTO, Geneva, 2005) 42–43. The TRIPS Agreement also established the Council for Trade-Related Aspects of Intellectual Property Rights ('Council for TRIPS') to oversee the implementation of the Agreement and facilitate the ongoing negotiations.

[6] *For elaboration see EC—Trademarks/GIs* (US), paras 7.762–7.767. (The panel rejected the claim that certain EC requirements force Members to adopt a particular set of rules to implement the TRIPS Agreement in a manner contrary to Art 1.1.)

TRIPS Agreement also contains provisions providing for extended transitional periods, such as granting LDCs until January 2006 to comply with the TRIPS Agreement and giving developing countries that had not previously protected IPRs until January 2000 to legislate for the application of the TRIPS Agreement, while giving those same Members until January 2005 to apply other provisions, including several provisions of particular importance to pharmaceuticals (see Articles 65 and 66). The TRIPS Agreement also includes a number of exceptions to the exclusive rights of the patent holder. The most important of these in terms of patents are the general exceptions provided by Article 30, the compulsory licensing provision of Article 31 and the clause relating to parallel importing/exhaustion contained in Article 6.[7] The TRIPS Agreement also contains other important exceptions, including those for copyright (Article 13) and trade marks (Article 17).

In addition to the substantive legal provisions, the TRIPS Agreement contains provisions relating to domestic procedures and remedies for the enforcement of IPRs. In this regard, the TRIPS Agreement generally sets out the procedures and remedies that must be available to right holders for the effective enforcement of their rights by detailing certain general principles on civil and administrative procedures and remedies, provisional measures, special requirements related to border measures and criminal procedures. The Agreement also provides for dispute settlement as well as various other institutional and other matters.

(b) General Structure

The TRIPS Agreement is divided into seven Parts. Parts I and II contain the substantives rules that WTO Members must implement and apply domestically. Part III sets out the enforcement obligations of Members. Part IV details the provisions for acquiring and maintaining IPRs. Part V provides dispute settlement rules for the TRIPS Agreement and makes clear that disputes between WTO Members regarding the obligations set out in the Agreement are subject to the dispute settlement procedures of the WTO. Part VI provides for transitional arrangements. Part VII details various institutional and other matters.

At the outset, the Preamble to the TRIPS Agreement requires WTO Members to provide adequate standards and principles (ie minimum standards) concerning the availability, scope and use of IPRs as well as mechanisms for parties to obtain these rights. Importantly, the Preamble also reinforces the long-held belief that IPRs are 'private rights', meaning that rights holders (such as individuals or companies), rather than governments (unless, of course, the government is the rights holder), are responsible for enforcing their own IPRs (ie by bringing actions in national court systems for injunctions, damages, etc). In the WTO context, of course, governments are the ones filing the claims, usually in

---

[7] Art 73 also provides several security exceptions, stating that 'nothing in the Agreement shall be construed: (a) to require a Member to furnish any information the disclosure of which it considers contrary to its essential security interests; or(b) to prevent a Member from taking any action which it considers necessary for the protection of its essential security interests;(i) relating to fissionable materials or the materials from which they are derived;(ii) relating to the traffic in arms, ammunition and implements of war and to such traffic in other goods and materials as is carried on directly or indirectly for the purpose of supplying a military establishment;(iii) taken in time of war or other emergency in international relations; or(c) to prevent a Member from taking any action in pursuance of its obligations under the United Nations Charter for the maintenance of international peace and security.'

response to the demands of private companies who have been thwarted in their attempts to claim or enforce their rights.

Members are required to comply with the entirety of the TRIPS Agreement but it is important to note that the Agreement only sets minimum standards, which allows Members to provide more extensive IP protection if they desire. Additionally, Members are free to determine the appropriate method of implementing the provisions of the Agreement within their own legal system and practice.

Part I of the TRIPS Agreement sets out a number of general provisions and basic principles. In the rest of this sub-section, we discuss key aspects of these provisions. In the ensuing sections, we discuss the other Parts of the agreement.

(c) National Treatment and Most Favoured Nation Treatment

Similarly to the GATT and several other WTO agreements, the TRIPS Agreement establishes the basic principles of national and most-favoured-nation treatment in the area of IP protection. Due to the slightly different wording of the provisions and the specific nature of IP, the TRIPS Agreement rules differ slightly from the non-discrimination provisions discussed elsewhere in the book.

(i) National Treatment

The National Treatment provision (Article 3) requires that a Member accord to the nationals of other Members treatment no less favourable than that it accords to its own nationals with regard to the protection[8] of IP, subject to certain explicit exceptions and limitations. In *US—Section 211*, the Appellate Body noted that the national treatment obligation is a 'fundamental principle' underlying the TRIPS Agreement and found section 211(a)(2) of the US Omnibus Appropriations Act of 1998 to be a violation of the national treatment obligations in Article 2(1) of the Paris Convention[9] and Article 3(1) of the TRIPS Agreement by treating foreign successors-in-interest to original trade mark owners that are non-US nationals less favourably than US nationals.[10] More specifically, the Appellate Body found an 'additional obstacle' and an 'extra hurdle' in the form of an additional licensing procedure being imposed by section 211(a)(2) of the US Act on successors-in-interest who are non-US nationals. The Appellate Body went further and, while referring to the GATT panel report in *US—Section 337*, concluded: 'even the *possibility* that non-US successors-in-interest face two hurdles is *inherently less favourable* than the undisputed fact that US successors-in-interest face only one'.[11]

---

[8] A footnote to Art 3 states: 'For the purposes of Articles 3 and 4, "protection" shall include matters affecting the availability, acquisition, scope, maintenance and enforcement of intellectual property rights as well as those matters affecting the use of intellectual property rights specifically addressed in this Agreement.'

[9] As incorporated into the TRIPS Agreement, Art 2(1) of the Paris Convention reads: 'Nationals of any country of the Union shall, as regards the protection of industrial property, enjoy in all the other countries of the Union the advantages that their respective laws now grant, or may hereafter grant, to nationals; all without prejudice to the rights specially provided for by this Convention. Consequently, they shall have the same protection as the latter, and the same legal remedy against any infringement of their rights, provided that the conditions and formalities imposed upon nationals are complied with.'

[10] Appellate Body Report, *US—Section 211*, paras 233–34, 244.

[11] *Ibid*, paras 261–65.

The Appellate Body also found that both sub-sections 211(a)(2) and 211(b) of the US Omnibus Appropriations Act of 1998 violated the national treatment obligations in Article 2(1) of the Paris Convention and Article 3(1) of the TRIPS Agreement by treating 'original owners' that are 'designated nationals' less favourably than US nationals. The Appellate Body found both sub-sections 211(a)(2) and 211(b) to be 'discriminatory on their face' as they applied less favourable treatment only to 'designated nationals' who were asserting rights relating to certain trade marks, defined in section 515.305 of Title 31 of the Code of Federal Regulations as 'Cuba and any national thereof including any person who is a specially designated National'; thus, the provisions apply to 'original owners' who are Cuban nationals, but not to 'original owners' who are US nationals.[12]

The above dispute is a relatively straightforward example of a violation of the national treatment principles of the TRIPS Agreement. *In EC—Trademarks / GIs*, by contrast, the issue of national treatment was more complicated. In that dispute, the panel dealt with several issues relating to the obligations contained in Article 3.1 (and correspondingly, Article 2 of the Paris Agreement), including the availability of protection, application procedures, objection procedures, regulatory committee, inspection structures and labelling requirements.[13] The following journal extract on the dispute provides an overview of the issues relating to Article 3.1 and the panel decision.

M Handler, 'The WTO Geographical Indications Dispute' (2006) 69 *Modern Law Review* 70

Australia and the US's first complaint was that Article 12(1) of the Regulation, which deals with the registration of GIs from non-EC countries, violated the principle of national treatment in Article 3.1 of the TRIPS Agreement, namely that '[e]ach Member shall accord to the nationals of other Members treatment no less favourable than that it accords to its own nationals with regard to the protection of intellectual property'. Article 12(1) of the Regulation provides as follows:

. . . this Regulation may apply to an agricultural product or foodstuff from a third country provided that:

–the third country is able to give guarantees identical or equivalent to those referred to in Article 4,

–the third country concerned has inspection arrangements and a right to objection equivalent to those laid down in this Regulation,

–the third country concerned is prepared to provide protection equivalent to that available in the Community to corresponding agricultural products for foodstuffs coming from the Community.

Australia and the US claimed that these conditions made registration of non-EC GIs under the Regulation contingent on the governments of those non-EC countries providing reciprocal and equivalent protection for EC GIs under their own laws. Given the standards of protection for

---

[12] *Ibid*, paras 274–77. For a dispute where Art 3.1 was claimed but unproven see Panel Report, *Indonesia—Autos*, paras 14.264–14.274.

[13] *See Panel Report, EC—Trademarks/GIs (Australia), paras 7.89–7.425 and Panel Report, EC—Trademarks/GIs (US), paras 7.38–7.499.*

GIs in Australia and the US, this meant that GIs from those countries could not be registered in the EC, arguably affording Australian and US nationals less favourable treatment under EC law than that provided to European GI owners. It was also alleged that other provisions of the Regulation setting out registration procedures for non-EC GI owners and allowing non-EC parties to object to the registration of a GI violated the national treatment provisions of TRIPS by requiring non-EC governmental authorities to intervene in these processes.

In its defence the EC first argued that none of the above provisions discriminated on the grounds of nationality. Rather, it suggested that the Regulation merely set out different application and registration procedures based on whether the GI was located within or outside the EC, which it argued was unrelated to the nationality of the applicant for the GI. Second, the EC contended that the mere existence of these different procedures did not mean that it was applying less favourable treatment to non-EC nationals; rather, it claimed that the obligations placed on non-EC governments relating to applications and objections in fact corresponded with those placed on EC Members.

The main problem with the EC's first argument was that it glossed over the peculiar nature of GIs. Unlike other forms of intellectual property, which may first subsist in one country under the ownership of the national of another, there would seem to be a virtually inseparable link in the case of GIs between the territory corresponding with the GI and the nationality of the party entitled to use the property. For example, only producers of goods from particular regions in the US would seek to use the corresponding regional name as a GI and these producers would almost invariably be US nationals. Thus the creation of different registration procedures for EC and non-EC GIs would seem in effect to discriminate on the basis of nationality. This was recognised by the Panel, which considered that in practice the Regulation accorded differential treatment to EC and non-EC nationals.

The Panel also gave short shrift to the EC's second argument. Drawing on earlier WTO jurisprudence on national treatment, the Panel considered that the key issue was whether the Regulation provided for the 'effective equality of opportunities' for EC and non-EC nationals. In relation to Article 12(1), it held that this was clearly not the case since the 'equivalence and reciprocity' conditions imposed a significant extra hurdle for non-EC nationals to overcome in attempting to register their GIs within the EC. As for the Regulation's imposition of obligations on non-EC governments in relation to registration and objection procedures, the Panel considered these also to be problematic. It held that these requirements inflicted a burden on such governments that they were not obliged to fulfil under any international agreement and involved an impermissible delegation of the EC's responsibility of ensuring that that no less favourable treatment was afforded to non-EC nationals.

... ...

(ii) Most Favoured Nation

The Most Favoured Nation provision (Article 4 of the TRIPS Agreement) states that any advantage, favour, privilege or immunity granted by a Member to the nationals of any other country (whether that country be a Member of the WTO or not) shall be accorded immediately and unconditionally to the nationals of all other Members, subject to certain exemptions and limitations. The most favoured nation principle featured in *US—Section 211*, where the Appellate Body found sub-sections 211(a)(2) and 211(b) of the US Omnibus Appropriations Act of 1998 to violate Article 4 of the TRIPS Agreement due to the fact that a Cuban national (defined as a 'designated national' in the US regulations) who is an 'original owner' is subject to the measures of the Act whereas a non-Cuban national is not subject to the measures of the Act.[14] In that dispute, the Appellate Body explained:

> 297. Like the national treatment obligation, the obligation to provide most-favoured-nation treatment has long been one of the cornerstones of the world trading system. For more than fifty years, the obligation to provide most-favoured-nation treatment in Article I of the GATT 1994 has been both central and essential to assuring the success of a global rules-based system for trade in goods. Unlike the national treatment principle, there is no provision in the Paris Convention (1967) that establishes a most-favoured-nation obligation with respect to rights in trademarks or other industrial property. However, the framers of the *TRIPS Agreement* decided to extend the most-favoured- nation obligation to the protection of intellectual property rights covered by that Agreement. As a cornerstone of the world trading system, the most-favoured-nation obligation must be accorded the same significance with respect to intellectual property rights under the *TRIPS Agreement* that it has long been accorded with respect to trade in goods under the GATT. It is, in a word, fundamental.

The most favoured nation clause operates in a relatively unqualified way because, unlike Article XXIV of the GATT, which may serve to exempt free trade agreements (FTAs) from the operation of MFN, the TRIPS Agreement does not contain a similar provision; thus, the principle of MFN in the TRIPS Agreement applies to the provisions of FTAs. Therefore, if FTAs are negotiated containing TRIPS-plus provisions, these provisions will essentially become the new minimum standard from which any future WTO trade negotiation will proceed.[15]

(d) Exhaustion

'Exhaustion' of IPRs refers to the principle that 'once the owner of an intellectual-property right has placed a product covered by that right into the marketplace, the right to control how the product is resold within that internal market is lost'.[16] Exhaustion of rights is important in the IP framework as it leads to the possibility of parallel importation (also called 'grey market goods'). For example, the owner of a shampoo manufacturing and bottling company may sell their product at a premium in their own territory (Country A), but may sell the product at a lower price to a distributor abroad with the intention (perhaps contractually) that the product be sold only in another territory (Country B). Parallel importation occurs when the distributor or any one else decides to buy the product for the lower price in Country B and re-export it to Country A. While the item is not counterfeit, the rights holder has not authorised its sale or marketing in Country A.

Traditionally, countries have had wide scope to set their own rules on exactly when IPRs are exhausted. Three options exist: national exhaustion, regional exhaustion or international exhaustion. *National exhaustion* means that upon the sale of a product only domestic rights are exhausted. Thus, the rights holder (or authorised licensee) may oppose the importation of legitimate, original goods marketed and sold abroad. In other

---

[14] Appellate Body Report, *US—Section 211*, paras 308–18. The issue of MFN also featured in *EC—Trademarks/GIs*: see paras 7.689–7.729.

[15] For detailed analysis see P Drahos, 'Expanding Intellectual Property's Empire: the Role of FTAs' (2003), available at www.grain.org..

[16] *Black's Law Dictionary*, 8th edn (2004).

words, under national exhaustion, a rights holder can effectively prevent the importation and sale of legitimate merchandise coming from abroad if the rights holder intended it for sale abroad only. In the case of *regional exhaustion*, the first consensual sale of the IP protected product by the rights holder exhausts any IPRs over these products not only domestically, but within the whole region, and parallel imports within the region can no longer be opposed based on the IPRs. *International exhaustion* extends this concept and exhausts all IPRs once the product has been sold by the rights holder in any part of the world, and thus parallel importation cannot be prevented.

Article 6 provides that, for the purposes of dispute settlement, nothing in the TRIPS Agreement shall be used to address the issue of the exhaustion of IPRs. In other words, the TRIPS Agreement allows Members to adopt their own policies and laws relating to national or international exhaustion of IPRs and, thus, on whether to allow or prohibit parallel imports/grey market goods. Following some commentators' and governments' assertions to the contrary, the Doha Declaration on the TRIPS Agreement and Public Health reiterated this interpretation. Paragraph 5(d) states:

> The effect of the provisions in the TRIPS Agreement that are relevant to the exhaustion of intellectual property rights is to leave each member free to establish its own regime for such exhaustion without challenge, subject to the MFN and national treatment provisions of Articles 3 and 4.

Based on these rules, it is clear that Members can choose to allow parallel importation of any and all items or legislate to ban parallel imports in all or certain product lines.

For those countries allowing parallel imports, the practical effect of Article 6 is that it allows companies in such countries to purchase and import goods through a third country at a cheaper rate than that charged in the importing country. Allowing parallel imports to compete with authorised merchandise is likely to result in a decrease of the price of the product. For instance, until recently Australia banned the parallel importation of most products, including books and music CDs, thus giving a distribution and sale monopoly to the rights holder or authorised licensee. Recently, however, the market in these products was opened to parallel imports, allowing importers to purchase and import lower priced books and music CDs manufactured or licensed to be sold in another country (normally the US or UK in the case of books and Thailand or Malaysia in the case of CDs) and re-sell them to consumers in Australia. The effect of this was, as imagined, lower prices of these products to consumers. Obviously, parallel imports have less of an effect where the price of the goods abroad is comparable to the price in the domestic market.

On the other hand, parallel imports in certain products are banned in most nations. One example of this is pharmaceuticals, where strict efficacy and safety standards exist and where drug companies routinely discount or donate drugs and medical products to the developing world. There is a fear that if exporting members (or others) allowed for parallel imports of these products, then the governments or other corrupt officials could re-export the drugs to another market for profit in lieu of distributing them to its populace. On the other hand, consumers in countries that do not allow re-importation are often upset at having to pay higher prices than those in foreign countries where prices are lower (ie consumers in the US who see Canadian consumers paying significantly less for prescription pharmaceuticals).

(e) Objectives and Principles

Articles 7 and 8 are entitled 'Objectives' and 'Principles', respectively. Article 7 sets out the 'Objectives' of the TRIPS Agreement:

> The protection and enforcement of intellectual property rights should contribute to the promotion of technological innovation and to the transfer and dissemination of technology, to the mutual advantage of producers and users of technological knowledge and in a manner conducive to social and economic welfare, and to a balance of rights and obligations.

This provision is a restatement of one traditional view of IPRs; that is, that the rules on IPRs are designed to balance the interests of private rights holders, so as to provide an incentive for creativity and invention, with those of rights users, or society, that benefit from access to creations, the transfer and dissemination of technology and a thriving public domain.

Article 8 sets out certain 'Principles' of the Agreement. Article 8.1 provides that Members 'may adopt measures necessary to protect public health and nutrition, and to promote the public interest in sectors of vital importance to their socio-economic and technological development, provided that such measures are consistent with the provisions of this Agreement'.[17]

Article 8.2 grants Members the right to take 'appropriate measures . . . to prevent the abuse of IPRs by right holders or the resort to practices which unreasonably restrain trade or adversely affect the international transfer of technology', as long as such action is consistent with the Agreement. For instance, the provision recognises the right of Members to take actions to combat anti-competitive practices relating to IP.

To date, Articles 7 and 8 have played a limited role in dispute settlement and, while they have been invoked to assist interpretation of the Agreement, they have not been determinative in any dispute. For instance, the Panel in *Canada—Pharmaceutical Patents* addressed the issue as part of its analysis of the object and purpose of Article 30. The Panel stated:

> 7.24 In the view of Canada, [Article 7] declares that one of the key goals of the TRIPS Agreement was a balance between the intellectual property rights created by the Agreement and other important socio-economic policies of WTO Member governments. Article 8 elaborates the socio-economic policies in question, with particular attention to health and nutritional policies. With respect to patent rights, Canada argued, these purposes call for a liberal interpretation of the three conditions stated in Article 30 of the Agreement, so that governments would have the necessary flexibility to adjust patent rights to maintain the desired balance with other important national policies.

> 7.25 The EC did not dispute the stated goal of achieving a balance within the intellectual property rights system between important national policies. But, in the view of the EC, Articles 7 and 8 are statements that describe the balancing of goals that had already taken place in negotiating the final texts of the TRIPS Agreement. According to the EC, to view Article 30 as an authorization for governments to "renegotiate" the overall balance of the Agreement would involve a double counting of such socio-economic policies. In particular, the EC pointed to the last phrase of Article 8.1 requiring that government measures to protect important socio-

---

[17] The requirement that measures be consistent with the Agreement is a slightly different wording of similar provisions in the GATT and GATS (Arts XX and XIV, respectively), with each providing for measures that are necessary and otherwise *inconsistent* with the Agreement.

economic policies be consistent with the obligations of the TRIPS Agreement. The EC also referred to the provisions of first consideration of the Preamble and Article 1.1 as demonstrating that the basic purpose of the TRIPS Agreement was to lay down minimum requirements for the protection and enforcement of intellectual property rights.

7.26 In the Panel's view, Article 30's very existence amounts to a recognition that the definition of patent rights contained in Article 28 would need certain adjustments. On the other hand, the three limiting conditions attached to Article 30 testify strongly that the negotiators of the Agreement did not intend Article 30 to bring about what would be equivalent to a renegotiation of the basic balance of the Agreement. Obviously, the exact scope of Article 30's authority will depend on the specific meaning given to its limiting conditions. The words of those conditions must be examined with particular care on this point. Both the goals and the limitations stated in Articles 7 and 8.1 must obviously be borne in mind when doing so as well as those of other provisions of the TRIPS Agreement which indicate its object and purposes.

…… …… ……

Therefore, the panel agreed with the EC, the complainant in that case, that Articles 7 and 8 reflect the balance already achieved in the Agreement and that they do not require a dispute settlement panel to re-balance the agreement between IPRs and national policy. These provisions may, however, feature more prominently if and when 'non-violation' disputes are allowed under the Agreement.

IV. THE SCOPE AND COVERAGE OF THE TRIPS AGREEMENT

The substantive scope of the TRIPS Agreement covers a number of different areas of IPRs. As set out in Part II of the Agreement, the following forms of IP are included: copyright and related rights; trade marks; geographical indications; industrial designs; patents; lay-out design (topographies) of integrated circuits; protection of undisclosed information; and control of anti-competitive practices in contractual licences. In terms of the substantive rules in each area, the title of Part II indicates that the rules govern the 'availability, scope and use' of these rights.[18]

In this section, we examine in detail the areas that have been the focus of disputes and negotiations: copyright and related rights, trade marks, geographical indications and patents.

(a) Copyright and Related Rights

(i) Copyright

Copyright has been defined as:

---

[18] In this regard, it should be noted that the agreement provides negative rights—that is, the right to exclude others from exploiting the protected subject matter—as opposed to positive rights—that is, a right to make or sell a product containing protected IPRs.

The right to copy; specifically, a property right in an original work of authorship (including literary, musical, dramatic, choreographic, pictorial, graphic, sculptural, and architectural works; motion pictures and other audiovisual works; and sound recordings) fixed in any tangible medium of expression, giving the holder the exclusive right to reproduce, adapt, distribute, perform, and display the work.[19]

Accordingly, the TRIPS Agreement extends copyright protection to expressions and not to ideas, procedures, methods of operation or mathematical concepts as such.[20] As noted earlier, copyright protection in the TRIPS Agreement is based upon the latest version of the Berne Convention (1971). Article 9.1 of the TRIPS Agreement begins by incorporating the substantive parts of the Berne Convention (Articles 1 to 21 and the Appendix thereto, with one exception, noted below), such as those dealing with the subject-matter to be protected, minimum term of protection and rights to be conferred, permissible limitations to those rights and certain provisions regarding developing countries.[21] However, the TRIPS Agreement expressly excludes the portion of the Berne Convention (Article 6*bis*) pertaining to moral rights (the right to claim authorship of the work and to object to any distortion, mutilation or other modification of, or other derogatory action in relation to, the work, which would be prejudicial to the author's honour or reputation) and of the rights derived therefrom.

Numerous articles in the Berne Convention have featured in a number of WTO disputes. For instance, the panel in *China——IPRs* found that China's law which denied copyright protection to works that are prohibited from being published or disseminated in China— for instance, works that would disrupt public order or social stability or 'jeopardize social ethics or fine national cultural traditions'—is inconsistent with Article 5(1) of the Berne Convention, as incorporated into the TRIPS Agreement by virtue of Article 9.1.[22]

In accordance with Article 7(1) of the Berne Convention, Article 12 of the TRIPS Agreement provides that the term of protection for copyright is the life of the author plus (at a minimum) 50 years after death, subject to the shorter terms allowed by Article 7(2)–(4). However, Article 12 of the TRIPS Agreement further provides that the term of protection of a work, other than a photographic work or a work of applied art, is calculated on a basis other than the life of a natural person, that is, it shall be no less than 50 years from the end of the calendar year of authorised publication, or, failing such authorised publication within 50 years from the making of the work, 50 years from the end of the calendar year of making.

The TRIPS Agreement, however, goes beyond the standards of the Berne Convention by adding to and clarifying the Convention in several respects. For example, Article 10.1 provides that computer programs, regardless of whether the form is in source or object code, are to be protected under copyright as literary works under the Berne Convention. To explain further, the treatment of computer programs as literary works means that the general term of protection of 50 years applies to computer programs and that the possible

---

[19] *Black's Law Dictionary*, 8th edn (2004).

[20] TRIPS Agreement, Article 9.2.

[21] For discussion of the relationship between the Berne Convention and the TRIPS Agreement see Panel Report, *US—Copyright*, paras 6.42–6.70. The panel concluded that: 'Article 13 of the TRIPS Agreement applies to Article 11*bis*(1)(iii) and 11(1)(ii) of the Berne Convention (1971) as incorporated into the TRIPS Agreement, given that neither the express wording nor the context of Article 13 or any other provision of the TRIPS Agreement supports the interpretation that the scope of application of Article 13 is limited to the exclusive rights newly introduced under the TRIPS Agreement': see Panel Report, *US—Copyright*, para 6.94.

[22] Panel Report, China—IPRs, paras 7.161–7.181.

shorter terms applicable to photographic works and works of applied art are not to be applied to computer programs. Furthermore, Article 10.2 provides copyright protection for compilations of data or other material, whether in machine readable or other form, which by reason of the selection or arrangement of their contents constitute intellectual creations. The provision adds further clarity by providing that such protection does not extend to the data or material itself and is without prejudice to any copyright subsisting in the data or material itself.

Article 11 grants authors (and their successors in title) the right to authorise or to prohibit the commercial rental to the public of originals or copies of their copyright works, in respect of at least computer programs and cinematographic works. The provision further excepts Members from this obligation in respect of cinematographic works unless such rental has led to widespread copying of such works which is materially impairing the exclusive right of reproduction conferred in that Member on authors and their successors in title (the so-called impairment test). In respect of computer programs, this obligation does not apply to rentals where the program itself is not the essential object of the rental.

Finally, Article 13 provides for certain limitations and exceptions to the general rights granted by the protection of copyright (such as 'fair use' or 'fair dealing' provisions). More specifically, the provision states that Members (1) confine limitations or exceptions to exclusive rights to certain special cases (2) which do not conflict with a normal exploitation of the work and (3) do not unreasonably prejudice the legitimate interests of the right holder. Article 13 has been discussed at length in *US—Section 110(5) of the US Copyright Act* and features prominently in the extract from the case below.[23]

The dispute concerned certain provisions of US copyright law providing limitations on the exclusive right 'to perform the copyrighted work publicly' (section 106 of the US Copyright Act) in the form of an exemption for broadcast by non-right holders of certain performances and displays (section 110 of the US Copyright Act). Section 110(5), the purpose of which was 'to exempt from copyright liability anyone who merely turns on, in a public place, an ordinary radio or television receiving apparatus of a kind commonly sold to members of the public for private use',[24] applies to specified retail and food establishments that transmit radio or television broadcasts for the enjoyment of their customers.[25] More specifically, section 110(5) provided for two exceptions: paragraph (A)—the 'homestyle exception'—exempted people using 'homestyle' broadcasting equipment in a public place ('communication of a transmission embodying a performance or display of a work by the public reception of the transmission on a single receiving apparatus of a kind commonly used in private homes'); paragraph (B) —the 'business exception'—exempted certain small businesses from section 106 of the US Copyright Act. Paragraph (A) was a codification of the 1976 US Supreme Court decision in *Twentieth Century Music Corp v Aiken* (referred to in the extract below as 'Aiken')[26] while paragraph (B) was first enacted as part of the Fairness in Music Licensing Act (1998).[27] In other words, the US law provided an exemption from normal copyright protection in the two circumstances described.

---

[23] See Panel Report, *US—Section 110(5) of the US Copyright Act*, paras 6.71–6.272.
[24] *Ibid*, para 2.5, quoting from HR Rep No 94-1476 (1976).
[25] 17 USC 110(5)(B).
[26] 422 US 151 (1975).
[27] Pub L No 105-298, 112 Stat 2830 (1998) (codified at 17 USC 110(5) (B) (2001)).

The Panel explained the rationale of the exceptions by quoting directly from a US House Report and a Conference Report:

2.5 A House Report (1976) accompanying the Copyright Act of 1976 explained that in its original form Section 110(5) "applies to performances and displays of all types of works, and its purpose is to exempt from copyright liability anyone who merely turns on, in a public place, an ordinary radio or television receiving apparatus of a kind commonly sold to members of the public for private use". "The basic rationale of this clause is that the secondary use of the transmission by turning on an ordinary receiver in public is so remote and minimal that no further liability should be imposed." "[The clause] would impose liability where the proprietor has a commercial 'sound system' installed or converts a standard home receiving apparatus (by augmenting it with sophisticated or extensive amplification equipment) into the equivalent of a commercial sound system." A subsequent Conference Report (1976) elaborated on the rationale by noting that the intent was to exempt a small commercial establishment "which was not of sufficient size to justify, as a practical matter, a subscription to a commercial background music service".

The EC complained that the 'homestyle' and 'business' exemptions violate Article 9 of the TRIPS Agreement, which obliges WTO Members to comply with certain copyright protection obligations set out in the Berne Convention.[28] As a defence, the US argued that the measure fell within the exception of Article 13. The following extract from the Panel Report sets out the panel's reasoning and decision on the 'business exemption' set out in subparagraph (B) of section 110(5) of the US Copyright Act.

Panel Report, *United States—Section 110(5) of the US Copyright Act*, Adopted 15 June 2000, WT/DS160/R

2.1 The dispute concerns Section 110(5) of the US Copyright Act of 1976, as amended by the Fairness in Music Licensing Act of 1998 ("the 1998 Amendment"), which entered into force on 26 January 1999. The provisions of Section 110(5) place limitations on the exclusive rights provided to owners of copyright in Section 106 of the Copyright Act in respect of certain performances and displays.

...

2.9 The 1998 Amendment has added a new subparagraph (B) to Section 110(5), to which we, for the sake of brevity, hereinafter refer to as a "business" exemption. It exempts, under certain conditions, communication by an establishment of a transmission or retransmission embodying a performance or display of a nondramatic musical work intended to be received by the general public, originated by a radio or television broadcast station licensed as such by the Federal Communications Commission, or, if an audiovisual transmission, by a cable system or satellite carrier.

2.10 The beneficiaries of the business exemption are divided into two categories: establishments other than food service or drinking establishments ("retail establishments"), and food service and drinking establishments. In each category, establishments under a certain size limit are exempted, regardless of the type of equipment they use. The size limits are 2,000 gross square feet (186 m2) for retail establishments and 3,750 gross square feet (348 m2) for restaurants.

2.11 In its study of November 1995 prepared for the Senate Judiciary Committee, the Congressional Research Service ("CRS") estimated that 16 per cent of eating establishments, 13.5

---

[28] The rights alleged to have been infringed are contained in Arts 11(1)(ii) and 11*bis*(1)(iii) of the Berne Convention, as incorporated into TRIPS by Art 9(1).

per cent of drinking establishments and 18 per cent of retail establishments were below the area of the restaurant ran by Mr. Aiken, i.e. 1,055 square feet. Furthermore, the CRS estimated that 65.2 per cent of eating establishments and 71.8 per cent of drinking establishments would have fallen at that time under a 3,500 square feet limit, and that 27 per cent of retail establishments would have fallen under a 1,500 square feet limit.

2.12 In 1999, Dun & Bradstreet, Inc. ("D&B") was requested on behalf of the American Society of Composers, Authors and Publishers (ASCAP) to update the CRS study based on 1998 data and the criteria in the 1998 Amendment. In this study, the D&B estimated that 70 per cent of eating establishments and 73 per cent of drinking establishments fell under the 3,750 square feet limit, and that 45 per cent of retail establishments fell under the 2,000 square feet limit.17

2.13 The studies conducted by the National Restaurant Association (NRA) concerning its membership indicate that 36 per cent of table service restaurant members (those with sit-down waiter service) and 95 per cent of quick service restaurant members are less than 3,750 square feet.

2.14 If the size of an establishment is above the limits referred to in paragraph 2.10 above (there is no maximum size), the exemption applies provided that the establishment does not exceed the limits set for the equipment used. The limits on equipment are different as regards, on the one hand, audio performances, and, on the other hand, audiovisual performances and displays. The rules concerning equipment limitations are the same for both retail establishments and restaurants above the respective size limits.

… … …

(a) General introduction

6.97 Article 13 of the TRIPS Agreement requires that limitations and exceptions to exclusive rights (1) be confined to certain special cases, (2) do not conflict with a normal exploitation of the work, and (3) do not unreasonably prejudice the legitimate interests of the right holder. The principle of effective treaty interpretation requires us to give a distinct meaning to each of the three conditions and to avoid a reading that could reduce any of the conditions to "redundancy or inutility". The three conditions apply on a cumulative basis, each being a separate and independent requirement that must be satisfied. Failure to comply with any one of the three conditions results in the Article 13 exception being disallowed. Both parties agree on the cumulative nature of the three conditions. The Panel shares their view. It may be noted at the outset that Article 13 cannot have more than a narrow or limited operation. Its tenor, consistent as it is with the provisions of Article 9(2) of the Berne Convention (1971), discloses that it was not intended to provide for exceptions or limitations except for those of a limited nature. The narrow sphere of its operation will emerge from our discussion and application of its provisions in the paragraphs which follow.

(b) "Certain special cases"

(i) General interpretative analysis

6.102 In invoking the exception of Article 13, as an articulation and clarification of the minor exceptions doctrine, the United States claims that both subparagraphs (A) and (B) of Section 110(5) meet the standard of being confined to "certain special cases".

6.103 The United States submits that the fact that the TRIPS Agreement does not elaborate on the criteria for a case to be considered "special" provides Members flexibility to determine for themselves whether a particular case represents an appropriate basis for an exception. But it acknowledges that the essence of the first condition is that the exceptions be well-defined and of limited application.

...

6.107 We start our analysis of the first condition of Article 13 by referring to the ordinary meaning of the terms in their context and in the light of its object and purpose. It appears that the notions of "exceptions" and "limitations" in the introductory words of Article 13 overlap in part in the sense that an "exception" refers to a derogation from an exclusive right provided under national legislation in some respect, while a "limitation" refers to a reduction of such right to a certain extent.

6.108 The ordinary meaning of "certain" is "known and particularised, but not explicitly identified", "determined, fixed, not variable; definitive, precise, exact". In other words, this term means that, under the first condition, an exception or limitation in national legislation must be clearly defined. However, there is no need to identify explicitly each and every possible situation to which the exception could apply, provided that the scope of the exception is known and particularised. This guarantees a sufficient degree of legal certainty.

6.109 We also have to give full effect to the ordinary meaning of the second word of the first condition. The term "special" connotes "having an individual or limited application or purpose", "containing details; precise, specific", "exceptional in quality or degree; unusual; out of the ordinary" or "distinctive in some way". This term means that more is needed than a clear definition in order to meet the standard of the first condition. In addition, an exception or limitation must be limited in its field of application or exceptional in its scope. In other words, an exception or limitation should be narrow in quantitative as well as a qualitative sense. This suggests a narrow scope as well as an exceptional or distinctive objective. To put this aspect of the first condition into the context of the second condition ("no conflict with a normal exploitation"), an exception or limitation should be the opposite of a non-special, i.e., a normal case.

...

6.112 In our view, the first condition of Article 13 requires that a limitation or exception in national legislation should be clearly defined and should be narrow in its scope and reach. On the other hand, a limitation or exception may be compatible with the first condition even if it pursues a special purpose whose underlying legitimacy in a normative sense cannot be discerned. The wording of Article 13's first condition does not imply passing a judgment on the legitimacy of the exceptions in dispute. However, public policy purposes stated by law-makers when enacting a limitation or exception may be useful from a factual perspective for making inferences about the scope of a limitation or exception or the clarity of its definition.

6.113 In the case at hand, in order to determine whether subparagraphs (B) and (A) of Section 110(5) are confined to "certain special cases", we first examine whether the exceptions have been clearly defined. Second, we ascertain whether the exemptions are narrow in scope, inter alia, with respect to their reach. In that respect, we take into account what percentage of eating and drinking establishments and retail establishments may benefit from the business exemption under subparagraph (B), and in turn what percentage of establishments may take advantage of the homestyle exemption under subparagraph (A). On a subsidiary basis, we consider whether it is possible to draw inferences about the reach of the business and homestyle exemptions from the stated policy purposes underlying these exemptions according to the statements made during the US legislative process.

(ii) The business exemption of subparagraph (B)

6.114 As noted above, the United States argues that the essence of the first condition of Article 13 of the TRIPS Agreement is that exceptions be well-defined and of limited application. It claims that the business exemption of subparagraph (B) meets the requirements of the first condition of Article 13, because it is clearly defined in Section 110(5) of the US Copyright Act by square footage and equipment limitations.

6.115 In the US view, if at all the purpose of an exception is relevant, the first condition only requires that the exception has a specific policy objective, but it does not impose any requirements on the policy objectives that a particular country might consider special in the light of its own history and national priorities. As regards the business exemption, the United States claims that the specific policy objective pursued by this exemption is fostering small businesses and preventing abusive tactics by CMOs.

6.116 The European Communities contends that the business exemption is too broad in its scope to pass as a "certain special case", given the large number of establishments which potentially may benefit from it. For the European Communities, it is irrelevant that the size of establishments and the type of equipment are clearly defined, when the broad scope of the business exemption turns an exception into the rule.

6.117 It appears that the European Communities does not dispute the fact that subparagraph (B) is clearly defined in respect of the size limits of establishments and the type of equipment that may be used by establishments above the applicable limits. The primary bone of contention between the parties is whether the business exemption, given its scope and reach, can be considered as a "special" case within the meaning of the first condition of Article 13.

...

6.133 The factual information presented to us indicates that a substantial majority of eating and drinking establishments and close to half of retail establishments are covered by the exemption contained in subparagraph (B) of Section 110(5) of the US Copyright Act. Therefore, we conclude that the exemption does not qualify as a "certain special case" in the meaning of the first condition of Article 13.

... ...

As set out in the extract, in order to fall within the Article 13 exception, section 110(5) had to comply with all of the three listed requirements: (1) confine limitations or exceptions to exclusive rights to certain special cases (2) which do not conflict with a normal exploitation of the work and (3) do not unreasonably prejudice the legitimate interests of the right holder.

The panel began its analysis by determining whether section 110(5)(A) and (B) met the first prong of the test. In this regard, the panel found that subparagraph (B) did clearly define the size of the establishments and the kinds of equipment that can be used to qualify for the exception, thus meeting the 'certain' requirement in the first part of the test. However, pointing to a Congressional Research Service study which showed that 65.2 per cent of all establishments, 71.8 per cent of all drinking establishments, and 27 per cent of all retail establishments met the size requirements of subparagraph (B), the panel ruled that subparagraph (B) failed to meet the 'special' requirement of the first part of the test. Therefore, far from being a 'special' case, the statistics revealed that the exception was actually the norm. In addition, despite having effectively decided the validity of the business exception with its analysis on the first part of the three part test under Article 13, the panel nevertheless continued to analyse the exception under the second and third parts of the test (this portion is not covered in the extract). For both parts, it found that the measure did not satisfy the requirements of Article 13.[29] Accordingly, section 110(5)(B) could not be justified under this provision.

On the other hand, as to section 110(5)(A) (the 'homestyle' exception), the panel found that the exemption is confined to 'certain special cases' within the meaning of the first condition of Article 13 of the TRIPS Agreement. In support of its conclusion, the panel pointed to a Congressional Research Service study showing that only 16 per cent of US eating establishments, 13.5 per cent of US drinking establishments, and 18 per cent of US retail establishments fall within the parameters described in section 110(5)(A).[30] It also relied on the legislative history and subsequent US judicial opinions and decisions which considerably narrowed the application of the provision relating to the beneficiaries of the exemption, permissible equipment and categories of works.[31]

As to the second prong of the test under Article 13, the panel found that the homestyle exception does not conflict with a normal exploitation of the work by virtue of the narrowness of the exemption and the fact that the authors might not reasonably expect to exploit the works in the manner covered by the homestyle exemption.[32]

On the third criterion, the panel found that the homestyle exception does not unreasonably prejudice the legitimate interests of the right holder due to several of the factors already mentioned, including its narrow scope, the legislative history of the exemption, and the fact that no evidence had been presented demonstrating that right holders, if given the opportunity, would exercise their licensing rights.[33]

Thus, the panel found that section 110(5)(A)'s exception was narrow enough to fall within Article 13, whereas section 110(5)(B)'s exception was too broad to fall within Article 13.

(ii) Trade Marks

Trade mark has been defined as: '[a] word, phrase, logo, or other graphic symbol used by a manufacturer or seller to distinguish its product or products from those of others'.[34] Article 15.1 of the TRIPS Agreement sets out the scope of trade mark protection:

> Any sign, or any combination of signs, capable of distinguishing the goods or services of one undertaking from those of other undertakings, shall be capable of constituting a trademark. Such signs, in particular words including personal names, letters, numerals, figurative elements and combinations of colours as well as any combination of such signs, shall be eligible for registration as trademarks. Where signs are not inherently capable of distinguishing the relevant goods or services, Members may make registrability depend on distinctiveness acquired through use. Members may require, as a condition of registration, that signs be visually perceptible.[35]

[29] See Panel Report, *US—Section 110(5) of the US Copyright Act*, paras 6.193–6.211 and 6.237–6.266.
[30] *Ibid*, paras 2.11; 6.142; 6.195; 6.243.
[31] *Ibid*, para 6.159.
[32] *Ibid*, para 6.212–6.219.
[33] *Ibid*, para 6.267–6.272.
[34] *Black's Law Dictionary*, 8th edn (2004).
[35] It must also be noted that Members are required to publish each trade mark either before it is registered or promptly after it is registered and afford a reasonable opportunity for petitions to oppose or cancel the registration. In *US—Section 211*, the Appellate Body found that trade names are also covered by the TRIPS Agreement, through the incorporation of Art 8 of the Paris Convention in Art 2.1. *Black's Law Dictionary* 8th edn (2004)

Therefore, the Agreement grants a broad level of protection while also providing some level of discretion to Members (for instance, on whether to make visibility a registration requirement or, in the alternative, to register sound or smell marks). While Members may make registrability dependent on use, actual use of a trademark cannot be a condition for filing an application for registration and at least three years from the date of application must pass before an application can be refused solely on the ground that intended use has not taken place (Article 15.3).

Article 16.1 gives the owner of a registered trade mark the exclusive right to prevent all third parties not having the owner's consent from using in the course of trade identical or similar signs for goods or services which are identical or similar to those in respect of which the trade mark is registered where such use would result in a likelihood of confusion.[36] In case of the use of an identical sign for identical goods or services, a likelihood of confusion shall be presumed. Moreover, Article 16.2 provides for well-known marks by incorporating Article 6*bis* of the Paris Convention (1967)—which requires the refusal or cancellation of registration as well as the prohibition of use of a mark conflicting with a mark which is well known—*mutatis mutandis*, to services and additionally by providing that, in determining whether a trade mark is well-known, Members must take account of the knowledge of the trade mark in the relevant sector of the public, including knowledge in the Member concerned which has been obtained as a result of the promotion of the trade mark. Moreover, Article 16.3 states that Article 6*bis* of the Paris Convention (1967) applies, *mutatis mutandis*, to goods or services which are not similar to those in respect of which a trade mark is registered, provided that use of that trade mark in relation to those goods or services would indicate a connection between those goods or services and the owner of the registered trade mark and provided that the interests of the owner of the registered trade mark are likely to be damaged by such use.

Article 18 provides that initial registration, and each renewal of registration, of a trade mark shall be for a term of no less than seven years. In addition, the registration of a trade mark shall be renewable indefinitely.

However, while nothing in the TRIPS Agreement requires Members to condition continuing registration on use, Article 19 allows Members to make such a condition and cancel registration for non-use provided there has been an uninterrupted period of at least three years of non-use, unless valid reasons based on the existence of obstacles to such use are shown by the trade mark owner. Importantly, circumstances arising independently of the will of the owner of the trade mark which constitute an obstacle to the use of the trade mark, such as import restrictions on or other government requirements for goods or services protected by the trade mark, are not recognised as valid reasons for non-use.

Finally, Article 20 makes it clear that Members cannot unjustifiably encumber the use of a trade mark in the course of trade by special requirements, such as use with another trade mark, use in a special form or use in a manner detrimental to its capability to

---

defines a trade name as: '[a] name, style, or symbol used to distinguish a company, partnership, or business (as opposed to a product or service); the name under which a business operates. · A trade name is a means of identifying a business—or its products or services—to establish goodwill. It symbolizes the business's reputation.' In *US—Section 211*, the Appellate Body held that Art 15.1 merely defines the types of signs that are eligible for trade mark protection but does not create an affirmative obligation on Members to award registrations to all signs that meet the Art 15.1 criteria: see Appellate Body Report, *US—Section 211*, paras 149–78.

[36] For elaboration see Appellate Body Report, *US—Section 211*, paras 179–202.

distinguish the goods or services of one undertaking from those of other undertakings.[37] Furthermore, Article 21 allows Members to determine conditions on the licensing and assignment of trade marks, but at the same time prohibits the compulsory licensing of trade marks. The provision also provides that the owner of a registered trade mark has the right to assign the trade mark with or without the transfer of the business to which the trade mark belongs.

As with the other substantive provisions of the TRIPS Agreement, Article 17 provides that Members may provide limited exceptions to the rights conferred by a trade mark (such as fair use of descriptive terms) provided that such exceptions take account of the legitimate interests of the owner of the trade mark and of third parties.

To date, trademarks have featured in two prominent disputes: *EC—Trademarks and GIs* and *China—IPRs*. The former is discussed in the following section on geographical indications while the latter is discussed below in the section on enforcement.

(iii) Geographical Indications

Article 22.1 of the TRIPS Agreement defines geographical indications as follows:

> Geographical indications are, for the purposes of this Agreement, indications which identify a good as originating in the territory of a Member, or a region or locality in that territory, where a given quality, reputation or other characteristic of the good is essentially attributable to its geographical origin.

The WTO Secretariat further explains that:

> A product's quality, reputation or other characteristics can be determined by where it comes from. Geographical indications are place names (in some countries also words associated with a place) used to identify products that come from these places and have these characteristics (for example, "Champagne", "Tequila" or "Roquefort") . . ..[38]

It is important to understand that the above definition specifies that the quality, reputation *or* other characteristics of a product can be a sufficient basis to establish eligibility as a geographical indication, where the quality, reputation or other characteristic is essentially attributable to a geographical origin.

Article 22.2 provides for the standard level of protection required and directs Members to provide the legal means for interested parties to prevent:

(a) The use of any means in the designation or presentation of a product that indicates or suggests that the product in question originates in a geographical area other than the true place of origin in a manner which misleads the public as to the geographical origin of the product;

(b) Any use which constitutes an act of unfair competition within the meaning of Article 10*bis* of the Paris Convention (1967).

Additionally, Article 22.3 directs Members to refuse or invalidate the registration of a trade mark—*ex officio* if its legislation so permits or at the request of an interested party—which contains or consists of a geographical indication with respect to goods not

---

[37] For discussion on Art 20 see Panel Report, *Indonesia—Autos*, paras 14.275–14.279.
[38] Available at www.wto.org/english/tratop_e/trips_e/gi_background_e.htm.

originating in the territory indicated, if use of the indication in the trade mark misleads the public as to the true place of origin.

Article 23.1 provides additional, higher or enhanced protection for geographical indications for wines and spirits by requiring Members to provide the legal means for interested parties to prevent use of a geographical indication identifying wines/spirits for wines/spirits not originating in the place indicated by the geographical indication in question, even where the true origin of the goods is indicated and the public is not being misled or the geographical indication is used in translation or accompanied by expressions such as 'kind', 'type', 'style', 'imitation' or the like. Moreover, the provision also requires the refusal or invalidation of registration of a trade mark for wines and spirits which contains or consists of a geographical indication identifying wines or spirits, with respect to wines and spirits not having this origin.[39]

Consistently with the other substantive provisions in the Agreement, Article 24 provides for exceptions to the protection of geographical indications. The exceptions, numbering seven in total, generally apply to the additional protection for geographical indications for wines and spirits granted in Article 23. Moreover, Article 24.1 explicitly states that the exceptions cannot be used to diminish the protection of geographical indications that existed prior to the entry into force of the TRIPS Agreement, and Article 24.5 explicitly states that the provisions in the TRIPS Agreement shall not prejudice prior trade mark rights that have been acquired in good faith.[40] In addition, Members are not required to provide protection for a geographical indication where it has become a common name (generic term) for describing the product in question (for example, the term 'cheddar' now refers to a particular type of cheese that is not necessarily made in or associated with the town of Cheddar, UK) (Article 24.6). Members are also not obliged to provide protection for if a Member's nationals or domiciliaries have used a geographical indication of another Member identifying wines or spirits in a continuous manner with regard to the same or related goods or services either (*a*) for at least 10 years preceding 15 April 1994 or (*b*) in good faith preceding that date, continued and similar use is allowed (Article 24.4). Article 24.8 makes it clear that the geographical indications protected in the this section in no way prejudice the right of any person to use, in the course of trade, that person's name or the name of that person's predecessor in business, except where such name is used in such a manner as to mislead the public. Finally, there is no obligation to protect geographical indications which are not or cease to be protected in their country of origin, or which have fallen into disuse in that country (Article 24.9).

Paragraph 18 of the Doha Declaration raises two issues for the Council for TRIPS to address as part of the Doha Development Agenda. The first issue is the creation of a multilateral register for wines and spirits and the second issue is the extension of the higher, enhanced level of protection offered through Article 23 to products beyond just wines and spirits. Although they are discussed separately, some delegations see a relation-

---

[39] At the outset, however, Art 24.1 requires that Members must be willing to enter into negotiations about their continued application to individual geographical indications. It is also worth noting that Art 23.4 provides for negotiations to take place in the Council for TRIPS concerning the establishment of a multilateral system of notification and registration of geographical indications for wines eligible for protection in those Members participating in the system.

[40] It must be noted that the Council for TRIPS keeps under review the application of the provisions on the protection of geographical indications and can take such action that can be agreed upon to facilitate the operation and further the objectives of this section: see Art 24.2 of the TRIPS Agreement.

ship between the two. Like so many other issues in the Doha Round, the issues have proven controversial, with a number of countries wanting to negotiate the extension of higher levels of protection to other products, while a number of other Members oppose the extension and even question whether the Doha Declaration provides a mandate for the negotiations.

The original deadline for completing the negotiations was the Fifth Ministerial Conference in Cancún in 2003. However, the negotiations are now taking place within the overall timetable for the Doha Round. It is helpful to view these negotiations together with the first and thus far only dispute dealing with the subject matter: *EC—Trademarks / GIs*. The following extract reviews the dispute while also discussing the implications and party negotiating positions.

M Handler, 'The WTO Geographical Indications Dispute' (2006) 69 *Modern Law Review* 70.

The vast majority of the world's food GIs—and some of the most famous, such as 'Roqeufort', 'Feta' and 'Prosciutto di Parma'– are located within Europe. The EC, influenced by Member States such as France and Italy which have a long history of subsidising regional producers of agricultural and viticultural goods, has deemed the strong protection of its Members' GIs to be a vital part of its agricultural policy of sustaining the rural European economy. To this end the EC has established, through Council Regulation 2081/92, a Community-wide notification and registration system for Members' GIs for agricultural products and foodstuffs. This Regulation ensures that following registration of a GI, only parties from defined regions whose goods meet certain production criteria can use the registered denomination in marketing their goods within the EC. Other traders are prevented from using or evoking the registered term in respect of goods covered by the registration, even if no consumer confusion results. These measures are ostensibly designed to foster the production of quality regional produce for which significant premiums can be charged, although critics claim that the scheme protects established European businesses by shielding certain valuable product names from competition.

Australia and the US, on the other hand, are sceptical of the extensive rights afforded by the EC to its rural producers. Historically, the Australian and US governments have not sought to promote small-scale, artisanal and localised production through their agricultural policies. As such, these countries do not have registration schemes specifically to benefit regional, traditional producers: if such parties wish to identify their goods using geographical denominations, they must rely on passing off laws, consumer protection legislation or certification mark schemes for legal protection. Further, these countries have expressed little interest in providing stronger, express protection for food GIs. In particular, they have suggested that any change in their levels of GI protection would benefit European GI owners and adversely impact on local producers that use European geographical terms as generic product descriptors—for example, 'parmesan' cheese or 'kalamata' olives.

Over the past twenty years there has been considerable debate between the EC and Australia/ the US over the international protection of GIs. In the late 1980s in negotiations in the Uruguay Round of GATT, the most on which these parties could agree was that, in principle, GIs should be included in a multilateral agreement on intellectual property. The incoherence of the final, compromised form of the TRIPS Agreement—in which WTO Members are obliged to provide EC-levels of protection for wine and spirit GIs but lower levels for other GIs and in which various issues were left open for further negotiation—is testament to the deep divisions over how GIs ought to be protected. In more recent discussions in the WTO over whether the TRIPS standards of protection ought to be increased and whether famous European GIs should be unconditionally protected worldwide, the positions taken by these countries have been both predictable and intransigent. Yet Australia and the US's [commencement] of dispute settlement proceedings at the WTO in relation to the EC's Regulation 2081/92 represented a more aggressive step in the international conflict over GIs. It was not only the first occasion on which a domestic system of GI protection was challenged over its alleged non-compliance with international law. It also demonstrated the tactics that Australia and the US were prepared to employ in the context of a much larger, ongoing battle: to prevent the EC model of GI protection from becoming a de facto global standard, privileging European agriculture in international trade at the expense of Australian and US businesses.

ARGUMENTS AND OUTCOMES IN THE WTO DISPUTE

The WTO dispute was initiated by the US in June 1999. At this time the Regulation provided that only parties within Member States could apply for or oppose the registration of a GI in the EC and that only the rights of owners of earlier *registered* trade marks would remain unaffected by the registration of a conflicting GI. The EC, implicitly accepting that the Regulation might not have been in compliance with its international obligations, amended the Regulation in April 2003. The amendment established GI registration procedures and rights of objection for non-EC nationals and provided safeguards for the interests of owners of earlier unregistered trade marks. Notwithstanding this, the US remained concerned about the Regulation and continued with its complaint, while Australia commenced concurrent proceedings in April 2003, leading to the dispute being heard by a Panel of the Dispute Settlement Body in 2004.

Australia and the US raised numerous arguments before the Panel in claiming that the amended Regulation was inconsistent with various international instruments. Two of these, both relating to alleged non-compliance with TRIPS, are particularly significant: first, that the Regulation did not accord national treatment to non-EC nationals with regard to the protection of non-EC GIs; and second, that the Regulation denied owners of earlier registered trade marks the exclusive right to prevent third parties using later, conflicting GIs.

The national treatment argument

[ed. this portion of the article is extracted in the earlier section on national treatment]

The trade mark argument

Australia and the US also argued that the Regulation was inconsistent with the provisions of TRIPS guaranteeing the rights of registered trade mark owners. More specifically, they argued that Article 14(2) of the Regulation breached Article 16.1 of TRIPS by allowing the co-existence of a later GI with an earlier registered trade mark. This was said to deprive the trade mark owner of the exclusive right to prevent the use of a confusingly similar GI. In reply, the EC claimed that prejudice to the trade mark owner's interest was avoided by Article 14(3) of the Regulation. This provision prevents the registration of a GI where, in light of an earlier trade mark's 'reputation and renown and the length of time it has been used', such registration would be liable to mislead consumers. It also argued that the co-existence of GIs and earlier registered trade marks was justified by either Article 24.5 or Article 17 of TRIPS.

The EC's reliance on Article 14(3) of the Regulation was surprising given the limitation of protection in that Article to a subset of trade mark owners, which would seem to fall short of the EC's obligations under Article 16.1 of TRIPS. It might be argued in the EC's defence that the only trade marks likely to be affected by later GIs would be for geographical terms and that such marks would only be registrable upon evidence of acquired distinctiveness (that is, they are likely to have some degree of reputation and have been substantially used at the time of registration). It would thus follow that under Article 14(3) no GIs conflicting with an earlier mark would ever be registered. This is unconvincing for two reasons. First, it overlooks the fact that not all GIs protected under the Regulation are, or need be, geographical terms—'Feta' being the best known example. It also pays insufficient regard to ECJ trade mark jurisprudence stating that a geographical sign may be registered without evidence of use if it does not designate a place that consumers currently associate with the goods in question or are likely in the future to do so. There may thus be instances, albeit rare, where inherently distinctive but little known or used registered marks come into conflict with later GIs. Second, Article 14(3) has not in the past filtered out problematic GIs. Both 'Bayerisches Bier' (German for 'Bavarian beer') and 'Budijovické pivo' (Czech for 'Budweiser beer') have been registered as GIs notwithstanding the EC's acknowledgement that their use might result in a likelihood of confusion with the earlier registered trade marks BAVARIA and BUDWEISER. The Panel's decision that the EC could not rely on Article 14(3), and that the Regulation was prima facie inconsistent with Article 16.1 of TRIPS, was thus well-founded.

More controversial was whether Article 14(2) of the Regulation was justified on the basis of a specific exception to Article 16.1 of TRIPS. Article 24.5 provides that a WTO Member's implementation of GI protection 'shall not prejudice . . . the right to use' an earlier trade mark that is similar or identical to the later GI. The EC argued that it was implicit in this Article that WTO Members could prejudice *other* rights of trade mark owners, such as the exclusive right under Article 16.1 'to prevent all third parties' from using confusingly similar signs, thus justifying the co-existence provisions in the Regulation. This argument was certainly open to the EC given the different language used in Articles 16.1 and 24.5. However, it disregards the essentially negative nature of the trade mark property right, in which the concepts of 'use' and 'prevention' are intertwined. That is, the scope of the right to use the mark is determined by the extent of the duties on others to exclude themselves from the property, which is the correlative of the right to prevent others from the property. Any attempt to prejudice this right of prevention will thus invariably prejudice the right to use the mark. This would suggest that Article 24.5 ought to be interpreted to ensure that prior trade mark owners could, as a result of Article 16.1, prevent the use of later, confusingly similar GIs. Unfortunately, the Panel considered, without elaboration, that nothing could be implied from Article 24.5 beyond its strict terms. That is, since the Article stipulated merely that Members were not to prejudice the 'right to use' an earlier mark, it neither preserved the right of prevention in (the apparently unrelated) Article 16.1 nor authorised Members to prejudice such a right. The effect of the Panel's decision is that Article 24.5 provides no guidance as to the scope of a trade mark owner's rights in relation to later, confusingly similar GIs, an issue which fell to be considered solely under Article 17.

Article 17 allows Members to provide 'limited exceptions' to Article 16.1, such as 'fair use of descriptive terms', provided that such exceptions take account of the interests of the trade mark owner and third parties. Australia and the US contended that the 'fair use' example suggested that exceptions were to be confined to those circumstances where third parties *needed* to use the mark, such as for denominative purposes, but not to indicate commercial trade origin. Implicit in this argument is the idea that if origin confusion were permitted, this would unacceptably harm both the interests of the trade mark owner and consumers in being able clearly to distinguish the owner's goods from those of other traders. This, however, raises the question as to whether an exception ought to be available where the defendant has used the registered mark in a way that is *both* descriptive and indicative of trade origin, as the use of a registered GI would seem to be. The US and the EC have taken different approaches to this question in their domestic laws on trade mark infringement. In the US the statutory 'fair use' defence permitting the good faith use of a mark to describe the geographical origin of goods is unavailable where the use is 'as a mark'. In contrast, the ECJ has held that a defendant's use of a GI that also denoted trade origin and was confusingly similar to an earlier registered trade mark could fall within the defence allowing for use in accordance with 'honest practices' of indications of the geographical origin of goods. For the ECJ it is the 'honesty' of the defendant's use that brings this exception within Article 17 of TRIPS—there is no additional requirement that the use must not threaten the origin-identification function of the mark.

It would have been helpful if the Panel had engaged with the above controversy in the context of the co-existence provisions of the Regulation. Instead, it again relied on a formalistic interpretation of TRIPS, concluding that Article 14(2) of the Regulation was a permissible exception under Article 17 of TRIPS. It first held that Article 14(2) was a 'limited' exception because it restricted a trade mark owner's rights only in relation to those goods in respect of which the GI is registered, those parties entitled to use the GI, and the use of the GI in the precise form registered (that is, not in translation). This finding seems reasonable but fails to address the issue of whether an exception allowing for the possibility of third party use of an earlier trade mark, post-registration, that leads to origin confusion can ever be considered to be 'limited' given that this arguably eviscerates the trade mark right in such circumstances. The Panel also held that the safeguards in Article 14(3), outlined above, combined with the right to object to the registration of confusingly similar GIs, meant that the trade mark owner's interests in being able to preserve the distinctiveness of its mark had been taken into account. Again, while the effect of these provisions might be that in practice few trade marks and GIs will ever co-exist under Article 14(2), the question remains as to whether the limitations imposed on the rights of the owners of those marks that *are* caught by Article 14(2) are acceptable. In other words, is a degree of origin confusion tolerable if the use of the GI is honest and, if so, why does the latter interest take priority over the former? This is not to suggest that the Panel reached an incorrect conclusion on this point but rather to demonstrate that the compatibility of the Regulation with TRIPS involved more complicated doctrinal considerations than were explored by the Panel.

THE SIGNIFICANCE OF THE DISPUTE

…

Following the release of the Panel's Reports, the Australian Minister for Trade commented that the decision:

Makes clear that it is not up to the EU to decide whether a particular term claimed by EU producers should be protected within Australia's territory as a GI—that is an issue to be determined according to Australian law.

This comment suggests that the complainants' greater concern with the 'equivalence and reciprocity' conditions in the Regulation was that they represented a clandestine attempt to impose European standards of GI protection for foodstuffs throughout the world. This might go some way to explaining why the EC did not amend the 'equivalance and reciprocity' conditions in the Regulation in 2003, notwithstanding the US's initiation of the WTO dispute in 1999 and the fact that such conditions were manifestly in breach of its national treatment obligations. This concern helps to locate the WTO proceedings within the broader context of the ongoing dispute between the EC and Australia/the US taking place in the WTO's Council for TRIPS, Trade Negotiations Committee and Committee on Agriculture, in which the EC is openly seeking to increase the scope of protection that WTO Members must afford to GIs.

The EC's extension objectives are threefold. First, it has argued that WTO Members should be required to extend the level of protection currently afforded only to wine and spirit GIs to GIs for all other products. This would oblige Members to proscribe the use of a GI where the goods in question do not originate in the place so indicated, even where such use does not mislead consumers. Second, the EC is aiming to establish a binding multilateral system of registration for GIs. Under its proposed scheme, Members not opposing another Member's attempt to register a GI, as well as those that fail in opposition proceedings, would be obliged to protect the GI under their domestic laws and would no longer be able to rely on any of the exceptions to protection under TRIPS. Third, the EC is seeking to 'claw-back' 41 European GIs that it claims are being 'abused' worldwide, including such contested terms as 'Feta', 'Parmigiano Reggiano' and 'Prosciutto di Parma'. This would require non-EC countries to proscribe the commercial use of these terms, even in translation, regardless of how they have been traditionally used or are generally understood. The overarching aim of the EC's agenda is to ensure that all WTO Members afford European levels of protection to European GIs, while minimising the impact of any exceptions to such protection, for example that the GI has become a generic product name or is an earlier registered trade mark. Countries including Australia and the US have strongly opposed the EC's demands, claiming that they would impose additional costs on domestic administrative authorities, consumers and producers without affording any countervailing benefits. In short, they fear that increased GI protection would constitute a non-tariff barrier to trade, primarily for the benefit of established European businesses.

The WTO dispute proceedings can thus be seen as a tactical, retaliatory response by Australia and the US to the EC's expansionist agenda and the protectionism that they believe it represents. Most obviously, by using the mechanism of WTO dispute settlement, Australia and the US sought to force the EC into a position where, if found to be in breach of its international obligations (however technical), it was required to amend its laws or face the prospect of Australian and US countermeasures. In effect, this would mean that Australia and the US could counteract the EC's discriminatory laws by imposing prohibitively high tariffs on targeted European goods or services, as has been done in previous WTO disputes. It is also arguable that Australia and the US used these proceedings to embarrass the EC politically by exposing deficiencies in its GI regime, potentially diminishing the credibility of the EC as an advocate for greater international GI protection. At present, the vast majority of WTO Members have not taken a firm stance on GIs: only approximately 35 other countries have expressly aligned themselves with or opposed the EC on this issue. Australia and the US might thus have hoped that a positive outcome in the dispute would lead to increased support for their GI policies amongst those otherwise agnostic countries. This might in turn lead to such countries more actively supporting related agricultural policies targeted at the EC, such as those calling for greater access to European markets and the removal of export subsidies.

It is unclear whether the WTO dispute will in fact have any of the above effects. Indeed, it is perhaps unlikely that the EC will refuse to comply with the Panel's findings, given that it did not seek to appeal them to the Appellate Body and in light of its previous experiences in dealing with US countermeasures. It also seems somewhat implausible that undecided countries would adopt a particular stance on GIs as a consequence of the dispute, unless they were to obtain certain political or trade advantages for themselves in the process. What the dispute does demonstrate is how convoluted the current debate on GIs has become and the lengths to which WTO Members are prepared to go to further their agendas on the issue. While the Panel has done a commendable (if somewhat formalistic) job of dealing with the complex questions raised in the course of the dispute, its decision does not provide a platform for the resolution of the outstanding issues of contention relating to the international protection of GIs. These issues span much larger concerns such as the relative importance of GIs to rural economies, the preservation of existing agricultural, industrial and cultural practices and, more fundamentally, whether EC-style GI protection would enhance or distort global trade in agriculture. As such, they are unlikely to be resolved other than by serious political compromise.

... ...

(b) Patents

A patent has been defined as:

> The right to exclude others from making, using, marketing, selling, offering for sale, or importing an invention for a specified period (20 years from the date of filing), granted by the federal government to the inventor if the device or process is novel, useful, and non-obvious.[41]

The TRIPS Agreement requires Members to make patents available for a period of at least 20 years from the date of filing for any inventions, whether products or processes, in all fields of technology provided that they are new, involve an inventive step and are capable of industrial application ('non-obvious' and 'useful').[42] Article 27.1 also requires patents to be made available and patent rights enjoyable without discrimination as to the place of invention, the field of technology and whether products are imported or locally produced.

There are exclusions from the patentability of inventions. The first exception, set out in Article 27.2, is for inventions that are necessary to protect *ordre public* or morality, including to protect human, animal or plant life or health or to avoid serious prejudice to the environment. The mere fact that exploitation is prohibited by national law is not sufficient justification for this exception. Secondly, Members can exclude from patentability diagnostic, therapeutic and surgical methods for the treatment of humans or animals (Article 27.3(a)). Finally, Members can exclude from patentability plants and animals other than micro-organisms, and essentially biological processes for the production of plants or animals other than non-biological and microbiological processes. However, Members must provide for the protection of plant varieties either by patents or, if the Member excludes plant varieties from patent protection, by an effective *sui generis* system, or by any combination thereof (Article 27.3(b)).[43]

The rights conferred by the grant of a patent are extensive. In terms of product patents, Article 29 grants the patent holder the right to prevent third parties from making, using, offering for sale, selling or importing the product. In terms of a process patent, the patent holder can prevent third parties from using, offering for sale, selling or importing for these purposes at least the product obtained directly by that process. Patent owners also have the right to assign, or transfer by succession, the patent and to conclude licensing contracts.

Similar to the manner in which Article 13 provides exceptions to copyright and Article 17 provides exceptions to trade marks, Article 30 allows Members to provide limited exceptions to the exclusive rights conferred by a patent, provided that such exceptions do not unreasonably conflict with a normal exploitation of the patent and do not unreasonably prejudice the legitimate interests of the patent owner, taking account of the legitimate interests of third parties. In practice, this provision authorises limited exceptions to patent rights for such things as research, prior user rights and pre-expiration testing. This provision is commonly used by countries to advance science and technology by allowing researchers to use a patented invention to gain a better understanding of the technology. In addition, the provision is also used by countries to allow manufacturers of generic

---

[41] *Black's Law Dictionary*, 8th edn (2004).
[42] See Art 27.1, 33 of the TRIPS Agreement.
[43] The Art also provided for a review of these provisions 4 years after the date of entry into force of the WTO Agreement.

drugs to apply for marketing and safety approval without the patent owner's permission and before the patent protection expires. The generic producers can market the drug upon expiry of the patent. This practice, often called the 'regulatory exception', was one of the issues in the *Canada—Pharmaceutical Patents* dispute. The panel in that case also made several important findings relating to the scope of the Article 30 exception in this context, and also to its relationship with Articles 27 and 28.

Panel Report, *Canada—Patent Protection of Pharmaceutical Products*, Adopted 17 March 2000, WT/DS114/R

VII. FINDINGS

A. MEASURES AT ISSUE

7.1 At issue in this dispute is the conformity of two provisions of Canada's *Patent Act* with Canada's obligations under the *Agreement on Trade-Related Aspects of Intellectual Property Rights* (the "TRIPS Agreement"). The two provisions in dispute, Sections 55.2(1) and 55.2(2) of the Patent Act, create exceptions to the exclusive rights of patent owners. Under Article 28.1 of the TRIPS Agreement, patent owners shall have the right to exclude others from making, using, selling, offering for sale or importing the patented product during the term of the patent. According to Article 33 of the TRIPS Agreement, the term of protection available shall not end before the expiration of a period of 20 years counted from the filing date of the application against which the patent was granted. Sections 55.2(1) and 55.2(2) allow third parties to make, use or sell the patented product during the term of the patent without the consent of the patent owner in certain defined circumstances.

(1) SECTION 55.2(1): THE REGULATORY REVIEW EXCEPTION

7.2 Section 55.2(1) provides as follows:

"It is not an infringement of a patent for any person to make, construct, use or sell the patented invention solely for uses reasonably related to the development and submission of information required under any law of Canada, a province or a country other than Canada that regulates the manufacture, construction, use or sale of any product."

Section 55.2(1) is known as the "regulatory review exception". It applies to patented products such as pharmaceuticals whose marketing is subject to government regulation in order to assure their safety or effectiveness. The purpose of the regulatory review exception is to permit potential competitors of the patent owner to obtain government marketing approval during the term of the patent, so that they will have regulatory permission to sell in competition with the patent owner by the date on which the patent expires. Without the regulatory review exception, the patent owner might be able to prevent potential competitors from using the patented product during the term of the patent to comply with testing requirements, so that competitors would have to wait until the patent expires before they could begin the process of obtaining marketing approval. This, in turn, would prevent potential competitors from entering the market for the additional time required to complete the regulatory approval process, in effect extending the patent owner's period of market exclusivity beyond the end of the term of the patent.

(2) SECTION 55.2(2): THE STOCKPILING EXCEPTION

7.7 Section 55.2(2) of the Patent Act, which is referred to as "the stockpiling exception", reads as follows:

"It is not an infringement of a patent for any person who makes, constructs, uses or sells a patented invention in accordance with subsection (1) to make, construct or use the invention, during the applicable period provided for by the regulations, for the manufacture and storage of articles intended for sale after the date on which the term of the patent expires."

The provision allows competitors to manufacture and stockpile patented goods during a certain period before the patent expires, but the goods cannot be sold until the patent expires. Without this exception, the patent owner's right to exclude any person from "making" or "using" the patented good would enable the patent owner to prevent all such stockpiling.

7.8 The exception created by Section 55.2(2) does not become effective until implementing regulations are issued. The only regulations issued to date under the stockpiling exception have been regulations making the exception operative with regard to pharmaceutical products. The period during which pharmaceutical products can be made and stockpiled is six months immediately prior to the expiration of the patent.

7.9 The text of Section 55.2(2) gives permission only to "make, construct or use" the patented product for purposes of stockpiling. In answer to a question from the Panel, however, Canada has taken the position that the exception will be construed also to allow the "sale" of patented ingredients that have been ordered by a producer who is stockpiling the final patented product—for example, with regard to pharmaceuticals, sales by fine chemical producers of active ingredients ordered by the generic producer.

7.10 The stockpiling exception is available only to persons who have invoked the regulatory review exception in Section 55.2(1). This limitation has the effect of limiting the exception to products that are subject to the kind of government marketing regulations referred to in Section 55.2(1). As a practical matter, only persons who have actually obtained regulatory permission to market such regulated products would be able to benefit from the stockpiling exception, because there would be no commercial advantage in having a stock of goods on hand when the patent expires unless one also has regulatory permission to sell those goods as of that date. Conversely, the stockpiling exception does complement the competitive effects of the regulatory review exception. Without the additional permission to stockpile during the term of the patent, competitors who obtain regulatory permission to sell on the day the patent expires would still not be able to enter the market on that day, because they would first have to manufacture a sufficient stock of goods.

E. SECTION 55.2(2) (THE STOCKPILING EXCEPTION)

(1) APPLICATION OF ARTICLE 28.1 AND ARTICLE 30 OF THE TRIPS AGREEMENT

(a) Introduction

7.17 The Panel began by considering the claims of violation concerning Section 55.2(2), the so-called stockpiling provision. It began by considering the EC claim that this measure was in violation of Article 28.1 of the TRIPS Agreement, and Canada's defence that the measure was an exception authorized by Article 30 of the Agreement.

7.18 Article 28.1 provides:

"Rights Conferred

1. A patent shall confer on its owner the following exclusive rights:

(a) Where the subject-matter of a patent is a product, to prevent third parties not having the owner's consent from the acts of making, using, offering for sale, selling, or importing for these purposes that product;"

There was no dispute as to the meaning of Article 28.1 exclusive rights as they pertain to Section 55.2(2) of Canada's Patent Act. Canada acknowledged that the provisions of Section 55.2(2) permitting third parties to "make", "construct" or "use" the patented product during the term of the patent, without the patent owner's permission, would be a violation of Article 28.1 if not excused under Article 30 of the Agreement. The dispute on the claim of violation of Article 28.1 involved whether Section 55.2.(2) of the Patent Act complies with the conditions of Article 30.

7.19 The TRIPS Agreement contains two provisions authorizing exceptions to the exclusionary patent rights laid down in Article 28—Articles 30 and 31. Of these two, Article 30—the so-called limited exceptions provision—has been invoked by Canada in the present case. It reads as follows:

"Exceptions to Rights Conferred

Members may provide limited exceptions to the exclusive rights conferred by a patent, provided that such exceptions do not unreasonably conflict with the normal exploitation of the patent and do not unreasonably prejudice the legitimate interests of the patent owner, taking account of the legitimate interests of third parties."

7.20 Both parties agreed upon the basic structure of Article 30. Article 30 establishes three criteria that must be met in order to qualify for an exception: (1) the exception must be "limited"; (2) the exception must not "unreasonably conflict with normal exploitation of the patent"; (3) the exception must not "unreasonably prejudice the legitimate interests of the patent owner, taking account of the legitimate interests of third parties". The three conditions are cumulative, each being a separate and independent requirement that must be satisfied. Failure to comply with any one of the three conditions results in the Article 30 exception being disallowed.

7.21 The three conditions must, of course, be interpreted in relation to each other. Each of the three must be presumed to mean something different from the other two, or else there would be redundancy. Normally, the order of listing can be read to suggest that an exception that complies with the first condition can nevertheless violate the second or third, and that one which complies with the first and second can still violate the third. The syntax of Article 30 supports the conclusion that an exception may be "limited" and yet fail to satisfy one or both of the other two conditions. The ordering further suggests that an exception that does not "unreasonably conflict with normal exploitation" could nonetheless "unreasonably prejudice the legitimate interests of the patent owner".

...

(c) "Limited Exceptions"

7.27 Canada asserted that the word "limited" should be interpreted according to the conventional dictionary definition, such as "confined within definite limits", or "restricted in scope, extent, amount". Canada argued that the stockpiling exception in Section 55.2(2) is restricted in scope because it has only a limited impact on a patent owner's rights. The stockpiling exception, Canada noted, does not affect the patent owner's right to an exclusive market for "commercial" sales during the patent term, since the product that is manufactured and stockpiled during the final six months of the term cannot be sold in competition with the patent owner until the patent expires. By "commercial sales", Canada clearly meant sales to the ultimate consumer, because it acknowledged that sales of patented ingredients to producers engaged in authorized stockpiling is permitted. Thus, Canada was arguing that an exception is "limited" as long as the exclusive right to sell to the ultimate consumer during the term of the patent is preserved. In addition, Canada also claimed that the exception is further limited by the six-month duration of the exception, and by the fact that it can be used only by persons that have made, constructed or used the invention under Section 55.2(1).

7.28 The EC interpreted the word "limited" to connote a narrow exception, one that could be described by words such as "narrow, small, minor, insignificant or restricted". The EC measured the "limited" quality of the proposed exception by reference to its impact on the exclusionary rights granted to the patent owner under Article 28.1. Applying that measure, the EC contended that the stockpiling exception is not "limited" because it takes away three of the five Article 28.1 rights—the rights to exclude "making", "using" and "importing". The EC argued that the impairment of three out of five basic rights is in itself extensive enough to be considered "not limited". The EC further contended that limitation of the exception to the last six months of the patent term does not constitute a limited impairment of rights when six months is taken as a percentage of the 20-year patent term, and especially not when taken as a percentage of the actual eight to 12-year period of effective market exclusivity enjoyed by most patented pharmaceuticals. In addition, the EC noted, there was no limitation on the quantities that could be produced during this period, nor any limitation on the markets in which such products could be sold. Finally, the EC pointed out that no royalty fees are due for such production, and that the patent holder does not even have a right to be informed of the use of the patent.

7.29 In considering how to approach the parties' conflicting positions regarding the meaning of the term "limited exceptions", the Panel was aware that the text of Article 30 has antecedents in the text of Article 9(2) of the Berne Convention. However, the words "limited exceptions" in Article 30 of the TRIPS Agreement are different from the corresponding words in Article 9(2) of the Berne Convention, which reads "in certain special cases". The Panel examined the documented negotiating history of TRIPS Article 30 with respect to the reasons why negotiators may have chosen to use the term "limited exceptions" in place of "in special circumstances". The negotiating records show only that the term "limited exceptions" was employed very early in the drafting process, well before the decision to adopt a text modelled on Berne Article 9(2), but do not indicate why it was retained in the later draft texts modelled on Berne Article 9(2).

7.30 The Panel agreed with the EC that, as used in this context, the word "limited" has a narrower connotation than the rather broad definitions cited by Canada. Although the word itself can have both broad and narrow definitions, the narrower being indicated by examples such as "a mail train taking only a limited number of passengers", the narrower definition is the more appropriate when the word "limited" is used as part of the phrase "limited exception". The word "exception" by itself connotes a limited derogation, one that does not undercut the body of rules from which it is made. When a treaty uses the term "limited exception", the word "limited" must be given a meaning separate from the limitation implicit in the word "exception" itself. The term "limited exception" must therefore be read to connote a narrow exception—one which makes only a small diminution of the rights in question.

7.31 The Panel agreed with the EC interpretation that "limited" is to be measured by the extent to which the exclusive rights of the patent owner have been curtailed. The full text of Article 30 refers to "limited exceptions to the exclusive rights conferred by a patent". In the absence of other indications, the Panel concluded that it would be justified in reading the text literally, focusing on the extent to which legal rights have been curtailed, rather than the size or extent of the economic impact. In support of this conclusion, the Panel noted that the following two conditions of Article 30 ask more particularly about the economic impact of the exception, and provide two sets of standards by which such impact may be judged. The term "limited exceptions" is the only one of the three conditions in Article 30 under which the extent of the curtailment of rights as such is dealt with.

7.32 The Panel does not agree, however, with the EC's position that the curtailment of legal rights can be measured by simply counting the number of legal rights impaired by an exception.

A very small act could well violate all five rights provided by Article 28.1 and yet leave each of the patent owner's rights intact for all useful purposes. To determine whether a particular exception constitutes a limited exception, the extent to which the patent owner's rights have been curtailed must be measured.

7.33 The Panel could not accept Canada's argument that the curtailment of the patent owner's legal rights is "limited" just so long as the exception preserves the exclusive right to sell to the ultimate consumer during the patent term. Implicit in the Canadian argument is a notion that the right to exclude sales to consumers during the patent term is the essential right conveyed by a patent, and that the rights to exclude "making" and "using" the patented product during the term of the patent are in some way secondary. The Panel does not find any support for creating such a hierarchy of patent rights within the TRIPS Agreement. If the right to exclude sales were all that really mattered, there would be no reason to add other rights to exclude "making" and "using". The fact that such rights were included in the TRIPS Agreement, as they are in most national patent laws, is strong evidence that they are considered a meaningful and independent part of the patent owner's rights.

7.34 In the Panel's view, the question of whether the stockpiling exception is a "limited" exception turns on the extent to which the patent owner's rights to exclude "making" and "using" the patented product have been curtailed. The right to exclude "making" and "using" provides protection, additional to that provided by the right to exclude sale, during the entire term of the patent by cutting off the supply of competing goods at the source and by preventing use of such products however obtained. With no limitations at all upon the quantity of production, the stockpiling exception removes that protection entirely during the last six months of the patent term, without regard to what other, subsequent, consequences it might have. By this effect alone, the stockpiling exception can be said to abrogate such rights entirely during the time it is in effect.

7.35 In view of Canada's emphasis on preserving commercial benefits before the expiration of the patent, the Panel also considered whether the market advantage gained by the patent owner in the months after expiration of the patent could also be considered a purpose of the patent owner's rights to exclude "making" and "using" during the term of the patent. In both theory and practice, the Panel concluded that such additional market benefits were within the purpose of these rights. In theory, the rights of the patent owner are generally viewed as a right to prevent competitive commercial activity by others, and manufacturing for commercial sale is a quintessential competitive commercial activity, whose character is not altered by a mere delay in the commercial reward. In practical terms, it must be recognized that enforcement of the right to exclude "making" and "using" during the patent term will necessarily give all patent owners, for all products, a short period of extended market exclusivity after the patent expires. The repeated enactment of such exclusionary rights with knowledge of their universal market effects can only be understood as an affirmation of the purpose to produce those market effects.

7.36 For both these reasons, the Panel concluded that the stockpiling exception of Section 55.2(2) constitutes a substantial curtailment of the exclusionary rights required to be granted to patent owners under Article 28.1 of the TRIPS Agreement. Without seeking to define exactly what level of curtailment would be disqualifying, it was clear to the Panel that an exception which results in a substantial curtailment of this dimension cannot be considered a "limited exception" within the meaning of Article 30 of the Agreement.

7.37 Neither of the two "limitations" upon the scope of the measure are sufficient to alter this conclusion. First, the fact that the exception can only be used by those persons who have utilized the regulatory review exception of Section 55.2(1) does limit the scope of the exception both to those persons and to products requiring regulatory approval. In regard to the limitation to such persons, the Panel considered this was not a real limitation since only persons who satisfy regulatory requirements would be entitled to market the product. In regard to the limitation to such products, the Panel considered that the fact that an exception does not apply at all to other products in no way changes its effect with regard to the criteria of Article 30. Each exception must be evaluated with regard to its impact on each affected patent, independently. Second, the fact that the exception applied only to the last six months of the patent term obviously does reduce its impact on all affected patented products, but the Panel agreed with the EC that six months was a commercially significant period of time, especially since there were no limits at all on the volume of production allowed, or the market destination of such production.

7.38 Having concluded that the exception in Section 55.2(2) of the Canadian Patent Act does not satisfy the first condition of Article 30 of the TRIPS Agreement, the Panel therefore concluded that Section 55.2(2) is inconsistent with Canada's obligations under Article 28.1 of the Agreement. This conclusion, in turn, made it unnecessary to consider any of the other claims of inconsistency raised by the European Communities. Accordingly, the Panel did not consider the claims of inconsistency under the second and third conditions of Article 30, the claim of inconsistency with TRIPS Article 27.1, and the claim of inconsistency with Article 33.

F. SECTION 55.2(1) (THE REGULATORY REVIEW EXCEPTION)

(1) APPLICATION OF ARTICLE 28.1 AND ARTICLE 30 OF THE TRIPS AGREEMENT

7.39 Both parties agreed that, if the regulatory review exception of Section 55.2(1) met the conditions of Article 30 of the TRIPS Agreement, the acts permitted by that Section would not be in violation of Article 28.1 of the TRIPS Agreement. Canada argued that Section 55.2(1) complies with each of the three conditions of Article 30. The European Communities argued that Section 55.2(1) fails to comply with any of the three conditions. We now turn to the respective arguments for applying these three Article 30 conditions to Section 55.2(1).

(a) "Limited Exceptions"

7.40 Canada's arguments pertaining to the "limited" character of the regulatory review exception of Section 55.2(1) started from the same premises as its arguments with regard to the "limited" character of the stockpiling exception of Section 55.2(2). Canada again asserted that the regulatory review exception of Section 55.2(1) can be regarded as "limited" because the rights given to third parties do not deprive the patent holder of his right to exclude all other "commercial sales" of the patented product during the term of the patent. As noted above when discussing this argument in relation to Section 55.2(2), Canada evidently intended the term "commercial sales" to refer to sales to the ultimate consumer, rather than sales by suppliers of ingredients. As before, Canada was taking the position that an exception is "limited" as long as the exclusive right to sell to the ultimate consumer during the term of the patent is preserved.

7.41 In the case of the regulatory review exception, however, Canada added two further arguments based on the negotiating history of Article 30 and on the subsequent practices of certain WTO Members. Canada pointed out that in 1984 the United States had enacted a regulatory review exception similar to Section 55.2(1) of Canada's Patent Act, known as the "Bolar exemption". Canada asserted that the United States "Bolar exemption" was well known during the negotiation of Article 30, and that governments were aware that the United States intended to secure an exception that would permit it to retain its "Bolar exemption". Canada further asserts that it was known that the United States agreed to the general language of Article 30 on the understanding that the provision would do so. Canada called attention to subsequent statements by United States officials stating that "[O]ur negotiators ensured that the TRIPS Agreement permits the Bolar exemption to be maintained."

7.42 With regard to subsequent practice, Canada pointed out that after the conclusion of the TRIPS Agreement four other WTO Members (Argentina, Australia, Hungary and Israel) adopted legislation containing similar regulatory review exceptions, and that both Japan and Portugal adopted interpretations of existing patent law which confirmed exemptions for regulatory review submissions. Canada argued that these actions are subsequent practices by parties to the agreement, within the meaning of Article 31(3)(b) of the Vienna Convention, that confirm its interpretation that regulatory review exceptions are authorized by TRIPS Article 30.

7.43 In arguing that the regulatory review exception was not "limited", the EC again focused on the extent to which that exception diminishes the patent owner's rights of exclusivity required by Article 28.1 of the TRIPS Agreement. The EC pointed out that Section 55.2(1) permits third parties to perform all five of the activities which the patent owner may otherwise exclude under Article 28.1. The EC acknowledged that the permission to conduct these activities was subject to the condition that the final purchaser of the patented product has the intention to use the product for supplying information to regulatory authorities, but the EC argued that the terms of Section 55.2(1) allowed "wide-ranging activities by a wide range of operators" and "infringing acts of a significant extent". The EC called particular attention to the fact that Section 55.2(1) authorizes the commercial sale of ingredients by fine chemical producers who often supply generic drug manufacturers with the ingredients needed to make test products. The EC also noted that regulatory requirements often require applicants or their suppliers to produce commercial quantities of drugs in order to demonstrate their ability to maintain the required level of quality at such production levels. The EC also stressed the fact that infringing activities are authorized at any time during the 20-year term of the patent. And finally, the EC called particular attention to the fact that Section 55.2(1) applied to regulatory submissions anywhere in the world, suggesting that the number and variety of such foreign regulatory procedures, as well as Canada's inability to supervise or influence them, would further enlarge the range of excluded activities permitted by this exception.

7.44 In the previous part of this Report dealing with the stockpiling exception of Section 55.2(2), the Panel concluded that the words "limited exception" express a requirement that the exception make only a narrow curtailment of the legal rights which Article 28.1 requires to be granted to patent owners, and that the measure of that curtailment was the extent to which the affected legal rights themselves had been impaired. As was made clear by our conclusions regarding the stockpiling exception, the Panel could not accept Canada's contention that an exception can be regarded as "limited" just so long as it preserves the patent owner's exclusive right to sell to the ultimate consumer during the patent term.

7.45 In the Panel's view, however, Canada's regulatory review exception is a "limited exception" within the meaning of TRIPS Article 30. It is "limited" because of the narrow scope of its curtailment of Article 28.1 rights. As long as the exception is confined to conduct needed to comply with the requirements of the regulatory approval process, the extent of the acts unauthorized by the right holder that are permitted by it will be small and narrowly bounded. Even though regulatory approval processes may require substantial amounts of test production to demonstrate reliable manufacturing, the patent owner's rights themselves are not impaired any further by the size of such production runs, as long as they are solely for regulatory purposes and no commercial use is made of resulting final products.

7.46 The Panel found no basis for believing that activities seeking product approvals under foreign regulatory procedures would be any less subject to these limitations. There is no a priori basis to assume that the requirements of foreign regulatory procedures will require activities unrelated to legitimate objectives of product quality and safety, nor has the EC provided any evidence to that effect. Nor is there any reason to assume that Canadian law would apply the exception in cases where foreign requirements clearly had no regulatory purpose. Nor, finally, is there any reason to assume that it will be any more difficult to enforce the requirements of Canadian law when Canadian producers claim exceptions under foreign procedures. With regard to the latter point, the Panel concurred with Canada's point that the government is not normally expected to regulate the actual conduct of third parties in such cases. The enforcement of these conditions, as with other enforcement of patent rights, occurs by means of private infringement actions brought by the patent owner. The patent owner merely has to prove that the challenged conduct is inconsistent with the basic patent rights created by national law. Once that initial case is made, the burden will be on the party accused of infringement to prove its defence by establishing that its conduct with respect to foreign regulatory procedures was in compliance with the conditions of Section 55.2(1).

7.47 In reaching this conclusion, the Panel also considered Canada's additional arguments that both the negotiating history of Article 30 of the TRIPS Agreement and the subsequent practices of certain WTO Member governments supported the view that Article 30 was understood to permit regulatory review exceptions similar to Section 55.2(1). The Panel did not accord any weight to either of those arguments, however, because there was no documented evidence of the claimed negotiating understanding, and because the subsequent acts by individual countries did not constitute "practice in the application of the treaty which establishes the agreement of the parties regarding its interpretation" within the meaning of Article 31.3(b) of the Vienna Convention.

7.48 A final objection to the Panel's general conclusion remains to be addressed. Although the point was raised only briefly in the parties' legal arguments, the Panel was compelled to acknowledge that the economic impact of the regulatory review exception could be considerable. According to information supplied by Canada itself, in the case of patented pharmaceutical products approximately three to six-and-a-half years are required for generic drug producers to develop and obtain regulatory approval for their products. If there were no regulatory review exception allowing competitors to apply for regulatory approval during the term of the patent, therefore, the patent owner would be able to extend its period of market exclusivity, de facto, for some part of that three to six-and-half year period, depending on how much, if any, of the development process could be performed during the term of the patent under other exceptions, such as the scientific or experimental use exception. The Panel believed it was necessary to ask whether measures having such a significant impact on the economic interests of patent owners could be called a "limited" exception to patent rights.

7.49 After analysing all three conditions stated in Article 30 of the TRIPS Agreement, the Panel was satisfied that Article 30 does in fact address the issue of economic impact, but only in the other two conditions contained in that Article. As will be seen in the analysis of these other conditions below, the other two conditions deal with the issue of economic impact, according to criteria that relate specifically to that issue. Viewing all three conditions as a whole, it is apparent that the first condition ("limited exception") is neither designed nor intended to address the issue of economic impact directly.

7.50 In sum, the Panel found that the regulatory review exception of Section 55.2(1) is a "limited exception" within the meaning of Article 30 of the TRIPS Agreement.

(b) "Normal Exploitation"

7.51 The second condition of Article 30 prohibits exceptions that "unreasonably conflict with a normal exploitation of the patent". Canada took the position that "exploitation" of the patent involves the extraction of commercial value from the patent by "working" the patent, either by selling the product in a market from which competitors are excluded, or by licensing others to do so, or by selling the patent rights outright. The European Communities also defined "exploitation" by referring to the same three ways of "working" a patent. The parties differed primarily on their interpretation of the term "normal".

7.54 The Panel considered that "exploitation" refers to the commercial activity by which patent owners employ their exclusive patent rights to extract economic value from their patent. The term "normal" defines the kind of commercial activity Article 30 seeks to protect. The ordinary meaning of the word "normal" is found in the dictionary definition: "regular, usual, typical, ordinary, conventional". As so defined, the term can be understood to refer either to an empirical conclusion about what is common within a relevant community, or to a normative standard of entitlement. The Panel concluded that the word "normal" was being used in Article 30 in a sense that combined the two meanings.

7.55 The normal practice of exploitation by patent owners, as with owners of any other intellectual property right, is to exclude all forms of competition that could detract significantly from the economic returns anticipated from a patent's grant of market exclusivity. The specific forms of patent exploitation are not static, of course, for to be effective exploitation must adapt to changing forms of competition due to technological development and the evolution of marketing practices. Protection of all normal exploitation practices is a key element of the policy reflected in all patent laws. Patent laws establish a carefully defined period of market exclusivity as an inducement to innovation, and the policy of those laws cannot be achieved unless patent owners are permitted to take effective advantage of that inducement once it has been defined.

7.56 Canada has raised the argument that market exclusivity occurring after the 20-year patent term expires should not be regarded as "normal". The Panel was unable to accept that as a categorical proposition. Some of the basic rights granted to all patent owners, and routinely exercised by all patent owners, will typically produce a certain period of market exclusivity after the expiration of a patent. For example, the separate right to prevent "making" the patented product during the term of the patent often prevents competitors from building an inventory needed to enter the market immediately upon expiration of a patent. There is nothing abnormal about that more or less brief period of market exclusivity after the patent has expired.

7.57 The Panel considered that Canada was on firmer ground, however, in arguing that the additional period of de facto market exclusivity created by using patent rights to preclude submissions for regulatory authorization should not be considered "normal". The additional period of market exclusivity in this situation is not a natural or normal consequence of enforcing patent rights. It is an unintended consequence of the conjunction of the patent laws with product regulatory laws, where the combination of patent rights with the time demands of the regulatory process gives a greater than normal period of market exclusivity to the enforcement of certain patent rights. It is likewise a form of exploitation that most patent owners do not in fact employ. For the vast majority of patented products, there is no marketing regulation of the kind covered by Section 55.2(1), and thus there is no possibility to extend patent exclusivity by delaying the marketing approval process for competitors.

7.58 The Panel could not agree with the EC's assertion that the mere existence of the patent owner's rights to exclude was a sufficient reason, by itself, for treating all gains derived from such rights as flowing from "normal exploitation". In the Panel's view, the EC's argument contained no evidence or analysis addressed to the various meanings of "normal"—neither a demonstration that most patent owners extract the value of their patents in the manner barred by Section 55.2(1), nor an argument that the prohibited manner of exploitation was "normal" in the sense of being essential to the achievement of the goals of patent policy. To the contrary, the EC's focus on the exclusionary rights themselves merely restated the concern to protect Article 28 exclusionary rights as such. This is a concern already dealt with by the first condition of

Article 30 ("limited exception") and the Panel found the ultimate EC arguments here impossible to distinguish from the arguments it had made under that first condition.

7.59 In sum, the Panel found that the regulatory review exception of Section 55.2(1) does not conflict with a normal exploitation of patents, within the meaning of the second condition of Article 30 of the TRIPS Agreement. The fact that no conflict has been found makes it unnecessary to consider the question of whether, if a conflict were found, the conflict would be "unreasonable". Accordingly, it is also unnecessary to determine whether or not the final phrase of Article 30, calling for consideration of the legitimate interests of third parties, does or does not apply to the determination of "unreasonable conflict" under the second condition of Article 30.

(c) "Legitimate Interests"

7.60 The third condition of Article 30 is the requirement that the proposed exception must not "unreasonably prejudice the legitimate interests of the patent owner, taking into account the legitimate interests of third parties". Although Canada, as the party asserting the exception provided for in Article 30, bears the burden of proving compliance with the conditions of that exception, the order of proof is complicated by the fact that the condition involves proving a negative. One cannot demonstrate that no legitimate interest of the patent owner has been prejudiced until one knows what claims of legitimate interest can be made. Likewise, the weight of legitimate third party interests cannot be fully appraised until the legitimacy and weight of the patent owner's legitimate interests, if any, are defined. Accordingly, without disturbing the ultimate burden of proof, the Panel chose to analyse the issues presented by the third condition of Article 30 according to the logical sequence in which those issues became defined.

7.61 The ultimate issue with regard to the regulatory review exception's compliance with the third condition of Article 30 involved similar considerations to those arising under the second condition ("normal exploitation")—the fact that the exception would remove the additional period of de facto market exclusivity that patent owners could achieve if they were permitted to employ their rights to exclude "making" and "using" (and "selling") the patented product during the term of the patent to prevent potential competitors from preparing and/or applying for regulatory approval during the term of the patent. The issue was whether patent owners could claim a "legitimate interest" in the economic benefits that could be derived from such an additional period of de facto market exclusivity and, if so, whether the regulatory review exception "unreasonably prejudiced" that interest.

(i) Primary EC claim of legitimate interest

7.62 The European Communities argued that the regulatory review exception in Section 55.2(1) fails to satisfy the third condition of Article 30. The primary EC argument on this point rested on an interpretation that identified "legitimate interests" with legal interests. The EC asserted that the "legitimate interests" of the patent owner can only be the full enjoyment of his patent rights during the entire term of the patent. Given that starting point, it followed that any exception to Article 28.1 rights would constitute "prejudice" to the legitimate interests of a patent owner. Consequently, the remainder of the EC's argument concentrated on whether the prejudice was "unreasonable", an issue which in turn focused on whether the "legitimate interests of third parties" outweighed the patent owner's interests in full enjoyment of his legal rights. The EC first argued that the only relevant "third parties" for the purpose of Article 30 are the patent owner's competitors—in the case of pharmaceutical patents the generic drug producers, because they were the only parties with interests adverse to those of patent owners. According to the EC's view, the TRIPS Agreement constitutes a recognition that patent systems serve the interest of the society, including the multiple interests of its health policy. That being so, the patent rights granted by that Agreement, being a part of the balance of rights and obligations that governments have agreed to as beneficial, cannot be found to be adverse to, or in conflict with, the interests represented by general social welfare policy. And that, in turn, means that the only adverse third party interests to patent owners are the interests of those firms with whom they compete.

7.63 Then, following its position that "legitimate interests" are essentially legal interests, the EC went on to argue that the legitimate interests of competing producers are essentially the same as those of patent owners—that is, the full enjoyment of their legal rights. The legal rights of the patent owner's competitors, the EC argues, are the rights to make, use or sell the patented product on the day after the patent expires. Such competitors, therefore, could have no "legitimate" interest in the rights granted by the regulatory review exception of Section 55.2(1), because they could have no legal right to "make" or "use" (or "sell") the patented product during the term of the patent.

7.64 Given these interpretations of the third condition of Article 30, the EC concluded: (1) that the impairment of the patent owner's Article 28 legal rights by the regulatory review exception amounts to "prejudice" to the patent owner's legitimate interests; and (2) that in the absence of any legitimate third party interest to the contrary, the abrogation of rights authorized by Section 55.2(1) is substantial enough to be characterized as "unreasonable".

...

(ii) Definition of "legitimate interests"

7.68 The word "legitimate" is commonly defined as follows:

(a) Conformable to, sanctioned or authorized by, law or principle: lawful; justifiable; proper;

(b) Normal, regular, conformable to a recognized standard type.

Although the European Communities' definition equating "legitimate interests" with a full respect of legal interests pursuant to Article 28.1 is within at least some of these definitions, the EC definition makes it difficult to make sense of the rest of the third condition of Article 30, in at least three respects. First, since by that definition every exception under Article 30 will be causing "prejudice" to some legal rights provided by Article 28 of the Agreement, that definition would reduce the first part of the third condition to a simple requirement that the proposed exception must not be "unreasonable". Such a requirement could certainly have been expressed more directly if that was what was meant. Second, a definition equating "legitimate interests" with legal interests makes no sense at all when applied to the final phrase of Article 30 referring to the "legitimate interests" of third parties. Third parties are by definition parties who have no legal right at all in being able to perform the tasks excluded by Article 28 patent rights. An exceptions clause permitting governments to take account of such third party legal interests would be permitting them to take account of nothing. And third, reading the third condition as a further protection of legal rights would render it essentially redundant in light of the very similar protection of legal rights in the first condition of Article 30 ("limited exception").

7.69 To make sense of the term "legitimate interests" in this context, that term must be defined in the way that it is often used in legal discourse—as a normative claim calling for protection of interests that are "justifiable" in the sense that they are supported by relevant public policies or other social norms. This is the sense of the word that often appears in statements such as "X has no legitimate interest in being able to do Y". We may take as an illustration one of the most widely adopted Article 30-type exceptions in national patent laws—the exception under which use of the patented product for scientific experimentation, during the term of the patent and without consent, is not an infringement. It is often argued that this exception is based on the notion that a key public policy purpose underlying patent laws is to facilitate the dissemination and advancement of technical knowledge and that allowing the patent owner to prevent experimental use during the term of the patent would frustrate part of the purpose of the requirement that the nature of the invention be disclosed to the public. To the contrary, the argument concludes, under the policy of the patent laws, both society and the scientist have a "legitimate interest" in using the patent disclosure to support the advance of science and technology. While the Panel draws no conclusion about the correctness of any such national exceptions in terms of Article 30 of the TRIPS Agreement, it does adopt the general meaning of the term "legitimate interests" contained in legal analysis of this type.

7.70 The negotiating history of the TRIPS Agreement itself casts no further illumination on the meaning of the term "legitimate interests", but the negotiating history of Article 9(2) of the Berne Convention, from which the text of the third condition was clearly drawn, does tend to affirm the Panel's interpretation of that term. With regard to the TRIPS negotiations themselves, the meaning of several important drafting changes turns out to be equivocal upon closer examination. The negotiating records of the TRIPS Agreement itself show that the first drafts of the provision that was to become Article 30 contemplated authorizing "limited exceptions" that would be defined by an illustrative list of exceptions—private use, scientific use, prior use, a traditional exception for pharmacists, and the like. Eventually, this illustrative list approach was abandoned in favour of a more general authorization following the outlines of the present Article 30. The negotiating records of the TRIPS Agreement give no explanation of the reason for this decision.

7.71 The text of the present, more general version of Article 30 of the TRIPS Agreement was obviously based on the text of Article 9(2) of the Berne Convention. Berne Article 9(2) deals with exceptions to the copyright holder's right to exclude reproduction of its copyrighted work without permission. The text of Article 9(2) is as follows:

"It shall be a matter for legislation in the countries of the Union to permit the reproduction of [literary and artistic] works in certain special cases, provided that such reproduction does not conflict with a normal exploitation of the work and does not unreasonably prejudice the legitimate interests of the author."

The text of Berne Article 9(2) was not adopted into Article 30 of the TRIPS Agreement without change. Whereas the final condition in Berne Article 9(2) ("legitimate interests") simply refers to the legitimate interests of the author, the TRIPS negotiators added in Article 30 the instruction that account must be taken of "the legitimate interests of third parties". Absent further explanation in the records of the TRIPS negotiations, however, the Panel was not able to attach a substantive meaning to this change other than what is already obvious in the text itself, namely that the reference to the "legitimate interests of third parties" makes sense only if the term "legitimate interests" is construed as a concept broader than legal interests.

7.72 With regard to the meaning of Berne Article 9(2) itself, the Panel examined the drafting committee report that is usually cited as the most authoritative explanation of what Article 9(2) means. The drafting committee report states:

"If it is considered that reproduction conflicts with the normal exploitation of the work, reproduction is not permitted at all. If it is considered that reproduction does not conflict with the normal exploitation of the work, the next step would be to consider whether it does not unreasonably prejudice the legitimate interests of the author. Only if such is not the case would it be possible in certain special cases to introduce a compulsory license, or to provide for use without payment. A practical example may be photocopying for various purposes. If it consists of producing a very large number of copies, it may not be permitted, as it conflicts with a normal exploitation of the work. If it implies a rather large number of copies for use in industrial undertakings, it may not unreasonably prejudice the legitimate interests of the author, provided that, according to national legislation, an equitable remuneration is paid. If a small number of copies is made, photocopying may be permitted without payment, particularly for individual or scientific use."

The Panel recognized that the drafting committee's examples concern the area of copyright as opposed to patents, and that, even further, they deal with the situation as it was in 1967, and accordingly the Panel was reluctant to read too much into these examples as guides to the meaning of Article 30. But the Panel did find that the concepts of "normal exploitation" and "legitimate interests" underlying the three examples used by the drafting committee were consistent with the Panel's definitions of these concepts and of the differences between them.

7.73 In sum, after consideration of the ordinary meaning of the term "legitimate interests", as it is used in Article 30, the Panel was unable to accept the EC's interpretation of that term as referring to legal interests pursuant to Article 28.1. Accordingly, the Panel was unable to accept the primary EC argument with regard to the third condition of Article 30. It found that the EC argument based solely on the patent owner's legal rights pursuant to Article 28.1, without reference to any more particular normative claims of interest, did not raise a relevant claim of non-compliance with the third condition of Article 30.

(iii) Second claim of "legitimate interest"

7.74 After reaching the previous conclusion concerning the EC's primary argument under the "legitimate interests" condition of Article 30, the Panel then directed its attention to another line of argument raised in statements made by the EC and by one third party. This second line of argument called attention to the fact that patent owners whose innovative products are subject to marketing approval requirements suffer a loss of economic benefits to the extent that delays in obtaining government approval prevent them from marketing their product during a substantial part of the patent term. According to information supplied by Canada, regulatory approval of new pharmaceuticals usually does not occur until approximately eight to 12 years after the patent application has been filed, due to the time needed to complete development of the product and the time needed to comply with the regulatory procedure itself. The result in the case of pharmaceuticals, therefore, is that the innovative producer is in fact able to market its patented product in only the remaining eight to 12 years of the 20-year patent term, thus receiving an effective period of market exclusivity that is only 40-60 per cent of the period of exclusivity normally envisaged in a 20-year patent term. The EC argued that patent owners who suffer a reduction of effective market exclusivity from such delays should be entitled to impose the same type of delay in connection with corresponding regulatory requirements upon the market entry of competing products. According to the EC,

"[T]here exists no reason why the research based pharmaceutical enterprise is obliged to accept the economic consequence of patent term erosion because of marketing approval requirements which reduce their effective term of protection to 12-8 years while the copy producer should be entirely compensated for the economic consequence of the need of marketing approval for his generic product, and at the expense of the inventor and patent holder".

Applied to the regulatory review exception, this argument called for the removal of such exceptions so that patent owners may use their exclusionary patent rights to prevent competitors from engaging in product development and initiating the regulatory review process until the patent has expired. The result of removing the exception would be to allow patent owners to create a period of further, de facto market exclusivity after the expiration of the patent, for the length of time it would take competing producers to complete product development and obtain marketing approval.

7.75 The normative claim being made in this second argument ultimately rested on a claim of equal treatment for all patent owners. The policy of the patent laws, the argument would run, is to give innovative producers the advantage of market exclusivity during the 20-year term of the patent. Although patent laws do not guarantee that patent owners will obtain economic benefits from this opportunity, most patent owners have at least the legal opportunity to market the patented product during all or virtually all this 20-year period of market exclusivity. Producers whose products are subject to regulatory approval requirements may be deprived of this opportunity for a substantial part of the 20-year period.

7.76 Under the Panel's interpretation of Article 30, this argument could be characterized as a claim of "legitimate interest" under the third condition of Article 30. It was distinct from the claim made under the second condition of Article 30 ("normal exploitation"), because it did not rest on a claim of interest in the "normal" means of extracting commercial benefits from a patent. Instead, it was a distinctive claim of interest, resting on a distinctive situation applicable only to patent owners affected by marketing approval requirements, asking for an additional means of exploitation, above and beyond "normal exploitation," to compensate for the distinctive disadvantage claimed to be suffered by this particular group of claimants.

7.77 The Panel therefore examined whether the claimed interest should be considered a "legitimate interest" within the meaning of Article 30. The primary issue was whether the normative basis of that claim rested on a widely recognized policy norm.

7.78 The type of normative claim put forward by the EC has been affirmed by a number of governments that have enacted de jure extensions of the patent term, primarily in the case of pharmaceutical products, to compensate for the de facto diminution of the normal period of market exclusivity due to delays in obtaining marketing approval. According to the information submitted to the Panel, such extensions have been enacted by the European Communities, Switzerland, the United States, Japan, Australia and Israel. The EC and Switzerland have done so while at the same time allowing patent owners to continue to use their exclusionary rights to gain an additional, de facto extension of market exclusivity by preventing competitors from applying for regulatory approval during the term of the patent. The other countries that have enacted de jure patent term extensions have also, either by legislation or by judicial decision, created a regulatory review exception similar to Section 55.2(1), thereby eliminating the possibility of an additional de facto extension of market exclusivity.

7.79 This positive response to the claim for compensatory adjustment has not been universal, however. In addition to Canada, several countries have adopted, or are in the process of adopting, regulatory review exceptions similar to Section 55.2(1) of the Canadian Patent Act, thereby removing the de facto extension of market exclusivity, but these countries have not enacted, and are not planning to enact, any de jure extensions of the patent term for producers adversely affected by delayed marketing approval. When regulatory review exceptions are enacted in this manner, they represent a decision not to restore any of the period of market exclusivity due to lost delays in obtaining marketing approval. Taken as a whole, these government decisions may represent either disagreement with the normative claim made by the EC in this proceeding, or they may simply represent a conclusion that such claims are outweighed by other equally legitimate interests.

7.80 In the present proceeding, Canada explicitly disputed the legitimacy of the claimed interest. As noted above, Canada appeared to interpret the term "legitimate interests" in accordance with the Panel's view of that term as a widely recognized normative standard. Canada asserted:

"[N]otwithstanding the private economic advantage that would be obtained by doing so, a patentee can have no legitimate interest deriving from patent law in exercising its exclusive use and enforcement rights within the term of protection to achieve, through exploitation of regulatory review laws, a de facto extension of that term of protection beyond the prescribed period, thereby unilaterally altering the bargain between the patentee and society. In this respect, the interests of a patentee of a pharmaceutical invention can be no different from those of patentees in other fields of technology."

7.81 Canada's argument that all fields of technology must be treated the same implicitly rejected the EC's argument that those fields of technology affected by marketing approval requirements should be given certain additional marketing advantages in compensation. Canada was asked by the Panel to explain the distinction between its decision in Section 55.2(1) to remove the delay in obtaining marketing approval for competitive producers seeking to enter the market after the patent expires and its decision not to correct or compensate for the similar delay encountered by the patent owner himself. Canada responded that the de facto diminution of the market exclusivity for patent owners was an unavoidable consequence of the time required to ensure and to demonstrate the safety and efficacy of the product, whereas the delay imposed on competitors by use of the patent rights to block product development and initiation of the regulatory review process during the term of the patent was neither necessary to product safety nor otherwise an appropriate use of patent rights. Canada's answer implied a further question as to the extent to which the marketing delays experienced by patent owners were in fact the result of government regulatory action, as opposed to the normal consequence of the necessary course of product development for products of this kind.

7.82 On balance, the Panel concluded that the interest claimed on behalf of patent owners whose effective period of market exclusivity had been reduced by delays in marketing approval was neither so compelling nor so widely recognized that it could be regarded as a "legitimate interest" within the meaning of Article 30 of the TRIPS Agreement. Notwithstanding the number of governments that had responded positively to that claimed interest by granting compensatory patent term extensions, the issue itself was of relatively recent standing, and the community of governments was obviously still divided over the merits of such claims. Moreover, the Panel believed that it was significant that concerns about regulatory review exceptions in general, although well known at the time of the TRIPS negotiations, were apparently not clear enough, or compelling enough, to make their way explicitly into the recorded agenda of the TRIPS negotiations. The Panel believed that Article 30's "legitimate interests" concept should not be used to decide, through adjudication, a normative policy issue that is still obviously a matter of unresolved political debate.

7.83 Consequently, having considered the two claims of "legitimate interest" put forward by the EC, and having found that neither of these claimed interests can be considered "legitimate interests" within the meaning of the third condition of Article 30 of the TRIPS Agreement, the Panel concluded that Canada had demonstrated to the Panel's satisfaction that Section 55.2(1) of Canada's Patent Act did not prejudice "legitimate interests" of affected patent owners within the meaning of Article 30.

(iv) Conclusion with regard to compliance of Section 55.2(1) with Article 30

7.84 Having reviewed the conformity of Section 55.2(1) with each of the three conditions for an exception under Article 30 of the TRIPS Agreement, the Panel concluded that Section 55.2(1) does satisfy all three conditions of Article 30, and thus is not inconsistent with Canada's obligations under Article 28.1 of the TRIPS Agreement.

(2) APPLICATION OF ARTICLE 27.1 OF THE TRIPS AGREEMENT

7.85 The EC claimed that Section 55.2(1) of the Canada Patent Act is also in conflict with the obligations under Article 27.1 of the TRIPS Agreement. Article 27.1 provides:

"Article 27

Patentable Subject Matter

1. Subject to the provisions of paragraphs 2 and 3, patents shall be available for any inventions, whether products or processes, in all fields of technology, provided that they are new, involve an inventive step and are capable of industrial application. Subject to paragraph 4 of Article 65, paragraph 8 of Article 70 and paragraph 3 of this Article, patents shall be available and patent rights enjoyable without discrimination as to the place of invention, the field of technology and whether products are imported or locally produced." (emphasis added)

7.86 The EC argued that the anti-discrimination rule stated in the italicized language in the text of Article 27.1 above not only requires that the core patent rights made available under Article 28 be non-discriminatory, but also requires that any exceptions to those basic rights made under Articles 30 and 31 must be non-discriminatory as well. Thus, the EC concluded, Article 27.1 requires that the exception made by Section 55.2(1) must be non-discriminatory. The EC contended that Section 55.2(1) does not comply with the obligations of Article 27.1, because it is limited, both de jure and de facto, to pharmaceutical products alone, and thus discriminates by field of technology.

7.87 Canada advanced two defences to the EC's claim of an Article 27.1 violation. First, Canada argued that the non-discrimination rule of Article 27.1 does not apply to exceptions taken under Article 30. Second, Canada argued that Section 55.2(1) does not discriminate against pharmaceutical products. The Panel examined these two defences in order.

(a) Applicability of Article 27.1 to Article 30 Exceptions

7.88 Canada took the position that Article 27.1's reference to "patent rights" that must be enjoyable without discrimination as to field of technology refers to the basic rights enumerated in Article 28.1 subject to any exceptions that might be made under Article 30. In other words, governments may discriminate when making the "limited" exceptions allowed under Article 30, but they may not discriminate as to patent rights as modified by such exceptions.

7.89 In support of this position, Canada argued that the scope of Article 30 would be reduced to insignificance if governments were required to treat all fields of technology the same, for if all exceptions had to apply to every product it would be far more difficult to meet the requirement that Article 30 exceptions be "limited". It would also be more difficult to target particular social problems, as are anticipated, according to Canada, by Articles 7 and 8 of the TRIPS Agreement. Conversely, Canada argued, requiring that exceptions be applied to all products would cause needless deprivation of patent rights for those products as to which full enforcement of patent rights causes no problem.

7.90 Canada acknowledged that there are certain textual difficulties with this position. It acknowledged that two of the primary purposes of Article 27.1 were to eliminate two types of discrimination that had been practised against pharmaceuticals and certain other products—either a denial of patentability for such products, or, if patents were granted, automatic compulsory licences permitting others to manufacture such products for a fee. Canada acknowledged that, in order to preclude discrimination as to compulsory licences, the non-discrimination rule of Article 27 was made applicable to Article 31 of the TRIPS Agreement, which grants a limited exception for compulsory licences under specified conditions. To defend its position, therefore, Canada was required to explain how Article 27.1 could apply to exceptions made under Article 31, but not to exceptions made under its neighbouring exception provision in Article 30. Canada argued that Article 31 was "mandatory" in character while Article 30 was "permissive," and that this distinction made it appropriate to apply the non-discrimination provision to the former but not the latter.

7.91 The Panel was unable to agree with Canada's contention that Article 27.1 did not apply to exceptions granted under Article 30. The text of the TRIPS Agreement offers no support for such an interpretation. Article 27.1 prohibits discrimination as to enjoyment of "patent rights" without qualifying that term. Article 30 exceptions are explicitly described as "exceptions to the exclusive rights conferred by a patent" and contain no indication that any exemption from non-discrimination rules is intended. A discriminatory exception that takes away enjoyment of a patent right is discrimination as much as is discrimination in the basic rights themselves. The acknowledged fact that the Article 31 exception for compulsory licences and government use is understood to be subject to the non-discrimination rule of Article 27.1, without the need for any textual provision so providing, further strengthens the case for treating the non-discrimination rules as applicable to Article 30. Articles 30 and 31 are linked together by the opening words of Article 31 which define the scope of Article 31 in terms of exceptions not covered by Article 30. Finally, the Panel could not agree with Canada's attempt to distinguish between Articles 30 and 31 on the basis of their mandatory/permissive character; both provisions permit exceptions to patent rights subject to certain mandatory conditions. Nor could the Panel understand how such a "mandatory/permissive" distinction, even if present, would logically support making the kind of distinction Canada was arguing. In the Panel's view, what was important was that in the rights available under national law, that is to say those resulting from the basic rights and any permissible exceptions to them, the forms of discrimination referred to in Article 27.1 should not be present.

7.92 Nor was the Panel able to agree with the policy arguments in support of Canada's interpretation of Article 27. To begin with, it is not true that being able to discriminate against particular patents will make it possible to meet Article 30's requirement that the exception be "limited". An Article 30 exception cannot be made "limited" by limiting it to one field of technology, because the effects of each exception must be found to be "limited" when measured against each affected patent. Beyond that, it is not true that Article 27 requires all Article 30 exceptions to be applied to all products. Article 27 prohibits only discrimination as to the place of invention, the field of technology, and whether products are imported or produced locally. Article 27 does not prohibit bona fide exceptions to deal with problems that may exist only in certain product areas. Moreover, to the extent the prohibition of discrimination does limit the ability to target certain products in dealing with certain of the important national policies referred to in Articles 7 and 8.1, that fact may well constitute a deliberate limitation rather than a frustration of purpose. It is quite plausible, as the EC argued, that the TRIPS Agreement would want to require governments to apply exceptions in a non-discriminatory manner, in order to ensure that governments do not succumb to domestic pressures to limit exceptions to areas where right holders tend to be foreign producers.

7.93 The Panel concluded, therefore, that the anti-discrimination rule of Article 27.1 does apply to exceptions of the kind authorized by Article 30. We turn, accordingly, to the question of whether Section 55.2(1) of the Canadian Patent Act discriminates as to fields of technology.

(b) Discrimination as to the Field of Technology

7.94 The primary TRIPS provisions that deal with discrimination, such as the national treatment and most-favoured-nation provisions of Articles 3 and 4, do not use the term "discrimination". They speak in more precise terms. The ordinary meaning of the word "discriminate" is potentially broader than these more specific definitions. It certainly extends beyond the concept of differential treatment. It is a normative term, pejorative in connotation, referring to results of the unjustified imposition of differentially disadvantageous treatment. Discrimination may arise from explicitly different treatment, sometimes called "de jure discrimination", but it may also arise from ostensibly identical treatment which, due to differences in circumstances, produces differentially disadvantageous effects, sometimes called "de facto discrimination". The standards by which the justification for differential treatment is measured are a subject of infinite complexity. "Discrimination" is a term to be avoided whenever more precise standards are available, and, when employed, it is a term to be interpreted with caution, and with care to add no more precision than the concept contains.

...

7.99 With regard to the issue of de jure discrimination, the Panel concluded that the European Communities had not presented sufficient evidence to raise the issue in the face of Canada's formal declaration that the exception of Section 55.2(1) was not limited to pharmaceutical products. Absent other evidence, the words of the statute compelled the Panel to accept Canada's assurance that the exception was legally available to every product that was subject to marketing approval requirements. In reaching this conclusion, the Panel took note that its legal finding of conformity on this point was based on a finding as to the meaning of the Canadian law that was in turn based on Canada's representations as to the meaning of that law, and that this finding of conformity would no longer be warranted if, and to the extent that, Canada's representations as to the meaning of that law were to prove wrong.

7.100 The Panel then turned to the question of de facto discrimination. Although the EC's response to the Panel's questions indicated that it did intend to raise the issue of de facto discrimination, the EC did not propose a formal definition of de facto discrimination, nor did it submit a systematic exposition of the evidence satisfying the elements of such a concept. Australia and the United States, third parties in the proceedings, referred to previous GATT and WTO legal rulings treating de facto discrimination, but primarily for the purpose of suggesting the mirror image principle—that not all differential treatment is "discrimination". Canada did not associate itself with the Australian and United States positions. Notwithstanding the limited development of the arguments on the issue of de facto discrimination, the Panel concluded that its terms of reference required it to pursue that issue once raised, and accordingly the Panel proceeded to examine the claim of a de facto discrimination violation on the basis of its own examination of the record in the light of the concepts usually associated with claims of de facto discrimination.

7.101 As noted above, de facto discrimination is a general term describing the legal conclusion that an ostensibly neutral measure transgresses a non-discrimination norm because its actual effect is to impose differentially disadvantageous consequences on certain parties, and because those differential effects are found to be wrong or unjustifiable. Two main issues figure in the application of that general concept in most legal systems. One is the question of de facto discriminatory effect—whether the actual effect of the measure is to impose differentially disadvantageous consequences on certain parties. The other, related to the justification for the disadvantageous effects, is the issue of purpose—not an inquiry into the subjective purposes of the officials responsible for the measure, but an inquiry into the objective characteristics of the measure from which one can infer the existence or non-existence of discriminatory objectives.

7.102 With regard to the first issue—the actual effects of the measure –, the EC had argued that, despite its potentially broad coverage of many industries, the exception created by Section 55.2(1) had "in effect" applied only to pharmaceutical patents. The Panel received no systematic information on the range of industries that have actually made use of Section 55.2(1). In the absence of such information, the critical question was whether there was some practical reason why the regulatory review exception would in reality work only to the disadvantage of producers of patented pharmaceutical products. The Panel asked the parties for an explanation of any practical considerations that would limit the scope of application of Section 55.2(1) to pharmaceutical products, but no such explanation was provided. Nor was the Panel able to find such a practical reason from the information before it. The Panel concluded that the EC had not demonstrated that Section 55.2(1) had had a discriminatory effect limited to patented pharmaceutical products.

7.103 On the issue of discriminatory purpose, the EC had stressed on several occasions that, in the public discussion of Section 55.2(1), all relevant participants had been exclusively concerned with the impact of the measure on pharmaceutical products, with both support and opposition to the measure being argued in terms of that one dimension. Canada did not contest this characterization of the public debates.

7.104 The Panel did not find this evidence from the debates on Section 55.2(1) to be persuasive evidence of a discriminatory purpose. To be sure, such evidence makes it clear that the primary reason for passing the measure was its effect on promoting competition in the pharmaceutical sector. This is also evident from Canada's justification for the measure presented in this dispute settlement proceeding. But preoccupation with the effects of a statute in one area does not necessarily mean that the provisions applicable to other areas are a sham, or of no actual or potential importance. Individual problems are frequently the driving force behind legislative actions of broader scope. The broader scope of the measure usually reflects an important legal principle that rules being applied in the area of primary interest should also be applied to other areas where the same problem occurs. Indeed, it is a common desideratum in many legal systems that legislation apply its underlying principles as broadly as possible. So long as the broader application is not a sham, the legislation cannot be considered discriminatory. In the absence of any proof that the broader scope was a sham, it must be found that the evident concentration of public attention upon the effects of Section 55.2(1) on the pharmaceutical industry is not, by itself, evidence of a discriminatory purpose.

7.105 In sum, the Panel found that the evidence in record before it did not raise a plausible claim of discrimination under Article 27.1 of the TRIPS Agreement. It was not proved that the legal scope of Section 55.2(1) was limited to pharmaceutical products, as would normally be required to raise a claim of de jure discrimination. Likewise, it was not proved that the adverse effects of Section 55.2(1) were limited to the pharmaceutical industry, or that the objective indications of purpose demonstrated a purpose to impose disadvantages on pharmaceutical patents in particular, as is often required to raise a claim of de facto discrimination. Having found that the record did not raise any of these basic elements of a discrimination claim, the Panel was able to find that Section 55.2(1) is not inconsistent with Canada's obligations under Article 27.1 of the TRIPS Agreement. Because the record did not present issues requiring any more precise interpretation of the term "discrimination" in Article 27.1, none was made.

... ...

Thus, the panel found that the regulatory review provision was consistent with Article 30 of the TRIPS Agreement but that the stockpiling provision failed to meet the requirements set out in Article 30 as it was not a 'limited exception'. The basic difference between the two was the scope of the exceptions: one exception was deemed to be broader than the other.

Finally, the panel's analysis of the discrimination issues under Article 27.1 is also noteworthy. In the dispute, the Panel based its conclusion that the regulatory review provision does not discriminate against pharmaceutical products as compared to other fields of technology under TRIPS Agreement Article 27.1 in part due to the representations made by the Canadian Government that, in fact, the regulatory review provision is not limited to only pharmaceuticals.[44] Thus, despite the fact that all Canadian discussion of the issue focused exclusively on pharmaceuticals, the panel relied on these representations and, while warning that its finding would no longer be warranted if Canada's representations were later overridden or incorrect, quickly discounted the EC's arguments regarding possible de facto discrimination.[45]

Moving away from Articles 27 and 30, the Agreement also provides for judicial review of any decision to revoke or forfeit a patent (Article 32) and sets out the framework for the burden of proof in process patent judicial proceedings (Article 34).

As a final point in this section, Article 31 permits Members to grant compulsory licences for patented products and processes under limited circumstances and upon satisfying certain conditions. This provision has been highly controversial. Article 31 conditions the granting of a compulsory licence and requires that certain minimum obligations be fulfilled on the following:[46]

(a) authorisation of such use shall be considered on its individual merits;

(b) such use may only be permitted if, prior to such use, the proposed user has made efforts to obtain authorisation from the right holder on reasonable commercial terms and conditions and that such efforts have not been successful within a reasonable period of time. This requirement may be waived by a Member in the case of a national emergency or other circumstances of extreme urgency or in cases of public non-commercial use. In situations of national emergency or other circumstances of extreme urgency, the right holder shall, nevertheless, be notified as soon as reasonably practicable. In the case of public non-commercial use, where the government or contractor, without making a patent search, knows or has demonstrable grounds to know that a valid patent is or will be used by or for the government, the right holder shall be informed promptly;

(c) the scope and duration of such use shall be limited to the purpose for which it was authorised, and in the case of semi-conductor technology shall only be for public non-commercial use or to remedy a practice determined after judicial or administrative process to be anti-competitive;

(d) such use shall be non-exclusive;

(e) such use shall be non-assignable, except with that part of the enterprise or goodwill which enjoys such use;

(f) any such use shall be authorised predominantly for the supply of the domestic market of the Member authorising such use;

(g) authorisation for such use shall be liable, subject to adequate protection of the legitimate interests of the persons so authorised, to be terminated if and when the circumstances which led

---

[44] For a similar ruling see *US—Section 301* (the Panel relied on 'undertakingss' by the US Government as to the manner in which the US would interpret the measure at issue). By way of contrast see *India—Patents* (where the Appellate Body disregarded India's pledge; however, the Indian law contained a *mandatory* requirement that the Patent Office violate India's obligations under the TRIPS Agreement and the courts were bound to follow the law, not the pledge).

[45] The decision by the panel to apply Article 27.1 to the exceptions contained in Article 30 has been heavily criticised in the literature. See eg GB Dinwoodie and RC Dreyfuss, 'International Intellectual Property Law and the Public Domain of Science' (2004) 7 *Journal of International Economic Law* 431, 443; R Howse, 'The Canadian Generic Medicines Panel: A Dangerous Precedent in Dangerous Times' (2000) 3 *Journal of World Intellectual Property* 493, 505–06.

[46] These conditions should also be read together with the related provisions of Art 27.1, which require that patent rights be enjoyable without discrimination as to the field of technology or whether products are imported or produced locally.

to it cease to exist and are unlikely to recur. The competent authority shall have the authority to review, upon motivated request, the continued existence of these circumstances;

(h) the right holder shall be paid adequate remuneration in the circumstances of each case, taking into account the economic value of the authorisation;

(i) the legal validity of any decision relating to the authorisation of such use shall be subject to judicial review or other independent review by a distinct higher authority in that Member;

(j) any decision relating to the remuneration provided in respect of such use shall be subject to judicial review or other independent review by a distinct higher authority in that Member; [and]

(k) Members are not obliged to apply the conditions set forth in subparagraphs (b) and (f) where such use is permitted to remedy a practice determined after judicial or administrative process to be anti-competitive. The need to correct anti-competitive practices may be taken into account in determining the amount of remuneration in such cases. Competent authorities shall have the authority to refuse termination of authorisation if and when the conditions which led to such authorisation are likely to recur.

One of the most important of these conditions is subsection (b), which permits the granting of a compulsory licence only if 'the proposed user has made efforts to obtain authorisation from the right holder on reasonable commercial terms and conditions and that such efforts have not been successful within a reasonable period of time'. Importantly, 'this requirement may be waived in the case of national emergency or other circumstances of extreme urgency or in cases of public non-commercial use'. However, 'in situations of national emergency or other circumstances of extreme urgency, the right holder shall, nevertheless, be notified as soon as reasonably practicable'.

Subsection (f) has played an important role in the controversy surrounding patent protection and access to medicines in the developing world. The reason is that subsection (f) restricts the issue of a compulsory licence unless it is used 'predominantly for the supply of the domestic market of the Member authorizing such use', meaning that a Member must have the means to produce the product itself or, since the exception is limited to use 'predominantly for the supply of the domestic market', the Member cannot get the benefit of this provision (although, as explained below, recent amendments have changed this).

In addition, subsection (h) requires that the patent holder must receive 'adequate remuneration' based on the 'economic value of the authorisation', but the text does not provide any interpretive guidance for this phrase. Unsurprisingly, Members can agree on the meaning of neither 'adequate remuneration' nor the 'economic value of the authorisation'.

Therefore, while Article 31 grants Members the right to issue a compulsory licence, it severely limits the circumstances under which such a licence can be issued and requires that adequate remuneration be paid for the licence. While it is argued that such limitations and conditions ensure against abuse, the practical effect of the limitations and conditions was that countries with manufacturing capabilities could make only very limited use of the provision, and those countries with insufficient or no manufacturing capabilities could not make use of the provision.

The flexibilities of the TRIPS Agreement and rights of Members to take measures to protect public health were reaffirmed on 14 November 2001, when the WTO Ministerial Conference in Doha adopted a Ministerial Declaration on the TRIPS Agreement and Public Health which expressly stated that the TRIPS Agreement does not limit the grounds on which compulsory licences may be granted, and acknowledged the right of each Member to determine when a national emergency or circumstance of extreme urgency exists in its territory. In other words, Members have the right to protect public health and implement the Agreement in a manner appropriate to its legal system.

The following extract details the Doha Declaration on Public Health, its failure successfully to resolve the problems of subsection (f) and subsequent efforts to clarify and resolve the situation in the form of a 'temporary waiver'.

B Mercurio, 'Resolving the Public Health Crisis in the Developing World: Problems and Barriers of Access to Essential Medicines' (2007) 5 *Northwestern University Journal of International Human Rights* 1

At Doha, Members adopted a Declaration on TRIPS and Public Health (Doha Declaration or the Declaration) which restated and affirmed the right of Member States to take measures to protect public health, clarified certain textual ambiguities contained in TRIPS and attempted to provide assistance to developing countries and LDCs in resolving the public health crises that are devastating many parts of the developing world. The Declaration is significant for a number of reasons. First, it "represented the first time international health and development was discussed at every level of WTO governance." Second, it was "the first significant victory for developing countries in the short history of TRIPS." Finally, the Declaration recognized that public health issues can take precedence over the rights of private intellectual property holders. India called the Declaration "the most important single achievement of the Doha Round," while the Philippines hailed the Declaration as being "the crowning glory of the WTO's contribution to global welfare and humanitarian concerns, especially for those who were gravely afflicted by the scourge of epidemics and other public health problems."

Broadly speaking, the Declaration sought to "clarify" the TRIPS Agreement while giving emphasis to the "flexibilities" already written into the agreement, including the right of Members to invoke those provisions when needed. Paragraphs 1 through 5 contain the Declaration's most significant conclusions. Paragraphs 1 through 3 outline the concerns of both developing and developed countries by providing context for the issue of intellectual property protection for medicines while recognizing the need to balance private property and public welfare interests. More specifically, paragraph 1 "recognizes the gravity of the public health problems afflicting many developing and least-developed countries, especially those resulting from HIV/AIDS, tuberculosis, malaria and other epidemics," while paragraphs 2 and 3 express the need for TRIPS to be part of the wider national and international action to address the problems and recognize that the link between intellectual property protection for the creation of new medicines as well as the concerns about the effect of intellectual property rights (IPRs) on prices.

Paragraph 4 affirms the principle that protecting public health and promoting access to medicines is a valid basis for Members to enact exceptions to patent protection in their domestic legislation. Specifically, paragraph 4 states that TRIPS "does not and should not prevent Members from taking measures to protect public health" and "affirms that the Agreement can and should be interpreted and implemented in a manner supportive of WTO Members' right to protect public health and, in particular, to promote access to medicines for all." Thus, paragraph 4 reinforces the plain meaning of Article 8 of the TRIPS Agreement, which permits Members to "adopt measures necessary to protect public health . . ."

Paragraph 5 provides Members with flexibilities in implementing TRIPS and reaffirms the right of WTO Members to use the provisions in TRIPS for the purposes of Paragraph 4. The paragraph sets out the "provisions," which may be used for this purpose:

(a) In applying the customary rules of interpretation of public international law, each provision of the TRIPS Agreement shall be read in the light of the object and purpose of the Agreement as expressed, in particular, in its objectives and principles.

(b) Each member has the right to grant compulsory licenses and the freedom to determine the grounds upon which such licenses are granted.

(c) Each member has the right to determine what constitutes a national emergency or other circumstances of extreme urgency, it being understood that public health crises, including those relating to HIV/AIDS, tuberculosis, malaria and other epidemics, can represent a national emergency or other circumstances of extreme urgency.

(d) The effect of the provisions in the TRIPS Agreement that are relevant to the exhaustion of intellectual property rights is to leave each member free to establish its own regime for such exhaustion without challenge, subject to the MFN and national treatment provisions of Articles 3 and 4.

Paragraph 6 "recognizes that WTO Members with insufficient or no manufacturing capacities in the pharmaceutical sector could face difficulties in making effective use of compulsory licensing under the TRIPS Agreement," but the paragraph left the issue unresolved, instead instructing the Council for TRIPS to find an "expeditious solution" to the problem and to report to the General Council before the end of 2002.

The failure to resolve the availability of compulsory licensing exceptions to patent protection for countries suffering a public health crisis with insufficient or no manufacturing capabilities tempered the success of the Declaration. As TRIPS Article 31(f) conditions the issuance of compulsory licenses on being "predominantly for the supply of the domestic market of the Member authorizing such use," a Member State could only override valid patent laws so long as it obtained the generic drugs from domestic producers. Whether intentionally or accidentally, Article 31(f) prevents a country from benefiting from the compulsory licensing provision if it does not have sufficient manufacturing capabilities because, in practice, the provision limits the licensee's ability to export medicines to a country with public health needs, thereby preventing countries with insufficient or no manufacturing capabilities from taking advantage of the provision. Additionally, as most countries needing to make use of the patent exceptions are economically troubled nations with insufficient or no manufacturing capabilities, Article 31 of TRIPS failed in its purpose of assisting those nations it was designed to benefit.

After several delays and weeks of constant negotiation in the days leading to the Fifth Ministerial Conference (Cancun Ministerial), a resolution to the issue was finally reached on August 30, 2003. In fact, when endless debate over technical points looked as if it would hamper an agreement being formed, a group of African countries reminded Ministers that while potential solutions had been discussed in the interim years, the situation of medicinal access in poor countries had worsened. During this time, those countries continued to lose the battle against such public health epidemics as tuberculosis, malaria, and HIV/AIDS. In a joint statement, the group poignantly stated that "8,480 people had died unnecessarily in Africa from HIV/AIDS and other diseases since the talks stalled over an accompanying document to the Agreement only two days earlier [Aug. 28, 2003]." The statement had the desired effect: the Ministers put their differences aside and reached agreement on a "temporary waiver" in the form of The Implementation of Paragraph 6 of the Doha Declaration on TRIPS Agreement and Public Health ("Implementation Agreement") and accompanying Chairperson's Statement. At the time, Canadian Ambassador Sergio Marchi commented: "[The African countries] showed that the poorest among us do make a difference in this organization . . . They helped the WTO find its heart and soul."

The Implementation Agreement resolved the Article 31(f) situation by creating an exception to Article 31(f) of TRIPS that allows nations with insufficient or no manufacturing capabilities to override intellectual property protection and import generic copies of patented drugs to combat public health crises. However, in order to be TRIPS compliant, the importing Member must abide by several procedural steps, namely that the importing Member:

(1) must notify the TRIPS Council of the "names and expected quantities of the products needed";

(2) must confirm that it is either a LDC or "establish[] that it has insufficient or no manufacturing capacities in the pharmaceutical sector for the products in question"; and

(3) confirm that, if the "product is patented in its territory, [that] it has granted or intends to grant a compulsory licence in accordance with [TRIPS] Article 31."

The Implementation Agreement also outlines several procedural conditions an exporting Member must fulfill when issuing a compulsory license:

2. The obligations of an exporting Member under Article 31(f) of the TRIPS Agreement shall be waived with respect to the grant by it of a compulsory licence to the extent necessary for the purposes of production of a pharmaceutical product(s) and its export to an eligible importing Member(s) in accordance with the terms set out below in this paragraph:

(a) the eligible importing Member(s) has made a notification to the Council for TRIPS, that:

(i) specifies the names and expected quantities of the product(s) needed;

(ii) confirms that the eligible importing Member in question, other than a least developed country Member, has established that it has insufficient or no manufacturing capacities in the pharmaceutical sector for the product(s) in question in one of the ways set out in the Annex to this Decision; and

(iii) confirms that, where a pharmaceutical product is patented in its territory, it has granted or intends to grant a compulsory licence in accordance with Article 31 of the TRIPS Agreement and the provisions of this Decision;

(b) the compulsory licence issued by the exporting Member under this Decision shall contain the following conditions:

(i) only the amount necessary to meet the needs of the eligible importing Member(s) may be manufactured under the licence and the entirety of this production shall be exported to the Member(s) which has notified its needs to the Council for TRIPS;

(ii) products produced under the licence shall be clearly identified as being produced under the system set out in this Decision through specific labelling or marking. Suppliers should distinguish such products through special packaging and/or special colouring/ shaping of the products themselves, provided that such distinction is feasible and does not have a significant impact on price; and

(iii) before shipment begins, the licensee shall post on a website the following information:

– the quantities being supplied to each destination as referred to in indent (i) above; and
– the distinguishing features of the product(s) referred to in indent (ii) above;

(c) the exporting Member shall notify the Council for TRIPS of the grant of the licence, including the conditions attached to it. The information provided shall include the name and address of the licensee, the product(s) for which the licence has been granted, the quantity(ies) for which it has been granted, the country(ies) to which the product(s) is (are) to be supplied and the duration of the licence. The notification shall also indicate the address of the website referred to in subparagraph (b)(iii) above.

While the Implementation Agreement goes some way in addressing the legal hole that existed, it is not a miracle solution and to hold it out as such would be extremely misleading. To some, the Implementation Agreement fails to satisfactorily resolve several issues, including: (i) the scope of diseases and product coverage; (ii) countries that would be eligible to use the system; (iii) ensuring adequate remuneration; and (iv) safeguarding the system against diversion of drugs into other markets. Health and policy advocates, meanwhile, have also criticized the Implementation Agreement, in particular the prerequisite that a drug supplied under compulsory licence must normally be clearly identifiable as a generic version. These critics often argue that even though the requirement may be met through a variety of features—such as labelling, marking, special packaging, or by the specific colouring of shaping of the drug—ensuring that such distinguishing characteristics are present could raise procedural and administrative costs in the export of generic versions. This could possibly render the process less cost-effective and efficient than initially presumed and lengthen the time it takes to get the generic drugs to countries where they are needed. Furthermore, many in the international community believe that meeting other requirements of the Implementation Agreement will also make the waiver hard to exploit.

In addition, and importantly as will be discussed below, both developing and developed countries have been slow to secure the necessary domestic implementing legislation operationalizing the Implementation Agreement. For instance, countries that may wish to take advantage of the provision in the future—that is, those which could possibly have insufficient or no manufacturing capability to meet a public health need—have by and large not passed domestic legislation which would override patent laws and allow them to import necessary medicines under a compulsory licence. In addition, countries which have pharmaceutical manufacturing capabilities have been slow to pass legislation allowing their respective industry to supply nations attempting to make use of the provision with the requested drugs under compulsory licence. For some time, only Canada and Norway had passed the necessary implementing legislation. At the time of this writing, China, the European Communities, India, Korea, the Netherlands, and Switzerland have also enacted comprehensive legislation implementing the 30 August decision. Even more worrisome is the fact that some developed nations do not appear interested in promoting and passing such legislation.

To date, there have not been any notifications to the TRIPS Council regarding the issuance of a compulsory licence. This is not surprising, as prior to 2005, developing country members such as India and Brazil could produce and supply generic versions of patented drugs without the need for the issuance of a compulsory license. TRIPS, however, is playing an increasingly bigger role and becoming more important in the expansion of access to medicines and public health in the developing world following the expiration of certain transitory flexibilities and implementation periods in January 2005. TRIPS now has the potential to become a barrier to access to affordable new medicines and vaccines as the rules on compulsory licensing become operational for a number of developing country Members who are now subject to totality of the TRIPS Agreement. The practical result of this is that TRIPS now affects generic producers' ability to provide existing medicines for developing countries without sufficient manufacturing capabilities. Thus, developed nations passing the necessary legislation operationalizing the Implementation Agreement takes on even more importance.

… … …

As mentioned in Chapter 2, the waiver detailed above has now been converted into the first amendment to a WTO agreement.[47] The amendment will come into force following ratification from two-thirds of WTO Members.

---

[47] See WTO, 'Amendment of the TRIPS Agreement: Decision on 6 December 2005', WT/L/641 (8 December 2005).

(c) Enforcement and Remedies

Part III of the TRIPS Agreement sets out rules for the domestic 'enforcement' of IPRs. According to Article 41.1 of the TRIPS Agreement, Members must ensure that enforcement procedures 'are available under their law so as to permit effective action against any act of infringement of IPRs covered by this Agreement, including expeditious remedies to prevent infringements and remedies which constitute a deterrent to further infringements'. In this regard, the panel in *China—IPRs* found that, where a Member denies copyright protection under its law in a manner inconsistent with its obligations under the TRIPS Agreement, that Members' enforcement measures are likewise not available to the rights holder as required by Article 41.1.[48]

Article 41 goes on to provide further that the procedures concerning the enforcement of IPRs must be fair and equitable, not unnecessarily complicated or costly, or entail unreasonable time-limits or unwarranted delays. Moreover, the procedures must be applied in such a manner as to avoid the creation of barriers to legitimate trade and to provide for safeguards against their abuse. Decisions on the merits of a case shall preferably be in writing and reasoned. They shall be made available at least to the parties to the proceedings without undue delay.

The article further declares a preference for written decisions and provides that for an opportunity for the parties to be heard, judicial review. It also explicitly states that Members are not obligated to provide an opportunity for review of acquittals in criminal cases. Importantly, Article 41.5 creates two important principles in terms of Members' obligations:

> It is understood that this Part does not create any obligation to put in place a judicial system for the enforcement of intellectual property rights distinct from that for the enforcement of law in general, nor does it affect the capacity of Members to enforce their law in general. Nothing in this Part creates any obligation with respect to the distribution of resources as between enforcement of intellectual property rights and the enforcement of law in general.

The first part of the provision makes it clear that Members are under no obligation to establish separate judicial systems for the enforcement of IPRs, as distinct from that for the enforcement of law in general. Additionally, the second part of the provision explicitly states that the Agreement does not require Members to distribute resources as between enforcement of IPRs and the enforcement of law generally. This seemingly innocuous provision essentially provides that if a Member does not have sufficient resources or adequate capacity to administer its laws and legal system, the Agreement does not obligate Members to focus on the enforcement of the TRIPS Agreement. This provision has significant ramifications regarding the 'effective' application of the TRIPS Agreement in any dispute settlement proceedings.

Articles 42 to 49 set out basic principles for the conduct of civil and administrative proceedings for the enforcement of IPRs. For instance, Article 42 provides that Members make civil judicial procedures concerning the enforcement of any IPRs available to rights holders. The Article also grants the right of defendants to timely written notice which contains sufficient detail, including the basis of the claims. Moreover, Article 42 requires that Members allow parties to be represented by independent legal counsel, a right of

---

[48] Panel Report, *China—Measures Affecting the Protection and Enforcement of Intellectual Property Rights*, WT/DS362/R, 20 March 2009, paras 7.161–7.181.

appearance and opportunity to present evidence, a prohibition on 'overly burdensome' procedural requirements concerning mandatory personal appearances and a conditional right to protect confidential information. The Agreement also provides for and regulates, to varying degrees, evidentiary issues (Article 43), injunctions (Article 44), damages (Article 45), other remedies (Article 46), a judicial right of information (Article 47), the indemnification of the defendant (Article 48) and administrative procedures (Article 49).

Article 50 then provides for certain 'provisional measures', and Articles 51–60 detail the measures that Members and their customs authorities must take to prevent the release of infringing goods into circulation. Finally, Article 61 requires Members to provide criminal penalties for 'trademark counterfeiting and copyright piracy on a commercial scale'. Additionally, the provision states that possible remedies include imprisonment and/or monetary fines 'sufficient to provide a deterrent, consistently with the level of penalties applied for crimes of a corresponding gravity'.

In *China—IPRs*, the panel clarified several uncertain aspects of enforcement standards in the TRIPS Agreement, including the meaning of 'commercial scale' (Article 61) and procedures dealing with the release of goods counterfeit goods (Article 59). The following short extract introduces some of the facts, circumstances and panel decision in the case. The case was not appealed.

J Mendenhall, 'WTO Panel Report on Consistency of Chinese Intellectual Property Standards' (2009) 13(4) *ASIL Insight*

Criminal Thresholds

Under Chinese law, acts of counterfeiting and piracy are criminal only if the amount of infringing material exceeds certain quantity or value thresholds, *e.g.*, 500 copies of a DVD or approximately $7,000 worth of counterfeit goods. The United States alleged that the thresholds create a safe harbor for businesses engaged in commercial activities such as distribution of infringing products and are inconsistent with Article 61 of the TRIPS Agreement, which requires the criminalization of "wilful trademark counterfeiting or copyright piracy on a commercial scale." In support of this claim, the United States provided, along with the measures themselves, industry reports detailing the volume of infringing material seized during police raids (which in many cases fell below the thresholds) and other anecdotal data.

The critical issue with respect to this claim was the meaning of the phrase "commercial scale," a term never before interpreted by a WTO panel or the Appellate Body. The panel concluded that "commercial scale" activity means something different than "commercial" activity. Specifically, the term "commercial scale" implies a certain size threshold and not a qualitative assessment of the purpose of the activity. Furthermore, according to the panel, the threshold cannot be interpreted in the abstract but varies with respect to individual products and markets. According to the panel, "counterfeiting or piracy 'on a commercial scale' refers to counterfeiting or piracy carried on at the magnitude or extent of typical or usual commercial activity with respect to a given product in a given market." In any given case, commercial scale "may be large or small. The magnitude or extent of typical or usual commercial activity relates, in the longer term, to profitability."

Despite the panel's reference to profitability, there is no indication that the panel believed that profitability is the critical defining characteristic for "commercial scale" activity. In fact, the panel appeared to conclude that the profitability or purpose of an individual operation is irrelevant. Under the standard enunciated by the panel, the critical question is whether the infringing activity is equal to or larger than the usual size of a business operation with respect to a given product or market. While the panel recognized that the Chinese measures "exclude certain commercial activity from criminal procedures and penalties," it found that this was insufficient to prove that the measures are inconsistent with TRIPS.

The panel emphasized the importance of evidence to establish a claim that quantitative thresholds are inconsistent with Article 61. It found that "the United States did not provide data regarding products and markets or other factors that would demonstrate what constituted 'a commercial' scale in the specific situation in China's marketplace." According to the panel, the press articles that the United States provided were merely anecdotal, while the raid data did not provide enough context to assess how the seized quantities related to typical or usual commercial activity with respect to the market and product at issue.

While the panel report provides a roadmap for litigating future claims, it possibly fails to provide clear guidance for governments seeking to ensure that national laws comply with their TRIPS obligations, at least to the extent that they wish to use thresholds. (In fact, very few countries use thresholds as opposed to more qualitative standards). If "commercial scale" differs for each product and market, then lawmakers attempting to comply with TRIPS Article 61 will seemingly be required to define criminal counterfeiting and piracy by (1) devising separate thresholds for each product and market; (2) setting a uniform threshold at the lowest level of commercial scale activity for any product or market covered by the law; or (3) eliminating thresholds altogether in favor of a qualitative definition of commercial scale activity.

The first option appears untenable as a practical matter, and any such system would be complex and inconsistent. Two acts of piracy or counterfeiting could involve *different* products, but result in *identical* levels of infringement. Under the standard adopted by the panel, the TRIPS Agreement might require that one type of activity be criminalized and the other not, depending on whether the activity was larger or smaller than usual commercial activity with respect to the product or market in question.

The second option—a single, least-common-denominator threshold—is likely more workable in that it only requires one threshold. However, unless the government could conduct a comprehensive review of all relevant products and markets within its jurisdiction to identify the lowest permissible threshold, the default threshold would likely need to be very low (or zero) to ensure that all commercial scale activity is captured. Those who support strong IP protection may prefer this policy, though it is not clear that this was the result the panel intended.

The third option—a qualitative threshold—may be the best way forward, though "commercial scale" does not readily lend itself to a simple qualitative definition if, as the panel suggests, the term is wholly divorced from the question of whether the underlying activity serves a commercial purpose.

…

Release of Seized Counterfeit Goods into the Stream of Commerce

China's customs regulations give customs authorities the following options for disposing of IPR-infringing goods seized at the border: (i) Customs may hand the goods over to public welfare bodies for public welfare undertakings; (ii) if the holder of the intellectual property wishes to buy the goods, Customs may sell them; (iii) if the first two options are not possible, and if Customs can "eradicat[e] the infringing features," then the goods may be auctioned; or (iv) when eradication is impossible, Customs may destroy the goods.

The United States argued that the customs regulations are inconsistent with Article 59 of the TRIPS Agreement, which requires that competent authorities have the authority to order destruction or disposal of infringing goods. The United States asserted that the Chinese regulations created a "compulsory scheme" that precluded destruction or proper disposal of infringing goods if one of the first two options listed above were possible. The panel rejected China's claim that customs authorities were not authorized to destroy or properly dispose of infringing goods in large part based on China's clarification of the powers granted to its authority.

The panel accepted the U.S. claim that the third option in the Chinese regulations is inconsistent with TRIPS Article 46, (as referenced in TRIPS Article 59), stating that "the simple removal of the trademark unlawfully affixed shall not be sufficient, other than in exceptional circumstances, to permit release of the goods into the channels of commerce."

One point in the panel's reasoning is of particular interest. TRIPS Article 59 requires that competent authorities "shall have the authority to order the destruction or disposal of infringing goods in accordance with the principles set out in article 46." The panel report made it clear that "[t]he obligation is to 'have' authority not an obligation to 'exercise' authority." According to the panel, "the obligation that competent authorities 'shall have the authority' to make certain orders is not an obligation that competent authorities shall exercise that authority in a particular way, unless otherwise specified." The United States had not challenged the manner in which China applied its customs regulations, but only the regulations as such. Thus, this statement does not preclude a future WTO claim, based on appropriate factual evidence, that the authority granted to an enforcement authority is never used and is effectively a nullity. Such a claim might be based not only on Article 59 but also Article 41 of the TRIPS Agreement, which requires that enforcement procedures be "available . . . so as to permit effective action against any act of infringement. . . ." Assembling the necessary evidence could be challenging, however.

… … …

(d) Acquisition and Maintenance of Intellectual Property Rights and Related *Inter Partes* Procedures

Article 62 of the TRIPS Agreement provides that Members may require reasonable procedures and formalities in connection with the acquisition or maintenance of IPRs (Article 62.1), that the procedures for the granting or registration of IPRs are undertaken within a reasonable period of time so as to avoid unwarranted curtailment of the period of protection (Article 62.2), and that service mark registrations are subject to the same Paris Convention procedures as trade mark registrations (Article 62.3). The provision also provides that administrative and *inter partes* (inter-parties) proceedings relating to the acquisition, maintenance, opposition, revocation or cancellation of rights are governed by similar due process protections to those applicable to enforcement proceedings (Article 62.4). Such procedures are subject to review by a judicial or quasi-judicial review concerning acquisition and revocation proceedings, with the caveat that there is no obligation to provide an opportunity for a review exists in cases of unsuccessful opposition or administrative revocation.

(e) Dispute Prevention and Settlement

Article 63 requires Members to have a high level of transparency in their laws and regulations, inter-governmental agreements, final judicial decisions and administrative rulings of general application, pertaining to the availability, scope, acquisition, enforcement and prevention of the abuse of IPRs. This provision requires publication, in a national language, but such publication must be in such a manner as to enable governments and right holders to become acquainted with them. In addition, Members must notify the laws to the Council for TRIPS in order to assist that Council in its review of the operation of the Agreement and must supply, in response to a written request from another Member, information of the sort referred to above. Moreover, a Member may also make a written request to be given access to or be informed in sufficient detail of any specific judicial decisions or administrative rulings or bilateral agreements if they have reason to believe that a specific judicial decision or administrative ruling or bilateral agreement in the area of IPRs affects its rights under the TRIPS Agreement.[49]

The TRIPS Agreement is subject to the dispute settlement provisions in the GATT, as elaborated and applied by the Dispute Settlement Understanding. That said, Members agreed in Article 64.2 that subparagraphs 1(b) and 1(c) of Article XXIII of GATT 1994 pertaining to non-violation and situation complaints should not apply for the first five years of the WTO's existence (1995–9). The purpose of this moratorium was to give the Council for TRIPS the time and opportunity to examine the scope and modalities for non-violation complaints in the context of the TRIPS Agreement and make recommendations to the Ministerial Conference. While the majority of Members favour keeping the moratorium in place (Egypt, Venezuela and the African Group have been vocal in making their case, as have Canada and the EC), other Members (most notably the US and Switzerland) believe that non-violation complaints should be allowed 'in order to discourage members from engaging in "creative legislative activity" that would allow them to get around their TRIPS commitments'.[50] The Doha Ministerial Decision on Implementation and Related Concerns directed the TRIPS Council to continue work on a recommendation to be considered at the Fifth Ministerial Conference held in Cancun in September 2003, and agreed that a moratorium on non-violation and situation complaints would remain in place until at least that meeting. A recommendation has not yet been agreed, however, and the 'moratorium' on non-violation complaints has simply been extended at each ministerial conference, with the most recent extension being the 2011 Geneva Ministerial Conference.

To date, there have been nine panel reports dealing with the TRIPS Agreement covering eight unique issues. One interesting interpretive issue of note stemming from the *India—Patents (US)* case was the panel's ruling that the 'legitimate expectations' of WTO Members concerning the TRIPS Agreement must be taken into account when interpreting the TRIPS Agreement. The Appellate Body reversed the panel's ruling and, in doing so, continued its reluctance to expand the concept of 'legitimate expectations' beyond the traditional GATT context of Articles XXIII:1(b).[51] The Appellate Body elaborates on the reasons behind its decision in the following extract.

Appellate Body Report, *India—Patent Protection for Pharmaceutical and Agricultural Chemical Products*, Adopted 19 December 1997, WT/DS50/AB/R

33. As one of the fundamental issues in this appeal, India has questioned the Panel's enunciation and application of a general interpretative principle which, the Panel stated, "must be taken into account" in interpreting the provisions of the *TRIPS Agreement*. The Panel found that:

---

[49] Art 63.4, however, explicitly states that Members do not have to disclose confidential information which would impede law enforcement or otherwise be contrary to the public interest or would prejudice the legitimate commercial interests of particular enterprises, public or private.

[50] Available at www.wto.org/English/tratop_e/trips_e/nonviolation_background_e.htm.

[51] See also, the Appellate Body's rejection of expanding the concept to Article II in *EC—LAN*.

... when interpreting the text of the TRIPS Agreement, the legitimate expectations of WTO Members concerning the TRIPS Agreement must be taken into account, as well as standards of interpretation developed in past panel reports in the GATT framework, in particular those laying down the principle of the protection of conditions of competition flowing from multilateral trade agreements.

India argues that the Panel's invocation of this principle caused the Panel to misinterpret both Article 70.8 and Article 70.9 and led the Panel to err in determining whether India had complied with those obligations.

34. The Panel stated that:

The protection of legitimate expectations of Members regarding the conditions of competition is a well-established GATT principle, which derives in part from Article XXIII, the basic dispute settlement provisions of GATT (and the WTO).

The Panel also referred to certain GATT 1947 panel reports as authority for this principle. The Panel noted that whereas the "disciplines formed under GATT 1947 (so-called GATT *acquis*) were primarily directed at the treatment of the goods of other countries", "the concept of the protection of legitimate expectations" in relation to the *TRIPS Agreement* applies to "the competitive relationship between a Member's own nationals and those of other Members (rather than between domestically produced goods and the goods of other Members, as in the goods area)".

35. In *Japan—Taxes on Alcoholic Beverages*, on the status of adopted panel reports, we acknowledged:

Article XVI:1 of the *WTO Agreement* and paragraph 1(b)(iv) of the language of Annex 1A incorporating the GATT 1994 into the *WTO Agreement* bring the legal history and experience under the GATT 1947 into the new realm of the WTO in a way that ensures continuity and consistency in a smooth transition from the GATT 1947 system. This affirms the importance to the Members of the WTO of the experience acquired by the CONTRACTING PARTIES to the GATT 1947 -- and acknowledges the continuing relevance of that experience to the new trading system served by the WTO. Adopted panel reports are an important part of the GATT *acquis*.

36. Although the Panel states that it is merely applying a "well-established GATT principle", the Panel's reasoning does not accurately reflect GATT/WTO practice. In developing its interpretative principle, the Panel merges, and thereby confuses, two different concepts from previous GATT practice. One is the concept of protecting the expectations of contracting parties as to the competitive relationship between their products and the products of other contracting parties. This is a concept that was developed in the context of *violation* complaints involving Articles III and XI, brought under Article XXIII:1(a), of the GATT 1947. The other is the concept of the protection of the reasonable expectations of contracting parties relating to market access concessions. This is a concept that was developed in the context of *non-violation* complaints brought under Article XXIII:1(b) of the GATT.

37. Article 64.1 of the *TRIPS Agreement* incorporates by reference Article XXIII of the GATT 1994 as the general dispute settlement provision governing the *TRIPS Agreement*. Thus, we have no quarrel in principle with the notion that past GATT practice with respect to Article XXIII is pertinent to interpretation of the *TRIPS Agreement*. However, such interpretation must show proper appreciation of the different bases for action under Article XXIII.

38. Article XXIII:1 of the GATT 1994 sets out the various causes of action on which a Member may base a complaint. A Member may have recourse to dispute settlement under Article XXIII when it considers that:

. . . any benefit accruing to it directly or indirectly under this Agreement is being nullified or impaired or that the attainment of any objective of the Agreement is being impeded as the result of

(*a*) the failure of another contracting party to carry out its obligations under this Agreement, or

(*b*) the application by another contracting party of any measure, whether or not it conflicts with the provisions of this Agreement, or

(*c*) the existence of any other situation.

39. Article XXIII:1(a) involves so-called "violation" complaints. These are disputes that arise from an alleged failure by a Member to carry out its obligations. During nearly fifty years of experience, Article XXIII:1(a) has formed the basis of almost all disputes under the GATT 1947 and the *WTO Agreement*. In contrast, Article XXIII:1(b) involves so-called "non-violation" complaints. These are disputes that do not require an allegation of a violation of an obligation. The basis of a cause of action under Article XXIII:1(b) is not necessarily a violation of the rules, but rather the nullification or impairment of a benefit accruing to a Member under a covered agreement. In the history of the GATT/WTO, there have been only a handful of "non-violation" cases arising under Article XXIII:1(b).25 Article XXIII:1(c), covering what are commonly called "situation" complaints, has never been the foundation for a recommendation or ruling of the GATT CONTRACTING PARTIES or the Dispute Settlement Body, although it has formed the basis for parties' arguments before panels in a small number of cases.

40. In the context of violation complaints made under Article XXIII:1(a), it is true that panels examining claims under Articles III and XI of the GATT have frequently stated that the purpose of these articles is to protect the expectations of Members concerning the competitive relationship between imported and domestic products, as opposed to expectations concerning trade volumes. However, this statement is often made *after* a panel has found a violation of, for example, Article III or Article XI that establishes a *prima facie* case of nullification or impairment. At that point in its reasoning, the panel is examining whether the defending party has been able to rebut the charge of nullification or impairment. It is in this context that panels have referred to the expectations of Members concerning the conditions of competition.

41. The doctrine of protecting the "reasonable expectations" of contracting parties developed in the context of "non-violation" complaints brought under Article XXIII:1(b) of the GATT 1947. Some of the rules and procedures concerning "non-violation" cases have been codified in Article 26.1 of the DSU. "Non-violation" complaints are rooted in the GATT's origins as an agreement intended to protect the reciprocal tariff concessions negotiated among the contracting parties under Article II. In the absence of substantive legal rules in many areas relating to international trade, the "non-violation" provision of Article XXIII:1(b) was aimed at preventing contracting parties from using non-tariff barriers or other policy measures to negate the benefits of negotiated tariff concessions. Under Article XXIII:1(b) of the GATT 1994, a Member can bring a "non-violation" complaint when the negotiated balance of concessions between Members is upset by the application of a measure, whether or not this measure is inconsistent with the provisions of the covered agreement. The ultimate goal is not the withdrawal of the measure concerned, but rather achieving a mutually satisfactory adjustment, usually by means of compensation.

42. Article 64.2 of the *TRIPS Agreement* states:

Subparagraphs 1(b) and 1(c) of Article XXIII of GATT 1994 shall not apply to the settlement of disputes under this Agreement for a period of five years from the date of entry into force of the WTO Agreement.

The meaning of this provision is clear: the *only* cause of action permitted under the *TRIPS Agreement* during the first five years after the entry into force of the *WTO Agreement* is a "violation" complaint under Article XXIII:1(a) of the GATT 1994. This case involves allegations of violation of obligations under the *TRIPS Agreement*. However, the Panel's invocation of the "legitimate expectations" of Members relating to conditions of competition melds the legally-distinct bases for "violation" and "nonviolation" complaints under Article XXIII of the GATT 1994 into one uniform cause of action. This is not consistent with either Article XXIII of the GATT 1994 or Article 64 of the *TRIPS Agreement*. Whether or not "non-violation" complaints should be available for disputes under the *TRIPS Agreement* is a matter that remains to be determined by the Council for Trade-Related Aspects of Intellectual Property (the "Council for TRIPS") pursuant to Article 64.3 of the *TRIPS Agreement*. It is *not* a matter to be resolved through interpretation by panels or by the Appellate Body.

43. In addition to relying on the GATT *acquis*, the Panel relies also on the customary rules of interpretation of public international law as a basis for the interpretative principle it offers for the *TRIPS Agreement*. Specifically, the Panel relies on Article 31 of the *Vienna Convention*, which provides in part:

1. A treaty shall be interpreted in good faith in accordance with the ordinary meaning to be given to the terms of the treaty in their context and in the light of its object and purpose.

44. With this customary rule of interpretation in mind, the Panel stated that:

In our view, good faith interpretation requires the protection of legitimate expectations derived from the protection of intellectual property rights provided for in the Agreement.30

45. The Panel misapplies Article 31 of the *Vienna Convention*. The Panel misunderstands the concept of legitimate expectations in the context of the customary rules of interpretation of public international law. The legitimate expectations of the parties to a treaty are reflected in the language of the treaty itself. The duty of a treaty interpreter is to examine the words of the treaty to determine the intentions of the parties. This should be done in accordance with the principles of treaty interpretation set out in Article 31 of the *Vienna Convention*. But these principles of interpretation neither require nor condone the imputation into a treaty of words that are not there or the importation into a treaty of concepts that were not intended.

46. In *United States—Standards for Reformulated and Conventional Gasoline*, we set out the proper approach to be applied in interpreting the *WTO Agreement* in accordance with the rules in Article 31 of the *Vienna Convention*. These rules must be respected and applied in interpreting the *TRIPS Agreement* or any other covered agreement. The Panel in this case has created its own interpretative principle, which is consistent with neither the customary rules of interpretation of public international law nor established GATT/WTO practice. Both panels and the Appellate Body must be guided by the rules of treaty interpretation set out in the *Vienna Convention*, and must not add to or diminish rights and obligations provided in the *WTO Agreement*.

47. This conclusion is dictated by two separate and very specific provisions of the DSU. Article 3.2 of the DSU provides that the dispute settlement system of the WTO:

. . . serves to preserve the rights and obligations of the Members under the covered agreements, and to clarify the existing provisions of those agreements in accordance with customary rules of interpretation of public international law. Recommendations and rulings of the DSB cannot add to or diminish the rights and obligations provided in the covered agreements.

Furthermore, Article 19.2 of the DSU provides:

In accordance with paragraph 2 of Article 3, in their findings and recommendations, the panel and Appellate Body cannot add to or diminish the rights and obligations provided in the covered agreements.

These provisions speak for themselves. Unquestionably, both panels and the Appellate Body are bound by them.

48. For these reasons, we do not agree with the Panel that the legitimate expectations of Members *and* private rights holders concerning conditions of competition must always be taken into account in interpreting the *TRIPS Agreement*.

… … …

(f) Transitional Arrangements

Article 65 of the TRIPS Agreement allowed for a one-year transition period for developed countries to bring their legislation and practices into conformity with the provisions of the Agreement. Therefore, developed countries had until 1 January 1996 to comply with the Agreement. Article 65 also granted developing countries and countries in transition from centrally planned economies (ie Eastern European countries) a five-year transition period (ending on 1 January 2000). In addition, developing countries which did not provide product patent protection in a specific area of technology (ie process patents) were given up to 1 January 2005 to introduce such protection. However, in the case of pharmaceutical and agricultural chemical products, certain conditions attach. For instance, those countries granted the additional transitional period must have maintained procedures to accept the filing of patent applications from the beginning of the transitional period. Thus, even though the patent need not have been granted until the end of the transitional period, the date of filing serves to preserve the novelty of the invention. Finally, if authorisation for the marketing of the relevant pharmaceutical or agricultural chemical was obtained during the transitional period, the developing country concerned must have offered an exclusive marketing right for the product for five years, or until a product patent is granted, whichever is shorter.[52]

Article 66 granted least-developed Members a transitional period of 10 years from the date of application of the TRIPS Agreement (until 1 January 2006). In addition, and in accordance with Article 66.1, the Council for TRIPS has extended this period until 1 July 2013 for trademarks, copyright, patents and other intellectual property,[53] and to 2016 for pharmaceutical products.[54] Therefore, least developing Members are at present under no obligation to comply with the provisions or obligations of the TRIPS Agreement (other than Articles 3, 4 and 5). Article 66.2 also directs developed country Members to provide incentives to their enterprises and institutions for the purpose of promoting and encouraging technology transfer to least-developed Members 'in order to enable them to create a sound and viable technological base'. Moreover, Article 67 seeks to facilitate the implementation of the Agreement by directing developed country Members to provide, on

[52] See Appellate Body Report, *India–Patents (US)*; *India–Patents (EC)*.

[53] See TRIPS Council, Extension of the Transition Period under Article 66.1 for Least-Developed Country Members, Decision of the Council for TRIPS of 29 November 2005.

[54] The Council for TRIPS adopted this decision pursuant to the instruction of the Ministerial Conference in the Declaration on the TRIPS Agreement and Public Health (WT/MIN(01)/DEC/2). See the minutes of the Council for TRIPS' meeting in IP/C/M/36. The text of the adopted decision can be found in IP/C/25. At the same meeting, the Council for TRIPS approved a draft waiver for least-developed country Members of obligations under Art 70.9 with respect to pharmaceutical products.

request and on mutually agreed terms and conditions, technical and financial cooperation in favour of developing and least-developed country Members. The Article also states that such cooperation 'shall include assistance in the preparation of laws and regulations on the protection and enforcement of IPRs as well as on the prevention of their abuse, and . . . support regarding the establishment or reinforcement of domestic offices and agencies relevant to these matters, including the training of personnel'.

(g) Criticisms of the Agreement

As IPRs had not been part of the international trading system prior to the negotiation and implementation of the TRIPS Agreement, considerable debate has taken place over their inclusion in the WTO Agreement. Such debate has focussed on such issues as the place of IPRs in the international trading system as well as the merits of specific provisions of the Agreement. Much of the debate has centred on the (perceived) effect of the Agreement on the developing world. The following extract is a useful illustration of some of the criticism levelled at the Agreement.

> **Asia Pacific Research Network,** *Re-thinking TRIPS in the WTO: NGOs Demand Review and Reform of TRIPS at Doha Ministerial Conference,* **27 May 2003**[55]
>
> The TRIPS Agreement (TRIPS) is facing a crisis of legitimacy. In the six years since it came into force, there has been ever-increasing evidence of social, environmental and economic problems caused by the implementation of TRIPS. Yet, little, if any, of TRIPS' promised benefits of technology transfer, innovation and increased foreign direct investment has materialised. Already there is worldwide public opposition to TRIPS for its role in patenting of life and in reducing access to medicines.
>
> For many hundreds of civil society groups and NGOs around the world, TRIPS represents one of the most damaging aspects of the WTO. The legitimacy of the WTO is closely linked to that of TRIPS. TRIPS has, in fact, given the multilateral trade system a bad name. Contrary to the so-called free trade and trade liberalisation principles of the WTO, TRIPS is being used as a protectionist instrument to promote corporate monopolies over technologies, seeds, genes and medicines. Through TRIPS, large corporations use intellectual property rights to protect their markets, and to prevent competition. Excessively high levels of intellectual property protection required by TRIPS have shifted the balance away from the public interest, towards the monopolistic privileges of IPR holders. This undermines sustainable development objectives, including eradicating poverty, meeting public health needs, conserving biodiversity, protecting the environment and the realisation of economic, social and cultural rights.
>
> We, the undersigned, call on WTO members to take action before more damage is done by TRIPS. We believe that a fundamental re-thinking of TRIPS in the WTO is required. We, therefore, urge WTO members to initiate a process of reviewing and reforming TRIPS at the Doha Ministerial Conference. For us, a major indicator of the success or failure of the Doha Ministerial Conference is whether WTO members take serious steps to reform TRIPS.

PATENTS ON LIFE, FOOD SECURITY AND BIOPIRACY

At the heart of debates surrounding the patenting of life and its adverse effects on food security, farmers' livelihoods, local communities' rights, sustainable resource use and access to genetic

---

[55] Available at www.aprnet.org/index.php?a=show&t=issues&i=21.

resources is the requirement of patent protection for life forms and natural processes in Article 27.3(b) of TRIPS.

Patents on seeds and genetic resources for food and agriculture threaten sustainable farming practices, farmers' livelihoods and food security. Farmers using patented seeds are deprived of their right to use, save, plant and sell their seeds. Article 27.3(b) also requires protection of plant varieties but gives WTO members the choice between patent protection, a sui generis system or a combination of both, for doing so. However, the option to protect plant varieties under a sui generis system is being reduced to compliance with the UPOV Convention, through pressure on developing countries from industrialised countries, the global seed and biotechnology industry, UPOV itself and the WTO Secretariat. Increasing consolidation of multinational corporations in the seed, agro-chemical and food processing industries has further concentrated the control over seeds, seed choices and ultimately, food security into the hands of a few corporations, and out of the hands of the farming communities. The patent system is also facilitating the theft of biological resources and traditional knowledge. The imposition of patent rights over biological resources and traditional knowledge unfairly deprive communities of their rights over, and access to, the same resources they have nurtured and conserved over generations. This contradicts the key principles and provisions of the Convention on Biological Diversity (CBD). The race to patent genes, cells, DNA sequences and other naturally occurring life forms has blurred the crucial distinction between discoveries and basic scientific information, which should be freely exchanged, and truly invented products or processes meriting patent protection.

Developing countries' attempt to undertake a substantive review of Article 27.3(b) is at a stalemate. The review process has opened up to issues of substance but the developed countries are not taking seriously developing country proposals for revision. The Africa Group, in particular, has voiced clear opposition to the patenting of life. The Group had called for a decision at the Seattle Ministerial Conference in 1999 to clarify that "plants and animals as well as micro-organisms and all other living organisms and their parts cannot be patented, and that natural processes that produce plants, animals and other living organisms should also not be patentable".

The Africa Group proposal has gained broad support from other developing countries in the WTO, as well as civil society groups and NGOs around the world. There is an urgent need to commence a serious, substantive review of Article 27.3(b).

NGO PROPOSALS FOR REVIEW OF ARTICLE 27.3(b)

We, therefore, call on the Doha Ministerial Conference to:

- agree to the immediate undertaking of the mandated and substantive review of Article 27.3(b). The review must be conducted on its own terms, outside of the review of Article 71.1 of TRIPS or the wider WTO negotiations, and should:
  - act on the Africa Group proposal to clarify that plants, animals, micro-organisms and all other living organisms and their parts cannot be patented, and that natural processes that produce plants, animals and other living organisms should also not be patentable;
  - respect the right of developing countries to determine the need for appropriate sui generis laws that effectively protect community and farmers' rights, and promote agricultural diversity and sustainability;
  - in line with the clarification that living organisms and their parts are not patentable, further ensure that the provisions of Article 27.3(b) of TRIPS are consistent with the CBD provisions on national sovereignty, prior-informed consent and benefit sharing, with regards to access to genetic resources and traditional knowledge; and
- take account of, and support the current negotiations in FAO's International Undertaking

on Plant Genetic Resources for Food and Agriculture to restrict or ban intellectual property rights on plant Genetic resources for food and agriculture within the multilateral system, in the interests of long-term food security and to prevent bio-piracy. In the interim, WTO members should:

– extend, with immediate effect, the implementation deadline for Article 27.3(b) for at least five years after the completion of the substantive review of Article 27.3(b);
– undertake not to apply bilateral pressure on developing countries to adopt the UPOV Convention as the sui generis model or other TRIPS-plus measures; and
– grant the CBD Secretariat observer status in the TRIPS Council.

TRIPS AND PUBLIC HEALTH

Strict patent regimes required by TRIPS allow pharmaceutical corporations to set prices of patented medicines at high, often exorbitant levels. Under TRIPS, the 20-year minimum patent protection period for products and processes confers exclusive monopoly for the manufacture, distribution and sale of medicines. The monopolies granted by TRIPS allow pharmaceutical giants to suppress competition from alternative, low-cost producers and to charge prices far above what is reasonable.

Appropriate national legislation, providing for compulsory licensing and parallel imports, is needed to ensure that chemical intermediates, raw materials and finished pharmaceutical products are available at competitive prices in the world market. Measures—such as compulsory licensing, parallel imports and other exceptions to patent rights—are allowed under TRIPS. Despite this, and the clear need for developing countries to exercise their rights for compulsory licensing and parallel imports to enable access to affordable medicines, bilateral pressures and bullying tactics have been used to prevent developing countries from implementing TRIPS provisions on compulsory licensing or parallel imports. Such bullying is outrageous and unacceptable.

WTO members are currently engaged in a series of Special Discussions on TRIPS and Public Health. Initiated by the Africa Group, the process is aimed at clarifying the role of intellectual property rights and their impact on public health and access to medicines. Developing countries, signalling their intent to ensure a tangible outcome to the process, have proposed that the Doha Ministerial Conference takes steps to endorse a clear and unambiguous affirmation that "the TRIPS Agreement does not in any way undermine the legitimate right of WTO Members to formulate their own public health policies and implement them by adopting measures to protect public health".

The overwhelming majority of developing countries in the WTO support this proposal. To give practical effect to the affirmation, the developing countries have further called for the Doha Ministerial Declaration to endorse the following elements; including the use of Articles 7 and 8 in the interpretation of all provisions in the TRIPS Agreement; the right of countries to determine the grounds on which compulsory licenses may be issued; recognition of compulsory licenses issued to a foreign manufacturer; the right to parallel importation; a moratorium on all dispute actions aimed at preventing or limiting access to medicines, or protection of public health; and the extension of transition periods for developing and least developed countries.

NGO PROPOSALS FOR TRIPS AND PUBLIC HEALTH

We fully support the developing countries' proposal that the Doha Ministerial Conference affirm the primacy of public health over TRIPS.

We call on all WTO members not to stand in the way of such an affirmation being made in Doha. We further call upon the WTO members to:

- strengthen the existing public-health safeguards within TRIPS to ensure that governments have the unambiguous right to override patents in the interests of public health.
- adopt a pro-public health interpretation of TRIPS through the flexible use of existing safeguards and exceptions. These include upholding the right of countries to grant compulsory licences for local manufacturing, import and export, and their right to implement parallel importation measures;
- remove the burdensome conditions that governments have to fulfil in the issuing of compulsory licences, so that licences can be granted on a 'fast track' basis for public-health purposes;
- extend the implementation deadlines within TRIPS for developing countries in relation to patent protection (both product and process) for medicines;
- agree not to exert bilateral or regional pressure on developing countries which take measures to exercise their rights under TRIPS to protect public health and promote access to medicines, nor to pressure them to implement necessarily strict and potentially harmful intellectual property protection standards or 'TRIPS-plus' measures;
- observe, with immediate effect, a moratorium on dispute settlement action against developing countries, which hinders their ability to promote access to medicines and protect public health including the use of compulsory licence and parallel importation measures);
- allow developing countries the options of restricting the scope and length of patent protection, including an outright exemption of medicines from patenting on humanitarian or public-health grounds, in order to meet the objectives of saving lives, countering and controlling epidemics, and ensuring that poor people obtain access to essential medicines for the treatment of poverty-related diseases.

DOHA: TIME FOR A FUNDAMENTAL RE-THINKING OF TRIPS

We believe that the protection of intellectual property rights is not an end in itself. The objectives of technological innovation and the transfer of technology (Article 7 of TRIPS) should place intellectual property rights protection in the context of the public interest of social and economic welfare. Furthermore, TRIPS also acknowledges the right of WTO members to adopt measures for protecting overarching public policy objectives, such as public health and nutrition, and socio-economic and technological development, and to prevent abuse of intellectual property rights, and anti-competitive practices (Article 8). Yet, these fundamental objectives and principles have been blatantly ignored by certain developed countries in their interpretation and implementation of TRIPS. Attempts by these developed countries to force developing countries to adopt such flawed interpretations will only perpetuate the crisis of legitimacy that TRIPS is already facing.

As can be seen above, civil society groups and NGOs have made specific demands relating to the issues of patenting of life and access to medicines. However, we note that common themes exist in the different campaigns relating to patenting of life, bio piracy and food security, and public health and access to affordable medicines. We all share the common view that TRIPS represents a significant shift in the balance in intellectual property rights protection that is too heavily in favour of private right holders and against the public interest.

NGO DEMANDS FOR THE REVIEW AND REFORM OF TRIPS

We, the undersigned organisations, call on the Doha Ministerial Conference to:

UNDERTAKE A FUNDAMENTAL REVIEW AND REFORM OF TRIPS

- Undertake a review of TRIPS under Article 71.1 to take into account new developments that may warrant modification or amendment of TRIPS. Such a review should include a critical impact assessment of TRIPS on food security, public health and nutrition, the environment, and its implications for social and economic development, with a view to revising TRIPS. An Article 71.1 review is mandated within TRIPS, and should therefore, be undertaken on its own merits so as not to be subsumed and traded-off as part of the wider WTO negotiations.

• As part of the review, clarify that all provisions of the TRIPS agreement must be interpreted in the context, and against the background, of Articles7 and 8 of the TRIPS Agreement. WTO members should put into operation the objectives and principles enshrined in Articles 7 & 8 of the TRIPS Agreement to ensure the primacy of public interests over the security of private intellectual property rights. Developing countries must be given maximum flexibility implementing TRIPS. They should not be restricted in their ability to adopt options or measures for implementing TRIPS that enable them to appropriately balance the overarching public policy objectives against private interests. Developing countries should also be given flexibility to reduce the scope and length of intellectual property right protection, including the right to exempt (or have a longer transition period for) certain products and sectors, on the grounds of public welfare and the need to meet development objectives.

END BILATERAL PRESSURES AND BULLYING TACTICS

• Affirm a commitment not to apply bilateral pressures or tactics on developing countries to give up the use of options available to them under TRIPS. Similarly, pressures should not be put on developing countries, either through bilateral means or regional arrangements or in the WTO accession process, to force them into implementing 'TRIPS-plus' measures or standards higher than those in TRIPS.

EXTEND IMPLEMENTATION DEADLINES FOR DEVELOPING COUNTRIES

• Extend the implementation deadlines within TRIPS for developing countries until after a proper and satisfactory review of TRIPS is carried out and appropriate changes are made.

MORATORIUM ON DISPUTE SETTLEMENT ACTION

• Agree to observe, with immediate effect, a moratorium on dispute settlement action, until there is a satisfactory resolution of the review. Many developing countries are facing difficulties in implementing TRIPS at the national level but the transition period for the implementation of Article 27.3(b) expired on 1 January 2000. This means that the majority of the developing countries are now legally obliged to implement the TRIPS Agreement within their national laws, or face the imminent threat of being taken to the dispute settlement body of the WTO.

REVIEW OF TRIPS' PLACE IN WTO

• Consider the rationale and desirability of TRIPS' location in the WTO.TRIPS is protectionist, promotes monopolistic practices and profits, and almost exclusively benefits developed countries. As part of the fundamental review and rethinking of TRIPS, WTO members should question TRIPS' place in a trade organisation that supposedly champions competition and consider the removal of TRIPS from the WTO.

... ...

V. INTELLECTUAL PROPERTY AND PREFERENTIAL TRADE AGREEMENTS

As foreshadowed in the above extract, the inclusion and regulation of IPRs in bilateral and regional free trade agreements is the latest in the contentious history linking IP and international trade.

The extension and increased protection of IPRs in PTAs (so called 'TRIPS-Plus' provisions) are now a common feature of PTAs, and certainly always now feature in PTAs negotiated by developed countries. While it is not feasible to detail or even list all of the TRIPS-Plus provisions in this forum, it is important to note that these types of provisions are being negotiated in every IP sector. For instance, both EC and US PTAs agreements commonly lengthen the period of copyright provided in Article 12 from 50 years to 70 years following the death of the author; EC agreements extend protection for GIs; and US agreements commonly link the granting of pharmaceutical regulatory approval to the status of a patent (thereby prohibiting the drug regulatory agency from approving the safety and efficacy of a generic manufacturers drug while a patent is still in force).

The following extract shows how and why this trend towards increasing IP protection through preferential trade agreements has been led by developed nations, most notably the US, and has the ability to shift dramatically the level and protection of IPRs globally. The extract also illustrates one example of a TRIPS-Plus provision regularly included in recent US PTAs.

B Mercurio, 'TRIPS-Plus Provisions in FTAs: Recent Trends' in L Bartels and F Ortino (eds), *Regional Trade Agreements and the WTO Legal System* **(Oxford University Press, Oxford, 2006) 215–37**

While the criticisms of TRIPS from a development perspective are well known, developed countries also failed to achieve all their goals in the Uruguay Round and, perhaps due to constant lobbying of IP holders, increasingly argue the multilateral standards are insufficient to protect their interests. Thus, as noted above, the US and other developed nations sought to negotiate higher levels of WTO IP protection in the late-1990s. Developing countries organised to resist these efforts, which not only led to the collapse of the Seattle Ministerial, but later the confirmation of the flexibilities built into TRIPS via the Doha Declaration on TRIPS and Public Health and a prolonged Doha Round (including the failure of the Cancun Ministerial in 2003). As a result of the strong and unwavering resistance, the US has again shifted its negotiating focus and sought to use bilateralism/regionalism to increase IPRs by requiring FTA partners to implement TRIPS-Plus provisions in the following form:

(a) inclusion of new areas of IPRs; or

(b) implementation of more extensive levels or standards of IP protection than is required by TRIPS; or

(c) elimination of an option or flexibility available under TRIPS.

On the one hand, the strategy of consolidating gains and then almost immediately moving to another forum to seek additional gains does make sense from a nationalistic policy perspective for a number of reasons. First, multilateral gains are always, to some extent, small and resemble the least common denominator that can be achieved when a large number of varied opinions and interests attempt to achieve consensus. This is especially the case at the WTO, where every Member, no matter the size or economic clout, essentially can use the consensus decision-making process to veto the entire process. In such a situation, the interests of a nation or lobbyist (such as the pharmaceutical industry) will never fully be placated through multilateralism. Thus, when the US is unable to gain concessions through multilateral negotiations due to, among other reasons, consensus-decision making, it simply shifts the parameters and sidesteps multilateral impediments (and the 'won't do' countries) through bilateral/regional agreements with those 'can do' countries willing to make concessions in order to secure a potentially lucrative agreement with, to many, the most important market in the world.

In addition, and intertwined to the above, is the fact that multilateral agreements also contain special and differential treatment and other opt-out clauses, resulting not only in unfulfilled negotiating goals but also scope for bilateral movement. As a result, Members find it advantageous to shift the forum. As one commentator stated of recent bilateralism:

From the United States' standpoint, the switch to bilateralism has at least two benefits. By changing the forum and reducing the number of negotiating parties, the United States can provide side payments that it would not be able to offer in a multilateral forum, given the diversity of interests the United States has vis-à-vis the contracting states. By switching to bilateralism, the United States can also prevent less developed countries from reopening the TRIPS negotiations with a better bargaining position.

Quite obviously, the TRIPS-Plus provisions and resulting standards are designed to best protect US domestic interests. While some commentators may disagree with this approach, it is in fact no different to any negotiation: the US is putting forth its position and the negotiation partner can choose to accept the demand, conditionally accept it in exchange for a US concession or outright reject the demand. It is also clear that the TRIPS-Plus provisions appearing in US FTAs (or, in other words 'internationalising') are identical to aspects of its domestic law. This is not hidden, and in fact can be seen in the US law providing the President with the power to conclude trade agreements ('Trade Promotion Authority' or so called 'fast track'), which states the promotion of an IP regime that 'reflect(s) a standard of protection similar to that found in United States law' is a US negotiating objective. This negotiating strategy can be seen in the similarities between recent US FTAs (such as, for instance, the US-Singapore and US-Australia FTAs).

The negotiation of similar, or in fact identical, standards is again not unexpected. As with any other system of standards, it is always more manageable if more than one country operates a similar system. In addition to administrative reasons for negotiating identical standards, developed countries are also meeting their own economic needs and persuading others to fit in with their cultural and philosophical traditions. In this regard, countries agreeing to such heightened standards must fully recognise they not only are agreeing to amend their IP laws, in most cases without full discussion and input of the IP community and, perhaps more importantly, any economic analysis as to the overall costs of the changes, but that they may be agreeing to standards that are far removed from their own the economic and social needs.

On the other hand, and unlike in the 1960s and 1970s when increased standards (such as investment and IP protection) were cast in terms of assisting development (ie encouraging investment), the current bilateralism unashamedly seeks to fragment developing country coalitions while at the same time taking advantage of unequal bargaining power in bilateral negotiations. It is apparent that such a strategy encompasses 'dividing' developing country coalitions and negotiating with those nations willing to compromise. It must be noted, however, that many developing countries do not hesitate to trade off IPRs in exchange for market access. In the vast majority of cases, such a trade off is not included nefariously by the larger trading nation but instead a conscious choice of the developing nation. This is why, despite protests from mainly Western NGOs purporting to represent the interests of the developing world, developing countries continue to negotiate FTAs. The reason for this is that bilateral agreements offer developing countries real gains instead of the mainly pyrrhic or symbolic victories of multilateralism (where the resulting gains may not flow to every country and must be divided among all competitors). It must be also noted that the practice of negotiating TRIPS-Plus provisions is not limited to FTAs with developing countries. For instance, the US-Australia FTA imposes a strict IP regime, modelled on the US-Chile and US-Singapore FTAs, requiring Australia to amend several laws.

All of the above illustrates how the US is supporting its overall trade agenda by strategically rebalancing the landscape and creating new norms for IPRs through multiple FTAs with both developed and developing countries. Peter Drahos refers to this as the 'global ratchet' for IPRs. According to Drahos, the 'ratchet' is dependent upon three factors. First, the standard setting agenda must be shifted from a forum where difficulty is being encountered to a more amenable forum. In IP, as with others aspects of international trade, this process has repeated several times. For instance, as explained above, in the early-1980s industrialized countries objected to the increasing domination of WIPO by developing countries and responded by including IPRs in BITs (and later FTAs) and pushing for IPRs to be included in the Uruguay Round. However, since the US does not have enough support to strengthen IPRs multilaterally, it has again shifted the forum to back to bilateralism in order to promote its agenda.

Second, there must be a co-ordination of bilateral and multilateral IP strategies. For instance, this could see the US negotiate BITs/FTAs requiring other parties to comply with certain multilateral IP standards. Such policies expedite compliance with TRIPS while at the same time force certain developing countries to relinquish their rights granted by the TRIPS (ie longer implementation periods). To illustrate, Nicaragua agreed to forego its implementation period and immediately comply with its TRIPS obligations in exchange for preferential access to the US market and increased prospects of foreign direct investment.

Finally, in order for the ratchet to take hold there must be a re-setting of minimum standards through multilateral entrenchment. In this regard, it is important to note that many of the US FTAs explicitly commit the parties to the agreement to provide adequate and effective protection of IPRs in accordance with 'the highest international standards'. The setting of minimum standards in each agreement is important because the minimum standards clauses can ratchet up the lowest level of protection with each subsequent bilateral or multilateral agreement. While such standards are not clearly defined, nor is the term mentioned in TRIPS, it has long been thought that such notations refer not to the standards existing at the time of negotiation but to any standards which subsequently emerge as a matter of international practice. In this regard, each bilateral agreement negotiated by the US not only further supports their framework of increased protection but also adds to it upon the completion of subsequent agreements.

Closely related is the fact that the MFN clause in TRIPS further assists the US in the process of recalculating and resetting international standards. The reason for this is that Article 4 of TRIPS states that any Member which grants 'any advantage, favour, privilege or immunity' to the nationals of *any* other country (whether that country be a Member of the WTO/TRIPS or not) must accord the same treatment to the nationals of other Members of TRIPS. The clause operates in a relatively unqualified way because, unlike Article XXIV of the GATT, which may serve to exempt FTAs from the operation of MFN, TRIPS does not contain a similar provision; thus, the principle of MFN applies to FTAs. To illustrate, if the US and a developing country Member negotiate an FTA, MFN will force the developing nation to make the same IP concessions it accepted in the FTA available to all nations. This provision clearly serves to 'ratchet up' international IP. Therefore, those nations negotiating for TRIPS-Plus provisions are at the same time utilising the MFN principle to harmonise the protection of IP rights, resulting in more far reaching implications than FTA provisions dealing with, for instance, goods. Therefore, if enough FTAs are negotiated containing TRIPS-plus provisions, these provisions will essentially become the new minimum standard from which any future WTO trade round will proceed.

…… …… ……

Patent term extensions

TRIPS requires Members to grant patent protection for a period of at least 20 years from the date of filing of an application for a patent. However, as medical products require lengthy testing periods and regulatory approval, pharmaceutical companies wishing to apply for patent protection must do so at a very early stage of basic research, many years before filing an application for regulatory approval. In total, the patent and regulatory approval process often lasts between eight and twelve years, meaning a company which has gained a patent for a drug will have its monopoly period significantly shortened.

TRIPS does not obligate Members to 'compensate' patent holders for 'unreasonable' delays in approving a patent or registering the product by extending the patent term. However, in order to rebalance the effects of the time delay, provisions in certain US FTAs 'compensate' the pharmaceutical companies for any 'unreasonable' delay caused by the national drug regulatory authority in examining an application for registration or from a patent office in assessing the application for a patent by extending the patent term in the same amount of time as the 'unreasonable' delay (often stated as a period extending beyond five years from the date of the filing or three years after a request for an extension). For example, article 15.9(6) of the CAFTA states:

> Each party, at the request of the patent owner, shall adjust the term of a patent to compensate for unreasonable delays that occur in granting the patent. For the purposes of this paragraph, an unreasonable delay shall at least include a delay in the issuance of the patent of more than five years from the date of filing of the application in the Party, or three years after a request for examination of the application has been made, whichever is later.

Similarly, Article 15.10(2) of the CAFTA relating to delays in market approval continues:

> With respect to any pharmaceutical product that is subject to a patent, each Party shall make available a restoration of the patent term to compensate the patent owner for unreasonable curtailment of the effective patent term as a result of the marketing approval process.

Proposals for the Andean FTA provide yet another avenue for extending the patent term by requiring signatory countries that have granted a patent on the basis of the patent being granted in another country to grant an extension if the term is extended in the granting country relied upon.

It should be noted that it is common international practice to grant extensions for delays caused by registration and examination, especially in developed countries. However, there is concern for developing countries from a public health perspective over what is considered 'reasonable'. Given the resource constraints on national drug regulation authorities and patent offices in developing countries, an arguably 'reasonable' delay could possibly exceed six years. But would the US view this delay as reasonable? The extra years added to a patent may not have serious implications in developed nations or even industrialised developing countries, but may have serious consequences for public health in poorer developing countries due to the fact that the provisions extend the time period drug companies are free from generic competition, thereby delaying significant reductions in price which follow the introduction of generic competition. Such delays could prevent large portions of the population from accessing needed drugs and further deepen the public health crises currently engulfing much of the developing world. Therefore, while it seems reasonable to extend patents when 'unreasonable' delay prevents the patent holder from exploiting their invention, and while it is easy to imagine abuse from patent offices and regulatory authorities, the undefined nature over what is considered 'unreasonable' is troublesome, especially given the complex applications coupled with resource constraints on patent offices and national authorities.

… …… …

VI. QUESTIONS

1. Are intellectual property rights a natural fit with the rest of the WTO Agreements? What role do they play in international trade?

2. Is it at all deceptive for the Agreement to be entitled 'Trade-Related Aspects' of Intellectual Property Rights? Isn't the Agreement broader than that? For example, in what sense is a minimum 20-year patent term requirement 'trade-related'?

3. What is the relationship between trade marks and geographical indications? What happens if there are competing claims between the two types of protection?

4. Would you view the panel's holding in *Canada—Pharmaceutical Patents* on stockpiling as narrow or broad? What about the regulatory review findings?

5. Why did the Panel focus on the economic impact of the Canadian measures in *Canada—Pharmaceutical Patents*?

6. How did the panel analyse the de facto discrimination claim against the Canadian measures in *Canada—Pharmaceutical Patents*? Is this analysis in line with other areas of WTO law and jurisprudence? Does the analysis leave you with any lingering questions?

7. What are the similarities and differences between the panel's analysis of the Article 30 issue in *Canada—Pharmaceutical Patents* and its analysis of Article 13 in *US—Section 110*? Why were the business exception and stockpiling exception held to violate the TRIPS Agreement but not the regulatory review and homestyle exception? Is the jurisprudence consistent?

8. Did the panel in *Canada—Pharmaceutical Patents* strictly follow the Vienna Convention in all of its reasoning? Where in its reasoning did it perhaps deviate?

9. Do the existing TRIPS Agreement rules set out an appropriate balance between IP protection and public health? There is clearly some flexibility in the existing provisions. Are the critics right that this flexibility is insufficient?

10. Who won the *China—IPRs* dispute? What interpretive guidance did this dispute provide in terms of IP enforcement under the TRIPS Agreement? Were China's measures regarding 'criminal thresholds' found to be consistent with the Article 61 of the TRIPS Agreement?

11. Should IPRs be included as a PTA negotiating topic? What are the arguments for and against their inclusion?

Part VIII

Social Policy Issues

18

Developing Countries in the Multilateral Trading System

I. INTRODUCTION

At its inception in 1947, the GATT was dominated by industrialised countries. Developing countries were few in number and some of these were still within the sphere of influence of the European powers. Not surprisingly, then, the original GATT trade rules did not have much to say about economic development concerns, although some provisions were added in the ensuing years. Over the years, however, more and more developing countries have joined the GATT, and they now make up a large majority of the WTO's membership.

As developing countries have grown in terms of membership numbers, their role has also changed. In the early years of the GATT, developing countries took on fewer obligations than did the industrialised world, and correspondingly played a less active role. However, as part of the Uruguay Round, developing countries made substantial commitments in a number of areas, including binding more tariffs and signing on to new agreements in intellectual property and services. As a result, developing countries are now much more active in the negotiations, as the current rules have a significant impact on them.

In this chapter, we examine a number of issues relating to the participation of developing countries in the WTO system. First, we address the question of how to identify 'developing' and 'least-developed' countries. Next, we examine the role of developing countries in the WTO, including: (1) the political realm, in particular the negotiation of the rules; (2) dispute settlement; and (3) the formal treatment of developing countries in relation to that of developed countries. Finally, we discuss whether the policies promoted under WTO rules are appropriate for developing countries.

II. CLASSIFICATION OF WTO MEMBERS AS 'DEVELOPING' OR 'LEAST DEVELOPED'

The WTO rules do not offer much guidance on which Members are 'developing'. As noted on the WTO website, '[f]or "developing countries" there is a degree of self-selection' as to which Members fall into this category. In this regard, 'Members announce for them-selves whether they are "developed" or "developing" countries', but 'other members can challenge the decision of a member to make use of provisions available to developing countries'.[1] By contrast, 'least developed countries' (LDCs) are defined according to a UN list[2] and there is no controversy surrounding which Members are in this category.[3] The term 'developing country' is often used loosely to cover both categories. In this chapter, unless otherwise indicated, we use 'developing country' in this manner.

It is rare that a country's self-selection as 'developing' is contested, but it does happen on occasion. At the DSB meeting where the *Korea—Beef* panel and Appellate Body Reports were adopted, the EC, which had not been a party to the case, made the following statement in relation to the treatment of Korea as a developing country:

> The representative of the European Communities said that his delegation did not wish to comment on the result or the substance of this case. However, it wished to note its disagreement with regard to the treatment of Korea as a developing country for the purposes of the Agreement on Agriculture. The EC noted with surprise that Korea had been treated as a developing country for the purposes of the Agreement on Agriculture. Although this issue did not seem to have been in dispute, the EC was compelled to underline its disagreement with Korea's self-characterization as a developing country. Korea's economic strength and its position as a major trading partner could not justify developing country status under any of the WTO Agreements.[4]

Korea's status as a developing country stems from its income and general development level at the time of accession to the GATT in 1967. At that time, Korea was relatively poor. However, Korea experienced rapid industrialisation and a consequential increase in wealth in the ensuing decades. It became a member of the Organisation for Economic Cooperation and Development in 1996 and, in terms of Gross National Income (GNI) per capita, is currently at similar levels to Western European countries like Greece and Portugal,[5] and it is now very competitive in a number of advanced industries. As a result, an argument could be made that Korea should no longer be considered to be 'developing'. However, countries that are in the mid-range of the development and industrialisation process may claim this status for certain sectors. Of course, if they do, they may face criticism from their trading partners, as evidenced by the EC comments quoted above. It

---

[1] WTO, 'Who Are the Developing Countries in the WTO', available at http://www.wto.org/english/tratop_e/devel_e/d1who_e.htm (accessed on 15 May 2012).

[2] In its triennial review of the list of LDCs in 2003, the Economic and Social Council of the UN used the following 4 criteria for the identification of LDCs, as proposed by the Committee for Development Policy (CDP): (1) a low-income criterion, based on a 3-year average estimate of the gross national income (GNI) per capita (under US$750 for inclusion, above US$900 for graduation); (2) a human resource weakness criterion, involving a composite Human Assets Index (HAI) based on indicators of: (a) nutrition; (b) health; (c) education; and (d) adult literacy; (3) an economic vulnerability criterion, involving a composite Economic Vulnerability Index (EVI) based on indicators of: (a) the instability of agricultural production; (b) the instability of exports of goods and services; (c) the economic importance of non-traditional activities (share of manufacturing and modern services in GDP); (d) merchandise export concentration; and (e) the handicap of economic smallness (as measured through the population in logarithm); and (4) the percentage of population displaced by natural disasters: UN Office of the High Representative for the Least Developed Countries, Landlocked Developing Countries and Small Island Developing States, 'The Criteria for the Identification of the LDCs', available at http://www.un.org/special-rep/ohrlls/ldc/ldccriteria.htm (accessed on 15 May 2012).

[3] WTO, 'Understanding the WTO, Least-Developed Countries', available at www.wto.org/english/ thewto_e/whatis_e/tif_e/org7_e.htm (accessed on 15 May 2012).

[4] See WTO Doc No WT/DSB/M/96 (10 January 2001) para 14.

[5] Based on World Bank country income classification statistics from 2010. Available at http://data.worldbank.org/indicator/NY.GNP.PCAP.CD (accessed on 15 May 2012).

is, in essence, a political issue, to be negotiated among the Members. There is always the possibility that the issue of whether a particular Member may claim 'developing' status will be challenged as part of dispute settlement, but it is not clear how the issue will be dealt with there.

To illustrate this point further, the issue of a Member's status as 'developing' was an important element of China's accession negotiations. In one of the last Working Party sessions addressing China's accession, the head of the Chinese delegation made the following statement:

> As we have emphasized consistently at various occasions in the past, although great progress has been made on China's economic development in the past two decades, we still firmly believe that China is a developing country. The position we have taken to accede to the WTO as a developing country is not only a reflection of the actual economic level of China at the present stage, but also our political choice. It has been one of the basic principles we stick to in the negotiations of the past 15 years. However, we have taken a pragmatic attitude towards the various treatments for the developing countries as embodied in the WTO agreements and practices. We have made specific commitments in different areas in light of our national situation, development level and capacity to implement these commitments.
>
> In some important areas, we insist on undertaking obligations in consistency with our own development level. We have rejected the request to reduce our average tariff level to that of developed countries and insisted that China's average tariff level should be comparable to the average level of the developing countries. In service areas, we insisted that we can not offer to open our market as a developed country and we can only base our commitments on the degree of market opening of the developing countries.
>
> In some areas, however, where China has already had the capability to implement the obligations as all WTO Members, we deem not necessary for China to enjoy preferential treatments to the developing countries as provided for in the relevant WTO agreements. For instance, the TRIPS Agreement provides a 5-year transitional period for developing countries. Since the Chinese government has been working hard to raise the IPR protection level by improving the legal system and enhancing law-enforcement, we have already obtained the capability of implementing the TRIPS Agreement fully. We, therefore, decided not to insist on the access to the transitional period. However, when we noted some developing countries are requesting for an extended transitional period due to their limitation on IPR protection, we support their request because of we believe [sic] that their request is reasonable. This is the approach that we have taken to deal with this matter—the approach of addressing different issues according to their specific situations.[6]
>
> ... ...

Thus, China insisted on being treated as 'developing' in some contexts, but not all. By contrast, as part of its accession, Chinese Taipei, despite an income per capita figure that is slightly above that of Korea,[7] stated that it 'would not claim any right granted

---

[6] Statement by HE Vice Minister Long Yongtu, Head of the Chinese Delegation, at the 16th session of the Working Party on China, available at www.wto.org/english/news_e/news01_e/china_longstat_jul01_e.htm. See also Report of The Working Party on The Accession of China, WTO Doc No WT/ACC/CHN/49 (1 Oct 2001) paras 8–9.

[7] According to World Bank statistics, Chinese Taipei had a GNI per capita of US$16,170 in 2005, whereas Korea had a GNI per capita of US$15,830. The statistics are available at http://web.worldbank.org/ WBSITE/ EXTERNAL/DATASTATISTICS/0,,contentMDK:20535285~menuPK:1192694~pagePK:64133150~piPK:6413 3175~theSitePK:239419,00.html (accessed on 29 July 2010).

under WTO Agreements to developing country Members or to a Member in the process of transforming its economy from a centrally-planned into a market, free-enterprise economy'.[8]

The treatment of China and Chinese Taipei appears to reflect an approach influenced by political and diplomatic considerations, which recognises the difficult issues involved and the differences in views. In essence, it implicitly says what is already known about 'developing country' status at the WTO: Whether to declare oneself to be 'developing' is a political decision to be made by a Member and reflects informal and formal negotiations with other Members on the issue.

III. THE ROLE OF DEVELOPING COUNTRIES IN THE WTO: NEGOTIATIONS, DISPUTES, AND SPECIAL AND DIFFERENTIAL TREATMENT

The eminent trade scholar John Jackson has distinguished between rule-oriented and power-oriented regimes, suggesting that the GATT/WTO system has moved towards a rule-oriented system. While this is no doubt true, power remains an important element in terms of Members' participation in the system. The following extract presents a picture of how power considerations affect developing countries' role in the current system. In this regard, it touches on three important aspects of developing countries' role in the WTO: the negotiating process; the dispute settlement system and the formal position of developing countries vis-à-vis developed countries. In the sub-sections of this chapter that follow the extract, we explore each aspect in more detail.

PM Gerhart and AS Kella, 'Power and Preferences: Developing Countries and the Role of the WTO Appellate Body' (2005) 30 *North Carolina Journal of International Law & Commercial Regulation* **515**

The WTO's primary purpose is to allow members to bargain with each other in order to obtain binding commitments to change policies that adversely affect the welfare of other member countries. This bargaining is inherently power-based. WTO members negotiate market access commitments, for example, based on the size and diversity of their economies. Members with the greatest economic wealth and most diversified economies, such as the United States and the EC, have more to offer in negotiations and less to lose in the event that negotiations break down. Thus, they have more bargaining power than other members. At the other end of the spectrum, members with little wealth and diversity in their economies have the least to offer in any given negotiation and the most to lose if the negotiations are unsuccessful. Consequently, in the absence of effective coalition building or other strategic considerations, these countries have the least bargaining power in the system and wealthy countries are significantly more likely to secure their desired outcomes under the WTO.

Over the years the GATT/WTO system has become increasingly subject to legal, rather than political, control. As members have taken on new commitments, the power of the wealthy countries has been decreased, and some commitments have been directly aimed at reducing

---

[8] Report of the Working Party on the Accession of the Separate Customs Territory of Taiwan, Penghu, Kinmen and Matsu, WTO Doc No WT/ACC/TPKM/18 (5 Oct 2001) para 6.

the use of unilateral power by the wealthy countries. Moreover, the new dispute resolution architecture allows each member to hold other members accountable for their commitments; this form of legalization has replaced the negotiated settlement of disputes (which is inherently power-based) with the level playing field of judicial review.

We should not, however, jump too quickly to the conclusion that in today's regime the relative power of countries is unimportant. Clearly, as WTO members undertake negotiations to work out the implementation of the GATS agreement or in the new Doha Round of multilateral negotiations, member's relative power continues to be an important force in determining the nature of the obligations that are undertaken and avoided. In these negotiations, the relative power of the members continues to shape the negotiations, both in process and in outcome. If nothing else, the search for ways to put together bargaining coalitions, and the counter-efforts to break up coalitions, shows that power remains the central ingredient of lawmaking by negotiation. Moreover, despite the efforts noted above, the WTO system has proven to be ineffective at eliminating the resort to unilateral power when powerful countries want to impose new obligations on others. Therefore it has proven difficult to address the power imbalance between developed and developing countries even within the WTO's current law-based system.

Although the legalization of the dispute resolution process is often thought to be a benefit to developing countries, the reality is not so simple. There is ample evidence that the dispute settlement system created under the Dispute Settlement Understanding (DSU) is not a meaningful source of power for developing countries; to the contrary, the system may asymmetrically favor the developed countries. Small countries often lack the incentive to seek redress. The level of a country's development still heavily influences the settlement of disputes before litigation, and enforcement of obligations depends on designing retaliation that imposes realistic costs on a non-complying country. Although the DSU has significantly improved the WTO dispute settlement process for developing country complainants by instituting a more timely "trial," removing the threat that a defendant could block a case, and providing the option of appellate review (to improve consistency and greater systemization), the reforms have also increased the transaction costs of settling disputes.

Whatever the reality now, over the last six decades developing countries have had a healthy distrust of the GATT/WTO regime and have maintained skepticism about the value of the WTO to their own interests. Integrating developing countries into the WTO regime has essentially been a task of finding a way to incorporate the powerless into a multilateral system whose benefits are distributed on the basis of power. This is required not only to bring developing countries into the regime, and to improve the universality of the regime, but also to maintain a power balance in the regime as it matures. The GATT/WTO regime is simultaneously strong and fragile. Its long run stability depends on insuring that all members continue to believe that the benefits of belonging to the WTO outweigh the costs, and this means that the powerless must continue to feel that they are better off within the organization than outside of it.

Historically, the primary issue between developed and developing countries has been whether the principle that governed GATT was to be one of formal equality (despite the differences between developed and developing countries) or real equality – recognizing that formal equality between countries that are unequal is not equality. Although the initial U.S. position on this question was that formal equality should be the rule, eventually the United States had to succumb to the view that if it wanted the GATT/WTO system to be attractive to all countries it would have to bend toward real equality. The developing countries had no interest in participating in a system that did not acknowledge the special position of poor countries, and the insistence of the United States that poor countries make the same sort of "concessions" as wealthy countries and accept the same sort of obligations made membership unattractive. Over time, the benefits of universality began to outweigh the desire for a uniform approach to rights and obligations, and the United States, as well as the rest of the developed world, began to understand the importance of creating special rules that would acknowledge the different status of the poorer countries. As Robert Hudec has written:

The history [of developing country involvement in the GATT/WTO system], begins with a legal relationship based essentially on parity of obligation, with only very limited, almost token, exceptions. Over the years, the relationship has gravitated, in seemingly inexorable fashion, towards the one-sided welfare relationship demanded by the developing countries.

Ultimately, the WTO implemented the concept of Special and Differential treatment – the notion that within the GATT/WTO system, poor countries would be given treatment that reflected their poverty, and thus their relative lack of bargaining power. Two types of special treatment developed. From the standpoint of avoiding obligations, commitments made by developed countries would be implemented more slowly, or less severely, for developing countries, and developing countries would not have to make the same concessions as industrial country members. From the standpoint of receiving special privileges, the industrial and developing countries negotiated the GSP program. Under this program, developed countries were allowed and encouraged to give preferential market access to the developing countries by lowering tariffs for developing countries below the level of tariffs for developed countries.

In the absence of any official authorization, preferences given under the GSP program to developing, but not developed, countries would have violated the prohibition on discriminatory treatment contained in the "cornerstone" most favored nation (MFN) obligation of Article 1 of GATT. Accordingly, the members created the necessary exception to the MFN requirement to allow such preferences in two ways: First, by way of a waiver of Article 1, known as the 1971 GSP Decision, and later by way of a 1979 decision that became known as the 1979 Enabling Clause. The Enabling Clause continues to provide the legal basis for the MFN exception allowing countries to give the preferences, thus serving as the instrument that determines whether preference programs are lawful.

In sum, the GSP system was instituted in the hope that developing countries could use the trade preferences to increase their national wealth and thereby increase their interest in, and allegiance to, the GATT/WTO regime. The underlying theory was that the preferences would hasten the economic development of less developed countries and would increase the power that these countries would derive from their own economic strength. This, in turn, would help to restore and maintain balance within the system. In this way, the preferences can be seen as a reflection of, and reaction to, the economic and political situation in the recipient countries. Nonetheless, the GSP system has unique characteristics that make it an imperfect tool for achieving that goal.

... ...

(a) The Negotiating Process

The role of developing countries in the negotiating process has been a particularly contentious issue. WTO negotiations have now moved far beyond a tariff-cutting exercise, leading to fairly complex negotiations. Even developed countries with vast resources are stretched thin trying to promote their interests in the midst of myriad rules and commitments being discussed. It goes without saying that developing countries, especially the least developed countries, are often completely overwhelmed. In addition to these difficulties, one of the criticisms of the WTO is that developing countries have been excluded from the process to a great extent. The process has improved in recent years, as at least some developing country nations are usually present at key negotiating meetings.

However, it is usually larger developing countries such as Brazil, China and India which play this role, rather than smaller and poorer countries. Below is an extract from a book by a researcher at Focus on the Global South, an advocacy group for developing country concerns, setting out some criticisms of the process:

A Kwa, *Power Politics in the WTO* (Focus on the Global South, Bangkok, 2003), 36–7

Decision-making essentially takes place in 'concentric circles'. First, the US and the EU come together to decide on a common position. The circle is then expanded to Japan and Canada. They make up the 'Quad'. After this, the circle is enlarged to include other developed countries, followed by friendly developing countries (e.g. South Africa, Chile, Singapore etc). This group is sometimes known as 'Friends of the Chair'. And finally, other influential developing countries, such as India and Malaysia are brought on board, since they carry weight, and it would be impossible for the 'majors' to leave them out. China, a new member, also falls into this category. The majority of developing countries never make it into this circle of decision-making.

This is achieved through informal meetings. Since Seattle, there has been more awareness of the need to include more countries than the usual 20-30 members. However, the choice of which countries to include is left entirely to the Chair. The Secretariat is often enlisted to help in this task, even though the Secretariat should be neutral. There are no rules binding the Chair. Members are invited for consultations. Those not invited would not even be informed and even if they did find out and wanted to join the meeting they may well find themselves stopped at the door.

This is how texts suddenly 'appear from nowhere' before important meetings, since consultations have been taking place without the knowledge or inclusion of many countries. When the Chair is sufficiently confident that his/her compromise package (supposedly coming out of the informal consultations) will not be openly objected to by the majority, informal general council meetings (of the entire membership) are convened. If objections remain strong, the decision goes back into informal consultations. Finally, a formal General Council meeting is convened and the decision is taken there by consensus i.e. no member present objects.

So, although the decisions of the WTO affect the lives of people in all member states, the process of decision-making is quite arbitrary and dependent on the Chair and those countries that have influence over her/him (usually the Quad).

This process of manufacturing consensus requires the developed countries to ensure that when the final package is brought to the larger membership, the ground has already been prepared so that no matter how unhappy the majority is, no single country will formally reject the package. This is achieved by an elaborate mixture of strategies of marginalisation, influence-peddling and even outright coercion, made possible by the huge differences in power between the players.

… … …

Although this piece was written by an organisation that is a harsh critic of many aspects of the WTO, and thus may exaggerate some of the points, most of what is said is at least close to an accurate description of the process. Even so, judging whether the negotiating process is fair and equitable for developing countries is a difficult task. Developed countries have taken a number of actions to help developing countries on their own, so, arguably, they do have developing countries' interests in mind to some extent. Thus, in theory, the process could be fair to developing countries despite their lack of participation in the negotiations. And groups in all countries complain about how badly they have fared in the negotiations, so claims of unfairness should be examined with a critical eye (in a sense, the fact that everyone complains may be a sign that a particular outcome was just about right). However, the discrepancy in the resources between rich and poor countries is very high, and the limited actual participation by many developing countries on the key negotiating points is almost certainly going to lead to some of their concerns being overlooked. So, even if the above extract overstates the concern, it is almost certainly true that there is a problem.

On the other hand, the current system may not be quite as bad as some critics imagine, as developing countries have been able to work together and form negotiating blocs. Thus, not all developing country Members need to participate to have their interests represented. Partly as a result, developing countries have been flexing their negotiating muscles in recent years, putting development concerns higher on the WTO's agenda than they have ever been (with the word 'development' now part of the title of the current negotiating round).

Unfortunately, if there is a problem, it is not clear what the solution is. If all 153 current WTO Members were to participate actively in WTO negotiations, it is hard to imagine how agreement would ever be reached, so this is probably not a viable option. Excluding some of the membership from key aspects of the negotiating process is unavoidable for this process to work.

(b) Dispute Settlement

The DSU, as discussed at length in Chapter 5, has been called the 'crown jewel' of the Uruguay Round negotiations. However, one persistent criticism of the DSU is that it does not work well for developing countries. There are two main aspects of this criticism. First, some argue that developing countries do not have the human or financial resources to participate effectively in dispute settlement. Secondly, some consider that the dispute settlement rules are skewed against developing countries (and small economies in general) because the impact of any retaliation they undertake pursuant to the DSU is limited. We explore each of these issues in more detail below.

(i) Limited Resources

While it is clear that developing countries are at a disadvantage, the extent of the disadvantage is hard to assess. There are a number of factors that hurt developing countries and others that help them. An overall assessment needs to weigh up all of these. We lay out some of these considerations below.

With regard to factors that hurt developing countries in dispute settlement, the number of government personnel that can be devoted to disputes is much higher in developed countries, especially the US and the EC. As a result, developed countries have a large contingent of well-trained government lawyers with expertise in WTO law. Furthermore, developed countries have greater financial resources to devote to the case. This includes the resources of the private companies with interests in the dispute, who can hire expensive private lawyers to work on the case, as well as the resources of the government itself to cover various litigation costs.

On the other hand, developing countries have some advantages as well. First, there is an intergovernmental organisation called the Advisory Centre on WTO Law ('ACWL') that was formed specifically to help developing countries with disputes (as well as understanding WTO law more generally). It operates as a law firm representing these governments at discounted rates, and also helps to defray the costs of hiring private lawyers where it cannot advise directly. As a result, it is sometimes the case that a developing country may end up being represented by an ACWL attorney who is one of the top lawyers in the field, whereas a developed country may only have a mid-level government staff attorney working on the case (the downside of this, of course, is that utilising outside help can inhibit the growth of in-house expertise). In addition, the heavy involvement of Members such as the US and EC in disputes stretches their resources thinly. Thus, while it is true that they have a lot of lawyers devoted to WTO issues, it is less clear which countries have the most lawyers per number of active disputes.

Finally, we note that the distinctions within developing countries are very important here. Some Members, while poor in terms of GNP per capita, have very large economies due to their population size. India and China are the prime examples of this group, but there are also Malaysia, Indonesia and others. In addition, countries like Brazil and Argentina are somewhat wealthier and also have large populations. Finally, some smaller countries like Chile and Costa Rica are relatively well off as compared to most developing countries. All of these countries, and some others, have the capacity to participate effectively in disputes that rival that of the Quad countries (US, EU, Canada and Japan).

(ii) Inherent Bias in the DSU Rules

Under the DSU, complainants that have brought a successful case have the right to retaliate with trade sanctions (ie, suspension of concessions) when the defending party does not implement a ruling properly. Clearly, retaliation by the US or EC is likely to have a greater impact than retaliation by a small country which only has a small amount of imports in absolute terms, as the US or EC will almost always be able to find imports from another Member that they can target effectively with sanctions. This is much less likely to be the case for developing countries.

Proposals have been made to address the problem, in particular by allowing developing countries to act as a group in this kind of retaliation, so as to have a better chance of finding an effective product or service on which to impose sanctions.[9]

On the other hand, while the rules are biased in the ways noted, they do offer developing countries some options when pursuing litigation. For example, the inclusion of rules on intellectual property in the WTO gives Members the ability to use intellectual property protection as a retaliatory tool. For example, allowing violations of music, film or software copyrights is something that developing countries could utilise to penalise the developed world, even where no imported goods are available for targeting.[10] Options such as this one, however, do have their limitations.[11]

---

[9] See, eg B Mercurio, 'Improving Dispute Settlement in the WTO: The DSU Review—Making It Work?' (2004) 38 *Journal of World Trade* 795. Others have proposed giving Members the ability to auction off retaliation rights: see K Bagwell, PC Mavroidis and RW Staiger, 'The Case for Auctioning Countermeasures in the WTO', NBER Working Papers 9920 (National Bureau of Economic Research, 2003).

[10] Such an approach was proposed by Ecuador against the European Communities in the *EC—Bananas* case (WT/DS27/52, 9 Nov 1999) by Brazil against the US in the *US—Cotton Subsidies* case (WT/DS267/21, 5 July 2005), and by Antigua against the US in the *US—Gambling Services* case (WT/DS285/22, 21 June 2007).

[11] See B Mercurio, 'Retaliatory Trade Measures in the WTO Dispute Settlement Understanding: Are There Really Alternatives?' in J Hartigan (ed) *Trade Disputes and the Dispute Settlement Understanding of the WTO: An Interdisciplinary Assessment* (London, Emerald/Elsevier, 2009).

(iii) Conclusions

As noted, conclusions on whether the dispute settlement system works for developing countries are difficult to draw. Views on this issue are often shaped by ideology and general worldview. We note that the following developing countries have all been fairly active in bringing complaints since the start of the WTO: Argentina (15 complaints), Brazil (25), Chile (10), China (eight) Costa Rica (five), Honduras (eight), India (21), Mexico (21) and Thailand (13). Korea, whose developing country status was challenged by the European Communities, has brought 15 complaints. By comparison, Japan and Australia, both of which are relatively wealthy developed countries, brought 15 and seven respectively.[12] In addition, it is no doubt true that, despite its flaws, developing countries are better off under the current system than they were under the GATT rules, where power and politics dominated.

(c) Special and Differential versus Equal Treatment

As noted above, there are many provisions in the WTO Agreement that provide for 'special and differential' treatment for developing countries. Not all of the provisions actually use these exact terms, but the common thread is that they offer looser rules for these countries. In general terms, according to the WTO's website, these provisions: offer 'extra time for developing countries to fulfil their commitments'; are "designed to increase developing countries' trading opportunities through greater market access'; require 'WTO members to safeguard the interests of developing countries when adopting some domestic or international measures'; and provide 'various means of helping developing countries'.[13] We note several examples here:

- GATT Article XVIII is entitled 'Governmental Assistance for Economic Development,' and allows developing countries more flexibility in using trade restrictions to address various issues related to economic development. (We examine below a WTO dispute related to this provision.)
- DSU Article 4.10 provides: '[d]uring consultations Members should give special attention to the particular problems and interests of developing country Members'.
- DSU Article 12.10 provides that in the context of consultations involving a measure taken by a developing country Member, the parties may agree to extend the relevant periods. In addition, it states: 'in examining a complaint against a developing country Member, the panel shall accord sufficient time for the developing country Member to prepare and present its argumentation'.
- DSU Article 21.2 provides: '[p]articular attention should be paid to matters affecting the interests of developing country Members with respect to measures which have been subject to dispute settlement'.
- AD Agreement Article 15 provides: '[i]t is recognized that special regard must be given by developed country Members to the special situation of developing country Members when considering the application of anti-dumping measures under this Agreement. Possibilities of constructive remedies provided for by this Agreement shall

---

[12] The figures are as of 15 May 2012.
[13] WTO, 'Understanding the WTO: Developing Countries: Overview', available at www.wto.org/english/thewto_e/whatis_e/tif_e/dev1_e.htm (accessed on 15 May 2012).

be explored before applying anti-dumping duties where they would affect the essential interests of developing country Members'.

SCM Agreement Article 27 provides, inter alia:

27.1 Members recognize that subsidies may play an important role in economic development programmes of developing country Members.

27.2 The prohibition of paragraph 1(a) of Article 3 shall not apply to:

(a) developing country Members referred to in Annex VII.

(b) other developing country Members for a period of eight years from the date of entry into force of the WTO Agreement, subject to compliance with the provisions in paragraph 4.

Many of these provisions are drafted in fairly vague terms, leaving the scope of the obligation somewhat unclear. For example, DSU Article 4.10 uses the term 'should', and it is not clear how it would be determined what constitutes 'special attention' and whether it was given.

Here, we review how the dispute settlement process has treated these issues in relation to one of these provisions, GATT Article XVIII, in the *India—Quantitative Restrictions* dispute. Special rules for developing country Members which are experiencing balance of payments difficulties are set out in Article XVIII:B of the GATT. The key paragraphs are quoted in the excerpt below (the normal rules on balance of payments which apply to other Members are found in Article XII of the GATT).[14] The term balance of payments refers to the payments that flow into and out of a country.[15] It is determined by a country's exports and imports as well as financial transfers. When the balance of payments becomes negative, which can be caused by a decline in exports or increase in imports, the country's foreign exchange reserves can become low. One approach countries have taken to addressing this issue is to restrict imports, and the GATT provisions on balance of payments difficulties recognise this option, allowing such restrictions as long as certain conditions are met. The *India—Quantitative Restrictions* dispute addressed a number of import restrictions purportedly taken for balance-of-payments reasons.

The factual background of *India—Quantitative Restrictions* is as follows: India had been consulting with the GATT/WTO Committee on Balance-of-Payments Restrictions ('BOP Committee') since 1957 in relation to its import restrictions, and claimed that the restrictions were justified under GATT Article XVIII as necessary to protect its balance-of-payments situation. During consultations held in November 1994, the Committee noted that India's 'aim' was to remove these restrictions by 1996–7. In May 1997, India notified these restrictions to the BOP Committee under GATT Article XVIII:B. At the same time, India notified the BOP Committee regarding a time schedule for the removal of its restrictions, under which removal would take place over a period of 10 years. On the basis of this proposal, consultations took place with the Committee. India's final proposal for the duration of the removal schedule was seven years. However, as set out

---

[14] More specifically, the provision applies to Members 'the economy of which can only support low standards of living and is in the early stages of development': see GATT Art XVIII:1 and 4(a).

[15] *Deardorff's Glossary of International Economics* defines it as: '[a] list, or accounting, of all of a country's international transactions for a given time period, usually one year. Payments into the country (receipts) are entered as positive numbers, called credits; payments out of the country (payments) are entered as negative numbers called debits': available at www-personal.umich.edu/~alandear/glossary/b.html (accessed on 15 May 2012).

in the report of the BOP Committee, no consensus among the Members of the Committee could be reached on the acceptability of this proposal. The US then brought a complaint against the Indian restrictions. At the time the dispute settlement panel was established in November 1997, India maintained quantitative restrictions on imports of products in 2,714 tariff lines within the eight-digit level of the Harmonised Tariff Schedule.[16]

The US claimed that the Indian restrictions violate, inter alia, GATT Article XVIII:11, which states:

> In carrying out its domestic policies, the Member concerned shall pay due regard to the need for restoring equilibrium in its balance of payments on a sound and lasting basis and to the desirability of assuring an economic employment of productive resources. It shall progressively relax any restrictions applied under this Section as conditions improve, maintaining them only to the extent necessary under the terms of paragraph 9 of this Article and shall eliminate them when conditions no longer justify such maintenance.

In response, India argued, inter alia, that the measures were justified by GATT Article XVIII:9, which is referred to in Article XVIII:11 and states:

> In order to safeguard its external financial position and to ensure a level of reserves adequate for the implementation of its programme of economic development, a Member coming within the scope of paragraph 4 (a) of this Article may, subject to the provisions of paragraphs 10 to 12, control the general level of its imports by restricting the quantity or value of merchandise permitted to be imported; Provided that the import restrictions instituted, maintained or intensified shall not exceed those necessary:
>
> (a) to forestall the threat of, or to stop, a serious decline in its monetary reserves, or
>
> (b) in the case of a contracting party with inadequate monetary reserves, to achieve a reasonable rate of increase in its reserves.

In this regard, India argued that the level of its 'monetary reserves' was low enough, and had declined enough, to justify restrictions under Article XVIII:9. We focus here on the panel's treatment of the issues under Article XVIII:9. The following extract contains the panel's analysis of whether India was, in fact, experiencing balance-of-payments difficulties:

Panel Report, *India—Quantitative Restrictions on Imports of Agricultural, Textile and Industrial Products*, Adopted 20 August 1999, WT/DS90/R

2. Is India experiencing balance-of-payments difficulties within the meaning of Article XVIII:9?

(a) Conditions under Article XVIII:9

5.158 As noted above, Article XVIII:11 requires Members to "progressively relax any restrictions applied under this section as conditions improve, maintaining them only to the extent necessary under the terms of paragraph 9 of this Article and shall eliminate them when conditions no longer justify such maintenance [. . .]". We recall that, under the terms of Article XVIII:9, "the import restrictions instituted, maintained or intensified shall not exceed those necessary:

---

[16] Panel Report, *India—QRs*, paras 2.1–2.8.

(a) to forestall the threat of, or to stop, a serious decline in monetary reserves, or

(b) in the case of a contracting party with inadequate monetary reserves, to achieve a reasonable rate of increase in its reserves"

due regard being paid to any special factors that may be affecting the reserves of the Member or its need for reserves.

(b) Date at which the situation of India's monetary reserves must be reviewed

5.159   The United States argues that the dispute began with the United States' request for consultations on 15 July 1997 and that the DSU treats consultations as the initiation of a dispute. Therefore, in its view, 15 July 1997 is the date as of which this Panel should determine whether India's measures were justified under Article XVIII:B. If the Panel disagrees, the United States considers that the latest date should be the date of establishment of the Panel. India generally considers that the Panel must determine the legality of the import restrictions under India's obligations "as of the date the United States submitted this request". However, India also considers that taking into account external or internal developments affecting India's economy since the establishment of the Panel would be appropriate because much of the evidence introduced by the United States in the dispute relates to the period after the establishment of the Panel.

5.160   With respect to the date at which India's balance-of-payments and reserve situation is to be assessed, we note that practice, both prior to the WTO and since its entry into force, limits the claims which panels address to those raised in the request for establishment of the panel, which is typically the basis of the panel's terms of reference (as is the case here). In our opinion, this has consequences for the determination of the facts that can be taken into account by the Panel, since the complainant obviously bases the claims contained in its request for establishment of the panel on a given set of facts existing when it presents its request to the DSB.5.161   In the present situation, the United States primarily seeks a finding that, at the latest on the date of establishment of the Panel (18 November 1997), the measures at issue were not compatible with the WTO Agreement and were not justified under Article XVIII:11 of GATT 1994. Therefore, it would seem consistent with such a request and logical in the light of the constraints imposed by the Panel's terms of reference to limit our examination of the facts to those existing on the date the Panel was established.

5.162   This result is also dictated by practical considerations. The determination of whether balance-of-payments measures are justified is tied to a Member's reserve situation as of a certain date. In fixing that date, it is important to consider that the relevant economic and reserve data will be available only with some time-lag, which may vary by type of data. This is unlikely to be a problem if the date of assessment is the date the panel is established, since the first written submission is typically filed at least two (and often more) months after establishment of a panel. However, using the first or second panel meetings as the assessment date is more problematic since data might not be available and, if the date of the second panel meeting were chosen, it could significantly reduce the utility of the first meeting.

5.163   We note that, in the case on *Korea – Beef*, the panel relied on the conclusions of the BOP Committee reached before its establishment, but also considered "all available information", including information related to periods after the establishment of the panel. In this case, the parties and the IMF have supplied information concerning the evolution of India's balance-of-payments and reserve situation until June 1998. To the extent that such information is relevant to our determination of the consistency of India's balance-of-payments measures with GATT rules as of the date of establishment of the Panel, we take it into account.

(c) Information provided by the IMF

5.164   The Panel put the following questions to the IMF which are relevant to our examination of India's balance-of-payments situation:

"1. (a)   (i) As of 18 November 1997, the date of establishment of the Panel, was India experiencing a serious decline in its monetary reserves, or facing a threat thereof? (ii) Was India experiencing an inadequate, or a very low level of monetary reserves? (iii) Was India experiencing a reasonable rate of increase in its monetary reserves?

(b)   In connection with responding to these questions, could the IMF indicate what would have constituted a serious decline in India's monetary reserves, what would have constituted an inadequate, or a very low level of monetary reserves for India, and what would have constituted a reasonable rate of increase in India's monetary reserves?"

5.165   The IMF's replies to the questions show that foreign currency reserves of India's monetary authorities stood at US$25.1 billion (excluding gold) on 21 November 1997, which represented an increase of US$5.6 billion from a year earlier, and of US$2.8 billion from end-March 1997. The IMF indicates that "[a]t about six months of imports of goods and non-factor services, India's reserves appeared to provide sufficient external liquidity and a reasonable degree of protection against unforeseen external shocks. In particular, reserves were sufficient to deal with debt service payments and potential outflows of portfolio investment, covering 2½ times the amount of maturing debt obligations in the next twelve months and 1½ times the stock of short-term debt and cumulative inflows of portfolio investment. Therefore, it was the Fund's view that India's level of foreign currency reserves on November 18, 1997 was adequate". The IMF notes that the establishment of the panel coincided with a period of turbulence in the foreign exchange market in India, but concludes that "with an appropriate macroeconomic response and the containment of contagion, India's foreign currency reserves on 18 November 1997 did not appear to be under a threat of a serious decline; since there was no threat, the question of whether an imminent threat existed is moot". Having noted that gross foreign currency reserves fell by US$1.9 billion in November 1997, the Fund nevertheless determines that "there has been a reasonable rate of accumulation of reserves since India's balance-of-payments crisis in 1991".

5.166   In response to question 1 (b), the Fund, noting the considerable degree of subjective judgment involved in an assessment of the adequacy of the level and rate of change of reserves, based its view on "the size of the existing and potential claims on reserves, examined in the context of the country's economic circumstances. In the case of India, policy had prudently aimed at ensuring that reserve coverage is ahead of the outstanding short-term liabilities (by remaining maturity) and potential outflows of portfolio investment. As of November 1997, short-term liabilities (by remaining maturity) and the stock of portfolio investment (after marking to market) were estimated at US$16 billion. A decline in reserves to significantly below this level would be considered serious, and such levels could be deemed inadequate or very low".

Table 1: Evolution of India's level of reserves (1995–98)

Year	31 March 1995	31 March 1996	31 March 1997	31 March 1998	30 June 1998
Level of reserves (US$ billions)	20.8	17	22.4	26	24.1

(Source: IMF)

5.167   India comments that the events described by the IMF in its answer to question 1(a) (i) constitute recognition by the IMF of the threat of a serious decline in India's reserves. India notes that the Reserve Bank of India (RBI) had to change its monetary policy goals in order to defend the rupee, and would not have done so had it not felt that it faced a threat of a serious decline in foreign currency reserves which it had been unable to control using other policy instruments. With regard to questions 1(a)(ii) and 1(b), India notes that experts have suggested alternative indicators to evaluate the adequacy of India's foreign currency reserves, which, in India's view, would be more appropriate than the standard measure used by the IMF. Using these measures, India calculated that its reserves should be at higher levels to ensure adequacy.

5.168   The United States comments that the IMF's replies are fully consistent with the evidence furnished by the United States to the Panel and make it clear that India's balance-of-payments situation does not meet the criteria of the proviso of Article XVIII:9. The United States also points out that the IMF's analysis of India's balance-of-payments situation is more complete than that presented by India, in that it considers the whole balance-of-payments situation, whereas India's analysis focuses mostly on its trade account, which is only one element of the analysis.

(d) Assessment of India's balance-of-payments situation in relation to the conditions of Article XVIII:9

(i). Article XVIII:9(a)

5.169   The issue to be decided under Article XVIII:9 (a) is whether India's balance-of-payments measures exceeded those "necessary . . . to forestall the threat of, or to stop, a serious decline in monetary reserves". In deciding this issue, we must weigh the evidence favouring India against that favouring the United States and determine whether on the basis of all evidence before the Panel, the United States has established its claim under Article XVIII:11 that India does not meet the conditions specified in Article XVIII:9(a).

5.170   The United States relies principally upon the following evidence and argument: it notes in the first instance that in the view of the IMF, as of 18 November 1997 India was not facing a threat of a serious decline in monetary reserves and that the IMF had expressed an identical view to the BOP Committee in January 1997 and June 1997. In addition, the United States notes the statement in the Annual Report of the Reserve Bank of India for the year July 1, 1996 to June 30, 1997 (para. 7.23), where it is stated:

"The level of foreign exchange reserves (including gold and SDRs) rose to US$ 29.9 billion by August 14, 1997 equivalent to seven months of imports and well above the thumb rule of reserve adequacy (three months of imports). In the context of the changing interface with the external sector and the importance of the capital account, reserve adequacy needs to be evaluated in terms of indicators other than conventional norms. By any criteria, the level of foreign exchange level reserves appears comfortable. They are equivalent of about 25 months of debt service payments and 6 months of payments for imports and debt service taken together. Thus, even if exchange market developments accentuate the leads and lags in external receipts and payments, the reserves would be adequate to withstand both cyclical and unanticipated shocks."

5.171   India responds that its monetary authorities had to change their monetary policy goals in the latter part of 1997 in order to defend the rupee during this period and argues that they would not have taken such actions if there had not been a threat of a serious decline in monetary reserves. Moreover, it contends that there are different ways to measure reserve adequacy. In this regard, it points to the answers of the IMF, where the IMF states that "A considerable degree of subjective judgment is involved in an assessment of the adequacy of the level and rate of changes of reserves". According to India, there are four other methods of assessing reserve adequacy:

(a)   import coverage of at least 6 months: US$22 billion;

(b)   import coverage of three months plus 50% of debt service payments plus one months' imports and exports to account for leads and lags: more than US$22 billion;

(c)   short-term debt and portfolio stock should not exceed 60% of reserves and incremental short-term debt and portfolio liabilities should be accompanied by equivalent increases in reserves: more than US$27 billion; and

(d)   foreign assets to currency ratio should not be less than 40% and a desirable level would be 70%: US$16 billion (minimum); US$28 billion (desirable).

5.172   In evaluating the evidence and arguments presented by the parties, we note India's argument that its monetary authorities changed their monetary policy goals in the latter part of 1997 to defend the rupee. However, the Indian authorities' action does not in itself demonstrate that there was a serious decline in India's monetary reserves or a threat thereof during that period, in terms of Article XVIII:9(a).

5.173   The question before us is whether India was facing a serious decline or threat thereof in its reserves (Article XVIII:9(a)) or had inadequate reserves (Article XVIII:9(b)). In analyzing India's situation in terms of Article XVIII:9(a), it is important to bear in mind that the issue is whether India was facing or threatened with a *serious* decline in its monetary reserves. Whether or not a decline of a given size is serious or not must be related to the initial state and adequacy of the reserves. A large decline need not necessarily be a serious one if the reserves are more than adequate. Accordingly, it is appropriate to consider the adequacy of India's reserves for purposes of Article XVIII:9(a), as well as for Article XVIII:9(b).

5.174   In this connection, we recall that the IMF reported that India's reserves as of 21 November 1997 were US$ 25.1 billion and that an adequate level of reserves at that date would have been US$ 16 billion. While the Reserve Bank of India did not specify a precise level of what would constitute adequacy, it concluded only three months earlier in August 1997 that India's reserves were "well above the thumb rule of reserve adequacy" and although the Bank did not accept that thumb rule as the only measure of adequacy, it also found that "[b]y any criteria, the level of foreign exchange reserves appears comfortable". It also stated that "the reserves would be adequate to withstand both cyclical and unanticipated shocks".

5.175   We have also considered the four alternative methods of assessing reserve adequacy cited by India. We note that India concedes that its reserves of US$25.1 billion would have been adequate under two of the alternatives (a and b). Under a third alternative (d), the reserves of US$25.1 billion were at the higher end of the range between the minimum (US$16 billion) and desirable (US$28 billion) reserve levels. Under the fourth method (c), reserves of US$27 billion would be considered adequate. While it might be following a prudential approach in suggesting method (c), India does not explain why it would be superior to the IMF method or to the other three Indian alternatives under which reserves could be considered adequate. Moreover, India's alternatives do not seem to be consistent with the approach of the Reserve Bank of India quoted above.

5.176   Having weighed the evidence before us, we note that only one of the four methods suggested by India for measuring reserve adequacy supports a finding that India's reserves are inadequate, and even under that method, the issue is a close one (US$25.1 billion vs. US$27 billion, or less than 10 per cent difference). Overall, we are of the view that the quality and weight of evidence is strongly in favour of the proposition that India's reserves are not inadequate. In particular, this position is supported by the IMF, the Reserve Bank of India and three of the four methods suggested by India. Accordingly, we find that India's reserves were not inadequate as of 18 November 1997.

5.177 Turning now to the question of whether India was facing a serious decline or threat thereof in its reserves, it is appropriate to consider the evolution of its reserves in the period prior to November 1997. As noted above, as of 31 March 1996, India's reserves were US$17 billion; as of 31 March 1997, India's reserves were US$22.4 billion. We note that at the time of the BOP Committee's consultations with India in January and June 1997, the IMF reported that India did not face a serious decline in its reserves or a threat thereof. As of 21 November 1997, India's reserves had risen to US$25.1 billion and the IMF continued to be of the view that India did not face a serious decline in its reserves or a threat thereof. In our view, in light of the foregoing evidence, and taking into account the provisions of Article XV:2, as of the date of establishment of the Panel, India was not facing a serious decline or a threat of a serious decline in monetary reserves as those terms are used in Article XVIII:9(a). In the event that it might be deemed relevant to add support to our findings concerning India's reserves as of November 1997, we have also examined the evolution of India's reserves after November 1997. We note that India's reserves fluctuated around the November level in subsequent months, falling to a low of US$23.9 billion in December 1997 and rising to a high of US$26.2 billion in April 1998. They were US$24.1 billion as of the end of June 1998.

5.178 The anticipated evolution of India's reserves after June 1998 shows that no serious decline was foreseen. Indeed, in response to a question as to whether there had been developments since November 1997 that could lead to a modification of the IMF's answers to the Panel's questions, the IMF responded:

"There has been a deterioration in the economic outlook and market sentiment over the past few months, and short-term risks have increased. [. . .] [O]n the basis of developments thus far, the balance-of-payments situation is expected to worsen and a decline in reserves ($2½-4 billion) is anticipated for 1998/99. Nevertheless, it remains the Fund view that the external situation can be managed using macroeconomic policy instruments and that quantitative restrictions are not needed for balance-of-payments adjustment."

Thus, not only the evolution until June 1998, but also assessments in relation to 1998 as a whole and 1999 support the view that no threat of serious decline existed as of November 1997.

5.179 As a result, the evolution of India's reserve situation in the seven months after November 1997 does not, in our view, call into question our conclusion that as of the date of the establishment of the Panel, India was not facing a serious decline or a threat of a serious decline in its monetary reserves as those terms are used in Article XVIII:9(a).

5.180 Accordingly, we find that as of the date of establishment of this Panel, there was not a serious decline or a threat of a serious decline in India's monetary reserves, as those terms are used in Article XVIII:9(a).

(ii) Article XVIII:9(b)

5.181 The issue to be decided under Article XVIII:9(b) is whether India's balance-of-payments measures fall into the category of those "necessary . . . in the case of a Member with inadequate monetary reserves, to achieve a reasonable rate of increase in its reserves". In deciding this issue, we must weigh the evidence favouring India against that favouring the United States and determine whether on the basis of all evidence before the Panel, the United States has established its claim under Article XVIII:11 that India does not meet the conditions specified in Article XVIII:9(b).

5.182   The United States relies upon the views of the IMF and the statement of the Reserve Bank of India, as cited in paragraph 5.170 above. As noted therein, in the view of the IMF, as of 18 November 1997 an adequate level of monetary reserves for India was US$16 billion. As noted above in paragraph 5.171, India suggests use of four other ways of measuring the adequacy of its reserves, which lead to a calculation of adequate reserves being between US$16 and US$28 billion.

5.183   For the reasons outlined in paragraphs 5.174-5.176 above, we find that as of the date of establishment of this Panel, India's monetary reserves of US$25.1 billion were not inadequate as that term is used in Article XVIII:9(b) and that India was therefore not entitled to implement balance-of-payments measures to achieve a reasonable rate of growth in its reserves.

(e) Summary

5.184   We find that, as of the date of establishment of this Panel, India's balance-of-payments measures were not necessary to forestall the threat of, or to stop, a serious decline in its monetary reserves and that its reserves were not inadequate. As a result, its measures were not necessary and therefore "exceed those necessary" under the terms of Article XVIII:9 (a) or (b). Therefore, India would appear to be in violation of the requirements of Article XVIII:11 by maintaining its measures. . . .

    . . . .

The panel therefore found that India's monetary reserves were adequate, and thus its restrictions were not 'necessary' under Article XVIII:9. As a result, the panel found a violation of Article XVIII:11. The panel then considered and rejected Indian arguments under an interpretive note to Article XVIII:11 and under the Article XVIII:11 proviso.

Special and differential treatment can also be seen in the more limited commitments made by developing countries in their GATT and GATS Schedules.[17] With regard to the GATT, Part IV, entitled 'Trade and Development', 'includes provisions on the concept of non-reciprocity in trade negotiations between developed and developing countries— when developed countries grant trade concessions to developing countries they should not expect the developing countries to make matching offers in return'.[18] The result is that developing countries have far fewer tariff lines that are bound (although that number was significantly increased as part of the Uruguay Round), as shown in Table 18.1.

Furthermore, developing countries have bound their tariffs at much higher rates on average than have developed countries, giving them flexibility to impose fairly high duties. In the agriculture sector, developing countries have committed to smaller percentage tariff reductions over a longer period of time than developed countries; and least developed countries were not required to make commitments at all.[19] Similarly, developing countries have made fewer GATS commitments. Thus, in the area of tariff concessions and services commitments, developing countries have less burdensome obligations than others.

On the other hand, despite the general incidence of lower tariffs in the developed world, rich countries maintain many of their highest barriers on the products of greatest export

---

[17] For the least developed countries WTO Agreement Art XI:2 explicitly provides for this: '[t]he least-developed countries recognized as such by the United Nations will only be required to undertake commitments and concessions to the extent consistent with their individual development, financial and trade needs or their administrative and institutional capabilities'.

[18] 'Understanding the WTO: Developing Countries: Overview', above n 13.

[19] 'Agriculture: Fairer Market for Farmers', available at www.wto.int/english/thewto_e/whatis_e/tif_e/agrm3_e.htm (accessed on 30 July 2007).

Table 18.1 Percentages of tariffs bound before and after the 1986–94 talks[a]

	Before	After
Developed countries	78	99
Developing countries	21	73
Transition economies[b]	73	98

[a]WTO, 'Goods Schedules, Members' Commitments',. available at www.wto.org/english/tratop_e/schedules_e/goods_schedules_e.htm (accessed on 15 May 2012).
[b]Transition economies are, generally speaking, former planned economies that are in the process of reducing the role of the state, so as to allow a greater role for the private sector.

interest to developing countries, such as textile and clothing products and agricultural products. As a result, despite some explicit favouritism towards developing countries, it is very difficult to judge the overall 'fairness' of the current system to them.

Finally, in addition to these scattered rules and policies, there is a specific mechanism established to promote the exports of developing countries: the Generalised System of Preferences (GSP). Under the GSP, rich countries are permitted to charge lower tariff rates on products imported from developing countries, even though this type of discrimination would normally violate the MFN principle. The goal of these preferences, of course, is to promote developing country exports, and thus industrialisation and income growth.

The origins of the GSP system are explained by the United Nations Conference on Trade and Development (UNCTAD) as follows:

> The idea of granting developing countries preferential tariff rates in the markets of industrialized countries was originally presented by Raúl Prebisch, the first Secretary-General of UNCTAD, at the first UNCTAD conference in 1964. The GSP was adopted at UNCTAD II in New Delhi in 1968.
>
> In 1971, the GATT Contracting Parties approved a waiver to Article I of the Agreement for 10 years in order to authorize the GSP scheme. Later, the Contracting Parties decided to adopt the 1979 Enabling Clause, Decision of the Contracting Parties of 28 November 1979 (26S/203) titled "Differential and More Favourable Treatment, Reciprocity and Fuller Participation of Developing Countries", creating a permanent waiver to the most-favoured-nation clause to allow preference-giving countries to grant preferential tariff treatment under their respective GSP schemes.
>
> There are currently 16 national GSP schemes notified to the UNCTAD secretariat. The following countries grant GSP schemes: Australia, Belarus, Bulgaria, Canada, the Czech Republic, the European Community, Hungary, Japan, New Zealand, Norway, Poland, the Russian Federation, the Slovak Republic, Switzerland, Turkey and the United States of America.[20]

As noted by UNCTAD, these schemes are run by individual governments. They are purely voluntary, as there is no requirement that they be undertaken. Nonetheless, most countries in the developed world maintain such a programme. A common feature of GSP systems is a 'graduation' mechanism. In essence, once a participating developing country

---

[20] UNCTAD, 'About GSP', available at www.unctad.org/Templates/Page.asp?intItemID=2309&lang=1 (accessed on 30 July 2007). See also Panel Report, *EC—Tariff Preferences*, para 7.64.

reaches a certain level of competitiveness for a particular industrial sector, it is no longer offered preferential treatment for these goods.[21]

As to the relevant WTO legal provisions relating to the use of GSP schemes, the UNCTAD summary quoted above refers to the 1971 GSP waiver and the 1979 Enabling Clause. The key provisions of the Enabling Clause are as follows:

1. Notwithstanding the provisions of Article I of the General Agreement, contracting parties may accord differential and more favourable treatment to developing countries, without according such treatment to other contracting parties.

2. The provisions of paragraph 1 apply to the following:

(a) Preferential tariff treatment accorded by developed contracting parties to products originating in developing countries in accordance with the Generalized System of Preferences,[3]

(b) Differential and more favourable treatment with respect to the provisions of the General Agreement concerning non-tariff measures governed by the provisions of instruments multilaterally negotiated under the auspices of the GATT;

(c) Regional or global arrangements entered into amongst less-developed contracting parties for the mutual reduction or elimination of tariffs and, in accordance with criteria or conditions which may be prescribed by the CONTRACTING PARTIES, for the mutual reduction or elimination of non-tariff measures, on products imported from one another;

(d) Special treatment on the least developed among the developing countries in the context of any general or specific measures in favour of developing countries.

3. Any differential and more favourable treatment provided under this clause:

(a) shall be designed to facilitate and promote the trade of developing countries and not to raise barriers to or create undue difficulties for the trade of any other contracting parties;

(b) shall not constitute an impediment to the reduction or elimination of tariffs and other restrictions to trade on a most-favoured-nation basis;

(c) shall in the case of such treatment accorded by developed contracting parties to developing countries be designed and, if necessary, modified, to respond positively to the development, financial and trade needs of developing countries.

[Fn. 3] As described in the Decision of the CONTRACTING PARTIES of 25 June 1971, relating to the establishment of "generalized, non-reciprocal and non discriminatory preferences beneficial to the developing countries" (BISD 18S/24).

In essence, the Enabling Clause permits WTO Members to provide better treatment to developing countries than to others, through actions that would otherwise violate GATT Article I:1. However, as a dispute relating to the EC GSP programme demonstrates, the exact parameters have been the subject of disagreement.

The *EC—Tariff Preferences* dispute was based on a complaint by India regarding certain aspects of the EC's GSP scheme as it stood from 1 January 2002 to 31 December 2004. The EC Regulation setting out the scheme[22] provided for five different tariff preference arrangements: (i) the General Arrangements; (ii) the Special Incentive Arrangements for

---

[21] See S Lester, 'The Asian Newly Industrialized Countries to Graduate from Europe's GSP Tariffs' (1995) 36 *Harvard International Law Journal* 220.

[22] EC Council Reg 2501/2001 [2001] OJ L346/1.

the protection of labour rights; (iii) the Special Incentive Arrangements for the protection of the environment; (iv) the Special Arrangements for least-developed countries; and (v) the Special Arrangements to combat drug production and trafficking (the 'Drug Arrangements'). Tariff preferences under the General Arrangements were the standard preferences that were offered to developing countries. The additional preferences under the Special Incentive Arrangements for the protection of labour rights and the protection of the environment were provided 'exclusively to countries which are determined by the European Communities to comply with certain labour and environmental policy standards'; the additional preferences under the Special Arrangements for least-developed countries were limited to the least-developed countries listed in Annex I to the Regulation. Finally, the preferences in the Drug Arrangements were awarded to certain countries determined by the European Communities to have problems controlling drug production and trafficking. India's complaint was based on this last aspect of the Regulation.[23]

With regard to the Drug Arrangements, Article 10 of the EC Regulation was entitled 'Special arrangements to combat drug production and trafficking'. The benefits under the Drug Arrangements applied to the following 12 countries: Bolivia, Colombia, Costa Rica, Ecuador, El Salvador, Guatemala, Honduras, Nicaragua, Pakistan, Panama, Peru and Venezuela. Thus, the beneficiaries were 11 South and Latin American countries, as well as Pakistan. India's concern was with the inclusion of Pakistan, with which its exports often compete (the inclusion of Pakistan was said to be as a reward for its cooperation in efforts to fight terrorism[24]).

Through the Drug Arrangements, the tariff reductions accorded to the 12 beneficiary countries were greater than the tariff reductions granted under the General Arrangements to other developing countries. For example, in respect of products that were included in the Drug Arrangements but not in the General Arrangements, the 12 beneficiary countries were granted *duty free* access to the EC market, while all other developing countries were required to pay the *full applicable duties*. As to products that were included in both the Drug Arrangements and the General Arrangements and that were deemed 'sensitive', the 12 beneficiary countries were granted *duty free* access to the EC market, while all other developing countries were entitled only to *duty reductions*.[25]

India claimed that the Drug Arrangements were 'inconsistent with GATT Article I:1' and were 'not justified by the Enabling Clause'. A majority of the panel[26] agreed with India on both counts. With regard to the Enabling Clause, the panel first found that the term 'non-discriminatory' in footnote 3 requires that '*identical* tariff preferences under GSP schemes be provided to *all* developing countries without differentiation' (emphasis added) except for the implementation of *a priori* limitations (ie import ceilings on certain imports where the products concerned reach a certain competitive level in the market of the preference-giving country) and the treatment of the least developed countries.[27] In

---

[23] In its panel request, India also made claims against the labour and environmental conditions, but these claims were withdrawn: see Panel Report, *EC—Tariff Preferences*, para 1.5.

[24] G Shaffer and Y Apea, 'Institutional Choice in the General System of Preferences Case: Who Decides the Conditions for Trade Preferences? The Law and Politics of Rights' (2005) 39 *Journal of World Trade* 977.

[25] Panel Report, *EC—Tariff Preferences*, paras 2.1–2.8.

[26] In a rare dissent, one panelist concluded that the dispute should have been brought as a complaint under the Enabling Clause rather than GATT Art I, and, because the complaint was not set out this way, the dissenting panelist concluded that it should be rejected. Panel Report, *EC—Tariff Preferences*, paras 9.1–9.21.

[27] *Ibid*, paras 7.117–7.176.

other words, the exceptions aside, if Pakistan and the other beneficiaries receive a duty exemption then India and all other developing country Members must receive it as well.

Turning to the measure at issue, the panel then found, inter alia, that 'the European Communities' Drug Arrangements, as a GSP scheme, do not provide identical tariff preferences to *all* developing countries and . . . the differentiation is neither for the purpose of special treatment to the least-developed countries, nor in the context of the implementation of a priori measures'. Such differentiation, it said, 'is inconsistent with paragraph 2(a), particularly the term "non-discriminatory" in footnote 3'[28] (earlier, in the context of GATT Article I:1, the panel had stated: '[t]he fact is clear that the tariff preferences granted by the European Communities to the products originating in the 12 beneficiary countries are not accorded to the like products originating in all other Members, including those originating in India'[29]).

On appeal, the EC challenged three of the Panel's findings:

(a) 'the term 'non-discriminatory' in footnote 3 [to paragraph 2(a) of the Enabling Clause] requires that identical tariff preferences under GSP schemes be provided to all developing countries without differentiation, except for the implementation of a priori limitations';

(b) 'the term 'developing countries' in paragraph 2(a) [of the Enabling Clause] should be interpreted to mean *all* developing countries, with the exception that where developed countries are implementing a priori limitations, 'developing countries' may mean *less than all* developing countries'; and

(c) the European Communities failed 'to demonstrate that the Drug Arrangements are justified under paragraph 2(a) of the Enabling Clause'.[30]

The Appellate Body addressed the key aspects of this appeal as follows:

Appellate Body Report, *European Communities—Conditions for the Granting of Tariff Preferences to Developing Countries*, Adopted 20 April 2004, WT/DS246/AB/R

B. Interpretation of the Term "Non-Discriminatory" in Footnote 3 to Paragraph 2(a) of the Enabling Clause

142. We proceed to interpret the term "non-discriminatory" as it appears in footnote 3 to paragraph 2(a) of the Enabling Clause.

143. We recall first that the Enabling Clause has become a part of the GATT 1994. Paragraph 1 of the Enabling Clause authorizes WTO Members to provide "differential and more favourable treatment to developing countries, without according such treatment to other WTO Members". As explained above, such differential treatment is permitted "notwithstanding" the provisions of Article I of the GATT 1994. Paragraph 2(a) and footnote 3 thereto clarify that paragraph 1 applies to "[p]referential tariff treatment accorded by developed contracting parties to products originating in developing countries in accordance with the Generalized System of Preferences", "[a]s described in the [1971 Waiver Decision], relating to the establishment of 'generalized, non-reciprocal and non discriminatory preferences beneficial to the developing countries'".

---

[28] *Ibid*, para 7.177.
[29] *Ibid*, para 7.58.
[30] *Ibid*, para 8.1(d).

144. The Preamble to the 1971 Waiver Decision in turn refers to "preferential tariff treatment" in the following terms:

> *Recalling* that at the Second UNCTAD, unanimous agreement was reached in favour of the early establishment of a mutually acceptable system of *generalized, non-reciprocal and non-discriminatory* preferences beneficial to the developing countries in order to increase the export earnings, to promote thefyyg industrialization, and to accelerate the rates of economic growth of these countries;

> *Considering* that mutually acceptable arrangements have been drawn up in the UNCTAD concerning the establishment of *generalized, non-discriminatory, non-reciprocal preferential tariff treatment* in the markets of developed countries for products originating in developing countries[.] (original italics; underlining added)

145. Paragraph 2(a) of the Enabling Clause provides, therefore, that, to be justified under that provision, preferential tariff treatment must be "in accordance" with the GSP "as described" in the *Preamble* to the 1971 Waiver Decision. "Accordance" being defined in the dictionary as "conformity", only preferential tariff treatment that is in conformity with the description "generalized, non-reciprocal and non-discriminatory" treatment can be justified under paragraph 2(a).

146. In the light of the above, we do not agree with European Communities' assertion that the Panel's interpretation of the word "non-discriminatory" in footnote 3 of the Enabling Clause is erroneous because the phrase "generalized, non-reciprocal and non discriminatory" in footnote 3 merely refers to the description of the GSP in the 1971 Waiver Decision and, of itself, does not impose any legal obligation on preference-granting countries. Nor do we agree with the United States that the Panel erred in "assum[ing]" that the term "non-discriminatory" in footnote 3 imposes obligations on preference-granting countries, and that, instead, footnote 3 "is simply a cross-reference to where the Generalized System of Preferences is described."

147. We find support for our interpretation in the French version of paragraph 2(a) of the Enabling Clause, requiring that the tariff preferences be accorded "*conformément au Système généralisé de préférences*". The term "in accordance" is thus "*conformément*" in the French version. In addition, the phrase "[a]s described in [the 1971 Waiver Decision]" in footnote 3 is stated as "*[t]el qu'il est défini dans la décision des PARTIES CONTRACTANTES en date du 25 juin 1971*". Similarly, the Spanish version uses the terms "*conformidad*" and "*[t]al como lo define la Decisión de las PARTES CONTRATANTES de 25 de junio de 1971*". In our view, the stronger, more obligatory language in both the French and Spanish texts—that is, using "as defined in" rather than "as described in"—lends support to our view that only preferential tariff treatment that is "generalized, non-reciprocal and non-discriminatory" is covered under paragraph 2(a) of the Enabling Clause.

148. Having found that the qualification of the GSP as "generalized, non-reciprocal and non discriminatory" imposes obligations that must be fulfilled for preferential tariff treatment to be justified under paragraph 2(a), we turn to address the Panel's finding that:

> . . . the term "non-discriminatory" in footnote 3 requires that *identical* tariff preferences under GSP schemes be provided to *all* developing countries without differentiation, except for the implementation of a priori limitations. (emphasis added)

149. The European Communities maintains that "'non-discrimination' is not synonymous with formally equal treatment" and that "[t]reating differently situations which are objectively different is not discriminatory." The European Communities asserts that "[t]he objective of the Enabling Clause is different from that of Article I:1 of the GATT." In its view, the latter is concerned with "providing equal conditions of competition for imports of like products originating in

all Members", whereas "the Enabling Clause is a form of Special and Differential Treatment for developing countries, which seeks the opposite result: to create unequal competitive opportunities in order to respond to the special needs of developing countries." The European Communities derives contextual support from paragraph 3(c), which states that the treatment provided under the Enabling Clause "shall . . . be designed and, if necessary, modified, to respond positively to the development, financial and trade needs of developing countries." The European Communities concludes that the term "non-discriminatory" in footnote 3 "does not prevent the preference-giving countries from differentiating between developing countries which have different development needs, where tariff differentiation constitutes an adequate response to such differences."

150.   India, in contrast, asserts that "non-discrimination in respect of tariff measures refers to formally equal [] treatment" and that paragraph 2(a) of the Enabling Clause requires that "preferential tariff treatment [be] applied equally" among developing countries. In support of its argument, India submits that an interpretation of paragraph 2(a) of the Enabling Clause that authorizes developed countries to provide "discriminatory tariff treatment *in favour of the developing countries* but not *between the developing countries* gives full effect to both Article I of the GATT and paragraph 2(a) of the Enabling Clause and minimises the conflict between them." India emphasizes that, by consenting to the adoption of the Enabling Clause, developing countries did not "relinquish [] their MFN rights [under Article I of the GATT 1994] as between themselves, thus permitting developed countries to discriminate between them."

151.   We examine now the ordinary meaning of the term "non-discriminatory" in footnote 3 to paragraph 2(a) of the Enabling Clause. As we observed, footnote 3 requires that GSP schemes under the Enabling Clause be "generalized, non-reciprocal and non discriminatory". Before the Panel, the participants offered competing definitions of the word "discriminate". India suggested that this word means "'to make or constitute a difference in or between; distinguish' and 'to make a distinction in the treatment of different categories of peoples or things'." The European Communities, however, understood this word to mean "'to make a distinction in the treatment of different categories of people or things, esp. *unjustly* or *prejudicially* against people on grounds of race, colour, sex, social status, age, etc'. "

152.   Both definitions can be considered as reflecting ordinary meanings of the term "discriminate" and essentially exhaust the relevant ordinary meanings. The principal distinction between these definitions, as the Panel noted, is that India's conveys a "*neutral* meaning of making a distinction", whereas the European Communities' conveys a "*negative* meaning carrying the connotation of a distinction that is unjust or prejudicial." Accordingly, the ordinary meanings of "discriminate" point in conflicting directions with respect to the propriety of according differential treatment. Under India's reading, any differential treatment of GSP beneficiaries would be prohibited, because such treatment necessarily makes a distinction between beneficiaries. In contrast, under the European Communities' reading, differential treatment of GSP beneficiaries would not be prohibited *per se*. Rather, distinctions would be impermissible only where the basis for such distinctions was improper. Given these divergent meanings, we do not regard the term "non-discriminatory", on its own, as determinative of the permissibility of a preference-granting country according different tariff preferences to different beneficiaries of its GSP scheme.

153.   Nevertheless, at this stage of our analysis, we are able to discern some of the content of the "non-discrimination" obligation based on the ordinary meanings of that term. Whether the drawing of distinctions is *per se* discriminatory, or whether it is discriminatory only if done on an improper basis, the ordinary meanings of "discriminate" converge in one important respect: they both suggest that distinguishing among similarly-situated beneficiaries is discriminatory. For example, India suggests that all beneficiaries of a particular Member's GSP scheme are

similarly-situated, implicitly arguing that any differential treatment of such beneficiaries constitutes discrimination. The European Communities, however, appears to regard GSP beneficiaries as similarly-situated when they have "similar development needs". Although the European Communities acknowledges that differentiating between similarly-situated GSP beneficiaries would be inconsistent with footnote 3 of the Enabling Clause, it submits that there is no inconsistency in differentiating between GSP beneficiaries with "different development needs". Thus, based on the ordinary meanings of "discriminate", India and the European Communities effectively appear to agree that, pursuant to the term "non-discriminatory" in footnote 3, similarly-situated GSP beneficiaries should not be treated differently. The participants disagree only as to the basis for determining whether beneficiaries are similarly-situated.

154. Paragraph 2(a), on its face, does not explicitly authorize or prohibit the granting of different tariff preferences to different GSP beneficiaries. It is clear from the ordinary meanings of "non-discriminatory", however, that preference-granting countries must make available identical tariff preferences to all similarly-situated beneficiaries.

155. We continue our interpretive analysis by turning to the immediate context of the term "non-discriminatory". We note first that footnote 3 to paragraph 2(a) stipulates that, in addition to being "non-discriminatory", tariff preferences provided under GSP schemes must be "generalized". According to the ordinary meaning of that term, tariff preferences provided under GSP schemes must be "generalized" in the sense that they "apply more generally; [or] become extended in application". However, this ordinary meaning alone may not reflect the entire significance of the word "generalized" in the context of footnote 3 of the Enabling Clause, particularly because that word resulted from lengthy negotiations leading to the GSP. In this regard, we note the Panel's finding that, by requiring tariff preferences under the GSP to be "generalized", developed and developing countries together sought to eliminate existing "special" preferences that were granted only to certain designated developing countries. Similarly, in response to our questioning at the oral hearing, the participants agreed that one of the objectives of the 1971 Waiver Decision and the Enabling Clause was to eliminate the fragmented system of special preferences that were, in general, based on historical and political ties between developed countries and their former colonies.

156. It does not necessarily follow, however, that "non-discriminatory" should be interpreted to require that preference-granting countries provide "identical" tariff preferences under GSP schemes to "all" developing countries. In concluding otherwise, the Panel assumed that allowing tariff preferences such as the Drug Arrangements would necessarily "result [in] the collapse of the whole GSP system and a return back to special preferences favouring selected developing countries". To us, this conclusion is unwarranted. We observe that the term "generalized" requires that the GSP schemes of preference-granting countries remain generally applicable. Moreover, unlike the Panel, we believe that the Enabling Clause sets out sufficient conditions on the granting of preferences to protect against such an outcome. As we discuss below, provisions such as paragraphs 3(a) and 3(c) of the Enabling Clause impose specific conditions on the granting of different tariff preferences among GSP beneficiaries.

157. As further context for the term "non-discriminatory" in footnote 3, we turn next to paragraph 3(c) of the Enabling Clause, which specifies that "differential and more favourable treatment" provided under the Enabling Clause:

> . . . shall in the case of such treatment accorded by developed contracting parties to developing countries be designed and, if necessary, modified, to respond positively to the development, financial and trade needs of developing countries.

158. At the outset, we note that the use of the word "shall" in paragraph 3(c) suggests that paragraph 3(c) sets out an obligation for developed-country Members in providing preferential

treatment under a GSP scheme to "respond positively" to the "needs of developing countries". Having said this, we turn to consider whether the "development, financial and trade needs of developing countries" to which preference-granting countries are required to respond when granting preferences must be understood to cover the "needs" of developing countries *collectively*.

159.   The Panel found that "the only appropriate way [under paragraph 3(c) of the Enabling Clause] of responding to the differing development needs of developing countries is for preference-giving countries to ensure that their [GSP] schemes have sufficient breadth of product coverage and depth of tariff cuts to respond positively to those differing needs." In reaching this conclusion, the Panel appears to have placed a great deal of significance on the fact that paragraph 3(c) does not refer to needs of "*individual*" developing countries. The Panel thus understood that paragraph 3(c) does not permit the granting of preferential tariff treatment exclusively to a sub-category of developing countries on the basis of needs that are common to or shared by only those developing countries. We see no basis for such a conclusion in the text of paragraph 3(c). Paragraph 3(c) refers generally to "the development, financial and trade needs of developing countries". The absence of an explicit requirement in the text of paragraph 3(c) to respond to the needs of "all" developing countries, or to the needs of "each and every" developing country, suggests to us that, in fact, that provision imposes no such obligation.

160.   Furthermore, as we understand it, the participants in this case agree that developing countries may have "development, financial and trade needs" that are subject to change and that certain development needs may be common to only a certain number of developing countries. We see no reason to disagree. Indeed, paragraph 3(c) contemplates that "differential and more favourable treatment" accorded by developed to developing countries may need to be "modified" in order to "respond positively" to the needs of developing countries. Paragraph 7 of the Enabling Clause supports this view by recording the expectation of "less-developed contracting parties" that their capacity to make contributions or concessions under the GATT will "improve with the progressive development of their economies and improvement in their trade situation". Moreover, the very purpose of the special and differential treatment permitted under the Enabling Clause is to foster economic development of developing countries. It is simply unrealistic to assume that such development will be in lockstep for all developing countries at once, now and for the future.

161.   In addition, the Preamble to the *WTO Agreement*, which informs all the covered agreements including the GATT 1994 (and, hence, the Enabling Clause), explicitly recognizes the "need for positive efforts designed to ensure that developing countries, and especially the least developed among them, secure a share in the growth in international trade commensurate with the needs of their economic development". The word "commensurate" in this phrase appears to leave open the possibility that developing countries may have different needs according to their levels of development and particular circumstances. The Preamble to the *WTO Agreement* further recognizes that Members' "respective needs and concerns at different levels of economic development" may vary according to the different stages of development of different Members.

162.   In sum, we read paragraph 3(c) as authorizing preference-granting countries to "respond positively" to "needs" that are *not* necessarily common or shared by all developing countries. Responding to the "needs of developing countries" may thus entail treating different developing-country beneficiaries differently.

163.   However, paragraph 3(c) does not authorize *any* kind of response to *any* claimed need of developing countries. First, we observe that the types of needs to which a response is envisaged are limited to "development, financial and trade needs". In our view, a "need" cannot be characterized as one of the specified "needs of developing countries" in the sense of

paragraph 3(c) based merely on an assertion to that effect by, for instance, a preference-granting country or a beneficiary country. Rather, when a claim of inconsistency with paragraph 3(c) is made, the existence of a "development, financial [or] trade need" must be assessed according to an *objective* standard. Broad-based recognition of a particular need, set out in the *WTO Agreement* or in multilateral instruments adopted by international organizations, could serve as such a standard.

164.   Secondly, paragraph 3(c) mandates that the response provided to the needs of developing countries be "positive". "Positive" is defined as "consisting in or characterized by constructive action or attitudes". This suggests that the response of a preference-granting country must be taken with a view to *improving* the development, financial or trade situation of a beneficiary country, based on the particular need at issue. As such, in our view, the expectation that developed countries will "respond positively" to the "needs of developing countries" suggests that a sufficient nexus should exist between, on the one hand, the preferential treatment provided under the respective measure authorized by paragraph 2, and, on the other hand, the likelihood of alleviating the relevant "development, financial [or] trade need". In the context of a GSP scheme, the particular need at issue must, by its nature, be such that it can be effectively addressed through tariff preferences. Therefore, only if a preference-granting country acts in the "positive" manner suggested, in "respon[se]" to a widely-recognized "development, financial [or] trade need", can such action satisfy the requirements of paragraph 3(c).

165.   Accordingly, we are of the view that, by requiring developed countries to "respond positively" to the "needs of developing countries", which are varied and not homogeneous, paragraph 3(c) indicates that a GSP scheme may be "non-discriminatory" even if "identical" tariff treatment is not accorded to "all" GSP beneficiaries. Moreover, paragraph 3(c) suggests that tariff preferences under GSP schemes may be "non-discriminatory" when the relevant tariff preferences are addressed to a particular "development, financial [or] trade need" and are made available to all beneficiaries that share that need.

166.   India submits that developing countries should not be presumed to have waived their MFN rights under Article I:1 of the GATT 1994 *vis-à-vis* other developing countries , and we make no such presumption. In fact, we note that the Enabling Clause *specifically* allows developed countries to provide differential and more favourable treatment to developing countries "notwithstanding" the provisions of Article I. With this in mind, and given that paragraph 3(c) of the Enabling Clause contemplates, in certain circumstances, differentiation among GSP beneficiaries, we cannot agree with India that the right to MFN treatment can be invoked by a GSP beneficiary *vis-à-vis* other GSP beneficiaries in the context of GSP schemes that meet the conditions set out in the Enabling Clause.

167.   Finally, we note that, pursuant to paragraph 3(a) of the Enabling Clause, any "differential and more favourable treatment . . . shall be designed to facilitate and promote the trade of developing countries and not to raise barriers to or create undue difficulties for the trade of any other contracting parties." This requirement applies, *a fortiori*, to any preferential treatment granted to one GSP beneficiary that is not granted to another. Thus, although paragraph 2(a) does not prohibit *per se* the granting of different tariff preferences to different GSP beneficiaries , and paragraph 3(c) even contemplates such differentiation under certain circumstances , paragraph 3(a) requires that any positive response of a preference-granting country to the varying needs of developing countries not impose unjustifiable burdens on other Members.

168.   Having examined the context of paragraph 2(a), we turn next to examine the object and purpose of the *WTO Agreement*. We note first that paragraph 7 of the Enabling Clause provides that "[t]he concessions and contributions made and the obligations assumed by developed and less-developed contracting parties under the provisions of the [GATT 1994] should promote

the basic objectives of the [GATT 1994], including those embodied in the Preamble". As we have observed, the Preamble to the *WTO Agreement* provides that there is "need for positive efforts designed to ensure that developing countries, and especially the least developed among them, secure a share in the growth in international trade commensurate with the needs of their economic development". Similarly, the Preamble to the 1971 Waiver Decision provides that "a principal aim of the CONTRACTING PARTIES is promotion of the trade and export earnings of developing countries for the furtherance of their economic development". These objectives are also reflected in paragraph 3(c) of the Enabling Clause, which states that the treatment provided under the Enabling Clause "shall . . . be designed and, if necessary, modified, to respond positively to the development, financial and trade needs of developing countries".

169.   Although enhanced market access will contribute to responding to the needs of developing countries *collectively*, we have also recognized that the needs of developing countries may vary over time. We are of the view that the objective of improving developing countries' "share in the growth in international trade", and their "trade and export earnings", can be fulfilled by promoting preferential policies aimed at those interests that developing countries have in common, *as well as* at those interests shared by sub-categories of developing countries based on their particular needs. An interpretation of "non-discriminatory" that does not require the granting of "identical tariff preferences" allows not only for GSP schemes providing preferential market access to all beneficiaries, but also the possibility of additional preferences for developing countries with particular needs, provided that such additional preferences are not inconsistent with other provisions of the Enabling Clause, including the requirements that such preferences be "generalized" and "non-reciprocal". We therefore consider such an interpretation to be consistent with the object and purpose of the *WTO Agreement* and the Enabling Clause.

170.   The Panel took the view, however, that the objective of "elimination of discriminatory treatment in international commerce" , found in the Preamble to the GATT 1994, "contributes more to guiding the interpretation of 'non-discriminatory'" than does the objective of ensuring that developing countries "secure . . . a share in the growth in international trade commensurate with their development needs." We fail to see on what basis the Panel drew this conclusion.

171.   We next examine the relevance of paragraph 2(d) of the Enabling Clause for the interpretation of "non-discriminatory" in footnote 3. The Panel characterized paragraph 2(d) as an "exception" to paragraph 2(a) and relied on paragraph 2(d) to support its view that paragraph 2(a) requires "formally identical treatment". In the Panel's view, if developed-country Members were entitled under paragraph 2(a) to differentiate between developing-country Members, then they would have been entitled under that paragraph alone to differentiate between developing and least-developed countries. Accordingly, "there would have been no need to include paragraph 2(d) in the Enabling Clause."

172.   We do not agree with the Panel that paragraph 2(d) is an "exception" to paragraph 2(a), or that it is rendered redundant if paragraph 2(a) is interpreted as allowing developed countries to differentiate in their GSP schemes between developing countries. To begin with, we note that the terms of paragraph 2 do not expressly indicate that each of the four sub-paragraphs thereunder is mutually exclusive, or that any one is an exception to any other. Moreover, in our view, it is clear from several provisions of the Enabling Clause that the drafters wished to emphasize that least-developed countries form an identifiable sub-category of developing countries with "special economic difficulties and . . . particular development, financial and trade needs". When a developed-country Member grants tariff preferences in favour of developing countries under paragraph 2(a), as we have already found, footnote 3 imposes a requirement that such preferences be "non-discriminatory". In the absence of paragraph 2(d), a Member granting preferential tariff treatment only to least-developed countries would therefore need to establish, under paragraph 2(a), that this preferential treatment did not "discriminate" against other

developing countries contrary to footnote 3. The inclusion of paragraph 2(d), however, makes clear that developed countries may accord preferential treatment to least-developed countries distinct from the preferences granted to other developing countries under paragraph 2(a). Thus, pursuant to paragraph 2(d), preference-granting countries need not establish that differentiating between developing and least-developed countries is "non-discriminatory". This demonstrates that paragraph 2(d) does have an effect that is different and independent from that of paragraph 2(a), even if the term "non-discriminatory" does not require the granting of "identical tariff preferences" to all GSP beneficiaries.

173.   Having examined the text and context of footnote 3 to paragraph 2(a) of the Enabling Clause, and the object and purpose of the *WTO Agreement* and the Enabling Clause, we conclude that the term "non-discriminatory" in footnote 3 does not prohibit developed-country Members from granting different tariffs to products originating in different GSP beneficiaries, provided that such differential tariff treatment meets the remaining conditions in the Enabling Clause. In granting such differential tariff treatment, however, preference-granting countries are required, by virtue of the term "non-discriminatory", to ensure that identical treatment is available to all similarly-situated GSP beneficiaries, that is, to all GSP beneficiaries that have the "development, financial and trade needs" to which the treatment in question is intended to respond.

174.   For all of these reasons, we *reverse* the Panel's finding, in paragraphs 7.161 and 7.176 of the Panel Report, that "the term 'non-discriminatory' in footnote 3 [to paragraph 2(a) of the Enabling Clause] requires that identical tariff preferences under GSP schemes be provided to all developing countries without differentiation, except for the implementation of a priori limitations."

C. The Words "Developing Countries" in Paragraph 2(a) of the Enabling Clause

175.   In addition to the Panel's interpretation of the term "non-discriminatory" in footnote 3 of the Enabling Clause, the European Communities appeals the Panel's finding that "the term 'developing countries' in paragraph 2(a) should be interpreted to mean *all* developing countries, [except as regards] a priori limitations". The Panel's interpretation of paragraph 2(a) is premised on its findings that (i) footnote 3 permits the granting of different tariff preferences to different GSP beneficiaries *only* for the purpose of *a priori* limitations , and (ii) paragraph 3(c) permits the granting of different tariff preferences to different GSP beneficiaries *only* for the purposes of *a priori* limitations and preferential treatment in favour of least-developed countries. We have concluded, contrary to the Panel, that footnote 3 and paragraph 3(c) do *not* preclude the granting of differential tariffs to different sub-categories of GSP beneficiaries, subject to compliance with the remaining conditions of the Enabling Clause. We find, therefore, that the term "developing countries" in paragraph 2(a) should not be read to mean "all" developing countries and, accordingly, that paragraph 2(a) does not prohibit preference-granting countries from according different tariff preferences to different sub-categories of GSP beneficiaries.

176.   Accordingly, we also *reverse* the Panel's finding, in paragraph 7.174 of the Panel Report, that "the term 'developing countries' in paragraph 2(a) [of the Enabling Clause] should be interpreted to mean *all* developing countries, with the exception that where developed countries are implementing a priori limitations, 'developing countries' may mean *less than all* developing countries."

D. Consistency of the Drug Arrangements with the Enabling Clause

177.   We turn next to examine the consistency of the Drug Arrangements with the Enabling Clause.

178.   We recall that, with respect to the Enabling Clause, the only challenge by India before the Panel related to paragraph 2(a) and, in particular, footnote 3 thereto. In response, the European Communities argued that it found contextual support for its interpretation of paragraph 2(a) in the requirement, contained in paragraph 3(c), to respond positively to the needs of developing countries. In rejecting the European Communities' interpretation of paragraph 2(a), the Panel did not determine whether the Drug Arrangements satisfy the conditions set out in paragraph 3(c), but, rather, limited its discussion of paragraph 3(c) to the relevance of that provision as context for its interpretation of paragraph 2(a). Thus, the Panel made a finding of inconsistency only with respect to paragraph 2(a) of the Enabling Clause. The European Communities appeals this finding of inconsistency with paragraph 2(a).

179.   Although paragraph 3(c) informs the interpretation of the term "non-discriminatory" in footnote 3 to paragraph 2(a), as detailed above , paragraph 3(c) imposes requirements that are separate and distinct from those of paragraph 2(a). We have already concluded that, where a developed-country Member provides additional tariff preferences under its GSP scheme to respond positively to widely-recognized "development, financial and trade needs" of developing countries within the meaning of paragraph 3(c) of the Enabling Clause, this "positive response" would not, as such, fail to comply with the "non-discriminatory" requirement in footnote 3 of the Enabling Clause , even if such needs were not common or shared by all developing countries. We have also observed that paragraph 3(a) requires that any positive response of a preference-granting country to the varying needs of developing countries not impose unjustifiable burdens on other Members. With these considerations in mind, and recalling that the Panel made no finding in this case as to whether the Drug Arrangements are inconsistent with paragraphs 3(a) and 3(c) of the Enabling Clause , we limit our analysis here to paragraph 2(a) and do not examine *per se* whether the Drug Arrangements are consistent with the obligation contained in paragraph 3(c) to "respond positively to the development, financial and trade needs of developing countries" or with the obligation contained in paragraph 3(a) not to "raise barriers" or "create undue difficulties" for the trade of other Members.

180.   We found above that the term "non-discriminatory" in footnote 3 to paragraph 2(a) of the Enabling Clause does not prohibit the granting of different tariffs to products originating in different sub-categories of GSP beneficiaries, but that identical tariff treatment must be available to all GSP beneficiaries with the "development, financial [or] trade need" to which the differential treatment is intended to respond. The need alleged to be addressed by the European Communities' differential tariff treatment is the problem of illicit drug production and trafficking in certain GSP beneficiaries. In the context of this case, therefore, the Drug Arrangements may be found consistent with the "non-discriminatory" requirement in footnote 3 only if the European Communities proves, at a minimum, that the preferences granted under the Drug Arrangements are available to all GSP beneficiaries that are similarly affected by the drug problem. We do not believe this to be the case.

181.   By their very terms, the Drug Arrangements are limited to the 12 developing countries designated as beneficiaries in Annex I to the Regulation. Specifically, Article 10.1 of the Regulation states:

> Common Customs Tariff ad valorem duties on [covered products] which originate in a country that according to Column I of Annex I benefits from [the Drug Arrangements] shall be entirely suspended.

182.   Articles 10 and 25 of the Regulation, which relate specifically to the Drug Arrangements, provide no mechanism under which additional beneficiaries may be added to the list of beneficiaries under the Drug Arrangements as designated in Annex I. Nor does any of the other Articles of the Regulation point to the existence of such a mechanism with respect to the

Drug Arrangements. Moreover, the European Communities acknowledged the absence of such a mechanism in response to our questioning at the oral hearing. This contrasts with the position under the "special incentive arrangements for the protection of labour rights" and the "special incentive arrangements for the protection of the environment", which are described in Article 8 of the Regulation. The Regulation includes detailed provisions setting out the procedure and substantive criteria that apply to a request by a beneficiary under the general arrangements described in Article 7 of the Regulation (the "General Arrangements") to become a beneficiary under either of those special incentive arrangements.

183.   What is more, the Drug Arrangements themselves do *not* set out any clear prerequisites —or "objective criteria" —that, if met, would allow for other developing countries "that are similarly affected by the drug problem" to be *included* as beneficiaries under the Drug Arrangements. Indeed, the European Commission's own Explanatory Memorandum notes that "the benefits of the drug regime . . . are given without *any* prerequisite." Similarly, the Regulation offers no criteria according to which a beneficiary could be *removed* specifically from the Drug Arrangements on the basis that it is no longer "similarly affected by the drug problem". Indeed, Article 25.3 expressly states that the evaluation of the effects of the Drug Arrangements described in Articles 25.1(b) and 25.2 "will be without prejudice to the continuation of the [Drug Arrangements] until 2004, and their possible extension thereafter." This implies that, even if the European Commission found that the Drug Arrangements were having no effect whatsoever on a beneficiary's "efforts in combating drug production and trafficking" , or that a beneficiary was no longer suffering from the drug problem, beneficiary status would continue. Therefore, even if the Regulation allowed for the list of beneficiaries under the Drug Arrangements to be modified, the Regulation itself gives no indication as to how the beneficiaries under the Drug Arrangements were chosen or what kind of considerations would or could be used to determine the effect of the "drug problem" on a particular country. In addition, we note that the Regulation does not, for instance, provide any indication as to how the European Communities would assess whether the Drug Arrangements provide an "adequate and proportionate response" to the needs of developing countries suffering from the drug problem.

184.   It is true that a country may be removed as a beneficiary under Annex I, either altogether or in respect of certain product sectors, for reasons that are not specific to the Drug Arrangements. Thus, Article 3 of the Regulation provides for the removal of a country from Annex I (and hence, from the General Arrangements and any other arrangements under which it is a beneficiary) if particular circumstances are met indicating that the country has reached a certain level of development. Article 12 provides for the removal of a country as a beneficiary under the General Arrangements and the Drug Arrangements with respect to a product sector where the country's level of development and competition has reached a certain threshold with respect to that sector. Neither Article 3 nor Article 12 appears to relate in any way to the degree to which the country is suffering from the "drug problem". Finally, Title V to the Regulation contains certain "Temporary Withdrawal and Safeguard Provisions" that are common to all the preferential arrangements under the Regulation. Although one reason for which the arrangements may be temporarily withdrawn is "shortcomings in customs controls on export or transit of drugs (illicit substances or precursors), or failure to comply with international conventions on money laundering" , this reason applies equally to the General Arrangements, the Drug Arrangements, and the other special incentive arrangements. Moreover, as the Panel appeared to recognize, this condition is not connected to the question of whether the beneficiary is a "seriously drug-affected country".

185.   We note, moreover, that the Drug Arrangements will be in effect until 31 December 2004. Until that time, other developing countries that are "similarly affected by the drug problem" can be included as beneficiaries under the Drug Arrangements only through an amendment

to the Regulation. The European Communities confirmed this understanding in response to questioning at the oral hearing.

186.   Against this background, we fail to see how the Drug Arrangements can be distinguished from other schemes that the European Communities describes as "confined *ab initio* and permanently to a limited number of developing countries". As we understand it, the European Communities' position is that such schemes would be discriminatory, whereas the Drug Arrangements are not because "all developing countries are potentially beneficiaries" thereof. In seeking a waiver from its obligations under Article I:1 of the GATT 1994 to implement the Drug Arrangements, the European Communities explicitly acknowledged, however, that "[b]ecause the special arrangements *are only available* to imports originating in [the 12 beneficiaries of the Drug Arrangements], a waiver . . . appears necessary". This statement appears to undermine the European Communities' argument that "all developing countries are potentially beneficiaries of the Drug Arrangements" and, therefore, that the Drug Arrangements are "non-discriminatory".

187.   We recall our conclusion that the term "non-discriminatory" in footnote 3 of the Enabling Clause requires that identical tariff treatment be available to all similarly-situated GSP beneficiaries. We find that the measure at issue fails to meet this requirement for the following reasons. First, as the European Communities itself acknowledges, according benefits under the Drug Arrangements to countries other than the 12 identified beneficiaries would require an amendment to the Regulation. Such a "closed list" of beneficiaries cannot ensure that the preferences under the Drug Arrangements are available to all GSP beneficiaries suffering from illicit drug production and trafficking.

188.   Secondly, the Regulation contains no criteria or standards to provide a basis for distinguishing beneficiaries under the Drug Arrangements from other GSP beneficiaries. Nor did the European Communities point to any such criteria or standards anywhere else, despite the Panel's request to do so. As such, the European Communities cannot justify the Regulation under paragraph 2(a), because it does not provide a basis for establishing whether or not a developing country qualifies for preferences under the Drug Arrangements. Thus, although the European Communities claims that the Drug Arrangements are available to all developing countries that are "similarly affected by the drug problem" , because the Regulation does not define the criteria or standards that a developing country must meet to qualify for preferences under the Drug Arrangements, there is no basis to determine whether those criteria or standards are discriminatory or not.

189.   For all these reasons, we find that the European Communities has failed to prove that the Drug Arrangements meet the requirement in footnote 3 that they be "non-discriminatory". Accordingly, we *uphold*, for different reasons, the Panel's conclusion, in paragraph 8.1(d) of the Panel Report, that the European Communities "failed to demonstrate that the Drug Arrangements are justified under paragraph 2(a) of the Enabling Clause".

... ...

Although both the panel and the Appellate Body reached the same result, the reasoning used was very different, in important ways. In its conclusions on the Enabling Clause, the Panel found a violation of paragraph 2(a), 'particularly the term "non-discriminatory" in footnote 3', because the Drug Arrangements 'do not provide identical tariff preferences to *all* developing countries and . . . the differentiation is neither for the purpose of special treatment to the least-developed countries, nor in the context of the implementation of a priori measures'.[31] These statements appear to indicate that, in the panel's view, it is

---

[31] Panel Report, *EC—Tariff Preferences*, para 7.177.

the existence of any discriminatory effect from the measure that is key, that is, whether identical preferences have actually been provided to *all* developing countries (aside from the least-developed countries). Thus, if any developing country Members do not receive the preferences, then there is a violation.

Such a rule would have important consequences, as many of the conditions that have been imposed through existing GSP programmes might be struck down as violations of WTO rules on this basis. These conditions are fairly common in GSP schemes, especially those of the US and the EC (as evidenced by the conditions in the EC scheme described above). If one or more developing country Members do not qualify for GSP benefits because of these conditions, the reasoning of the panel would be likely to lead to a finding that the conditions violate paragraph 2(a). This approach would make it extremely difficult for developed countries to impose *any* conditions on GSP benefits, and would call into question the legality of some existing GSP programmes. As a result, it could lead the developed world to abandon or scale back these preference schemes.

On appeal, the Appellate Body took a different approach. It reversed the panel's finding that 'the term "non-discriminatory" in footnote 3 [to paragraph 2(a) of the Enabling Clause] requires that identical tariff preferences under GSP schemes be provided to *all* developing countries without differentiation, except for the implementation of a priori limitations'. Instead, the Appellate Body concluded that GSP schemes may discriminate among countries that are not 'similarly situated'. It further explained that pursuant to paragraph 3(c) of the Enabling Clause, Members may discriminate among developing countries based on their different 'development, financial and trade needs'. The assessment of these needs, it said, must be based on 'objective' criteria, and the preferences must be 'available' to all developing countries that meet the established criteria. Applying this reasoning to the measure at issue, the Appellate Body emphasised that the Drug Arrangements 'do *not* set out any clear prerequisites—or "objective criteria"—that, if met, would allow for other developing countries "that are similarly affected by the drug problem" to be *included* as beneficiaries under the Drug Arrangements'. Rather, the benefits were available to only 12 countries selected by the EC, and the selection process for inclusion of countries as beneficiaries was non-transparent and did not involve objective criteria.[32] The Appellate Body noted that the 'closed list' of beneficiaries 'cannot ensure that the preferences under the Drug Arrangements are available to all GSP beneficiaries suffering from illicit drug production and trafficking'. On this basis, the Appellate Body found that 'the European Communities has failed to prove that the Drug Arrangements meet the requirement in footnote 3 that they be "non-discriminatory"'.[33]

Thus, under the Appellate Body's approach, the mere fact that some developing countries do not receive the preference appears to be insufficient to find a violation. Rather, the focus should be on whether the benefits are 'available' to all 'similarly-situated' developing countries based on 'objective' criteria relating to 'development, financial and trade' needs. In the case at hand, whether countries were 'similarly situated' was based on the existence of a problem with drug production and trafficking. It was the failure to make

---

[32] The inclusion of Pakistan illustrates the problems with the selection process, because evidence before the Panel indicated that there was at least one other developing country with more serious drug production/trafficking problems than Pakistan, but that country was not included as a beneficiary. Panel Report, *EC—Tariff Preferences*, para 7.228. As noted, it was the inclusion of Pakistan as a beneficiary that caused India to bring this WTO complaint, due to competition between Indian and Pakistani exports in the EC market.

[33] Appellate Body Report, *EC—Tariff Preferences*, paras 151–89.

benefits available to all such countries, based on objective criteria, that led to a finding of violation. (The issue of whether these kinds of drug related issues could constitute 'development, financial and trade' needs was not addressed.)

By allowing for differentiation based on 'development, financial and trade needs', as a means to determine whether countries are 'similarly situated', the Appellate Body took a more relaxed view than did the panel of the extent to which discrimination among developing countries is allowable. In effect, under the Appellate Body's approach, developed countries have a great deal of discretion as to which developing countries they will give benefits to, and they may even be able to select criteria that they know only specific countries will be able to meet (as long as they can show that these criteria are 'objective' and are based on 'development, financial and trade needs').

To illustrate the difference between the two approaches with an example, if the condition at issue is based on compliance with ILO labour standards, it is fairly clear that all developing countries will be eligible to benefit, in the sense that all countries can, in theory, comply with these standards if they so choose. If the panel's approach had been upheld, however, conditionality based on ILO standards would be likely to be in violation of the rules, because it is doubtful that all developing countries would actually adopt these standards and receive the preferences. By contrast, the Appellate Body's approach is much more accommodating, allowing conditions to be imposed as long as the benefits 'respond positively' to 'development, financial and trade needs' and are available to all similarly situated countries based on objective criteria. There is an argument that a condition based on compliance with ILO standards would be allowed under the Appellate Body's standard, although it is unclear exactly how the Appellate Body would view such a measure.

As noted, the inclusion of conditions to encourage the promotion of certain polices has become an established part of the US and EC GSP schemes. Some conditions in these programmes may pass the Appellate Body's standard, whereas others may need to be modified in order to conform.

In response to the findings in this dispute, the EC revised its GSP programme and eliminated the Drug Arrangements. In its new scheme, however, there was a special incentive arrangement for 'sustainable development' and 'good governance', which provided additional benefits for countries implementing certain international conventions in human and labour rights, environmental protection and good governance.[34] Under this new scheme, the benefits of additional tariff preferences were technically available to all developing countries, provided they had signed on to certain international agreements and had met various other requirements.

Whether the revised scheme satisfies the Appellate Body's standard is open to debate. While it clearly has the potential to have a discriminatory effect, as it is unlikely that all developing countries will satisfy the conditions, the Appellate Body's standard is not concerned with such a result. Rather, the Appellate Body focused on whether the benefits are 'available' to all developing countries that are 'similarly situated' based on 'objective criteria' relating to 'development, financial and trade' needs. It appears that the criteria involved in the revised scheme are 'objective', and the benefits are 'available' to all. However, the key question will be whether the criteria used relate to 'development,

---

[34] EC Reg 980/2005 [2005] OJ L169/1.

financial and trade' needs in a way that discriminates between countries that are 'similarly situated' in terms of these needs.

IV. ARE THE WTO'S GOALS APPROPRIATE FOR DEVELOPING COUNTRIES?

As discussed in Chapter 2, broadly speaking one of the main purposes of WTO rules is to promote trade liberalisation, that is, the elimination or reduction of barriers to trade. While there appears to be support for this goal among many, if not most, economists, the public at large is more evenly split on this issue, and there are many interest groups which strongly oppose it. With regard to whether a policy of trade liberalisation is right for developing countries, there is even greater opposition. Without getting into a detailed economic analysis of the issue, we present below some of the arguments relating to whether trade liberalisation is an appropriate policy for developing countries.

One argument that is made against the idea of having developing countries liberalise is that today's developed countries reached their current status not through open trade policies, but rather through protecting their domestic markets. Evaluating this claim is difficult, because it is hard to prove cause and effect. It is true that many of today's rich countries achieved industrialisation at a time when their markets for some products were heavily protected. But was that the cause of the industrialisation? Or would they have done even better without protectionist policies? Assessing what would have occurred in the counterfactual situation is a difficult task. Furthermore, the world was a different place during prior industrialisation periods. What may have made sense then, in a time of limited capital flows and foreign investment, may not be appropriate today.

A related claim is the idea that the trade liberalisation polices pushed by rich countries today are a form of 'neo-colonialism'. Some people take the view that rich countries promote this liberalisation so that their companies can take control of the economic resources of poor countries. In a limited sense, this claim is probably true. Governments of rich countries are looking out for the interests of their domestic companies. However, focusing on this motivation in isolation is probably not a fair assessment of the policy. In pushing for trade liberalisation, policy-makers in rich countries also have the interests of their own consumers in mind, as well as the general economic welfare of the world as a whole (they will benefit if the world is wealthier). Furthermore, some of the more altruistic leaders of the developed world are probably even thinking about the welfare of foreign consumers and workers in poor countries as well. Whether trade liberalisation policies actually promote all of those interests may be open to debate, but it is clear that many people believe they do and are not simply out to exploit the world's poor.

It is also important to note that any claims of harm to developing countries by trade liberalisation may be a bit exaggerated. The reality is that developing countries have not made extensive commitments to liberalise and they benefit from numerous exceptions to the rules. Moreover, few complaints are brought against them (especially the least-developed countries) under the WTO's dispute settlement process. Thus, the whole debate about the effect of trade liberalisation on developing countries is somewhat theoretical.

Much of the concern is really about what might occur if liberalisation were to progress considerably as opposed to what is actually happening now.

Finally, we recall an inherent contradiction in the WTO's negotiating process that was discussed above. WTO rules explicitly state in various places that trade liberalisation is a goal, and its substantive rules clearly promote this liberalisation. Thus, the assumption is that liberalisation is a good policy. Why, then, do the rules treat liberalisation as a 'concession' to be made? If it is such a good policy, should Members not just undertake it on their own? This applies generally, but especially to developing countries, which need economic growth the most. The answer, of course, lies in the uneven benefits that liberalisation engenders, as well as the nature of the trade negotiating process. With regard to the former, even if, on balance, most people benefit from trade liberalisation, there will be people who are hurt by it, at least in the short term, and their resistance makes it difficult for governments to adopt liberalising policies. As to the latter, given that governments are not likely to liberalise unilaterally, there is a need for a mechanism to provide incentives for them to do so. The negotiation process allows countries to use an 'I'll open my market if you open yours' approach, which arguably leads to the greatest overall reduction of trade barriers.

VI. QUESTIONS

1. According to World Bank statistics, over the years 2001–5 Korea had a Gross National Income per capita that was very similar to that of Greece and Portugal. Was it appropriate for Korea to be treated as a developing country for some sectors of its economy in the *Korea—Beef* dispute?

2. Given the controversy and contentiousness, should WTO Members address the issue of which countries can be classified as 'developing' in order to make the issue more clear and transparent? Or would it be better to let the current approach continue so as to avoid injecting further impediments into the already fragile WTO decision-making process?

3. There are some groups in the developed world that believe their governments have given too many concessions to developing countries, and as a result their industries will suffer due to competition with these low wage, low regulation countries. At the same time, some groups in developing countries believe that their governments have made too many concessions that benefit large transnational companies from developed countries, at the expense of their much smaller domestic companies. Is it possible to measure in an objective way who has actually conceded the most?

4. If trade liberalisation is a goal that is pursued by the WTO Members, presumably it is considered beneficial to the economies of its Members. Why, then, are developing countries permitted to liberalise more slowly than others? Should they not liberalise faster?

5. In the current Doha negotiations, there has been talk of ways to make the existing developing country exceptions more effective. What features could be added to the rules to accomplish this?

6. Are WTO panels capable of examining economic policy issues such as those arising under GATT Article XVIII:9? Should the IMF play a greater role in addressing such issues?

7. In the *EC—Tariff Preferences* case, the Appellate Body allowed Members to impose conditions on tariff preferences as part of their GSP schemes. As a result, it is clear that Members can use these schemes to encourage at least certain kinds of policies among developing country recipients (although the scope of the specific policies that can be encouraged is not clear). Is it a good idea to allow trade measures such as a lower tariff rate to be used to promote non-trade policies in developing countries? Do developing countries benefit from this? Is it fair for developed countries to use their economic power to make developing countries do what they want? Could developing countries ever be faced with conflicting demands by different trading partners? If it is permissible and sensible to allow this, what kinds of policies should be in play?

8. As noted, the key aspect of the Appellate Body's reasoning in *EC—Tariff Preferences* is whether the criteria used relate to 'development, financial and trade' needs in a way that discriminates between countries that are 'similarly situated' in terms of these needs. In practice, will this standard resolve conflicts over the use of GSP schemes to promote non-trade policies? Is the standard open to abuse?

9. Some GSP systems are based on 'positive' conditionality, in which benefits are granted only where certain conditions are met. Others are based on 'negative' conditionality, in which benefits are normally granted to all developing countries but are taken away where certain conditions are not met. Does the Appellate Body's reasoning in the *EC—Tariff Preferences* case make a particular approach more likely to be upheld?

10. How will the shift in power within the WTO over the years from developed to developing countries influence the future shape and accomplishments of the organisation?

11. Do the least-developed countries have the human and financial resources to participate effectively in WTO negotiations and the WTO dispute settlement system?

12. How would developing countries fare in trade negotiations and disputes without the WTO?

19

Linkages between Trade and Social Policies

When the modern trade debate began in the nineteenth century, trade policy was almost exclusively an economic issue. The free traders and protectionists each believed that their policies would improve their country's economic well-being.[1] There were additional aspects of the debate as well, such as national security (in relation to ensuring production of certain security related products). But on the whole, the debate centred on domestic economic policy.

Today, by contrast, the trade debate is intimately linked to a wide range of social policy issues. This change is the result of a number of factors, including: the expanded scope of trade agreements, which are no longer limited to reducing tariff duties; the integration of poor countries into the trading system, which has resulted in trade between countries of vastly different income levels; regulatory regimes and policy goals; the rise in importance of issues such as environmental protection and human rights, which were not prominent in the nineteenth century; and the general growth of the modern regulatory state.

In this chapter, we explore the various ways that trade agreements and trade policy intersect with, and sometimes come into conflict with, other policy issues. There are different elements to be considered in this regard. First, there are the specific policies that are involved: environmental protection, health and safety, labour rights, human rights, and culture, to name the key ones. Secondly, there are the ways these issues conflict or intersect with trade issues: use of trade measures to promote these policies abroad (unilaterally or pursuant to multilateral agreements); trade between countries which have adopted different policies and regulatory standards (including the possibility of harmonisation around low standards and the use of high domestic standards as a means of disguised protection); and the general effects of trade on industrialisation and growth. We address each of the specific policies in its own section, and in doing so explain how conflicts with other policies may arise in the ways described.

Before turning to these issues, it is worth recalling that the GATT Article XX and GATS Article XIV exceptions, discussed in earlier chapters, address issues related to balancing trade and other policies. In large part, these provisions attempt to draw lines between domestic measures that are legitimately used to pursue certain policies and policies that are discriminatory or otherwise trade restrictive. In addition, these provisions

---

[1] They did recognise that there was a trade off among different groups within the country. The free traders focused on the benefits to consumers and to producers who used foreign inputs, whereas protectionists emphasised the benefits to specific producers who would be protected from competition.

may also affect other kinds of measures, such as the use of trade sanctions. We will not repeat the discussion of the GATT and GATS exceptions in detail here, but do make occasional reference to them.

I. ENVIRONMENT

Concern for the environment has grown in recent decades, covering areas such as clean air and water, protection of endangered species, and climate change believed to be caused, in large part, by carbon emissions. A number of environment oriented concerns have been voiced.

First, to the extent that the economic policies promoted by WTO rules lead to growth and industrialisation, there is a concern that the Earth's resources will continue to be used in a way that is not sustainable. The current rate of consumption of resources is perceived by some to be too high t and policies that increase this consumption in developed countries and also bring developing countries up to the developed world's level of consumption will further deplete an environment that is already being strained. In reaction to this perceived threat, there are calls for the trade regime to be reformed to promote 'sustainable development', that is, growth which takes into account effects on the environment. Sustainable development is mentioned in the Preamble of the WTO Agreement, of course, and reference to this goal has even been made by the Appellate Body in the *US –Shrimp* case (paras 127–31). But in terms of substance, there is still a concern that WTO rules undermine, rather than promote, sustainable development.

Translating the general concept of sustainable development into precise rules is a bit difficult, as it may mean different things to different people. A well-known definition of sustainable development is: 'Development that meets the needs of the present without compromising the ability of future generations to meet their own needs'.[2] The concept has been further elaborated on the UK government's Department for Environment Food and Rural Affairs as follows:

> The goal of sustainable development is to ensure all people throughout the world are able to satisfy their basic needs, while making sure future generations can enjoy the same quality of life.

> Sustainable development recognises the interconnections between society, the environment, and economy—and aims to use a holistic approach to find solutions that deliver benefits for all of these whilst minimising negative impacts. Our long term economic growth relies on protecting and enhancing the environmental resources that underpin it.

> The past 20 years have seen a growing realisation that the current model of development is unsustainable.

> Our way of life is placing an increasing environmental burden on the planet through:

> - the consequences of unavoidable climate change
> - increasing stress on resources and environmental systems from the way we produce, consume and waste resources

---

[2] See the World Commission on Environment and Development Report (the Brundtland Commission), *Our Common Future* (Oxford, Oxford University Press, 1987).

• increasing loss of biodiversity, from the rainforest to fish stocks.

We are also living in a world where over a billion people live on less than a dollar a day, more than 800 million are malnourished, and over two and a half billion lack access to adequate sanitation. A world disfigured by poverty and inequality is unsustainable.

Unless we reconcile these contradictions, we face a less certain and less secure future. It is in our long-term best interests to make a decisive move towards more sustainable development.[3]

... ...

How to address such issues is unclear as a general matter, and, as a result, figuring out how to adapt trade rules to these concerns can be difficult.

A second, environmental, concern is that trade agreements are given precedence over environmental agreements and thereby undermine the effectiveness of the environmental agreements. For instance, environmental agreements may ban the trade of some products (eg, harmful chemicals); or they may rely on trade sanctions to enforce environmental rules in those agreement. The possibility that such provisions would violate trade rules worries environmentalists, as it would undermine the effectiveness of these agreements. This fear has not been realised in a specific instance as yet, but there is a concern that, if such a case arose, the trade officials who hear disputes under trade agreements would give short shrift to environmental concerns. As described in the following extract, environmentalists believe the problem has been mitigated by specific Appellate Body rulings, but it is still present to some extent.

H Mann and S Porter, *The State of Trade and Environment Law—2003: Implications for Doha and Beyond (IISD)* **(September 2003)[4]**

4. The relationship of WTO obligations to multilateral environmental agreements

Since the beginning of the trade and environment debates the relationship between the WTO rules and the MEAs (or, more broadly, international environmental law) has been central. What happens if a measure is challenged in the WTO, and that measure has been compelled by an MEA? What if the measure is not actually compelled, but rather simply enabled and promoted? Who decides those issues of law, and how?

When the WTO was created the few cases addressing these questions had yielded mixed results. In three cases (*Superfund*, and *Tuna—Dolphin I* and *II*), it was ruled that international law from sources outside the GATT was not relevant to the deliberations of a GATT panel. In one other case (*Canada—Salmon and Herring*), the answer was different; the panel in this case expressly used the conservation and fisheries management provisions of the Law of the Sea Convention to help it determine what policy options were available to Canada. In other words, it used non-trade law to help interpret and apply trade law obligations.

Since the creation of the WTO, and with it the system of dispute settlement, the state of trade law on these issues has been consistent, and generally closer to the understanding used by the Salmon and Herring panel. The AB in its first case—Reformulated Gas—stated that the new Dispute Settlement Understanding 'reflects a measure of recognition that the General Agreement is not to be interpreted in clinical isolation from public international law'. In the later Beef Hormones case, the AB did not shy away from using the precautionary principle (a non-trade law principle) as a source of input in the interpretation of WTO provisions.

---

[3] Available at http://sd.defra.gov.uk/what/ (last accessed May 2012).
[4] Available at http://www.iisd.org/pdf/2003/trade_enviro_law_2003.pdf (last accessed May 2012).

The *Shrimp—Turtle* case, discussed above, significantly expanded the scope for considering non-trade international law in matters of WTO law. In defining 'exhaustible natural resources'—a key phrase in the exception being sought by the U.S.—the AB turned to five international agreements related to the natural environment (even while recognizing that not all the parties to the dispute were Parties to the agreements in question). It also cited these agreements in establishing that common environmental problems should be, to the extent possible, addressed through international actions rather than unilateral action. And it used an inter-American agreement on turtle protection to help in its analysis of whether unilateral actions taken by the U.S. might be consistent with the requirements of Article XX of the GATT (again, noting that not all parties to the dispute were Parties to the agreement).

These rulings, taken together, mark a complete reversal of the exclusionary logic of the *Tuna—Dolphin* and GATT cases. The AB explicitly used MEAs to help it interpret the scope of the GATT obligations, and to assess the appropriate scope of unilateral action in the absence of an MEA. This second use comes close to analogizing MEAs to the role of international standards under trade law; under the TBT and SPS Agreements, unilateral actions based on an international standard are presumed to be consistent with trade law. While the AB did not go so far as to suggest this form of legal presumption, it did reason that measures consistent with an MEA, even where not all disputants were Party to the MEA in question, would have a strong basis for being consistent with trade law.

The important lesson from this analysis, particularly with respect to the ongoing Doha negotiations on the WTO-MEAs relationship, is that the relationship at its most critical point of potential conflict—the dispute settlement process—has been given specific and cogent direction; it is not a blank slate.

The Doha Declaration mandates negotiations on the relationship between MEAs and WTO, but limits the scope of those negotiations to cover only specific trade obligations in MEAs (i.e., not covering those trade measures that are not specifically mandated), to cover only those issues arising among Parties to the MEA, and to ultimately refrain from altering any existing WTO rights and obligations.

There is a real risk that the results of this negotiating mandate might be less supportive of a mutually integrative approach to trade and environment than the status quo. For example, the results might be read as limiting the AB's ability to use MEAs as interpretive guides to those cases where the parties to the dispute are also Parties to the MEA, a position already explicitly rejected by the AB. And creating a definition of specific trade obligations and rules on the use under trade law might simply invite WTO litigation that challenges whether these definitions and rules have been met—the very type of damaging WTO-MEA clash that has thus far been avoided.

... ...

Thirdly, there is concern that the laws of developed countries which create higher standards domestically or try to promote environmental goals abroad will be challenged as disguised protection that violates trade rules, and thus environmental protection will be undermined in this way as well. The *US—Gasoline* case is an example of the former; the *Tuna/Dolphin* and *Shrimp/Turtle* cases are examples of the latter.

Fourth is the concern that trade rules will lead to multinational companies (MNCs) seeking out countries with weak regulatory standards for products and production processes, often in developing countries, in order to lower their compliance costs. The result will be that more production takes place in areas with lower standards (eg, environment and labour). There is a further concern that this behaviour among MNCs will lead countries in a 'race to the bottom' in lowering standards to attract investment, as well as harmonisation of laws around these low standards. The following extract from an environmental group makes the case for this point.

Friends of the Earth International, *Activist Guide*
Corporate decision-making and environmental and social issues

Some economists argue that environmental factors do not play a part in the investment or relocation decisions of companies, implying therefore that governments will not need to offer lower standards as an incentive to attract companies. For a number of polluting industries, environmental control costs have been shown to be a small percentage of total costs, and not to significantly influence trade flows. However in the USA in the 1940s, '50s and '60s competition between states to attract investment resulted in some offering low pollution control requirements. With the increasing globalisation of the world economy there is every reason to think that such competition will affect environmental and social policy-making more widely.

This seems to be borne out by the number of companies moving from the USA to Mexico after the North American Free Trade Agreement (NAFTA) had been signed. Whilst the reasons for moving are often complex, the main attraction in this case was the ready supply of cheap semi- and unskilled labour. A number of firms also cited more stringent environmental standards in the US. Women now make up a significant proportion of the workforce within these newly 'relocated' manufacturing plants in Mexico (the so-called 'maquiladora' sector). Wages are low and working conditions are very poor (see impacts).

The movement of companies is by no means confined to the developing world. An article report in the Economist magazine (22/08/98) cites a Swedish firm, Ericsson, that was threatening to move its headquarters from Stockholm to London because of lower taxes and cheaper labour (the company subsequently announced a major reorganisation which included a new office in London). The article went on to say that,

"Faced with higher <u>energy costs</u> and little hope of labour-market reform, other big companies are also thinking of leaving Sweden". (Underlining added).

Also, research by the World Wide Fund for Nature (WWF) revealed that a number of large multinational companies in the Netherlands forced the Dutch Government to scale back plans for increasing energy and environmental taxes by threatening to take their new capital spending elsewhere.

This last example raises another question. If environmental costs are so insignificant, and thus unimportant in company decision-making, why do some companies and industries spend billions of pounds every year lobbying to keep environmental regulations in check? For example, when the US Clean Air Act came up for review in 1990, oil companies lobbied to have it weakened. In Canada, the forest industry of British Columbia (BC) has spent millions of pounds funding an organisation called the 'BC Forest Alliance' which, amongst other things, has actively campaigned against endangered species legislation. Also in Canada, the BC Forest Practices Code was twice amended following concerns expressed by the forest industry regarding the costs of implementation.

Natural resources such as forests may be of particular concern in terms of the 'race to the bottom' as environmental costs may actually constitute a greater proportion of company costs than those polluting industries considered in studies by, for example, Steininger (1994) and Tobey (1990). In Steininger's study of environmental expenditure in Austrian industry, the average was about 2% of production value, but in a resource extraction industry such as oil it rose to 8.63%. It is difficult to obtain figures on environmental expenditure as a proportion of production value in the forest industry. However, rough comparisons can be made in some circumstances. For example, the approximate environmental costs for the operations of MacMillan Bloedel (a Canadian forest products company) in BC in 1996 were 15% of the value of its BC-made products. According to a group of forest economists, when reforestation and forest rehabilitation requirements are strictly enforced,

". . . they can add significantly to the costs of timber extraction".

It is likely therefore that the environmental costs in an industry such as forestry are closer to (or beyond) the higher levels in Steininger's study than the lower levels (e.g. 0.57% of production value in the textile industry).

Such a view is supported by another economist who concludes that,

". . . the suggestion that environmental factors do not affect competitiveness (and should be ignored as a policy variable) is demonstrably untrue if one looks beyond the narrow category of pollution control spending. Specifically, broader environmental policies such as energy pricing unequivocally have competitiveness effects".[5]

This is borne out by calls from British Steel in January 1999 to be exempted from a proposed UK carbon energy tax (designed to help reduce greenhouse gas emissions) on the grounds that such a tax would undermine its competitiveness. [5]

... ...

This fourth concern (MNCs seeking out countries with weak environmental standards) has become especially significant in recent years. This significance has arisen from disparities in the extent to which states have undertaken (if at all) to reduce emissions of greenhouse gases under the Kyoto Protocol. The well-known economist Joseph Stiglitz has proposed using trade measures to promote environmental protection. Specifically, he advocates the imposition of tariffs on countries, such as the US, which had not signed the Protocol.

J Stiglitz, 'A New Agenda for Global Warming' (2006) 13(7)*The Economists' Voice***, Article 3**[6]
In Kyoto, nine years ago, the world took an important first step to curtail the greenhouse gas emissions that cause global warming. But in spite of Kyoto's achievements, the United States, the world's largest polluter, refuses to join in and continues to pollute more and more . . . .. It is now clear that something else is needed. I propose here an agenda to deal . . . with the United States' pollution . . .

Reducing United States emissions

The first step is to create an enforcement mechanism to prevent a country like the United States, or any country which refuses to agree to or to implement emission reductions from inflicting harm on the rest of the world. . . .

Fortunately, we have an international trade framework that can be used to force states that inflict harm on others to behave in a better fashion. Except in certain limited situations (like agriculture), the WTO does not allow subsidies—obviously, if some country subsidizes its firms, the playing field is not level. A subsidy means that a firm does not pay the full costs of production. Not paying the cost of damage to the environment is a subsidy, just as not paying

---

[5] Available at http://www.foei.org/trade/activistguide/globrace.htm.
[6] Available at http://www.bepress.com/ev/vol3/iss7/art3 (last accessed May 2012).

the full costs of workers would be. In most of the developed countries of the world today, firms are paying the cost of pollution to the global environment, in the form of taxes imposed on coal, oil, and gas. But American firms are being subsidized—and massively so.

There is a simple remedy: other countries should prohibit the importation of American goods produced using energy intensive technologies, or, at the very least, impose a high tax on them, to offset the subsidy that those goods currently are receiving. Actually, the US itself has recognized this principle. It prohibited the importation of Thai shrimp that had been caught in "turtle unfriendly" nets, nets that caused unnecessary deaths of large numbers of these endangered species. Though the manner in which the US had imposed the restriction was criticized, the WTO sustained the important principle that global environmental concerns trump narrow commercial interests, as well they should. But if one can justify restricting importation of shrimp in order to protect turtles, certainly one can justify restricting importation of goods produced by technologies that unnecessarily pollute our atmosphere, in order to protect the precious global atmosphere upon which we all depend for our very well-being.

Japan, Europe, and the other signatories of Kyoto should immediately bring a WTO case charging unfair subsidization. Of course, the Bush Administration and the oil companies to which it is beholden will be upset. They may even suggest that this is the beginning of a global trade war. It is not. It is simply pointing out the obvious: American firms have long had an unfair trade advantage because of their cheap energy, but while they get the benefit, the world is paying the price through global warming. This situation is, or at least should be, totally unacceptable. Energy tariffs would simply restore balance—and at the same time provide strong incentives for the United States to do what it should have been doing all along.

... ...

Stiglitz is not a lawyer, and perhaps as a result his characterisation of how such action should be taken seems at odds with WTO rules (for instance, failure to regulate green-house gas emissions is clearly not a 'subsidy' within the meaning of the SCM Agreement). While his argument that such trade measures could be justified under GATT Article XX(g) is not completely far-fetched, to succeed with such a defence would be quite difficult. This so-called 'green/carbon' tariff idea was also supported by some in France, but then rejected by the then EU Trade Commissioner Peter Mandelson. In doing so, Mandelson concluded that such a tax would be 'highly problematic under World Trade Organisation rules and almost impossible to implement in practice'.[7] Nevertheless, there are ongoing efforts in both the EU and the US to consider the use of trade measures to address the problems caused by carbon emissions.[8] The motivations for these ongoing efforts are described in the following extract:

P-E Veel, 'Carbon Tariffs and the WTO: An Evaluation of Feasible Policies' (2009) 12(3) *Journal of International Economic Law* **749, 751–55**

One rationale advanced for carbon tariffs is that they prevent 'leakage' of CO_2 emissions to foreign countries that do not have effective cap-and-trade systems or carbon tariffs. The notion here is that without carbon tariffs, firms—especially in those industries which have relatively high CO_2 emissions which cannot be abated at low cost—that are required to pay carbon taxes or purchase emission allowances when operating in that jurisdiction may relocate to a foreign

---

[7] A Bounds, 'EU Trade Chief To Reject "Green" Tax Plan', *Financial Times*, 17 December 2006.

[8] See P-E Veel, 'Carbon Tariffs and the WTO: An Evaluation of the Feasible Policies' 12 (2009) *Journal of International Economic Law* 749.

jurisdiction which does not impose similar charges on firms' CO_2 emissions. Producing in that foreign jurisdiction, the firm can then export its products back to consumers in the jurisdiction with the CO_2 emissions charges which it left. In these circumstances, the abatement of CO_2 emissions which the home jurisdiction's emissions charge was supposed to realize does not actually occur, as the firm has avoided the charges by relocating its operations and merely emitting the CO_2 in another jurisdiction. A carbon tariff is intended to lessen or negate this effect by ensuring that firms producing for markets in a particular jurisdiction cannot evade the charges by relocating their operations to a foreign jurisdiction.

A second and related economic rationale for carbon tariffs is that they ensure that foreign producers in countries without carbon taxes or equivalent schemes do not benefit from an artificial comparative advantage stemming from more lax regulations on greenhouse gas emissions. The notion of a comparative advantage rests on the idea that those countries that are able to produce certain goods relatively more efficiently than others should do so. While normally we view it as economically optimal for countries to exploit whatever comparative advantage they might have, the comparative advantage flowing from a more permissive regime for greenhouse gas emissions is different from other forms of comparative advantage, as it results in the negative externality of increased global warming. Although it remains desirable for those countries that are relatively most efficient at producing a particular good to produce it, the notion of efficiency necessarily needs to include those externalities which arise as a result of that production. Carbon tariffs effectively force foreign producers to internalize the externality of CO_2 emissions, at least to the same degree as do domestic producers.

While both of these rationales provide economic justifications for carbon tariffs, much of the increased focus on adopting carbon tariffs has undoubtedly stemmed more from political considerations rather than purely economic considerations. It is certainly politically difficult for developed countries to justify imposing additional costs on domestic manufacturers which are not similarly imposed on foreign manufacturers. This is because such costs can, as noted above, lead to the decreased competitiveness of domestic firms, which can then lead firms to relocate to more permissive jurisdictions, increasing domestic unemployment. These political considerations loom large in any consideration of domestic environmental regulations, but they are especially pronounced with the issue of greenhouse gas emissions. This is because, unlike is the case with environmental restrictions designed to protect the quality of local air of water, the harms of greenhouse gas emissions are a global problem, and it may be difficult to convince domestic constituencies to accept policies to address global problems without corresponding action from other states.

As Pauwelyn notes, the concern about the competitiveness of American firms vis-à-vis firms in developing countries is a major reason that the USA failed to sign on to the Kyoto Protocol. Indeed, given the increasingly precarious state of the manufacturing sector in developed countries in recent years—which is perceived by many to be caused at least in part by competition from developing countries—a scheme which is perceived to further handicap domestic manufacturers would be extremely difficult for any government to implement. An example of such views is provided in the testimony of Robert Baugh, the Executive Director of AFL-CIO Industrial Council, before a US Senate Subcommittee in relation to proposed US measures to limit domestic greenhouse gas emissions:

[China] and other major developing nations must be part of the solution or everything we the EU and other nations do to cut carbon emissions will be for naught . . . .. To put it bluntly, it is not in our national interest to see our efforts to reduce carbon emissions become yet another advantage that a developing nation uses to attract business. However, it is in our interest and the world's interest to have developing nations become part of the solution because the problem cannot be solved without them.

Carbon tariffs render the additional costs imposed on domestic manufacturers more politically palatable, thereby making domestic programs designed to curb greenhouse gas emissions and prevent global warming more politically feasible. Thus, perhaps the strongest policy argument in favour of carbon tariffs is that they provide a politically viable mechanism for states to implement a market-based mechanism to encourage their own producers to meaningfully lower their greenhouse gas emissions.

... ...

Trade officials are aware of the environment-oriented concerns described above, and much progress has been made over the past decade in bridging the gap between the environmental and trade communities. The following speech by the Director-General of the WTO, Pascal Lamy, attempts to bring the two groups closer together by proposing an 'environmental chapter' for the Doha Round.

P Lamy, *Globalization and the Environment in a Reformed UN: Charting a Sustainable Development Path*, 24th Session of the Governing Council/Global Ministerial Environment Forum, Nairobi (5 February 2007) [9]

Ladies and gentlemen,

"Gaia"—which means "mother earth" in Greek—is traversing a difficult phase: a zone of turbulence. It was as early as 1979 when James Lovelock published his famous work—**Gaia: A New Look at Life on Earth**—that we were warned that living matter is not passive, and that the Earth responds to provocation. We learned that the Earth's air, oceans and land surfaces react in the face of threats to their very existence. They fight to defend themselves. Today, as we face environmental challenges of an unprecedented magnitude, like we do with climate change, there is little doubt that Gaia will indeed react, and that humankind may suffer the consequences.

James Lovelock, for those of you who do not know him, was not only the originator of the Gaia theory, but was also the inventor of the electron detector. The device that made possible the detection of CFCs.

On 4 July 1994, when the United States awarded the Czech President, Vaclav Havel the Liberty Medal, Havel's words were:

According to the Gaia Hypothesis, we are parts of a greater whole (he said). Our destiny is not dependent merely on what we do for ourselves but also what we do for Gaia as a whole. If we endanger her, she will dispense with us in the interests of a higher value—life itself

UNEP's Governing Council meeting could not be more timely. It comes in the wake of many serious warnings that we have received about climate change, and other environmental problems. It suffices to glance through the UNEP Global Environmental Outlook for 2007 to see the full scale of the challenge before us.

In 1987, when the Brundtland Report coined the term "sustainable development", many of us saw it as *one* option. The other option was the business-as-usual scenario. Twenty years later no one can argue that sustainable development is a choice anymore. It has become a must.

Sustainable development should be the cornerstone of our approach to globalization and to the global governance architecture that we create. If I have come to this forum, it is to deliver a message: **the WTO stands ready to do its part**.

---

[9] Available at http://www.wto.org/english/news_e/sppl_e/sppl54_e.htm (last accessed May 2012).

When the WTO was established back in 1995, "sustainable development" was placed right at the heart of its founding charter. Governments vetoed the type of trade that is premised on the depletion of natural resources. Rather, they called for their "sustainable" use. They went further in their pledge to pursue a sustainable development path by launching environmental negotiations in the Doha Round. This is the first time in the history multilateral trade talks that such negotiations have been started. The credit for these negotiations must not only go to WTO member governments. The environmental community has, no doubt, played a decisive role in their launch through its repeated calls for greater mutual supportiveness between trade and the environment.

Ladies and gentlemen, there are many different ways to look at globalization. Some see it as an economic phenomenon, driven by a greater flow of goods, services and capital between countries. In this definition, the WTO plays a central part. Others see it as a technological phenomenon, driven by the revolution that we have witnessed in information technology, and so on. The one certain element in all of this, is that the world has become inter-connected to a point, that today it is impossible for a country to live and prosper in isolation of the rest of the world.

Clearly, globalization is a phenomenon that requires careful management. By connecting people from opposite ends of the planet, globalization offers tremendous potential, but it can also have drawbacks. As goods, services and people cross borders, so does pollution for example. The management of globalization would allow us to capture its benefits, while leaving behind its downside. There is no doubt that the world needs more effective "global governance"— governance at a level that transcends national boundaries. Our institutions of global governance must therefore be strengthened. They must also be made to function as a more coherent whole. This applies to the WTO, and to all other international institutions, which should complement each other.

Trade, no doubt, leads to a more efficient allocation of resources on a global scale. However, for this efficient allocation to truly materialize, we all know that resources must be properly priced to start with—that externalities would have to be internalized. In today's world, our policies are not fully synchronized. Greater awareness of the need for this synchronization is, first and foremost, required of governments.

We need to turn the page on the era in which governments would bring conflicting positions to different fora. The right hand of government should not compete with its left hand. The WTO, UNEP, and MEAs—as well as all other international institutions—must be put to work towards a shared sustainable development vision.

The Doha Round of trade negotiations contains a promise for the environment. A promise to allow for a more efficient allocation of resources—including natural ones—on a global scale through a continued reduction of obstacles to trade (tariffs and subsidies). But it also includes a promise to ensure greater harmony between the WTO and MEAs: a promise to tear down the barriers that stand in the way of trade in clean technologies and services; as well as a promise to reduce the environmentally harmful agricultural subsidies that are leading to overproduction and harmful fisheries subsidies which are encouraging over-fishing and depleting the world's fish stock.

The WTO needs the engagement of the environmental community in these negotiations. The engagement of environment ministers, of UNEP, of MEAs, and of civil society. As I said earlier, it is due, in large part, to the efforts of the environmental community that these negotiations have come about. But these efforts must be sustained, especially at this crucial phase of the Doha Round. As imperfect as the WTO may be, it continues to offer the only forum worldwide that is exclusively dedicated to discussing the relationship between trade and the environment.

Through Doha Round, decisions on that relationship can finally be made, influencing the way that the relationship is shaped. I call upon the environmental community to support the environmental chapter of the Doha Round, and to provide its much needed contribution.

The world must forge ahead with these negotiations as fast as it possibly can. Not because the negotiations are going to save the world's environment. But because they are the very modest start that the international community has agreed to make to address environmental challenges through the prism of trade. A failure of these negotiations would strengthen the hand of all those who argue that economic growth should proceed unchecked. That economic growth is supreme and need not take account of the environment. Trade, and indeed the WTO, must be made to deliver sustainable development. They are starting to.

This modest first step that governments have taken, would allow them in future to become bolder, addressing issues that have so far been left behind. The proper pricing of resources, the internationalization of externalities, and sound energy policy, are but some of the topics requiring much more serious attention.

The contribution of the Doha Round to the environment is but a drop in the bucket of the solutions required to address the world's environmental problems. But that drop needs to enter the bucket, so that governments are encouraged to begin looking at the bucket as a whole. A sustainable development strategy, linking all international actors, must become our goal. We must not wait for Gaia to react!

… … …

While there has been some criticism of the WTO's response to environmental concerns, others have defended it (to some extent).

E Neumayer, 'The WTO and the Environment: Its Past Record is Better than Critics Believe, but the Future Outlook is Bleak' (2004) 4(3) *Global Environmental Politics* 1–8

Negative Impact of the WTO on Environmental Protection is Over-Rated

The WTO has done much less to hinder or damage environmental protection policies than its critics believe. I will try to demonstrate this with respect to four main points.

(a) WTO Jurisprudence does not have a Bad Environmental Record

WTO jurisprudence has become increasingly environmentally friendly. There is, as Brack and Branczik note, "continued failure to make any substantial progress in rewriting WTO rules—but significant changes in the way in which existing rules have been interpreted to deal with environmental concerns." The WTO agreements put few restrictions on environmental regulation of consumption externalities, which refer to damage to the environment or human health connected to the consumption of goods. The one important exception is if the damage is highly uncertain and somewhat speculative, a point to which I will come back in the next section. Otherwise as long as these restrictions are applied fairly, even-handedly and without discrimination against foreign producers, they are compatible with WTO agreements even if they completely ban a certain product. This follows from the appellate body ruling on the case "European Communities—Measures affecting asbestos and products containing asbestos" from 2001. The appellate body rejected Canada's contention that asbestos fibers and non-asbestos fibers are to be considered "like products" in the meaning of GATT Article III. Just in case it also made clear that even if they were like products, the European Union would still be justified to ban asbestos products with recourse to the exception clause contained in GATT Article XX. Where WTO disputes have decided against measures aimed at consumption-externalities, this has been because the measures served more to protect domestic industries than the environment. Telling examples for this are the cases "United States— taxes on automobiles" and "United States—standards for reformulated and conventional gasoline." As DeSombre and Barkin have succinctly put it:

The reason that the WTO, and the GATT before it, usually ruled against regulation that claimed environmental exceptions to international trade rules is that the regulations were not particularly good; they were either clear attempts at industrial protection dressed up in environmentalist clothes, or they were poorly thought through and inappropriate tools for the environmental management intended.

Production externalities refer to damage to the environment or human health connected to the production of goods. GATT panels used to decide against regulations aimed at so-called process and production methods (PPMs) *outside* the regulating country's own proper jurisdiction—see the famous case of "United States—restrictions on imports of tuna" caught without dolphin-safe nets. However, the 1998 appellate body ruling and the follow-on 2001 arbitration panel decision in the by now equally famous case of "United States— import prohibition of certain shrimp and shrimp products" harvested without sea turtle excluder devices changed things fundamentally. The appellate body ruled that regulations aimed at PPMs in foreign countries need not necessarily violate WTO rules as long as the country imposing the restrictions has undertaken good-faith efforts at reaching a multilateral agreement, has applied the restrictions in a fair, non-arbitrary and non-discriminatory manner, giving affected countries some flexibility in how to achieve the aim of natural resource protection. Since the United States had not complied with these requirements at the date of ruling, the appellate body ultimately decided that the import ban was in violation of WTO rules. However, the arbitration panel dismissed Malaysia's complaint three years later that the efforts undertaken by the United States in the meantime were not sufficient steps into the direction of rendering the import ban compatible with WTO rules. The United States had started to negotiate in good faith international agreements on sea turtle protection and allowed shrimp to be imported on a shipment-by-shipment basis if it could be shown that sea turtles were not harmed even if these shipments came from countries, which had no comprehensive policy of sea turtle protection. With its ruling, the panel basically upheld for the first time trade restrictions aimed at PPMs outside a country's proper jurisdiction. That this ruling has not gained more widespread recognition among environmentalists, rightly prompted DeSombre and Barkin to contend that:

it was almost as though those campaigning against the WTO's record on trade and environment were loathe to admit that the organization could come up with a positive ruling in what had otherwise appeared to be a string of failures for environmental interests within the realm of free trade.

(b) Misunderstandings about the Dispute Settlement Process

In addition, there is some widespread misunderstanding about the dispute settlement process and its implications. Critics such as Thomas find fault with the provision that an appellate body cannot reconsider the fact finding process itself and are limited to examining whether the panel has interpreted the WTO rules adequately in the light of its own fact finding process. However, this is not so different from the judicial system of most countries where similarly higher courts often restrict themselves to examining whether the lower court has applied the law correctly, but will not commence a new fact finding process.

He also criticizes that the appellate body in the shrimp-sea turtles case made reference to the negotiation history of Article XX and has thus conferred an "open-ended validity to the perspectives of negotiators of that by-gone time." That dispute bodies resort to the negotiation history in interpreting rules is common practice, however. And to infer from this that the appellate body applied anachronistic arguments in its evaluations is highly misleading. To give an example: It is not without irony that the very same appellate body criticized by Thomas significantly extended the meaning of the terms "exhaustible natural resources," contained in GATT's Article XX. It noticed that while the term might have encompassed merely exhaustible mineral or other non-living natural resources by the time of drafting in 1947, the words of Article XX(g) "must be read by the treaty interpreter in the light of contemporary concerns of the nations about the protection and conservation of the environment." Emphasizing that the WTO's commitment to sustainable development in the preamble of the agreement establishing the WTO "must add colour, texture and shading to our interpretation of the agreements annexed to the WTO Agreement," it ruled that exhaustible natural resources should therefore encompass both living and non-living resources.

Critics like Thomas also often fail to recognize that even though WTO rulings become automatically authoritative unless consensually objected to by all its members, no country can actually be forced to remove the restriction that was found incompatible with WTO rules. What the country needs to be willing to do is to accept retaliatory trade sanctions in response, which it should if it is strongly committed to the environmental or health protection cause underlying the restriction. Admittedly, this is only possible for countries that are strong enough to weather the retaliatory trade sanctions. Thus, the EU has never lifted its import ban on beef from hormone-treated cattle and the United States has never lifted its import ban on dolphin-unsafe tuna. But this is not really an option for poor and small developing countries.

(c) WTO rules have not Deterred Multilateral Environmental Agreements

WTO rules have so far not hindered, let alone blocked, any multilateral environmental agreement (MEA). Most regional or international environmental agreements do not contain any trade-restrictive measures, but some do and they tend to be the more significant ones. It is important to note that no provision contained in a MEA or any trade restriction undertaken in (alleged) compliance with any MEA has ever been disputed at the WTO. This is despite the fact that some provisions in, for example, the Montreal Protocol, the Convention on International Trade in Endangered Species, the Basel and Rotterdam Conventions, the Agreement on Persistent Organic Pollutants and the Cartagena Protocol on Biosafety might well conflict with WTO rules. The same applies to the Kyoto Protocol and follow-up treaties. What this shows is that WTO members have shown great restraint in this area. Of course, the potential for clash creates some anxiety among negotiation parties. Those opposed to the MEA like to raise the concern of a potential clash with WTO rules to further their argument. Given the lack of agreement on how to resolve the potential for clash, recent MEAs are at pains to state that MEA rules do not supersede WTO rules and vice versa. However, to my knowledge it has yet to be shown convincingly that any recently negotiated MEA is less ambitious because of concern over a potential clash with WTO rules, let alone that a MEA was not successfully concluded for that reason. At the EU's insistence, the compatibility between MEA and WTO rules also forms part of the current negotiation agenda, a point to which we return below.

(d) WTO is not Responsible for Lack of Environmental Policies

Where trade exacerbates environmental degradation, the fault lies with non-existing or insufficiently ambitious environmental protection measures. However, the WTO cannot be blamed for this. Much of the anger and frustration of environmentalists is wrongly channelled at the WTO and its representatives, whereas policy-makers in the WTO member countries are truly to blame. As argued above, the WTO puts few hindrances in the way of those enacting strong environmental protection measures and it should not be blamed if policymakers fail to enact them. No doubt, we continue to observe environmental degradation on a large scale. There is also no doubt that trade liberalization can at times lead to increased environmental degradation if strong environmental policies are not in place. Where massive negative environmental externalities are allowed to exist, trade liberalization can be like a fresh breeze of wind on a house that is already set on fire. But it is the responsibility of the policy-makers from its member states, not the WTO itself, to put these policies in place.

... ...

II. CULTURE

Fear of a threat to 'culture' due to international trade is something felt more strongly in some countries than in others. For Americans, there is little concern when a foreigner occasionally wins a traditional US cultural 'prize', such as an Oscar (Nicole Kidman) or an NBA MVP award (Steve Nash). Perhaps this is because it happens only occasionally (generally speaking, Americans do quite well in the American 'culture' industry); perhaps the United States is more welcoming and accepting to foreigners; or perhaps it is the sheer size of the US market, which gives each particular aspect of the culture less overall importance. However, a problem arises because Americans also are very prominent in the 'culture' industries of other countries. For example, in foreign cinemas, American films are quite prominent. Small economy countries (and even some big ones) fear that reducing barriers in these industries will mean the loss of important aspects of their culture. Two countries in particular, Canada and France, have expressed strong concerns about the loss of their culture in the face of American or other cultural exports such as films, TV shows and magazines, as well as fast food restaurants and snack foods, among others.

The following extract discusses the relationship of trade policy and culture in the context of the US–Canada trading relationship.

WA Dymond and MM Hart, *Abundant Paradox: The Trade and Culture Debate* **(2005)**[10]

INTRODUCTION

The relationship between Canadian trade policy and cultural policy first burst into full public debate during the negotiation of the Canada-US Free Trade Agreement (CUFTA) in the 1980s. While there had been some isolated episodes of conflict between Canadian trade and cultural polices in the 1960s and 1970s, the CUFTA negotiations brought two well-armed protagonists together in hand-to-hand combat. The debate ended in a temporary truce with the cultural exemption in the CUFTA, and subsequently in the North America Free Trade Agreement (NAFTA). The truce broke down in the late 1990s in the face of serious disputes with the US over specific Canadian measures and the onset of multilateral negotiations on foreign investment, services negotiations in the World Trade Organization, and the negotiation of the Free Trade Agreement of the Americas (FTAA). As a result, the trade/culture nexus has assumed a place near the centre of public debate over the direction of Canadian international trade and investment policy. Like the CUFTA debate, the discussion is characterized by distrust and a

---

[10] Available at http://ctrc.sice.oas.org/geograph/north/dymond.doc (last accessed May 2012).

woeful lack of mutual comprehension between the advocates of cultural sovereignty and the defenders of trade and investment agreements.

Cultural sovereignty believers reject the notion that cultural goods and services should or can be treated as ordinary goods. In their view, subjecting trade in cultural goods and services to international trade rules denies the special characteristics of the cultural industries and the crucial role they play in defining national identity and reinforcing national attachment. Trade agreement supporters disagree that trade in cultural goods and services should be outside the bounds of international trade and investment rules. They contend that, like all internationally traded goods and services, cultural goods and services result from the application of capital, technology, and labour. Similar to other sectors, the cultural industries depend upon success in the commercial marketplace for their prosperity. A subtext for this debate is the controversy surrounding globalization. Cultural sovereignty advocates argue that international trade erodes the capacity of nation states to promote national cultural expression and that this erosion is aided and abetted by international trade rules. Supporters of the trade system retort that trade enriches economic and cultural choices for people around the world. While there are many variations and nuances in the presentation of arguments of both sides, essentially it is a debate between two solitudes. The government position, trapped between these solitudes, is heavy on posture and light on substance. As Queen Gertrude admonished Polonius, "more matter with less art" is required if the debate is to resolve itself into some practical negotiating positions.

The debate is replete with paradox. The argument of the cultural industries—that the production of cultural goods and services is so close to the national soul that it requires special treatment—echoes the haunting argument that international trade threatens the family farm. The demand by some in the cultural industries that the government support (i.e., subsidize) domestic production and consumption, their complaint that foreign products occupy too much shelf space in the national market, their pleading for tax exemptions, and their appeals for more content quotas, are reminiscent of the equally passionate pleas from the representatives of protected or threatened sectors in earlier years. Their long-standing demand that trade agreements provide a total exemption for cultural products and services is the polar opposite to a cardinal principle of Canadian trade and foreign policy: Canadian interests are best advanced and protected through international agreements.

Trade agreement supporters can make a strong economic case for the applicability of the rules. Their case is bolstered by the traditionally pragmatic approach governments have used in negotiating and in applying the rules. Multilateral and regional trade agreements have a long history of tolerating, even encouraging, special trade restrictive regimes for politically difficult sectors such as textiles and agriculture. If such regimes can exist within the architecture of international trade rules, there is every reason to believe that trade in cultural goods and services can be fitted within the system in a manner compatible with expanding trade and vibrant cultural expression.

... ...

One early WTO dispute, *Canada—Periodicals*, involved issues of Canadian culture in relation to magazines. Canada had taken a series of measures to support domestic magazines, including import restrictions on foreign magazines and lower postal charges on certain domestic magazines, as well as special taxes on foreign magazine publishers selling 'split-run' editions of their publications in Canada (a 'split-run' is a foreign-owned magazine that prints a second edition of a magazine issue in Canada, in order to qualify for treatment as 'Canadian'). With regard to the 'split-run' tax, the relevant measure imposed a tax equal to 80 per cent of the value of all the advertisements in the split-run edition. The goal of this tax was to protect the national periodical industry by undermining 'split-runs' and thus keep Canadian advertising dollars invested in Canadian publications. The United States challenged the consistency of these measures with various provisions of the GATT.

With no explicit cultural exceptions to consider, the panel and the Appellate Body focused narrowly on the claims made by the United States and found several violations. It did not go into any detail on the relevance of Canada's 'cultural' concerns. Indeed, the panel even stated: 'in order to avoid any misunderstandings as to the scope and implications of the findings above, we would like to stress that the ability of any Member to take measures to protect its cultural identity was not at issue in the present case'.[11]

The absence of any specific WTO exception for cultural matters has prompted some to propose an explicit provision in trade rules to this effect. The following extract from a speech by Catherine Trautmann, the French Minister for Culture and Communications, in 1999 offers an example.

Speech by C Trautmann, French Minister for Culture and Communication Press Release WTO, on the mandate given to the European Commission to preserve the cultural exception, Thursday, 28 October 1999

For several months now, there is no effort I have not made to further the preservation of the cultural exception [in multilateral trade negotiations]. I have been exposing my objectives in this matter, which are very ambitious, since the month of July 1999, during a council of Ministers of Culture in Finland. This was the principal reason for my trip to Mexico, to Oaxaca, in September, which allowed me to sensitize 16 Ministers of Culture from the entire world to what is at stake in the upcoming WTO negotiations, and to have a text adopted which asserts the right of States to freely carry out their own cultural and audiovisual policies. I also evoked these objectives from a recent journalistic platform in Le Monde. (The declaration and the article are in the press kit.)

The main difficulty lay in convincing all of our European partners of the necessity of giving a specific mandate to the Commission, who will be in charge of leading the negotiations, under the control of the member States.

Has this objective been reached with the text finally adopted? Have we diluted our wine with water in order to win the case? Are we abandoning cultural exception for the more diffuse notion of cultural diversity? To be clear, am I satisfied with the mandate given to the Commission, as Minister of Culture and Communications, having battled for months in order to obtain the preservation of the cultural exception?

I say to you most emphatically, it is without precedent that the member States of the European Union agree so clearly that the cultural exception should remain the rule. We are incontestably better off than during the previous round. What was acquired from the Marrakech round of negotiations is fine, but was obtained in extremis, at the end of a conflict with the Commissioner, Leon Brittan, who had only one idea in his mind: that the European Community renounce having recourse to the possibilities contained in the WTO treaty on services, to protect certain sectors from liberalization. These possibilities are twofold: that of not taking any obligation of liberalization, and that of requiring exceptions to the most-favored nation clause in order to allow for the preferential treatment of certain States.

---

[11] Appellate Body Report, *Canada—Periodicals,* para 5.45.

To the question: have we attained our objective without relinquishing any of our demands? I therefore answer, yes.

It is perhaps not useless to come back to the texts so that you can compare the results with the objectives that the professionals concerned, who as you know are watchful and have a sense of involvement, and myself have set. Read again, if you like, my speeches and discussion in the press that preceded the negotiation with the Council (in the press kit); also read again the press release "Vigilance Committee concerning the WTO and International Negotiations" of October 6, 1999. What did the vigilance committee want?

I quote: "that in the framework of the upcoming WTO negotiations, the European Union reasserts its refusal to undertake any obligations of liberalization as concerns audiovisual services and maintains its exemptions from the most-favored nation clause". This committee also described itself as "attached to the perpetuity of the European position during the next round of negotiations, whatever themes are to be debated (electronic commerce, subsidies for services, investments, etc.)". These expectations have, I believe, been heard and we are off to a good start in having them realized.

To achieve this end, we have taken the risk of slowing down preparation for the conference in Seattle by refusing an unacceptable text during the Council of General Affairs on October 11. The conflict could have been prolonged much longer, but fortunately our uncompromising attitude with the combined pressure of the timetable, has borne fruit. The last hesitaters preferred not to take the risk of ruining months of efforts, incidentally very productive, by opposing themselves to our legitimate claims.

The "compromise" version (this is the Community jargon used whenever a text is modified) that we refused to accept on October 11 was the following:

"The Council underlines the particular importance of cultural diversity and of maintaining the capacity of member States to promote and develop this diversity. The Union will work in this direction during the upcoming WTO negotiations."

You can imagine that such a version could not satisfy us. The reference to the capacity of the States to promote cultural diversity was much too vague. What we were hoping for was a guarantee that the negotiations would be led as during the previous round of negotiations. Because, for certain States, the obligations of partial liberalization are not incompatible with the necessity of preserving cultural diversity. This reference to the previous round of negotiations was difficult to get accepted.

We were also hoping to maintain the cultural exception whatever the subject debated may be. This is why recourse to a larger formulation than the single reference to the Uruguay negotiations imposed itself. We should obtain that the negotiations will not have a negative impact on the capacity of the Union and the member States to define and to put into practice their cultural and audiovisual policies.

I believe I can say, from the reading of the adopted text, whose content I will recall to you, that we have fully reached our objective, without compromise on the heart of the matter. This text is the following: "The Union will take care, during the upcoming WTO negotiations, to guarantee, as in the Uruguay negotiations, the possibility for the Community and its member States to preserve and develop their capacity to define and put into practice their cultural and audiovisual policies for the preservation of their cultural diversity" . . .

In practice, this means a non-offer of liberalization of the European Union in the cultural or audiovisual sectors, and protection of the latter exemptions from the most-favored nation clause, in order to allow for the preferential treatment of certain States. But the formulation retained offers us even larger guarantees, in particular if new matters should be touched upon, such as investment and subsidies.

Let us not be mistaken, cultural exception has never meant for the 134 member States a WTO legal exclusion for culture and audiovisuals. This objective would, moreover, be unrealistic and dangerous for cultural policies. Unrealistic because this would suppose that all the members States of the WTO are in agreement. This is a treaty which links sovereign States; the European Union can therefore not act on behalf of others. A minority of States wished to liberalize the audiovisual field (19 States out of 134 made offers of liberalization) and therefore, for them, the audiovisual field is in the WTO. For us, on the contrary, the audiovisual field is not and will not be in the sectors coming under the jurisdiction of the WTO, because we have not made liberalization proposals. To be clear, the WTO is an organization of varying geometry: it does not uniformly bind all the States to the same obligations.

... ...

This extract provides an insight into the negotiating position of the EU with regard to audiovisual services. The key point is that the EU has declined to assume any liberalisation commitments in this area so that obligations such as MFN treatment under the GATS are inapplicable. This emphasis on securing explicit exemptions when negotiating commitments is prescient in light of the *China—Publications and Audiovisual Products* case.

The case was brought by the US to challenge China's restrictions on the import and distribution of certain foreign cultural products, including books, magazines, newspapers, sound recordings, audiovisual entertainment products and films. At issue was China's obligation to liberalise trading rights under its Accession Protocol. The main commitment on trading rights is set out in Section 5.1 of the Protocol as follows:

> Without prejudice to China's right to regulate trade in a manner consistent with the WTO Agreement, China shall progressively liberalize the availability and scope of the right to trade, so that, within three years after accession, all enterprises in China shall have the right to trade in all goods throughout the customs territory of China, except for those goods listed in Annex 2A which continue to be subject to state trading in accordance with this Protocol. Such right to trade shall be the right to import and export goods.

The US claimed that, contrary to its commitment, the Chinese government has not allowed foreign entities and non-state-owned Chinese enterprises to import cultural products, and instead had reserved the right to import such products to certain state-owned enterprises (SOEs). In response, China submitted that its restrictions on trading rights fell under the opening clause of Section 5.1 as being within its 'right to regulate trade in a manner consistent with the WTO Agreement'. Specifically, China considered that the restrictions could be justified as necessary to protect public morals under GATT Article XX(a).

The background to the case, including China's possible oversight in securing explicit exemptions to the trading rights obligation, is explained in the extract below.

J Qin, 'The Challenge of Interpreting "WTO-Plus" Provisions' (2010) 44 *Journal of World Trade*

Prior to the accession, the government controlled the rights to engage in foreign trade in China. It did so by allocating trading rights to approved entities. Typically, the domestic companies receiving trading rights were state-owned. Although all foreign invested enterprises (FIEs) were also allowed to import and export, their rights to trade were generally limited to importation for their own production needs and exportation of their own products.

As part of the accession commitments, China agreed to completely change this trading system. Specifically, China promised that, within three years of its accession, all Chinese enterprises, regardless of their ownership, and all foreign individuals and enterprises, whether they invested in China or not, would have the right to import and export all goods except for a list of products the trading of which is reserved for specific SOEs. This commitment is "WTO-plus" because the WTO does not require its Members to limit the extent of their state trading activities. Rather, the WTO discipline on state trading focuses on the requirement of non-discrimination.

To implement the trading rights commitment, China amended its Foreign Trade Law in 2004. The new law did away with the government approval system and replaced it with a simple registration procedure for operating foreign trade businesses in China. Under the new system, any person—legal or natural, domestic or foreign—who wishes to engage in imports and exports of goods may do so simply by completing the registration process with the Ministry of Commerce. The implementation of this commitment, therefore, has fundamentally changed the way in which China conducts its foreign trade.

Despite the fact that cultural products were not among the listed products reserved for state trading, China has never liberalized the trading rights in foreign cultural products. Since the 2004 amendment of the Foreign Trade Law, the Chinese government has reiterated its policy of prohibiting non-state capital from engaging in the import of cultural products.

This prohibition is part of a long-standing policy of the Chinese government. In contrast with the extensive liberalization of economy in the past three decades, the government has kept a relatively tight political control over Chinese society. Such control is exercised through government censorship of press, media and the Internet, which is carried out to a large extent by maintaining state ownership in the media and publishing industries. Under this policy, private capital is prohibited from owning or operating news agencies, newspapers, publishing houses, radio broadcasting or TV stations, and from engaging in the import of foreign cultural products. Consistent with this policy, the government has strictly limited foreign investment in the cultural sector. The Industry Catalogue for Foreign Investment, which the government publishes periodically to guide foreign direct investment, has consistently listed news organizations, newspapers, publishing houses, radio and TV stations, and importation of various cultural products under the category of "Prohibited" sectors for foreign investment.

The dominance of state ownership in China's cultural sectors is undoubtedly a legacy of the centrally-planned economy, but it continues to serve an important function in preserving the political control of the Communist Party. Although the state-owned media have become increasingly commercialized, they remain the ideological tools of the Party and are entrusted with the missions of propagating government policies and educating and informing the public within the parameters set by the Party. In addition, ownership control is critical to China's censorship regime. Unlike censorship typically practiced in other countries, the Chinese authorities rely heavily on self-censorship and constantly adjust censorship criteria. By limiting the "sensitive" industries to a small number of SOEs whose management personnel are appointed and controlled by the government, the Chinese authorities are able to implement censorship policies in a highly flexible and non-transparent manner, which arguably has made censorship more effective and cost-efficient. While the ownership restriction is clearly anti-competitive—a small number of SOEs are guaranteed monopoly profits in the cultural industry—it is motivated by political rather than economic considerations . . .

. . . In light of the political nature of the policy, it seems curious that China failed to include cultural products in the Protocol list of products reserved for state trading. One plausible explanation is that the Chinese government had considered cultural products of sufficiently a political character that it would not be necessary to include them in the reserve list, just as it would not be necessary to include weaponry and military equipment in the list. Apparently, the issue of trading in cultural products was never discussed in the accession negotiations . . .

. . . What the WTO adjudicatory body encounters in this case are measures taken by the Chinese government for the purpose of keeping political control over its citizens. In maintaining exclusive state trading and import monopoly in foreign cultural products, the Chinese authorities can rely on the personnel of selected SOEs to police the imports. In other words, the Party can trust the personnel of selected SOEs in a way it cannot with private entities to carry out its opaque and capricious censorship policies. It is for this reason that I believe that China has never intended to liberalize trading rights in foreign cultural products and that the failure to explicitly exclude these products from the trading rights commitment was a major oversight on the part of China in the accession negotiations. While a partial reform of the system is possible (e.g., to allow private entities to import certain categories of products that are not politically sensitive, such as science and technology publications), complete liberalization of trading rights in the cultural sector is unlikely to happen in the foreseeable future no matter how this case is decided. In the event China loses, it may just accept the consequences of non-compliance, which would be an outcome similar to that of *U.S.–Gambling*. The ultimate challenge for the WTO adjudicatory body, therefore, is to determine where the boundary should be drawn between the jurisdictions of the WTO and China on regulating domestic measures of such political nature.

... ...

The panel found that China's measures restricting foreign entities and non-state-owned Chinese enterprises to import cultural products were in breach of the Accession Protocol obligation to 'liberalize the availability and scope of the right to trade'. The next issue was whether the GATT Article XX(a) 'public morals' exception was available to justify the breaches. In order to establish a link between its Accession Protocol obligations and GATT Article XX, China relied on the opening sentence of the Protocol. This provides that the obligations to provide the 'right to trade' is '[w]ithout prejudice to China's right to regulate trade in a manner consistent with the WTO Agreement'. China's position was therefore that the availability of GATT Article XX was an integral aspect of 'regulating trade in a manner consistent with the WTO Agreement'. On the availability in principle of Article XX, the panel used an arguendo approach. In other words, it applied Article XX on the assumption of its availability in principle, but without determining this point. The panel then found that Article XX, even if available in principle, was not satisfied by reason of China's failure to demonstrate that the measures were 'necessary' to protect public morals.

The Appellate Body confirmed the panel findings on the breach of the Accession Protocol obligation. However, it disapproved of the panel's methodology under GATT Article XX. For the Appellate Body, it was first necessary to decide upon the availability in principle of this provision before proceeding to whether it was satisfied with respect to the measures at issue. While the availability in principle of Article XX was confirmed, so too were the panel's findings on the application of the 'public morals' exception.

It is interesting to note the suggestion made by Julia Qin in the extract above that, should China lose, 'it may just accept the consequences of non-compliance, which would be an outcome similar to that of *US—Gambling*'. The adoption of the Appellate Body report in this case was later followed by compliance proceedings under DSU Article 21.5 and suspension of concessions proceedings under Article 22, with an authorisation for Antigua to suspend obligations under the TRIPS Agreement up to the value of US $21 million annually. In *China—Publications and Audiovisual Products*, the reasonable period of time for implementation expired on 19 March 2011. While the US subsequently expressed concern about the lack of progress in bringing the measures into compliance, this has not yet resulted in compliance and suspension proceedings. It is notable, however, that the parties have notified the DSB of agreed procedures under DSU Articles 21 and 22 applicable only to this dispute. It is therefore a reasonable assumption that negotiations towards compliance (or perhaps mutually agreed solutions short of full compliance) are taking place in the shadow of these agreed procedures. China reported to the DSB in February 2012 that it had completed amendments to most measures at issue, and that it had recently signed a Memorandum of Understanding with the US regarding measures concerning films.

III. LABOUR STANDARDS

Labour issues have been part of trade relations longer than most other social policy issues, mainly due to the significant impact trade policy can have on workers, particularly in the industrial and agricultural sectors. There are a number of ways that labour issues arise: the impact of trade on employment in specific industries, especially when trade is between countries of different development levels; the existence of varying degrees of labour rights in different countries, relating to such policies as the minimum wage, unionisation and safe working conditions; and the use of trade measures to coerce better labour practices in other countries.

The WTO has described some of the key aspects of the trade-labour relationship, and the WTO's role in it, as follows.

Understanding the WTO

Labour Standards: Consensus, Coherence and Controversy[12]

Consensus on core standards, work deferred to the ILO

There is a clear consensus: all WTO member governments are committed to a narrower set of internationally recognized "core" standards—freedom of association, no forced labour, no child labour, and no discrimination at work (including gender discrimination).

At the 1996 Singapore Ministerial Conference, members defined the WTO's role on this issue, identifying the International Labour Organization (ILO) as the competent body to negotiate labour standards. There is no work on this subject in the WTO's Councils and Committees. However the secretariats of the two organizations work together on technical issues under the banner of "coherence" in global economic policy-making.

However, beyond that it is not easy for them to agree, and the question of international enforcement is a minefield.

Why was this brought to the WTO? What is the debate about?

Four broad questions have been raised inside and outside the WTO.

---

[12] Available at http://www.wto.org/english/thewto_e/whatis_e/tif_e/bey5_e.htm (last accessed May 2012).

- **The analytical question**: if a country has lower standards for labour rights, do its exports gain an unfair advantage? Would this force all countries to lower their standards (the "race to the bottom")?
- **The response question**: if there is a "race to the bottom", should countries only trade with those that have similar labour standards?
- **The question of rules**: Should WTO rules explicitly allow governments to take trade action as a means of putting pressure on other countries to comply?
- **The institutional question**: is the WTO the proper place to discuss and set rules on labour—or to enforce them, including those of the ILO?

In addition, all these points have an underlying question: whether trade actions could be used to impose labour standards, or whether this would simply be an excuse for protectionism. Similar questions are asked about standards, i.e. sanitary and phytosanitary measures, and technical barriers to trade.

The WTO agreements do not deal with labour standards as such.

On the one hand, some countries would like to change this. WTO rules and disciplines, they argue, would provide a powerful incentive for member nations to improve workplace conditions and "international coherence" (the phrase used to describe efforts to ensure policies move in the same direction).

On the other hand, many developing countries believe the issue has no place in the WTO framework. They argue that the campaign to bring labour issues into the WTO is actually a bid by industrial nations to undermine the comparative advantage of lower wage trading partners, and could undermine their ability to raise standards through economic development, particularly if it hampers their ability to trade. They also argue that proposed standards can be too high for them to meet at their level of development. These nations argue that efforts to bring labour standards into the arena of multilateral trade negotiations are little more than a smokescreen for protectionism.

At a more complex legal level is the question of the relationship between the International Labour Organization's standards and the WTO agreements—for example whether or how the ILO's standards can be applied in a way that is consistent with WTO rules.

What has happened in the WTO?

In the WTO, the debate has been hard-fought, particularly in 1996 and 1999. It was at the 1996 Singapore conference that members agreed they were committed to recognized core labour standards, but these should not be used for protectionism. The economic advantage of low-wage countries should not be questioned, but the WTO and ILO secretariats would continue their existing collaboration, the declaration said. The concluding remarks of the chairman, Singapore's trade and industry minister, Mr Yeo Cheow Tong, added that the declaration does not put labour on the WTO's agenda. The countries concerned might continue their pressure for more work to be done in the WTO, but for the time being there are no committees or working parties dealing with the issue.

The issue was also raised at the Seattle Ministerial Conference in 1999, but with no agreement reached. The 2001 Doha Ministerial Conference reaffirmed the Singapore declaration on labour without any specific discussion.

… … …

In essence, the extract makes clear that labour issues, aside from prison labour, fall generally outside of the WTO, lying instead with the International Labour Organisation—a situation that primarily is due to the strong views of developing countries, whose exports often benefit from labour policies that do not comply with international standards. However, it does seem to recognise the close connection between trade and labour.

The following excerpt makes the case for building labour standards into the WTO's legal architecture.

R Chartes and B Mercurio, 'A Call for an Agreement on Trade-related Aspects of Labor: Why and How the WTO Should Play a Role in Upholding Core Labor Standards' (2012) *North Carolina Journal of International Law and Commercial Regulation* **665, 672–706**

I. Do Labor Standards Belong in the WTO?

Critics, such as Jagdish Bhagwati, argue that labor standards have no place in the WTO because it is an organization that exists primarily to promote mutually beneficial, non-coercive trade through reciprocal and mutually advantageous arrangements aimed at reducing barriers to trade. Under this view, the incorporation of labor standards for the purpose of upholding certain rights *within* a Member State is not a concern of the WTO, which has as its key objective the furtherance of *Member* rights regarding market access to other Members by upholding mutually agreed upon tariff rates and other concessions.

Bhagwati's view that the WTO's role is limited to regulating "pure" trade issues for the purposes of trade liberalization ignores that the GATT and WTO, as well as human rights treaties and organizations, were created for the purpose of increasing human welfare, and for the considerable evolution of the aims, objectives, and roles of the international trading regime, starting from the establishment of the GATT in 1947. For example, the preamble to the WTO Agreement cites "sustainable development" as an objective to be balanced against economic objectives. To most, human rights would be considered an element of "sustainable development" and thus implicitly included within the scope of the WTO. More directly, the WTO has expanded its coverage beyond "border measures," such as import tariffs, to include other policies which might *affect* trade—for instance, domestic policies concerning government regulation of investment, product and health standards, agricultural policy, and government procurement. The primary purpose of regulation on such topics has little, if anything, to do with trade, but instead concerns the fact that regulation in these areas *could* affect foreign producers and trade more generally. Furthermore, the Agreement on Trade-Related Intellectual Property Rights ("TRIPS Agreement") offers a cogent example of obligations imposed on *wholly* domestic activities, where such activities *may* affect international trade. Despite its name, the TRIPS Agreement sets minimum standards and requirements on a range of issues which until now, were considered purely domestic considerations (ranging from the term of protection for a patent to the availability of judicial review and the criminal sanctions for certain infringements).

It is therefore a gross overstatement—and, in fact, simply incorrect—to state that the WTO has an inherent institutional difficulty imposing obligations that could be viewed as wholly internal. Of course, the WTO cannot incorporate every area or subject matter which merely *may* have an effect on trade and traders; there must be some criteria upon which to assess the suitability of incorporation. This is not to say that whether a topic is "trade-related" or "affects" trade is irrelevant. On the contrary, it should be a factor upon which to assess the suitability of a topic for incorporation into the WTO. Using the inclusion of intellectual property rights ("IPRs") into the WTO as a guide, three other relevant factors emerge. First, IPRs were seen to "have a significant enough impact on the international economy that they should be regulated internationally even when no foreign party is directly involved." More specifically, since IPRs are a body of standards which *positively* affect trade flows, their under-enforcement was an impediment to the WTO's fundamental intention to *expand* international trade. Second, rights holders and governments alike realized that the existing international mechanism for enforcing international IPRs was insufficient. Those same parties also viewed the World Intellectual Property Organization ("WIPO") treaties as failing to adequately protect IPRs (both in scope and coverage), and realized that in order to increase protection to an acceptable level, the forum of negotiations must be shifted. Third, many simply believed that IPRs were inherently deserving of protection.

By applying the same reasoning to CLS, the following four criteria would need to be satisfied in order for one to consider incorporation of CLS into the WTO framework: (1) CLS must be "trade-related"; (2) protection of CLS would positively affect international trade flows; (3) CLS are not sufficiently protected and enforced; and (4) CLS would need to be viewed as inherently deserving of protection. Even if one is not convinced that satisfying the above four criteria is justification for incorporating CLS into the WTO, there are several textual-based arguments from the GATT which favor such incorporation. The remainder of this section explores both issues. Part A analyzes whether the CLS satisfy each of the four criteria. Part B explores additional GATT-based arguments supporting the incorporation of CLS into the WTO framework.

A. Core Labor Standards Deserve Protection

1. Core Labor Standards are "Trade-related"

The fact that labor directly affects market share and activity is relatively uncontroversial. Labor is by nature an "intrinsic part of the production process that culminates in the manufacture of goods and services for trade." Simply stated, the conditions under which a product is manufactured or produced impact the quantity and cost of the product in the world market. As such, it seems only natural that labor standards should be viewed as an indispensable part of the effective trade in goods.

Additional evidence of this can be seen by the fact that the drafters of the United Nations Havana Charter, which sought to establish the failed International Trade Organization ("ITO"), explicitly recognized the link and impact that labor has on international trade by including a provision on labor. Specifically, Article Seven of the Havana Charter (titled "Fair Labor Standards") stated that "unfair labor conditions, particularly in production for exports, create difficulties in international trade . . . [and] each member shall take whatever action may be appropriate and feasible to eliminate such conditions within its territory." Thus, not only did trade negotiators in the 1940s identify the link between labor and international trade, they also recognized that unfair labor conditions create difficulties or distortions in the market by lowering the price of goods below what would normally exist in a competitive market and should be eliminated. It is clear that the drafters explicitly recognized labor as being related to trade.

Finally, the major industrialized countries already link labor rights with trade in a similar fashion to the pre-TRIPS situation with regard to IPRs. For instance, the United States links labor and trade in at least three different ways. First, the United States requires GSP beneficiaries to observe "internationally recognized work rights" and be actively taking steps to implement certain labor rights (as determined under the Act, and slightly differing from the CLS) as a condition of receiving the preferential treatment. Countries that have not complied with international commitments to eliminate the worst forms of child labor are *per se* ineligible to receive GSP preferences.

Second, the United States includes labor provisions in its FTAs. Beginning with the North American Trade Agreement ("NAFTA") in 1994 and becoming standard practice since the U.S.-Jordan FTA in 2000, labor provisions were codified by the Bipartisan Trade Promotion Authority of 2002 ("BTPAA"), which, inter alia, directs the President and trade negotiators to (1) "ensure that a party to a trade agreement . . . does not fail to effectively enforce its . . .

labor laws, through a sustained or recurring course of action or inaction in a manner affecting trade"; (2) recognize that parties have the right to exercise discretion with respect to labor law enforcement and regulation; and (3) "strengthen the capacity of United States trading partners to promote respect for core labor standards."

The BTPAA expired in 2007, but was quickly replaced with a compromise agreement reached between leading Democrats in Congress and the Bush administration, which also directly linked labor with trade. Entitled "A New Trade Policy for America," the agreement begins with calls to "[e]nsure that U.S. free trade agreements raise standards of living [and] create new markets for U.S. goods," to require countries "to adopt, maintain, and enforce in their laws and practice, the basic international labor standards as stated in the 1998 *ILO Declaration*," and to "[e]nsure that government procurement promotes basic worker rights and acceptable conditions of work." The agreement further required the addition of four elements, pending and all future U.S. FTAs: (1) Fully enforceable commitments that the FTA partner countries would adopt and maintain in their laws and practices the ILO Declaration; (2) fully enforceable commitments against FTA partner countries that lower their labor standards; (3) new limitations on discretionary "prosecution" and "enforcement" of labor provisions; and (4) ensuring that labor provisions are subject to the dispute-settlement mechanisms (and any resulting penalties) of the FTAs.

Third, the United States links labor and trade through §301 of the U.S. Trade Act of 1974, which permits trade sanctions against states which fail to observe workers' rights. Under that Act, the administration can initiate an investigation, or any interested person can file a §301 petition requesting that the U.S. administration investigate claims regarding unfair trade practices, and take steps to remedy these practices. While an investigation has never been initiated or a petition filed, the point is that the U.S. Trade Act of 1974 already links labor with trade and, in doing so, tacitly deems labor to be "trade-related."

Likewise, the European Union ("EU") retains a similar scheme whereby GSP benefits from general and special incentive arrangements for sustainable development and good governance, with specific reference to certain human rights treaties. Unlike the carrot and stick approach of the United States, the EU's special incentive arrangements do not take a trade sanctions-based approach to the issue. Rather, special incentive arrangements offer additional incentives to beneficiaries who have ratified and effectively implemented sixteen specific human rights conventions and at least seven conventions related to environment and governance. Special preferences can be withdrawn if the beneficiary fails to implement human rights or labor rights. Moreover, the EU similarly furthers the labor-trade link in its FTAs with the majority of its agreements obliging FTA partner countries to, inter alia, conform to a comprehensive set of labor standards, or simply referencing labor conditions without any accompanying obligation.

2. Protection of Core Labor Standards Would Positively Affect International Trade Flows

The incorporation of IPRs into the WTO framework indicates that governments are willing to allow for the regulation of internal activity if such regulation has the net effect of expanding the volume of world trade and, in so doing, increasing the security and predictability of markets. Yet, developing country governments, industry associations, certain economists, and some developing country NGOs often argue that the inclusion of CLS into the WTO would not expand trade volumes, but would rather operate as disguised protectionism to undermine developing countries' comparative advantage in cheap labor vis-à-vis developed countries. Thus, it is claimed that allowing Members to impose restrictive measures on products manufactured in contravention of CLS would have the net effect of reducing world trade—a result that is irreconcilable with the WTO's objective to further promote trade-liberalization and the expansion of trade.

Some commentators pursue this trajectory even further and argue that the imposition of CLS is philosophically *incompatible* with the WTO's goal of removing barriers to trade. Under this logic, the imposition of CLS on Members implies that a "fixing" of standards between countries, incompatible with market principles as regulatory policy, is a matter of comparative advantage. In other words, some argue that the imposition of artificial international standards into the domestic regulatory structure interferes with the market and thus impedes efficiency and stifles competition.

Before responding to these arguments, it is useful to briefly return to the four CLS in the ILO Declaration: (1) Freedom of association and the effective recognition of the right to collective bargaining; (2) the elimination of all forms of forced and compulsory labor; (3) the effective elimination of child labor; and (4) the elimination of discrimination in respect of employment and occupation. Critically, these rights do not encompass a "fair minimum wage" or compliance with occupational health and safety measures. It is generally accepted that low wages are a legitimate comparative advantage in international trade and that developing countries should not be denied that advantage; thus, rather than seeking to "equalize" the comparative advantage related to labor standards, the CLS concern practices that are not determined or fixed by market mechanisms—the absence of regulations actually denies *workers* comparable rights to use the freedom they otherwise would have to enable them to seek out better conditions of employment. Therefore, in denying the workers the freedom to seek out better working conditions, the absence of worker rights actually forecloses any possibility of a "natural market correction." In this sense, far from being incompatible with market philosophy, the decision not to enforce CLS in a domestic market is itself an interference with the free market.

The realization that CLS are not about the *equalization* of domestic market regulations allows for a more rational analysis of the evidence available as to the economic effects of the enforcement of CLS for both world trade and developing countries. Significantly, the Organization for Economic Co-Operation and Development ("OECD") published a study in 1996 questioning much of the "evidence" regarding CLS "leveling the playing field" or undermining developing countries' comparative advantage. The OECD report concluded that "it is conceivable that the observance of core standards would strengthen the long-term economic performance of all countries." Furthermore, the report rejected the theory that countries which refuse to comply with CLS enjoy better export performance than those countries which do comply with CLS. Another OECD report published in 2000 was even more explicit in detailing what it saw as the source of the benefits of complying with CLS: "Countries which strengthen their core labor standards can increase economic efficiency, by raising skill levels in the workforce and by relating an environment which encourages innovation and high productivity." An OECD report in 2005 affirmed the earlier findings and concluded: "Countries do not gain sustained improvement in competitiveness by disregarding core labor standards. Indeed, to the contrary, improved working conditions are found to contribute importantly to growth and development, a point made in the final report by the ILO's World Commission on the Social Dimension of Globalization." These findings and conclusions are supported by independent economic analysis, as well as by ILO investigations, which find a positive correlation between long-term economic success within the world trading system and the observance of CLS. Indeed, the findings of the OECD and ILO correspond with the conclusions of a World Bank report published in 2001, stating: "Keeping labor standards low is not an effective way of gaining a competitive advantage over trading partners. Indeed low labor standards are likely to erode competitiveness over time because they reduce incentives for workers to improve skills and for firms to introduce labor saving technology."

Thus, three major international organizations and several leading economists all conclude that the imposition of fundamental worker rights can be pursued without necessarily injuring a nation's capacity to effectively export and trade with the world system. Furthermore, evidence suggests that many developing countries have (in taking a myopic view of the issue) completely ignored the benefits that acceptance of universal labor standards could bring and the correlative role that acceptance could play in the expansion of the world market.

3. Core Labor Standards Suffer from Significant Under-enforcement

Similar to the pre-TRIPS situation with regards to IPRs, CLS suffer from significant under-enforcement, with the existing international agency—that is, the ILO—seemingly impotent to enforce standards and curb widespread violations.

Despite being the body responsible for the protection of CLS, the ILO's enforcement record to date has proven to be consistently inadequate. This is not due to lack of effort; the ILO has adopted 188 binding conventions and approximately 200 nonbinding resolutions since its creation in 1919. While it is difficult to pinpoint the precise reasons for the lack of enforcement, several impediments can be identified. One such impediment is that the ILO suffers from a disparate, and sometimes rather low, rate of ratification of its treaties (including by leading developed countries such as the United States). This, in turn, creates a "patchwork of inconsistent legal obligations" and serves as a major impediment to the global enforcement of labor standards. Moreover, a number of ILO conventions are ratified but not implemented.

Another impediment is that while in theory the ILO Constitution authorizes sanctions in the event of non-compliance, in practice the organization prefers to adopt a "soft" approach to the enforcement of its norms, relying on public identification, embarrassment and shaming, and technical assistance to promote compliance. The ILO does not even do this very well, as the ILO's "special list" of transgressions of CLS garners little international publicity and even less government attention; in fact, the list has not produced any substantial improvements in compliance with CLS.

One recent example of the limitations of the ILO's enforcement capacities is the ILO's response to Myanmar's use of forced labor for both private and public purposes, which the ILO "has been considering for over thirty years." In the case of Myanmar, following a formal complaint by twenty-five worker delegates, an ILO Commission of Inquiry investigated and found extensive violations of the Forced Labor Convention, amounting to a "saga of untold misery and suffering, oppression and exploitation of large sections of the population inhabiting Myanmar by the Government, military and other public officers." The Commission of Inquiry made several recommendations, namely that Myanmar's government should bring several of its laws into compliance with the Forced Labor Convention by May 1, 1999 at the latest; that Myanmar should publicly renounce the practice of forced labor and take concrete steps to eliminate it in all its forms; and that it should strictly enforce a long-neglected provision of the Myanmar Penal Code that provides for the prosecution and punishment of those who exact forced labor. Importantly, the Governing Body took action under Article 33 of the ILO Constitution and recommended, for the first time in the ILO's history, that the International Labor Conference "take such action as it may deem wise and expedient to secure compliance" by Myanmar with the recommendations and with Myanmar's obligations under Convention Number 29 on Forced Labor. Nonetheless, no ILO Member State actually initiated any further sanctions (in large part due to concern that such an effort would violate WTO rules). It was not until 2003 that the United States banned all trade with Myanmar under the Burmese Freedom and Democracy Act. In passing the legislation, members of the U.S. Congress argued in the face of considerable opposition that sanctions were justified under Article XX of the GATT. By contrast, a number of Member States, including China and India, continued to engage with Myanmar while the EU's and Australia's trade restrictions continued to target only the military junta and their family members. Importantly, these sanctions cannot be considered a response to the ILO Resolution, but rather to the repressive political developments in Myanmar in 2007, including the detention of democracy leader Aung San Suu Kyi.

Myanmar remains in non-compliance with the Convention and the ILO continues to report that forced and compulsory labor remains prevalent in many areas of the country in circumstances of severe cruelty and brutality. In November 2010, the ILO reported that very few of the recommendations from the Commission of Inquiry had been effectively implemented.

Statistics on compliance with CLS provide further testimony as to the need for a stronger enforcement mechanism. Simply put, it is a generally accepted fact that large numbers of violations of CLS occur everyday. For instance, the ILO estimates that 153 million children aged five to fourteen are engaged in child labor, including an estimated fifty-three million in hazardous work. Furthermore, child labor makes up approximately 26% of the total workforce in Africa, with one in four children engaged in child labor (approximately sixty-five to eighty million children) and 15% of all Sub-Saharan African children engaged in some form of hazardous work. In Asia, an estimated one in eight children are child laborers, with a total of 5.6% of Asian children engaged in hazardous work. Moreover, an OECD study found that only nine out of sixty-seven non-OECD countries complied with the right to freedom of association and fifteen out of sixty-seven countries upheld the right to collective bargaining. It is also clear that bonded labor continues to be widely practiced in several countries, and that organizing and bargaining rights are repressed or otherwise absent in export processing zones across the world. Indeed, this body of evidence led the OECD to conclude that there is "no indication in recent years of substantial progress overall in reducing non-compliance with respect to freedom of association and the right to collective bargaining across the sample of sixty-nine countries that have ratified the two corresponding ILO fundamental conventions."

4. Core Labor Standards are Inherently Deserving of Protection

The fact that CLS are human rights is uncontroversial; no Member State voted against the ILO Declaration when it was put forth at the 86th Session of the General Conference of the ILO in June, 1998. The ILO Declaration itself acknowledges CLS have a special status within the international labor law hierarchy in that the CLS are imposed upon ILO Members by virtue of them simply being Members of the organization. Thus, Member States that have not ratified the relevant conventions are nevertheless bound to promote and realize the basic principles concerning the four CLS. Regardless of this requirement, all of the respective seven Conventions dealing with the standards currently enjoy almost universal acceptance, with the highest rate of ratification among all ILO conventions. The four principles are also broadly articulated in the Universal Declaration of Human Rights ("UDHR"), the International Covenant on Civil and Political Rights ("ICCPR"), the International Covenant on Economic, Social and Cultural Rights ("ICESCR"), and a number of other key human rights conventions, which signify the commitment of Members to protect workers on a much wider scale than that proposed by the CLS.

With such a high ratification rate and widespread endorsement within the broader international human rights system, the CLS do not simply constitute rights that belong to workers, but rather constitute rights that belong to individuals as human beings. Thus, child labor is prohibited not because the labor is cheaper than adult labor, but rather because the growth and development of children should not be undermined through labor; the operative principle is that children should be shielded from the burdens of labor, and concerns regarding the rate of pay a child receives are irrelevant by comparison. Similarly, forced labor is prohibited not because it creates an economic distortion, but rather because it denies workers their freedom. While prohibition of discrimination reaches beyond wage costs to protect workers' equal right to work and the right to equal treatment as part of the human right to be treated equally, freedom of association serves broader political and social goals than merely permitting unionization.

Given the above, any comparative advantage gained by non-compliance with these standards is not an advantage that should be shielded or trumped by liberalized trade. This is not a controversial statement; in fact, the vast majority of countries agree with such an edict. It is, therefore, extremely rare (if not completely unheard of) for a trade representative to publicly state that their country's comparative advantage is in child labor and the prohibition of unionization.

As human rights, the CLS are worthy of inclusion as a GATT-protected norm. By viewing CLS as human rights and not merely as an attempt to level the playing field, the case for the WTO incorporating the rights and correspondingly playing a role in their enforcement becomes clear for at least two reasons. First, when viewed as basic human rights, CLS can be seen to be promoting human freedom of choice. Such freedom of choice is entirely consistent with a liberal trading regime that seeks to ensure other human freedoms, particularly the right of individuals to engage in market transactions without discrimination on the basis of country of origin. Indeed, on a practical level, the sovereignty argument does not stand up to scrutiny when one considers that all Members of the WTO (including developing countries) allow some degree of sovereignty erosion by virtue of membership in the organization (or, in fact, by membership in any international organization). In exchange for the reduced sovereignty, Member States receive the benefits of membership in an organization which assists in making trade more stable, predictable, and free, and in improving the overall wealth of its citizens.

Second, the human rights approach shows that imposing trade restrictions on products manufactured in a manner that fails to comply with universally acknowledged human rights is not an *economic* regulation per se, but rather a form of international social regulation driven by the fundamental premise that human rights are universal and indivisible. Viewed in this manner, it becomes clear that the enforcement of human rights is not merely a convenient opportunity to engage in protectionism, but an obligation to *respect, protect, and fulfill* their responsibilities under international human rights treaties, including the ILO Declaration. It is thus no answer to claim that the imposition of trade restrictions for products manufactured in violation of CLS interferes with the internal regulatory policy of another state; in the contemporary world, human rights concerns are matters of international, rather than domestic, concern. All states have an interest in compelling compliance with human rights norms, regardless of whether the violating state's conduct directly impacts other states' interests in the traditional sense. As Michael Trebilcock and Robert Howse observe, linking trade rights to compliance with CLS will not impose a discriminatory set of conditions on Members' exercise of their trading rights; rather, the "condition" is, in effect, something that they are all already committed to do, inasmuch as they are Members of the ILO and signatories to the ICCPR and the ICESCR human rights treaties.

... ...

IV. HUMAN RIGHTS

There is a long-standing and natural concern held by many people with regard to trade with countries who have policies that are considered to violate basic human rights. Of course, there are many different understandings of what constitute human rights, so the concerns may vary. But that does not make people's concerns any less strong. One of the most famous examples is the widespread revulsion at South Africa's Apartheid policy. South Africa was way out of step with the world when it continued racial discrimination and segregation practices into the 1980s. The result was widespread boycotts of

South Africa and of foreign companies doing business there. Similar concerns have been expressed in relation to other countries with undemocratic governments and repressive regimes. For years, the United States required annual reviews of trade with countries such as China and the Soviet Union before granting them most-favoured-nation treatment. How these human rights concerns play out in trade relations varies depending on the countries involved and the nature of the alleged abuses.

To take a recent real world example, in the 1990s the US state of Massachusetts decided not to purchase from companies doing business in Burma/Myanmar because of that government's alleged human rights abuses. Global Trade Watch, a frequent critic of the WTO and other trade institutions, described the situation and how it led to a WTO complaint against the US.

Public Citizen, Global Trade Watch, Massachusetts Burma Procurement Law Challenged at WTO[13]

The serious human rights violations and the deliberate suppression of democracy perpetrated by the military junta ruling Burma (which the junta has renamed Myanmar) since it came to power in 1988 are well known throughout the world. The International Labor Organization issued a scathing report on the human rights violations of the Burmese dictatorship. The ILO found that the Burmese military dictatorship was systematically violating the basic human rights of Burmese citizens and non-Burmese minorities. It ordered the Burmese dictatorship to reform its laws and practices regarding labor rights. "There is abundant evidence before the Commission showing the pervasive use of forced labor imposed on the civilian population throughout Myanmar by the authorities and the military for portering, the construction, maintenance and servicing of military camps, other work in support of the military, work on agriculture, logging and other production projects undertaken by the authorities or the military, sometimes for the profit of private individuals. . . . none of which comes under any of the exceptions of the Convention. . . . Forced labor in Myanmar is widely performed by women, children, and elderly persons as well as persons otherwise unfit for work. . . . All of the information and evidence before the Commission shows utter disregard by the authorities for the safety and health as well as the basic needs of the people performing forced or compulsory labor."

Burma's pro-democracy movement, led by Nobel Peace Prize holder Aung San Suu Kyi, has called for South Africa-style foreign divestment from Burma to financially starve the military dictatorship. Some two dozen U.S. municipal and county governments, and the state government of Massachusetts, have acted on this request and terminated purchasing contracts with companies doing business in Burma. The selective purchasing laws are designed to ensure that public money is not used to indirectly support a regime whose conduct taxpayers find repugnant. A goal of such policies is to create incentives to encourage transnational corporations to divest from Burma. The selective purchasing laws are based on the effective divestiture and selective purchasing initiatives that animated the anti-apartheid movement in the U.S. in the 1980s and which are widely credited for helping to facilitate the successful transition to democracy in South Africa.

The attack on the Massachusetts selective purchasing law was two-pronged. Japan and the EU filed a case at the WTO. In parallel, the National Foreign Trade Council (NFTC), a coalition of corporations, challenged the measure in the U.S. District Court in Massachusetts as a violation of the U.S. Constitution. NFTC's law suit was part of a larger campaign by a corporate front

---

[13] Available at http://www.citizen.org/trade/issues/burma/articles.cfm?ID=11103 (last accessed May 2012).

group called USA*Engage to eliminate human rights considerations from U.S. international commercial policy.

The EU and Japan challenged the law at the WTO in the summer of 1997. The EU argued that Massachusetts' procurement policy had to conform to the WTO rules and that the Burma law contravened the WTO procurement agreement by imposing conditions that were not essential to fulfill the contract (Art. VIII(b), imposed qualifications based on political instead of economic considerations (Art. X), and allowed contracts to be awarded based on political instead of economic considerations (Art. XIII).

Massachusetts officials were flummoxed to learn they were required to comply with WTO procurement rules that they had never approved. They later learned that a previous governor had sent a letter to the USTR during the Uruguay Round without legislative consultation, much less approval which was the basis for the claim that the state was bound to the WTO procurement rules.

However, the EU and Japan suspended the WTO case pending the outcome of a federal lawsuit filed against that state by the NFTC in U.S. District Court. The NFTC argued that the Massachusetts law "unconstitutionally infringed on the federal foreign affairs power, violated the Foreign Commerce Clause, and was preempted by the federal Act." The District Court permanently enjoined enforcement of the state law, ruling that it "unconstitutionally impinge[d] on the federal government's exclusive authority to regulate foreign affairs." Massachusetts appealed, but the U.S. Court of Appeals for the First Circuit affirmed the District Court's decision.

Massachusetts appealed to the Supreme Court. Seventy-eight Members of Congress, 38 state and local governments, all eight major state and local government associations, and 66 non-profit organizations filed *amicus curiae* ("friend of the court") briefs supporting the Massachusetts law. Nonetheless, the Supreme Court affirmed the lower courts' decisions, although on narrower grounds, holding that a state or local selective purchasing law sanctioning a nation is preempted only when Congress has passed a corresponding law sanctioning that nation—as Congress had done in the case of Burma—and only when the two laws differ. This leaves the door open for state and local governments to pass several other types of laws.

For example, state and local governments could enact general laws to avoid purchasing goods and services from companies that violate human rights or labor standards as long as the laws do not apply specifically to companies doing business in a country where Congress has adopted *different* sanctions. Thus, states and cities could divest their holdings in companies that do business in Burma or could require companies to disclose whether they do business in Burma as a condition for selling goods or services to the government because these actions do not conflict with the federal Burma law. Under the Supreme Court ruling, state and local governments also could use preferential purchasing policies regarding countries about which Congress has not passed conflicting legislation. Thus, the Supreme Court decision, in contrast to WTO Agreement on Government Procurement (AGP) rules, does not rob state and local governments of all their options.

The U.S. Supreme Court ruling is more permissive of human rights links to procurement decisions than the relevant WTO rules. The WTO AGP forbids consideration of any non-commercial factors in governments', even sub-federal governments', procurement decisions.

The EU and Japan suspended their WTO challenge pending the outcome of the domestic case, thus the provisions of the AGP were never interpreted. Given the WTO has decreed that labor rights are solely in the jurisdiction of the ILO, it would have been revealing to see how a WTO tribunal treated the ILO's clear position on Burma's labor rights violations.

... ...

As described in the extract, the WTO challenge was not pursued because the Massachu-setts law was struck down by the US Supreme Court on the basis that federal action in the area of Burma sanctions had 'pre-empted' the states from addressing the issue. Nonethe-less, the case illustrates the potential for future conflict between WTO rules, in particular the Government Procurement Agreement, and the pursuit of human rights causes. The issue of how such a conflict should be addressed remains unresolved.

At least one prominent scholar, Ernst-Ulrich Petersmann, has argued strongly for better integrating human rights and WTO law. His views in this regard are set out in the following extract:

EU Petersmann, 'Time for a United Nations "Global Compact" for Integrating Human Rights into the Law of Worldwide Organizations: Lessons from European Integration' (2002) 13(3) *European Journal of International Law* 621

1. Introduction: Time for Reconsidering the `Washington Consensus' and for Strengthening Human Rights in Global Integration Law

Everyone is entitled to a social and international order in which the rights and freedoms set forth in this Declaration can be fully realized.

The human rights obligations in the UN Charter and in the Universal Declaration of Human Rights (UDHR) of 1948 were negotiated at the same time as the 1944 Bretton Woods Agreements, the General Agreement on Tariffs and Trade (GATT) of 1947 and the 1948 Havana Charter for an International Trade Organization. All these agreements aimed at protecting liberty, non-discrimination, the rule of law, social welfare and other human rights values through a rules-based international order and 'specialized agencies' (Article 57 of the UN Charter) committed to the economic principle of 'separation of policy instruments':

- *foreign policies* were to be coordinated in the UN so as to promote 'sovereign equality of all its Members' (Article 2(1) of the UN Charter) and collective security;
- *liberalization of payments* and *monetary stability* were collectively pursued through the rules and assistance of the International Monetary Fund (IMF);
- GATT and the Havana Charter aimed at mutually beneficial *liberalization of international trade and investments*;
- *development aid and policies* were coordinated in the World Bank Group; and
- *social laws and policies* were promoted in the International Labour Organisation (ILO) and other specialized agencies (such as UNESCO and WHO).

Apart from a few exceptions (notably in ILO, UNESCO and WHO rules), human rights were not effectively integrated into the law of most worldwide organizations so as to facilitate functional international integration (such as liberalization of trade and payments), notwithstanding different views of governments on human rights and domestic policies (such as communism). The focus on enlarging equal liberties was in accordance with prevailing concepts of 'justice' in the United States whose government had elaborated the blueprints for the post-war international order.

Regional integration law, by contrast, has moved towards a different 'integration paradigm' linking economic integration to constitutional guarantees of human rights, democracy and undistorted competition. For instance, the 'human rights clauses' in the European Union (EU) Treaty, in the association and cooperation agreements between the EU and more than 20 countries in eastern Europe and the Mediterranean, and in the EU's Cotonou Agreement with 77 African, Caribbean and Pacific states make 'respect for human rights, democratic principles and the rule of law . . . essential elements' of these agreements. The Quebec Summit Declaration of April 2001 and the Inter-American Charter of Democracy of September 2001, adopted by more than 30 member states of the Organization of American States, similarly link the plans for a Free Trade Area of the Americas (FTAA) to the strengthening of human rights and democracy. The regular civil society protests at the annual conferences of the IMF, the World Bank and the WTO, and the WTO Ministerial Declaration of November 2001 envisaging additional WTO competition, health and environmental rules, are further illustrations of the need to examine whether the European and FTAA 'integration paradigm' should not also become accepted at the worldwide level in order to promote a new kind of global integration law based on human rights and the solidary sharing of the benefits and social adjustment costs of global integration.

The proposed change from international functionalism to constitutionalism does not put into question the economic efficiency arguments for 'optimizing' and separating policy instruments. However, European integration confirms that the collective supply of public goods (such as the global division of labour) may not be politically feasible without comprehensive 'package deals' including solitary responses to 'market failures' and redistributive 'principles of justice'. Less developed countries, for instance, often perceive market competition as a 'licence to kill' for multinational corporations from developed countries as long as liberal trade rules are not supplemented by competition and social rules (as in the EC) promoting fair opportunities and the equitable distribution of gains from trade.

In order to remain democratically acceptable, global integration law (e.g. in the WTO) must pursue not only 'economic efficiency' but also 'democratic legitimacy' and 'social justice' as defined by human rights. Otherwise, citizens will rightly challenge the democratic and social legitimacy of integration law if it pursues economic welfare without regard to social human rights, for example the human right to education of the 130 million children (aged from 6 to 12) who do not attend primary school; the human right to basic health care of the 25 million Africans living with AIDS, or of the 35,000 children dying each day from curable diseases; and the human right to food and an adequate standard of living for the 1.2 billion people living on less than a dollar a day. The new opportunities for the worldwide enjoyment of human rights created by the global division of labour (such as additional economic resources, job opportunities, worldwide communication systems, and access to new medicines and technologies) must be accompanied by the stronger legal protection of social human rights so as to limit abuses of deregulation (e.g. by international cartels, trade in drugs and arms, and trafficking in women and children), help vulnerable groups to adjust to change without violation of their human rights, and put pressure on authoritarian governments to protect not only business interests but also the human rights of all their citizens.

...

9. Conclusion: The Need for Multi-Level Constitutionalism Protecting Human Rights More Effectively

Since the Greek republics in the fifth century BC, constitutionalism has emerged, in a process of 'trial and error', as the most important 'political invention' for protecting equal liberties against abuses of power. Today, virtually all states have adopted written or unwritten national constitutions. Even though national constitutionalism differs from country to country, constitutional democracies tend to recognize six interrelated core principles: (1) the rule of law; (2) the limitation and separation of government powers by checks and balances; (3) democratic self-government; (4) human rights; (5) social justice; and (6) the worldwide historical experience that protection of human rights and 'democratic peace' cannot remain effective without international law providing for the collective supply of international 'public goods' (such as collective security) and for reciprocal international legal restraints on abuses of foreign policy powers.

The legal concretization of these core principles in national constitutions (e.g. in national catalogues of human rights), and increasingly also in international 'treaty constitutions' (such as the EC Treaty and the ILO Constitution), and their mutual balancing through democratic legislation, legitimately differ from country to country, from organization to organization, and from policy area to policy area. There are also valid 'realist' reasons why 'democratic peace' may be possible only among constitutional democracies, and power politics may remain necessary to contain aggression from non-democracies where human rights are not effectively protected. Yet, are there convincing arguments that 'constitutionalism' is a 'fallacy', and 'constitutionalizing the WTO a step too far'?

The universal recognition and legal protection of inalienable human rights at national, regional and worldwide levels requires a new human rights culture and a citizen-oriented national and international constitutional framework different from the power-oriented, state-centred conceptions of traditional international law. In Europe, the emergence of 'multi-level governance' has led to 'multi-level constitutionalism' and 'divided power systems' that have succeeded in overcoming Europe's history of periodic wars and of the 'constitutional failures' of nation-states to protect human rights and the peaceful division of labour across frontiers. Just as within federal states 'the federal and state governments are in fact but different agents and trustees of the people, instituted with different powers, and designated for different purposes', so international organizations must be understood as a 'fourth branch of government' which is indispensable for protecting human rights and democratic peace across frontiers. In view of their 'constitutional functions', international guarantees of freedom, non-discrimination, the rule of law and human rights should be seen—as within the EC—as integral parts of the constitutional limitations on abuses of foreign policy powers. National constitutional law and human rights cannot achieve their objectives of promoting personal self-development and democratic self-governance unless they are supplemented by international constitutional law protecting human rights across frontiers in the economy no less than in the polity.

The promotion and protection of human rights is the task of national and international human rights law and of specialized human rights institutions. The law of regional and worldwide organizations (such as EU law, UN law and WTO law) also serves 'constitutional functions' for protecting freedom, non-discrimination, the rule of law and social welfare across national frontiers. Historical experience confirms that, without such multilateral rules, national parliaments can neither effectively supervise foreign policies among 200 sovereign states nor ensure that foreign policy decisions respect human rights and the rule of law at home and across frontiers. European and global integration law further demonstrates that the different layers of national and international rule-making, and executive and judicial processes, must be subject to effective democratic controls and to the constitutional safeguards of 'subsidiarity', 'necessity' and 'proportionality' of regulatory limitations of human rights (cf. Article 5 of the EC Treaty).

The democratic legitimacy of national as well as international constitutionalism, and the various levels of governance, derive from respect for human rights and from the democratic participation of citizens in the exercise of national and international government powers. Just as national citizenship and EC citizenship are complementary (cf. Article 12 of the EC Treaty), citizens must also be recognized as legal subjects of international law and international organizations. Their democratic participation and more effective representation in international organizations require far-reaching constitutional reforms of the state-centred international legal system so as to enable, for example, 'UN citizens' and 'WTO citizens' to invoke international guarantees of freedom before domestic courts and to participate more actively in parliamentary and civil society institutions at national and international levels.

The German Constitutional Court, for example, has rightly interpreted the creation of the European Central Bank as an act that redefines the guarantee of private property in money, protected by the German Constitution (Article 14) as a fundamental right. From such a human rights perspective, the state-centred interpretation of the agreement establishing the IMF as an exclusively monetary agreement on the rights and obligations of governments in the field of monetary policy, without legal relevance for the human rights obligations of governments and of UN agencies, appears too one-sided. International guarantees of freedom, non-discrimination and the rule of law, such as the UN guarantees of human rights and the WTO guarantees of liberal trade and property rights, should be seen as part of the domestic constitutional systems of WTO members which need to be protected by domestic courts so as to safeguard human rights across frontiers. Human rights law requires that the delegation of regulatory powers to national, regional and worldwide institutions must always remain constitutionally limited. Democratic sovereignty remains, as proclaimed in the Preamble to the UN Charter, with 'We the Peoples of the United Nations'. The protection of human dignity and human rights across frontiers through global integration law based on mutually coherent legal guarantees of 'state sovereignty', 'popular sovereignty' and 'individual sovereignty' remains the biggest constitutional challenge of law and governance in the twenty-first century.

... ...

Petersmann's support for a global constitution encompassing a wide range of rights is almost certainly not something that will be achieved any time soon. Nevertheless, it shows that there is at least some support for pushing forward with the integration of human rights and trade law. There is also a great deal of opposition. A critical response to Petersmann's proposal was provided by Philip Alston:

P Alston, 'Resisting the Merger and Acquisition of Human Rights by Trade Law: A Reply to Petersmann' (2002) 13(4) *European Journal of International Law* **815**

Ernst-Ulrich Petersmann and other like-minded commentators have responded to the end of the Cold War and the ascendancy of a form of neo-liberal economic orthodoxy by calling for a fundamental realignment of international human rights law in order to give appropriate priority to what they call 'economic liberties'. Petersmann has made an important and distinctive contribution to the debate by suggesting that the entrenchment of these values can best be done at the international level, using the well-established techniques of international law, and by urging that the principal locus of action should be the international economic institutions such as the WTO and the IMF rather than the UN's human rights bodies. If one takes an ordo-liberal starting point then these proposals, which would have the effect of prioritizing property and free trade over virtually all other values and would do so by giving them the imprimatur of human rights, make perfect sense. There is also a powerful instrumentalist motivation as Petersmann acknowledges when he says that 'human rights law offers WTO rules moral, constitutional and democratic legitimacy that may be more important for the parliamentary ratification of future WTO agreements than traditional economic and utilitarian justifications'.

Petersmann is in fact far from being the first to advocate a human right to free trade. In his 1944 State of the Union address, President Franklin D. Roosevelt put forward an economic bill of rights which included: 'The right of every businessman, large and small, to trade in an atmosphere of freedom from unfair competition and domination by monopolies at home or abroad.' Ironically, when the American Law Institute subsequently adapted the long list of economic and social rights proposed by Roosevelt for possible inclusion in the UDHR they omitted this right but retained virtually all of the standard economic and social rights that were subsequently recognized in the relevant provisions of the Universal Declaration. Moreover, Petersmann's proposal to privilege the right to property recalls the arguments put forward over the years by Richard Epstein, who has long advocated an interpretation of the fifth amendment to the US Constitution (the so-called 'takings clause' which prohibits the taking of private property 'for public use without just compensation'), which would give far greater protection to property rights than they currently enjoy and would result in the overriding of many of the social and labour rights which currently exist under US law. In these respects, Petersmann's proposals are hardly novel.

The principal problem with his approach, however, is that it is presented as though it were simply a logical development of existing policies, rather than representing a dramatic break with them. In a form of epistemological misappropriation he takes the discourse of international human rights law and uses it to describe an agenda which has a fundamentally different ideological underpinning. Thus, his proposals are presented as: involving a relatively minor adaptation of existing human rights law; amounting to little more than the transposition of a balanced and proven EU policy on human rights and trade; being entirely consistent with widely accepted conceptions of constitutionalism and the rule of law; being fully compatible with the recognition of a wide range of social rights; and being a straightforward application of Kantian principles. But as the preceding analysis has sought to show, none of these characterizations is accurate.

The proposed agenda is in fact a revolutionary and radical one which, if adopted, would have far-reaching consequences for the existing international human rights regime as well as for the balance of values reflected in the vast majority of existing constitutional orders. The most fundamental change is that human rights would, despite all of the Kantian rhetoric, become detached from their foundations in human dignity and would instead be viewed primarily as instrumental means for the achievement of economic policy objectives. Individuals would become the objects rather than the holders of human rights. While their broader range of human rights would continue to be protected through ineffectual institutional arrangements, they would become empowered as economic agents acting to uphold the WTO agenda. More specifically in terms of changes, a very large number of national constitutions, only a handful of which recognize anything approaching a right to free trade, would have to be amended. International human rights instruments, which have proved notoriously difficult to amend, would have to be substantially revised if the rights to property, contract and freedom of trade are to be recognized and made judicially enforceable in the way Petersmann envisages. Economic actors, such as corporations, would be empowered far beyond existing practice to invoke the protection of human rights instruments. The various limitations upon the right to property, which have been prominent in the application of that right by international human rights organs, would be dramatically curtailed. At the political level, the reluctance to incorporate any human rights dimension within the WTO framework, a position which the vast majority of governments have consistently manifested in that context, would need to be overcome. Finally, there is the paradox implicit in a project which proceeds on the basis of the constant reiteration of the importance of democratic values being achieved through measures designed to put the principle of free trade, repackaged as a human right to be enforced by international economic agencies, effectively beyond the reach of all domestic constituencies.

Rather than waiting for these radical changes to occur within our lifetimes it would seem to be more productive to pursue the debate over the appropriate relationship between trade and human rights in two directions. The first, which focuses on the ways in which the two separate bodies of law can best be reconciled and made complementary to the greatest extent possible, is already well under way (the 'trade and . . .' debate), although Petersmann's writings show a reluctance to place much store upon this approach. The second is to begin a more sustained and critical debate that focuses upon the agenda that Petersmann describes, but does so in a systematic and intellectually open way which acknowledges the underlying assumptions and imposes a high scholarly burden of proof on the proponents of the different positions. Petersmann is correct when he says that the human rights community has so far been reluctant to take such proposals seriously and perhaps one very constructive result of his many writings will be to compel the sort of debate which is required. But it cannot be based on flimsy assertions such as those put forward by another commentator who has also called for 'economic freedoms, including property and contract rights [to] be placed at the top of a new agenda for international human rights' and asserts that empirical studies vindicate the efficiency of such an approach in order to guarantee 'wealth, social stability and civil rights'. Human rights proponents, on the other hand, can no longer dismiss the strong version of claims made on behalf of property rights and free trade without engaging with them in a more convincing and incisive manner.[14]

... ...

V. HEALTH AND SAFETY

Whereas a few of the conflicts between trade and other policies, such as the environment and labour, are treated sceptically in some circles, most people would agree that governments should have the ability to take appropriate action to promote human health and safety, and that trade policy and agreements should not undermine this. Nevertheless, conflicts do arise in a number of contexts.

As seen in Chapter 10, GATT Article XX(b) has a specific exception for measures necessary to protect human (and animal or plant) life or health. We will not repeat that discussion here, but we note that the interpretation of certain GATT obligations and the Article XX(b) exception has an important impact on how much discretion is given to governments to promote health and safety. Similarly, interpretation of the SPS and TBT Agreements also affects governments' abilities in this regard (Chapter 14).

Recently, access to essential medicines has been a very controversial issue at the WTO. As discussed in Chapter 18, in response to concerns that the TRIPS Agreement imposed too many constraints on the availability of cheap, generic medicines in times of a public health crisis or public emergency and, more specifically, on the rules regulating compulsory licensing of pharmaceuticals, the relevant provisions were modified to encourage increased access.

Another example of issues related to consumer safety is a set of EU regulations on chemicals, as discussed in the following excerpt.

DA Mottal, 'Reaching Reach: The Challenge for Chemicals Entering International Trade' (2009) 12(3) *Journal of International Economic Law* 643, 643–46, 649–57

I. WHAT IS REACH?

'Registration, Evaluation, Authorisation and Restriction of Chemicals' (REACH) is the new toxic chemicals regulation that has entered into force in the European Union (EU) on 1 June 2007 with the intention of replacing over 40 existing directives and regulations. According to the European Commission (EC), the reason it presented a proposal for REACH in 2003 was to address what was an 'inadequate legislative framework' for chemicals management in the EU. Another stated objective was to enhance the competitiveness of the EU chemicals industry by

---

[14] It should be noted that Professor Petersman replied to Alston. See EU Petersmann, 'Taking Human Rights, Poverty and Empowerment of Individuals More Seriously: Rejoinder to Alston' (2002) 13 *European Journal of International Law* 845.

fostering innovation and ensuring high safety standards for its products. REACH was perceived as a measure necessary to deal with the growth of chemicals production, globally. While global chemicals production was at 1 million tons in 1930, it has rise to over 400 million tons today. This growth was not perceived to have been accompanied by adequate safety measures. It is said that in 2004, the World Wildlife Fund for Nature tested the blood of the government ministers from 13 EU Member States for chemicals that could negatively affect human health, and found that, on average, 37 of the 103 substances that it had tested for, were present. These safety concerns, together with environmental and animal welfare concerns, propelled the Commission to take action.

Under prior directives and regulations, chemical manufacturers and importers were required to register certain high-volume substances with EC regulatory authorities. However, it was the regulatory authorities themselves that had to determine whether there was a need (i) to conduct a risk assessment for a particular chemical and (ii) to themselves do so, if such an assessment was deemed necessary.

The EC argued that this system had proved to be slow, cumbersome and extremely costly for regulatory authorities. While EC regulatory bodies had earmarked a total of 140 high-volume chemicals for assessment in 1993, only 10 of these chemicals had actually been assessed for many years. The authorities were unable to gather sufficient information about their health and environmental impact and, therefore, to recommend risk-management measures. This situation was seen as a danger for public health and the environment and, the slowness of the process, as an obstacle to innovation.

When proposing REACH, the EC estimated that its overall cost would fall in the range of €2.8–5.2 billion over a period of 11–15 years, with a negligible impact on the EU's Gross Domestic Production. The benefits to health and the environment were considered to outweigh these costs. For instance, one estimate suggested that benefits of REACH for occupational skin and respiratory diseases could range from €21 to 160 billion in the next 30 years.

So how does REACH work then? Contrary to what the title of this legislation suggests, 'registration', 'evaluation' and 'authorization' are not required for all chemicals. In other words, the title is not intended to denote a series of steps through which all chemicals must pass. Rather, the vast majority of chemicals are only required to be 'registered' under REACH, with the process going no further. It is the potentially new chemicals on which little information is available, or existing sources information are inappropriate, that must go through an evaluation. Authorization, which is an independent process, is only required for a pre-determined set of substances that are already known to be highly toxic. So, substances that are harmless must simply be registered, substances that may be harmful must be evaluated and substances that are known to be harmful must be authorized.

Registration is the basis of REACH. All manufacturers or importers of chemicals into the EU are required to register any substance brought into the EU at a volume of 1 ton or more. Full registration, when it occurs, will take place on the basis of the one substance, one registration rule, requiring different manufacturers of the same chemicals to collaborate. REACH has resulted in the creation of a new regulatory authority at the European level (the European Chemicals Agency, otherwise known as ECHA), to which applications have to be made.

The objective of the registration phase is to have manufacturers and importers (i) gather information on the properties of their substances, (ii) indicate how they intend to manage them safely and (iii) turn all of this information over to the EC for the creation of a 'central chemicals database'. This reverses the burden of proof, but perhaps more importantly the 'burden of work', from the regulator to the manufacturer or importer. Registration is primarily intended to help EC regulators gather information that they were not able to do before. For information that was not already available to a manufacturer or importer, the EC proposes computer modelling, epidemiological studies or further testing. As all of these options may be costly, it encourages the sharing of information among companies for joint registrations. Furthermore, animal testing is to be kept to a minimum under REACH through the mandatory sharing of animal test data by applicants.

The registration process has been planned in such a way as to be phased in slowly. Very harmful substances that meet the volume requirement need to be registered first but less harmful ones can do so over longer timeframes. All chemicals existing in the marketplace prior to 1981 do not have to be registered at all (even if the volume threshold applies); they are 'grandfathered' under the legislation. According to the EC, 100 substances existed prior to 1981 but a total of 3,000 new ones have been placed on the market since.

Evaluation is a process that is triggered for chemicals that meet one of the two requirements: (i) they are found to require further animal testing, in which case REACH intervenes to explore ways of minimizing this testing or (ii) if there is reason to believe that a substance may present a high risk to human health or the environment. It is the individual EC member states that will need to conduct evaluations. Authorization, on the other hand, only kicks in for a set of pre-determined chemicals that are known to be highly toxic. Authorization will only be granted if the applicant can demonstrate that the risks from use can be adequately controlled. Carcinogens fall into this category.

In terms of the scope of REACH, it is important to note that the legislation covers not only chemical substances as they exist in isolation but also 'articles' containing chemicals from which there may be 'release'. This basically means that everything from textiles to automobiles can be covered by REACH. Food additives, however, are explicitly carved out of REACH. While the regulation contains broad exemptions for pesticides and pharmaceuticals, there remain important regulatory obligations in these areas. There is some room for interpretation of the exemptions.

In terms of practical implementation, the EC had mandated that all chemicals be 'Pre-Registered' under REACH by 1 December 2008, ahead of a complete first 'Registration' by 30 November 2010. The idea behind this was to publicize information on chemicals used within the EU, allowing manufacturers of the same substances to collaborate for the purpose of submitting one dossier per substance for the first complete registration.

...

IV. RANGE OF TRADE CONCERNS EXPRESSED AT THE WTO AND BEYOND

Numerous concerns have been expressed by WTO members about the 'practical' aspects of complying with REACH. In other words, at this particular point in time, members seem to be more concerned with their ability to access REACH and to fulfil its registration requirements, than they are with the 'standard of proof' to which their scientific evidence will be held in an eventual evaluation or authorization phase. This was particularly evident at the last meeting of the WTO's Committee on Technical Barriers to Trade (TBT), held in November 2008. The bulk of members' concerns stem from the 'data generation' requirements of the REACH. They do not know how their industry and, in particular, small- and medium-sized enterprises (SMEs) will be able to generate the necessary data. Some have pointed to the fact that their degree of concern is directly proportional to their degree of dependence on the EU market for their chemical exports. Egypt, for instance, stated at the last TBT Committee meeting that as more than 50% of its chemical exports were destined for the EU, it was seriously concerned about the impact of REACH. The United States expressed the fear that its $4 billion worth of cosmetics exports to the EC could be adversely affected.

As previously stated, REACH envisaged a pre-registration procedure, that has now closed in December 2008. The only possibility at this stage for substances that failed to pre-register would be to follow what is called a 'late' pre-registration procedure. Pre-registration entailed the electronic submission to ECHA of certain basic information on the chemical and the pre-registrant. In January 2009, ECHA already started to publish on its Website the list of the pre-registered substances. The list does not identify the pre-registrants but the other information is available to all companies that have pre-registered the same substance. This year, the companies are required to participate in Substance Information Exchange Fora (SIEFs) to facilitate the sharing of existing data on their chemicals, the collective identification of data gaps and cost sharing for the purposes of generating new data.

Chemicals can be registered under REACH either by the EU importer or the Only Representative (OR) office that an exporter may designate. The OR must be a 'natural or legal person established in the EU'. Thus, only an EU-based individual or an EU entity can function as an OR. An OR must have sufficient background in the practical handling of chemicals and in information related to them. In other words, it must be a technically qualified individual or entity with a developed understanding of REACH. The OR has an obligation to keep available and up-to-date information on the quantities of the chemicals imported and the customers that the chemicals are sold to. In case an exporting country chooses to designate an OR, the OR, rather the importer, would carry out the registration, and the importer would be regarded as a downstream user of the substance.

The following section provides an overview of the different categories of concerns expressed by WTO members, whether in the WTO or other fora, in relation to REACH. It demonstrates the continued desire of some WTO members to influence the post-legislative process on REACH.

A. Broad coverage or excessive registration

Several WTO Members have criticized REACH for its excessively broad coverage, calling on the EC to 'prioritize' the chemicals that are of greatest concern using a risk-based approach. REACH is perceived as being too ambitious and as potentially leading to stopping the chemicals industry in its tracks. Criticisms have been made of the use of the 'volume threshold' as the trigger for registration, with the argument being that volume is an imperfect surrogate for risk. Certain highly toxic chemicals may be imported in very low quantities, but less toxic ones in greater volumes. REACH would discriminate against high-volume imports, it has been stated.

The EC has offered a number of arguments in response. First, it has objected to the notion that REACH is triggered by volume. The volume threshold only applies for 'registration'. Chemicals that are suspected of being dangerous will be evaluated, and highly toxic chemicals must be authorized. The EC believes that it is prioritizing chemicals since it phases in the registration process over many years, and has created a list of those chemicals that must absolutely be authorized.

B. Uncertainty in registration

It has been argued by several WTO Members that there are numerous uncertainties concerning the pre-registration and registration processes. For instance, one uncertainty argued by China is that it will be very difficult to establish whether imports meet the volume requirement of REACH, particularly when substances are contained in 'articles'. For instance, how many metres of a particular textile must the EC be importing to trigger a registration for an 'azo dye' used in the production process?

Furthermore, the only articles that require registration under REACH are those articles from which substances may be released. It has been argued that it is impossible to determine with certainty the articles from which there may be 'release'. The fear is that liability provisions could kick in for situations in which producers genuinely did not known about the possibility of release. A number of countries have also called on the EC to simply create a list of substances requiring registration to resolve the uncertainty—a 'positive list'— as it has been called.

Others have questioned how REACH would apply to specific substances, saying that it lacked clarity. For instance, some oil and petrochemical exporters, such as Qatar, expressed concern about the applicability and impact of REACH on the petrochemicals industry, in particular. Reflecting further confusion at the last TBT Committee meeting, the United States posed the following questions: 'blood and blood derivatives were covered by the regulation. Do re-imported substances need to be pre-registered a second time? What substances in articles such as autos are intended for release? Where does the dividing line between a substance and a preparation lie?'

Several have also wondered what a chemical would need to do if it has missed the pre-registration deadline of the last year or if it misses the final registration deadline of this year. Similarly, at the last TBT Committee meeting, the United States, in particular, argued that REACH lacked transparency, and that the EC had deliberately kept REACH off the agenda of the Transatlantic Economic Council, despite various requests for bilateral talks on the subject that had been made by the United States.

The EC has not perceived these criticisms as justified and has argued that countries must first see how REACH will be 'applied' in practice, before identifying problems. It has argued that volumes of chemicals incorporated in products can be assessed, just as can their release. As far as a 'positive list' is concerned, the EC has argued that this would discriminate against substances for which information is available today, since the list would be established based on what is 'already known'. The unknown would be ignored. It, therefore, preferred to gather information on all substances.

It attempted to clarify the exact coverage and scope of REACH in various TBT Committee meetings and pointed members to the existence of REACH Help Desks. It also drew the attention of members to existence of a late pre-registration procedure for substances that would have missed the initial deadline.

C. Animal welfare

A number of other countries have argued that the EC is imposing its animal welfare concerns extraterritorially. They have argued that whether substances are tested on animals or not outside the EC, should be the decision of other countries. A more specific concern has also been expressed on whether REACH breaches intellectual property rights through its sharing of animal test data. Under REACH, applicants must submit to the EC any information concerning animal tests that they have conducted. That information becomes available to subsequent applicants through the SIEFs. Therefore, any SIEF member can obtain another member's study data on vertebrate animals, and all studies submitted over 10 years earlier, would automatically be made public ECHA.

The EC has given a mixture of different responses to these concerns, the most significant of which is that it has come under very heavy pressure from its animal welfare groups to make the legislation even more stringent. In fact, the final outcome embodied in REACH is a compromise that relaxes some of the initial provisions. In addition, in its response to WTO members, the EC argued that all intellectual property rights were respected.

D. The SIEFs

Under REACH, manufacturers and importers are encouraged to form SIEFs to pool their resources in the generation of data on chemicals. SIEFs are intended to offer what the EC perceives as a practical way of complying with the heavy-data requirements of the legislation. Many concerns have been expressed regarding the ability of foreign producers to join EC-established SIEFs, run by what would essentially be an industry's local 'competitors'. The heavy-data requirements of REACH have been seen by several WTO members as necessitating some pooling of resources, with SIEFs regarded as vital. The fear of anti-competitive practices by SIEFs, as well as concerns over how they would be likely to protect confidential data, have led some to question their viability.

At the last TBT meeting, for instance, Japan wondered whether the opinions of foreign-based firms would be respected when participating in SIEFs, suggesting that they could suffer discrimination.

The EC has explained that one of the objectives of REACH is to limit vertebrate-animal testing as far as possible, while balancing that with the generation of necessary information to identify the hazard of substances. The purpose of a SIEF is to help registrants of the same substance share information about it and to avoid duplication of testing.

Therefore, duplicate animal testing has to be avoided and tests on vertebrate animals for the purposes of REACH can only be undertaken as a last resort. Before new tests are conducted to comply with the identified information needs, potential registrants have to take part in the data-sharing mechanisms set up for tests on vertebrate animals. They may use those mechanisms for other tests not involving vertebrate animals to save time and money.

The EC added that summaries of tests would only be protected for 10 years from their Registration, after which they would be made freely available to all potential registrants asking for them. For other tests, the mechanisms set up would encourage manufacturers and importers of substances to come to an agreement on the sharing of tests and costs. Forced sharing of tests involving vertebrate animals would be a measure of last resort.

E. The OR Office

A number of WTO members have wondered how the ORs would operate in practice, raising concerns about (i) how these offices would be set up, (ii) whether it would be possible to change an OR once appointed and (iii) the impact of ORs on the confidentiality of information. Questions have been posed on whether it would be possible to find alternative systems to ORs by having the EC conduct inspections extra-territorially, in the exporting country instead, so that exporters would then be able to register the chemicals themselves (a point stressed by Mexico, in particular). Some have also wondered whether the burdensome procedures required to find and establish and OR would lead European importers to begin sourcing their inputs domestically instead. Certain developing countries, such as Egypt, asked the EC to provide a list of recommended or accredited ORs, in order to facilitate the process for developing countries.

The EC has explained that ORs are not an obligation under REACH but rather a possibility given to non-EU manufacturers. 'In fact', the EC stated, 'the OR provision was introduced in REACH to address some of the concerns that had been expressed by trading partners, particularly regarding the protection of confidential business information'. Countries could let the EU importers, rather than ORs, bear the responsibility of registering the chemical but in that situation they could then have to turn what they consider 'confidential information' over to the importer. The EC added that the relationship between the OR and the exporting country was not governed by REACH, allowing exporting countries to establish the confidentiality requirements of their choosing.

On the proposal for inspections outside the EU, the EC argued that that would violate various principles of international law, since the EC could only impose its laws in territories under its jurisdiction. Mexico and Australia responded that they would not see a violation of international law or of WTO rules if inspections were to be carried out in their countries, in particular urging the EC to consider provisions of the TBT provisions on conformity assessment that call on countries to 'permit participation of conformity assessment bodies located in the territories of other Members in their conformity assessment procedures' (Article 6.4 of the TBT Agreement).

F. Impact on SMEs

The impact of REACH on SMEs has been an issue of particular concern to countries (also linked to the fee structure discussed below). Many countries, in particular developing countries, have questioned how SMEs could comply with such a complex regulation and have requested technical assistance in its implementation. China, for instance, called for making staff head-count, one of the operational criteria under REACH. Others stated that the net effect of REACH would be to drive SMEs off the EC chemicals market.

The EC responded that SMEs were a vital part of the EU chemicals industry and that it had, for that reason, endeavoured to make the regulation work for them (through lower registration fees for instance). However, safety was a concern, regardless of company size, the REACH information requirements were related to production volumes, uses and properties of chemicals and not to the turnover or the number of employees in a company.

G. Fee structure

Various concerns have been raised about the fee structure for applications made under REACH. For instance, Japan stated that it was unfair that fees depend on 'business size' as they currently do, since many businesses were not only servicing the EC market but various others too. Therefore, Japan suggested the EC to modify its fee structure so as to calculate only the business taking place within the EU market. The United States argued that the registration and testing fees, even with the reduced registration fees for SMEs, could easily exceed $50,000 per substance. It was not uncommon, it added, that companies use up to 400 chemicals in the manufacture of a single fragrance in the cosmetics industry. The cost of registration of each of these individual ingredients would then be prohibitive.

In response, the EC noted that the requests from some delegations that fees and charges be applied equally to EC-based and non-EC-based companies showed that there could be a misunderstanding about who had to register and who was a member of the SIEFs. It recalled that registrants (and, consequently, members of SIEFs) were only EC-based companies, be they manufacturers, importers or ORs. These would all be treated in the same way as manufacturers and importers established in the EU.

H. Confidential information

Under Articles 39(1) and (2) of the TRIPS Agreement, Members are required to protect undisclosed information and data submitted to governments or regulatory agencies. Many WTO Members that intervened in the EC's Trade Policy Review in the WTO on REACH have argued that data likely to be disclosed by REACH would fall within this zone. Furthermore, as previously stated, some have questioned how SIEFs and ORs would also be made to protect confidential information.

The EC has responded that there is a specific article in REACH that provides for the protection of confidential information, and which tries to strike a balance between the need to protect intellectual property and to allow access to health and environmental information. It has maintained that: 'Certain information will always be considered confidential, whereas information related to health and environmental risks will always be publicly available'.

I. Harmonization and conformity assessment

Many countries have called on the EC to harmonize REACH with existing regional and international standards or to await the outcome of certain harmonization efforts that are currently underway. References have been made to the Global Harmonized System for Classification and Labelling, to the Stockholm Convention on Persistent Organic Pollutants and to the work of the OECD Task Force on Endocrine Disrupters, for instance. In addition, questions have been raised, in particular by developing countries, about the extent to which the EC is likely to accept test data generated outside the EC, and whether OECD's 'Good Laboratory Practice' would be applied.

The EC has responded that REACH complements, rather than supplants, existing international and regional regulations, and that it has every intention of complying with these norms. Furthermore, it has reassured its trading partners that test data generated by bodies located outside the EC would be accepted. Data that is not generated under Good Laboratory Practice can be accepted in certain circumstances under particular provisions of REACH.

J. Other concerns

Several other concerns have also been expressed by WTO Members. They include: how the EC would ensure consistent application of REACH by different member states; how REACH would interact with other pieces of EC legislation (such as the Waste Electrical and Electronic Equipment Directive); how product liability would be affected by REACH; how the sanctions for non-compliance with REACH would be devised and how the 'precautionary principle' would be applied under the legislation. The latter, some have argued, is a concern that is likely to grow once countries settle the practicalities of 'registration'. Furthermore, some concern has been expressed about this regulation leading to a shifting of polluting activity to developing countries due to excessive stringency within the EU.

REACH appears to have also triggered fears about substances progressively requiring 'authorization' under the regulation—'authorization-creep'. This was evidenced at the last meeting of the TBT Committee, where lengthy discussions took place on how the EC was regulating nickel under the 31st Adaptation to Technical Progress (ATP) to the Dangerous Substance Directive. The EC has classified hundreds of nickel substances under the ATP, prompting questions about the relationship between the ATP and REACH. The African Caribbean and Pacific group of states expressed the fear that the stringent risk assessment methodology applied by the ATP to nickel could spill-over into REACH: 'the read-across methodology used for the reclassification of nickel could set a precedent for regulating other substances under REACH thereby amplifying the impact of the methodology across numerous products and economic sectors'.

In terms of the compliance of REACH with WTO rules, much will depend on the specific set of WTO rules that a country may invoke to challenge the legislation (whether under the TBT Agreement, for instance, or the Agreement on Sanitary or Phytosanitary Measures or a provision of the General Agreement on Tariffs and Trade), as well as the specific portion of REACH that is contested. Having said that, the overall WTO integrity of REACH would likely be assessed against two main question: (i) whether it represents an arbitrary or disguised restriction on trade and/or (ii) an unnecessary obstacle to trade.

In other words, the WTO compatibility of REACH would likely be determined by whether there is any protectionist intent behind the legislation (a desire to privilege a domestic industry for instance) or to unnecessarily discriminate against a foreign chemicals supplier, and/or whether REACH can simply achieve its objectives easier, with less hindrance to trade. The jury is out on these questions, since REACH has never been formally challenged before the WTO's dispute resolution mechanism.

... ...

VI. QUESTIONS

1. If you believe economic growth and industrialisation are bad for the environment, does it make sense to protest trade agreements based on the view that trade promotes growth and industrialisation?

2. Analyse the trade measures proposed by Joseph Stiglitz, and similar 'green' tariffs, under Article XX(g). Does his analogy to the *Shrimp* case work? What if the EC just taxed all goods, domestic and foreign, made by a process that had high emissions, rather than targeting imports?

3. Would harmonisation of various laws reduce conflict resulting from different regulatory standards? Would there be negative consequences from such harmonisation?

4. How far does Pascal Lamy's proposed 'environment chapter' go in terms of addressing trade–environment conflicts?

5. Are trade sanctions effective as a way to coerce better behaviour on non-trade policies? Are there any alternatives that could be used?

6. When developed countries propose high labour and environmental standards, to what extent do you think their domestic industries support these standards in order to gain advantage against imports from developing countries?

7. Are 'cultural' industries really any different from other industries? Is there a difference between Canada losing market share to foreign car-makers and declining broadcasts of 'Canadian' programming?

8. Are there clear human rights standards that can be applied universally? Can we define a level of abuse that merits trade sanctions against a country?

9. Are there clear labour rights standards that can be applied universally? For example, if we want to establish a minimum wage, can the level be set fairly and accurately across different countries?

10. Sex tourism is travel to engage in sexual intercourse or sexual activity with prostitutes, and is typically undertaken internationally by tourists from wealthier countries. Based on standard definitions of 'trade', it would appear that such behaviour constitutes trade in services. Should WTO rules and other trade agreement rules try to address this issue?

11. While trade and other policies often come into conflict, there are times where they can come together. For example, trade and environmental groups have recently begun working together to eliminate or reduce fisheries subsidies, a policy that both groups oppose (trade groups due to the economic distortions, environmental groups due to the harm to the environment). What other areas of cooperation can you envision?

12. Food miles are the measure of the distance a food travels from field to plate. It has been argued that this travel adds substantially to the carbon dioxide emissions that are contributing to climate change. To address such concerns, are laws that favour local agricultural products appropriate?

Index